MASTERING

NETWARE 5.1

MASTERING™
NETWARE® 5.1

James Gaskin

SYBEX®

San Francisco • Paris • Düsseldorf • Soest • London

Associate Publisher: Neil Edde
Contracts and Licensing Manager: Kristine O'Callaghan
Acquisitions & Developmental Editor: Brenda Frink
Editors: Linda Recktenwald, Emily K. Wolman
Production Editor: Leslie E. H. Light
Technical Editors: Robert Abuhoff, Tami Evanson
Book Designers: Pat Dintino, Catalin Dulfu, Franz Baumhackl
Graphic Illustrator: Tony Jonick
Electronic Publishing Specialist: Robin Kibby
Proofreaders: Laurie O'Connell, Andrea Fox, Nancy Riddiough
Indexer: Matthew Spence
Cover Designer: Archer Design
Cover Illustrator/Photographer: FPG International

Library of Congress Card Number: 00-102841

ISBN: 0-7821-2772-X

An earlier version of this book was published under the title *The Complete Guide to NetWare® 4.11/IntranetWare, Second Edition,* copyright © 1997 SYBEX Inc.

Manufactured in the United States of America
10 9 8 7 6 5 4 3 2 1

As always, this is for Wendy, Alex, and Laura.

ACKNOWLEDGMENTS

Every book of this size includes a large, unseen, yet valuable team to transform ideas into reality. My name as author may be on the front of the book, but their work behind the scenes made it all possible.

I'd like to thank Brenda Frink for starting this project with me. The editors, Linda Recktenwald and Emily Wolman, applied a light yet experienced touch to maintain consistency and make me appear to be a better writer than I may actually be. They changed no jokes; groaners must be blamed on me, not them. Leslie E. H. Light, production editor, with help from Teresa Trego, kept polite (but firm) pressure to keep the words flowing. Technical editing by Robert Abuhoff and Tami Evanson served as a strong safety net for catching missteps and technical details. Robert Abuhoff also provided valuable help with Chapters 13 and 16.

And lastly, I'd like to mention the proofreaders and indexer, their expertise helps to ensure a quality product comes to you, the reader.

CONTENTS AT A GLANCE

PART V • APPENDICES 1123

CONTENTS

PART II • MANAGING THE NETWORK

6 Creating and Managing User Objects

7 Handling More Than One User at a Time

10 NetWare 5.1 Administrator Duties and Tools 469

17 Using NetWare 5.1 Enhancements and Special Features   1019

INTRODUCTION

NetWare 5.1 is the latest version of the world's most popular network operating system, developed by the world's most successful networking company. With NetWare 4 and intraNetWare 4.11, Novell engineers took the file and print services that have defined networking for the past decade and added new components: directory services, messaging, routing, security, and management. They then took the best of the Internet (Web server, Web client, and TCP/IP communications software) and rolled it into the NetWare 5.0 package.

NetWare 5.1 builds upon exciting new features recently introduced by Novell: native TCP/IP support, the Netscape Enterprise Web Server, distributed print services, multiprocessor support, application preemption, memory protection, virtual memory, Domain Name Service support, Dynamic Host Configuration Protocol server support, a new tape backup system, a robust and scalable development environment supporting Common Object Request Broker Architecture (CORBA), JavaBeans, JavaScript, and Perl scripting, and public-key cryptography. These services are what will define networking as we move into the new millennium.

Gee, this all sounds pretty fancy. What does it mean to you? If you're new to NetWare, it means that NetWare 5.1 is the best network for companies small and large. If you're a current NetWare user, it means that NetWare 5.1 builds upon the solid NetWare foundation you're familiar with and adds features necessary for the continued growth of your network.

Just as there are some new features in NetWare, there are some new features in this book. I've worked hard to present this huge wad of information in digestible chunks, ready when you need specific information.

Who Should Read This Book?

If you're a NetWare user already, this book builds on what you know from earlier versions of NetWare and adds the new features in steps. A new management architecture, NetWare Management Portal, is introduced with NetWare 5.1. This Web browser utility provides a ton of new information displayed in a friendly, easy format. It complements ConsoleOne, the interface that provides a common environment for Novell and other developers to build management tools. For seasoned NetWare administrators, one change that will not come as a surprise is that the DOS utilities used for server and network administration (such as PCONSOLE, NETADMIN, and PARTMGR) have finally been retired. All these utilities' functions are now included in either NetWare Administrator, NetWare Management Portal, or ConsoleOne.

I've been working with NetWare for more than a dozen years, and I believe I have a good understanding of its "feel." I place these new features in perspective so that you, experienced in NetWare but new to version 5.1, will understand where these features came from and how they fit into the current version of NetWare.

NetWare neophytes will find "ground-up" explanations for NetWare 5.1 features and utilities. As a PC networking consultant working with a variety of customer networks, I have learned to explain networking logically and clearly to people who don't have a background in NetWare. I regularly work with people new to networks and NetWare and can relay networking concepts to users familiar only with their PCs. I have also learned that most people don't care a whit about the networking technology we provide. They just want to get their work done with less hassle. These guidelines have served me well over the years; the users don't care what we go through, they just want their lives to be easier.

Advanced users, especially those who are performing some network administration for their departments, will find quite a bit of interest here. I recommend recruiting subadministrators and point out the many areas where they are useful. If you fall into the power user or subadministrator category, you will like this book.

Those of you managing small networks will find clear directions on installing and configuring NetWare 5.1 for your company. Novell answered one criticism of earlier NetWare versions by adding a new, simple-to-use, Java-based graphical installation program. This streamlined installation-and-configuration process makes NetWare 5.1 as easy to install as pointing and clicking. For us old-timers, using a mouse and working with a graphical user interface at the server console may seem odd at times, but they do work.

Those of you managing large networks will find many details about the advantages NetWare 5.1 offers administrators. This book includes all you need to know about managing users by large groups, both when you're importing them into NetWare 5.1 and when you're controlling them afterward. Options for NetWare Directory Services suitable for large companies are provided with illustrations and recommendations.

The "real" side of networking, dealing with users and bosses, appears regularly in these pages. Your network clients aren't computers and printers—they are people. Forget that at your own peril. Remember that people have jobs to do; the network will help them do those jobs and your career will be fine.

How This Book Is Organized

To help you find the information you need, this book is divided into five major sections:

Part I: Setting Up the Network, Chapters 1 through 5   The chapters in this part cover what you need to know about installing your network. The first three chapters walk you through planning your installation and the nitty-gritty of the installation itself, and Chapter 4 is devoted to planning and expanding Novell Directory Services. This part takes you up through connecting workstations to the network.

Part II: Managing the Network, Chapters 6 through 13   The first two chapters in this part are about those who are using the network: your users. The next chapter deals with a service those users take advantage of frequently (much too frequently in my opinion), network printing. Security, an important topic for many networks; is the subject of Chapter 9. The next chapter is a complete guide to network management and the NetWare 5.1 utilities that make those tasks easier than ever. Chapters 11 and 12 cover two basic user needs: applications and network training. The last chapter in this part is an overview of integrating NetWare with Windows NT and 2000.

Part III: Integrating NetWare with TCP/IP, Chapters 14 and 15   This part teaches you how to take advantage of NetWare's native IP support and to use NetWare 5.1 in a TCP/IP world. Chapter 14 introduces IP networking and shows you how to plan and administer a TCP/IP network with NetWare. Chapter 15 shows you how to manage IP addresses with the new DNS and DHCP utilities integrated with NDS. We can no longer think of TCP/IP and Internet tools as some "new parts" of NetWare; these technologies now weave through the core of NetWare and are just as integral as file and print services.

Part IV: Taking Advantage of Special Network Features, Chapters 16 through 18   In this part, you'll find coverage of Novell's remote access capabilities and NetWare 5.1 enhancements, which include the advancements in the NetWare product other than NDS features. The final chapter is where you turn when you (I'm sorry to say, inevitably) have a problem with your network (or a network user or your boss).

Part V: Appendices and Glossary

- Appendix A provides instructions for upgrading to NetWare 5.1 from earlier versions of NetWare.

- If you want to compare the features in NetWare 5.1 with earlier NetWare versions and with other networks in general, see Appendix B for the details on what's new and what the new features can do for you.

- Appendix C contains some of the useful NetWare 5.1 server SET commands, for those of you who would prefer the command-line route to setting server parameters.

- Appendix D shows you how to handle legacy DOS-based NetWare clients that do not use the new Novell Client32 software. Also included are a few of the DOS utilities still available in NetWare 5.1

- Appendix E gives you some background on using Macintoshes with NetWare 5.1. Novell has unbundled the Macintosh file and print services and the new support product being developed by Prosoft Engineering (www.prosofteng.com). You'll find updated information on the companion Web pages to this book on the Sybex Web site (www.sybex.com).

 NOTE You'll find more information about the companion Web pages to *Mastering NetWare 5.1* a little later.

- If you're interested in my sources, and perhaps would like to take a look at a few of them yourself, you'll find a reading list of the books I referred to for some of my information in Appendix F.

- Finally, at the back of the book is a glossary of the terms used in this book. When you're not sure what I mean by a particular word, turn to the glossary for a quick definition.

I don't expect you to read this book straight through, cover to cover. (In fact, if you did, I might worry about you a little bit.) You are expected to skip around and dip in and out of the book regularly.

Network management functions can now be performed using NetWare Administrator in Windows 95/98, Windows NT, and Windows 2000, or using the new Console-One Java-based management utility. Newly introduced, the NetWare Management Portal brings browsers into the management toolbox. Because I think most of you will prefer one or the other and will read just the information about your preferred utility, management explanations and procedures are sometimes repeated, once for each option. If you read both, you will get the same background information with minor variations, along with the precise procedure for the specific utility being discussed. Keep in mind that ConsoleOne is still new (two versions into development, but still new) and doesn't have all the features of the more mature NetWare Administrator program; some functions may only be done in NetWare Administrator.

Special Features in This Book

Throughout the book, you will find several interesting features. For your reading convenience, you'll find a topics list at the beginning of each chapter that lists the subjects featured within.

The In A Hurry instructions supply the basic steps of a procedure without the embellishments. They appear throughout the chapters, just under the section heading and before the discussion of that task. These steps are here for quick-and-easy reference, for those times when you want to check yourself before a procedure.

If the In A Hurry instructions give you everything you need, that's great. If you need more information about how or why to do the procedure (or maybe you're just interested), read the following text for the details. And, for extra convenience, all of the In A Hurry instructions are gathered in a printable quick reference available from the Sybex Web site (see the next section).

Another bonus you get with this book is extra networking wisdom, in the form of sidebars. Scattered throughout the book, you'll find special sections with advice about the politics of networking, some historical background on the topic at hand, and any other information I thought you might find interesting or helpful (or both).

And, as you may have grown used to if you read a lot of computer books, you'll see tips, warnings, and notes in the appropriate spots.

The Companion Web Pages

To provide you with useful extras and updated information, Sybex and I have created companion Web pages to go along with *Mastering NetWare 5.1*. Visit `www.sybex.com`, click Catalog, and search for this book to find its companion pages. There you'll find:

- The In A Hurry Quick Reference in `.PDF` format. We've gathered together all of the book's In A Hurry sidebars—which show you the basic steps of all important procedures described in the book—into a quick reference for your convenience. You can easily view and print these pages in Acrobat Reader. If you don't have Acrobat Reader, you can also download it from these Web pages.

- Updated information and the Macintosh support product developed by Prosoft Engineering (see Appendix E) when they become available.

- Links to sites where you'll find useful information on NetWare, hardware and software, training, and more.

Hardware and Software Used for This Book

Many companies provided hardware or software to help me with this book. The generosity of these companies goes past just the equipment; many provided help and information above and beyond the call of duty. Without their help, this book would have been nearly impossible.

Hardware

Here's a list and some brief descriptions of the equipment I used creating the examples for this book. This extensive list is a testament to the robust design of NetWare 5.1 and its ability to run on practically any PC.

- Compaq ProLiant 3000 tower server (called PROLIANT in the book), including:
  - Dual 600MHz Intel Pentium III XEON processors
  - 128MB RAM
  - Three 9.1MB hot-swappable disk drives
  - 24x CD-ROM drive
  - Compaq Net100 Fast Ethernet Adapter
- Compaq ProLiant Cluster Server for NetWare, including:
  - Four PL6400R/550MHz servers, each with four 2MB Pentium III XEON processors (four quad-processor servers)
  - One RA41000 Storage Enclosure (Storage Area Network)
  - Twenty 9.1GB Ultra2 drives (two drives per server and one populated array)
  - Four 64-bit/66MHz StorageWorks fibre channel Host Bus Adapter Kits (Persian)
  - One seven-port FC hub
  - One seven-port FC hub mounting kit
  - One 22U rack (9122)
  - One six-port KMM Switch box
- NetWinder OfficeServer from Rebel.com, including:
  - 275MHz StrongArm processor
  - 64MB of RAM
  - 6GB hard drive
  - Linux operating system
  - Complete office software package, including Web, e-mail, and DHCP servers

- Two Gateway2000 P5-120s, each with the following:
  - 120 MHz Pentium processor
  - 128MB RAM
  - 1.6GB hard disk
  - 8x CD-ROM drive
  - 3Com 3C509 10BaseT Ethernet network adapter

The Gateway2000 systems were used in all four versions of this book. They have all run various beta versions of all sorts of strange software products. None of the three systems have as much as hiccuped.

Gateway2000 was the primary server for most of the first version of this book. When it came time to test OS/2, this machine was reformatted and ran OS/2 Warp without a problem. The addition of NetWare Server for OS/2 still didn't strain the speed and performance of Gateway2000, even though we were technically exceeding the stated capabilities of the box. It just kept on running.

- Acer Altos 4500, with the following:
  - EISA bus
  - 33MHz 486 processor
  - 32MB RAM
  - 500MB SCSI hard disk
  - Thomas Conrad TC5043-T 10BaseT Ethernet network adapter
  - Adaptec 1542 SCSI controller
  - MDI SCSI Express 600CDX2, dual CD-ROM drive attached

This machine, dubbed ALTOS486, is a repeat performer: it first appeared in my book *Integrating UNIX and NetWare Networks* (Novell Press, 1993) as both a Unix host and NetWare server (running Altos NetWare for SCO). It performed for both books without a single blip or anomaly, no matter how much I abused the poor thing. Gone now but not forgotten, it still appears in a few old screenshots.

- A variety of home-built 386/33, 486/66, Pentium, and Pentium II machines with a variety of internal hardware:
  - Up to 128MB RAM
  - 340MB hard disks
  - Up to 4GB IDE disks
  - 3Com 3C509 10BaseT Ethernet network adapter

- Macintosh Performa 6400, with the following:
  - 96MB RAM
  - 1.4MB hard disk
  - CD-ROM
  - Internal 10BaseT Ethernet network adapter
- Other hardware:
  - LinkSys 24-port managed wiring concentrator from LinkSys Corporation

Software

The software I used includes the following packages:

- NetWare 5.1 from Novell, Inc.
- Netscape Navigator and Netscape Communicator for testing Web server connectivity and directory services access via LDAP.
- Collage Complete screen capture and catalog software from Inner Media, Inc.
- Windows 2000, Windows 98, Windows 95, Windows NT, and Windows 3.1, from Microsoft.
- Word 7 (for writing the book).

How to Contact the Author

Use this address to reach me electronically:

james@gaskin.com

Relax and have fun with NetWare and this book. This isn't a Harry Potter book, and you aren't an orphaned Wizard, but sometimes, if you work hard and threaten your servers with a big enough sledgehammer, magic happens.

PART I

Setting Up the Network

LEARN:

- *Planning your network before installation*

- *Installing NetWare 5.1*

- *Installing a NetWare 5.1 server*

- *Using Novell Directory Services*

- *Connecting PC clients to your network*

CHAPTER 1

Planning Your Network Before Installation

Every new network and installation must have a complete, detailed plan describing every particular. One customer once told me, "We plan monthly and revise daily." Although he said it as a joke, a lot of networking truth is in that statement. Since a network is a collection of people, things will change because people change. That's a guarantee.

But even though things will change, you need a plan to provide a network framework. Once you have a plan, you can deviate from the plan. If you don't have a plan, you will wander about, getting more lost every day.

We'll get to what you need to plan for your network before you install NetWare, but first, let's set the scene. Let's begin with a look at the various types of networks, so you'll know how yours fits into the overall picture.

Physical Network Types

The early days of NetWare were marked by a profusion of different types of network interface cards (NICs). Novell took an unusual approach to this proliferation: they supported every NIC they could find. Although the early 3Com and Corvus networks ran only on their own NICs, NetWare ran on all these, as well as on Western Digital's and SMC's and Datapoint's and Proteon's, and on and on.

I once counted (in 1985) about 35 versions of NetWare available for 35 different NICs. Now more than 200 NICs are available, but they break down neatly into Ethernet, legacy Token Ring, and Other. The "Other" space is adding new categories seemingly every full moon.

If you are mostly Unix, you are also almost completely Ethernet. Many people believe that "Open Systems" means Unix over Ethernet, but that's not exactly true. You will probably hear that from vendors of both Unix and Ethernet, however.

The majority of PC-only LANs are Ethernet as well. Ethernet was available before Token Ring, and the price of Ethernet cards has often been hundreds of dollars less than that of Token Ring cards. For these reasons, Ethernet got a big head start over Token Ring for NetWare networks. As more Token Ring vendors compete with IBM, the price difference between the two is declining. But Token Ring still costs more than Ethernet.

If you are mostly IBM, you are also mostly Token Ring, at least if you followed their party line. IBM introduced Token Ring for the PC in 1984 and has had great success. By making it easy to connect Token Ring networks to 3270 cluster controllers, mainframes, AS/400s, and the like, IBM has made Token Ring the technical equal, if not the sales equal, of Ethernet.

IBM now supports Ethernet in a major way and had effectively stopped making Token Ring interface cards by the end of 1999. Some Unix vendors support Token Ring, but that support will die with attrition. IBM's RS/6000 Unix system shipped from the factory with an Ethernet adapter from day one, a first for Big Blue. Sun, DEC, HP, and other manufacturers now have Token Ring boards available for virtually their entire product lines.

That doesn't mean the two systems are interchangeable—not by any means. In fact, technically and philosophically, the two systems are as different as they could be, especially now as Ethernet speeds up and Token Ring heads to the computer museum.

Ethernet Networks

Developed by Xerox, Intel, and DEC in 1976, Ethernet was created where? You got it, PARC (Palo Alto Research Center). Credit for Ethernet belongs to Robert Metcalfe and David Boggs. Starting at 3Mbps (megabits per second), Ethernet was soon bumped to 10Mbps. At the beginning, its main purpose was to connect host systems to printers to provide quicker PostScript graphics printing, much faster than the speeds possible with serial lines. Metcalfe later founded 3Com, one of the earliest providers of Ethernet interface cards. Boggs also stayed in the industry, working to implement Ethernet at Xerox. Later he joined Digital Equipment Corporation, where he worked on RISC computing.

As defined in the IEEE 802.3 standard documents, Ethernet is a nondeterministic network access control method. This means that the network is available at all times for every node. When a node has information ready to transmit, it listens to be sure no one else is using the network and then sends a packet. Hence, the private car on the highway analogy. Leave when you want, and travel fast when the highway is empty.

The technical jargon for this access method used by Ethernet is CSMA/CD, which stands for carrier sense multiple access/collision detect. This just means that a node listens to the net (carrier sense), that any node can get on at any time (multiple access), and that when a collision occurs, it will be detected. Collisions occur when two nodes send information at the same time and the two electrical signals get garbled. When a collision is detected, both stations wait a random number of microseconds before retransmitting. Users never know if a packet is being retransmitted; it happens randomly, and the retransmission scheme is so good that noticeable delays are avoided.

Ethernet nodes are strung together into an electrical bus, where each node connects to all other nodes. Visualize coax (coaxial cable), with the wire running from one node to the next, to the next, and so on. The improved (over coax) 10BaseT specification details how to run Ethernet over UTP (unshielded twisted-pair) cabling, like telephones use. This is still a bus topology electrically, even though every node must be connected to a central hub—as with Token Ring and its MSAUs (Multi-Station Access Units). Inside the hub, the electrical signals still act as if they were on good old (okay, brittle, capricious, and prone-to-failure) coax. Figure 1.1 shows Ethernet on coax.

FIGURE 1.1

Ethernet on coax

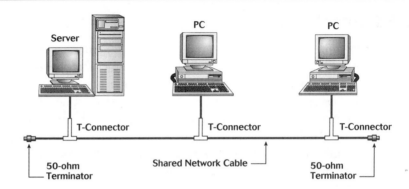

Ethernet packets carry anywhere between 46 and 1500 bytes of data. With routing and error-checking bits added, the smallest Ethernet packet is usually 64 bytes; the largest is 1518 bytes.

Every Ethernet interface card has a unique, 12-byte address assigned by the manufacturer. This address cannot be changed.

NOTE For more information on Ethernet, visit www.ots.utexas.edu/ethernet.

TIP After you install NetWare, you can see the Ethernet NIC address by typing **NLIST USER /A /B** at a DOS prompt. Under the NODE heading, you will see the 12-byte address (with leading zeros replaced by spaces) for every active connection. To obtain the server's NIC address(es), type **CONFIG**.

Switched Ethernet

Ethernet is a wonderful, high-performance technology until the network gets about 40 percent saturated with packets. With a high number of packets, more collisions occur, and more packets must be resent. The more you load standard Ethernet, the more problems you have.

Some people say that Ethernet doesn't really offer 10Mbps throughput, since you can't reach 10Mbps of data transfer by placing 20 systems, all spitting out 500Kbps, on the network. There are too many collisions and retransmissions, resulting in an actual throughput of 4- to 5Mbps in this situation. This is technically true, but I feel the test is rigged to show the poorest side of Ethernet.

If you have only two systems on Ethernet, one sending and one receiving, you get close to a full 10Mbps throughput. With send and receive packets from only two machines, few packet collisions will occur. Also, the shorter the physical network, the less chance of two packets corrupting each other. With a short network and two stations, I can get over 9Mbps throughput from off-the-shelf Ethernet.

Some smart people decided that the problem with Ethernet was not the CSMA/CD access method, but the constant collisions. If they could figure out how to offer each computer on the network a dedicated Ethernet network—Eureka! Enter switched Ethernet. *Switched Ethernet* is a system whereby an "intelligent" switching hub sends packets only to the port on the hub that is connected to the destination MAC address. It is then possible for different nodes to communicate independently without causing unnecessary collisions. Hence, each pair of computers in a conversation has in essence a dedicated channel for communications.

With an intelligent "matrix switch" bridge in the center of this picture, switched Ethernet can provide a dedicated network for high-performance systems such as servers. The earliest manufacturer of this equipment is Kalpana, so I copied that company's illustration (with permission), which is shown in Figure 1.2.

With switched Ethernet, shared network segments run at typical Ethernet speeds, but they are subject to overloading and multiple packet errors, just as with typical Ethernet. On the exclusive network segments used by the servers, there are virtually no collisions, so throughput approaches Ethernet's "theoretical maximum" of 10Mbps.

Devices such as the Kalpana EtherSwitch and those of Kalpana's now-numerous competitors may easily extend the life of Ethernet an extra decade. Prices on Ethernet switches are reasonable and prove to be an excellent value under the proper circumstances.

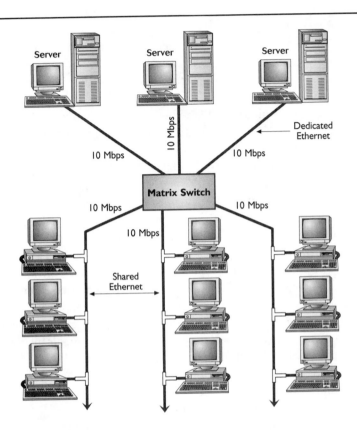

Fast Ethernet (100BaseT, 802.3u)

In the infant years of Ethernet, the speed was bumped from the original 3Mbps to 10Mbps. More recently, Ethernet was bumped again, this time to 100Mbps. This new technology, *Fast Ethernet*, can be called Ethernet because, other than speed, most of its specifications are the same as those for 10BaseT.

Fast Ethernet networks are built on distributed hubs that have dedicated lines to each network device so that control can be centered in the hubs. Fast Ethernet ignores the Ethernet standards for coax cable, so the shorter network cable requirements imposed by the higher speed aren't a problem. Like 10BaseT, Fast Ethernet is limited to about 100 meters (330 feet) between powered devices. A diameter of about 200 meters (660 feet) from a hub in a wiring closet supports more than 90 percent of desktops in corporate America today.

Two common Fast Ethernet types for copper cables are 100BaseTX and 100BaseT4. The big difference between 100BaseTX and 100BaseT4 is that the TX variation uses two of the four pairs of wires in standard UTP, whereas the T4 variety uses all four pairs of wires (hence the name). This was useful for sites with older, sub-Category 5 wiring installed, but it didn't have a great life span because those sites rarely had four pairs of wires available. Fiber fans can use 100BaseFX, linking devices with multimode fiber. Poor suckers stuck with shielded wire could use 100BaseST, if they could find adapters supporting that wire type.

Fast Ethernet continues to use the CSMA/CD mechanism for controlling network access. The MAC (Media Access Control) specifications of Ethernet describe everything in a speed-independent fashion. Only the interpacket gap is given in absolute time measurements; everything else is done on the basis of bits versus time. Nothing in the CSMA/CD specifications ties Ethernet to 10Mbps.

Fast Ethernet is currently a local transport option only. Many people consider it unsuitable for real-time uses such as video, since collisions will still be a factor. Without a guarantee of regularly scheduled packets, video over Fast Ethernet may jerk and waver on occasion. Switch vendors are working on priority schemes to guarantee certain (streaming) packets. However, most computer applications used today will happily scream along at 100Mbps. Of course, it only makes sense to put such speedy network connections on systems that can support them, such as high-speed buses inside servers and the like. All Fast Ethernet backbone products include a bridge to standard Ethernet. Add to all the benefits of the higher speed a similar cost to 10BaseT, and you have a great product to deploy today. The cost of the NICs is comparable (many cheap NICs now support both speeds), and hubs cost only a little more.

Token Ring Networks

For our purposes, Token Ring became a network option when IBM released the first 4Mbps Token Ring cards in 1984, along with its PC Network software. Token-passing technologies had been examined and somewhat standardized by that time. Some IBM systems used a type of Token Ring before 1984, but the draft documents for IEEE 802.5 mark the beginning of Token Ring for this discussion. IBM's Token Ring Standard was the basis for the IEEE and is almost completely interoperable with 802.5 systems.

For our further purposes, Token Ring died when IBM stopped making adapters at the end of 1999.

Token Ring is a deterministic network access control method. This means that each node has a certain time slot when it can access the network to transmit a packet of information. An electrical signal goes from one station to the next, and if nothing is appended to that signal, the network is available. No matter when a node has information, it must wait for an empty token to come by. Hence, the bus and bus stop analogy. Whether the highway is busy or not, you must wait for the next bus before starting your travels. If the highway is busy, however, you have a special bus lane that avoids congestion problems.

Packets on 4Mbps Token Ring can be as large as 4096 bytes. You should consider the packet size difference when considering Token Ring and Ethernet. On 16Mbps Token Ring, packets can be even larger, as much as approximately 18 kilobytes. The maximum size depends on how long a node may keep a token and the speed of the network.

Token Ring sends signals from one node to the nearest active upstream neighbor (NAUN). Each node must be connected to a central hub called a *multistation access unit* (MSAU, often shortened to MAU). Each MSAU has an input and output port (Ring In and Ring Out) for connection to other MSAUs. The electrical wire path is circular, with the signal going to each active node in sequence before returning to our original station, hence Token Ring. Figure 1.3 shows the Ring In (RI) and Ring Out (RO) connections.

FIGURE 1.3

Token Ring network with Ring In and Ring Out connections

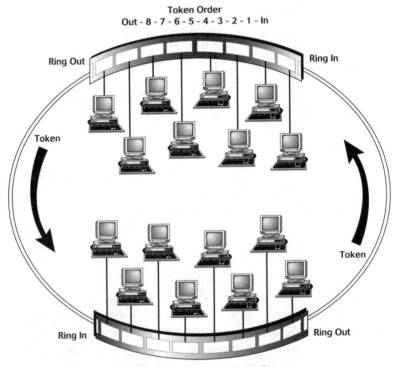

Like Ethernet, Token Ring interface cards are assigned a unique address when they are built. However, a feature called LAA (locally administered address) can override the built-in address with an address assigned when the NIC drivers are loaded. This address is sometimes used to list a location code for each Token Ring card, but the network administrator must then track all assigned numbers and make sure no duplicates are created.

 NOTE For more technical information on Token Ring, visit www.8025.org.

Token Ring and Ethernet: Practical Similarities

Although they have different speeds (10- or 100Mbps for Ethernet; 4- or 16Mbps for Token Ring), different topologies (bus for Ethernet; ring for Token Ring), and other technical differences, today's networks look amazingly similar. Both Token Ring and Ethernet installations often have powered intelligent hubs with UTP wire pairs running from the hub directly to a workstation.

Take a look at Figure 1.4 and tell me which technology, Ethernet or Token Ring, is being illustrated. Can't, can you? The practical installation of Token Ring and Ethernet over UTP cable is almost exactly the same.

Does this physical similarity somehow violate the "spirit" of the two networking protocols? Not at all. The situation merely acknowledges the influence of the market toward cleaner and neater solutions to common network problems.

Both Ethernet and Token Ring, in their traditional guise, have plenty of aggravations. But if you isolate each workstation on its own cable from the other workstations, limiting the effect a bad connection has on the network, you will have fewer headaches. Now when a cable or NIC goes bad, it doesn't take the entire network with it. If Joe kicks the wire loose under his desk, only Joe loses his network connection.

Management of the physical plant (fancy talk for wires and hubs) is easier with the scenario shown in Figure 1.4 as well. Each hub can be managed down to the individual port with the proper software. The ability to turn each hub port on or off from a remote location is old hat, as is the ability to monitor traffic levels by port.

As a general rule for both UTP Ethernet and Token Ring, the distance between powered devices can only be about 100 meters (330 feet). Powered devices include hubs, PCs, bridges, routers, matrix switches, and the like. If you run cables north and south from a hub, you have a network diameter of more than 180 meters (600 feet). Since most buildings are much smaller than that, placing hubs in the middle of the area works well.

FIGURE 1.4

Which is it—Token Ring or Ethernet?

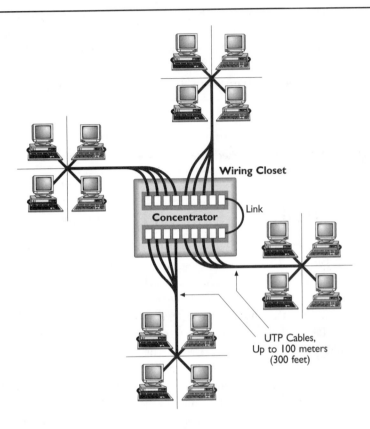

Hubs are connected with UTP, coax, or fiber-optic cable. If fiber-optic cable is used, the distance between hubs can be as much as 2 kilometers (more than a mile). Your mileage may vary; check with the manufacturer of your premise's wiring equipment, and stay within the manufacturer's guidelines if you want product support.

Other Physical Network Options

You can never be too rich, have too big a hard drive, or have too much network bandwidth. The eternal quest for speed means other, faster networks are vying for the space now controlled by Ethernet and Token Ring.

Users strongly prefer UTP cabling for all network connections. Only if the speed is tremendously better will users consider more expensive cable with shielding, more pairs inside the wire sheath, or the price jump to fiber optics.

On the flip side are those users who are dying to find an application, such as video and audio, that requires fiber-optic cabling all the way to the desktop. Vendors pushing technology such as full-motion video want users to have enough fiber-optic cable installed so that the software runs well.

Fiber-optic cable is popular because it is immune to electrical noise and is almost impossible to tap without being detected. All the new, fast technologies work on fiber-optic cabling first and then gradually learn how to suppress electrical noise well enough to run over coax, STP (shielded twisted-pair), or UTP cables. Another benefit of fiber-optic cable's electrical isolation is that it allows longer cable runs (up to 2 kilometers, or more than a mile) between hubs in a campus environment. The telephone companies run fiber-optic connections for dozens of miles between signal repeaters but use single-mode fiber-optic cable rather than the dual-mode used in LAN connections.

One important consideration when discussing the "networks of the future" is that they no longer are data-only networks. Previously, voice and video traffic was analog, and this traffic needed a transport mechanism that was different from that for digital data. Today, everything either is digital or it will be when upgraded; your LAN server may run your telephones before long. All the mess of the analog world (hundreds of shades of blue, increasing volume of a sound, and so on) has been replaced by the precision of digital transformation into ones and zeros. At least everything is digital once it gets into the computer system.

The successful networks of the future will deliver high bandwidth on a reliable basis. High availability leans toward small, fast packets of data so that transmissions can occur the instant they're needed. A delay of as little as 10 milliseconds introduces annoying echo into voice conversations and is unacceptable. For video to become an everyday part of the computer world, it must be clean and clear and deliver at least 24 complete new images per second, just like the television that so enthralls us.

100VG and AnyLAN

The competitors of Fast Ethernet wanted to fix what they considered the problem of Ethernet: the CSMA/CD network access method. Although both groups called themselves Fast Ethernet at one time or the other, cooler heads prevailed, and the CSMA/CD camp was declared Fast Ethernet. The other vendors, primarily IBM and HP, rechristened everything into AnyLAN (also known as 100VG[Voice Grade]), which now includes both Token Ring and 10BaseT Ethernet-style networks. This design has been standardized in IEEE 802.12.

Despite the purported advantages and a level of standardization, Fast Ethernet became 100BaseT and 802.3u, not 802.12. 100VG and AnyLAN are now candidates for the computer museum.

Wireless Networking

A fact of network troubleshooting: cables will kill you. They break, they get unplugged, they get cut, and they cause problems. So let's dump 'em!

Wireless networks have come a long way over the past few years. They will go even further to become a vital part of your network as wireless speeds increase.

The fastest growth in the wireless business is with laptops and PDAs (Personal Digital Assistants, such as Apple's Newton or 3Com's PalmPilot). PC Card (formerly PCMCIA) slots have become popular as a connection point to your LAN across a wireless link. Other common uses for wireless connections include hard-to-wire locations and buildings protected by historical designations that make modifications less desirable, if permissible at all.

As Figure 1.5 shows, you can connect wireless stations into your existing LAN in several ways. Since wireless components are two to six times the cost of their wire-bound cousins, it's rare to see a completely wireless network.

FIGURE 1.5

A variety of wireless networking options

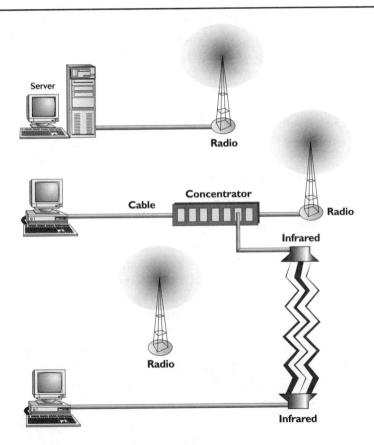

The wireless grouping also includes infrared products that use light pulses rather than radio waves. Most people assume that wireless means radio, but it only means "without wires."

Some of the improvements with wireless products include support for standard protocols such as TCP/IP and support for NetWare clients. Packet burst technology in NetWare 3.12 and higher greatly improves performance. Be aware, however, that the transmission speed for wireless products is only about 2Mbps for older products to approximately 10Mbps today. Plan your software distribution to put as much of the executable software as possible on the wireless client, to minimize user frustration.

Frequency hopping (technically called Spread Spectrum) technology splits the send and receive frequency (either 900MHz or 2.4GHz) into as many as 100 subchannels. Each transmission pair (the wireless network card and the access point to either the file server or LAN to wireless bridge) jumps around the subchannels in a predetermined pseudo-random pattern. This considerably reduces the chance of collisions and retransmissions and increases the difficulty of eavesdropping.

As networks go into the home and become consumer devices, wireless will be more and more important. Apple scored big with their AirPort wireless connections for the portable iBooks. All major vendors are working to make wireless the choice of home networkers everywhere, and even standard cell phones and pagers can now browse the Web.

FDDI

FDDI (Fiber Distributed Data Interface) is another method for reaching transmission speeds of 100Mbps, developed before Fast Ethernet got rolling. Products are available and in general distribution, although the prices remain high because of low volumes and the complexity of FDDI.

Based on Token Ring ideas, FDDI uses a timed token-passing access method. The physical layout is a dual ring, with the token rotating around the ring in the opposite direction. The dual counter-rotating rings provide redundancy if a cable is damaged, and the protocol includes quite a bit of management support.

Despite the *fiber* in the abbreviation, FDDI wasn't even a standard when companies started implementing FDDI over STP and UTP cabling. The specifications for UTP and STP support are now built into the protocol specification to enhance FDDI's use in workgroup situations. FDDI on UTP cabling is known as CDDI (Copper Distributed Data Interface), and over STP it is known as SDDI (Shielded Distributed Data Interface). CDDI and SDDI are also sometimes called TPDDA (Twisted-Pair Distributed Data Interface).

Systems can be attached to the dual counter-rotating ring cabling directly, or they can be connected by a single-attached cable to a concentrator. Again, this design helps lower the cost of connections and encourages smaller groups to participate. With a network length of 100 kilometers (yes, that's more than 60 miles), FDDI can connect as many as 1000 stations on a single ring.

FDDI has lost the PR war against Fast Ethernet on the low end and against ATM (Asynchronous Transfer Mode) on the high end. It is now doomed to niche applications.

ATM

ATM is one of the newest high-bandwidth network options. Developed by the telephone companies as much as the data networking industry, ATM is a radical departure from Token Ring and Ethernet-type networks.

Based on a matrix-switching technology similar to giant telephone exchanges and switched Ethernet, ATM uses 48-byte "cells" of data preceded by five bytes of routing information. These cells are fixed in length, and each cell's header contains all the information needed to route the cell to its destination. ATM fools the higher-level applications into believing they have a dedicated connection between nodes.

ATM speeds are flexible, and technically they can range between 1Mbps and 2.488Gbps (gigabits per second), with proposals to modify the upper limit to 10Gbps. The most common speeds mentioned for ATM are 155Mbps and 622Mbps. The numbers are related to the SONET (Synchronous Optical NETwork) standard for North America and the corresponding SDH (Synchronous Digital Hierarchy) international standard. These higher speeds above 155Mbps will likely be supported only in the long-haul network system.

Anything digital can be stuffed into ATM cells. Advocates of ATM predict an end-to-end system of nothing but ATM cells whizzing about. Realistically, however, the cost and complexity of such high-speed interfaces will be applied to backbones, WANs, and special applications. In fact, more recently, the ATM Forum has focused less on the desktop and is focusing attention on the network backbone instead.

Fiber-optic cable is the transmission medium of choice for ATM. However, ATM will also work on 10BaseT-quality UTP.

Routers will connect LANs to an ATM WAN framework, rather than having ATM come to the desktop. The overhead of ATM is high (one byte of overhead for every 10 bytes of data in a cell), and only at high speeds does ATM make good sense.

 NOTE For more information, visit www.atmforum.com.

A Short History of NetWare

NetWare was developed by Novell Data Systems in the late 1970s, in the hills of Utah. Using CP/M (Control Program for Microprocessors, the operating system of choice before the PC solidified DOS) and Unix as the guidelines, a multiuser microcomputer was being built. This was a typical time-sharing system, with dumb terminals attached by serial cables to a central box containing the CPU, disk, memory, and printer attachments.

This idea was not particularly original, and the graveyards are full of similar companies started about the same time. The difference between the living and the dead was each company's approach to the Hot New Item: the IBM PC. Novell embraced it, believing a system that utilized the intelligence of the end node would always be better than one using dumb terminals. (At least this is the story told around campfires.)

Another stroke of genius was the search for a "file" server, not a disk server. In the early 1980s, Novell's competitors offered a way to split a large hard disk (maybe 50 whole megabytes!) into 5- or 10MB partitions, one for each user and perhaps a common partition. Although this did help contain the capital budget for hardware, it did not allow any better communications between people, applications, or computers than the then-current rage, SneakerNet.

Once the folks at Novell moved to include the PC as a file server in all their future plans, they made another good decision. Rather than offering the NOS (Network Operating System) as a way to sell hardware, as did 3Com and Corvus, they concentrated on the NOS itself. They also made deals with every hardware vendor they could, helping to port NetWare to their hardware. This gave Novell a win-win situation whenever two hardware vendors were bidding on the same business. No matter which of them won, Novell won as well.

Taking the early lead with NetWare/86 (for the Intel 8088/8086 processors), Novell also started the concept of a remote file system for PC networking. Not just a file repository any more, the file server actually began to control and secure files. Security became stronger, and the file-access controls allowed Unix software vendors to port their applications to NetWare. This allowed true multiuser programs to help push the sales of NetWare into typically Unix installations, particularly accounting systems and databases.

By 1986, network hardware independence was a given for NetWare, to the point that the file server could support multiple types of interface cards at the same time. Even more amazing, packets could be routed between network segments without the user being involved.

Continued ▐▶

The push for more NetWare-aware applications was paying off as well. More than 2000 multiuser applications existed for the NOS.

With the advent of the PC AT, Novell focused most of its NOS development attention on the Intel family of processors. There had been an earlier PC file server, but the AT was such a hot machine that it outstripped the current workhorse, the Motorola 68000-powered S-Net server. As the S-Net server gradually waned, an S-100 bus system using nine-pin RS422 connectors (which look exactly like CGA or Token Ring connectors), the PC server era began. With the new support of the AT and Intel 80286 processor, NetWare officially became Advanced NetWare/286.

In 1988, NetWare for VMS made its appearance, and Portable NetWare (later called NetWare for Unix) appeared in early 1989. Macintoshes could be supported by NetWare version 2.15 (late 1988), filling the Mac server hole left by Apple.

In 1989, NetWare/386 (also known as version 3) was released; version 3.20 is currently shipping. The majority of current Novell users are connected to at least one NetWare 3.1x server. The rewriting done for NetWare 386 is what made NetWare for Unix and Processor Independent NetWare (PIN) possible. Modularity of the NOS was underway, continuing a trend Novell started back when the software engineers wrote support for more than one NIC in a server.

Released in early 1993, NetWare 4 continued the improvements to operating system modularity and introduced the object-oriented NDS (NetWare Directory Services, now renamed Novell Directory Services, as NDS is available on non-NetWare platforms). One network, one login, many servers.

With NetWare 4.10, the tools that network managers asked for, and more, were included. The network manager now had complete control over the NDS tree, able to prune, graft, split, and merge sections of the tree from the graphical NetWare Administrator program. With the Simplified and Custom Installation options, new networks were installed and running in about 10 minutes of hands-on work. Novell set the pricing to match NetWare 3.12, making smaller companies that avoided NetWare 4 because they didn't feel they needed NDS at a premium happy to try it on a "free" basis. Add the extra disk space provided by the file compression and other storage enhancements, and NetWare 4.10 actually cost less than a comparable NetWare 3.12 system.

NetWare 4.11 did three important things: made application support manageable with the NetWare Application Launcher (finally fixed and working well), further improved all the graphical management tools, and infused NetWare with TCP/IP and technology derived

Continued

CONTINUED

from the World Wide Web. Novell went so far as to coin a new name, IntranetWare, for the combination of NetWare 4.11, the Web Server, the new IPX/IP Gateway, and NetWare/IP. To emphasize the "Web-ization" of NetWare, Novell sold the bundle of all the intranet and Internet goodies for the same price as "basic" NetWare 4.11.

All of which brought us to NetWare 5 (the old, familiar NetWare name returned instead of IntranetWare). The biggest change was with TCP/IP support. Yes, Novell had been talking about it for a long time, and, yes, it had supported TCP/IP to varying degrees for years, but, finally, with version 5 we had true support for TCP/IP. In the past, all requests of the file server were submitted in IPX. True, there may have been a TCP/IP connection to the server, but inside each TCP/IP packet was an IPX packet (a technology called *tunneling*).

In NetWare 5, we also received a GUI (graphical user interface, pronounced "gooey") on the server, support for hot-swappable PCI (which allows components to be upgraded, exchanged, and so on without bringing down the server), and support for multiple processors. As if these features weren't enough, NetWare 5 supported memory protection and virtual memory and included a new format for storing files called Novell Storage Services (NSS). NSS allowed for larger volumes, more files per volume, less overhead per volume on the physical medium and in RAM, and faster recovery from errors when they do occur. The last major new features were ZENworks (which stands for Zero Effort Networking), which made managing the network and individual stations much easier, and Novell Distributed Print Services (NDPS), which greatly simplified the printing process.

Today, NetWare 5.1 turns a NetWare server into a complete e-commerce powerhouse, including all the server software necessary for full Web site building. Management through a browser interface is part of this package. People may claim that Windows NT or 2000 is a better application server than NetWare, but not if they honestly examine all the software inside the red box.

Planning for an Efficient File System

Your network users don't care about cabling, but they do care about their files. Let's look at some basic file system plans. There are all sorts of "systems" recommended for handling the directory structure of hard disks. Unfortunately, no one system works for everyone.

There are two main philosophies of network file structure. One is *user*-centric and revolves around user home directories and subdirectories for each application. The second is *application*-centric and provides group directories where users can share files. Figure 1.6 illustrates the differences between the two philosophies.

FIGURE 1.6

User-centric and application-centric file structures

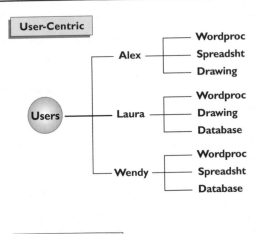

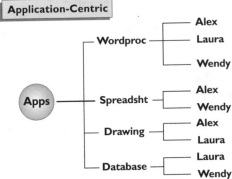

Circumstances, not network administrator whims, will dictate which system your network should follow. No matter which way you begin, you will wind up with a combination of both systems, because some software will force you into a new direction. Your only real choice is which system comes first.

Home Sweet Home Directory

One decision you must make when creating a user is whether to create a "home" directory for that user. The home directory is a private subdirectory on the server for each user. This is the user's private area, and access to this directory is typically limited to the owner. It is the place where the user will typically store all of his or her data.

Users like the home directory, because it's their own private space. They are free to create subdirectories underneath their home directory, just as on a personal hard drive. I encourage home directories, because it gives people a feeling of ownership on the network. If you can convince users to store their important information in their home directory, that information will be safely archived when you back up the server. With this backup, you can help them out when they accidentally type DEL *.* in the wrong place. You generally can't help them when they screw up their own hard drive.

No matter which file directory system you prefer, user-centric or application-centric, one piece of good advice comes directly from the Novell engineering group. Their strong recommendation is to keep applications and data in separate directories. Most administrators prefer the user-centric model because it makes backups easier and is much simpler to set up.

NetWare System Directories

During installation, NetWare creates 20 or more special directories. A few more specialized directories may also be installed that are for the server's use only. These are referred to as the *system directories*, and you should move the files in these directories only under the most compelling circumstances. Never move system directories, even the documentation files, on a whim. The documentation can be moved, but there's no reason to do so. It will be less confusing in the future if you leave them in their default locations.

If you're familiar with earlier versions of NetWare, you know most of these directories already. The big four directories, there since the early days of NetWare, are SYSTEM, LOGIN, MAIL, and PUBLIC. The hidden DELETED.SAV directory showed up in NetWare 3.1, along with the ETC directory if you installed any of the Unix connection software. When the manuals went electronic, separate directories (DOC and DOCVIEW, if you installed the electronic documentation) appeared to keep the information from being lost in a large PUBLIC directory. NetWare 5.*x* keeps the documentation in a directory called NOVDOCS instead of DOC, and the viewer is now any Java-enabled Web browser.

Here's a summary of the directories created during installation:

SYS:DELETED.SAV A hidden, system directory that holds deleted files from deleted directories before they're purged.

SYS:CDROM$$.SYS CD-ROM control files, including one 8.4MB file.

SYS:ETC Contains files to help you configure the server, especially for TCP/IP support and functionality with Unix.

SYS:LOGIN Includes programs that are necessary for users to log in to the network, such as LOGIN.EXE. The subdirectory is NLS (NetWare Language Support), containing subdirectories for login message files in the languages configured on the server.

SYS:MAIL   May or may not contain subdirectories or files. Bindery servers (those before version 4) included one subdirectory with a unique ID for each configured user. NetWare 4 and higher servers have this directory for compatibility only and are used only in Bindery emulation mode.

SYS:SYSTEM   Contains NetWare operating system files as well as NetWare utilities and programs for the administrator. SYSTEM also has an NLS subdirectory, among many others, containing subdirectories for message files.

SYS:PUBLIC   Contains NetWare utilities and programs for all network users. SYS:PUBLIC has special subdirectories for Windows 95 and Windows NT utilities, and the usual NLS subdirectory, containing the message files for utilities. Placing the client installation software in a subdirectory of PUBLIC makes automated installations of the client easy.

SYS:NOVDOCS   Contains electronic versions of the NetWare manuals in HTML format and installation files for Netscape, K server (the knowledge server, which is the searching and printing engine for the documentation), and Adobe Acrobat.

SYS:JAVA   Contains the code for the new server-based GUI. It functions like an extension to SYS:SYSTEM.

SYS:NDPS   Tools, utilities, and drivers to enable NDPS support.

SYS:NETBASIC and SYS:PERL   Files that enable NetBasic and Perl scripts on Web pages.

SYS:JAVASAVE   Small information files for Java on the server.

SYS:NI   Java files and control programs.

SYS:NOVONYX   More Java, Perl, and communication control files.

SYS:NSN   Novell Script for NetWare files and program examples.

SYS:ODBC   Open Data Base Connectivity files for expanded application programs on the server.

SYS:PVSW   Pervasive SQL Client installation and configuration files.

SYS:README   Various README.TXT files describing software on the system.

SYS:SENLM   Load files and the NLMs for Script Ease.

SYS:TMP   Storage place for odd files and an installation workspace.

SYS:UCS   Universal Component System, a bunch of developer tools.

NetWare takes precautions so the files in these directories aren't destroyed by accident. The SYSTEM, PUBLIC, and LOGIN directories are set to make it nearly impossible to delete or rename the files they contain (the files are set to Read-Only, Delete Inhibit, and Rename Inhibit). If someone does manage to erase a few of these files, the installation process can copy them back out to the server for you (see Chapter 3 for details). Individual files can be copied from the CD-ROM disk.

Companies with tape backup systems that can't quite cover the full disk contents often have an "operating system" tape with just the bare system files. Since the system files don't change except after updates, it's safe to not back them up every day.

Physical Space and Protection for Your Server

Personal computers today are built to run in an office environment. No special air-conditioning, raised floors, or expensive fire-dampening foam is needed. Even if you buy a superserver or cluster of servers all crammed into a 19-inch rack, an office environment is fine. So why should we make a big deal out of the physical space for your server?

Physical Security Considerations for Your Server

The biggest reason to lock up your server is security. The first part of any security program is to limit accessibility to what you are protecting. What people can't see, they don't try to steal or vandalize. Why do you think the police always tell you to lock packages in your car trunk, rather than leaving them in the back seat? Out of sight, out of their hands.

Mischief is possible from the file server. From a worst-case angle, a malcontent with access to your server can reformat the server hard disk without problem. Even if the malcontent happened to forget a DOS bootable disk, he or she could still cause trouble because the tools to format and partition the PC hard disk are included with the NetWare installation utilities. The NetWare partition on the disk can be erased even more quickly, which does just as much damage to your network. Either way, you have a long day ahead of you, and your tape backup procedures will be severely tested.

Separate from actual harmful intent to your server, accidents happen more often to equipment out in the open. If your server is on a table, the table will get knocked over. Someone will "borrow" the monitor or the keyboard. Someone will spill coffee directly into the chassis air holes. If bad things do happen, let them happen to someone else's computer; keep your server safe.

One customer had five servers clustered together, and they went down every evening. No diagnostics cleared up this mystery until someone spent the night in the office.

The cleaning crew unplugged one server for the vacuum cleaner (from the UPS), and the noise on the line sent the other servers into terminal weirdness.

Controlled environments are easier to make static-proof and generally safer for sensitive electronic equipment. Yes, this is contrary to the idea that the computers on every desk are safe, but they're really not. In the owner's manual of every computer is a warning about static electricity and how to avoid it. We all ignore that warning, with little consequence. However, since your file server may support dozens to hundreds of excitable people, crashing the server because of static buildup in the carpet will bring all those excitable people to an even higher level of agitation. Better to keep the server in a locked room with a tile floor than risk that one-in-a-million, server-killing, static discharge from the carpet and your wool sweater.

Any repair manual will go into detail about wearing static wrist-straps while working on a computer. It will give directions for ways to slowly bleed static away from your server (ground equipment through a one mega-ohm resistor). It also reminds us to never open the chassis on a system with the power turned on.

You wouldn't do anything so stupid, would you? Well, I did, once, by accident. Take it from me, unplugging an Ethernet board from a powered PC will fry the mother...board.

Power Conditioning and Protection for Your Server

While you have the server in a locked room with tile floors, run dedicated power lines to that room. It's safest to run every network device from these dedicated lines, but that may not be possible. Propose a dedicated line for every network printer, server, and wiring device to scare your boss into providing a dedicated circuit, at least for your server.

Ground the server (or all these dedicated circuits) to an earth ground if at all possible. Weird things happen with what's called a "floating ground," multiple grounds, and circuits that get cross-wired somehow. If your systems get flaky for no reason, an electrician may be a good person to call.

Always, always, always put the server on a UPS (Uninterruptible Power Supply). There is no excuse for not doing so. UPS systems are cheap today, and many are smart enough to gently shut down your server.

The system works like this: a cable from the UPS connects to a server serial port. When a power blackout or brownout activates the UPS, the server software will communicate with the UPS over the connecting cable. When the UPS battery is in danger of being discharged completely, leaving the server without power, the monitoring software will down the server so all files are closed properly.

Few sites need to worry about power dropping out for more than a few seconds. Many sites do need to worry about power that has malformed signals and constant fluctuations. A good UPS will take care of these problems as well.

All powered network devices, such as wiring concentrators, modems, communication servers, bridges, routers, and tape backup systems, should be on a UPS. Remember to plug the server console monitor into the UPS as well, unless you have memorized all the proper shutdown keystrokes. Figure 1.7 shows the setup for a properly protected server.

Repeat: there is no excuse for having a server without a UPS. None.

FIGURE 1.7

*The properly pro-
tected server*

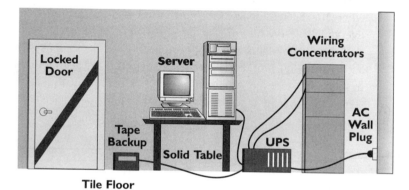

Proper Tape Backup Precautions for Your Server

Your file server must have a tape backup system. That's just as, if not more, important than a UPS system. You will use the tape backup system more than you ever imagined.

Many people believe that a tape is used to restore the entire file server disk contents after a catastrophic failure. That's not the most common use. You will constantly be replacing files for users, a single file or directory at a time. Users delete the wrong files for many reasons, but the result is the same: a needed file is gone.

Yes, NetWare tracks all deleted files, some for quite a long time, and you can sometimes reclaim them with a minimum of time and aggravation. Don't count on that. If it happens that way, count your blessings. Don't give up your tape backup system.

RAID (redundant array of inexpensive disks) systems are great and work well, but they are no replacement for tape backup systems. How does RAID help when a person types DEL *.* on drive G: instead of drive C:? Get that tape backup system working today.

Some people use long, involved tape-backup schedules and tape-rotation schemes. Some software relies on complicated file tracking along with tape-rotation schedules to keep current files on as few tapes as possible. These are all too complicated and make me nervous. I'm sure the software accurately tracks every file and when it was last changed and backed up to tape, but I don't want to use five tapes to restore one directory.

The single-best tape backup system is to back up your entire server disk every night. Period. Any day you need to reclaim a file that was deleted accidentally, you know exactly where that file is—on last night's tape. No logs are consulted to find where the deleted file went into the rotation, no "grandfather" rotations, nothing. Every night, every file.

Some file problems don't appear for quite awhile, such as garbled or deleted accounting files. You don't need these files until the year-end reporting, so you need to keep some tapes for a long, long time. I recommend 13 months of monthly tapes, six weeks of weekly tapes, and four weeks of daily tapes. See Figure 1.8 for a quick map of tapes moving through a daily, weekly, and monthly schedule.

FIGURE 1.8

Every night, every file backup and long-range safety system

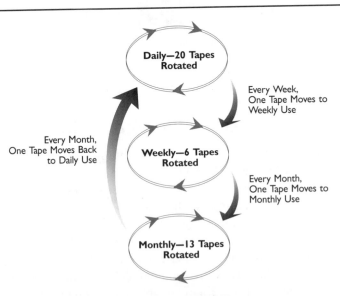

The plan is simple: move a daily tape from daily use to weekly use every week (say Friday or Monday). Move a weekly tape to monthly use every week (last Friday or Monday of the month, for instance). After 13 months, move a monthly tape back into the daily rotation. After a tape has been used 25 times, retire that tape to long-term storage. Don't press your luck and use tapes past their effective age.

Some newer tapes can now store as much as 50GB per tape, which means that you can often back up multiple servers on one tape. That's fine to do, and smarter tape-backup software now backs up multiple servers all at one time, interspersing files from each server along the tape. If you have more servers than even that system can handle, get a second or third tape-backup machine. You really are safer taping each file each night, and if you automate that procedure, people won't forget.

This system takes 40 tapes to start, and more as tapes get used 25 times and retired. Your boss may well complain about the cost of a large-capacity tape system and so many tapes. This is an excellent example of penny-wise and pound-foolish. Explain to your boss the true cost of re-creating files and the downtime costs for all people waiting for the information being re-created. Explain to your boss how this is the single cheapest insurance your company has. Explain to your boss that the majority of small companies go out of business if all their data records are lost through a catastrophe. If all this fails, divert a PC purchase order into a tape-backup system anyway. You absolutely must have one.

Some tapes must be kept off site. Which tapes you ship away depend on how inconvenient the off-site storage is. Last week's tape may be too soon, but last month's tape may be too late. If your building has a bank in the lower floor, quickly get a safety deposit box. If not, pick a date you can live with for tape delay and send some tapes somewhere safe. I guarantee that if your server burns, the box of backup tapes next to it will burn as well. I repeat: keep copies off site. You might also consider the use of CD-WORM (Write Once, Read Many) or CD-RW (Read/Write) drives rather than tape as their capacities grow and prices drop.

If your information is sensitive, remember that each tape is a copy of your company's secrets. There are services that use armored cars to pick up and deliver backup tapes on a regular schedule. Check your Yellow Pages.

The last, and perhaps most important, topic in this section is verification of the data on the tape. All the foregoing procedures, ideas, precautions, and so on are of little consequence if the data on the tape is not restorable. I once had a client faithfully make nightly backups for six months only to realize that the data was not restorable from the tape due to an incompatibility. I suggest that you try to restore a file or two periodically. Pick something that, if lost, is of little consequence. Something like the ATTACH.BAT file in SYS:LOGIN is easily re-created and is a good test of the tape's restorability.

Planning Cabling Installation

Your network is most likely already up and running to some degree. You probably have inherited the cabling with all its faults and quirks. If so, take this information and store it for when you add to your network.

Installing New Cabling

Stop right now. If you have a telecommunications department, go talk to those technicians before you do anything else. The people running the phones have been running cable since before you were born, and much of what they know through experience can help you. At best, you want to coordinate all cabling through one overseer; at worst, you should know when and where the phone people are running cable, and they should know the same about your plans.

Regardless of whether you are using Ethernet, Fast Ethernet, Token Ring, or something else, you probably are using UTP wiring. This means you have wiring concentrators within about 100 meters (330 feet) of the computers they serve. Therefore, you will become familiar with all the wiring closets in your building.

If you are not using UTP cabling, why not? You can run up to 1,000Mbps on UTP now. Don't delay.

Those still using coax Ethernet, please see a doctor. If your application is important enough to justify spending thousands of dollars on networking hardware and software, it's important enough to justify a few hundred more dollars for UTP cable and equipment (eight-port 10BaseT hubs are under $50 now and still dropping). Bad or poorly installed cable is the source of the majority of network problems (90 percent at fault if you ask vendors of new cable). Use Category 5 UTP at a minimum. Pay the extra few cents for Category 5 connectors.

New installations give you an opportunity not to be missed: an up-to-date map of which wires go which way. Your existing cabling is already a mass of confusion, and more wires are lost or mislabeled every week. New cable will become another mass of confusion if you don't plan ahead and push your cabling contractor to do a good job of documentation.

Before you decide on a cabling contractor, get blueprints of your office. These don't need to be construction blueprints exact down to the inch, but they would work. These blueprints must at least have office walls to scale and proper labeling. Provide a set of these drawings to each prospective cable contractor.

As part of the installation price, require four items:

- Digital testing of each link
- Labels on each wall plate, wiring concentrator port, and physical cable at *both* ends

- A map with "as-installed" wiring routes and distances to each wall plate
- A warranty

The "as-installed" drawings need not be works of art or exact engineering documents. You just need an idea of where wires are going and the length of each cable run. Placing the labels on the drawing helps you check the work during installation and makes troubleshooting easier for you over the coming years. Figure 1.9 is an example of an adequate wiring plan document. The more notes you put on the drawing during installation, the better chance you'll have of tracking down problems later on.

FIGURE 1.9

An acceptable wiring plan

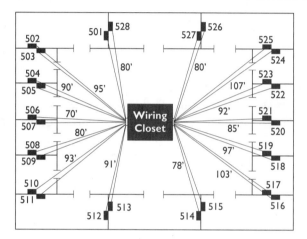

5th Floor
Two Connections in Every Office
Two Wire Exits from Wiring Closet
Four Pair Wires to Every Connector
Back-to-Back Wall Plate Wires
Pulled Together-Same Length
Distance-Tested with Digital Ethernet Tester

You must participate in the partnership between the cabling contractor and the customer (you). Decide what you want before the bidding starts. Get your boss to sign off on the requirements, and stress that changing plans during installation will cost more and create future problems. Decide on the time for the wiring installation: during work hours is cheaper but more disruptive.

If there is any question whether a location will need a network connection in the future, put one there. The big cost in cabling is the hardware and labor, not a few extra feet of wire. You'll never add extra network drops more cheaply than during installation.

Planning the Rest of Your Wiring Closets

Remember the discussion of dedicated power circuits? The wiring closets are good candidates for dedicated wiring because more and more networking hardware is going into the wiring closet.

If you can't get dedicated power, at least make sure there *is* power in the wiring closets. Telephone intermediate distribution frames (connections for bundles of phone wires to the floor and on to other floors) don't need power, so many wiring closets do not have AC wall outlets, especially the older ones. It's a bad feeling to hold a plug in one hand and suddenly realize there is no wall outlet.

At the least, you should add a small UPS to each wiring closet. Wiring concentrators take little power, but you should provide power backup for them in case the building's power supply drops or goes off. There's little advantage to having the server and your management workstation on standby power if the network cabling is dead.

Wiring closets have become good places to put servers, bridges, routers, communications gateways, and modems. The closets are usually locked, or locks can be added easily. Mechanical rooms like these closets are usually near the center of the building, making it easy to run cable to computers in all corners. Larger ones often have space for a rack to hold lots of equipment. Lacking that, the walls are lined in plywood to better attach telephone wiring connectors. That plywood is a good anchor for shelves to hold modems, bridges, routers, and even smaller PCs. One important note about your wiring closet: it needs to be kept cool. UPSs, hubs, modems, and so forth all generate heat. Enclosed areas need to have adequate cooling to live long, healthy lives. This can be achieved with special cooling systems or just a large AC vent in the room.

 TIP   Respect any telephone equipment and cabling in the wiring closets. Once again, working with the telecommunications people will make your life easier. Networking is hard enough without asking for extra headaches. Eliminate one headache for yourself by being on good terms with the folks in the telecom department.

Network Protocols Used by NetWare 5.1

A *protocol* is a formal description of message formats and the rules that two or more machines must follow to exchange those messages. Protocols are often compared to languages. If two people want to communicate, they must speak a common language. If one person speaks only English, and another speaks only Spanish, they can't talk;

they must either both speak a third language, such as French, one must be bilingual, or an interpreter must be present. In networking, we speak of protocols all the time, such as IPX/SPX (Internetwork Packet exchange/Sequenced Packet exchange), which is used by all versions of NetWare, and TCP/IP (Transmission Control Protocol/Internet Protocol).

Protocols can be complex, but all you need now is enough information to get started building your network. If you run a NetWare 5-only network or support access to the Internet or an intranet, or if you need to support Unix hosts, TCP/IP is the only protocol you will need. If your network involves previous versions of NetWare, you will need to understand IPX/SPX. Let's get started with a brief introduction to the OSI (Open Systems Interconnection) and DOD (Department of Defense) models, followed by a brief history of IPX/SPX and TCP/IP.

The OSI and DOD Models

The OSI model was created to provide a theoretical reference model to guide in the development of protocols and standards and to give us a framework for studying networking. As shown in Figure 1.10, this model comprises seven layers.

FIGURE 1.10

The OSI and DOD models

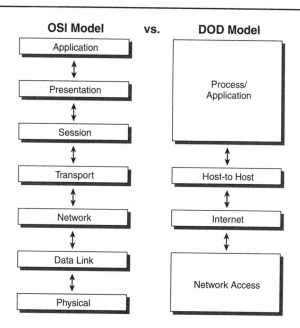

There is not enough space in this book to cover this model in detail; in fact, entire books have been written on the subject. However, a brief introduction to each layer and its functions will suffice for our purposes. From bottom to top the layers are:

Physical   This layer is responsible for the electrical and mechanical details of the actual cabling (or other media) and network card connectors. An example of a protocol at this level is Ethernet.

Data Link   This layer's responsibilities include creating packets (usually called *frames* at this layer) and controlling access to the physical media. Many common networking protocols span both the Data Link and the Physical layers, for example, Ethernet and Token Ring.

Network   This layer has two major functions—addressing and routing. *Addressing* refers to how a node is identified on the network (for example, an IP address in the TCP/IP protocol suite). *Routing* is the process of determining how a packet will be moved, or routed, through a network. Protocols at this layer include both IP and IPX.

Transport   This layer's functions are related to the transfer of the data. It may be reliable (meaning that the receiver will let the sender know if the transmission contains errors) or unreliable, also known as *best effort* (in other words, no guarantee of the data arriving the way it was sent; another layer must do this). The protocols at this layer may be connection oriented (in which case, the details of the transmission are worked out before transmission starts and are used for the entire transfer) or connectionless (in which case, each packet may use a different route and may get lost, out of sequence, and so on). Examples of protocols used here include TCP, UDP (User Datagram Protocol), and SPX.

Session   This layer creates a connection at the beginning, monitors a connection in the middle, and destroys a connection at the end. It also is responsible for security during the connection. Few protocols are purely Session-layer protocols, but a few examples of protocols that operate at this layer as a major part of their function are NetBIOS (Network Basic Input/Output System) and NetBEUI (NetBIOS Extended User Interface), both of which are associated with Microsoft networking.

Presentation   This layer is responsible for the format of the data. It is responsible for converting character formats (for example, EBCDIC [a character format on some mainframes] to and from ASCII), compressing and uncompressing data, and encrypting and decrypting information. There are few, if any, true Presentation-layer-only protocols; rather, they usually span the Application and Presentation (and sometimes Session) layers. An example of a protocol that has functionality at this level is FTP (File Transfer Protocol).

Application This layer provides the interface to the network for applications. This layer does not include actual end-user applications (such as Microsoft Excel or Corel WordPerfect), but rather provides network services to those applications. Examples of services provided here include e-mail, file transfer, mainframe connectivity, and network management. Examples of protocols at this level include SMTP (Simple Mail Transport Protocol) for e-mail, FTP (File Transfer Protocol) for file sharing, and HTTP (HyperText Transfer Protocol) for access to the World Wide Web.

Once you know what the layers are responsible for and on which layer or layers a protocol resides, you have a good idea what it does. We will refer to this model throughout this section.

The DOD Model

This model actually predates the OSI model and is the one used for the creation of the TCP/IP protocol suite. As you can see from Figure 1.10, this model correlates closely with the OSI model and, in many cases, more accurately reflects what protocols actually do. Since we have already reviewed the OSI model, we will not spend much time here other than to note the correlations between the layers.

The top layer is the Process/Application layer and encompasses the same functionally as the Application, Presentation, and Session layers in the OSI model. The Host-to-Host layer is equivalent to the Transport layer, and the Internet layer is similar to the Network layer. The bottom layer, the Network Access layer, is comparable to the Physical and Data Link layers.

Now that we have reviewed the models that networking is based on, let's look at where the protocols used in NetWare, namely IPX/SPX and TCP/IP, came from.

XNS: The Primordial Protocol

Once again, history takes us back to Xerox and PARC. The XNS (Xerox Network Services) protocol was developed along with Ethernet, which makes sense. What good is hardware without software?

Several assumptions were made when XNS was developed. First, every user in the network was expected to be using Ethernet. Since there was no other network transport media at PARC at the time, that was a safe bet. But multiple Ethernet networks were assumed to exist. That meant there must be intelligent devices to link networks. This was the beginning of the router industry. The first information about XNS was published in 1980, well before the IBM PC even appeared.

Continued ▐▶

CONTINUED

Routers are intelligent devices that send packets to the proper LAN segment based on Network-layer protocol-dependent addresses (such as IP or IPX) within the packet. Routers must read the packet up through the Network layer of the OSI model to make the proper routing decision.

Several major protocols were created for XNS, including IDP (Internet Datagram Protocol), which is a Network-layer protocol, and RIP (Routing Information Protocol), which maintains a list of reachable networks, calculates the difficulty in reaching a specific requested network, and is also a Network-layer protocol. There is also the RPC (Remote Procedure Call) protocol, which provides a framework for client/server programming across a network and operates at the Application and Presentation layers, and the SPP (Sequenced Packet Protocol) protocol, which is a Transport-layer protocol.

As you can see from the description above, XNS was a complete network system from the beginning. The designers of XNS made sure that support for X.25 packet networks, leased telephone lines, and dial-up lines were included in the specifications. At one time, Xerox had the largest worldwide corporate network, and XNS was the only protocol in the entire system.

In biblical terms, XNS begat IPX/SPX. Simply put, Novell's IPX is virtually identical to IDP (Internet Datagram Protocol).

IPX/SPX and NCP

IPX handles all the addressing, routing, and switching of packets to their destinations. Each IPX datagram contains all the information needed for routing to its target. This avoids invoking virtual connections with the server, sapping server resources. Instead, IPX packets are not guaranteed.

 NOTE When packets contain all the information necessary for their delivery, they are often called *datagrams*, although some people use the terms *packet* and *datagram* interchangeably.

SPX packets are guaranteed. The protocol sets up a direct connection between the two stations involved. Based on SPP (Sequenced Packet Protocol), SPX guarantees a connection by having the destination node send an acknowledgment for received packets. If no acknowledgment comes within a certain time, the packet is re-sent.

Too many missed packets, and SPX informs the user. SPX uses IPX's network I.401 capabilities for routing.

NCP (NetWare Core Protocol) is a higher-layer protocol, encompassing the Session through the Application layers of the OSI model, that is proprietary to Novell. It is used for file access, print sharing, and application program support. For the casual user, NCP *is* NetWare. NCP runs over IPX or NCP *and* SPX, depending on the application. NCP can also be used with TCP/IP, notably for the first time in NetWare 5. (More on TCP/IP shortly.) IPX functions include:

- Create service connection
- Request (to server)
- Reply (from server)
- Destroy service connection
- Request being considered response (from server)

Some people, especially TCP/IP people, complain about IPX/SPX and its problems. While no one says IPX/SPX is the world's ultimate protocol, be sure to complain about the right things.

First, the constant (every minute from every server) broadcasts are not due to IPX/SPX but to RIP (Routing Information Protocol) and SAP (Service Advertising Protocol). RIP requires broadcasts to figure out routing but is being replaced with NLSP (NetWare Link State Protocol), which should dramatically reduce the number of broadcasts. SAP is required to allow NetWare clients to know what services are available on the network. TCP/IP handles this notification differently, which reduces broadcasts but increases setup and management complexity. NetWare has a new protocol for use with TCP/IP that is essentially SLP (Service Location Protocol), which functions very much like SAP.

Second, the "ping-pong" packet trait is not due to IPX, but to NCP's DOS file service. Often called the "ack-ack" syndrome, NCP requests acknowledgment from receiving stations when packets are sent. This has roots in the fact that IPX is a non-guaranteed transport, meaning a higher-level protocol (such as NCP) must check that all packets are present and accounted for. In addition, performance over a LAN is fast, and the "ping-pong" packets are not noticeable. When used over slow WAN links, this asynchronous packet performance does become a problem. That's why we now have Packet Burst Protocol.

In Figure 1.11, there are a couple of new things. ODI (Open Data-Link Interface) was released in 1989 to separate the NIC device drivers from the software that connects the workstation to the network. By adding a layer of abstraction with ODI, one NIC can now support multiple protocols concurrently.

How NetWare protocols stack up on a PC workstation

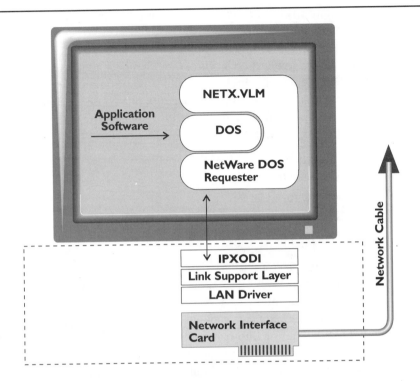

In the old days, each NIC needed a specific program generated for it for each configuration. This was called "genning a shell," as in generating a shell program. If you changed something on the NIC, such as the IRQ (interrupt request), a new shell had to be generated. ODI did away with all this. More details will follow in Chapter 5, when we talk about connecting clients to your network. For now, here's a quick summary of how ODI fits together, for your legacy connections:

LSL (Link Support Layer)   Interface layer between the device driver and the protocol stack(s). Any ODI LAN driver can communicate with any ODI protocol stack through the LSL.

MLID (Multiple Link Interface Driver)   Handles sending and receiving packets to and from the network. In older versions of NetWare clients, it included the MSM, TSM, and HSM described below. The MLID will be named 3C5x9.COM or NE2000.COM or the like. With the newer Client32 architectures, they are separated into the following three separate components:

MSM (Media Support Module)   Interfaces ODI HSMs to the LSL and to the operating system.

TSM (Topology-Specific Module)   Controls operations specific to a particular network media type, such as Ethernet.

HSM (Hardware-Specific Module)   Program normally provided by the network interface card vendor that contains details particular to that network card, such as initialization routines, reset, shutdown, packet reception, timeout detection, and multicast addressing. In the Client32 architecture, they have a .LAN extension, with names such as 3C5x9.LAN.

IPX, the standard protocol included with NetWare from the earliest versions, provides enormous benefits during installation and setup. NetWare handles the entire client addressing and routing information, unlike other protocols that require tables of address information to be created during installation. With IPX, the unique serial number on each NIC, in conjunction with the network number assigned during server installation, is used for identification.

If your network contains older versions of NetWare or if you want the simplicity offered by IPX, you will spend less than two minutes during installation dealing with protocol issues. That's the beauty of IPX: it doesn't have the installation and management overhead of other protocols.

TCP/IP

Speaking of other protocols, TCP/IP has now received the U.S. government's blessing as an "open protocol for open systems." Officially, as of mid-1994, TCP/IP replaced the OSI (Open Systems Interconnection) protocols as the acceptable protocol (without special exemptions) on new government systems. How did TCP/IP get to this point?

First, it was developed to be a protocol for packet-switching WANs. In fact, it was developed to also support packet radio and packet satellite networks, two other media with shared communication channels and a penchant for lost packets.

Second, TCP/IP was under development at PARC. Robert Metcalfe and David Boggs were busy adding TCP/IP support to their newfangled Ethernet. David Farber at the University of California, Irvine, was also working on TCP/IP, but on a ring concept network.

Third, the government was involved at the beginning. The original push for developing TCP/IP was from DARPA (U.S. Defense Advanced Research Projects Agency) in 1973. The ARPAnet (Advanced Research Projects Agency Network) had been started in 1969, and in October 1972 it was publicly demonstrated.

This is all fine, but those events took place well over 20 years ago. What inside the development process gave TCP/IP its tremendous staying power in an industry known for having a short attention span?

Since the developers knew that packets would be lost across the early networks, TCP/IP was split into TCP (Transmission Control Protocol) and IP (Internet Protocol), and UDP (User Datagram Protocol) was added. IP is a Network-layer protocol in the OSI reference model (or the Internet layer in the DOD model), responsible for inter-network considerations. The Network Access level takes care of the actual Ethernet, X.25, or other physical transport details. TCP, a Transport (OSI) or Host-to-Host (DOD) layer protocol, provides sequenced, guaranteed transmission by relying on IP. UDP provides nonsequenced, transaction-like applications, such as packet voice.

 NOTE The Internet made its appearance in 1973 in the guise of these early WAN experiments. The term *internet* will be used when speaking of any collection of networks that may or may not use official Internet standards. Internet, with a capital letter, will refer to the officially sanctioned network of networks.

Figure 1.12 shows the TCP/IP protocol suite and how it fits into the OSI reference model. Table 1.1 lists some of the major components of the TCP/IP protocol suite (there are literally hundreds, if not thousands, of protocols in the suite).

FIGURE 1.12

The TCP/IP protocol suite referenced with the OSI and DOD models

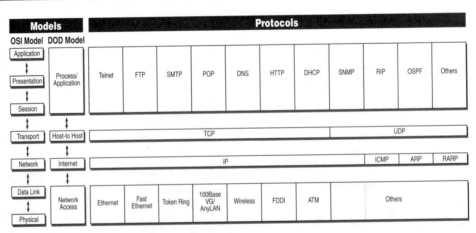

TCP/IP has the broadest support of any protocol today or tomorrow. If you say "open systems," many people hear "TCP/IP."

TABLE 1.1: COMPONENTS OF THE TCP/IP PROTOCOL SUITE

Component	Function
IP (Internet Protocol)	Unreliable internetwork routing of datagrams.
ICMP (Internet Control Message Protocol)	Reports errors and responds to queries about remote conditions. This is an integral part of IP.
ARP (Address Resolution Protocol)	Maps Internet (IP) address to physical network (MAC) address.
RARP (Reverse Address Resolution Protocol)	Maps physical network address to Internet address.
TCP (Transmission Control Protocol)	Provides reliable, connection-oriented delivery between clients; full-duplex connections; runs over IP.
UDP (User Datagram Protocol)	Provides unreliable, connectionless packet delivery service between clients over IP.
Telnet	Provides remote terminal connection services.
FTP (File Transfer Protocol)	File transfer protocol between hosts; supports ASCII, binary, and EBCDIC file formats.
SMTP (Simple Mail Transfer Protocol)	Rules for exchanging ASCII e-mail between different systems; can be extended with MIME for binary, video, and other files as well.
POP (Post Office Protocol)	Protocol for getting e-mail from an e-mail server.
RIP (Routing Information Protocol)	Protocol that keeps a list of reachable networks for Internet packets. This protocol is distinct from, but analogous to, IPX's RIP.
DNS (Domain Name System)	Hierarchical naming scheme, with domain sub-names separated by periods, for example, www.sybex.com.
OSPF (Open Shortest Path First)	A newer, Link State routing protocol, replacing RIP.
HTTP (HyperText Transfer Protocol)	Protocol used in accessing the World Wide Web (WWW).
DHCP (Dynamic Host Configuration Protocol)	A protocol to automatically assign IP addresses, DNS information, and so on.
SNMP (Simple Network Management Protocol)	Method for managing network devices and getting information (including warning or error messages, called traps) remotely.

Setting Up the Network

DOS and Windows versions of TCP/IP used to be memory-hungry and slow, but the situation today is greatly improved. Small and fast TCP/IP software packages for DOS and Windows are available from more than a dozen vendors, besides being included in Windows 95, 98, NT, and Win2000.

Many companies have worldwide TCP/IP networks, including systems from mainframes down to tiny handhelds. SNA (Systems Network Architecture) users by the boatload are busy moving to a combination TCP/IP and SNA network or are replacing SNA completely. There is nothing in computing today that can't be accomplished across TCP/IP, and the situation is constantly improving.

A Note of Appreciation

Great thinkers and developers stand on the shoulders of previous generations. The compression of technical development time is so intense today that great thinkers stand on the shoulders of other great thinkers in the next cubicle.

The advancements in computer networking are hard to see, because we're part of them. Think of the time from the first powered airplane flight (1903) to the first moon landing (1969). Many noted that this enormous technological leap occurred in one lifetime. Technology has never moved so far so fast.

Following that reasoning, the development of computer networking has happened during the working life of people you and I can meet at conventions. Many of the people who drafted the plans to start the Internet are still working and pushing new technological boundaries today.

Imagine Wilbur and Orville Wright developing their first airplane from bicycle parts and pushing technology the same way. Not only would Wilbur and Orville still be working, they would be part of the design team for the space station.

Does this mean networking (and flight) is as advanced as it can be? Of course not. We're on the brink of enormous leaps in technology, and the speed of new developments is increasing. Our children will pity us as technological cave people, as their children will pity them.

Take a moment to silently nod in appreciation for all the hard work that has gone before. Some of the smartest people in the world have pushed us this far, and they are still pushing. They deserve some appreciation.

CHAPTER 2

Preparing Your NetWare 5.1 Server Machine

FEATURING:

I nstalling NetWare for the first time may give you pause. If you have never installed NetWare before, your anxiety about a new procedure is compounded by all your questions about NetWare particulars. If you have installed NetWare before, you may be concerned because NetWare 5.1 doesn't look much like NetWare 4.x or any other earlier version.

Although it may give you little comfort now, NetWare 5.1 is the easiest version of NetWare to install in the history of the product. It's now shipped on a nice, shiny set of CD-ROMs. The older versions of NetWare took a bushel basket of floppy disks and constant attention to feed those same disks in mind-numbing repetition. Mistype or forget something with earlier NetWare? Start all over, and feed those flippin' floppies in one after another.

The new GUI (Graphical User Interface) installation screens are pretty but not necessarily faster or better than the earlier text screens. Be forewarned, if you're used to NetWare 3.x, that you NEED a mouse for NetWare 5.1 installation.

The automated installation process has been improved over NetWare 4.x, especially if you're using a server equipped with Plug-and-Play capabilities. The installation routines more often understand the drivers for disks and network adapters, meaning that the installer (that's you) doesn't need to re-enter driver information and parameters.

Do you have a dual-processor server? When Novell introduced SMP (Symmetrical Multi-Processor) support, the modified NetWare operating systems were licensed to the manufacturers. This allowed vendors to make minor modifications to support their particular hardware. NetWare 5.1 incorporates these improvements, so the software detects multiple processors during installation and adds the proper code.

You'll see the other improvements in NetWare 5.1 described in the appropriate places here and there throughout the book. In many cases, however, what went for version 4.1x will also apply to version 5.1.

 NOTE You don't want to run a mixed network of 5.x and 3.x or 4.1x servers if you can help it, although, of course, this is fully supported (with NDS 8). See the online documentation for issues, procedures, and so on.

New and Improved NetWare Installation

The biggest advantages of NetWare 5.1 installation are:

- With the CD-ROM, you spend only a few minutes at the computer; the installation program automatically does the rest.
- You can easily correct all installation mistakes.

- You can easily make any changes you think of during or immediately after installation.

- The installation program is GUI-based, so you have point-and-click access to most options.

Let's take each item and squelch any remaining nervousness on your part. First, since there are no floppies to feed during installation, you can actually install a new server with only a few minutes of your time spent at the keyboard. It will probably take you longer, at least the first time, because you will read all the help screens and peruse every word on each screen. If you are a typical NetWare administrator, you also won't fill out the worksheets completely, so you'll need to look up some information. That will take additional time.

Later installations will take less time, because you will know the answers to the questions that appear during installation. Let me also offer hope for those of you installing from slow (less than 8x) CD-ROMs: you can easily install the second (and third, fourth, and so on) NetWare 5 server in your network by copying information from the first server. If you have a slow CD-ROM, you will need it only twice: once to install the first system, and the second time to load all the installation files onto the server hard disk for easy future installations.

Second, any time you make a mistake during installation, you can correct that mistake with little trouble. The installation program offers you several chances to stop and start all over or to go back. You have opportunities at every section to go back and redo any piece of that section.

Third, you can run a separate installation program in text mode (NWCONFIG.NLM) at any time to fix any mistake or installation confusion. With the new graphical NetWare administration tools, you can easily correct common installation mistakes, such as typos (there is no spelling checker in the installation program).

Of course, the "few-minute install" works best when you take the approach of the cooking shows on TV. You should have all the necessary ingredients (information) at hand, so fill out those worksheets or at least gather all the specific details needed about your network. You should have a working oven (server) all preheated and ready to go (properly configured with the correct disk drives and NICs). And, you should know the recipe, which means that you should read over the entire installation process once or twice to understand where you're heading with each step.

Okay, if you don't plan on filling out the worksheets, keep a pad and pencil beside the server during installation. Every time you must make a choice and every time the installation program provides a randomly generated number for you, write it down. Save that paper, because you will forget the information. With luck, you won't need to refer to this information, or at least you won't lose the paper.

Requirements for NetWare Servers

NetWare 5.1 operates on a wider range of server hardware and network peripherals than most other network operating systems. According to Novell, your server must meet these minimum requirements:

- A PC or PC-compatible with a Pentium or better processor
- 128MB of RAM (Novell recommends more.)
- 256MB of RAM for servers running WebSphere Application Server (512MB recommended)
- 750MB hard disk space free (and unpartitioned) for standard NetWare
- 2GB of space on a volume for NetWare and WebSphere Application Server (SYS: can be only 400MB, with other NetWare products put on another volume.)
- One (or more) network board(s) connected to a functioning network cabling system (NE2000, 3Com, Intel, SMC, and so on)
- 50MB DOS partition
- A CD-ROM drive that can read ISO 9660 formatted CD-ROM disks (if you're installing from the CD-ROM and not from another server)
- 3.5-inch disk drive
- VGA monitor and video board (SVGA recommended)
- Keyboard
- Serial or PS/2 mouse (optional, but *highly* desirable, at least for the installation)

Technically, these elements will make a server. Practically, this server will be worthless for supporting many users. Your choice for server components should read like this:

Option	Recommendation
CPU	Intel Pentium II, III, or XEON
RAM	256MB minimum, more is much better.
Hard disk	2GB minimum, more is better. In all but the smallest environments, I would start with at least a 10GB hard disk.
NIC	PCI bus-mastering 100BaseT NIC
CD-ROM	24x speed CD-ROM drive minimum
Monitor	VGA card and cheap monitor (unless you plan on spending much time at the server)

Each item on the list is necessary, but choosing some items demands more critical decision-making skills than others. The items requiring some soul-searching depend on your needs for this server. Our goal in this section is to discern which options best fit your situation for each server you will install.

If your company is like most companies, there is a constant struggle between what is wanted and what is affordable. Every network administrator would love to have nothing but superservers with more RAM and hard disk space than the company's mainframe. However, budget constraints exist in every situation. You may well talk your boss into a superserver, but you must justify that expenditure.

The only way to justify expenditures for most bosses is to give clear pictures of the options, with the good and bad points of each option. Normally, the equation is simple: here are the good points, here are the bad points (usually price tag or required resources). Then you and your boss argue about the list of good/bad points for each portion of the server until some compromise is reached.

A question for you and your boss: What are the three most important functions for your planned server? The answers from you and your boss may be different. If so, problems will be your constant companion. Only when you and your boss are in agreement regarding the network will you both be happy with the choices you must make.

Living with Your Networking Decisions

The question, What are the three most important functions of x? will reappear in various places throughout this book. If you are uncomfortable making decisions, I have one bit of advice: get over it. Business management, and especially networking, is nothing but decisions regarding the conflict between goals and constraints.

Let me help take the fear out of decisions: every single one you make will be wrong next year. By this, I mean that technology will change, and better options will appear. If you make the same decision next year as you made yesterday, you will be overlooking better options. Better equipment will be available, prices will be lower, or both, but things will change.

Don't beat yourself up over decisions made in the past that didn't work out as well as hoped. No one can blame you if you had the right priorities at the time you made that decision. The only action you can be blamed for is not revisiting poor decisions as time makes more options available.

Choosing the Server's CPU

As with all your server decisions, if money is no problem, select the high-end option each time. If money is an issue, as it normally is, you might be interested in a ranking of which server functions require the most CPU power. Here is a list of common server uses, ranging from supporting the clients with occasional file access to running large database applications (involving NLMs, or NetWare Loadable Modules) directly on the server:

Section 1: Low-End Requirements (1 point each)

- Standard client-support file service, with clients having local hard drives
- File service for clients without local hard drives
- File service for PC clients who run Windows locally but store applications on the server

Section 2: Mid-Level Requirements (2 points each)

- Shared database application files on the server with clients doing all the processing
- Communications gateway NLM applications on the server
- Shared CD-ROM support on the server
- E-mail processing functions execute on the server

Section 3: High-End Requirements (4 points each)

- WAN connections made from modems attached directly to the server
- Network and client management software NLMs
- Several NLM database application programs on the server
- One busy database application with heavy activity on the server

You can use this list to help you decide which type of CPU your server needs. Check each function that applies. Add up the number of points for all the questions (combine all groups into one total).

- If your total is less than 5, the low-end server (a Pentium 90) will do fine.
- If your total is between 6 and 11, go with the mid-range option (a mid-range Pentium [133–200]).
- If your total is more than 12, get the high-end system (a high-end Pentium [233 or better or Pentium II, preferably with MMX]).

Actually, if your point total is close to the maximum in the first two categories, you should go with the higher-end server because it's cheaper than upgrading.

If you're not comfortable with a lower-powered processor because of the server workload today or what may happen tomorrow, buy more horsepower. Your server demands will only increase, not decrease. Better to have too much horsepower than not enough.

Figuring the Needed RAM (Buy More)

Novell has a complicated method for calculating the necessary server RAM and a "short-form" version of the same calculation. The short version is:

Server Function	RAM Recommended
Operating system, disk, and LAN drivers	128MB
Running Java applications (like ConsoleOne); acting as a database server or Web server	256MB each

Personally, I say you should buy all you can afford. NetWare 5.1 can support up to 4GB of RAM and 32TB (terabytes) of hard disk space with traditional NetWare volumes, plus up to 255 NSS volumes at a maximum size of 8TB each, for a total of 2072TB (or 2 pentabytes [PB]) in hard drive space.

NetWare 5.1 makes this requirement even stronger. Although the base operating system has grown, the extra goodies (such as the Web Server, WebSphere Application Server, and Oracle 8i) will tempt many into loading a lot more than the basic system. When you try that, your realistic minimum memory balloons past 128MB to 384MB or more.

Choosing the Hard Disk (Buy a Bigger One)

No one complains about too much storage space, whether we speak of closets, car trunks, or server hard disks. My friend David Strom has this recommendation for beginning NetWare administrators: "Buy twice as much disk space as you think you'll ever need. Better yet, buy three times as much."

Today, three types of disk interfaces are suggested for servers:

IDE (Integrated Drive Electronics)   A common, fast, low-cost controller that supports two drives per controller. Minimal, barely acceptable except for small workgroups.

IDE Ultra DMA   33MB worth of data transfer per second.

SCSI (Small Computer System Interface)   A parallel adapter interface running 4Mbps or more, seven devices per SCSI adapter, data transfer path up to 32 bits wide. New variations include Fast and Wide SCSI, SCSI-2, and SCSI-3 up to Ultra2 SCSI-3 with a data transfer rate up to 80MB per second. Popular for tape backup and CD-ROM drive support as well. This is the recommended interface for servers.

Let's talk about IDE and SCSI, along with RAID systems. Before we begin, however, just a quick note for those familiar with previous versions of NetWare. The big change in hard drive drivers is the end of support for .DSK-type drivers. NetWare 4 introduced the NetWare Peripheral Architecture (NPA or sometimes NWPA) but allowed both types of drivers. NetWare 5.*x* supports only NPA-type drivers. NPA drivers are split into two parts, .HAM and .CDM files. The .HAM portion interfaces with the controller directly, and the .CDM controls the devices on that controller, such as hard drives and CD-ROMs. Be careful when upgrading to ensure that your controller cards have NPA drivers available.

IDE Disk Controllers and Drives

If you buy a PC with an installed hard disk, chances are it will be an IDE system. IDE controllers are usually located directly on the motherboard. Early versions of IDE controllers were limited to 525MB, but now drives up to many GB are supported.

NetWare 5.1 support of IDE controllers is strong. The standard IDEATA.HAM driver included in the installation process works with almost all brands of IDE controllers. With the larger capacity available today, IDE drives are now decent choices for servers. PCI IDE controllers now support 32-bit access, making disk performance even better. Novell also includes .CDM files for hard drives (IDEHD.CDM) and CD-ROMs (IDECD.CDM).

SCSI Disk Interfaces and Drives

Another technology "borrowed" from the world of Unix hardware, SCSI adapters and drives are the choice for serious servers and large server disks. Technically, SCSI (pronounced "scuzzy") is an ANSI standard that details an I/O bus capable of supporting as many as seven devices.

The old-style SCSI adapters use a short, 50-pin connecting cable. The newer, faster SCSIs use a high-density 68-pin cable. IDE drives, in comparison, use a 40-pin cable. Since SCSI devices are "chained" together, a terminator must be used on the last device to anchor the chain. SCSI is a popular adapter for CD-ROM drive connections. This popularity helps make SCSI devices more affordable.

The high-performance needs of Unix workstations and servers are advancing the performance of SCSI devices every day. SCSI-2, Fast SCSI, Wide SCSI, Fast and Wide SCSI, and Ultra2 SCSI-3 are improvements being advanced by various parties. The world of SCSI is also being pushed to support longer cable lengths to make disk clusters more convenient.

Adaptec SCSI adapters have the longest history in the PC hardware market. Years of experience making drivers for Intel-based Unix systems have been leveraged into a similar leading position in the NetWare server world. NetWare 5.*x* includes support for many Adaptec, and other SCSI, adapters.

SCSI drives are excellent choices for servers. SCSI works better for servers than IDE, however, because SCSI drives have more flexibility and more throughput, and SCSI taxes the CPU much less than IDE.

RAID Disk Systems

Coming into popularity in the 1990s, *RAID* (redundant array of inexpensive disks, although some references now say *independent* rather than *inexpensive*) uses several disks to replace the storage capacity of a single disk. The advantage of RAID is fault tolerance; one disk can die, but because the information is spread across all disks, no data is lost.

How the data is spread determines the RAID level of a disk system. The levels range from 1 to 5, but RAID levels 1, 4, and 5 are generally used for servers, with RAID levels 1 and 5 the most popular. The best RAID systems allow bad disks to be replaced without downing the server, maintaining server uptime for users despite what is ordinarily a catastrophic failure, a technology called *hot swapping*. Some vendors build cabinets with multiple power supplies and cooling fans to emphasize the fault-tolerant nature of RAID.

Two warning notes are attached to this rosy scenario, however. RAID systems do not, in any way, make a tape backup obsolete. Although a RAID disk system will continue if one drive goes bad, catastrophic (multiple disk) failures can occur. More important, tape backup is most often used to replace files accidentally deleted. If you delete a file on a RAID disk system, the system will happily delete the file no matter how many disks hold part of that file.

The second warning is that reconstruction of a RAID system is not transparent. As the new disk in the system is populated to take the place of the failed drive, your server will be involved. The performance for clients will drop drastically.

Despite the warnings, RAID systems perform better in critical systems than any single drive available. No system is perfect, but RAID is a step in the right direction. These systems will become more commonplace as prices settle and companies realize the value of the data on their server disks.

Choosing the Server's NIC

Whether your network runs Ethernet, Token Ring, or something else, the card in your server must carry the largest load. Each client talks to one system: the server. The NIC for the server is no place to save money.

Get the fastest PCI network board you can. PCI (Peripheral Component Interconnect) now supports 64-bit data paths at 33MHz. Unless your network supports few people, get a 100BaseT interface board for every server and your tape backup system.

Early advice was to add several NICs in each server to handle higher network traffic loads. Now that switched Ethernet and Token Ring are available, my advice is to avoid multiple NICs. When you add the second network adapter in the server, the operating system turns on the software necessary to route traffic between the two (or more) network segments. This means that each and every packet coming to each network adapter must be examined and routed to either the server itself or to another network adapter. This overhead actually tends to slow server processing of packets in heavy network situations. If at all possible, do not use your server as a local router for your network segments. Figure 2.1 shows the possible and preferred setups.

FIGURE 2.1

Handling high net-work traffic levels

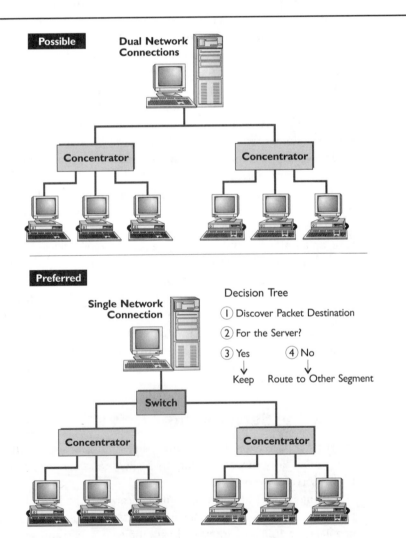

To paraphrase the old adage, put all your eggs in one basket, and then really watch that basket. Put a stout network adapter in your server, and make sure it has been certified by Novell. Make doubly sure the card has the proper driver for not just NetWare, but for NetWare servers.

The NetWare operating system supports more than 60 LAN drivers right out of the box. You can add drivers for any other interface card during installation by reading the vendor's configuration diskette.

One more suggestion: check your NIC vendor for new server drivers now and then. You can improve your server's performance by upgrading your drivers, and vendors regularly supply new driver files.

Choosing the Server's CD-ROM Drive

The trick with CD-ROM drives is not the drive itself, but the controller card that sits in the server. Since SCSI is an accepted standard, a NetWare-supported card in the server can easily run any new CD-ROM drive. So NetWare doesn't care about the drive, just the controller.

More than 20 drivers for various SCSI adapters are included in the NetWare installation program. Just as with NICs, any vendor can supply its own Novell-certified drivers with their own SCSI card. Because NetWare servers are big business, most SCSI-board manufacturers provide Novell drivers.

If you plan to use your CD-ROM drive as a NetWare volume after the server is installed, get at least a 24x drive. If you're not going to use the CD-ROM as a volume, it makes little difference; here's one place you can save some money, though the installation will take longer. Just make sure the interface card for the CD-ROM drive doesn't interfere with the network adapter and disk controller.

IDE CD-ROM support started in NetWare 5, if that's important. The performance doesn't promise to be better than SCSI drives, however, so there's little reason to go out of your way to get an IDE drive and controller if you are already using SCSI. If you are using IDE on the other hand, there is nothing wrong with using an IDE CD-ROM.

 WARNING   There are problems with some SCSI adapters when running both the hard disk and the CD-ROM drive from the same adapter. During installation, the adapter may become unstable and lock up the console keyboard. If that happens, take all the SCSI references out of your CONFIG.SYS file that boots your server under DOS before restarting the installation process. Then load the proper SCSI driver supplied by NetWare to load the CD-ROM as a NetWare volume, and use that volume as the installation files source. More details on resolving SCSI conflict problems during installation are in the section about disk driver setup, in Chapter 3.

Choosing the Server's Floppy Drive

This is an easy selection, because any DOS floppy controller and drive will work under NetWare.

 NOTE Upgraders from previous versions please note: it is no longer possible to boot from a floppy drive. You must boot from the hard drive now.

Choosing the Server's Monitor

This is another easy choice—any VGA video board and low-end monitor would work fine on your server. Now that NetWare has a GUI, the video card and monitor are more important. Choose one that is on Novell's approved list, or at least a name-brand card.

Once installation is complete, server console operations are done infrequently. All normal console operations can be done across the network using the RCONSOLE.EXE or ConsoleOne program.

Setting Interrupts, DMA, I/O Ports, and ROM Addresses

Each of the interface cards discussed in this chapter so far requires some special configuration. The more of these cards in the server, the more difficult it may be to configure each one to work with the others. PCI cards and new Plug-and-Play-enabled systems are reducing these headaches, but they are not gone completely.

Keep track of these settings for each server, and keep track of the paper with the final settings for each server. Having this paper handy will save you time when you add to or modify the equipment in your server. Some people keep the setting information in a notebook, some keep it by the server, and some track the settings in a small database. Just remember to track them somewhere, and your life will be easier.

Interrupts

Interrupts are signals to the CPU in a system from a device under CPU control. Abbreviated IRQ for *interrupt request*, the hardware lines that carry the signals to the CPU are required for every device in the system. The ISA bus has only eight IRQs, numbered 0 to 7, available. AT-class machines and above have 16 IRQs (minus IRQ 2, which functions as a link between the first interrupt controller chip that handles IRQs 0 through 7 and the second interrupt controller chip that manages IRQs 8 through 15). Table 2.1 lists the IRQs and their devices.

TABLE 2.1: IRQS AND THEIR DEVICES

IRQ	Device
0	Timer
1	Keyboard
2	Second IRQ controller chip
3	COM2
4	COM1
5	LPT2
6	Floppy disk
7	LPT1
8	Clock
9–11	Available
12	PS/2 mouse (or available)
13	Math coprocessor
14	Hard disk (Primary IDE) or available
15	Hard disk (Secondary IDE) or available

DMA

DMA (dynamic memory access) is the quick method for transferring information from a mass-storage device of some kind into memory without using the CPU as a traffic cop. Because the processor does not need to be involved, performance is better. Network adapters rarely use DMA, but SCSI adapters often do. There are only five DMA channels, but these are plenty for NetWare servers.

I/O Ports

I/O (Input/Output) describes the transfer of data between the computer and its peripheral devices. Disk drives, printers, tape storage systems, and CD-ROM drives are considered I/O. A hexadecimal number describes a particular I/O port location for those peripherals in the server. Network adapters, SCSI adapters, and disk controllers require a particular I/O port number during installation. Examples are I/O port 300 for the 3Com 3C509 interface card and I/O port 330 for the Adaptec 1540 SCSI adapter.

ROM Addresses

ROM (read-only memory) addresses are necessary for those adapters that store their own operational code in hardware on the adapter. Expressed in large hexadecimal numbers, such as D000 or C800, these addresses are used most commonly in Token Ring interface cards and older Ethernet cards. Any device may require a specific ROM address, but usually you have only one or two of these devices in a file server. If you assemble the server yourself, make note of the settings for each card you place in the server. Although the CONFIG command on the server console tells you the network adapter settings, it doesn't give the details for SCSI adapters, video boards, or anything else in the server. Even worse, if settings conflict, your server won't start.

Preparing for Installation

Before starting the actual NetWare installation process, you must verify that your server-to-be is properly configured. It must boot, have access to the hard disk and CD-ROM drive, and connect to the network. In other words, before a PC can be a server, it must be a functioning workstation.

If your system came loaded with DOS and Windows and various applications, these will all be wiped out. If you want to keep the application software on the system, verify that you have all the disk or CD-ROMs necessary to reload the applications elsewhere. Everything on the hard disk will be history.

Creating the Server Installation Boot Disk

A server installation boot disk is optional and not required by the NetWare installation when you boot the server from a DOS partition on the server hard disk. However, this working installation boot disk comes in handy. What we must create is a floppy containing all the necessary files to boot the machine and activate the CD-ROM. You can also copy this floppy onto the hard drive for all future access.

Tables 2.2 and 2.3 show the CONFIG.SYS and AUTOEXEC.BAT files from a Gateway 2000 Pentium machine used in my lab for this book. As many retail systems do, this machine came with extensive software. What we are worried about now, however, is just enough software to make the CD-ROM usable for our forthcoming NetWare installation. These files were copied from the root directory of the Gateway 2000 PC and modified for use on the boot disk. Modifications were made with an ASCII text editor (like EDIT) before the server boot disk was used to begin the installation process. Where a subdirectory is referenced to reach a file, the file is copied to the root directory of the boot disk. The best example is the last line of the CONFIG.SYS file. In fact, I like to put all the files in the root directory and remove all references to drive letters in CONFIG.SYS and AUTOEXEC.BAT, so I can boot from the floppy or the hard drive with no modifications to either file.

TABLE 2.2: CONFIG.SYS MODIFIED FOR SERVER INSTALLATION

Original Line	Reason for Change or Function of Line
REM DEVICE=\DOS\HIMEM.SYS	NetWare will manage the PC's extended memory.
REM DEVICE=C:\DOS\EMM386.EXE NOEMS X=F000-F7FF	No DOS memory management can be used on NetWare servers.
REM DEVICEHIGH=C:\DOS\SETVER.EXE	NetWare ignores the DOS version.
REM DEVICEHIGH=C:\WINDOWS\IFSHLP.SYS	Windows is erased from the system.
REM DOS=HIGH,UMB	This can be removed because HIMEM.SYS wasn't loaded.
STACKS=9,256	Common command for environment space control; not needed for the server and can be removed.
FILES=50	This will have no impact after the server is installed but must be at least 20 for the installation to work.
BUFFERS=30	This will also have no impact but must be present for the server to install.
REM LASTDRIVE=K	This setting was for the now-deleted Windows for Workgroups software.
LASTDRIVE=Z	This setting works for NetWare clients; necessary if you install across the network.
DEVICEHIGH=MTMCDAE.SYS /D:MSCD001/ P:340 /A:0 /M:30 /T:S /I:11	This is the important line; it's the driver for the CD-ROM drive. Yours may vary, but it must be here.

The boot disk was created by making a formatted, bootable floppy (from C:, type **FORMAT A: /S**). The entire root directory of the Gateway 2000 PC was then copied to the boot disk (**COPY *.* A:**). The COPY command does not copy subdirectories, so there's no worry about copying a subdirectory to the floppy and filling it up before we get the files needed.

Every line in both files could have been cut except for the seventh, eighth, and last lines in CONFIG.SYS and the second line in AUTOEXEC.BAT, but that wouldn't illustrate the point as well. NetWare needs no memory-management help from DOS, disk caching, mouse drivers, or anything else along that line. Only the lines necessary to start the CD-ROM to function as drive D: are needed on this boot diskette, along with the files and buffer statements for the installation process to run.

TABLE 2.3: AUTOEXEC.BAT MODIFIED FOR SERVER INSTALLATION

Original Line	Reason for Change or Function of Line
REM @ECHO OFF	I prefer to see all messages to help with troubleshooting.
MSCDEX.EXE /D:MSCD001	Important file: Microsoft CD-ROM Extension program for CD-ROM control (placed in the root directory of the floppy).
PROMPT PG	DOS prompt showing current working directory.
REM LH C:\DOS\SMARTDRV.EXE	NetWare provides its own server cache program.
REM LH C:\WINDOWS\NET START	Unneeded command to start Windows for Workgroups networking software.
REM SET MOUSE=C:\MSMOUSE	Server has its own mouse driver.
REM C:\MSMOUSE\MOUSE	Server has its own mouse driver.
REM PATH=C:\;C:\DOS;C:\WINDOWS;	DOS path is unnecessary during server installation, and these subdirectories are not on the boot floppy.
REM SET TEMP=C:\TEMP	No temp directory is needed.
REM WIN	Unneeded command to start Windows—it's gone.

Two other files are necessary from the DOS directory: FDISK.EXE and FORMAT.COM, which are on the installation floppy. Both will be used to prepare the hard disk in the server machine. You will need to also place MSCDEX on the floppy from the DOS directory if it's not already there. You may also want some of the following files: SYS.COM (in case you forget to format C: /s), EDIT.COM and QBASIC.EXE (for a basic text editor [if EDIT.COM is bigger than 1K, you don't need QBASIC.EXE]), and ATTRIB.EXE (in case you forget to change the attributes on a file and need to do so later). I also like XCOPY.EXE (in case subdirectories need to be copied later) and DELTREE.EXE (to take unused subdirectories out).

You can use the supplied Novell license disk and boot the soon-to-be server from its own hard disk that contains all the CD-ROM driver files. If the installation goes perfectly, you will not need this bootable installation disk. However, if you stop somewhere in the installation and turn the machine off after you have modified the hard disk partitions, the bootable installation disk will save you 30 minutes of frustration. All the files needed to start the PC and activate the CD-ROM will be in one place, rather than scattered who knows where.

Where Do We Go from Here?

Well, at this point we have our server configured, hardware installed, boot floppies made, and we are ready for the big event. Installation is covered from beginning to end in Chapter 3. Before you begin, get ready all of the hardware settings you were told about. You did write them down, didn't you? Now is the time to take a quick breather, gather any missing paperwork, drivers, settings, and so on, and prepare to take the plunge. When you're ready, move on to the big event in Chapter 3, "Installing a NetWare 5.1 Server."

PART

I

Setting Up the Network

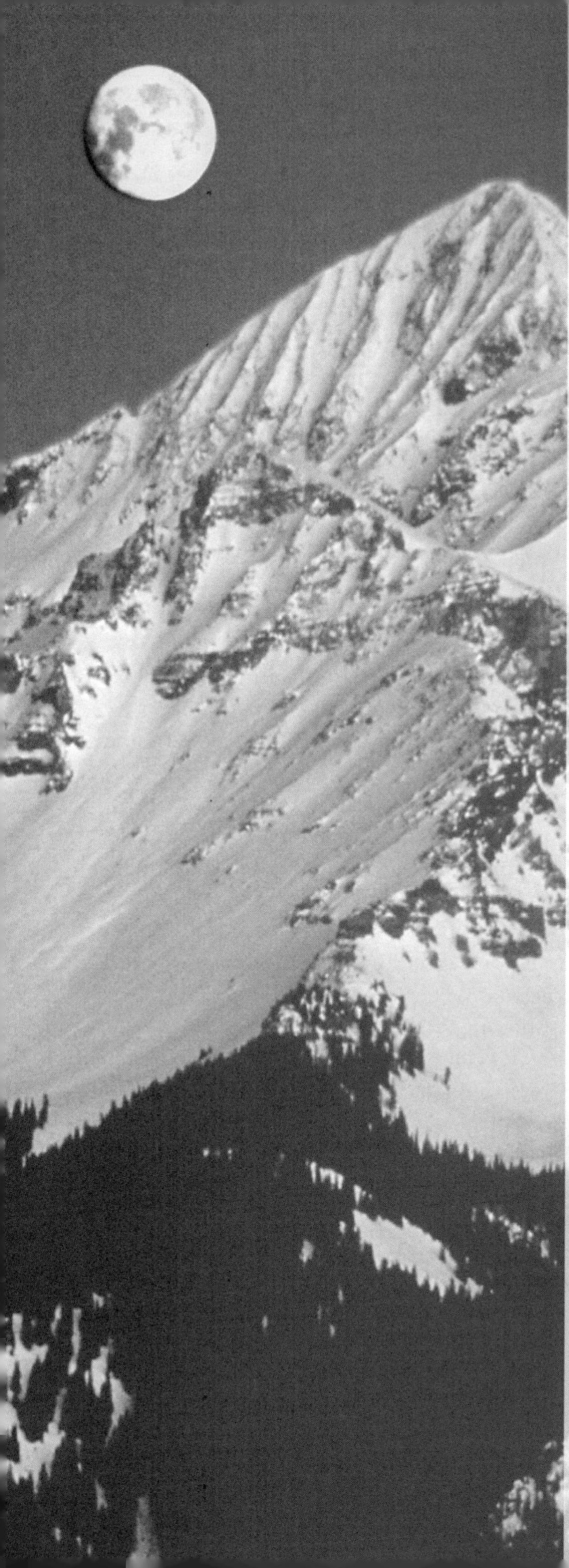

CHAPTER 3

Installing a NetWare 5.1 Server

FEATURING:

N ow that you have prepared the hardware (as described in Chapter 2), it is time to begin the installation. After you have finished this chapter, you will have your server installed (or at least you will have read about installing it). Plan to spend about an hour or so for the installation, if you don't encounter any major problems. That's the bad news. The good news is that most of that time will be spent copying files to your server, requiring no intervention or effort on your part. Are you ready? Let's begin.

Booting Your Server from the Hard Disk

With a brand-new server PC, there may be nothing on the hard disk. Novell and I *strongly* recommend that you create a DOS partition of 50MB or so and boot the server from the hard disk.

If there are files on the hard disk (as is often the case with systems bought from retail outlets eager to add "value" by adding strange software of all types), all those files will be erased. When you run FDISK (and rework your DOS partition), everything on your hard disk will be deleted. Has this PC been backed up? If not, do a backup now if there is even the smallest chance you or someone else will one day want some of the files.

To boot your server from the hard disk, there must be a DOS partition. Novell recommends 50MB for the partition. This allows enough room for all DOS files, the NWSERVER directory for the NetWare files, and a little space for other server utilities.

With a configured and working PC, you will need to use FDISK.EXE to make the adjustments to your disk partitions. It's painful to press the Y key to say, "Yes, completely wipe the disk contents, never to be seen again," even when you know there is nothing valuable on the disk. I suppose you need to accidentally erase a disk or two before you become paranoid about partitioning a disk. If you haven't wiped away valuable files, you haven't been playing with computers long enough.

Follow these steps to prepare the hard disk of your future server:

1. Boot the system from a DOS floppy disk or your server installation floppy (better).

2. Run FDISK.EXE.

3. Delete the existing DOS partition (and any others you may find).

4. Create a DOS partition using 50MB of disk space.

5. Set the new partition as the active partition.

6. Exit FDISK.EXE by pressing Escape.

7. Format the small DOS partition (type **FORMAT C: /S**) from the server installa-tion floppy. DO NOT use DOS from a Windows 95/98/NT system.

8. Create the CONFIG.SYS file on the new hard drive with these two lines (you can, if you prefer, simply copy the server installation floppy to the hard drive, but be sure to place these two statements on the hard drive's version of the file):

   FILES=40
   BUFFERS=30

9. Reboot the system and boot from the hard disk to verify the previous steps.

10. If the CD-ROM drive will be used for installation, copy and verify that CD-ROM drivers initialize the drive. If a network connection is needed for installation, copy and verify that NIC drivers connect to the network. If you have an existing network, ensure that you can see and connect to a server.

Before you begin installation, make sure that you know the settings for all the net-work interface cards in your machine, as well as the necessary names and passwords. Also, if you are installing into an existing NetWare 4.*x* or 5.*x* system, you should know the design of your NDS tree.

 TIP   Starting the file server is much faster with a DOS partition and booting from the hard disk. I prefer letting the installation program modify the AUTOEXEC.BAT program so that the NetWare server starts every time the system is booted. If something happens to stop the server, such as a power failure, it's nice that the server can restart without some-one typing a command or two. You'll see where you can choose this option a bit later in this chapter, when we get to running the INSTALL batch file program.

Use the CD-ROM driver files you saved from the hard disk and placed on the installation boot floppy before you wiped the server hard disk. If your CD drive sup-ports bootable CDs, life will be slightly easier during the NetWare installation process.

If a network connection is necessary for installation, copy the minimum client files needed from a working network client. You don't need a full-featured client. You can probably use a DOS Shell (NETX) client if you have one; you can definitely use the DOS Requester (VLM) or Client 32 for DOS client (see Appendix D for more informa-tion about DOS-based clients).

Setting Up Your Installation Files

If you are installing your first NetWare server, you have no choice about where your server installation files are located. They must be loaded into a CD-ROM drive on your server.

If you are installing your second or seventeenth NetWare server, your installation files can come from the CD-ROM drive on the server or from a remote server across the network. Installing from a remote server requires an existing network and a server with space for the installation files or the NetWare 5.1 CD mounted as a NetWare volume.

There is little difference in the actual installation between loading your network operating system from a CD-ROM drive in the server or from another server three floors away. Most of the installation time is spent watching a seemingly endless list of filenames zoom by. After answering a few questions at the beginning and in the middle, you have little to do during the installation of NetWare 5.1.

Installing from a Server-Based CD-ROM

IN A HURRY

3.1 Install NetWare from an Internal CD-ROM Drive

1. Install and configure a CD-ROM drive on the target server.
2. Boot the server-to-be, loading only DOS and the CD-ROM drivers.
3. Make the CD-ROM drive, with the NetWare 5.1 operating system CD loaded, your current drive.
4. Type **INSTALL** in the root directory (unless your bootable CD drive takes care of this for you).
5. Skip to the section about running INSTALL.

The server-to-be machine must be functioning properly as a DOS system before it can be a server. Test the CD-ROM drive initialization files by rebooting the system, loading only DOS and the CD-ROM startup drivers. These files are all you need for your server installation boot disk. If all is well, you can make your CD-ROM drive (normally drive D:) your active directory and scan the CD just as you can your hard disk. Now you can start the NetWare 5.1 installation process with confidence.

After you switch to your CD-ROM drive, you will see the batch file INSTALL.BAT. You now can skip ahead to the "Running the Installation Program" section of this chapter.

Installing from a Remote Server across the Network

The fastest way to install NetWare may be to use a remote NetWare server as your installation source. You can install from a NetWare volume (the fastest choice here) or from a remote CD mounted as a NetWare volume. Even if this is the first NetWare 5.1 server you are installing, a remote server can be the source of all the installation files, saving you time and aggravation, if you have another NetWare 3 or 4 server available.

How Can a Network Be Faster Than a CD-ROM?

If you're new to networking in general or NetWare in particular, you may wonder why transferring files from another PC over the network is faster than reading an internal CD-ROM drive. How can you send information through a bunch of network cabling, involve two different servers, and worry about other network traffic during your file transfer, yet still believe it's faster than an internal CD-ROM drive?

PCI bus-master network cards running at 100Mbps move buckets o' bits quickly. Internal CD-ROM drives, although getting faster, are almost always based on IDE hard drive controller chips. Not as fast.

The next boost of performance comes with the file caching that NetWare does. Even when reading a fast CD-ROM drive, NetWare reads file blocks beyond the information needed to fill the current request. The file stays in the cache of the source NetWare server, so many of the file requests by the target server will be serviced by server RAM rather than the server CD-ROM drive. If you have copied the installation CD onto the server hard drive, the performance boost by file caching is even more pronounced. Server hard drives are much faster than the fastest CD-ROM drive.

The moral of this story is simple: install from a remote server if practical. If not, you may have a chance to read three magazine articles rather than two during the installation.

Installing from a NetWare Volume

This is probably the first NetWare 5.1 server you are installing into your network. I base that assumption on your attention to the installation chapter. Since you're reading this section about running the installation process across the network, I assume that you already have a NetWare server or servers available. NetWare 5.1 is actually fairly simple to install, so as a good NetWare administrator, you probably won't need instructions more than the first time or two.

Copying the Installation Files from the CD-ROM   The easy way to get the installation files from the CD-ROM drive to the NetWare server is by copying everything from a workstation with a CD-ROM drive. There are more than 4000 files and directories that collectively use about 535MB of space on the operating system CD, so make sure that you have room on your target server before you start. If you add the clients and documentation CDs, the totals balloon to more than 8500 files and about 875MB of space. The copying process will take a quite a while, so start at lunchtime or at the end of the day.

Here are the requirements for making a copy of the NetWare 5.1 operating system CD on a different NetWare server:

- An existing NetWare server with 550MB disk space available (If you need only the operating system CD; add 300MB for the clients CD and another 250MB for the documentation if desired.)

- The target server configured as a NetWare workstation, with at least 1.3GB of free, unpartitioned space available

- A workstation with a CD-ROM drive that can read ISO 9660 formatted CDs (Almost all CD-ROM drives can read this format.)

- A functioning network supporting all three machines

Follow these steps to make the copy:

1. Log in to the host server with proper rights to create a subdirectory.

2. Change to the root directory of the NetWare volume (not SYS: unless you will have plenty of disk space available after copying the CD to the server).

3. Type **MD NETWARE51** (or give it a more descriptive name, such as **NW510PSYS**).

4. Type **CD NETWARE51** (or whatever you named the directory).

5. Type **NCOPY D: /S /E /V** (assuming D: is the CD-ROM drive).

 NOTE   The switch options on the NCOPY command are /S for subdirectory, /E for empty directories, and /V to verify. Use NCOPY rather than XCOPY so that all the NetWare attributes on the files are copied properly.

Setting Up the Target Server as a Workstation   Once the files from the CD-ROM drive are copied on your host server, you can begin installation. The target server must load the files necessary to log in to the host server. This requires loading the NetWare client shells, the NetWare DOS Requestor, or the Client32 for DOS used by your other NetWare clients to connect to the server. Older NetWare shells using the NETX client files will work for installation, but they can't use NDS resources, so you will need to use Bindery Emulation (details on this are in Chapter 4). If you need to install Client32 for DOS, place the client installation files on the server or use the clients CD on the target server and run the INSTALL.EXE program from the \PRODUCTS\ DOSWIN32 directory (again on the clients CD) to configure the server-to-be as a NetWare client. (For further details on this process, see Appendix D.)

Log in to the host server as Admin (if it's a NetWare 4 server or above) or the user you used above. Map a drive from your workstation, er, server-to-be to the directory on the host server containing the NetWare 5.1 files. Change to that drive and type **INSTALL**. You can now skip ahead to the "Running the Installation Program" section of this chapter.

Installing from a Remote CD-ROM

For those of you with existing NetWare servers already containing CD-ROM drives, your job is simple. Place the NetWare 5.1 operating system CD in the drive and mount the new volume; any NetWare client can now reference that volume.

Once again, the server-to-be must be configured as a workstation. Log in from the target server as SUPERVISOR (for NetWare 3.*x*) or Admin (for NetWare 4.*x*) or any other account that has rights to the CD volume, and make a connection (in other words, map a drive) to the CD volume. Follow these steps to mount the NetWare 5.1 operating system CD on a remote server:

1. Dismount the current CD (if any) by typing either **DISMOUNT** *volume-name* if you are using NetWare 5.1 or **CD DISMOUNT** *volume-name* if you are using NetWare 3 or 4. Then remove the disk.

2. Place the NetWare 5.1 operating system CD in the drive.

3. Type **CD MOUNT NW51** if you are using NetWare 3 or 4, or load the CDINST.NLM module and then type **MOUNT NW51** if you are using NetWare 5.*x*.

4. From the workstation/server-to-be, log in to the host server as SUPERVISOR (for NetWare 3) or Admin (for NetWare 4 or 5) or another user with rights to the volume.

5. Map a drive letter to the CD volume by typing **MAP N:= *host_server*\NW51**. (Note that you can use any drive letter; I just like to use N: to remind myself it is the NetWare CD.)

6. Type **INSTALL**.

This procedure brings you to the same point in the installation process as if the CD were inside the target server's CD-ROM drive. You can now continue to the next section.

Running the Installation Program

You begin the installation process on the server-to-be machine as follows:

1. Boot DOS on the PC (without memory managers or other resident programs).

2. Load the CD-ROM drive or network client drivers (as needed).

3. Type **INSTALL** to start the batch file.

It may seem odd, but your PC technically becomes a server the minute the SERVER.EXE program starts. This program is the NetWare kernel.

Of course, loading the SERVER.EXE program without any of the disk drivers and LAN connection software makes a useless server. As it sits now, the server can't communicate with anyone or anything else across the network or even with its own internal hard drives. These details are configured during this portion of the installation process. If you are loading the system from a remote server, the installation program will know which LAN drivers are being used. You will have the option to verify the drivers and accept them for the new server.

The first screen you see (after the initial screen) is a fairly standard license screen. After you have read it, press F10 to move on.

 NOTE If you leave the computer idle on some screens for more than a few minutes, NetWare may automatically blank the screen for you. Don't be alarmed; simply press any key to get it back.

Many things in life force a choice—you can make it powerful or you can make it easy, but not both. NetWare changed the rules starting with version 5. You now have an industrial-strength, enterprise operating system with a relatively easy-to-use GUI (graphical user interface) to guide you through installation (although you are currently looking at a TUI, or textual user interface, to get you started).

Those of you who are using NetWare 5.1 as your first NetWare server or have a typical LAN application will pick the New Server choice to configure the server for your environment. The default choice is Upgrade, for those who want to upgrade their server from NetWare 3 or 4 to 5.1 (wishful thinking on the part of NetWare sales, no doubt). For now, select the New Server choice (see Appendix A for information about upgrading options). You can also choose your installation directory here. The default is C:\NWSERVER, and I see little reason to change it. The options are explained, albeit poorly, by pressing F1. Figure 3.1 shows this installation screen.

FIGURE 3.1

The first fork in the installation road

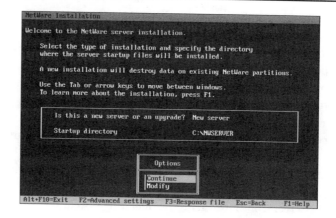

Notice the important message in the second paragraph. New with NetWare 5.1, Novell provides a Deployment Manager to get NDS up to spec before installing a new server in the network.

Another option presented here is for a response file. If you have set up Windows 95 or NT computers in the past, you may have heard of the MSBATCH.INF file (for 95) or unattended installation files (for NT). These allow you to set some or all of the options needed for an installation, so no user input is needed when the operating system is installed. NetWare 5.1 offers the same capability. For large installations, you can simply create the response file and let relatively untrained people set up servers at other locations without knowing the intricacies of server installations, NDS, and so on. If this sounds like something you could use, refer to the online documentation.

Yet another option from this screen is to set Advanced Settings, discussed next. The instructions for Advanced Settings appear on the screen when you choose a New Server installation.

Advanced Settings

If you press F2 from the installation choice screen, you'll see the Advanced Settings dialog box:

The first of these options, CD-ROM Driver To Access Install, lets you decide if the operating system CD should be mounted as a NetWare volume and accessed as such for the remainder of the installation or if the DOS drivers that you have used to this point should continue to be used. You should leave the default unless you have a problem accessing the CD and finishing the installation. Pressing Enter on this choice toggles between the two options.

The Server ID number is what Novell called in former days (and what the console command CONFIG still calls) the IPX internal network number. The IPX internal network number (called the internal network number in NetWare 3.*x*) provides a unique reference number for the server operating system. Since your server may have two (or more) network interface cards or support more protocols than just IPX/SPX or TCP/IP, the Server ID number helps the operating system know which packets go to which interface card using which frame type and protocol. It is used only by the server.

The number must be unique (on the network), and it must be in the range 0 through FFFFFFFF (hex). One quick note here: if you set this number to zero, the installation process will create a new random number later in the process and ask you to accept that number. The odds of duplication are slim, but it has happened before. This is a good time to verify that no other server has that number. (You do have the documentation on all your other servers, don't you?) Unless you like to be cute (BABE is a popular address relying on hexadecimal characters) or have a conflict with another server, take the recommendation. The number cannot match any other Server ID numbers or external IPX network numbers, so don't be cute more than once.

In rare cases, you may need this number, so write it down. You're supposed to have a pad and pencil beside the server during installation, remember?

You will rarely, if ever, change the Server ID number, which is why it is included under Advanced Settings.

The third setting, Load Server At Reboot, is not what I would consider an Advanced Setting. This setting has been debated fiercely in administrator circles. The debate is essentially this: when your computer boots, should NetWare automatically be loaded?

There are those who say, "No, if there is a problem, you want to be able to deal with it before the server loads." The other camp asks, "What happens when you aren't around to reboot the server? Who will do it?" Novell has changed the default on this from Yes to No and back with almost every version. I set it to Yes. The server should automatically restart after a power failure, a critical error, or whatever, without me (or potentially an end user) having to get involved. If there is a problem, I will be there to address it, and I can always boot with a floppy or press F5 when DOS starts to skip CONFIG.SYS and AUTOEXEC.BAT. Anyway, the default is now "Yes, automatically start NetWare with each reboot." The choice is yours; start the debate.

The final Advanced Setting is Server Set Parameters. The purpose of this option is to allow you to enter any SET parameters needed for the server to boot properly. (SET parameters are listed in Appendix C.) These parameters will then be stored in STARTUP.NCF. STARTUP.NCF is similar in purpose to CONFIG.SYS, in that server parameters needed can be set when the server first boots. You will not normally need to enter anything here. If you do need to enter parameters here, however, be sure to spell them correctly. If you don't, NetWare will not recognize them and will ignore them, negating the setting you were trying to make.

Regional Settings

The next screen presents Regional Settings with defaults that you will probably be using. You can use this screen to set your Country Code. See your DOS manual (you still have a DOS manual, don't you? Oh well. . .) under the heading COUNTRY.SYS for more information on this setting.

In addition, you can modify the Code Page you will be using. For more information on Code Pages, see DOS Help under MODE.

The last setting on this screen allows you to change your keyboard type for many countries. If you are installing in the United States in English, simply choose Continue to move on.

Mouse Type and Video Mode

After you choose your regional settings, you can select your video and mouse settings. Let's explore both options.

Now that NetWare 5.1 has a GUI-based installation (coming up after the file-copy process), it only makes sense to have mouse support as well. You don't need to have a mouse for the installation, but it makes the process much easier. (Have you ever used Windows without a mouse?) NetWare supports the PS/2-style mouse, as well as the serial mouse on COM1 or COM2. I recommend that you put a mouse on the server, if only for the installation. You may choose to leave it there if you will be using the GUI on the server for additional administrative tasks after installation.

NetWare's video support is simple: Basic VGA or Super VGA. Novell recommends that you use the Super VGA setting unless your video card is not VESA-2-compliant (and most are today). Be sure to check Novell's Web site for a compatible video card. However, most basic video cards will work.

As the help screens point out, these two parameters are *not* autodetected, so you must be sure you supply the correct settings, or you may encounter problems later. Cursor keys replace the mouse in the GUI but are horrendously slow. Better to restart your installation with the correct mouse setting than to continue without a mouse, believe me.

Device Drivers

Without drivers, NetWare can't speak to any hardware component. Because the NetWare software is a server, there are two main types of drivers that need to be loaded: disk and network. Novell has split driver selection among these two broad categories, with some other options on both screens. Let's begin by looking at storage drivers.

PSM, HotPlug, and Storage Adapters

The next screen, which takes a few minutes to appear as many driver files are copied, allows you to choose a Platform Support Module (PSM), a PCI-Hot Plug Support Module, and the storage adapters that you will be using. This screen is shown in Figure 3.2.

FIGURE 3.2

Choosing drivers

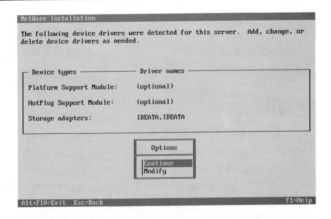

A *PSM* is a hardware abstraction layer used when you have multiple CPUs in your server to isolate the details on how the multiple CPUs are implemented from the operating system. The system will check the hardware settings to see if there are multiple CPUs and then attempt to detect which PSM is needed. If you have only one CPU, a PSM isn't necessary, and the field will be blank. If you buy a server with multiple CPUs from a major supplier (such as Compaq, Dell, or IBM), the drivers will certainly be there when you need them.

The second item on this screen is the HotPlug Support Module. Here you can choose (if NetWare doesn't detect it for you automatically) the module you need to load to support HotPlug. HotPlug technology allows you to unplug storage and network interface cards while the server continues running and replace them as needed. This great benefit keeps the server up when a card needs to be replaced. Rather than shut down the entire server, you can simply remove the card and put in the new one.

The third item that NetWare will attempt to detect and display for your approval or modification is the choice of storage adapters. NetWare needs to know what type of disk and disk controller are in the server. A large number of controller definitions come with NetWare. New drivers certified by Novell are available through technical support channels, such as Novell's Web site or your dealer.

Vendors that add NetWare support for disk controllers include the proper drivers on a disk or their Web site. The installation program allows you to add vendor drivers to your system. To modify the list, choose Modify, select Storage Adapters, and press Enter. In the dialog box that appears, shown in Figure 3.3, you can use a standard NetWare convention: press the Insert key to add something or open a pick list (a list of options available at that point). In this case, pressing the Insert key will display a list of drivers that ship with the product. Press Insert a second time to open a window that asks the source drive of the new driver. Place the disk in the server's floppy drive, and the installation program will pick up the driver and save it on the server.

FIGURE 3.3

*Add, edit, or delete
storage drivers as
needed.*

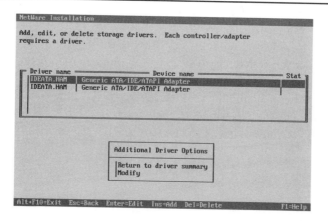

You can modify the properties of a driver by selecting it and pressing Enter. If NetWare incorrectly detects a driver, simply select it and press Delete. When finished making changes, choose Return To Driver Summary.

New in NetWare 4, and mandatory in version 5.*x*, are NWPA (NetWare Peripheral Architecture) drivers. They replace the drivers with the .DSK extension used in previous versions. The DSK drivers were *monolithic* drivers, which meant that a single driver controlled the disk controller and all devices attached to that disk controller.

NWPA drivers continue with Novell's move toward modularity in the operating system. Rather than a single driver that controls all devices, NWPA drivers are in two parts: HAMs and CDMs. HAM (Host Adapter Module) drivers control the interaction between the NetWare operating system and the physical host adapter plugged into the server bus. These drivers use the extension .HAM. There will be one HAM driver for each adapter. CDM (Custom Device Module) drivers, on the other hand, control the devices connected to the host adapters. There may be multiple CDM drivers for a single host adapter, since each device connected to the host adapter must have a specific driver. Table 3.1 shows the details.

TABLE 3.1: NWPA DISK DRIVERS, HAMS, AND CDMS

Server Architecture	Controller	HAM to Load	CDM to Load
ISA, EISA	AT, IDE (ATA)	IDEATA.HAM	IDEHD.CDM (for hard disk) or IDECD.CDM (for CD-ROMs)
SCSI	Adaptec 1540 and others	AHA154x.HAM	SCSIHD.CDM (hard disk), SCSICD.CDM (CD-ROM), or others depending on the device

NWPA uses the Media Manager as the storage management layer of the NetWare 5.1 operating system, providing a storage management interface between applications and storage device drivers.

New drivers will show up first with the devices they control. Remember to use the Insert key to redirect the installation program to look for new driver files in the floppy drive.

After selecting the adapter driver, you have the chance to verify the parameters for that driver. Any changes to adapter settings should be made here. Once the parameters are set, you will have a chance to repeat the process for any number of additional drivers.

WARNING Beware of problems upgrading old disk drivers. The DSK drivers are not supported. You will need to find equivalent HAM drivers for your devices before you upgrade.

As you continue past the storage adapter screen, you will be presented with a screen (see Figure 3.4) on which you can confirm the NetWare storage devices and network cards that were found. The storage device drivers are the .CDM files I just discussed, so let's move on and review the network card issues.

Network Boards, Storage Devices, and NLMs

Like disk controllers, network interface cards need a driver. Network adapter drivers have .LAN as their filename extension. The next step in the installation process: choosing and configuring this LAN driver.

FIGURE 3.4

Storage device, network board, and NLM selections

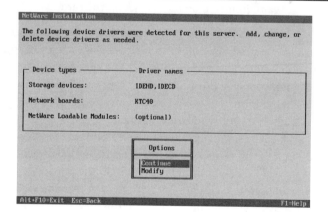

You must have at least one network adapter in the server for it to communicate with network clients and other servers. You may have multiple LAN adapters in a server. They may all be the same type of adapter, such as Ethernet, or you may have four different topologies represented. It's possible to have Ethernet, Token Ring, FDDI, and WAN connectors in one server (possible, but not likely or practical). NetWare 5.1 does include the updates to the TCP/IP stack that allow two network cards to share the same subnet.

NetWare commands great respect among network-adapter vendors because of the large market share. Novell supplies many drivers as part of the installation process.

One interface card will probably have different drivers for use in a NetWare client or a NetWare server. Make sure you verify that a card vendor provides a driver for more than just "NetWare." If it goes into the server, the vendor must provide a server (LAN) driver.

Once again, you can load drivers not detected or supplied with NetWare by choosing Modify, selecting Network Boards, and pressing Enter. In the dialog box that appears, you can select any card, press Enter, and modify that card's properties. You should do this for all of your cards to ensure that NetWare is using the proper settings to interface with each card.

You need to verify, or change if necessary, the following attributes:

Is the card an ISA card? Set this to Yes if it is a legacy (in other words non-Plug-and-Play) ISA card; otherwise, choose No.

Interrupt number Verify (and change if necessary) the number (IRQ) if needed so that the actual settings on the card match those here.

Port value Verify (and change if necessary) the port used to access the card. Again, it must match those set on the card.

One quick note on the last two parameters: they are usually supplied in hexadecimal. Be sure that you enter the parameter in the correct format and that you know the values for those two settings in both hexadecimal and decimal.

When you have finished, choose Return To Driver List and then repeat this process for all remaining network interface cards. When you have finished all the interface cards, choose Return To Driver Summary.

Back at the summary screen, you'll notice the Storage Devices choice. A reasonable question at this point is, "What's the difference between a storage device and a storage driver?" Recall from our discussion in the previous section (and Table 3.1) that there are now two components you need to load: an .HAM file and a .CDM file. You have already chosen the .HAM file on the previous screen. Here is where you choose the .CDM file. Remember that these drivers are for the various devices (hard drives, CD-ROMs, and so forth) that you have attached to your storage adapter. NetWare will usually detect them for you and have this list filled in correctly here, but you could modify these drivers if necessary.

The last thing that you can specify here is any NLMs that are needed for the server to boot. Typically, none are needed, but if you have special hardware, the drivers for it can be loaded here.

When you have finished with the settings on this screen, choose Continue to move on.

Partitions and the SYS: Volume

Now that you have loaded the disk drivers, you can configure one to support the SYS: volume. The rest of the partitions and volumes will be created later in the process. You can select the device you are interested in, change the size of the NetWare partition and SYS: volume, and so forth.

The only thing that you need to know to create the SYS: volume is that it must be at least 900MB, and preferably 1.3GB or more. If you press F1 for help at this point, you will see the minimum size recommendations from Novell (1.3GB). You may notice that Novell left some 5.0 information about a 250MB minimum, and another place talks about 750MB for NetWare 5.1, but don't fall for it. The smallest size the installation program will allow you to choose is 790MB (it's a good thing disks keep getting cheaper). Table 3.2 lists some of the possible scenarios and both Novell's and my own minimum recommended size for each. My recommendation: 2GB for SYS: and put everything else on other volumes.

TABLE 3.2: MINIMUM RECOMMENDED SYS: VOLUME SIZES		
Scenario	**Novell's Recommendation**	**My Recommendation**
NetWare 5.1 Minimum Install	900MB	2GB
NetWare 5.1 Default Install	1.3GB	2GB
All but Documentation	800MB	2GB
All and Documentation	1.3GB	2GB

You must make a number of important choices here, so I will go slowly through the options and their effects. To repeat, for those of you who have multiple disks or desire multiple volumes, these choices are made later in the installation process; here, we are just getting the SYS: volume set up. As you can see in Figure 3.5, Novell presents a lot of information in a simple, well-designed manner, with defaults that greatly simplify the installation process.

FIGURE 3.5

*Configuring partitions
and volumes*

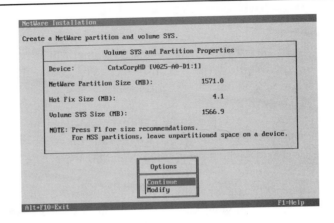

FIGURE 3.5

*Configuring partitions
and volumes*

NetWare Disk Partitions

By default, NetWare selects a suitable place for SYS: (or tells you at this point that one can't be found and that you must stop the installation, make space—*unpartitioned* space—for NetWare, and then restart the process) and asks you to confirm the details. By default, it chooses the first hard drive with at least 790MB space for SYS: and uses all the unpartitioned space for a NetWare partition.

Your first choice concerns the size of the partition. The default, as mentioned, is all the available unpartitioned space on that drive. Unless you plan to use some of that space for another operating system (such as might occur in a lab situation) or for NSS (Novell Storage Services) partitions, use all the space available. In fact, I suggest reserving about 2GB for the SYS: volume, leaving the rest for the new, improved file format found on NSS volumes. You'll learn more about NSS volumes in the "File System Configuration" section, coming up later in the chapter.

A Partition Isn't a Volume

There is a difference between partitions and volumes. A *partition* of a hard disk is a portion that the *operating system* treats as a separate drive.

DOS supports two partitions on a drive (for DOS-based files), but only one can be the primary, bootable partition. All hard disks, including the ones in a NetWare server, can have four partitions.

Continued

CONTINUED

Only one NetWare partition can exist on any given hard disk. Boot disks have a DOS partition along with a NetWare partition. Imagine the disk as a pizza, with one slice DOS and the rest NetWare. Non-boot disks in the server, whether internal or part of an external disk system, usually have one NetWare partition filling the entire disk (unless NSS volumes are desired).

A *volume*, on the other hand, is a logical portion of disk space created and controlled by the *NetWare operating system*. There can be up to eight volumes per partition, or volumes may span several physical disks.

Hot Fix Settings

The Hot Fix Size item allows you to expand or decrease the number of megabytes of disk blocks set aside. Hot Fix is a Novell utility that protects your information by marking bad spots on the hard disk as unusable. Any information already written to one of these bad spots is moved to a redirection area maintained by the Hot Fix utility. You can change the redirection area size, but there's little reason to go to the trouble. If you need to increase the size because your disk is developing more trouble areas, you need to replace your disk.

SYS: Volume Setup

The SYS: volume (and name) is mandatory. It must be at least 800MB in size. Novell and I recommend 2GB as a minimum for NetWare because if you add any of the extra files to support client installation, access to the Internet or an intranet, and the like, 800MB is not enough. Print jobs that sit in the print queue may get spooled to SYS: (although it is not recommended; more on this in Chapter 8), and bad things happen if a print job—or anything else for that matter—fills the SYS: volume. Give yourself some room for growth and make the volume 2GB.

Think about your network setup before you create your SYS: volume. You have three options for volume placement:

Several volumes per disk   The advantages of this setup are that security is easy to control by volume and you have descriptive naming options. The disadvantages are that artificial segmentation chops up available data space and it takes extra work to configure your backup system by volume.

One volume per disk   This setup makes it easy to back up and restore the volume if the drive fails, but it can still limit file space for large data sets.

One volume across two or more disks   With this setup, there is an increase in performance since each segment will have its own disk. You'll also have almost unlimited file space as disks are added. However, one drive fault means restoring the entire multi-disk volume.

Some companies structure the SYS: volume to hold application files. This is easy to set up, because the NetWare operating system files are already on the SYS: volume. Once configured, the SYS: volume won't need to be backed up often, since the information rarely changes. NDS replicas are also stored on the SYS: volume, but they aren't backed up with the data on this volume; instead, replicas are part of an NDS backup.

A problem with keeping application files in the SYS: volume is that applications are constantly upgraded, and each new upgrade takes more space than the one before. This means that you need to back up regularly. Also, since Windows applications often write files all over your local and server hard disks, you may not be able to exclude the users of those applications from writing to the SYS: volume. If you write to the volume, sometimes you will need to delete from that volume. If you don't give users the ability to delete files on at least some parts of the SYS: volume, they may come to you with application problems caused by this security feature. If you do give users the ability to delete files on the SYS: volume, you need to back up that volume every single day. I strongly suggest that the SYS: volume be reserved for the NetWare operating system and the files needed to support it. Store the rest of your applications and data on other volumes.

The advantages of multiple volumes on a single disk include making separate volumes that support non-DOS name spaces. The long names from other operating systems (Windows 95/98/NT/2000, Macintosh, Unix, and OS/2) supported in the name spaces are controlled by extended attributes in the FAT (file allocation table). If you add, for instance, Macintosh name space support after a volume has been in use for a while, the FAT will be fragmented as it marks the old filename locations and makes room for the new. This fragmentation will slow performance when files are read. However, this is only a concern if you are using the standard NetWare volumes rather than NSS volumes, which handle these differently.

The backup and restore concerns come into play once again with the third option: one volume spanning two or more disks. When you use this method, you must replace the entire volume if any one of the disks crashes. For this reason, volumes that span multiple drives are excellent candidates for mirrored or duplexed drives (allowing data stored on one disk to be simultaneously maintained on another disk). If one of the drives does crash, the fault tolerance built into the system keeps the server up and working. When the drive is replaced, it merely needs to be synchronized with the remaining good drive of the pair to be ready for service once again. If the drive is big, this process may take a while, but not nearly as long as restoring files for the entire volume from tape. One of the advantages of a name-brand server with RAID storage is fault tolerance, for instance with the Compaq ProLiant server family, the ability to replace a disk while the server keeps running.

Along with deciding where to place your SYS: volume, you can also set volume block size and enable or disable file compression, block suballocation, and data migration. You can make these changes for the SYS: volume by pressing F3 to display the volume properties (see Figure 3.6). These properties are discussed in the following sections. After you've finished making volume changes, press the F10 key to save your volume changes, then choose Continue. The volume setup time is much less than formatting the same size disk, so you won't wait long.

FIGURE 3.6

*Modifying the SYS:
volume's properties*

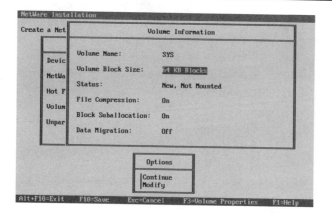

Volume Block Size   The first changeable parameter in the Volume Information screen is the Volume Block Size. Volume blocks set the size of pieces of data stored in a volume. NetWare 5.1 sets the default block sizes based on the size of the volume. (If you take my advice and store your data on NSS volumes, leaving SYS: for system files, this setting will have little effect.)

Larger block sizes (on the traditional NetWare volume) use less server RAM, since there are fewer blocks to track. Unfortunately, the larger blocks waste more disk space. A single file is stored in each block, meaning an 87-byte batch file may "fill" an entire 64KB disk block. To eliminate this waste, turn on block suballocation. We'll be there in just a second.

Unless your volume will hold large files, such as large database files, graphics files, or other consistently large data files, the defaults will work fine. If server memory is more limited than disk space, you may want to bump the block size up a bit, but it's much better to buy more memory.

Another reason to go with the defaults and not guess about your block sizes is that these can't be changed after the volume is up and running. Changing the block size requires backing up the volume files and information (several times if you're the least bit paranoid, which you should be), deleting the volume, and re-creating the volume with the new settings. And keep in mind that going through this for the SYS: volume, where the operating system resides, is much more difficult and time-consuming than with the other volumes.

However, if you absolutely must change the volume block size, highlight that line in the Volume Information screen and press the Enter key. A pick list of your options will appear. Press Enter on your choice, and that block size will fill in. The highlight bar will move to the next option.

File Compression   The next option, File Compression, enables or disables file compression for the volume being configured. You cannot turn this setting off on existing volumes once it is turned on. All is not lost, however. Using NetWare's utilities, you can set individual files to be compressed or never to be compressed, as well as disable all new file-compression activity via various SET parameters (more information on them is in Appendix C).

File compression is one of the big advantages of NetWare 5.1. Working intelligently in the background, file compression is applied to files that have not changed for a certain amount of time. The default setting is two weeks without being accessed, but you can change that setting.

At a predetermined time (the default is midnight), all files ready for compression will be crunched by the operating system. The algorithm for compression tips the scales for fast decompression rather than being balanced; you don't care how long the file takes to shrink since it happens when you're not using the server. You do care that a previously compressed file, when accessed again, responds as quickly as any other file.

The details of compression times are set after the server is up and running. Now we're just concerned about whether to support compression on this particular volume. The default is On, as your answer should be. If you press the Enter key on this field, you will toggle between On and Off.

 NOTE   Note: NSS volumes do not (yet) support compression. If disk space is tight and compression helps, stick with regular volumes. Or add more disks, and make those volumes NSS.

Block Suballocation   Block suballocation, another feature of NetWare 5.1, is a fancy name for "let's pack in these files like a vacation suitcase." Rather than limiting you to a large block size that wastes lots of space when a small file is stored there, block suballocation splits the remaining space of a partially used block into 512-byte segments. If an 87-byte batch file is placed into a new block, 63.5KB will then become available for other file remainders. New files won't be placed here, just the ends of other files that are just a little larger than the configured block size. If the next file sent to the server is a 65KB file, the first 64KB of that file will fill a new block, and the remaining 1KB will take two 512-byte suballocation blocks in the block with our 87-byte batch file, leaving us with 62.5KB free for another file.

You can see how this space savings will add up. Rather than wasting almost 128KB in the examples just discussed, NetWare block suballocation works to keep these left-over corners of disk blocks full and under control.

Data Migration   A common problem with large groups of data files is the need to keep them handy but not necessarily immediately available. Hard disks, while coming down drastically in price, still cost more per megabyte of storage than optical disk platters.

Imagine a newspaper's situation: many new stories every day that need instant file response. While reporters are writing and working on stories, those stories must be on the server's hard disk and readily available. What about last month's stories? They must be kept, but the chances of needing any particular story are low. They become excellent data migration candidates.

To a user looking for an old story, the files appear to all be on the volume. In reality, however, NetWare tracks which files have been migrated and which have not, and NetWare will get the file wherever it is currently located. The retrieval time will be a few seconds slower, but the user (or more important to you, the network administrator) doesn't need to do anything special when accessing these migrated files.

NetWare uses some hard disk space as a staging area for files going to or coming from (properly called *migration* and *demigration*) the near-online storage. An optical jukebox, an excellent example of near-online storage, will extend the capacity of a volume using data migration. Files are moved based on a configuration profile listing the age of the file and the storage capacity threshold of the hard disk space.

Remote Server Login

If you are installing from a local CD-ROM drive, you can skip right to the "NetWare File-Copy Process" section. If you are installing NetWare from a remote server, you'll be prompted to log in once again.

During the installation of network drivers, the connection to the remote server gets broken. Reestablishing the connection takes just your login name (on the host server, not the server you are installing) and the password. This step is a necessary security precaution. Under no circumstances do you want someone to be able to connect to and take files from your system without going through security.

NetWare File-Copy Process

Now it's time for the installation program to copy NetWare files. Notice the information in the main window. If you are installing from an internal CD-ROM drive, the source may be drive D: rather than the name of a remote server and volume.

This process will take a while, so be patient. The installation program will copy many, many files to your SYS: volume, and several times during the process it will tell you that control has been passed to another NLM. It expands compressed files just copied from the CD. Also, at this point, the installation program copies the files needed to set up the GUI for the GUI installation portion of the installation process.

When the process is almost finished, it will tell you that it is "Launching NetWare 5.1 Installation Wizard!" You are now entering the world of the GUI installation. Welcome, I think.

The Age of the GUI Has Arrived

We now have, for the first time with NetWare 5.0, a GUI on the server. From now until you finish the installation, you will be using the GUI to answer all the questions needed to set up your server.

You probably can figure out how to get around in this new environment. You can, of course, use the mouse if you have one. This is the preferred (and simplest) method. However, the GUI allows you to use the standard keyboard-navigation techniques. (You will die of boredom. Get a mouse.) You can use the Tab key to move between fields, the spacebar to check or uncheck boxes, and the Enter key to perform the highlighted action (for the buttons on the bottom of the screen). Choose Next to move to the next dialog box, Back to go to the previous dialog box, Cancel to end the installation process, or Help for information about the current dialog box.

Server Name

The first question you will be asked in the GUI, as you can see in Figure 3.7, is what you would like to name your server. It's generally recommended that you choose a short, easily typed name. The default, FS1 in earlier versions of NetWare, resulted in thousands of servers named FS1.

FIGURE 3.7

*The age of the GUI
has arrived, and it
begins with the prompt
for a server name.*

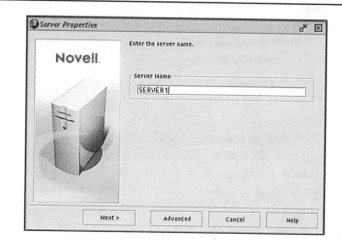

With NetWare 5.1, there are few places a user will need to type the server name. In both DOS and Windows utilities, the names of all available servers are shown in a pick list. Choosing a server means either moving the highlight bar and pressing Enter in DOS or clicking with the mouse in Windows. There is no typing involved.

Choose a name that means something to your users, say SALES1 or 4_FLOOR or EMAIL1. Most users do not interact with the file server but with the volumes on that server, as in SALES1_SYS or EMAIL1_GROUPWISE. You can change the name of the server later, but that may create a bit of work if you have referenced the server's SYS: volume (or any other volume, for that matter) in login scripts. Rather than go to that trouble, you can just provide an alias for the volume or reference certain directories with a simple directory map name. We'll get to aliases, directory maps, and login scripts later; this is just to let you know that naming a server is less restrictive than it used to be. That said, choose carefully to save yourself many headaches later.

The official naming instructions are 2 to 47 alphanumeric characters, plus the hyphen and underscore. No spaces are allowed; use the underscore or hyphen instead. And go with the urge to use meaningful names for your servers. It's tough to tell your CEO his main server is BOINGO.

After you click Next, the installation will take a few seconds to check for duplicate server names. Remember, these names must be unique network-wide. If there is a duplicate, you will get an error message and will have to choose another name. The file system will also be initialized at this point. If you have unpartitioned space available, you will be given the chance to configure it now; otherwise, skip to "Protocol Selection."

Just in case you wondered, NetWare 5.1's installation graphic shows the server and a swoosh of some kind (see Figure 3.7). In real life, the green swoosh looks like swamp gas. I much prefer the NetWare 5.0 graphic showing a CD-ROM heading for the server like a UFO landing at the mothership.

File System Configuration

In the File System Properties dialog box, you can set up the file system any way you like. As shown in Figure 3.8, you will see all the partitions you created, including their types and sizes, the SYS: volume, and any free or unpartitioned space you have on any drives. You can delete existing partitions, create new partitions and volumes, and edit the settings of your SYS: volume (in a limited way) and all the other volumes you choose to create at this point.

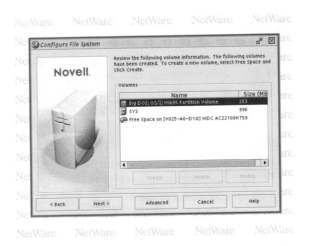

Your options include all the ones described earlier for the SYS: volume, in the "Partitions and the SYS: Volume" section. Refer to those earlier descriptions for help in setting the Hot Fix, block size, block suballocation, file compression, and data migration items.

Here, I will concentrate on how to create new volumes and extend existing volumes. Let's begin with type of volume choice—traditional or NSS?

NSS, the New File System

The biggest change in the file system in NetWare 5.1 over versions 3 and 4 is the addition of NSS, a 64-bit file system with many advantages over the traditional 32-bit file system. Table 3.3 summarizes the differences between the two file systems.

TABLE 3.3: TRADITIONAL FILE SYSTEM VERSUS NSS

Feature	Traditional File System	NSS File System
Character format	ASCII double-byte	Unicode (the international standard)
Time to mount a volume	Up to several minutes (depending on volume size)	Typically only seconds
Utility used to repair damaged volumes	VREPAIR	REBUILD
Ability to access DOS partitions on the NetWare server	N/A	Accessible; treated as a standard NSS volume (load DOSFAT.NSS)
Time to repair a volume	Up to several hours (depending on volume size)	From a few seconds to a few minutes (depending of volume size)
Memory required	Increases with volume size	1MB or less for any size volume
Maximum file size	2GB	8TB (8192GB)
Maximum number of files per volume	16 million (with one name space), 8 million (with two name spaces), 4 million (with three name spaces), etc.	16 trillion files per volume, with any number of name spaces
Volume limitations	64 volumes 32 segments per volume 1TB total volume size	256 volumes (total, counting traditional and NSS volumes); no limit on segments per volume; 8TB (8192GB) total volume size
Features not supported	N/A	Data migration File compression TTS Disk duplexing Auditing

Unfortunately, you can't make the SYS: volume the NSS type. NSS doesn't support the Transaction Tracking System (TTS), and TTS is the component that protects the NDS database from corruption. This limitation will be removed in the future, but for now, SYS: must be the traditional type. NSS works great with RAID storage, eliminating the need for data duplexing, disk mirroring, or disk striping. No file compression (as mentioned earlier), and no NFS (Network File System), FTP (File Transfer Protocol), or filename locks, either. OK, toss a coin whether you want NSS or the 32-bit file system on a single disk, but always use NSS on RAID.

Volume Management

To create a new volume, select free space and then choose New Volume. You will be prompted for a volume name (see Figure 3.9). You can change the size of the volume here, if desired. The default is all available space that you assigned to this volume. Select the desired file system and choose OK.

FIGURE 3.9

Creating a new volume

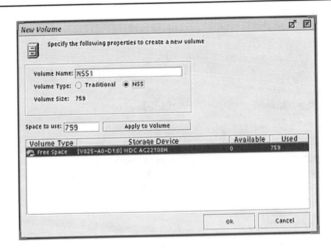

To change the size of an existing volume, select it from the main dialog box, select Modify, and then modify the parameters as desired in the bottom half of the dialog box. Be sure to choose the Apply To Volume button before choosing OK, or none of your changes will be saved to disk.

To delete a volume, select it and choose Delete. You need to be aware of a couple of things about deleting volumes. First, there is no confirmation of the deletion. You select it, choose Delete, and it's simply gone. Second, and a major mitigating factor on the first point, is that you can delete only items you have created here. You cannot delete DOS, other non-DOS (like HPFS, NTFS, or Unix) partitions, or the SYS: volume.

When you have finished making all the changes you want to any volume, choose OK to return to the File System Properties dialog box. When you have the file system set up the way you want, click Next. You will see a dialog box asking when you would like to mount those volumes you just created.

The volume mounting choices are simply Yes or No. Yes or No what? The Yes answer means mount them after the installation is finished and the server is rebooted. No means mount them all now. You will need to choose No if you want to place some of the product options on these other volumes. If you keep all of the system files on SYS:, however, stick with the default of Yes. After you have made your choice, click Next to move on to the Protocols dialog box.

Protocol Selection

The next task at hand is to select the protocol or protocols that you want to use in your network. You can choose IP, IPX, or both. A screen similar to Figure 3.10 will appear, where you can see all of your NICs. To select the protocol or protocols you want for a particular NIC, simply select it, then check the box in front of the desired choice or choices (see Figure 3.11). Repeat this process for every network interface card installed in your server.

FIGURE 3.10

*The initial Protocols
dialog box*

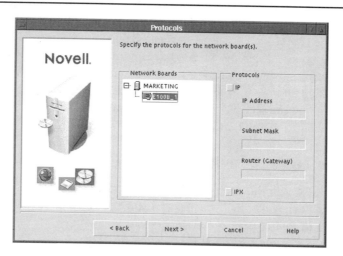

FIGURE 3.11

*The Protocols dialog
box with a NIC
selected*

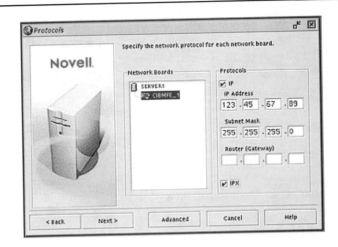

If you choose to add IP, you will need to fill in the IP Address, Subnet Mask, and Router (Gateway) settings for this node. The Router setting is optional, but you will need to fill it in unless there are no routers in your network. If you are not sure what these are, *do not make up an address* and type it in. If you do, you will have many problems because wrong addresses will likely play havoc with your network. You can add IP support later. You'll find more information on TCP/IP in Chapter 14.

If you want to use IPX, NetWare will automatically detect the IPX frame type(s) on your network. If it can't detect any, it will default to installing support for the Ethernet_802.2 frame type (as all versions of NetWare since 3.12 have done). If you don't want all these frame types to be bound, at the end of the installation you will be given a chance (when you choose Customize on the Summary screen) to choose the ones you want and/or to set the addresses of each.

You can set up DNS here, but let's wait until Chapter 15. There's more to explain about DNS and DHCP than we want to put here.

Time Zone Selection

The next installation task is to choose a time zone for the server site. Figure 3.12 shows the dialog box that will appear. (Note the capability to automatically adjust for Daylight Saving Time!) You can choose from 54 time zone settings, covering 29 time zones (some are in half-hour increments).

FIGURE 3.12

*Choosing your time
zone*

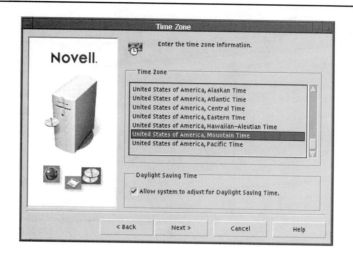

NetWare engineers made a Daylight Saving Time (DST) adjustment automatic in NetWare several versions ago. Check this box if DST applies to your location. Novell made defaults for each time zone. If most places in your time zone support it, it is checked; if not, it isn't checked. Notice, however, that when DST comes and goes, the local time will be affected, but the time that NetWare uses internally will remain the same.

Installing Novell Directory Services

The next question you will be asked is if you want to use an existing tree or create a new tree. Figure 3.13 shows the dialog box where you must make this important choice. I'll assume that you are creating the first server in the tree; hence, you will need to choose New NDS Tree. If you already have a tree (or trees), you can skip to the "New Server in an Existing NetWare 5.1 Network" section.

Before continuing with creating your NDS tree, there are some things you need to know about NDS. This installation isn't difficult; in fact, you made harder decisions earlier in the installation process. However, your choices here will shape what your NDS tree will look like. Read through this section before you install NDS, and if you have further questions, refer to Chapter 4 before you continue.

FIGURE 3.13

A very important fork in the installation process—create a new tree or use an existing one?

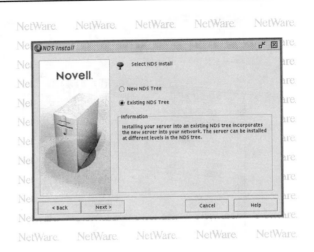

Some Definitions

Before you begin, scan these brief definitions of the NDS terms you'll be seeing:

Tree   The hierarchical organization of the network. Like a directory structure for a hard disk, an NDS tree has a single root with multiple branches (directories) containing other directories and/or files (other branches and/or leaf nodes).

Container   An object that can hold or contain other objects. The Tree (a special container), Country, Organization, and Organizational Unit objects are containers.

Organization   A high-level container just below the Country level (if used) or the [Root] of the Tree and just above the Organizational Unit. There must be at least one Organization object in every NDS tree.

Organizational Unit   The smallest container, below Organization. This container is not required, but it's often used for better management of workgroups, departments, or project teams.

Context   A way to describe the position of an object within containers in an NDS tree. The context is a position reference point, similar to a user's home directory being a reference point in a file system tree.

Admin   A User object created during NetWare 5.1 installation, similar to the SUPERVISOR in NetWare 3.*x*. Admin has the rights to create and manage all objects in the newly installed NDS tree.

Leaf objects   Objects that don't contain any other objects. Leaf objects include users, printers, servers, server volumes, and the like. Leaf objects are effectively the bindery contents from NetWare 3.*x*.

What You Need to Know

To install NDS on a NetWare 5.1 server, you need to know the following:

- The name of your NDS tree
- Your time zone
- Your company (Organization) name
- Any company divisions (Organizational Units) (optional)
- The NDS location for the server (the default Organization or Organizational Unit)
- The password for your Admin user (or provide the password for new installations)

You'll need this information whether you are creating a brand-new NetWare 5.1 network or plugging this server into an existing NDS tree. The process is remarkably similar in either case.

When you're installing your first NetWare 5.1 server, you must create an NDS tree and the context for the server being installed. For your subsequent servers, you must decide where in the existing NDS tree they should live.

When you're installing a new server in an existing NDS network, you can still create new NDS trees, Organizations, and Organizational Units during installation. The installation process will offer you the choice of installing the server into an existing context or creating a new context.

Although the best time to fix a mistake is immediately, if you make a mistake during server installation, it's not going to cause you any long-term trouble. If you later decide you don't like the name for a particular Organization or Organizational Unit, you can change it—no big deal.

Figure 3.14 shows four NDS tree arrangements. Each Organization or Organizational Unit is a context. The Simple Installation method follows the first illustration, with only a single Organization containing leaf objects. During NDS installation, you can create as many Organizations and Organizational Units as you desire.

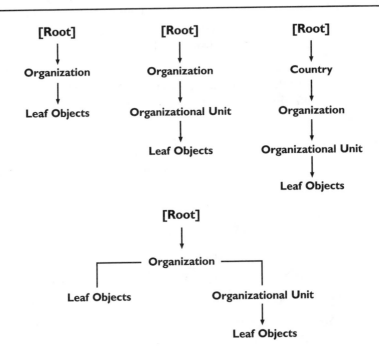

FIGURE 3.14

NDS tree examples, from simple to less simple

NDS Tree Naming

Since this is your first NetWare 5.1 server, you need to give your NDS tree a name and create it. Figure 3.15 shows the dialog box where NDS is configured, including where the tree name is entered. Here are the NDS tree-naming rules:

- Must be unique across all connected networks
- May use letters A–Z
- May use numbers 0–9
- May use a hyphen (-)
- May use an underscore (_)
- May be any length, as long as the complete context name does not exceed 255 characters

FIGURE 3.15

*Entering your tree
name, the context for
your server and Admin
user, the name of your
Admin user, and the
initial password for
that user*

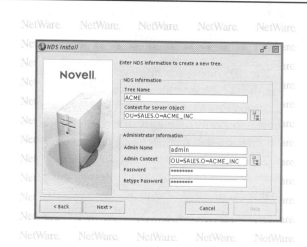

There's no reason to give a long, descriptive name to the tree, because the Tree and [Root] objects are always implied (not shown) when listing contexts. This is not a problem, since Novell recommends only a single NDS tree per organization, and the client usually uses only one tree at a time.

NDS trees aren't easily renamed. Trees can be merged, but this is a more advanced topic. Pick a unique name.

The Server's Context

You must tell the server its location in the NDS tree. Every server is installed into a context, so the first server must define its own context. The server can change contexts later, but go ahead and get it right the first time.

As you can see in Figure 3.15, we have chosen a name for our new NDS tree, ACME, and set the server's context to OU=SALES.O=ACME_INC. The only default user for this new NDS tree is Admin (although the name can be changed at this point), the manager of the entire newly created tree. Admin will be the equivalent of SUPERVISOR for NetWare 3.*x* users. Notice also that the Admin user account's context is the same as the server context; this also represents a change from the past, where the Admin account was installed near the top of the tree. One more thing to notice in Figure 3.15: any time a context is needed, the Browse buttons to the right of the text boxes allow you to graphically choose (and/or create) the desired context.

Organization and Organizational Unit Naming

To finish the installation, you need at least one Organization name. Organizational Unit names are optional, both during installation and when your network is up and running. The NDS dialog box displays the Context For Server Object text box and the location in the tree. Next to the text box is a Browse button, where you can graphically create the structure of your tree. Click it and then select Add to create a new container.

You can choose only a Country or Organization as your top-level container. For a discussion on container types, see Chapter 4. Typically, you will begin with an Organization. The Organization name can be the same as the name you gave the NDS tree itself, but that might be confusing to some users later. That's why the lab network tree has the name ACME and the Organization is also named ACME. Clearly, they are different, but the relationship between ACME and ACME isn't clear. To clarify that relationship, you might want to call the tree ACME_Tree and the top-level organization ACME. This would make it clear that it all belongs to the same company but would eliminate any possible confusion with duplicate names for the Organization and the tree. The Organization name you type in and save will appear in the Context For Server Object field. This naming standard, *TopLevelOrganization*_Tree, is commonly used when naming trees.

As you install your first server, keep in mind that this information pertains not to just this particular server; you are creating a basic NDS framework. Maybe only one server is involved right now, but your network may contain many more servers over time.

Each field can contain a maximum of 64 characters. Legal characters in this section are A–Z and a–z (uppercase and lowercase), along with 0–9 and the underscore (_) character. The limit for the total server context name is 255 characters.

The Admin Password

Passwords are an art in themselves, and your company may have guidelines set already. If not, and you need to make up a password here, try to follow these guidelines:

- It should contain at least five characters.
- It should include both letters and numbers.
- It is not case sensitive.
- It is not the name of a loved one or your birthday.
- Do not tape the password to your monitor, desk, or any other place near the computer. (Yes, people still do that.)

Select the Password field, type your password, select Retype Password, and retype the password for verification. Remember, someone logging in as Admin has full run of your network. Please use a decent password. Notice in Figure 3.15 that the password's characters all appear as asterisks, so type carefully.

One final note before we move on: once you click Next, you're committed. The installation program will create the NDS structure you have chosen, and there is no going back (although changes can be made after installation is complete).

For Your Information: All the Details in One Screen

After you click Next, the installation program will verify that the tree name is unique, and then it will create the structure you just created in the previous dialog box. The tendency of network administrators to be distracted during installation and forget vital information is well known at Novell. Remember the pad and pencil you're supposed to have beside you during the installation process? Well, go find it, because you do need to write down the information shown in the summary screen. All this information is easy to forget while NetWare 5.1 is still new.

The only information you don't have on-screen that you will need is the password for Admin. Jot that down now while you're thinking of it (but please don't leave it next to the server).

You can now skip ahead to the section concerning the NetWare License information.

New Server in an Existing NetWare 5.1 Network

There are some differences between installing the first server and adding a second, third, fourth, and so on server into an existing NetWare 5.1 network. Some of the differences are obvious, but others are not. For example, when installing a second or third server, you may want to add another container for that server by creating another Organizational Unit. These added pieces require a few more decisions during installation, but nothing serious.

As soon as you begin the NDS installation, you must decide whether to include the new server in an existing NDS tree or to create a new tree. To install it into an existing tree, simply choose Existing NDS Tree and click Next.

In the next dialog box, you need to fill in a user name and password with the appropriate rights to install this new server in the tree (specifically, the Create right to the selected context, as explained in Chapter 9). This is another security feature—you wouldn't want just anybody to be able to install a server and replicate data or NDS information anywhere.

To choose your tree, click the Browse button to the right of the text box that prompts you for your tree name. NetWare will then compile a list of all known trees and ask you to select one. You can select an existing tree or choose Not Listed (the other buttons allow you to add, delete, or edit the context for your server). Choosing Not Listed displays another dialog box that asks you to enter the tree name and the target server's TCP/IP address or its Server ID. This should not normally be necessary; the option is here for those with advanced needs and those who are using address filtering.

Once you choose your tree, you can then set the server's context, as described earlier. When you've finished, a dialog box with summary information appears. You will notice that it is a little bit different from the one that appears when you create a new tree; this one shows only the tree name and context.

 NOTE Each NDS tree has its own database of objects that is not visible from another tree. If you're using the Client32 software, multiple trees are not a problem. As you'll see in a bit, Network Neighborhood in Windows 95/98, after being enhanced by Client32, can see multiple trees. But this doesn't mean that your users won't get confused, so don't go tree crazy. One tree remains best.

The NetWare License Software

One of the disks included with your software is labeled as the license disk. It will also have a user count, such as 5 User, 100 User, and so on. The installation program will ask you to insert that disk. Notice in Figure 3.16 that you can choose another location, for example from a hard drive or a server. This is not usually done, but it can be good backup policy to protect the license disk's contents in case the disk itself gets damaged. You can also check the box Install Without Licenses if you want to do this later or are installing the two-user version to practice with at home.

Novell has rejected some of the onerous copy-protection schemes other vendors use. If the license file from another operating system is used, error messages will appear on the servers and on workstations.

License management doesn't take very much time but does require care. Leaving licensing until later works for an existing network, since you'll want to put the license files in your regular spot. For new networks, however, go ahead and feed in the disk when requested.

FIGURE 3.16

Entering the location of the license

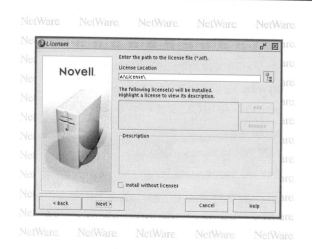

WARNING   Software piracy is a multibillion-dollar criminal market. Every piece of stolen software used takes money from the developer of the software that could be used to improve the product. Besides that, using software that you didn't purchase is no different from using an automobile that you didn't buy: it's theft.

Installing Optional Products

There is one last major set of choices to make. These are optional products that can be installed at this point. I will give a brief description of each here, along with references to the places later in the book where they are described in more detail. Your choices are:

- Novell Certificate Server
- LDAP Services
- NetWare Management Portal
- Storage Management Services
- Novell Distributed Print Services (NDPS)
- NetWare Enterprise Web Server

- NetWare News Server
- NetWare Web Manager
- NetWare FTP Server
- IBM WebSphere Application Server
- NetWare Web Search
- Novell DNS/DHCP Services
- Novell Internet Access Server
- WAN Traffic Manager Services
- NetWare Multimedia Server

A dialog box similar to that shown in Figure 3.17 allows you to make your optional product choices. To choose a product or a service, simply check the box in front of the selection (or uncheck a box if you don't want to install that component). When you have made all your selections, choose Next. Many of the components will bring up additional dialog boxes where they can be individually configured.

FIGURE 3.17

Choosing your optional components

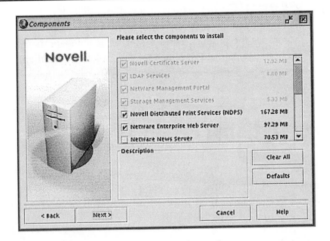

Let's begin with a brief introduction to each of these optional products or services. Adding them all takes approximately half a gigabyte, in addition to the space needed by the operating system, which is 144MB. As I mentioned earlier in this chapter, a 2GB SYS: volume is not too large.

Novell Certificate Server

New with NetWare 5.1 is the Certificate Server, pushed by an increased need for internal security but blasted onto your NetWare server by the need to certify and authenticate Web transactions. The Certificate Server gives you, for free, the ability to mint, issue, and manage digital certificates. These are key for the NetWare Web Manager and NetWare Enterprise Server.

If the server being installed is your first NetWare 5.1 server, it will host the Certificate Server. Therefore, put your best, long-term, and most reliable server box up for the first server on the network. This will hold the Certificate Server for your network.

If other servers already populate the network, you probably won't be reading this deep into the installation process. If so, for some reason, feel free to reference the existing Certificate Server via the NDS Lookup button.

LDAP Services

LDAP (Lightweight Directory Access Protocol) Services allow you to connect to your tree and view and update data in your NDS database from any Web browser. As its name implies, LDAP is the lightweight version of DAP, the X.500 Directory Access Protocol on which NDS is based. Once you set up this service, you can define who can see what in your NDS tree. For example, you might make names and phone numbers available to anyone on the Internet; allow the employees in the company to see names, work addresses, phone and fax numbers, and title information; and allow administrators complete control over all properties of all users.

To allay security concerns, LDAP supports the use of NDS rights, as well as LDAP Access Control Lists to define who can do what. What about security concerns in getting authenticated? You don't want your name and password crossing the Internet unencrypted, right? LDAP also supports SSL, the Secure Sockets Layer, which encrypts all that information to help keep it secure.

If you check this box, after you click Next, a dialog box will appear asking you to configure it. You will be asked if you want to enable use of the LDAP catalog on this server (it is an NDS object like any other). If you do, indicate whether requested information should come from the catalog only or if NDS should be checked when the data is not in the catalog. Typically, you will use only the information in the catalog to make LDAP more secure. You'll find more information on LDAP and how to implement it in Chapter 14.

NetWare Management Portal

An extremely cool new feature for NetWare 5.1 is full management via a Web browser. Well, not everything, but all the physical details of any server. This option is definitely recommended, especially since so little disk space is involved. Get it, you'll love it. You'll see it plenty of network management in Chapter 10.

Storage Management Services

You use Storage Management Services (SMS) when backing up and restoring data. This basic technology now included in NetWare can get your backups rolling. Remember how important I said backups are? Now you have no excuse for not doing them. The basic software is included.

That said, most companies buy a third-party backup package that has more features, such as ArcServe or Legato NetWorker. No matter which package you get, however, be sure it has the capability to back up and restore the file system, including the new NSS volumes.

Novell Distributed Print Services

Novell Distributed Print Services (NDPS) is Novell's improvement and gift to the world of printing. By adding a certain level of intelligence to printers, NDS can shuffle queues automatically after failure and the like.

NDPS allows for bi-directional flow of information between the printer and the server. The printer can report information such as status (online or offline), features, and capabilities. If this information is reported (and stored) in NDS, users can search for printers with specific traits, such as all the printers that support color printing, 11 by 17 paper, and duplexing and then have a printer automatically download and install the needed drivers. You can notify the person when the print job is done, as well as schedule print jobs. NDPS is also protocol independent, so it works well with IP and/or IPX.

This feature takes an awful lot of disk space for a program that doesn't thrill me much anyway (read more of my griping in Chapter 8). If you have printers or print servers that are NDPS-enabled, this service is great. If you have normal, rather stupid printers, stick with print queues for now.

NetWare Enterprise Web Server

Well, surprise! This is the Netscape Enterprise Web Server, with more features and raw power than most other Web servers. Millions of Web sites around the world owe their existence to a Netscape server.

Earlier NetWare versions just shipped the FastTrack server from Netscape, but NetWare 5.1 upgraded to the Enterprise Server. If you know a webmaster, ask him or her to come over and help you start the Web server, then watch your friend's eyes light up with excitement.

NetWare News Server

Want Groupware? Want Groupware without the expense of Notes or even GroupWise? Want every conversation concerning projects to remain on the server, so new members to the project team can get up to speed quickly? Think News Server.

Some 50,000 newsgroups on Usenet can't all be wrong. Weird at times, yes, but not all wrong. The technology powering Usenet now comes free in the red box. Take a few minutes (literally) to set up a News Server, start using it for the IT group, and watch people start begging for their own newsgroups. Happens every time.

NetWare Web Manager

You don't use this to manage the Web per se, but to manage many of the places where your network interacts with the Web. Web Manager, a browser-based management tool, comes almost completely from Netscape via Novonyx (the Novell and Netscape joint venture now largely gone). At least the Web Manager now says NetWare everywhere instead of Netscape.

Connect to the Web Manager software on the appropriate server by using the address `https://servername.com:2002`. Why `https` rather than `http`? For the security; the `https` tag calls SSL security for communication.

The Web Manager comes in handy for managing the News Server, Web Server Search, and Multimedia Server.

NetWare FTP Server

Novell included a File Transfer Protocol server component back with NetWare 4.*x*, so you shouldn't be surprised. Yes, it can be used to handle FTP requests across the Internet. Yes, you can also configure the server to communicate with other NetWare servers without TCP/IP or the FTP Server software running. More on that later.

IBM WebSphere Application Server

Here we get into a serious e-commerce component and one of the main reasons NetWare 5.1 takes its place as a leading Web-server platform. The IBM WebSphere Application Server Standard Edition, now free in the red box, provides an outstanding framework for deploying and managing Java applications on the NetWare server.

WebSphere connects the Web Server (oriented toward display, not processing) to a variety of programming and processing interfaces. Need JavaBean applications? WebSphere handles that for you. Need servelets? Ditto. Connection servelets for CORBA applications? Got it.

A five-user version of Oracle 8i also appears in the red box. Together with the Enterprise Web Server, WebSphere, and Oracle 8i, you or your webmaster can run one serious Web site.

NetWare Web Search Server

Piling plenty of content into a Web server becomes self-defeating when you can't find what you want. That's where the NetWare Web Search Server comes in.

As you already guessed, the Web Search Server indexes Web server content and controls searches. This service is free, simple to configure through the Web Manager, and necessary for serious Web sites, whether for external public use or the company intranet.

Novell DNS/DHCP Services

As I mentioned in Chapter 1, DNS (Domain Name Service) and DHCP (Dynamic Host Configuration Protocol) are important protocols in the TCP/IP protocol suite. DNS allows you to enter a name, such as www.sybex.com, and have that translated into an IP address, instead of forcing you to memorize 150.65.75.35, for example, for each site that you want to go to. If you will be using IP, having DNS set up will allow your users to do the same thing for your intranet. If you will create Web servers, they will need DNS entries and DNS servers in place.

DHCP is another important component (at least for you) as you migrate to TCP/IP. In the old IPX days, you assigned network addresses on the server (and you have seen them in this chapter already if you checked the box to install IPX), and the protocol had a mechanism to automatically assign each computer's individual node address. TCP/IP has no such mechanism. You must touch each computer and assign an IP address, subnet mask, and (in all but the smallest of networks) a default gateway (or router). There are other parameters as well, such as an IP address for a DNS server, that you may want to assign. All this is done manually, and you must keep track of each IP address assigned to make sure that it is assigned only once. This is a lot of work and has a high probability of error as you repeat the process many times, which is tough to accomplish.

Enter DHCP. With DHCP, you install the protocol on a server, configure the range of IP addresses you want to give out, fill in a subnet mask and router, and let the clients come and get the information from the server. You don't have to touch each computer.

If you check the box to install Novell DNS/DHCP Services, a dialog box for more information will appear after you click Next. You must set up three NDS contexts for the objects that are needed to support these services. There are many implications and considerations that must be taken into account, so read Chapter 15, which is dedicated to these subjects.

Novell Internet Access Server

Slightly misnamed, this software consists mostly of the NIASCFG utility. Although NIASCFG hints at controlling user access to the Internet, that job remains with Border-Manager. NIASCFG concentrates on protocol and routing configuration for your NetWare servers.

Just about everything to do with IPX, TCP/IP, routing, tunneling, and filtering comes under the Novell Internet Access Server heading. We'll spend some time with this utility later, so install this software whether or not you know why you're doing so at this time. You'll need it later.

WAN Traffic Manager Services

WAN Traffic Manager is another NetWare 5.1 innovation. In version 4, whenever NDS had a change to be sent out, it sent that change. Sounds great, right? In a LAN environment, this setup worked fine, but as more and more WAN links were added to the picture, more and more traffic started to cross those links. So what?

WAN links usually have much less total and available bandwidth than LAN links. The more NDS data had to be replicated, the less bandwidth that was available for users to do whatever the links were installed for, such as getting their e-mail. With WAN Traffic Manager, however, you can schedule when NDS synchronizes, such as only at night when WAN traffic is usually much lighter.

NetWare Multimedia Server

Here's another new goodie within NetWare. Ever want to stream audio or video to your Web browser customers, internally or externally? Multimedia Server is the software you need.

It's easy to add later, so don't lose sleep if you don't plan on using this feature and later must go back and add the software. By the way, streaming works better across the company LAN than across the Internet. Be aware that streaming media on your network, such as video, tap into the couch potato syndrome for many users. In other words, they watch, open their mouths, turn off their minds, and turn on their drool. Just like TV. So use it with care.

Customizing Your Installation

You have probably been reading this for quite a while, and it sounds hard to install a server. There is nothing to fear, however. After you have installed a few servers, it will be almost second nature. The GUI will help you throughout the process, and Help is abundant, both in the TUI and the GUI. You are almost finished at this point.

If you suddenly realize that you forgot one of the optional networking products just after hitting the Finish command button, fear not. All these extra products are easy to install later. See their individual sections later in the book for the details.

After you make your optional product selections, you'll see the Summary screen illustrated in Figure 3.18. To make final selections, choose Customize. Here's another dialog box of choices; we'll now cover any not listed in the optional products list just discussed.

FIGURE 3.18

The last chance to customize your choices before installation begins

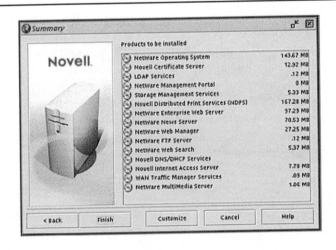

The NetWare Operating System

If you choose NetWare Operating System, then Properties, you will get a dialog box where you can set the Server ID number, discussed previously, and review the license settings. You can also set the language for the server, as well as the Admin Language field for the Admin user. These settings both default to English, but if you are installing a server and sending it elsewhere, this would be the place to change the language so that console messages would appear in the local language. The same would be true if someone other than yourself would be administering the server and didn't speak English.

The Components tab here does effectively nothing, as it shows choices that can't be modified and that each choice takes no disk space, with the exception of NDPS, which takes 82.51MB. Clicking the + next to NetWare Operating System reveals four more choices that can be customized:

- File System
- Protocols
- NDS
- Novell Distributed Print Services (NDPS)

You can choose each of these, make selections, and then click OK to return to the main Product Customization dialog box. This screen summarizes and helps rework mistakes. You can always rework mistakes later; further into the book we'll discuss how.

TimeSync Details

Every PC includes a clock function, so every NetWare server has a clock built into the supporting hardware. Servers have always used these clocks for certain operations (file access for instance), but the time of an event within a single server is not critical.

When you expand your network across multiple servers, time becomes more of a concern. Some applications use time stamps on files or records, so a consistent time source is important to them. If there is only one server, you have a single time source. If you have two NetWare 3.*x* servers and you are attached to both, the time from one system may not match the time from the other one. If they don't match, time stamps on files and records across the two servers will not be reliable.

When you go a step further and spread your network Directory system across multiple servers, you have even more need for a single, reliable time source. Directory functions such as security changes and new user creation now require the participation of multiple individual servers. The most reliable means of tracking changes in a distributed network is by time stamps for each operation. Since multiple servers are involved, there must be a reliable time source for all servers to reference.

When you set up your first NetWare 5.1 server, you chose the Single Reference time server type, since there is only a single server on the network. That same choice is valid for only one server on the network; no other servers can be this type (that's why it's called a *Single Reference* time server). All remaining servers will be Secondary time servers by default.

All time servers provide time to clients, but some time servers communicate to decide the proper network time. The following sections describe each type of time server in more detail.

Single Reference Time Servers   A Single Reference time server provides time information to all other servers and clients. You must configure other servers as Secondary time servers, not Primary or Reference servers. The network administrator sets the time on a Single Reference server, although time can also be checked against an outside source, such as a radio clock. With a single-server network, time is rarely so critical as to require outside verification.

A Single Reference time server network has no time fault tolerance. If all other servers rely on one server and the server goes down, time will slip. Smaller networks with few servers are more likely to have a Single Reference time server. Other servers, if they exist, do not negotiate with a Single Reference time server to set the time; they just accept the time given.

Reference Time Servers   More restrictive than the Single Reference time server, the Reference time server is often tied to an outside source for accurate time. While the Reference time server communicates with other servers (in particular, Primary time servers) to discuss the actual time, the Secondary time servers must accept the time from the Reference time server.

It is advisable to have multiple time servers if your network is geographically distributed. The delay in transmitting time information will skew your time settings across a WAN. The best plan is to have a Reference time server and an additional Primary server in each geographical location to provide time information for those clients and servers. The fewer time packets you have crossing your WAN, the better.

Primary Time Servers   The Primary time server synchronizes time settings with at least one other Reference or Primary time server. Each server offers its time and then learns the time of the other servers; then an agreed-upon time is set for all Reference and Primary time servers.

Large networks use Primary time servers to offer alternative paths to other Secondary time servers. In WANs, a Primary time server will handle the long-distance connection to another time server source and pass that time along to local Secondary time servers.

Secondary Time Servers   Secondary time servers obtain time from a Single Reference, Reference, or Primary time server and pass that time to clients. The Secondary time server does not vote with other time providers to set the time.

Most servers will be Secondary time servers, especially in a large, distributed network. For best time-keeping, make time server connections across the fastest network links possible.

Sorry for the diversion on time, but this is the only place during installation where you can change these settings, and you need to know what each type is for before you start making changes.

Protocols

When you choose Protocols, you can verify and/or modify your IP address, subnet mask, and router, as you could earlier in the installation process, but you have more control over IPX. Earlier, all you could do was select IP and/or IPX. Now, you can choose the frame types you want supported and see what NetWare has picked up for the IPX addresses for those frames it has detected. If it didn't detect any, there would simply be made-up numbers here with 802.2 the only selected frame type. You can change the numbers NetWare generated to other numbers if need be.

Use the tabs in this dialog box to set other IP-related parameters, such as DNS name servers and the domain to which this server belongs. This is an advanced topic, and I'll discuss it in much greater detail in Chapter 15. You can also set up SNMP (Simple Network Management Protocol) information here, and you can specify where to send traps (potential issues or problems that may need to be addressed) for both IPX and IP servers. (I'll cover this topic in Chapter 17.) You can also set some information about this server, such as a description and location to help you make sense of traps returned. The IPX Compatibility tab applies to issues concerning the migration of IPX to IP. I'll talk about the issues surrounding the change and/or coexistence of IP and IPX in Chapter 14.

NDS

The third set of operating system parameters that you can modify during installation relates to Novell Directory Services. The Directory Services Properties dialog box provides one last chance to write down the NDS summary information. If you have not written it down already, do it now! If you forget this information, you may be forced to reinstall NDS, which will waste your time and make you feel stupid.

You can also set time zone parameters here. You can select a preconfigured time zone from the list. If you don't see your time zone, you can invent one or use the normal abbreviation for your time zone and specify the offset from GMT (Greenwich Mean Time) and the direction of the offset (ahead or behind). You can also set the Daylight Saving Time (DST) information—when it starts and ends—and the offset while in use.

Greenwich Mean Time (GMT) is the world time reference site in Greenwich, England. It's rare to need to change the GMT offset from that supplied by the installation program when you choose a time zone.

If you are east of GMT and create your own time abbreviation, use AHEAD with the number, since you're ahead of GMT. For example, in Germany, you would use an offset of 1 and select AHEAD. If your time zone is west of GMT, toggle to BEHIND since your time is behind GMT.

Novell Distributed Print Services (NDPS)

When you select NDPS and choose Properties, you can choose to use an existing broker or to create a new one. If you choose to create a new one, you specify the context and the services it will provide. Usually, the defaults will work well here (as in just about every other place in this customization area). Remember also that you can modify these settings later with the administration tools. For more information on NDPS, brokers, and so forth, see Chapter 8.

Additional Products and Services

To change a selection you made in the previous dialog boxes, choose Additional Products And Services, then choose Properties. If you click the + next to this selection, the section will expand. Only the LDAP Services, Storage Management Services, and Novell Documentation CD-ROM components can be configured here. To customize any of them, select it and choose Properties.

Selecting LDAP Services gives you the same choices explained earlier. Now you can change any of the configuration options you've already selected.

The final component that you can modify is Storage Management Services. When you click the Properties button, you will see a dialog box that allows you to choose which tree you are using and the context for the server. These choices are necessary to specify where the SMS-related objects will appear. You can also choose the context for the SMDR (Storage Management Data Requestor) object and the queue name and context. These settings will be described in Chapter 19.

Finishing the Installation

When you have finished making modifications to the components, click Close to leave the Product Customization dialog box and then Finish to begin installing all of the options you selected.

Congratulations, you have just installed a NetWare 5.1 server! That wasn't so hard, was it? While you are watching the file-copy progress, notice all the information that Novell provides. It looks a lot more like a Windows product installation than a server installation.

As is typical of almost all Windows programs you install today, there is a progress indicator toward the bottom of the screen. It will (slowly) move to 100%. Along the way, you will see ads for various new features and capabilities in the background, another feature common to most modern Windows programs.

The copying process will take quite a long time, depending on the options you have chosen, the speed of your CD-ROM drive, and so on. Sooner or later you will see the final dialog box, which contains a quick summary and informs you of any errors. You should review this file when you are finished. You are also told that you should restart the computer now, so that all of the selected options and configuration options may take effect. If you like, you may also read the readme file now. No, really, that's not a joke. You should read it. I'm serious.

Removing Novell Directory Services

IN A HURRY

3.2 Removing NDS from a Server

1. At the server console prompt, type **NWCONFIG**.
2. Highlight Directory Options and press Enter.
3. Highlight Remove Directory Services From This Server and press Enter.
4. Read the NDS warnings.
5. Verify your intent to delete Directory Services.
6. Log in as Admin or equivalent.
7. Read the NDS warnings concerning the single NDS tree.
8. Verify your intention to delete the Directory.
9. Read the messages about further actions.

Paranoia about planning your NDS tree was rampant when NetWare 4 first hit the streets, because it was new. The tools to recover from mistakes were incomplete, and some customers deleted NDS rather than try to fix it.

That's no longer true, even for the most paranoid of administrators. But if you do want to remove NDS, right at installation is a good time to do so. Installation is so quick with NetWare 5.1 that it actually may be faster to reload NDS than to rework a mangled tree.

Once again, we're back to the Installation Options screen. Type **NWCONFIG** at the server console prompt to reach this screen. Highlight Directory Options and press Enter to see the Directory Services Options menu. Highlight Remove Directory Services From This Server and press Enter. Depending on the situation in your network, you will see various warning messages.

Warning, Warning

NDS removal is a big deal and should be done only under the *rarest* of circumstances after the server has been put in use. However, during initial installation, you may want to play with different NDS arrangements. If one plan doesn't work well, it's little trouble to delete a basically empty NDS tree and reinstall. These instructions are only for situations in which NetWare 5.1 is in a pilot network test mode, no valuable information is contained on the server, and no users are going to be stranded.

However, and this is serious, *deleting a working NDS tree erases all users, objects, printers, print queues, and groups.* Sorry for yelling, but this is an important point. When you remove the directory, you perform a lobotomy on your server. This is the same as erasing the bindery files on a NetWare 3.*x* server.

No, it's actually worse than erasing bindery files. Bindery files concern only one server at a time. If you erase a bindery, only one server's users are inconvenienced. With NetWare 5.1, hundreds of users may suffer some aggravation.

Directories that are part of a large network may be referenced in scores or hundreds of object descriptions. Some users may not discover the loss of the directory information for that one server for weeks or months, but that just amplifies the hassle when they do realize it's gone.

Be careful about removing NDS from an existing network. Try *everything* else before you dump the directory.

Removing NDS from a One-Server Network

After you run INSTALL and select Remove Directory Services from the Directory Options menu, you'll reach the first warning. You must confirm again that you want to delete Directory Services. Figure 3.19 shows one of the warning screens.

FIGURE 3.19

Warning! Warning!

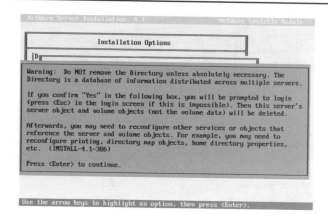

PART

I

You cannot delete the directory without proving you have the authority to do so. This would be a big security hole if just anyone could trash your server. Figure 3.20 shows the Admin password screen.

FIGURE 3.20

Authenticating Admin before directory deletion

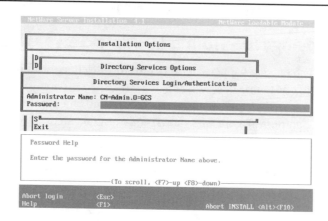

Once you are past the Admin login stage, you can delete Directory Services. Figure 3.21 warns you of the consequences for deleting the single replica of an NDS tree.

Setting Up the Network

FIGURE 3.21

One more warning

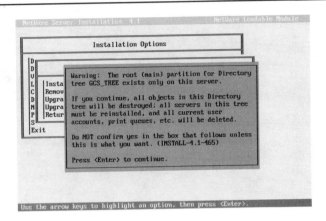

This warning appeared on a single-server network. The default installation routines make the second server in an NDS tree a replica holder automatically. Although it would take some extra work, it might be possible for you to delete a single directory installation and undo a network of several servers—possible, but unlikely. You might just take a deep breath and think again before you continue, however.

Removing NDS from a Multiple-Server Network

Much of what happens during a directory deletion on a single-server network happens with one of many servers. NDS is a serious service, and you shouldn't delete it cavalierly.

When multiple servers are involved, time synchronization becomes another sticking point. As Figure 3.22 shows, you must take steps to continue time-keeping for the remaining servers and users in the tree.

FIGURE 3.22

Time synchronization settings after NDS deletion

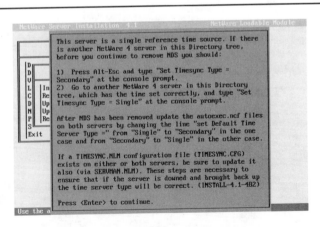

Remember, there are better ways to fix an NDS tree than chopping it down. These options are described in Chapter 10, which covers network management. Removing it is a last resort.

Installation Is Good, but It Will Get Better

When Novell included the Simple Installation process for NetWare 4.10 (it actually got into 4.02), some network resellers were unhappy. How can you charge a customer for installation when the customer knows the installation process is a snap? With the addition of the GUI for the installation program for NetWare 5.x, the procedure can even be considered "user-friendly."

Customers, of course, are happy with these new installation features. Installing NDS is simple, and any NDS tree mistakes can be easily corrected. What could be wrong?

What if this is too easy? What if customers figure, "no pain, no gain?" After all, NetWare is now almost as easy to install as DOS. It's much easier to configure than Windows of any version. How can this product be any good?

But only those with experience might take the "too-easy" view. Most people today *expect* things to be easier. You and I are in the computer business, and we know how much easier things are today than five years ago. People in the "real" world just see how computers are still more difficult to use than they should be.

Amazingly, the most difficult areas are those that home computer users most want. Have you installed a sound board and CD-ROM drive lately? Not simple. Modems are still killers, especially if they're cheap (and even worse if the cheap bundled software isn't configured for that particular modem). The result of these problems is that people think computers are getting harder to understand, not easier. They may be right.

I'm waiting for the installation procedure that listens to the network and configures itself. The first disk that loads the SERVER.EXE program would start a network monitor, listen for the NDS information, and fill out several proposed configurations. You then choose your favorite and get another cup of coffee. That's the kind of installation routine I want. It would also make books like this shorter.

CHAPTER 4

Novell Directory Services: Overview, Planning, Expansion

Some people believe, mistakenly, that NDS (Novell Directory Services) is the only improvement that NetWare 4.*x* and 5.*x* have over NetWare 3.*x*. Many people may also believe, mistakenly, that NDS is some terribly complicated technology that bears no relationship to earlier NetWare software.

Put your fears to rest. NDS is the next step in network organization and administration, grouping servers the way NetWare 3.*x* groups users. NetWare 5.1 provides user access and simplified management to a single department as well as an enterprise containing hundreds of servers.

In fact, notice the name of the directory service: *Novell* Directory Services. The name used to be *NetWare* Directory Services, but it was changed to reflect that NDS runs not only on NetWare, but on other platforms such as multiple flavors of Unix, Linux, and NT.

The Global Network View

Officially, NDS is a relational database distributed across your entire network. All servers in the network can take part in supporting NDS, making all network resources available to NetWare clients. NDS provides global access to all network resources (users, groups, printers, volumes, and so on), regardless of where they are physically located. Users log in to a multiserver network and view the entire network as a single information system.

Fancy official words boil down to this: every client can see everything in the network from a graphical program provided by NetWare 5.1 (assuming they have the assigned rights to do so, of course). More exciting for you as the administrator is that this single network view works for management as well. You can view, change, add, or delete network resources anywhere in the network (assuming appropriate rights), without logging in to each server where the resource is located.

You've heard about how the old phones worked: you picked up the handset, an operator asked the name of the person you wanted to connect to, and then the operator took care of the rest. NDS works in a similar manner. Instead of picking up the phone, you execute the NWUSER (Windows 3.*x*-based NetWare User Tools) program or browse Network Neighborhood (in Windows 95/98). Instead of asking for a person by name, you highlight the resource name with a mouse, then click, and you're connected.

Many users already think things are almost this easy, which is testimony to all your hard work managing your network. The reality is, of course, that NetWare 3.*x* and earlier focused on each server in the network. We call this the *server-centric* view of networking. The NetWare 5.1 network focuses on the entire network, thus creating what is known as the *network-centric* view. NDS is the database, and associated programs help track all the pieces of the entire network.

 NOTE Some procedural notes before our foray into NDS. References to *the Directory* (uppercase D) assume the NDS Directory structure; *directory* (lowercase d) references a file directory on a disk or volume. The word *tree* refers to the NDS tree (I won't be talking about the oak, willow, or pecan type). And, while you might think Novell Directory Services is plural and should be referred to in that manner, we've decided that it's a singular object and should be referred to in that manner. I will say "NDS is" rather than "NDS are." Although made of many pieces, NDS is a single logical item.

Advantages of NDS

Stretching the earlier telephone example a bit further, NDS looks like a giant network switchboard. Everything that happens in your network goes through the central authority of NDS.

Another analogy (in case you're collecting them) is that of a card catalog in a library. Each object in the library is listed on a card in the card catalog. If you want a library resource, such as a book, a map, a picture, a tape, a reference book, or a meeting room, the card catalog is the place to start. To make a stronger analogy for us, the card catalog should be used as the inventory-tracking database as well. NDS tracks the location and disposition of all network resources.

NDS is a fundamental network service. A client (such as a user, an application, or a server) requests network information, services, or access. NDS finds the resource information and provides information, network services, or resource access based on the information contained in the Directory.

NDS provides the following:

- A global database providing access to, and management of, network information, resources, and services

- A standard method of managing, viewing, and accessing network information, resources, and services

- A logical organization of network resources that is independent of the physical characteristics or layout of the network

- Dynamic (on-demand) mapping between an object and the physical resource to which it refers

The "global" aspect of the database will help you, even if your network doesn't span continents. This ensures that NDS is available to every client and every server and that it tracks every network resource.

Let's clarify two of the earlier points. The way that NDS handles network requests and activity is not much different from the way they were handled by the bindery, but some people insist on making things more difficult than they really are. The bindery is just as important in earlier versions of NetWare as NDS is in NetWare 5.1, but NDS has a larger scope.

NDS does have the ability to handle resources that are physically distant from the file server where you are connected. Since earlier NetWare versions were completely server-centric, the idea of separating the logical object location from the physical object location never came up. With NetWare 5.1, the server-centric network has been replaced by NDS. Therefore, the physical location of a particular object in relation to a particular server is handled by NDS.

All these benefits come from having a single login name/password concept. This is the advantage of having all the servers work through NDS rather than individually. Before, you needed to connect to each server to use the resources controlled there. Now, you log in to the *network*, and all the NetWare 5.1 servers work together to provide services.

Quick Summary of NDS

All network requests go through NDS. Looking for a printer? Sending mail to another user? Looking for a file? Any client wanting information about or access to any (that means *any*) network resource must use NDS.

NDS contains logical resource information about network resources. The Directory contains information about each object connected to the network. The location of each object within the Directory tree may be different than the physical location would indicate. NDS is a logical, not a physical, concept.

Here's how it works with the common network task of printing:

1. **Client requests resource.** You need to print. You request a printer by its NDS object name.

2. **A NetWare server responds.** A NetWare server, participating in NDS as they all do, looks for the printer object with that name in the Directory.

3. **NDS locates object in Directory.** The particular printer object is located in the Directory database.

Continued

CONTINUED

4. **Resource location is identified.** Based on the property values found for the object, NDS discovers the physical location of the printer.

5. **Client validity and authority are checked.** Your user name and rights are checked and referenced against the list of those eligible to use that particular printer.

6. **Client is connected to resource.** You are connected to the requested printer.

Everything that happens in NetWare 5.1 goes through NDS. Every network resource is tracked by NDS, and every network client uses NDS to find those resources.

Objects Are Everywhere, and All Things Are Objects

I've mentioned objects many times. If you're wondering what objects are and why they matter, you're not alone. In the world of computing, and especially in networking, things are gradually becoming objectified. (Yeah, we made it a word because it's more fun than "object-oriented.")

An *object* is a distinct, separate entity, in programming or in networking. NetWare uses objects in the NDS structure to store information about a network resource, such as a user, group, printer, file server, or volume.

Directory objects are data structures that store information, not the entity they represent. Each object consists of properties. A *property* is a category of information that you can store about an object. Some properties are required to make an object unique; those are mandatory when you create the object. The name of an object is a required property; for example, a User object name property might be "James."

The name of an NDS object can be a maximum of 64 characters, but there is a limit of 256 characters for any complete NDS name. This should not be a problem, unless you give very long names or have way too many levels in your NDS tree.

Other properties are available in the object but not mandatory. There are many, many properties for each object, and different types of objects have different properties. For instance, the description property for James can contain "author," or it can be blank.

The information within the property is called a *value*. In the example just given, the description property value for object James is author. Some properties may have multiple values. If the property is telephone number, for instance, both office and home numbers can be listed.

Objects, properties, and their values are stored in the Directory database. Some objects represent physical objects, such as the User object James. Some objects represent logical, not physical, entities, such as the group Marketing. See Figure 4.1 for a graphical representation.

USER

PROPERTY	VALUE
LOGIN NAME	MARCY
TITLE	EXEC. ASST.
TELEPHONE	555-1234
	555-4321

PRINTER

PROPERTY	VALUE
NAME	HPACCT
DESCRIPTION	HPIIP
LOCATION	ROOM 305
NET ADDRESS	ED043F43

Whether the object represents a physical or logical entity, remember that the *object* we speak of is itself only a structure for storing information. There are no objects you can touch and manipulate physically in this definition.

The object for a device is not the device. That's easy to remember when speaking of printers, but it can become confusing when speaking of logical items such as groups. The object describes the device, but it is not the device.

The category of an object is important. There are three categories, although one is slightly cheating. The *leaf* category of objects represents the actual network resources represented by the bindery in earlier NetWare. Examples are users, printers, servers, and volumes. Leaf objects cannot contain any other objects. They are similar to files in the file system. They are the reason that everything else exists, and you can't place a file inside a file as you could place a file inside a directory.

The *container* category of objects performs that job. Container objects hold, or contain, other objects. Examples of container objects are the Organization and Organizational Unit objects. Container objects are called *parent* objects if there are actually objects inside the container. One container object is mandatory per tree. They are similar to directories in the file system. They are useless in and of themselves, but they are crucial for the organization they give to files.

Finally, there is the *[Root]* category, a "super" container category at the very top of your NDS tree. This category is created during installation, is mandatory, and slightly stretches the category metaphor. There can be only one [Root]. Each tree must have at least one Organization object. Remember naming your Organization during installation? That's when at least one mandatory Organization is created. You can create other Organizations (and other container objects) during installation or later.

Here's a quick review of the NDS terms related to objects:

Object   A unit of information about a resource; for example, a user.

Property   The information category stored about an object; for example, first name.

Value   The specific information within the property; for example, Ashley.

Hierarchical Tree Structure and Schema

Official stuff here: NDS is consistent with the international standard, X.500. This specification, drawn by the CCITT (Consultative Committee for International Telegraphy and Telephony, now officially the ITU, International Telecommunications Union; it is part of the United Nations) and the ISO (International Organization for Standardization), provides a global standard for organizing Directory information.

The X.500 specification describes a global "telephone book" that can be used with the e-mail specifications detailed in X.400.

The Directory *schema* are the rules defining how the NDS tree is built. The schema define specific types of information that dictate the way data is stored in the Directory database. The following information is defined:

Attribute Information   The type of additional information an object can or must have associated with it. Attribute types are defined within the schema by specific constraints and a specific syntax for their values.

Inheritance   Determines which properties will flow down the tree to objects below the current object.

Naming   Determines the structure of the NDS tree.

Subordination   Determines the location of objects in the NDS tree.

These are all technical terms for how the standard objects, such as servers, users, and print queues, are technically defined by NDS. The NDS schema can be modified to suit your network, which is exactly what we'll be doing soon.

[Root]: The Base—and Top—of Your NDS Tree

It sounds backwards to call the top of a hierarchical structure "root," but that's what we do. A statement such as "[Root] is automatically placed at the top of the NDS tree during installation" is true, but sounds weird. So what is this [Root], anyway?

The [Root] object contains everything, which is why the icon for [Root] is a globe. The name of the tree, the only property of the [Root] object, is entered during installation.

The [Root] object is the very first object in the Directory tree and cannot be deleted, although it can be renamed. All other objects, including Country and Organization objects, are contained within the [Root] object. Characteristics of [Root] include:

- Mandatory
- One per Directory
- Forms the top of the NDS tree
- Holds only Country, Organization, and Alias objects (of Country and Organization objects only)
- Created only during installation of Directory Services when creating a new tree
- Cannot be moved or deleted
- Has only one property—the name of the tree

Analogies are fully stocked in our inventory room. In fact, that's a good analogy right there. The storeroom is [Root], the shelves are containers, and things on the shelves are leaf objects. You may have one wall for canned goods (an Organization) and two shelves named Peas and Lima Beans (Organizational Units, or OUs) on that wall.

Or, your conglomerate's entire global network is [Root], with each individual subsidiary an Organization (container). Departments are Organizational Units (containers) made of file servers, file server volumes, users, printers, and all your other leaf objects.

NOTE Do not confuse [Root] with the root directory of a file system. When you see [Root] with the brackets and the capital letter, it refers to the top level of your NDS tree. The root directory is the first directory of a volume or other hard disk and has no relationship to the [Root] object.

For nature lovers, the tree trunk is [Root], branches are containers (with many containers from [Root]), and leaves are, well, leaf nodes. A single tree supports multiple branches, which support multiple leaf objects. Similarly, a single [Root] can support multiple Organizations and Organizational Units, which can in turn support multiple leaf objects.

Objects with rights to the [Root] object have those same rights all the way down the NDS tree. Unless blocked, a trustee of [Root] can have authority over the entire network. The Admin user, created at the same time as [Root] during installation, has a trustee assignment including Supervisor rights to the [Root] object. This allows Admin all rights to all objects in the NDS tree. This roughly equates to the SUPERVISOR user created during installation of earlier NetWare versions. Admin, as SUPERVISOR before, uses those rights to set up the network and create the framework for all users and other network resources.

 WARNING   If you make any other user or group a trustee of [Root], that user or group may have the same rights as the Admin user. I recommend adding another user or group (besides Admin) as a trustee of [Root]. This is useful in case the Admin object becomes damaged, deleted, and so on. During NetWare 5.1 installation, the Public object is granted the Browse object right at the [Root] object of the NDS tree. This setting allows all users to see the entire NDS tree.

Container Objects Go in the [Root] Object

Since [Root] contains everything, the next question is, What is everything? Everything, in terms of NDS, is containers, more containers, and leaf objects. Here's a summary:

- The [Root] object can hold Country and Organization objects.
- The Country objects can hold Organization and Locality objects.
- The Organization objects can hold Organizational Units, Localities, and leaf nodes.
- The Organizational Units can hold other Organizational Units, Localities, and leaf nodes.
- The Locality objects can hold Organizations, Organizational Units, and other localities.
- Leaf nodes are not containers and cannot contain any other object.

In Figure 4.2, you see a simple NDS design. Everything in the figure is a container except for the User and Printer objects.

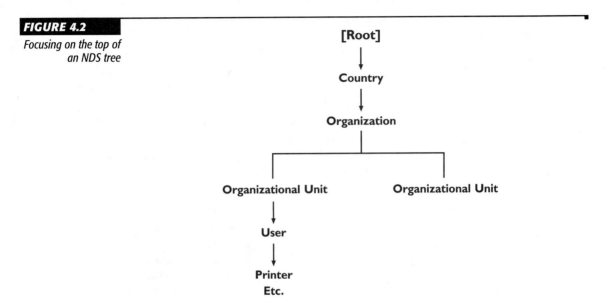

FIGURE 4.2

Focusing on the top of an NDS tree

The "official" suggestion is to keep container names short. There are times when users must type a full path (called a *distinguished name*) to an NDS object. The location of an object in the tree is called its context, much as we call a file's place in the directory tree its path. In Figure 4.2, the name for the user would be typed

```
.USER.ORGANIZATIONAL UNIT.ORGANIZATION.COUNTRY
```

The [Root] name is always assumed to be included, since there can be only one [Root] per NDS tree. Country is rarely used, as you'll see.

Although the example for the user in Figure 4.2 looks like a lot of typing, it's rare for a user to type that much. There are programs for Windows 3.*x* (NWUSER) and Windows 95/98 and NT/2000 (Network Neighborhood) that allow a user to move around the NDS tree without lifting a finger from the mouse or cursor keys.

For the few times a user must type a distinguished name, keep the names of the Organizations and Organizational Units fairly short. (You might also offer typing tutorial programs, but that's a diatribe for another time.) Don't, however, sacrifice clarity for a few keystrokes. Use the common abbreviations used elsewhere in your company, such as Eng for Engineering. Don't truncate Marketing to Mg; use Mktg.

The Country (C) Container

Characteristics of the Country container include:

- Optional for most networks
- Designates the country for your network
- Organizes all Directory objects within the country
- Must use a two-character country abbreviation
- Can only exist in [Root]
- Holds Organization, Locality, and Alias objects only (plus a few special leaf objects described later)

NetWare 5 is a global network operating system, and the inclusion of a Country object makes that distinction clear. But the Country container is optional, even for those networks that do cross international lines.

If you can avoid using the Country object, do so. Using it when you don't need to will only complicate things for your users and administrators. Country objects are included mainly for compatibility with X.500 and would rarely be used. How often do all of a department's functions fit solely in one country, while another's is only in another country? Novell's recommendation is to use Organizations, Organizational Units, and Localities instead. Besides, with these objects you can spell out the names of countries if you want to refer to them.

If you do use a Country object, it can contain only Organization, Locality, and Aliases of those objects. The only leaf objects allowed are the special leaf objects LAN Area, SLP Directory Agent, and SLP Scope Unit (more on these objects later).

If you're in doubt about needing the Country object, you don't. Remember that even multinational networks don't require (and rarely use) the Country object to function. In fact, even in those rare situations where a Country object is desirable, an Organization object is used instead. Why? Using an Organization object, the name of the country can be spelled out, instead of using an obscure two-character code.

The Organization (O) Container

An Organization container has these characteristics:

- Mandatory (at least one per tree)
- Created under [Root], Country, or Locality only
- Typically represents a company, university, or department
- First level that can support leaf objects
- Can contain Organizational Unit, Locality, leaf, and Alias objects
- Named during installation, but subsequent Organizations can be created during installation or later

The next mandatory object after [Root] is the Organization container, indicated by the O abbreviation. There must be one Organization object per NDS tree. Novell recommends one Organization per tree if possible, but more may be created if each Organization object represents a completely separate and distinct business unit. Smaller networks get along perfectly well with a single Organization object, using Organizational Units to separate workgroups or divisions. You may give the Organization the same name as your tree, but it's much clearer during network use if you don't. In the lab network, the Organization is named GCS, while the tree is GCS_TREE. This pattern works easily and avoids confusion the few times you or a user may need to type the entire tree name and context of an object.

The Organization object is the first container that can hold leaf objects. It can also hold Organizational Unit, Locality, and Alias objects. You could create an NDS tree with a single Organization object, place all network resources in that single container, and have a flat network design modeled on NetWare 3.*x* layouts. The big advantage that this design has over a NetWare 3.*x* network is the ability to support multiple servers and their resources for all users with a single login. In fact, this design is common in small networks and works quite well.

Multiple Organization objects can exist in [Root], and each can contain as many Organizational Unit or leaf objects as you wish. However, users must be able to search the container without being overwhelmed.

Organization objects usually contain either Organizational Unit or leaf objects, with networks tending to lean toward one or the other. If your network is large, you may have several Organization objects, each containing multiple Organizational Units, each containing leaf objects. If your network is small, you may have many of your leaf objects in the Organization object, with few or no Organizational Units. Neither way is better than the other, and the choice is usually determined by company organization rather than philosophy.

The Template object is a convenient object for providing similar services for groups of users. This object holds information you can apply to new User objects as they are created. Common details for groups of users, such as file restrictions, language used, and the like, are put in the Template object. More information on this will follow in the section on leaf objects.

The first Organization must be named during the installation of the first NDS server in the tree. Later servers can be installed into the existing Organization or in a new one created for them. Organizations may also be created in the administrator utility (NWADMIN for Windows).

The Organizational Unit (OU) Container

Characteristics of the Organizational Unit container are:

- Optional
- Created in Organization, Locality, or other Organizational Unit objects
- Typically represents a division, department, workgroup, or project team
- Can contain Organizational Unit, Locality, leaf, and Alias objects
- Created during installation or later

The Organizational Unit (OU) object is optional but helpful in grouping leaf objects. If you have a single Organization in your network but many users and resources, the Organizational Unit objects will be valuable in keeping straight which resources belong closest to which users. If you have multiple Organization objects, your user base is large enough to subdivide each Organization into multiple Organizational Unit objects.

Organizational Unit objects are created within Organization objects or within other Organizational Unit objects. Organizational Unit objects can hold other Organizational Unit objects, Locality objects, leaf objects, and Alias objects.

Organizational Unit objects can be created during installation or later through normal administration utilities. They are also useful as anchors for User login scripts.

One early approach of short-sighted administrators was to create an OU for every NetWare 4 file server. They felt more comfortable pushing NDS into the same role as NetWare 3's bindery. But they lost many time-saving advantages and didn't let their users benefit from NDS's single view of the network. That's why I called them short-sighted.

The Locality (L or S) Container

Characteristics of the Locality container are:

- Optional
- Created in Country, Organization, Locality, or Organizational Unit objects
- Typically represents a physical location or geographic area
- Can contain Organization, Organizational Unit, other Locality, and Alias objects (plus a few special leaf objects described later)
- Created during installation or later

The final container, Locality, is optional but helpful in grouping geographic areas. When you create a Locality object, it may take on two forms: the generic Locality (L) or the State or Province (S). It was new in NetWare 5.0. Previous versions mentioned this object in the documentation, but it was never implemented until then. If you have a single site, you will probably never use Locality objects. If you have multiple sites, you may choose to use Locality objects to represent geographic regions, states, counties, and so on, or individual sites. However, many (including myself) prefer to use the Organizational Unit instead, as it can also hold leaf objects, such as servers, directory map objects, and other useful objects.

Locality objects are created within Organization, Country, Locality, or Organizational Unit objects. Locality objects can hold other Locality objects, Organization objects, Organizational Unit objects, and Alias objects.

Locality objects can also be created during installation, like most of the foregoing objects, or later through NWADMIN.

The Licensed Product (LP) Container and Its Leaf Objects

This container is for tracking licenses to various products, including the operating system itself. The licenses you purchase for a product appear as License Certificate leaf objects under this container. This container type and its associated leaf objects have a special purpose, and it is not for general use. Therefore, we won't discuss these License objects until Chapter 11.

Container Rules

Each container has rules defining where it must reside and which objects it can contain. Table 4.1 summarizes these rules.

TABLE 4.1: RULES OF CONTAINMENT FOR NDS OBJECTS

Object	Can Exist in	Can Contain	Sample Names
Country	[Root]	Organization, Locality, Alias objects	US, FR
Organization	[Root], Country, Locality	Organizational Unit, Locality, Alias, leaf objects	GCS, UTDallas
Organizational Unit	Organization, Organizational Unit, Locality	Organizational Unit, Locality, Alias, leaf objects	Marketing, Integration, South Central Region, Dallas
Locality	Country, Locality, Organization, Organizational Unit	Organization, Organizational Unit, Locality, Alias objects	South Central Region, Dallas

Figure 4.3 shows four examples of NDS trees that illustrate the rules of containment. The first example shows the simplest tree possible. All the other examples could have multiple Organization objects, spreading the network horizontally (remember, however, that Novell recommends only one Organization per tree). There's no practical limit on the number of Organization objects that [Root] can hold, but there are reasons to keep the network from spreading too far. I'll cover many of those reasons when we look at NDS replication and how to take advantage of the fault-tolerant nature of the NetWare 5.1 NDS tree (Chapter 10).

FIGURE 4.3

Some sample structures

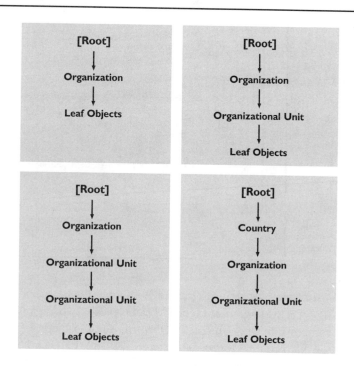

Container objects hold (contain, get it?) other Directory objects. A container object that holds other objects, regardless of level, is officially called a *parent* object.

Leaf Objects and the Bindery They Replace

Now we've come to the point of all the new objects and containers and global NDS trees: *leaf objects*. These are the network resources that make networking worthwhile.

Yes, these are all the bindery components (and more!) that you learned to love in earlier versions of NetWare.

Figure 4.4 is an image from early in the NDS development process of my lab network. The line divides the new NDS containers from the older bindery-type elements familiar to NetWare 3.*x* users.

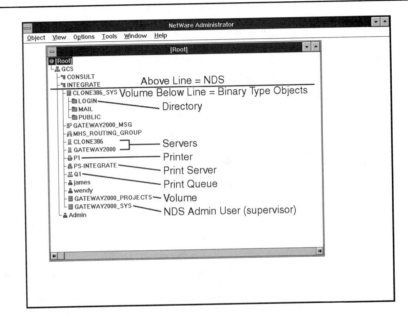

In Figure 4.4, you can see the [Root] object, with a globe icon, highlighted. Below [Root] is the Organization object named GCS. Two Organizational Unit objects are contained in GCS. The first, CONSULT, is not expanded. The second, INTEGRATE, is the main context for the lab network.

Labeled for you are a few of the leaf objects that directly correspond to earlier NetWare versions. You can see NetWare volumes, NetWare servers, users, and some standard NetWare system directories (such as LOGIN and PUBLIC).

Later, you will see many pictures of the lab network as it grows and changes and transmogrifies to illustrate the flexibility of NetWare 5. But now, let's see what new spin NetWare 5.1 has put on our old friends such as users and groups. We'll also look at some new items that didn't exist until NetWare 4 (and in some cases later versions) hit the market.

The name of a leaf object can contain a maximum of 64 characters, but be aware of your limits and your users. The distinguished name of an object cannot exceed 256 characters. Painfully long names for leaf objects will aggravate your users.

 NOTE Remember that each item discussed here is represented by an icon for the object, not the device itself. That's the trick with object-oriented systems, you know. You always speak of the object representing some physical or logical item, not necessarily the item itself.

User

 The entire reason for the network: *users*. The icons of the User objects represent the people who log in to the network and use the network resources.

There are many User object properties that you can set; among them are login restrictions, login scripts, password and password restrictions, and security equivalencies. In fact, there are 18 screen pages full of properties that you can set, and more may be added depending on what other services (such as e-mail) you add to the network.

When you create a User object, you may create a home directory, just as in earlier NetWare versions. You can create User objects anywhere in the NDS tree, but your users typically must know that location in order to log in. However, with the new catalog services, the system can locate the user objects that match the user's login name and display a list of possible contexts. This having been said, it's best to create them in the context in which they will spend most of their time. It is only a matter of clicking one context or another in the NWADMIN program.

Group

 Just as in earlier NetWare versions, a *Group* is a collection of users with common network requirements. Now, however, they are members of the Group object.

The Group object is a list of User objects that can be located anywhere in the NDS tree. There is no requirement to limit Group object members to a particular context.

Group objects act as management shorthand. Rather than make many similar trustee assignments to individual User objects, applying these same trustee assignments to a Group object does the job for each User object listed in the Group object. Many of these same statements can be made for members of the same container too. If you prefer groups, you can include members of different containers. Groups are most useful for sub- or supersets of a container.

NOTE   Remember, the Group object is a *leaf* object, *not* a container object, in much the same way that you may be a member of an auto club, but the auto club doesn't contain you in any way.

NetWare Server

Also called NCP (NetWare Core Protocol) Server objects, the NetWare Server object represents some machine running NDS on your network. The server can be a Net-Ware, Unix, or NT server, or any other operating system that has NDS ported to it. The Server object is created automatically when the NetWare Server software is installed.

The NetWare Server object is used as a reference point for several other objects, such as NetWare volumes. The Server object's properties hold a great deal of information, such as that particular server's physical location, services provided, and the error log.

A bindery-based server (as in a NetWare 3.*x* server) must have a Server object created for the server in order to access the server's volumes in NWADMIN. The bindery server must be up and running when this happens, so the Add New Object routine in NWADMIN has a server to use for verification and reading during the installation process. Or, you can use the Novell Upgrade Wizard and upgrade your 3.*x* servers, as Novell is pushing you to do.

NetWare Volume

The Volume object represents a physical NetWare volume on the network, automatically created during the NetWare 5.1 server installation. You may, however, need to create the Volume object inside NWADMIN to display the volume's icon. Double-clicking the volume icon in NWADMIN displays the volume's file system.

The Volume object's properties include information such as the name of the host server, volume location, space limits for users, and available disk space, among many others.

You can create multiple Volume objects that refer to a single physical volume, for example, to refer to it easily in other contexts. You can also create Volume objects to refer to volumes on NetWare 2.*x* or 3.*x* servers.

Print Objects

NetWare 5.0 included a new method for printing, called Novell Distributed Print Services (NDPS), but 5.1 supports the old queue-based system for backward compatibility. I'll discuss printing in detail in Chapter 8. There are separate objects for both types.

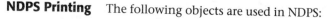

NDPS Printing   The following objects are used in NDPS:

NDPS Broker   Brokers are used to enable the advertising of printer services, to handle printer events, and to deal with resource issues (such as printer drivers for clients). NDPS creates one by default.

NDPS Manager   Used to create and maintain NDPS Printer Agents. They are central to the entire NDPS scheme.

NDPS Printer   A printer in the NDPS system. NDPS printers come in two types: public access and controlled access. Public access printers are available to anyone on the network and are not represented by NDPS printer icons in the tree. A controlled access printer can be limited and is associated with NDPS printers in the Directory. You can search through the list of controlled access printers for a printer with certain characteristics; they have a broad range of security, event notification, and status notification options.

Queue-Based Printing   The NetWare print objects for queue-based printing include:

Printer (non-NDPS)   Represents a physical network printing device. One Printer object is required for each printer in the network.

Print Server (non-NDPS)   Represents a network print server, whether located on a NetWare server or separately. One Print Server object is required for every network print server.

Print Queue   Represents a network print queue. A Print Queue object is required for every network print queue.

You create the print objects using the NWADMIN utility program. Some third-party print server devices may create the Printer object for you, but you should verify this before trusting that it is done correctly with NDS.

Leaf Objects That Have No Equivalent in the Bindery

All of the above leaf objects (except for the NDPS printing objects) existed in the old bindery (a.k.a. NetWare 2.x and 3.x) days. The rest of the objects in this section are unique to NDS. Most of them have existed since NetWare 4 days, but a few were new in NetWare 5.0.

Directory Map

The Directory Map object points to a particular directory on a volume. This works like the MAP command by representing what could be a long path name as an easily remembered label.

Directory Map objects help you manage your login scripts. In the login script, use a Directory Map object to refer to a particular directory. Then, if the path name changes, you won't need to update each and every login script that includes the directory.

A common example is a product upgrade. Say you use Visual Kumquat Designer version 2.4. As is their wont, the software makers release a new version, 2.401, which is not compatible with version 2.4. If you have a Directory Map object pointing to the directory holding Visual Kumquat Designer, you can place the new software in a newly created VKD_2401 directory. Then make a single change in the Directory Map object. That's all it takes to point all Directory Map requests from the old VKD_24 directory to the new VKD_2401 directory. You won't need to change a single login script; all users will automatically access the VKD_2401 directory. This is a very versatile object when implemented correctly.

Organizational Role

Perhaps my favorite NDS object, the Organizational Role object represents a position or role within the company organization. It is typically used for jobs that have well-defined requirements but that are performed by a rotating group of individuals rather than a single person.

For instance, team leader may be a position that needs some access rights above and beyond those of the rest of the workgroup. Granting those rights to the Organizational Role rather than to individuals makes it easy to track which person has these extra rights at any one time. When the team leader changes, the next person can be assigned the Organizational Role. That user will immediately inherit all the team leader rights. You may even have multiple users assigned to the role, for example, in the case of co-team leaders. Although this object is great and can make your life much easier, conceptually, it functions like a Group. The big difference between a Group and an Organizational Role is that Groups have members but Organizational Roles have occupants.

Profile

The Profile object contains a Profile login script, a special login script used by individuals with common needs but little else in common. If the Profile object is listed as one of a User object's properties, the Profile object's login script is executed when that User object logs in.

The Profile object provides a way for users who don't belong to the same context, such as accounting payroll clerks from multiple divisions, to share common login script commands. For example, the Profile login script may provide these users with access to particular directories or special printers. This process also works for a subset of users in the same container. The biggest caveat with profiles is that each User object may have a maximum of *one* assigned.

Computer

A Computer object represents any computer on the network that is not a server, such as a workstation, a router, an e-mail gateway, or the like.

Use the Computer object properties to store information about the system, such as network address, configuration, serial number, the person it's assigned to, and so on. The Computer object is informational only; it has no effect on network operations. Because it is for documentation purposes only, it is rarely used. When was the last time you had time to document your server configuration, much less that of all your workstations? If you have done it, when was it last updated? I thought so.

Alias

The Alias object points to another object in the NDS tree in a different context. When you use the Alias object, objects appear to be in places they really aren't. Using an Alias object is an easy way to allow users to access an object in another context.

This is fun: the Alias object is a representation of a representation of an entity. In other words, the Alias object takes the form of another object and makes it appear that the second object is in a place it's not really in.

When an object is moved or renamed, you have the option of leaving an Alias object in its place. This keeps resources in the (seemingly) same place for the users who rely on those resources, even after the resource has been moved. If you delete or rename an Alias object, the Alias itself is affected, not the object it's pointing to.

WARNING Be careful when modifying an Alias object or an object that has an Alias. The Alias object takes the shape of the object it replaces or points to, so changes made to either affect both. Look for the small Halloween mask beside the Alias object.

If you want to access the Alias object and the properties of the object it refers to, you need the Read right to the Alias name and the Read right to the properties of the object it refers to. You can set these options in NWADMIN in Windows.

Bindery and Bindery Queue Objects

The Bindery object represents an object placed in the NDS tree by an upgrade or a migration utility (such as the Novell Upgrade Wizard).

The Bindery Queue object is exactly what you might expect: a print queue from a NetWare 3.*x* server placed in the NDS tree by an upgrade or a migration utility.

Both of these objects are used by NDS to provide compatibility with bindery-based utilities. Many third-party print servers still expect the bindery and its capabilities and require it to function. You'll find more on bindery emulation at the end of this chapter.

Unknown

The Unknown object is an NDS object that has been invalidated or corrupted. The NDS tree does not recognize the object. These Unknown objects appear when changes are made to NDS, such as when a NetWare server is deleted and the administrator forgets to delete the volumes for that server. The volumes will then appear as Unknown objects.

During large-scale changes to the NDS, some objects may briefly appear to be "unknown." This is caused by changes being made faster than NDS can synchronize. If you make changes and see Unknown objects, wait awhile. However, the best action is to delete Unknown objects that persist. You can also try the maintenance utilities discussed in Chapter 10 to see if they fix the problem. In the case of orphaned volumes, re-create them if they belong to a server that has been re-created or modified.

Template

This object is used to create users with common properties. This is a very powerful object, because you can modify all the users based on the template at once if needed. For example, let's say that your accounting department is moving from an outpost in Houston to corporate headquarters in Dallas. Do you want to edit the location property for 100 accountants? Me neither. All that you need to do is select the template, choose Details On Multiple Users in NWADMIN, change the location, click OK, and *voila*! They are all updated. It also helps when you have many properties that are the same for a bunch of users (like a department), users who need the same restrictions placed on them, etc. Try it, you'll like it.

Miscellaneous Objects

You will see some other objects as you use NetWare 5.1. Some of the objects are standard, and some will show up when you install optional components, upgrades, and so on. I'll discuss those that appear when you install optional components later, as they come up. The other standard objects provide advanced functionality:

- The SLP (Service Location Protocol) Directory Agent object and SLP Scope Unit object are used for the new Service Location Protocol (the replacement for SAP when using TCP/IP). I'll discuss them in Chapter 14.

- The Key Material object is used for cryptography services. I'll discuss it in Appendix B.

- The NDSCat: Master Catalog object and NDSCat: Slave Catalog object are the NDS entries that make up Catalog Services, which allow contextless login, among many other things. I'll discuss them in Chapter 11.
- The LAN Area object is used like the Groups object for servers, in that all servers that belong to this object have a common WAN policy applied to them. I'll discuss WAN policies later in this chapter.

Planning Your NDS Tree

NetWare 5.1 uses building blocks in network design that were not available in Net-Ware until version 4.0. These include the NDS tree, Organizations, and Organizational Units. Only when we speak of the leaf nodes, such as users, printers, servers, and volumes, do we overlap the pieces used by NetWare 3.x and earlier versions.

Although some administrators new to NetWare 5.1 fear these building blocks, many others understand the advantages that the NDS tree offers to network architects. How many NetWare customers have a single server to handle every job? A few, but the normal sequence is to get one server, then have an application or two grow beyond that one server. Suddenly, the workgroup that started with one server has four servers.

With previous versions of NetWare, the management overhead quadrupled (and more) as the new servers arrived. With NetWare 5.1, however, each server is just another object in the NDS tree. More important, each disk volume is just another object, and any one user can easily reference a dozen volumes with a single network login.

Some Goals for Your NDS Tree Design

Plan your large NDS tree to perform the following functions:

- Fault-tolerance for the Directory database
- Decreased traffic on the network, especially over WAN links
- Easy lookup of information and resources for users
- Simplified network administration and maintenance

Keep these goals in mind, but let me say something: there is no one, perfect way to plan your NDS tree. The design that works for your network may not work for another network. The design for one division of your network may not work for another division. How your tree begins may not be how it ends. There are tools to modify the NDS structure, and I'll discuss them in due course. Expect your network to change; expect to change NDS as a result.

Before I get into specific planning and installation ideas, remember that adding NetWare 5.1 will be an adjustment for both you and your users, especially if coming from NetWare 3.*x*. The more comfortable the users feel, the easier the transition to the new network. Here are some tips for improving your rollout process:

- Run NetWare 5.1 in a lab environment.
- Demonstrate NetWare 5.1 to your power users before the upgrade.
- Train users before the upgrade (but not too long before).
- Draw NDS designs until everyone's priorities are covered.
- Coordinate with all other network administrators during the planning process.

Work with all other network administrators to develop an NDS tree that everyone can accept. No network design suits everyone perfectly, but you need to cover the priorities. This will require input from all the other network administrators and representative users during the NDS design stage. The more closely everyone works together, the more successful your network will be.

When Novell implemented NDS on its global corporate network, managers met and talked (argued) about the design for months. Those wanting a purely geographical design disagreed with those wanting a design modeled strictly along job function lines. Finally, a hybrid network was designed and built. If the people at Novell themselves don't have a "magic" design that suits everyone, why should you?

When we speak of planning NDS design, we get into some gray areas, since each company and network is different. The process differs considerably depending on whether you will be doing all the setup and management or whether you are one of many network administrators. If you do it all, your plans can be less detailed, because you will be the one making all the decisions as new questions arise. If you're working with a group of administrators, planning is the most important part of the process. You and all other administrators must be in sync about NDS before starting.

The goal is supporting your users in the most efficient manner (for them) possible. Making resources easy for your users to find will speed their workday and, more selfishly, keep them from bothering you all the time. A good network design can save hours of network training.

Semantics can cause arguments in this section. Is a "bottom-up" design the same as a "logical" design? Is "top-down" the same as "managed" or "preplanned"? Who cares? The important part is making the network fit your situation.

The focus here is on designing networks based on user function or user location. These roughly correspond to the top-down and bottom-up labels. As you might guess, a large network, or one that covers several geographic areas, will use a combination of both methods.

Setting Up a Pilot System

It will save you time and aggravation to have a pilot NetWare 5.1 server up and running before you begin the rollout, particularly if coming from NetWare 4.11 or earlier. It will also help immensely if you can have representative samples of your clients set up as well. Include the different architectures, models, brands, and so on of computers and the operating system(s) that you plan to run on them. I know this sounds like a lot of work, but it will save you a lot of time and grief later on (not to mention embarrassment when something doesn't work right in front of the user). Even if the pilot server is running for only a week or two, the experience will be invaluable.

Build some sample users with different rights and let people experiment. User 1 may have the run of the server, while Users 2 and 3 can only use specific areas. Place instructions in the test area so that users can log in and tour the network under each user name already created for them.

Be sure to make the pilot system available to the power users in your organization. You know the users I'm speaking of: those who read all the computer magazines, haunt the Internet, and informally help all the users in their area. They will be interested in the workgroup management facilities, since that kind of authority will verify what they've been doing unofficially for quite a while.

NDS Design Phases

Each network design, regardless of the architecture, has two phases: logical and physical.

Logical Phase

The *logical phase* focuses on the Directory structure and the process for implementing that structure. The steps in the logical design sequence are:

1. Determine the NDS tree structure.

2. Identify the naming conventions for your network.

3. Plan your implementation method.

Physical Phase

The *physical phase* focuses on how users access the Directory during their workday. This phase also considers how information is stored on the servers and how it is coordinated to provide accurate Directory and time information. The steps in the physical design sequence are:

1. Determine security considerations.

2. Set up Directory replication.

3. Synchronize Directory time.

The departmental design that served so well with earlier versions of NetWare also works fine with NetWare 5.1. But NetWare 5.1 gives you many more options than the basic "one department, one server" design strategy. Even better, you can take the departmental strategy and fold it into a bigger, more client-friendly framework.

Designing for Users: Who Works with Whom, and for How Long?

Don't get timid when designing your new company network. You must have the courage to ask questions. Some people you must question don't normally get involved in the network. You must, if no one else in your company ever has, make some sense of which people really work on which projects with which other people.

This may sound easy, but if it is easy, you haven't dug down deep enough. You may have set up your existing network to mirror groups of people sitting close together in departments all in one building. That worked well with the limitations forced on large companies by departmental, server-centric networking. Although you can still set up your network in this manner, you are no longer limited to a departmental design.

Are you familiar with the futurists (and network designers) and their new definitions of work? According to sources as varied as Alvin Toffler and developers of workgroup software such as GroupWise and Lotus Notes, people regularly shift and change their internal work partners. A project begins; a team is gathered. A project ends; the team members go in various directions.

This is cleaner than what usually happens, of course. Theories, no matter how outlandish, pale beside the mess we people make of plans. If your life as a network administrator is typical, you are a member of 10 ad hoc groups. You have meetings to choose new software, to review current vendors, and to get authorization for a new server or two, in addition to managing personnel, marketing support, remote computing, and network security. If you ever dream of pieces of yourself being pulled apart and flying in all directions, save the psychological counseling fees. You're just dreaming about your normal workday.

E-mail and groupware help us deal with the mess we've worked ourselves into, but they can't do it all. Your network design for NetWare 5.1 will go a long way in helping improve the ease of user interaction. The easier it is for users to share information, the better the resulting project.

Design versus Implementation

Your network *design* is planning the NDS structure. Your network *implementation* is creating the NDS structure. You might think that the "design" component always comes before the "implementation" component. That's not true. The best designs always consider the problems of implementation and maintenance. The key here is simple: the more time you spend *planning* your tree, the less time you will spend *re-creating* your tree later (which can be very time consuming).

Are you upgrading from an earlier version of NetWare? If so, some of the design choices will be made for you. The users, tied to a particular server throughout their NetWare experience, may want to remain tied to that server. Create a comfortable environment for them by intelligent NDS design, and their transition will be smoother.

If you are upgrading, are you upgrading all servers at once? With a small network, it's possible to upgrade all servers in one pass, usually over a weekend. The user leaves an office with one network design and returns to the same office with a different network design. If you aren't upgrading all the servers at once, you may wind up creating multiple NDS trees and merging those trees later, although this is not usually recommended.

Are you "seeding" the network with one NetWare 5.1 division and gradually expanding the NDS reach through the rest of the company? This method offers more time for training users and coordinating departments, but it isn't magic. You must provide Bindery Services for those users caught between two departments that upgrade at different times.

If you create multiple NDS trees, a consistent naming convention must be agreed upon before the rollout begins. If a single NDS tree is created and expanded when each part of the company is connected, the naming consistency is just as important but a bit easier. The only advantage is that you will know about name conflicts as they arise during each department's installation, rather than all at once during the upgrade procedure. More work will be necessary to combine multiple trees into one tree than to create one tree and add to it.

Developing Naming Standards

With earlier NetWare versions, a "naming standard" generally meant using the last name and first initial for user login or the first name and last initial. Large companies focused on the last name, while small companies and departments favored the first name.

With NetWare 5.1 and the global Directory database, you must develop a more complete naming standard. Names are needed for User, Printer, Print Queue, Server, Volume, Group, Organizational Role, Directory Map, and Distribution List objects, to name a few. Lots of names will be needed before all is said and done.

Naming standards provide a framework for naming all network users and resources. These standards work best with consistency and a goal of making users comfortable while navigating a large network full of resources. The new search capabilities, as well as Catalog Services, in NetWare 5.1 NDS work best when simple wildcard searching is possible. If all servers are named SRVsomething, a search with SRV* provides usable results. The same is true with printers: name all laser printers LASsomething, and searching for a printer becomes simple.

Name length for any object is the same: 64 characters. The caveat is that the total length for the distinguished NDS name of an object cannot exceed 256 characters including periods, equal signs, and name type designators. Long names or deep NDS trees will cause users to work unnecessarily hard and may bump against your namelength limit. Short but descriptive names have these characteristics:

- Make names easier to remember
- Simplify logins
- Use capitalization to increase readability
- Use hyphens rather than spaces
- Reduce NDS traffic across the network

If you are using Bindery Services, keep in mind the naming restrictions of NetWare 3.x. Keep names particularly short to fit all systems the user will be encountering.

Sample Naming Standards

If you are migrating some NetWare 2.x or 3.x users, there may be some renaming necessary. If you have been planning to redo your naming standards, the transition to NetWare 5.1 is a good time to make your move. Even if it's not technically true, everyone will believe you when you tell them they must change names because of the new network.

Table 4.2 shows some naming standards and the rationale behind them, along with some suggestions.

TABLE 4.2: SOME SUGGESTIONS FOR NAMING STANDARDS

Object	Naming Standard	Examples
User	Limit names to eight characters (eight-character names make good home directories). Choose names that work with both the network and your e-mail package. This is particularly true if you have clients that run DOS and/or Windows 3.x. For other operating systems, however, you may want to allow more characters. Using middle initials will greatly reduce the number of duplicate names in your tree. Decide now how to handle duplicate names if they still occur.	James E. Gaskin becomes JEGASKIN; Brenda D. Frink becomes BDFRINK.
Server	Server names must be unique on the network. Use a set of three- or four-letter codes for the location, department, and server. Airline city codes are good location designators (DFW for Dallas Ft. Worth; LAX for Los Angeles) because they are unique, but they can be difficult for non-travelers to recognize. (Do you know that YYZ is Toronto, Ontario?)	SRV-LAX-ACCT-001
Group	Base group names on the group function.	GP-ACCT for the accounting group
Printer	Use city codes as for servers, along with building location codes and printer type. Preface the name with P for queue-based printers or NDPS for NDPS-based printers to distinguish them.	NDPS-DFW-HP-LJ4SI
Print Queue and Print Server	Start with PQ or PS. Include the host server name and the numeric ID of each.	PS-GATEWAY2000-1
Organization and Organizational Unit	Use your company's internal abbreviations if possible. Reference a short version of the company name for the Organization object.	OU=SALES.OU= WEST.O=ACME
Organizational Role	Base the name on the job function. Always grant administrative rights to the Organizational Role rather than to particular users for ease of control when job descriptions or people change.	OR-ACCT_MGR
Profile	Base the name on the job function.	PR-PTRS-Y
Directory Map	Base the name on the application being mapped.	DM-WP, DM-EMAIL

Some may complain about the extra characters needed for the "type" designator at the beginning of each name, such as DM-EMAIL. This is not a requirement, of course, just a suggestion from Novell. If your company wants to rely on the icons under Windows to provides those clues, that's fine. But be consistent: don't label some groups GP-EMAIL and other groups just ACCT. Your users may be more aggravated by the confusion than they are about typing the extra characters.

NDS Example: Organizing by User Location (Bottom-Up)

This tree organization is often labeled the *departmental* or *workgroup* method, but the terms *bottom-up* or *user-location* method work just as well. The key point is that this is an independent group that will later be part of a larger group.

Some references assume this bottom-up plan can only be done by creating separate NDS trees for each department and joining them later. That method will work and may make sense when the NDS trees that the department will later join are geographically dispersed. Instead, you can make the department a self-sufficient Organizational Unit inside an existing NDS tree. The important consideration in the user-location method is to set the department as a distinct entity from the rest of the corporate network, whether it is NetWare 3, 4, or 5. A group of users who share a location and a set of resources fits this profile, regardless of whether these users have their own tree or just their own Organizational Unit.

Departmental Design

Focusing on the department when designing your NDS tree makes sense under several circumstances. Especially with the new NDS utilities offered with NetWare 5, there is no longer an administrative penalty to pay for developing a network design that must be changed later.

When the departments will stay isolated from one another, the bottom-up (figuring the department is the bottom of the organization chart) design works well. This design also works well if there is no strong central administration group dictating standards. Even if there is a central group, it may not yet be prepared with a comprehensive plan that supports all departments. It wouldn't be the first time the people doing all the work are inconvenienced by the HQ folks trying to figure out what they're doing, would it?

There are benefits of the departmental design, whether each group is a completely separate tree or just containers that don't interact. Each department can maintain the names used in earlier NetWare versions for ease of learning and minimal disruption. Although duplicate names in the same context are not allowed when the trees are merged, separate trees spread the learning curve out a bit. However, if you do your job right, this shouldn't be much of a problem. Forcing users to learn NetWare 5.1 at the same time as renaming all their network resources (again, if you do your job right, this will be at most their user name) is a lot to handle all at once, but it may make sense. Why have them learn three or four transitional schemes? Plan up front and get all the pain out of the way at once.

NetWare 5.1 users running Client32 software will be able to see multiple trees at one time. If each department is its own container, some sharing can be introduced gradually. This situation is perfect for Alias objects, which allow you to refer to other container resources. You don't need to teach the users all about contexts and the NDS hierarchy until they're ready to learn, if ever. If you do your job well, most users will never know about context, NDS, and so forth anyway.

If you set up separate trees before a central plan is established, you'll need to use the DSMERGE.NLM utility (a server utility) to combine trees. Remember that servers must have a unique name across the entire tree. Some minimal guidelines must be available for server names before you can integrate each department into the larger network. To help ease context issues after you merge, consider having a common Organization under the [Root] and placing all your other objects under it. When you merge the trees, simply rename one of the Organizations and merge the trees; there are no context issues.

Physical and Logical Views

Network diagrams are handy, at least until they're outdated (which happens constantly). With NetWare 5.1, two types of network diagrams become obsolete: physical and logical views of your network.

The physical view of your NDS tree shows the branches clearly, with all network resources of that branch grouped together. Once the department tree is merged into the larger network, the current administrator may well continue to be the container administrator. The authority of the container administrator is similar to that of a full administrator, except that this authority is over only a specific container or branch of the tree.

Figure 4.5 is a physical diagram of a departmental design network in its own tree. Both servers and volumes are represented, as are users, printers, and the like.

The physical diagrams are not what you are used to: the wire and all users, servers, and printers attached to that wire. You may have one diagram for each floor of your building or just one large diagram for everything. Those are *wiring diagrams*, which prove useful when expanding and troubleshooting your physical network. What we mean by a *physical view* here is the icons strung together.

FIGURE 4.5

*A departmental NDS
tree, physical view*

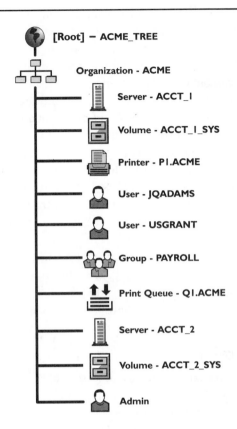

This is less important in small networks than in larger ones. However, if you have no naming designators (as is the case for the items in Figure 4.5), the icons help clarify which name refers to a Group, a Directory Map, or an Alias object.

Figure 4.6 shows the same information as Figure 4.5 but uses block diagrams and NDS abbreviations rather than icons. Admittedly, there is not a lot of difference when showing small networks.

Notice that the naming designators would help clarify some details in the logical view that didn't really need clarification in the physical view. Quick, without looking back at Figure 4.5, what is PAYROLL? Is it a group, a volume, or a directory map?

FIGURE 4.6

A departmental NDS
tree, logical view

[Root]

O=ACME

ACCT_1

ACCT_2

ACCT_1_SYS

ACCT_2_SYS

P1.ACME

Q1.ACME

JQADAMS

USGRANT

PAYROLL

NDS Example: Organizing by User Function (Top-Down)

The top-down design model works well when a central MIS (Management Information Services) or LAN control group is in charge of the network. If your HQ folks
know their business, this is the model you will likely use. If you are the MIS department, as often happens in smaller companies, this is a good option.

It's a delicate balancing act to design by user function. If the network is geographically wide, your WAN connections may be too slow to provide good service if half
your network traverses the WAN for normal business. If the network is physically in
one place but contains too many servers to upgrade all at once, it may be difficult to
use this model as well. However, this is a great design for networks that are mostly local
and have clearly defined job descriptions that stretch across internal departments.

Organizational Design

During the past few years, the trend in business has been to place support functions
(such as accounting, sales, design, engineering, human resources, and the like) directly
in the departments they support. Earlier, the model was to always group like job functions, as in the bottom-up design method previously described. With the business pen-
dulum swinging, however, your company may well decide to disperse these functions.

Figure 4.7 shows our mythical Acme Corporation built around a top-down model, grouping the various functions in separate Organizational Units. This design requires that you know and make sense of your company's organization.

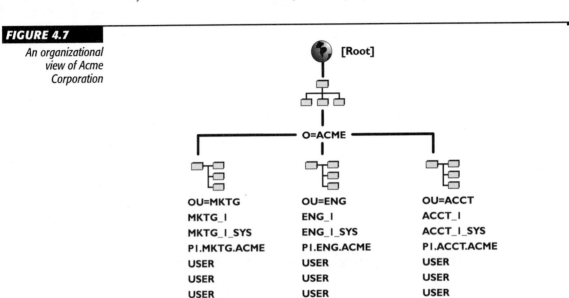

This illustration makes good sense for central planners, who don't need to worry about which user sits in which cubicle. If you are responsible for maintaining the connection of user Guy H. Davis in cubicle 4-E-2, you may need an additional map, like the one shown in Figure 4.8.

The cable contractor who installed your network cabling was supposed to leave an "as-built" map showing each connection in each physical location. You probably can't find that now, so get the cubicle layout from the human resources space-planning department. On copies of the floor plan, label each user and his or her context in the NDS tree. This type of planning and forethought is rewarded during emergencies but is difficult to maintain. Make an effort to start and maintain such a map for the feeling of self-satisfaction if nothing else. Again, this idea is wonderful on paper and in theory, but don't beat yourself up if you don't have the time to document all aspects of your network. If you have done what was suggested earlier in the process and have a good naming standard, you simply ask the user in cube 4-E-2 what his or her name is (if you don't already know that his name is Guy H. Davis), then search for GHDAVIS in the tree.

FIGURE 4.8

A cubicle view of the organizational design

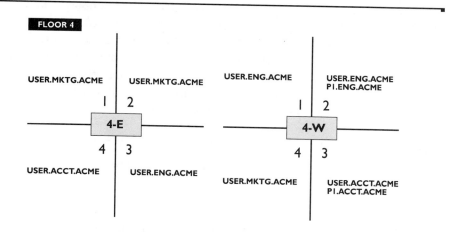

Notice that engineers are sitting next to marketing people, who are next to accounting people. This is slightly fictionalized, to enhance the contrast. If this were real life, translators would be needed between each cubicle.

The printers for two of the groups are in the west cubicle. Printers can be physically located anywhere on the network, either by connecting them to workstations or by using print servers that attach directly to the network cabling. By the way, I highly prefer the latter approach, which will make your life much simpler.

Even if your company begins the year by placing each group in the same physical location, normal business chaos will mangle that plan before long. People get promoted, people change jobs, the accounting department runs out of room so the managers place a few people in the marketing area, and so on—things just change. The type of map shown in Figure 4.8 helps monitor that change. Can you track each cubicle user to their spot on the map in Figure 4.7? See, context names do help, don't they?

NDS Example: Distributed Organization Chart with a WAN (Mixed)

Let's say Acme Corporation has grown beyond its founders' wildest dreams. Hey, when marketing people and engineers learn to communicate, great things happen.

The new layout for Acme will probably be a mix of departmental and user-function designs. WAN considerations particularly push this mixed design, since small, remote offices often don't have enough personnel to keep job functions separate. But the slow WAN connections limit the practicality of using a top-down design.

Figure 4.9 shows the expanded Acme Corporation spreading across the country. The designers have chosen not to use the Country level, even though the company has grown from the United States into both Canada and Mexico. The design is clearly discernible without needing the extra layer of name contexts that the Country object introduces. Notice the lack of planning in designing the naming standard for locations. There is Corp (a business unit located where?), Mexico (a country), and Toronto and San_Jose (cities). Doesn't make much sense, does it?

FIGURE 4.9

A global corporate/division/ department/ workgroup design

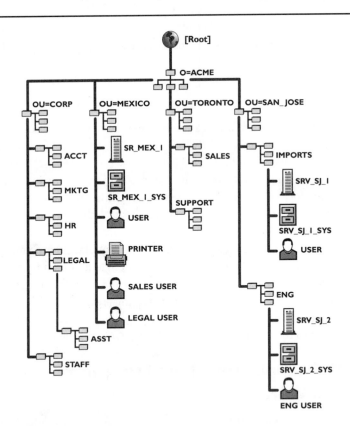

You should notice that OU=CORP is the largest and is not labeled by location. Each department has clearly defined groups, since more people in the corporate office tend to have specific job functions.

The other cities are labeled geographically, since that made the most sense during the design phase. In Mexico, the small office has no departmental subgroups or OUs within the Mexico OU. Toronto, a larger office, contains an OU for both Sales and

Support. San Jose includes two OUs, labeled Imports and Eng. Although there are defined groups in San Jose, the file servers are named incrementally by the location.

Does this all make sense? Probably not, but it's a common situation. In fact, it is one of the most common designs for a network. This is also a tree that follows Novell's recommendations, namely design the top of the tree (the first two to three layers) to reflect your WAN topology and the bottom of the tree (all the rest) to cover departments and other corporate organizational structures. And the lesson to learn from this is twofold:

- NDS is flexible enough to cover your crazy company.
- No NDS design is inherently better than another.

NDS Context Control and Management

As you may recall, *context* refers to the location of an object within the NDS tree. Not the physical location, but the logical position.

In the earlier example in Figure 4.9, the context of the first file server in San Jose (SRV_SJ_1) is:

`IMPORTS.SAN_JOSE.ACME`

The context here is given in *typeless* format. The formats are:

Typeful   Includes abbreviations for all containers and leaf objects (if appropriate). The object types were listed earlier in the section on containers, and all leaf objects are CN. The typeful method of referring to the above context is:

`OU=IMPORTS.OU=SAN_JOSE.O=ACME`

Typeless   No container abbreviations as was illustrated above.

The translation of the above typeless name is "Organizational Unit Imports in the Organizational Unit San_Jose in the Organization Acme." The typeful, distinguished name of that server would be written as:

`CN=SRV_SJ_1.OU=IMPORTS.OU=SAN_JOSE.O=ACME`

Personally, I prefer the typeless names and am glad they are available. With typeless names, the trick to remember is that typically the Organization is to the far right, and the object (CN stands for the Common Name of the object, remember?) is at the far left. Anything in the middle is usually an Organizational Unit.

See Table 4.1, earlier in this chapter, for the complete, official list of the rules of containment. For a shorthand and simplified list, remember that [Root] contains Organizations, and Organizations hold Organizational Units, which can hold other Organizational Units but not Organizations. Remember that most leaf objects go in Organizations or Organizational Units.

Why Current Context Is Important

Knowing where you are is important in every endeavor, especially when we're speaking of something like NDS, with the capacity for a global network. Think of your current context as the map with a red arrow saying, "You are here."

Current context and knowing how to change your context are just as important in the NDS tree as in a file system's directory tree. The biggest difference is that with NetWare 5.1, you can have many drives mapped to different points in the file system tree but only one active point in the NDS tree.

Let's break this into components. First, the far-left name is the common name, with the abbreviation of CN. The common name denotes a leaf object, such as a user, printer, server, or volume.

In Figure 4.10, PAT is the user name for both users. Although PAT by itself doesn't help us differentiate the two users, the rest of the object's distinguished name (that is, its context) will always let us know which PAT is which. (Of course, using PATD or PJONES instead works without confusion.)

FIGURE 4.10

Find and describe PAT in as many ways as possible.

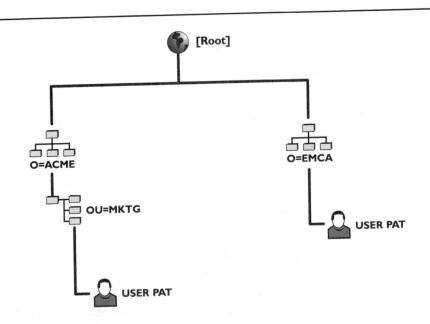

Since we don't know anything about PAT or even if it's Ms. PAT or Mr. PAT, we need a better way to describe this PAT object. Hence, we have *distinguished names*, another label for the complete context of an object.

Current context works similarly to the current directory context in a file system. The context acts as the CD command might work, by referencing where an object is located. People don't use this function of the CD command often, but just typing CD by itself will list your current directory. The Unix command pwd (for Print Working Directory) does the same thing. If you are in the same directory as the file you're looking for, just the filename is enough to reference the file. If you are in another directory, you must give the path to the file.

The distinguished name for the PAT on the right is PAT.EMCA; the PAT on the left has the distinguished name PAT.MKTG.ACME. However, if you are currently in the EMCA Organization with PAT, you can merely reference the name PAT without any of the extra identifiers for context.

What if PAT.EMCA wants to send a message to the other PAT? How should that be addressed? The distinguished name is PAT.MKTG.ACME. A subset of this is the *relative distinguished name*. Are you comfortable using the CD (Change Directory) DOS command to move up one directory level, then going down from there? If so, using a relative distinguished name should be comfortable for you as well.

When a network administrator with a context of O=ACME needs to refer to PAT.MKTG.ACME, there is a shortcut. Use either CN=PAT.OU=MKTG or just PAT.MKTG, since both refer to the same object. If the administrator is already in the MKTG container, the reference would be either CN=PAT or just PAT.

A beginning period in a name tells the system that the following name is complete and referenced from the [Root] of the current NDS tree. This is, in fact, the definition of a distinguished name. The period works the same as a leading backslash in DOS path names for file designations.

The last trick is the trailing period in object naming. A name with a trailing period tells the system to start the partial naming one level up from the current context. This method is rarely used, although those familiar with the command prompt and bad typists use it more frequently. You are effectively removing one object name from the *left* side of the current context. Note that this works only for relative distinguished names. For example, if your current context is

    OU=MKTG.O=ACME

and you enter the relative distinguished name

    CN=Admin.

NDS will remove the OU=MKTG object from the current context and prepend the relative distinguished name to the remainder:

    .CN=Admin.O=ACME

Of course, looking at Figure 4.10, you will see that NDS will not be able to locate that object, and you will get an error.

Using CX to Change Your Context

Changing contexts is as easy as changing directories from the DOS command line. The CX command stands for Change conteXt just like CD stands for Change Directory, but the acronym is more of a stretch.

Typing CX on the DOS command line will display your current context. In our example, if PAT on the left types CX, the result will be

```
mktg.acme
```

Somewhat underwhelming, but often helpful.

The CX command with no options is used more than the CD command with no options, because there is no "Context" prompt like the DOS prompt that automatically shows your file system location.

The easiest way to use CX is to always type

```
CX distinguished_name (.MKTG.ACME)
```

replacing *distinguished_name* with your desired context name, of course, although relative distinguished names are permissible.

For ease of use when logging in to a server, the CX.EXE command is included in the LOGIN directory. If you connect to any NetWare server in the desired tree, you can then change your context before logging in to the system.

How To Use Contexts to Your Advantage

Current context is most important when a user logs in to the system. As we just saw, several people may well have the same name. When PAT wants to log in, how will the system know which PAT is being referred to?

Context helps here. NDS looks for objects in the following order:

1. The user's distinguished name or relative distinguished name plus current context

2. During login only, the context of whatever server the user is currently attached to

There is no "search path" as in DOS and NetWare. If the user who wants to access any object doesn't provide the necessary context, the object will remain unfound. The exception is with the LOGIN program: if you start to log in from the wrong context, NDS will search the container of the server you are communicating with. If that context is not correct and you don't have Catalog Services, you'll get the error message "User not found." You must try again. With Catalog Services, however, a list of users with the specified name will appear, and the user can choose the right one.

Let's take that login problem PAT had just a moment ago. Some suggestions require you to type the full distinguished name every time a user logs in, looks for a printer, or references a network resource. This is a lot of typing, however, and you are likely to meet a lot of resistance and anger from users who must now type 150 characters to log in, instead of the old eight. However, if everyone is in the same container, including all the various file servers for that department, full distinguished names aren't necessary.

When PAT logs in, NDS searches the current context. *Voila!* The file server holding PAT's object is in that current context, and login continues without a hitch.

The advantages of grouping similar users in Organizations or Organizational Units together with their file servers and other network resources make NetWare 5.1 feel more comfortable. Users of earlier NetWare versions don't need to make a drastic leap of faith to take advantage of many of NetWare 5.1's strong points.

Setting a User's "Home," or Default, Context

Part of the reason some advisors make a big deal of using the shortest container names possible is to avoid having users enter many characters when typing their distinguished name. Since NetWare allows a user to log in from any machine on the network (very handy for network administrators, this ability to gain your full rights from any desktop), worrywarts and concerned users will get confused if they need to type a long distinguished name.

This is a problem for few networks today, because most users log in on their own computer almost all the time. When networks started, it was more common for companies to have several users share a computer. Today, at least in the larger companies, almost every employee has full access to his or her own computer or two.

The advantage of this situation is the ability to place user-specific commands in the NET.CFG file on the client PC workstation if the user is running DOS and/or Windows 3.1. In the NET.CFG file, the NetWare DOS Requester section will probably already exist. If so, use a text editor to add the name context line that applies to the particular user. In PAT's case, the following will show up in the NET.CFG file:

```
NetWare DOS Requester
 name context="MKTG.ACME"
 preferred tree=ACME_TREE
 first network drive=f
```

The preferred tree line is only necessary if your company has multiple NDS trees active on the network. That's very rare.

When the client is loaded, the NET.CFG file will set the default context. NDS won't need to search for PAT's user object, since the system will assume PAT belongs in MKTG.ACME before the LOGIN command appears.

If and when PAT does wander to another desk, there's still not much to remember to log in to the proper context. Have PAT type

```
LOGIN PAT.MKTG.ACME
```

and then give the proper password when asked. PAT will be connected in the proper context without any problems.

If PAT uses Windows 95/98 or Windows NT and the Client32 software, you must use the Network Properties page to set a context.

Using Bindery Services to Emulate the Old Bindery

NDS supports Bindery Services to allow users still using the NETX client shells to connect to NDS and to support third-party products, such as tape backup programs and print servers. Until all third-party products are current with the latest NetWare 5.1 release or are at least NDS aware (most are already), Bindery Services will continue to be used.

If you have slipped into a comfortable mode with NDS over the last few chapters, give that up and remember what it used to be like. Bindery Services provides only some access to leaf objects on a server-centric basis within NDS. The global, distributed NDS database pretends to be a flat, limited structure for server resources and users. Only the leaf objects in specified containers can be seen under Bindery Services.

How Bindery Services Works

The *bindery context* refers to the container object where the Bindery Services feature is set. The bindery context is normally set during server installation, but only the first three servers automatically receive a replica of the NDS partition during installation. Without the replica, the server can't support NetWare 5.1's Bindery Services feature. When you upgrade a NetWare 3 server to NetWare 5.1, its bindery context is automatically set, and the server will automatically receive a replica of the container it is in.

You may add replicas to any NetWare 5.1 server you wish in order to support Bindery Services. Check Chapter 10 for details on using the NDS Manager program to add replicas.

Once the server in question is ready, you can set as many as 16 bindery contexts for a single NetWare 5.1 server. The contexts are then added together, in the order they were listed in, to form one large, emulated bindery. This is done by using the Monitor utility at the server console or by directly modifying the AUTOEXEC.NCF file. The activation of Bindery Services is limited to the specific server modified.

Once active, Bindery Services responds to NETX requests (or NetWare 5.1 clients using VLM files with the /B switch at the end of their LOGIN command, Client32 users with the Bindery Connection box checked, or Windows 95/98's Microsoft Client for NetWare without their NDS services installed) from clients or applications. Leaf objects—and only leaf objects that meet the bindery's naming conventions—are presented by Bindery Services as if they were a standard NetWare 3.*x* bindery. Containers are not presented under Bindery Services.

Information contained in NDS but not in the bindery is not visible under Bindery Services. The invisible items include:

- E-mail names
- Phone numbers
- Aliases
- Profiles
- NDS, though not bindery, login scripts
- Directory maps

Why Bindery Emulation May Be Necessary

Even the most gung-ho NDS advocate may be forced to use Bindery Services sometimes. During the transition to NetWare 5.1, some NetWare 3.*x* or NetWare 4.*x* servers may not be upgraded immediately. Some computers may not have the prerequisite hardware to upgrade, or you may not have time to reach them all at once to upgrade the client connection software to be NDS-aware.

Print servers from some third-party vendors use Bindery Services to verify user access to the printers. Although most companies are moving, if they haven't already moved, to support NDS, it takes time.

Make no mistake: there's no advantage for a NetWare 5.1 server to run Bindery Services except under the circumstances listed above. NDS has far too many advantages to emulate a server-centric bindery system.

Installing Bindery Services

If you are upgrading a NetWare 3.*x* server, or it's one of the first three NetWare 5.1 servers, Bindery Services will be installed automatically. The appropriate lines, such as

```
SET BINDERY CONTEXT=MKTG.ACME
```

will be written into the AUTOEXEC.NCF file during installation.

You may later add Bindery Services by typing the SET command at the server console and listing the server's context in the command. To engage Bindery Services each time the server is restarted, you must add the SET command to the AUTOEXEC.NCF file manually (or choose to save the change in MONITOR). Remember that an NDS replica must be stored on this server to support Bindery Services.

The other option for adding Bindery Services is through the MONITOR console utility. At the console, follow these steps:

1. Type **MONITOR.**

2. Choose Server Parameter in the Available Options window.

3. Choose Directory Services in the Select A Parameter category.

4. Scroll down to Bindery Context.

5. Press Enter to modify the bindery context setting.

6. Enter as many as 16 valid bindery context listings (remember, you must have replicas on this server for each context listed), separated by semicolons.

7. Press Escape three times, and then save the changes to your SYS:\SYSTEM\ AUTOEXEC.NCF file.

8. Exit MONITOR.

9. Verify that the context was set correctly by typing **CONFIG** at the console prompt; it should match.

The single-container NDS tree makes sense for the first NetWare 5 server in a network, especially as a way to roll out a pilot server. With this setup, clients can test the new NDS features while keeping the server resources available to all the bindery clients.

Bindery clients can see only the NDS leaf objects that are covered by a bindery context. What if there are two Organizational Units in a company, and one of them is running Bindery Services? What can bindery clients see? Figure 4.11 illustrates this example.

As you might guess, leaf objects that do not exist in a container running Bindery Services are invisible to bindery clients. If Joe Bindery wants to connect to the Acme NDS tree, the only part he will see is the container OU=ACCT.O=ACME.

Don't let your users push you into postponing the best parts of NDS by installing Bindery Services. Bindery Services was a short-term solution as all vendors got rolling with NDS-compliant products and as you upgraded your servers and clients. The present and future is NDS, because the future of our networks is distributed. Trying to avoid the short-term pain of upgrading workstation clients will only lead to long-term agony when the change is forced on you. Has any onerous job ever gotten better the longer it festered? No. If you (or your bosses) are still unconvinced about the value of NDS and the advantages of a global, distributed directory, just try it for a month. I guarantee that you won't go back.

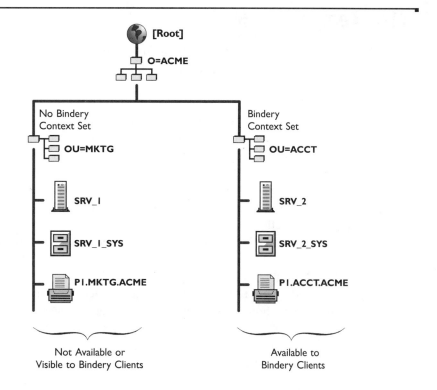

FIGURE 4.11

A bindery context that covers a portion of the NDS tree

Maintaining Bindery Services

If a bindery client uses a User login script from a NetWare 3.*x* server or a NetWare 4.*x* or 5.*x* server with Bindery Services, any changes to that User login script will not be replicated to any other servers. Only the text file on the authenticating server in the user's MAIL directory will be changed. The replication of user information changes is one of the big advantages of NDS and a major improvement over the server-centric bindery in earlier NetWare. In fact, NetWare helps make the transition from version 3.*x* to version 5.1 by automatically placing the login script in its new home in the user object during migration. Once upgraded, maintain it there, and it will be replicated to all the other NetWare 5.1 servers, keeping them in sync.

If you want System login scripts for these clients, you will need to create and maintain them on each server. The simplest way to do this is with SYSCON (which you will have to obtain from an old copy of NetWare 3.*x* or download from Novell's Web site; NetWare 5.1 doesn't ship with it), and then replicate it where it is needed.

New Features of NDS 8

Novell is putting much of their brainpower behind NDS, since directory services remains one area where they have a substantial lead over Microsoft (Active Directory is about NDS version 1.5 or 2). Their eagerness resulted in the release of NDS 8 and shipping that and NDS 7.3 with NetWare 5.1.

I don't think this is a good idea, personally, but Novell didn't ask me about it. Put the best NDS in the box and let fly, I say. Oh well.

Novell released NDS 8 in the middle of 1999 and made it available for NetWare 5.0 users. We'll cover each of the major improvements to NDS in NDS 8 in their appropriate places (mostly management sections), but let's at least mention them now.

First, and in keeping with Novell's new file-system philosophy, NDS 8 doesn't use TTS (Transaction Tracking System) to ensure that database transactions are completed accurately or rolled back in case of a problem. These fixed-length records weren't as scalable, and Novell has moved to a new, flashy, indexed database with log files tracking transactions for possible rollback.

Second, there are several new ways to manage NDS, including via Web browsers. We'll look at those in detail in the management chapters.

Third, NDS now directly supports standard LDAP version 3 (Lightweight Directory Access Protocol), an improvement in speed over earlier support. This may be the final piece of the puzzle that makes Novell the leading candidate for corporate directory service for all types of systems, from the tiniest synchronized palmtop to the largest Unix Web cluster.

New NDS Data Structure

Novell hides all the NDS control and index files, which is smart. Even smarter are the upgrades with NDS 8 that allow unlimited numbers of NDS items to remain under control.

Think you have a large network? Novell has claimed for some time that they could store the Internet inside NDS. During NDS 8 rollout, they demonstrated an NDS structure managing over a billion (yes, that's a *b*) objects.

With NDS 8, Novell moved from using their long-time TTS for transaction control to a new journaling file system. This new indexed database uses log files to back out transactions that can't be fully performed because of a system failure of any type, so the transactions can be completely performed when the system is right again. Let's look at these files briefly:

NDS.DB Control file, which also contains the rollback log.

NDS*.LOG Tracks transactions until completed, storing information until interrupted transactions can be completed.

NDS.01, 02, etc   All records and indices found on the server. Size limit is 2GB; when NDS.01 gets that big, NDS.02 is created for new data, followed by NDS.03, and continuing as far as necessary.

Stream files   Have .NDS extensions and hold such information as login scripts and print job configurations.

Indices in the NDS.01 file (and siblings) include substring indices for many of the most important object properties. Attribute indices for strings beginning with the CN (Common Name), uniqueID, Given Name, and Surname fields make locating people faster. Separate indices for just the CN and uniqueID fields help find any network object. LDAP connections have their own indices to improve LDAP coordination and performance.

NDS schema management is improved for both the network manager and any third parties making NDS-enabled products. Some have criticized Novell's deliberate rollout and control of third-party NDS products, but this control has been critical to NDS's success. Anyone here feel that Microsoft's Windows Registry database, with all the extensions available to any third party with no control or structure, is anywhere close to reliable? Didn't think so. And Active Directory will suffer several embarrassing meltdown problems until Microsoft puts out some patches. NDS has avoided these problems and will continue to be the safest place for network object information.

Do you need to worry about these files? Not at all. You should avoid them unless directed by Novell support technicians to use them. But these details are listed here so you better understand how NDS 8 has upgraded NDS to handle billions and billions (thank you, Carl Sagan) of network objects.

NDS eDirectory

For a company long castigated for poor marketing execution, Novell sure changes product names a lot. Maybe there's a connection.

Anyway, NDS eDirectory is the new name (as of NetWare 5.1) for native NDS 8 on Solaris, NT, Linux, and even NetWare. This is a corporate backbone directory, supporting other directories such as Active Directory from Microsoft or Netscape's directory (excuse me, that will probably become AOL's Enterprise Extended Keyword, or EEK, one of these days).

NDS eDirectory lives and functions on the host, replacing the need for a separate NetWare server. Novell has finally started selling NDS separately from NetWare. Let's hope lots of people buy it, because that will help Novell in many ways.

NDS Corporate Edition

The traditional method of redirection, such as NDS for NT where NDS supplanted the cludgy NT domain database management scheme, has been relabeled NDS Corporate Edition. This is the product for companies wishing to integrate other NOSs, such as NT, into NetWare.

NDS eDirectory is the guts of NDS Corporate Edition and relies on the standard NetWare tools such as NWADMIN and ConsoleOne to interface with the directory.

Directory Designs and Discussions

"Are we there yet?" If you've ever taken children on a car trip, you've heard those words too often.

In NetWare 5.1, the Directory answers those questions. Are we there yet? Yes, we are. NetWare 4.x wasn't quite there, but now we are there.

Where is there? That's the important network question. Where is there? What's there? Where is anything? Where is everything?

It's all around the network, that's where. Everything now has a place, and there's a place for everything, just as your mother told you. The bindery of NetWare 3.x was always "there," on the file server, and only on one file server at a time. So why didn't Novell call NetWare Directory Services something like Bindery Plus?

My friend Art Wittman has a great analogy for this: we no longer refer to cars in terms of being carriages without horses (horseless carriages); we refer to them as cars. We no longer care about the previous technology of horses; we only care about our current technology of self-powered automobiles.

We will soon come to that point with NDS. NDS isn't an expanded bindery; it's a whole new network ball game. Soon we'll speak of the "Directory" the same way we speak of the "Disk" and the server "Memory." In other words, just another part of every good network.

Will users like this? Sure, if the tools that make NDS simple for users are in place for them. Will all the users like this? No. All users never like all things. You will have some users complaining because of the change just because it is a change. Can't help those folks.

The trick is that complaining users will need to use the new network, whether they like it or not. Over time, they will all start complaining about something else and will deny they complained about the network at all.

Change is constant, and so are complainers. Don't let a few ruin your work for the many. Go forth and set NDS loose upon your users. Realize that the complainers will complain, but they are few and the Directory advancements are many.

CHAPTER 5

Connecting PC Clients to Your Network

t's easy to forget that the word *server* originated from *service*. In our situation, a server is something that is of use, available, and convenient. The person being served in a network is the client, or user.

NetWare provided a client/server system long before the term became a buzzword. In the early days, the only things a client needed were file and printer service. Today, much of a server's time is still spent providing controlled and shared access to files and printers.

But the client of today needs more than just access to files and printers. There are seven services that the modern client requires. In addition to file and print services, the client needs directory, management, routing, messaging, and security services.

NetWare 5.1 supports DOS, Windows of every type, and soon Macintosh and Unix clients (more about DOS and Macintosh clients in the Appendices). The majority of NetWare clients are PCs with Intel microprocessors running some version of Windows. All these various clients can be connected to the same server at the same time and share all the server resources. To be a NetWare client, a PC must:

- Be IBM PC-compatible.
- Have one of these types of processors: Intel 8088, 80286, 80386 (SX or DX), 80486 (SX or DX), Pentium, Pentium II, or Pentium III (or equivalent).
- Have a 1.44MB disk drive. (A CD-ROM drive is handy, but not mandatory; a 1.2MB floppy will work, but only after much pain.)
- Have a network interface card and suitable network cabling.

Using Client32 software for Windows 32-bit client operating systems (Windows 95, 98, NT, or 2000) changes the rules quite a bit from the struggles of the past, as you'll see in this chapter. But before we get to the client installation procedures, let's take care of the last item in the requirements list, your network interface card (or cards).

Installing Network Interface Cards

Before installing any of this nice networking software, the PC must have a *network interface card*. The network interface card has many names, depending on what you're reading:

- Network board
- NIC (network interface card)
- Board
- Adapter
- Driver (the software that handles the communication between the computer and the interface card)

A network interface card connects your PC to the network cabling system. Every PC must have at least one network interface card (or other means of communication) before the client software will load. Up to four adapters may be placed in a single PC running NetWare client software.

The adapter files provided with NetWare 5.1 or by the adapter manufacturer include all the default settings for each card. There are literally hundreds of driver files included with NetWare 5.1, and the adapter vendor should also supply a driver file. In case the files are not the same, try the newest one first.

 TIP Adapter driver files are often upgraded. New driver files can make a tremendous improvement in workstation performance. Contact your vendor for details, or watch the Novell Web site (www.novell.com) or the Internet newsgroup (comp.sys.novell) for upgrade information.

Check the adapter's documentation for specific details on any jumper or switch settings for each adapter. Newer interface cards may not have hardware jumpers or switches; all settings are done by software. This is especially true with PCI (Peripheral Component Interconnect) Plug-and-Play adapters.

Before opening a PC case to install any device, turn the computer off and unplug the system. The documentation with many adapters will warn you to work in a low-static environment (no carpet), and to work on a grounded pad with a wrist strap if you want to really be safe. That's great, but unrealistic for most situations. A clean desk and some care will generally be enough.

Adapters in your PC must work together with existing peripherals. There are four areas of connection between your adapter and your PC:

- Hardware interrupts
- Base I/O port addresses
- Memory addresses
- DMA channels

 NOTE Each of these settings is required by the NetWare client installation program. If you don't know the following information for your network adapters, find the manuals for each adapter type you plan to use on your network (if that's possible).

Go PCI Whenever Possible

Much of the next section details how to work with older style network interface cards in computer systems that don't have a PCI bus. Every personal computer built since about 1997 (including Apple, believe it or not) supports PCI cards.

Do yourself a favor: use PCI cards and Plug-and-Play computers and cut yourself some slack. Windows 95 and 98 don't do as much as they should to automatically find and correctly configure adapters, but Microsoft did force vendors to provide proper drivers for PCI cards in more recent computer systems. Take advantage of Microsoft's arm-twisting, and save yourself the headaches in the rest of this section.

Hardware Interrupts

Hardware interrupts, or *IRQs*, are used by a device to request services from the PC's processor. These are normally shown as integers, but hardware IRQs are occasionally shown as hexadecimal numbers. Eight-bit interface cards (the old ones, which I hope you don't have anymore) have interrupts 2, 3, 4, 5, and 7 available. Sixteen-bit cards have additional interrupts 9, 10, 11, 12, 13, 14, and 15 (or 9, A, B, C, D, E, and F). Interrupts support only one device (until you get to PCI cards). Standard PC interrupts and their assignments are listed earlier in the book, in Chapter 2 (Table 2.1).

With eight-bit interface cards, and PC and XT systems that have only eight bits available, interrupts are rare and valuable. Only interrupts 0 through 7 are available, and 0, 1, 2, 4, 5, 6, and 7 are already in use in most systems. The default for these eight-bit cards is often IRQ 3; a few still try to use IRQ 5 as the default. If you have a mouse on COM1 and a modem on COM2, there is no open interrupt for the network interface card. It's a good thing most of these old machines have been flushed out of the system. You have my deepest sympathy if you still have some left in your network.

Starting with the IBM AT with 16-bit slots, interrupts 8 through 15 become available, although IRQ 2 is lost as the bridge to the higher interrupts. The hard disk in AT and newer machines tends to use IRQ 14, leaving IRQ 5 open. However, the recent multimedia push requires more peripheral devices that need interrupts. CD-ROM drive controllers like IRQ 5 and sound boards often need an interrupt as well. Interrupts are becoming scarce again. ISA (Industry Standard Architecture—really old cards from the early days) network interface cards often come with a default of IRQ 10, which is generally available.

Base I/O Port Addresses

Once the peripheral device has an interrupt assigned to request services from the CPU, it needs a specific address to send and receive messages from the CPU and other devices. Addresses are normally three-digit hexadecimal numbers (such as 280h or

340h) and are often expressed as a range bound by the low and high addresses. Most network interface cards, however, request a single address, such as 320h.

Each device must use a *base I/O address*. There are more addresses available than there are interrupts, so this setting is generally less trouble than the interrupt setting. The adapter documentation will specify the default I/O address and the options supported by the adapter card.

Memory Addresses

The *memory address* is the exact location in memory that stores a particular data item or program instruction. When installing network interface cards, only the first megabyte of RAM is available.

Not all network interface cards use a memory address. If your card will be started by a remote boot PROM (programmable read-only memory) chip, a memory address will be necessary. Token Ring and ARCnet adapters often use these memory addresses; Ethernet cards rarely do.

The memory address must be unique to the adapter. The addresses are expressed in hexadecimal with three- or four-digit numbers, such as D000 or C400 or 280h or 340h. Your adapter documentation will state whether a memory address is required and what the default address is.

DMA Channels

DMA (dynamic memory access) is a method of transferring information from a device such as a hard disk or network adapter directory into memory without passing through the CPU. Because the CPU is not involved in the information transfer, the process is faster than other types of memory transfers. The DMA channel must be unique for each device.

Ethernet adapters make more use of DMA channels than Token Ring adapters, but you must check the adapter documentation. Other devices that transfer large amounts of information—such as hard disks, CD-ROM drives, and sound boards—will compete for DMA channels with the network adapter. The DMA channels are labeled with decimal integers.

Installing and Configuring Client32

Forgive an old-timer's musings, but I miss the days when a person actually knew what software did when it was installed, where the files were located, and how to fix a problem. Today, particularly with Windows 95/98/NT/2000, you start the process, hear the hard disk churn, and cross your fingers, hoping the process works properly. Because if it doesn't, you have no simple way to find the problem and fix the installation. Uninstall if possible, and reinstall until the operating system magic amulet you bought from the witch doctor at NetWorld+InterOp works its spell correctly.

You can download software from the Novell Web site (www.novell.com) if you would like to get started with Client32 before upgrading to NetWare 5.1. If you copy the files, just run the SETUP.EXE file from the local or network hard drive that holds the Client32 files.

Let's get started with the Windows 3.1 software.

The Story Behind Novell's 32-Bit Windows Clients

Microsoft's move to real 32-bit client operating systems (Windows NT/2000) and pseudo 32-bit (Windows 95/98) operating systems meant that Novell had to make some major changes in the Windows 95 and NT client software. Of course, Microsoft developers made their own 32-bit NetWare clients, hoping to freeze Novell out of the loop. Microsoft's lack of a decent directory service caused the designers to ignore NDS in their Windows 95 client, implying that directory services aren't really all that important.

Well, NDS turned out to be important to NetWare users, and folks were upset. Their aggravation was aimed in equal parts at Microsoft for making such an underpowered 32-bit client and at Novell for being so slow in bringing out its own client for Windows 95.

Novell protested that Microsoft was making it impossible to bring out a good client, and Microsoft protested that wasn't true, and they went round and round until nobody cared. The fact that Novell took more than two years to deliver its first (nearly worthless) Windows NT client makes me suspect that Novell political infighting was just as much to blame for the late Windows 95 drivers as Microsoft's bad attitude. Either way, customers of both companies were being poorly served.

NetWare 4.11 was released 13 months after Windows 95, so Novell had no excuses for the client shortcomings and installation hassles. Luckily for NetWare users, Novell has made a good Windows 95 client. If you don't believe me, check the various PC and network magazines; all agree Novell's client is better than Microsoft's. Of course, a NetWare client that's only "better than Microsoft's" doesn't mean it's a wonderful client. There are still installation hassles, so be wary.

With the continued update of Novell's Client32 software, excellent clients for Windows 95/98/NT/2000 are available with NetWare 5.1. If you haven't upgraded to NetWare 5.1 yet, you may want to download the client files from Novell's Web site.

Continued ▯▶

CONTINUED

In the licensing terms for the new client, you'll notice that you may freely use these client files *only* when connected to a Novell operating system. If that seems strange, you must have missed Microsoft's File and Print Services for NetWare product running under Windows NT. To encourage the use of Windows NT servers as replacements for NetWare servers, Microsoft copied the basic NetWare 3.1 file and print services, but running under Windows NT. The idea was that users could use their own NetWare client files to connect to the Windows NT server—the same files they used for connecting to the NetWare server.

I have the dubious honor of being the person who pointed out (in a review in *Information Week*) that Microsoft, a stout defender of their own product licensing, was somewhat sleazy in encouraging the misuse of Novell client software. It turns out Novell's lawyers thought the same thing, and Microsoft was forced to release their own pseudo-NetWare client software for their own pseudo-NetWare server clone. Don't you love legal retribution?

Client32 for Windows 3.1*x*

Since the Client32 software must load in DOS before Windows 3.1*x* gets started, the installation of the DOS files is the most important part. The DOS installation looks almost exactly like that of the VLM file process network administrators struggled with after the release of NetWare 4.

For some variety, we'll look at the Windows 3.1 installation screens. First, we're assuming the computer has a network connection, and so we'll load the Client32 files from a network server (assuming that these files were copied there when the server was installed). This is a good way to install clients, even for brand new machines. Keep a boot disk that loads the proper drivers for your brand of network adapter card from the floppy disk, and use that disk to get connected to the network. Then, using the Run option on the Windows 3.1, run the SETUP.EXE program from the \PUBLIC\CLIENT\DOSWIN32\NLS\ENGLISH subdirectory. You know, the one you copied from the Client and ZENworks CD-ROM to your server. If you haven't installed ZENworks, you can use the ZENworks CD to run SETUP.EXE in the \PRODUCTS\ DOSWIN32\NLS\ENGLISH subdirectory, or choose the Windows 3.x Client after activating WINSETUP in the CD's root directory.

First comes a progress screen showing files being copied from the server to your client workstation. Yawn. Temporary files will be created and then deleted on your workstation during this process.

The next thing you'll see when loading Client32 software is a license agreement. This was new for Novell starting with NetWare 4 and reflects the increasing legal climate chilling the computer business.

You'll notice you have no option concerning the licensing of Client32 software. You either accept the license agreement or you don't run the software. I'm not sure if this stand is completely legal, but that's not our problem in this book. Since you're using the client software to connect to a NetWare server, you have nothing to worry about, so click Yes and continue.

Another screen appears with details about the readme file and the like. Ignore it. If the information was important, wouldn't they show it on screen? Okay, read it if you're new at this or slightly paranoid.

Something new in the Windows 3.1*x* installation routine is a list of optional modules to load on this workstation. Figure 5.1 shows all your choices, waiting for your approval. When you make this installation automatic, which you can do with the Automatic Client Upgrade feature, you can preselect your choices.

FIGURE 5.1

New optional features for your Windows 3.1 workstation

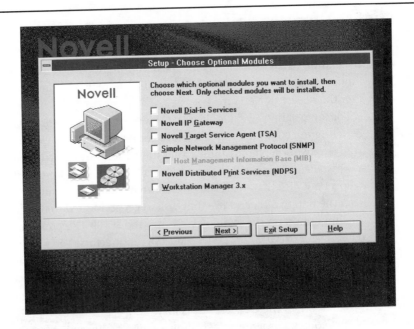

There is no mention of TCP/IP on this screen, although you have a choice to use Novell's IP Gateway if you wish. In another screen or two, you'll get a chance to select TCP/IP and/or NetWare/IP.

The next dialog box sets the file target directory (\NOVELL\CLIENT32) and the location of your Windows 3.1*x* files (generally \WINDOWS). If you have moved either, you must direct the installation routine to the proper place. However, there's no good reason to move these directories.

Disk space is checked, and an information screen shows how much space you have now and how much you will have. The important command button reads Begin Copy, so click it already. More files are copied here and yon.

Next, you start making decisions about network details. Choose your first network drive letter (usually F:). Choose the program group name or accept the default choice of Novell Client. Watch as the setup program modifies your configuration files, or rather, see the notice that it's doing so.

Another new screen appears, this one with an artsy (out-of-focus) picture of a network interface card. Figure 5.2 shows this new screen, which offers choices for your adapter.

FIGURE 5.2

*Specifying LAN
adapter details*

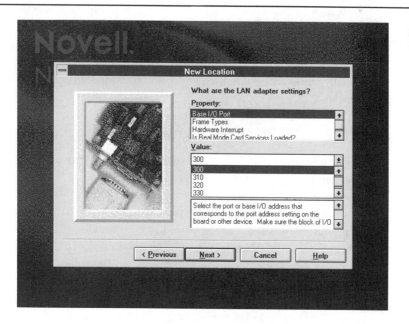

The illustration really doesn't show this, but you need to supply all the details yourself. Figure 5.2 shows a pick list of I/O port memory addresses, but it doesn't pick the one you have as the default (at least it didn't for me, but you may be lucky). Just be sure you know the I/O port, interrupt, and frame types you want to use on your workstation before you start.

You will have a choice to select TCP/IP and/or IPX frame types for this workstation. Both or either is acceptable, depending on your network. The default for NetWare 5.1 is TCP/IP, but Novell promises to support IPX for the next 100 years (like any of us will be around to complain if they don't).

Next come the network details: tree, context, and favorite server. If you don't remember these, go find out. It's easier to put them in correctly than to change them later.

The penultimate screen allows your choice of TCP/IP or IPX for this workstation. If you choose TCP/IP, have your IP network details handy. You'll need to know the IP address for this station or the IP address of the server providing the networking information. If your network is still using NetWare/IP, that option will be available here as well.

Finally, your work is finished, and you learn that a reboot is necessary. If you know you need to modify one of the configuration files, you can do so before rebooting. If not, cross your fingers and reboot.

When the planets are aligned correctly, your old Windows 3.1x workstation will become a workstation on your new NetWare 5.1 network. If you are being punished for sins in a past life, you'll need to tweak things and make changes. Luckily, Novell engineers realize few NetWare users have sins needing repentance, so the installation usually works without a hitch. Well, you hitch to your network, but you know what I mean.

Client32 for Windows 95/98

Yes, Microsoft includes NetWare client files with Windows 95/98 systems, but I bet you will be happier with the Novell client files. After all, if you're installing NetWare 5 clients, you probably want the best NDS support possible, plus tools for NDPS (Novell Distributed Print Service). All these work better with the Novell client software. Some details are missing completely from the Windows 95/98 client software, such as tight integration with NDS, which is another good reason to stick with the Novell software.

If you've installed ZENworks on the server, client files for Windows 95/98 are located in \PUBLIC\CLIENT\WIN95\IBM_ENU. For now, let's assume that you're installing your first Windows 95/98 client from the ZENworks CD or upgrading in the same way. This is a good idea, even if you plan to use one of the automated methods later (see the "Automated Client Installations" section later in this chapter and Appendix A for details on automating Windows 95/98 client installation). There are a few differences between the NetWare 5 and NetWare 4 installation routines, and you'll need to see the NetWare 5 choices at least once.

The `WINSETUP.EXE` file is in the root of the ZENworks CD, which replaces the file on NetWare 4's Client CD. This provides you a sample of the ZENworks program, a worthwhile way to spend just a few extra dollars and get plenty of network client management horsepower.

If you prefer, you may go down to the `\PRODUCTS\WIN95\IBM_ENU` directory on the ZENworks CD and run the SETUP program from there. Running the SETUP program three directory levels deep skips the first two screens, where you choose English (or whatever language this book is written in for my non-English-speaking friends) and then click to install the Windows 95/98 workstation components. Whether changing directories is worth clicking through the first two screens is up to you.

Oops, if your Windows 95 client doesn't have Service Pack 1 installed, you will have no joy. My copy of Windows 95 didn't, so I downloaded the file from Microsoft and installed it. Windows 98 machines don't have this problem, although Microsoft did release a Service Pack pretty quickly after the official release, so be ready for your own Service Pack download.

Standard screens go by, beginning with the license agreement (say Yes or get dumped from the installation program). When you get to the Typical or Custom installation screen, choose Typical for now (see the next section on Windows NT installation for a look at the Custom installation choices). Then watch the scary part: removing the existing client. That always makes me nervous. Even Novell smart guys, like my friend Henry Sprafkin, get nervous when doing this for customers to demonstrate new products.

Again will appear a choice of protocols: TCP/IP or IPX or both. Pick according to your network. Even if you're a big fan of IPX as I am, we both know TCP/IP won the protocol battle. Sigh and click TCP/IP or both.

Windows 95/98 churns for a time, building driver databases and the like, then finally we start copying files to the local Windows 95/98 system. You don't have any choice about where to put these files, so lean back and enjoy the ride—it can take some time. Time for coffee?

Then reboot, and cross your fingers as the machine comes back with—we all hope—the new Novell client software properly installed and configured.

 TIP One of the best ways to upgrade multiple Windows 95/98 machines to Novell's Client32 at the same time is to use the server-based Windows 95/98 installation routine (`ACU.EXE` for Automatic Client Update). See Appendix A for details.

There's one more important point about the Windows 95/98 client that must be mentioned: Client32 software adds a network file cache, speeding access to and from network resources by using part of your workstation RAM. If some software turns out to be touchy about the local cache, set it to 0 (zero) to disable the local cache. (Some third-party software will not work with file caching; you may want to check with your software vendor to avoid problems.) Many reports have come from disgruntled users who have seen huge amounts of memory gobbled up by their Client32 software. These reports have slowed after the early versions of Client32 software, but you need to understand the goal here is local caching of network information. The more RAM dedicated to local caching, the better most network interactions.

Balance this RAM gobbling depending on the user's needs, especially on workstations without enough RAM (and who really has enough RAM?). The way to curtail RAM grabbing by Client32 software is one level deeper in the Network Control Panel below the properties of the NetWare client. The File Cache Level setting is on the Advanced Settings tab of the Novell Client Configuration dialog box, as shown in Figure 5.3.

FIGURE 5.3

Slowing the RAM grab

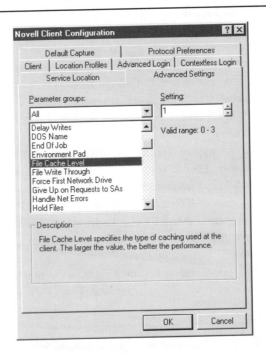

As you can see in the figure, never one to avoid a speed improvement if possible, I've set the lowest level of file cache, 1. Setting the number to 0 (zero) eliminates the RAM file cache completely. Raising the number to 4 guarantees that no application will have enough memory. Okay, that's a slight joke, but never underestimate an application's desire for RAM. Can you say "code bloat"?

Windows 98 isn't the ultimate desktop operating system, but it's what we have to work with today. It's harder to control in many ways than Windows 3.1x, but it also works better most of the time. The extra pain of support may or may not be balanced by the new capabilities.

Client32 for Windows NT/2000

Microsoft used to put forth the (now obvious) untruth that much of Windows 95/98 and Windows NT shared a common code base. Regardless of semantics about the number of lines of code in one version or another overlapping, the physical communication details in Windows 95/98 are vastly different than those in NT (and Windows 2000 has been rewritten from scratch). Most critically, applications can't communicate directly with the hardware in NT and 2000; all access is under the control of the operating system. This means the network client guts must be different.

The differences in the code don't mean that the user interface of the network clients must vary wildly. Novell has done a good job making the Windows 95/98 and NT/2000 clients look and feel much the same. In fact, some of this chapter may feel like deja vu all over again, as we see the NT/2000 client so soon after the Windows 95/98 client.

Follow the directions from the previous section: put the CD in the NT/2000 Workstation or Server destined to be a Novell client, and let auto-run do its stuff. You have other alternatives. You could direct your network pointer to the server directories holding the NetWare files for across-the-wire client upgrade. You could also set the /ACU (Automatic Client Upgrade) command in the login scripts that the NT/2000 Workstations will use, letting the system interrogate the client and upgrade any files necessary, but that's covered in the next section. For now, let's put a CD in the drive for consistency.

Choose your language, then choose your option. Since the heading above here says "Windows NT/2000," I suppose that's the choice for now, so click on the Windows NT Client option on this screen. Choose this option for both NT Workstation and NT Server machines used as workstations. Then click on Install Novell Client to finally start something.

Your first choice is whether this is a Typical or Custom installation. Since we did a Typical installation last time, let's choose Custom this time around. Figure 5.4 shows the Custom installation screen's choice of components.

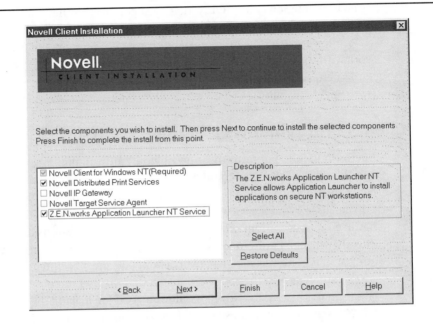

FIGURE 5.4

*Windows NT client
Custom installation
options*

Notice that the Novell Client for Windows NT (Required) box is checked and grayed out. As the screen says, this is required, so you don't have a choice. Also notice the description area with information about ZENworks. If you haven't played with this outstanding desktop system management utility, you should do so soon.

Next is your choice of protocols. The default is IP only, unless the installation routine discovers you are already running IPX (which you will be if you're performing any automatic or other type of network installation). Then the default is both IP and IPX. If you choose IP only, you may also choose to delete IPX (this seems rather drastic to Novell old-timers, but those are your options).

NDS or Bindery? NDS, of course, so choose that on the next screen. Then read that you have finished the custom portion of the installation, and click the Finish command button to continue.

Hear disks churn and see the progress bar inch left to right as filenames zoom by too fast to read. Notice how many are forced into \WINNT\SYSTEM32 or \WINNT\SYSTEM, and you see one of the main problems with Microsoft's method of cramming so much into one directory.

More information dialog boxes stream past your screen, then you should notice bindings being set and configured. Then, as always, choose to reboot.

Novell has so much experience now with these automated client installation routines that you have a great chance of success. When your NT station finally reboots, you'll see the new Novell Client login screen, shown in Figure 5.5.

FIGURE 5.5

*New login, new
security, but same old
control*

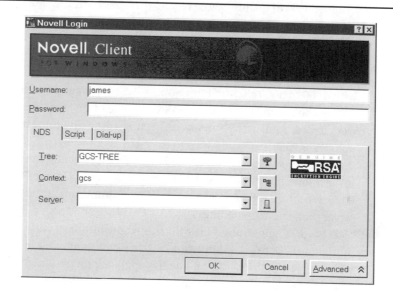

You can probably almost read that this screen says "For Windows NT" under the Novell Client heading at the top left of the screen. The only difference in this screen's appearance and the Windows 95/98 client screen on my test systems is that this one has a Dial-up option. Since RAS (Remote Access Services) is hard-wired into NT, this pops up whether I want it or not.

Clicking any of the Browse buttons to the immediate right of the Tree, Context, or Server text fields opens a browse window (how handy). You may scroll around to your heart's content to find your context, tree, or server, although speed and the ability to do context-less logins now seem to make this browsing capability less useful than in the past.

NOTE   If you need full-scale integration of your NT and NetWare 5 systems, you can use either of two products: Novell Administrator for Windows NT or NDS for NT. See Chapter 13 for details.

Automated Client Installations

Novell employees really learned to "eat their own cooking" during the development of NetWare 5 and 5.1. There was more time spent testing NetWare 5 and pushing it to a higher level of quality before release than has been the case for any other NetWare product release I can remember (and I've been watching for nearly 15 years). NetWare 5.1 is no different, although the move from 4.11 to 5.0 was bigger than the move from 5.0 to 5.1 in terms of network changes.

A minimum of 5000 client updates were made per week in Novell headquarters, with 1500 to 3000 clients at once upgraded an average of twice a week, for several months before the release of NetWare 5. Some of the upgrades were optional; some were forced. Some were NetWare client upgrades only; some included GroupWise 5.5 updates as well.

The method used by Novell, and one you should consider before any other group installation option, is the ACU, or Automatic Client Update. This option assumes that you have some level of client-to-server communications already, such as a NetWare 4.11 server that you're upgrading.

ZENworks helps quite a bit with this whole business, and all the files you need are on that disk. Here's the skinny on ACU: a single command in the login script (/ACU with very few options) can handle the upgrade process for you.

Here are the four steps to automated client installation:

1. Copy the Novell client files from the ZENworks CD and the Windows installation files to the same directory on a NetWare server.

2. Create a group called ACU (no changes allowed) and give all members read and scan rights to that folder.

3. Edit the NWSETUP.INI file in the directory along with the SETUP.EXE file for Windows 95. Directions can be long and involved and subject to change, so check Novell documentation for the latest details.

4. Add the @*SERVER**VOLUME*\PUBLIC\WIN95\SETUP/ACU command to the login scripts that the workstations will use.

There, you've done it. Novell recommends that you warn your users before you set this up the first time, so you don't get a call from every single user as each of their workstations takes off during the login process and starts copying files without their permission. Or you can schedule this for a day you're out of the office, and let the fun begin (that's a joke—don't even think about it).

Configuring Windows Clients

There are more configuration options available with the new NetWare Client32 software for Windows 95/98 and NT/2000 than ever before. Luckily, you don't need to check but a few to get the clients up and running just as well as ever. In fact, you will rarely need to change any of them, because the defaults for NetWare 5.1's client software give just about everything you need.

Novell Client Options

If you right-click the red *N* in the system tray, you will see many options. Some duplicate Windows offerings, such as Network Neighborhood, which has its own semi-useful icon on the Desktop, and options to map and disconnect network drives. These options are available under Windows Explorer's Tools menu, but the Novell options here are easier to find and seem to work slightly faster.

Some of the options in the pop-up menu are old Novell utilities still rattling around inside the product, such as the Send Message option. Plop a message onto the center of your friends' screens using the Novell instant one-way messaging option. Plop enough messages and you won't have any friends left (hint).

New options on the menu include NetWare Connections, which is a pop-up screen, not the magazine. Click this menu item, and a box labeled NetWare Connections appears, showing the resources you are authorized to see and use. Other information includes your user name, the connection number, the authentication method (usually NDS), the tree holding the resources, the transport protocol used, and the NetWare address. This information is helpful for troubleshooting, but the average user won't spend much time perusing it.

Printer port capturing and configuring are also available from the Novell pop-up menu, although these options are still available through Windows Explorer as well. You may also start the login process again, which is handy for workstations alternating between administrative use and standard client operation.

Novell Client Properties

The last Novell pop-up menu option, Novell Client Properties, is a shortcut to drilling down through the Control Panel, Network, and the Novell Client properties box. Figure 5.6 shows the default view when you choose this option.

*More client control
than ever before*

You have seen some of this before, of course, in earlier login screens. Until Novell Client32-equipped clients could see multiple trees, there was no reason to make room to show more than one tree at a time. Now there is.

Little functional difference can be found between the Windows 95/98 and NT/2000 versions of the Novell client properties. The NT client has some extra options in the Advanced Login page, but these only give you a chance to change the welcome screen and caption. There is no File Cache Level setting for Windows NT/2000, as there is for Windows 95/98 clients. Many other Advanced Settings options differ between the two clients, but few (if any) administrators will ever need to mess with any of these, so don't worry too much about them.

The Default Capture options help set the stage for each client's use of the printer, but this is not a good place to put those details. Unless it's impossible, you should put printing details into the default printer configuration on the print server. As you know, individual client changes are to be avoided whenever possible.

Other options, such as mapping NetWare drives, are handy at the client for power users but become nightmares for less-experienced users. Rather, they become nightmares for you trying to manage those newbies gleefully changing every setting they can find in their Novell menus and never understanding why you aren't excited by their constant voyages of discovery. If only a real voyage were an option for about two users out of every hundred, life would be much, much better.

Too Many Client Options, Too Little Time

When I have a problem with my car, I pull up the hood and look for a button that's labeled, "Push this and all will work again." Unfortunately, there isn't one of those, at least not on any of the cars I've owned.

When I have a problem with a computer or a network, I want to open the manual and see a heading that says, "James, here is the answer to your question." Unfortunately, there isn't one of those, either.

NetWare clients used to require almost as much compiling (yes, compiling) as the NetWare server itself. Those weren't happy days.

Now you'll see better networking and easier client configurations with NetWare 5.1 than ever before. Of course, you still need to be careful. The added client complexities of Windows 95/98 and NT/2000 add a new layer of confusion and potential disaster, especially with the Microsoft habit of hiding everything inside the Registry. But the automated client installations have become much better, and NetWare 5.1 makes these installations almost foolproof.

Speaking of Microsoft, you may be wondering why I haven't said anything about Microsoft's clients in this chapter. After all, Microsoft went to all that trouble to put these clients inside its operating systems, so I should describe how to use them. Well, not necessarily. If you want to use Microsoft's mediocre, bindery-based, NDS-unaware clients for your network, I can't stop you, but I can try to talk you out of it.

Use Novell clients for NetWare networks. You can keep the Microsoft clients for Microsoft networks, although you'll find that the Novell client for NT/2000 works better by itself than the Microsoft NetWare and Microsoft network clients do. Who knows the most of anyone about high-speed, highly reliable network clients? Novell, that's who. Don't accept the pale imitation of Microsoft clients when there are NetWare servers involved.

PART II

Managing the Network

LEARN:

- *Creating user objects*

- *Handling multiple users*

- *Arranging network printing*

- *Securing your network*

- *Administering your network*

- *Providing applications for clients*

- *Teaching your clients to use the network*

- *Integrating NetWare 5.1 with Windows NT*

CHAPTER <u>6</u>

Creating and Managing User Objects

I n network support departments, this is the first joke that rookies learn: *user* is a four-letter word. If your boss hears you, explain that this joke mines the same humor vein as college professors who love teaching but hate students, salespeople who love selling but hate customers, and editors who love books but hate authors. The things we know best, we both love and hate, depending on the stress of the moment.

For those few moments when the stress overwhelms you and user *does* become a four-letter word, just remember that users require administration, which requires you. When users are a pain, it's often because they are untrained and ill-equipped for their job as network clients.

The smart network user needn't like computers, but smart network administrators like both the business they're in and networking. Since users won't come to you until it's too late or something is broken, you must go to them. Learn their job function goals and provide them the proper tools to reach those goals, and your users will be happy and productive.

But first, before they can be a pain in the neck, users must be created on your new file server. With some management help, users will pain you less. Except for that one user who drives everybody crazy; there's one on every network.

Users and NetWare 5.1

The User object in NetWare 5.1 is the fundamental object in NDS. It contains information about the person it represents, and as the system administrator, you can set or control every aspect of the User object's interface to the network. The only requirements for the User object are:

- A user name that is unique within the container
- A completed Last Name field (not empty)

That's it. Everything else for a User object is optional, but much is recommended. Each physical user on the network should have a unique User object, but that's not mandatory either.

If you are coming to NetWare 5.1 from NetWare 4.*x*, you will be familiar with user properties. If you are coming from an earlier version of NetWare, you will be familiar with many of the User object properties. User object details are as follows:

Group Membership   When added to a group, the User object inherits the rights assigned to that group.

Home Directories   Serve as personal disk space on the server. It's best if the directory is placed under an umbrella directory and uses the person's name for the directory name, as in SYS:\USERS\CORI.

Security Equivalences   This is a quick way to assign the same rights to one User object as the rights held by another. This makes administration slightly more difficult, however, so verify the string of equivalent rights all the way through for each User object. If you assign Riley the same rights as Katie, Riley suddenly has access to everything Katie controls. Be sure that's what you want before granting this equivalence.

User Login Scripts   Configurable network batch files that customize the User object's network environment by setting environment variables, mapping drives, attaching printers, and the like.

User Account Restrictions   Security restrictions that limit a person's access to the network or limit the use of certain network resources. For example, you can place limits on disk space used, connection times, and network computers from which to connect. You can make passwords mandatory and force the user to change them at specified intervals.

User Trustee Rights   Allow the user to access other NDS objects. Must be granted by the Admin user, by the equivalent, or by any user with the necessary rights.

Print Job Configurations   Specific print job details for each User object, or a container may have configurations for all the User objects within.

Account Manager   The configuration of one User object with the necessary rights (usually Supervisor right) to other objects. This allows the supervised object's rights to be modified. Without having to assign full Supervisor rights, one object can be granted rights to other objects to fulfill certain functions, such as modifying phone numbers for each User object.

If you are the first user connecting to a NetWare 5.1 server, you will see only one configured user: Admin. The Admin User object is the NDS counterpart to the user SUPERVISOR from the bindery (NetWare 3.*x* and earlier versions). Everyone else must be created using either the NetWare Administrator (NWADMN32) or ConsoleOne. The DOS-based NETADMIN utility is not included with NetWare 5.1. In this chapter, I will discuss how to use NWADMN32, Novell's latest NetWare Administrator for 32-bit Microsoft desktops, and ConsoleOne.

For new installations, you must log in as the Admin User object to have the proper rights to create new users. Later, subadministrators can be allowed to create User

PART

II

Managing the Network

objects in parts of your network. Workgroup administrators granted Admin equivalence can, of course, also create any NDS object.

You can create and manage users with any of the three NetWare administration programs, and you can modify any user information you enter during setup of the User object in the same manner.

This is not a linear chapter: if you prefer NetWare Administrator, keep reading from here. If you would like to learn more about using ConsoleOne, skip ahead to the "Creating User Objects with ConsoleOne" section. The explanations are remarkably similar in both places.

Creating User Objects with NetWare Administrator

Once you are connected to the network and have the proper client programs loaded for your workstation, you can run the NetWare Administrator program, NWADMN32. Novell manuals and technical support people call this program NetWare Administrator rather than NWADMN32. Look at it longingly, because ConsoleOne will take over soon.

Most NetWare 5.1 administrators will use a Windows 95/98/NT/2000 system. So, when I reference NetWare Administrator, I'm speaking of the version specific for 32-bit Windows platforms. I'm also using it in conjunction with Novell's Client32.

Loading Client Software and the NetWare Administrator Program

Detailed instructions for client installation were in the previous chapter. If you've skipped ahead and are in a hurry to log in to the NetWare 5.1 server and start administrating, follow these steps:

1. Load the WINSETUP.EXE program from the Client CD-ROM and follow the instructions on the screen.

2. Exit the installation program and reboot your workstation.

3. Log in to the appropriate directory tree as Admin.

4. Browse Network Neighborhood to your server, to the SYS: volume, to the PUBLIC directory, and to the WIN32 subdirectory.

5. At this point, you can double-click the NWADMN32.EXE program to launch NetWare Administrator.

NOTE   To avoid all the browsing in the future, map a drive to the WIN32 subdirectory, and/or create a shortcut on the Windows desktop.

Upon login, the Admin user has access to the root of the SYS: volume, to SYS:SYSTEM, and to SYS:PUBLIC, just as in earlier NetWare versions. The LOGIN command for Admin assumes the Admin object was placed in the main Organization container.

Basic User Object Setup with NetWare Administrator

IN A HURRY

6.1 Create a Basic User Object

1. Open NetWare Administrator and move to the context for the new User object.
2. Press Insert to open the New Object list box.
3. Choose the User object and press Enter.
4. Provide the Login Name and press Tab.
5. Provide the Last Name and press Enter.

PART

II

Managing the
Network

When I say basic, I mean basic. The bare-bones User object created using the minimum configuration has no login script and no rights except those granted to the [Public] trustee object.

The first thing to do, as when performing any administrative task while in Windows, is to load the NetWare Administrator program. When the program opens, you will see the [Root] object with the globe icon. Each container you open displays the objects contained inside, both container and leaf objects. You can open a container by double-clicking the container object or by choosing View ➤ Expand. (If you ask me, double-clicking is easier.) You can also press Alt+V+X if you don't want to use the mouse.

Before we can create the User object, we must reach the context in which it will reside. Technically, you can create a User object in any context you wish, and the user will have access to the NDS tree. The trick is that the individual user must know his or her context when logging in, or the context must be placed in the Login prompt. Practically, it's easiest to create each user in the same context as that user's primary server.

Non-NetWare 5.x or 4.1x users (those using NetWare 3.x or earlier NETX shells on their workstations) must be created in the containers where Bindery Services is enabled. Their context is not important when they log in, because those users log in through Bindery Services. They log in directly to their target NetWare 5.1 server (which must be running Bindery Services).

Once all the containers are open, or at least the container in which you plan to create a new User object, highlight the Organization or Organizational Unit name. To create a new object, you have several choices to start the process:

- Press the Insert key.
- Right-click the container name, and then left-click the Create button.
- Press Alt+O or click Object on the main menu, then highlight Create and press Enter.

Old NetWare hands will no doubt press the Insert key, since that's the time-honored NetWare tradition. No matter which method you choose to start the Create process, you wind up with what's shown in Figure 6.1.

FIGURE 6.1

Beginning the process of creating a User object

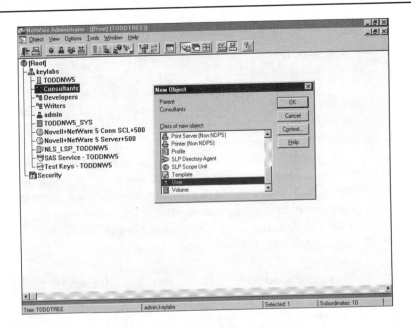

The NetWare Administrator program runs as a multiple-document interface (MDI) application. The main, full-screen NetWare Administrator window becomes the background for multiple secondary windows.

NOTE In Figure 6.1, I have moved the New Object subwindow to the right so that it does not cover the NDS tree. For many of the illustrations in this book, I moved the windows for clarity. So don't be alarmed when your screen doesn't look exactly like the one shown in the picture.

In typical Windows fashion, you can left-click the scroll bar to the right of the window until User comes into view, as it is in the screen in Figure 6.1. In typical NetWare fashion, you can also press the first letters of your choice until that choice appears under the highlight bar. In Figure 6.1, pressing U was all that was necessary to highlight User.

When the proper object is highlighted, press Enter or click OK. You can cancel the process by clicking Cancel or pressing Escape. Clicking the Context button displays the context, which echoes the listing under Parent at the top of the New Object window. Clicking the Help button or pressing F1 pops open the standard Windows hypertext Help system, with information for your specific topic.

After you choose the User object and confirm your choice in the manner you feel most comfortable, the Create User window opens. This window has two mandatory fields, Login Name and Last Name, along with four options. Figure 6.2 shows the Create User window.

FIGURE 6.2

Creating Mackenzie

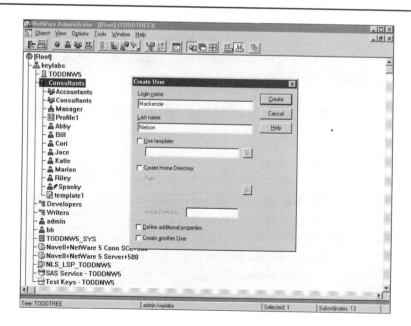

The login name can contain spaces. Names are not case-sensitive, but they will be displayed as typed in the Login Name field (Mackenzie will display that way, but NDS regards it as identical to mackenzie and MACKENZIE).

The requirements for login names are:

- Must be fewer than 64 characters
- Must be unique within the container

These restrictions aren't onerous and are much more liberal than earlier NetWare versions, which brings up an important point. If your NetWare 5.1 server must support non-NDS clients or work with earlier NetWare server versions, you must be mindful of the restrictions placed on login names by the bindery:

- Names longer than 47 characters are truncated.
- Spaces are shown as underscores.
- Non-NDS clients cannot see the following characters: slash (/), backslash (\), colon (:), comma (,), asterisk (*), and question mark (?).

The special characters above are legal within NDS but not within bindery systems. These characters also create problems in DOS names. The path of least trouble is to develop a naming standard for users that allows only alpha and numeric characters. If e-mail is important to your company, verify names with that system before assigning them inside NDS. You want names that work across all applications and systems.

The Last Name field is mandatory, but it has no restrictions except making the name fit into the field. You might wonder why this is here, looking so much like a database entry field. What about searching for users at a later date? This will be done, and last name is certainly an excellent search field. That's why this information is mandatory.

Specifying Optional User Object Details with NetWare Administrator

Notice in Figure 6.2 the four checkboxes below the Last Name field. Much more information is suggested for each user, even if it isn't mandatory.

Use Template   The user template is a file containing default information applied to new User objects, giving them predetermined property values within that container.

Create Home Directory   Makes a personal directory for this user and grants this user all rights to that directory.

Define Additional Properties Opens a window with fields for more details about the User object.

Create Another User Saves this User object and lets you immediately create another.

Of these four options, Define Additional Properties and Create Another User are mutually exclusive. If you choose one, the other option turns gray, indicating it's no longer valid.

Let's take a look at some of these. The first option, Use Template, is blank because we have yet to define a user template. We'll get to that soon.

Creating a Home Directory

IN A HURRY

PART

II

6.2 Create a Home Directory for a User

1. Click the Create Home Directory checkbox.
2. Open NetWare Administrator and create a new User object.
3. Click the Browse button to display the available file systems.
4. Choose the proper location for the home directory, and then click OK.
5. Enter the name of the home directory in the Home Directory field, or accept the default (same as the User object name).
6. Click Create, and the home directory is created immediately.

Managing the
Network

I'm all in favor of the Home Directory concept that's been in use from the earliest days of NetWare. It encourages two important habits in your users:

- Placing personal working files on the server so they are easy to back up and restore
- Developing a sense of "ownership" of the server, since users have a personal stake

These habits may not be earthshaking, but they are important. Although backup systems are becoming more sophisticated, client backup is still difficult. The easiest backup system for you as the administrator is to back up only the server, knowing the user files will be taken care of at the same time.

The ownership feeling is a bit more ephemeral but just as important. When Net-Ware networks were bought and supported by the department, the department "owned" the server and often felt protective toward it. The trend today is for servers to be centrally administered, making them more distant from the departments. The department now has less control of the network composition, mission, and administration. Some of the aggravation formerly directed at the mainframe people is now being aimed at the central network authority. If each person has a direct connection to a little piece of the network he or she "owns," that user has more positive feelings about the network.

Creating the home directory is not at all difficult. Figure 6.3 shows the creation of a home directory for user Mackenzie.

FIGURE 6.3

Selecting the home directory location

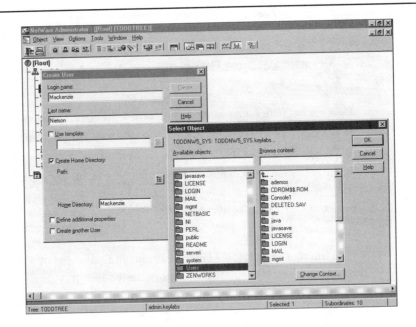

It's smart to group all users under an "umbrella" directory (named Users in the example in Figure 6.3). It makes for neater file systems, easier management, and smoother expansion. If all users are on the same volume, and the volume grows, you can add another disk and spread the volume across both disks without inconveniencing the users.

Users can use their home directory as if it were the root of their personal hard disk. They can create and delete files and subdirectories to their hearts' content. No user has, by default, the right to see or manipulate the contents of another user's home directory.

Don't put the user home directories on the SYS: volume if at all possible. That's been the tradition with NetWare administrators for years, but it's not a good idea. User-controlled space can grow quickly, filling the volume. If the SYS: volume becomes full, your server gets weird and will likely shut down. If some other volume gets full, a few users call and complain that they can't save any more files. Of the two error conditions, the second is by far preferable.

When you click the Browse button (the one that looks like a tiny map of the NDS tree) in the Create User dialog box, the Select Object dialog box, the active one in Figure 6.3, opens. Remember, directories and file systems are treated as objects now.

When the Select Object dialog box opens, the Browse Context box in the lower right shows the list of available servers and volumes in the context. To move around the NDS tree, double-click objects in the Browse Context list box. In this example, double-clicking the TODDNW5_SYS volume displays the list of available directories. When the umbrella directory appears, you must click the name in the Available Objects list. Doing so activates the OK button.

The Change Context button at the bottom of the dialog box allows you to see a different context. No Browse button is available; you must type the new context name. Clicking Cancel clears everything and returns you to the previous dialog box.

Clicking OK closes the Select Object dialog box. Back in the original Create User dialog box, the home directory name, with its full context, is copied into the Path section. The Home Directory field contains the User object name. You can accept that name or type a different name in the field. Clicking Create will immediately create the home directory and grant all rights to that directory to the user.

Adding User Identification Information

If you click the Define Additional Properties checkbox in the Create User dialog box, you will find tons of things to fill out about this particular User object. Don't be overwhelmed; none of this information is mandatory. But many items are helpful, and you are probably already familiar with such things as the Login Script properties from earlier NetWare versions.

Figure 6.4 shows the main user Identification screen, identified in two ways. First, the screen name appears in the upper-left corner, just under the main title bar. Second, the Identification button on the right side is pressed and has black borders.

FIGURE 6.4

Entering Mackenzie identification information

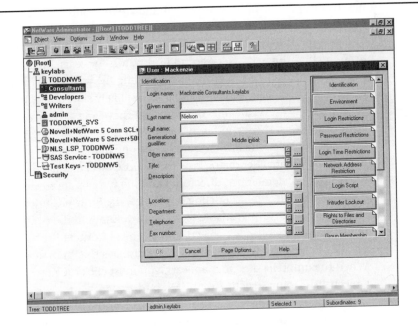

Let's take a quick look around this screen. The title bar shows the object class and name of the object. Here, it's User:Mackenzie (I told you the system remembers exactly how you typed the name). The page title shows just under the left side of the title bar. Page buttons line the right side, with the active one sporting a dark bar across the top and left side. The 3-D effect makes the active button look as if it's pressed.

By default, 15 pages are represented by the buttons; 17 pages are available. Clicking the scroll bar to the right of the buttons pulls the rest into view. When the turned-down corner of a page button is black, changes have been made to that page, but those changes are not yet saved. Clicking OK saves all the pages at once.

NetWare 5.1 allows you to choose which command buttons appear on the screen when you ask for details about an object. I don't recommend subtracting command buttons from the list. But as more and more NDS-aware applications become available, the number of command buttons may grow. If the list grows too much, paring it down may be worth the time and effort.

If your mouse arm is just too tired to reach all the way over to the command buttons, there is a shortcut if you're running Windows 95, believe it or not. Put your cursor anywhere on the foreground box, and click the right mouse button. The entire list of all command buttons will pop up in menu form.

WARNING The OK and Cancel buttons across the bottom of Figure 6.4 work on all the pages represented by the buttons on the right. Each button represents at least one page of information. Do not click the Cancel button unless you mean to cancel every change made on every field on every page during this session.

Notice the More buttons to the right of the fields, starting with Other Name and running through the end. The three little dots on the button are really an ellipsis (Latin for "three little dots"). At the end of a sentence, the ellipsis indicates there is more not explicitly stated. The same is true here. Every field with a More button can hold multiple values, such as several phone numbers, titles, or the like.

When you start, the only information filled in is the Login Name (with full context) and Last Name fields. If you remember, these are the only two mandatory fields when creating a User object. However, the WHOAMI command-line utility presents the information in the Other Name, Title, and Description fields if they are not blank.

The fields in the Identification page contain plenty of information that can be useful when searching for particular people or locations on the network. The list of field names and uses are:

Given Name   User's first name

Last Name   User's last name (filled in automatically)

Full Name   User's complete name

Generational Qualifier   Jr., Sr., II, III, and so on

Middle   User's middle initial

Other Name   Nickname, job function name, or other identification information (60 characters maximum per entry; duplicates are not allowed)

Title   Position or function of user (60 characters maximum)

Description   Function the user performs (30 lines of 37 characters each maximum)

Location   Physical location, such as floor, wing, or mail stop

Department   User's department, division, or workgroup

Telephone   User's telephone numbers

Fax Number   User's fax numbers or those available to the user

Why should you enter all these things? Seems like a lot of extra work, doesn't it? Well, what if your boss asks for all the network users on the third floor? How many network users are senior editors? How many network users will use the new fax modem when we replace the fax machine with the number 214-555-2599? These answers are easy to find if the database information is available.

PART

II

Managing the Network

NOTE Of course, if anyone had bothered to ask me, I would have replaced the fax number slot with an e-mail address. But then, I hate faxes and prefer e-mail. I'm surprised that Novell didn't add a spot for e-mail in NetWare 5.1, but perhaps they're expecting all NetWare customers to buy GroupWise. Nothing stops you from adding e-mail addresses in one of the fields that takes multiple entries, like Location, but it would have been nice to have e-mail.

Entering User Environment Information

The Environment page is strictly informative. None of the information you set here changes the User object's setup or configuration. Figure 6.5 shows this page. Notice that the second button along the right side of the dialog box is pressed.

FIGURE 6.5

Environment information

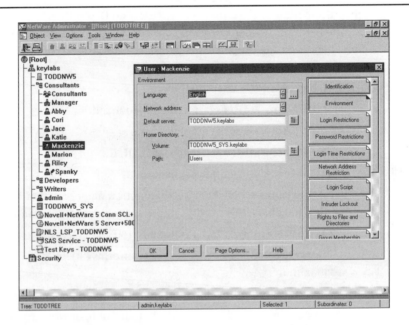

The fields on the Environment page are:

Language   From the SET command, shows the language for system messages.

Network Address   Address or addresses of the workstation this user is currently using to connect to the network. This will change when the user connects from a different station.

Default Server   NetWare server the user tries to connect to when logging in. This information is supplied by NDS.

Home Directory   The volume and path of the user's home directory. You can add or change a home directory through this field.

Specifying Print Job Configurations

> ### IN A HURRY
>
> ### 6.3 Create a Print Job Configuration
>
> **1.** Open NetWare Administrator and locate the User object in the NDS tree.
> **2.** Open the User dialog box by double-clicking the User object name.
> **3.** Click the Print Job Configuration button.
> **4.** Click the New button.
> **5.** Fill in the appropriate fields for this print job configuration, including a unique name for this user.
> **6.** Click OK in the Print Job Configuration dialog box, then again in the User dialog box.

The Print Job Configuration (Non-NDPS) button is no longer a default button in NetWare 5.1, probably due to the release of Novell Distributed Print Services (NDPS). But this is still an option, and you can add the command button to NetWare Administrator.

You usually create print job configurations at the container level so that they are available to all users in the container. You can, however, create a personal print job configuration.

Any print job configuration is activated by using the Job option (J=) in the CAPTURE and NPRINT print utilities. You must specify which print job configuration you want to engage by naming it as part of the CAPTURE or NPRINT command, as in:

```
CAPTURE J=PJ1
```

If you have a default print job configuration, those parameters will be in effect each time you invoke CAPTURE or NPRINT. You can override any of the defined parameters by using a command-line parameter with either print utility.

Figure 6.6 shows the Print Job Configuration page, with a new print job configuration being created. This screen is identical to the screen used to set up print job configurations for Organizations or Organizational Units.

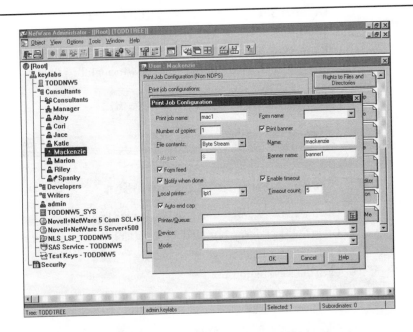

Here we are adding a new print job configuration in addition to the one already listed in the background dialog box. The foreground dialog box opened when the New button was clicked. Beside the New button (but unseen because of the foreground dialog box) are buttons for Modify, Delete, and Default.

The Print Job Configuration dialog box field names and acceptable values are:

Print Job Name   Must be unique for this user. You cannot change the name, although you can modify all other fields later.

Number of Copies   The default is 1, but you can enter any number up to 65,000.

File Contents   Text or Byte Stream. Byte Stream is the default and also is the safest choice for general printing.

Tab Size   Active only when the file contents are listed as Text. Refers to the width in characters each tab character should be when printed.

Form Feed   When checked, the CAPTURE or NPRINT software sends a form feed to flush the job out of the printer.

Notify When Done   When checked, the system sends the user a message when the print job is spooled to the printer. It does not guarantee that the printer has successfully printed the job itself.

Local Printer Chooses the parallel port to which your print job will be sent.

Auto End Cap When checked, tells the CAPTURE command to print the job when the application says it is finished.

Printer/Queue Designates the printer or print queue for this print job configuration. Clicking the Browse button opens the Select Object dialog box, but the dialog box displays only printers and print queues.

Device Specifies a named print device for this print job configuration.

Mode Specifies a defined mode (such as Re-initialize) for the print device specified in the previous field.

Form Name Specifies a defined form for this print job configuration, chosen from a list that appears when the down arrow button is clicked.

Print Banner When checked, includes a banner page at the beginning of the print job.

Name Active only when Print Banner is checked. When this field is blank, the user name is inserted. The name listed in this field and the next can be a maximum of 11 characters.

Banner Name Active only when Print Banner is checked. When this field is left blank, the printer port is inserted on the banner page. The name listed in this field and the previous can be a maximum of 11 characters.

Enable Timeout When checked, forces CAPTURE to consider a print job finished if there is no activity for a defined number of seconds.

Timeout Count Active only when Enable Timeout is checked. Range is from 1 to 1000 seconds. For typical word-processing print jobs, a short value (5–10) will be fine. For print jobs requiring lots of computer calculations, such as large reports or spreadsheets, the time should be longer. If a print job comes out in two or more pieces, this value is too low.

 TIP The ability to specify print job configurations for particular users is good, but don't get carried away. You're better off configuring printing for groups of users at a time. A print job configuration for a container works much better than this one for individuals.

PART

II

Managing the
Network

Specifying the User's Postal Address

6.4 Set Postal Address Information

1. Open NetWare Administrator and locate the User object in the NDS tree.
2. Open the User dialog box by double-clicking the User object name.
3. Click the Postal Address button on the right.
4. Fill in the fields in the top half of the window.
5. To copy the information to the Mailing Label Information, click the Copy to Label button.
6. Click OK to save the information.

You can use the Postal Address page to track either the home or business address for each user. You can use the fields for searching and to create a mailing label format. Figure 6.7 shows the Postal Address dialog box with information for user Mackenzie.

FIGURE 6.7

Addresses the old-fashioned way

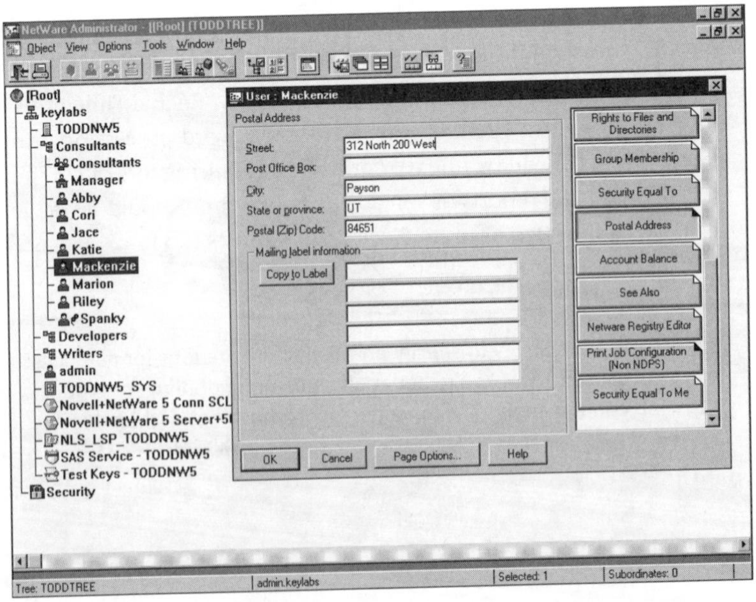

After opening the NetWare Administrator program, find the user you want to give a physical address listing. Double-click that name, or open the User dialog box in one of the other ways: select from the Object menu, right-click and press Enter, or simply press Enter when the User object is highlighted. From the User dialog box, click the Postal Address button on the right side. You will need to scroll down to find this particular button. After you click, the screen shown in Figure 6.7 appears.

No particular secrets here; no Browse buttons or pick lists. The only concern is if you plan to use this information for searching your NDS database later. Only the top half of the dialog box will be searched, not the bottom.

These fields accept all international postal codes. If you have international addresses, simply supply the appropriate codes and countries in the Postal (Zip) Code field.

Setting the Account Balance

IN A HURRY

6.5 Set the Account Balance for a User

1. Open NetWare Administrator and locate the User object in the NDS tree.
2. Open the User dialog box by double-clicking the User object name.
3. Click the Account Balance button on the right.
4. Click to disable the Allow Unlimited Credit box to enable accounting.
5. Set the current Account Balance and the Low Balance Limit.
6. Click OK to save your settings.

NetWare was the first network operating system to allow accounting. By tracking such details as connect time, disk space used, and service requests to a file server, NetWare accounting moved away from a PC LAN level toward mainframe-type control. Accounting is used by some network administrators to charge company departments and by others to track when resources are being used more heavily than in the past.

If accounting is enabled on a server, the users of that server can be assigned a value for each server operation. The screen shown in Figure 6.8 tells you how simple it is to track the server resources consumed by a user.

The Account Balance field shows the credits available for this user. The credits are set on the network resource itself, not here (see Chapter 10 for details). The Low Balance Limit field shows the credit level to warn the user before the account is disabled.

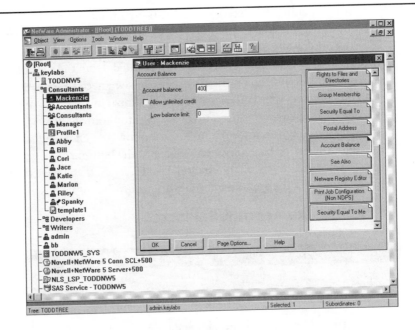

FIGURE 6.8

Accounting for user Mackenzie

If you want to track the accounting information for charge-back or overhead calculations but don't want to prevent users from reaching their network resources after they've used up their allotted credit, click the Allow Unlimited Credit box. This will track the information needed for the accounting reports but never lock out users.

 NOTE If a user's credits do drop to the level of the Low Balance Limit field and that user is locked out of the system, nothing happens to the user's information. The user will regain access as soon as an administrator changes the Account Balance field.

Adding Reference Information

IN A HURRY

6.6 Track Related Objects for a User

1. Open NetWare Administrator and locate the User object in the NDS tree.

2. Open the User dialog box by double-clicking the User object name.

Continued

IN A HURRY CONTINUED

3. Click the See Also button on the right.

4. Click the Add button to list more objects related to the user.

5. Choose the related objects from the Select Object dialog box.

6. Click OK to move the selected objects to the See Also page.

7. Click OK to save the information.

The See Also page is strictly informational. It does not affect any network configurations. Figure 6.9 shows the process of adding new related objects to the user Mackenzie. This page is a handy place to put items you may need for reference, such as the Computer object type used by Mackenzie.

FIGURE 6.9

*Showing Mackenzie–
alias Spanky*

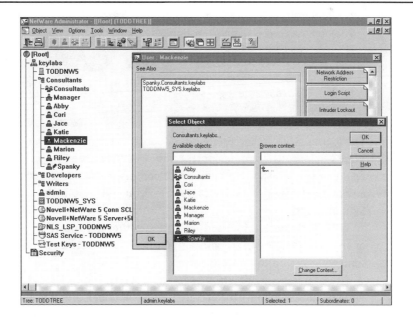

Managing the
Network

You cannot enter text in the See Also page. You can choose multiple objects in the Select Object dialog box. Simply hold down the Ctrl key as you click the left mouse button on each object you want to select.

Configuring User Object Security with NetWare Administrator

So far, most of the user configuration options we've covered have been informational. The last 11 entry/information screens in the User section involve network security.

We'll get into more serious security discussions in later chapters. Now, however, we'll focus on the particular security information that is necessary to set up and manage individual User objects through the NetWare Administrator program.

Adding a User Login Script

IN A HURRY

6.7 Create or Modify a User Object Login Script

1. Open NetWare Administrator and locate the User object in the NDS tree.
2. Open the User dialog box by double-clicking the User object name.
3. Click the Login Script button on the right.
4. Enter login script commands.
5. Click OK to save the login script.

The login script was the single place to manage user configuration in the earliest NetWare versions. Later, more control was available in the System login script, but there could be only one System login script per server. That limited what could be done for any particular user or groups of users (or you ended up with a huge and unwieldy System script).

With NetWare 5.1, four scripts work together to control the network configuration of any one user. The User login script, once the most important, has now become somewhat less important.

The User login script executes last and overrides all previous settings. This is the same relationship as with NetWare 3.*x*'s System and User login scripts. But the extra scripts available in NetWare 5.1 make the User login script necessary only for unique needs of a particular user. We'll discuss the various types of login scripts in the next chapter, but if you do need individual User login scripts, the User dialog box's Login Script button is the one to click.

After starting NetWare Administrator and selecting the User object to examine, open the User dialog box by double-clicking that User object. You'll notice that the Login Script button is toward the bottom of the screen shown in Figure 6.10. It may be completely hidden in your Windows display.

FIGURE 6.10

*Adding a test login
script for user
Mackenzie*

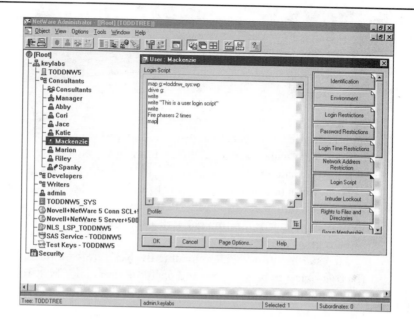

 NOTE See the Profile field toward the bottom of the dialog box in Figure 6.10? That will become important soon. Since we haven't created a Profile login script yet, we can't include it in the User login script here.

In the Login Script page, enter the login script commands. See the next chapter for information about login script commands and syntax.

Setting Login Restrictions

IN A HURRY

6.8 Set Login Restrictions for a User

1. Open NetWare Administrator and locate the User object in the NDS tree.

2. Open the User dialog box by double-clicking the User object name.

3. Click the Login Restrictions button on the right.

4. Check the boxes to disable the account, set the account expiration date, or limit concurrent connections.

Continued ▌▶

IN A HURRY CONTINUED

5. Read the last login time and date (if applicable).

6. Click OK to save the restrictions.

Login restriction setup focuses on the individual user. Normally, any configuration that can be done for a particular user can be done better working with a group. Restrictions on a particular user are useful at times, however, and this is where you set some of those restrictions.

Login restriction sounds like a way to stop someone from connecting to the network. That's only part of the value of the restrictions here. Maintaining tight network security often means limiting network access for users and tracking the resources used by each user.

After starting Windows and loading the NetWare Administrator program, choose the User object to be restricted and open the User dialog box. You will see a screen similar to the one shown in Figure 6.11, which contains three action boxes and one piece of information.

FIGURE 6.11

Restricting a user's access to the network

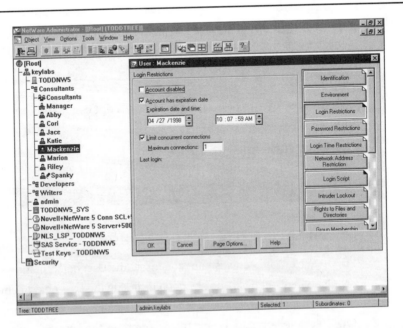

Since users tend to share passwords and login names even when the manager yells at them not to, security heads south. One way to slow this trend is to use login restrictions.

The Account Disabled checkbox is an excellent security tool when dealing with a shifting user base. This stops anyone from using this account but does not erase the applicable login scripts, change passwords, or delete data.

When a user goes on vacation, check this box. It will prevent co-workers from borrowing this user account while the user is gone. This also works well for temporary users. Let's say you bring in accounting help at the end of every month. Do you want to create and delete these users each month? No way. Create some generic accounting users, such as ACCT_1 and ACCT_2, and use the Account Disabled checkbox. When the temporary workers are gone, no one will be able to log in with the ACCT_1 or ACCT_2 names. When they come back, one click of the mouse sets everything back into place for them.

Account Has Expiration Date works similarly to Account Disabled. Once the expiration date is reached, the account disappears as far as any login attempts are concerned. The date can always be extended by changing it here. Have a group of visitors who need network access during their two-week stay? Set their user names with an expiration date, and you won't need to worry about other users getting access to their information after they're gone.

Limit Concurrent Connections controls one of the advantages developed in the early days of NetWare: the ability to log in from two or more places on the network but have the exact same rights and access for each login. Novell had this feature before any of its competitors.

If security is important in your network, however, this should always be set to only one concurrent connection per user. Limiting concurrent access is a good way to slow down the sharing of passwords among the users. If a second person tries to access the account of a person already connected, that user will get an error message.

You can limit connections in other places, and we'll cover them later in the book (in Chapter 9). If your default is to allow multiple connections, you can use the Login Restrictions page to limit particular users to a set number of connections.

The Last Login field displays the last time this user connected to the network. Only one historical connection is listed here.

Setting Password Restrictions

IN A HURRY

6.9 Set Password Restrictions

1. Open NetWare Administrator and locate the User object in the NDS tree.
2. Open the User dialog box by double-clicking the User object name.
3. Click the Password Restrictions button on the right.
4. Set the desired password restrictions.
5. Click OK to save the restrictions.

The single most important user security tool is a good password system. If security is important to your company, password restrictions will be important as well.

Click the Password Restrictions button on the right side of the User dialog box to display the screen shown in Figure 6.12.

FIGURE 6.12

Tightening password parameters

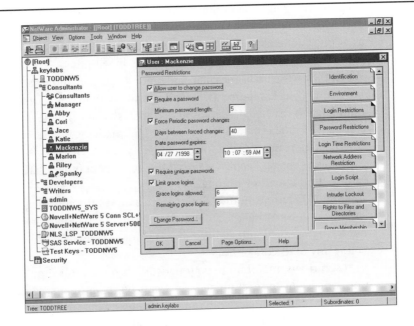

Providing passwords for users usually isn't a good idea. Users like to feel their password is known to only them. Even though, as the administrator, you most likely have access to all their data files, users still feel more secure if they set their own passwords. A good compromise allows users to make their own passwords within certain restrictions.

Here, for the sake of our example, we have poor Mackenzie restricted every which way. This looks like an enormous amount of extra work for the network administrator, and it may be. However, tight security takes time. Few networks use all these options. Most network administrators prefer to train users and teach them why security is important. Let's take a look at each option and see what choices we have.

Allow User To Change Password   If your security is extremely tight, you may not allow the user to change his or her own password. This is both good and bad. It's good, because the passwords you choose will be better than the ones non-security-minded users will choose. You will not select his wife's name; users often choose a family name as the password. It's bad, however, because users will not easily remember the passwords you choose. This leads to passwords written on calendars or desk blotters, which is not secure either. Pick your poison, but remain consistent.

Require A Password   If this box is unchecked, everything else in this dialog box turns gray to show it's unavailable. Checking this box allows you to set the minimum password length and choose whether to force periodic changes. The password can be between one and 999 characters, although setting this larger than 11 characters makes it impossible for Macintosh clients to log in. For security reasons, most experts recommend a password length of at least five characters. The longer the password, the harder it is to remember.

 TIP   Although NetWare doesn't demand mixing alpha and numeric characters, some Unix systems do. Following the Unix example and requiring a minimum of five characters including at least two numeric characters makes passwords much more difficult to guess. It also cuts down on using family names, unless someone on your network is related to 007. John007 is more secure than Marsha.

Force Periodic Password Changes   When this box is checked, the user will be forced to change his or her password at the interval you specify. The default for days between forced changes is 40 days (and 40 nights). The date the password will expire is listed on the screen for you. Changing that date does not change the Days Between Forced Changes field.

Require Unique Passwords   When password changes are forced, the option to require unique passwords becomes available. If you choose not to have unique passwords, users can simply alternate between their son's name and their daughter's name for passwords. If you require passwords to be unique, NetWare tracks each user's last 20 passwords and does not allow duplication.

Limit Grace Logins   If you force password changes, NetWare allows each user a few grace logins. In other words, even though the password is expired, NetWare will allow that password for a certain number of times. The default is six, and this dialog box displays how many grace logins are left. This is a friendly thing to do when forcing users to change passwords. If users must make up their own new passwords, they may not feel creative the morning their old password expires. The grace logins allow them to carefully consider their next password. If you or your department parcels out passwords, the users will interrupt you constantly.

Change Password   If you do want to change users' passwords for them, here's the place. Click this button, and a smaller dialog box pops open with three fields. If you logged in as an Admin-equivalent user, you must type the old password, type the new password, and retype the new password for verification. The Admin user doesn't need to enter the old password. Asterisks appear for each letter you type. This feature also works when a user forgets a password; you assign a new one here, then force them to change it quickly.

Setting Up Group Membership

IN A HURRY

6.10 Add or Delete User Objects from a Group

1. Open NetWare Administrator and locate the User object in the NDS tree.
2. Open the User dialog box by double-clicking the User object name.
3. Click the Group Membership button on the right.
4. To add a user, click the Add button, choose a group or groups in the Select Object dialog box, and click OK.
5. To delete a user, highlight the group name and click Delete.
6. Click OK to save your changes.

Groups are a marvelous tool when administering networks. Instead of dealing with each user, you can maintain a list of similar users and deal with the Group object. User objects inherit all the property rights of their Group objects.

Be careful—a Group object is *not* a container. A Group object merely keeps a list of User objects. When some action is taken with that Group object, it is also taken with each User object listed as part of the group.

After opening the NetWare Administrator program and selecting the User object to be added to a group, click the Group Membership button on the right (you may need to scroll down past the other buttons). The Group Membership page will open, showing all the groups of which this particular user is a member. There is no practical limit to the number of groups one user can belong to, although making a group of two users may wind up being more trouble than it's worth.

If this particular user is not a member of any groups, click the Add button. That calls the Select Object dialog box, as shown in Figure 6.13.

FIGURE 6.13

Adding Mackenzie to the Consultants group

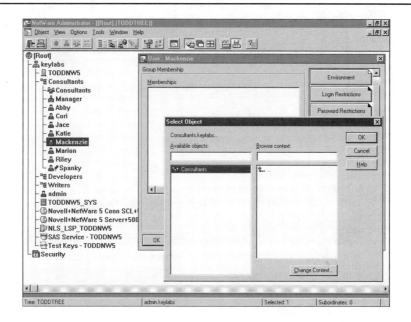

In the example, you can see that the context is currently Consultants.keylabs and that the only group contained in this context is Consultants. In the Objects pick list, Consultants is highlighted. Clicking OK pops the group name into the Memberships listing in the Group Membership page.

The Delete button works as expected. After highlighting a group name, clicking Delete erases the User object's name from the Memberships list. This screen is not where you delete the Group object itself; it just allows you to take this particular User object out of the Group object.

Setting Security Equal To

IN A HURRY

6.11 Set Security Equivalence

1. Open NetWare Administrator and locate the User object in the NDS tree.
2. Open the User dialog box by double-clicking the User object name.
3. Click the Security Equal To button on the right.

Continued

IN A HURRY CONTINUED

4. To add security equivalence, click the Add button, choose objects in the Select Object dialog box, and click OK.

5. To delete security equivalence, highlight the Security Equivalent object and click Delete.

6. Click OK to save your settings.

Security equivalence grants one User object the same rights as another object. This is the same idea as Group objects, in which the members of the group all have the rights of the group itself. However, granting security equivalence of a User object to another User object is more dangerous than putting users into groups. We'll look at security equivalence and other security-related topics in Chapter 9.

Open the NetWare Administrator program and choose the User object to make equivalent to another object. In the User dialog box, click the Security Equal To button, and then click the Add button. The Select Object dialog box will open, as in Figure 6.14. Notice that, in our example, Mackenzie already has security equal to the group Consultants. That's the result of our last operation, when we added a User object to a Group object.

FIGURE 6.14

Modifying a User object's security equivalency

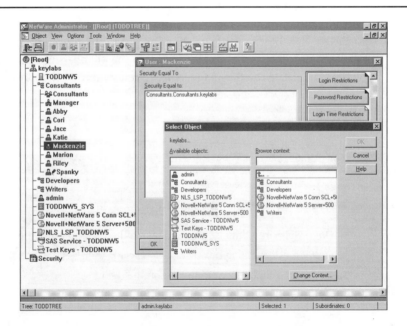

As an example, I have changed the context to keylabs and am now able to make Mackenzie equivalent to file servers or volumes as well as to other User objects. This inappropriate type of assignment would be dangerous, since Mackenzie could suddenly have rights and access privileges of the server TODDNW5.

Deleting equivalence is simply a matter of highlighting the equivalent object in the Security Equal To box and clicking Delete.

Setting Login Time Restrictions

IN A HURRY

6.12 Set Login Time Restrictions

1. Open NetWare Administrator and locate the User object in the NDS tree.

2. Open the User dialog box by double-clicking the User object name.

3. Click the Login Time Restrictions button on the right.

4. On the grid, indicate the times to lock out the User object.

5. Click OK to save the restrictions.

PART

II

Managing the Network

You'll want to restrict access to your network for several reasons. First, and most common, is to allow tape backup systems to work properly. Most backup systems skip open files. If users are logged in and still have applications open, the files in use will likely be skipped. Closing all connections before the backup starts eliminates that problem.

Security is another reason to restrict access. If no one in your company works the night shift, any user on your network at 1:13 a.m. is probably up to no good. Locking out all the users during the night and early morning limits your exposure to network tampering. If a user had forgotten to exit an application and log out, this setting will take care of that by closing the file so it can be backed up.

If you use login scripts to inform users of upcoming events with an MOTD (Message of the Day), you want them to log in to see it. If they stay connected overnight, the login script can't call the MOTD and display it. So set the Login Time Restrictions to force users to disconnect from the server during the night.

The name of this feature is slightly misleading. Along with restricting logins, this feature of NetWare 5.1 disconnects those users who are still connected at the beginning of the blocked time. Think of this as Connection Time Restrictions rather than Login Time Restrictions.

Open the NetWare Administrator program, choose the User object for your restriction operation, and click the Login Time Restrictions button. This is one utility that really takes advantage of the graphical interface, as you can see in Figure 6.15.

FIGURE 6.15

Blocking out time

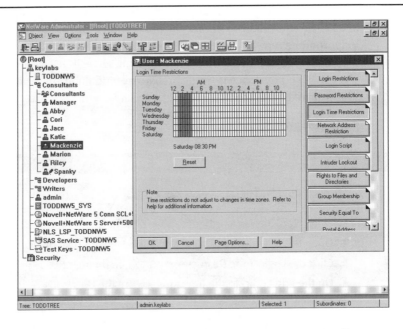

Each block on the time grid represents a half-hour. White blocks allow connection; dark blocks restrict. Clicking each block toggles its state: click a white block and it turns dark, click a dark block and it turns white.

Clicking each half-hour block is cumbersome, so you can use a shortcut. Click the first block of time to restrict, hold down the left mouse button, and drag the rectangle to the last time to restrict. When you release the mouse button, all the blocks within the rectangle will change state. You can also use your cursor keys: press the Shift key while pressing the arrow keys to go across the grid.

Setting Network Address Restrictions

IN A HURRY

6.13 Set Network Address Restrictions

1. Open NetWare Administrator and locate the User object in the NDS tree.

2. Open the User dialog box by double-clicking the User object name.

3. Click the Network Address Restriction button on the right.

4. Choose the protocol the User object uses for connection to the network.

5. Provide the protocol address for the allowable workstation.

6. Click OK to save your settings.

As you saw earlier (Figure 6.11), the Login Restrictions page for a user has a Limit Concurrent Connections checkbox. The second step in restricting the number of concurrent logins users can have is to restrict the workstations from which they can connect to the network. This is drastic and makes more work for the network administrator, but it is possible.

There is one good way to use this option to improve security without inconveniencing your users: make the restriction for your tape backup system. If your tape backup system runs from a network node, as most do, tie the backup User object to the address of the machine with the tape backup attached.

The User object for backup (usually called BACKUP or something equally creative and inviting to hackers and snoopers) has full rights over the network file systems, which could be a serious security breach if a person got hold of the backup user's user name and password. If that happens, but you have restricted the address for the backup User object, the thieving user must gain access to that physical workstation to cause problems.

After opening the NetWare Administrator program and choosing the User object to restrict, click the Network Address Restriction button on the right to open the Network Address Restriction page.

To add a restriction, click the protocol for that user, and then click the Add button. A dialog box pops up asking for the specific address of that particular machine, as you see in Figure 6.16. Each protocol has different address requirements.

PART

II

Managing the Network

FIGURE 6.16

Tying the user to a particular network address

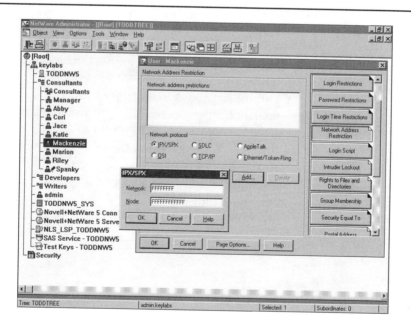

If you don't know the address for a particular user machine, start the `WINIPCFG.EXE` program on a Windows 95/98 station and read it there. ZENworks and other network inventory programs will also find this number for you.

Resetting Intruder Lockout

IN A HURRY

6.14 Reset Intruder Lockout

1. Open NetWare Administrator and locate the User object in the NDS tree.
2. Open the User dialog box by double-clicking the User object name.
3. Click the Intruder Lockout button on the right.
4. Click the Account Locked checkbox to reopen the account.
5. Click OK to save the settings.

The intruder lockout function is a "gotcha" from NetWare, special delivery to hackers. If the intruder-detection feature is active, you will always know when someone connects to your network while guessing a password. Of course, you will also know when users forget their password, possibly even before they come crying for help.

Intruder detection must be set for the container (see Chapter 10) before this dialog box becomes active for the User object. Detection can be active on some containers but not on others.

Once again, start the NetWare Administrator program and open the dialog box for the user whose account has been locked. Click the Intruder Lockout button on the right side; the page you'll see appears as Figure 6.17.

There is nothing to do here except clear the workstation by clicking the Account Locked checkbox. You can't lock the account by clicking this checkbox. To lock an account, use the Account Disabled checkbox in the Login Restrictions dialog box (Figure 6.11), as explained earlier.

FIGURE 6.17

Intruder lockout activated by using the wrong password

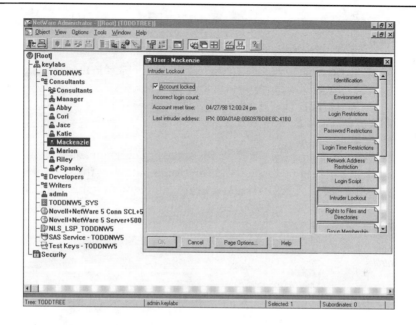

Setting Rights to Files and Directories

IN A HURRY

6.15 Change Rights to Files and Directories

1. Open NetWare Administrator and locate the User object in the NDS tree.

2. Open the User dialog box by double-clicking the User object name.

3. Click the Rights To Files And Directories button on the right.

4. Click Find beside the Volumes box to display file systems to which the user has access.

5. To view assigned rights, click the Find button, highlight the volume or directory in the Volumes box, and click Add. Highlight the directory or volume in the Files And Directories box.

6. To grant access, click the Add button and choose the volume or directory to grant access.

Continued

IN A HURRY CONTINUED

7. To delete access, highlight the volume and click the Delete button.

8. To grant or modify rights, highlight the object in the Files And Directories box and toggle the checkboxes in the Rights box.

9. Click OK to save your settings.

After opening the NetWare Administrator program and choosing your User object, click the Rights To Files And Directories button in the stack of buttons on the right. The page you see in Figure 6.18 appears, without volume and directory listings.

FIGURE 6.18

Directory and volume access control

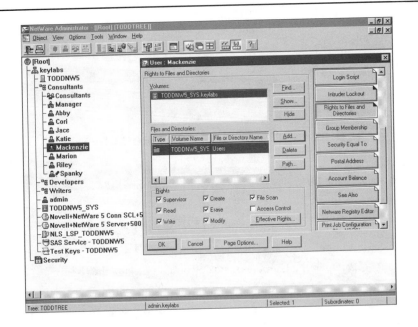

This looks like the busiest page we've seen in all the User object information, but it's not too bad. However, rather than controlling access this way, when possible, assign rights to volumes and directories to groups, not to individuals. When we get to Group object setup (in Chapter 7), you'll see that its screen looks just like this. You'll also get full definitions of all the trustee rights and other access controls in Chapter 9, which covers securing your network.

To find out which volumes and directories the user already has access to, click the Find button. You will be asked where in the NDS tree you want to search. The default is your current context, but you can request a search of the entire tree. If your NDS tree is large, you may be warned to expect a delay.

The Find button operates like a Browse button with a shortcut. When you click Find, a small dialog box appears, asking for the context you want to search. If you know exactly where you want to look, it's easy to type in the name of the context. If you're not sure or if you feel like doing less typing, you can click a Browse button to open the Select Object dialog box.

When the list of volumes returns, the Volumes box will have an entry for each volume containing a directory of which the user is a trustee. When you highlight each directory, the Rights box just below the Files And Directories box will reflect the user's rights to that file or directory.

To delete trustee assignments, highlight the volume or directory and click Delete. To modify rights to a particular directory or file, check the appropriate boxes in the Rights box. All the checkboxes are toggles, so if one is blank, checking it grants that right to that object.

The Effective Rights button displays the actual rights for the highlighted directory or volume object located in the Files And Directories box. When you click this button, you'll see a small dialog box that includes the actual directory under examination, along with a Browse button to help you search more areas of the network. Figure 6.19 shows this Effective Rights dialog box.

PART

II

Managing the Network

FIGURE 6.19

Browsing around, checking rights

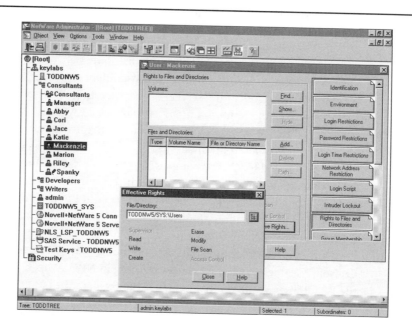

Notice in this example that the Volumes box and the Files And Directories box are empty. To check rights, I clicked Effective Rights and used the Browse button from there. From the Select Object dialog box, I moved to the other Organization, keylabs, and looked down into the TODDNW5\SYS: directory. Take another look at Figure 6.19, especially at the Supervisor and Access Control rights. Notice how these rights are grayed out? User Mackenzie has all rights except Supervisor and Access Control in the TODDNW5\SYS:\USERS directory. In other words, she can do about anything except grant access control to this directory.

Creating User Objects with ConsoleOne

As I mentioned earlier, ConsoleOne is a Java-based program with which you can browse and organize network resources, set up users and group accounts, control access to network resources, and configure and monitor the network for optimum efficiency. Because it is Java-based, ConsoleOne can be run from any system with Java Virtual Machine software, including the NetWare server console.

Since the beginning of NetWare, the server console has not been a pretty picture for network administrators. In the early days, nobody knew any different. Everything was DOS-based—ugly, but functional. But somewhere along the line, mainly influenced by Windows, the world turned GUI (Graphical User Interface). Everybody and everything, that is, except the NetWare server console and other utilities.

Why the resistance? Well, issues such as server performance and the ability to use existing hardware have long been big selling points for NetWare. The Novell model with NDS and NWADMIN32 has been to distribute network administration to a separate workstation. A GUI interface at the server might entice the administrator to spend more time doing work at the server console, affecting server performance. Besides, a GUI interface would require companies to throw away the cheap VGA monitors connected to all their NetWare servers, causing companies to upgrade their monitors and putting an incredible strain on landfills.

I won't pretend to know what goes into Novell product direction, but I would bet that ConsoleOne was created to appease the clamor coming from "eye-candy" addicts—not a bad tactic in the perception war. But I'm personally for substance over style, and there is no doubt that NetWare has provided, and continues to provide, substance to the networking industry.

At any rate, ConsoleOne can be used on the NetWare 5.1 server or from a workstation. ConsoleOne doesn't yet duplicate everything in NWADMIN32, but soon it will push the Windows program out the door. Let's go through the basics of creating User objects with ConsoleOne from the server console, or highlight areas where ConsoleOne includes more features than NWADMIN32.

Setting Up User Objects with ConsoleOne

IN A HURRY

6.16 Create a User Object with ConsoleOne

1. Start ConsoleOne.
2. Expand Entire Network and browse to the tree you want to access.
3. Click the tree and log in as Admin.
4. Expand the organization and highlight the container where you want to create the user.
5. Select the Create User icon in the toolbar or choose File ➤ New ➤ User.
6. Provide the Name and press Tab.
7. Provide the Surname and press Enter.
8. At the Create Tokens screen, enter a password for the user and click OK.

You will notice some similarities between this way of adding a user and the way we did it with NetWare Administrator. Even though there are many differences, if you understand the basics of adding a user in NWADMIN32, you won't have any problem adjusting to this new tool.

Open ConsoleOne by navigating to NetWare's GUI screen—the server lists "current screens" when you press Ctrl+Esc. It's referred to as X Server—Graphical Console. Click the Novell icon at the bottom-left corner of the screen and choose ConsoleOne from the pop-up menu.

With ConsoleOne open, expand Entire Network by clicking on the little round tab next to the Entire Network icon. Repeat to expand the Trees object.

Notice that when you select the tree you want to work in, you must first authenticate to NDS. A Login dialog box appears, prompting you for a Username, Context, and Password. You will want to log in as Admin or as another user with rights to add users to a container.

Once you've authenticated to the tree, the tree expands, showing the container objects. Browse through the tree until you find the container where you want the new User object to exist.

The toolbar changes depending on what is highlighted in the left pane. With a container highlighted, four icons appear on the toolbar:

- Groups
- User
- Organizational Units
- New Object (cube)

To add a user, you can either click the Create User icon, represented by the single individual on the toolbar in Figure 6.20, you can choose File ➤ New ➤ User, or you can choose New Object and pick from the list of applicable objects. Notice the Unique ID field—new in the improved ConsoleOne.

FIGURE 6.20

Adding Sandi

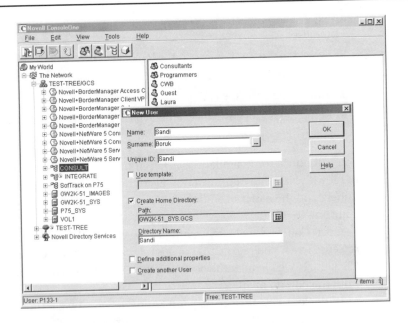

The New User dialog box that appears should look familiar if you are used to NetWare Administrator. The two mandatory properties, Name and Surname, are required before the Create button is activated. You can also choose to define additional properties or create another user (one or the other), as shown in Figure 6.20.

The NDS conventions that applied to objects created using NWADMIN32 will apply here. The user name, though not case-sensitive, will appear as it is typed. If you type it in all caps, that is how it will appear in ConsoleOne.

The requirements for login names are:

- Must be fewer than 64 characters

- Must be unique within the container

If your NetWare 5.1 server must support non-NDS clients or work with earlier NetWare server versions, you must be mindful of the restrictions placed on login names by the bindery:

- Names longer than 47 characters are truncated.

- Spaces are shown as underscores.

- The following characters can't be seen by non-NDS clients: slash (/), backslash (\), colon (:), comma (,), asterisk (*), and question mark (?).

The special characters above are legal within NDS but not within bindery systems. These characters also have problems in DOS names. The path of least trouble is to develop a naming standard for users that allows only alpha and numeric characters. If e-mail is important to your company, verify names with that system before assigning them inside NDS. You want names that work across all applications and systems.

The Surname field has no restrictions except making the name fit into the field. My example, Sandi Boruk, is my oldest niece and I'll give her this tiny bit of fame for a high school graduation present.

Once you've filled in the Name and the Surname, you can click Create to create the object. Or you can click Define Additional Properties before creating the object. If you create the object and then want to define the properties, simply right-click the User object and select Properties. You will see the same property page that you would if you had checked the Define Additional Properties checkbox.

With NetWare 5.0, you were finished when you clicked OK to create the user. No more. Now a new screen pops up, as shown in Figure 6.21.

Create Authentication Secrets, new with NetWare 5.1's version of ConsoleOne, ratchets up the security level. This option used to be called Create Tokens. Utilized by BorderManager, tokens initiate a challenge-response authentication, much safer than traditional passwords. NWADMIN32 on my test system didn't offer this; ConsoleOne starts to pull ahead in the development race. Passwords can be empty, but don't cancel the box in Figure 6.21.

PART

II

Managing the
Network

FIGURE 6.21

Creating Sandi Boruk

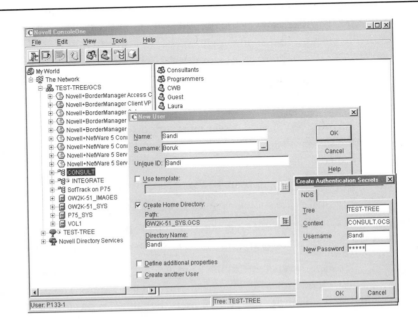

Adding User Property Information

If you click the Define Additional Properties checkbox in the New User dialog box, you will have the option to include a lot of information for this User object. Or you can double-click the object after creation to pop up this page. Don't be overwhelmed; none of this information is mandatory, but some is helpful.

Figure 6.22 shows the Properties subwindow for user Sandi. The NDS Rights tab is active and is displaying the Effective Rights option. I probably shouldn't let Sandi edit her own login script—a good security option change for everyone.

Let's take a quick look around this screen. The ConsoleOne object properties screen looks different from NetWare Administrator, but as we go through the tabs, you will see that you have access to the same object properties. Rather than placing the property buttons down the right side of the screen, ConsoleOne groups the objects into the following tabs:

Security Includes controls for Certificates and Entrust Information.

General Includes Identification, Environment, Postal Address, and See Also.

Restrictions Includes Account Balance, Login Restrictions, Time Restrictions, Address Restrictions, Intruder Lockout, and Password Restrictions.

FIGURE 6.22

Properties for user
Sandi

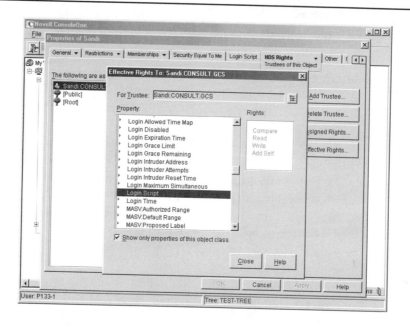

Memberships   Includes Group Membership and Security Equal To.

Security Equal To Me   Used to be located under Memberships, but Net-Ware 5.1 offers both Security Equal To still under Memberships and Security Equal To Me as its own tab.

Login Script   Includes the Login Script property page.

NDS Rights   Includes Effective Rights, Inherited Rights Filter, and Trustees of This Object.

Other   New, contains "Leftover attributes that are not handled by custom pages," according to Novell.

Rights To Files And Folders   Another example of ConsoleOne catching up to NWADMIN32.

When you select a tab, it becomes active and moves to the foreground on your screen. Under the tab title is the name of the property page you are viewing. If additional property pages exist on that tab, you will see a down arrow to the right of the tab title. To display the other available property pages, click and hold the down arrow. Continue to hold down the left mouse button and drag the mouse to highlight the page you want to display. Release the mouse button, and you are taken to the new property page.

The General Tab

Let's look at the General Tab first. The options here are Identification, Environment, Postal Address, and See Also.

Entering Identification Information When you open the Identification page in the ConsoleOne Properties screen, the only information filled in is the Last Name field. NetWare Administrator included the Login Name with full context, but Console-One just puts the object name in the title of the property page and assumes you know the context. The WHOAMI command-line utility presents the information in the Other Name, Title, and Description fields if they are not blank.

The fields in the Identification page contain plenty of information that can be useful when searching for particular people or locations on the network.

Why should you enter all these things? Seems like a lot of extra work, doesn't it? Well, what if your boss asks for all the network users on the third floor? How many network users are senior editors? How many network users will use the new fax modem when we replace the fax machine with the number 214-555-2599? These answers are easy to find if the database information is available.

Notice the last field: E-Mail Address. Finally! The address in Figure 6.23 isn't legal, but it expresses my feelings.

FIGURE 6.23

Identification information

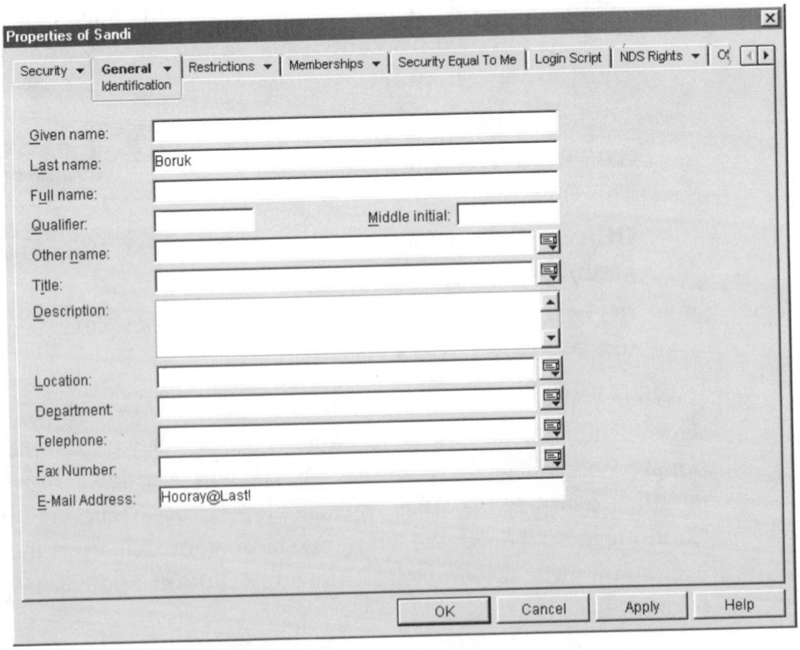

Entering Environment Information   The Environment page (Figure 6.24) used to be strictly informative but now is fully functional.

FIGURE 6.24

Environment information

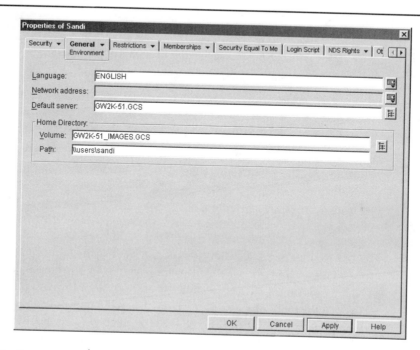

The Environment page includes the following fields:

Language   From the SET command, shows the language for system messages.

Network Address   Address or addresses of the workstation this user is currently using to connect to the network. This will change when the user connects from a different station.

Default Server   The NetWare server the user tries to connect to when logging in. This information is supplied by NDS.

Home Directory   The volume and directory of the user's home directory. You can add or change a home directory through this field, but you cannot create a home directory from here. You can point the object to a home directory, but if the directory doesn't exist in the file system, you will have to create it using NetWare Administrator or some other way. ConsoleOne still doesn't allow you to create the directory.

Notice that the buttons to the right of the fields are somewhat different from those in NetWare Administrator, which uses an ellipsis, or three little dots, in the button to indicate there is more information. ConsoleOne employs a drop-down menu icon that expands.

PART

II

Managing the
Network

Specifying the User's Postal Address

6.17 Set Postal Address Information

1. Open ConsoleOne and locate the User object in the NDS tree.
2. Open the user's property page by right-clicking the User object name and selecting Properties.
3. Select the General tab.
4. Click and hold the down arrow and select Postal Address.
5. Fill in the fields in the top half of the window.
6. To copy the information to the Mailing Label Information, click the Copy To Label button.
7. Click OK to save the information.

The Postal Address page allows you to track either the home or the business address for each user. You can use the fields for searching and to create a mailing label format.

After opening ConsoleOne, find the user you want to give a physical address listing. To open the user's property page, right-click that name and choose Properties, or you can highlight the user and choose File ➤ Properties. From the user's property page, click the General tab. Then click and hold the down arrow and select Postal Address.

No particular secrets here; no Browse buttons or pick lists. The only concern is if you plan to use this information for searching your NDS database later. Only the top half of the dialog box will be searched, showing Mailing Labels.

These fields accept all international postal codes. If you have international addresses, just supply the appropriate codes and countries in the Zip Code field.

Adding Reference Information

6.18 Track Related Objects for User

1. Open ConsoleOne and locate the User object in the NDS tree.
2. Open the user's property page by right-clicking the User object name.
3. Select the General tab.

Continued ▮▶

4. Click and hold the down arrow and select See Also.

5. Click the Add button to list more objects related to the user.

6. Choose the related objects from the Select Object dialog box.

7. Click OK to move the selected objects to the See Also page.

8. Click OK to save the information.

The See Also page is strictly informational. It does not affect any network configurations. This page is a handy place to put items you may need for reference, such as the Computer object type used by Sandi.

You cannot enter text in the See Also page. You can choose multiple objects in the Select Object dialog box. Just hold down the Ctrl key as you click the left mouse button on each object you want to select.

Configuring User Object Security with ConsoleOne

So far, many of the user configuration options we've covered have been informational. The rest of the properties in this section involve security.

I'll get into more serious security discussions in later chapters. Now, however, let's focus on the particular security information that is necessary to set up and manage individual User objects through ConsoleOne.

The Memberships Tab

You use the Memberships tab to add a user to a particular group and to set the user's security rights equal to that of another object. Let's look at each of these options individually.

Setting Up Group Membership

6.19 Add or Delete User Objects from a Group

1. Open ConsoleOne and locate the User object in the NDS tree.

2. Open the user's property page by right-clicking the User object name and selecting Properties.

Continued

PART

II

Managing the
Network

IN A HURRY CONTINUED

3. Select the Memberships tab.

4. Click and hold the down arrow and select Group Membership.

5. To add a user, click the Add button, choose a group or groups in the Select Objects dialog box, and click OK.

6. To delete a user, highlight the group name and click Delete.

7. Click OK to save your changes.

Groups are a marvelous tool when administering networks. Instead of dealing with each user, you can maintain a list of similar users and deal with the Group object. User objects inherit all the properties of their Group objects.

Be careful—a Group object is *not* a container. A Group object merely keeps a list of User objects. When some action is taken with that Group object, the same action is taken with each User object listed as part of the group.

After opening ConsoleOne and selecting the User object to be added to a group, right-click the User object and select Properties. Click the Memberships tab on the user's property page. Click and hold the down arrow, and select Group Membership if it isn't already selected. The Group Membership page will open, showing all the groups of which this particular user is a member. There is no practical limit to the number of groups to which one user can belong.

If this particular user is not a member of any groups, click the Add button to open the Select Objects dialog box, as shown in Figure 6.25.

By clicking the down arrow in the Look In box, you can see what context the user is in, or you can browse to a different context to find the group to which you want to add the user. In the example, you can see that the context is currently Consultants.gcs, and the only groups contained in this context are Consultants and Programmers. In the Objects pick list, Consultants is highlighted. Clicking OK will pop the group name into the Memberships listing in the Group Membership page.

The Delete button works as you would expect. After highlighting a group name, clicking Delete erases the User object's name from the Memberships list. This screen is not where you delete the Group object itself; it just takes this particular User object out of the Group object.

FIGURE 6.25

*Adding Sandi to the
Consultants group*

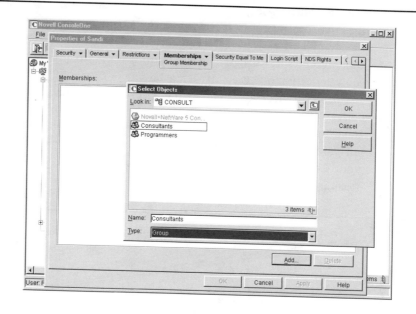

Setting Security Equal To

IN A HURRY

6.20 Set Security Equivalence

1. Open ConsoleOne and locate the User object in the NDS tree.

2. Open the user's property page by right-clicking the User object name and selecting Properties.

3. Select the Memberships tab.

4. Click and hold the down arrow and select Security Equal To.

5. To add security equivalence, click the Add button, choose objects in the Select Objects dialog box, and click OK.

6. To delete security equivalence, highlight the Security Equivalent object and click Delete.

7. Click OK to save your settings.

Security equivalence grants one User object the same rights as another object. This is the same idea as Group objects, where the members of the group all have the rights of the group itself. However, granting security equivalence of a User object to another User object is more dangerous than putting users into groups. We'll cover security equivalence and other security-related topics in Chapter 9.

Open ConsoleOne and choose the User object to make equivalent to another object. In the user's property page under the Memberships tab, select the Security Equal To page. Click the Add button to open the Select Objects dialog box, as shown in Figure 6.26. Notice that, in our example, Sandi already has security equal to the group Consultants. That's the result of our last operation, when we added a User object to a Group object.

FIGURE 6.26

Modifying a User object's security equivalence

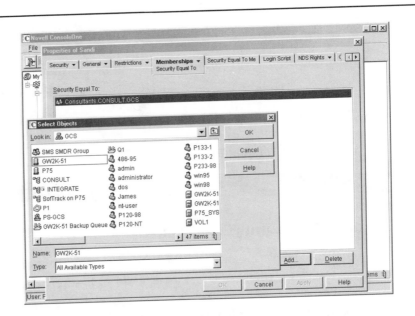

As an example, I have changed the context to GCS and am now able to make Sandi equivalent to file servers or volumes as well as to other User objects. This inappropriate type of assignment would be dangerous, since Sandi could suddenly have rights and access privileges of the server GW2K-51, the Gateway2000 box.

Deleting equivalence is simply a matter of highlighting the equivalent object in the Security Equal To box and clicking Delete.

Setting Security Equal To Me

The Security Equal To Me option allows you to specify the users who are security-equivalent to this object. This is the opposite of the Security Equal To option described above, which allows you to specify this object as security-equivalent to other objects.

You can follow the same steps you took in Setting Security Equal To, except instead of the Membership tab, you select the Security Equal to Me tab. The rest of the steps are identical. You can view which objects have security equivalence to this object, or you can grant or remove security equivalence by using the Add or Delete buttons, just as illustrated in Figure 6.26.

The NDS Rights Tab

The NDS Rights tab replaces the Rights to Files and Directories button in NetWare Administrator. You have three options under this tab:

- Trustees Of This Object
- Inherited Rights Filters
- Effective Rights

Chapter 9 covers these options in detail. For our purposes here, I'll explain how you can set these items from ConsoleOne.

Effective Rights

IN A HURRY

6.21 **View Effective Rights**

1. Open ConsoleOne and locate the User object in the NDS tree.
2. Open the user's property page by right-clicking the User object name and selecting Properties.
3. Select the NDS Rights tab.
4. Click and hold the down arrow and select Effective Rights.
5. View the trustee's effective rights to this object.

The Effective Rights To: page is an informational page that allows you to view a trustee's effective rights to this object. You can't make any changes here, but it is a good way to get a report on the effective rights of a trustee to any given object. Figure 6.27 provides a good view of this page.

PART

II

Managing the
Network

FIGURE 6.27

Trustee James'
Effective Rights to
Sandi

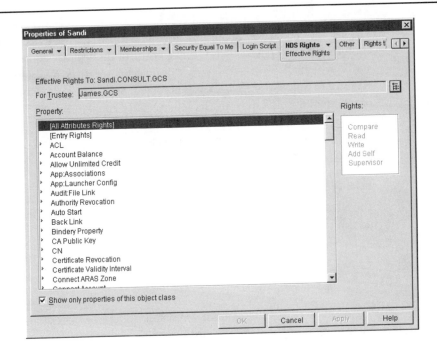

The Effective Rights To field shows the distinguished name of the target resource, in this case Sandi.CONSULT.GCS. Sandi is the object to which the trustee has effective rights. You cannot edit this field. If you want to see the effective rights trustees have to another object, you must open that object's Effective Rights property page.

The For Trustee field shows the distinguished name of the trustee whose effective rights are displayed on this page. In this case, the trustee is James.GCS. Notice the Browse button to the right of the field. You can browse for another trustee and view its effective rights to the target resource.

The Object Rights field shows the trustee's effective object rights to the target resource. These rights include the following:

- Supervisor

- Browse

- Create

- Delete

- Rename

- Inheritable (container objects only)

In this case, James has all applicable object rights to Sandi (as the James user, I am an Admin equivalent). Notice that if the trustee has that right it appears on the right in the Rights box. Also notice that the Create right does not appear. The reason for this is that you cannot create an object within a User object, so that right is not applicable here.

The Property Rights field shows James' effective property rights to Sandi. These rights include the following:

- Compare
- Read
- Write
- Add Self
- Supervisor

Admin (and an equivalent) has all these rights, but another trustee would have fewer property rights.

In the Property Rights field in the corresponding screen in NetWare Administrator, you have the option to view Admin's effective rights to All Properties or to Selected Properties. All Properties is the default. Here in ConsoleOne, the question changes to a checkbox asking whether you want to show only properties of this object class to help narrow the pick list that appears. To view a trustee's effective rights to a single property, click that property in the Property pick list, and the listing of the effective rights in the Rights box on the right of the dialog box will change accordingly.

Inherited Rights Filters

IN A HURRY

6.22 View or Set Inherited Rights Filters

1. Open ConsoleOne and locate the User object in the NDS tree.
2. Open the user's property page by right-clicking the User object name and selecting Properties.
3. Select the NDS Rights tab.
4. Click and hold the down arrow and select Inherited Rights Filters.
5. View or set inherited rights filters (IRFs) for this object.

You can use the Inherited Rights Filters page (see Figure 6.28) to view or set inherited rights filters (IRFs) on this object.

Here some things to remember about IRFs:

- IRFs don't give rights to anyone and then take rights away. If a user is granted rights at a certain level of the directory or container structure, the only way to keep those rights from flowing down through the subdirectories and subcontainers is by setting up an IRF or by reassigning that user rights at lower directories.

- IRFs can block only inherited rights, or those rights that are flowing down because of granted rights somewhere up the line. Rights that are granted at the current level by explicit assignment cannot be blocked.

- When you set an IRF for an object, it applies to all trustees.

FIGURE 6.28

Setting an inherited rights filter to Sandi

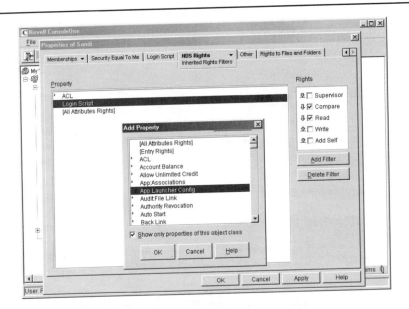

 TIP If you need to brush up on IRFs, see Chapter 9.

The Inherited Rights window for Sandi shows the target resource, in this case, Sandi.CONSULT.GCS, that the IRFs shown on this page are affecting. You cannot browse and view IRFs for another object without closing the property page and opening the properties for another object.

The Object Rights section allows you to view or set the IRF that blocks object rights from being inherited by the current object.

It is easy to block an object right. You can block the following five rights:

- Supervisor
- Delete
- Browse
- Rename
- Create

Figure 6.28 shows that when the box next to the object right is checked, the flow down arrow is large. But when the box is unchecked, the large arrow is replaced with a stumpy arrow with a line underneath, signifying the object right has been restricted or filtered to this object. So to block an object right, uncheck the corresponding checkbox.

The Property Rights section allows you to view or set the IRF that blocks property rights from being inherited by the current object.

Again, you can block the property rights by unchecking the box next to the specific right. You will get the same stumpy arrow and line, indicating that right has been filtered. The property rights are Supervisor, Compare, Read, Write, and Add Self.

Again, with property rights, you have the option to set the IRF for all properties or for selected properties.

To block the property rights to all properties, click the top menu option for [All Attribute Rights] and uncheck the box next to the right you want to restrict. Notice that I took away Sandi's right to modify her own login script, to counteract my earlier mistake.

To block the property rights to individual properties, press the Add Filter button to open the menu, highlight a property or multiple properties (hold the Ctrl key down to select more than one property), and uncheck the box next to the right you want to restrict.

Trustees Of This Object

IN A HURRY

6.23 View or Change Trustees

1. Open ConsoleOne and locate the User object in the NDS tree.
2. Open the user's property page by right-clicking the User object name and selecting Properties.
3. Select the NDS Rights tab.
4. Click and hold the down arrow and select Trustees Of This Object.
5. View or change the trustees for this object.

The Trustees Of This Object page allows you to view or change the list of trustees for this object. This property page gives you several options. You can add a trustee, delete a trustee, assign or change the rights of a trustee, and view the effective rights of a trustee, as shown in Figure 6.29.

FIGURE 6.29

The Trustees Of This Object page

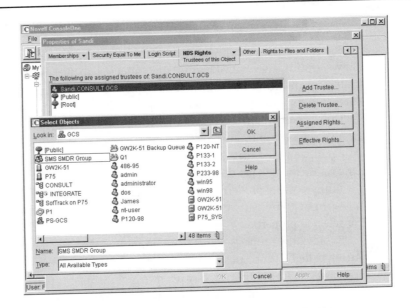

To add a trustee, simply click the Add Trustee button and select a new trustee object. Use the Select Objects dialog box to browse the tree until you find the object you want to add as a trustee (I left it open for illustrative purposes). Highlight the user, and click the OK button. The object will now appear as a trustee of the object.

Delete a trustee by highlighting the trustee and clicking the Delete Trustee button.

To assign rights or view previously assigned rights for a trustee, highlight the trustee and click the Assigned Rights button. You will know how to get around this screen. It should look familiar to you.

Remember that just because you delete a trustee or remove rights doesn't necessarily mean that object doesn't still have rights to this object. The trustee may still have rights granted through security equivalence. By clicking the Effective Rights button, you will be able to see what effective rights a trustee has to this object. This screen should also look familiar to you. You can use the browse function to view the effective rights of other objects as well.

NOTE When you finish making changes on this page or any other page, you must click the OK button or the Apply button for the changes to take effect.

The Restrictions Tab

The Restrictions tab contains all the property pages that you can use to limit or restrict users' access to certain parts of the network. These properties are similar to corresponding properties in NetWare Administrator. Remember, you are making the same changes to objects whether you use NetWare Administrator or ConsoleOne.

Password Restrictions

IN A HURRY

6.24 Set Password Restrictions

1. Open ConsoleOne and locate the User object in the NDS tree.
2. Open the user's property page by right-clicking the User object name and selecting Properties.
3. Select the Restrictions tab.
4. Click and hold the down arrow and select Password Restrictions.
5. Set the desired password restrictions.
6. Click OK to save the settings.

The single most important user security tool is a good password system. If security is important to your company, password restrictions will be important as well.

Select the Password Restrictions page from the Restrictions tab of the user's property page to see the screen in Figure 6.30.

Providing passwords for users usually isn't a good idea. Users like to feel that their password is known to only them. Even though you have access to all their data files as the administrator, users still feel more secure if they set their own passwords. A good compromise is to allow users to make their own passwords within certain restrictions.

FIGURE 6.30

*Tightening password
parameters*

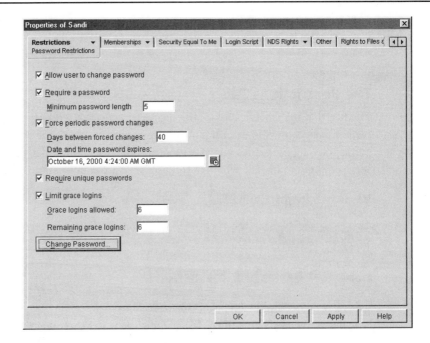

Here, for the sake of our example, we have poor Sandi restricted every which way. This looks like an enormous amount of extra work for the network administrator, and it may be. However, tight security takes time. Few networks use all these options. Most network administrators prefer to train users and teach them why security is important. Let's take a look at each option and see what choices we have.

Allow User To Change Password   If your security is extremely tight, you may not allow the user to change his or her own password. This idea is both good and bad. It's good because the passwords you choose will be better than the ones non-security-minded users will choose. You will not choose the user's wife's name; users often choose a family name as the password. It's bad, however, because users will not easily remember the passwords you choose. This leads to passwords written on calendars or desk blotters, which is not secure either. There's no good way to cover both these contingencies.

Require A Password   If this box is unchecked, everything else in this dialog box turns gray to show that it's unavailable. Checking this box allows you to set the minimum password length and choose whether to force periodic changes. The password minimum length can be between one and 999 characters, although setting this field larger than 11 characters makes it impossible for Macintosh clients to log in. Most security experts recommend a password of at least five characters. The longer the password, the harder it is to remember.

 TIP   Although NetWare doesn't demand that you mix alpha and numeric characters, some Unix systems do. Following the Unix example and requiring a minimum of five characters including at least two numeric characters makes passwords much more difficult to guess. It also cuts down on using family names, unless someone on your network is related to 007. John007 is still more secure than Marsha.

Force Periodic Password Changes   When this box is checked, the user is forced to change his or her password at the interval you specify. The default for days between forced changes is 40 days (and 40 nights). The date the password will expire is listed on the screen for you. Changing that date does not change the Days Between Forced Changes field. ConsoleOne with NetWare 5.1 pops open a real calendar dialog box rather than forcing you to push the up or down arrows to slide the date. Nice improvement.

Require Unique Passwords   When password changes are forced, the option to require unique passwords becomes available. If you choose not to have unique passwords, users can simply alternate between their son's name and their daughter's name for passwords. If you require passwords to be unique, NetWare tracks each user's last 20 passwords and does not allow duplication.

Limit Grace Logins   If you force password changes, NetWare allows each user a few grace logins. In other words, even though the password is expired, NetWare will allow that password for a certain number of times. The default is six, and this dialog box displays how many grace logins are left. This is a friendly thing to do when forcing users to change passwords. If users must make up their own new passwords, they may not feel creative the morning their old password expires. The grace logins allow them to carefully consider their next password. If you or your department parcels out passwords, the user will need time to contact you to obtain a new one.

Change Password   If you do want to change users' passwords for them, here's the place. Click this button, and a smaller dialog box pops open with three fields. If you logged in as an Admin-equivalent user, you must type the old password, type the new password, and retype the new password for verification. The Admin user doesn't need to enter the old password. You will see only asterisks for each letter you type. This feature also works when a user forgets a password; you can assign a new one here.

Login Restrictions

IN A HURRY

6.25 Set the Login Restrictions for a User

1. Open ConsoleOne and locate the User object in the NDS tree.
2. Open the user's property page by right-clicking the User object name and selecting Properties.
3. Select the Restrictions tab.
4. Click and hold the down arrow and select Login Restrictions.
5. Check the boxes to disable the account, set the account expiration date, or limit concurrent connections.
6. Read the last login time and date (if applicable).
7. Click OK to save your settings.

Login restriction setup is one situation in which NetWare 5.1 focuses on the individual user. Normally, any configuration that can be done to a particular user can be done better working with a group. Restrictions on a particular user are useful at times, however, and this is where you set some of those restrictions.

Login restriction sounds like a way to stop someone from connecting to the network. That's only part of the value of the restrictions here. Maintaining tight network security often means limiting network access for users and tracking the resources used by each user.

After starting ConsoleOne, choose the User object to be restricted and open the user's property page. Select the Restrictions tab, and click and hold the down arrow and select Login Restrictions. You will see a screen similar to the one in Figure 6.31, which shows three action boxes and one piece of information.

Since users tend to share passwords and login names even when the manager begs them not to, security heads south. Login restrictions provide one way to slow this trend.

The Account Disabled checkbox is an excellent security tool when dealing with a shifting user base. This stops anyone from using this account but does not erase the applicable login scripts, change passwords, or delete data.

When a user goes on vacation, check this box. It will prevent coworkers from borrowing this account while the user is gone. This method also works well for temporary users. Let's say you bring in accounting help at the end of every month. Do you want to create and delete these users each month? No way. Create some generic accounting users, such as ACCT_1 and ACCT_2, and use the Account Disabled check-box. When the temporary workers are gone, no one will be able to log in with the ACCT_1 or ACCT_2 names. When they come back, one click of the mouse sets everything back into place for them.

FIGURE 6.31

Restricting a user's access to the network

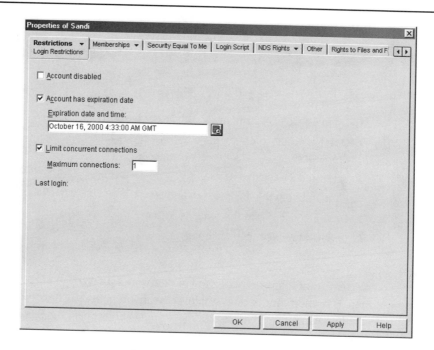

Account Has Expiration Date works similarly to Account Disabled. Once the expiration date is reached, the account disappears as far as any login attempts are concerned. The date can always be extended by changing it here. Have a group of visitors who need network access during their two-week stay? Set their user names with an expiration date, and you won't need to worry about other users getting access to their information after they're gone. Again, this is a nicer calendar dialog box than with earlier versions.

Limit Concurrent Connections controls one of the features NetWare developed in the early days of NetWare: the ability to log in from two or more places on the network but have the exact same rights and access for each login. Novell had this feature before any of its competitors.

If security is important in your network, however, this field should always be set to only one concurrent connection per user. Limiting concurrent access is a good way to slow down the sharing of passwords among the users. If a second person tries to access the account of a person already connected, that user will get an error message.

PART

II

Managing the
Network

There are other places to limit connections, and I'll cover them later in the book (in Chapter 9). If your default is to allow multiple connections, you can use the Login Restrictions page to limit particular users to a set number of connections.

The Last Login field displays the last time this user connected to the network. Only one historical connection is listed here.

Time Restrictions

IN A HURRY

6.26 Set the Time Restrictions for a User

1. Open ConsoleOne and locate the User object in the NDS tree.
2. Open the user's property page by right-clicking the User object name and selecting Properties.
3. Select the Restrictions tab.
4. Click and hold the down arrow and select Time Restrictions.
5. On the grid, indicate the times to lock out the User object.
6. Click OK to save the restrictions.

You may want to restrict access to your network for several reasons. First, and most common, is to allow tape backup systems to work properly. Most backup systems skip open files. If users are logged in and still have applications open, the files in use will likely be skipped. Closing all connections before the backup starts eliminates that problem.

Security is another reason to restrict access. If no one in your company works the night shift, any user on your network at 1:13 a.m. is probably up to no good. Locking out all the users during the night and early morning limits your exposure to network tampering.

If you use login scripts to inform users of upcoming events with an MOTD (Message of the Day), you want them to log in to see it. If they stay connected overnight, the login script can't call the MOTD and display the same. So set the Login Time Restrictions to force users to disconnect from the server during the night.

The name of this feature is slightly misleading. Along with restricting logins, this feature of NetWare 5.1 disconnects those users who are still connected at the beginning of the blocked time. Perhaps Novell should call this Connection Time Restrictions (they should have asked me).

Open ConsoleOne, choose the User object for your restriction operation, select the Restrictions tab, click and hold the down arrow, and select Time Restrictions. This is one utility that really takes advantage of the graphical interface, as you can see in Figure 6.32.

FIGURE 6.32

Blocking Sandi out during backups

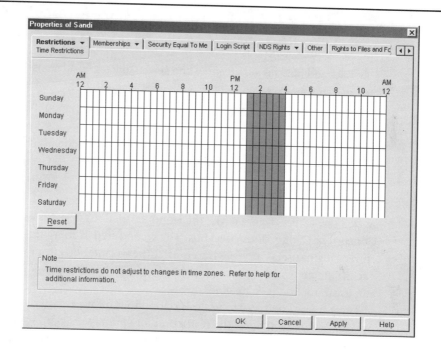

Each block on the time grid represents a half-hour. White blocks allow connection; dark blocks restrict. Clicking each block toggles its state: click a white block and it turns dark, click a dark block and it turns white.

Clicking each half-hour block is cumbersome, so you can use a shortcut. Click the first block of time to restrict, hold down the left mouse button, and drag the rectangle to the last time to restrict. When you release the mouse button, all the blocks within the rectangle will change state.

Address Restrictions

IN A HURRY

6.27 Set the Address Restrictions for a User

1. Open ConsoleOne and locate the User object in the NDS tree.

2. Open the user's property page by right-clicking the User object name and selecting Properties.

Continued

IN A HURRY CONTINUED

3. Select the Restrictions tab.

4. Click and hold the down arrow and select Address Restrictions.

5. Click the Add button.

6. Choose the protocol the User object uses for connection to the network from the NetAddress Type field.

7. Provide the protocol address for the allowable workstation.

8. Click OK to save the settings.

As you saw earlier (Figure 6.31), the Login Restrictions page for a user has a Limit Concurrent Connections checkbox. The second step in restricting the number of concurrent logins users can have is to restrict the workstations from which they can connect to the network. This action is drastic and makes more work for the network administrator, but it is possible.

There is one good way to use this option to improve security without inconveniencing your users: make the restriction for your tape backup system. If your tape backup system runs from a network node, as most do, tie the backup User object to the address of the machine with the tape backup attached.

The User object for backup (usually called BACKUP or something equally creative and inviting to hackers and snoopers) has full rights over the network file systems, which could be a serious security breach if a person got hold of the backup user's user name and password. If that happens, but you have restricted the address for the backup User object, the thieving user must gain access to that physical workstation for mischief.

After opening ConsoleOne, choose the User object to restrict, open the user's property page, and select the Restrictions tab. Click and hold the down arrow and select Address Restrictions to open the Network Address Restriction page.

To add a restriction, click the Add button to open the Create Network Address dialog box. In the NetAddress Type field, click the protocol button to select the protocol for that user, as you see in Figure 6.33. In the NetAddress field, enter the specific address of that particular machine. Each protocol has different address requirements.

FIGURE 6.33

List of protocols for tying a user to a particular network address

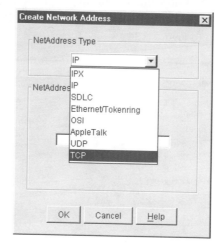

Intruder Lockout

IN A HURRY

6.28 Reset Intruder Lockout

1. Open ConsoleOne and locate the User object in the NDS tree.
2. Open the user's property page by right-clicking the User object name and selecting Properties.
3. Select the Restrictions tab.
4. Click and hold the down arrow and select Intruder Lockout.
5. Click the Account Locked checkbox to reopen the account.
6. Click OK to save the settings.

The intruder lockout function is a "gotcha" from NetWare, special delivery to hackers. If the intruder-detection feature is active, you will always know when someone connects to your network while guessing a password. Of course, you will also know when users forget their password, possibly even before they come crying for help.

Intruder detection must be set for the container (see Chapter 10) before this dialog box becomes active for the User object. You may have detection active on some containers but not on others.

Once again, start ConsoleOne and open the Intruder Lockout property page found under the Restrictions tab of the user whose account has been locked. The page you'll see is shown in Figure 6.34.

FIGURE 6.34

Intruder Lockout activated by using the wrong password

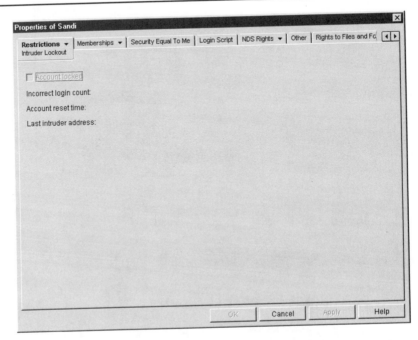

There is nothing to do here except clear the workstation by clicking the Account Locked checkbox. You can't lock the account by clicking this checkbox. You lock accounts using the Account Disabled checkbox in the Login Restrictions dialog box (Figure 6.31), explained earlier in this chapter.

Yeah, this boring screen looks worthless. But it will be exciting when a user comes crying about a lost password. And you'll know about the blunder before the user has the nerve to call or drop by.

Account Balance

IN A HURRY

6.29 Set the Account Balance for a User

1. Open ConsoleOne and locate the User object in the NDS tree.
2. Open the user's property page by right-clicking the User object name and selecting Properties.

Continued ▶

IN A HURRY CONTINUED

3. Select the Restrictions tab.

4. Click and hold the down arrow and select Account Balance.

5. Set the current Account Balance and the Low Balance Limit.

6. Click OK to save your settings.

NetWare was the first network operating system to allow accounting. By tracking such details as connect time, disk space used, and service requests to a file server, NetWare accounting moved away from a PC LAN level toward mainframe-type control. Some network administrators use accounting to charge company departments, and others use accounting to track when resources are being used more heavily than in the past.

If accounting is enabled on a server, the users of that server can be assigned a value for each server operation. The screen in Figure 6.35 shows you how simple it is to track the server resources consumed by a user.

PART

II

FIGURE 6.35

*Accounting for user
Sandi*

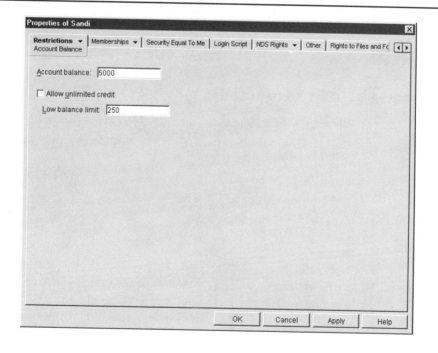

Managing the
Network

The Account Balance field shows the credits available for this user. The credits are set on the network resource itself, not here (see Chapter 10 for details). The Low Balance Limit field shows the credit level at which to warn the user before the account is disabled.

If you want to track the accounting information for charge-back or overhead calculations but don't want to prevent users from reaching their network resources after they've used up their allotted credit, click the Allow Unlimited Credit box. This field will track the information needed for the accounting reports but never lock out users.

NOTE If a user's credits drop to the level of the Low Balance Limit field and the user gets locked out of the system, nothing happens to the user's information. The user will be back in business as soon as an administrator ups the Account Balance field.

The Login Script Tab

The Login Script tab has only one available option—to add a login script.

Adding a Login Script

IN A HURRY

6.30 Add a Login Script

1. Open ConsoleOne and locate the User object in the NDS tree.
2. Open the user's property page by right-clicking the User object name and selecting Properties.
3. Select the Login Script tab.
4. Enter the login script commands.
5. Click OK to save the login script.

The login script was the single place to manage user configuration in the earliest NetWare versions. Later, more control was available in the System login script, but there could be only one System login script per server. That limited what could be done for any particular user or groups of users (or you ended up with a huge and unwieldy system script).

With NetWare 5.1, four scripts work together to control the network configuration of any one user. The User login script, once the most important, has now become somewhat less important.

The User login script executes last and overrides all previous settings. This is the same relationship as with NetWare 3.*x*'s System and User login scripts. But the extra scripts available in NetWare 5.1 make the User login script necessary only for unique needs of that particular user. We'll discuss the various types of login scripts in the next chapter, but if you do need individual User login scripts, the User dialog box's Login Script button is the one to click.

After starting ConsoleOne and selecting the User object to examine, display the user's properties by right-clicking that User object. Select the Login Script tab, as shown in Figure 6.36.

FIGURE 6.36

Adding a test login script for User Sandi

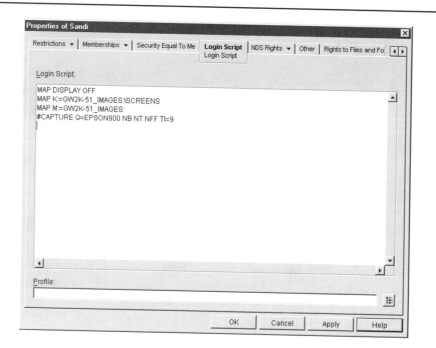

 NOTE See the Profile field toward the bottom of the dialog box in Figure 6.36? That will become important soon. Since we haven't created a Profile login script yet, we can't include it in the User login script here.

In the Login Script page, enter the login script commands. See the next chapter for information about login script commands and syntax.

The Users and You

As stated at the beginning of the chapter, *user* is a four-letter word. So is *work*. The two are closely related.

Think of how the users on your network see you. If your company charges an internal budget for network hardware, software, and personnel, you're seen as an overpriced leech. If your company considers you overhead, you're seen as part of the group that sucks profits out of the profit-sharing plan, and hence out of the user's very own pocket. None of this is flattering, is it? Do you want to change this perception?

First, realize that you can't change everyone's mind. Some people won't like you or your job because they don't like computers. You'll never convert them, so be friendly but realistic.

Second, let users know that the internal prices for services are competitive or better than services purchased on the "outside." If they aren't competitive, figure out why not and fix the problem. If corporate management has set some outrageously high figure for labor or markup, you have a problem. It won't be easy to convince that same management to lower the internal rates; but if you don't, you'll never look good compared with the outside world.

Finally, let the users do some of your work for you. Believe it or not, they will love the opportunity.

This works especially well with vocal users and non-computer management. Most people believe their own job is rougher than anyone else's. If you offer them a chance to apply their business experience to your "deficiencies," they will quickly discover the problems you face every day. Let some of those bean-counters (excuse me, those esteemed accountants) debate the need between more server hard disk space, a new laser printer, a better tape backup system, or training for the new guy in the tech department. Maybe then they will appreciate your position a bit more. You might even offer to help them out a bit or volunteer to handle your own payroll. Can't hurt to ask.

Seriously, the bottom line is this: the users are your job; the network is not. The network is a business tool for the users, supported by you. The activities of the users matter more than you and your network.

Is this terrible? Not if you adopt the proper viewpoint. Mechanics love cars, veterinarians love animals, and you love computers and networking. The first two groups need customers to support their favored occupation. So do you.

CHAPTER **7**

Handling More Than One User at a Time

n the old days, it was easy to manage each user individually. Early NetWare systems often had a dozen or fewer attached workstations. The big network started at about 25 workstations. PCs were new; only a few people in each company had access to a PC full time. No applications required more complexity than file and record sharing. The network stopped at the department; at the most, it went to the walls of the building.

Today, a large network starts at 500 users supported by 10 servers (according to the guidelines for the Simple Installation option). Most people connected to the network have full-time access to a computer, whether it's a PC running Windows, Linux, or even OS/2, a Macintosh, or a Unix system. Applications are mutating and replicating across the company, often with tools and technologies not yet fully developed. A logical workgroup may now include several continents.

You, the network manager, still have only 24 hours in your workday. Luckily, improvements in technology make it possible for one lonely administrator to keep up with more users in more places than ever before. Early NetWare had a single group function to gather users; NetWare 5.1 has a variety of ways to organize and manage network users and resources.

Who Manages the Users?

The assumption during this chapter is that the person managing network users is either the Admin or an Admin-equivalent user.

NetWare 5.1 allows more flexibility than early NetWare versions. A User object may be granted rights to create objects but not be able to access the information contained in the object. For that capability, the Supervisor right must be given to that person, or property rights must be granted along with the object rights. These new rights and how they relate to earlier NetWare versions and to each other will be explained in detail in Chapter 9. For now, do the work as the Admin user or equivalent, and there will be no surprises.

NetWare 5.1 Tools for Managing Users and Resources

NetWare 5.1 provides six ways to organize and manage network users and resources:

Organization object   The largest grouping option. Your company may have one or several Organizations defined in an NDS tree. You can assign trustee rights, login scripts, and user defaults to all the User objects in the Organization object.

Organizational Unit object   The second-largest grouping option and the subunit for an Organization. A network will typically have many more Organizational Units than Organizations. Once again, you can assign trustee rights, login scripts, and user defaults to all the User objects in the Organizational Unit object.

Group object   Similar to the earlier NetWare idea of groups, meaning a list of users sharing common items such as directory access rights. Objects in the same group may be from any part of the NDS tree. The Security Equal To property in the User object lists the groups connected to the User object.

Profile object   Depending on your NDS design, you can place many users requiring similar work environments in different containers. The Profile object login script can be executed just before the User object login script. Each User object can belong to only one profile; hence, each User object can have only one Profile login script.

Organizational Role object   A leaf object that defines a specific operational role, such as operations manager or team leader. The expectation is that the person or persons filling this role will change regularly, but the responsibilities and rights needed for the position will not change. The difference between a Group object and an Organizational Role object is that a Group object usually has many members and an Organizational Role object usually has only one or two.

User Template   Technically a limited User object, the User Template functions as a list of properties that can be applied to newly created leaf objects. You can place common information, such as a fax number, login time restrictions, addresses, password restrictions, and language, in the User Template for easy replication. When a User Template is created, you can take information from the parent container's User Template (if one exists).

 NOTE   The NDS tree itself is not considered a grouping resource for our examples. Resources can't be used across trees, and users can't be NDS clients in multiple trees at one time, unless you're running Client32 software.

Before you can manage more than one user, you need to have a group of users. Although there are alternative options to the old NetWare implementation of a group, let's start with the Group object for old times' sake.

PART

II

Managing the
Network

Creating and Managing Group Objects

Technically, the *Group object* is a leaf object, like a User object or a Printer object. The Group object, unlike Organization and Organizational Unit objects, is not a container. Seems like it should be, but the joke's on us.

Many of the group functions performed in earlier NetWare versions are more easily managed using rights and login scripts assigned to containers. The Group object is still, however, an efficient way to manage only one object (the Group object) instead of many individual User objects.

Practically, the Group object will do most of what is necessary in the area of granting file and printer rights to users listed as group members. After all, the group idea came from earlier versions of NetWare, in which there were no object and NDS rights to worry about. The Group object in NetWare 5.1 carries the idea of a group of users into the new operating system by focusing on the file system and printer access rights accorded to Group object members.

Plenty of third-party products make extensive use of groups, especially the ability of groups to contain members from multiple containers. Services such as e-mail, faxserver, modem pool, and host-access gateways need groups. The applications generally build the groups themselves, but be prepared to help now and then.

Just as you can use the NetWare Administrator program from Windows or ConsoleOne to create and manage User objects, you can use these administration utilities to work with Group objects. If you prefer to work with NetWare Administrator, continue with the next section. If you're a ConsoleOne user, you can skip to the section titled "Creating and Modifying Group Objects with ConsoleOne." In case you haven't noticed, Novell's stated direction is to make everyone a ConsoleOne user, although NetWare Administrator runs faster right now.

Creating and Modifying Group Objects with NetWare Administrator

IN A HURRY

7.1 Create a Group Object

1. Open NetWare Administrator, highlight the Organization or Organizational Unit container that will hold the new Group object, and press the Insert key.

2. Choose the Group object from the list, provide the Group object name, and press Enter.

3. Click OK to create the new Group object.

Before you can place users in a Group object, you must create a Group object. This process is remarkably similar to that of creating a User object, as we did in the last chapter. The similarity is planned. Both groups and users are leaf objects, so the process should be almost identical. The differences appear as we configure the objects for their different roles.

First, we must open the NetWare Administrator program. In Chapter 6, we assumed that most people would be using Windows 95/98/NT to do their network administration. We logged in to a server and mapped a drive to the NWADMN32 folder in the Public directory on the SYS: volume. We also created a shortcut to the NWADMN32.EXE file. The NetWare Administrator icon should still be on your desktop.

Log in again to your server using the Client32 software, and double-click the NetWare Administrator icon. If you look closely, you will see that the icon shows a figure before a wall map of an NDS tree. Appropriate.

Once NetWare Administrator is started, I prefer to double-click each container to open each of the Organizational Units. This allows me to see all the objects in each container, making it easier to avoid duplications. NetWare does not require you to open the container that will contain the new Group object before starting the process, but you may feel more comfortable if you can see everything in the container before you begin.

While the container name is highlighted, you can do one of three things to begin the creation of a new object:

- Press the Insert key.
- Click the right mouse button, and then click Create in the menu that appears.
- Choose Object ➢ Create.

NetWare vets will be comfortable with pressing the Insert key, a common function in earlier NetWare versions. If you are new to NetWare, pressing the Insert key whenever you're not sure of the next step can't hurt; in fact, it will often help.

Hard-core mousers will appreciate the increasing use of the right mouse button in NetWare 5.1. The NetWare Administrator program is even more mouse-friendly than it appears in the listing above. If you hold the left button while sliding the highlight bar down the menu items, releasing the button while highlighting Create opens the New Object dialog box.

Hard-core keyboard users will appreciate the Alt-key functions that speed menu operations. Most of the menu shortcuts available in earlier NetWare versions are still available in NetWare 5.1. If you have some keystroke combinations memorized, try them. The keystrokes may work.

The result of any of the three options mentioned above is to open the New Object dialog box. From there, you can choose any of the new object classes listed. Since we want to create a Group object, highlight the Group entry by using the cursor keys, by using the mouse, or by pressing the G key. Figure 7.1 shows the result.

PART

II

Managing the Network

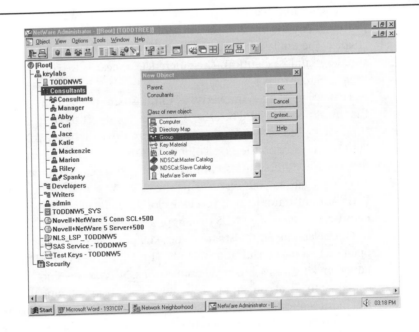

Once you begin to create your new Group object, a two-step process starts. The creation of the Group object takes little time and requires almost no detail. If you remember creating a User object, the process will be familiar.

When creating new User objects, the only information needed is the login name and the last name of the user. Since Group objects don't have last names, the only information required before creating the Group object is the name of that Group object. Figure 7.2 shows the Create Group dialog box that appears after you choose Group from the New Object dialog box.

The naming rules for the Group object are the same as those for the User object (and all other leaf objects for that matter). Here is a short recap of naming rules:

- Names must be fewer than 64 characters. Names longer than 47 characters are truncated for non-NDS clients.

- Names must be unique within the container.

- Names are not case-sensitive but will be displayed as they were typed in the Group Name field (SalesSupport will display that way, but NDS regards it as identical to salessupport and SALESSUPPORT).

- Spaces can be used and will be displayed as spaces within NDS. Spaces are shown as underscores for non-NDS clients.

- The following characters can't be seen by non-NDS clients: slash (/), backslash (\), colon (:), comma (,), asterisk (*), and question mark (?).

FIGURE 7.2

Choosing to configure this group before creating another

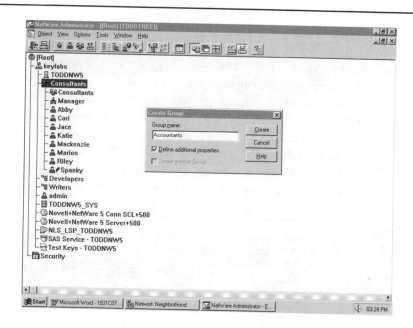

You can check one, but not both, of the two boxes below the name in Figure 7.2. If you choose Create Another Group, the Create Group dialog box will clear and be ready for the next name. If you choose Define Additional Properties, as we did in Figure 7.2, the new object is immediately created and placed into the NDS tree. The process for defining Group object properties remains the same, whether done immediately after creating the object or by modifying an existing object.

Modifying the Identification of a Group Object

IN A HURRY

7.2 Identify a Group Object

1. Open the NetWare Administrator program, highlight the Group object to modify, and press Enter.

2. Fill in the optional information for the Other Name, Owner, Description, Location, Department, and Organization fields.

3. Click OK to save the information and exit the Group dialog box.

Identification for a Group object is not required, but it is helpful when searching a large NDS system. All the fields in the Group dialog box can be searched.

If you're not currently running the NetWare Administrator program, start Windows 95/98/NT. Double-click the NetWare Administrator program icon. Once the program is running and the main browser screen is open, you must expand the container to see all the objects inside. Double-click the container name, or press Alt+V+X to expand the list. Highlight the Group object to modify and press the Enter key, or double-click the Group object to open the Group dialog box.

Figure 7.3 shows the Identification page of the Group dialog box. The name is listed across the top, and the current page appears in two places: by the button pressed on the right and by the name in the top-left corner of the dialog box.

FIGURE 7.3

Providing searchable information for the Accountants group

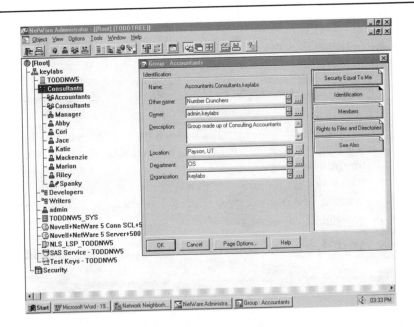

Notice that all the fields on the Identification page for the Group object are a subset of the User object fields. The information here is optional, as is the corresponding information for User objects. You can fill in the fields as follows:

Other Name Allows more descriptive or alternative names for the Group object. Multiple entries are allowed, and you can view them by clicking the More button at the end of the field. Each entry in this field can be searched.

Owner   Provides space to list owners or administrators for this group. NetWare 5.1 allows multiple subadministrators, a feature that will save you time once each subadministrator understands what they can and can't do. Multiple owners are allowed; to see them, click the More button at the end of the field.

Description   Holds free-form text, a maximum of 30 lines of 37 characters of any text you find helpful concerning this Group object. Long description fields are scrollable. Unfortunately, the search program does not parse each word, so only a complete match of the Description field contents helps. The scroll arrows display any text beyond the limits of the small field, if you stupidly get wordy.

Location   Provides space to indicate the physical location of this Group object. Multiple entries are allowed. This field allows any information (maximum of 64 characters) and can be searched. With dispersed companies, this field is helpful when looking for all group members in a particular place, such as a building, a wing, or a state.

Department   Shows the company department to which this group reports. Multiple entries are allowed. Like Location, this field has a 64-character limit.

Organization   Shows the organization to which this group reports. Multiple entries are allowed.

As in other dialog boxes, several buttons and screen areas can speed things along. First, the page buttons take you to different pages of the same dialog box. The five page buttons shown in Figure 7.3 all pertain to information about the Group object named Accountants. You can move up and down the page buttons using the Ctrl+Page-Up and Ctrl+Page-Down key combinations, or you can just place the pointer on the desired page button and click with your mouse.

The More buttons at the end of the fields allow multiple entries in those fields. Clicking the More button once pops up a dialog box for the other field entries. The up and down scroll arrows included in the field make it easy to check other values in the field without using the More button.

As in all object dialog boxes, the OK and Cancel buttons at the bottom apply to all the pages of the dialog box. Don't click OK when you finish modifying the first page if you plan to modify more pages. There is no penalty if you do, but you will need to go through the steps necessary to return to the dialog box, wasting a bit of time and increasing your frustration level because you forgot, once again, that you shouldn't click OK until you've finished all your work here.

When providing the owner name on the Group Identification page, you must supply the full name for the User object, even if the current context is set to the container for the Group object and User object to be labeled as Owner. Clicking the More button opens the Owner dialog box. Click the Add button, and then locate the User object you want to make an owner of the group.

Modifying the Member List of a Group Object

7.3 Add or Delete Group Members

1. Open NetWare Administrator, and locate and choose the Group object to modify.

2. Click the Members page button.

3. To add a user, click the Add button. In the Select Object dialog box, choose one or more User objects to add to the group.

4. To delete a user, highlight the User object name in the Group dialog box, and then click Delete.

5. Click OK in the Group dialog box to save your changes.

If you're not currently running the NetWare Administrator program, double-click the NetWare Administrator program icon. Once the program is running and the main browser screen is open, you must expand the container to see all the objects inside. Double-click the container name, or press Alt+V+X to expand the list. Highlight the Group object to modify and press the Enter key, or double-click the Group object to open the Group dialog box. Click the Members page button or press Ctrl+Page-Down.

To add a new User object to the list of group members, click the Add button. The Select Object dialog box opens, with the current context listed. If the current context does not contain the User object you want to add to this group, click the up arrow in the Browse Context box. When you see the container holding the User object you want to add to the group, double-click that name. The applicable objects for inclusion in a list of users will appear on the left side of the box.

NOTE These sections concerning group setup look amazingly like those for user setup. If you read the user information, you will be able to perform the same procedures with groups as you do with users. If you did not read the user information first, excuse this note (but shame on you).

Figure 7.4 shows the Group dialog box, with Accountants listed as the current Group object under examination. You can see the Members label in the upper-left corner of the dialog box, and notice that the Members page button is pressed.

FIGURE 7.4

Browsing and selecting new Accountants Group members

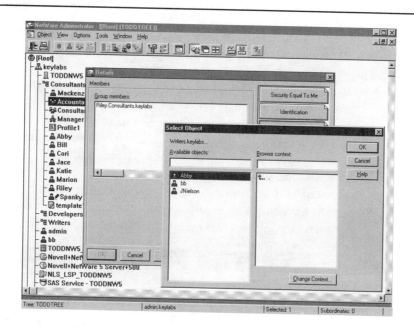

Please notice several things about Figure 7.4. First, you see we have already added one user. The full name Riley.Consultants.keylabs appears in the Group Members list.

In the Select Object dialog box, the User object representing user Abby is highlighted. The Current Context is listed as Writers.keylabs, meaning Abby is in a different context from that of our previous user, Riley. No problem. This is one reason groups are still around, even though many of the group functions can be handled by Container login scripts. Users from any container can be members of the same group. Repeat: users from any container can belong to the same group.

Once you click the OK button, user Abby will become part of the group Accountants, joining Riley. By holding down the Ctrl key while clicking with the left mouse button, you can choose multiple objects.

To delete a User object from the group listing, highlight the User object in the Group Members box. The Delete button will become active (no longer gray and faded). Click the Delete button once, and the highlighted User object will be deleted from the list.

WARNING There is no undo feature when you delete a User object from a group, so do this carefully. If you delete the wrong User object, click the Cancel button rather than the OK button. Oops, too late. Reinstall it.

Remember, this screen does not delete the User object itself, just the inclusion of that User object in the Group object membership list. See Chapter 10 for details on how to delete a User object entirely.

Here is something for you to consider at this point—the difference in the User object names. The naming option I've used is the first name. The first name, and first name only, makes up the entire User object name. While this is friendly, first names tend to be duplicated quite a bit, forcing changes. Another naming option is to use three initials, such as CWB. This method is handy and works well with the User variables set in some network-aware programs, such as the WordPerfect word processor. The final naming option I'll mention is using the first two initials and the first six letters of the last name. This method became popular because you seldom see duplicate user names this way, and IBM mainframes used it.

Job Description for Assistant Network Administrators

Adding members to, or subtracting them from, a group is a good job for assistant administrators. In fact, this is one area where the idea of workgroup administrator that first appeared in NetWare 3.x makes great sense. NetWare 5.1 takes this idea further, allowing added security constraints for the main Admin user to truly separate a container from the rest of the NDS tree.

The assistant administrator, charged with responsibility for this group, can add and subtract members as necessary for the needs of the department. This can be done without bothering the main network administrator.

Positive benefits happen two ways: the primary network administrator goes about his or her business, while the people in the department feel they have much more control over their own network destiny.

This job is also one that doesn't take constant administration and worry time. People tend to stay in particular groups for a long time. When a user leaves and you delete that user, the name is deleted from the User object list of members. When someone transfers, that user often keeps some of the old job's responsibilities, meaning the user will stay in the old group and become a member of an additional group as well.

Modifying the Rights to Files and Directories for a Group Object

IN A HURRY

7.4 Manage File and Directory Access for the Group Object

1. Open NetWare Administrator, and locate and choose the Group object to modify.
2. Click the Rights To Files And Directories page button.
3. To view assigned rights, click the Add button, and then highlight each volume or directory you want to view.
4. To add a volume, click the Add button to open the Select Object dialog box and choose the new volume.
5. To delete access, highlight the volume and click the Delete button.
6. To grant access, click the Add button to open the Select Object dialog box and choose the volume or directory.
7. To grant rights, highlight the object in the Files And Directories box and toggle the checkboxes in the Rights box. To modify rights, toggle the checkboxes for each volume or directory.
8. Click OK to save your settings.

This section is exactly like the corresponding section for the User object we worked with back in Chapter 6. There's a good reason for the similarity: here we are granting access to a single group, but the group includes many users. Although we modify only a single object, we affect anywhere from a few to hundreds of users all at once.

If you're not currently running the NetWare Administrator program, double-click the NetWare Administrator program icon. Once the program is running and the main browser screen is open, you must expand the container to see all the objects inside. Double-click the container name, or press Alt+V+X to expand the list. Highlight the Group object to modify and press the Enter key, or double-click the Group object to open the Group dialog box. Click the Rights To Files And Directories page button.

First, you will want to check which rights the Group object has before granting any more rights. Find this information by clicking the Add button once. Select the volume and click OK. Highlight each directory, and the Rights box just below the Files And Directories box will reflect the group's rights to that file or directory.

To delete all trustee assignments from a particular volume, highlight the volume or directory and click the Delete key. To modify rights to a particular directory or file, check the appropriate boxes in the Rights box. All the checkboxes are toggles, so if one is blank, checking it grants that right to that object.

The Effective Rights button displays the actual rights for the highlighted directory or volume object. When you click this button, a small dialog box pops up, listing the actual directory under examination. It also has a Browse button to help you search more areas of the network.

Figure 7.5 shows the Select Object dialog box open in order to grant trustee rights to another directory. This dialog box appears after you click the Add button.

FIGURE 7.5

Choosing the directory before granting rights

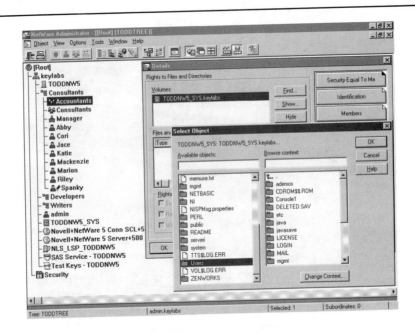

You can browse up and down the NDS tree in the Directory Context box to locate the Users directory. The Users directory is copied to the Files And Directories box in the Rights To Files And Directories page.

As before, you can select multiple directories by holding down the Ctrl key while clicking the file or directory name with the left mouse button. If you choose multiple items, each name appears in the Files And Directories box.

Once you choose the files or directories, you must grant the rights. Figure 7.6 shows the changed checkboxes, allowing the group Accountants near omnipotence over the Users directory. Omnipotent accountants? Oops!

FIGURE 7.6

Granting Accountants trustee rights to the Users directory

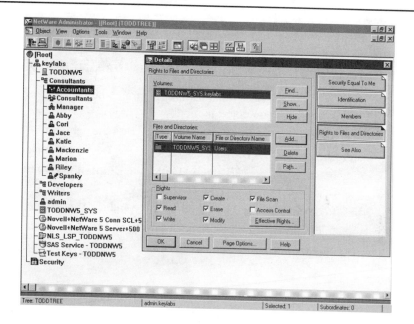

As far as file rights are concerned, each user in the Accountants group now has complete control over the Users directory and all subdirectories. Accountants also have Read, Write, Create, Erase, Modify, and File Scan rights. The only rights withheld are Supervisor and Access Control, neither of which affects the handling of files and directories.

Subsequent members of the Accountants group automatically receive these rights. Once you click the OK button, the changes to these rights take place immediately, or at least as quickly as the information zooms around the NDS tree.

To remove a right, click the checkbox to toggle the setting. If the group has Modify rights and you clear the checkbox, no member of the group will be able to modify an existing file.

When a group no longer needs access to a volume or directory, this same page handles that change as well. Highlight the directory or filename in the Files And Directories box, and the Delete button becomes active. Clicking the Delete button removes the file or directory from the trustee list of the Group object. The users in the group

PART

II

Managing the Network

no longer have access to those files or directories. This action does not delete the files or directories themselves.

Modifying the NDS Trustees for a Group Object

IN A HURRY

7.5 Modify the NDS Trustees for the Group Object

1. Open the NetWare Administrator program and browse through the NDS tree to locate the Group object to modify.
2. Highlight the desired Group object and click the right mouse button.
3. Choose Trustees Of This Object to open the Trustees Of dialog box.
4. To add a trustee, click the Add button to choose the new trustee from the Select Object dialog box.
5. To delete a trustee, highlight the trustee and click the Delete button.
6. To modify rights, highlight each trustee and toggle the appropriate checkboxes.
7. Click OK to save the settings.

Groups have trustees, and Accountants is no exception. Trustees are those network users or resources that have some control over the group. For more information about trustee rights and what they involve, see Chapter 9.

After opening NetWare Administrator, highlight the Group object whose trustee list you want to modify, and click the right mouse button. The same Trustees Of dialog box can be summoned by using the Object menu.

If you must add a trustee or two, you will once again use our friend the Select Object dialog box. Scroll through the dialog box to find the user (most likely) or other resource to make a trustee of the Accountants group. Figure 7.7 shows user Cori gaining control over the group.

This screen should look familiar by now, since the process here is the same as adding trustees to volumes, servers, users, and so on.

 WARNING Be careful in deleting trustees from a resource or group, because the users may have some procedures that require access to a resource for which they no longer have trustee rights. This can cause some aggravation later, so think hard before granting or deleting individual trustee rights.

FIGURE 7.7

Gaining more control over Accountants

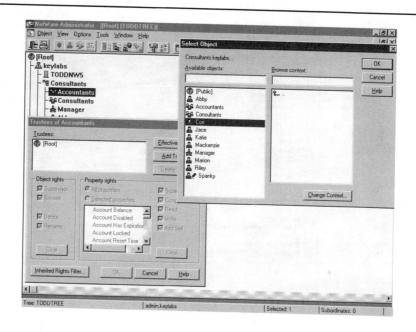

Modifying the See Also Page for a Group Object

IN A HURRY

7.6 Add or Delete See Also Page Information

1. Open NetWare Administrator, and locate and choose the Group object to modify.
2. Click the See Also page button.
3. Click the Add button, select the related objects from the Select Object dialog box, and click OK.
4. Click OK to save the information.

Purely informational, the See Also page holds references for your group to other network resources. Which printer is the primary printer for the group? Place that printer name here. You can place any other related resource here, but not by typing in its name. You must choose each object through the Select Object dialog box, as shown in Figure 7.8.

FIGURE 7.8

*Relating other objects
to Accountants*

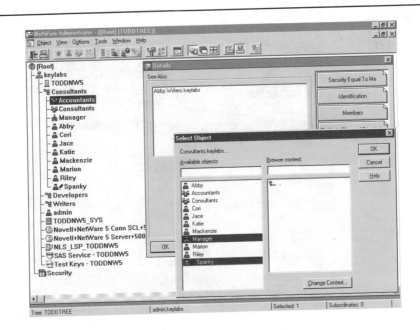

After opening NetWare Administrator, browsing, and choosing the Group object, click the See Also page button. Click the Add button to open the Select Object dialog box. To select multiple items, hold down the Ctrl key while clicking with the left mouse button.

You can see in Figure 7.8 that both the Manager Organizational Role object and the Spanky Alias object have been selected for inclusion in the Select Object box at the top of the screen. They will join the object already in the See Also list, user Abby.Writers.keylabs.

Modifying the Security Equal To Me Page for Group Objects

IN A HURRY

7.7 Add or Delete Objects on the Security Equal To Me Page

1. Open NetWare Administrator, and locate and choose the Group object to modify.

2. Click the Security Equal To Me page button.

3. To add an object(s), click the Add button, select the object(s) from the Select Object dialog box, and click OK.

4. To delete an object(s), click the object(s) in the list, click the Delete button, and click OK.

The Security Equal To Me page displays a list of users with security equivalent to that particular object. You can add or delete users from here.

Just as users can use the Security Equal To page button to display all the objects to which they are security equivalent (as mentioned in Chapter 6), the Security Equal To Me page looks at the same information from the object's point of view. It displays all objects that are security equivalent to the object.

To add a user to the list, click the Add button. The familiar Select Object dialog box appears. We should all be experts in using this by now. Remember, browse on the right, select on the left. Highlight one or multiple users in the left box.

Click OK to add the object or objects to the Security Equal To Me page. Notice when you add a user to the list, the full name of the user appears, as shown in Figure 7.9.

To delete a user from the list, highlight the user and click the Delete button.

FIGURE 7.9

Adding users to the Security Equal To Me page

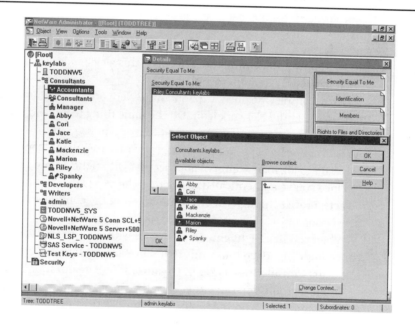

Creating and Modifying Group Objects with ConsoleOne

You can use ConsoleOne to create and modify Group objects from the server console or from a workstation. As you will see, the process closely mirrors creating and modifying groups in NetWare Administrator.

Setting Up Group Objects with ConsoleOne

IN A HURRY

7.8 Create a Group Object with ConsoleOne

1. Start ConsoleOne.
2. Expand Entire Network and browse to the tree you want to access.
3. Click the tree and log in as Admin.
4. Expand the organization and highlight the container where you want the group created.
5. Select the Create Group icon in the toolbar or choose File ➤ New ➤ Group.
6. Provide the group name and press Enter.

You will notice some similarities between this way of adding a group and the way we did it with NetWare Administrator.

With ConsoleOne open, expand Entire Network by clicking the little round tab next to the Entire Network icon. Do the same thing to expand the Trees object.

When you select the tree you want to work in, you must first authenticate to NDS. A Login dialog box appears, prompting you for a user name, context, and password. You will want to log in as Admin or another user with rights to add groups to a container.

Once you've authenticated to the tree, the tree expands showing the container objects. Browse through the tree until you find the container where you want the new Group object to exist.

When you first highlighted a container within a tree, did you notice that the toolbar changed? It added four icons that represent the four objects you can add to the tree using ConsoleOne—Groups, Organizations, Organizational Units, and Users.

To add a group, you can either click the Create Group icon, represented by the multiple individuals on the toolbar in Figure 7.10, or you can choose File ➤ New ➤ Group.

The New Group dialog box that appears should look familiar if you are used to NetWare Administrator. There is no difference between this box and the Create Group dialog box in NetWare Administrator. They are identical and accomplish the same tasks. The only mandatory property for groups, the Group Name, is required before the OK button is activated. You can also choose to define additional properties or to create another group (one or the other), as shown in Figure 7.10.

FIGURE 7.10

Creating the Techies
group

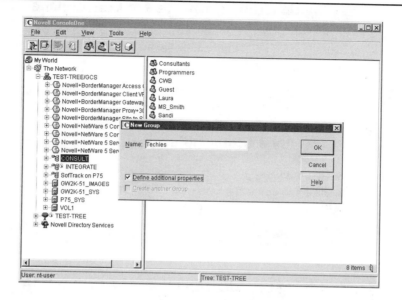

The naming rules for the Group object are the same as those for the User object (and all other leaf objects for that matter). The same rules apply in ConsoleOne as applied in NetWare Administrator. Again, here is a short recap of naming rules:

- Names must be fewer than 64 characters. Names longer than 47 characters are truncated for non-NDS clients.

- Names must be unique within the container.

- Names are not case-sensitive but will be displayed as they were typed in the Group Name field (SalesSupport will display that way, but NDS regards it as identical to salessupport and SALESSUPPORT).

- Spaces can be used and will be displayed as spaces within NDS. Spaces are shown as underscores for non-NDS clients.

- The following characters can't be seen by non-NDS clients: slash (/), backslash (\), colon (:), comma (,), asterisk (*), and question mark (?).

Once you've filled in the Group Name, you can click OK to create the object. Or you can select Define Additional Properties before creating the object. If you create the object and then want to define the properties, simply right-click the Group object and select Properties. You will see the same property page that you would if you had checked the Define Additional Properties checkbox.

PART

II

Managing the
Network

Setting Up Group Properties in ConsoleOne

The property page in ConsoleOne, as you probably have gathered by now, differs drastically from the Group dialog box in NetWare Administrator. For this reason, it warrants some attention.

IN A HURRY

7.9 Identify a Group Object

1. Open ConsoleOne, right-click the Group object to modify, and select Properties.
2. Fill in the optional information for the Other Name, Owner, Location, Department, Organization, and Description fields.
3. Click OK to save the information and exit the Group properties dialog box.

Modifying the Identification of a Group Object

Identification for a Group object is not required, but it is helpful when searching a large NDS system. All the fields in the Group property page can be searched.

If you're not currently running ConsoleOne, start it from either the server console or a workstation. Once the program is running and the main browser screen is open, expand the Entire Network icon, the Trees icon, and the specific tree in which you want to work. Double-click the tree, and you will be prompted to authenticate by entering your user name, context, and password. Be sure to log in as either Admin or another user who has rights to modify the Group object.

Once you are authenticated, the tree expands to display the objects contained within it. Navigate to and right-click the Group object to modify. Select Properties to open the group's property page. Select the General tab, click and hold the down arrow, and select Identification.

Figure 7.11 shows the Identification property page for the Techies group.

The information here is optional, as is the corresponding information for User objects. You can fill in the fields as follows:

Other Name   Allows more descriptive or alternative names for the Group object. Multiple entries are allowed, and you can display them by clicking the More button at the end of the field. Each entry in this field can be searched.

Owner   Provides space to list owners or administrators for this group. NetWare 5.1 allows multiple subadministrators, a feature that will save you time once each subadministrator understands what they can and can't do. Multiple owners are allowed; to display them, click the More button at the end of the field.

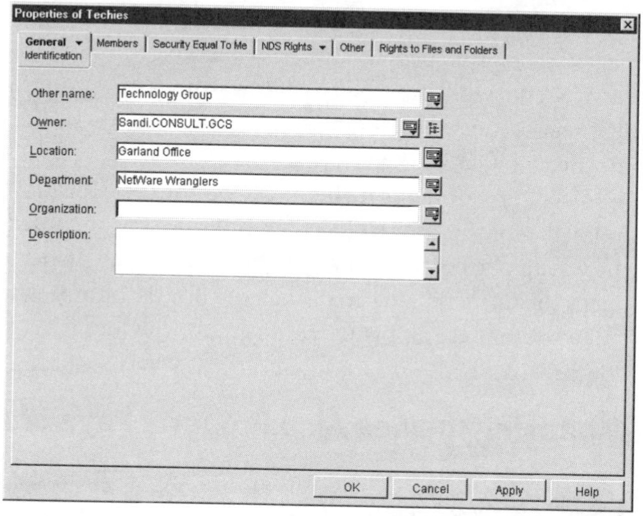

PART

II

Managing the
Network

FIGURE 7.11

*Providing searchable
information for the
Techies group*

Location   Provides space to indicate the physical location of this Group object. Multiple entries are allowed. This field allows any information (maximum of 64 characters) and can be searched. With dispersed companies, this field is helpful when looking for all group members in a particular place, such as a building, a wing, or a state.

Department   Shows the company department to which this group reports. Multiple entries are allowed. Like Location, this field has a 64-character limit.

Organization   Shows the organization to which this group reports. Multiple entries are allowed.

Description   Holds free-form text, with a maximum of 30 lines of 37 characters of any text you find helpful concerning this Group object. Long description fields are scrollable. Unfortunately, the search program does not parse each word, so only a complete match of the Description field contents will result in a successful search. The scroll arrows are provided to help you if the text goes beyond the limits of the small field.

As in dialog boxes in NetWare Administrator, several buttons and screen areas can speed things along. First, the page button on the Description field takes you to different pages of the same box. You can move up and down the page buttons by placing the pointer on the desired page button and clicking with your mouse.

The More buttons at the end of the fields allow multiple entries in those fields. Clicking the More button once pops up a dialog box for the other field entries. The

OK and Cancel buttons at the bottom apply to all the pages of the property page. Don't click OK when you finish modifying the first page if you plan to modify more pages. There is no penalty if you do, but you will need to go through the steps necessary to return to the property page, wasting a bit of time and increasing your frustration level because you forgot, once again, that you shouldn't click OK until you've finished all your work here.

When providing the owner name on the Identification page, you must supply the full name for the Group object, even if the current context is set to the container for the Group object and User object to be labeled as Owner. Clicking the More button opens the Owner dialog box. Click the Browse button, and then locate the User object you want to make an owner of the group. Previous Group Owners appear in the drop-down list.

Modifying the See Also Property Page of a Group Object

IN A HURRY

7.10 Modify the See Also Property Page

1. Open ConsoleOne, right-click the Group object to modify, and select Properties.
2. Select the General tab.
3. Click and hold the down arrow and select See Also.
4. Click the Add button. Browse and select objects related to the group by highlighting the object and clicking OK.
5. The object appears in the main See Also property page.
6. Click OK to save the information and exit the property page.

Purely informational, the See Also page is a place to make references for your group to other network resources. Which printer is the primary printer for the group? Place that printer name here. You can place any other related resource here, but not by typing in its name. You must choose each object through the Select Objects dialog box, as shown in Figure 7.12.

After opening ConsoleOne, browsing, and choosing the Group object's property page, select the General tab, click and hold the down arrow, and select the See Also page. Click the Add button to open the Select Objects dialog box. To select multiple items, hold down the Ctrl key while clicking with the left mouse button.

FIGURE 7.12

Relating other objects to Techies

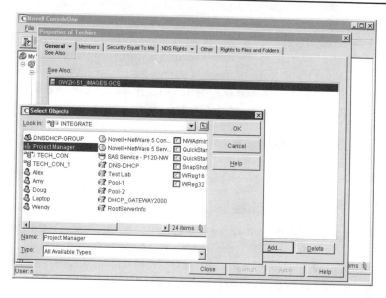

You can see in Figure 7.12 that the Project Manager Organizational Role object has been selected for inclusion in the Selected Objects box at the top of the screen. It will join the IMAGES volume object already in the See Also list. Yes, we pulled something from another Organizational Unit.

To delete an object from the See Also property page, simply click the object and click the Delete button.

The Members Tab

The Members tab contains only one option. Therefore, when you select the tab, you go directly to the Members property page.

IN A HURRY

7.11 Modify the Members Property Page

1. Open ConsoleOne, right-click the Group object to modify, and select Properties.
2. Select the Members tab.
3. To add objects as members of the group, click the Add button.
4. Browse and select an object to be added to the group by highlighting the object and clicking OK.
5. The object appears in the Members property page.
6. Click OK to save the information and exit the Members property page.

PART

II

Managing the Network

Adding members to a group works identically to adding objects to the See Also page. When an object is added as a new member, it receives all rights assigned to the group object.

To reiterate, if you aren't tired of hearing it by now, managing NetWare can be simplified if you learn to manage groups instead of individual users.

To add a new member to the group, click Add, browse and select the object by clicking it, and then click OK. The object now appears in the Members property page.

Remember, even though you add the user to the property page, that user is not yet a member of the group. You must always click the OK button or the Apply button to save your changes.

To delete an object, highlight the object and click the Delete button.

The NDS Rights Tab

The NDS Rights tab replaces the Rights To Files And Directories button in NetWare Administrator. The three options you have under this tab are Effective Rights, Inherited Rights Filters, and Trustees Of This Object. Chapter 9 covers these in detail. For our purposes here, let's look at how you can view and set these items from ConsoleOne.

IN A HURRY

7.12 View Effective Rights

1. Open ConsoleOne and locate the Group object in the NDS tree.
2. Open the group's property page by right-clicking the Group object name and selecting Properties.
3. Select the NDS Rights tab.
4. Click and hold the down arrow and select Effective Rights.
5. View the trustee's effective rights to this object.

The Effective Rights page is an informational page that allows you to view a trustee's effective rights to this object. You can't make any changes here, but it is a good way to get a good report on the effective rights of a trustee to any given object. Figure 7.13 provides a good view of this page.

The Effective Rights To field shows the distinguished name of the target resource, in this case Techies.CONSULT.GCS. Techies is the object to which the trustee has effective rights. You cannot edit this field. To see the effective rights that trustees have to another object, open that object's Effective Rights property page.

FIGURE 7.13

The trustee nt-user's
effective rights to
Techies

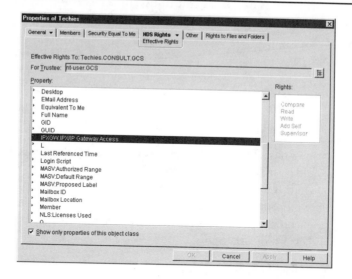

The For Trustee field shows the distinguished name of the trustee whose effective rights are displayed on this page. In this case, the trustee is nt-user.GCS. Notice the Browse button to the right of the field. You can browse for another trustee and view its effective rights to the target resource.

The Rights display box shows the trustee's effective object rights to the target resource. This field used to be called Property Rights in NetWare 5.0's ConsoleOne, but the field name changed in 5.1. These rights include the following:

- Compare
- Read
- Write
- Add Self
- Supervisor
- Create
- Delete
- Rename

In this case, nt-user has all applicable object rights to Techies. The Create item doesn't apply because you can't create an object within a User object.

The Rights field shows the nt-user's effective property rights to Techies. These rights include the following:

- Compare
- Read
- Write
- Add Self
- Supervisor

Nt-user has all these rights because of administrator equivalence, but another trustee would have fewer property rights.

On this page, you have the option to view nt-user's effective rights or to "Show only properties of this object class," the default. To view a trustee's effective rights to a single property, uncheck the box and choose the desired right from the seemingly endless list of NDS rights.

Setting Inherited Rights Filters

IN A HURRY

7.13 View or Set Inherited Rights Filters

1. Open ConsoleOne and locate the Group object in the NDS tree.
2. Open the group's property page by right-clicking the Group object name and selecting Properties.
3. Select the NDS Rights tab.
4. Click and hold the down arrow and select Inherited Rights Filters.
5. View or set Inherited Rights Filters (IRFs) for this object.
6. Click OK to save the settings.

You can use the Inherited Rights Filters page (see Figure 7.14) to view or set Inherited Rights Filters (IRFs) on this object. Here are some things to remember about IRFs:

- IRFs don't give rights to anyone; they take rights away. If a user is granted rights at a certain level of the directory or container structure, the only way to keep those rights from flowing down through the subdirectories and subcontainers is to set up an IRF.

- IRFs can block only inherited rights, or those rights that are flowing down because of granted rights somewhere up the line. Rights that are granted at the current level by explicit assignment cannot be blocked.

- When you set an IRF for an object, it applies to all trustees.

 TIP   If you need to brush up on IRFs, see Chapter 9.

FIGURE 7.14

Setting an Inherited Rights Filter to Techies

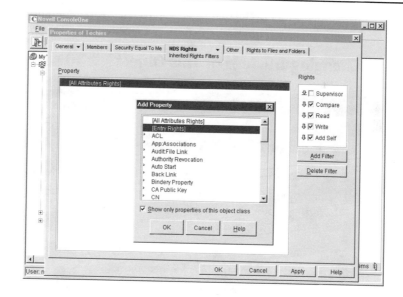

The Inherited Rights Filters field shows the distinguished name of the target resource, in this case Techies.CONSULT.GCS, that the IRFs shown on this page are affecting. You cannot browse and view IRFs for other objects without closing the property page and viewing the properties for another object in the tree.

The Rights section allows you to view or set the IRF that blocks object or property rights from being inherited by the current object.

It is easy to block an object right. The five rights that can be blocked are Supervisor, Delete, Browse, Rename, and Create. Figure 7.14 shows that when the box next to the object right is checked, the flow down arrow is large. But when the box is unchecked, the large arrow is replaced with a stumpy arrow that has a line underneath, signifying that the object right has been restricted or filtered to this object. So to block an object right, uncheck the corresponding checkbox.

Again, you can block the property rights by unchecking the box next to the specific right. You will get the same stumpy arrow and line, indicating that right has been filtered. The property rights are Supervisor, Compare, Read, Write, and Add Self.

Again, with property rights, you can set the IRF for all properties or for selected properties.

To block the property rights to properties, uncheck the box next to the right you want to restrict.

To block the property rights to individual properties, highlight a property or multiple properties (hold the Ctrl key down to select more than one property) in the Add Property box, and uncheck the box next to the right you want to restrict.

Changing Trustees of This Object

IN A HURRY

7.14 View or Change Trustees

1. Open ConsoleOne and locate the Group object in the NDS tree.
2. Open the group's property page by right-clicking the Group object name and selecting Properties.
3. Select the NDS Rights tab.
4. Click and hold the down arrow and select Trustees Of This Object.
5. View or change the trustees for this object.
6. Click OK to save the settings.

You use the Trustees Of This Object page to view or change the list of trustees for this object. This property page gives you several options. You can add a trustee, delete a trustee, assign or change the rights of a trustee, and view the effective rights of a trustee, as illustrated in Figure 7.15.

FIGURE 7.15

The Trustees Of This Object page

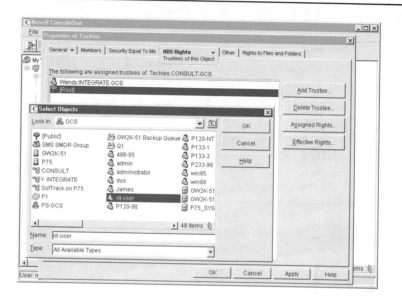

To add a trustee, simply click the Add Trustee button and select a new trustee object. Use the Look In field to browse the tree until you find the object you want to add as a trustee. Highlight the user and click the OK button. The object will now appear as a trustee of the group object.

To delete a trustee, highlight the trustee and click the Delete Trustee button. If you added Wendy.INTEGRATE.GCS by accident, meaning to add nt-user.GCS, highlight Wendy and press the Delete Trustee command button.

To assign rights or view previously assigned rights for a trustee, highlight the trustee and click the Assigned Rights button. You will know how to get around this screen by now. It should look familiar to you.

Remember, even though you delete a trustee or remove rights, that object may still have rights to this object. The trustee may still have rights granted through security equivalence. By clicking the Effective Rights button, you will be able to see which effective rights a trustee has to this object. This screen should also look familiar to you. You can use the browse function to view the effective rights of other objects as well.

 NOTE When you finish making changes on this page or any other pages, you must click the OK button or the Apply button for the changes to take effect.

Saving Time with the Template

Now that you've gone through and created both User and Group objects by hand, so to speak, you're probably ready for some shortcuts. The first one to explore is the template. The name clearly indicates the purpose and function of this object: to provide a template of information for use when creating users.

 NOTE A template is a leaf object that provides a basic set of properties and setup procedures to apply to new, but not existing, users. In NetWare 4.10, these were called user templates. In NetWare 5.1, the name is shortened to template.

Technically, the template is an NDS object holding default information common to many users. Here is some of the information you might include in a template:

- Login time restrictions
- Password restrictions
- Language
- Phone, location, and department information
- Print job configuration details
- Login scripts
- Group memberships
- Security equivalence settings
- Account balance information

You can create a template in any Organization or Organizational Unit objects. If a template exists in the container above, you can copy information from that template. In our example, if there were a template in GCS, the template created in INTEGRATE.GCS could include all the parent information as a starting point.

The template information is passed to a new User object if you check the Use Template option when you create the User object. The information in the template may change later, but that change will not be reflected in the User object information. There is no live link between the template and the User object; there is just a one-time copy process from template to user. Rights may not be granted via template.

No one may log in as the template, but it appears to be a normal User object during setup and modification. This anomaly is a helpful utility, not a security hole.

Creating a Template with NetWare Administrator

IN A HURRY

7.15 Create a Template with NetWare Administrator

1. Open NetWare Administrator and highlight the Organization or Organizational Unit container that will hold the template.

2. Open the Object drop-down menu and choose Create, or press Insert.

3. Select Template to open the Create Template dialog box.

4. Check Use Template or User if you want to use another template or user as a baseline. Browse for the template or user.

5. Check the Define Additional Properties checkbox.

6. Provide information as you would for a User object.

7. Click OK to save the template.

PART

II

When you're creating a template, a small dialog box opens, asking for the name of the template. Type in a name. The next option is Use Template or User. This allows you to use another template or user as a baseline for the new template, rather than starting from scratch. Next, you can choose whether to create another template or define additional properties. When you indicate (by checking the proper checkbox) that you want to define additional properties, the dialog box opens, presenting the standard information for new objects.

Fill in the various pages of the dialog box exactly as you would for any other User object. In Figure 7.16, you can tell by the turned-down corners that information has been added to the Identification, Login Restrictions, Login Time Restrictions, and Password Restrictions. Some buttons don't appear in the normal user property page, such as New Object's DS Rights, New Object's FS Rights, Trustees Of New Object, Volume Space Restrictions, and Member Of Template. Fill out the Template Members fields just as you would to add members to a Group object.

When the information is complete, click OK to save it. When you create a new User object, the system adds these details into the proper properties. See Figure 7.17 to see how the template is accessed as you add a user.

Managing the
Network

FIGURE 7.16

User Template
configuration

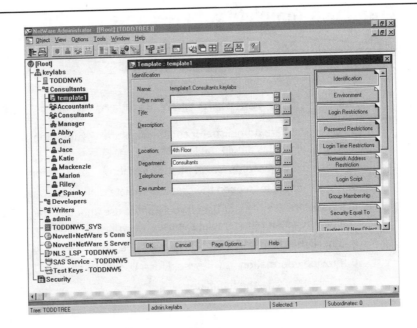

FIGURE 7.17

Using the Use
Template checkbox

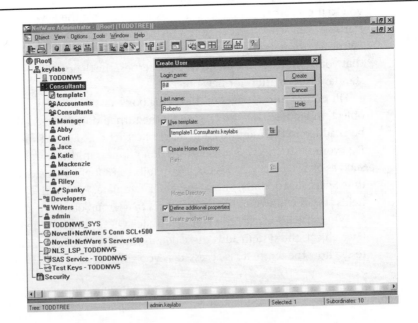

When you check the Use Template checkbox, you can then browse for a template to use. Once you select a template and click Create, the user is created with all the template information imbedded in the account.

Does this work? See for yourself. Figure 7.18 shows a new User object in the process of being installed. The information from the user template shown in Figure 7.17 has been copied into the fields for our new user Bill. This is the result of providing the user's last name, accepting the default values, and using the template.

FIGURE 7.18

Applying the template to a new user

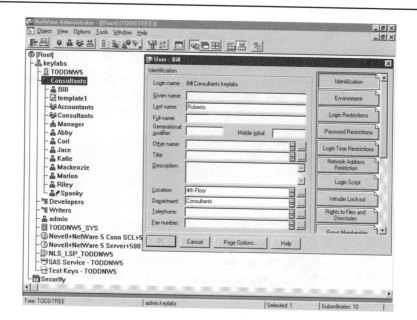

PART

II

Managing the
Network

 NOTE Remember, a template is meant to be used to create users who work in a similar environment. All properties set in the template should be common to all users. For example, if you put information about the template in the Description field or a specific phone number in that field of the Identification page, that information will be carried over to each user created using that template. That will require you to go in to each user and change the information. Suddenly you are doing the work you had hoped to avoid by using the template.

Using Login Scripts

Login scripts are files that contain instructions to configure the networking environment for users. These scripts are read and executed when a user logs in to the network. A login script is similar to an AUTOEXEC.BAT file for an IBM-compatible PC. Login scripts are properties of objects.

Login scripts are excellent tools for shielding computer-phobic users from the network. With a well-designed login script, a user may never need to know any details concerning application locations and data file directories.

The most popular way to use login scripts is to map a drive to a particular directory. Using the MAP command dedicates a particular network drive letter, such as drive H:

```
TODDNW5_SYS:\Public\Win32
```

The users merely change to drive H:, and they are automatically connected to the folder that contains NetWare Administrator on the server TODDNW5. The user does not need to type anything.

There are four types of login scripts:

- Container
- Profile
- User
- Default

As with earlier NetWare versions, the last login script to execute has the last word, meaning it can change any and all information from previous scripts.

With four scripts available, you may wonder how to keep them all straight. It's not difficult, and you will see how each type of login script makes sense. Besides, all login scripts are optional.

The order of execution for these four login scripts is:

- Login begins
- Container object login script

    EXISTS = Execute and continue

    DOES NOT EXIST = Continue
- Profile object login script

    EXISTS = Execute and continue

    DOES NOT EXIST = Continue
- User object login script

    EXISTS = Execute and stop

    DOES NOT EXIST = Continue

- Default login script

  Executes if there is no User object login script

The User login script and the Default login script are an either/or situation. If you have a User login script, the Default script will not run. If you don't have a User login script, the Default login script will run. There are two exceptions:

- When a user has a NO_DEFAULT line in a Container or Profile login script, which prevents the Default login script from executing

- When an EXIT statement exists in the Container or Profile login script, causing the user to exit that script

The primary use of the login script is to set different drive letters to provide users with an easy way to reach their applications. It is true that the entire network is open to users, and they can use any resource to which they have been granted trustee rights. It is also true that most users do not know how to navigate even a small network. Our job is to make network applications and other resources available to users with as little work on their part as possible. Login scripts go a long way in making the network easy for users to navigate.

Users, Login Scripts, and You

The effectiveness of login scripts is evident when you speak to most users and ask them where any of their application directories are. Word processing is on drive G:, and the database is on drive M:. Does this answer tell you anything of value? No. It tells you that the user doesn't understand how NetWare handles drive redirection and has no clue about the network environment.

You can take this two ways. You can regard the user as stupid and computer-phobic, since he or she is unaware of fundamental network processes. This guarantees you will burn out and become bitter toward the users before much longer. You can also regard this as a successful network setup on your part, since the user is able to function perfectly well without worrying about network technical details. This mental approach will make you much happier in your work.

Perhaps the second method is the best way to approach network support in general and login scripts in particular. Your job is to provide a network foundation that supports the users' primary jobs without drawing attention to the underpinnings. Login scripts are your most direct tool to make the network an invisible connection between people and the resources they need.

Types of Login Scripts

Since the login scripts execute in the same order each time, there are some guidelines for each script's role. Container login scripts should focus on access to resources used by most network users, such as volumes and printers. Specific group needs can be answered by the Profile login script. Individual requirements belong in the User login script. You cannot configure the Default login script.

The Container Login Script

The Container login script has the following characteristics:

- It is a property of an Organization or an Organizational Unit.
- Each user can execute only the Container login script.
- The user will execute the login script for the container to which his or her User object belongs.

The Container login script is executed first. This replaces the System login script from earlier NetWare versions. The System login script was server-based; the Container login script is a property of the user's container. Whether the container is an Organization or Organizational Unit makes no difference. If the parent container for a User object does not have a login script, no other Container login script will be available for that user.

Use Container login scripts to do the following:

- Establish network drive mappings to horizontal application directories.
- Establish a link to the user's home directory.
- Connect each user to the PUBLIC directory for NetWare utilities.
- Connect a default printer for the entire container.
- Activate menus or applications used by all members of the container.
- Send login messages to all container users.

You can use conditional IF statements based on login times, group membership, or other variables to make your Container login scripts more versatile.

The Profile Login Script

The Profile login script has the following characteristics:

- It is a property of a Profile object.
- A person can belong to only one profile and, hence, can have only a single Profile login script.
- Many users can execute the same Profile login script.

The Profile login script works differently from an IF MEMBER OF statement referencing a group in a login script. (Using the IF MEMBER OF statement in login scripts is covered a little later in the chapter.) One important difference is that a User object can belong to many groups but can have only one Profile login script. The Profile login script executes after the Container login script.

Use Profile login scripts to do the following:

- Establish drive mappings to special data and/or application directories.
- Set specific search mappings for application directories.
- Connect to special-purpose printers (such as color or high-speed printers) unique to a group.
- Send login messages to a specific group.

The User Login Script

The User login script is a property of the User object. The User login script executes after both the Container and Profile login scripts. It is normally used for specific network details for one user only. There can be only one User login script per User object.

Use User login scripts to do the following:

- Establish drive mappings to specific user directories.
- Send user-specific login messages.
- Activate menus or applications for each particular user.

The Default Login Script

The Default login script has the following characteristics:

- It is contained in the LOGIN.EXE program.
- It cannot be edited.
- It executes in the absence of the User login script.
- It provides minimal functionality.

The Default login script executes last, but only if there is no User login script. There is only one Default login script for the network.

The Default login script does not exist as a text file to be edited. It is contained within the LOGIN.EXE program and cannot be changed. Since so little happens in this login script, few (if any) networks use only the Default login script.

The three ways to avoid the Default login script are:

- Exit from an earlier login script.
- Have a User login script.
- Use the NO_DEFAULT command in a Container login script.

PART

II

Managing the
Network

As an introduction to login scripts in general and some sample commands used, the following are the lines in the Default login script, along with a quick explanation for each one:

```
MAP DISPLAY OFF
```

MAP redirects a local drive letter to a network resource, either a regular drive or a search drive (similar to the DOS PATH command). MAP DISPLAY OFF prevents map commands from displaying on the screen, similar to the DOS command ECHO OFF.

```
MAP ERRORS OFF
```

Prevents mapping errors and the resulting messages from displaying on the screen.

```
MAP *1:=SYS:
```

Maps the first drive to volume SYS:. The *1 indicates a wildcard symbol for mapping the first non-local drive letter. This avoids possible problems in mapping particular drive letters (F: or G:) that may not be available for all clients.

```
MAP *1:=VOL1:USERS\%LOGIN NAME
```

Maps the first drive to the user's home directory, if LOGIN_NAME is the same as the user's home directory. If the user has no home directory, the first drive is still mapped to SYS:. The %LOGIN_NAME is an identifier variable and will be interpreted differently for each person who logs in. The value given by the user as the login name will be captured by the login process and passed to this variable.

```
IF %1=Admin THEN MAP *1:=SYS:SYSTEM
```

If the login name is Admin, the first drive is mapped to SYS:SYSTEM instead of to the user's home directory. This is an example of the IF THEN statement.

```
MAP P:=SYS:PUBLIC
```

For OS/2 workstation clients only (have any left?). With OS/2, drive P: is mapped to SYS:PUBLIC. If the user is not using an OS/2 workstation, this drive mapping is ignored during execution of the Default login script.

```
MAP INS S1:=SYS:PUBLIC; MAP INS S2:=SYS:PUBLIC\%MACHINE\%OS\ %OS_VERSION
```

The INS stands for insert, which places S1 (first search drive) into the DOS PATH statement in a way that does not overwrite any of the existing PATH commands.

If the user is using a DOS or a Windows workstation, the first search drive is mapped to SYS:PUBLIC, where DOS-based NetWare utilities are stored. The second search drive is then mapped to the directory where DOS is stored. The two MAP commands are joined by a semicolon. The default has always been a single command per line, and it's still safer to write login scripts in that manner. If the user logs in from an

OS/2 workstation, these drive mappings are ignored during the execution of the Default login script.

```
MAP DISPLAY ON
```

This command allows MAP commands to display.

```
MAP
```

When the MAP command is used alone from the DOS command line or inside a login script, it displays a list of all drive mappings on the user's screen.

The Most Common Login Script Commands

You know the old story: 80 percent of the work is done by 20 percent of the blank. Fill in the blank with people, tools, circus elephants, or login script commands.

The complete list is located with the other commands in the online documentation. There are more login script commands than any one company will ever use. As you look over the list, you may think some commands seem strange. But remember that each command solves a problem for some customers. Every command has a use, no matter how specialized.

Most of your login scripts will use the following few commands over and over. These descriptions show the command, the explanation, and a usage example.

 WARNING Always place a final carriage return at the end of each login script. The cursor should be on a line by itself, beyond the final login script command line, before saving the script. This will save you much troubleshooting; unless you do this properly, the last line may not execute.

The ATTACH Command

The ATTACH command connects to bindery-based NetWare servers (NetWare 2.*x* or NetWare 3.*x*). This command can be used with NetWare 5.1 servers to bypass NDS. This external ATTACH.EXE no longer works from the command line. It has been replaced by the LOGIN/NS command. Do not confuse the ATTACH command native to LOGIN .EXE with the external executable program. ATTACH only works from a login script.

An example is:

```
ATTACH 312_NW/JAMES
```

PART

II

Managing the Network

The # Command

The # command indicates an external program that will execute and return control to the login script. The example here is the most common, setting the print redirection from a local printer port to a network system printer using the CAPTURE command:

```
#CAPTURE Q=LASER_Q1 NB NFF TI=9
```

The EXIT Command

EXIT stops execution of the LOGIN utility and executes an external program. This command doesn't apply to OS/2 workstations. An EXIT command placed in any login script stops any subsequent login scripts from running.

An example is:

```
EXIT "NMENU ACCOUNTING"
```

The FIRE PHASERS Command

The FIRE PHASERS command emits an electronic space gun sound that may fire as many as nine times. Two is the tasteful limit, as in:

```
FIRE PHASERS 2 TIMES
```

This command is helpful to signal login messages or the conclusion of a login process.

The IF THEN Command

IF THEN is a conditional statement used to perform an action only under certain conditions. Earlier NetWare versions with a single System login script often used IF THEN statements to check the user for group membership before mapping certain drive connections. Although it is still useful, some conditions requiring IF THEN statements in the past can now be done with a combination of the Container and Profile login scripts.

The following example specifies that members of the group WIN95 will have the next available search drive (S16 tells the system to start with the highest possible search drive number, 16, and count down until it finds the next open search drive letter) mapped to the \APPS\WIN95 directory. The interior part is generally indented for clarity.

```
IF MEMBER OF "WIN95" THEN
  MAP INS S16:=SYS:\APPS\WIN95
END
```

The MAP Command

The MAP command maps drives and search drives to network directories and NDS objects. Examples are:

```
MAP G:=TODDNW5_SYS:\REPORTS
MAP INS S16:=SYS:\APPS\WIN95
```

The PAUSE Command

PAUSE stops the execution of the login script until a key is pressed. It provides a handy way to force a user to look at the screen, since FIRE PHASERS tends to be ignored after the novelty wears off.

The SET Command

The SET command sets a DOS or OS/2 environment variable. For OS/2 workstations, SET commands affect the environment only while the login script is running. Values must be enclosed in quotation marks, as in:

```
SET PROMPT="$P$G"
```

$P sets the drive letter, and $G sets the symbol >.

The WRITE Command

WRITE displays messages on the workstation screen while the login script is running. It's best to put these commands at the end of the login script so that they stay on the screen or to use them in conjunction with the PAUSE command.

All values, including special characters, must be in quotation marks. Special characters that help you control text strings are:

\r	Inserts a carriage return
\n	Starts a new line
\	Displays quotation mark
\7	Beeps the internal speaker

An example is:

```
WRITE "Welcome to the Corporate Network \7"
```

The Most Common Login Script Identifier Variables

Identifiers personalize login scripts. They work by using variables known to the NetWare client programs as information to fill in the blank of the identifier variable. For example, the user gives a login name as part of the login process. This name identifies

PART

II

Managing the
Network

that user to the system. After checking NDS for authentication, the system asks for that user's password. With the proper password, the user gains access to the network. By the time a user gets access to the network, the network knows everything about that user. Since this happens before the login script is started, the information about every user is available to personalize the login script using a common set of variables. The most familiar to many people is the greeting often used by network administrators. It's nice to see:

```
Good morning, Mackenzie!
```

as you prepare for work in the morning. More important, it's easy for the administrator to make this happen. Table 7.1 describes the most commonly used login script identifier variables. When you use an identifier variable in a WRITE statement, it must be within quotation marks, typed in all capital letters, and preceded by a percent sign (%). In NetWare 3.*x*, the identifier variable didn't need to be within the WRITE statement's quotation marks, but this is a requirement in NetWare 5.1.

 NOTE The requirement for identifier variables to be in uppercase letters suggests that you should always use capital letters in all your login scripts. This looks a bit garish, especially to people with a Unix background. Using all capitals is, however, the easiest way to avoid potential problems with your login scripts.

TABLE 7.1: COMMON LOGIN SCRIPT IDENTIFIER VARIABLES

Identifier Variable	Function	Example
%GREETING_TIME	Uses the workstation clock to determine morning, afternoon, or evening time frame. Supplies the proper term for the time of the day upon login.	WRITE "Good %GREETING_TIME"
%LOGIN_NAME	The variable for the client's unique login name.	MAP
F:=GATEWAY2000_SYS: USERS\%LOGIN_NAME. %MACHINE	Determines and displays the type of non-OS/2 computer used by the client.	WRITE "Your computer is: %MACHINE"
%OS	Determines and displays the operating system used by your system, such as MSDOS or DRDOS.	WRITE "Your %MACHINE is running %OS"

Continued

TABLE 7.1 (CONTINUED): COMMON LOGIN SCRIPT IDENTIFIER VARIABLES		
Identifier Variable	**Function**	**Example**
%OS_VERSION	Determines and displays the version of DOS, such as 3.3, 6.0, or 6.2.	WRITE "You are using version %OS_VERSION of %OS"
%STATION	Determines and displays your workstation connection number.	WRITE "You are connection number %STATION"

TIP The %LOGIN_NAME identifier variable works well when first names are used for login names, less well if the naming system uses initials or name combinations. Being greeted by "Hello, CWB" is not particularly warm or friendly. However, this variable is great for mapping a drive to the user's home directory. Since the home directory name is the same as the login name, this variable will reliably map every user to that user's particular directory.

Creating and Managing Login Scripts

Now that you know what login scripts are and the commands that are available, let's get scripting. We'll use NetWare Administrator. You must have the trustee rights to create and modify the login scripts for each object. The easiest way to be sure of this capability is to be the Admin or equivalent.

The login script is an object property. Not all objects have login scripts, just users, profiles, and containers. There are no mandatory login scripts or even mandatory login script commands for containers, profiles, or User objects. The Profile script is stored in Organizations or Organizational Units as an NDS leaf object. Container scripts are stored in their respective containers. The User object login script is stored as a property of each User object. See Figure 7.19 for a graphical look at these storage locations.

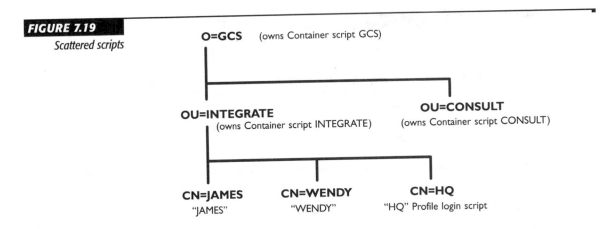

FIGURE 7.19

Scattered scripts

As Figure 7.19 illustrates, you must go to the particular object that owns the login script you want to create or modify. No central database exists for login scripts. Before we get to the specifics of creating and editing login scripts with the NetWare Administrator program, let's take a look at some examples of login scripts and see how they work.

A Sample Container Login Script

Let's look at our sample Container login script in Figure 7.20.

FIGURE 7.20

A sample Container login script in NetWare Administrator

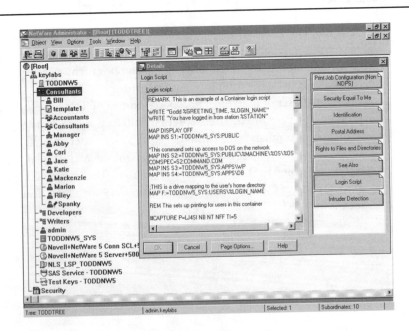

Since the login script is longer than the text box (not unusual for Container login scripts), let me expand on it. Each line is followed by comments and clarifications.

`REMARK This is an example of a Container login script`

REMARK allows you to add comments that are not executed. Four commands (REMARK, REM, ;, and *) perform this same function.

`WRITE "Good %GREETING_TIME, %LOGIN_NAME"`

Displays the information inside the quotation marks. The resulting line will look something like:

`Good morning, Riley`

Variables must be within quotation marks and in all uppercase letters.

`WRITE "You have logged in from station %STATION"`

Displays the connection number for this login.

`MAP DISPLAY OFF`

Turns off the information display to avoid multiple MAP statements clogging the screen. A later Profile or User login script will provide the MAP DISPLAY ON command.

`MAP INS S1:=TODDNW5_SYS:PUBLIC`

Inserts the first network search drive into the DOS path statement, allowing the NetWare utilities in the `PUBLIC` directory to be available to the user from anywhere on the system.

`*This command sets up access to DOS on the network`

Shows a different way to exclude lines from executing with the login script. Comments such as this are helpful to other administrators who work on the network. They are also helpful to you a year later when you have no idea what you were thinking when you set up this system.

`MAP INS S2:=TODDNW5_SYS:PUBLIC\%MACHINE\%OS\%OS_VERSION`

Inserts the second network search drive into the DOS path statement. This drive uses variables to point to the particular machine type and DOS version necessary for each user.

`COMSPEC=S2:COMMAND.COM`

Sets the DOS pointer to the correct `COMMAND.COM` file on the network. This command must follow the network mapping to DOS in the login script, but it doesn't need to be the next command. It can also be set locally. This command rarely gets used anymore because Windows 95/98/NT/2000 demands control over this value.

`MAP INS S3:=TODDNW5_SYS:APPS\WP`

Inserts the third network search drive into the DOS path and gives access to the WP directory.

```
MAP INS S4:=TODDNW5_SYS:APPS\DB
```

Inserts the fourth network search drive and points to the DB directory.

```
;This is a drive mapping to the user's home directory
```

Another comment line that doesn't execute.

```
MAP F:=TODDNW5:USERS\%LOGIN_NAME
```

Sets drive F: to the user's home directory. However, if another MAP command later uses drive F:, this entry will be overwritten. Since Windows setup demands constant drive letters, using a variable such as *1 for this mapping may not work.

```
REM This sets up printing for users in this container
```

The last, and most popular, line-exclusion command. REM works just as it does in a DOS AUTOEXEC.BAT file.

```
#CAPTURE P=LJ4SI NB NT NFF TI=9
```

The crosshatch or number sign (#) starts execution of a .COM or an .EXE file. Once the program is finished, control returns to the login script. Larger programs may not work, since the login script remains in memory during this procedure, taking about 70KB of RAM.

```
#COMMAND /C CLS
```

Executes the external command to clear the screen and then returns to the login script.

```
;This command displays a DOS text file the administrator
;creates for daily messages
FDISPLAY TODDNW5:Admin\MESSAGE.TXT
```

Displays the file MESSAGE.TXT during the login process. FDISPLAY can handle word processing files. DISPLAY works only with text files.

```
PAUSE
```

Stops the login script until a key is pressed. It is identical to the DOS PAUSE command.

```
SET PROMPT="$P$G"
```

Same as the DOS SET statement, but the variable must be enclosed in quotation marks.

```
IF MEMBER OF
```

Adds conditional statements based on group memberships. For example:

```
IF MEMBER OF DEVELOPERS THEN MAP P:=TODDNW5:\APPS\SRC_CODE
```

You can see the ways in which this script is tailored to a large group of users: it sets the default printer, sends messages to the group, and maps drives to the user's home directory and the most generic applications.

A Sample Profile Login Script

Some coordination must happen between the Container and Profile login scripts. If you include User login scripts as well in your network, you must coordinate all three. Figure 7.21 shows a sample Profile login script.

FIGURE 7.21

Profile login script details in NetWare Administrator

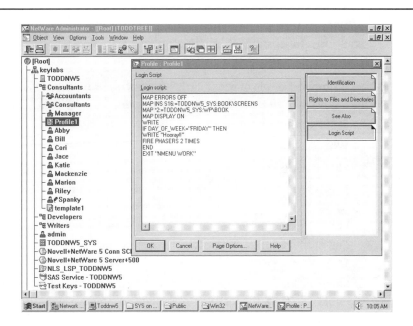

Let's take a line-by-line look at this Profile login script.

```
MAP ERRORS OFF
```

If any drive-mapping errors occur, they won't show on the screen. Even if MAP DISPLAY OFF is set, errors will still display unless you specifically exclude them with this command.

```
MAP INS S16:=TODDNW5_SYS:BOOK\SCREENS
```

Uses the highest search drive number, rather than relying on a specific drive letter designation.

```
MAP *2:=TODDNW5_SYS:WP\BOOK
```

Also uses a wildcard to set the actual drive letter, although we are assuming there is only one other mapped so far.

```
MAP DISPLAY ON
```

Remember that in the Container login script we turned MAP DISPLAY OFF but never turned it back on? Here it is.

```
MAP
```

Executes the MAP command, listing all configured drives for this user.

```
WRITE
```

With no text, the WRITE command inserts a blank line on the screen. This is generally used to separate information.

```
IF DAY_OF_WEEK="FRIDAY" THEN
```

A simple example of the IF THEN statement, using a date variable picked up by the NetWare client software from the workstation.

```
WRITE "Hooray!!"
```

What's to explain?

```
FIRE PHASERS 2 TIMES
```

Makes some noise for Friday, but only IF it is Friday, or THEN goes to the END statement.

```
END
```

End of the IF THEN structure.

```
EXIT "NMENU WORK"
```

Stops the login script execution and runs the specified program if there is one. This example goes from the login script straight to a menu, bypassing any lower login scripts, including the User/Default.

A Sample User Login Script

Here we have a User login script that works well with the previous Container login script. Take a look at it in graphic format in Figure 7.22 and then in text with some explanations.

FIGURE 7.22

A User login script
with conditional
commands in NetWare
Administrator

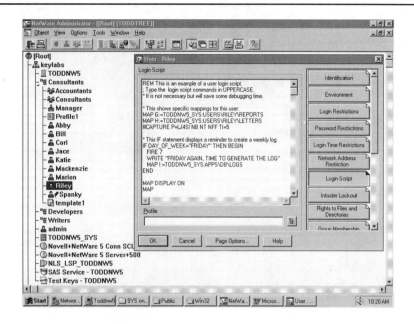

```
REM This is an example of a User login script.
; Type the login script commands in UPPERCASE;
*it is not necessary but will save some debugging time.
```

More comments, and the beginning of each line shows different ways to exclude comment lines from the login script. The line about using capital letters states a good idea. The commands themselves don't need to be in uppercase, but identifier variables must be. By getting in the habit of putting everything in uppercase except comments, you avoid a potential problem.

```
*This shows specific mappings for this user.
```

Comment line for a section of the login script.

```
MAP G:=TODDNW5_SYS:USERS\RILEY\REPORTS
MAP H:=TODDNW5_SYS:USERS\RILEY\LETTERS
```

Maps specific drive letters to specific directories.

```
#CAPTURE P=LJ4SI NB NT NFF TI=5
```

Redirects all printing to the LJ4SI printer.

PART

II

Managing the
Network

```
*This IF statement displays a reminder to create a weekly log.
IF DAY_OF_WEEK="FRIDAY" THEN BEGIN
 FIRE 7
 WRITE "FRIDAY AGAIN, TIME TO GENERATE THE LOG"
 MAP I:=TODDNW5_SYS:APPS\DB\LOGS
END
```

This use of the IF THEN structure is based on a variable, Friday. When DAY_OF_WEEK does equal Friday, too many phasers are fired (FIRE and FIRE PHASERS are the same command to the system), and a new drive mapping is set. On Friday, drive I: becomes available to the user in order to write the necessary log.

```
MAP DISPLAY ON
```

Turns on the map information display. If on already, no problem.

```
MAP
```

Executes the MAP command, listing all the drive mappings in place for this user.

Creating and Editing Login Scripts with NetWare Administrator

IN A HURRY

7.16 Create or Edit a Login Script in NetWare Administrator

1. Open the NetWare Administrator program and click the container, profile, or user that has the login script to be modified.
2. Open the Properties dialog box by pressing Enter or by double-clicking on a Profile or User object.
3. Click the Login Script button.
4. Create or edit the login script.
5. Click OK to save the script.

In the NetWare Administrator program, you can create or edit login scripts for containers and users. Browse down your NDS tree to find the object of your scripting endeavors. Once you've found it, open the Properties dialog box. For containers, you must press Enter or choose Object ➤ Details. For Profile and User login scripts, you can simply double-click the object to open the Properties dialog box.

The Login Script button is with the other page buttons in the dialog box. If you do not find such a button, the object does not support the Login Script property. Printers and NetWare volumes, for instance, don't have login scripts.

When you click the Login Script button, the dialog box is dominated by a text box. Type your login script, or edit the existing one, using the standard Windows text-editing commands and keystrokes. To copy a login script from one user to another, use Windows Cut and Paste commands.

Creating or Editing a Container Login Script

Once you locate the container needing a login script inside the NetWare Administrator program, open the Properties dialog box by pressing Enter while the container is highlighted or by choosing Object ➤ Details. Then click the Login Script page button to open the Login Script text box. From there, you can create a new Container login script or modify one that already exists.

Creating or Editing a Profile Login Script

The Profile login script executes after the Container login script but before the User login script. This type of script is still general, but more narrowly targeted to a smaller group of users within a larger container. Open NetWare Administrator and find the Profile object. Since this is not a container, double-clicking will open the Properties dialog box, as will pressing the Enter key. Then click the Login Script button to open the Login Script text box. From there, you can create a new Profile login script or modify one that already exists.

If you haven't already assigned a user to the profile, you can do this by following either of the two processes below:

1. Select the User object, choose Details, and then choose Login Script.

2. Type the name of the Profile object in the Profile field or use the browse option to find the Profile object, located below the login script box.

3. Click OK to save the settings.

Or

1. Right-click the Profile object (located by browsing through the main NetWare Administrator window). Choose Trustee Of This Object, and then choose Add Trustee.

2. Click Add Trustee, select the user or users, and assign the appropriate object and property rights.

3. Click OK to save the settings.

Creating or Editing a User Login Script

Once the most-used login script, the User login script has become less important in NetWare 5.1. It is still useful, however, and some situations can be handled only by a User login script. The main problem with individual login scripts is the time it takes to manage them in any kind of a dynamic network environment.

Open the NetWare Administrator program and browse until you find the User object to get the login script. Open the Properties dialog box by double-clicking the User object, or highlight the object and press Enter. You will probably need to scroll down the buttons to see the Login Script button. When you find it, click once to open the Login Script text box, and then create or modify the User login script.

Swear Off Single Users

Let's get this title right: swear *off*, not swear *at*, single users. This slogan tells you to never make changes to a single User object on your network (unless forced). This has nothing to do with marital status, but everything to do with maximum management. Anything done for a single User object will be repeated in the future. Why? If one user needs some part of his or her network fixed, another user will need the same thing done. Maybe not today, maybe not this week, but sometime. You can bank on that.

So, if you bend this rule and make a change to user ALEX today, you will do something similar for user LAURA in the future. After a time, you'll discover you've done the same thing for users NICHOLAS, NATALIE, and BRADLEY.

One day, the fix you put in quickly "for one user" will blow up. A directory will be moved, an application will be upgraded, a printer will move to another print server, or something equally as innocent will happen. Then Alex, Laura, Nicholas, Natalie, and Bradley will all come to visit you in your office, loudly proclaiming "our network is broken."

So you'll scramble around for awhile looking for the problem. After a time, you'll remember you did something special to Alex's login script. Then you'll realize you did it to everyone's login script. Then you'll need to fix each individual login script. Then you'll swear not to do the same thing again.

Go ahead and swear that today, and avoid the trouble.

CHAPTER **8**

Arranging
Network Printing

Printing on paper has been a wonderful technology for centuries. In fact, you're holding some of that technology at this moment. Books have been excellent knowledge-transfer agents for 500 years.

Today, however, newer technologies highlight the disadvantages of printing on paper as the primary way to transmit information. Change is nearly impossible on paper; the content of this book can be changed only with great difficulty, and no changes will be reflected in existing copies of the book. It's likely that some of the data in the report you received yesterday has already changed, but the printed copy of the report you have has remained the same. Business assumptions you make tomorrow based on that report could be mistaken. Even worse, when you check your paper files, you'll probably find several copies of the same report, each with slightly different information. Which copy is correct? Does this copy match the report your coworkers are using for their assumptions?

Even when you receive accurate printed information, the printed paper format makes it difficult to use that information. Most computer applications today allow you to share data between different files. Developing standards such as the OLE (Object Linking and Embedding), COM (Component Object Model), and OpenDOC technologies make it possible to view a memo that contains graphs that change based on the current information. When you print that memo and graph, however, the information is locked and won't ever be accurate again.

Some people object more to paper printing because of the waste. Companies today discard tons of used paper every month, and paper consumption goes up 40 percent when a new e-mail system hits a company. The idea of leveling a forest to turn trees into quickly discarded paper seems ridiculous, yet paper consumption is higher today than ever.

Your users will complain more about printing than any other single network component. Why? Many people don't consider what's inside the computer "real" until it appears on paper. If you are new to the network administration game, you will soon hate paper because of the hassles printing causes you.

Whatever your personal reasons, controlling printing will save your company time and money. In the dynamic swirl of information, paper has been left behind. The less your company relies on paper to transfer knowledge, the more dependable that knowledge will become.

However, since we're stuck with all this printing, we might as well do it right. NetWare 5.1 offers several advantages over earlier NetWare versions in the setup and control of the printing process but also retains compatibility with older network printing methods. First, let's all agree on how the network printing process works in general; then we'll get to setting up and managing NetWare 5.1 printing in particular. This chapter covers the print objects and properties. The client side of printing is covered in Chapter 12.

NetWare Printing System Overview

Early PCs printed to an attached printer containing little or no intelligence. The printer was often a small Epson dot-matrix unit, connected to the PC by a 10-foot cable. A diagram of this relationship is simple and uncluttered. Figure 8.1 re-creates the scene on many corporate desks in the 1980s. Millions of home computers and attached printers are still configured this way today.

FIGURE 8.1

Printing the old way

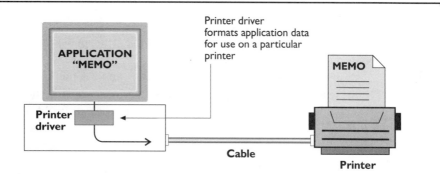

PART

II

Managing the Network

The components of this process are straightforward:

1. An application sends data (print stream) through the print driver to the designated printer.

2. The PC directs the print stream to the printer port.

3. A printer cable carries the print stream (now formatted by the driver) to the printer.

4. The printer puts characters on paper and responds to the PC, indicating when the print stream can continue.

5. The printer cable carries the acknowledgment and request for more data to the PC.

6. The PC directs the request to the application.

7. The process repeats.

This process can look overly complicated for a single PC connected to a single printer, but even simple processes often require complicated underpinnings. Some details that cannot be clear in the diagram and text also impact the user sitting at this PC. For instance, notice that there is a direct connection between the printer and the application. The application sends data through the printer driver and must wait for the printer to request more data. Printer cache buffers were tiny in the old days, so the application would patiently wait for each request for more data until the entire print stream had been delivered to the printer. Unfortunately, the user was staring at a screen that flashed "Wait Wait Wait" or "Printing Printing Printing." Both meant the same thing.

Several things happened over the space of two or three years. First, people forgot how much time the PC saved them and grew impatient with the slow printing process. The printers were slow, the applications were slow, and the PC was useless until the print process was finished.

This problem was solved with stand-alone print spoolers, little devices that contained memory (sometimes as much as 256KB!) that sat between the PC and the printer. The application would send the print stream, and the print buffer would accept it all quickly and tell the PC application everything was printed. The buffer would then wait for the slow printer to finish printing, but the user could go back to work.

Print buffers helped, but each person still had his or her own printer, which was expensive. Worse, the printers were often dot-matrix printers, which produced crude characters and lots of noise. The loud BZZZZZZ of tiny pins hitting paper still sends chills up my spine.

Then laser printers appeared and changed the world of printing forever. The quality was a thousand-fold better than the dot-matrix printers, but laser printers were expensive. Companies couldn't justify spending many thousands of dollars per PC to add laser printers for everyone.

The push to share laser printers probably had more to do with the growth of Novell than any other single factor. Thousands and thousands of networks were cost-justified by sharing one or two laser printers among the members of a workgroup.

Novell's Queue-Based Printing System

NetWare has traditionally used a queue system to route print jobs through the network. Figure 8.2 shows our previous application's print stream reaching the printer through the network.

FIGURE 8.2

Printing the NetWare way (the queue system)

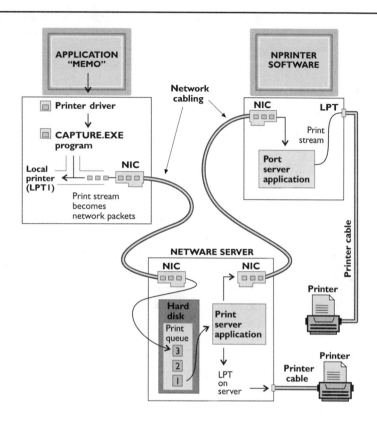

The components of the process in Figure 8.2 are a bit more involved. First, at the workstation:

1. The application generates print output "Memo" to the print driver.

2. The CAPTURE.EXE or Windows spooler program checks the destination: local or network printer?

3. If the destination is local, CAPTURE ignores the print stream, and it goes to the local printer, or the Windows spooler directs the job to be printed on the local printer.

4. If the destination is network, CAPTURE or the Windows spooler converts the print stream into packets that the network understands.

5. The network interface card addresses the packets and transfers them to the network cabling system.

6. If an existing file is being printed with NPRINT, the CAPTURE or the Windows spooler program is bypassed, and NPRINT feeds the print stream to the network card.

NOTE The DOS utility CAPTURE is covered in Appendix E. It is almost obsolete today since many network workstations now use Windows. Windows programs send their print jobs to a program called the *spooler*, which makes the decision about which printer should service a print job.

Most applications are network-savvy and print directly to the network client software, especially through Windows of some flavor. A few applications may still have a default of printing to a locally attached printer. For these packages, the NetWare client software program CAPTURE redirects the print stream from the local printer port to the network. Windows clients can set the default printer to a network printer using the Windows spooler instead of using the CAPTURE program, but the effect is the same: the application doesn't know about the network printer; only the network client software does.

The DOS CAPTURE utility works by intercepting the print stream for particular printer ports and converting that print stream into packets that can travel over the network. These packets are sent to the network interface card, which addresses them to the server running the print server software. (We'll set up the client side of the print process in Chapter 12.)

If the printer port addressed by the application is still a local port, not controlled by CAPTURE, the NetWare software stays out of the way. It's possible to reference two printers in many applications and in Windows. Making one printer local and one printer available through the network is no problem. Multiple network printers are even allowed.

The network cabling transports the print stream (now converted into data packets) across the wire to the file server running the print server software. The specific print server is referenced when the CAPTURE program is started or the Windows printer is chosen. There is no practical limit on how many clients can feed print jobs to a print server. The number of clients is not limited to the number of concurrent licenses allowed by the file server software. Any NetWare client can send a print job to any NetWare print server, attached to a server or linked via network cabling.

Once the print stream (now split into data packets) leaves the workstation, the following occur:

1. The packets travel across the network cabling to the addressed file server hosting the print queue.

2. The server strips the addressing information from each packet and saves the print stream as a file on the server hard disk.

3. When the last packet of the print stream is received, the application and the user running it are able to go back to work.

4. The file is closed and the filename (assigned by NetWare) is fed into the queue with any other waiting print jobs.

5. The print server polls the queue for the next available job. When other jobs in the queue have printed (or sooner if the priority level for this print job is higher than the priority of the other waiting jobs), the file is transferred to the control of the print server.

6. If the specified printer is locally attached to the file server, the print server software and the printer negotiate concerning forms and availability, and printing starts.

7. If the specified printer is attached to a remote print server or to a workstation running the NPTWIN95 or NPRINTER software, the print server passes the print job to the network card.

8. The network card splits the print stream into packets, addresses them, and sends the packets on their way.

When the print stream (once again split into data packets) reaches the remote workstation supporting the remote printer, the following occur:

1. The network card strips the address information from the packets and passes them to the NPTWIN95 or NPRINTER software.

2. The port server software included in NPTWIN95 or NPRINTER reassembles the print stream from the packets and initializes the printer port.

3. NPTWIN95 or NPRINTER negotiates with the locally attached printer. If it is printing in the background, time slicing is used to avoid disturbing the primary application.

This process sounds much more convoluted than it seems to the users if everything is working properly. The users neither know nor care what happens underneath the surface. All they want is for their printouts to appear more quickly.

PART

II

Managing the
Network

Be careful because the Novell manuals often include remote links and routers in their printing diagrams to emphasize NetWare's global reach. Nothing stops your printing setup from looking like that, of course. But no company today can get away with forcing users to traverse a great distance when looking for their printouts. In the old days, mainframe users often went from one building to another in search of their paper. Huge printouts were stacked by the operations staff in cubbyholes waiting for the departmental wheelbarrow (okay, cart) to come and fetch paper by the dozens of pounds.

Today, an employee forced to walk more then five cubicles away for a printout might file a labor grievance. Users want fast printers close by. People will walk the length of the building for the fax machine without complaining, but they've been spoiled by personal printers. Most network users prefer a laser printer beside their desk and will put up with a walk to the next cubicle for the color laser.

You can physically connect a printer to the network in four ways:

- Plug a network-attached printer into the network cabling system directly.
- Plug a printer into a network-attached print server.
- Connect a server-attached printer by serial or parallel port to a file server.
- Connect a workstation-attached printer by serial or parallel port to a workstation.

There is nothing new in these physical methods of connecting printers. However, larger networks and smarter printers make the choice of a network-attached printer more practical for more networks today than ever before. Printers with their own network connection provide, by far, the best performance, because Ethernet runs faster than a printer port.

Many companies are working to make printing faster and easier. The client software for Windows 95/98 workstations takes advantage of Microsoft's pseudo-multitasking for quicker printing. Third-party vendors make print server boxes that attach directly to the network cabling and eliminate the need for a PC running the NPTWIN95 software (nope, Novell hasn't changed the name to NPTWIN98 yet). These print servers cost less than a PC and speed up printing. Some print servers plug directly into the printer, and some need a printer cable to connect the printer and the network.

Even though things are better than they were, printing will still be your largest network hassle. As you can tell from Figure 8.2, plenty of software and hardware pieces must mesh for printing to work properly. Any slip in any part of the journey can send your print job to the print job burial ground. Even though many print problems will have nothing to do with the network (how does the network know a person sent data to a printer without the right fonts?), you, as the network administrator, will be called upon to make things work again.

Network-Attached Printers and Print Servers

As early as 1989, I started seeing devices that allowed a network printer to be attached directly to an Ethernet or a Token Ring network. These devices had print server software that connected them to a NetWare server and allowed them to service a NetWare print queue.

These devices generally sped up the printing process quite a bit. They also removed the restriction that printers be physically close to a workstation or file server. You could get around this, of course, with serial or parallel port extenders, but I had terrible luck with those.

Hewlett-Packard released its JetDirect printer interfaces that plugged directly into the network. Most Hewlett-Packard printers, starting with the HP LaserJet II, had ports that allowed you to plug these JetDirect devices into the printer. These JetDirect devices had separate management programs that were used to configure the JetDirect print server software.

Recent advances such as NAS (Network Attached Storage) include print servers. LinkSys (www.linksys.com) released its Instant GigaDrive 20 in late 1999, combining a 20GB hard drive with one of its print server modules. It doesn't emulate NetWare, like the Snap! Server does (albeit only NetWare 3.x), but it uses Windows networking to connect PCs and Macintoshes to the 20GB drive. Any TCP/IP or Windows-enabled printer software can send print jobs through the network to the GigaDrive via its built-in 10/100 Base-T connection. Linux controls the box, with administration through a browser interface. Very slick and fast.

Novell Distributed Print Services

Novell started developing *Novell Distributed Print Services* (NDPS) as an add-on product for NetWare 4.11. Novell has now bundled NDPS with NetWare 5.1. When I first looked at the specifications for NDPS, I was impressed and suspected that this was the way network printing would be handled in the future. Now I'm not so sure. Few manufacturers have jumped onto the NDPS bandwagon, the code takes 184.32MB to install on existing servers, and third-party gateways for non-HP and Xerox printers are dicey.

Novell Distributed Print Services remains the party line, however, and we'll respect that. Don't be surprised, however, if some nice, smart Internet-driven printing spec comes and blows NDPS out of the red box. Oops, the Web site touts NetWare Enterprise Print Services—sounds like an upgrade, but the price is $995 for each two-server license and five NetWare users, plus another $9 for every additional user. The NetWare 5.1 manual and administration tools still focus on NDPS, so we will as well.

PART

II

Managing the
Network

Developed jointly with Xerox and Hewlett-Packard, NDPS streamlines NetWare printer management. Some of the advantages of NDPS include:

- Bi-directional communication with newer printers allows proactive management of printers by allowing printer administrators to receive messages and errors related to events such as paper jams, low toner, out of paper, and so on. Administrators can be notified of as many events as the printers are capable of reporting; for some printer types this is more than 100 events. Administrators can obtain printer status information in real time.

- Interoperability with queue-based printing makes upgrading go more smoothly.

- Networked printers can be centrally administered through a single management interface, the NetWare Administrator program. This includes managing functions formerly built into utilities such as Hewlett-Packard JetAdmin, PCONSOLE, PRINTDEF, PRINTCON, and NetWare Administrator.

- Printers are easier to set up than the queue/printer/print server model used by NetWare 4. Newer HP printers can also be set up automatically when you first plug them into the network.

- Vendors can develop plug-in applications for NDPS to further extend the management capabilities of their own printers.

- Printer device drivers can be automatically downloaded if a user selects a printer, even if the user has never before used that printer. This feature alone can save network administrators hundreds of hours of configuration time. This is supported for Windows 3.1, Windows 95/98, and Windows NT clients that had the NDPS software installed when the NetWare 5.1 client software was installed.

- Printers can be filtered based on capabilities, location, or type.

- Banner pages are customizable.

- NDPS supports ISO (International Organization for Standardization) 10175 Document Printing Architecture and SNMP (Simple Network Management Protocol) MIB (Management Information Base) RFC 1759.

- Job scheduling is customizable.

- Print jobs can easily be moved from one printer to an alternate printer.

- Drag-and-drop printing is supported for ASCII text and PostScript files without launching the application that created the file.

Comparing NDPS and Queue-Based Printing

Sometimes sharing printers on a network can be inconvenient. If the printer you select has run out of paper, you discover that only when you make the trip to pick up your non-existent print job. Then you load the paper and wait for the printer to finish jobs that were sent earlier to that print queue. If you need to print in a hurry, your best bet is to call someone sitting near a printer or to make a trip to see if the printer is available.

NDPS allows users to find out the current condition of a printer through software. In other words, without leaving your desk, you can find out if a particular printer is out of paper or low on toner, if a print job is complete, or the location of a color printer on the system that is not busy at a particular time. NDPS printers can be connected to the network through third-party gateway products, such as Hewlett-Packard's print servers. NDPS printers can also be connected as remote printers using LPR (for Unix or TCP/IP printers), attached to the file server or attached to local ports on network workstations.

Novell's traditional queue-based system required that administrators create and manage three objects—a Print Server, a Print Queue, and a Printer—for each printer device on the network. An appropriate printer driver was needed on each client computer for a particular type of printer so that the user could print. Novell's CAPTURE utility or the Windows spooler redirected a client application's print job to a queue stored on the file server, which would hold it until the printer assigned to that queue was available to print it.

With the advent of NDPS, all those functions have been built into one Printer Agent object. The DOS-based PCONSOLE.EXE utility has been discontinued, and the NLM program loaded at the file server, PSERVER, has been replaced by NDPSM.

Intelligent printers will arrive soon. Novell teamed with smart printer folks at HP and Xerox to push printers further up the intelligence scale. Is NDPS the end result or a mid-step? I tend to be wary of technologies that promise to simplify our lives, then start talking about necessary strategy and planning. So let's talk about planning NDPS.

Planning an NDPS Deployment

If you have been working with versions of NetWare prior to NetWare 4, you are familiar with the process of "unlearning." After working with numerous Advanced NetWare through NetWare 2.x networks, I found NetWare 3 a bit of a shock (in a good way). I had to learn a lot of new features and capabilities in order to properly design and maintain NetWare 3 networks. I had eagerly anticipated NetWare 4 and NetWare Directory Services, but it was a shock to me also; I had to "unlearn" my notions of managing bindery-based NetWare servers since NetWare Directory Services used an entirely different management approach to NetWare.

PART

II

Managing the Network

The same can be said for Novell Distributed Print Services. Although they are supported for backward compatibility, you must "unlearn" the concepts of print queues, printers, and print servers in order to grasp some of the new NDPS concepts such as agents, brokers, and managers. OK, Novell people have moved on, so let's admit queue-based printing isn't all that bad, especially with the quick setup options inside NetWare Administrator. Oops, here they come again. Take a deep breath and dive right into the wonderful world of NDPS; you'll be glad you did.

Printer Agents are at the center of NDPS. Printer Agents represent the printers on the network, and there is one agent for each device. The agent combines the functions of the print server, queue, printer, and spooler. It provides information to users regarding features and status of the printers and their print jobs, and it sends data directly to the printer. The Printer Agent can be software or firmware embedded in the printing device, or it can be software running on a print server that connects the printer to the network.

Printer Agents provide access to the two types of printers available in the NDPS environment:

- Controlled-access printers
- Public-access printers

Controlled-access printers are specified as NDS objects, with rights defined for certain users or groups, and can provide bi-directional feedback to users.

Public-access printers are available to anyone on the network, but they lack the extra functionality of NDPS. A public-access printer would appear on the network, for example, if a Hewlett-Packard printer were installed and set to automatically configure itself. Users can find it easier to access public-access printers on their own, but they need an administrator to set them up to use controlled-access printers.

Table 8.1 describes the differences between public-access printers and controlled-access printers.

TABLE 8.1: PUBLIC-ACCESS PRINTERS VS. CONTROLLED-ACCESS PRINTERS

Controlled-Access Printers	Public-Access Printers
Have an NDS printer object associated with them.	Do not have an NDS printer object associated with them.
Rights can be assigned and usage can be restricted.	Anyone can use a public-access printer.
Security can be administered through NDS.	No security associated with public-access printers.

Continued ▶

TABLE 8.1 (CONTINUED): PUBLIC-ACCESS PRINTERS VS. CONTROLLED-ACCESS PRINTERS	
Controlled-Access Printers	**Public-Access Printers**
Must be configured through the NetWare Administrator program.	Printers that support automatic configuration can automatically configure themselves as public-access printers.
Event notification through e-mail, pager, event logging, or pop-up messages.	Event notification only for job-related events.

In planning your printing environment, use a diagram to indicate where individuals and printers are physically located. You can determine access by matching the following:

- Job function, particular needs (large volume, duplex, color, forms)
- Location
- Printer characteristics

Other important variables include whether you are supporting NetWare 4.1 or older servers; DOS, OS/2, and Macintosh clients; and older printers, which will require queues. Which network protocols are in place—IPX, TCP/IP, or both? In a mixed environment, you can assign queues to an NDPS printer, or you can reserve specific printers to handle queues.

Novell offers an Upgrade Wizard on its Web site (www.novell.com), which upgrades a queue system to NDPS. Or, you can install NDPS and manually reconfigure clients and printers as needed.

Understanding the Architecture of NDPS

The *NDPS Broker,* BROKER.NLM, supervises three services that run on the NetWare file server:

The Service Registry Service (SRS)   Stores information about public-access printers on the network, including type, manufacturer, and model.

The Event Notification Service (ENS)   Can send customizable messages about printer events and status to managers or users if, for example, a printer is out of paper or is low on toner. These messages can be in the form of pop-up messages, e-mail, or log files.

The Resource Management Service (RMS)   Centralizes storage of printer resources such as drivers, fonts, banner pages, and printer definition files (NPD), facilitating client installations.

BROKER.NLM runs on a server on the network, storing information on a specified volume and supervising printing activities anywhere on the system. When a file

PART

II

Managing the
Network

server is first installed, an NDPS Broker can be created automatically. NDPS requires that at least one broker be active on the system. If you have a larger NetWare network, you should plan to have at least one NDPS Broker per subnet.

NDPS Managers (NDPSM.NLM) are entities that communicate with the modules running on the file server. They can supervise any number of printer devices attached to a network. At least one NDPS Manager must be present on the network, but there can be only one NDPS Manager per server. NDPS Managers also manage the Printer Agents.

Gateways (such as HPGATE) are software modules that manage communications between NDPS and a printer device. These are provided either by the printer manufacturer (for example, Hewlett-Packard or Xerox) or by Novell.

Novell's gateway employs the *Printer Device Subsystem* (PDS), which accesses the printer through a Port Handler that you specify when you set up the Agent object. You use the Novell gateway to communicate with printers attached to parallel and serial ports as well as remote printers such as those connected via NPRINTER.EXE or NPTWIN95.EXE.

NDPS Embedded Printers are printing devices that the NDPS Printer Agent software built directly into the printer's firmware. Administrators and users can communicate directly with printers that have this software embedded in them. Many printer manufacturers are working to incorporate NDPS technology in their next generation of printers. If you want NDPS to work correctly, spend the money to get real NDPS-enabled printers.

An *NDPS enabled client* is a Windows 3.1, Windows 95/98, or Windows NT client that has had the NetWare 5.1 client software installed with the Novell Distributed Print Services option checked during custom installation (see Figure 8.3). If the NDPS client software is not installed, the client will be able to print only to queue-based printers.

Figure 8.4 shows the three ways that an NDPS printer can be attached and configured on the network and how an NDPS client can access that printer.

In the first configuration, the client communicates directly with a printer in which the NDPS software is embedded. In the second configuration, the printer is attached directly to the server (through the parallel or serial port), and the Printer Agent redirects the job through the Novell Printer Device Subsystem, which is one of the components of the Novell gateway. In the third configuration, the printer communicates through a gateway product such as Hewlett-Packard or Xerox's printer gateway.

Managing the
Network

FIGURE 8.3

The Novell Distributed
Print Services client
installation option

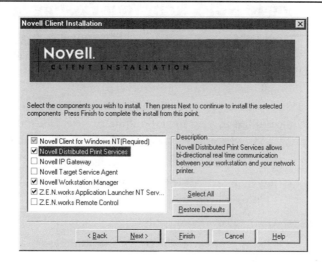

FIGURE 8.4

How NDPS printers
can be attached to the
network

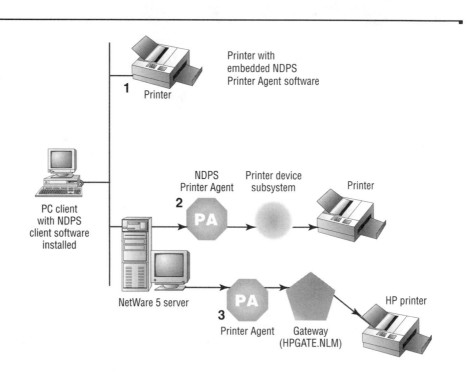

Migrating to NDPS from Your Existing System

There is no single "best" way to migrate from your existing older printing system to the Novell Distributed Print System. The only thing I can tell you for sure is that NDPS is Novell's recommended path for network printing. NetWare 5.1 supports the traditional queue/printer/print server system.

When you start planning your move to NetWare 5.1, you need to make sure you include printers in your migration plan. Your migration path is going to depend on a number of factors, and you need to answer the following questions:

- How many printers need to be migrated?
- How many clients will need to have their software upgraded to the NetWare 5.1 client software?
- Which network protocols will you be using? TCP/IP? IPX/SPX? Both?
- What is your current network operating system version?

Should I Migrate Immediately?

Before I start talking about interoperability between the queues and NDPS, let me first jump into the line of fire and make some firm recommendations.

- If you have fewer than 25 queues and your clients will all be upgraded to NDPS client software, plan to upgrade immediately. I don't have hard-core data to support the "25" number; to me it is just a manageable number of print queues to migrate simultaneously.
- If you have fewer than 200 workstations and can easily deploy the NetWare 5.1 client software (including the NDPS option), go ahead and migrate to NDPS.
- If you are currently using NetWare 3.x, you will have to convert from the NetWare 3 printing model anyway. For fewer than 25 print queues, start over from scratch. For more than 25, use the NetWare 5.1 Upgrade Wizard that ships with NetWare 5.1 to upgrade your NetWare 3.x printing objects "across the wire." Again, there is nothing magical about the 25 number; for me, that is a manageable number. You have to select your own realistic and manageable number.
- If you are migrating from another operating system such as Windows NT Server or Unix, you will have to redo your printing architecture anyway. Go ahead and get the printers configured using NDPS.

If you have decided that it is necessary to use both NDPS and the traditional NetWare 4 printer system, you need to be aware of the interoperability that is provided between NDPS printers and NetWare 4 queues. NetWare 4 Queue, Printer, and Print Server objects can coexist on the same server as NDPS Brokers, Agents, and Managers.

Of course, if you don't have many printers, and they're all working fine, you can postpone NDPS installation. There's no law that you have to change your printer arrangement. If this task falls way down on your priority list, so be it. But if you will benefit from NDPS, let's get going.

Designing Your New NDPS System

As part of your upgrade or network design process, Novell says you should have written records of the following (no, this isn't a joke, really):

- All printer types and physical locations.

- How each printer connects to the network (through a network printer interface card, workstation, print server, NetWare server, or some other type of server such as Unix or Windows NT).

- Restrictions that need to be placed on any specific printers (for example, the Marketing department may not want the Sales department using their snazzy new color laser printer).

- Management responsibilities for each of the printers. Does the help desk manage all the printers, or is there a person in each department or area who should be given that task?

As you start planning your NDPS system, remember that at least one server should be an NDPS Manager. On multiple-segment or multiple-location networks, I suggest a server with an NDPS Manager in each segment or location. Because the Printer Agents communicate with the NDPS Managers, you want the NDPS Managers to be near their Printer Agents. You will create one Printer Agent for each printing device on your network. Each Printer Agent is assigned to an NDPS Manager.

Network Protocols

An important design issue concerns which network protocols will be used. Novell Distributed Print Services uses IPX/SPX and TCP/IP—you can use either protocol or both. The NCP (NetWare Core Protocol) requests on a NetWare 5.1 network that is based on TCP/IP are transported natively in IP packets. Earlier versions of NetWare supported TCP/IP clients, but the NCP data were transported across the TCP/IP network as encapsulated IPX frames in an IP datagram. For more information on TCP/IP in NetWare 5.1, see Chapter 14.

PART

II

Managing the
Network

Interoperability with NetWare Queues

As stated earlier, no single "correct" way exists to migrate from a queue-based printing system to an NDPS system. Let me offer one path for a large system with many network printers.

Your clients must run the NetWare 5.1 version of the client software before you can move from a queue-based system to an NDPS system. Until you have upgraded these clients, you must maintain your queues, and your clients will continue to print as they have in the past (see Figure 8.5). You can continue to operate your printers in this manner indefinitely if you decide that you don't want to move to NDPS.

FIGURE 8.5

A non-NDPS client printing to a NetWare queue that is serviced by a print server

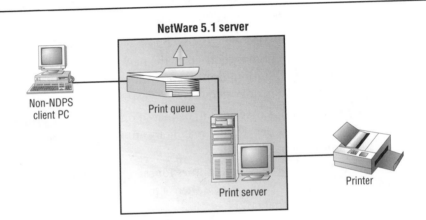

Next, create NDPS Managers and NDPS Brokers on the servers near the printing devices, and create NDPS Printer Agents for each printer on the network. Then you can test your newly created Printer Agents before putting them into production.

 NOTE Now both the queue system and the NDPS Printer Agent send jobs to the same printing device.

Reassign printing responsibility for your queues; instead of having the print server managing print jobs from the queue, assign the Printer Agent to manage print jobs. Figure 8.6 shows non-NDPS clients using the traditional queue, NDPS clients using the Printer Agent, and all print jobs being delivered to the same print device. For details, see the section "Assigning an NDPS Printer Agent to Service a NetWare Print Queue," later in this chapter.

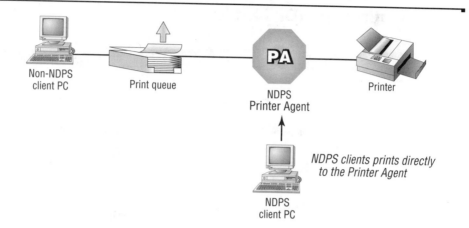

Now you're almost there! All printers are configured with Printer Agents, so you can start upgrading clients slowly. Once all clients that depend on using queues are upgraded, delete the NetWare queues. Delete your queues only a few at a time. There could possibly still be users on your network who are printing to queues rather than to NDPS printers. If you delete them all at the same time, your phone calls will only be drowned out by irate users yelling and cursing at you.

For an in-depth discussion of NDPS migration options, see Novell's AppNote "Migrating to NDPS and IP" at `http://developer.novell.com/research/appnotes/2000/february/04/04.htm`.

Setting Up and Managing NDPS with NetWare Administrator

In a typical scenario, you need one NDPS Broker, one or more NDPS Managers, and as many Printer Agents as there are actual printers attached to the network. You must create a manager for each file server attached to a printer. You might also create multiple managers if you are assigning operator rights to specific departments. You can take care of all the tasks required for creating and managing NDPS in NetWare Administrator, but you can optionally do some of the work at the file server console with `NDPSM.NLM`.

Creating the NDPS Broker

IN A HURRY

8.1 Create an NDPS Broker

1. Open NetWare Administrator and highlight the appropriate container for the new NDPS Broker object.
2. Choose Object ➢ Create.
3. Choose NDPS Broker.
4. Fill in the Broker name.
5. Browse to indicate a volume to store the NDPS Resource database.
6. Click Create to exit and create the NDPS Broker object.

If you chose the Typical Install option when you set up NetWare 5.1, an NDPS Broker was created for you. You can optionally choose to create or add new brokers later. If you chose Custom Install, you may have decided not to copy the NDPS Resource Database, which saved about 60MB of storage space on your server. To add this service later, you need to run the GUI on the server console (using C1START), click Start, choose the Install option, then follow the directions to install the appropriate files (184MB of files) for Novell Distributed Print Services.

If you are used to working with NetWare 4, you will immediately notice in the Create New Object dialog box several new object types that can be created, including NDPS Broker, NDPS Manager, and NDPS Printer.

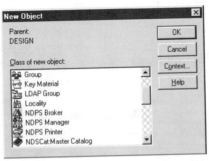

Choose NDPS Broker to open the Create NDPS Broker Object dialog box:

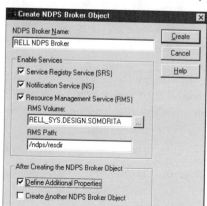

At the very minimum, you need to supply a Broker name such as RELL NDPS Broker. You can also specify whether to enable the Service Registry Service (SRS), the Notification Service (NS), and the Resource Management Service (RMS). In addition, you can provide the volume name and path that contain the Resource Management Service data. If you don't provide data for these fields, the defaults apply.

Check the Define Additional Properties checkbox and click Create to open the NDPS Broker object properties dialog box:

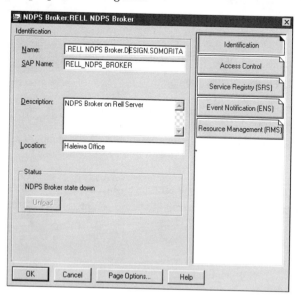

The Identification tab includes location and description boxes, which are details for the administrator. The Access Control tab allows you to assign individuals or groups to manage this object. The other tabs indicate the status of the three modules on the server—SRS, ENS, and RMS—which will become active when you complete this procedure.

Activate the NDPS Broker modules at the server by typing the following at the System Console and then adding it to the AUTOEXEC.NCF to load automatically when the server is restarted (this line is automatically inserted if NDPS was installed on the server during initial installation):

```
LOAD BROKER "RELL NDPS Broker.DESIGN.SOMORITA"
```

The NDPS Broker is called RELL NDPS Broker and is located in the OU=DESIGN .O=SOMORITA context. This loads the BROKER.NLM and initializes a screen at the server console. From this screen, you can view broker events and disable the Service Registry, Event Notification, and Resource Management Services.

Creating the NDPS Manager

IN A HURRY

8.2 Create an NDPS Manager

1. Open NetWare Administrator and highlight the appropriate container for the new NDPS Manager object.
2. Choose Object ➤ Create.
3. Choose NDPS Manager.
4. Fill in the NDPS Manager name.
5. Browse to indicate a server and volume to store NDPS data.
6. Click Create to exit and create the NDPS Manager object.

Next, we need to create an NDPS Manager in NetWare Administrator that will interact with the services running at the server. From NetWare Administrator, choose the NDS context in which the NDPS Manager should exist, and then choose Create ➤ NDPS Manager to open the Create NDPS Manager Object dialog box:

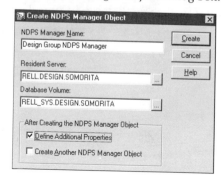

At the very least, you need to supply a name for the NDPS Manager. You should also choose a resident server that will store the database of driver files and configurations, and you should choose a volume on that server. Servers that have shared printers attached directly to their local ports must run an NDPS Manager.

Check the Define Additional Properties checkbox and click Create to open the Design Group NDPS Manager properties dialog box:

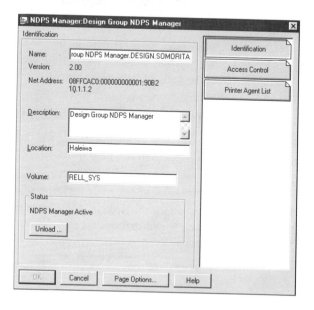

The Identification tab, as you saw when we created the NDPS Broker, includes Location and Description boxes, which are details for the administrator. You can set up access control by clicking the Access Control tab:

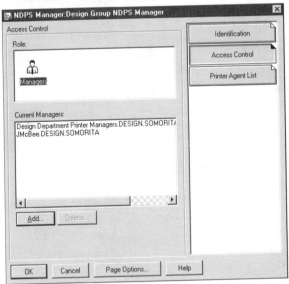

Select users or groups from the NDS tree. Our system will indicate that only the user JMcBee and the group Design Department Printer Managers can manage the Broker object Design Group NDPS Manager.

You need to load the NDPS Manager on the server where you want it to run. For example, to do this at the server console type:

```
LOAD NDPSM ".DESIGN GROUP NDPS MANAGER.DESIGN.SOMORITA"
```

Put this statement in the server's AUTOEXEC.NCF file (you don't need the quotation marks unless you have spaces in the name).

 WARNING You can use the NetWare Administrator to delete NDPS Manager objects, but if you do, NetWare Administrator will also delete any Printer objects associated with that NDPS Manager object.

Creating Printer Agents

8.3 Create Printer Agents

1. Open NetWare Administrator and highlight the appropriate container for the new NDPS Printer Agent object.
2. Choose New Object ➤ Create.
3. Choose NDPS Printer.
4. Fill in the NDPS Printer name.
5. Select Create a New Printer Agent.
6. Choose the NDPS Manager.
7. Specify a gateway type and click OK.
8. Select a printer model and Port Handler.
9. Select the connection type and port.
10. Select an IRQ or polled mode.

PART

II

Printer Agents represent the actual printers on the network. You can create and manage them at the file server console with the NDPS Manager (NDPSM.NLM) or at a workstation with NetWare Administrator. We'll look at using NetWare Administrator first. Locate the NDS context in which you want the Printer Agent to be located. Choose Create ➤ NDPS Printer to open the Create NDPS Printer dialog box:

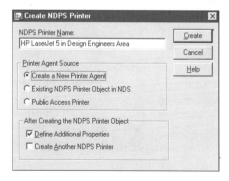

Managing the Network

Enter the name of the printer and select the Printer Agent source. You have three choices.

Create a New Printer Agent   Creates a new Printer Agent in the NDS directory.

Existing NDPS Printer Object in NDS   Allows you to select a previously configured NDPS Printer Agent.

Public Access Printer   Allows you to select a previously created public access printer. If none has been created, the list will be cleared.

Select the Printer Agent source, enter a name for the Printer Agent, and then click Create to open the Create Printer Agent dialog box:

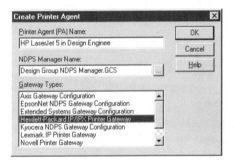

In this dialog box, you browse to select the NDPS Manager name and the gateway type. Choose Novell Printer Gateway for printers that are attached to workstations or that are attached directly to the server, or to send output of this printer to an existing NetWare print queue.

NetWare 5 included three gateways, one each from Novell, HP, and Xerox. NetWare 5.1 includes so many that a scroll bar is needed. All the ones you see, except for the Epson gateway I added, were in the red box.

 NOTE   You must create the NDPS Manager prior to creating Printer Agents.

Did you notice that our new Design Group NDPS Manager indicated that it was unavailable? Since this is the first Printer Agent we are adding to the network attached to that manager, the system will automatically load the NDPS Manager at this point in our installation.

When you select the printer type in the Configure Novell PDS for Printer Agent dialog box, the Configure Port Handler For Printer Agent dialog box opens. The Port

Handler represents the interface between the Print Device Subsystem (PDS), which stores information pertaining to the printer's capabilities, and the physical printer. The Port Handler manages the details of each print job, regardless of the port or protocol.

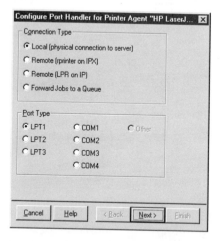

Connection Type and Port Type refer to how the printer is connected to which computer, whether on the server, on a workstation, or on the network. From here, the installation branches out significantly, depending on the connection type you choose.

- If you choose Local (physical connection to server), you need to choose a port type, and then on the next screen, you need to choose the parameters for that port. I recommend leaving the controller type at Auto Select and the IRQ parameters at None (polled mode).

- If you choose Remote (rprinter on IPX), you can configure this agent to use printers that are running in remote printer mode, such as printers on workstations that are running NPRINTER.EXE or NPTWIN95.EXE or on NetWare servers running NPRINTER.NLM. You must provide an SAP (Service Advertising Protocol) name. The number refers to the internal network number assigned to the server when IPX is bound to a network adapter, and the hexadecimal address refers to the address of that adapter. You can also provide restrictions on which IPX networks can send jobs to this remote printer and which MAC addresses can send jobs to this remote printer. If you do not want to restrict access, leave the fields blank.

- If you choose Remote (LPR on IP), you must specify the host name or IP address of a system running the LPD (line printer daemon) and the name of the printer.

- If you choose Forward Jobs To A Queue, you must specify a NetWare queue name. All print jobs to the Printer Agent will be forwarded to the queue. Whatever mechanism services the queue will actually print the job. You use this choice if you are setting up TCP/IP print servers or redirecting print jobs to Unix-based printers.

The Printer Agent has been created on the system. Now NDPS needs information about the printer drivers at the client workstations. The Select Printer Drivers dialog box will automatically appear next:

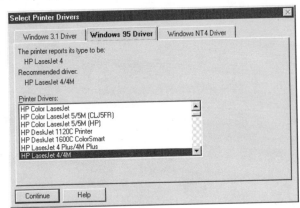

You identify printer drivers for your clients according to the operating systems in use, including Windows 3.1, Windows 95/98, and Windows NT.

If you prefer to set up or manage NPDS Printer Agents at the server console, follow these steps:

1. To load the NLM for the NDPS Manager, type **LOAD NDPSM** at the command prompt.

2. To select an NDPS Manager, highlight it.

3. To add a printer, press Insert.

4. To modify a printer, highlight it and press Enter.

The information is presented a bit differently from the NetWare Administrator screens. The Scheduler option allows you to identify the order of print jobs. Configuration Utilities refers to the NDPS gateway. When you select a storage volume, you can provide a size restriction and a timeout period in Job Wait Time. Press Escape to accept the entries, and press Enter on the printer to view its status.

Configuring an NDPS Printing Device

To view the NDPS Printer Control Panel, using NetWare Administrator, browse the NetWare Directory Services directory and locate the printer you want to control. Highlight the printer, right-click, and choose Details to open the Printer Control property page of the NDPS Printer. At this point, you are ready to use the bi-directional features of NDPS.

NOTE Not all printer types and printer configurations will support bi-directional printing.

Click the various buttons to familiarize yourself with the Printer Control property page. The Printer Control property page shown in Figure 8.7 describes a Hewlett-Packard printer.

FIGURE 8.7

The Hewlett-Packard Printer Control properties

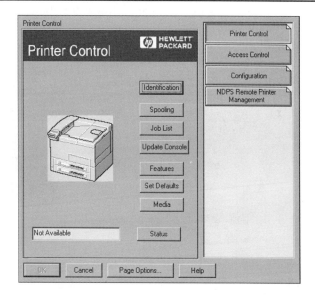

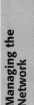

PART

II

Managing the Network

The Printer Control property page has eight buttons:

Identification Properties include the NDPS Manager and the Printer Agent name, as well as optional information that can be helpful to you as the Administrator, including description and location boxes.

Spooling Allows you to direct the location of the spool files on your server and restrict their size if you have constraints. You can also change the order of the print jobs—the default is first in, first out. Another item allows you to direct printer queues to this device.

Job List Displays current print jobs. You can view details of the spooled jobs.

Update Console Requests current information from the printer.

Features Contains information about the printer, including document formats (PostScript or PCL), speed, memory installed, duplex capabilities, resolution, and mechanism type (for example, laser).

Set Defaults   Allows you to add customized banners, select printer drivers, and set up pauses. This is also where the Notification options are located. Click the objects to notify a user when a print job has been completed.

Media   Refers to paper types to which you might want to restrict the printer. For example, you might designate a certain printer to print labels or forms.

Status   Allows you to view the printer's current status.

NDPS Printer Agent Access Control

A really nice feature in NetWare printing is the ability to set different levels of access to a network printer. NDPS printers are no exception. To set access to a particular printer, highlight the printer in NetWare Administrator, choose Object ➤ Details, and select the Access Control tab, as shown in Figure 8.8.

FIGURE 8.8

Printer access control entries

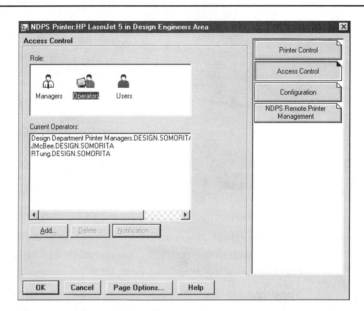

Notice that the group Design Department Printer Managers, user JMcBee, and user RTung have been assigned Operator permissions to this printer.

Users and groups can be assigned three roles:

Managers   Can perform any function required on the printer such as printing, managing others' print jobs, and changing device drivers. The person who created the printer is automatically a Manager.

Operators Can print to the printer as well as manage other people's print jobs and pause the printer. The person who created the printer is automatically an Operator.

Users Can send print jobs to the printer and delete their own print jobs from the printer. By default, when a new printer is created in an NDS container, the container is given User permissions to that printer. This means that all users located in that NDS container will have the User permission. The person who created the printer is automatically a User.

Configuring Print Jobs

If you were an administrator of any earlier version of NetWare, maybe at some point you had to create a print job configuration using the old DOS utility PRINTCON. You can also assign print jobs to NDPS Printer Agents, and I think you will find these much easier to set up and manage.

NDPS just calls these *configurations*. Configurations are properties assigned to NDPS Printer Agents that will control the default behavior of all print jobs or specific print jobs. To create a configuration for a Printer Agent, locate the agent in the NDS directory, display the Printer Agent's details, and then choose the Configuration tab to open the Configuration dialog box. Figure 8.9 shows a list of printer configurations for the NDPS printer HP LaserJet 5 in Design Engineers Area. To modify an existing configuration, highlight the configuration you want to modify and click the Modify button:

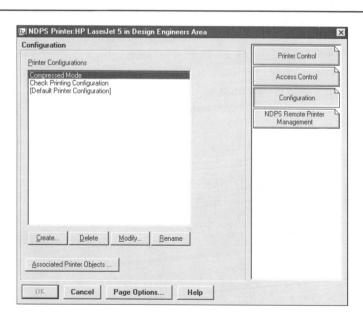

FIGURE 8.9

The Configuration dialog box

PART

II

Managing the Network

From this dialog box, you can create new printer configurations, modify and/or rename existing printer configurations, or delete printer configurations you no longer need.

To create a new printer configuration, click the Create button to open the Printer Configuration dialog box:

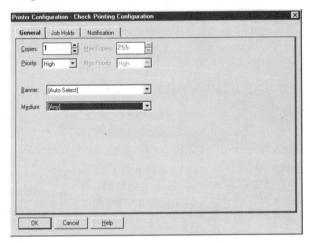

This dialog box has three tabs:

- General
- Job Holds
- Notification

From the General tab, you can set the number of copies, maximum number of copies, job priority, maximum priority, banner type, and the medium (form) on which jobs can print. Specifying a medium that is different from the current form mounted on the printer will pause the printer.

Using the Job Holds tab, as shown in Figure 8.10, you can specify the following options:

Operator Hold   Specifies that print jobs that use this configuration do not print until the operator releases them.

User Hold   Specifies that print jobs that use this configuration do not print until the user who printed them releases the job.

Pause Printer On Job Start   Causes the printer to pause before the print job starts. Only a printer operator or manager can restart the printer. The printer will remain paused for 15 minutes by default. You can also specify a notification message you want to see when the job causes the printer to pause.

Pause Printer On Job End   Is much the same as Pause Printer on Job Start except that this occurs when the job is completed. Both options might be useful when a particular form is required.

Retain Job For   Causes the print job to be retained after it is printed. You can control the length of time that the job is retained.

FIGURE 8.10

The Job Holds tab

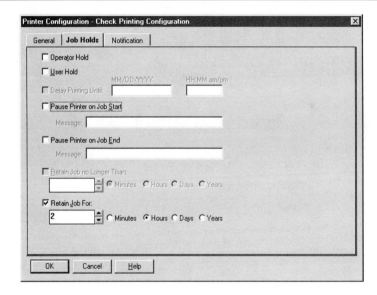

Some choices displayed in Figure 8.10 are available only when working with individual print job properties. These grayed-out choices include Delay Printing Until and Retain Job No Longer Than.

 NOTE   All options on the Job Holds tab are optional.

The events on the Notification tab, as shown in Figure 8.11, work in conjunction with the Event Notification Service to notify users or operators of specific events that can occur on the printer—low toner, out of paper, paper jams, and so on.

FIGURE 8.11

The Notification tab

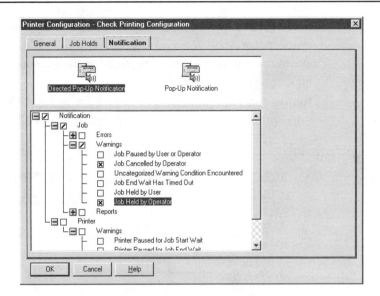

The Event Notification Service uses three types of delivery mechanisms:

- Pop-up messages
- E-mail
- Log files

The NDPS system provides an open architecture for vendors to develop other notification systems. How would you like to be paged every time a printer runs out of toner or gets a paper jam? The way I look at it, if my job is fixing paper jams, I am going to hear about it whether the printer beeps me or the user calls me. I would rather be on top of things and on my way to fix the problem when the user calls.

TIP Individual print jobs can have a unique print job configuration assigned to them through the Novell Printer Manager, discussed later in this chapter in the section "Managing Print Jobs from Windows Clients."

Assigning an NDPS Printer Agent to Service a NetWare Print Queue

If you are making a phased migration from traditional NetWare queue-based printing to NDPS Printer Agents, one feature you should be aware of is the ability to assign a

Printer Agent to service NetWare print queues. This is done from the Spooling Configuration dialog box, which is easy to miss if you don't know exactly where to look for it:

1. In the NDS tree, select the Printer Agent, and display the Printer Agent's details.

2. Select the Printer Control tab.

3. Choose Jobs ➤ Spooling Configuration to open the Spooling Configuration dialog box:

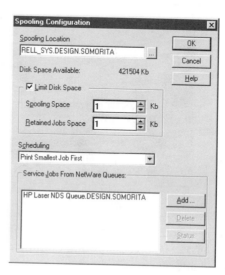

4. In the Service Jobs From NetWare Queues section, click the Add button and select the NetWare print queue that you want this Printer Agent to service.

From the Spooling Configuration dialog box, you can also set the maximum amount of disk space that the Printer Agent will use for spooling and the scheduling priority of jobs. The Scheduling drop-down list gives you three options:

- Print Smallest Job First
- Minimize Media Changes
- First In, First Out

Administering the NDPS Broker and Manager

You can perform a few tasks at the server console. The two NDPS NLMs that run at the server are the NDPS Broker (BROKER.NLM) and the NDPS Manager (NDPSM.NLM). Both have a console screen.

PART

II

Managing the
Network

Managing the NDPS Manager at the Console

As Figure 8.12 shows, you have two options:

- Printer Agent List
- NDPS Manager Status And Control

FIGURE 8.12

The NDPS Manager console main menu

Choose Printer Agent List to display a list of agents that have been assigned to this NDPS Manager. You can also create additional Printer Agents from this screen.

Choose NDPS Manager Status And Control to display the NDPS Manager Status And Control menu:

From the NDPS Manager Status And Control menu, you can see how long the NDPS Manager has been up and running as well as the number of Printer Agents assigned to this NDPS Manager. If you choose Status, you have four options:

Cancel Unload   Cancels a previously requested unload request.

Unload Immediately   Shuts down the NDPS Manager even if print jobs are currently printing.

Unload After Active Print Jobs   Stops the NDPS Manager after the currently active print jobs have completed. No new print jobs will be started.

Unload After All Print Jobs   Stops the NDPS Manager when no more print jobs are waiting to be printed.

Finally, you can choose Database Options to open the NDPS Manager Database Options menu:

From this menu, you have eight choices.

Examine Database   Allows you to view the database statistics and the number of objects within each object class.

Backup Database Options   Allows to you specify how often the database is backed up. The default is to back up the database daily at 1:00 A.M.

Backup Database Files   Backs up the current database.

Restore Database From Backup   Restores the database from the most recent backup.

Resynchronize Database Files   Rebuilds the database index file using the current database file.

View Log File   Displays the log file from the resynchronize operations. The log file is stored in SYS:SYSTEM\DPREPAIR.LOG.

Delete Log File   Deletes the SYS:SYSTEM\DPREPAIR.LOG file.

Uninstall Database   Removes the NDPS Manager database and supporting directories.

Managing Brokers from the Console

The BROKER.NLM also has a console screen. It doesn't contain many options, but I didn't want it to feel left out (see Figure 8.13).

You use the Supported Services menu to enable or disable the three services that a Broker provides:

- Service Registry
- Event Notification
- Resource Management

PART

II

Managing the
Network

FIGURE 8.13

*The NDPS Broker
console screen*

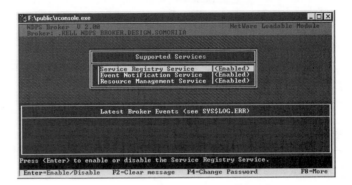

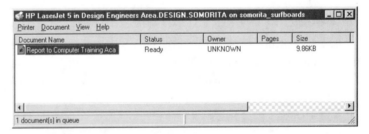

WARNING Don't disable services unless you know *exactly* what results to expect.

You can also notice in Figure 8.13 the Latest Broker Events field. This field contains error and warning messages for the five most recent events that were reported to the NDPS Broker; these events will also appear in the SYS:SYS$LOG.ERR file. To clear events from this screen, press F2.

Managing Print Jobs from Windows Clients

When a Windows 95/98 or Windows NT client prints, you can manage print jobs from the Windows Print Manager:

To display print jobs for a specific printer, choose Start ➤ Settings ➤ Printers, and double-click the desired printer.

From this interface, users can delete (cancel), restart, pause, or resume their own jobs. If they have Manager or Operator access control to this particular printer, they can also delete, restart, pause, or resume other people's print jobs.

Novell provides a better interface for managing NetWare printers—the Novell Printer Manager. For Windows 3.1 clients, the Novell Printer Manager program is SYS:PUBLIC\NWPMW16.EXE. For Windows 95/98/NT clients, the program is SYS:PUBLIC\WIN32\NWPMW32.EXE. Figure 8.14 shows the Details view for this program.

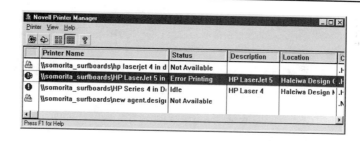

From this program, you can connect to other NDPS printers, manage print jobs, and browse or search for printers that will meet your requirements. Obviously, clients must have NDPS printing enabled to run this utility.

Supporting Queue-Based Clients

If NDPS is so new and improved, why would Novell continue to make the legacy queue-based system available? Particular circumstances make NDPS backward compatibility important for OS/2 and Macintosh clients, for older printers, and for third-party gateways that cannot send print jobs directly to Printer Agents. Or for people like me, who still have plenty of non-NDPS printers and well-established print queues that work quite well.

You can resolve this situation in two ways:

- By setting up printers that use only queues
- By adding queue services to an NDPS printer

The three print system objects' mandatory values relate this way:

- The Print Server object must know the name of the Printer object.
- The Printer object must know the name of the Print Queue object.

Before any printing can be initiated, you must create all three parts as objects inside NDS. The Name property of a Print Queue object is added to a Printer object's Print Queue list to identify the print queue servicing the printer. The Name property of a Printer object is added to a Print Server object's Printer list to establish that the

PART

II

Managing the Network

printer is servicing that print server. As you saw earlier with User objects, you can set several properties for each object in NetWare, but you must define a few critical properties before the objects will work.

Using Quick Setup in NetWare Administrator

IN A HURRY

8.4 Define New Print Objects with NetWare Administrator's Quick Setup

1. Open NetWare Administrator and highlight the container for the new printer and print queue.
2. Choose Tools ➤ Print Services Quick Setup (Non-NDPS).
3. Change any defaults.
4. Click OK to save the settings.

In NetWare Administrator, choose Tools ➤ Print Services Quick Setup (Non-NDPS) to create all three objects, or select them manually—NetWare Administrator adds the comment (non-NDPS object) to each. Fill in the details in the properties box. NetWare will use generic default names such as P1 and Q1 if you do not modify them. In the example in Figure 8.15, I added a queue-based printer that is attached to the parallel port of a workstation.

FIGURE 8.15

Quick queue setup

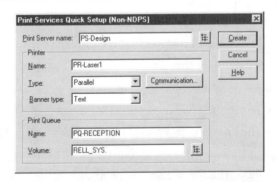

Click the Communication button to select a printer port and to specify whether it is hooked to an IRQ or is in polled mode.

TIP Use Auto Load only if the printer is connected directly to the print server.

NetWare Administrator adds these three objects—Printer, Print Server, and Print Queue—to your current NDS context.

Reviewing the Quick Setup Defaults

The Print Server, New Printer, and New Print Queue fields are filled in automatically. The default names are based on whether these are the first print objects that have been created in this context. If you want to change these names to something more descriptive, now is a good time to do so. Keep in mind the restrictions for naming objects, especially objects that can be referenced by NetWare 3.*x* clients or servers. I like longer names because they are more descriptive, but short names keep you out of trouble.

PART

II

Managing the
Network

 TIP Consider developing a naming standard so that you can easily look at an object name and figure out what the object actually does. I like to put PS- in front of print server names, PR- in front of printer names, and PQ- in front of print queue names.

If there is an existing print server, that name will be placed in the appropriate field. If there are several, you can choose the one you want by pressing Enter and selecting the desired Print Server object from the pop-up list that appears.

Two other values need specific attention at this point. The first field to think about is Print Queue Volume, RELL_SYS in Figure 8.15.

This question never came up in earlier versions of NetWare. The print queues have always been on the SYS: volume, no matter how many volumes your server had. This led to problems at times, since print queues can overrun the space allotted to them. If that overloaded volume is SYS:, bad things can happen, such as your server shutting down. When there is no open disk space on the SYS: volume, the operating system loses its mind.

Starting with NetWare 4, you were given the choice of placing the printer queues on any volume you want. This will not prevent print queues from clogging up now and then and overflowing (sounds like a sink, doesn't it?). But when they do overrun the available disk space, the volume that shuts down won't be SYS:. Your network will continue to operate, and you can fix the print queue problem without the added pressure of trying to restart the file server operating system with a full SYS: volume.

Let's pretend server RELL has only one hard disk volume; one of the three volumes is a CD-ROM drive, and one is the NSS_Admin volume. Since I've always put print queues on SYS:, that is where I like to put them. I'm not as paranoid about this as about some things. If your network must be up every minute possible, however, the placement of the print queues is just one small detail to consider. Moving the print queues off of the SYS: volume can save you a network crash, and it's worth the move for that reason. I have had servers in the past that had their SYS: volumes filled because of printing large quantities in a very short period.

The second item you may want to change is the Connection Type field, found by looking in the Printer Type section and clicking the Communication button. By default, the printer is loaded manually. If this printer is attached directly to a file server, you can change to Auto Load so that the NPRINTER.NLM is loaded automatically when the print server starts. This is handy and is encouraged if you have the printer hanging directly from the server, though I tend to discourage connecting printers directly to the server.

The defaults will work for most users. If you're not sure they'll work, the quick setup offers an easy way to set them and see if any modifications are necessary.

Saving the Setup

Once you make your peace with the defaults or change those that bother you, press F10 to save the setup. You will see a message stating that the printer information is being saved and that this could take as long as 60 seconds. The creation process won't really take 60 seconds unless your network is huge or you're setting up a Printer object for a remote context.

Once this is finished, all users in the context with the new Printer, Print Queue, and Print Server objects will have the rights to use them. Users outside the context of the Printer object must be granted the rights to use your new setup. This comes later.

Creating the Print Queue Object with NetWare Administrator

IN A HURRY

8.5 Create a Print Queue Object

1. Open NetWare Administrator and highlight the container for the new Print Queue object.
2. Press Insert to open the New Object dialog box, and choose Print Queue (highlight it and press Enter).
3. Keep the Print Queue object as a Directory Service Queue or click Reference A Bindery Queue.

Continued

> ## IN A HURRY CONTINUED
>
> **4.** Provide a name for the Print Queue object.
>
> **5.** Supply a name for the Print Queue volume (type it or click the Browse button to select a volume).
>
> **6.** Click Create to exit the dialog box and create the Print Queue object.

As always, these administrative chores should be performed by either the Admin user or equivalent. Or if you prefer (as I often do), a user with security equivalence to Admin (or with supervisory authority in the container) will work just as well for all NetWare administrative activities.

After logging in as an appropriate user, start NetWare Administrator. Open the NDS tree and highlight the container that will be the context for your new Print Queue object. Press Insert to open the New Object dialog box. Your screen should approximate the one shown in Figure 8.16. The New Object dialog box shows your container in the upper-left corner. Our goal now is to create a Print Queue. Choosing this option opens the Create Print Queue dialog box, which is a typical dialog box for creating a new object.

FIGURE 8.16

Preparing to produce the printing system

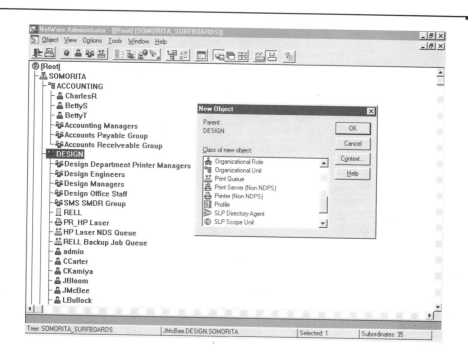

Fill in all fields by clicking, typing, or browsing. The first two options at the top of the dialog box offer a choice of making this Print Queue object a Directory Service Queue or a Bindery Queue, for NetWare 3.x. The default is Directory Service Queue, and the setting should stay that way for all new queues created inside NDS, unless you must support NetWare 3.x printing devices.

The Print Queue Name field is mandatory. The Print Queue name must be unique for the context. Keep in mind the restrictions for object names, especially objects referenced by NetWare 3.x clients or servers.

The Print Queue Volume field must be filled in as well. You can type the volume name, but it's easier to click the Browse button (the button at the right end of the field), which pops open the Select Object dialog box. In Figure 8.17, the dialog box shows the applicable objects in our current context, DESIGN.SOMORITA.

FIGURE 8.17

Configuring our new Print Queue object

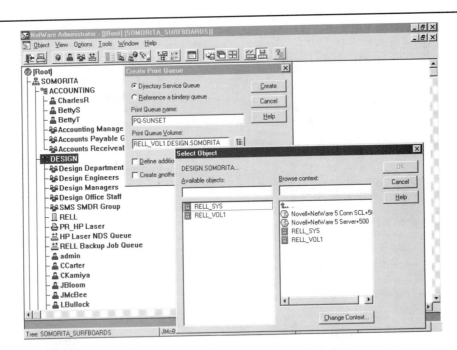

This dialog box illustrates an important point: The Print Queue object for DESIGN .SOMORITA can exist on a volume and even in another context if necessary. The right side of the Select Object dialog box has a Browse Context window, showing the volumes in our current context. You can click the up arrow and search for other volumes on the network. When the Volume object you want shows in the Available Objects box on the left side, highlight that volume and click OK. As mentioned earlier, in early NetWare versions, print queues were always on the SYS: volume. NetWare 5.1

allows you to place printer queues on any volume. There are two volumes on server RELL. I chose the volume called VOL1.

The last two lines in the Create Print Queue dialog box are either/or choices. When you check Define Additional Properties (the default) and click OK, the system takes you to the Properties dialog box. If you are creating multiple print queues and plan on defining them later, you can check Create Another Print Queue. When you exit this dialog box, a new Create Print Queue dialog box will appear, awaiting the name of the next print queue to be created.

These two checkboxes are mutually exclusive, and they are both optional. (Don't you think that these checkboxes should be radio buttons? Hello? Novell? Is anyone listening?) I find it easier to configure an object immediately upon creation, but you cannot. If you are creating multiple objects, you will certainly need to return later for configuration.

When you've finished with this dialog box, click Create. If you checked the Define Additional Properties box, NetWare Administrator will immediately open the Print Queue: dialog box for the Print Queue object you just created.

PART
II

Managing the
Network

Taking Advantage of Power Users

Since a print queue is a workgroup-type item, decentralized management makes a great deal of sense. Any time users can control their part of the network, they feel more in control of their networking environment. Printing, since it's so localized and important to most groups, is a great area in which to grant some level of management authority to the workgroup. Besides that, it keeps you from being interrupted every time someone sends a PostScript file to a non-PostScript printer, causing it to go crazy. That kind of problem is best handled by an area workgroup manager.

Power users, the ones who know more about computers and networking than anyone else in the department, are good candidates for providing administrative help. Whether you make these men and women official helpers or they do it on an unofficial basis, the service they provide will always be more timely than that from a central support group.

Does that hurt your feelings? It shouldn't, if you understand how close-knit departments work. When a problem appears, everyone in the department turns to their expert, the power user, first. If he or she isn't available, they call the official support people. If the power user can't solve the problem, he or she is expected to make contact with the support department.

In the early days, there was no network career path and certification. The folks who became the network support group were all power users who found computers more fun than bookkeeping or inventory management or payroll or chemistry. Power users are a valuable resource for you; work with them rather than against them.

Creating the Printer Object with NetWare Administrator

8.6 Create a Printer Object

1. Open NetWare Administrator and highlight the container for the new Printer object.
2. Press Insert and choose Printer (Non-NDPS) from the New Object dialog box.
3. Provide a name for the printer (the name must be unique in this context).
4. Click Create to exit the dialog box and create the Printer object.

As an appropriate user, start the NetWare Administrator program. Choose the container to hold the new Printer (Non-NDPS) object and press Insert to open the New Object dialog box. Highlight Printer and press Enter.

Figure 8.18 shows the sparse dialog box labeled Create Printer. Here you can see another advantage of NDS in general and better NetWare printing in particular. The name for a printer can be short and sweet, because it will be identified in its context (PR-LASER1.DESIGN.SOMORITA). In earlier NetWare versions, each printer defined on a server needed to be uniquely named. With the hierarchical naming conventions of NDS, for example, PR-LASER1 is a valid name a dozen times across the network, as long as each PR-LASER1 is in a different context. All users in their home context can reference PR-LASER1 and get to their default printer. That said, keep in mind the restrictions for naming objects, especially objects that can be referenced by NetWare 3.x clients or servers.

You must configure more items for a Printer object before it can be used. You will need to check the Define Additional Properties box now and define these values immediately, or you'll need to remember to come back and provide the values later. If you plan on setting up more printers now, check the Create Another Printer box.

Neither of these boxes must be checked to create the Printer object. But if you get interrupted during your workday, it's better to define the object as soon as you create it. Otherwise you can get dragged away from your desk if you forgot to configure a critical value.

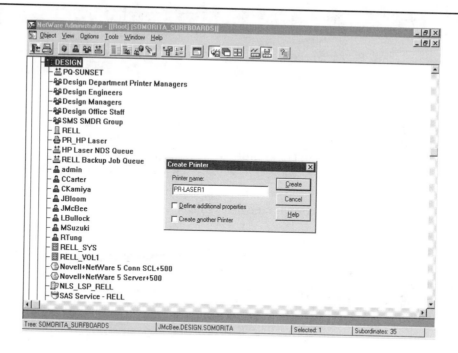

FIGURE 8.18

Naming your new printer

You must define the following mandatory values for this printer before it will be operational:

- Printer type (parallel or serial)
- Printer port (LPT or COM)
- Whether to use interrupts or the new polling method
- Whether to load the print server software manually or automatically

Creating the Print Server Object with NetWare Administrator

IN A HURRY

8.7 Create a Print Server Object

1. Open NetWare Administrator and highlight the container for the new Print Server object.
2. Press Insert and choose Print Server (Non-NDPS) from the New Object dialog box.

Continued

IN A HURRY CONTINUED

3. Provide the Print Server object name.

4. Click Create to exit the dialog box and create the Print Server object.

Once again, log in as an appropriate user to administer your network. Start the Net-Ware Administrator program. Highlight the container in which to place your Print Server object, and press Insert to open the New Object dialog box.

This dialog box lists the objects you have the authority to create in this context. Highlight Print Server (Non-NDPS) and press Enter. Figure 8.19 shows the Create Print Server dialog box with the name filled in.

FIGURE 8.19

Creating the PS-DESIGN Print Server object

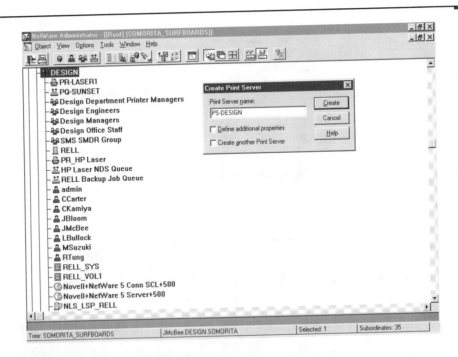

You must supply a proper object name for the print server. Remember the object-naming considerations for NDS, and remember the restrictions that apply to objects that can be accessed by NetWare Bindery Services clients.

The name for a Print Server object can be anything but often starts with PS, as in PS-DESIGN. The icons for all the print devices are different, but the icons are small.

Labeling the Print Server object distinctively will help you find it in the NDS tree. The users never reference the Print Server object, so a longer name will not be an inconvenience.

The Define Additional Properties and Create Another Print Server checkboxes are optional items. There's little reason to have more than one or two print servers active in a context, so you'll probably move right on to Define Additional Properties.

When you click the Create button, the dialog box closes. The new Print Server object will appear in your NDS tree immediately. You still have a few things to take care of before it's operational, however. Continue, you're almost finished.

Specifying Print Queue Object Details with NetWare Administrator

The Print Queue object has many of the same properties as other objects in NetWare 5.1, plus a few extras. The queue was once the item most users identified with, since earlier NetWare versions forced users to direct print output to the queue and not to the printer. In NetWare 5.1, the user is free to address either the printer or the print queue and get the same result.

The next five sections go through all the areas of Print Queue object management. However, queues tend to get running and stay running. You shouldn't need to spend much time managing your print queues.

Print Queue Object Identification and Operator Flags

IN A HURRY

8.8 Identify the Print Queue Object and Set Operator Flags

1. Open NetWare Administrator and double-click the Print Queue object to be configured.

2. On the Identification page, supply Other Name, Description, Location, Department, and Organization values.

3. Change any of the Operator Flags options as necessary.

4. Click OK to save and exit.

The Print Queue Identification page has the same properties that most other objects have. What is new on this page is the Operator Flags section, with a set of checkboxes.

While connected to the network as a user with appropriate permissions, start the NetWare Administrator program. Move through the NDS tree until the Print Queue object you want to manage is visible. Double-click the Print Queue object, or highlight the object and press the Enter key. Either way, the Print Queue object dialog box appears, with the Identification page showing.

The first two lines on this screen, Name and Volume, cannot be changed. These match the two mandatory fields entered during the creation of the Print Queue object. The other fields set the standard Identification values:

Other Name   Any other identification labels used for this object. Multiple entries are allowed.

Description   Free-form text window. Searches must match the entire contents of the Description field to succeed.

Location   Physical location of this object. Multiple entries are allowed.

Department   Shows the company department to which this object reports. Multiple entries are allowed.

Organization   Shows the Organization to which this object reports. Multiple entries are allowed.

Figure 8.20 shows the Print Queue object dialog box for the queue we set up in the previous section. The values in the fields are strictly informational; they do not affect your network settings.

FIGURE 8.20

Identifying a Print Queue object

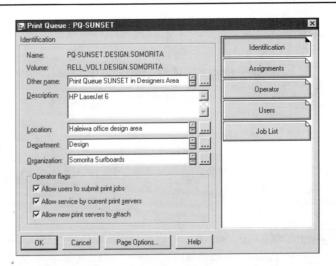

The Operator Flags choices are in the bottom-left corner of the dialog box. The choices and definitions are:

Allow Users to Submit Print Jobs   When checked, queue users can submit print jobs to the queue.

Allow Service by Current Print Servers   When checked, assigned print servers can transfer jobs in the print queue to the proper printer.

Allow New Print Servers to Attach   When checked, allows print servers to attach to the queue.

You might remove the check for the first flag so that users can't send jobs to clog a full or problematic print queue. If a print server is being replaced or modified, these flags will unhook the connection between server and queue.

Viewing Print Queue Assignments

IN A HURRY

8.9 View Print Queue Assignments

1. Open NetWare Administrator and double-click the Print Queue object to be configured.
2. Click the Assignments button.
3. View the information.
4. Click Cancel to exit.

You can't make your print queue assignments from the Print Queue object, but you can see the assignments that have been made. The Assignments page is purely informational. Take a look at Figure 8.21 and see the blank screen. In a bit, we'll see how the information has been filled in for us on the Printer and Print Server screens.

While connected to the network as an appropriate user, start the NetWare Administration program. Move through the NDS tree until the Print Queue object of interest is visible. Double-click the Print Queue object, or highlight the object and press Enter. Click the Assignments tab on the right side of the dialog box.

The top section of the dialog box, Authorized Print Servers, will be filled with print servers supporting this queue. Those assignments will be made in the Print Server dialog box.

PART

II

Managing the
Network

FIGURE 8.21

*An empty
Assignments screen*

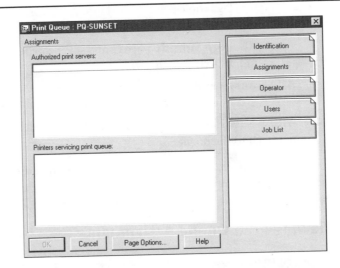

The lower section of the dialog box, Printers Servicing Print Queue, will be filled with the printer (or rarely, printers) being fed by this print queue. That connection will be made in the Printer dialog box.

If you are doing this in order, don't feel like you've overlooked something when you see this screen. The OK button at the bottom-left corner never becomes active, because you can never do anything here. Again, this dialog box is strictly for your information, not for making changes.

Managing Print Queue Operators

IN A HURRY

8.10 Add or Delete Print Queue Operators

1. Open NetWare Administrator and double-click the Print Queue object to configure.

2. Click the Operator button.

3. To add an operator, click the Add button. Choose the User object to add as an operator, and click OK in the Select Object dialog box.

4. To delete an operator, highlight the User object name in the Operators list and click Delete.

5. Click OK to save your changes.

A print queue operator can manage other users' print jobs, change the order of print jobs serviced, or delete those jobs from the print queue. A user listed as a print queue operator can also change the print queue status by modifying the three operator flags on the Identification page of the Print Queue dialog box. The Admin user or equivalent can assign users to be print queue operators.

As an appropriate user, such as the Admin user or equivalent, log in to the network and start the NetWare Administrator program. Browse the NDS tree listing until you find the Print Queue object to be modified. Double-click the Print Queue object, or highlight the object and press Enter. You can also open the Object drop-down menu and choose Details. Once the Print Queue dialog box is open, click the Operator button on the right side of the dialog box.

The list of current operators will appear in the Operators box that takes up the bulk of the dialog box. If the box is empty or if you want to add another User object to the list of operators, click the Add button.

The Select Object dialog box will open, with a view of the current context. The objects that can become print queue operators—User objects and Group objects—will appear in the Available Objects side of the dialog box. Even though they're listed, you cannot make Group objects into print queue operators. Notice that a user from another context can be designated as an operator. Highlight the desired user or users, and press Enter or click the OK button. The selected User objects will be copied into the list of print queue operators. Figure 8.22 shows this process. In the example, I added user CharlesR to the list because he is one of the power users from Accounting.

FIGURE 8.22

Adding User object CharlesR to the approved list of print queue operators

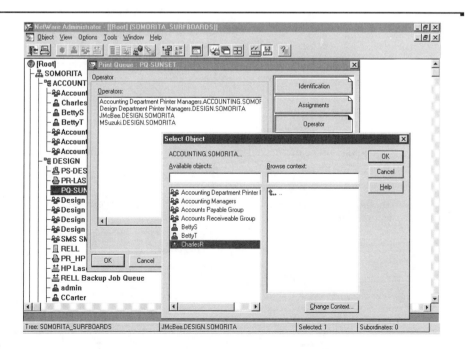

PART

II

Managing the Network

If you want to remove an existing print queue operator from the list, highlight that user name in the Operators box. When a name in the box is highlighted, the Delete button will become active. Click that Delete button, and the user will no longer have the authority to operate the print queue. The user is not deleted; only that user's ability to affect the print queue is removed.

Did you notice someone missing in the list of operators? The print queue was set up not by the Admin user, but by an Admin-equivalent user, JMcBee.DESIGN.SOMORITA. Unlike in earlier NetWare versions, the Admin user doesn't automatically control every piece of the network. Figure 8.23 shows the trustee rights of the Print Queue object PQ-SUNSET.DESIGN.SOMORITA. Notice that the Admin user does not have the Supervisor rights. Since an Admin-equivalent user, JMcBee.DESIGN.SOMORITA, created print queue PQ-SUNSET, that user has all those rights in place of Admin.

FIGURE 8.23

The Admin user's rights aren't absolute.

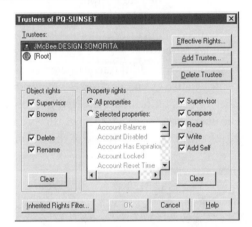

This never happened in NetWare 3.*x* systems. SUPERVISOR was always in control of each part of the network, no matter if a SUPERVISOR equivalent created the particular piece of the network under discussion. Thanks to NetWare Directory Services and the new Admin user profile in NetWare NDS networks, distributed networks can be administered by groups of managers, with more power going to the manager who creates objects than some (possibly) remote super-manager such as SUPERVISOR.

Managing Users in the Print Queue List

IN A HURRY

8.11 Add or Delete Print Queue Users

1. Open NetWare Administrator and double-click the Print Queue object to configure.

2. Click the Users button.

3. To add a user to the print queue's Users list, click the Add button, choose the User object, and click OK in the Select Object dialog box.

4. To delete a user, highlight the User object name in the Users list and click Delete.

5. Click OK to save your changes.

The list of approved users for a print queue automatically includes those users in the same context as the print queue. Others, both individual users and groups, can also use the print queue when listed on the Users page of the Print Queue dialog box.

While connected to the network as an appropriate user, start NetWare Administrator. Move through the NDS tree until the Print Queue object to be managed is visible. Double-click the Print Queue object or highlight the object and press Enter. Click the Users button on the right side of the dialog box.

In Figure 8.24, three objects are listed as users of the print queue. Since DESIGN .SOMORITA is the context where the print queue was created, all members of that context have access automatically. JMcBee.DESIGN.SOMORITA is the Admin-equivalent user who created the print queue, so he has access. I added the Accounting Managers group from the ACCOUNTING.SOMORITA context.

The Group object Marketing Managers, highlighted in the Select Object dialog box in Figure 8.24, includes users from other contexts besides DESIGN.SOMORITA. It's always easier to grant access to an object to a group rather than to each user individually.

CharlesR, seen in Figure 8.24, is a member of the Accounting Managers group and so should have access to the print queue in DESIGN.SOMORITA. The fact that he is not in the DESIGN.SOMORITA context doesn't matter. He can still be added to the print queue access list. Who else is a member of the Accounting Managers group? Is BettyT? Doesn't matter, nor does it matter who joins the group in the future. If the group has access to a network resource, all the users in the group also have access.

FIGURE 8.24

Adding a group to the list of users approved to use queue PQ-SUNSET

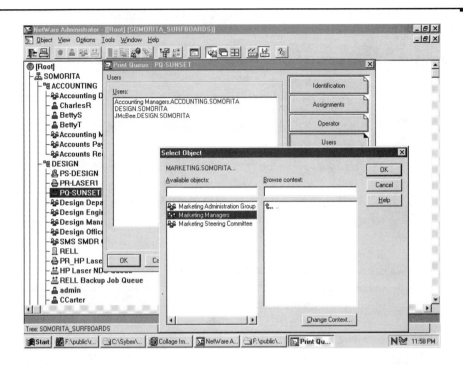

Deleting User objects from the access list to the print queue works the same as deleting objects from any other dialog box: highlight the user or users and click the Delete button. The button will become active when one or more users are highlighted in the Users box area. The User objects are not deleted; this just removes their ability to use the print queue.

Managing the Print Queue Job List and Job Details

IN A HURRY

8.12 View or Modify the Print Queue Job List

1. Open NetWare Administrator and double-click the Print Queue object to configure.
2. Click the Job List button.
3. To see details about a specific print job, highlight it and click the Job Details button.
4. To hold, resume, or delete the highlighted print job, click the appropriate button.
5. Click OK to save and exit.

When there is a problem with a printer or a print queue, the Job List page is the screen you will need to see. Print jobs stuck in limbo can be deleted, shuffled, postponed, or have their instructions modified. If you think that is a lot for one screen, you're right. The Job Details button opens another dialog box with lots of this information.

As an appropriate user, such as the Admin user or equivalent, log in to the network and start the NetWare Administrator program. Browse the NDS tree listing until you find the Print Queue object of interest. Double-click the Print Queue object, or highlight the object and press Enter. Once the Print Queue dialog box is open, click the Job List button on the right side.

A screen similar to Figure 8.25 appears. The waiting jobs are listed in the Job List box, in the order they were received. When a print job is highlighted, the four buttons below the list box become active.

FIGURE 8.25

*The print job control
screen*

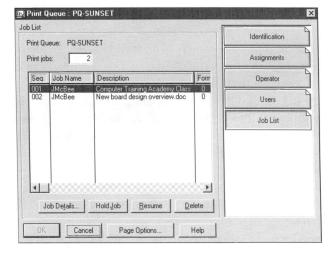

The buttons do the following:

Job Details   Opens another dialog box with specific details for each print job.

Hold Job   Holds a print job in the queue, postponing printing.

Resume   Releases a held job, allowing it to print.

Delete   Erases the highlighted print job or jobs.

Clicking the Job Details button opens another world of print job information. Figure 8.26 shows the details for a print job.

FIGURE 8.26

*Controlling every
aspect of a print job*

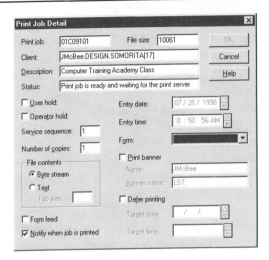

In the upper-left corner of the Print Job Detail dialog box is the Print Job number, an eight-digit hexadecimal number. This is the random number assigned by NetWare to a print job to track the job through the system. The number also appears in the Job List page shown in Figure 8.25. The print job ID is the sixth column, after Status, and is not even visible in Figure 8.25. You need to use the scroll bar to see the ID, but this number does you little good until you need to start troubleshooting.

Users can change the details of their own jobs only. If they highlight someone else's print job and look at the detail screen, the options will be gray and inactive. Administrators of the print queue have access to all options. The details for each print job are set by the user who submitted the job or by the default print configuration information for the user. For instance, a print job that is particularly important to a user can have a request for the user to be notified when printing is complete, but the default is for no notification.

Table 8.2 explains the fields on the Print Job Detail screen.

TABLE 8.2: FIELDS ON NETWARE ADMINISTRATOR'S PRINT JOB DETAIL SCREEN

Field	Description
Print Job	Unique system-assigned ID number for this job.
File Size	Size in bytes of this print job.
Client	User who submitted this job.
Description	Descriptive information, which typically shows captured printer port.

Continued ▶

TABLE 8.2 (CONTINUED): FIELDS ON NETWARE ADMINISTRATOR'S PRINT JOB DETAIL SCREEN

Field	Description
Status	Descriptive line about the print job. Ready, Held, or Active in the Job List dialog box translates to more information on this screen.
User Hold	Job held by original submitter.
Operator Hold	Job held by the print queue operator or administrator.
Service Sequence	This job's position in the print queue.
Number Of Copies	Instructions per print job for duplicates.
Byte Stream	Indicates the existence of non-ASCII data in the print file.
Text	Indicates the existence of only straight ASCII text in the print file.
Tab Size	Used only with text files, indicates the number of spaces used to represent the tab character inside the print stream.
Form Feed	Indicates whether a form-feed command is sent to the printer at the end of the print job.
Notify When Job Is Printed	Uses a system message to notify the user this print job is finished.
Entry Date	The date the print job was submitted.
Entry Time	The time the print job was submitted.
Form	Indicates whether a particular form will be used for this job. If a specific form was requested by the user when this job was submitted, that name will appear. In this screen, you can click the down arrow and choose any defined form.
Print Banner	Indicates whether the user wants this print job to print an identification banner as the first page of this print job.
Name	If Print Banner is checked, the name of the user submitting the print job.
Banner Name	If Print Banner is checked, the name of the print job. If not specified by the user, the printer port used by the CAPTURE program will be listed.
Defer Printing	Delay printing until the specified Target Date and Target Time. This provides an easy way to postpone long or graphically complex print jobs to a less-disruptive time.

PART

II

Managing the
Network

 NOTE   The File Contents section of the Print Job Detail dialog box is not a security breach. This concerns only the type of file data: byte stream or text. Actual file information does not appear on this screen.

Few print jobs require this level of control and intervention. These screens are valuable when dealing with a user who doesn't understand the printing process or who sends huge jobs that get in the way of other users. These two screens are also handy in a heavy printing environment, since users can hold or delete print jobs if they realize there is a mistake or potential problem. In a normal network with a decent printing system, the print jobs are done before anyone can think to change any details. But if you need to change details, this is the place.

Specifying Printer Object Details with NetWare Administrator

There are more reasons to manage the Printer object than the Print Queue object. The mandatory settings are quick and simple:

- Print Queue(s)
- Port
- Interrupt
- Location
- Printer type
- Name

The optional fields cover areas of description similar to those we saw with the Print Queue objects. Using at least some of these optional fields will help you track and manage network resources. Older versions of NetWare didn't offer any search capabilities to the manager, but NetWare 4 and NetWare 5.1 provide quite powerful search features.

Printer Object Identification

IN A HURRY

8.13 Identify the Printer Object

1. Open NetWare Administrator and double-click the Printer object to configure.
2. On the Identification page, supply values in the fields.
3. Click OK to save the information and exit.

The only field that is mandatory on the Printer Identification page is the one that can't be changed: the printer name. Everything else is useful for management and tracking, but not required.

After logging in to the system as the Admin user or equivalent, start the NetWare Administrator program. Browse the NDS tree until the desired Printer object is located. Double-click the Printer object name, or highlight the object and press Enter. The Identification page appears when the dialog box opens. Figure 8.27 shows some of the fields completed.

FIGURE 8.27

Printer object identification information

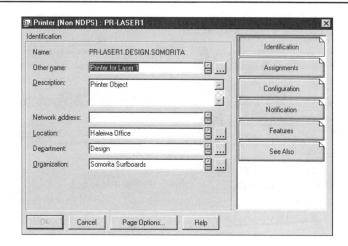

The fields on the Identification page are:

Other Name Any other identification labels used for this object. Multiple entries are allowed.

Description Free-form text window. Searches must match the entire contents of the Description field to succeed.

Network Address The eight-digit hexadecimal number of the file or print server hosting this printer.

Location Physical location of this object. Multiple entries are allowed.

Department The company department to which this object reports. Multiple entries are allowed.

Organization The organization to which this object reports. Multiple entries are allowed.

After you've filled in the Identification page information that you want to record, click OK to save your settings and exit.

NOTE Remember that the OK and Cancel buttons apply to every page of the dialog box, not just to the Identification page. If you have made changes on other pages and cancel this page, all changes will be lost if you proceed with the Cancel request. Fortunately, you will be warned by the system before this happens.

Tying the Printer Object to a Print Queue

IN A HURRY

8.14 Add or Delete a Print Queue Object from the Printer Object's List

1. Open NetWare Administrator and double-click the Printer object to modify.

2. Click the Assignments button.

3. To add a Print Queue object to the Printer object, click the Add button, highlight the desired Print Queue object, and click OK in the Select Object dialog box.

4. To delete a Print Queue object from the Printer object, highlight the Print Queue object and click Delete.

5. Click OK to save and exit.

The Assignments page is the spot where you tie the Printer object to the Print Queue object. This step is necessary before anything will print. We'll take the final step in activating the printer when we connect the printer and the print server in the next section.

While logged in as Admin or equivalent, start the NetWare Administrator program. Browse your NDS tree until you find the Printer object to set up or modify. Highlight the object and press Enter, or double-click it to open the Printer dialog box. Click the Assignments button on the right side of the dialog box to open a dialog box similar to the one shown in Figure 8.28.

Notice that something is missing: an entry for Print Server. We'll take care of that in the next section. Just below the empty Print Server field is the Print Queues box, also currently empty. This shows that the order in which you configure your print system doesn't really matter; some fields will stay empty for a time.

You can define many Print Queue objects in the Print Queues box, even queues from other containers. For now, we're adding the previously defined queue PQ-SUNSET to our printer PR-LASER1. Click the Add button to open the Select Object dialog box (as shown in Figure 8.28), find your desired Print Queue object, and double-click to assign it to the printer.

FIGURE 8.28

Tying a Printer object
to a Print Queue object

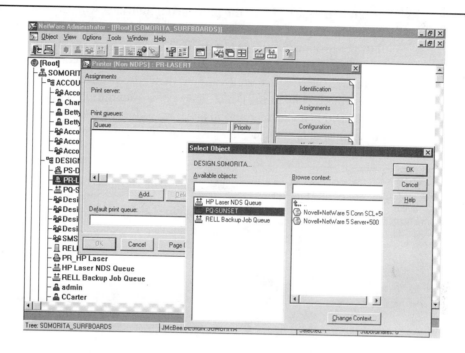

Once a highlighted Print Queue object is in the Printer dialog box, the Delete button becomes active. To delete (unhook) a print queue from this printer, just highlight the Print Queue object and click Delete. This action does not delete the Print Queue object; it just disconnects this queue from this printer.

Modifying Printer Object Configuration

IN A HURRY

8.15 Modify a Printer Object

1. Open NetWare Administrator and double-click the Printer object to modify.
2. Click the Configuration button.
3. Supply the Printer Type, Banner Type, Service Interval, Buffer Size, Starting Form, and Service Mode For Forms values, or accept the defaults.
4. Click the Communication button to configure the Printer Type values.
5. Click OK to save and exit.

The physical details of how the printer communicates with the network are set on the Configuration page. All manner of communication and printer details are controlled on this page of the Printer object dialog box.

Log in to the network as either Admin or equivalent. Start NetWare Administrator, and browse the NDS tree until you find the desired Printer object. Double-click the Printer object, or open the Details dialog box from the Object drop-down menu. Figure 8.29 shows the Configuration page. The values shown here are the defaults for a printer physically connected to a NetWare file server.

FIGURE 8.29

The default printer configuration information

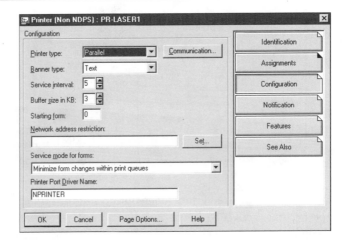

NOTE The server is not the best place to hang a printer in a busy network, but it used to be the only option NetWare gave you. Now, with workstation printers available to the entire network and third-party print servers doing so well, the server should be the last place to put a printer. Of course, a lightly loaded server or installation where every dollar counts will gladly use the server-attached print devices.

The first option, Printer Type, has seven possible values:

Other/Unknown OS/2 printers or those configured by NPRINTER.

Parallel Standard Centronics parallel printer, the most common option.

Serial Asynchronous serial printers, attached to a server or workstation via a serial port.

XNP eXtended NetWare Printer protocol, a high-performance system for shared network printing.

AppleTalk   Support for printers developed for the Macintosh network protocol.

Unix   Designates printers attached to Unix systems.

AIO   Asynchronous Input/Output. Designates printers attached to an asynchronous communications server or a multiple-port serial adapter.

The configuration details for each printer type will appear when you change the Printer Type field. They also appear when you click the Communication button next to that field. All printer types, except Other/Unknown and XNP, require unique settings in the Communication dialog box. Other/Unknown and XNP printers are configured at the devices that connect them to the network cabling or remote system. XNP supports Macintosh and Unix printing; printer details are set on that end.

The second field, Banner Type, has two options. Text is the default. The other choice is PostScript. Use the default of Text, even if you do have a PostScript printer. Most PostScript printers sold over the last few years handle text in this manner, but problems loom large if you send PostScript files to a non-PostScript printer. Keep the default until you can check your printer for problems, and then change the setting to PostScript if necessary.

The Service Interval field sets how many seconds go by before the print server checks the print queue for print jobs belonging to this printer. The default is five seconds; the range is one to 255 seconds.

The Buffer Size in KB field shows the maximum size a piece of data can be for this printer. The default is 3KB; the range goes to 20KB.

If printer forms are used, the Starting Form field sets the form number to make active when the print server brings the printer online. Any form value in the range zero through 255 is allowed.

If your security requirements demand that you restrict a printer to a particular address, set that address in the Network Address Restriction field. In extremely rare cases, print output can be copied to a recording device as well as printed. The two fields that pop up when you select this option (one each for the network and node) require you to list the network number and physical address of the print server or host.

The Service Mode For Forms field dictates how often the print server will demand that you change printer forms (predefined page length and width setups) to accommodate print output to forms that are not mounted. When a print job calls for such a form, the print server holds that print job until the form can be mounted. The options in this list are:

Minimize Form Changes within Print Queues   Requires you to change forms when print jobs demand a new form within this particular print queue, even if other print jobs in lower-priority queues for this printer are waiting to use the currently mounted form. This is the default setting.

PART

II

Managing the
Network

Change Forms As Needed   Forces the form changes for each print job as they appear. You will hate this setting, so don't use it if you can avoid it, unless you love servicing printers all day.

Minimize Form Changes Across Print Queues   The printer will print all print jobs for the mounted form before stopping and requesting a form change. High-priority print jobs with a different form will be placed behind low-priority print jobs using the mounted form.

Service Only Currently Mounted Form   The printer never requests a new form. All print jobs requiring a different form than the one mounted will be held indefinitely.

As you can see, multiple forms on one printer will always cause you grief. If there's any way to restrict your printing requirements so that no form changes are required on any printers, your life will go much more smoothly. Life is hard enough; don't make it worse by trying to print different forms on the same printer.

When you choose a Printer Type and click the Communication button, you see settings for the port, interrupts, and connection type for the chosen type of printer. Figure 8.30 shows the Communication dialog box with the default settings for a parallel printer.

FIGURE 8.30

Parallel connection details for the file server printer

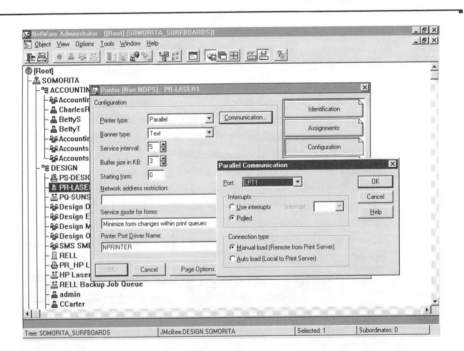

Parallel Printer Communication Settings For parallel printers, there are three choices for the Port field: LPT1, LPT2, and LPT3. The second area, Interrupts, offers a choice of the original LPT interrupt mode or the new polled printer communications.

Polled communications let the operating system check on the status of the print queues without requiring a hard interrupt from the print server. In most cases, the performance is as good as the interrupt method, without the potential of conflicting interrupt settings. There are only so many interrupts to go around in a PC file server, as you saw during the installation chapters. While the IRQ for the first parallel port is generally available (IRQ 7), LPT2 and LPT3 use IRQ 5, a popular number. More than one printer hanging from the file server, demanding an IRQ, can squeeze your installation options. This squeeze doesn't happen with the Polled setting.

The Connection Type refers to port driver loading (NPRINTER.NLM and NPRINTER.EXE are port drivers). Printers connected to the file server can have PSERVER.NLM load automatically, which also loads the NPRINTER.NLM at the same time. You can also load these port drivers manually at the server console.

Printers connected to workstations must always use the Manual Load option. Printers attached to the network cabling via internal or external print servers load their own port drivers.

Serial Printer Communication Settings For a serial printer, the Communication dialog box has these settings:

Port COM1 through COM4

Interrupts Use Interrupts or Polled

Connection Type Manual Load or Auto Load

Line Control - Baud 300 to 38,400

Data Bits 5 to 8

Stop Bits 1, 1.5, or 2

Parity None, Even, or Odd

X-on, X-off Yes or No

AppleTalk Printer Communication Settings AppleTalk printer settings require Macintosh services. See Appendix F for more information. For an AppleTalk printer, the Communication settings are:

Names Seen by Macintosh clients

Type of Printer LaserWriter, ImageWriter, L.Q., DeskWriter, PaintWriter XL, or PaintJet XL300

Zone AppleTalk zone number

Hide Printer (from direct Macintosh access) Yes or No

PART

II

Managing the
Network

Unix Printer Communication Settings   You must have the optional NetWare-to-Unix printing support installed, which is discussed in Chapter 14. The Communication dialog box settings for a Unix-type printer are:

> **Host Name**   Unix system host name
>
> **Printer Name**   Unix printer name as described on Unix host

AIO Printer Communication Settings   For an AIO printer, the Communication settings are:

> **Port**   Supplied by manufacturer
>
> **Hardware Type**   Supplied by manufacturer
>
> **Board Number**   Supplied by manufacturer
>
> **Line Control - Baud**   300 to 38,400
>
> **Data Bits**   5 to 8
>
> **Stop Bits**   1, 1.5, or 2
>
> **Parity**   None, Even, or Odd
>
> **X-on, X-off**   Yes or No

Notifying Users of Printer Problems

IN A HURRY

8.16 Specify Users to Notify of Printer Problems

1. Open NetWare Administrator and double-click the Printer object to modify.
2. Click the Notification button.
3. To add a user to the Notification list, click Add and select the user(s) to be notified about this printer's problems; then click OK in the Select Object dialog box.
4. To delete a user from the Notification list, highlight the user and click Delete.
5. Click OK to save and exit.

When a printer has a problem, you have two choices: wait until someone calls and complains, or use the printer notification option. The normal printer problems are lack of paper, jamming, or going offline. The quicker someone knows about these problems, the quicker the remedies.

That someone can be anyone on the network, not just you. The owner of the print job, along with any other users you specify, can get a message. Hey—another job for your workgroup administrator helper.

After connecting to the network as either Admin or equivalent, start the NetWare Administrator program. Browse through the NDS tree until you find the particular printer you want to send notifications.

 NOTE It's a good idea to decide your policy for printer notifications and configure the notification details during initial printer setup.

Add users to the list by clicking on the Add button, which opens the Select Object dialog box, as usual. The eligible objects to be notified appear in the Objects portion of the dialog box. Highlight your choice or choices, and click OK. Figure 8.31 shows an example of adding a user to the Notification list.

PART

II

FIGURE 8.31

The print job owner is on the notification list, and MSuzuki is being added.

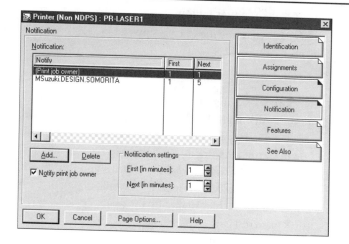

Managing the Network

Delete users from the list the same way you delete any item from a list in NetWare Administrator. Highlight the object and click Delete. The item is immediately deleted from the list but not from the system.

The Notification Settings box sets the length of time before the first notification is issued and also sets the delay between each subsequent alert. In a nice bit of programming, the NetWare developers support different settings for each user on the list.

When user MSuzuki is added to the Notification list, he will be given his first notice in one minute and the next notice in five minutes, by default. The print job owner is assumed to be more interested in the print job than anyone else on the list, so that user's notifications are more frequent by default. The one-minute delay before the first notification allows almost enough time to change a font cartridge or add paper.

If someone turns off a printer that lists you as one of its people to notify, you will be bombarded with messages about the printer being offline. Fortunately, these notification settings are easy to change.

Describing Printer Object Features

IN A HURRY

8.17 Describe Printer Features

1. Open NetWare Administrator and double-click the Printer object to modify.
2. Click the Features button.
3. Type the information in each applicable field; multiple values are allowed.
4. Click OK to save and exit.

In support of creating manageable networks, each Printer object has several Features properties. Although these have nothing to do with running the network or the printers, they are handy for inventory and tracking purposes.

Log in to the network as either Admin or equivalent. Start the NetWare Administrator program. Browse the NDS tree until you find the desired Printer object. Double-click the Printer object, or open the Details dialog box from the Object drop-down menu. Once the Printer dialog box is open, click Features. See a partially complete Features page in Figure 8.32.

None of this information is read from the printer itself. You must enter all the information in the format that makes sense for later searching. For instance, if you care only about HPGL (Hewlett-Packard Graphics Language) and not the differences for HPGL4 or HPGL5, type only HPGL in the Page Description Language field.

Each field with a "..." button to the far right supports multiple values. Click the "..." button to open a small dialog box, allowing you to add more values.

FIGURE 8.32

*Describing your
printer*

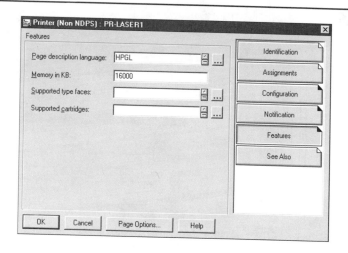

Listing Objects Associated with the Printer Object

IN A HURRY

8.18 Add Printer Object See Also Details

1. Open NetWare Administrator and double-click the Printer object to modify.
2. Click the See Also button.
3. Click Add, browse the NDS tree, and select objects for the See Also listing.
4. Click OK in the Select Object dialog box.
5. Click OK to save and exit.

Like many other objects, the Printer object includes a See Also page to list associated objects. These objects have no impact on the workings of the printer or the network. They are simply here to remind you of some connection between your current object and those listed.

Log in as an appropriate user and start NetWare Administrator. Browse the NDS tree and select the Printer object you want to modify, double-clicking to open the dialog box. Click See Also to open the page shown in Figure 8.33.

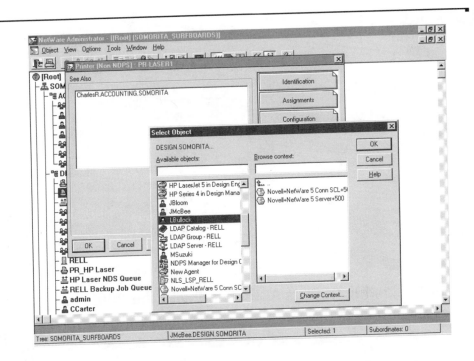

To add objects, click the Add button to open the Select Object dialog box. Browse and choose as many items as you want to place on the page. To delete objects from the box, highlight them and click Delete.

Specifying Print Server Object Details with NetWare Administrator

Now we're to the point of managing the Print Server object. You can do some of this from the server console hosting the print server software, but you can do more from within NetWare Administrator.

Some items in this section should look familiar by now. That's one of the advantages of NetWare Administrator: learn to manage one object, and you've learned to manage them all. Well, some details change, but the NetWare Administrator program makes those details easier to handle.

Print Server Object Identification

IN A HURRY

8.19 Identify the Print Server Object

1. Open NetWare Administrator and double-click the Print Server object to modify.
2. Provide information in the descriptive fields of the Identification page.
3. Click the Unload button to stop the Print Server.
4. Click Change Password to add or modify the Print Server password.
5. Click OK to save and exit.

Most Identification pages have helpful, but not active, buttons and information. The page for the Print Server object offers a few extras.

Connect to the network as either the Admin user or equivalent. Start the NetWare Administrator program. Cruise your NDS tree until you locate the Print Server object. Double-click the object, or highlight it and press Enter. You will see an Identification page, similar to the one in Figure 8.34.

PART

II

Managing the Network

FIGURE 8.34

The Print Server Identification page

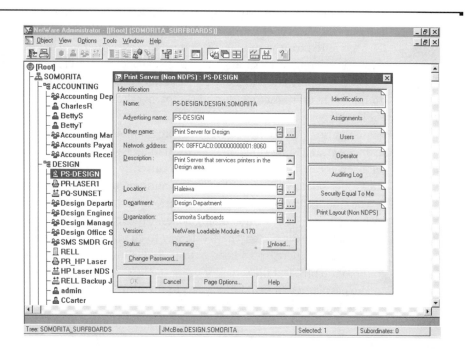

Some new things are tucked into the standard object properties:

Name   Full NDS name for this print server.

Advertising Name   The SAP (Service Advertising Protocol) name broadcast across the network every 60 seconds to tell the network this print server is available.

Other Name   Any other identification labels used for this object. Multiple entries are allowed.

Network Address   Protocol, internal address, and network address of the host server for this print server.

Description   Free-form text window. Searches must match the entire contents of the Description field to succeed.

Location   Physical location of this object. Multiple entries are allowed.

Department   The company department to which this object reports. Multiple entries are allowed.

Organization   The organization to which this object reports. Multiple entries are allowed.

Version   The PSERVER.NLM version running this print server.

Status   Print server status (Running, Down, or Going Down).

The last two fields on this page, Version and Status, are not fill-in-the-blank items. The running version of PSERVER.NLM for this server is the NetWare Loadable Module (NLM) referred to as version 4.170. Novell makes regular updates of NLMs available through the company's support Web site at support.novell.com or through NSE Pro (Network Support Encyclopedia, Professional Version). This information saves you from looking up the actual file and comparing the release date and file size to figure out if your NLM is in need of updating.

Status also refers to the PSERVER.NLM program. Although the Running and Down states are clear, Going Down may seem strange. The reason for this odd state is that the print server can be told to finish the jobs currently in the queues and then shut down. The Going Down state can last for many minutes, depending on the queue backlog.

The Change Password and Unload buttons on this Identification page are two that we haven't seen in any other dialog boxes. Unload refers to stopping the PSERVER.NLM program on the file server. That's one way to change the state from Running to Down. Unfortunately, there isn't a Load button. Restarting the print server requires either going to the physical file server or using the RCONSOLE program.

The password will help limit access to the print server. Every time the print server is loaded, the password must be entered.

When clicked, the Change Password button opens a dialog box allowing you to type the old password (for verification that you actually know the old password), type the new password, and retype the new password (for verification of your typing). If a password exists and you want to erase it, type the old password and then press Enter on the New Password line. A message box will ask you to verify that you are serious about eliminating the password.

Changing Print Server Assignments

IN A HURRY

8.20 Change Print Server Assignments

1. Open NetWare Administrator and double-click the Print Server object to modify.
2. Click the Assignments button.
3. To add a printer, click the Add button and double-click the printer to add.
4. To delete a printer, highlight the printer in the Printers box, then click Delete.
5. To change the printer number, highlight the printer in the Printers box, click the Printer Number button, type the new printer number, and click OK.
6. Click OK to save and exit.

PART

II

Here's the deal: Print Server objects work with Printer objects. Print Queue objects also work with Printer objects, even though Print Server objects take print jobs from Print Queue objects and feed them to Printer objects. Get all that? See why I recommend less paper and more e-mail?

For our purposes, it's enough to remember that print servers serve printers, and print queues handle print job traffic. So let's work with a print server.

To get to a print server, log in to the network as either Admin or equivalent. Start the NetWare Administrator program, and browse through your NDS tree until you find the Print Server object to investigate. Either double-click that object, or highlight it and press Enter. Then click the Assignments button on the right. Something akin to Figure 8.35 will appear.

To add a new printer, click the Add button to summon the Select Object dialog box. As before, cruise around the NDS tree and double-click the Printer object to add to the Print Server assignment list.

Deleting a printer assignment requires you to highlight the printer in the Printers box and click Delete. This eliminates the Printer object from this list but doesn't delete the object itself.

Managing the Network

FIGURE 8.35

Viewing and changing
print server printer
assignments

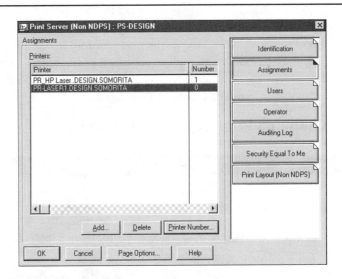

As you can see in Figure 8.35, you can change a printer number within the Print Server object by clicking the Printer Number button. Although most people don't know or care about this, the NPRINTER.NLM program requires, and NPRINTER.EXE allows, the loading of a port driver by specifying the print server name and logical printer number. This number can be referenced in batch files or applications requiring special printers. After the number is changed, the print server must be unloaded and reloaded for the changes to take effect.

Don't believe me? Check your server console, and after the line

```
Loading Module PSERVER.NLM
```

you will see version and language details, then:

```
Network printer PR-LASER1 (number 0) loaded
and attached to print server PS-DESIGN
```

This information goes by quickly when the server is loading, and it's easy to miss. It makes sense, when you think about it, that NetWare will need some unique numeric way to identify printers supported by each print server. So if you want to change these, you now know how. When finished, click OK to save the page and exit the Print Server dialog box.

Managing Print Server Users and Groups

Rights to use the Print Server object are not necessary in order to print. Only rights to the Print Queue object are necessary for printing; the rights to the Print Server object go along with that automatically.

Here are the advantages to being a user of a particular Print Server object. You can:

- Monitor the print server
- See the print server status
- Learn whether the print server needs some type of attention (rare, but possible)

IN A HURRY

8.21 Add or Delete Print Server Object Users and Groups

1. Open NetWare Administrator and double-click the Print Server object to modify.
2. Click the Users button.
3. To add a user or group, click the Add button and mark the User and Group objects.
4. To delete a User or Group object, highlight the object in the Users box, and click Delete.
5. Click OK to save and exit.

As the Admin or equivalent user, start the NetWare Administrator program. Browse the NDS tree until the proper Print Server object is spotted, then highlight it and press Enter, or right-click it, highlight Details, and press Enter. The Print Server object dialog box appears, print server name at the top. Figure 8.36 shows the Print Server object PS-DESIGN.

Assigning and Modifying Print Server Operators

IN A HURRY

8.22 Add or Delete Print Server Operators

1. Open NetWare Administrator and double-click the Print Server object to modify.
2. Click the Operator button.
3. To add a user or group, click the Add button, mark the User and Group objects to add, and click OK in the Select Object dialog box.
4. To delete a User or Group object, highlight the object in the Operators box, and then click Delete.
5. Click OK to save and exit.

PART

II

Managing the
Network

FIGURE 8.36

Adding a group to the
Print Server PS-
DESIGN access list

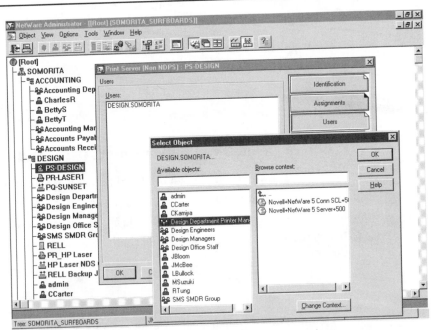

To add or delete a print server operator, log in to the network as Admin or equivalent, and start the NetWare Administrator program. Browse the NDS tree to find the print server of interest. Double-click the Print Server object name. Click the Operator button to see a screen similar to the one shown in Figure 8.37.

FIGURE 8.37

Adding a print server
helper

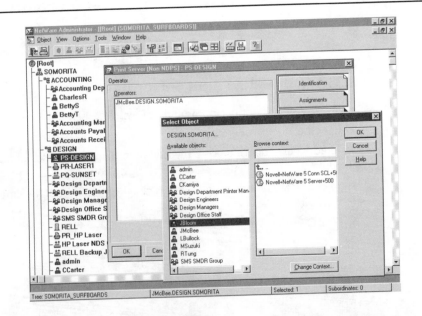

To add an operator, click the Add button and cruise the Select Object dialog box. Users and groups can be operators. Find the object(s) you want to list as a Print Server object operator, and click the OK button. This adds the chosen object(s) to the Operators box in the Print Server dialog box, as shown in Figure 8.37. Operators can see the print server status and shut down the print server. They also have authority to control the printers attached to the print server. Dead printer? An operator can reroute the printer output and the print jobs to a different print server until repair or replacement is finished.

Having a power user be a print server operator makes good sense. Having help with the print system from anyone makes more sense than trying to do it yourself. Notice that the only other operator listed so far is the user JMcBee. If this were you, would you want to answer every call for every paper jam and every form change?

Managing the Print Server Log

IN A HURRY

8.23 Manage the Print Server Auditing Log

1. Open NetWare Administrator and double-click the Print Server object to modify.
2. Click the Auditing Log button.
3. View the Auditing Log for the print server, or click View if the text box is empty.
4. To start logging, click the Enable Auditing button.
5. To turn off logging, click the Disable Auditing button.
6. To delete the log, click Delete.
7. Limit the log size by checking the Limit Size box and setting the maximum size.
8. Click OK to save and exit.

Log files, listings of what happened where and when, are a staple of the mainframe and Unix worlds. They are late getting to the PC world, but items such as the log for the print server help rectify that oversight. The Print Server object log file tracks information such as:

- The internal ID number the operating system assigned to the print job
- The form used (if any)
- The print job name (if any)
- The print queue name

- How many bytes a job took to print
- The user submitting the job
- When the job entered the print queue
- When the job actually printed
- Which printer serviced this job

Macintosh and Unix printers often supply this additional information:

- How long the print job took
- How many pages were printed

To see this information, connect to the network as either Admin or equivalent. Run the NetWare Administrator program and browse through the NDS tree until you find the print server whose log you want to check. Double-click the Print Server object, and click the Auditing Log button. Figure 8.38 shows the Auditing Log page for Print Server object PS-DESIGN.

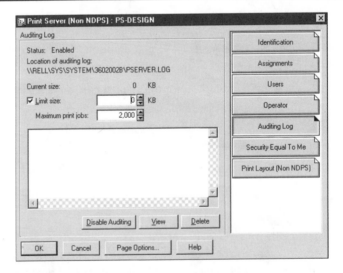

The top line, Status, indicates whether auditing is enabled. The status listed will be the opposite of the button in the bottom-left corner of the interior dialog box. If Status is Enabled, the button offers a choice to Disable.

The information in the Location Of Auditing Log field is important and not something you can change. It's important because Novell engineers realize that people who want this auditing information probably have a format they want to use. Since it's impossible to guess what that format will be, the log is kept as a fixed-record-length ASCII file. The log can be read with any text editor and can be managed by any database application that can import ASCII files.

By checking the Limit Size box, you can keep the log from growing forever and taking over your hard disk. But keep in mind, if the maximum size is reached, the log stops recording instead of overwriting the earlier information. If limits are necessary, put this task on your weekly checklist to keep the log from filling the space allotted and shutting down. You can change the size of the log by using the KB or Maximum Print Jobs text box scroll arrows. You can track nearly two million print jobs using 2GB of disk space. Audit to your heart's content.

The actual audit log is read through the scrolling text window in the bottom portion of the dialog box. The entire log will scroll through the text box, but no changes can be made. If you view the log once and then come back to view it before another print job has gone through, the log may not appear in the window. Run a small print job through the print server to restart things.

Speaking of restarting things, you must unload and restart the print server software after the log is enabled (the default is disabled). Once the software is started, run a quick print job through to make sure the log picks up the information.

PART

II

Managing the
Network

The Auditing Log and Your Quest for a New Printer

How could you use the numbers in the print server auditing log? Say you want another printer, and your boss doesn't want to pay for it.

Track all the print jobs for the time going into the queue and the time coming out of the printer. If this is more than a minute or three, whip out your lost productivity argument. Paint visual images of high-priced employees waiting in line at the printer, cursing and complaining. Try to find a huge graphics file printout that backed up the queue for 20 minutes as your example. If your boss weakens, add a request for more file server memory. You always need file server memory, and more memory helps everything.

If this doesn't work, ask your boss to list the workgroup personnel in order of printing importance. Lower-rated folks can be shunted to a print queue with a lower priority than the important printer people. Bosses hate to make this kind of decision and will often authorize new hardware to avoid making this list. Remember to ask for more server memory while your boss staggers on the ropes.

Viewing the Print Layout in NetWare Administrator

IN A HURRY

8.24 View the Print Layout

1. Open NetWare Administrator and double-click the Print Server object.
2. Click the Print Layout (Non-NDPS) button.
3. To update the diagram, click Update.
4. To check the status of a listed object, highlight the object and click Status.
5. Double-click any object to collapse subordinate objects if the display is crowded.

The connections between printers, print queues, and print servers are somewhat abstract and hard to visualize. That's why Novell included a graphical representation of the print system interrelationships.

To see this grand diagram, log in as either Admin or equivalent. Start the NetWare Administrator program, browse the NDS tree until the Print Server object you want to check appears, and double-click it. Click the Print Layout button. A diagram similar to Figure 8.39 appears (the Status box appears after highlighting an object and clicking Status).

FIGURE 8.39

The three legs (Print Server PS-DESIGN, Printer PR-LASER1, and Print Queue PQ-SUNSET) supporting shared printing and status information

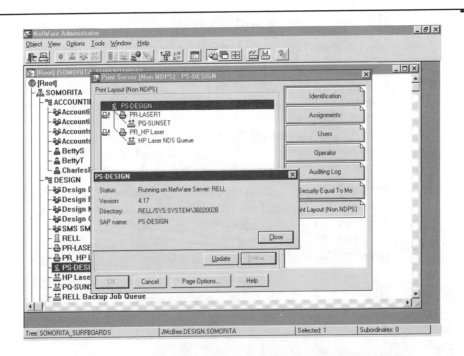

The Print Layout box shows standard icons for the Print Server object, the Printer object, and the Print Queue object.

PR-LASER1.DESIGN.SOMORITA has an exclamation point beside it, indicating trouble. Perhaps one of our programmers has sent some output there that locked it up, or perhaps it's just out of paper (or maybe I just unplugged it!). The printer can be rerouted to another Print Server object so that users addressing that printer can still print. I used the Assignments page to make this happen. This movement is temporary, as shown by the dashed lines connecting printers and print queues.

To see the status of any print object, highlight the object and click the Status button. If you prefer, you can click the print object with the right button to open the Status box automatically. The box on display in Figure 8.39 is showing us some details for PS-DESIGN.DESIGN.SOMORITA.

This same information can be seen through the Organization dialog box. Open the dialog box for an Organization object with printing defined, and click the Print Layout button. The resulting page will look almost exactly like what is shown in Figure 8.39.

Viewing and Understanding Printer Status with NetWare Administrator

IN A HURRY

8.25 View and Change the Printer Status

1. Open NetWare Administrator and double-click the Printer object to modify.
2. Click the Printer Status button.
3. Use the Pause, Start, Mount Form, Eject Page, or Abort Job command buttons, as necessary.
4. Click OK to save and exit.

Now that we know about the three components that are part of every print job (the printer, the print queue, and the print server), we can better understand the Printer Status information. Although you won't spend lots of time checking this screen, it's handy when someone calls with a problem. If the problem is the wrong form or a huge job clogging the printer, you can tell immediately.

The NetWare Administrator program stays in communication with the servers after the program is started. This makes the Printer Status page real-time. When your printer goes from Waiting For Job to Printing as you watch, you'll understand the advantages of real-time management.

PART

II

Managing the
Network

Start as an appropriate user on the network, and run NetWare Administrator. Browse the NDS tree until you find the printer to check, and double-click the Printer object. Click the Printer Status button. If you are not logged in as an administrator or user with authority to see printer information, the screen will look more like Figure 8.27 (the Printer Identification page), earlier in this chapter, than Figure 8.40. Notice that the buttons on the right side include Printer Status here, but not in the earlier figure. Table 8.3 explains the fields listed on the Printer Status page.

FIGURE 8.40

Checking a printer while printing

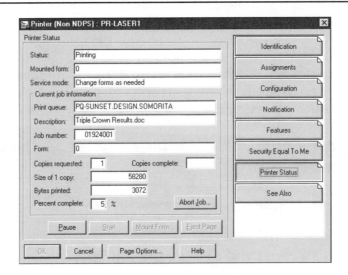

TABLE 8.3: FIELDS ON NETWARE ADMINISTRATOR'S PRINTER STATUS PAGE

Field	Description
Status	The printer status: Not Connected, Waiting For Form, Out Of Paper, Printing, Paused, Stopped, Offline, Private, Waiting For Job, or Ready To Go Down.
Mounted Form	Defined form now loaded. If another form is needed, click Mount Form for a dialog box listing all defined forms.
Service Mode	How jobs in the queue are processed according to forms usage.
Current Job Information	Listing of details about the current print job.
Print Queue	Queue submitting this print job.
Description	Filename or port captured.
Job Number	Internal number assigned to this print job.

Continued ▶

TABLE 8.3 (CONTINUED): FIELDS ON NETWARE ADMINISTRATOR'S PRINTER STATUS PAGE	
Field	**Description**
Form	Form used to print this job (if any).
Copies Requested	Requested copies per print job owner.
Copies Complete	If multiple copies are in process, which copy is currently printing.
Size Of 1 Copy	Same as File Size field in the details portion for the Print Queue object.
Bytes Printed	Bytes processed by the printer for this print job.
Percent Complete	Ratio, listed per individual print job even for multiple-copy jobs.

The Printer Status page has four command buttons:

Pause   Stops the current job or changes printer from Waiting For Job to Stopped.

Start   Moves from Paused to Printing, Stopped to Printing, or Stopped to Waiting For Job.

Mount Form   When clicked, opens a dialog box that lists the available forms and allows the form to be changed.

Eject Page   A long-distance form-feed command to push a page from the printer.

Figure 8.41 shows the same type of printer status information from the PSERVER.NLM console at the file server. However, opening the Printer Status page for the Printer object is easier than going to the server physically. It's also more friendly and usable than running the PSERVER screen with RCONSOLE.

PART

II

Managing the Network

FIGURE 8.41

Printer PR-LASER1 status as viewed from the PSERVER.NLM at the server console

Creating and Modifying Printer Forms with NetWare Administrator

8.26 Manage Printer Forms

1. Open NetWare Administrator, highlight the container to hold the Printer Form object, and press Enter.

2. Click the Printer Forms (Non-NDPS) button.

3. To create a Printer Form object, click Create and fill in the form name, number, paper length, and width.

4. To modify a Printer Form object, click Modify and change the form name, number, paper length, or width.

5. To delete a Printer Form object, highlight the object and click Delete.

6. Click OK to save and exit.

All this talk about printer forms might lead you to believe they are some complex, amazing, outstanding feature of the printing world. Alas, they only set the paper boundaries. You can set length and width, but that's it.

Still, if you hate to print a regular letter on legal-sized paper or sometimes make the mistake of printing a legal-size document on letter-sized paper, these forms can be useful. The NetWare Printer Forms feature can prevent these types of errors.

Different forms can certainly be the same length and width, of course. Just because the Request for Office Supplies form is the same size as the Request for Overtime form doesn't mean the two are interchangeable. The form is created at the container level, and once created, it is available to all printers in the container.

 TIP Life is too short—don't use forms if you can avoid them. Printers are cheaper than management time for something as common as printing. If you have a need for both letter and legal printing, dedicate a printer to each. This might not make much sense in the capital budget, but it will certainly save management time, user time, frustration, and probably wasted paper.

After connecting to the network as either Admin or equivalent, start NetWare. Since Printer Form objects are a container feature rather than a printer feature, highlight the container to hold the form. Once the container is highlighted, either press Enter or right-click to open the menu for the container, and then click Details. Click the Printer Forms button on the right side to open the dialog box shown in Figure 8.42.

FIGURE 8.42

Modifying a printer form for the DESIGN.SOMORITA container

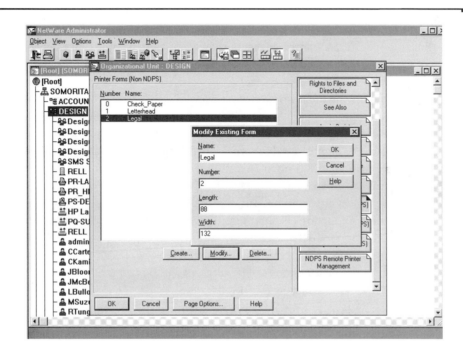

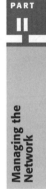

PART

II

Managing the Network

The Name field can contain a maximum of 12 alphanumeric characters. The first character must be a letter, and the name must be unique. If you use spaces, they appear as underscores.

The limits for the other printer form fields are:

Number   0 to 254

Length   1 to 55

Width   1 to 999

These numbers are for your reference only. This information doesn't force any action or limitations on your printer; it only provides a way to reference different paper sizes and hold printing until the right-sized paper is loaded.

Creating and Modifying Print Devices with NetWare Administrator

Here is another throwback feature, back to the time the laser printer was new and applications didn't know how to exploit all the features available. As a result, Net-Ware offered ways to set different print modes for printers with the few crude fonts and features available at the time.

Today this is less necessary, since the GUI has overwhelmed both the desktop and applications. Printer drivers have become more complex for the vendors to support, while making life easier for users and network administrators (after getting the clients working correctly, of course).

Knowing life is not perfect, however, Novell provides 60 printer definitions. Known as *print devices* inside NetWare, they can be modified to suit your situation. The included device files cover the popular printers, and they provide a good starting place if you must modify some printer functions. These functions are controlled by files with a .PDF (Printer Definition File) extension, located in the PUBLIC directory.

Functions are actions, such as bold text or landscape orientation, that a printer can use. *Modes* are combinations of functions defined for specific printing needs. The string of functions is often sensitive to presentation order, so check your printer documentation for details.

You import devices (printers) using the NetWare Administrator program. During printing, the functions can be combined into print modes before being fed to the print device. The dance works this way:

Print functions Printer Reset, Landscape Orientation, and Typeface–Lineprinter

Combined into mode Report

Print to printer device HP LaserJet 4

Importing Devices

IN A HURRY

8.27 Import or Delete a Print Device

1. Open NetWare Administrator, highlight the container to hold the printer device, and press Enter.
2. Click the Print Devices (Non-NDPS) button.

Continued

IN A HURRY CONTINUED

3. Click Import, choose a Printer Definition File (*.PDF) from the File Open dialog box, and click OK.

4. To delete a print device, highlight it and click Delete.

5. Click OK to save the container Print Devices page settings and exit.

With five dozen predefined devices, you should be able to find the one for your printer, or a compatible printer, without too much trouble. If your printer is not represented, check with your NetWare dealer for new .PDF file releases, or check with the printer manufacturer. If your applications have the printer drivers you need, the network files aren't necessary. It's better for your application to have the proper drivers than for you to set up the appropriate .PDF file.

Open the NetWare Administrator program after logging in to the network as Admin or equivalent. Highlight the container that will hold the created print device and press Enter. Click the Print Devices (Non-NDPS) button on the far right of the dialog box. If Print Device objects exist, you can modify or delete them by clicking the appropriate buttons. To import a new print device, click the Import button. The dialog box shown in Figure 8.43 will open.

FIGURE 8.43

Importing another print device into the DESIGN Organizational Unit

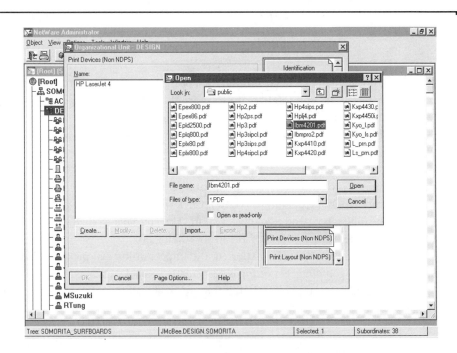

The Open dialog box in Figure 8.43 will display only files with the .PDF extension. As you can tell by the existence of the Open dialog box, you can easily browse any directory or disk drive that you have access to for more .PDF files.

You need not do any configuring at this time. If the printer works with your applications, no further configuring is necessary.

If you must create or modify print functions, a pop-up dialog box appears asking for the Function Name and Control Sequence. The unique name can be a maximum of 32 alphanumeric characters, including spaces. The control sequences are the <Esc> <E> type codes sent to printers to control various functions, such as reset, orientation, and font. The Help screen includes a listing of acceptable codes and good explanations.

Exporting Devices

IN A HURRY

8.28 Export a Print Device

1. Open NetWare Administrator, highlight the container to hold the print device, and press Enter.
2. Click the Print Devices (Non-NDPS) button.
3. Click Export, choose a location to save the Printer Definition File (*.PDF), and click OK in the File Save As dialog box.
4. Click Cancel to exit the container Print Devices dialog box.

If one container has a definition for a print device, especially one that you have created or modified, you might want to share that device. The Export option on the Print Devices page will create the official Novell System .PDF file for you. You can copy this file, including all modifications, anywhere you want. This export feature makes it simple to import the copied file into other containers.

After connecting to the network as Admin or equivalent, run the NetWare Administrator program. Highlight the container where the print device export will take place (the source) and press Enter. Click the Print Devices button on the right side of the dialog box, and then click Export. The File Save As dialog box opens, and you can type the name of the .PDF file in this dialog box.

Once the .PDF file is exported, the Import utility can pick the file up and use it in another container. Exporting is particularly valuable when a device has been customized. This allows you to copy, rather than re-create, all the work done setting up the print device.

Defining Print Modes

IN A HURRY

8.29 Define a New Print Mode

1. Open NetWare Administrator, highlight the container holding the print device, and press Enter.
2. Click the Print Devices (Non-NDPS) button.
3. Click the Create button, enter a name for the new print device, and press Enter.
4. Highlight the new print device, click Modify, and then click Create Mode.
5. Type a unique name (eight alphanumeric characters or less, starting with a letter).
6. Highlight a function listed in the Device Functions list, and click Add Above or Add Below.
7. Click OK when the proper functions are listed in the Mode Functions list.
8. Click Cancel to exit the container Print Devices dialog box.

Print modes define the font style, size, boldness, and page orientation. Although you can modify or delete modes for the existing printer list, these are dangerous actions and rarely needed. The safest, and most common, usage of print modes is to create new ones that set up the page to be printed in a special way.

Remember that specifying print modes means specifying new printer forms. This will require either separate printers for each form or extra printer management to load the proper forms. Better yet, take the path of least resistance and let the fancy design programs handle their own printing without requiring you to get in the middle of the transaction.

 WARNING Print modes are not casual items to create and modify for fun. Check your printer's documentation carefully. The proper commands in the wrong order will lock up your printer just as tight as the wrong commands. These lockups require turning the printer off and back on to clear. Luckily, most users don't tend to play with these settings and cause trouble, even if they could find them buried in the NetWare Administrator program.

PART

II

Managing the
Network

If you still need a printer form or two, log in to the network as Admin or an equivalent user. Start the NetWare Administrator program and highlight the container with the print device that needs a new print mode and press Enter, or right-click and click Details. Highlight a print device and click Modify. In the Modify Existing Device dialog box, click Create Mode to open the Create New Mode dialog box, shown in Figure 8.44.

FIGURE 8.44

Creating a new print mode

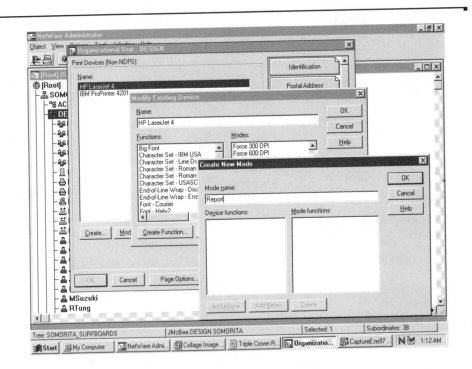

The list of printer function commands is in the left box, and the right box is empty until you choose the functions needed to make your new print mode. The name is first, so type a NetWare 3.*x* type name. This means eight letters or numbers, but beginning with a letter. This name must be unique. If you give an existing name (as in Report in the example shown in Figure 8.44), the error message will list several items that might be the error, and the system won't accept the duplicate name.

Select each item from the Device Functions list, and click Add Above or Add Below to move the function to the Mode Functions list. The entry will be placed above or below the highlighted mode function already in the box, if there is one.

Setting Up Print Job Configurations with NetWare Administrator

IN A HURRY

8.30 Manage Print Job Configurations

1. Open NetWare Administrator, highlight the container holding the print job configuration, and press Enter.
2. Click the Print Job Configuration button.
3. To create a new configuration, click New and enter the information.
4. To change an existing configuration, highlight the print job configuration name and click Modify.
5. To set the default configuration, highlight that print job configuration name and click Default.
6. Click OK to save the settings.

Now that we've gone through lots of printing details, you can appreciate the labor-saving device known as a print job configuration more than you did previously. Although I haven't covered the user side of printing yet (that's in Chapter 12), almost every printing detail I've covered so far can be specified by the users. They can set their printing environment using command-line parameters every time they need to print, or you can create some print job configurations they can use. Since users will wear out your beeper if the printing system has problems, these print job configurations are a wonderful network-management tool.

As with the other printing details, a good application will eliminate the need for most of this information. Applications today, routed to the proper printer, can quickly create beautiful and/or complex pages. Our job here is to make sure the minimum details are configured and to offer other print configurations for those applications that haven't gotten their printing support up-to-date.

Earlier versions of NetWare had only private print job configurations. Each of the configuration details could be the same, but the same configuration had to be copied to each user's individual SYS:MAIL directory. In addition, there was a limit of 37 unique configurations that could be stored by the system.

PART

II

Managing the Network

NetWare 5.1 allows group configurations to be shared, while still allowing private configurations for users if necessary. But you, as the administrator, need only create a default configuration, one time, for everyone. Users can create multiple configurations for different circumstances and easily reference them.

Each user in this container has access to the default Print Configuration object. If no instructions are issued to the contrary, the default Print Configuration object will provide the printing instructions for the user. Any of the defined print configurations can be declared the default configuration. In Figure 8.45, notice that the Laser configuration has the little printer icon beside it. That says Laser is the default, and Default is not the default. See how flexible this is? To set the default, highlight one of the configurations and click the Default button.

Figure 8.45 shows the Print Job Configuration page for the DESIGN.SOMORITA container. The field names and acceptable values for the print job configurations are listed in Table 8.4.

FIGURE 8.45

The default print job configuration for a container

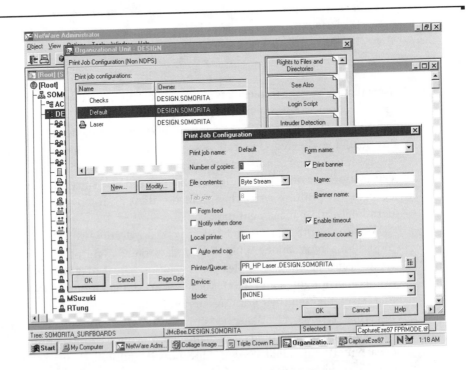

TABLE 8.4: FIELDS ON NETWARE ADMINISTRATOR'S PRINT JOB CONFIGURATION SCREEN

Field	Description
Print Job Name	Must be unique for this user. You cannot change the name, although you can modify all other fields.
Number Of Copies	The default is 1, but you can enter any number up to 65,000.
File Contents	Text or Byte Stream, with Byte Stream the default and safest choice for general printing.
Tab Size	Active only when the File Contents is listed as Text. Refers to the width in characters each tab should be when printed.
Form Feed	Used with older DOS clients. When this option is checked, the CAPTURE or NPRINT software sends a form feed to flush the job out of the printer.
Notify When Done	When this option is checked, the system will send the user a message when the print job is finished being spooled to the printer. It does not guarantee that the printer has successfully printed the job itself.
Local Printer	Used with older DOS clients. Chooses which parallel port will be captured. NetWare expands on DOS by allowing as many as nine LPT designations. You must modify the user's NET.CFG file to allow more than three LPT ports.
Auto End Cap	When checked, tells the CAPTURE command to print the job when the application says it is finished.
Printer/Queue	Designates the printer or print queue for this print job configuration. Clicking the Browse button opens the Select Object dialog box, which shows only printers and print queues.
Device	Specifies a named print device for this print job configuration.
Mode	Specifies a defined mode (such as Report) for the print device specified in the previous field.
Form Name	Specifies a defined form for this print job configuration, picked from the list that appears when you click the down-arrow button.
Print Banner	When checked, includes a banner page at the beginning of the print job.
Name	Active only when Print Banner is checked. When this field is blank, the user name is inserted. The name listed in this field and the next can be only 11 characters.
Banner Name	Active only when Print Banner is checked. When this field is blank, the banner page names the printer port. The name listed in this field and the previous one can be only 11 characters.
Enable Timeout	When checked, forces CAPTURE to consider a print job finished if there is no activity for a defined number of seconds.
Timeout Count	Active only when Enable Timeout is checked. Range is from one to 1000 seconds. For typical word-processing print jobs, a short value (five to 10) will be fine. For print jobs requiring lots of computer calculations, such as large reports or spreadsheets, the time should be longer. If a print job comes out in two or more pieces, this value is too short.

PART

II

Managing the
Network

NPRINTER Updated

8.31 Assign a Remotely Attached Printer to an NDS Printer

1. From a Windows 95/98 client, run the (still named for W95) `SYS:PUBLIC\ WIN95\NPTWIN95.EXE` program.
2. Click the NDS Printer radio button.
3. Browse the NDS directory, select an NDS Printer object, and click OK.
4. Click the OK button to create the printer.

Time marches on, as any parent will tell you. Time even applies to workstation-attached system printers, as NPRINTER gives way to NPTWIN95. Well, "gives way" might be an overstatement. After all, NPRINTER is still available, but now you have a good reason to never use it with a non-dedicated system. Windows 95/98, on the other hand, no matter how Novell may curse it behind the scenes (heck, I curse it regularly, as you probably do as well), does function well enough to act as a decent non-dedicated remote print server.

How hard is this to accomplish? Not too hard, actually.

First, find `NPTWIN95.EXE`. You might think that this file is in the set that was copied with your Windows 95/98 client files, but it isn't. The program is located in the `SYS:\PUBLIC\WIN95` directory, and the `NPTWIN95.EXE` file will be there, begging to be run.

Second, copy the `NPTWIN95.EXE` program to each local Windows 95/98 workstation acting as a remote print station, or make a reference to the program on the server in your Startup folder. Either way will work. If you decide to copy NPTWIN95 to the local hard disk, you need to copy some files so that `NPTWIN95.EXE` runs properly. These include:

From the `SYS:PUBLIC\WIN95` directory   NPTWIN95.EXE, NPTR95.NLM, NPTDRV95.NLM, DPCMN32.DLL, BIDS45F.DLL, CW3215.DLL, and OWL252F.DLL

From the `SYS:PUBLIC\WIN95\NLS\ENGLISH` directory   NPTWIN95.DLL, NPTWIN95.HLP, NPTDRV95.MSG, and DPCMNR32.DLL

I recommend creating a separate subdirectory for these files, such as `C:\NPRINTER` or something similar.

Third, run the program on the aforementioned Windows 95/98 workstation and configure important details as shown in Figure 8.46.

FIGURE 8.46

Configuring
NPTWIN95

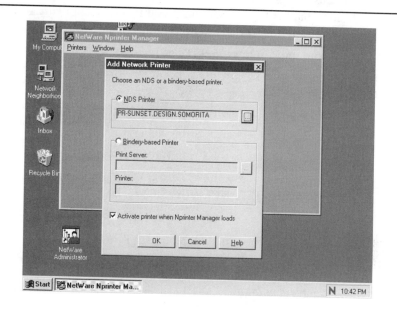

In Figure 8.46, I'm adding the printer PR-SUNSET that I previously created and assigned to a print server in NetWare Administrator. Nothing fancy here—just look around until you hit the right context, and then select your printer. Notice that the NDS Printer button is active, as evidenced by the little black dot. Clicking the Browse button (the one at the end of that line with the three dots) displays the Select Object dialog box.

Save the information, and verify that the printer will be activated when the NPRINTER manager program starts.

The program will retreat to the Taskbar, staying out of the way on your desktop. All this is fine, and it works better than the old NPRINTER, but be careful. Users will turn off their systems, leaving your newly configured printer out of reach. Network print servers such as the Hewlett-Packard JetDirect are cheap (cheaper than upgrading PCs to handle Windows 95/98), and they don't turn themselves off. It's your choice, but at least you have a choice.

You can configure NPTWIN95.EXE to automatically load when users log in by putting a shortcut in their Startup folder. If you don't want the NetWare Nprinter Manager to load each time you initialize NPTWIN95.EXE, load it with the /EXIT switch. This will

PART

II

Managing the
Network

load the printing support, but not the NetWare Nprinter Manager program. You can also configure NPTWIN95.EXE to run automatically before the user logs in. To do this, you must modify a setting in the Registry. You must have copied the required files to the local hard drive, for example C:\NPRINTER. To configure NPTWIN95.EXE to load automatically, follow these steps:

1. Run the Windows 95/98 Registry Editor (REGEDIT.EXE).

2. Select the key in HKEY_LOCAL_MACHINE \SOFTWARE\Microsoft\Windows\ Current Version.

3. Locate the RunServices key and highlight it.

4. Choose Edit ➤ New ➤ String Value.

5. Assign a name to the String Value, such as NPTWIN95, and press Enter.

6. Double-click the new String Value, and in the Value data field, enter **C:\NPRINTER\NPTWIN95.EXE /EXIT**.

7. Click OK.

The next time the computer reboots, NPTWIN95 will automatically load. You can adjust settings for NPTWIN95 in an .INI file called C:\WINDOWS\NPRINTER.INI. For more information on this file and how to modify it, see the Novell Knowledgebase article 2907959 found on the Novell Support Web site at support.novell.com.

Potshots on Printing

The prognosticators lied to us all: the paperless office prediction is not only wrong, but more paper is sold today than ever before. You have as much chance of winning the lottery as your office does of going completely paperless in the next three years.

Should we say phooey and buy printers for everyone? No. Despite what people want, the time for information primarily stored on paper is past. You make your children eat vegetables when they don't want to, and you must gently but firmly push your network into the uh-ohs (00s), when paper starts dying.

Don't be hard on your users when they complain, "My report doesn't look right. The graphic looked great on the screen, but the printed version stinks! Why don't we have color lasers for everybody?"

Why not blow your top the seventeenth time you hear that type of remark in one day? Because to most people, what the computer does is not real. Paper is real. Until information from the computer appears on paper, they are not sure if it exists.

Someday, when everyone is carrying their PDA that connects over a wireless network to the company Web server holding every document on magneto-optical disks rather than paper, users will understand. But some of them will still print things when you're not looking.

No doubt some Novell people will take offense because I'm not thrilled with the advantages of NDPS. Hey, if a printer works, queue-based or not, I'm happy. Those who need the added intelligence of NDPS, and the intelligent printers able to communicate, will learn enough about NDPS here to make things work. NDPS-enabled printers are worth the money, if you plan to push forward. But if you don't, and stick with queue-based printing or add network print servers, you'll still get your printout.

CHAPTER 9

Securing Your NetWare 5.1 Network

Security—What does it mean to you? Hackers sneaking in and deleting entire volumes? Illegal software on the system?

What does security mean to your boss? Inventory asset tags on all the computers, so you know the location of every piece of hardware? Competitors tapping into your system and stealing the plans for the rollout of your new product line?

Security, like much of life, is a desirable abstract state sought through the use of material items. No two people think of the same thing when they hear the word *security*. Regardless of the situation, some people never feel secure. Other people may feel content and secure when actually their systems are vulnerable. The trick is to develop a sense of appropriate paranoia, without becoming obsessed.

Security: A Definition

Each company must make a decision about what security means and about the amount of effort that it will expend to reach a comfortable level of security. Securing your network, including all the physical and virtual items, will be expensive. This brings up another management decision point: how much security is enough?

How about a definition: security is an aspect of networking administration concerned with ensuring that the data, circuits, and equipment on a network are used only by authorized users and in authorized ways. This comes from the *Complete Encyclopedia of Networking* by Werner Feibel, published by Sybex (the folks who bring you this book).

Notice the order of items to be secured: data, circuits, equipment. Management often focuses security measures on physical items, such as computer hardware and telephone connections and modems. But if a computer is stolen, all that's necessary to replace that computer is money. Circuits must be protected from tampering and eavesdropping, and they must be available when needed.

If data is destroyed, years of work, effort, and thought are gone. Unfortunately, work, effort, and thought are not easily replaced.

Mr. Feibel suggests four threat areas to manage for your system security:

Threats to hardware Theft, tampering, destruction, damage, unauthorized use, and ordinary equipment wear and tear.

Threats to software Deletion, theft, corruption, and bugs.

Threats to information Deletion, theft, loss, and corruption.

Threats to network operations Interruption, interference, and overload.

Can you and your boss agree on these items? Do some of them seem outside the realm of security, such as ordinary equipment wear and tear? What about the threat of overload?

Some network managers think of security from a negative aspect only. Something is stolen or deleted. I don't believe that definition is wide enough to support the network needs of today.

Let's agree that system security means that the system is available to authorized users doing their job. Anything that interferes with this is a security problem. If a file server is stolen, people can't do their work. What if the file server is overloaded or erratic? Isn't the result the same? People can't do their work. What if the file server is safe and running well, but someone deletes (either accidentally or on purpose) some of the system files? The result is the same once again: people can't do their work.

Where Is Your Security Plan?

In 1988, the Internet Worm ran amok, clogging thousands of computers and data circuits for days. The Worm was not destructive but caused disruptions in computer services all across the Internet. Front-page stories were copied by paranoid managers and handed to network technicians with a question: "Where is our security plan?"

One of the responses of the Internet community to the Worm of 1988 was to establish CERT (Computer Emergency Response Team). This group responds to and helps resolve Internet security incidents. Part of the group's job is to help network administrators protect their systems against intruders before an attack is attempted.

The good news is that upgrading security takes surprisingly little work for most systems. Unfortunately, that's also the bad news. CERT estimates that 60 to 75 percent of network problems are caused by the following:

- Accounts with no passwords

- Poor passwords

- Unwatched guest accounts

- Poor user security management, especially giving users more rights than necessary

Are the listed problems familiar to you? Do you understand how easy these problems are to fix? I covered the user password details earlier; I'll talk about user rights in this chapter.

Before doing anything else, check the easy things. Many cars are stolen simply because the keys are left dangling from the ignition switch. Don't make things that easy in your network.

The Site Security Handbook

To help you devise your security plan, RFC 1244 was developed. Here is the opening:

```
Network Working Group     P. Holbrook
Request for Comments: 1244 CICNet
FYI: 8     J. Reynolds
ISI
Editors
July 1991
Site Security Handbook
Status of this Memo
```

This handbook is the product of the Site Security Policy Handbook Working Group (SSPHWG), a combined effort of the Security Area and User Services Area of the Internet Engineering Task Force (IETF). This FYI RFC provides information for the Internet community. It does not specify an Internet standard. Distribution of this memo is unlimited.

As is the norm, the information in this RFC may be freely copied and distributed. I'll quote two small sections, skipping most of the valuable information in this handbook.

```
1. 7 Basic Approach
```

Setting security policies and procedures really means developing a plan for how to deal with computer security. One way to approach this task is suggested by Fites, et. al. [3, FITES]:

- Look at what you are trying to protect.

- Look at what you need to protect it from.

- Determine how likely the threats are.

- Implement measures which will protect your assets in a cost-effective manner.

- Review the process continuously, and improve things every time a weakness is found.

This handbook will concentrate mostly on the last two steps, but the first three are critically important to making effective decisions about security. One old truism in security is that the cost of protecting yourself against a threat should be less than the cost of recovering if the threat were to strike you. Without reasonable knowledge of what you are protecting and what the likely threats are, following this rule could be difficult.

Continued ▯▶

CONTINUED

The last two sentences apply to everyone in the computer business but are difficult to quantify at times. You know what you have is valuable, but how valuable? How do you put a price on a database or spreadsheet templates or transaction history? Someone, preferably management, must assign some value to the information stored in your network. Quick estimate: how long will it take you to replace the database? (Multiply that by twice as long, then figure a high rate per hour, and you're on your way to setting a value). You know what's coming from all this, don't you? Audit—inventory every server, workstation, network component, remote access device, wiring diagram, and each module of application and system software. Your manager will probably ask you to do this in your "spare" time. If you don't have a value assigned to what you're protecting, you don't know when the protection is more expensive than what's protected.

Another set of management decisions is described in this section:

```
2. 3 Policy Issues

There are a number of issues that must be addressed when developing a
security policy. These are:

1. Who is allowed to use the resources?

2. What is the proper use of the resources?

3. Who is authorized to grant access and approve usage?

4. Who may have system administration privileges?

5. What are the user's rights and responsibilities?

6. What are the rights and responsibilities of the system administrator
vs. those of the user?

7. What do you do with sensitive information?
```

RFC 1244 may be retrieved from many places on the Internet. The source for these quotes is the "Internet Info" CD-ROM, December 1997 release, available from Walnut Creek CD-ROM, Walnut Creek, California. This CD includes more than 17,000 documents (including many more on security topics) for a price of $39.95. Check it out, along with their other products, at www.cdrom.com.

Should I Be Concerned Since My NetWare Network Is Connected to the Internet?

Yes, of course you should worry. Bad things sometimes happen to networks connected to the Internet. But you shouldn't be overly paranoid.

Your boss, however, will be overly paranoid. That's because the non-technical press latches onto every hacker story like a starving pooch on a pork chop. You and I know these stories are poorly researched and written by journalists who either don't understand computers or don't trust them, so we ignore them. Bosses can't ignore them because their bosses read the same articles in the same papers, and misinformed hysteria feeds upon non-technical misunderstanding, and everyone gets all worked up.

Prepare yourself every time the *Wall Street Journal* or *New York Times* runs a computer hacker or system crash story—your boss will come and ask how nervous you are about the horrible state of Internet security. If you're of a certain type of mind, that is the time to increase your budget considerably under the guise of improving security. Even if you're not of that type of mind regularly, chances like that don't come around often, so you should take a shot and ask for enough money to get a new server or firewall or software upgrade.

The truth is that connecting any part of your network to the Internet requires plenty of extra work, caution, and responsibility. You must keep the bad people out and keep the irresponsible people in.

No intelligent network manager will connect to the Internet without some type of firewall in place to provide security. If your company already has an Internet connection and you are adding your own NetWare network to the list of Internet-aware networks, a firewall is in place already. Talk to the network administrator in charge of your TCP/IP network, and get the details you need to feel good about network security.

If your network is the corporate network, check out Novell's BorderManager software. You aren't familiar with this product? It adds a complete security- and performance-enhancing software server to any NetWare 4.*x* and NetWare 5.*x* server. You can run both the NetWare 5.1 server and BorderManager on the same hardware. Larger networks will want to separate the BorderManager software to its own server for performance reasons. One BorderManager server protects your entire network when configured correctly. Feel free to look up my *IntranetWare BorderManager* book, also from Sybex, at your local bookstore or favorite online shopping destination.

The Internet and Firewalls

Firewall is an unusually descriptive term, even for the term-spewing computer industry. In construction, a firewall stands against disasters by forming an impenetrable shield around the protected area (I got the impenetrable shield slogan from my deodorant). Most disasters in buildings revolve around fires; hence, the term *firewall*.

The goal of a firewall is simple: to control access to a protected network. Firewall managers use two philosophies during configuration:

- Allow everything except designated packets
- Block everything except designated packets

Today, the proper attitude is to block everything except designated packets. Novell's products come this way straight from the box. When you enable filtering, everything is blocked, and you must designate what is allowed to pass through the firewall and/or filtering software.

The four types of firewalls are:

- Packet filters (FILTCFG)
- Circuit-level gateways
- Application-level gateways
- Stateful inspection firewalls

As illustration, let's look again at the OSI seven-layer model and see where these firewall functions line up. Table 9.1 shows how this works.

TABLE 9.1: MATCHING SECURITY FILTERS AND NETWORK LAYERS

OSI Model Layer	Internet Protocols	Firewalls
Application	HTTP, FTP, DNS, NFS, Ping, SMTP, Telnet	Application-level gateway, stateful inspection firewall
Presentation		
Session	TCP	Circuit-level gateway
Transport	TCP	
Network	IP	Packet-filtering firewall
Data Link		
Physical		

The lowest level, packet filters, was once enough to protect your network, but that is no longer true. IP addresses are used to allow or deny packets, and IP address spoofing (disguised packets) has ruined the idea of this level of protection being enough to protect your network.

Circuit-level gateways do more to control internal traffic leaving your protected network than to keep outsiders at bay. Rules for users, such as allowable hosts to visit and time limits, are handled at this level.

Application-level gateways are specific to network services, such as FTP or e-mail. These are most common today with Web browsers, used by software meant to monitor or block Web access to certain sites.

Finally, the most critical area is the stateful inspection firewall, used by Novell and few others. This software examines incoming packets to match them to appropriate outgoing packets and is able to examine packet contents to maintain control. The more options you have, the better your security, and NetWare gives you plenty of options. Of course, you'll need more time to configure more settings, but NWAdmin will help with that chore.

Keeping Up with Security Threats

Can one person, namely you, keep up with all the network miscreants out there? No, but there are more people on your side than you might imagine.

First, enlist the resources of your firewall vendor, whether Novell for BorderManager or another vendor. Keep up-to-date on all bug fixes, patches, and upgrades for your firewall software. Maintain proper security for the physical firewall system (lock it up in the server room or equivalent).

Second, watch the trade magazines and Web sites pertaining to security. Security information is all over the place if you keep your eyes open. Please don't be one of those who become paranoid *after* you get burned. Go ahead and start being paranoid, or at least well informed, before something serious happens to your network.

Finally, and this is a regularly repeated warning, *watch your users carefully*. Some companies are using "internal" firewalls to keep employees out of sensitive areas. A serious security breach, where valuable information is stolen or compromised, almost always includes help from the inside. Every user is a potential thief. Always provide new services with tighter rather than looser security, and then loosen the leash as you and your management feel more comfortable with the security situation on your network. Most data thieves walk out rather than break in.

Common-Sense Security Measures

Along with file system and NDS security, security practices include passwords, login restrictions, virus precautions, and other common-sense measures.

Passwords and Login Restrictions

In our discussion of user creation and setup, I spoke at length about the value of login and password security. Much of Chapter 6 concerns these very topics. Rather than repeat all that information here, I'll provide a quick synopsis. For more details, you can thumb back to Chapter 6 and review it with a new understanding of security.

Passwords   Each user must have a password. Here are some tips for your passwords:

- The longer the password, the better. Novell's default minimum is five characters; try for six or lucky seven.
- Encourage the use of mixed alpha and numeric characters in the password.
- Set passwords to expire (the default is 40 days).
- Let the system keep track of passwords to force unique ones. The limit is 20.
- Limit the grace logins; two is enough.

Login restrictions   Using login restrictions, you can limit users' network access and track the resources they use. Here are some tips for setting login restrictions:

- Limit concurrent connections for all users.
- Set an account expiration date for all temporary workers.
- Disable accounts for users away from the office who don't communicate remotely to your network.

There are a few more common-sense ideas to combat the problem of slipping security. When the network is new, or a security problem has occurred, everyone is conscientious. After a time, however, human nature takes over and everyone gets sloppy.

Your network changes constantly, and each change is a potential security disaster. Add a new user? Did you take care to match the new user to an existing group with well-defined security and access controls? How about new files created by the users themselves? Do you have a plan for watching the access level of those files? Do users have the ability to allow other users access into a home directory? If so, no private file will be safe. Don't allow file sharing within each person's private directory. Send the file by e-mail or have a common directory in which users can place files to share. Do *not* allow them more file rights to the \PUBLIC directory, even though some will ask for it.

Watch new applications. Many vendors have modified NetWare rights for files and directories for years, especially during installation. Are these loopholes closed in the new application directories you created just last week? Better check.

NetWare 5.1 Admin Compared to NetWare 3.x SUPERVISOR

There are two main security areas for NetWare 5.1: file system and NDS security. If you are familiar with NetWare 3.x, you will be familiar with file system security. NetWare 4.1x added some attributes to support data compression and data migration features and changed a bit of the terminology. But most of the details and the security goals are still the same. The main goal is to provide users access to and control of the proper files and directories.

The only user created with NetWare 5.1 is named *Admin*, short for Administrator. (I suppose this is to save time typing over Windows NT 4, which makes the default user Administrator.) If you just climbed up the version tree from NetWare 3.1x, don't bother looking for SUPERVISOR because Admin replaced SUPERVISOR.

Make the mental note that the Admin user is separate from the Admin rights over the network operating system and included objects. As you'll see later, the more advanced management techniques that arrived with object management and the Admin user are a way to block this SUPERVISOR equivalent from managing parts of the network. Oops.

NDS security was new with NetWare 4, as was NDS itself. Just as file system security controls which users can control which files, NDS security controls the same functions for the NDS objects. The two security systems are not in any way related. Let me repeat: having control over the NDS attributes of an object (let's say a disk volume) does not grant the rights to the files contained in that volume.

The Admin user is a supervisor's supervisor, able to control the network completely as the old SUPERVISOR did in earlier NetWare versions. The Supervisor right, however, may be granted to any user for particular NDS objects or containers. Being able to set up subadministrators for specific tasks, as I have spoken of before, can be a great help.

This flexibility of supervision is an important feature of NetWare 5.1—one of the many features that place NetWare ahead of the competition. With global enterprise networking the norm for many companies today, the job of supervision is far beyond the abilities of any one person. NetWare 5.1 allows the supervision chores to be distributed in whatever method you prefer.

You can have different administrators for different parts of the tree, as well as different volumes, directories, or files. Admin may control the NDS design and overall setup but have no control over the files. File system supervisors in each container will handle those chores. Admin in Chicago may share duties with Admin in Cleveland, with each responsible primarily for his or her own city but able to support the other network across the WAN if necessary.

File System Security

NetWare files are protected in two ways:

- Users must be granted the right to use files and directories.
- File and directory attributes provide hidden protection.

What is hidden protection? Suppose that Doug has the right to create and delete files in the \LETTERS directory. If he writes a letter named SLS_GOAL.OCT and decides he doesn't like that file, he can delete it. Files can be deleted from within applications or from the DOS prompt. He can use the Windows File Manager.

What if Doug's mouse slips a fraction within File Manager, and he tries to delete the SLS_GOAL.PLN file, the template for all the sales goal letters? Is the file doomed?

Not necessarily. If the network administrator (probably you) has set the attribute to SLS_GOAL.PLN as Read Only or Delete Inhibit, Doug can't delete the file. However, if Doug also has the right to modify the file attributes (a bad idea, knowing Doug), he could change the Read Only or Delete Inhibit designation and delete the file anyway. But he would need to work at deleting the file; he couldn't do it by accident.

When granting Doug rights to use the \LETTERS directory, we call him a *trustee* of the directory, given to him by way of a *trustee assignment*. He has been trusted to use the directory and files properly. The trustee concept works with objects and NDS items, as we'll soon see.

Someone in authority must grant Doug, or a group or container Doug is a member of, the rights to use the file, directory, or object in question. The administrator is the person who places trust in Doug, making him a trustee of the rights of the object. This is referred to as making trustee assignments to a directory, file, or object. The trustee assignments are stored in the object's ACL (Access Control List) property.

The rights granted to users flow downhill. This means that the rights Doug has in one directory apply to all subdirectories. This idea works well, and the official name is *inheritance*. If your system is set up with \LETTERS as the main directory, and Doug has rights to use that directory, he will automatically have the same rights in the \LETTERS\ SALES and \LETTERS\PROSPECT subdirectories. He will inherit the same rights in \LETTERS\SALES as he has in \LETTERS.

One way to stop Doug from having full access to a subdirectory is to use the IRF (Inherited Rights Filter). The IRF filters the rights a user may have in subdirectories and will be covered later in this chapter. The other way is to explicitly make a new trustee assignment to this subdirectory. A new assignment always overrides the inherited settings.

[Public] is a special trustee, for use by all the users on the network, and can always be specified as a trustee of a file, directory, or object. Although it sounds similar to the

PART

II

Managing the
Network

group EVERYONE in earlier NetWare versions, containers act more like the EVERY-ONE group than [Public] does.

The rights to use directories and files are similar, so we'll take a look at the directory situation first. User's rights in dealing with files and directories are also similar, making explanations fairly simple.

There are reasons to grant rights to directories rather than files, not the least of which is the time savings. Even with wildcards available, I would rather set the rights of users to use a directory and all subdirectories than set their rights to the files in each directory.

Directory Rights for Users and Groups

What are these rights that users can have over a directory? And did that last sentence in the previous section mean subdirectories? Yes it did.

The directory rights available to users are summarized in Table 9.2.

TABLE 9.2: DIRECTORY RIGHTS IN NETWARE 5.1

Right	Description
Supervisor (S)	Grants all rights to the directory, its files, and all subdirectories, overriding any restrictions placed on subdirectories or files with an IRF. Users with this right in a directory can grant other users Supervisor rights to the same directory, its files, and its subdirectories.
Read (R)	Allows the user to open and read the directory. Earlier NetWare versions needed an Open right; Read now includes Open.
Write (W)	Allows the user to open and write files, but existing files are not displayed without Read authorization.
Create (C)	Allows the user to create directories and files. With Create authorization, a user can create a file and write data into the file (authority for Write is included with Create). Read and File Scan authority are not part of the Create right.
Modify (M)	Allows the user to change directory and file attributes, including the right to rename the directory, its files, and its subdirectories. Modify does not refer to the file contents.
File Scan (F)	Allows the user to see filenames in a directory listing. Without this right, the user will be told the directory is empty.
Access Control (A)	Allows the user to change directory trustee assignments and the IRFs for directories. This right should be granted to supervisory personnel only, because users with Access Control rights can grant all rights except Supervisor to another user, including rights the Access Control user doesn't have. The user can also modify file trustee assignments within the directory.

Let's see how these directory rights appear in ConsoleOne. Figure 9.1 shows the group Consultants and the file and directory rights the members have. Why use ConsoleOne rather than NetWare Administrator? To get ready for the future, since ConsoleOne gets the Novell developer's attention today, while NetWare Administrator remains static.

FIGURE 9.1

An example of the rights a group can have

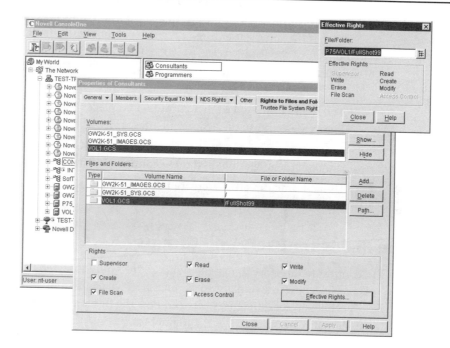

The Effective Rights listing is in the separate dialog box in the upper-right corner of Figure 9.1. This dialog box appears when you click the Effective Rights command button in the Group: Consultants dialog box. Notice that on the top of the dialog box, the Rights To Files And Folders tab is active, which opened the main dialog box. The odd arrangement here helps show all the pieces without blocking the parent window. Unlike NetWare Administrator, ConsoleOne requires you to drill down through the volume to the directory in the Select Object dialog box (not shown here).

The Supervisor and Access Control checkboxes are clear in the Rights area. This means the group Consultants does not have those two rights. Giving a group of users the Supervisor right could be dangerous. Giving a person or group the Access Control right is equally dangerous. With the Access Control right, the user or group member can change his or her own rights and add more rights without your knowledge or consent.

These rights apply to the directory where they are granted and to all subdirectories. Rights are inherited from the top directory levels through all the existing subdirectory levels.

The rights are displayed (in DOS with the RIGHTS command) as a string of the initials within brackets: [SRWCEMFA]. If some are missing, a space is put in their place. For instance, the most rights non-administrative users generally have are [_RWCEMF_]. As you can see, underscores were put in place of the S (Supervisor) and A (Access Control) rights. If the generic user listed previously didn't have the rights to Erase in a particular directory, the listing would look like [_RWC_MF_].

There are three minor differences in how the rights are handled in NetWare 3.*x* and in NetWare 5.1:

- The name Inherited Rights Filter (IRF) replaces the earlier name of Inherited Rights Mask (IRM); the actions are the same.

- New attributes were added to files in NetWare 4.1*x* to accommodate compression and file migration, and these continue in NetWare 5.1.

- Users' home directories created during the initial user setup now include all rights, including Supervisor.

File Rights for Users and Groups

In contrast to directory rights, file rights address only specified files. Sometimes the files are specified individually, sometimes by a wildcard group (*.EXE, for example).

There are minor differences between how the rights are applied to a directory and to a file. Table 9.3 summarizes the file rights.

TABLE 9.3: FILE RIGHTS IN NETWARE 5.1

Right	Description
Supervisor (S)	Grants all rights to the file, and users with this right may grant any file right to another user. This right also allows modification of all the rights in the file's IRF.
Read (R)	Allows the user to open and read the file.
Write (W)	Allows the user to open and write to the file.
Create (C)	Allows the user to create new files and salvage a file after it has been deleted. Perhaps the latter should be called the Re-create right.
Erase (E)	Allows the user to delete the file.

Continued ▶

TABLE 9.3 (CONTINUED): FILE RIGHTS IN NETWARE 5.1	
Right	**Description**
Modify (M)	Allows the user to modify the file attributes, including renaming the file. This does not apply to the contents of the file.
File Scan (F)	Allows the user to see the file when viewing the contents of the directory.
Access Control (A)	Allows the user to change the file's trustee assignments and IRF. Users with this right can grant any right (except Supervisor) for this file to any other user, including rights that they themselves have not been granted.

You might notice that the Create right is a bit different, and the Supervisor and Access Control rights apply to individual files. Why do we have the differences between directory and file rights?

The IRF and File and Directory Rights

Let's pretend that your file system is set up so that all the accounting data is parceled into subdirectories under the main \DATA directory in the volume ACCOUNTING. Many people on your network will need access to the information in these accounting files. Some will need to use the accounting programs, some will need to gather the information into reports, and others may need to write applications that use those data files.

Since directory rights flow downhill, this will be easy: give the group ACCOUNTING rights to use the \DATA directory, and the information in \DATA\AR, \DATA\AP, \DATA\GL, and \DATA\PAYROLL is available to everyone. But suddenly your boss realizes that giving everyone rights to see the information in \DATA\PAYROLL is not smart.

This is what the IRF was made for. The IRF controls the rights passed between a higher-level directory and a lower-level directory. In our example, that would be \DATA to \DATA\PAYROLL. The IRF does not grant rights; it strictly revokes them. The IRF default is to let all rights flow down unless otherwise instructed.

Figure 9.2 shows a simple look at our example. Everyone has access to all directories except for \DATA\PAYROLL. The IRF is blocking the rights for everyone in that directory.

There's a problem here: how does anyone see the \DATA\PAYROLL directory? The network administrator must specifically grant rights to the \DATA\PAYROLL directory for those users who belong there. The IRF filters between the parent directory and subdirectory. It does not dictate the rights assigned specifically to the subdirectory.

FIGURE 9.2

Keeping prying eyes out of PAYROLL

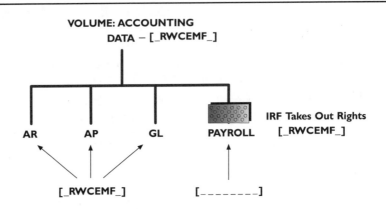

VOLUME: ACCOUNTING
DATA — [_RWCEMF_]

AR   AP   GL   PAYROLL

IRF Takes Out Rights
[_RWCEMF_]

[_RWCEMF_]   **[_____]**

When you type RIGHTS from the DOS command line, you see your rights in the current directory listed with an explanation. If you have all rights in a directory, such as your home directory, the RIGHTS command will show something like the display for user ALEX in Figure 9.3.

FIGURE 9.3

Results of the RIGHTS command

```
[Novell DOS] I:\HOME\ALEX>rights
GATEWAY2000\PROJECTS:\HOME\ALEX
Your rights for this directory:  [SRWCEMFA]
     Supervisor rights to directory.          (S)
     Read from a file in a directory.         (R)
     Write to a file in a directory.          (W)
     Create subdirectories and files.         (C)
     Erase directory and files.               (E)
     Modify directory and files.              (M)
     Scan for files and directories.          (F)
     Change access control.                   (A)

[Novell DOS] I:\HOME\ALEX>
```

If you have no rights in a directory, such as if our friend ALEX typed the RIGHTS command in the HOME directory above his own, the result would look something like this:

```
GATEWAY2000\PROJECTS:\HOME
Your rights for this directory: [   ]
```

Like the old screenshot using Novell DOS? Yes, they had it for a while until they sold it to Caldera. Yep, the Linux people.

You can approach the IRF in two ways: ignore it and set your file system up so that inheritance is never a problem, or take a minute to figure out how it works. The problem with the first option is that reality always rises up and bites you when you try to ignore problems, such as the previous example with the \DATA\PAYROLL directory. Since inheritance is always going to be with us, and the IRF makes good sense in certain situations, let's look at another view of the IRF.

First, let's add a complication: group rights. Users can be assigned rights directly, or they can get them through group memberships. The individual and group rights are additive. If you have one right granted individually and another granted through group membership, you effectively have both rights.

The IRF works against both the individual and group rights. The results of the individual plus group rights minus those taken away by the IRF are called the *effective rights*. Figure 9.4 stacks up the individual and group rights, subtracts the IRF, and shows the effective rights.

FIGURE 9.4

Stacking and subtracting rights

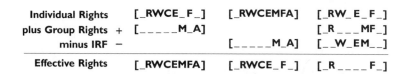

Individual Rights	[_RWCE_F_]	[_RWCEMFA]	[_RW_E_F_]
plus Group Rights +	[_____M_A]		[_R___MF_]
minus IRF –		[_____M_A]	[__W_EM__]
Effective Rights	[_RWCEMFA]	[_RWCE_F_]	[_R____F_]

Notice that the Supervisor (S) rights aren't mentioned anywhere. The IRF does not block the Supervisor rights, whether granted to the individual or a group. This is true only of the directory and file rights IRF. Later, we'll see that the object rights are a different story.

Directory and File Security Guidelines

No two networks are alike or use the same security profile. However, some general guidelines are applicable:

- Design your network top-down, from tighter security at the higher directories to looser security in the lower directories.

- Fight the urge to grant trustee rights to individuals. Always look for groups first, second, and third before you work with the individual user.

- Plan for inheritance. Grant Read and File Scan rights high, and Create, Erase, and Modify rights lower in the NDS tree.

- Avoid granting any destructive rights high in the directory structure.

- Remember that the Supervisor right for the file system cannot be blocked by the IRF. Grant that right carefully, if at all.

Using File Attributes as a Security Enhancement

File attributes in NetWare, as in DOS and OS/2, detail the characteristics of a file or directory. NetWare administrators often call these attributes *flags*, from the NetWare DOS command-line utility (FLAG.EXE) that views and modifies those attributes.

Since we've decided that security includes making sure all network resources are available, the safety of files on the file server is important. Someone besides you deleting or renaming files is a security problem.

File and directory attributes are not a defense for cases of willful destruction and sabotage. They are a defense against mistakes and typos by innocent users. Haven't you ever had a user type DEL *.* in a directory on drive G: instead of drive C:? Having some of the files set as Read Only or Delete Inhibit may lessen the damage from a confused user.

Attributes control what can and can't be done with files and directories. They are also a limited form of virus protection. Since most viruses work by modifying executable files, keeping those executables Ro (Read Only) will stop viruses from trying to rewrite files and save them back with the same name.

 WARNING Of course, Ro flags won't help with the new genre of Word macro viruses or with many of the other multitude of viruses out there. Flagging files Ro is never enough virus protection; it just helps a little.

File System: Directory Attributes

As is the case with much of NetWare, there are attributes for directories as well as files. Again, this makes sense. Unlike the rights to use an object, most directory rights don't directly affect the files in the directory. The attributes dealing with compression and data migration obviously do impact individual files. Since compression may be set by volume, the Immediate Compress attribute may be used more often than the Don't Compress attribute.

Table 9.4 lists the directory attributes with their abbreviations and descriptions.

TABLE 9.4: DIRECTORY ATTRIBUTES IN NETWARE 5.1	
Attribute	**Description**
All (All)	Sets all available directory attributes.
Don't Compress (Dc)	Stops compression on any files in the directory. This overrides the compression setting for the volume. New when NetWare 4 added compression.
Delete Inhibit (Di)	Stops users from erasing the directory, even if the user has the Erase trustee right. This attribute can be reset by a user with the Modify right.
Don't Migrate (Dm)	Stops files within the directory from being migrated to secondary storage. New when NetWare 4 added advanced storage features.
Hidden (H)	Hides directories from DOS DIR scans. NDIR will display these directories if the user has appropriate File Scan rights.
Immediate Compress (Ic)	Forces the file system to compress files as soon as the operating system can handle the action. New when NetWare 4 introduced compression.
Normal (N)	Flags a directory as Read/Write and non-shareable. It removes most other flags. This is the standard setting for user directories on the server handling DOS programs.
Purge (P)	Forces NetWare to completely delete files as the user deletes them, rather than tracking the deletions for the SALVAGE command to use later.
Rename Inhibit (Ri)	Stops users from renaming directories, even those users who have been granted the Modify trustee right. However, if the user has the Modify trustee right, that user can remove this attribute from the directory and then rename the directory.
System (Sy)	Hides directories from DOS DIR scans and prevents them from being deleted or copied. The NDIR program will display these directories if the user has appropriate File Scan rights.

PART

II

Managing the Network

Most of these directory attributes are seldom used to protect a directory from confused users. The options you will probably use the most are those that concern the operating system, such as Don't Compress and Immediate Compress. The Normal attribute will be used most often, if your network follows true to form.

File System: File Attributes

Most flagging happens at the file level and doesn't get changed all that often. After all, once you set the files in a directory the way you want (all the .EXE and .COM files Read Only and Shareable, for instance), few occasions require you to change them.

The time to worry about file attributes is during and immediately after installation of a new software product. Many product vendors today advertise, "Yes, it runs with NetWare," and they normally set the flags for you during installation. However, it's good practice to check newly installed applications, just in case the developers forgot to set a flag or three.

The available file attributes are listed in Table 9.5, with their abbreviations and meanings.

TABLE 9.5: FILE ATTRIBUTES IN NETWARE 5.1

Attribute	Description
All (All)	Sets all available file attributes.
Archive Needed (A)	DOS's Archive bit that identifies files modified after the last backup. NetWare assigns this bit automatically.
Copy Inhibit (Ci)	Prevents Macintosh clients from copying the file, even those clients with Read and File Scan trustee rights. This attribute can be changed by users with the Modify right.
Don't Compress (Dc)	Prevents the file from being compressed. This attribute overrides settings for automatic compression of files. New when . . . you know.
Delete Inhibit (Di)	Prevents clients from deleting the file, even those clients with the Erase trustee right. This attribute can be changed by users with the Modify right.
Don't Migrate (Dm)	Prevents files from being migrated from the server's hard disk to another storage medium. New with NetWare 4.
Hidden (H)	Hides files from the DOS DIR command. The NDIR program will display these files if the user has appropriate File Scan rights.
Index (I) (NetWare 4.0 and 4.1)	Forces the NetWare operating system to index this file's FAT (file allocation table) entries in the server memory for faster file access. This happens automatically on any file with more than 64 FAT entries.
Immediate Compress (Ic)	Forces files to be compressed as soon as the file is closed. New again with NetWare 4.

Continued ▮▶

TABLE 9.5 (CONTINUED): FILE ATTRIBUTES IN NETWARE 5.1	
Attribute	**Description**
Normal (N)	Shorthand for Read/Write, since there is no N attribute bit for file attributes. This is the default setting for files.
Purge (P)	Forces NetWare to automatically purge the file after it has been deleted.
Rename Inhibit (Ri)	Prevents the filename from being modified. Users with the Modify trustee right may change this attribute and then rename the file.
Read Only (Ro)	Prevents a file from being modified. This attribute automatically sets Delete Inhibit and Rename Inhibit. It's extremely useful for keeping .COM and .EXE files from being deleted by users, and it helps stop a virus from mutating the file.
Read Write (Rw)	The default attribute for all files. Allows users to read and write to the file.
Shareable (Sh)	Allows more than one user to access a file simultaneously. Normally used with the Read Only attribute so that a file being used by multiple users cannot be modified. All the utility files in the \PUBLIC directory are flagged Sh (and Ro, Di, and Ri).
System File (Sy)	Prevents a file from being deleted or copied and hides it from the DOS DIR command. NetWare's NDIR program will display these directories as System if the user has appropriate File Scan rights.
Transactional (T)	Forces the file to be tracked and protected by the Transaction Tracking System (TTS).
Execute Only (X) (NetWare 4.0 and 4.1)	Prevents a file from being copied, modified, or backed up. Used for .EXE or .COM program files, this attribute cannot be removed unless the file is deleted. Take care with this attribute. It can cause problems during updates (files can't be written over by a newer version), and some older backup software handles an Execute Only file by stopping.

PART

II

Managing the
Network

File attributes are normally assigned to the files using a wildcard with the FLAG command, such as the command:

```
FLAG *.EXE RO Sh
```

This command says, "Change the file attributes of all files with the .EXE extension to be readable, but not writable, and to share the file by allowing multiple clients to use the program file concurrently."

TIP When a user has a problem with a file, the first two things to check are the user's rights in that directory and the flags set on the problem file. One of these two settings, mismatched in some way, accounts for 80 percent or more of user file problems.

Let's look at how to type an exploratory FLAG command and examine the results. Figure 9.5 shows the command and result.

FIGURE 9.5

Checking the FLAG setting in the \PUBLIC directory

```
[Novell DOS] Z:\PUBLIC>flag t*.*

Files        = The name of the files found
Directories  = The name of the directories found
DOS Attr     = The DOS attributes for the specified file
NetWare Attr = The NetWare attributes for the specified file or directory
Status       = The current status of migration and compression for a file
               or directory
Owner        = The current owner of the file or directory
Mode         = The search mode set for the current file

Files                DOS Attr NetWare Attr         Status Owner         Mode
----------------------------------------------------------------------------
TEXTUTIL.IDX         [Ro----] [---ShDi--Ri------]         .GATEWAY200... N/A
TOSHP321.PDF         [Ro----] [---ShDi--Ri------]         .GATEWAY200... N/A
TYPEMSG.EXE          [Ro----] [---ShDi--Ri------] Co      .GATEWAY200... 0
TLIST.BAT            [Ro----] [---ShDi--Ri------]         .GATEWAY200... N/A
TCLASS31.DLL         [Ro----] [---ShDi--Ri------]         .GATEWAY200... N/A
TLI_SPX.DLL          [Ro----] [---ShDi--Ri------] Co      .GATEWAY200... N/A
TLI_TCP.DLL          [Ro----] [---ShDi--Ri------] Co      .GATEWAY200... N/A
TLI_WIN.DLL          [Ro----] [---ShDi--Ri------] Co      .GATEWAY200... N/A
TESTING.BAK          [Rw---A] [-----------------] Co      .Admin.GCS    N/A
TESTING.DAT          [Rw---A] [-----------------] Cc      .Admin.GCS    N/A

[Novell DOS] Z:\PUBLIC>
```

In this example, we can see the file attributes for a few of the NetWare utility files. Most are Ro (Read Only), meaning they also have the NetWare attributes of Di (Delete Inhibit) and Ri (Rename Inhibit) set as well. Looking at the second set of attributes, you see this is true.

The TESTING.DAT and TESTING.BAK files have been modified by the Admin user. You can tell because the flag is set to Rw (Read Write) and the Archive attributes are set, meaning they have changed since the last backup. The owner of these modified files is the Admin user. The rest of the files in the screen shot are owned by the server, GATEWAY2000. The ownership for these files was set during installation.

To check for all the various FLAG command-line switches, from the DOS command line, type:

FLAG /? ALL

You'll see six screens' worth of information.

NOTE Don't think that FLAG is the only way to change file attributes. FILER, Console-One, and NetWare Administrator utilities allow these same functions, just not as quickly and easily (in my opinion).

ConsoleOne's new beefy manifestation, like the weakling working out after being embarrassed, impresses me with its progress. Early versions of ConsoleOne couldn't get to the file level, but Novell engineers whipped that problem. See Figure 9.6 for ConsoleOne's new file-control features.

FIGURE 9.6

ConsoleOne now displays file attributes

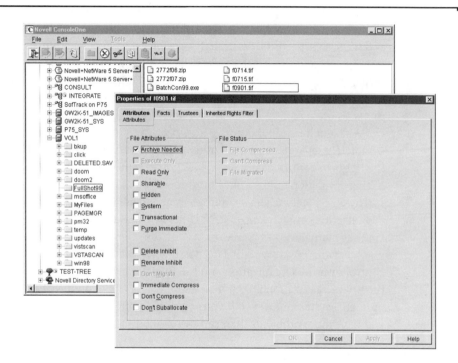

PART

II

Managing the Network

Notice the strange icons? The red X means delete, the scissors mean cut, the pages mean copy, and the A with a strike-out and the B means rename. Not the best iconography for rename, I grant you, but new and impressive overall.

NDS Security

Since NDS was new to NetWare 4, the idea of NDS security was new to old NetWare hands at the time and may still be new to those just jumping up from good old Net-Ware/386. NDS security is concerned with the management and protection of the NDS database and its objects.

The SUPERVISOR user in NetWare 3.*x* was concerned about both file security (as we just discussed) and network resources security. The second part of the job included creating and managing users, setting network access privileges for all network users, and creating and managing network resources, such as printers and volumes.

The Admin user has, by default, all the rights and power of the SUPERVISOR user. In NetWare 5.1, however, the management can easily be split between NDS security and file system security. It's entirely possible to have one administrator with no control over file and user trustee rights and another administrator with no control over containers, Organizations, or Organizational Units. You can also set up subadministrators with complete control over their containers, having both file and property rights.

Let's be quite clear about this: file system and NDS security systems are (almost) completely separate from each other (the Supervisor right crosses the line). Having the rights to control a container gives you no authority over a file kept on a volume in that container, unless rights are granted to that volume.

The NDS database allows multiple management layers. You can create as many Organizations and Organizational Units as you want, nesting the Organizational Units as many levels as you want. As you'll see when I talk about how the IRF works on object and property rights, it's possible for the Admin of a network to have full control over the Organization and the first Organizational Unit, but no control over the final Organizational Unit. Make sure this is what you have in mind before setting up such a system, however. If you can't trust your Admin with access to everything, you have more problems than can be solved by NetWare.

Object Rights versus Property Rights

There are two types of rights in NDS:

- *Object rights* determine what a trustee (user with the proper rights) can do to an object, such as creating, deleting, or renaming the object.
- *Property rights* determine whether a trustee can examine, use, or change the values of the various properties of an object.

Only in one case does an object right intrude into the property rights arena: the Supervisor right. A trustee with the Supervisor right to an object also has full rights to all properties of that object. But unlike with file and directory rights, the Supervisor right can be blocked on object and property rights by the IRF.

The opposite of the Supervisor right is the Browse right. This is the default right for users in the network. It allows users to see, but not modify, objects in the NDS tree.

Object rights concern the object as a whole in the Browser. Actions taken on an object in the Browser, such as moving a User object from one context to another, exemplify object rights.

Property rights concern the values of all the properties of an object. The User object that was moved in the last paragraph has hundreds of properties. The ability to change a property value, such as Minimum Account Balance or Telephone Number, requires property rights.

Objects have inheritance rights, meaning a trustee of one object has the same rights over a subsidiary object. If a trustee has rights over one container, that trustee has the same rights over any container objects inside the main container.

Let's play "Pick Your Analogy." Object rights are like moving boxes, and the box contents are properties. The movers have authority over the boxes (object rights) but not over the contents of the boxes (property rights). A mover supervisor, however, has the rights to the boxes and to the contents (property rights) of those boxes for management situations.

When you turn your car over to a parking lot attendant, you give that attendant object rights: your car can be placed anywhere in the parking lot. The attendant has full control over where your car is and if it needs to be moved while you're gone. You probably exclude the Delete right from the attendant, however. The property rights to your car, such as the items in your trunk, glove compartment, and back seat, do not belong to the parking lot attendant. You have granted the attendant some object rights to your car, but no property rights. Do you think armored car drivers have object rights or property rights to the money bags? Which would you prefer if you were a driver? Which if you owned the bag contents?

To keep things consistent, object rights and property rights overlap only in the Supervisor right. The trick is to remember that sometimes a C means Create and sometimes it means Compare. Take a look at the official list of object rights in Table 9.6.

TABLE 9.6: OBJECT RIGHTS IN NETWARE 5.1

Right	Description
Supervisor (S)	Grants all access privileges, including unrestricted access to all properties. The Supervisor right can be blocked by an IRF, unlike with file and directory rights.
Browse (B)	Grants the right to see this object in the NDS tree. The name of the object is returned when a search is made, if the search criteria match the object.
Create (C)	Grants the right to create a new object, below this object, in the NDS tree. No rights are defined for the new object. This right applies only to container objects because only container objects can have subordinates.
Delete (D)	Grants the right to delete the object from the NDS tree. Objects that have subordinates can't be deleted unless the subordinates are deleted first, just like a DOS directory can't be deleted if it still contains files or subdirectories.
Rename (R)	Grants the right to change the name of the object. This officially changes the Name property of the object, changing the object's complete name.

The object rights tend to be used by managers, not by users. Create, Delete, and Rename rights are not the type of things normally given to users. The Browse object right is granted automatically to [Root], meaning everyone can browse the NDS tree. Remember, the Supervisor object right automatically allows full access to all property rights. The property rights are listed in Table 9.7.

TABLE 9.7: PROPERTY RIGHTS IN NETWARE 5.1

Right	Description
Supervisor (S)	Grants all rights to the property. The Supervisor right can be blocked by an IRF, unlike with file and directory rights.
Compare (C)	Grants the right to compare any value with a value of the property for search purposes. With the Compare right, a search operation can return True or False, but you can't see the value of the property. The Read right includes the Compare right.
Read (R)	Grants the right to read all the values of the property. Compare is a subset of Read. If the Read right is given, Compare operations are also allowed.
Write (W)	Grants the right to add, change, or remove any values of the property. Write also includes the Add or Delete Self right.
Add or Delete Self (A)	Grants a trustee the right to add or remove itself as a value of the property, but no other values of the property may be changed. This right is meaningful only for properties that contain object names as values, such as group membership lists or mailing lists. The Write right includes Add or Delete Self.

The Access Control List (ACL)

The *ACL* (Access Control List) is the object property that stores the information about who may access the object. Just as Joe is a value of the Name property, the ACL contains trustee assignments for both object and property rights. The ACL also includes the IRF.

To change the ACL, you must have a property right that allows you to modify that ACL value for that object. Write will allow this, as will the Supervisor object right. Add or Delete Self is for users to add or remove themselves from a Members List property of a Group object.

Want to grant object or property rights to another object? You must have the Write, Add or Delete Self, or Supervisor right to the ACL property of the object in question.

Although it sounds as if the ACL is some list somewhere, it's really just one of many properties held by an object. Each object has an ACL. If a user is not listed in the ACL for an object, that user cannot change the properties of that object.

How Rights Inheritance Works

As I said before, rights flow downhill (ask a plumber what else flows downhill). Directory rights pass down to subdirectories, and container rights flow down to subcontainers. The only way to stop rights from flowing to a subcontainer is to use the IRF in the subcontainer. This forces users with rights to the parent container to also get the trustee rights to the subcontainer in a separate operation. That means the network supervisor (probably you) must go back and grant trustee rights to those users who need access to the subcontainer.

The system works well, with one exception: selected property rights are not inherited. If a user is granted trustee rights to an object for selected property rights only, those rights do not move down to the subcontainer or other objects. Figure 9.7 shows the process of granting user Wendy selected property rights to the IMAGES volume of server GW2K-51.

Selected property rights always take precedence over inherited rights. Even without an IRF, setting particular trustee rights in one container puts those rights in effect, no matter which rights are assigned to the container above. ConsoleOne shows these rights assignments in a different way than we're used to, but you can see that we just added property rights to the ACL property for the IMAGES volume for Wendy. I had to click the Add Property button on the foreground dialog window to pop up the long list of rights to choose for Wendy.

PART

II

Managing the
Network

FIGURE 9.7

*Granting limited rights
that cannot be
inherited*

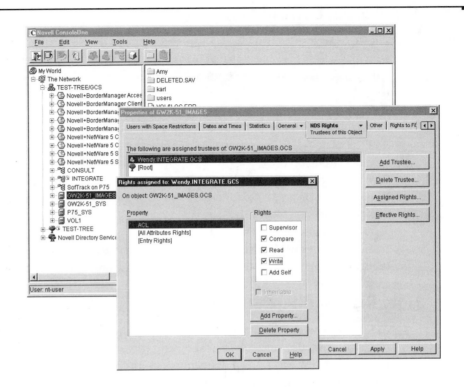

The IRF and Object and Property Rights

The IRF works the same with object and property rights as it does with file and directory rights. The IRF doesn't give rights to anyone; it only takes rights away.

You, as network manager, set the level of rights users should have to an object. If a particular user has more rights than that, the IRF will filter that particular user to the level of access you set.

The big difference in the IRF when dealing with the NDS object and property rights is the ability to block the Supervisor object right. This gives some departments a warm fuzzy feeling, since no one except their administrator can control their part of the NDS tree. But care must be taken in organizing your system.

NetWare helps safeguard against accidentally eliminating all supervision for part of your tree by not allowing you to block the Supervisor object right to an object unless at least one other object has already been granted the Supervisor right to that object. The problem comes if the other Supervisor object is deleted. Deleting the sole Supervisor for part of your NDS tree leaves part of the system without management, which is not a good thing.

This is a good reason to never delete the Admin user, even if you have one or two Admin-equivalent users. Over time, something will happen to both equivalent users, and suddenly your network will not have anyone able to perform supervisory functions over the entire tree. Some paranoid people have both Admin-equivalent users and users not set as Admin-equivalent but granted the full set of rights. Why? If Admin is deleted or the properties are garbled, the Admin equivalency may be worthless as well.

So, when you grant someone the Supervisor trustee right to a section of the NDS tree, also grant them all other trustee rights. This precaution allows that person to maintain the ability to create, delete, rename, and modify objects, even if the Supervisor right is blocked by the IRF.

NDS Security Guidelines

Security management is not the most exciting stuff in the world, 99 percent of the time. The goal of this section is to help you ensure that the one percent of security management that is exciting—a security breach—happens only in the mildest way possible. Maybe only a bad joke breach.

Realize that few users need to create, delete, or modify objects (users, printers, etc.) during their normal workday. Those users who have occasion to need these trustee rights should be made an official or unofficial helper. The designation of "Power User for Marketing" will help that person feel better about spending extra time helping other users without getting paid for it. At least recognize those power users, since recognized helpers will help keep security strong, not tear it down. The big problems come when someone accidentally gets too many rights, not when the department's power user has defined a new printer.

A CNI (Certified NetWare Instructor) friend of mine offers these guidelines for granting rights:

- Start with the default assignments. Defaults are in place to give users access to the resources they need without giving them access to resources or information they do not need.

- Avoid assigning rights through the All Properties option. Avoiding All Properties will protect private information about users and other resources on the network.

- Use Selected Properties to assign property rights. This will allow you to assign more specific rights and avoid future security problems.

- Use caution when assigning the Write property right to the ACL property of any object. This right effectively gives the trustee the ability to grant anyone, including himself or herself, all rights, including the Supervisor right. This is another reason to use extreme care when making rights assignments with All Properties.

- Use caution when granting the Supervisor object right to a Server object. This gives Supervisor file system rights to all volumes linked to that server. This object rights assignment should be made only after considering the implication of a network administrator having access to all files on all volumes linked to a particular server. Furthermore, granting the Write property right to the ACL property of the Server object will also give Supervisor file system rights to all volumes linked to that particular server.

- Granting the Supervisor object right implies granting the Supervisor right to all properties. For some container administrators, you might want to grant all object rights except the Supervisor right and then grant property rights through the Selected Properties option.

- Use caution when filtering Supervisor rights with an IRF. For example, a container administrator uses an IRF to filter the network administrator's rights to a particular branch of the NDS tree. If the network administrator (who has the Supervisor right to the container administrator's User object) deletes the User object of the container administrator, that particular branch of the NDS tree can no longer be managed.

Here's my security slogan: grant to containers or groups; ignore the individuals. The more individual users you administer, the more time and trouble it will take. I've known some NetWare managers to make groups holding only one person. That sounds stupid, but consider the alternative: when a second person comes, and then a third person, you'll find yourself handling each one by hand. If a group is in place, each new person who arrives takes only a few seconds to install and to apply all the necessary trustee rights and network resource mappings.

Whenever possible, handle security (access to network resources) through the container. If not a container, then a group. If not a group, look harder to make the need fit an existing group or develop a new group. The more adamant you are about securing your network by groups rather than by individual users, the lighter your network management burden. The more you use the container to grant rights, the neater things are.

Security Management with ConsoleOne (Mostly)

When NDS is first installed, there are two objects: Admin and [Public]. The default rights, and the reasons for the rights, are:

Admin	Supervisor object rights to [Root]	Allows Admin to create and administer all other network objects.
[Public]	Browse object rights to [Root]	Allows all users to see the NDS tree and all objects on the tree.

When you create User objects, each has a certain set of default rights. These rights include what the User object can do to manage itself, such as Read and Write the user's login script and print job configuration. To get around in the NDS tree, users are also granted limited rights to [Root] and [Public].

Here's a summary of the default User object trustee, default rights, and what these rights allow a user to do:

[R]   Read right to all property rights, which allows the reading of properties stored in the User object.

[RW]   Read and Write property rights to the user's own Login Script property, which allows users to execute and modify their own login scripts.

[RW]   Read and Write property rights to the user's own Print Configuration property, which allows users to create print jobs and send them to the printer.

The [Root] object has this default property right:

[R]   Read property right to Network Address and Group Membership, which identifies the network address and any group memberships.

And the [Public] object has this property right by default:

[R]   Read property right to the Default Server property, which determines the default server for the User object.

As you can see, the default NDS rights are fairly limited. A new user can see the network, change his or her own login script and printer configuration, and wait for help.

If that's too much—perhaps you don't want users to have the ability to change (and mess up) their own login scripts—change it. Merely revoke the User object's Login Script property right. Figure 9.8 shows the User object details, with the Write capability for the Login Script property revoked. The Read capability is necessary so that the user can log in.

PART

II

Managing the
Network

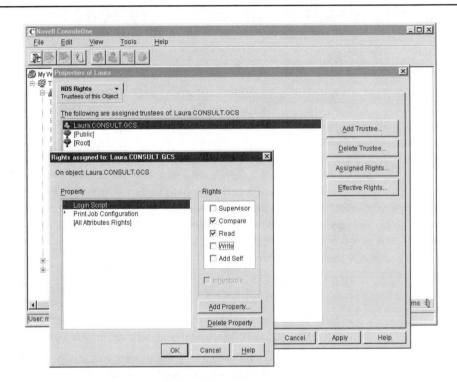

FIGURE 9.8

Preventing Laura from changing her login script

Revoking a Property Right

9.1 Prevent a User from Modifying His or Her Own Login Script

1. Open ConsoleOne from some Java Virtual Machine–enabled system.
2. Highlight the User object to modify, and click the right mouse button.
3. Select Properties.
4. Click the NDS Rights tab and choose Trustees Of This Object.
5. Highlight the User object and click the Assigned Rights button.
6. Click the property to modify (you may have to click the Add Property button).
7. Clear the Write checkbox while Login Script is highlighted.
8. Click OK to save and exit.

Think of this process as a prelude to the other security-management tasks we're going to do in the following sections. First, you must start ConsoleOne from some Java Virtual Machine-enabled system and highlight the User object that you want to modify. You must either click the right mouse button and then choose Properties or use the File ➣ Properties menu choice.

When we get to the dialog box for the User object (as you can see in Figure 9.8 in the previous section for user Laura), we want to change the Property Rights setting. It may sound odd, or at least different, but with ConsoleOne we want to check the Trustees Of This Object right under NDS Rights. Drill down to Laura.CONSULT.GCS. Then click the Assigned Rights command button, which opens the Rights Assigned To dialog box. Scroll through the list, find Login Script, highlight it, and review the rights.

The default is to have both Read and Write capabilities. By clicking the Write checkbox, that right is cleared from our user. The change will become active after the dialog box is saved with the new setting and the NDS database has a second to digest the change.

In Figure 9.8 (shown earlier), I also opened the Effective Rights dialog box by clicking the Effective Rights button. When I highlighted Login Script, the rights for user Laura to her own login script were shown: Compare and Read appeared in the Rights box. So now we know user Laura has the capability to read and therefore execute the login script but not to change it.

 TIP The other way to prevent users from playing with their login scripts is to bypass them entirely. Remember the sequence of login script execution? The User object's login script comes last. Just use the EXIT command in the Container login script, and the personal login script for everyone in the container will be bypassed. Users can then make all the changes they want in their login scripts, but it won't make a bit of difference.

Setting or Modifying Directory and File Rights

You can allow a user or group of users access to a directory in two ways:

- You can go through the user side and use the rights-to-files-and-directories approach.

- You can go to the directory to be accessed and use the trustees-of-this-directory angle.

PART

II

Managing the Network

Which method you use depends on whether you're making one directory available to lots of users or granting trustee rights to one set of users to lots of other network objects. We'll take a look at both angles.

First, let's take a different view of the network inside NetWare Administrator. Each time we've seen it before, there has been one big window with the network objects running down the left side. This view is the quickest and works well with a small network. But for some tasks and some networks, other views are handy. NetWare Administrator is very flexible in its presentation of your NDS tree.

Figure 9.9 shows the use of the Browser utility. With the Browse function, you can divide the network into as many views as you want. In fact, you can look at the same information in so many ways that you might get confused if you're not careful.

FIGURE 9.9

Browsing and exploding our network view

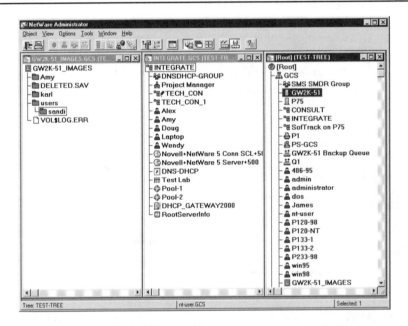

This is the same network we've seen before with NetWare Administrator, but sliced a different way. The far-right window is the [Root] view, which has been the only view we've seen so far. The middle window is the INTEGRATE Organizational Unit, shown in its own window instead of underneath the CONSULT Organizational Unit. The far-left window is the GW2K-51_IMAGES directory, expanded from the [Root] window to show all the directories. The highlighted directory, USERS, is expanded to show the subdirectory we made for user Sandi earlier. No, ConsoleOne can't do this, at least not yet. It's still locked into the two-window configuration because the multi-window within an open window remains Windows-specific and has yet to be emulated in Java.

Opening a Browser Window

IN A HURRY

9.2 Open a Browser Window in NetWare Administrator

1. Open NetWare Administrator.
2. Double-click the Organizations and Organizational Units you want to expand.
3. Highlight the object to place in a new Browser window.
4. Click the right mouse button to open a floating menu.
5. Click Browse.

Officially, each display window in NetWare Administrator is a Browser window. But since the first window always opens in full-screen mode when you start NetWare Administrator, it's hard to think in terms of the display being just one of many windows.

After opening NetWare Administrator from Windows, double-click all the container objects you want to expand. (I have always expanded both Organizational Units, INTEGRATE and CONSULT, in the main window for each screen copy.) Then highlight the object you want to place in its own Browser window. Click the right mouse button to open a "floating" menu. Left-click Browse to see the previously highlighted container in a new window. The container expands automatically and displays its contents in the new window.

You can also use a drop-down menu to start a Browser window. Highlight the object to set in its own window and click the Tools menu. The drop-down menu contains the Browse option, which you can click to open a new Browser window.

 NOTE   If the item highlighted cannot be browsed, as is the case with a User object, you cannot open a Browser window for it. The Browse choice in both the Tools menu at the top of the screen and the floating menu will be gray and unavailable.

PART

II

Managing the
Network

From the Group or User's Point of View

IN A HURRY

9.3 Grant Trustee Rights to a Volume or Directory

1. Open ConsoleOne.
2. Drill down in the left window to the CONSULT organizational unit.
3. Right-click the Programmers group and choose Properties.
4. Click the Rights To Files And Folders tab.
5. Click the Show command button and choose the correct volume in the Select Object dialog box.
6. Click the Add command button, and drill down to the correct directory or file.
7. Check the boxes near the rights you wish to grant.
8. Click the OK command button, or the Apply button if you have more changes to make.

You can easily grant trustee rights for a single object to multiple volumes, directories, or files. The object gaining the rights should be a group of some kind, such as an Organization, Organizational Unit, or Group object, but it works for single User objects as well.

Start ConsoleOne as either the Admin user or another user with the Supervisor right to both the user side and the network resource side of this equation. Drill down until the group Programmers appears on the right side of ConsoleOne. Right-click that group, choose Properties, and you'll see most of what appears in Figure 9.10.

First, click the Show command button to find and select the correct volume (GW2K-51_IMAGES in this case). Then click the Add command button, select down to the directory level, and choose the \SRC-CODE directory. Programmers demand access to source code, so let them have it.

Notice that all rights are being granted to Programmers. If you don't give them all rights, they'll just whine and complain until you change your mind and upgrade their rights. Give them all rights the first time, then let them worry about what happens if they screw up. They're programmers, so if they do screw up, they'll never admit a thing. That's what I'm doing in Figure 9.10, giving them all rights to the \SRC-CODE directory.

PART

II

Managing the
Network

FIGURE 9.10

*Granting
Programmers access
to the \APPS\
SRC-CODE
directory*

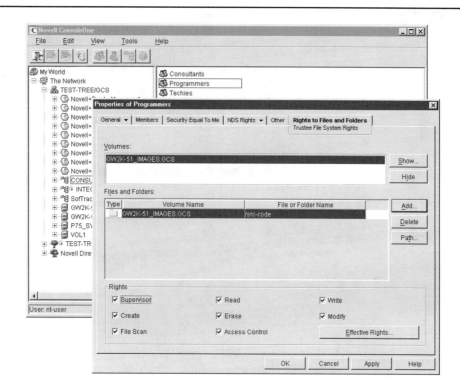

The chosen directories are in a different context than the Programmers group. This is not a problem, but you will need to create an Alias object for the remote volume to enable the group to connect to these directories during login. We'll get to that in the management chapter coming right up (Chapter 10).

Unlike in NetWare Administrator or other Windows utilities, ConsoleOne won't allow you to select multiple files or directories for the Files And Folders section of Properties Of Programmers. You can change utilities, but I'd rather you take the hint and not change one file at a time.

The default rights to any new volume, directory, or file are Read and File Scan. These rights are probably not enough for your purposes. For Programmers, all rights are given. See Figure 9.11 for a display of the effective rights in the far-right window.

You can grant trustee rights to a Volume object rather than to a directory or file. If you do, the object with those rights has complete access to the root directory, meaning the entire volume. If you have enough volumes to parcel them out in that manner, that's great, but many networks grant rights to a directory. That allows plenty of accessibility for the users, since they can build a full directory structure while still maintaining an easy method of control.

FIGURE 9.11

Granted rights are bold; excluded rights are gray.

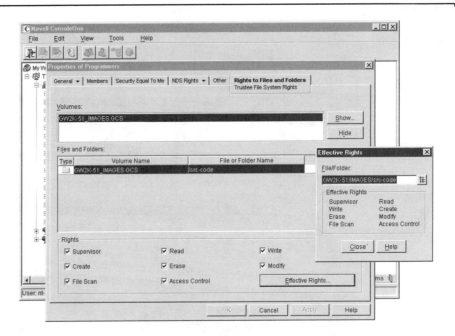

Granting rights to a directory in another container is not a problem, but one more step may be needed. If the users want to map a drive to another container in their login script, they can't get there from here. You must create an Alias object for the remote volume and then map the groups and users to the Alias.

From the Directory or File's Point of View

IN A HURRY

9.4 Grant Trustee Rights to a Group or User

1. Open ConsoleOne.
2. Drill down to the volume or directory desired.
3. Right-click the directory and choose Properties.
4. Click the Trustees tab to check current trustees. Click the Add Trustee command button to add another trustee.
5. Drill down to the object to become a trustee of the SRC-CODE directory. In this case, it's the group Techies.

Continued

6. Highlight the groups and/or users in the Select Object window and click OK.

7. To modify the rights, check to add or uncheck to delete rights in the Rights section at the bottom of the dialog box. Repeat as necessary for each group or user.

8. Click OK to save and exit.

This is the best method to use when granting several users or groups trustee rights to the same volume, directory, or file. One screen allows you to choose multiple trustees at once and yet assign different rights to each of them. Although this technique can work with volumes and files, let's use a common scenario: making a group of users trustees to a directory.

Start the ConsoleOne program. Browse through the NDS tree as necessary to highlight the object to make available to the new user or users. In our example, the IMAGES\ SRC-CODE directory is the one to be shared with the Programmers and now the Techies groups.

Once the volume is highlighted in the left pane, the directories will appear in the right pane. Pressing Enter will display the directories in the left pane, leaving the right pane still empty. Right-click the directory name (in either pane you prefer) and choose the Properties menu item.

We added Programmers earlier, so that group appears as a trustee of the directory. Click the Add Trustee command button to open the Select Object dialog box to find the Techies group, as shown in Figure 9.12.

Once you've found it, click OK to add the Techies to the list of trustees for the IMAGES directory. Check the proper Access Rights boxes on the right side of the Trustees window, and click OK.

Once the new trustees are copied to the list, checking the Access Rights for each group will set the level of control the group has over the directory. Since few groups should ever have Supervisor rights, leave that and the Access Control box unchecked.

Using NetWare Administrator, checking the Effective Rights requires more work. In ConsoleOne, however, the Access Rights checkboxes do an excellent job of showing the Effective Rights. In Figure 9.12, you can see that the Programmers group has all rights to the directory.

PART

II

Managing the
Network

Adding Techies to the
\IMAGES\SRC-CODE
Trustees list

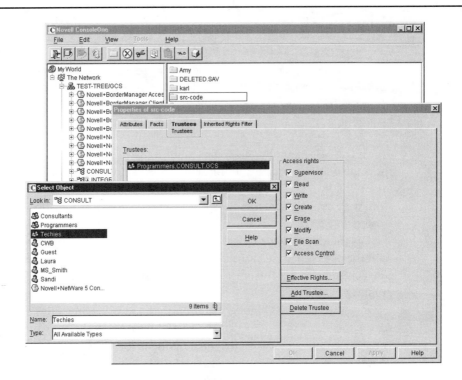

Techies tend not to be as demanding as programmers, so they don't need all the same rights. As you can see in Figure 9.13, I granted them all the rights except Supervisor and Access Control. This way, I can still blame the programmers if something happens, since the Techies won't have as many rights and therefore have fewer chances to mess up something.

Click OK to save and exit, or just click Close since the rights have already been changed, and then reenter to check that all the rights you planned to grant have in fact been granted. It's easy to skip a mouse-click here and there, so make it a habit to check yourself.

Once again: granting rights to a directory in another container is not a problem, but one more step may be needed. If the users want to map a drive to another container in their login script, they can't get there from here. You must create an Alias object for the remote volume and then map the groups and users to the Alias.

FIGURE 9.13

The effective rights to
\IMAGES\SRC-CODE
for Techies

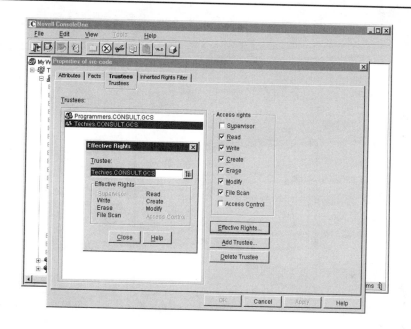

Setting or Modifying Object and Property Rights

NetWare Administrator offers drag-and-drop trustee assignments to some NDS objects. That means you can, for instance, drag a User icon over to a network object such as a Volume and drop that User object there. Trustee rights are granted from the dropper to the droppee, although only the basic Read and File Scan rights are included. Granting any more rights requires going through the Trustees Of This Object menu item.

This drag-and-drop feature is far ahead of NetWare 5.1's competition. Although the mouse can't manage your network by itself, easier administration means more time for you to stay ahead of your users.

Let's take a look at drag-and-drop in action. Figure 9.14 shows the Browser window in two pieces: the left one with the [Root] display we've used almost exclusively, and the right window showing the INTEGRATE Organizational Unit display. Notice that User object Laura is highlighted. This is the first part of the drag-and-drop activity. The tiny User object icon, a Lego-like head-and-shoulders drawing, is floating close to the printer P1.

PART

II

Managing the
Network

FIGURE 9.14

Dragging Laura into Trustee Rights to P1

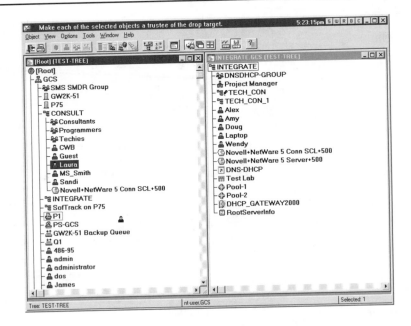

While the Laura User object icon is floating up and down the NDS tree, several things happen. As the object moves, the dotted box that surrounds P1 in the example moves along with the icon. If the dragged object has the ability to become a trustee of the object being indicated by the dotted box, the status line on the very top of the screen announces the ability to make each of the selected objects a trustee of the drop target. In other words, you can drop and gain some control over the target.

Once the target is reached and the icon released, the Trustees Of This Object menu item is automatically checked, popping open the dialog box of the same name.

From the Target Object's Point of View

IN A HURRY

9.5 Drag-and-Drop Trustee Rights

1. Open NetWare Administrator.

2. Highlight the object to be given the trustee rights.

3. Click and hold down the left mouse button on the object.

4. Move the object icon over the NDS tree until the target object is indicated by the dotted line.

Continued

5. Release the left mouse button.

6. Modify any of the object or property rights using the checkboxes.

7. Click OK to save and exit.

Dragging-and-dropping is a handy way to grant object and property rights from one object to another. Even if you have multiple objects that need rights to the target object, this is a fun way to open the Trustees Of dialog box.

After connecting to the network as an appropriate user, start NetWare Administrator. In this example, we have the two Organizational Units displayed in one window, and the INTEGRATE Organizational Unit is opened separately in the right window.

Find the object to make a trustee of our target object, and click and hold down the left mouse button on that object. As you move the mouse up and down the NDS tree, you'll see the icon for the object move along with you (as in Figure 9.14, shown earlier). The dotted-line box will surround each object you pass over, indicating exactly which object is your target at that second.

When the dotted line surrounds your target, drop the object by releasing the left mouse button. The Trustees Of dialog box will open, with the trustee object added to the Trustees list and highlighted. The Browse object right and the Compare and Read property rights are granted automatically in this process. Take a look at Figure 9.15 for the status of this operation.

FIGURE 9.15

Click and save, or grant more rights for Laura to P1.

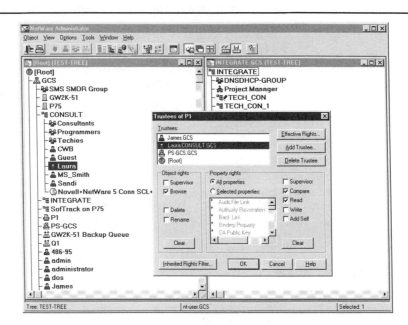

PART

II

Managing the Network

If you want to change any of the trustee rights, this is the time to do so. Use the checkboxes to add or delete rights. Click OK to save and exit.

You can add more trustees to this screen by clicking the Add Trustee command button. This opens the Select Object dialog box once again, and all the objects that can be a trustee of the target object are displayed. Change context by using the Change Context button or the up arrow in the Directory Context box. The process is exactly like that of adding more directory and file trustees.

You can skip the drag-and-drop operation if you want. To open the Trustees Of dialog box (as shown in Figure 9.15), highlight the target object and click the right mouse button. This opens the floating menu containing a Trustees Of This Object choice. Click there, and the dialog box opens, without any assignments. All the trustees must be added through the Select Object dialog box. After choosing the trustees you need, highlight each and modify any of the object and/or property rights for each trustee. Finally, click OK to save and exit.

From the Trustee Object's Point of View

IN A HURRY

9.6 Give an Object Trustee Rights to Other Objects

1. Open ConsoleOne.
2. Highlight the object to be given trustee rights to another object.
3. Click the right mouse button and open the Properties menu item.
4. Choose NDS Rights, then Trustees Of This Object.
5. Click the Add Trustee command button to open the Select Objects dialog box.
6. Click the down arrow to open the NDS tree listing, or click the folder icon with the up arrow to move up one context level.
7. Move up or down the tree as necessary to find the object to become an assigned trustee.
8. Click OK to save your selection into the Properties dialog box, then click OK to save and exit.

Want to give an object trustee rights to more than one other object at a time? Here's the place. This procedure allows you to grant trustee rights to multiple objects from one screen.

As the Admin user or equivalent, start ConsoleOne. Highlight the object, such as a user, a group, or a container, that you want to make a trustee of one or more other objects. Click the right mouse button to open the menu, then choose Properties.

The first step is to discover what the object already has rights to. This requires our first real search operation. Figure 9.16 shows the Select Objects dialog box open, with the Properties Of Laura dialog box in the background showing Laura's trusteeship of P1. The Select Objects dialog box offers two ways to cruise the NDS tree, and Figure 9.16 shows one of them.

PART

II

Managing the
Network

FIGURE 9.16

*Searching for other
objects for Laura to
control*

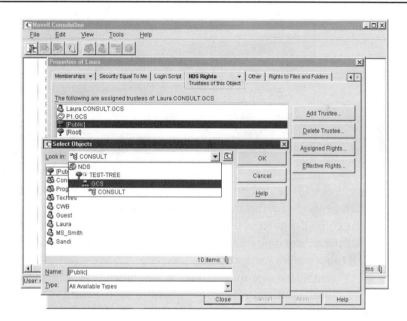

When the dialog box opens, the current context displays. Use the down arrow at the end of the Look In text line to display the full NDS tree down to your current context, or press the up-arrow icon if you need only go up one context level. Drill down, or slide up, the NDS tree until you find what you need. Since we're going to let Laura control some servers in a minute, we need to move up to the GCS organization level.

Our goal is to Add Trustee, so we must click that command button. Now your friendly Select Objects dialog box appears, as shown in Figure 9.17. Browse through the NDS tree and highlight the object or objects to gain trustee rights over. In our example, Laura now takes over the P75 and GW2K-51 servers.

FIGURE 9.17

*Laura selects servers
to control.*

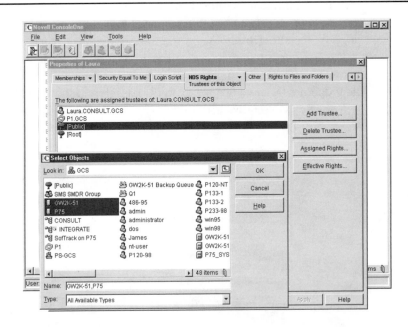

Notice that we may once again tag several objects in one screen by using either the Ctrl-key-and-multiple-click or the Shift-key-and-inclusive-click technique. We can see the current context of the items we're choosing, not the context of the objects gaining the trustee rights. Click OK to save your choices and move them to the Properties Of Laura box for final configuration.

Figure 9.18 shows the final step in this process. We can configure both of our chosen objects concurrently. As long as one or more items in the Rights Assigned To list is highlighted, the checkboxes will apply to all. Check the rights you want the object to have over the target object (in our example, the rights of Laura over GW2K-51 and P75). When you've finished, click OK to save and exit.

The same process works for modifying existing rights to objects. In that case, making sure you search the entire network for all objects is even more important. If you want to delete the assignment, highlight Assigned Rights and click the Delete Assignment command button. The rights assignment, not the object itself, will be deleted.

FIGURE 9.18

Granting trustee rights
to more than one
object at a time

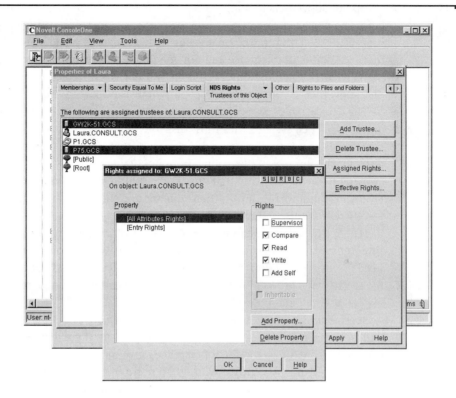

Virus Precautions

Viruses are always a concern, even if they are statistically insignificant. People worrying about viruses waste more time than viruses waste. But knowing that a virus attack is rare doesn't make you feel any better or get your network back to normal any faster if it does happen. Time spent preventing viruses is much more fun than time spent cleaning up after a virus attack.

You can take some precautions without adding optional software to your network or much time to your day. Mark all .EXE and .COM files as Read Only. Viruses generally function by modifying executable files. If all your executable files are read-only, viruses have a much harder time getting started.

Keep a tight watch on users' access rights to system areas—there shouldn't be any. Only managers, with a proper understanding of virus prevention, should have access to system files.

Do not allow users to bring disks from outside and load them to the network before being tested. Some companies go so far as to lock floppy drives, not so that users can't steal from the company, but so that users can't load infected software. This method is difficult to enforce and not good enough to be your only prevention step. Better to offer a virus-free check station for users to test floppies than try to ban floppies altogether. If you ban them, people will just sneak them into the building.

The days when users regularly downloaded unknown files from bulletin boards and booted their systems with those disks are long gone. That's good. Commercially sponsored download sites now pride themselves on running a clean site. That's good also. But the number of files copied from unknown sources across the Internet is growing tremendously, and that's bad. Unix administrators often don't know which DOS and Windows files are on their systems, and they don't have the time or tools to test them for viruses. That's also bad.

Feel free to restrict or eliminate FTP (File Transfer Protocol) programs from your Internet suite of applications, except for those trustworthy users who understand the need for virus protection. Although you can't always stop users from downloading files with a Web browser such as Netscape, keeping the FTP programs away from the general user population can't hurt.

Special virus-protection software is available for networks, often in conjunction with software metering or network user management. If your company is overly concerned with a virus attack, the software may give some peace of mind. However, virus software used inconsistently is worse than none at all. When you have none, people are more careful. When you have virus software used poorly, people develop a false sense of protection.

Some of the virus-protection features the optional programs provide are:

- Install and configure easily. NetWare versions are run as NLMs (new Java versions have yet to appear).
- Block unprotected clients from logging in to a protected server.
- Distribute protection to multiple servers and clients.
- Include an administration program for Windows as well as DOS.
- Send alerts to specified users when a questionable event occurs.
- Schedule when and how security sweeps are made.
- Report on status and other statistics.

There are two major camps regarding the primary means of protection against the virus-developer community. One idea is to track the signature of all viruses. The *signature* is a piece of code inside the virus that identifies that virus, usually included by the virus criminal as an ego enhancer. As more viruses are discovered, the signature database must grow. Those systems that scan for known virus signatures should receive regular database updates.

The other option is to register a *CRC* (cyclical redundancy check) of every executable file on the server when the file is installed. The CRC is checked each time the file is read from the server. If the CRC value changes, this means that the file has been tampered with. The alert sounds, and the software shuts down the use of that file.

I lean toward the CRC method, for several reasons. First, a new virus obviously can cause you problems, and this threat is eliminated with a CRC. Second, the overhead of checking a large virus database with every file-read request will only get heavier. As the demands on servers grow, this overhead will become burdensome. Finally, my friend John McCann was one of the first programmers to make quality add-on NetWare utilities, and he says the CRC method is better. Since he knows more about NetWare programming than anyone else I know, I'll take his word for it. (It's especially easy when I agree with his conclusion anyway.)

Some of the major NetWare-specific virus-protection vendors are:

- Dr. Solomon's Software, Inc.
- Computer Associates (they bought Cheyenne Software, Inc.)
- Intel Corporation
- Symantec Corporation, maker of Norton AntiVirus
- McAfee Associates, Inc.

Do you have a favorite anti-virus program? Do I? Not really. Be sure to check each of these major brands if you don't have virus protection already (and why don't you have protection already?). Those readers with multi-vendor networks (which usually means some Windows NT servers) will find that many of the companies in this list make virus products for both NetWare and NT.

Some people ask about the values of server-based versus client-based virus protection. We could even have separate sections extolling the virtues of both types of protection.

But we won't, because I feel strongly that you can't trust users to do your job for you. Yes, the users will suffer if they have a virus attack on their personal system, but they will demand that you fix things for them. So, asking them to protect against virus attacks on the client is asking them to do your job for you. Even if they were willing, they don't have the mental discipline to do a good job. They'll trust a file from a friend, assuming their friend knows the file's history. Bad move every time.

A critical part of virus protection is regular updates. Server-based products need a single update session to protect hundreds of clients. This is much more efficient (and reliable) than upgrading hundreds of clients individually.

Verify that your virus protection works on the client when the user logs in. Kicking off a check of the client during the login process catches most of the viruses introduced by careless users. You won't catch them all, unfortunately, because if you make the process idiot-proof, your company will hire a better idiot. Just make sure the virus doesn't spread.

 TIP If your manager is particularly scared of a virus attack, use that fear to your advantage. Clip an article about a virus attack and the resulting damage to the company. Nearly every single report includes a line about how the company had an inadequate backup procedure in place, meaning extra loss. If you've been angling for a bigger tape backup system or an upgrade, play the cards you're dealt, and hit your manager with the tape backup request in one hand while waving the virus attack article in the other hand. Is this dishonest? Not at all. Some people need to be pushed into doing the right thing. You should take care to push your manager when he or she is already staggering. This way, you don't need to push noticeably hard, but you still get what your network needs.

Using AUDITCON

Who watches the watchers? That question first appeared concerning the Roman army. How do you monitor a person who has all the power? In our case, the network administrator has full control of the network. You can limit that authority in some cases, but generally the administrator controls the network countryside as completely as the Roman soldiers controlled their territory.

We in the modern world know who watches the watchers: auditors. NetWare 4 was the first network operating system that allowed true auditing of network events by a person with power only to watch, not to change. The network administrator has always been the network auditor, but that leaves a security hole. Would your bank trust the branch manager with all that money without checking the books regularly? Of course not. Now your network can be audited by an outside individual with full access to network events but no control to change the network in any way.

Officially, auditing examines records to verify that transactions are accurate and that confidential information is handled securely. NetWare auditing allows independent auditors, separate from the regular NetWare administrators or users, to audit network transactions. Changes to NDS, to a volume's content, files, or directories, and to server status are considered transactions for auditing purposes. Table 9.8 shows the auditable network events.

TABLE 9.8: AUDITABLE EVENTS IN NETWARE 5.1

Category	Event
File or directory events	File and directory creation, modification, or deletion File and directory salvage, move, or rename operations Print queue creation, service, and deletion
Server events	Server going down Bindery object creation or deletion Volume mounting and dismounting Security rights changes
NDS events	Object create, move, rename, and delete operations Security equivalence changes User object logins and logouts
External auditing	Auditing of some workstation events for NetWare 5.1 clients

Because NetWare did not include auditing in earlier versions, some third-party products are available for this task. Ask your dealer for names of popular audit and management programs.

In fact, I suggest those of you serious about network auditing to ignore AUDITCON and go straight to a third-party product. Novell hasn't upgraded their auditing program past their old DOS C-Worthy interface, they don't secure audit files automatically, and their reporting options are limited. Check out ManageWise if you really want to know what happens on your network.

Starting AUDITCON

IN A HURRY

9.7 Start the Volume-Audit Process

1. While connected as the Admin or equivalent user, create an auditor user and a home directory for that user.
2. Assign the auditor Browse rights in all containers to be monitored.
3. Verify that the auditor has Read and File Scan trustee rights in SYS:PUBLIC to run the AUDITCON program and support files.

Continued

IN A HURRY CONTINUED

4. From the DOS command line, type **AUDITCON** to start the program.

5. Change the server or volume if desired. Current information is listed at the top of the screen.

6. Choose Enable Volume Auditing from the Available Audit Options menu and press Enter.

7. Enter a password for the volume if asked, and then verify the password.

8. Notify the auditor of the password.

Setting up auditing doesn't take much work on your part as the network administrator. The user account doesn't need to be named AUDITOR, and in fact it will be more secure if it isn't. One important part of security is to keep valuable things hidden; the user name AUDITOR draws attention, while LKGASKIN doesn't get a second look.

As Admin or equivalent, create a new user to be the auditor, giving this user all rights to a home directory. This is necessary for the auditor to store reports from the audit process. Since the AUDITCON program and supporting files are in the SYS:PUBLIC directory, Read and File Scan rights are necessary, but those trustee rights are standard for the network.

Start AUDITCON from a DOS prompt. If you did not start the program from the server or volume you want to audit, change that with the opening menu options. A list will appear offering you the available servers or volumes, as shown in Figure 9.19. Highlight one and press Enter. Once you've decided on the server and volume, choose Enable Volume Auditing from the main menu.

FIGURE 9.19

The opening AUDITCON screen

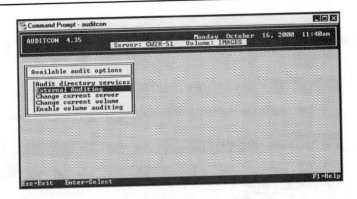

If the "Enter volume password" prompt appears, provide a new password for the auditor.

After verifying the password by retyping if necessary, your job is finished. The auditor will take over from here and should change the password immediately. Once that password is changed, you (the network supervisor) have no way of knowing what it is. If the auditor forgets the password, you can't be of any help, except to create a new auditor and do this all over again.

The described process sets up auditing on a volume. To start auditing for a container, choose Audit Directory Services, rather than Enable Volume Auditing, from the Available Audit Options menu, and set a password for the container. Each container is audited separately; subcontainers aren't audited with their parent container.

Setting the New Auditor Password (If Necessary)

IN A HURRY

9.8 Secure the Auditor's Password

1. As the assigned auditor user, start AUDITCON from the DOS prompt.
2. Choose Auditor Volume Login and type your password.
3. Select Auditing Configuration from the Available Audit Options menu.
4. Select Change Audit Password from the Auditing Configuration menu.
5. Enter the current password, enter the new password, and then retype it to verify.

When the auditor changes his or her password, the NetWare administrator no longer knows the password for AUDITCON.

This must be the first act of the auditor. If this step is not taken, the audit results will not be regarded as accurate by most auditing procedures. Allowing one of the audited people to access the audit procedure does resemble having a fox guard the hen house, doesn't it? Don't take a chance on your auditing work being criticized for something so easy to fix. Have the auditor change passwords immediately.

Performing Audits

IN A HURRY

9.9 Audit File System Events

1. As the assigned auditor user, start AUDITCON from the DOS prompt.
2. Select the proper volume if necessary (you will start on the volume of the DOS prompt).
3. Choose Auditing Configuration and set the audit by event, file/directory, or user.
4. Choose the details for events, files and directories, or users from the submenus.
5. Enable volume auditing if that has not been done.
6. Press Escape to save your changes and exit.

There are more options to monitor and audit than you want to know about. You will likely configure the system to audit almost everything the first time. After you wade through pages and pages of dull details, you will then focus your auditing quite a bit more.

Figure 9.20 shows just a few of the options to track on one volume of one server. If you activate each of these options, plus the other pages not shown in the figure, you will spend your life deciphering file activities.

FIGURE 9.20

Just a few of your audit options for the file system

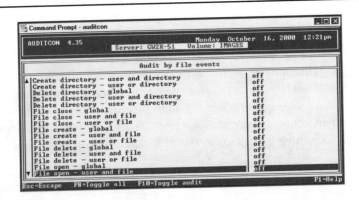

Most of the activity for the file system will be created by users during their normal user jobs. As you might guess by the listing, you can track file activity for all files, no matter who does what, with the global option. The user or file option tells the system to track that particular user or file, no matter where it is in the volume or who instigates the action. You might watch all files in the \APPS\SRC_CODE directory, for instance, or track all files deleted by user CWB.

This section should be entitled "Watching the Watcher," since most events being tracked by this configuration screen can only be done by the NetWare administrator. Feeling just a bit paranoid?

The arrows at the top and bottom on the left side of the event listing indicate there is more in each direction.

 NOTE Being audited may make you unhappy, but companies under strict guidelines must do this. Don't take it personally if a big audit of all computer systems is under way, and you, the network administrator, are in the spotlight as well. After all, if you weren't so honorable and noble as you are, you could really trash the network. Read the Internet newsgroup comp.sys.novell sometime, and you'll see plaintive requests for ways to undo damage done by departed, and angry, network managers.

Viewing Audit Reports

IN A HURRY

9.10 Configure and View Audit Reports

1. As the assigned auditor user, start AUDITCON from the DOS prompt.
2. Select the proper volume if necessary (you will start on the volume of the DOS prompt).
3. Select Auditor Volume Login and type the password if necessary.
4. Choose Auditing Reports, and then choose View Audit File to see the current file. Other choices allow viewing old files and setting report filters.

The variety of trackable items is nearly matched by the variety of ways to view the resulting report. As you can see in Figure 9.21, AUDITCON gives you flexibility in viewing audit files and the reports from those files.

FIGURE 9.21

*Reports ready to slice
and dice your way*

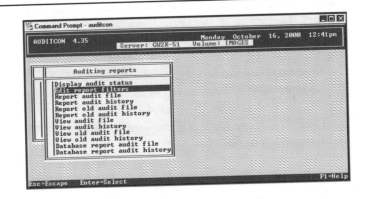

The amount of archived audit file history is configurable, as are the report formats. The submenu for Edit Report Filters offers:

- Report by date/time
- Report by event
- Report exclude paths/files
- Report exclude users
- Report include paths/files
- Report include users

Finding a way to view the audit trails won't be a problem, even if finding the time to do so is. If these options aren't enough for you, the reports are exported as .TXT files. You can then bring them into another program and slice and dice them any way your heart desires. Have fun.

NetWare 5.1 Security Improvements

Ever-evolving features required Novell to add some bang to the security section of NetWare 4.1*x* and NetWare 5.*x*. Novell could have done this by adding a few extra security screens everyone ignores, marked the security matrix as "improved," and gone on with their business.

Security became much more prominent than that. Novell hired one of the original developers of the U.S. Government's "Red Book" security project. That developer, and other work done by Novell deep inside the operating system, helped certify NetWare 4.11 as a "C2 Red Book" network. This is a big deal. NetWare 5.1 must also be certified, but Novell officials declared this rating important and will submit NetWare 5.1 as soon as they can.

First of all, it's a big deal because Microsoft made so much noise about Windows NT getting C2 security. The Novell folks can't stand for Microsoft to beat them in any purchase order check-off category, and that's what was happening. The fact that Windows NT was only C2 secure in stand-alone mode left the door open for Novell to top Microsoft, at least in the PR war. Not that the government followed their own regulations; departments regularly ignored the security guidelines to buy NT.

Second, it's a big deal for customers who support and use such security systems already, such as the government, the armed forces, and paranoid corporations. It's true that the government has a sizable NetWare installed base, and huge areas of some departments can't run computer equipment rated lower than C2.

Does C2 security do much for you? Probably not. Realistically, C2-level security is a giant hassle, and few companies go to that much trouble. If your company is one of the C2 adherents, you know of what I speak.

I will be amazed if your company increases your NetWare security profile up to the C2 level, unless you work for one of the aforementioned groups such as the military. For one thing, only C2-authorized software can run on a NetWare NTCB (Network Trusted Computing Base). All those NLMs you have? Gone, unless they've been certified.

Are you and the other administrators certified? Gone. Do you have NetWare 3.*x* networks still running on your corporate network? Gone. Only secure systems can run on a secure network. Do you have your server under lock and key? Gone until that's done. Have you limited access to remote console programs, such as RCONSOLE? Gone. See what I mean? It's more trouble than it's worth.

Adding the Java Virtual Machine will make your NetWare 5.1 server more popular for all types of utilities for the server, including security. Distributed applications are all the rage today, and security is becoming a consideration in the design phase. This falls under the heading of "a good thing," as Martha Stewart would say.

NetWare 5.1 includes a certificate authority for added security, but don't get confused. Those certificates guarantee that traffic across the Internet came from whom you think it came from and have nothing to do with normal, intracompany network business. We won't go into much depth with the Internet security options, because that topic deserves a book or two or ten devoted to ways to secure Internet traffic.

When Security Stinks, Management Smells the Worst

A "rock and a hard place" describes security. The tougher the security, the more people will hate the network. Looser security makes for happier users but more virus problems and file mishaps.

PART

II

Managing the Network

Remember that your company routinely allows access to every room of your building to the lowest paid, and least monitored, employees: cleaning crews. The biggest risk is crews employed by the building management, especially those who use temporary helpers. Do you have any idea what these people are doing? Does your management? Probably not.

This is one of the areas where hard choices must be made, and your management must make them. If your bosses won't do their jobs, push a little. If they still refuse, document the security measures in place, the reasons for those measures, and apply them absolutely. When users complain to their bosses, and their bosses complain to your boss, let your boss modify the procedure. Then get your boss to sign any changes. Accountability is shared; blame is yours alone.

Don't let management overcompensate for lousy security elsewhere by tightening the screws on the network. That's like a bank with a vault full of cash, while the bearer bonds, cashier checks, and negotiable securities are lying out in the open, ready to be picked up and carried away.

Force management to define a consistent security profile. It makes no sense to restrict network users to the bone while leaving the president's file cabinet unlocked. People looking to steal information, both from the inside and outside, will happily take paper or computer disks. While it isn't legal to steal a report off your computer system, it is legal to grab a printout of that same report out of the Dempsey Dumpster.

Inconsistent security control runs both ways. I once had a customer so worried about security that he refused to have a fax server on the network. The owner was afraid of dial-in hackers going through the fax-modem into the computer system. We finally convinced the owner that this was impossible.

The flip side was a major oil company in the mid-1980s that had the typical tight security on its mainframe. Terminal and user IDs were tracked, users were monitored, and passwords were everywhere—the whole bit. Then someone noticed it was possible to copy information from the mainframe to a PC connected with an IRMA board (an adapter in the PC that connected via coax to an SNA cluster controller, effectively making the PC a 3270 terminal).

A management committee studied the matter and verified that yes, anyone could copy any information from the mainframe to disks and paper. The information could then be dropped in the trash, carried home, or sold to a competitor. All these options obviously violated the company's security guidelines.

What did the managers do? They decided to ignore the problem and placed no security on PCs with IRMA boards beyond what they had on the terminals the PCs replaced. It may be noble to trust the employees, but it was inconsistent security. Those users with PCs deserved security training and a warning about the severity of potential security leaks. They got nothing because corporate management was too lazy to do its job. If a problem developed, who would be blamed? Yep, the computer managers who had no control over the decision.

More security concerns will be addressed later when we get to the Web portions of NetWare. If you thought your managers were paranoid before, wait until they come to you waving copies of the *Wall Street Journal* predicting doom and gloom because hackers stopped another Web site for a few minutes. Realistic threat to your servers? Very low. Realistic threat to your schedule because of paranoid managers? High—your whole day will be wasted chasing non-existent loopholes and manager security blankets.

CHAPTER 10

NetWare 5.1 Administrator Duties and Tools

What are administrator duties? The short answer is that if you're the administrator, anything you do on the network is an administrator duty. When you're playing a network game such as Duke Nukem or Arena Quake, you're not wasting time; no, you're the network administrator using a network-intensive application to test the network's performance under load.

The long answer to the question of administrator duties is to list everything that is expected of you. Take a look at the standard list of administrator duties:

- Plan the network.
  - Design the cabling.
  - Decide on server location and other equipment placement.
  - Devise the NDS structure.
  - Create the user list and appropriate access privileges.
  - Define application and data storage requirements.
- Install the network.
  - Perform or oversee the physical cabling installation.
  - Configure server machines.
  - Install NetWare on the servers.
  - Install or upgrade workstation software.
- Support the network users.
  - Make all network resources available to authorized users.
  - Provide protective, but not restrictive, security.
  - Train the users as necessary.
  - Protect network files and data from mishaps.
  - Maintain a high level of network performance.
  - Leap tall buildings in a single bound.
  - Plan for the future.
  - Understand network growth.
  - Foresee and avoid network bottlenecks.
  - Watch new technologies and investigate ones appropriate for your network.

If you're a perfectionist or can't live with chaos, get another job. Likewise, leave if you're sensitive to real or imagined criticism. Need constant praise to maintain your self-esteem? Good luck, and tell your therapist "Hello" for me.

NetWare administration is a thankless job about 90 percent of the time; 5 percent of the time, it's worse. However, the rest of the time makes up for everything. When the network hums along and nothing can disrupt either the network or your good mood, no job in the world can beat the life of a network jockey. The light that goes on in people's eyes when they start to understand how the network can help them is wonderful to see.

 NOTE Other, more specific administration topics are scattered about the book. Check the chapter about printing (Chapter 8) if you have questions about printing not covered here. You'll find plenty of information about setting up users and other objects in Chapter 6. If you don't find your topic here, check the index or the table of contents, and I bet you'll find what you're looking for.

Managing Your Network with a Plan

Now that you've seen the list of what a "good" network manager should be doing, you may feel like taking up a career in something less challenging, like brain surgery or astrophysics or juggling chainsaws. No one can do everything on that list of standard administrator duties, can they?

No, of course not. All you can do is work hard and work smart. I can't help you with the work hard part, but perhaps we can make some progress in the working smarter department.

If the network is new to your company, everyone will be thrilled for a few weeks. No matter how poorly the network is running, it's still a thousandfold better than *no* network.

If your company has just moved up to NetWare from some other network, such as a peer-to-peer workgroup solution that was outgrown much too quickly, people will still think this is amazing. Again, even a poor NetWare network is a hundredfold better than the best peer-to-peer system whose capabilities have been surpassed. Most peer-to-peer networks reach the end of their rope at about eight users, but most companies won't justify the cost of a server and separate operating system like NetWare until at least 20 users are screaming for improvements.

The supervision and plans for stand-alone workstations, or even for a small, underpowered workgroup network, are not sufficient for a NetWare network. If you are new to this, you must upgrade your thinking quite a bit.

Some books go into long, detailed plans on how to manage your network. I've even seen books with timesheets, planning every hour for you. There used to be a trend where company management tried to make the network a "utility," such as that provided by the electric company or telephone company. Flip a switch, there's the network. Of course, this was before the electrical service started fluctuating widely enough to reset everyone's VCR at home, and a few software problems downed large parts of the national long-distance network.

Management doesn't use the utility example as much anymore. But it's not a bad idea to emulate, with slight provisions.

Having electrical and telephone service available at every moment is a fact of modern life we have grown to love. But both these services spent decades as monopolies. There are advantages to monopolies, not the least of which is the ability to mandate the infrastructure and set rules for the users. The disadvantages include the Department of Justice and far too many angry lawyers, but that's another story.

Translate the electrical grid throughout a city into a plan for supporting network connections in every corner of your company. When management complains about building the network for sections of your company that are not yet inhabited, point to the growth trends and economy of wiring as many connections as possible to maximize every labor hour by the cabling contractor. If they're building a new building, are they expecting to see the electrical company executives standing in the street, scratching their heads and wondering how to get power to it? Of course not. Don't let that be the case with your network.

Managing Your Future Network

This may seem like an odd section heading. How do you manage a network you don't have yet? By making sure the network you want is the one you eventually build, of course.

If you're driving from Baltimore, Maryland, to San Francisco, California, how do you get there? By driving west. You may drive north or south for a bit now and then, but most of the time, you keep driving west. When you come to an intersection, you want to go west if at all possible.

You get to your future network the same way. You must decide what your future network will look like and move in the direction of that vision with every network decision. There are choices to make every day when running a large network, and you want to choose the option that will get you closer to your future network.

Decisions about what your network of the future will be must be made with your management. We can always say that tomorrow's networks must be larger and faster, have more disk storage, and be more fault-tolerant than the networks of today, but those guidelines are a little too vague to serve as directions.

What does "larger" mean for your future network? Does it mean more users? Does it mean more locations? Does it mean more types of clients to service? More types of data to carry across the network? If it means geographically larger, then a method of WAN connections and data distribution may be necessary. More clients, or different types of clients, need support in the physical cabling and network protocol area. Is your boss hot to run video across the LAN? Does she want to teleconference across a campus using desktop-mounted cameras and microphones? Then you must move toward a network transport layer that guarantees support for priority packet types and real-time data streams.

What type of storage will be needed? Do you want more hard disk space, stringing together dozens of gigabytes? Or does your network information better suit a plan using HSM (Hierarchical Storage Management)? Do you keep some data on server hard disks for immediate access, some other data on magneto-optical jukebox platters with a few seconds of delay, and other data on tape? Or does your company need to move more toward a large disk cluster, with every byte available instantly through any file server? Each option has a learning curve and a foundation that can be laid today.

Does "fault-tolerant" mean absolutely no service interruptions? Or does it mean that you must recover from a hardware failure within a certain number of minutes? How about two hours? How much does it cost your company when the network is completely down? Can you work with your management to set that number? If you don't know how much it costs when your network is broken, how will you know how much you can spend to make sure it doesn't break? Should you plan for an extremely well-protected central server cluster, or should you maintain high network availability by distributing network access and replicating the data? These two options are directly opposed to each other and will make a difference in every network plan and hardware purchase over the next few years.

Many of these questions can only be answered after you (and your management) develop a network philosophy. Once everyone agrees on the philosophy of your network and the services that will be provided to your network clients, you have a decision framework. Is your philosophy to move toward a single network protocol (TCP/IP) for every client? Then you want to start learning about NetWare 5.1's TCP/IP software (now used as the standard client-to-server communication protocol), MacTCP, and details about the TCP/IP protocol stacks in Windows 95/98/NT/2000. Do you prefer to make the fewest changes possible on the clients and force your servers to support multiple protocols? Then your learning curve is different, as are your choices in WAN equipment.

Perhaps this section could be called "Developing Your Network Philosophy" rather than "Managing Your Future Network." A well-developed network philosophy today helps you make decisions concerning all parts of your network for tomorrow.

A Sampler of Management Slogans

If you're currently running a network, you know that "interrupts" happen not only to computer CPUs but to your day. Every phone call may be a disaster on the other end. Your day is not your own.

Make a mental change, and make it simple: you run your network, not the other way around.

Sure, you say, that's easy for me to say, sitting back in Texas. Nobody's hollering for my head because the laser printer goes offline every time the president sends it a spreadsheet.

Let me give you some network advice as stated by your grandmother. Sayings that are simple, short, and clear, but echo longer and louder than you would expect. Perhaps we can get Granny to stitch these slogans onto some pillows for the office.

"Up Is Good, Down Is Bad"

Every network resource should be available at all times. That's a "good" thing. Unavailable network resources are "bad" things. This seems amazingly simple, but it needs to be said.

However, sometimes the definition of "up" needs to be slightly reworked. The users will complain that the network is terrible when the only problem is that their favorite network printer is not working properly. Show them the other network printers, and they will rephrase their network complaint. Instead of "not printing," it becomes "print over there." The printing system itself is working, even if their particular printer is not.

"Maximize Uptime by Scheduling Downtime"

Maintenance time should be scheduled for your network every day or every week. If your network is smaller, there is probably time every night or early morning for the network downtime.

Downtime need not be serious, with major overhauls of server and hard disk. You may want to reorganize the print servers. You may need to add a new protocol to a network segment. You may need to readjust the physical wiring and add an extra concentrator or two.

This type of network maintenance isn't serious, but it is necessary. Even more necessary is making sure that your management understands that the network is always available when people need the network. If no one is in the office at 5:00 A.M., who cares if the network is down? If you need to shut down a database running on a server to get every system file on a backup tape, shut it down.

Continued

There will always be reasons to take the network offline for maintenance. If you schedule regular downtimes, it never becomes a question or a concern to management. When your network has been running for 86 days and you say it must be taken offline, people will think the reason for the downtime is more serious than it really is. Perhaps we should say this is an example of managing not the network, but your management's expectations.

"Promote Confidence through Paranoia"

To make your users confident in your network, you must be slightly paranoid. You must have a constant, nagging worry in the back of your mind, forcing you to examine every inch of your network for flaws and weaknesses.

Like the old joke says, you're not really paranoid if they really are out to get you. If you run a network, fates are actively conspiring to make it break. So you're not paranoid; you're just doing your job.

Spare parts are a good example of paranoia. Does your boss demand an HA (High Availability) system—not quite fault-tolerant and able to continue in the face of hardware failure, but able to resume operations fairly quickly? Then keep available spare parts for all the servers that must keep running. If your main server's main data lives on a Maxtor 12GB drive, you better have another one on the shelf or another server ready to take the backup files and start running immediately.

Do you imagine a server's power supply is making some kind of strange noise, but you're not quite sure? Replace it. That's an example of paranoia that will enhance your network by minimizing downtime.

"Every User Is an Honored Guest and a Potential Criminal"

The chapter about security (Chapter 9) should make this warning clear, but it's worth restating. Your worst security problems are the people at the end of your network wires.

Retail executives will tell you that much more stolen property goes out the back door with the employees than out the front door with the shoplifters. While you would like to think your fellow employees will not knowingly harm your network or steal your data, the sad truth is that one or more of them will. The man in the elevator with you yesterday evening may have had an illegal copy of WordPerfect in his briefcase. The woman beside him may have had the marketing plan for the next quarter in her purse.

You must provide network access to all users in order for them to perform their jobs. Any more access than necessary will only lead to trouble.

PART

II

Managing the
Network

Selling Your Network Plan to Your Boss

One problem with network (or personal) philosophies is that everyone has his or her own. While this makes for a more interesting society at large, it makes it more difficult for you to plan and run your network unless some agreement is reached.

No matter how brilliant your network plan or how comprehensive your network philosophy, all is lost unless your boss agrees. I've met some wonderful network administrators who failed because they and their bosses never agreed on the network. I've also met some very "un-technical" network administrators who built amazing, complicated networks with the full support of their bosses in particular and their company in general.

The key here is for you and your boss to share the same network vision and philosophy. If you have been hired to support an existing network, the boss's philosophy is probably well set, and you must go with that. If you built the network from nothing, your philosophy has been the guide. The trick is to get your boss to agree with the work you've already done and to help you continue on the same path.

Just as *you* get pressure from higher up the management chain, so does your immediate manager. So you are now in a situation where you must sell to not only one layer of management, but to another layer or two above that.

Yes, *sell*. Your boss must be sold on the facts that you know what you're doing technically and that your ideas for network growth make sense. Don't assume that your boss will understand the technical parts and agree because your choice of technology is superior to all other options. It's not, and your boss won't.

I prefer to lay out the network choices in such a way as to "lead" people to the conclusion I have already reached. This only works when the facts support my idea, so it helps if, before I present the case to anyone, I verify that I'm on the right track. We can call this method the "Pros-and-Cons Weighing of Technical Alternatives," but in sales, it's called the "Ben Franklin Close." Evidently, old Ben used this trick on the other Founding Fathers to sell them life insurance during the Revolutionary War.

This method works by listing three columns: the decision to be made, the pros, and the cons. In sales, you actually sit with the customers and write down each element of the chart, letting them come up with some of the pros and cons. If you think this won't work with your boss, think again. It works every time, because your boss helps list the pros and cons for the decision with you. If your boss picks the "wrong" decision, you'll know why, because you went over the reasons together. Either you didn't know your facts or your boss feels differently about the situation than you do. Better to find out during a discussion than from a rejected proposal.

Let's say that you feel the need for a software-metering product, but your boss doesn't want to spend the money. Sit down together and draw a line separating a page into two columns labeled Pro and Con. Write the decision to be made across the top of the page, such as Start Software Metering Y/N. Now ask your boss for the primary objection, and write that down. Ask for the next, and the next. You may have a list like this:

- Too expensive.
- Too much management time.
- Current software inventory system works okay.
- Inconveniences the users.

After your boss is finished, you can write down a list similar to the following:

- $5 per user.
- Installation reads the NetWare user list and automatically builds access tables.
- No one knows how many copies of each program have been purchased.
- Users are now copying software illegally and trying to install it themselves.
- Tracks application use.
- Forces all applications onto the server, meaning consistent backup and easier upgrades.
- Lists software that users may not know is available, especially between departments.
- Demonstrates compliance with software-use laws to auditors.

In case the pros and cons don't line up exactly, draw lines between each. If you're careful with the two lists, your columns will look like this when you're finished:

Too expensive.	$5 per user.
Too much management time.	Installation reads the NetWare user list and automatically builds access tables.
	Demonstrates compliance with software use laws to auditors.
	Forces all applications onto the server, meaning consistent backup and easier upgrades.
Current software inventory system works okay.	No one knows how many copies of each program have been purchased.
	Tracks application use.
Inconveniences the users.	Lists software that users may not know is available, especially between departments.
	Users are now copying software illegally and trying to install it themselves.

PART

II

Managing the Network

Every objection from your boss has at least one response. Several of your responses apply to more than one of the objections. For example, to the objection "Too expensive," you can say that the cost of the metering software is a new cost, but it reduces the cost of software purchases, since everyone can share better. It also saves time (money) with better backup and upgrades, and it tells which applications are really used. If you have 20 copies of presentation software that only six people are using, you'll save money when it's time to upgrade by upgrading only six copies.

Will Ben Franklin come to your rescue every time your boss gives you a hard time? No, but the idea of selling your boss rather than arguing will help. Everyone needs to be sold on ideas—and often resold several times. The sooner you understand that selling is a big part of network management, the better off you'll be.

Selling Your Network Plan to Your Users

You're not through with sales when you convince your boss of your positions. You must still convince the users that the way you run the network provides them the best support within the constraints dictated by management.

What constraints? Generally money. The network would run faster if you had a row of superservers, like those shiny Compaq ProLiant systems, stacked against the wall, and maybe a rack of quad-servers in the computer room. Storage space wouldn't be a problem if you had an extra 100GB of hard disk for every workgroup. User applications would run better if each desktop came equipped with a fast Pentium III (heck, let's ask for 1GHz dual Pentium III) computer with 256MB of RAM (okay, 512MB of RAM).

The users understand these types of constraints. Each of them wants more desk space in a bigger office, a company car, more vacation time, paid trips to conventions, and a bigger bonus. They're probably so worried about their constraints that they haven't given much thought to your problems.

This is where your network philosophy can help clarify exactly what the network can and can't do. If you (and your boss, of course) can condense your network philosophy into a mission statement, your users will better understand what to expect from the network today and tomorrow. The shorter the mission statement, the better. Two paragraphs is too much.

How would your users like this: "Our network will be available a minimum of 20 hours every business day, providing secure access to applications, data, printers, and host access services." This tells the story quickly, but doesn't promise 24-hour satisfaction of every tiny network desire they may have. This also excludes 24/7 systems such as Web servers, but those are generally for outside users.

Unless there is an immediate network problem, unhappy users are expressing a conflict between their expectations and your network reality. Align the users' expectations to the network you can provide, and everyone will be happier.

Daily Administration Tasks

Those readers new to the world of network administration may wonder if their day will be so full of idle time that they will need to follow a daily checklist to keep from falling into a deep sleep caused by their workday boredom. If you are one of those people, take this book to an experienced network administrator and let him or her read the first sentence of this paragraph. Be sure and stand back, because when people laugh hysterically they often drop things, and this book hurts your foot when it lands on it.

Perhaps you detect the wry smile I'm sporting as I write this. The trick is not how to spend your idle moments as a network administrator; it's finding some of them in the first place.

Yes, the workload's too large in most situations. If you're a good administrator, you're more nervous when things are going well than when they aren't, because you know disaster is sneaking up behind you. So, it isn't that checklists aren't needed. There are still a few things that, regardless of how busy you are, you must—repeat, *must*—do on a daily basis. I discuss them in this section.

System Backups (Have a Plan and Follow It)

The title is "system backups," but it could be "data" or "file" backups, because that's what we're discussing here. Files will disappear all too often, and a good backup is your only defense. Certainly, plan for the catastrophic disaster, such as a fire in the computer room that melts all your servers (but that will never happen—well, almost never), but also plan for the daily screw-ups that accompany life.

File security means several things, but right now it means file safety. Your files are secure if they are copied to a reliable backup system a minimum of once per day. Many companies copy critical file sets several times per day, having determined that recovering a crashed or lost file at any expense is cheaper than taking the network down for any reason.

Way back in Chapter 1, you saw a plan for rotating backup tapes in order to keep files close at hand, yet safe from localized disaster. You know, like that computer room fire that never happens (until it does). The rotation details back in Chapter 1 may not

PART
II

Managing the
Network

be the best ever, but they will work. If you have a better rotation plan, feel free to use it. But use something.

Here's the payoff for this section: back up your critical files every day, or even more often if possible. Do not trust the fact that your server hard drive has a mean-time-between-failure rating of over 125,000 hours and so should last over 14 years. "Mean" time between failures means the average time, and if one drive happens to be good enough to work for 28 years, another drive must quit in three days to balance things out. Unfortunately, drive manufacturers don't label the drive that will fail in three days.

Besides, you will not face a file crisis because a drive fails nearly as often as a user will screw up. That's why "user is a four-letter word" to some network administrators. Files *will* be deleted by accident, and they must be recovered. Normally this means tape, but if you want to push the envelope and copy all critical files to writeable CDs (now a fairly cheap option), feel free. Just back up the files to some reliable device every day that any files change. Every day. Period.

Checking Your System Log Files

There should probably be a separate heading for "Weekly Administration Tasks," but then you might believe a free moment is rarer than an honest politician. Free moments are rare, but not that rare.

Checking log files should be a habit if you have a Web server open to the public, because you want to know who has come to your Web site. Checking log files in NetWare isn't that much fun, but at least you have a fighting chance of seeing some errors develop over time rather than having them sneak up on you. The following are NetWare's log files:

SYS$LOG.ERR   The main file is SYS$LOG.ERR, found in the SYS:\SYSTEM directory. When you use NetWare Administrator to see the Error Log by clicking that command button, this is what you see. And see and see and see. There's lots of stuff in this file, especially if you're adding new servers and you get an IPX address wrong on one server segment. This happens to me a lot, and it fills the server log up quickly with meaningful and descriptive, but soon-to-be-rectified, information. Often the file is too long to fit inside the viewer, so clean out this log file now and then.

BOOT$LOG.ERR   This file, also in the SYS:\SYSTEM directory, holds comparatively little information. I wouldn't worry too much about this one.

VOL$LOG.ERR   Volume-specific and file-specific log files are kept in the root directory of each volume. The VOL$LOG.ERR file shows each time the volume is mounted and dismounted (started and stopped). Check this file when file errors start to mount, in case something is taking your volumes offline.

TTS$LOG.ERR   This is the log for the Transaction Tracking System (TTS). Under normal circumstances, this file shows information similar to the volume log file. Normally, all you'll see in here are times when TTS starts or stops. These times should correspond with those recorded in the volume log file, starting a few seconds after, and stopping a few seconds before, the timestamps in the volume log file.

ABEND.LOG   This is one error file I hope you never see. ABEND.LOG is moved to the SYS:\SYSTEM directory when the server is restarted after an ABnormal ENDing. This term is an old mainframe term, believe it or not. How it got loaded into NetWare in the early versions is anyone's guess.

Keeping Anti-Virus Software Up-to-Date

This is critical, and surprisingly easy. The reason to keep your virus software up-to-date is simple: more social misfits make more viruses every week. Each virus has a "signature" code pattern within the software that identifies it and can be used to identify that particular virus. Adding these virus signatures to your anti-virus software's signature table gives you protection against these viruses. Not complete protection, but a good start.

The highest-quality virus-protection software offers free updates, either forever or for a subscription period. These updates normally happen on a scheduled basis across the Internet—a good approach.

I recently reviewed Symantec's Norton Anti-Virus for Microsoft Exchange Servers. That product may apply to your situation, but the item that illustrates my point was Symantec's "Live Update" feature. Inside the software is a schedule program to specify how often the anti-virus software itself should go out through an Internet connection and download the most recent virus signature files. Options range from as frequently as once a day to as infrequently as never (not a good choice).

Demand that your anti-virus software vendor provide capabilities similar to Symantec's: easy updates. Is time short? If your vendor doesn't have an automatic schedule, train an assistant in the technical department or a secretary to download the file regularly. Just make sure that file is downloaded and applied to your anti-virus software regularly.

PART

II

Managing the Network

Supervisory Functions and the Necessary Rights

When the first NetWare 5.1 server is installed in a new network, the Admin user is created. Granted the Supervisor right to the [Root] level of the network, Admin controls the entire new network through inheritance.

Let's take a quick look at what rights go where:

Directory rights	Apply only to the directory in the file system where they are assigned. Directory rights are part of the file system, not of NDS. Unless blocked or redefined, directory rights are inherited by subdirectories and files. A User object may be granted directory rights to any directory on a volume.
File rights	Apply only to the file to which they are assigned. Trustees inherit rights to a file from the directory rights above the file.
Object rights	Apply to NDS objects. Object rights are inherited from higher objects or are assigned directly. Inherited object rights continue to be passed down to lower objects. Assigned object rights do not flow down the NDS tree.
Property rights	Apply to the properties of NDS objects. Rights can be assigned to specific properties of a given object. Rights to a specific property do not flow down the tree through inheritance.
All Property rights	Allow the trustee assignment to apply to all rights of the given object with one assignment. The All Property rights trustee assignment, unlike Property rights, *does* flow down the NDS tree, through inheritance.

Trustee Assignments

A *trustee* is a user or group granted rights to a directory, file, or object. This user or group is then called a trustee of that directory, file, or object. Although this naming reminds me of bad prison movies, the root of the term *trustee* comes from *trust*. A trustee is trusted to properly use the objects placed in his or her trust.

Trustee assignments grant rights for one object to another object. The trustee rights assignments are kept as part of the object to which they grant access.

The trustee assignments are stored in a trustee list. The trustee list for an object is stored in the ACL (Access Control List) property. Every object in the network has an ACL property.

[Public] is a special trustee and acts somewhat like the group EVERYONE in earlier NetWare versions. Rather than granting EVERYONE rights to a directory in NetWare 5.1 as you did in NetWare 3, you might instead specify the rights of [Public] in that directory. [Public] may also be a trustee of a file or other object, besides just a directory.

If a user has no specific trustee rights to an object, directory, or file, that user automatically has the same rights as the [Public] trustee. [Public] is assigned the Browse right to the [Root] of the NDS tree and so has the ability to read the entire tree. This allows all users to see the available network resources.

 NOTE More coverage of rights across the network can be found in Chapter 9, which discusses security. If you've skipped to here and bypassed Chapter 9, skimming back through that information may eliminate any confusion.

Workgroup Managers to the Rescue

Although I'm wary of granting workgroup administrators complete control with no Admin supervision, I think they are a valuable tool in your network management toolkit. In fact, proper use of workgroup administrators will keep you closer to your end users than a crowded elevator.

To restate one last time: please do not lock Admin out of parts of your NDS tree. Some departments will cry and moan how they need "security" from prying eyes in the "corporate" computer room. Don't fall for it, and be ready when they go over your head to your boss. Then be ready when they go over your boss's head.

Use the argument about training and maintaining a support staff as a starting point. You and your group (if you have one) are trained to know all parts of the network and are supposed to be able to support each other. If a department has its own administrator and has locked you out, what do those employees do when this person is on vacation or is out sick? What about when that person quits or transfers?

Say a directory gets deleted accidentally (hey, it happens all the time). Assuming the department has a good backup plan in place and follows that plan, replacing the directory's files is no problem. But what if the only administrator with access to the tape backup software is in the Cleveland airport? If Admin is not blocked, you can step in and save the day. If Admin is blocked, you can call the airlines and get the

PART

II

Managing the
Network

estimated arrival time for the wandering administrator. But you can't retrieve the files until you've got the administrator on the phone. If you are able to help out by still maintaining access to that departmental branch of the NDS tree when that branch's administrator is unavailable, none of these situations are a problem.

Let's get back to the good side of workgroup administrators. They are closer to the department's problems and hence are quicker with easy solutions than you are. More than that, they serve as your cheerleader in the department. If you make them feel special by sharing information and responsibility, the workgroup administrators can help make the network better. How? Let's take a look at some ways the workgroup administrators, and by extension the user community, can work with you:

- Involve them in pilot projects. Two great benefits come from their involvement. First, they know more about how your end users work than you do and will make sure all the bases are covered. Second, they will spread the word about your new project and generate positive word-of-mouth among the groups that will most likely need to pay for the new service. This makes your job of selling the benefits much easier.

- Have them let you know how the users really feel. Your network clients won't tell you the truth. This is not really their fault; it just works that way. Formal questionnaires and focus groups help, but the little things won't get passed along. Your workgroup administrator will know what users are happy about and what they hate.

- Let them help you define training goals and courses. Generic application training is always helpful. Specific job-related training on those same applications is invaluable but difficult to identify and develop. Your workgroup administrator will know where your training courses are falling short and how to stretch them back out again.

- Ask them to explain the computer decisions made by you (or your department) to the users. No one likes hearing pronouncements handed down from above, and your network users are no exception. Having one of their own able to translate "HQ" talk into "people" talk will soften the resistance to network changes. Of course, if you're involving them in pilot projects, there won't be any surprises.

Are there more ways in which the workgroup administrator can help? Many more methods are available, but they depend on your situation. Remember, power users are your friends.

Installing NetWare Administrator

Now it's time to get out your primary management tool and unleash it. Let's install NetWare Administrator and look at how the program itself works, with all the options.

In the version of this book for NetWare 4.11, I described how to install NetWare Administrator in Windows 3.1. I don't think it's a good idea at all anymore, even if you managed to make it work well. Everything from Novell is now optimized for a more powerful operating system. Windows 3.1 doesn't fall into anyone's description of a "powerful" operating system (if you can call Windows 3.1 an operating system with a straight face).

Configuring Windows 95/98 (Running Client32) for NetWare Administrator

Here's where all the work will happen: 32-bit clients. It's also where we'll spend most of our time in this chapter. Client32 appeared during the early days of NetWare 4.11, and so people made a big deal about Client32 software. Today, with NetWare 5.1, all the clients are built using Client32 software, so you needn't worry about whether you have it or not. All NetWare 5.1 client software is Client32.

There's nothing difficult about running the NetWare Administrator program, once you discover where on the file server it resides. If you search \PUBLIC first, you will be disappointed. Check the \PUBLIC\WIN32 directory; NWADMN32.EXE and supporting files are hiding there.

Make a shortcut on your Windows 95/98/NT/2000 workstation to this directory and filename. I put this file in the NOVELL folder, but you may put it on the desktop or in any folder you wish. You might even choose to put it on the Start menu.

Configuring Windows NT/2000 for NetWare Administrator

Running NetWare Administrator on Windows NT Workstation or Server (makes no difference to this application) or Windows 2000 is just as easy as running it on Windows 95/98. So you'd think the first thing you'd want to do is go to the \PUBLIC\WINNT directory and start looking for it, wouldn't you? But it's not there, is it? Used to be. Even in the beta versions of NetWare 5.0, that's where you would have found it, as there were different NetWare Administrator programs for Windows 95/98 and NT. But in the shipping version, you'll find that things are a little different.

Go back to the \PUBLIC\WIN32 directory and run the NWADMN32.EXE program just like you were instructed in the last section. This one program works for Windows 95/98/NT/2000.

Many companies are standardizing on Windows NT/2000 as their network management platform of choice. Fine with me—and Novell. NT seems more stable and better at handling memory (fewer memory leaks) than Windows 95/98, and it's what I use for my personal workstation now. By "now," though, I mean only after memory became cheap enough that I could afford 128MB of RAM. With this much memory, Windows appears almost (but not quite) snappy. Windows 2000 Professional improves upon NT, although not as much as Microsoft's PR department would have you believe. But Windows 2000 will become the administrator's tool of choice before long.

Getting Familiar with NetWare Administrator

Using NetWare Administrator is quite a bit different from using the old SYSCON program in earlier NetWare versions. Although everyone familiar with SYSCON will have a nostalgic twinge for the old days, I predict you will grow comfortable with NetWare Administrator within a short time.

Go ahead and play with the program. Click, drag, drop, expand, collapse, and search. The amount of information that can be packed into the NetWare Administrator screen makes it far more useful than the old SYSCON and more informative than the current NETADMIN DOS-based program.

Although the largest difference between NetWare Administrator that shipped with NetWare 4.10 for Windows 3.1*x* and the version shipping with NetWare 5.1 concerns the look and feel of the interface, there are some substantive changes as well. For example, there's the ability to add or remove items from the toolbar, which is the result of increased functionality in the improved Windows 95/98/NT/2000 interface. Better Help screens mean quicker productivity for network managers new to NetWare. Besides all that, the Windows 95/98/NT/2000 interface offers a more polished and three-dimensional look. Some companies feel it's better to look good than work good; fortunately, here you get both.

 NOTE No one will say so officially, but my guess is that DOS utilities have reached the end of their life spans. A few are included in NetWare 5.1, but none of them have been upgraded, and programs like NETADMIN have disappeared. Since DOS has vanished from new computer shipments, there will be little reason for Novell engineers to continue upgrading products for a non-existent operating system. My guess is that Windows 2000 will eventually corner the market on management applications.

So far in this book, you've seen a few pictures of the NetWare Administrator program from the earlier, 16-bit version. Take a look at Figure 10.1 to see an expanded view in the 32-bit version that comes with NetWare 5.1.

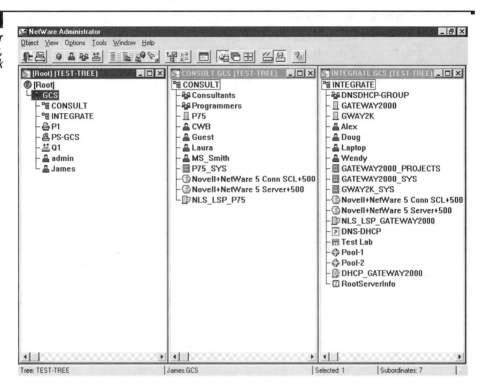

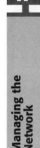

In the far-left browser window, the [Root] view is collapsed to show the minimum information. Our two Organizational Units, CONSULT and INTEGRATE, are all that are listed, along with the Admin user and James (that's me) in the GCS container. The middle browser window shows CONSULT.GCS. On the far right is INTEGRATE.GCS. You may have up to nine browser windows open at one time.

Many of the menu options depend on which object is highlighted in the browser window. When the program opens, what looks like the entire program is really just the first browser window, open to your current context. Most operations in NetWare Administrator require you to highlight an object in a browser window, then take some action using a menu choice.

The menu bar has six options: Object, View, Options, Tools, Window, and Help. When you highlight a menu or a menu item, the description displays just above the menu bar. Menu choices that are grayed are not available for the highlighted object. Each menu option is described in the following sections.

The Object Menu

The Object menu has these commands:

Create (Ins)   Opens a dialog box to create a new object, or creates a directory if used on a Volume object. Insert is this option's shortcut key.

Details (Enter)   Opens an information dialog box about the object, file, or directory highlighted. The same dialog box opens when you double-click a leaf object.

Details On Multiple Users   Starting with NetWare 4.11 and now continued in NetWare 5.1, you may choose multiple objects and take some action on all highlighted objects at one time.

Rights To Other Objects   Shows which rights the highlighted object has to other objects. You must specify which part of the NDS tree you wish to search to gather this information.

Trustees Of This Object   Shows which other objects have rights to the selected object. This option is also used to set the object's Inherited Rights Filter (IRF).

Move (F7)   Moves selected leaf objects or files to other locations. Destinations are selected in a dialog box that appears.

Copy (F8)   Allows you to make copies of single or multiple files. A destination dialog box appears once the Copy option is chosen.

Rename   Opens a dialog box to rename the selected object. You have the option to keep the old name to maintain existing references to the object.

Delete (DEL)   Deletes and purges the selected object. There is no recovery available. Containers must be empty before they can be deleted.

Browse   Opens a new browser window with the selected object at the top. Right-clicking a container is an easier way to open a new browser window.

Search   Opens a Search dialog box to help find objects in the NDS tree matching the specified pattern. Found objects are listed for further action.

Print (Ctrl+P)   Prints the objects in the browser window. NetWare Administrator can wrap long listings into two columns.

Print Setup   Opens a standard Windows 95 Printer Setup dialog box.

Exit   Closes the NetWare Administrator program.

The View Menu

The View menu has these choices:

Show Hints   When checked, shows hints above the main menu bar.

Show Toolbar   When checked, displays the toolbar under the menu bar.

Show Status Bar   When checked, displays the status bar on the last line of the screen.

Show Quick Tips   Pops open the little help line beside the cursor when you linger on an icon.

Configure Toolbar And Status Bar   Opens a Preferences dialog box that allows you to pick the icons that appear on the toolbar and the information panels that are on the status bar.

Set Context   Changes the context shown at the top of the browser window or panel.

Go Up A Level (Backspace)   Sets the root of the browser window up one level in the NDS hierarchy.

Sort And Include   Includes or excludes certain object classes from the browser window and sets sort preferences.

Expand (keypad +)   Displays objects in the selected container or volume. You can also either press the + key or double-click the + symbol next to the selected container or volume for the same result.

Collapse (keypad –)   Hides all objects contained in the selected object. You can also either double-click the – symbol next to the object or press the – key for the same result.

The Options Menu

The following are Options menu choices:

Save Settings On Exit   When checked, opens to the same network view when the program is restarted.

Confirm On Delete   Verifies that you wish to delete the object. (Deleted objects are not salvageable.)

Get Alias Trustees   When checked, this option allows you to manage the trustees of an Alias object rather than the actual object the Alias is representing.

Get Aliased Object Trustees   When checked, this option allows you to manage the trustees of the actual object, not the Alias referring to the object.

The Tools Menu

You'll find these tools among those listed on the Tools menu (snap-ins change the Tools menu):

Internet Connections   Starts your favorite Web browser and displays bookmarks for quick Internet connections (at least with the Novell-logo version of Netscape).

Salvage   Allows you to recover or permanently trash previously deleted files.

Remote Console   Opens a DOS box and starts the Remote Console utility program.

Pure IP Remote Console   Opens the Java-based JConsole using only the TCP/IP protocol (no IPX packets are used).

NDS Browser   Starts a new browser window.

Query Catalog   The Catalog, new in NetWare 5.1, is a flat-file database containing a snapshot of part or all of the NDS database, optimized for fast lookup.

DNS-DHCP Management Console (optional)   Java-based control and configuration utilities to handle TCP/IP addressing.

NDPS Public Access Printers   Browser window of all configured NDPS printers.

NDPS Remote Printer Management   Remote management utility for all the new NDPS printer objects.

Novell License Services   Submenu provides the following three listings:

Add Licenses   Apply new licenses.

Move Selected License Certificates   New feature with NetWare 5.1 that allows network managers to shuffle licenses around for the best coverage.

Generate License Reports   Several options for creating reports listing license usage and assignments.

Print Service Quick Setup (Non-NDPS printers)   Starts the Quick Setup routines for easy printer installation, which were formerly only inside the PCONSOLE command-line utility. See Chapter 8 for details.

The Window Menu

Here are the choices on the Window menu:

New Window   Starts a new browser window, copying the same settings as in the existing browser window.

Cascade (Shift+F5)   The traditional Windows Cascade command, to arrange all open windows in such a way that they are overlapping, with only the titles showing.

Tile (Shift+F4)   The traditional Windows Tile command, to arrange all open windows to display without any overlap. The size of each window will be adjusted automatically to fit the space available.

Arrange Icons   The traditional Windows Arrange Icons command, to straighten the icons.

Close All   Shuts all open browser windows. Open browser windows are listed by the name of their container.

The Help Menu

The Help menu lists these options:

Help Topics   Presents a Windows 95/98/NT-style tabbed Help page listing Help topics and index. Error messages for NetWare and NDS are included in the Help topics.

Novell Support   Calls your Web client software and connects to the Novell support Web site.

Show Welcome Screen On Startup   Allows you to continue or cancel the "Did You Know?" tips each time you open NetWare Administrator.

About NetWare Administrator   Displays traditional version and copyright information, including the version of NetWare Administrator in use.

PART

II

Managing the
Network

NDS Administration with NetWare Administrator

The move to a graphical utility for management reinforced the object-oriented foundation of NetWare 4 when it appeared. Perhaps it's just me, but the ability to open containers, and see their containers, which might hold even more containers, helps emphasize the idea of inheritance. Drilling down through your network from the highest [Root] context through an Organization, and through one or more Organizational Units, and through a Volume object, and through a directory, down to an individual file, displays the organization like a giant network x-ray.

NOTE A distributed database takes a while to "ripple out" the changes. Just as the waves from a pebble splash take a moment to reach the bank of the pond, so too does NDS take a bit of time to synchronize all servers. The control over user information is quick, just as it was with SYSCON. The control over NDS takes a bit longer. Try to wait for results twice as long as you think is possible, and you'll be about right.

Creating Container Objects

IN A HURRY

10.1 Create a Container

1. Log in to the network as the Admin user or equivalent and start NetWare Administrator.
2. To create an Organization, highlight the [Root] level. To create an Organizational Unit, highlight the Organization or Organizational Unit that will hold the new container.
3. Press the Insert key.
4. Choose to create an Organization or Organizational Unit.
5. Type the name of the new container. You can check either Define Additional Properties or Create Another Organizational Unit (or Create Another Organization), but not both. Check Define User Defaults if you want the container to inherit the parent container's template.
6. Click Create, then Yes or No for the template if the Define User Defaults box was checked in the previous step.

An *Organization* can contain anything except another Organization. Only [Root] can contain an Organization. All leaf objects may be contained in an Organization. Single-server NetWare 4 networks may easily be a single Organization holding all servers, users, and network resources, mimicking a flat, NetWare 3 network.

Used more often is the *Organizational Unit*. Any container, including another Organizational Unit, can contain an Organizational Unit. Typically, there are multiple Organizational Units per Organization.

The process of creating either container is exactly the same. The difference is only where you put the container. Figure 10.2 shows the creation process for a new Organizational Unit, TECH_CON, being added within INTEGRATE.GCS. The name for this Organizational Unit will be TECH_CON.INTEGRATE.GCS.

FIGURE 10.2

Creating a new Organizational Unit

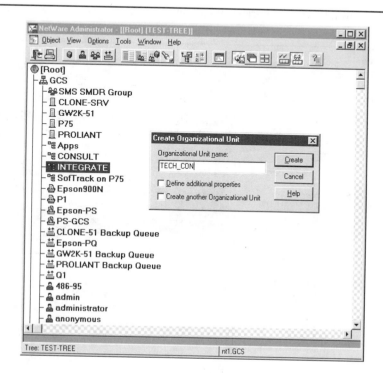

The Country container object is rarely used and should be avoided if possible. The hierarchy is as follows:

1. The Organization container can exist in a [Root] or Country container. It can contain Organizational Unit, Alias, and all leaf objects. Some examples of Organization names are GCS and UTDallas.

2. The Organizational Unit container can exist in an Organization or another Organizational Unit container. It can contain Organizational Unit, Alias, and all leaf objects. Some examples of Organizational Unit names are INTEGRATE and TECH_CON.

PART

II

Managing the
Network

Containers have as many details about themselves as do User and Group objects. In fact, the dialog box for the Organizational Unit INTEGRATE.GCS has as many pages as there are in the User and Group object dialog boxes. Check out Figure 10.3 to see what I mean. The screen in this figure should be familiar, since it's the same as for a User object or Group object. The users in INTEGRATE.GCS have rights to files and directories, because their container has rights to those files and directories.

FIGURE 10.3

Showing that a container has access to directories and files, just like a user

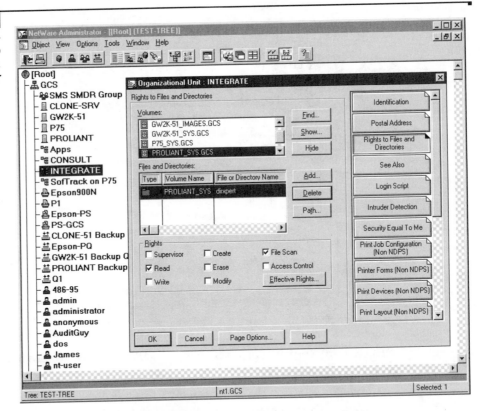

This is an advantage of NetWare 5.1 over NetWare 3 versions. Using container objects similarly to how you used a group in NetWare 3 allows you to grant trustee rights to files and directories without modifying any of the User object's rights individually. NetWare 5.1 Group objects do have the advantage of being able to grant trustee rights to User objects from different containers, and so they are still useful.

The only improvement in this screen from the similar screen in NetWare 4.11 came with NetWare 5.0. This is the addition of the Path command button beside the

Files And Directories list. When you click this button, a little information box appears to inform you of the full path name of the volume highlighted in the Files And Directories list.

Guidelines for NDS Objects

Let's take a second to reiterate the naming rules and guidelines for NDS objects:

- Must be less than 64 characters long. Names longer than 47 characters are truncated for non-NDS clients.

- Must be unique within the container.

- Names are not case-sensitive but will be displayed as typed in the Name field. (For example, although "SalesSupport" will display as you see here, NDS regards it as identical to "salessupport" and "SALESSUPPORT".)

- Spaces can be used and will be displayed as spaces within NDS. Spaces are shown as underscores for non-NDS clients.

- The following characters cannot be seen by non-NDS clients: slash (/), backslash (\ ), colon (:), comma (,), asterisk (*), and question mark (?).

Setting Intruder Detection

IN A HURRY

10.2 Set Intruder Detection

1. Log in to the network as the Admin user or equivalent and start NetWare Administrator.
2. Highlight the container to modify, or immediately modify a new container with the Define Additional Properties box checked during setup.
3. Click the Intruder Detection command button on the right side.
4. Check Detect Intruder and accept or modify the default settings.
5. Check Lock Account After Detection and accept or modify the default settings.
6. Click OK to save and exit.

Every new container deserves some security from the first moment of creation. You should get in the habit of thinking of security every time you create an object. Maybe you should stay ahead of the curve by considering security even *before* you create the object.

If you are setting up a new container, you may wish to select the Define Additional Properties checkbox in the Create Organizational Unit dialog box (see Figure 10.2, shown a bit earlier in the chapter). If you are creating several containers at one time, that's not an available option. If you want to set intruder detection for an existing container, open that container object's dialog box, click the Intruder Detection command button, and adjust the settings from there.

Intruder Detection works on the idea that anyone trying the same user name with multiple password attempts is up to no good. We've talked about the simple passwords people choose if you let them choose their own, and other employees and crooks know to try the obvious choices first when trying to break into accounts. Figure 10.4 shows the setup screens for Intruder Detection, along with NetWare's much too lenient default settings.

FIGURE 10.4

Stopping the pass-word guessing game

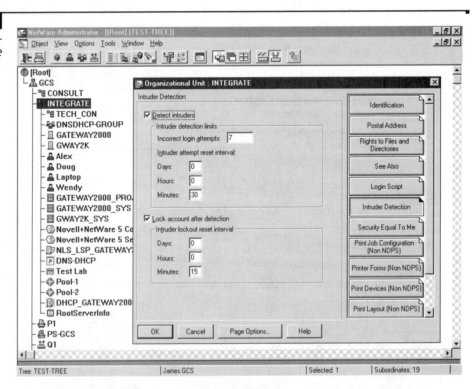

As you can see, the default setting for Incorrect Login Attempts is 7. This is way too high. If an employee coming back after a liquid lunch can't type a password in three tries, send that person home in a cab. The reset interval is 30 minutes, meaning three bad password guesses in 29 minutes will be counted as a possible intrusion. Since someone trying to crack the password will probably try several at a time, 30 minutes is enough for employees. But it isn't enough for outside attackers, who know about these detection settings. Set the time longer, such as one or two days.

The second checkbox tells the system what to do after the maximum password retries is exceeded. When the proper password isn't given in the set number of tries, the server console will beep, and the account will be locked. Again, the default (15 minutes) is far too short. Some recommend that the account be locked for a day or more. What if someone is trying to break the account on Friday evening? Locking it for only one day lets the perpetrator try again on Saturday and Sunday evenings without detection. Since you can reset the locked account easily by clicking the Intruder Lockout command button for the user, set the lock to last for three days and protect your system through the weekend. Also, keep notes of users who consistently come and ask for help clearing their messed up login attempts so that you start a paper trail of potential intruders.

Creating Leaf Objects

IN A HURRY

10.3 **Create a Leaf Object**

1. Log in to the network as the Admin user or equivalent and start NetWare Administrator.
2. Highlight the container for the new leaf object and press the Insert key.
3. Choose the leaf object to create from the New Object list.
4. Name the new leaf object. If necessary, provide file or location information.
5. Check a box to either Define Additional Properties or Create Another leaf object if you wish.
6. Click Create to save the new object.

The process for creating a leaf object is basically the same for all types of objects. The differences are related to whether the new object depends on a directory or volume path or on some other reference to the NDS tree that a User or Group object won't need.

As an example, let's create a Directory Map object, since we haven't done one of these before. A Directory Map represents a particular directory in the file system. In login scripts, it's helpful in two ways:

- It references a specific directory in the file system without requiring the entire path name.
- You can move the directory and change only the Directory Map description, not every login script that uses the Directory Map.

After highlighting the container for the object and pressing the Insert key, the New Object list box opens. Choose your object by double-clicking or by highlighting it and clicking OK. Then the Create dialog box opens. (The dialog box title always indicates which type of object you are creating.) Figure 10.5 shows us creating a Directory Map object.

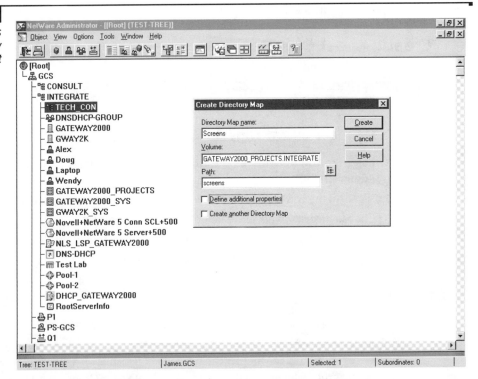

FIGURE 10.5

Setting the particulars for a new Directory Map leaf object

Since a Directory Map object works with the file system, the Create Directory Map dialog box has more information than usual. Here, we need to detail the volume used and the path within that volume. The Select Object dialog box is called by clicking the Browse button on the right side of the Path field.

Now that we've taken a quick look at Directory Map object creation, let's switch over to the setup of another leaf object that needs some rights. Suppose that new user Laura is now part of the CONSULT Organizational Unit. Her job is to help out with the graphics work. To do this, she needs access to the \SCREENS directory and all sub-directories under that directory.

Open up the Laura object by double-clicking the name. Scroll down the User dialog box until you can see the Rights To Files And Directories command button. Click that button to display that page of information for user Laura.

Figure 10.6 shows the process of granting Laura rights to the directory in question. Being a member of the CONSULT Organizational Unit, she is automatically granted access to the volumes you see listed in the upper-left part of the dialog box, but \SCREENS is in the INTEGRATE container. I highlighted the GATEWAY2000_PROJECTS: volume, then clicked the Add button to open our old friend, the Select Object dialog box. By scrolling through the directory context list, I found and highlighted the \SCREENS directory.

PART

II

Managing the
Network

FIGURE 10.6

Giving Laura access to
\SCREENS

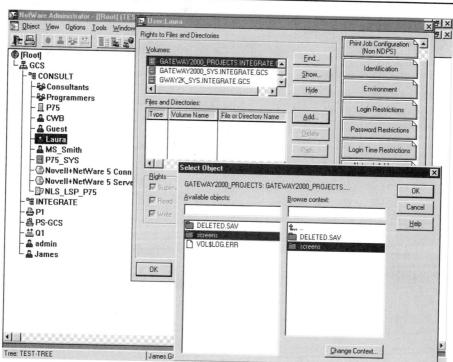

Once you've closed the Select Object dialog box and accepted the specified directory path, click the OK button. The last step is to grant the trustee rights for the directory. This is accomplished by clicking the checkboxes in the Rights section of the main dialog box (User:Laura in Figure 10.6). To give all the necessary user rights to the directory (and all subdirectories through inheritance), check Read, Write, and (hidden by the Select Object dialog box in the foreground of Figure 10.6) Create, Erase, Modify, and File Scan.

NetWare 4.10's NetWare Administrator program required you to highlight the volume(s) in question and click OK in the Select Object dialog box. In the spirit of productivity, NetWare 5.1 only requires you to double-click the directory name. Don't squander all your saved time at once.

Moving Objects

IN A HURRY

10.4 Move an Object

1. Log in to the network as the Admin user or equivalent and start NetWare Administrator.
2. Highlight the object to be moved and press the F7 key.
3. Type the new location or use the Browse button to open the Select Object dialog box.
4. Choose the new location and click OK to exit the Select Object dialog box.
5. If available (NetWare 4.10), check the Create Alias In Place Of Moved Container box.
6. Click Create to save the settings.

When you move a leaf object, all NDS references to the moved object are changed. The common name of the object will remain the same, but the full name showing the context will change.

 NOTE Early versions of NetWare 4 allowed the moving of leaf objects only. Now, however, you may move any container object as well, but with some caveats. A container object can be moved only if it is the root of an NDS partition that has no subordinate partitions. Check the NDS Manager information coming up soon for more details.

Let's correct a mistake of mine made just a bit ago. There's no reason to put the Directory Map object into a container three levels deep, especially since all network users may want access to the files referenced by the Directory Map object Screens.

After logging in to the network as Admin or equivalent, open the NDS display so you can see the Directory Map object Screens. Your first thought might be to drag and drop the object into its new location, but that won't work. If you do grab an object and start to move it, notice the help information that appears above the menu line: "Make each of the selected objects a trustee of the dropped target." Oops, this isn't what we want. So before letting it go, drag your object to the top or bottom of the screen, or you will wind up creating a trustee assignment that you don't want.

 TIP Here's the correct drag-and-drop approach to move this same object: hold down the Ctrl key while you're dragging and dropping. (This isn't in the manual, so don't tell anyone, okay? What is in the manual is wrong, because the manual tells you to simply drag and drop objects to move them. You'd think after four versions of NDS and corresponding versions of the manual, they'd get this straight in the online documentation, but the CD I have is still wrong. Nice new presentation format, but still wrong.)

The official way to move an object is to highlight the object and either press F7 or choose Move from the Object menu. This opens the Move dialog box, showing the current location and a text box awaiting the destination. You can type the destination or use the Browse button. Figure 10.7 shows the Select Object dialog box being used to move Screens to a more reasonable location. Once I click OK in each dialog box, SCREENS.TECH_CON.INTEGRATE.GCS will become SCREENS.GCS, a much more manageable handle. I have now corrected the "mistake" I made previously.

If you remember NetWare 4.10's NetWare Administrator program, you may recall that the Move dialog box included an option to create an Alias object in place of the moved object. That option no longer exists. Either Novell's research showed that people didn't use that function or the designers forgot to upgrade those lines of code. Either way, once you move an object, the only way to leave an Alias in its place is to create one yourself.

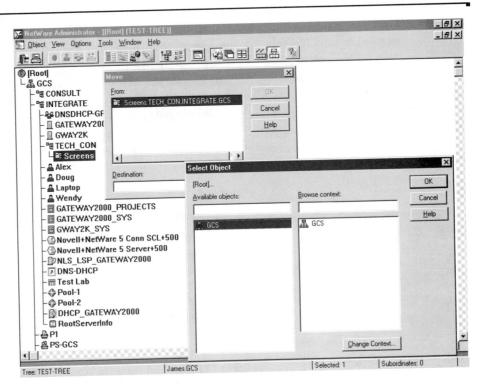

FIGURE 10.7

Moving Screens up two NDS tree levels

Renaming Objects

IN A HURRY

10.5 Rename an Object

1. Log in to the network as the Admin user or equivalent and start NetWare Administrator.

2. Highlight the new leaf object to be renamed.

3. Pull down the Object menu and choose Rename.

4. Type the new name.

5. Indicate whether to save the old name and whether to create an Alias if renaming a container.

6. Click Create to save.

This may come as a shock to you, but things in your network will change. Some brilliant VP will decide that SLS+MKTG must become MKTG+SLS, and every reference in the company, including the network Organizational Unit, needs to change. Luckily, this is easier and much cheaper than getting new business cards (quicker, too).

To change an object's name, you just highlight the object that needs the name change and pick Rename from the Object menu. A small dialog box appears, asking for the new name. Figure 10.8 shows the process of renaming TECH_CON to TECH_CON_1.

FIGURE 10.8

Renaming a container and taking all the proper precautions

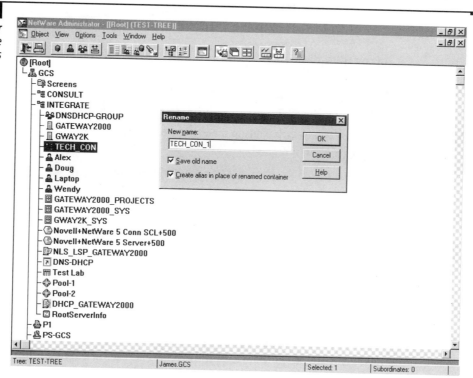

PART

II

Managing the Network

With this step, all references to TECH_CON will become TECH_CON_1, throughout the entire NDS tree. What about the users who will go looking for TECH_CON, only to be disappointed? As you can see in Figure 10.8, there are two ways to make sure the users can find the container.

The first checkbox asks if you wish to save the old name. This will keep the name as an Alias in the NDS database, so searches for the old name will work. The search results will tell the users (or other network administrators) what the new name for the object is. Now, see why I think this would have been a good thing to keep in the Move Object feature?

The second checkbox creates an Alias object with the name of the original object. The Alias object points to the object with its new name. Users with references to the newly renamed object in their login script will be connected properly.

Searching for Objects

IN A HURRY

10.6 Search for Objects

1. Log in to the network as the Admin user or equivalent and start NetWare Administrator.
2. Highlight the container from which to start the search (optional).
3. Pull down the Object menu and choose Search, or click the flashlight icon.
4. Choose your search filters in the dialog box, or open a previously saved search filter.
5. Click OK to start the search.
6. Use the search results in their own browser window.

As your network and NDS database both get larger, finding objects with specific properties will get tough. Your users will be okay, since they spend most of their time in specific containers using a small set of servers and volumes. You, however, must patrol the entire network.

The Search option on NetWare Administrator's Object menu (you could click the flashlight icon on the toolbar instead of going to the menu) makes life much simpler. You can list search requirements based on an enormous number of options and save the search query for reuse. Once the search is finished, the results appear in their own browser window, so they are easy to keep in one place and remain available for quick reference.

Make sure you run the search utility as a user with as many trustee rights as possible. The minimum rights required for a search are the Browse rights to objects, so you can see the entire network, and the Read and Compare property rights, so you can match a particular value to the object of your search profile.

Figure 10.9 shows a search about to start. Since NetWare 5.1 no longer has the SECURITY.EXE file that NetWare 3 used to list security settings for all users, this search operation will list all users who are equivalent to Admin. One of the most serious security breaches occurs when the wrong person has the ultimate network access privileges, and this type of search can tell you if this has happened.

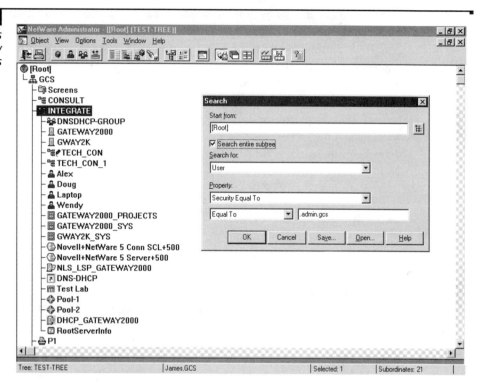

FIGURE 10.9

Searching for users who may be security risks

Setting a Search Filter

There are several steps in setting up a search filter. Here are some suggestions for the Search dialog box fields:

Start From   The context you have highlighted when calling the Search dialog box is placed in the Start From field. If you don't wish to start from that point, click the Browse button at the end of the field and move through the NDS tree until you find your preferred context.

Search Entire Subtree   Checking this option searches the current container and all subordinate containers. When it isn't selected, the search utility looks only in the current container.

Search For   Every leaf object, plus additions such as volume, Organization, and Organizational Unit, may be searched for. The default is User, figuring that some network client will be causing the problem you are searching to resolve.

Property   Specifies the property value to search, based on the item in the Search For field. None is the default, somehow meaning all.

The field directly below Property could be called the Boolean field, since the contents tend to be Equal To or Not Equal To, Present or Not Present, Greater Than or Less Than, and the like. If you use this field to indicate a number or text, such as Equal To or Greater Than, enter the value in the text box to the right. In our example in Figure 10.9, "Equal To .admin.gcs" is specified for the search.

Search results appear in a separate browser window, waiting for you to take some action. You may minimize the window, keeping it available for use but out of your way while you go about your business within NetWare Administrator. Using the defaults of the Search window gathers all users in the container in one tidy spot. If your container is getting so large that these searches are used regularly, you need to rethink your network design.

Saving Search Criteria

The search results always inhabit their own browser window entitled Search. There's no way to save the search results for reuse later, but you can save the search criteria.

Notice the command buttons across the bottom of the Search dialog box in Figure 10.9. We expect OK, Cancel, and Help, but Save and Open are a surprise in NetWare Administrator. Once you have the search questions set the way you want them, click Save. A Save As dialog box appears, prompting you to put the saved procedure files in the \PUBLIC directory with an .SCH extension.

If you later click Open, the File Open dialog box arrives, aimed at the \PUBLIC subdirectory. The File Name list box is set for the .SCH extension, so you merely need to double-click the name of the procedure you want to retrieve.

Once summoned, the Search dialog box waits for you, with all the previously configured information in the proper places. You may then click OK and either conduct the same search operation or modify any of the fields' contents before starting the search.

Using NDS Manager to Manage Partitions and Replicas

The NDS database tracks all the network objects and their rights to use the network. The database is spread around the network for two main reasons: fault-tolerance and speed of execution. The closer the database is to a user requesting services, the sooner those services can be provided. Having more copies of the database running on the network prevents one dead server from locking everyone out of the network.

NetWare 5.1 divides the Directory into *partitions*. Each partition is a distinct unit of data in the NDS tree. A partition includes a container object, all objects contained therein, and the data about those objects. No file system information is included in a partition. An object can only be in one partition, but copies of the partition allow the object to be accessed from anywhere in the network. Subordinate partitions are labeled *child* partitions; the partition above that is called the *parent* partition.

A *replica* is a copy of one partition. Replicas provide fault-tolerance within each partition by copying the database to multiple file servers. A lost partition can be re-created by using a replica. There are four types of replicas:

Master replica   The primary replica of a given partition. Used to create new Directory partitions or to read and update Directory information. The Master replica should be near the NetWare manager responsible for maintaining the partition. Only one Master replica of any partition can exist.

Read/Write replica   Reads and updates Directory information, such as the addition or deletion of objects. This replica should be near the workgroup serviced by that partition. If a Master replica is lost, a Read/Write replica must become the Master. If the first Master comes back online, the replica currently serving as Master will be deleted automatically in deference to the Master with an earlier time stamp.

Read-Only replica   Primarily a backup that speeds information by allowing users to view the information, without allowing any changes.

Subordinate Reference replica   Placed automatically by NDS on a server if the parent Directory partition has either a Master, Read/Write, or Read-Only replica on the server and the child Directory partition does not. Subordinate Reference replicas are maintained by NDS.

In NetWare 4.10, you can manage partitions and replicas with Partition Manager, accessed from the Tools menu of NetWare Administrator. In NetWare 4.11, Partition Manager was still available as a DOS utility, but NDS Manager handled the Windows-based work. You may run NDS Manager on its own or add the NDS Manager option to your NetWare Administrator Tools menu. In NetWare 5.0, the DOS utility disappeared. (See why I say DOS is dead as a management tool?)

During partition operations, you may see some unknown icons as the synchronization between different Directory databases settles down and stabilizes. There is no reason to worry unless this continues for a day.

During installation, a replica of the partition containing the server's context is added to each new server, unless there are already three replicas. Servers with bindery files will get a replica, regardless of how many replicas are there already. Extra partitions or replicas are controlled by the NDS Manager utility, NDSMGR32.EXE, which works under Windows 95/98/NT/2000.

Partition and Replica Management Guidelines

Here are some guidelines for managing partitions and replicas:

- Make sure you replicate the partition that includes the [Root] object. If this partition dies, your NDS tree is worthless. Make an extra copy or two while you're at it.

- For NDS fault-tolerance, plan for three replicas of each partition. If your network design allows it, keep replica copies in different physical locations.

- Create partitions to group your network users in their natural boundaries. If users from the partition are spread far and wide, move the replicas close to them. The closer the replicas are to the workgroup using them, the better.

- Servers that need to run Bindery Services must have either a Master or a Read/Write replica of the partition.

- Changes to the replicas, such as adding or deleting objects or redefining a partition, send little traffic across the network. Only the changed information is sent across the network. However, placing or rebuilding a replica requires the system to copy the entire replica across the network. Enough traffic is generated to impact the users slightly. It's better to leave these operations for low-traffic times if possible. Each object in a replica takes about 1KB of disk space.

Follow these guidelines and use your common networking sense, and the management of replicas and partitions will go smoothly. High-speed connections between partitions and replicas, as in a purely local or campus network, will never show a significant performance drop because of replica placement. When you start crossing WANs, however, especially those with slow connections, pay extra attention to replica and boundary placement.

When You Mess Up NDS

During research for this section, my lab network (TEST-TREE) somehow got quite messed up. Perhaps the fact that I deleted the SYS: volume holding the Master replica of the [Root] partition for the network had something to do with the problem. Kids, do not try this at home, or when folks with tender ears are within screaming and cursing distance.

NetWare 3 offered a well-defined process for restoring the server resource information: you retrieved the bindery files from your backup tape. If your backup tape did not copy the bindery files (i.e., was a cheap backup system), you copied the bindery files from the disk you created by telling NetWare to back up the entire server to floppy disks, stopping at the first disk since that one held the three bindery files. Then you hoped you remembered all the network users and printers added since the backup.

The good news with NetWare 5.1 is that the NDS information is distributed and current. The bad news is that the NDS information is distributed, and it will take a while to recover from major surgery or ham-fisted management. The Read/Write replicas will eventually propagate the information to the newly installed NDS files on the butchered server. During that time, however, you will have to do the following:

- Try to make a Read/Write replica a Master replica (using DSREPAIR). The delay will become interminable, and you will try to do the same thing again, then try to force another replica into Master mode.

- Try to reinstall NDS on the afflicted server, getting error messages when you provide the Admin password. Press Alt+F10 to get out of the loop by stopping the installation.
- Try to redo the replica status again.
- Go to the hardware store and decide which sledgehammer will make the best adjustment tool for your servers.
- Notice that the replicas are starting to settle down.
- Try again, without success, to resurrect NDS on the afflicted server.
- Read the employment classifieds.
- Actually get NDS installed once again on the less-afflicted server.
- Be amazed at how much of your network returns in good working order.

The key element in this sequence is the time needed for NDS to heal itself. Of course, a busy network is not a relaxed place. Users want access to their services, and they want them 10 minutes ago. Reject the urge to do something, especially something drastic. Help your users find ways to get the resources they need. Check the NDS status and use DSREPAIR a time or two (more details on DSREPAIR soon).

If possible, make your mistakes on a weekend, so the system has a chance to settle down before the users appear. Just don't make any social plans for that weekend.

Before starting any work on NDS, take a moment to verify that your partitions and replicas are well distributed. Keep Master replicas away from the target of any changes. Make a new Master replica if necessary, and give the network time to settle down before the next step. If you don't, you may need my list of colorful adjectives for describing recalcitrant replicas. E-mail for details, but don't let any children see the list. And before you e-mail (I've gotten some from readers of earlier versions of this book), you can get the list by hanging around constructions sites or Navy shipyards and listening to sailors.

Putting NDS Manager on the NetWare Administrator Tools Menu

First, you need to know where to find the NDS Manager program. If you're running Windows 95/98/NT/2000, run NDSMGR32.EXE in the \PUBLIC\WIN32 directory. (If you're looking for a way to run this under Windows 3.1*x*, give up, because Novell stopped including the 16-bit version in NetWare 5.0.)

Second, there's a trick to getting NDS Manager to show up in the NetWare Administrator Tools menu. With NetWare 4.*x*, you had to edit the Windows 95 Registry and all sorts of nonsense, but with NetWare 5.1, you have one step to take before NDS Manager shows up in the Tools menu: copy the NMSNAP32.DLL file from the \PUBLIC\WIN32 directory to the \PUBLIC\WIN32\SNAPINS directory. There. Done. When you restart NetWare Administrator, the NDS Manager option will appear on the Tools menu. Or, if you wish, you can avoid the extra copying by running the NDS Manager program separately from NetWare Administrator.

Taking a look at Figure 10.10, notice how flexible the columns are on the NDS Manager screen. I've rearranged the bottom columns so that they are completely different from the default settings on the top. This allows me to put the information I want first. In this case, I put the little pictures of the servers, showing that the P75 server is the Master replica for the [Root] partition, but PROLIANT contains only a Read-Write replica (see the bottom pane of the screenshot). How do I know that there are two partitions? Well, the upper-left window, labeled Partitions, lists two containers. Each container has the small partition icon to its left.

FIGURE 10.10

Rearranging the management furniture

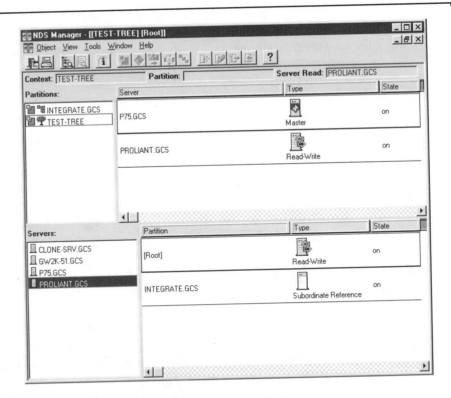

Clicking the icon at the top of the screen containing the lowercase *i* displays information about the highlighted object. Figure 10.11 shows information about the [Root] partition.

Checking partition details

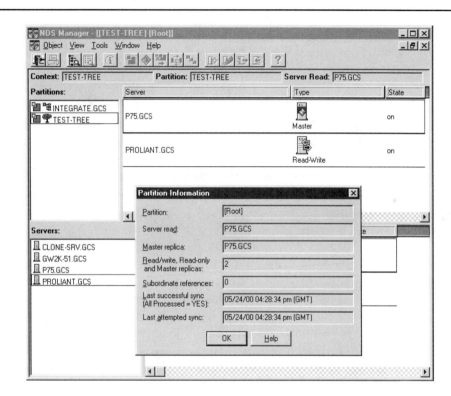

There is one new field shown here from the information in NetWare 4.11. Previously, the dialog box showed only the Master Replica information, but Novell added (with NetWare 5.0) the Server Read field to duplicate the Server Read text box at the upper-right of the screen.

Notice that the last attempted sync and last successful sync coincide. This is a good feeling, and one you should enjoy when it happens.

Creating a New Partition

IN A HURRY

10.7 Create a Partition

1. Log in to the network as the Admin user or equivalent and start NetWare Administrator.
2. Highlight the container in which to make a new partition.
3. Start NDS Manager from the Tools menu or as a separate program.
4. In NDS Manager, switch to Tree view and highlight the container you want to make into a new partition.
5. Click Create As A New Partition and confirm by clicking Yes in the warning dialog box.
6. Click Yes in the information box that appears during the partition operation.
7. Refresh the screen to see the new partition icon.

The [Root] is the first partition in your new network. Any new partition from that becomes a child partition. Any new partition from that becomes another child partition, and the middle partition becomes both a parent and a child partition (sort of what you become when you turn your parents into grandparents).

A new partition must consist of a container and its objects, both leaf objects and other containers. The partition replicas remain on the same servers they were on before you made the new partition, but the information for the partition will be moved to the appropriate replica for the new partition.

Figure 10.12 shows partition creation about to begin, so the CONSULT Organizational Unit, holding the Programmers and Consultants groups, will have some directory service fault-tolerance. There is no strain in creating a partition, but large networks may take some time for NDS to become synchronized once again. Your network traffic will increase slightly, since there will be communication between partitions and replicas across the network.

Using the Abort Partition Operation command button that appears after you approve the new partition is usually not a good idea. If you had a sudden attack of conscience and decided that giving the programmers in CONSULT their own partition was a bad idea, you could click the Abort button quickly. But partition operations are so fast on LANs that you probably wouldn't catch the operation in time to stop it.

FIGURE 10.12

*Giving the program-
mers and consultants
their own partition*

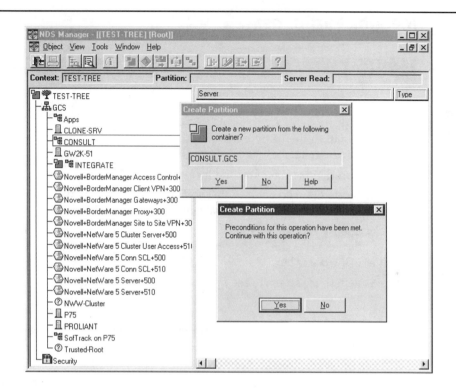

I wouldn't even try to stop a partition operation unless I realized a WAN link was down. In a case like that, where a WAN break stopped an operation from completing, you would need to abort the partition operation. Otherwise—i.e., on local connections with all servers present and accounted for—wait for the partition operation to finish, and then undo it, as described in the next section.

After you click Yes to create the new partition, a nice box labeled Create Partition says that all preconditions have been met and you may create the partition. This dialog box appears in Figure 10.12. Click Yes once more, and your partition will be created. Things happen so fast in NetWare 5.1 that you don't even get a warning about how long the operation may take. In a LAN setting, your partition appears before you could read the screen saying the partition is being created.

Merging Partitions

IN A HURRY

10.8 Merge Partitions

1. Log in to the network as the Admin user or equivalent and start NetWare Administrator.
2. Start NDS Manager from the Tools menu.
3. Locate the child partition that you want to merge back with its parent partition in the NDS Manager browser window.
4. Choose Partition from the Object menu, then select Merge, or highlight the partition and click the Merge Partition icon on the toolbar, and confirm by clicking Yes in the dialog box.
5. Refresh the screen to see the new partition alignment.

If you change your mind after creating a new partition, you can easily merge it back with its parent partition. This makes sense if the two partitions serve essentially the same Directory structure and their information is similar. Your only choice is whether or not to merge a partition back with its parent partition; you're not offered the choice of picking some other partition to merge.

Partitions are not deleted; they are just merged. All the information in one partition is absorbed into the parent partition.

Figure 10.13 shows the dialog box you'll see when you choose to merge partitions. A warning box appears to tell you that this operation may take up to an hour. In large networks with WAN links, merging may take quite a bit of time. Eventually the warning dialog box will go away, and things will look like they are finished—possibly before they actually are. Wait an extra minute or two between operations so partitions and replicas don't get confused halfway through the first operation when you start a second one.

Although you can create a partition only while in the hierarchical (Tree) view, you can merge partitions from the flat view, as in Figure 10.13. Once you click Yes in the Merge Partition dialog box, an informational box appears. This box includes a Cancel command button, if you feel the urge to un-merge immediately.

FIGURE 10.13

A child partition returns home to its parent partition.

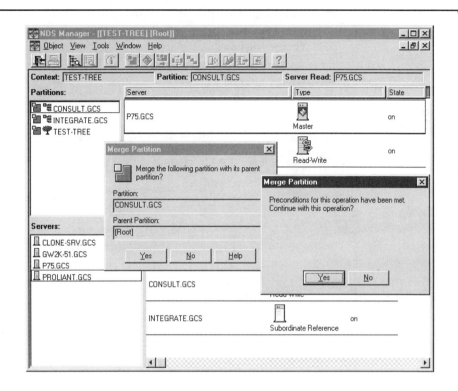

Viewing or Modifying Replicas

IN A HURRY

10.9 View or Modify a Replica

1. Log in to the network as the Admin user or equivalent and start NetWare Administrator.

2. Start NDS Manager from the Tools menu or as a separate program.

3. Click the Replicas button on the right side of the toolbar. Explanatory balloons (hints) will appear to tell you which icon is which as your cursor touches the icon.

4. Click the toolbar buttons to Add Replica, Delete Replica, Change Type, Send Updates, or Receive Updates.

5. Verify the server name and the type of replica you wish to add before clicking OK.

6. Click Close to exit the finished dialog box.

PART

II

Managing the Network

Replica management is generally necessary when you make changes to the NDS design. The Partition Replicas dialog box appears after you click any of the replicas in NDS Manager. This dialog box gives you a look at the replicas for the partition that was highlighted. Figure 10.14 shows a good view of the replica information for the [Root] partition of the GCS network.

FIGURE 10.14

Checking the replica status

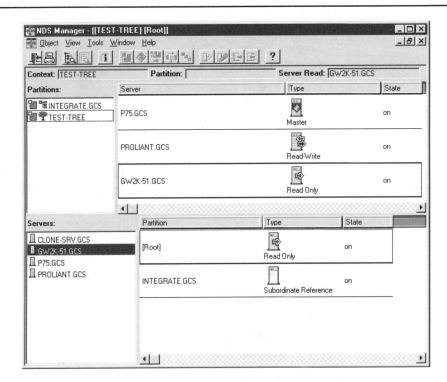

Notice in Figure 10.14 that we're showing the NDS Manager flat view. This is important, as some changes can be made only in the flat view, such as adding a replica. The top window shows the partitions (only [Root] now), and the bottom window shows the status of each server when its name is highlighted. All three types of replicas are on display in Figure 10.14, since I added a Read-Only replica for GW2K-51. Notice that it also gets a Subordinate Reference automatically, new with NetWare 5.1.

The toolbar buttons for the NDS Manager, shown in Figure 10.14, include all the obvious options for replicas: Add, Delete, Change, and Update. The display shows that there is one Read-Only replica on server GW2K-51. Figure 10.15 shows the Add Replica dialog box that appears when you click the Add Replica toolbar button (or when you highlight the partition display, right-click, and choose Change Type).

FIGURE 10.15

Getting server GW2K-51 into the partition replication business

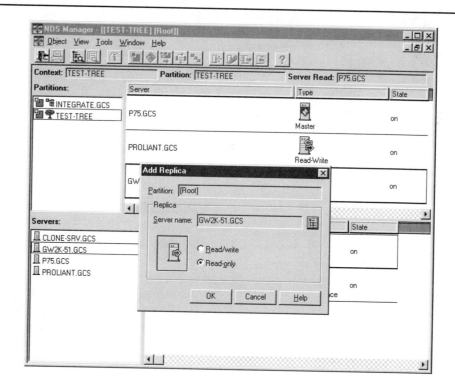

There are two types of replicas that could be installed on GW2K-51; for this example, I opted for the Read-Only type. The copy operation will take a moment, but not much longer with a small network and all LAN connections between the servers. If there are WAN links in the path, it will take longer. The more objects in the partition, the more time it will take to add a partition replica.

What if you want to change the replica type? Let's say that I realized it would be better to make GW2K-51 a Read/Write replica rather than a Read-Only replica. All I need to do is right-click the server name and click the Change Type button. This opens the Change Replica Type dialog box in Figure 10.16.

Actually, it really is better to have Read/Write replicas. Read-Only replicas are not recommended, because they can't help re-create your NDS structure in case of damage to parts of the database. When you click OK in the Change Replica Type dialog box, the replica is immediately changed, with little or no network impact.

PART

II

Managing the
Network

FIGURE 10.16

*Changing server
GW2K-51's replica
from Read-Only to
Read/Write*

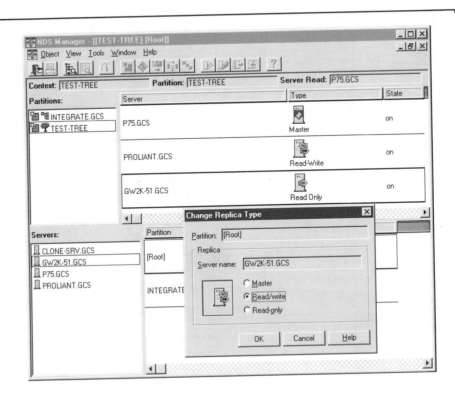

When a replica is changed to Master, the current (and replaced) Master replica automatically downgrades to Read/Write. So if you wish to make your Master replica a Read/Write replica, you must set up the new Master replica first.

When you right-click while pointing at a replica, you'll see many choices. If you wish to delete the replica, highlight the Delete menu option, then verify that you know what you're doing. The system won't let you delete the Master replica. (It's certainly embarrassing when you kill the Master replica. Don't ask me how I know this.)

The Update toolbar buttons (the last two on the right, before the question mark icon) depend on the highlighted replica as well. If the replica you have highlighted is the one you want to update with some recent change from another replica, click the Send Updates command button. If you have a feeling that the highlighted replica has a problem and needs to be updated, click the Receive Updates button. You may also send and receive updates by right-clicking while pointing to a server. These operations shouldn't be necessary often, but they're handy in case a WAN connection has just been restored.

Viewing Server Partitions

IN A HURRY

10.10 View a Server Partition

1. Log in to the network as the Admin user or equivalent and start NetWare Administrator.

2. Start NDS Manager from the Tools menu or as a separate program.

3. Highlight the server with the replica of interest.

4. Double-click the server name to view the server information, or right-click and choose Information from the menu. This screen is read-only (nothing in the Replica Information box may be changed here).

Let's say we wish to verify that the GW2K-51 server is, in fact, now supporting Read/Write replicas for our partition. Plus, we want to know how the server and its replica are doing. That's where the Information button on the toolbar comes in handy.

Switching back to the hierarchical view (I can never make up my mind) and opening the replica display is our first step. When you want information about a server, it really doesn't matter whether the NDS Manager's display on the left is flat or hierarchical. Highlighting one of the server replicas in the main window area is the second step. The final step is to either right-click for the menu and choose Information or click the toolbar's Information button. Either way, this step pops open what you see in Figure 10.17.

The information in the Server Information window is Read-Only, in case you were thinking of making changes here. But it's so easy to make a change with the NDS Manager utility—with a right-click or a toolbar choice—that you won't mind.

If you've been a network manager for any length of time, you may notice something unusual here for NetWare: the Network Address, the last field in the dialog box, shows TCP:204.251.122.51. What kind of joke is this?

No joke. It's just that NetWare servers can now be identified by TCP/IP addresses. In fact, the list also shows a UDP (User Datagram Protocol) address as well, but it's the same as the TCP/IP address. Get used to it.

 NOTE IPX addresses are still available with a click of the scroll button.

PART

II

Managing the
Network

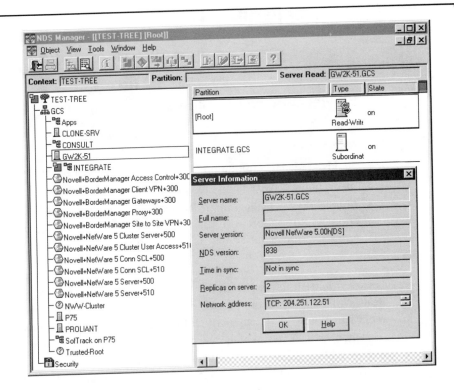

FIGURE 10.17

Checking the status of GW2K-51

Deleting a NetWare Server Object from NDS

IN A HURRY

10.11 Delete a Server

1. Go to the NetWare server to be deleted and type **DOWN** at the console.
2. Log in to the network as the Admin user or equivalent.
3. Start NetWare Administrator.
4. Start the NDS Manager from the Tools menu or as a separate program.
5. Highlight the server object to be deleted and press the Delete key.
6. Click Yes to delete.

Getting rid of a server is serious business. When you press the Delete key, the high-lighted server bites the dust, never to rise again. There is no SALVAGE utility to resurrect the server. Gone are all the server's resources, which are now out of reach for all network clients. Still available, thankfully, are all the files and directories on the server volume(s). When (and if) you reinstall NDS on the server, the data will still be there, waiting for your return.

Taking out a server may corrupt your NDS database, so move all partition replicas away from the server before proceeding. If you delete a server holding your only replica, that partition is in deep trouble. There will be a pass/fail test of your tape backup system immediately, which it will most likely fail. If it fails, you must re-create the partition by memory, and by hand.

If you are taking a server out of commission and have removed all replicas from the server, highlight the server and press the Delete key. If the server is still up, you'll see something like the warning shown in Figure 10.18. Simply down the server and try once more to delete it.

PART

II

FIGURE 10.18

You forgot a step before deleting the server.

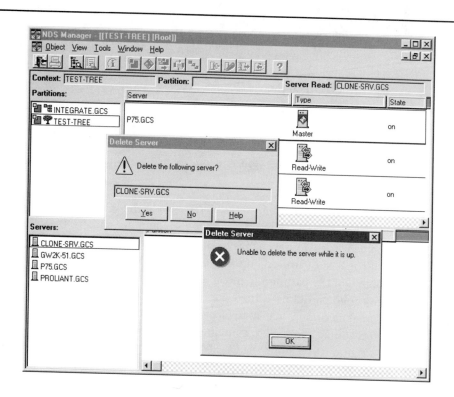

Managing the Network

In the tree view on the left side of the screen, be sure to highlight the server itself rather than the large Partition block just above the Delete Server dialog box. If you highlight the latter and press Delete, you will see a different dialog box asking if you're sure that you want to delete the replica. That should be done earlier; now you're taking a physical server out of NDS.

You don't need to delete a server to move the object to another context; just use the techniques described earlier to move the Server object. If you need to move a partition, keep reading.

Moving a Partition (and Its Container)

IN A HURRY

10.12 Move a Partition and Container

1. Log in to the network as the Admin user or equivalent and start NetWare Administrator.
2. Start NDS Manager from the Tools menu, or start it as a separate program.
3. Highlight the partition to be moved and click the Move Partition toolbar icon, or right-click and choose Move from the menu.
4. Type the new partition location or use the Browse button to move through the NDS tree.
5. Be sure to check the box to leave an Alias object in place of the moved container.
6. Click Yes to move, save, and exit.

When a container is moved, all references in the Directory database for the container are changed. The common name of the container remains the same, but the full name will obviously change to reflect the container's new location in the NDS tree.

The Move Partition button is on the NDS Manager toolbar. You must pick and highlight the partition to move, and it must be the root of an NDS partition, without any child partitions. If there are child partitions, you must merge each of them to the parent partition you plan to move before continuing. This is why you must go through NDS Manager to move a container: the container must be a partition.

Figure 10.19 shows the INTEGRATE Organizational Unit highlighted in NDS Manager. You can still see the partition icon to the left of INTEGRATE within the NDS Manager hierarchical display. CONSULT can't be moved until a new partition is created with that container as the root of the partition.

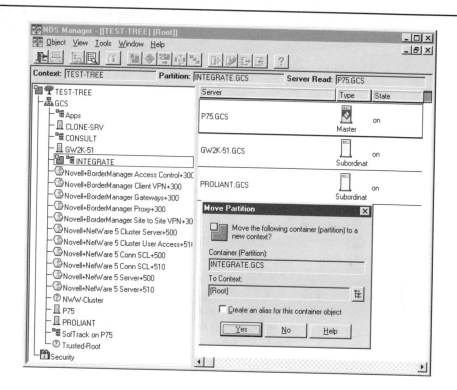

FIGURE 10.19

Threatening to move INTEGRATE.GCS

User Management

Most of the information about individual user creation and management is back in Chapter 6. Turn to Chapter 7 for managing users in groups of one type or another, including how to set up menus and login scripts. What may be called the traditional user management information has thus already been covered.

But tradition isn't worth much in the days approaching the new millennium, is it? So we still have a few things worth covering about user management in this chapter.

Using NetWare Accounting

NetWare was the first network operating system to allow accounting. By tracking such details as connect time, disk space used, and service requests to a file server, NetWare accounting moved away from a PC LAN level toward mainframe-type control.

Accounting is used by some network administrators to charge back company departments and by others to track when resources are being used more heavily than in the past.

NetWare accounting is set per server, giving you a way to track the usage of network resources on that server alone. Tracking users of the entire network, through the distributed NDS database, would generate enormous extra network traffic. Since the licenses for NetWare are set per server, accounting is set per server. This may change when the user licensing changes to a network model, although most likely the report gathering will change, leaving the accounting set per server. I sure wouldn't want to be in charge of making accounting work across a distributed network, however. My guess is that if the user licensing changes, accounting will still track users per resource.

Some companies use this information to charge their network clients for a portion of the server cost, based on a cost value per network resource used. Some companies use this information to track the amount of server usage over time, to see whether usage is growing, shrinking, or staying the same. How you use the information, if at all, is up to you.

Accounting is not mandatory, and it's not necessary to activate accounting to manage any server user or resource. Since accounting does add slightly to the server overhead, some network administrators prefer to charge users by total disk space used, not connect time or disk blocks read and written. Applying charged values generated by the accounting system to users and their departments requires constant attention and maintenance.

The information tracked by the system is displayed by the DOS ATOTAL utility. Many companies use accounting to generate usage levels per server, viewed by the ATOTAL command, without any of the charge-back information per user. The information that is gathered, along with the names of the related command buttons in the Server dialog box, includes:

- Total disk blocks read (Blocks Read)
- Total disk blocks written (Blocks Written)
- Total minutes of connect time (Connect Time)
- Total disk blocks used for storage per day (Disk Storage)
- Total service requests (Service Requests)

Servers that have the accounting feature activated have five extra command buttons in their dialog box, labeled as shown in the list. Servers without accounting do not have these buttons in their dialog box.

Activating Server Accounting

IN A HURRY

10.13 Activate Server Accounting

1. Log in to the network as the Admin user or equivalent and start NetWare Administrator.

2. Double-click the target server, and then click the Accounting command button at the bottom of the dialog box.

3. Verify that you wish to start accounting. The server's bindery context must be set for accounting to begin.

Accounting is activated per server, so you must double-click the particular server in the NetWare Administrator tree diagram. In the Server dialog box, the Accounting command button is the one on the bottom right. Click the button, and you will have a choice about starting or stopping accounting, depending on the accounting status (this is a toggle button).

Setting the Charge Rates for Resources

IN A HURRY

10.14 Set the Blocks-Read Rate for Server Accounting

1. Log in to the network as the Admin user or equivalent and start NetWare Administrator.

2. Double-click the target server to open the dialog box, and then click the Blocks Read command button at the bottom of the dialog box (you may have to scroll down within the box to see it).

3. Click Add Charge Rate and define a charge if an acceptable one is not listed.

4. Click and drag the cursor across the boxes that define each half-hour slot of the day. Chosen blocks will change to the color of the applied charge.

5. Click OK to save and exit.

PART

II

Managing the
Network

Once you determine that you will charge your users for server resources, you must decide how much to charge them. The user's account balance is kept in cents, so it's easiest to use cents as a basis for your charges.

NetWare accounting uses a charge rate that is denoted as a fraction. The charge rate screen will ask for a multiplier (the top number) and a divisor (the bottom number). The multiplier is the amount that you are charging for each unit or resource. For whole cents, place the number of cents over 1, such as 5/1 for a charge of 5 cents for the resource. For fractions, such as 1.5 cents, you must multiply by 10 enough times to make the number a whole number (in this case, $1.5 \times 10 = 15$). Then add that 10 to the divisor. If the number is something like 1.55 cents for some strange reason, multiply by 10 twice to reach 155, then place 100 (the "10 twice") in the divisor. For whole cents, the divisor is always 1. For fractions, the divisor is always 100, with a whole number in the multiplier.

The charge rates may vary according to day and time of the week. Setting the rate is always the same, however, no matter how many rates you have for a resource. Accounting can keep track of as many as 20 rates per resource.

Unfortunately, there isn't a database of charge rates. You must define each charge rate in the pages of the Accounting dialog box.

If you want to charge a penny (or any other amount) for each disk block read from this file server, the Blocks Read page of the NetWare Server dialog box is the place to do so. Figure 10.20 shows a one-cent charge for each block read, but only on weekdays between 6:00 A.M. and 6:00 P.M. Since the book you're reading reproduces all the screens in shades of gray, you can't see what color it is that fills the blocks on Saturday and Sunday, when two-cents per disk read is charged, but you can see that the different rates are readily distinguishable.

The Time and Charge Rate fields, just below the day and week grid, reflect the time and day pointed to by the cursor. Notice that the mouse arrow is now pointing to some time on Thursday. The fields let us know we are looking at 2:00 P.M.

 TIP Users reading disk blocks from the server shown in this example during the times indicated will be debited one cent for each disk block read. If you have 64KB block sizes defined, this won't be too much. A utility of 220KB will need only three blocks read to load. A 4KB block size, however, means that same utility will require 55 blocks read. This realization may require you to go back and rethink some of your charge rates. It also means it will be difficult to maintain a stable charge rate across multiple servers if they have different block sizes.

FIGURE 10.20

Checking the charge
rate on Thursday at
2:00 P.M.

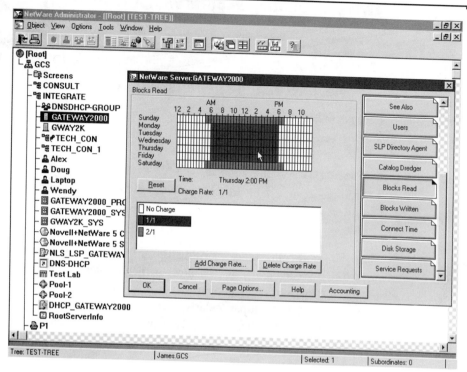

The other options for accounting are set exactly the same way as in this example. Some managers use the Disk Storage option to tag only one block for the week, such as Monday at 6:00 A.M., to get a single charge for the week. This method tracks the use of the resource, but without as much time and trouble involved.

After you've set the charge rates, you cannot delete a charge rate that's currently on screen. You can click the Reset button to cancel the latest charge rate change, but that doesn't work often enough. Your other choice is to cover the offending charge rate with a No Charge rate, effectively blanking out the charges. Then you can delete the charge rate. Since no modifications of the charge rates are possible, deletion and re-creation is your only option.

PART

II

Managing the
Network

Viewing Accounting Reports with ATOTAL

IN A HURRY

10.15 View Accounting Reports with ATOTAL

1. Log in to the network as the Admin user or equivalent.
2. Move your current DOS command line to the SYS:SYSTEM directory of a server with accounting enabled.
3. Type **ATOTAL** from the command line.
4. Read the report on the screen, or redirect the information to a file (for example, ATOTAL > OCTOBER.REP).

Once you start collecting accounting information, there are two things you can do. One is to charge each user's credit balance, which we'll get to next. The other option is to view the totals by day and by week.

This information is not particularly secret, but it's placed in the SYS:SYSTEM directory in a file named NET$ACCT.DAT. This file will grow until you delete it. Here's an example of ATOTAL's display of accounting data:

```
H:\SYSTEM>atotal
ACCOUNTING SERVICES TOTAL UTILITY


10/11/2000:
   Connect time:   99      Server requests:    466
   Blocks read:    148     Blocks written:
   Blocks/day:     399



10/12/2000:
   Connect time:   1717    Server requests:    107333
   Blocks read:    12426   Blocks written:     18863
   Blocks/day:     15771



10/13/2000:
   Connect time:   1742    Server requests:    370
   Blocks read:    111     Blocks written:
   Blocks/day:     24450
```

```
Totals for week:
   Connect time:      3558   Server requests:    108169
Press any key to continue ... ('C' for continuous)
```

When used by itself, the ATOTAL information provides a way to track server usage over time. Plotting this information will quickly show server activity. The results will help you to better reallocate resources among servers so that one server won't be overloaded. It is not necessary to set charge rates for users to get the information in this table.

Yeah, this accounting method dates back to NetWare 3 days. I figure that if accounting issues were a priority to users, the DOS ATOTAL utility would be upgraded by now.

Network-Usage Charges: Friend or Foe?

Personally, I don't care for this accounting business and charging rates on resources. Finding ways to justify the budget for new network technology and to keep up with growing demand is a problem for some companies. However, I don't feel that penalizing users for relying on the network to do their job will encourage them to think fondly of the network. What's next, a butt tax for office chairs?

You don't need to charge users to track server usage. I much prefer the server-usage method of justifying network budgets. You can show that the usage trend per server, such as connect time or disk reads and writes, is up. If it isn't up, you can blame the old, slow network that the server is on and claim that people are avoiding the network because the poor performance is hurting their productivity. Improvements are needed either way.

Claims that charging for resources forces users to keep personal information and games off the network don't wash. It doesn't cost the *user* money; it just costs the *department* some of its (funny money) budget. If you force departments to pay for such things as disk space, they're likely to go outside and buy their own hard disks and possibly even servers.

Bottom line: our job as network computing providers is not to police what goes across the wire; the department managers must do that. If the employees are slacking off of their work to play games, their performance will suffer and their boss, not you, should investigate. If you allow personal phone callers to leave voicemail messages at no charge, how can you justify charging for server disk space?

Setting User Account Balances

10.16 Set the User Account Balance and Low Balance Limit

1. Log in to the network as the Admin user or equivalent and open NetWare Administrator.
2. Open the User dialog box by double-clicking the User object name.
3. Click the Account Balance button.
4. Click the Allow Unlimited Credit box, to enable accounting for the user.
5. Set the current Account Balance and the Low Balance Limit.
6. Click OK to save and exit.

If accounting is enabled on a server, the users of that server can be assigned a value for each server operation. The screen shown in Figure 10.21 tells you how simple it is to track the server resources consumed by a user.

FIGURE 10.21

Accounting for User WENDY

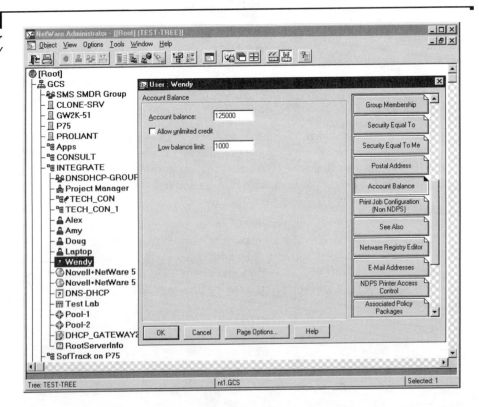

The Account Balance field shows the remaining credits available for this user. The credits are set on the network resource itself, as described in the previous sections. The Low Balance Limit field shows the credit level that will trigger a warning to the user before the account is disabled. If the Allow Unlimited Credit box is checked, the Account Balance field will show a negative number. This reflects the amount of resources used by that user since accounting was enabled or since the previous number was cleared.

If you wish to track the accounting information for charge-back or overhead calculations, but you don't wish to disable users from reaching their network resources, click the Allow Unlimited Credit box. This tracks the information for the accounting reports but never locks out users.

Nothing bad happens to the user's *information* if a user is locked out of the system because of dropping to the level of the Low Balance Limit field. What happens with the *user*, on the other hand, is a matter for concern—obviously for him or her, but also for you. The user will be back in business as soon as an administrator changes the Account Balance field (that means another interruption for you), but that might not happen as quickly as the user will demand. Of course, if the person who runs out of credit occupies a higher position in the company hierarchy than you do, and it happens while you're out of town, you may wish you had never agreed to activate accounting. Before your boss forces accounting on you, make sure all the possible problems, such as locking users out at the worst possible time, are covered and have an answer waiting.

Limiting User Disk Space

IN A HURRY

10.17 Set the User Disk Space Limit

1. Log in to the network as the Admin user or equivalent and open NetWare Administrator.
2. Locate the Volume object in the NDS tree, highlight it, and press Enter to open the Volume Information page.
3. Click the User Space Limits command button (check the Page Options command button to add the necessary button if User Space Limits is not displayed).
4. Use the Browse button to choose the search context.
5. Click Search Entire Tree to check for all volume disk space users, regardless of context.
6. Highlight a user and click Modify to set or change that user's volume space restrictions.
7. Click OK to save and exit.

Here's where you catch the disk hogs and tie them up if you desire. Setting disk space limits has a much more direct effect than charging back to the department, since the user will personally run out of disk space. The effect of reaching your disk limit is the same as emptying your bank account: no more. The disk will be full as far as that particular user is concerned. This limit is set on a per-volume basis, which is even more focused than the server.

NOTE The capabilities of NDS will allow watching the disk space for users scattered about the network, but that will take quite a bit more development. I would be surprised if some third-party software developer isn't busy at this moment, working on software to query NDS and put this information into a report.

There are some interesting touches in the example shown in Figure 10.22. First, notice that the Search Context field is set to GCS, at the top of the network's Organization. This means that when we check the Search Entire Subtree box, we'll get this container and all subcontainers. Since both of our lab Organizational Units are under the GCS container, this search catches everyone in the network allowed to use this volume.

FIGURE 10.22

Checking (and potentially clamping) a disk hog

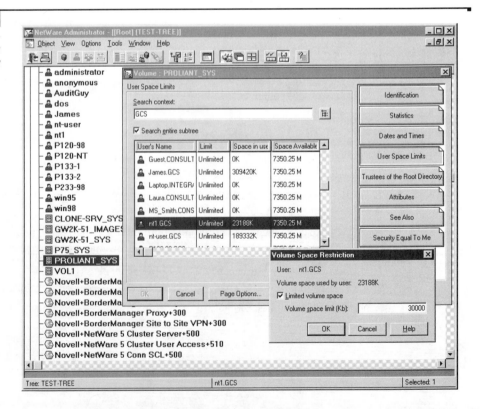

All the disk space numbers are in kilobytes. The default is to allow all users unlimited disk space, and that works fine for most networks. However, when space is getting tight, taking an inventory of disk space per volume may show a user consuming hundreds of megabytes. The Space In Use column shows the amount of disk space owned by the user, even when that user's space is not limited.

The Space Available column shows the same amount, 7350.25 in this example (M here stands for megabytes), available for everyone. That's because any *one* person can use that much space, not because *each* person can use that much space. NetWare makes no space restrictions by default; you must make those changes here. If you don't change the settings, the first users to fill the gigabyte that's available will get that gigabyte to themselves, and everyone else will go without.

The Volume Space Restriction dialog box opened for our friend nt1 is about to make a maximum of 300MB (30,000KB) of disk space available. When nt1 uses the DIR command anywhere on the PROLIANT_SYS volume, it will display the disk space available as 6812KB (30,000KB–23,188KB).

In larger networks, it's much faster to check one container than to check the current container and all containers below that. However, the query doesn't generate enough traffic to noticeably slow the network, and it's much easier to look at all users of a volume at once.

 TIP Currently, NetWare provides no way to print this information. Check your reseller for third-party report software that can do this.

Using UIMPORT to Move Employee Database Records into NDS

UIMPORT (User Import) feeds ASCII data from an existing database into the NDS database. Do you have thousands of students enrolling into your school who need network access? This utility will help you with these tasks:

- Create User objects in the NDS database.
- Update existing User object properties in your NDS database.
- Delete User objects from the NDS database.

There are some considerations, of course, when creating your ASCII file. Every database can create an ASCII file, but the separators used to tell NDS where one record stops and the next record starts can be a problem. If you have punctuation such as commas in your database, you can't use comma-delimited ASCII files. If you do, NDS won't know which comma is for a new record and which is for, for example, the last-name and first-name separator. To avoid this problem, you can use the caret (^) as a separator rather than a comma or question mark. Once the ASCII file is clean and you've inserted your record separators consistently, and you have the records selected, you must tell NDS which of the many properties for the new User objects will be filled in and which will be skipped and left empty. You do this by means of the Import Control File. This file can be created by any text editor under DOS, Windows, or OS/2, as long as it will create an ASCII file. There are two types of information in the Import Control File:

- Control parameters, which define the characters used in the data file and dictate how the data is updated
- Field definitions, which determine which fields in the NDS database will be given the data

Control parameters go first, followed by the field definitions. A small Import Control File might look like this:

```
Import control
  Name context=.freshman.students
  Separator=^
  User template=y
Fields
  Last name
  Name
  Telephone
```

This file tells the NDS database that the field separator is the caret and that we will apply the template for the container.

 NOTE The parameters for the Import Control File are not case sensitive, but the format is important. Just like the NET.CFG file, the headings must be flush left, with the entries indented at least one tab or space. (I suggest that you make it at least two spaces so you don't miss one and cause yourself extra problems.)

Just as when you're creating a new user with NetWare Administrator, two fields are mandatory: the user's login name (Name) and last name (Last Name). If you are updating existing users, only the Name field is mandatory. The fields can be any or all properties of a user. The list includes Account Balance, Account Has Expiration Data, Allow

Unlimited Credit, Grace Logins Allowed, Group Membership, Home Directory, and every other user information field.

Some of these fields are single-valued, meaning only one bit of information (for example, a name) can be entered. Other fields are multi-valued, meaning multiple entries are allowed (for example, Group Membership). Check the manual and the readme files for the latest information on the fields and their allowable entries.

You can't have data without a corresponding field definition in the Import Control File.

 NOTE If you have used the Import Control File with an earlier version of NetWare 4, be aware that many of the field names have changed. Check the manual and the readme files once again for the latest information.

The syntax for the DOS command is:

```
UIMPORT [control_file] [data_file] [/C]
```

This assumes you have both files in the same directory. If they are not, you'll need to use the full path names for the files. The /C says to write the screen output continuously (without it, you'll be hitting "any key" forever). If you prefer to route the output to a file, use this syntax:

```
UIMPORT [control_file] [data_file]
>users\james\uimport.log
```

UIMPORT will take hours to run large files and will slow your server performance because of the amount of NDS churning required. Run this at night and come in early to repair any server malfunctions that occur. (Nothing should go wrong, of course, but gremlins bite everyone now and then.)

During the first pass or two, you might have some problems getting the separators and field information correct. No automatic program transfer like this works the first time or every time. Using commas as separators guarantees you extra aggravation, because the exported database will contain spurious characters all over the place. If you have a large database to import, you should definitely begin by bringing in just a few records at first in order to get the bugs worked out.

Server Management

NetWare 4 moved from the server-bound approach used in NetWare 3 to a network-wide, global approach. NetWare 5.1 extends that even more. But the engines for all

PART

II

Managing the
Network

this worldliness are still the servers, busily supporting the replicated NDS database, managing the disk drives that make up the volumes, and connecting to the clients across the network cabling.

A Hollywood director would move the viewpoint from the server to the enterprise network, like pulling the camera up and away from a single car to show the entire highway. Soon, however, the focus would come back down to the hero, forcing his car ever faster. In our movie, that hero is you, forcing the server ever faster. If the car dies, the traffic backs up, and something bad happens to our hero. Similarly, if the server dies, then the network backs up, and your phone rings with calls from angry users.

Just as the movie hero must check the car gauges, so must you check the gauges of your network. Your primary gauge on the server console is the MONITOR.NLM program. Your turbo-booster is the SERVMAN.NLM program, which was included within the MONITOR program starting with NetWare 4.11. Your toolkit includes DSMERGE.NLM, DSREPAIR.NLM, the DSTRACE function, INSTALL.NLM, and a few other assorted commands. NetWare 5.0 shipped with a group of immature but promising control programs, all written in Java, that will change NetWare if the lack of speed doesn't kill our hero. Luckily, with NetWare 5.1, the Web browser rocketed onto the scene and may become the management interface of choice.

RCONSOLE and RConsoleJ for Remote Console Control

Unless you enjoy hunkering down in a small computer room squatting over and around several servers, learn to use the remote console (RCONSOLE) utility. This client/server application runs both on the server (REMOTE.NLM and RSPX.NLM) and on your local workstation (RCONSOLE.EXE) in a DOS box.

RConsoleJ, the Java version, does the same remote connection trick using a Java client application and TCP/IP for a network transport layer. If you don't run IPX, you must use RConsoleJ for connection. Once connected, the utilities are identical, so we'll talk about RCONSOLE first to make experienced NetWare managers comfortable.

The server part must be started before the client can make a connection. If you have the RCONSOLE.EXE and supporting files on your local workstation, you are not required to be logged in to NDS to run RCONSOLE.

RCONSOLE allows you to:

- Execute all console commands remotely
- List directories in the NetWare and DOS partitions of the server
- Edit text files in either the NetWare or DOS partitions of the server
- Transfer files from your workstation to the server, but not vice versa

- Down and/or reboot the server
- Install or upgrade NetWare

There's nothing you can do at the server console that you can't do with RCON-SOLE. Using remote access in this manner allows you to leave the keyboard and monitor off the server, increasing the server's security. Taking care of catastrophic failures will require an attached keyboard and monitor, but most of the time, you'll be fine without them, assuming your server PC boots without a keyboard attached.

Configuring REMOTE at the Server

There are two steps in configuring the server for remote access. You must start the REMOTE program, with or without a password. A password is preferred, and you have an option of using an encrypted password. You must then start either the RSPX.NLM program for access across the network, or AIOCOMX.NLM (or other communication port driver, depending on your server hardware), AIO.NLM, and RS232.NLM. The earlier ACONSOLE.NLM (Async Console) available in NetWare 3 has given way to the beefed-up RCONSOLE.

To start REMOTE, at the server console colon prompt, type **REMOTE** *<password>* and press Enter. Then type **RSPX** and press Enter.

Until you encrypt the password, the password you give at the console is the one you must type when making a remote connection. NetWare 5.1 no longer allows the Supervisor password to unlock the REMOTE program, so if you want a password, you must specify that password. These commands should be placed at the end of the AUTOEXEC.NCF program so that remote access is configured every time the server starts.

For an encrypted password, you must run the REMOTE program and provide your password, letting the system generate the encrypted password. For connection, you must then provide the encrypted password result. (The password *good* came out as 0A137773E4AEAFFA3B on my system.) Every time you load REMOTE on that server, you must use the encrypted password. A better idea is to let the system save the command to load the REMOTE program and the encrypted password automatically by placing it in a specially created SYS:\SYSTEM\LDREMOTE.NCF file. Then, rather than typing **REMOTE -E 0A137773E4AEAFFA3B**, you can type **LDREMOTE**.

Since LDREMOTE is a batch file-type program, you don't need the LOAD command. You must then add the appropriate command to enable LAN or async connections. You can add those commands to the LDREMOTE.NCF program, but if you generate another encrypted password, the new file will overwrite your modified file.

To disable remote connections, you can use the following command:

```
REMOTE LOCK OUT
```

PART

II

Managing the
Network

This is best done at the physical console, although it does work from a remote connection. Once that remote connection is broken, however, the console remains locked and you can't get back in. To enable remote connections, use this command:

```
REMOTE UNLOCK
```

RCONSOLE from the Client Side

Once the remote connection software is loaded at the server, the client part is fairly simple. From a DOS prompt, type **RCONSOLE** and press Enter. A screen will appear, asking for your choice of connection type: asynchronous or LAN. On LANs, the answer is (surprise) LAN. A screen similar to Figure 10.23 will appear, listing all the servers answering the broadcast request from the RCONSOLE program. The screen in this figure replaced another screenshot from mid-1997, which looked exactly the same. RCONSOLE doesn't change much.

FIGURE 10.23

The server list for RCONSOLE connections

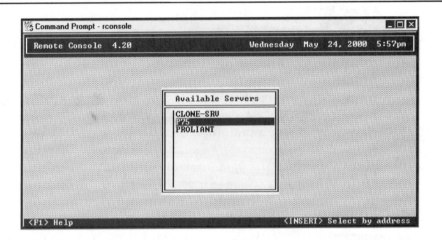

Notice that there is no mention of containers or contexts with the server names. RCONSOLE bypasses NDS and speaks directly to the server. You can connect directly to a specific server, skipping the pick list in Figure 10.23 by giving its name with the command, as in

```
RCONSOLE PROLIANT
```

Whether you pick from the list or go directly to the server, the next step is to provide the password configured for that server. Type in the password given when you loaded REMOTE on the server, and you will immediately become a remote console.

Here are some keystrokes that you need for your remote console work:

Alt+F1 Opens the Available Options menu overlay.

Alt+F2 Exits RCONSOLE.

Alt+F3 Moves to the next server console screen.

Alt+F4 Moves to the previous server console screen.

Alt+F5 Shows the network address of the RCONSOLE workstation.

The Ctrl+Escape combination on the server that opens the Current Screens menu does not work with RCONSOLE. Neither does the Alt+Escape combination to roll through the screens. However, the up and down arrows to scroll through previously entered commands do work remotely.

RCONSOLE Available Options Menu

Everything you need in RCONSOLE can be done from the Available Options menu called by the Alt+F1 combination. (If you're like me and have trouble remembering which keystrokes work with which program, write Alt+F1 somewhere on your cubicle wall.)

Figure 10.24 shows the Available Options menu, overlaying the Help screen for the REMOTE console command. Move the highlight bar with the cursor keys and press Enter to activate any menu item.

PART

II

Managing the
Network

FIGURE 10.24

*The RCONSOLE
Available
Options menu*

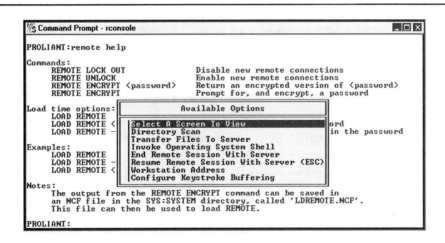

The menu items are fairly straightforward. Let's take a quick look at each option:

Select A Screen To View   Opens a submenu of all active console screens. Move the highlight bar to a screen and press Enter to move immediately to that screen.

Directory Scan   Lists the files and subdirectories in any directory on the server, both the NetWare and DOS partitions. To reference the DOS partition, use C:\<*directory_name*>.

Transfer Files To Server   Copies files from any local or mapped workstation drive to any directory on any server partition. Long files show the progress of the amazingly slow transfer process.

Invoke Operating System Shell   Exits to the DOS shell, but RCONSOLE takes so much memory that this has limited value.

End Remote Session With Server   Disconnects with server (same function as Alt+F2).

Resume Remote Session With Server   Clears the menu off the screen and returns you to the remote connection (same function as Escape).

Workstation Address   Shows the network and local address of your workstation (same function as Alt+F5).

Configure Keystroke Buffering   Normally, each keystroke is sent immediately to the server. Because of async connections, you may wish to control the delivery of your text. The options are:

> **No Keystroke Buffering**   Send each keystroke immediately.
>
> **Keystroke Delay**   Send when keyboard is idle.
>
> **Manual Keystroke Send**   Press Alt+F8 to send.
>
> **On-Demand Buffering**   Press Alt+F9 to enter a buffered command.

Most of the time, you'll use RCONSOLE across the network to connect to a server in your building. You'll connect to the server, check the status of one or more NLMs (NetWare Loadable Modules), check the MONITOR program, and disconnect. If your servers are 10 floors up and the elevator is broken, this utility will save you a workout.

When DOS is removed from the server memory, the EXIT command forces a reboot. If your server is configured to boot DOS and go straight into NetWare, this system works great. And there are no stairs to climb.

RConsoleJ Makes Its Appearance

The new remote console connection program is RCONSOLEJ.EXE, also available as RCONJ.EXE, and typed RConsoleJ by Novell in the documentation. There is a batch file, RCONJ.BAT, full of Java runtime commands that make little or no sense to non-programmers, but it all seems to work.

Instead of the old C-Worthy interface screen shown in Figure 10.23, we get a nice Java screen as shown in Figure 10.25. If you can't tell at this size, the little icon in the upper-left corner is the official Java coffee-cup logo.

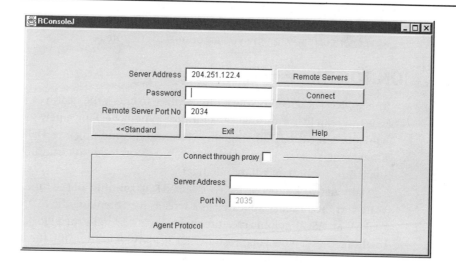

If you click the Remote Servers command button, a pick list will appear that contains similar information to that shown in Figure 10.23, except that it will include only servers running TCP/IP that have the proper support NLM running.

RCONAG6.NLM is that proper NLM to run and configure. You may encrypt the remote password with RConsoleJ just as you do with RCONSOLE, following the same process, except that you must type **RCONAG6 –E** and the password.

Of course, the big difference is that this Java remote console uses TCP/IP for communications, rather than SPX. RConsoleJ sessions won't even recognize servers running the SPX version of RCONSOLE.

Nothing stops you from loading the earlier REMOTE and SPX versions on a Net-Ware 5.1 server, but Novell needed this for those customers wanting to run all client-to-server communications over TCP/IP. This makes life easier for multi-protocol shops, since RConsoleJ will run from any Java-enabled system, including Unix hosts.

Once connected, the new remote console looks amazingly like the old. Rather than the Alt+F1 and Alt+F2 control keys to pop open a menu or exit the program, a status bar over the RCONSOLE text screen appears. A pick list of active server screens, arrow keys (to cycle up and back through those screens; Alt+F3 still works, too), and a Sync checkbox (to keep the remote and server screens in sync if you wish) are all there. The last three command buttons on the status screen are Activate, Disconnect, and Help. Activate helps kick-start applications running on the server that don't respond properly; Disconnect and Help are easy to figure out.

There are ways to use RConsoleJ with SPX, but they're not worth covering. The Java version is slower than the DOS version, so keep using the DOS version for IPX-based servers. You can have both the DOS and Java support programs running on one server concurrently, giving you an option for remote access.

MONITOR Almost Everything

The MONITOR screen is your primary place to check the health of your server. You may only rarely use another server utility. When checking a new server on a new network, use the MONITOR program before you do anything else. Half the time, it will provide the answers to your questions (and when it doesn't, running it gives you some time to think of what to do next).

Many network supervisors leave MONITOR running all the time. With earlier NetWare versions, a snake appeared as a screensaver, blanking the MONITOR display. The snake is an ASCII-graphic creature made of various red-tinted blocks following a bright red head. Now you must use the SCRSAVER utility. Still, the longer and faster the snake goes, the busier the network.

It's a good idea to check the MONITOR information now and then. Some network managers take screenshots of server-information screens, such as those that show redirected blocks, cache utilization, and processor utilization, to have a benchmark for later reference. You're a busy person; don't believe you can remember your cache utilization statistics from four months ago. Make notes or make screenshots, but keep some record of the health of your network as shown by MONITOR.

The General Information Screen and What It Means

IN A HURRY

10.18 View Server Information with MONITOR

1. Type **MONITOR** from the console prompt.
2. Press Tab once or twice to get to the Available Options menu.
3. From the Available Options menu, choose the menu option for the utilization data you want to view: Cache, Memory, Processor, or Resource Utilization.

The opening screen of MONITOR holds the most useful information. See Figure 10.26 for a look at the screen from PROLIANT.

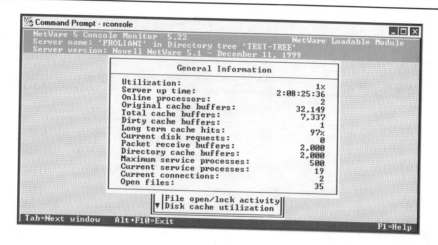

```
Command Prompt - rconsole                                    _ □ ✕
NetWare 5 Console Monitor  5.22            NetWare Loadable Module
Server name: 'PROLIANT' in Directory tree 'TEST-TREE'
Server version: Novell NetWare 5.1 — December 11, 1999

                        General Information
        Utilization:                              1%
        Server up time:                     2:08:25:36
        Online processors:                         2
        Original cache buffers:               32,149
        Total cache buffers:                   7,337
        Dirty cache buffers:                       1
        Long term cache hits:                    97%
        Current disk requests:                     0
        Packet receive buffers:                2,000
        Directory cache buffers:               2,000
        Maximum service processes:               500
        Current service processes:                19
        Current connections:                       2
        Open files:                               35
                    ┌──────────────────────┐
                    │File open/lock activity│
                  ▼ │Disk cache utilization │
                    └──────────────────────┘
  Tab=Next window    Alt+F10=Exit                          F1=Help
```

The PROLIANT server in this example has 128MB of RAM and a 9100MB (9.1GB) hard disk. This equates to 32,149 buffers of 4KB each, of which just over 15,000 are usually available. The number fluctuates as NLMs take and return server RAM for various operations. Running the ConsoleOne program takes quite a few of these, but luckily NetWare allows you to unload the server GUI, unlike Windows NT, which sucks CPU cycles with the GUI whether you want the GUI or not. The NetWare Enterprise Web Server, and brethren like the FTP Server and News Server, sucks up quite a few resources as well.

The ALTOS486 server used during the first iteration of this book had a 500MB disk with 32MB of RAM. The original cache buffer number there was 7620, with about 5450 available. NetWare 4.10 was slightly more conservative than NetWare 4.11, but not that much.

Server CLONE386, the underpowered server with only 8MB of RAM and a 312MB disk that lived out its usefulness just after finishing the 4.10 version of this book, had 1487 original cache buffers, of which only 740 or so were available. (Warning: that server was a test to show it can be done, not an attempt to sell an 8MB server to unsuspecting users.)

Across the top of the MONITOR screen, the version of the NetWare server (5) and of the MONITOR program (5.22) are listed, along with the fact that this is an NLM, in the upper right. The server name and tree are also listed at the top. The last line in the top information section gives the server operating system version again (actually correctly on this line), along with the date of manufacture. This information will be important as you upgrade pieces of your server operating system over time and Novell support asks what versions you have.

You expand the General Information window by pressing the Tab key, or just waiting 10 seconds. The window will expand itself, covering some of the Available Options menu. Press Tab again (or Escape) to return it to a smaller size. The fields on the MONITOR General Information screen are described in Table 10.1.

TABLE 10.1: FIELDS ON MONITOR'S GENERAL INFORMATION SCREEN

Field	Description
Utilization	Percentage of time the CPU is busy. This normally hovers under 5 percent, unless you have NLMs that do active processing, such as Web servers and databases.
Server Up Time	Days, hours, minutes, and seconds since the server was started.
Online Processors	The number of CPUs in this server that are in use.
Original Cache Buffers	The number of 4KB buffer blocks contained in your server memory, minus room for the operating system and DOS. This number is rarely high enough.
Total Cache Buffers	The number of buffers available for file caching after loading all the NLM programs and other server housekeeping programs. This number is never high enough.
Dirty Cache Buffers	Buffers waiting to be written to a server disk.
Current Disk Requests	Number of disk requests waiting for service.
Packet Receive Buffers	1KB buffers that hold client requests while the server processes them. The default is 10, but the server allocates more as needed. Web service bumps this up to 2000.
Directory Cache Buffers	Buffers dedicated to holding the server directory entries, speeding access to files since the directory need not be read from the disk when a request comes. The server allocates more as needed, and Web service again bumps this up to 2000.
Maximum Service Processes	Largest number of task handlers, or processes, available for servicing client requests. Once the server allocates this maximum number, the number cannot be reclaimed. This number can be lowered in SERVMAN or by using a SET command, freeing memory for cache buffers. When there is no more memory to allocate more processes, performance suffers. Web service bumps this up to 500.
Current Service Processes	Current processes available for servicing client requests.
Open Files	Number of files accessed by the server and other clients.

Some of these numbers have a direct impact on server performance. The more memory, the better the performance. How much is enough? Superserver manufacturers are advertising the ability to support 4GB of server RAM. My guess is that 1GB is enough—for a while. The ProLiant Cluster I tested shipped with 1GB of RAM for each of the four 4-processor servers in the box.

If you're used to earlier versions of NetWare Administrator, you may be looking for the detailed information for Maximum Licensed Connections now. It has moved to the Licensing server item inside NetWare Administrator. Current Licensed Connections has made the same move, as you might expect, leaving those experienced with earlier NetWare versions feeling just a bit lost until they remember the new Licensing menu option in NetWare Administrator.

If your total cache buffers number is suffering because of many NLMs, you need more memory. The amount of total cache buffers available is probably the quickest indicator of server health and performance. Plus, you always need more memory, no matter what.

Cache Utilization (now Disk Cache)

Cache use by NetWare is one of the biggest performance advantages of the operating system over its competitors. The cache is a temporary storage area for files read from the disk. Once a file is read from the disk, it stays in the server memory for a time, guessing that you may need that same information again. If you do, then the next request comes from server RAM rather than being read from the disk, saving tremendous amounts of time. It's common to sort a large database from your workstation and have all of the database file stay in the cache, finishing 20 times faster than reading the file from the disk.

The RCONSOLE Available Options menu option to get to the important cache information is labeled, clearly enough, Disk Cache Utilization. Highlight it and press Enter, and you will see a screen much like the one shown in Figure 10.27.

PART

II

Managing the
Network

FIGURE 10.27

Checking the cache

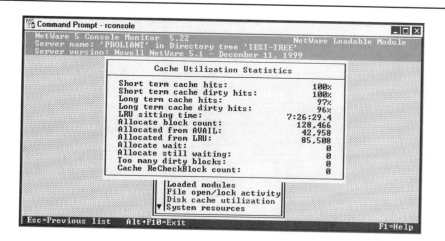

Before NetWare 5.1, cache always meant RAM. Now, with NetWare 5.1's virtual memory support, cache means a combination of RAM and disk space. RAM is used first, so more RAM still helps, because writing memory out to disk means slower performance.

The most important indicator for more RAM is the Long Term Cache Hits listing. If this number was below 98 percent in NetWare 4.11, Novell engineers suggested that you should add more RAM. (Of course, Novell engineers suggest that you add more RAM for almost every problem, but statistically they will be right once in a while). Now, they suggest that you add more RAM if the number falls below 90 percent.

The Long Term Cache Hits number is averaged for every cache request since the server has started. It is the most accurate reflection of cache utilization, much better than the Short Term Cache Hits and even the Total Cache Buffers number from the previous screen. After all, if all the file requests are being handled from cache, whatever amount you have must be enough.

The fields on the Cache Utilization Statistics screen are described in Table 10.2.

TABLE 10.2: FIELDS ON MONITOR'S CACHE UTILIZATION STATISTICS SCREEN

Field	Description
Short Term Cache Hits	Percentage of disk-block requests serviced by the cache in the last second.
Short Term Cache Dirty Hits	Percentage of disk blocks requested in the last second that were in cache, but changed since being read from the disk.
Long Term Cache Hits	Your trigger to get more memory. Below 90 percent is a failing grade.
Long Term Cache Dirty Hits	Percentage of disk blocks requested since the server started that were in cache but waiting to be written to the disk.
LRU Sitting Time	LRU = Least Recently Used. This field indicates the age of the block that is the oldest in the LRU list. Higher times are better, indicating that there is plenty of memory to service the clients. Time is in days, hours, minutes, and seconds, including tenths.
Allocate Block Count	Total block requests since the server was started.
Allocated From AVAIL	Number of cache-block requests filled by available (i.e., not being used) blocks.
Allocated From LRU	Number of cache-block requests filled by blocks from the LRU list of used cache blocks.

Continued ▌▶

TABLE 10.2 (CONTINUED) : FIELDS ON MONITOR'S CACHE UTILIZATION STATISTICS SCREEN	
Field	**Description**
Allocate Wait	Number of instances where a cache request waited while a block from the LRU list was made available. If this number increases regularly, you need more RAM.
Allocate Still Waiting	Number of times the operating system was forced to wait for an LRU block in the last 10 minutes. If the number is greater than 7, your blocks are being reused too quickly. Add more RAM.
Too Many Dirty Blocks	Number of block-write requests delayed by an overloaded write queue. This can be caused by a busy disk channel. Add more RAM.
Cache ReCheckBlock Count	Number of times a cache request had to try again because the target block was still being used. If this number is steadily increasing, add more RAM.

Add More RAM

As you look over the descriptions in Table 10.2, you should recognize a recurring theme in the recommendations. I hate to sound like a broken record (or a CD with a tracking error, for you kids), but more RAM cures many server ills. The move toward huge disks eats RAM, since directory file cache settings are based on disk size; though, granted, using the NSS file system leaves lots more RAM for other server uses. More applications running on the server take more RAM, since the program must have a segment of RAM in which to run.

The move that replaced two or three NetWare 3 servers with one NetWare 4 server meant that one server must have the RAM of the earlier three, plus some to support NDS. There is a trend, mostly because NetWare 5.1's NDS now has a cache and responds much more quickly, to consolidate three NetWare 4 servers onto two NetWare 5.1 servers in some companies. This is why I advise you to put RAM on every budget request for everything else.

RAM needs go up over time, but not because the software changes. Every server adds disk space and NLMs now and then. Each time you add something, you check the RAM and it doesn't look too bad. Then you add another NLM and another few users, and it doesn't look much worse than it did last time. Unfortunately, your available RAM for file cache is now about half what you had when you started the server the first time. Your server gets gradually slower and flakier until you fix things. And how do you fix things? Add more RAM.

Processor Utilization

Some people worry constantly about the server CPU. Part of this worry comes from competitors, such as Banyan's VINES and Microsoft's NT Advanced Server, who claim that their multiprocessor versions give them an advantage over NetWare's single processor. Unfortunately for Banyan and Microsoft, this isn't necessarily true, especially when you consider the price and performance of these multiprocessor servers versus a single CPU server running NetWare. In fact, Novell's internal tests show that NetWare 5.1 runs faster with one processor than Windows NT Server 4 does with two processors.

But to keep up in the RFP (Request For Proposal) checkbox feature war, Novell released SMP (Symmetric MultiProcessing) NetWare as part of NetWare 4.11. Previously available with NetWare 4.10, but only from the hardware vendors directly, SMP support now appears in every NetWare 4.11 package. NetWare 5.1 ships with support for up to four symmetrical processors right out of the box, for no extra charge. Part of the move to virtual memory was to support easier engineering for multiple processor support.

Most network bottlenecks happen at the disk channel. The server CPU is rarely loaded, unless you are running NLMs on the server that execute as databases and gateways. Even then, people misunderstand the utilization number. When it reaches 100 percent, it doesn't mean that things are going to blow up; it just means that the CPU is working on all barrels. It isn't uncommon to see utilization spike above 100 percent, because your server processor is probably faster than the benchmark processor used to set the percentages.

Virtual Memory Information

Available memory is another performance indicator. NLMs use memory as they load and release it when they unload. However, like Microsoft Windows 3.1x (and Windows 95/98, for that matter), occasionally some of the memory never gets released. Unlike Windows, NetWare 4 provided an easy way to reclaim that lost memory. NetWare 5.1 does away with that need, with the combination of physical and virtual memory allocation and regular collection of "orphaned" memory segments.

When discussing memory, this new technology makes a decision necessary—are you speaking of physical memory (RAM) or virtual memory (RAM plus disk space)? For some extra confusion, Novell adds a memory display for both Address Spaces and Swap Files, since both are so important now.

Figure 10.28 shows some of the information you may want to check now and then just for personal reassurance. Some of the details within MONITOR have become so obscure that they don't help, but memory use is always worth watching.

FIGURE 10.28

Tracking system virtual memory use

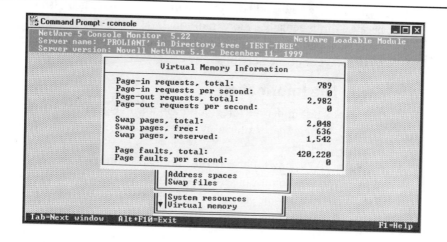

Table 10.3 describes the fields on the Virtual Memory Information screen.

TABLE 10.3: FIELDS ON MONITOR'S VIRTUAL MEMORY INFORMATION SCREEN

Field	Description
Page-in Requests, Total	Number of memory moves in from swap files since the server was started.
Page-in Requests Per Second	Number of requests to move one of the 4KB virtual memory pages from the swap files in the last second.
Page-out Requests, Total	Number of memory requests out to swap files since the server was started.
Page-out Requests Per Second	Number of requests to move 4KB virtual memory pages for file swap space.
Swap Pages, Total	Number of 4KB blocks currently used.
Swap Pages, Free	Number of 4KB blocks available for use.
Swap Pages, Reserved	Number of 4KB pages set aside for use by the memory system.
Page Faults, Total	Number of virtual memory retrievals from a swap file since the server came up. ("Fault" doesn't mean error in this situation.)
Page Faults Per Second	Number of times in the last second information was retrieved from the swap files (meaning the information wasn't in RAM).

PART

II

Managing the Network

It's a whole new world of NetWare memory management, isn't it? Don't worry, because this is actually a more traditional way to handle memory. Unix servers, especially high-performance systems running huge databases and Internet Web servers, have always done memory this way.

Swap File Information

If you look just under the foreground window in Figure 10.28, you'll see two menu choices, Address Spaces and Swap Files. Swap Files offers some information that is worth a quick look.

Figure 10.29 shows the Swap file information for the file created during installation on the SYS: volume of server PROLIANT. You may delete the Swap volume on SYS: and create it somewhere else using the SWAP command from the colon prompt, but I didn't do that here.

FIGURE 10.29

Swap file details

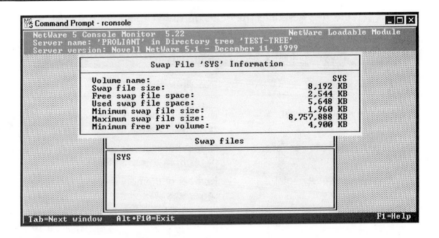

Most of what you see in Figure 10.29 is easy to understand. The penultimate listing, Maximum Swap File Size, is the total space of the volume holding the swap file, in this case SYS:. The last entry, Minimum Free Per Volume, shows the threshold below which NetWare can't go to protect free space on the volume. In other words, this space is kept away from the Swap file, no matter how hungry the file becomes.

System Resource Utilization

When you choose System Resources from MONITOR's Available Options menu, the Server Memory Resource Utilization screen appears. Although this screen looks like more server memory information (the main window titled Server Memory Statistics is a good clue), the memory tracked here is used by NLMs only. The operating system forces NLM programs to use a resource tag when they allocate resources, somewhat like tracking books taken from the library. This way, the system can track which module has which memory page.

In Figure 10.30, the top window shows the summary of all server memory with the information displayed two ways. First is the number of bytes allocated to the pool, and second is the percentage of total server memory allocated to the pool.

FIGURE 10.30

Server memory resource utilization

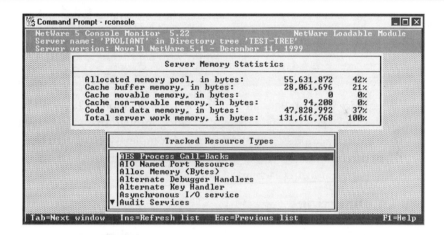

```
Command Prompt - rconsole                                          _ □ X
NetWare 5 Console Monitor  5.22                 NetWare Loadable Module
Server name: 'PROLIANT' in Directory tree 'TEST-TREE'
Server version: Novell NetWare 5.1 - December 11, 1999

                      Server Memory Statistics
      Allocated memory pool, in bytes:        55,631,872    42%
      Cache buffer memory, in bytes:          28,061,696    21%
      Cache movable memory, in bytes:                  0     0%
      Cache non-movable memory, in bytes:         94,208     0%
      Code and data memory, in bytes:         47,828,992    37%
      Total server work memory, in bytes:    131,616,768   100%

                       Tracked Resource Types
      AES Process Call-Backs
      AIO Named Port Resource
      Alloc Memory (Bytes)
      Alternate Debugger Handlers
      Alternate Key Handler
      Asynchronous I/O service
    ▼ Audit Services

Tab=Next window    Ins=Refresh list    Esc=Previous list         F1=Help
```

Table 10.4 describes the fields in the Server Memory Statistics window of the System Resources screen.

TABLE 10.4: FIELDS ON MONITOR'S SYSTEM RESOURCES SCREEN

Field	Description
Allocated Memory Pool	Memory reserved for NLM programs. The cache buffer pool allocates memory to NLMs (and hence to this allocated memory pool) dynamically. When the NLM is unloaded, the memory is returned to the cache buffer pool. The Memory Utilization option (see Table 10.3) offers a look at the NLM programs and the memory they have allocated.
Cache Buffer Memory	The pool of memory currently being used for file caching. This used to be the largest pool, and if it fell below 50 percent, more RAM was needed ASAP. With the new virtual memory scheme, this goes up and down without a call to buy RAM.

Continued ▶

PART

II

Managing the Network

TABLE 10.4 (CONTINUED): FIELDS ON MONITOR'S SYSTEM RESOURCES SCREEN

Field	Description
Cache Movable Memory	Memory directly allocated from the cache buffer pool. It returns to that pool when released. The memory manager of the operating system may move the location of these memory blocks to optimize memory usage, unlike the non-movable pool.
Cache Non-Movable Memory	Used when large blocks of memory are needed. Allocated directly from the cache buffer pool and returned there when released.
Code And Data Memory	Memory used by the operating system and other NLM programs to store their executable code and data.
Total Server Work Memory	Sum of the memory pools in RAM, not counting the Swap files.

Once you highlight an item in the Tracked Resource Types list, press Enter to see specific details for that resource. Scrolling through these lists is fascinating only if you want to be impressed by the depth and complexity of modern NetWare. Little if any of this information will ever be of direct use to network managers, so don't worry about memorizing each list of options.

Connections

IN A HURRY

10.19 Check Connections with MONITOR

1. Type **MONITOR** from the console prompt.
2. Choose Connection Information from the Available Options menu.
3. From the Active Connections screen, choose the connection to view.

The choices in MONITOR we've covered so far have to do with serious server management. The last few may be the ones you use more often. What do you think will happen more often: tracking the memory usage of one NLM or clearing a connection because a user locked up Windows again?

When a user does lock up a program, or leaves for the day with his or her system still connected, the Connections screen is the place to take care of the problem. There are ways to see which files are still open, to check how long the user has been connected, and to disconnect that user, all from your desk.

When you open MONITOR, the default choice of the Available Options menu is Connections, which is first in the list (this was labeled Connection Information in earlier versions). The list is not alphabetical, so Novell engineers obviously felt this was the option you would use the most often.

After opening the Connections screen, you will see a list of the active connections. The number to the left of each entry is the connection number, assigned when each user or resource logs in. The names are kept in alphabetical order. Connections with the asterisk in front of the name are NDS connections, not counted against the server license count. They access the NDS database of information on this server, but they don't use the file and print resources specific to the server. The Not-Logged-In connection is a user workstation that has not logged in to this server or has not used a specific resource of this server. Take a look at Figure 10.31 and notice the starred connections versus the normal connection.

FIGURE 10.31

*Active connections on
PROLIANT*

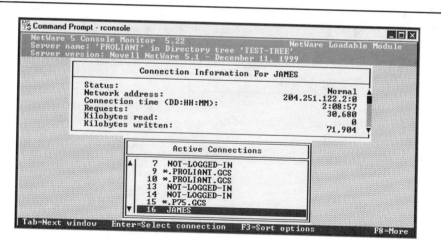

To view details of one of the active connections, highlight the connection and press Enter. To delete a connection, highlight it and press Delete. You can choose multiple connections with the F5 key before pressing the Delete key. Press F6 to clear all the unused connections.

Figure 10.32 shows the information for my workstation. The top window shows connection information, while the bottom window shows open files. (When you first press Enter, the two windows don't overlap. If they do overlap, you can press the Tab key to open the information screen.)

FIGURE 10.32

Checking on my connection

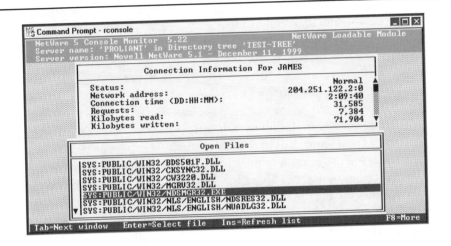

 NOTE In the Connection Information window, you'll see the term "Semaphores." A *semaphore* is an interprocess communication signal used to control access to resources such as multiuser data files. NetWare supervisors never need to worry about semaphores; developers set and control them within programs. NLMs use lots of semaphores.

Table 10.5 describes the fields on the Connection Information screen.

TABLE 10.5: FIELDS ON MONITOR'S CONNECTIONS SCREEN

Field	Description
Status	Possibilities are: Not Logged In (client is not authenticated and so does not count against the licensed user count), Authenticated (client authorized by NDS but cannot access other resources on the server), Normal (authenticated by NDS and currently using a server resource, so this connection counts against the server license count), Waiting On A Lock (normal connection waiting for a locked resource, generally a file, to become available), Waiting On A Semaphore (normal connection waiting for access to a semaphore-controlled resource).

Continued ▌▶

TABLE 10.5 (CONTINUED) : FIELDS ON MONITOR'S CONNECTIONS SCREEN

Field	Description
Network Address	Logical address of the client. Format is *network:node:socket* on the server. The socket number is used to separate server processes or programs in use by each client. The socket number may be the same or different depending on the client. Clients using TCP/IP will have an IP address in this space.
Connection Time	Days, hours, and minutes the user has been connected to this server. If the user isn't logged in to this server, the number will be zero.
Requests	Service requests sent to the server from the client during this connection.
Kilobytes Read	Number of kilobytes read from all the server disks on all volumes during this connection.
Kilobytes Written	Number of kilobytes written to any of the server disks on any volume during this connection.
Semaphores	Number of semaphores in use by the client.
Logical Record Locks	Locks used by the client to restrict access by other users to a file in use by the client.
Supervisor (or Equivalent)	Yes or No, depending on the client's configuration.

The bottom window in Figure 10.32 shows the files currently open for the client. The first file opened winds up at the bottom of the list, since all subsequent files appear from the top of the list. If you choose one of the open files and press Enter, another window opens and shows the physical file lock status. More details on file locking will be explained in the "Seeing File Open/Lock Activity" section, coming up in just a bit.

Wonder what some of those files are? The \PUBLIC\WIN32 directory holds files to support the management programs, such as the NDSMGR32.EXE file highlighted on the list.

Storage Devices

IN A HURRY

10.20 View Disk Information in MONITOR

1. Type **MONITOR** from the console prompt.
2. Choose Storage devices from the Available Options menu.

Continued

IN A HURRY CONTINUED

3. From the Registered Storage Objects screen, choose the adapter module, partition, or CD-ROM drive to view.

4. Press Tab to expand the Drive Information window.

5. View the information in the Drive Status window. If you can highlight an item, you can press Enter to display further details about it.

When you choose Storage Devices from the Available Options menu, you enter the disk drive information section of MONITOR. There's not a lot you can change in this section, but it's a great way to check the status of the server drives. One critical item to review is the number of disk blocks used by the Hot Fix feature because of a failing disk. If this number increases slowly, your disk may be failing. If this number increases drastically, perform a backup immediately and buy another disk today.

When you go into this section, you will see Registered Storage Objects in the bottom window. This is much different from NetWare 4.11 and earlier. Just another example of finer-grained control and feedback available in NetWare 5.1.

Most of this information for the drive was set during installation and has not changed, and you can't change it here. But to check for Hot Fix usage, you must drill down past the screen shown in Figure 10.33.

FIGURE 10.33

Hard disk details

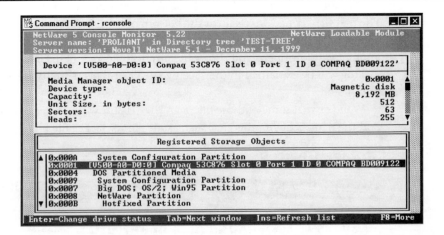

> **NOTE** If you have installed disk mirroring, check here regularly. You may not know if the disks are mirroring properly unless you look into this section of MONITOR. I've seen systems where one disk died, but no one knew it until we checked the console MONITOR screen!

This new screen shows more information about your hard disk than any previous version of NetWare. But in this section we're most interested in the status of your Hot Fix drive sections, to make sure things are all right.

NetWare 5.1 is kind enough to put this information right into the menu window, rather than forcing you to look around. Do you see Hotfixed Partition at the bottom of the window in Figure 10.33? That's what we want, and when I highlight that line and press the Tab key, the screen in Figure 10.34 appears.

FIGURE 10.34

Hot Fix check, all is well.

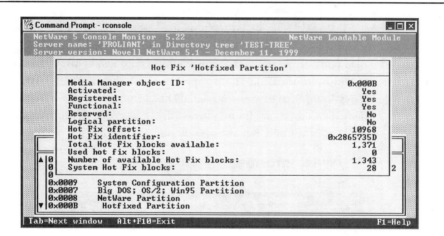

The key number is Used Hot Fix Blocks, three up from the bottom of the top window. So far, so good: no Hot Fix blocks are in use on my server. If that number increases, however, trouble is on the way.

Volumes

What little disk information that used to be in one area in NetWare 4.11 and earlier versions is now spread over two sections. The next area to check is Volumes, to check all the volume settings in one quick, easy location.

Figure 10.35 shows the Volume information for server PROLIANT volume SYS:. I reached this screen by pressing Enter on the Volumes option from the main menu,

PART
II

Managing the
Network

then expanding this information in the Mounted Volumes listing. I then highlighted my choice and pressed the Tab key.

FIGURE 10.35

Volume details galore

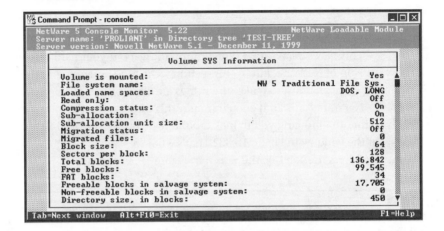

```
Command Prompt - rconsole                                              _ □ ×
NetWare 5 Console Monitor  5.22                    NetWare Loadable Module
Server name: 'PROLIANT' in Directory tree 'TEST-TREE'
Server version: Novell NetWare 5.1 - December 11, 1999

                         Volume SYS Information

     Volume is mounted:                                            Yes  ▲
     File system name:                      NW 5 Traditional File Sys. ▐
     Loaded name spaces:                                   DOS, LONG
     Read only:                                                   Off
     Compression status:                                           On
     Sub-allocation:                                               On
     Sub-allocation unit size:                                    512
     Migration status:                                            Off
     Migrated files:                                                0
     Block size:                                                   64
     Sectors per block:                                           128
     Total blocks:                                            136,842
     Free blocks:                                              99,545
     FAT blocks:                                                   34
     Freeable blocks in salvage system:                       17,705
     Non-freeable blocks in salvage system:                        0
     Directory size, in blocks:                                   450 ▼

 Tab=Next window    Alt+F10=Exit                                  F1=Help
```

Do you need to know that this volume is not Read-Only? Probably not, but that's the type of information on display. If you page down, you uncover three more entries: Total Directory Entries, Used Directory Entries, and Extended Directory Space. The first two totals are found more easily in NetWare Administrator, under Statistics for a chosen volume. But at least you now know what's down here.

LAN/WAN Information

IN A HURRY

10.21 View LAN/WAN Information in MONITOR

1. Type **MONITOR** from the console prompt.
2. Choose LAN/WAN Drivers from the Available Options menu.
3. From the Available LAN Drivers screen, choose the LAN driver to view.

There are three fields to check on each LAN/WAN driver when giving a network the once over. When you choose LAN/WAN Drivers from MONITOR's Available Options menu, you'll see the Available LAN Drivers screen. From there, pick the LAN driver of interest to see details. Figure 10.36 shows the top part of this screen for the Compaq N100 interface card in my PROLIANT server.

FIGURE 10.36

More details about the network board than you can really use

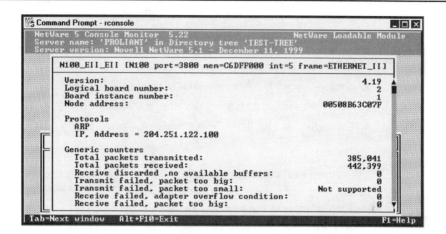

```
MS  Command Prompt - rconsole                                    _ □ ×
NetWare 5 Console Monitor  5.22                 NetWare Loadable Module
Server name: 'PROLIANT' in Directory tree 'TEST-TREE'
Server version: Novell NetWare 5.1 - December 11, 1999

    ┌ N100_EII_EII [N100 port=3800 mem=C6DFF000 int=5 frame=ETHERNET_II] ┐
    │                                                                    │
    │  Version:                                             4.19  ▲      │
    │  Logical board number:                                   2  █      │
    │  Board instance number:                                  1         │
    │  Node address:                                 00508B63C07F        │
    │                                                                    │
    │  Protocols                                                         │
    │    ARP                                                             │
    │    IP, Address = 204.251.122.100                                  │
    │                                                                    │
    │  Generic counters                                                  │
    │    Total packets transmitted:                      385,041        │
    │    Total packets received:                         442,399        │
    │    Receive discarded ,no available buffers:             0         │
    │    Transmit failed, packet too big:                     0         │
    │    Transmit failed, packet too small:       Not supported         │
    │    Receive failed, adapter overflow condition:          0         │
    │    Receive failed, packet too big:                      0  ▼      │
    └                                                                    ┘
Tab=Next window    Alt+F10=Exit                              F1=Help
```

The first fields you want to check are Total Packets Transmitted and Total Packets Received. These give a good clue to your network health. The statistics are kept from the time the server starts; when it goes down, these numbers are cleared.

The information at the top of the screen shows the version of the driver, the node address of the server, a list of the protocols supported on this board, and the board's network address. Other boards in the server will show similar information, with different addresses. Notice that this board, although it's only one of two logical boards based on one physical 3Com board, shows its address in TCP/IP, which started with NetWare 5.0.

Although this information is overkill for the typical network, you should appreciate the complexity of the information tracked for each network adapter card. Management software for your network and server uses these values to determine network health. For this Compaq N100 board, there are tons of statistics gathered for the Desktop Management standards and Compaq's own hardware monitors. It doesn't bother us to have all these extra details, although I wouldn't want to explain them all right now. Try F1 for the Help screen, and you'll be fine.

PART

II

Managing the Network

Loaded Module Information

IN A HURRY

10.22 View NLM Information in MONITOR

1. Type **MONITOR** from the console prompt.
2. Choose Loaded Modules from the Available Options menu.
3. From the Loaded NLMs screen, choose the NLM program to view.
4. Choose an item from the Resource Tags list to see details.

"System modules" is a fancy name for NLM programs running on the server. The System Module Information option on the Available Options menu shows you the list of all loaded NLMs and information about each one.

Figure 10.37 shows the screen several options deep. The Resource Tags list is one layer deeper, but I stopped here, because I covered this list a few sections ago. This screen looks at the memory usage of each NLM, and it allows you to check the resource usage of every NLM.

FIGURE 10.37

Details for every loaded NLM on your system

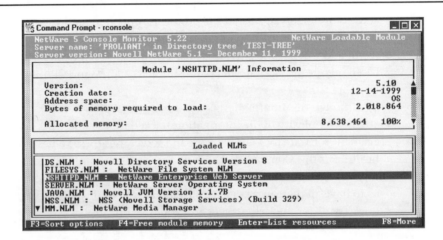

In Figure 10.37, I have chosen the NetWare Enterprise Web Server NLM (a new one for NetWare 5.1). *Allocated memory* is that memory set aside by the operating system exclusively for use by this one NLM. If I had pressed the Enter key on the NSHTTPD.NLM

(Netscape HyperText Transfer Protocol Daemon) option, it would drill down and show that of the 100 percent of allocated memory, 96 percent of the bytes were in use, 0 percent were not in use, and 4 percent of the bytes were declared overhead.

Do you have a suspect NLM or two? Do some of your server-based programs go crazy now and then? These screens will give you a chance to track the memory usage of each problem NLM, as well as all the subsidiary NLMs called by the main programs. But don't head to this screen at the first hint of trouble; these things are far down the troubleshooting list. However, they do give you some great ammunition against a vendor saying that its "NLM software is perfect, so all the problems must come from another program."

Locking the File Server Console

IN A HURRY

10.23 Lock the File Server Console

1. Type **SCRSAVER** from the console prompt.
2. Set the delay time and enable the lock feature.
3. To unlock the file server console, type the administrator name and password.

It used to be that you locked the MONITOR display with MONITOR's Lock File Server Console option to address security concerns once again. Knowing that easy access to the server console can cause damage to your network (the villain can disconnect users or take drives offline, not to mention change all the other server parameters), Novell engineers offer a lock for the MONITOR screen. In NetWare 5.0, this moved out of the MONITOR area and now has its own program called SCRSAVER.

After typing **SCRSAVER** at the colon prompt, type **SCRSAVER HELP** to see all the new details you must learn. To set the console to start the snake after about two minutes, type **SCRSAVER ENABLE; DELAY=120; ENABLE LOCK**. Figure 10.38 shows the password screen used to verify access to the console, whether local or remote.

This option is useful when many people can reach your server. Not everyone has the ideal situation of keeping the servers in a locked room. If the console is in a location where you can see it, or if you are using MONITOR remotely from your workstation, you want to be able to see the information or the snake whenever you look in that direction. Taking the keyboard and monitor away is more secure, but that approach may be inconvenient.

PART

II

Managing the
Network

FIGURE 10.38

Protecting MONITOR
in an unsafe
environment

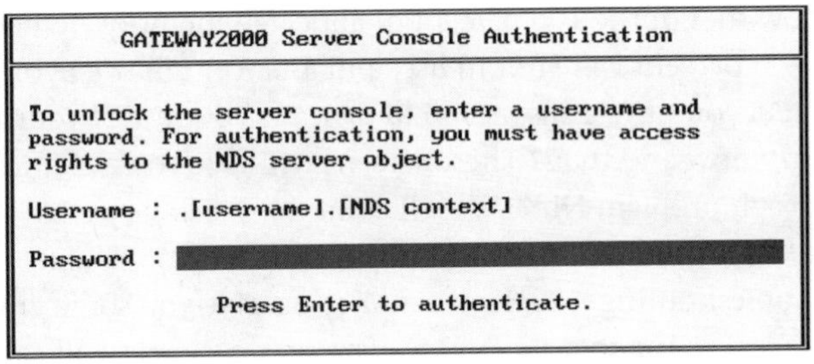

```
        GATEWAY2000 Server Console Authentication

 To unlock the server console, enter a username and
 password. For authentication, you must have access
 rights to the NDS server object.

 Username : .[username].[NDS context]

 Password : ▓▓▓▓▓▓▓▓▓▓▓▓▓▓▓▓▓▓▓▓▓▓▓▓▓▓▓▓▓▓▓▓▓▓▓▓

             Press Enter to authenticate.
```

In a clever bit of programming, even the RCONSOLE and RConsoleJ connections are locked when this option is used. Now you can leave the display running in your cubicle without fear of someone with malicious intentions getting his or her hands on your server, or just someone clumsily pressing the wrong key.

Seeing File Open/Lock Activity

IN A HURRY

10.24 View Files Opened and Locked Activity in MONITOR

1. Type **MONITOR** from the console prompt.
2. Choose File Open/Lock Activity from the Available Options menu.
3. Use the Select and Entry list to find the specific file, and then choose that file to view the lock information.

The File Open/Lock Activity option on MONITOR's Available Options menu is a companion to the Connections screen that shows the files in use by each individual user. Here, you can check on a particular file to see the lock status and which connection number is using the file.

Figure 10.39 shows the end of the file hunt, reaching down to a particular file and seeing those particulars. In this case, it's the NDSMGR32.EXE file from the PUBLIC/WIN32 directory.

The lock information is shown in two windows. The fields are described in Table 10.6.

FIGURE 10.39

Checking out who has
a file checked out

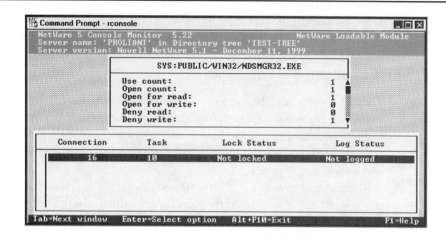

PART

II

Managing the
Network

TABLE 10.6: FIELDS ON MONITOR'S FILE OPEN/LOCK ACTIVITY SCREEN

Field	Description
Use Count	Number of connections using this file by having it open, locked, or logged.
Open Count	Number of connections with this file open.
Open For Read	Connections reading this file.
Open For Write	Connections using this file with access to write to the file.
Deny Read	Connections that have opened this file and requested that other stations not have the right to open the file for reading.
Deny Write	Connections that have opened this file and requested that other stations not have the right to open the file for writing.
Open Status	Lock status of the file.
Connection	Number of the connection on the Connection Information screen. Use this field to find out who has the file open or locked.
Task	A task number defined by the NLM and of little use.
Lock Status	Shows whether the file is in use and how the file is configured (Shareable, Read-Only, etc.).
Log Status	Whether the file activity is logged.

This information is useful when a particular file is giving you problems and you can't track down the user holding the file open or locked. However, it's more common to track the files a user has open in the Connection Information screen.

SET Command Overview

The SET commands allow you to change almost every server parameter you can imagine. There are well over 100 SET commands, and most of them have from two to one million options. The number of possible commands at your fingertips is greater than the United States federal deficit, believe it or not. For a discussion of some of these commands, see Appendix C.

Great power lives in the SET commands, but it's like a medieval fantasy in which our hero finds a magic sword that can conquer the dragons. Unfortunately, he usually destroys half the town before he learns to manage the power of the sword. Keep that in mind as you look over the SET commands.

Fortunately, the default SET command parameters have been honed over the years to a point where few, if any, changes are needed. Even more fortunate for us, the SERVMAN utility will help make those decisions that are necessary for the SET parameters, as well as for AUTOEXEC.NCF and STARTUP.NCF. (See the section "Using SERVMAN to Fine Tune Your File Server" later in this chapter for more information on the SERVMAN utility.)

Figure 10.40 shows the server console with the SET command categories. After the list, the help information for SET is displayed, showing the format used by all the SET commands.

FIGURE 10.40

A set of SET categories

```
SET [parameter_name] [= parameter_value]
   View or set current operating system parameters.  Most parameters do not need
   to be changed, however they may be configured to fit your situation.
   Example:  set replace console prompt with server name = off
Type HELP SET [TIME | TIME ZONE] to display specific help.

GATEWAY2000:set
Settable configuration parameter categories
      1. Communications
      2. Memory
      3. File caching
      4. Directory caching
      5. File system
      6. Locks
      7. Transaction tracking
      8. Disk
      9. Time
     10. NCP
     11. Miscellaneous
     12. Error Handling
     13. Directory Services
     14. Multiprocessor
     15. Service Location Protocol
     16. Licensing Services
Which category do you want to view:
```

The example given with the Help command is a small detail that wasn't under our control with earlier NetWare versions, but it is now. As you can see, the server name is displayed as part of the server console prompt. The command

```
SET replace console prompt with server name = off
```

overrides the default setting of On. The format, just as shown, is

```
SET [parameter_name] [=parameter_value]
```

SET commands have long names, as this one illustrates: Mirrored Devices Are Out Of Sync Message Frequency. Yes, that's one command, and one long command name.

The following sections provide a quick summary of each of the 16 categories listed in Figure 10.40 and what types of details are available in each. The complete list of each parameter and all the options that go with it is in Appendix C. As I've said before, and as the manuals and Help screens say, the SET parameters are not something to play with when you're bored by Solitaire. The Help text options on the server are a little sparse, but the full Help screens and other details in SERVMAN and the NetWare Management Portal (discussed later in the chapter) make those programs the way to go.

NOTE I don't present the SET command descriptions and details in this section for two reasons. One is that the NetWare Management Portal and even SERVMAN do a better job with Help screens and information than the SET commands on the console. The other is that both options relieve you of the necessity of typing the SET command and parameter at the console prompt. I always make a typo or forget a word when typing the long command, so I prefer the NetWare Management Portal. Nonetheless, SET commands are discussed in Appendix C.

Communication Parameters

Communication parameters manage the communication buffers. Of the twenty parameters available, four of them control packet receive buffers, and four control the watchdog.

Packet receive buffers hold data packets in the server's memory while they are being processed. Use MONITOR to view the number of packet receive buffers allocated.

Making sure stations are connected is the job of the watchdog packets. If the client doesn't communicate with the server within a certain time (configurable, of course), the server sends a watchdog packet.

Over another configurable time (59.3 seconds is the default), a default of 10 packets is sent to the station. If the workstation doesn't respond to 10 minutes of requests,

PART
II

Managing the
Network

the server assumes that the station is disconnected and clears the internal connection for that workstation.

Memory Parameters

The Memory section holds six commands that control the dynamic memory pool and work with EISA servers for proper memory registration. The command you are most likely to use is Set The Number Of Reserved Buffers Below 16MB. With NetWare 4, you had to also Register RAM Above 16MB, but that is no longer necessary.

File Caching Parameters

Caching is one of the most important parts of NetWare server performance, and the six commands in this section control cache size and behavior. You can set details such as the minimum number of file cache buffers to have on hand when starting the server or the delay before changed buffers (dirty disk cache buffers) are written to disk. These options are helpful for optimizing the performance of servers that focus on reading or writing information.

Directory Caching Parameters

One way that NetWare speeds up file access is by keeping the location of recently used files and directories in server RAM as a *directory cache*. The directory cache buffers are separate from the file cache buffers. When the server starts, a minimum of 20 cache buffers are set aside for directory caches. Entries stay in the cache for a default of 33 seconds but can be overwritten if the directory cache buffers can't handle the activity load.

If enough directory cache buffers are allocated for the amount of files on the system, all directory entry tables may be cached in memory. However, the more directory cache buffers, the fewer file cache buffers. You must find a balance between increasing performance through more directory buffers and decreasing performance because of too few file cache buffers.

File System Parameters

There are 25 SET commands for the file system, three of which control warnings about almost full volumes. File-purging parameters set how long files must be kept under the Minimum File Delete Wait Times setting, and that affects other files. Since deleted files remain on the disk for a time, the system must calculate how much free space is available by taking deleted but not purgeable files into consideration.

File compression has 10 parameters to set, including items such as when compression should start, when it must end, and how much disk space a compressed file should save to warrant compression.

Lock Parameters

Three lock parameters control the number of open files per workstation, the number of open files for the system, the number of record locks for each connection, and how many total record locks are supported. The three types of locks are as follows:

File locks   These locks secure a file or files by a workstation, keeping other stations from accessing any of those files.

Physical record locks   Enforced by the system, these control data access by more than one user at a time. While locked, other users cannot access or change a range of bytes (a record) in a file. When another station tries to access the lock record(s), the system sends an Access Denied message.

Logical record locks   Also enforced by the system against multiple-user access. The locking application assigns a name to each section of data that must be locked. Access for other users is checked against the named sections before the application unlocks the section.

Transaction Tracking Parameters

The five transaction tracking parameters help the TTS (Transaction Tracking System) guarantee that a transaction is written completely to disk or backed completely out again if there is a problem. No harm can come to any record if a failure stops the database; half-finished transactions will not cause a data-integrity problem.

Disk Parameters

The three parameters in the disk area control one part of the Hot Fix feature:

Write redirection   The disk sees an error during a write operation. The Hot Fix system writes the data to a redirection block and tags the original block as a problem.

Read redirection   A disk error appears during a read operation. The block is marked "bad," and the data in that block is lost unless the disk is mirrored. If there is a mirror disk, the data is read from the second disk and redirects the data to a redirection block on the first disk. This keeps the mirroring intact.

Read-after-write redirection   During the read operation that is done to verify the data just written, this parameter specifies that a data mismatch should force the system to mark the block as bad and rewrite the data to a redirection area.

Redirection as part of Hot Fix may now occur during a write or read request or during a read-after-write verification.

Time Parameters

The 20 parameters concerned with time synchronization help configure the TIMESYNC .CFG file. Time zone settings, time synchronization to other servers, and time source references are covered as well.

NCP (NetWare Core Protocol) Parameters

These 12 parameters help configure NCP details, such as NCP packet particulars and server packet security levels between the workstation and server. For example, you can set the security option for packet signatures (a NetWare exclusive) to guard against counterfeit stations impersonating authorized stations. The ability to support LIPs (Large Internet Packets) is also set here.

Miscellaneous Parameters

This catchall area is composed of 24 parameters, including the Replace Console Prompt With Server Name choice we saw earlier. Maximum Service Processes, Allow Unencrypted Passwords, and Automatically Repair Bad Volume illustrate the range of choices in this section.

Error Handling Parameters

These 12 options control the log files, the size of the log files, and what happens when the log files reach the configured maximum size. For example, you can set the log file size for the volume log, server log, and TTS log (if TTS is enabled).

Directory Services Parameters

Another baker's-dozen options for NDS support. These include setting the bindery context, NDS synchronization intervals and restrictions, and time intervals for maintenance processes. Maintenance items include reclaiming disk space and controlling the NDS trace file. This group of SET parameters is new since NetWare 4.0.

Multiprocessor Parameters

This is a new area, because NetWare 5.1 handles multiprocessor systems differently than NetWare 4 did. Three parameters handle load-balancing questions, when to start secondary processors, and how to handle certain details when a processor is taken offline.

Service Location Protocol (SLP) Parameters

These parameters are new with NetWare 5.1, because the need to use a TCP/IP protocol required Novell to locate services without the broadcasts used by IPX. SLP is an

Internet standard now, and NetWare 5.1 is the first large commercial product to use this (as far as I can tell, anyway). But since all the NetWare TCP/IP innards will take care of these details, you shouldn't have to deal with these parameters too much if at all.

Licensing Services Parameters

This category is so new that the NetWare 5.1 documentation still thinks licensing is an entry in the Miscellaneous category. It's not, although with only two entries it certainly could have stayed there without inconveniencing anyone. But with digital certificates ensuring authentication with other companies across the Internet, licensing is important, so Novell engineers evidently decided to set aside a new SET category for licensing.

Using SERVMAN to Fine Tune Your File Server

The SERVMAN (Server Manager) utility, introduced with NetWare 4, was a one-stop control program. With NetWare 5.0, SERVMAN was completely folded into MONITOR. To call the SERVMAN menu, choose the Server Parameters menu option in Available Options in MONITOR.

Don't be at all surprised if NetWare 5.1 is the last iteration of SERVMAN in any form within MONITOR. The NetWare Management Portal does a much better job using the browser interface than SERVMAN does. I just hope Novell executives don't keep pushing ConsoleOne as the utility of choice and put SERVMAN into Java's molasses.

We'll be looking at the server parameters later in this chapter.

 NOTE Earlier NetWare versions included a means of configuring IPX/SPX, but that has now been folded into INETCFG.NLM with all the other protocol support.

Copying SET Parameters to a File

Before you start changing anything, it might be wise to CYAWP (Cover Your A** With Paper). Press Enter while the highlight bar is on Server Parameters, opening the menu labeled Select A Parameter Category. This list shows the same 16 items we just reviewed in the SET parameter list.

When you make a change in SERVMAN in NetWare 5.1, there is no more rework of the file causing you to save a file and even reboot. This was a much more cumbersome process in the old days. This is another reason why a separate big utility program is no longer needed to handle these parameters—and another nail in the SERVMAN coffin.

Setting Server Parameters in SERVMAN

10.25 Set Server Parameters in SERVMAN

1. Type **MONITOR** from the console prompt.
2. Choose Server Parameters, then the category to view or modify.
3. Scroll through the parameter listing to see current settings. Help information will be displayed for every choice.
4. If necessary, reboot the server to allow the new parameter(s) to take effect.

Peruse SERVMAN for a time, if for no other reason than to appreciate how complicated NetWare could be if you had to make all those decisions about all those parameters yourself. Then look later in the chapter for the section called "NetWare Management Portal," which does a better SERVMAN than SERVMAN does and should take over these SET chores.

However, refer to Appendix C before you get carried away and start changing things just for grins, because some of these parameters control obscure but critical operating system functions. Scared enough not to change anything just to see what happens? Good.

DSTRACE Tracks NDS Synchronization Processes

NetWare's TRACK ON console command has always been helpful. Watching server communications as clients connect to servers, and servers exchange network routing information, gives a nice, warm feeling that things are working as they should be.

That same warm feeling is now extended to the NDS communications between servers. The DSTRACE (Directory Services Trace) utility, run from the server console or in SERVMAN, will display server chat concerning NDS. Figure 10.41 is a screen full of (luckily) boring (and almost incomprehensible) NDS communications.

Notice the nice ending to all the processes: A11 processed = YES. This was the tail end of a DSREPAIR automatic repair session. All the directory services details, including all the Schema operations, were caused by the DSREPAIR utility.

FIGURE 10.41

Successful replica repair

```
LocalSetServerVersion succeeded, for server .P75.CONSULT.GCS.TEST-TREE..
request DSAResolveName by context 6 succeeded
ncp request, verb: 104 by context 6 succeeded
request DSAStartUpdateSchema  by context 6 succeeded
Local Time Vector:
    --> 1998/09/07 19:02:02, 1, 0
    --> 1998/09/06 12:31:39, 2, 0
    --> 1998/08/31 17:52:24, 3, 0

Remote Time Vector:
    --> 1998/09/06 12:30:38, 1, 0
    --> 1998/08/31 13:20:03, 65534, 190
    --> 1998/09/07 19:02:03, 2, 0
    --> 1998/08/31 17:52:24, 3, 0

Sending deleted classes...
Sending deleted attributes...
Sending present attributes...
Sending present classes...
request DSAEndUpdateSchema  by context 6 succeeded
Schema update end.
1998/09/07 19:02:03 * SchemaPurger processing deleted classes.
1998/09/07 19:02:03 * SchemaPurger processing deleted attributes.
DCFreeContext context 00000006, idHandle 00000600, connHandle 0000f00
All processed = YES.
```

You can't see it here, but the computer names are all in bright blue. The word "succeeded" is in bright green. Purger operations are in hot pink. This isn't exactly graphical, but it certainly is colorful.

The reasons you may wish to watch such a boring but colorful display are:

- To check whether the NDS replicas are finished with a process

- To watch for NDS errors, especially during and/or soon after adjusting or moving NDS objects

NDS-related system messages are numbered –601 through –699 and F966 through F9FE. Not all NDS system messages are bad news, just like regular NetWare system messages. However, you know the old story: no news is good news. If you see system messages that don't clear up as NDS settles down after changes, they are usually error messages. The System Messages section of the documentation describes all the system messages in mind-numbing detail.

To see the NDS synchronization information using DSTRACE, go to the server console or start an RCONSOLE session. At the console prompt, type **SET DSTRACE TO SCREEN = ON**. To stop, replace the ON with OFF. (Use the up arrow on the console to repeat the command, then just backspace over the ON to make it OFF.)

If you wish to save this information for your server archives, or send the file to a support person, use this command at the server console:

```
SET DSTRACE TO FILE = ON
```

The file will be sent to DSTRACE.LOG in the SYS:SYSTEM directory. To write the file elsewhere, use

    SET DSTRACE FILENAME = path\filename

When you feel there is enough information in your file, repeat the DSTRACE TO FILE command, adding OFF. If you don't stop it, the file will wrap at about 500KB. Old information will be overwritten with new information as long as the log file is open.

 NOTE As with most log files, not everything is written faithfully to the log. If your log and screen information look good but things are still strange, trust your feelings rather than the log file.

DSREPAIR Means Directory Services Repair

If you read the computer magazines, you know that distributed database technology is fraught with peril for database vendors. Trying to manage database pieces spread across multiple computers is beyond the ability of most commercial database vendors today. Part of the problem is the learning curve for database designers just starting to investigate using the network as a constant, reliable communications platform to tie all the database pieces together.

Novell has a considerable head start over database vendors in the network communications area. Servers have been negotiating with each other across the network since 1986. And as we saw with the DSTRACE utility, the NDS database must keep things synchronized through regular cross-network communication.

But things can still go wrong. Some customers (and network administrators as well) can tear up a ball bearing with a powder puff. When the unlucky object of these attentions is the NDS database, DSREPAIR will put things right once again.

DSREPAIR works on one single-server database at a time. There is no option to repair all the databases from remote servers in one operation from one server console. However, you can easily run DSREPAIR on multiple servers sequentially using RCONSOLE.

Here's what DSREPAIR can do for you:

- Repair the local database. The DS.NLM file on a server will be addressed by the DSREPAIR utility.

- Repair the local replicas. Examine and repair replicas, replica rings, and server objects. You can also verify that each replica has the same data as the others.

- Search for local database objects. A browser function helps you locate and synchronize objects in the local database.

- Analyze the servers in each local partition for synchronization problems. View errors and list the partition name, server name, synchronization time, and errors with error codes.

- Write replica details to a log file. Detailed information about local partitions and servers is made available to check for database damage. If the local server has a wrong address for a remote server, you can check that here.

- Create a dump file of a damaged database. A compressed file is dumped, so you must use DSREPAIR to work with the file.

- Check the remote server ID list. Verify identification numbers for all remote servers and change those numbers as necessary.

Some NDS problems are less serious than others, and your Directory may continue to function. However, if you see a message saying that the server can't open the local database, go directly to DSREPAIR and start to work. Reinstalling the NDS database from a tape backup is more trouble, and that backup is probably slightly out of date. Try DSREPAIR before anything else.

Now that you know what DSREPAIR can do, here's what it can't do:

- Repair a remote NDS database

- Recover Unknown objects that do not have the mandatory object properties

DSREPAIR looks a lot like all the other NetWare utilities. Its opening screen shows the current version in the upper-left corner above the name of the tree and server being examined. The bottom of the screen shows helpful keystroke information and a brief description of the highlighted menu choice. Figure 10.42 shows the opening menu of DSREPAIR.

FIGURE 10.42

Preparing to repair the NDS database with DSREPAIR

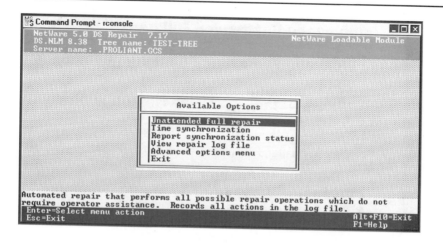

Following are the DSREPAIR menu options:

Unattended Full Repair Most of your work in DSREPAIR will be quick and simple, accomplished with this menu choice. In fact, if you start DSREPAIR and press Enter, your Directory will probably be back in shape in just a few seconds. Then you can press Enter again after reading the results of the operation and press Escape to exit DSREPAIR altogether.

Time Synchronization Contacts every server in the local database and checks NDS and time synchronization details. If this server holds a replica of the [Root] partition, every server in the tree will be polled. Each server will be listed with its DS.NLM version, type of replica code, time source, whether time is synchronized, and the difference in time to the remote server. This process starts immediately when this option is selected, and the results are written to the DSREPAIR.LOG file.

Report Synchronization Status Determines whether the NDS tree is healthy by checking the synchronization status of each replica on each server. You must provide the Admin name and password to start this function. A log entry is added to the DSREPAIR.LOG file.

View Repair Log File Shows the entire DSREPAIR.LOG file, allowing you to view all entries. The log file is controlled with the Log File Configuration option in the Advanced Options menu.

Advanced Options Menu Opens another menu allowing you to manually perform each of the automatic repairs done by the first menu option. The Advanced options give you more power and flexibility, as well as more potential for disaster. Use them carefully.

Exit Exits DSREPAIR; you can cancel by entering No or pressing the Escape key.

Running the Unattended Full Repair

IN A HURRY

10.26 Repair the NDS Database Automatically with DSREPAIR

1. Type **DSREPAIR** from the console prompt.
2. Choose Unattended Full Repair (the default) and press Enter to start the repair operation.
3. Press Enter after reading the automatic repair results to view the log.
4. Press Escape to return to the main DSREPAIR menu.

When you press Enter on this first option, you won't be asked to verify your choice or to provide any information. The option is labeled Unattended and means just that. Press Enter, and the repair starts immediately.

During the repair process, the NDS database must be closed for obvious reasons. Just like any database record, if the file can be written to while it's being overhauled, dangerous things can happen.

Because the locking of the directory database will inconvenience users, it stays locked the shortest time possible. Repair of the GATEWAY2000 server took seven (yes, 7) seconds. Obviously, a small network with no real problems will take less time than a large network with a reason to use DSREPAIR.

Figure 10.43 shows the DSREPAIR process under way. The lines whiz by so quickly you can't read any of them during the process. The whizzing stops a time or two, but not long enough to consider the pause as a breakdown in the process. Although the display in the upper-right corner shows no errors, seven minor errors of no consequence to anything except the database were found and listed in the log file.

PART

II

Managing the Network

FIGURE 10.43

Repair work in progress

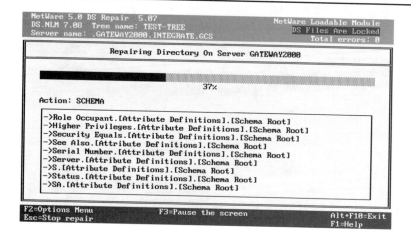

The bottom of the screen shows three interesting options:

F2=Options Menu   Shows the DSREPAIR Options menu.

F3=Pause the screen   Stops the screen and the repair so you can examine the process.

Esc=Stop repair   Abandons the repair and returns to the menu.

NOTE Little of what zooms by is helpful to a network administrator. But what great technical names: External synchronizer and attribute definitions are some of the functions that scroll by. I can almost hear Scotty now, yelling over the warp engines, "Cap'n, I canna keep the External Synchronizer up much longer! Our Attribute Definitions are blown!"

Using the Advanced Options Menu and Submenus

If the automatic full repair procedure doesn't fix your Directory problem, the Advanced Options menu is the next choice. You have little to lose at this point. Alternatively, your next step after the unattended repair is to restore from tape (not generally a good idea for directory services) or to delete the local database and copy it from another server. You might as well try a few advanced options before searching through the tape library.

Figure 10.44 shows the Advanced Options menu that appears as a submenu to the opening DSREPAIR program. The look is consistent with what you've seen before, including the identification information on the top and the help information at the bottom of the screen.

FIGURE 10.44

Serious DSPREPAIR tools

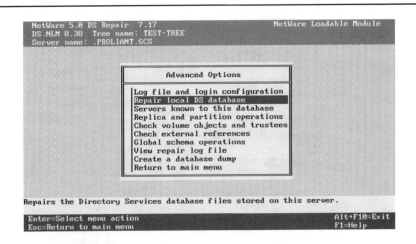

Remember that each of these options locks the Directory database. No one can be authenticated by NDS on this server during that time, since the database will be unavailable.

Log File And Login Configuration The default DSREPAIR log file, which will be created automatically for you, is SYS:SYSTEM\DSREPAIR.LOG. If you wish to delete the log file, the first menu choice is one place to do so. Figure 10.45 shows the process in progress.

FIGURE 10.45

Combo screen: log file configuration and directory login

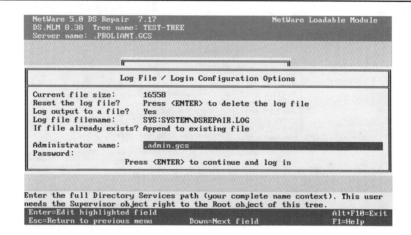

The first field, Current File Size, cannot be changed here. The Reset The Log File? option, to delete the current log file, is the first choice you have. Pressing Enter by accident as you go into this submenu may teach you the value of the Salvage option in FILER.

The option to log output to a file (coincidentally named Log Output To A File?) of your own choosing is the same as is available in DSTRACE, but it provides a more complete capture of information. This file will be helpful if your Directory gets so messed up that you need help from Novell support technicians. You can send a copy of this file for their perusal. In the Log File Filename option, you may rename the log anything you wish or leave the default name. In the next option, if the named log file already exists, you can append or overwrite the file. If you don't want to specify the log file, a temporary one will be created during repair operations. This will be shown to you after the repairs are finished.

To continue, you must provide the Admin user's name and password. The name and password will be authenticated by the NDS database before you can save your log file changes.

Repair Local DS Database This option does much of the same work as the Unattended Full Repair option on the main menu, with a few extra choices. One important

PART

II

Managing the Network

distinction is that this option performs the repairs on a temporary file set, and you have the opportunity to back out before the temporary files become permanent. Figure 10.46 shows the choices you'll be able to make.

FIGURE 10.46

NDS database repair options

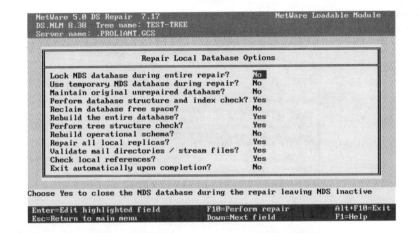

```
NetWare 5.0 DS Repair  7.17                    NetWare Loadable Module
DS.NLM 8.38  Tree name: TEST-TREE
Server name: .PROLIANT.GCS

                    Repair Local Database Options

    Lock NDS database during entire repair?        No
    Use temporary NDS database during repair?      No
    Maintain original unrepaired database?         No
    Perform database structure and index check?    Yes
    Reclaim database free space?                   No
    Rebuild the entire database?                   Yes
    Perform tree structure check?                  Yes
    Rebuild operational schema?                    No
    Repair all local replicas?                     Yes
    Validate mail directories / stream files?      Yes
    Check local references?                        Yes
    Exit automatically upon completion?            No

Choose Yes to close the NDS database during the repair leaving NDS inactive

Enter=Edit highlighted field      F10=Perform repair        Alt+F10=Exit
Esc=Return to main menu           Down=Next field           F1=Help
```

Here are the questions and what your answers mean:

Lock NDS Database During Entire Repair?   You used to have no choice, but now you have some. Keep it locked (choose Yes) if you're doing this when traffic should be light; keep it unlocked otherwise (choose No).

Use temporary NDS database during repair?   Saying Yes locks the database so a copy can be worked on and then can replace the original.

Maintain original unrepaired database?   If the old database has problems, why keep it? It eats lots of disk space. Your answer here should be No.

Perform database structure and index check?   Yes—these are two areas that must be checked.

Reclaim database free space?   This should really say "Delete unused database records?" because that's what it does.

Rebuild the entire database?   Repairs, cleans, and rebuilds the database, but this can take a while on a large network.

Perform tree structure check?   Verifies connectivity for all tree points to the appropriate database entries.

Rebuild operational schema?   The operational schema is the schema required for basic operation of NDS, making things very messy if rebuilt unnecessarily. Do this only under orders by Novell technical support; it's rarely needed.

Repair all local replicas?   Fixes all replicas stored on this physical server. A good idea.

Validate mail directories/stream files?   Mail directories are not required by NDS; those were necessary in NetWare 3 for storing login scripts. If you have mail directories for an e-mail program built like the old bindery mail system, make sure this is Yes. If you have users who access the server through Bindery Services, they will need their login directories for login scripts as well. Stream syntax files, like login scripts, are a type of object property. These are stored in a special reserved area of the SYS: volume, along with the NDS database. If you choose Yes, orphaned stream syntax files are tagged and deleted.

Check local references?   This option takes more time, because it verifies the information within the local database. In large networks, it will extend the repair time, but this option should be set to Yes whenever time permits.

Exit automatically upon completion?   If you know enough or are so incurious as to not care what happens with the rebuild, change this to Yes. Otherwise, leave it alone. Even if you don't know a lot about how NDS works, you will be able to understand some of the log files and explanations given at the end.

After you've answered these questions, press F10 to perform the repair.

Servers Known To This Database   Here we can fine-tune the local NDS database per server and see what the local server knows about the remote servers. Each of the known servers is listed, with its status and its local ID. See Figure 10.47 for a look at the server display as seen from PROLIANT.

FIGURE 10.47

Know thyself and thy fellow servers in the NDS database.

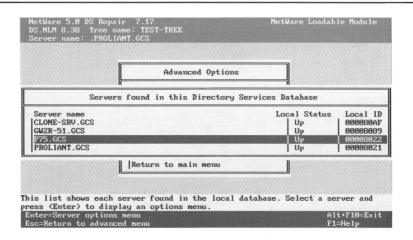

The information imparted in this screen is easy to understand. The three servers listed are those in the NDS database of PROLIANT. Each server, according to the local database, is up. The local ID for each server is listed.

It's possible for a server to be listed as up on this screen but really be down. It's possible to go the other way, with a server really active though shown as down here. Once the servers exchange some information, the display will match reality.

Pressing Enter while highlighting any of the listed servers opens up a new menu, named Server Options. The action occurs immediately after you press Enter, so if you're unsure, check the Help screens first by pressing F1.

The Server Options menu has these choices:

Time Synchronization And Server Status   Contacts every server in the local database and requests time and NDS information. If this server contains a replica of [Root], it will poll every server in the tree. The information presented here is exactly like that shown from the main DSREPAIR menu choice of Time Synchronization.

Repair All Network Addresses   There needs to be an entry for each remote server in the local SAP tables. These tables match the remote server object's IPX network address and the address in the replica. If the addresses don't match, the RNA (Repair Network Address) function updates the local tables. If there is no name for an SAP address entry for a remote server, there is little else to be done.

Repair Selected Server's Network Address   Same as above, but for the highlighted server only.

View Entire Server's Name   Shows the full distinguished server name for the highlighted server; for example, PROLIANT.GCS.

Return To Server List   Backs out of this menu.

Replica and Partition Operations   This innocent-looking entry hides multiple submenus and powerful processes. Figure 10.48 shows the first of the submenus. After you choose this option, the Replicas Stored On This Server box opens, showing all the replicas on our local server.

The first menu option, View Replica Ring, brings up a new term: *replica ring*. As you can read on the lower part of the screen, a replica ring is basically a group of replicas within a partition. Remember all the copies of replicas you can spread everywhere? These functions help keep them coordinated and functional.

FIGURE 10.48

*Specific replica
options for PROLIANT*

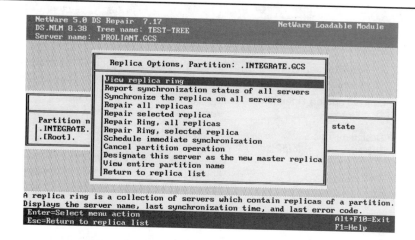

You're not missing anything interesting in the background box, which explains that the INTEGRATE.GCS partition on this server holds a Subordinate replica type and that it is On.

Table 10.7 describes the options on the main Replica Options menu.

TABLE 10.7: OPTIONS ON DSREPAIR'S MAIN REPLICA OPTIONS MENU

Option	Description
View Replica Ring	Brings up a box labeled Servers That Have Replicas Of This Partition. Choose a server to see another submenu of choices.
Report Synchronization Status Of All Servers	Runs a quick report and details time synchronization status of partitions.
Synchronize The Replica On All Servers	Reads the table of remote servers and replicas on the local server and forces all servers to synchronize with all other servers.
Repair All Replicas	Checks the replica information on each remote server defined in the local Directory database tables and makes any modifications necessary. If the local database hasn't been repaired in the last 30 minutes, repair it before trying this option.
Repair Selected Replica	Same as above, but for one highlighted replica rather than all.
Repair Ring, All Replicas	Repairs all the replicas on the ring, validating remote ID information. Run the Repair Local Database option before doing this.
Repair Ring, Selected Replica	Repairs the selected replica on the ring. Again, make sure you run Repair Local Database first.

Continued ▶

TABLE 10.7 (CONTINUED) : OPTIONS ON DSREPAIR'S MAIN REPLICA OPTIONS MENU

Option	Description
Schedule Immediate Synchronization	Provides a good way to force synchronization, especially if you're watching the DSTRACE screen and are tired of waiting.
Cancel Partition Operation	Stops the partition operation on the selected replica, if the process hasn't gone too far.
Designate This Server As The New Master Replica	If the original Master replica is damaged or lost, this option makes this replica the Master replica. If the old Master replica comes back from a hardware failure, there will be two Master replicas, causing some confusion until the synchronization checks and forces the issue by deleting the original Master replica.
View Entire Partition Name	Shows the entire partition name, regardless of its length.
Return To Replica List	Backs up one menu (same as pressing Escape).

These operations force repairs and synchronizations while writing full details to the log file. They provide a rifle approach, as opposed to the shotgun approach of the Unattended Full Repair option.

As with VREPAIR in past NetWare versions, you may need to perform some operations several times. While the replica and partition information is updated throughout the network, small errors here and there may be magnified, or they may not appear until later in the process. So don't expect any of these options to be able to work magic and quickly fix your problem. Things take longer when working across a distributed network, and this is no exception.

Choosing the View Replica Ring choice, the first option on the Replica Options menu, brings up a list of servers. In our case, all three servers have replicas of this partition.

Highlight the server and replica type of your choice, and still another new menu appears: Replica Options, Server (and the name of the current chosen server). Here we have nothing but actions, with no pause for reflection. If you've come down this many levels in your server operating system, you might as well go for it. These are your choices:

Report Synchronization Status On The Selected Server   Gathers partition details on a specific server and replica.

Synchronize The Replica On The Selected Server   Same as above for a single, highlighted replica.

Send All Objects To Every Replica In The Ring   This may create high network traffic. All other replicas are relabeled as new replicas, and the old replicas are destroyed. The host server sends a new copy of the replica to the remote servers that had their old replicas deleted. Modifications made to the now-deleted replicas that didn't have time to get back to the host replica are gone.

Receive All Objects From The Master To This Replica   Again, this may create high network traffic. This option is the reverse of the above. The old replica is marked deleted, and any objects are deleted. The Master remote replica replaces the host server replica.

View Entire Server Name   Another look at the server name, for those servers with names that can't fit in the small box of text in the earlier menu.

Return To Servers With Replicas List   Backs up one menu (same as pressing Escape).

Check Volume Objects and Trustees   This menu choice tests and verifies that everything on the server's volumes is correctly listed in NDS, as illustrated in Figure 10.49. If a volume object can't be found, an attempt will be made to create one.

All mounted volumes are checked for compliance. You must log into NDS to perform these checks.

FIGURE 10.49

Verifying volumes

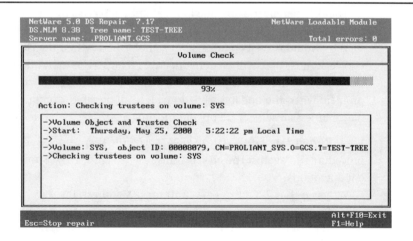

Check External References   Each external item referenced is checked to see if a replica containing the object can be located. If there is no joy, a warning will be given, but nothing dire happens immediately. Just keep working on your NDS repair until everything matches.

Global Schema Operations   The *schema* consists of the rules governing objects and their relationships to NDS. It's important to have all servers on the same schema. Think of the schema as somewhat like the NDS program that tracks and controls all the objects. Having all servers on the same version of the program is smart, and it's also necessary. Figure 10.50 shows your choices in the submenu.

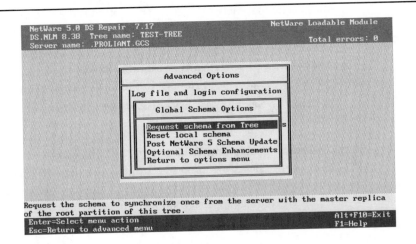

FIGURE 10.50

Choosing your global schema update options

The first step in the upgrade looks at known servers in the tree and checks their schema version. If it's current, nothing happens, and the next server is checked.

Why would Novell engineers put a choice here, when the Help screen for the choice admits there will be network errors if all servers aren't up to the same level? The answer is that this is placed here for servers that were down or having an NDS problem when the updates were done. If at all possible, don't do any NDS maintenance unless all servers are up and running.

View Repair Log File   The DSREPAIR.LOG file keeps track of every result from every procedure run against the NDS on this server. Figure 10.51 shows parts of some different operations.

Why is it that PROLIANT has only an IPX address, but P75 has TCP/IP and UDP addresses (the same address) as well? This is because P75 is running on PROLIANT, so it doesn't need TCP/IP for communications. As we've seen before, PROLIANT has a TCP/IP address.

When you've finished viewing this file, press Escape and select to save the log file under the same name, or just exit.

FIGURE 10.51

Viewing the DSREPAIR log file

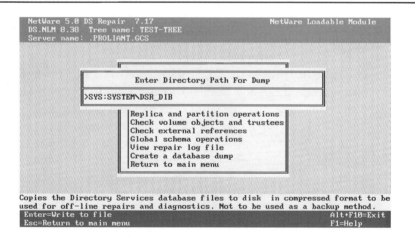

```
NetWare 5.0 DS Repair   7.17                NetWare Loadable Module
DS.NLM 8.38  Tree name: TEST-TREE
Server name: .PROLIANT.GCS
┌──────────────────────────────────────────────────────────────────┐
│          View Log File: "SYS:SYSTEM\DSREPAIR.LOG"  (23064)         │
├──────────────────────────────────────────────────────────────────┤
│Checking server: .P75.GCS                                         ▲│
│Found a Network Address Property on the server object and through SAP :│
│Address Type = (IPX), data[12] = 0AAD0D910000000000010451         │
│Found a Network Address Property on the server object and through SLP :│
│Address Type = (TCP), data[6] = 204.251.122.12:524                │
│Found a Network Address Property on the server object and through SLP :│
│Address Type = (UDP), data[6] = 204.251.122.12:524                │
│Checking server address in Replica ID : 1, .INTEGRATE.GCS         │
│The Replica Property for this server has been updated             │
│                                                                   │
│Checking server: .PROLIANT.GCS                                    │
│Found a Network Address Property on the server object and through SAP :│
│Address Type = (IPX), data[12] = 0F4D3C890000000000010451         │
│Checking server address in Replica ID : 1, .INTEGRATE.GCS         │
│                                                                   │
│** Automated Repair Mode **                                      ▼│
│Repairing replica ring                                            ►││
└──────────────────────────────────────────────────────────────────┘
Esc=Exit the editor          F1=Help              Alt+F10=Exit
```

Create A Database Dump File   If you send your dump file to the Novell support team, they can make sense out of it. The file is compressed, so looking at it yourself does no good. Since security is important to many customers, the file format keeps prying eyes from being able to easily read your Directory database. If not for security, why would the dumped file be almost five times larger than the ASCII log file?

You have a choice about dump file placement. The only restriction is that it be placed on a NetWare volume. Figure 10.52 shows the path name redirection option box.

FIGURE 10.52

Place your dump file where you want it.

```
NetWare 5.0 DS Repair   7.17                NetWare Loadable Module
DS.NLM 8.38  Tree name: TEST-TREE
Server name: .PROLIANT.GCS



        ┌─────────────────────────────────────────────────┐
        │          Enter Directory Path For Dump          │
        ├─────────────────────────────────────────────────┤
        │>SYS:SYSTEM\DSR_DIB                               │
        └─────────────────────────────────────────────────┘
              ┌──────────────────────────────────────┐
              │Replica and partition operations      │
              │Check volume objects and trustees     │
              │Check external references             │
              │Global schema operations              │
              │View repair log file                  │
              │Create a database dump                │
              │Return to main menu                   │
              └──────────────────────────────────────┘

Copies the Directory Services database files to disk  in compressed format to be
used for off-line repairs and diagnostics. Not to be used as a backup method.
Enter=Write to file                              Alt+F10=Exit
Esc=Return to main menu                          F1=Help
```

If a dump file is there already, you may change the name or the path. The dump file zooms to disk, and before you know whether it's started or not, the success screen tells you to press Enter and head back into the menu system once again.

Return to Main Menu   Believe it or not, we are finished wandering in the world of partitions, replicas, schemas, and Directory databases. At least, we are for a while. Once you choose the Return To Main Menu option or press Escape, you're out of the Advanced Options section. Back at the main menu, you'll see that we're out of DSREPAIR altogether.

Using a Graphical DSREPAIR

IN A HURRY

10.27 Use DSREPAIR from NDS Manager

1. Log in as Admin or equivalent and open NDS Manager.
2. Highlight a partition in the upper-left window.
3. Click the Partition Continuity toolbar button (in the middle group, the far-right icon, showing three descending boxes).
4. Highlight the server to be repaired.
5. Click the Repair Local Database toolbar button.

Hidden within NDS Manager is a fully graphical, almost complete copy of DSREPAIR. Novell marketing managers haven't made much noise about this utility, but they should; this is pretty cool.

Figure 10.53 shows the DSREPAIR window you can get to from NDS Manager. If you can squint at the middle section of toolbar icons in your NDS Manager window, you will be able to see that the far-right icon of that group is three boxes arranged diagonally. On your own system, you'll see they are three different colors, making a nice transition effect (at least when that option is available, unlike in this screenshot). Since they are representing Partition Continuity, the transition is important. With a partition highlighted in the left window, click the three boxes, and the featured window appears. The default heading is Partition Continuity, but DSREPAIR appears when you move the cursor over the button showing the wrench laying under some blocks.

FIGURE 10.53

DSREPAIR goes
Hollywood

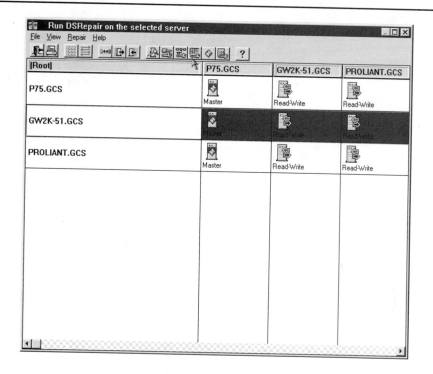

Why would you use the console DSREPAIR if this version is here? Because the console version is more complete and may work on systems too crippled to support users. Besides, the more you use the console version, the more you appreciate the graphical option.

Running DSREPAIR functions from NDS Manager provides the same log file as the console version. You also have a choice of saving the log to an external file right on the viewing window. While DSREPAIR is running, the standard screens and repair details fly by on the server console in question, but, as you can see in Figure 10.54, the NDS Manager program stays graphical.

You can see the Save As command button in the View Log window in Figure 10.54. If you have young eyes, you can read the warning telling you that running DSREPAIR requires closing of the partition and so on.

PART

II

Managing the
Network

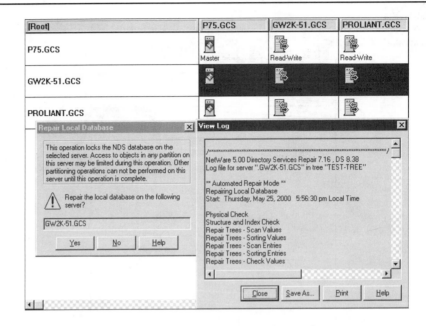

FIGURE 10.54

DSREPAIR warning and resulting log within NDS Manager

The other icons within the Partition Continuity windows of NDS Manager allow you to do the following:

- Close the active window (DSREPAIR)
- Print partition information
- View all replica lists for the partition
- View transitive synchronization information for the partition
- Schedule an immediate synchronization of the highlighted partition
- Send replica updates from the highlighted replica to all others
- Update the highlighted server's replica from the Master replica
- Check remote server IDs on the highlighted server
- Repair a single replica
- Repair network addresses on the selected server
- Run DSREPAIR on the selected server
- Reassign the current replica to be the Master replica
- Repair volumes and trustees on a selected volume

As you can see, there a few items missing from the NDS Manager version that are present in the console version of DSREPAIR, but the main options are available. You may never have to mess with DSREPAIR if you're lucky.

 TIP There are a few more fun things hiding in NDS Manager, and you should take some time to check it out yourself. The Help screen includes hundreds of error codes and their meanings, which is worth the price of admission all by itself. Not that you should expect to see error codes, but the only thing worse than seeing an error code at night is seeing one the morning your trip out of town starts. At least this way, you'll quickly know what the error is, and you may be able to fix it without taking a later plane.

Using DSMERGE for NDS Tree Management

Companies with large networks often assume that they need multiple NDS trees to handle their network design. Part of this feeling is misguided security, and part is a misunderstanding of how well the Organizations and Organizational Unit containers do their jobs.

After the company has multiple trees, the network managers realize that it's difficult for users to see or take advantage of resources outside their own tree. With the first version of NetWare 4, merging two trees into one wasn't possible. This caused some consternation.

Novell engineers developed a DSMERGE (Directory Services Merge) program. Using information gained at customer sites during DSMERGE development, the program was improved in parallel with the client software, so clients can connect to multiple trees at once. But there are reasons to merge trees, and that's exactly what DSMERGE does.

DSMERGE allows you to prune and graft your tree at the highest level imaginable: [Root]. This program is not used to move containers or partitions (use NetWare Administrator for these functions). The program works with only two trees at one time. Your players in this tree drama are:

Local Source tree   The tree that will be folded into another tree. Start the operations from the server holding the Master replica of this tree's [Root] partition.

Target tree   The eventual new tree, with your local source tree folded in. The target tree name will be the same as the new tree's name.

PART
II

Managing the
Network

Here are some details you should know before starting a DSMERGE operation:

- DSMERGE does not change container names or contexts within containers. The merged objects are retained. The file system is not touched at all, except for changed names of containers holding the volumes.

- The [Root] of the target tree becomes the new [Root] for objects in the source tree. Tree names for all servers and other objects in the source tree are changed to reflect their new tree name.

- During the merge, all replicas of the [Root] partition are removed from servers in the local tree. After the merge, the local tree replica is replaced by a replica of the combined trees.

Figure 10.55 shows the opening screen of the DSMERGE program. You see that there are few options, and the listings are straightforward.

FIGURE 10.55

Major tree surgery upcoming

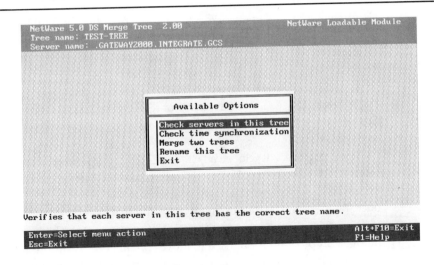

The prerequisites are fairly stiff before a DSMERGE operation. If you think about it, there's nothing more extensive you can do to your NDS network. Every object in your source tree will be changed, and many of your target tree objects will require some adjustment. Here are the prerequisites:

- No active network connections are allowed. Close all connections on both trees. If there are users around who may try to log in, disable login on all affected servers.

- No leaf or Alias objects are allowed in the [Root] of the local source tree. Delete or move any Alias or leaf objects in the [Root] before starting. Give the Directory time to digest those changes.

- No similar names are allowed at the top of both trees. You may have identical container objects in both trees if they are not immediate subordinates of [Root]. The immediate container sets their identification. The full distinguished name will let your users tell the difference between ACME.ACCTNG.P1 and ACME.MFG.P1.

- NDS must be the same version on both trees. Upgrade all pre-Directory or NDS7 servers that have a replica of the [Root] object, but be prepared to upgrade all servers. Having all servers running the same version will eliminate some problems and make management less complicated. It's worth the time to get every server on the same version before starting your network redesign.

- All servers must be up and running in both trees. If WAN links are involved, verify the servers on the remote side of the link. Technically, only those servers containing a replica of the [Root] must be up, but any down servers will delay the total integration of the two trees. It's best to have every server running.

- Schema on both trees must be the same. Any products installed on one tree that modify the schema must be installed on the other tree before merging. Check carefully, since many products are starting to take advantage of NDS features and may change the schema.

- Time reference must be the same. Verify that each server in both trees is synchronized within 10 seconds of the other. If both trees have either a Reference or Single Reference time server, change one of them to a Secondary or Primary time server. All servers in both trees should then reference the same time source.

- The two trees must have different names. If both trees have the same name, one must be renamed before starting DSMERGE.

You start DSMERGE from a server console or RCONSOLE session. Although you don't log in as the Admin user at the console or through RCONSOLE, you will need the Admin passwords for both trees. At the console colon prompt, type **DSMERGE**. Now you've reached DSMERGE's Available Options menu. These choices are described in the following sections.

Checking the Servers in This Tree

Before you start merging trees here and there, all the servers must be up, running, and current on their software versions. The first option on the DSMERGE menu is Check

Servers In This Tree. Press Enter to scan the tree and list all servers. Figure 10.56 shows the results of this check on my lab network.

FIGURE 10.56

Servers in the tree, awaiting DSMERGE

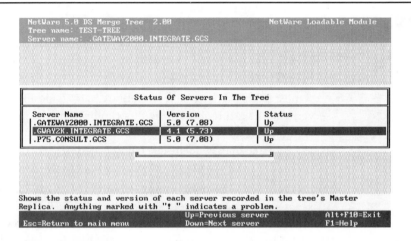

What is this telling us? First, the servers are up, and they are in the tree where they belong. If the field shows an error or a status of down, check that before proceeding with the merge operation. The same goes if you see DS Locked, meaning the NDS database is probably still trying to digest some earlier change. The only problem is that one server, GWAY2K, is still running NetWare 4.11 and an old version of Directory Services.

The worst news is if a server has an exclamation point in front of the name, as in !P75. If this is the case, fix that server's problem before attempting the merge.

Checking Time Synchronization

IN A HURRY

10.28 Check Time Synchronization with DSMERGE

1. Type **DSMERGE** from the console prompt.
2. Choose Check Time Synchronization.
3. Check the server name, time server type, whether it's synchronized, and the time difference.
4. Press Escape to return to the menu.

"Synchronize your watches!" is a cliché of spy movies and comedies spoofing them, but it makes sense here. NDS relies on timestamps to control the database; events in dispute are settled by examining the timestamps. The merge may not continue if time is not properly configured on all involved servers.

When you press Enter on the Check Time Synchronization menu choice, a progress bar displays the query process to all servers. After all servers have responded to the NDS query, the server name and information are displayed. Figure 10.57 shows the screen with this information.

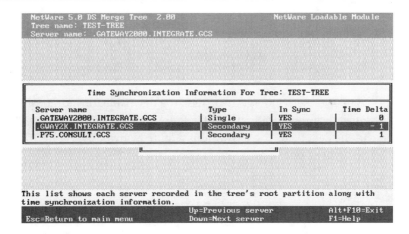

The first column shows the names of all servers in the tree. The second column shows the type of time server each is running. In our example, GATEWAY2000 is a Single Reference server, advertising the time, and GWAY2K and P75 both listen for time information. They are not quite in sync, with the time variance between the servers at zero, or less than two seconds difference. The three servers have a slightly larger variance, but nothing so drastic that synchronizing time won't fix before the tree merge.

Just because this screen looks good doesn't mean your time troubles are over. The report here does not check which time servers are referring to which time source. The time arrangement for the new, merged tree must be planned and configured before merging. If the other tree has a Single Reference time server, as does GATEWAY2000, one of the two must be downgraded to a Secondary or Primary time server before the merge.

PART

II

Managing the
Network

Merging Two Trees

IN A HURRY

10.29 Merge Trees with DSMERGE

1. Type **DSMERGE** from the console prompt.
2. Choose Merge Two Trees and press Enter.
3. Provide the Admin name and password for the local tree.
4. Choose the target tree from the list and provide the Admin name and password for that tree.
5. Press F10 to start the merge.

When you select Merge Two Trees, the tree name for your local source tree will be filled in automatically. The full administrator's name, not just Admin, must be placed in the next field. The password is required, obviously. Figure 10.58 shows this screen being filled out.

FIGURE 10.58

Authenticating Admin users in both trees

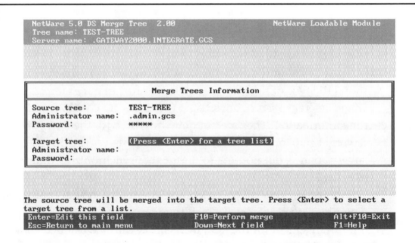

If the target tree name you want isn't on the list that appears when you press Enter, press the Insert key and provide the network address of any server in the target tree. To get that address, type **CONFIG** at the server console prompt, and make a note of the IPX internal network number. Use that address to latch onto the target tree.

The Admin user password is required for the target tree as well. When all this is filled out, press F10 to perform the merge. The time the merge will take will vary depending on the size of the network, but it will be longer than when you organized the partitions earlier.

Renaming Trees

IN A HURRY

10.30 Rename a Tree with DSMERGE

1. Type **DSMERGE** from the console prompt.

2. Choose the Rename This Tree option.

3. Provide the Admin name and password for the tree.

4. Type the new name and press Enter.

Although you should give serious thought to naming your tree before you finish the installation, names do change at times. Merging a small tree into a large tree is the most efficient method, but you may prefer the name of the small tree. Your company or division may change names, necessitating a change of your network. You can change the name of a tree here. The physical process of changing the tree name is not difficult.

We covered tree naming in Chapter 3, but here's a refresher of the rules, which are a bit more restrictive than those for a regular object:

- Tree names must be 32 characters or less.

- Tree names may only include A–Z and 0–9; the _ and - (underscore and dash) are allowable, but multiple adjacent underscores are not.

- Tree names cannot start or end with an underscore (_).

After starting DSMERGE on the server console or RCONSOLE session, select the Rename This Tree option. You must then type the Admin name and password before you can type the new name. Figure 10.59 shows this process in progress.

After you press F10, it will take a few minutes to replicate the new tree name across the network. Don't do any other administrative tasks during that time, since NDS will be busy and may behave slightly oddly during the process.

PART

II

Managing the
Network

FIGURE 10.59

Soon to be a new tree name

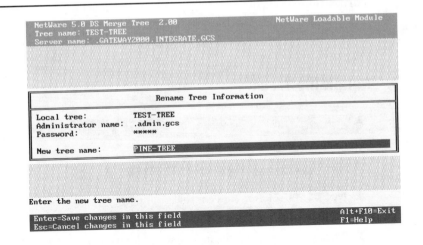

```
NetWare 5.0 DS Merge Tree  2.00              NetWare Loadable Module
Tree name: TEST-TREE
Server name: .GATEWAY2000.INTEGRATE.GCS



                         Rename Tree Information

   Local tree:          TEST-TREE
   Administrator name:  .admin.gcs
   Password:            *****

   New tree name:       PINE-TREE



 Enter the new tree name.

 Enter=Save changes in this field              Alt+F10=Exit
 Esc=Cancel changes in this field              F1=Help
```

 NOTE   Remember, if you change the tree name, you'll need to reset bunches of application references on all your user workstations. Make sure you really, *truly*, want to rename a tree before doing so.

Exiting and Cleaning Up

After you've finished with DSMERGE (choose Exit on the menu, and say Yes to exit DSMERGE), there are some things that you'll need to do immediately. Whether you merged trees or renamed one or two, a lot of users are suddenly lost in the woods, unable to find their favorite tree.

The bad news: client details must be changed to find the correct new tree. If you've gone to a single tree, there shouldn't be much problem. If you still have multiple trees on the same physical network segment, users will have to know which tree they need.

One more bit of administrivia: when merging multiple trees, the first tree's Admin user will lose all rights. For example, say you have Tree A merging into Tree B. No problem; both Admin users are fine. Say you now merge Tree B into Tree C. Problem: Admin from the original Tree A finds itself without rights. The Admin from either old Tree B or new Tree C must manually grant rights again to Admin A.

Installing Additive Server Licenses

10.31 Install an Additional License on a NetWare Server

1. Type **NWCONFIG** from the console prompt.
2. Choose License Option from the menu.
3. Insert the license disk into the appropriate server drive and press Enter.
4. Move to the console prompt (press Alt+Escape on the console or Alt+F3 in RCONSOLE to cycle forward through all open screens).
5. Type **VERSION** to verify the new license count.
6. Move back to the NWCONFIG screen and exit by pressing Escape.

This process, new in NetWare 4.10 and continued in 4.11, 5.0, and on to 5.1, allows you to add the number of user licenses per server you need, but not more than you need. Earlier NetWare versions required you to choose the number of concurrent users from specified options: 5, 10, 20, 50, 100, 250, 500, or 1000 users. Obviously, if you needed 105 users, you wasted a lot of licenses.

Options for Novell included moving to a client-licensing arrangement. However, this turns out to be more unfair than a server license. It's common for NetWare users to have a 50-user license, but have 65 users. The trick is that only 50 users are ever logged in at any one time. If you forced each user, even those who only connect to a particular server once a month, to buy a client license, the extra cost for the company wouldn't be trivial.

So NetWare 4.10 added *additive licensing*, often called "bump disks," for multiuser software. Now if a company has 105 clients, it can buy one license for 100 users and another for 5 users. That covers the total needs, while still buying licenses in bulk rather than one at a time.

Yes, you may do this as well through NetWare Administrator. After opening NWAdmin, highlight the license object and see if there is a serial number certificate attached. Figure 10.60 shows adding a new license. We got to this point in the figure by choosing Tools ➢ Novell Licensing Services ➢ Add Licenses ➢ Add License File ➢ OK, and then looking to drive A: for the file.

PART

II

Managing the
Network

FIGURE 10.60

*Configuring a network
license envelope*

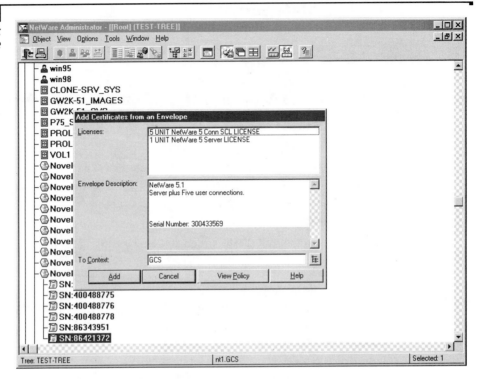

Novell ships license files on floppy disks, which is why the License Envelope File shows the floppy drive as a source. There's plenty of information inside one of these little license files, if you care to look. Figure 10.61 shows the License Policy details, including the number of users available and the like.

Novell provided the licenses for this book, for which I thank them. But for the NetWare 5.0 revision, Novell gave me a Master License Agreement disk for a sample. Their little trick: the license expired on Halloween. Isn't that a scary thought?

Commonly Used Console Commands

This section contains the eight commands typed at the console most often. The command frequency was determined by pure happenstance: I asked some friends which console commands they used, if any. These eight came up more than any other, but each network and network administrator is different.

FIGURE 10.61

License information

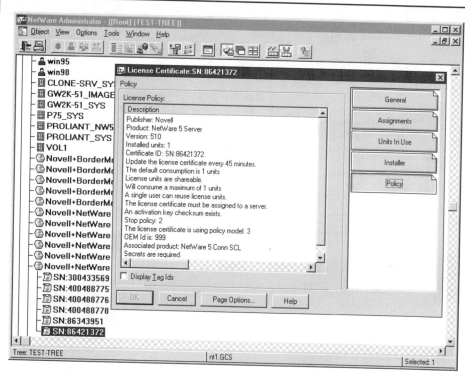

The "top eight"—DISPLAY NETWORKS, DISPLAY SERVERS, DOWN, EXIT, MOD-ULES, TRACK ON, VERSION, and VOLUMES—are described in the following sections; they're listed in alphabetical order, not ranked by importance.

Displaying a Network List

The DISPLAY NETWORKS command lists all networks and network IDs known to the server's internal router. Figure 10.62 shows an example at the top of the screen.

The first number is the external network number of recognized networks. One of these numbers belongs to every server adapter card, as well as every configured proto-col on every adapter card. The three physical servers in the lab generate six known networks, even though none has more than one network adapter card.

The second number indicates how far away the other network is. The first number of what looks like a fraction is the number of hops to the remote network. The second number is the time in ticks (about 1/18 second) required to send a packet to that address.

PART

II

Managing the Network

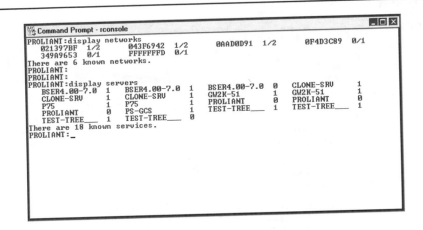

Displaying a Server List

The DISPLAY SERVERS command shows servers in the network. Toward the middle of the display in Figure 10.62, you can see the output of DISPLAY SERVERS. The server name is shown, and the number afterwards is the number of hops between your server and the referenced server. Your server always shows 0 hops.

Each NetWare 5.1 server advertises at least two services: file service and NDS service. Print servers show up as servers in this display (PS-GCS), as do NDS trees.

Shutting Down the Server

The DOWN command writes information in the server cache to disk, closes files, updates directory entry tables and file allocation tables, and shuts down the server in an orderly manner.

When you use DOWN, warnings are sent to each connected workstation, after which you'll see a message saying that it's safe to reboot or power off the server.

Using EXIT to Unload NetWare

EXIT unloads NetWare from server memory after the server is down. When you use EXIT, you'll end up at the DOS prompt from the server DOS partition. EXIT removes NetWare memory and applications from the server, making the unit a DOS machine once more.

If restarting your server is the goal, you may type **RESTART SERVER** after using DOWN. This saves the steps of using EXIT and then running the SERVER.EXE program from the DOS partition.

Listing NLMs

The MODULES command lists all loaded NLM programs, along with version information. Figure 10.63 shows an example of the result.

FIGURE 10.63

Using the MODULES command

```
MS Command Prompt - rconsole                                          _ □ ×
PROLIANT:modules
XENGNUL.NLM      (Address Space = OS)
  NICI NULL XENG from Novell, Inc.
  Version 1.02      October 1, 1999
  Copyright 1995-1999 Novell, Inc. All rights reserved. Patent pending.
CDBE.NLM        (Address Space = OS)
  Loaded from internal nlm list [C:\NWSERVER\]
  NetWare Configuration DB Engine
  Version 5.10      September 27, 1999
  Copyright 1998-1999 Novell, Inc. All rights reserved.
NWKCFG.NLM      (Address Space = OS)
  Loaded from internal nlm list [C:\NWSERVER\]
  NetWare Kernel Config NLM
  Version 2.05      December 7, 1999
  Copyright 1996-1999 Novell, Inc. All rights reserved.
PVER500.NLM     (Address Space = OS)
  Loaded from [C:\NWSERVER\]
  NetWare 5.00 Version Library
  Version 2.10      November 4, 1999
  Copyright 1996-1999 Novell, Inc. All rights reserved.
<Press ESC to terminate or any other key to continue>_
```

This list normally takes several pages, and the modules don't seem to appear in any particular order. However, they are listed in the order loaded. When modules are unloaded, they leave a slot open for the next module. If no free slots exist, later modules are appended to the end of the list.

Dates of modules can become critical when chasing stubborn problems. Rest assured, whatever date you have on your system modules, at least two will be out of date already (or at least that will be the problem according to technical support).

There are other places to list these modules, such as within MONITOR or the NetWare Management Portal, that actually give you useful information—like memory usage, which is always critical.

In fact, let's jump the gun a bit on the NetWare Management Portal and show the modules loaded on PROLIANT organized by the allocated memory of each module. Reach NetWare Management Portal through your browser by typing a URL of the server IP address, colon, and the port number 8008. In PROLIANT's case, you would type http://204.251.122.100:8008. When you log in (with an administrator-level name and password to be authenticated by NDS), a secure connection begins, changing the URL to https://204.251.122.100:8009. Notice that it doesn't say http: like most URLs, but https: to trigger security.

Figure 10.64 shows the modules on PROLIANT organized by the Allocated Memory heading. The bottom of the list shows column totals.

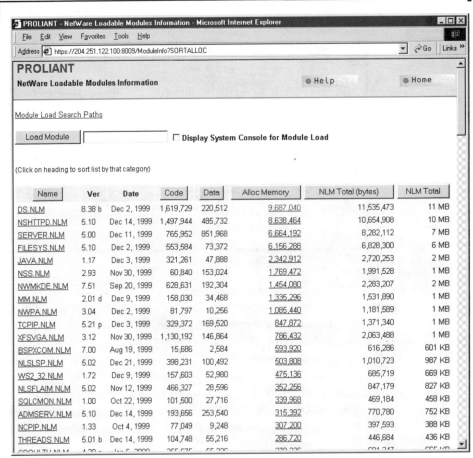

Name	Ver	Date	Code	Data	Alloc Memory	NLM Total (bytes)	NLM Total
DS.NLM	8.38 b	Dec 2, 1999	1,619,729	220,512	9,687,040	11,535,473	11 MB
NSHTTPD.NLM	5.10	Dec 14, 1999	1,497,944	485,732	8,638,464	10,654,908	10 MB
SERVER.NLM	5.00	Dec 11, 1999	765,952	851,968	6,664,192	8,282,112	7 MB
FILESYS.NLM	5.10	Dec 2, 1999	553,584	73,372	6,156,288	6,828,300	6 MB
JAVA.NLM	1.17	Dec 3, 1999	321,261	47,888	2,342,912	2,720,253	2 MB
NSS.NLM	2.93	Nov 30, 1999	60,840	153,024	1,769,472	1,991,528	1 MB
NWMKDE.NLM	7.51	Sep 20, 1999	628,631	192,304	1,454,080	2,283,207	2 MB
MM.NLM	2.01 d	Dec 9, 1999	158,030	34,468	1,335,296	1,531,890	1 MB
NWPA.NLM	3.04	Dec 2, 1999	81,797	10,256	1,085,440	1,181,589	1 MB
TCPIP.NLM	5.21 p	Dec 3, 1999	329,372	169,520	847,872	1,371,340	1 MB
XFSVGA.NLM	3.12	Nov 30, 1999	1,130,192	146,864	786,432	2,063,488	1 MB
BSPXCOM.NLM	7.00	Aug 19, 1999	15,686	2,584	593,920	616,286	601 KB
NLSLSP.NLM	5.02	Dec 21, 1999	398,231	100,492	503,808	1,010,723	987 KB
WS2_32.NLM	1.72	Dec 9, 1999	157,603	52,980	475,136	685,719	669 KB
NLSFLAIM.NLM	5.02	Nov 12, 1999	466,327	28,596	352,256	847,179	827 KB
SQLCMON.NLM	1.00	Oct 22, 1999	101,500	27,716	339,968	469,184	458 KB
ADMSERV.NLM	5.10	Dec 14, 1999	193,656	253,540	315,392	770,780	752 KB
NCPIP.NLM	1.33	Oct 4, 1999	77,049	9,248	307,200	397,593	388 KB
THREADS.NLM	5.01 b	Dec 14, 1999	104,748	55,216	286,720	446,684	436 KB

Me? I'll never use the console MODULES command again. Not only are there too many modules to scroll through, but they can't be sorted. MONITOR sorts by the default Allocated Memory listing and offers a way (F3=Sort options) to sort by date or name. However, the window showing the listings is small and requires lots of Page Down keystrokes to cover all the modules.

Tracking RIP and SAP Information

TRACK ON displays RIP and SAP tracking information sent between servers on the console screen. Figure 10.65 shows an example of the result.

FIGURE 10.65

Using TRACK ON to track advertised services

```
SAP Tracking Screen
OUT [349A9653:FFFFFFFFFFFF] 23:32:29      GATEWAY2000  1   TEST-TREE____  1
       GATEWAY2000   1    TEST-TREE____  1
OUT [00000001:FFFFFFFFFFFF] 23:32:29      GATEWAY2000  1   TEST-TREE____  1
       GW2K-NT       2    GATEWAY2000   1  TEST-TREE____  1
IN  [00000001:0020AFD82229] 23:32:50      P75          1   GW2K-NT        2
       TEST-TREE____  1
IN  [349A9653:0020AFD82229] 23:32:50      P75          1   TEST-TREE____  1
IN  [00000001:0020AFD8227F] 23:33:13      GWAY2K       1   GWAY2K         1
       P75           2    TEST-TREE____  1  GATEWAY2000   2   GW2K-NT    2
       PS-GCS        1
IN  [349A9653:0020AFD8227F] 23:33:13      GWAY2K       1   GWAY2K         1
       TEST-TREE____  1    PS-GCS        1  TEST-TREE____  2
IN  [00000001:0020AFD8227F] 23:33:13      GATEWAY2000  2   TEST-TREE____  2
       TEST-TREE____  2
IN  [349A9653:00A0248F095D] 23:33:14      GW2K-NT      1
OUT [349A9653:FFFFFFFFFFFF] 23:33:29      GATEWAY2000  1   TEST-TREE____  1
       GATEWAY2000   1    TEST-TREE____  1
OUT [00000001:FFFFFFFFFFFF] 23:33:29      GATEWAY2000  1   TEST-TREE____  1
       GW2K-NT       2    GATEWAY2000   1  TEST-TREE____  1
IN  [00000001:0020AFD82229] 23:33:50      P75          1   GW2K-NT        2
       TEST-TREE____  1
IN  [349A9653:0020AFD82229] 23:33:50      P75          1   TEST-TREE____  1
<Use ALT-ESC or CTRL-ESC to switch screens, or any other key to pause>
```

This display has now been split into SAP and RIP screens. Earlier versions had both RIP and SAP on the same screen, but growth changed that setup. Two screens keep the information from scrolling by so fast, which was a problem in a busy network.

Each packet is labeled IN if the server is receiving information and OUT if the server is broadcasting information. Servers also receive and respond to connection requests from clients attempting to log in to a server. These requests show up as Get Nearest Server requests and Give Nearest Server responses. Clients attempting to log in will send a packet labeled Get Nearest Server, and the server will send its name and address in a packet labeled Give Nearest Server.

This chatty screen, and the less-chatty RIP screen, used to bug WAN users to no end. These packets are broadcast every 30 seconds, day and night, eating up (they claimed) valuable bandwidth.

The IPX detractors have won the day, and NetWare 5.1 has completely installed TCP/IP and replaced SAP and RIP over IPX. TCP/IP-enabled systems won't have any activity in these screens.

To turn off this display, use the TRACK OFF command.

TIP Use TRACK ON when you can't understand why a client is unable to log in to a particular server (if you're using IPX). While watching the console screen, either directly or through RCONSOLE, have the user log in again. Assuming that the server can even see the client, the activity of the server may help you isolate the problem.

Listing Version Information

Use VERSION to list the NetWare operating system license information. This command used to show a decent amount of information, but NetWare 5.1 cuts down the detail considerably. All you see now is the NetWare version, with the date stamp, which is useful when you're checking for needed upgrades or patches. No longer does this command show the number of licensed connections and serial number of the operating system. Shame.

Listing Volume Information

VOLUMES shows mounted volumes on the server, including CD-ROM volumes. Figure 10.66 shows an example of the result, with VERSION at the top of the screen and VOLUMES at the bottom.

FIGURE 10.66

Using VOLUMES to see server volumes (and VERSION at the top)

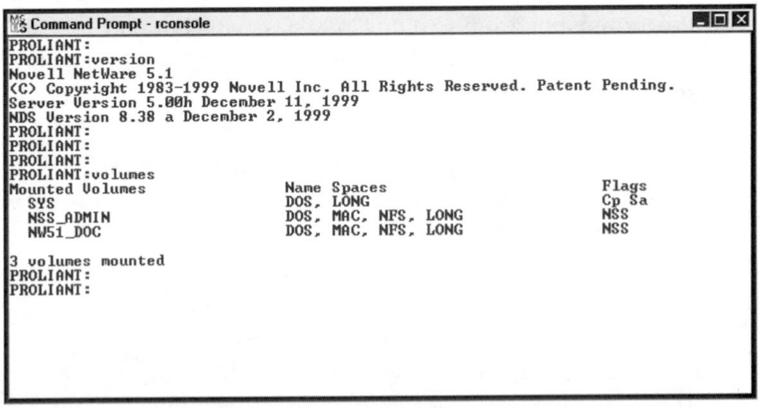

```
Command Prompt - rconsole                                    _ □ ×
PROLIANT:
PROLIANT:version
Novell NetWare 5.1
(C) Copyright 1983-1999 Novell Inc. All Rights Reserved. Patent Pending.
Server Version 5.00h December 11, 1999
NDS Version 8.38 a December 2, 1999
PROLIANT:
PROLIANT:
PROLIANT:
PROLIANT:volumes
Mounted Volumes              Name Spaces              Flags
  SYS                        DOS, LONG                Cp Sa
  NSS_ADMIN                  DOS, MAC, NFS, LONG      NSS
  NW51_DOC                   DOS, MAC, NFS, LONG      NSS

3 volumes mounted
PROLIANT:
PROLIANT:
```

The Name Spaces section shows DOS here, but includes Mac, NFS, and OS/2 when those name spaces are supported on the volume. Name spaces are set per volume, not per server.

The Flags column shows volume characteristics: Cp means compressed, Sa means block suballocation, and Mg means data migration is enabled (which isn't the case for the volumes shown in Figure 10.66).

Managing Protocols and Remote Server Access with INETCFG

The INETCFG (InterNetworking Configuration) utility is the focal point of all protocols on your server. The LOAD and BIND commands in the AUTOEXEC.NCF file, configured when you installed your server, can be moved under control of INETCFG. This makes it possible to configure multiple protocols in this one utility. Figure 10.67 shows the opening menu for INETCFG.

FIGURE 10.67

Opening menu for protocol and other network configurations

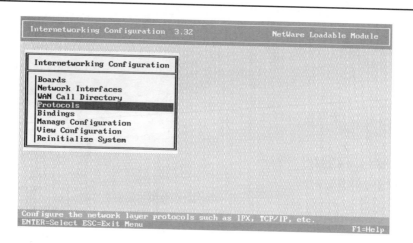

PART

II

Managing the Network

Yes, Novell should have converted this utility out of C-Worthy and into NetWare Administrator by now, shouldn't they? No timetable for this conversion that I've heard of. I really wish they had converted this to a GUI rather than the installation routines, but they didn't ask me. Sometimes you're forced to dig down six or seven levels in here, and it gets a bit thick and confusing. Maybe by NetWare 5.1.1 they'll have this utility converted, but I've been hoping for a change, without success, for three versions. Alas, the NetWare Management Portal doesn't yet cover this area.

The menu options work as follows:

Boards   Adds a new hardware network board, or modifies the hardware parameters of an existing board.

Network Interfaces   Configures WAN boards, if you have one in your server. Don't use this menu item for LAN boards.

WAN Call Directory   Specifies connection parameters for remote site connections.

Protocols   Enables and configures protocols for your server.

Bindings   Links protocols to network interfaces.

Manage Configuration   Sets up SNMP parameters, exports copies of your configuration to disk, imports them back from a disk, enables remote access to the server, and edits the AUTOEXEC.NCF file.

View Configuration   Displays the commands used by INETCFG to set the network configuration of your server. The submenu breaks down the presentation various ways, so you can check just one section or get an overview of the entire configuration.

Reinitialize System   Makes your newly configured settings the active settings (new with NetWare 4.11).

When you first run INETCFG, the LOAD and BIND statements are moved from your AUTOEXEC.NCF file to a special file under control of INETCFG exclusively. These files should not be edited directly or interfered with in any manner:

- AURP.CFG
- TCPIP.CGF
- IPXSPX.CFG
- NLSP.CFG
- NETINFO.CFG
- INITSYS.NCF (new with NetWare 4.11)

INETCFG offers one-stop protocol shopping for your server. This program configures the network boards, sets up different protocols, and hooks them to the proper boards.

NetWare has a great history of support for the Macintosh computer. Novell was the first network operating system vendor to support AppleTalk and is now supporting Macintosh systems over IPX as well. As an example of the importance of Macintosh support to Novell, the installation program offers a chance to support AppleTalk. Turn to Appendix E for the entire Macintosh and NetWare story. That appendix includes the installation and configuration details necessary to support Macintosh clients.

Just as important to Novell as AppleTalk, TCP/IP also has a switch for support during server installation. Whether you set that switch or not, you'll need some TCP/IP details to configure this protocol on your NetWare server.

Configuring IPX

10.32 Configure IPX with INETCFG

1. Type **INETCFG** from the console prompt (or RCONSOLE).
2. Choose Boards to verify the initial setup done during installation.
3. Choose Network Interfaces to verify the initial setup done during installation.
4. Choose Protocols to open the Protocol Configuration menu.
5. Choose IPX to set any advanced options.
6. Press Escape twice to return to the main menu.

IPX is the workhorse protocol for 100 percent of all NetWare networks up through version 4.1. Although it's now possible to run a NetWare server without IPX by using native IP, there's a good reason to keep IPX going for existing clients.

Supporting a second protocol doesn't interfere with the server's ability to maintain IPX support. And as we've seen, IPX is well suited for the LAN, providing excellent performance without requiring any management, installation, or configuration time.

The default IPX configuration doesn't add any extra bells and whistles. Figure 10.68 shows the entry screen behind the Protocols and IPX menu choices. If you wish to set advanced options, you may do so here by enabling the Advanced IPX option. If you don't enable Advanced IPX, there isn't a single active field in this or the next screen.

FIGURE 10.68

Advanced IPX is still fairly simple.

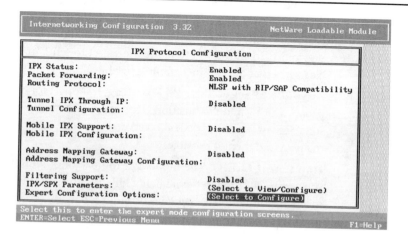

There are a few options in Expert Configuration Options you will want to check into. The Expert Configuration Options choices aren't particularly complex, either. Take a look at Figure 10.69, which appears when you press Enter on the Expert Configuration Options field.

FIGURE 10.69

Expert IPX defaults and explanations

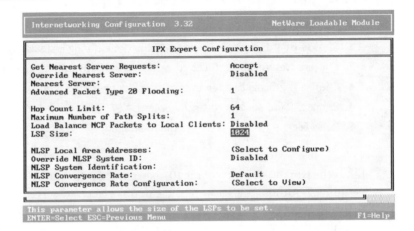

This screen also provides NLSP options. This is the NetWare Links Support Protocol, a feature introduced in NetWare 4.10 that replaces RIP and SAP. The other fields on the IPX Expert Configuration screen that you can configure include the following:

Get Nearest Server Requests Accepts or ignores packets requesting the name of the nearest server. These are usually clients trying to log in. The default is to accept.

Override Nearest Server When enabled, responds to Get Nearest Server packets with the name of another server. This is useful with Novell's MPR (Multi-Protocol Router), which can't accept more than one connection. If enabled, the previous field allows you to name the server to send, in response to the Get Nearest Server query. The default is disabled.

Advanced Packet Type 20 Flooding Support for NetBIOS (IPX Type 20) packet routing and propagation. This may place multiple NetBIOS packets on some legs of the network. For a NetWare network, any NetBIOS packets are too many. Avoid them if possible.

Hop Count Limit The number of routers (or other NetWare servers) a packet can go through before being killed. Although this sounds harsh, the reasoning is sound: if a packet goes through too many servers and routers, it must be lost. Packets, being male, hate to ask for directions (and actually can't if they want to). Novell recommends setting this value to the maximum diameter of your network, up to 16 hops (127 if you have enabled NLSP).

Maximum Number Of Path Splits   Sets the number of equal-cost paths NLSP will consider when forwarding packets. Be aware that paths set to equal cost, but with unequal speeds, may cause IPX problems due to packets arriving at "inopportune" times. In other words, don't count two paths equal in cost unless they're roughly equal in performance.

Load Balance NCP Packets To Local Clients   NetWare 4.11 allows load balancing from the server, meaning faster performance and maximized high-performance links rather than slower connections.

LSP Size   Least Sized Packet, in bytes. These can't be larger than your minimum frame size for all types of frames enabled.

More detailed IPX information is available in IPXCON, which we'll cover soon. Keep in mind that the level of configuration we have just covered is not necessary for the vast majority of networks.

Configuring RCONSOLE Parameters

IN A HURRY

10.33 Configure RCONSOLE with INETCFG

1. Type **INETCFG** from the console prompt (or RCONSOLE).
2. Choose Manage Configuration, and then choose Configure Remote Access To This Server.
3. Enable Remote Access, and provide an appropriate password.
4. Enable RCONSOLE Connection.
5. Press Escape twice to return to the main menu.

Remote access to your server means more than just RCONSOLE, although that utility is used the majority of the time. If you have Unix systems on your network, you can run RCONSOLE from any terminal that supports vt100 emulation. This is the XCONSOLE program, and the Unix protocol support is Telnet. This screen also allows you to install software from a remote server.

This utility is being expanded and/or replaced with RConsoleJ, remember, for TCP/IP clients. XCONSOLE still works, so there are several ways to communicate with and configure a NetWare server over TCP/IP.

As we did in the RCONSOLE section earlier, we must load both REMOTE.NLM and RSPX.NLM. We can also do this through INETCFG. As you can see in Figure 10.70, we have enabled remote access and provided a password. Following my instructions earlier, this password is longer than six characters and includes numeric characters as well.

FIGURE 10.70

Configuring the server side of RCONSOLE

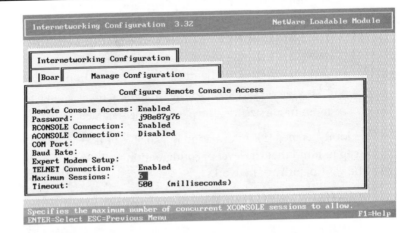

WARNING Notice that the password for RCONSOLE is not hidden here, as it is for user passwords. Just another reason to keep the server away from curious hands and eyes. Anything that can be done at the console can be done through RCONSOLE, making this a security hole you must keep plugged.

Configuring ACONSOLE Parameters

IN A HURRY

10.34 Configure ACONSOLE with INETCFG

1. Type **INETCFG** from the console prompt (or RCONSOLE).

2. Choose Manage Configuration, then Configure Remote Access To This Server.

3. Enable Remote Access and provide an appropriate password (if a password hasn't already been defined).

Continued

4. Enable ACONSOLE Connection.

5. Set the COM port, baud rate, and any Expert Modem Setup parameters, as necessary.

6. Press Escape twice to return to the main menu.

Remote access through a modem directly to the server was a great innovation in the mid-1980s but seems far less important today. For one thing, resetting the COM port when the modem locks up requires a server reboot. Managers try to minimize these reboots, but modems have a mind of their own.

Another reason this has fallen out of favor is the wide availability of remote-control software for PCs, allowing a user to remotely control a station on the network. This station can certainly run RCONSOLE, so that if the modem locks and a reboot is necessary, it happens to a workstation rather than to the server. Of course, Telnet and RconsoleJ work across the Internet, if your NetWare server can be reached through the Internet or an internal TCP/IP network.

If you need a modem connection to the server, INETCFG provides a place to set it up. You use the same screen as you do for RCONSOLE configuration. Figure 10.71 shows the new ACONSOLE information configured.

FIGURE 10.71

Multiple remote-access options to this server

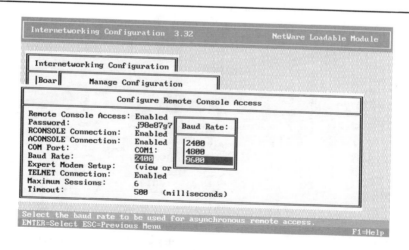

The only options for server COM ports are COM1 and COM2. The modem Baud Rate options are 2400, 4800, and 9600. (Yes, the default really is 2400; I told you this was an ancient utility.) There are patches available on Novell's Web site to speed up this connection.

PART

II

Managing the Network

The screen painting in ACONSOLE is not at all optimized, and the color palette takes longer than you would think to transmit. If you have particular modem initialization parameters to set, the Expert Modem Setup option will let you type in all you want.

Activating ACONSOLE requires RS232.NLM to be loaded in the AUTOEXEC.NCF file. This NLM controls the COM port for the modem.

Viewing Advanced IPX Statistics with IPXCON

IN A HURRY

10.35 View IPX Protocol Details with IPXCON

1. Type **IPXCON** from the console prompt (or RCONSOLE).
2. View the packet statistics on the opening screen.
3. For more details, choose IPX Information ➢ Detailed IPX Information.
4. For IPX internal router statistics, choose the Circuits, Forwarding, and Services options.
5. Press Escape to exit.

For those never satisfied with standard information, IPXCON should satiate your desire for numbers and numbers that have little value in normal networks. IPXCON, as you can see in Figure 10.72, duplicates some of the information from the MONI-TOR program, but the menu hints at so many more numbers.

FIGURE 10.72

Tracking the packets as they whiz by

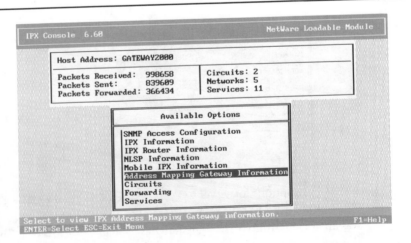

Useful functions of IPXCON include the following:

- Monitor IPX routers and network segments
- View IPX router and network segment status
- View all IPX packet paths
- Locate the IPX routers on your complete network
- Monitor remote IPX routers running NetWare IPX router software

These options aren't of much interest if you have a small network with just a few servers, all in one location. If you have a large internetwork, however, knowing details about the status and throughput of your IPX routers will become more and more important to you.

Notice the highlighted option, Address Mapping Gateway Information. Security features abound in NetWare 5.1, and this is one of them. If you have the Address Mapping Gateway enabled within INETCFG, you can check some of the details here. Hiding your internal network numbers from the outside world is one good way to increase your network's protection.

Viewing TCP/IP Statistics using TCPCON

IN A HURRY

10.36 View TCP/IP Protocol Details with TCPCON

1. Type **TCPCON** from the console prompt (or RCONSOLE).
2. View the packet statistics on the opening screen.
3. For more details, choose Statistics, and then choose the protocol of your choice.
4. Press Escape to exit.

I'm sure you knew this was coming: if NetWare 5.1 has an IPXCON, it should also have a TCPCON. And it does, but it has had TCPCON for several versions. This utility isn't new, but it is suddenly more popular.

Figure 10.73 should remind you strongly of Figure 10.72, since they both show lots of statistics and details you'll rarely if ever need when managing a network. One day, however, you'll need to check out the TCP/IP packets zooming through one of your servers, and Figure 10.73 will appear when you type TCPCON at the colon prompt.

PART

II

Managing the
Network

FIGURE 10.73

FIGURE 10.73

Tracking TCP/IP whizzing packets

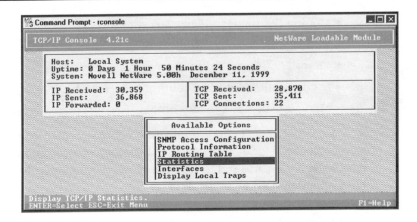

This screen shot was taken after the server had been up only two hours, as the Uptime label shows. The IPXCON screen shot came after several days of uptime, which is why the IPX packets look so much more popular. If your NetWare 5.1 network is running only IP, you may never see any activity on IPXCON. Conversely, a typical NetWare 4 network will show nothing but zeros for TCP/IP packet counts.

The IP Routing Table option, one above the highlighted bar in Figure 10.73, may actually come in handy one day. Pressing Enter twice brings up the IP routing table, where the next hop (my router for my lab network) must be configured. If the gateway is not set (that's the next hop), your TCP/IP packets may have trouble leaving the network. If you can load the PING command from a server and ping internal stations but not any of those past your router, check the Next Hop setting.

WAN Traffic Manager

The WAN (wide area network) Traffic Manager utility included with NetWare 5.1 does a wonderful job that I hope you don't have to worry about: conserving bandwidth. Like money, bandwidth is only precious to those who don't have enough. WAN Traffic Manager helps you reserve your bandwidth for data and schedule server-to-server NDS traffic for the time most convenient for you—rather than most convenient for NDS.

Of course, when everyone has T3 lines pumping 45Mbps between every branch office, bandwidth conservation won't be necessary. Just watch out that the flying pigs don't poop on your head.

Seriously, NDS is pretty efficient and won't drag your traffic to a standstill anytime. Okay, I suppose if you have 28.8K links between offices and you start a complete NDS replica reconstruction, traffic would be clobbered. But normal operations won't kill your communications.

But you don't always know when something out of the ordinary will happen, do you? Maybe you just like being in control and only want traffic to route through the servers you dictate, rather than building a typical mesh network. Then WTM (WAN Traffic Manager) is for you.

More important, this shows another area where NDS is far ahead of the pack. Policy control has been a solid foundation of NDS from the beginning, but it was called things like login time restrictions and rights to files and directories. All those things are policies, and now the buzzword police have decreed that "policy" is the name for all these things.

Starting WAN Traffic Manager (WTM)

There may be some type of auxiliary installation program for WTM, but I couldn't find it. If you miss this checkbox during installation, you can reinstall that portion or try to hack through it, as I did. I started the program the old-fashioned way, by copying files from the server installation CD-ROM disk to the server hard disk. Better for you to go through NWCONFIG and start the program properly.

When you restart NetWare Administrator, you'll see several new command buttons: Lan (sic) Area Membership, WAN Policies, and Cost. Take a look at Figure 10.74 to see these new buttons.

PART

II

Managing the
Network

FIGURE 10.74

New options for NetWare servers

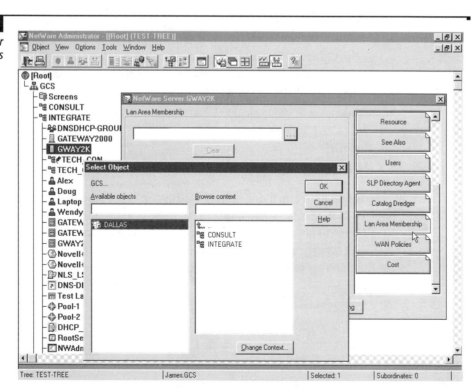

These new buttons are visible on the server detail page only until you make the server part of a LAN Area. After that, these functions are controlled through the detail page for the LAN Area itself.

What you can't see in Figure 10.74 is the long list of Predefined Policy Groups that are available (though you can peek at them if you skip ahead to Figure 10.75). Here, with a short description, are the items in the predefined policy group list. Each is also a filename, with .WMG for Wan Man Group. I prefer Blue Man Group, but they didn't ask me.

1–3A.M. Two policies are used to restrict traffic to those hours. This one requires NA, for No Address, applying to five NDS properties. 1–3A.M. by itself limits the rest of the NDS traffic to those hours. To section off all traffic to those hours, both the 1–3A.M. option and the 7A.M.–6P.M. option must be used.

7A.M.–6P.M. The companion to the 1–3A.M. option discussed above, this one is for the hours of 7:00 A.M. to 6:00 P.M.

CostLT20 Limits traffic-defined links that have a price values set of less than 20.

IPX This blocks all traffic that's not IPX.

NDSTTyps A group of variables used to define the properties passed by NDS to the Traffic Type Query.

ONoSpoof This blocks all traffic to existing WAN connections. How? It stands for, somehow, "Already Open, No Spoofing," blocking all traffic.

OpnSpoof This turns off all connections to WAN links open more than 15 minutes, figuring that those that are open that long are being spoofed rather than actually being connected.

SameArea This blocks all traffic that's local only, based on an assumed Class C TCP/IP address.

TCPIP This blocks all but TCP/IP traffic.

TimeCost Sets priority links by assigning a cost to connections over time.

Instructions are included in the Help files for those who wish to write their own policies. Not being a programmer, I get lost between IF and THEN, but if you or a friend want to get involved, the instructions are there. More than that, the Policy Editor won't save the new policy until all the syntax is checked, and it oh-so-snidely lists the line number of every mistake. Enjoy.

Setting Policies

This is, unfortunately, not a graphically dazzling section. The policies don't look particularly stunning on screen, and unless you start DSTRACE properly, you may not even know they're running.

Your NetWare Administrator program will have three new buttons now, called Servers Belonging To LAN Area, Cost, and WAN Policies. These will be just about the only command buttons on the page when you create your LAN Area.

Ah, what's that, you ask? A smart option from Novell, allowing you to set the policies for a group of servers at one time. Do your normal tricks to create an object, and notice the new LAN Area icon that appears when you start the Create process from a container or individual server. Since we're going to put a group of servers into our new LAN Area, create this LAN Area in an organization or organizational unit. In Figure 10.75, I chose to create a single LAN Area for my organization.

FIGURE 10.75

Choosing policies for your new LAN Area

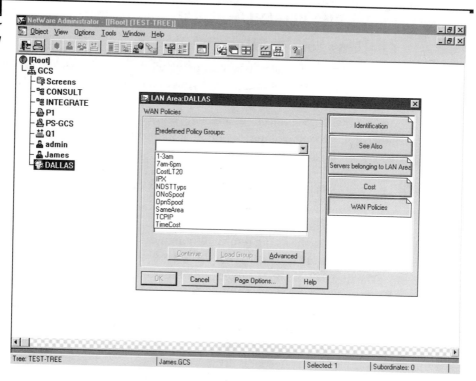

Since you've already created quite a few objects by now, I skipped over that easy part. This is the LAN Area object I created, and I've already added some servers to the list. Notice the Servers Belonging To LAN Area command button? That's the way to add servers.

In Figure 10.75, you can see the Predefined Policy Group items we discussed in the previous section. If you pick a policy, such as the 1–3A.M. policy at the top of this list, the name will appear in that top text box. What you can't see in Figure 10.75 is an informational window titled Policy Load Results that shows that the policy load operation proceeded with no errors. Since Novell created these, you shouldn't have any errors.

Yes, each policy is listed twice, the second time with NA afterwards. This stands for No Address and is necessary to make the policy valid in all circumstances. Luckily, you and I don't have to worry about this at all.

After setting a policy, it will take 24 hours for the policy to ripple out to all the servers involved. If that's too long (and I think it is, too), go to the server console and type **WANMAN REFRESH IMMEDIATE**. This reloads the policies without waiting.

Checking Your Policies

As I said, there's no real notice that these policies are working. You may put a traffic analyzer on the network and see that your traffic has dropped, but that's a lot of work.

Being rather lazy when possible, my method is to start a directory services trace and see that NDS connections are being refused. This says that the policies are working, because the refusal means potential traffic has been stopped. Ergo, less traffic on your WAN links.

Go again to the server console (in one form or another) and type **SET DSTRACE = +WANMAN**. This tells DSTRACE to show WANMAN messages. The next step is to start DSTRACE with the SCREEN ON options, so you can see the information echoed to the server console.

Figure 10.76 shows the results, although the stuff is a little hard to read at first. Take a look, and I'll explain what's going on.

The first six lines on the screen don't matter to us. There are five operations, the last of which wraps around to line six.

Ah, but lucky line seven tells us our policy is working. What looks like an error (Sync Failed To Communicate…) is really a successful policy implementation. I know this because error number 720 means "connection denied" rather than something terrible like "the coffeepot is dry."

This trace is nice and colorful, making it easy to pick out these messages. You may also send these to a trace file, but then you get just black and white again.

FIGURE 10.76

DSTRACEing your new
policy setting

```
Start state transitions for .TEST-TREE., current state 0
Finish state transitions for .TEST-TREE.
Start state transitions for .TEST-TREE., current state 0
Finish state transitions for .TEST-TREE.
Sync - Start outbound sync with (#=2, state=0, type=1 partition .P75.CONSULT.GCS
.TEST-TREE.) .TEST-TREE..
* Sync failed to communicate with server <.P75.CONSULT.GCS.TEST-TREE.>, error co
nnection denied (-728).
Sync - Start outbound sync with (#=3, state=0, type=1 partition .GWAY2K.INTEGRAT
E.GCS.TEST-TREE.) .TEST-TREE..
* Sync failed to communicate with server <.GWAY2K.INTEGRATE.GCS.TEST-TREE.>, err
or connection denied (-728).
DCFreeContext context 00000008, idHandle 00000700, connHandle ffffffff
SkulkPartition for .TEST-TREE. succeeded.
Sync - Partition .TEST-TREE. All processed = NO
Calling DSAReadEntryInfo conn:12 for client .James.GCS.TEST-TREE.
Calling DSAReadEntryInfo conn:12 for client .James.GCS.TEST-TREE.
DSAReadEntryInfo failed, no such entry (-601).
Calling DSAReadEntryInfo conn:12 for client .James.GCS.TEST-TREE.
Process IPX Watchdog on inconn = 12
DCDuplicateContext oldContext 7, newContext 8, flags 00000000
Calling DSAGetServerAddress conn:1 for client .GATEWAY2000.INTEGRATE.GCS.TEST-TR
EE.
request DSAGetServerAddress by context 8 succeeded
DCFreeContext context 00000008, idHandle 00000703, connHandle 00000001
```

We have successfully limited some of our WAN traffic by setting a policy dictating that to NDS. Let's just see if you can do this with Active Directory, now that it's shipping and people realize the problems dealing with a supposedly enterprise directory tool in a 1.0 version.

NetWare Management Portal

Here we go with one of the best new features included with NetWare 5.1: the NetWare Management Portal. Please, Novell, forget MONITOR, forget ConsoleOne (pretty please), forget RconsoleJ, and move everything under the server's management banner to NetWare Management Portal.

See Figure 10.77 for a look at the NetWare Management Portal opening browser screen.

When you have the NetWare Enterprise Web Server installed on a server, you must use the port number in the address (for example, http://204.251.122.100:8008). It won't hurt to give the port address even if the Enterprise Web Server isn't loaded, but if you forget on servers with the Web Server, you'll pull up a general screen of little use.

An opening screen that provides good information portends great value from the NetWare Management Portal. From the top of the page down, you know the application (NetWare Management Portal says the banner), the server name (PROLIANT), the NetWare version generally (5.00) and specifically (revision H), the NetWare Management Portal version (1.3), and server uptime.

FIGURE 10.77

*The new face of
NetWare management
(I hope)*

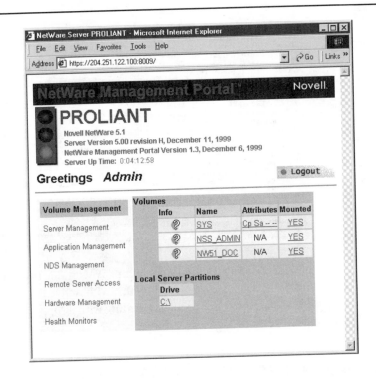

See the traffic light? A new touch, and used to great effect later. One glance tells you all is well (green light), something should be checked (yellow light), or something must be fixed (red light).

The Greetings *Admin* line comes after clicking the Login command button that sits under the traffic light at the beginning. Users without a high security clearance may view many details from the NetWare Management Portal, just as they have limited use of various NetWare utilities with earlier NetWare versions. However, once an administrator or equivalent logs in, everything inside NetWare Management Portal (from here on to be called Portal because I'm tired of typing the whole phrase) opens and awaits your command.

Novell's own literature from before the launch of NetWare 5.1 proclaimed the Portal similar in functionality to:

- NWAdmin

- ConsoleOne

- RCONSOLE (and RconsoleJ)

- NWCONFIG

- SERVMAN (the SET parameters)
- MONITOR
- Filer

There are a few things Portal can't yet do from the above list. In addition, the first version of Portal can't do the following:

- Handle alerts
- Set thresholds on reported values
- Manage NetWare 3.*x* servers
- Access the DOS partition on NetWare 4.*x* servers

The list of Nos seems to be shorter than the Yeses, so we'll assume that Portal represents a step forward in NetWare management. In fact, it's a giant step forward and a direction I implore Novell to travel in the future. For a long future.

Portal provides quite a bit of functionality, especially for a version 1.0 product. Almost all the server and volume management can be handled via Portal, lots of hardware details can be controlled via Portal, all sorts of remote access starts with Portal, and a new feature, Health Monitors, will gladden many a network administrator's heart.

Management tools are scattered through seven lucky areas inside Portal: Volume Management, Server Management, Application Management, NDS Management, Remote Server Access, Hardware Management, and Health Monitors. Let's start at the top.

Volume Management through Portal

Since Volume Management holds the top spot, Novell must believe it's the most used utility section. If it were up to me, I'd put the Health Monitors at the top, but they didn't ask me (that never stops me from telling them, however).

Notice back in Figure 10.77 that Portal gives you access to the DOS partition on the server. That can be handy at times, especially when you need to add a new management utility for safety's sake. Notice that entries in the Name, Attributes, and Mounted columns are underlined. As you'd expect, these are hyperlinks, and clicking them drills down into more details.

Figure 10.78 shows the information screen that appears when you click the question mark icon under the Info heading. Who needs to load NWAdmin to check storage statistics when this resource is only one click away?

FIGURE 10.78

*Volume SYS:
information via Portal*

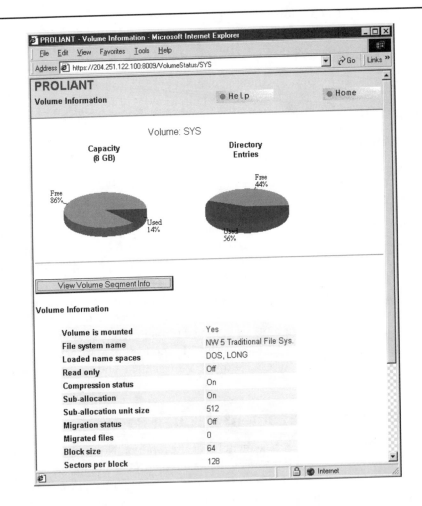

Notice the Help command button. The Help screens in Portal are more useful than most of Novell's Help screens, and Novell's screens tend to be more useful than other network vendors'. Your questions will be answered more often than not. The general background for the Help topic continues into specific details about the options on the screen.

The Help screen writers must have enjoyed the opportunity to point out what each screen in Portal replaces from other NetWare utilities. In this case, if you click the Help button, the Help screen points out that the Volume Information table shows the same information presented about the volume by MONITOR.

View Volume Segment Info looks inviting, so feel free to click that button. Then feel free to be disappointed when the information about starting and ending sectors doesn't help you all that much.

Back at the home page for Portal (Figure 10.77), notice that the items about each volume contain a hyperlink. Clicking the YES entry under the Mounted column pops up a warning message asking if you're really sure you want to dismount the SYS: volume and lose almost all server functionality. Since this YES option is a toggle, just click Cancel to avoid dismounting SYS:.

Clicking the hyperlink under the Attributes heading opens another screen with explanations about possible attributes and checkboxes showing which attributes are in effect. We'll see more about this once we drill down into the SYS: volume, as shown in Figure 10.79.

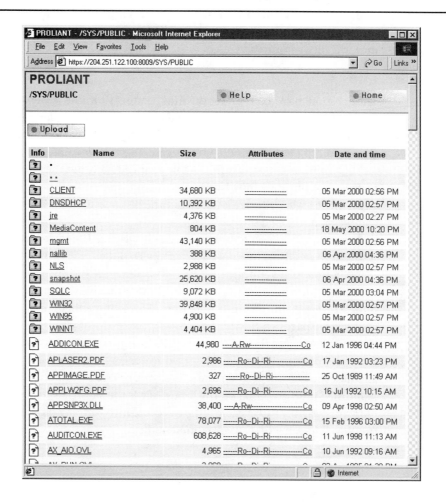

FIGURE 10.79

All /SYS/PUBLIC details on display

There are two indicators showing your location on this page. On the Address toolbar, the URL lists /SYS/PUBLIC after the port number 8009. Under the server name, Portal again provides your current location. Nice of Novell, don't you think?

In this screen's header, along with the server name and current directory location, are two command buttons. The Help button pops up the (actually helpful) Help screen. The Home button zooms you back to Portal's home screen (shown in Figure 10.77).

Click the Upload command button, and a browser screen opens so you can search for your file if you can't type the name directly into the space provided. After providing the filename one way or the other, click the Upload command line on the second screen, and away goes the file.

Downloading files are easy: click the filename, and your browser asks if you want to run the program from the current location or save the program to disk. Make your choice, click OK, and the file-copy process starts immediately.

But I'm getting ahead of myself (usually it's my wife and kids ahead of me). Let's check out the Info and Attributes headings and see what happens when you link to more detailed information.

Info

The question mark icons under the Info heading sit inside folders for a directory, inside of which are pages of paper for a file. Clicking the underlined filename triggers your browser into trying to run or download the file. Clicking the question mark fetches information about the (in this case) file, as shown in Figure 10.80.

The File Information details can't be changed here, but they do give a pretty complete look at the file. Think NetWare disk compression works? Look at the last two entries. The logical file size is 733K, but the disk space used is only 218K. Pretty good compression ratio, I'd say.

At the bottom of the screen, you may click Delete File to delete the file (go figure). If the attributes listed in Figure 10.79 show Di (Delete Inhibit), the Delete File command button won't appear.

Similarly, the Rename File command button and New Name text box won't appear if the Ri (Rename Inhibit) attribute is set. This tells me that Portal generates intelligent display pages on the fly.

When you check the information for a directory, a couple of other options appear when appropriate. When you check a directory, a note tells you whether you have any files you can salvage, rename a directory, or create a subdirectory. Handiest when ham-fisted users go postal on the Delete key is the Salvagable (sic) Files entry. I might more properly say Salvageable Files, in accordance with my dictionary, but perhaps the Novell screen writers used a different dictionary.

FIGURE 10.80

A Portal view of file information

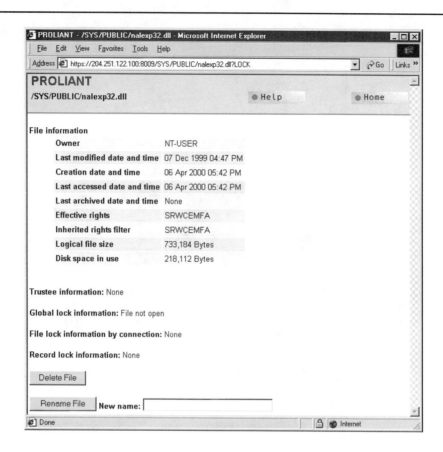

If you have some files that can be salvaged in that directory, a hyperlink saying Select For List will be shown. If you have no files available for salvage operations, there will be no hyperlink under the word None. Since I want to show you this neat function, I picked a directory with some files to salvage, and the result is shown in Figure 10.81.

Too bad you don't have a color page in this book. The Purge All Files and Purge command buttons are bright red, and the Salvage command buttons are green. Hope I don't get salvaged files for Christmas, although sometimes, a recovered file ranks at the top of a user's wish list.

Again, Novell displays your current location in two places, although the /SYS/ PUBLIC/WIN32 beneath the giant server name (PROLIANT in this case) is the most obvious and clear. The hyperlink just above the Purge All Files button goes back one screen, just as if you used the browser's Back button or the Alt+Back Arrow key combination. A Salvage All Files command button beside the Purge All Files button would be nice, but there's not one (yet?).

FIGURE 10.81

Salvage operations underway

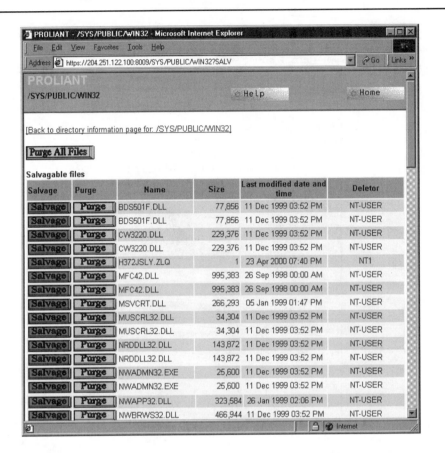

Next to the Purge buttons, you can see the Name, Size, Last Modified Date And Time, and Deletor under the appropriate headings. Deletor sounds like the name for a WWF wrestler in training, doesn't it?

Notice that Deletor for almost all the files in Figure 10.81 is NT-USER, the name my Windows NT Server system used for a time. Unfortunately, hyphenated names aren't tolerated by the Linux NetWinder server I'm also running on the network, so I changed the name to NT1. Perhaps hyphenated names should be avoided in multi-vendor networks. (See? Learn from my mistakes, and you'll be way ahead of the game).

While you can delete and rename files on their information pages, directories come with an extra option: Create Subdirectory. Under the Salvagable (sic) Files link, the command buttons are Delete Directory, Rename Directory, and Create Subdirectory. The Rename Directory and Create Subdirectory buttons offer text windows for you to provide the new names.

Is it quicker to create a subdirectory inside a DOS window with the MD (Make Directory) command? Yes, but a DOS box scares many new network managers born with a silver mouse. Acknowledging that fact, Novell makes life easier for the command-line impaired.

Attributes

Curious about attributes? Figure 10.82 shows the page created by clicking the Attribute listing for a file.

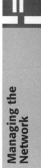

PART

II

Managing the Network

FIGURE 10.82

Attributes clearly explained and changeable

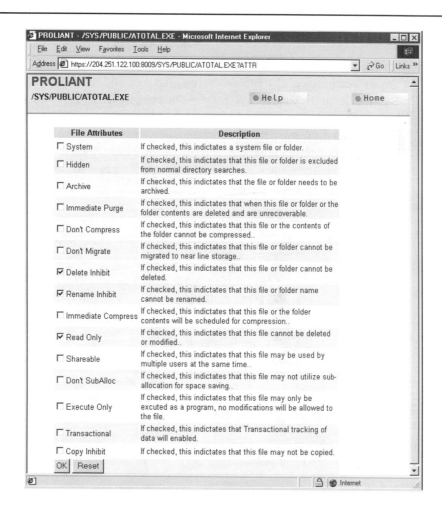

Yes, we covered directory and file attributes earlier, but this is a great page detailing attributes, their explanations, and an easy way to change them.

Check (or uncheck it, as the case may be) a box to change the corresponding attribute. Click the OK command button to make your changes. If you check or uncheck boxes carelessly, use the Reset command button to undo all your changes.

These same attribute changes are possible on the DOS files on your NetWare DOS partition. However, DOS has far fewer attributes than NetWare. Also, there's no question mark icon for file details, because DOS doesn't store those either. Since there's so little information on one screen, Novell went ahead and put a Delete hyperlink for each DOS file on the main page of the DOSDRV listing. Yes, you still have a chance to cancel the deletion if you hit your mouse button by accident.

Server Management through Portal

This Portal section contains the most options and will be the tool of choice to manage items such as SET parameters, connections, and remote console screens. You can even down the server from this page, but you still must go to the server to turn it off.

As you can see in Figure 10.83, Server Management includes eight categories, most of which get regular attention from network managers. Frankly, System Resources doesn't provide a lot of help, and the Down Server Options are used rarely (since NetWare almost never needs to reboot to incorporate new features).

FIGURE 10.83

Server Management provides many options.

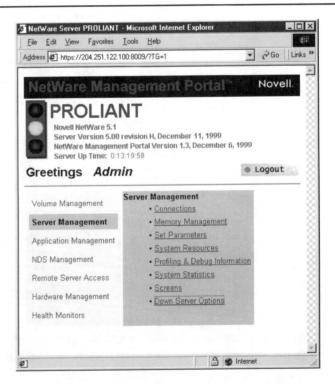

Did you like how I cleverly manipulated the server into showing a yellow light now? Too many NLMs are eating too many cache buffers—a common problem. That's why I always say you need more memory.

The eight categories and their primary uses are as follows:

Connections   Displays which users and/or processes are connected to this physical server, and shows ways to clear connections.

Memory Management   Pie graph of Current Memory Usage, along with drill-down details of NLM Memory, Swap File Size, and Virtual Memory Pages.

SET Parameters   The 16 SET parameter groups, including good help information, descriptions and ranges for each setting, and easy ways to modify parameters.

System Resources   Scores of highly technical and rarely used resource details including Alternate Debugger Handlers, Interrupt Time Call-Backs, and Processor Exception Handlers. Each has a drill-down to a list of (and details about) the NLMs involved.

Profiling & Debug Information   A dynamic listing of the Execution Profile Data By Thread, showing threads, their NLM parents, and the execution time percentage used. Additional Debug Options offers literally hundreds of debug operations to perform and complete stack listings of NLMs in those threads. These listings will excite only sophisticated developers.

System Statistics   Opens to four subheadings with more options, including Network Management Information (number of service processes, cache buffers, NLMs loaded, etc.), Kernel Statistical Information (Event Counter By CPU shown by processor), LSL Statistical Information (packets in and out, including a handy Packets Per Second Graph option), and Media Manager Statistical Information (Input/Output requests and data transfer rates).

Screens   One-click connection to echo each server console screen, except for the X console running the GUI.

Down Server Options   Big red buttons yelling Down, Restart, and Reset for server control options.

Let's take a look at two of these screens in a bit more detail. Figure 10.84 shows the Connections screen, one of the places you may visit regularly.

PART

II

Managing the
Network

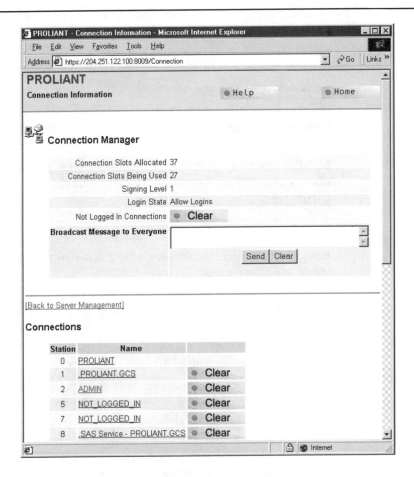

See the handy Broadcast Message To Everyone text box? It's easier than using the SEND command from the console, I promise.

Just above that text box, Not Logged In Connections offers just about the easiest way to clear these pesky non-authenticated connections that stick, barnacle-like, to every NetWare 5.*x* server. One click on the Clear command button beside Not Logged In Connections, and all clearable connections are disconnected. You may also take the time to clear connections one at a time or use the Connections section to drop connected users as necessary.

In the bottom half of the Connections screen, clicking any of the actual user names opens another sub-screen with connection details such as Login Time, Protocol Used, and Address. This sub-screen also offers a way to send a message to just that user. Any open files are listed and hyperlinked to file details. This screen shows more details (more easily) than the similar screen in MONITOR.

The first thing I do with a new server is turn off the stupid bell for alerts that beeps with every non-essential blurb to the console screen. Portal makes this easy, since the Sound Bell For Alerts parameter setting is located under the Miscellaneous setting, as shown in Figure 10.85.

FIGURE 10.85

This bell will not toll for thee.

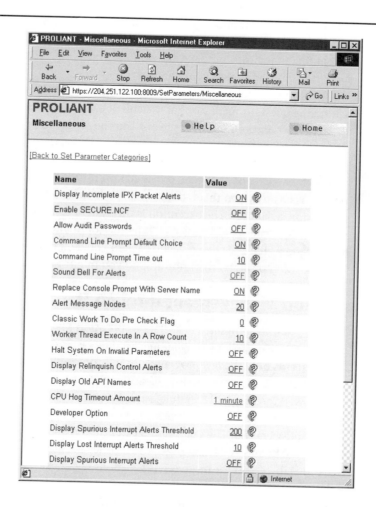

See this offending parameter in the sixth row from the top of Figure 10.85? That's the one—Sounds Bell For Alerts. You change this toggle setting by clicking the value listed (another hyperlink, of course) and making the setting fit your needs. The default for the danged bell is ON; I turn mine to OFF immediately.

The earlier SET Parameter Categories screen (Figure 10.40), where you choose Miscellaneous by choosing the eleventh entry in a list of 16, also shows where to save the settings. NetWare's default is, and should remain, SETTINGS.TXT.

The Set Parameter Categories page also has a new option in NetWare 5.1, View Hidden Set Parameters. If you thought some of the parameter settings were obscure before, turn on the hidden settings and take a look. Dozens more parameters, none of which should ever be changed in normal operations, appear out of nowhere. Take a look at them for curiosity's sake, but don't start playing with them unless a NetWare support technician directs your changes.

Also on the Miscellaneous page (back in Figure 10.85), the Help screens hide behind the question mark icons at the end of each parameter. Ranges, when appropriate, are shown in both the Help screens and the screen where the values are actually changed.

What looks like a tremendous help, the Screens option, turns out to offer less than expected. The screens only echo to the station running Portal; they can't be changed. You can keep an eye on them, but to change them, you have to fire up a remote console session separately. The exception is the System Console screen, which has a text box for single command-line input. Type the command, hit the Execute command button, and watch the changes echo back to you. Not exactly interactive or thrilling, is it? But it can be better than nothing, so you might give it a try.

Application Management through Portal

There are four headings inside Portal's Application Management section, but we're going to take a quick look only at one: Module List. Address Spaces/Memory Protection concerns only the few programs run in protected memory, and both Registry and Winsock 2.0 Management go into areas rarely if ever visited on standard networks.

Your NetWare Loadable Module list, however, can be a regular source of frustration when something goes out of whack. One bad NLM can ruin your whole day, even your whole weekend. The quicker you can find out about a troubled NLM, the better.

Figure 10.86 shows the first page of 156 loaded NLMs on PROLIANT, organized by NLM Total (bytes). As the on-screen instructions say, clicking a heading sorts by that list.

Know what strikes me? The DS.NLM, for Directory Services, now takes much more memory than the server operating system (number four on our memory hit parade). Anyone else need a graphic representation of the importance Novell now puts on NDS, perhaps even higher than NetWare?

FIGURE 10.86

The big NLM eaters of server memory

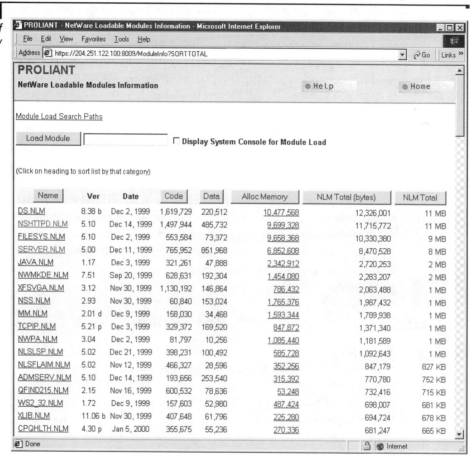

PART

II

Managing the Network

As you can see in Figure 10.86, each listing shows the NLM name (the default listing is alphabetical), followed by the version and date. These details are often critical when troubleshooting a problem, since an old NLM will ruin all your other troubleshooting. The Code and Data headings show how much of your precious server memory gets sucked up the program code versus the data controlled by the NLM. Notice that number two on the list, NSHTTPD.NLM (the NetWare Enterprise Web Server), actually includes quite a bit more data than anything except the server operating system. And this Web server has nothing installed except a little bit of test code. Allocated Memory shows the memory actually taken by the NLM to function properly.

Drilling down by clicking the name of the module pops open a new page full of interesting, if not particularly useful, information. Version number and date are on the first page, where they belong. Copyright, the address space used, and other details fill about a page of information. The only really useful info is the line listing other modules currently using the NLM in question. For NSHTTPD.NLM, the answers are WEBDAV.NLM and NHWDIR.NLM. Dependencies such as these can be helpful, and this is one good place to find those.

In case you don't want to check out AUTOEXEC.NCF to see the server search paths for NLMs, the details are here on this page. A hyperlink cleverly named Module Load Search Paths occupies the upper-left side of the page, just under the banner (see it there in Figure 10.86?).

Perhaps it's just me, but it seems that many of the drill-downs in this section of Portal die without a way back up the page list. Luckily, the Home command button always awaits on the upper-right corner of the banner. However, it does get frustrating to hit a dead end, not be able to back up, and then have to start all over again with the drilling. Especially when you know you'll just get caught again after you drill down another path. Sigh!

NDS Management with Tree Walker

Novell people often make a big deal about Tree Walker, although it sounds to me like a slang term for Tarzan. Regardless, this NDS Management option inside Portal offers a unique look at your NDS system.

Traversing NDS Tree politely tells you the screen you reach after clicking the Tree Walker hyperlink from the front screen. One list, Objects, shows active trees available to the server supporting the Portal application; in this case, the server is PROLIANT.

Click the name of an active tree, and you reach a screen showing the objects in your tree inside NWAdmin, as seen from the [Root] level. In other words, you don't see much. In my case, I can see .GCS.TEST-TREE and .Security.TEST-TREE. Check out Figure 10.87 for a look at a dull screen.

One more click shows you a list—written ungainly in full, distinguished NDS notation, including the leading periods and full context paths—of every object in the container. Containers, such as CONSULT and INTEGRATE, have little plus signs in front of them to tell you that more information is hiding inside. The same plus signs appear before License objects, so you can drill down and see individual certificates.

FIGURE 10.87

Graphical display of NDS text

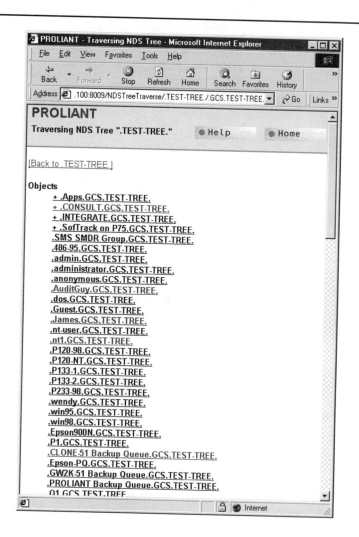

Figure 10.88 shows a wealth of obscure but never before uncovered NDS information for user .James.GCS.TEST-TREE, including all attributes and values. Nothing can be changed from here, but it's interesting nonetheless.

What you can't see below the Public Key field includes Security Equals, Surname, Last Login Time (in unusable format), and Equivalent To Me, which can be helpful. Yes, you can get some of this information through NWAdmin pages, but here it's much easier to see. It's also much easier to print: one click of the Print key, and all NDS details for an object slide out of the printer.

PART

II

Managing the
Network

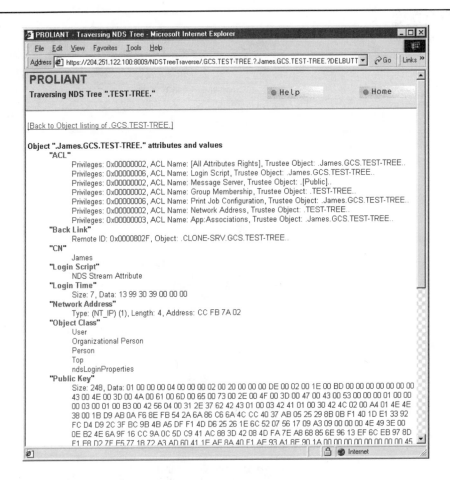

One last thing, at the bottom of the page (also not visible in Figure 10.88), is a command button, to be used almost never, that says Delete Object in black letters. My advice: don't do it, at least not through this interface. But the fact that you can delete the object here gives me hope that more of the functions from NWAdmin will find their way into a browser interface sooner rather than later.

The second option from the first screen under NDS Management is NDS Partitions. There's nothing of interest here, just a bare listing of each Partition/Replica Name stored on the host server. Not really helpful—at least, not yet.

Remote Server Access

Your Portal session anchors to one server, of course, because you start the session by giving an IP address of that server. Yet that one server communicates constantly with all other NetWare servers—and will allow you to do the same.

Two options appear when you highlight Remote Server Access on the Portal home screen: Portal Servers and NetWare Servers. Portal servers, as you might guess, are other servers running NetWare Management Portal software. The NetWare Servers option links you to other NetWare servers via the NCP (NetWare Core Protocol), even if they aren't running Portal software.

When you link to Portal Servers, the focus changes from your current server to the new server, just as if you typed the new IP address as the URL. If you haven't logged in to NDS through the Portal server yet, you may still make connections to the remote server, but you're limited in what you can see. If you have logged in, you still have to log in to the other server (yeah, I thought NDS would take care of that, too).

NCP connections to other servers are limited to file access only. You can delete and rename files, but information on attributes doesn't pass through. File upload still works, however, so that's something handy.

Hardware Management through Portal

Since Portal ties directly into an individual server, plenty of hardware details are close at hand. On the Portal home screen, click the Hardware Management menu item, and four submenus pop up: Hardware Adapters, Processor Information, Hardware Resources, and PCI Device Information.

Hardware Adapters

An advantage of tying certain information directly to hardware comes when trying to monitor that hardware. The Hardware Management section of Portal provides several nice graphs showing throughput of one kind or another, as illustrated in Figure 10.89.

PART

II

Managing the
Network

FIGURE 10.89

*A simple but useful
packet graph*

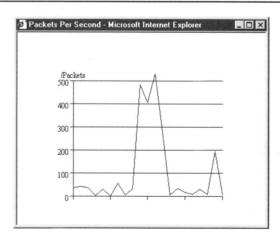

Fancy? No, but handy. To reach this point, click the Hardware Adapters link on the front page of Hardware Management, and then click the Network Statistics command button. Lots of numbers show up; a refresh rate of 10 seconds changes those numbers, and you can set the rate at 2, 5, 10, 30, or 60 seconds, or 5 minutes.

If you go back one screen from here, you can gather all types of details on installed storage and network adapters. Rather than pulling open a server and checking, you can use this screen to see which adapters are in which slots. It's quicker this way, and it doesn't take down the network. Sure, you can get most of the information through MONITOR, but this is more fun.

Processor Information

The Processor Information screen provides basic processor details. PROLIANT has dual 600MHz Pentium III XEON processors, and I see from the details that they are from Family 6, Model 7, and Stepping 3, if that helps anyone reading along. The second processor entry provides an option to stop the processor or restart it if it's already stopped. Why you would need to stop one processor I'm not sure, but if you come up with a reason, you can do it here.

Hardware Resources

Hardware Resources opens a page with five items linked to informational pages: Interrupts, Slots, Ports, DMA, and Shared Memory. You should rarely, if ever, need this information on a running server. When you have port or interrupt conflicts, you can't get the operating system running enough to get to this point and find out where the conflict resides. That's called a *Catch 22*, after the wonderful novel of the same name by the late Joseph Heller. I'll try to put it in the recommended reading list although my editors will probably delete it, but if you ever want to see how screwed up managers and bosses can really be, read that book.

PCI Device Information

For some reason, you must be logged in to the system to read the PCI Device Information pages. Seems odd to me, but many things do. You can drill down to great depths of PCI slot minutia, including the Vendor ID, Device ID, Subsystem Vendor ID, and Subsystem ID. More thrilling information of this type awaits; why it's secured, I have no idea.

Health Monitors: A Big Portal Plus

This heading should be at the top of the Portal home page, because more value hides in here than anywhere else in the Portal utility. Let me show you why immediately, in Figure 10.90.

FIGURE 10.90

*Server health sum-
mary supreme*

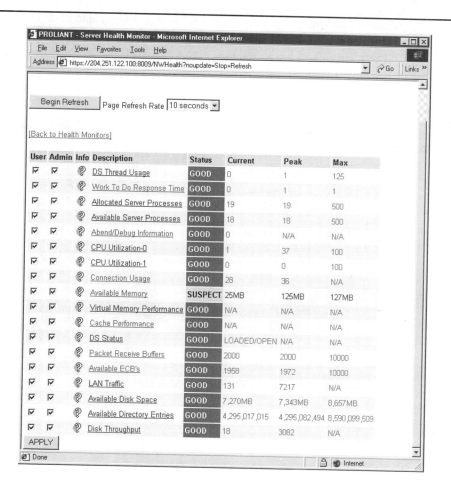

Sorry I had to roll up the screen so you can't see the banner across the top, but it looks the same as every other screenshot in this section. The important detail I needed to get is the Apply command button at the lower-left corner of the screen.

This screen may be customized to display different information to users and administrators. See the checkboxes on the left of each entry? There are two types: User and Admin. If you clear the User checkbox for an item, that item won't be displayed unless the viewer has Admin or equivalent rights. Similarly, clear the Admin box, and only the item name appears, even for administrators. I guess some people just don't appreciate good summary screens.

First troubleshooting things first: the ninth entry from the top, Available Memory, glows SUSPECT in bright yellow. (A nice contrast with the deep green of the GOOD status flags, but you probably can't see much difference in black and white.) Why does Available Memory show as SUSPECT? Because you always need more memory, as I've mentioned a few times. Figure 10.91 shows the result of clicking the Available Memory hyperlink.

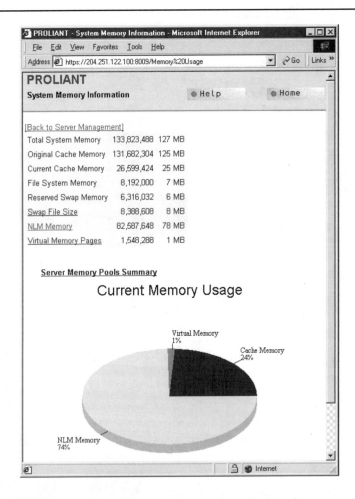

Aha! The NLMs have eaten all of my memory! No surprise there, with the Web server and other things running.

If you want to see exactly which NLMs are sucking up the memory, click the NLM Memory hyperlink. It will take you directly to the screen you saw back in Figure 10.86, so you can click a heading and sort the NLMs by memory usage if you desire.

Notice the Server Memory Pools Summary link above the pie chart? How could you miss it, right? Figure 10.92 shows what you'll see if you click it: an excellent breakdown of server memory, where it is, and how it's used.

FIGURE 10.92

Concise memory-use summary

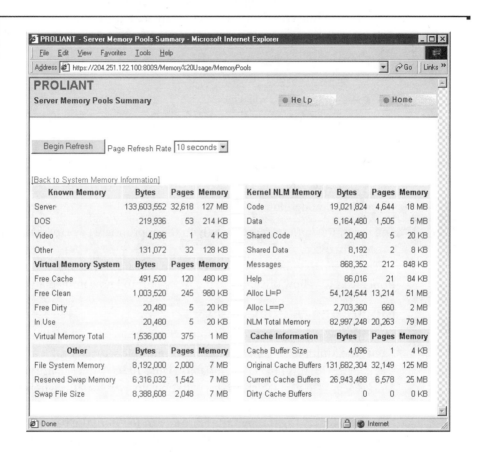

Again, notice the Begin Refresh button, with the Page Refresh Rate settings ranging from two seconds to five minutes. Unless your server dynamically handles wide load swings, the refresh option won't show you too much. But it's nice to have, just in case.

Critical information, and why PROLIANT shows as SUSPECT for memory, can be seen in the Cache Information details in the lower-right corner. The story screams out when looking at the number of original cache buffers versus current cache buffers. The reason? Just above the Cache Information heading, look at NLM Total Memory. 79MB of NLMs are too many when a server has only 128MB of RAM. Of course, you can see this on the summary screen displayed in Figure 10.91, as well.

PART

II

Managing the Network

Back on the Server Health Monitor page (Figure 10.90), each item comes equipped with a question mark icon at no extra charge. Click that and get information more valuable than usual from an online Help system.

As we did when checking out the Available Memory problem, clicking a hyperlink in the Description column takes you directly to that page or chart. Charts pop up for the following items:

- DS Thread Usage
- Allocated Server Processes
- Available Server Processes
- CPU Utilization (0 and 1)
- LAN Traffic
- Available Disk Space
- Available Directory Entries
- Disk Throughput

The rest of the options zoom directly to the appropriate page, perhaps one we've already discussed.

This screen does have value for a regular, repeated refresh rate. If something goes from green to yellow or yellow to red, you want to know immediately.

Monitoring Multiple Servers

The other option under Health Monitors is Multiple Server Monitor. True to the name, the Multiple Server Monitor shows multiple servers' health at one time.

The setup for this fun feature inhabits Figure 10.93. Rather sparse yet useful, the plan for this page is to pick which servers will show up with a traffic light beside them.

This screen shot came when I still had the wonderful Compaq ProLiant Cluster for NetWare overflowing through the lab. You can tell from the banner that the active server is SERVER1, so we can't put that into the monitoring page. I don't know why, exactly, but we can't.

Click the Select All command button to save time, unless you plan to pick and choose the displayed servers. That's fine if you want to, but I say pick 'em all.

Figure 10.94 glows green with signs of successful servers. Perhaps it's monochromatic, but that's exactly what you want.

FIGURE 10.93

Pick your servers for group display here.

FIGURE 10.94

Good servers glowing green

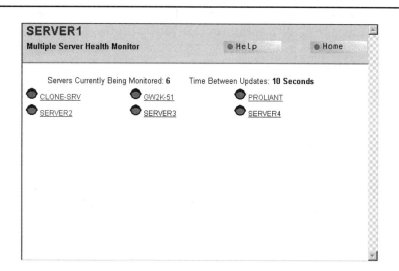

All green, all good. Click any of the hyperlinked names to go directly to the main Portal page of the server in question.

Wouldn't it be wonderful to see a server go red, drill down to the problem, fix it, then wait and laugh at the users calling to report the problem? Well, maybe you shouldn't laugh. But having a clue about the problem before your desktop auditory trouble-reporting tool (a.k.a. telephone) starts ringing and ringing will definitely make your life easier.

Thus we reach the end of our journey through the NetWare Management Portal. Cool, right? I just hope that the Novell executives start focusing their programming teams on improving Portal and letting ConsoleOne slide quietly away. Or at least push Portal to the top of the development list, ahead of ConsoleOne. Because I'm convinced, and I hope I convinced you, that Portal takes the server management prize.

NetWare Enterprise Server

Yes, here's the new Web server sitting on top of the best file server in the business. Since Web service consists of serving lots of files to many users as quickly as possible, NetWare should have a tremendous performance edge. Not to hide the light under a basket, but Novell's tests, and those administered by other firms, show that performance with NetWare and Enterprise Server far outstrips anything from Microsoft.

Under the Enterprise Server umbrella stands the NetWare News Server, NetWare Multimedia Server, and NetWare Web Search Server. There's even a link to the NetWare Management Portal on the front page of the Web Manager General Administration screen. All management goes through the NetWare Enterprise Web Server interface at the URL https://server-IP:2200 (as opposed to port 8008 for Portal).

If the Enterprise Server wasn't installed with the rest of the NetWare server, use the GUI Console Install routine to add the server. Follow these steps:

1. Put the CD-ROM holding NetWare into the server drive.

2. Mount the CD (type **CDROM** at the colon prompt), and use the file browser to select the PRODUCT.INI file that holds the details about installable products. Files will churn and copy.

3. Select the NetWare Enterprise Web Server from the list of products. If the system automatically selects other products to install along with the Web server, don't worry about it.

You're set. Files will copy, messages will come and go, and then your Web server will be ready for use.

NOTE Sorry, but I can't explain all (or even a few) of the details needed to set up and run a Web server in the space we have in this book. NetWare details take precedence over Web server details. Besides, you'll find no shortage of books on building Web servers at your bookstore, and there are a few recommendations in the Recommended Reading appendix. Instead, here I'll show you the entry points to managing your Web server from a NetWare point of view. Filling your Web server with fascinating content is up to you.

NetWare Web Manager and General Administration

Novell—or, technically, Novonyx, a joint venture between Novell and Netscape before AOL swallowed Netscape—ported the standard and comprehensive General Administration utility to NetWare. More than just running the utility on top of NetWare, Novonyx infused Netscape with NDS, making a powerful server for intranet use. No other Web server offers NetWare customers so much control over access, authentication, and content control.

The first screen for General Administration appears after authentication triggered by using a secure connection via the URL https://server-IP:2200. Figure 10.95 shows the General Administration screen, which looks the same regardless of which browser platform you use.

This utility/screen will not appear if the Web Manager is not running on your server. The NetWare Web Manager screen, an old-style C-Worthy interface screen, must be up on your server before the General Administration page will appear. If you don't need to make changes, you can unload the Web Manager to eliminate one entry point for hackers.

The Contact Novell hyperlink at the upper-left corner of the screen takes you to www.novell.com, which provides lots of nice information but no help managing your particular Web server at this time. The Help hyperlink on the upper-right corner opens a new browser window full of a complete online documentation system that's fairly helpful, although redundant in all the NDS areas.

The existing Web servers stack down the left side of the screen under the headline Servers Supporting General Administration. If you look closely, you can see which servers are ON or OFF. Click the command button under the server description you're interested in, and away you go.

Want a demonstration of NDS weaving through Web Manager? Take a look at Figure 10.96. Find this screen yourself by clicking the Users And Groups hyperlink from the banner in Web Manager General Administration.

PART

II

Managing the Network

FIGURE 10.95

*All Web management
starts here.*

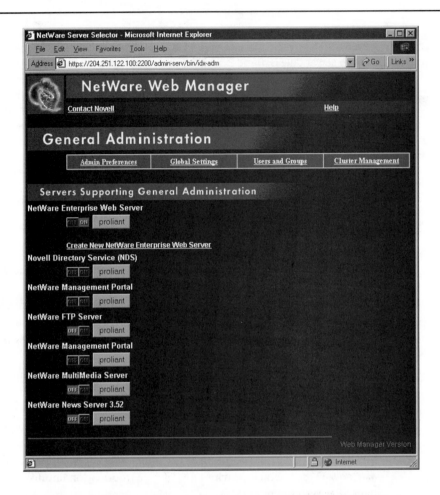

No, I'm not a fan of Web screens done predominantly black, either. A little too artsy and hard to use for my taste. Remember that when helping put up your company's Web sites.

Notice that everything you expect from NDS appears to be on the screen. Want to create a new user? Click the New User hyperlink. New Group? Find it right under New User.

You can drill down the volumes to see file lists, but you can't open a file and see the contents as you can with NWAdmin or Portal. Score another one for the Web-based administration movement.

Does all NDS information make it to the General Administration page? Not quite, as you can see in Figure 10.97.

FIGURE 10.96

Another view of NDS

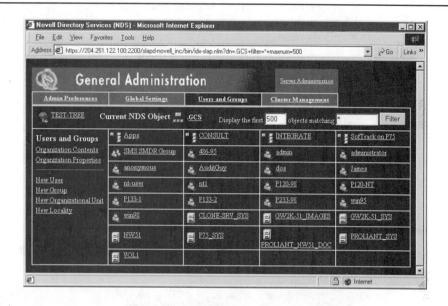

FIGURE 10.97

User administration
with a Web flair

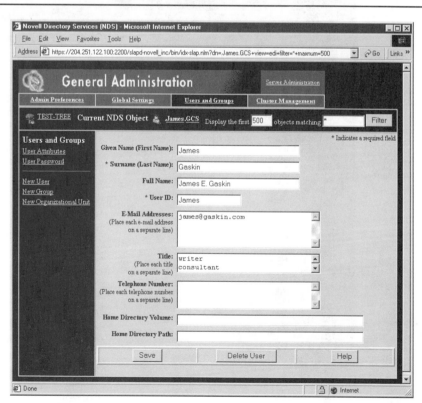

The critical new user information appears, but not full NDS details. Enough to be usable? Barely. But the Portal doesn't give enough user NDS details either, so fans of Web-based administration still yearn for satisfaction.

Interested in actual Web server control screens? From the General Administration home page, click the first command button under the Servers Supporting General Administration heading (in Figure 10.95). In this case, it's the command button marked PROLIANT under NetWare Enterprise Web Server.

OK, this is a trick, because the first screen shown is downright dull. It's the Server On/Off screen, and that's about all. Two buttons: Server On, and Server Off. Another command button for Help. A wee bit of information About This Server, if you care.

Click the View Server Settings hyperlink in the left frame. This starts the fun, as you can see in Figure 10.98.

FIGURE 10.98

Server info, Netscape style

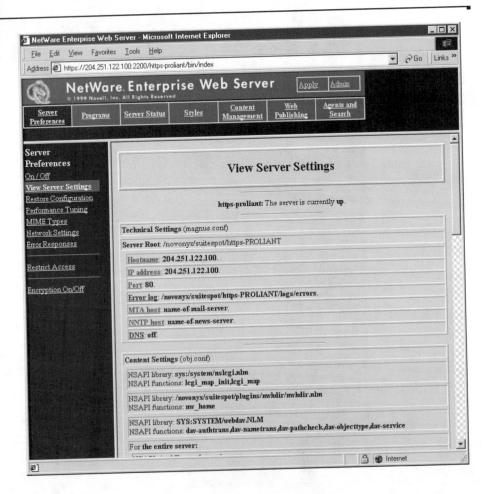

Do you understand everything they ask? MTA host? NSAPI library? NSAPI functions? Neither do I, at least not completely. My job stops when the NetWare server runs great and users don't complain (see, our job never stops). Building and configuring Web servers remains "outside my purview," according to Captain Picard.

Web Server Management from the Server Console

Interestingly enough, Novell/Novonyx also includes console controls, or at least Web server status information, on the NetWare console. The screens look just like the MONITOR screen, and they work the same way.

Figure 10.99 shows the main screen from the Web Manager on the server console. Unlike MONITOR, the top screen doesn't expand when you make it active by pressing the Tab key.

FIGURE 10.99

Old-fashioned management of a new-fangled Web server

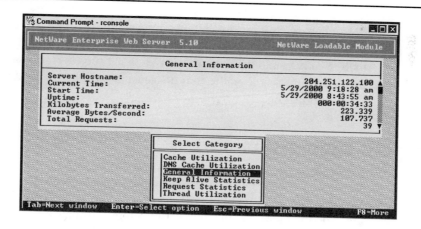

PART

II

Managing the Network

Since the Netscape General Administration page doesn't show any throughput figures for the Web server itself, this screen on the NetWare server console comes in handy. Even the information in Portal doesn't break down the Web server parts of throughput and file activity.

Handy breakdowns include the Request Statistics screen, shown in Figure 10.100. The different numbers (2xx, 3xx, etc.) are status report numbers, defined by the World Wide Web Consortium (www.w3.org). You're no doubt as familiar with the 404: Not Found message as I am and just as tired of cursing it when it appears.

FIGURE 10.100

*Quick HTTP status
information*

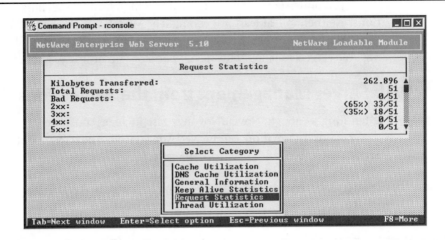

Do these screens provide as much information as a good Web site-monitoring package? Not at all. Do they help? Yes. Are they free? Yes, making them good, usable tools to carry you to the point where Web server success requires better tools to keep up with the marvelous traffic your site generates. Until then, C-Worthy yourself some status information.

Superb Supervision

You don't administer a network, you administer people. Please don't forget that fact. Your users are not computers, they are people. The network is just a tool the people use to do their jobs. I've mentioned this before, but some of you don't believe me. Let me restate: your job is to help the users.

Does this make you a doormat, subservient to every weird whim of any user? Not at all. The network is there to serve, but certain rules of conduct apply. The users on a network are similar to diners in a fine restaurant: proper dress (decorum) is necessary if the diners (users) wish to be served. Politeness is important. Tips are appreciated (yet so rarely received).

It's easy to get bogged down in the technical details of administering a network, but those details obscure the people on the network. Which do you think your boss would prefer: a network tweaked to the last bit where the users feel left out, or an acceptable network with users who feel like owners of the network?

My friend Stan has a good example of bad network management, and the moral is "keep your opinions to yourself." A user bought a flimsy (though name brand) laptop and had a problem. The tech told the customer the problem came about because the laptop was crap. The customer pointed out that the technical department approved the purchase. In fact, Stan's boss had done so. The problem did turn out to be hardware, because the laptop is the low-priced entry system and the docking station didn't work. Put yourself in that tech's shoes: did mouthing off to the user fix the problem? No. Did it make the tech look stupid, since his department approved the purchase? Yes. Is the user a friend of the network support department today? Not on your life; imagine the stories of support department stupidity swirling around the water cooler.

When you have a team of technical personnel, make sure that all the members know their place in the team and that their place makes the best use of their abilities. Don't put an irresponsible person in charge of critical backup operations. Bad things will happen sooner rather than later.

Unfortunately, you will never catch up with all that your job requires of you. It's mathematically impossible to cover every possible variable for every possible user, especially when those users want entirely different, contradictory support. Then there is the conflict between your network clients, who want everything possible to make the network faster and more fun, and your boss, who wants to spend less money.

The best chance you have to succeed in a conflict-ridden environment like this is to have your own idea of what the network should be. Your vision, if articulated to your boss and your clients, can bridge the gap between what your boss will pay for and what your clients need. If there is a vacuum, and you have no clear idea of your network, everyone will feel free to force the network into what they want. In that case, I just hope that what they want is something you can (1) provide and (2) live with comfortably.

Before I grew into computers, I worked for a manufacturer. At trade shows, people would come to the booth and ask, "Why don't you have this feature?" It would bother me, because everyone wants their product to make people happy. But I couldn't add every suggestion; the unit price would triple. We were making a low-end, entry product, not the top of the line.

Finally, I came up with a response. After a person asked about a new feature, I said, "That's a good idea. How much would you be willing to pay for that?" Most of the time, the response was the same: "Nothing." Those suggestions I disregarded. I listened to the people with ideas they were willing to pay for.

When a department begs to have a new network wrinkle, ask the same question: How much are you willing to pay for this? That weeds out most of the suggestions right there.

CHAPTER <u>11</u>

Providing Applications for Your Network Clients

As much fun as network utilities are, sometimes you must provide applications for your network clients. Your network might need to support a single multiuser application for all the users or many applications for every user. The normal case, fortunately, is for most users to share the core applications. Specific projects will require different software, but most of your users will need access to the same programs.

Some might go so far as to suggest that providing applications is the primary reason for the network. I think that is a bit shortsighted, since I prefer to believe the network is sharing information rather than just programs. But trying to follow the paths of applications begetting information begetting sharing the information begetting using the information in new applications can make you dizzy. Suffice it to say that applications are bound into everything that happens on the network.

Applications have changed over the years, but not enough. Early PC applications were hard-pressed to do a good job supporting a single user on a dual-floppy PC or single hard drive. Each printer was tied directly to the computer. The need for multiple configuration files, remote printer control, dispersed applications, and data directories never arose.

Today, even the smallest freeware program must understand how to install to remote server hard disks and run with separate data and applications directories. If it does not, we throw it away in disgust. Shareware programs routinely support multiple print queues, shared files, and NetWare-controlled record locking. It looks like the application software developers are far ahead of the network.

As if this were not enough, now the new wave of client/server applications is upon us: Web server systems. Fortunately, Novell and AOL/Netscape have teamed up to provide the Netscape-based NetWare Enterprise Web Server for NetWare 5.1. Although you may currently have another type of Web server on your network, you should install the Enterprise Web Server and become familiar with its advantages. As users who are shuffled off to Web applications start realizing how slow other Web servers are, they will begin demanding NetWare-level performance.

 TIP For more information on the Netscape-based NetWare Enterprise Web Server for NetWare 5.1, see Chapter 14.

Application Categories

Novell's former application group (now the Corel WordPerfect Suite) divided applications into three categories:

- Network-aware
- Network-enabled
- Network-integrated

Network-aware applications are programs that can run on the network, but that do not use any special network features. They cannot use messaging or other communication options.

Network-enabled applications are programs that run well on the network, but that use proprietary solutions for services such as messaging and user authorization. These application services, such as the user database in an e-mail program, cannot be shared with other applications. This approach is wasteful because it adds extra cost to each program, because services aren't shared (often even between applications by the same company), and because the cost of managing all these different systems is high. Do you want to add a new user to the network database, then to the e-mail, scheduling, and database user lists?

Network-integrated applications are excellent choices for today's network. They do not have the shortcomings of network-aware or network-enabled applications. They provide good communication and collaboration features. Also, they are well integrated into the advanced services of the network operating system, such as the NDS directory database. This makes them easier to manage, keeping down the cost of ownership.

 NOTE This is a long way from some applications available in the mid-1980s, which I called *network-hostile*. They hard-coded drive C: into the installation program. Almost as bad were the programs stored on the server hard disk that required a single-license floppy at the workstation to start but were sold as multiuser. Does that make sense? This evolution of applications compares to the leap in medicine from leeches to antibiotics.

Unfortunately, almost all PC LAN applications are stuck in level two, network-enabled. We can't really blame the software developers, however. The tool they need to share communication channels and the user database is, in fact, a better user database. NDS provides a strong global directory with extensions available for developers. Now the smart developers are moving to take advantage of these features with applications that are integrated into the network.

A good example of network-enabled control is the ability for software to store the bulk of the application on a server, requiring minimum disk space on the workstation. Keeping individual configuration files for the software on the individual workstation is acceptable, but it's better to keep configuration files on the server. Having them under control on the server allows the network administrator to change and update those files quickly and easily. Keeping them on the server also helps protect them from user mistakes. Microsoft, for example, doesn't like this, but does provide this capability with most of their products.

Beyond the three levels defined by WordPerfect years ago, we must add a new term: *collaborative software*. Many examples abound on the Internet, such as group calendars, scheduling software, and discussion forums. Each of these products runs perfectly well within a local network and local Web server. Third-party products appear every day, such as the Linux-based NetWinder from Rebel.com, an Internet appliance providing collaboration, Web and e-mail servers, and at least 6GB of storage in a cute package the size of a hardback book. You can also run these products directly on NetWare servers, as we'll see in later chapters.

On the Server or on the Workstation?

One of the important decisions you will make when deploying your network is where to store the application programs. When I first started installing Novell LANs, in a fit of network enthusiasm, I would install every application I could on the file server's hard disk. This was in the days when I was lucky if a workstation even had a local hard disk. If it did have a local hard disk, it was 10 or 20MB. Of course, WordPerfect 5 could also be installed in less than 1MB of disk space.

The debate has raged on over the last 10 years. Where do we install the networked applications? A lot has changed. Applications have become more network-savvy. The cost of hard disk space for workstations has dropped (and continues to drop) rapidly. Tools have become available to allow you to more easily manage applications installed on a local hard disk.

I continued to come down on the server-based application side of things. They were centrally located, easier to manage, easier to license, and users could not delete something off the server. Recently though, Novell has begun their Zero Effort Networks initiative that they call ZENworks. ZENworks has made me reconsider my position on the location of shared applications. When you read about it, I think it will make you revisit this issue as well.

What Is an Application Server?

The term *application server* means different things to different people. Many people use the term to designate the NetWare server that stores all their end-user applications such as Microsoft Office, Netscape, GroupWise, and so on. When a server is used to store shared applications, I still call it a file server but refer to the applications as *server-based applications*.

Others, myself included, use the term *application server* to indicate a file server or other computer that is providing the server component of a client/server application. For example, if you installed Oracle 8i on your NetWare server, that server would become an application server.

Zero Effort Networks (ZENworks)

Network administrators today face the challenge of coping with the growth of their workgroups and with the increasing complexity of desktop Windows systems. Novell's answer to this challenge? ZENworks (yeah, I know it used to be Z.E.N.works, but Novell changed it). The ZENworks Starter Pack is a NetWare 5.1 feature that I am excited about. I know many network administrators and help desk people whose daily routines are going to change dramatically due to ZENworks. Perhaps yours will, too.

As excited as I am about ZENworks, I am also faced with a dilemma. When I began writing about ZENworks, I realized I could easily fill up several hundred pages of information about it as well as nifty examples, tips, and suggestions. To keep you from getting a strained back, this book just can't get much bigger. I want to give you an idea of what the ZENworks product can do for you and point you to references that will get you started, but this is by no means a complete ZENworks reference. Who knows, maybe I will write an entire book about it some day.

 TIP   This chapter includes a basic overview of ZENworks. For more information, including some excellent white papers and "How to" guides, see Novell's ZENworks home page at www.zenworks.com.

Basic ZENworks includes functionality of two earlier Novell products: Workstation Manager and the NetWare Application Launcher (NAL). Workstation Manager lets you track workstations on your network, and the NetWare Application Launcher lets you assign program icons to users or groups and place them on those users' desktops. Further, it takes advantage of built-in capabilities of Windows 95/98/NT/2000 called *policies*. Windows administrators would have to create a *policy file* using the System Policy Editor; ZENworks incorporates this functionality into the Novell Directory Services (NDS) database (a much more manageable and secure spot).

ZENworks takes advantage of the power of NDS to centralize desktop configurations so that network administrators can keep track of their users' desktop setups and application needs and so that they can distribute, configure, and update software without visiting each workstation. User details such as printers and printer drivers, applications, and desktop configurations (screen background, screen savers, startup applications) are linked to the user in NDS, so they are portable. User and workstation details are enforced through Application and Workstation policy objects.

 TIP ZENworks administration tools are actually snap-in tools in NetWare Administrator; thus you are already familiar with the user interface for managing ZENworks objects.

Locality-specific information such as preferred server, printers, and context are stored in NDS to configure workstations dynamically when a user logs on and selects a location. This means that users can log on to any computer on the network and view the same interface they are accustomed to in their own offices. If a user on a WAN based in Chicago travels to New York and logs on to the network, the server will recognize her by her login, setting up the same access rights she had in Chicago and making locale-specific adjustments such as New York's servers and printers.

Remote access configurations can be saved in NDS, as well. You can update client configurations by scheduling a distribution with ZENworks that is activated at a certain date and time when the workstation logs on to the network.

ZENworks also maintains a hardware inventory of each PC, which is updated whenever the computer is connected to the network. This includes:

- Desktop OS version
- Workstation RAM
- Hard drive capacity
- I/O ports, DMA, IRQs
- Services and peripheral devices (printers, scanners, modems)

Don't Touch That!

ZENworks policy packages allow administrators to control users' desktops, preferences, and workstation settings. Furthermore, the administrator can turn off features of Windows 95/98 or Windows NT that can be a security risk, such as the ability to run programs from the Start menu, to access My Computer or Network Neighborhood, and other such features.

These policies are similar (sometimes exactly the same) as policies that are provided with Windows NT/2000 and Windows 95/98 for use with the Microsoft System Policy editor, but Novell has instilled a lot more versatility and punch in the ZENworks policies.

These policies basically modify the Local Computer and Local User portions of the computer's Registry. If you have ever attempted to use the Windows 95/98 or Windows NT/2000 Registry editors, you will appreciate the improvement to these policies.

Everybody Say "Cheese"!

The snAppShot utility is installed with the ZENworks Starter Kit. In a nutshell, it allows you to take a "picture" of a system prior to installing a new application and after the application is installed. It records any differences such as Registry changes, changes to .INI files, as well as new files that have been copied to the system.

You can then place this application in the NetWare Application Launcher. The first time an authorized user attempts to use the application, it automatically installs on that user's desktop.

Physician, Heal Thyself!

We have all seen this problem. An end user thinks he can tweak his own settings. He edits an .INI file, modifies a value in the Registry, or even deletes a file. Then his application no longer works. He calls you and whines, "Why has my program stopped working? What did *you* do to it? My boss says this needs to be fixed immediately!"

Can you tell I have had this happen to me a few times? No, I'm not bitter or sarcastic.

If you have used the ZENworks snAppShot utility to install your applications, if the application is configured with the NetWare Application Launcher desktop, and if Auto Verify is enabled, the application will automatically be verified and rebuilt if there are problems.

PART

II

Managing the
Network

The Two Flavors of ZENworks

ZENworks comes in two flavors:

- The ZENworks Starter Pack
- The full version

The NetWare 5.1 Client CD includes the ZENworks Starter Pack, which offers the following features:

- Software can be distributed, maintained, updated, and repaired automatically, even if the applications are stored on a workstation's local hard disk.
- It automatically runs applications for a user when that user logs in or schedules programs to run at specified times.
- Program items can be placed on a user's desktop, Start menu, or system tray or in the Novell Application Launcher menu.
- It allows users' desktop profiles and configuration information to be stored on a server and therefore accessible from any computer on the network.
- It centrally enforces restrictions on users, such as not allowing users to view Network Neighborhood, removing the Run option from the Start menu, or restricting a user's ability to access certain drive letters.

The full version of ZENworks is available from your reseller or systems integrator, and in addition to the above features, it:

- Provides users with a help request application
- Includes remote-control capabilities
- Allows NDS to be used to track workstation hardware inventory

Shaping Up NDS for ZENworks

ZENworks will only adequately meet your needs if your Novell Directory Services (NDS) design is solid. If you have not already spent some time thinking through your NDS design, you should do so before deploying ZENworks. A well-designed NDS structure is one of the primary elements of a successful NetWare network. For more information on NDS and NDS design, see Chapters 3, 4, and 10.

 TIP When you install ZENworks, you are going to be adding several new objects to the NDS database and new properties to many existing objects. This will increase the size and complexity of the NDS database.

For the sake of review, let me say that you should focus your NDS design efforts on three areas:

- Replicas
- Partitions
- The tree as a whole

Of course, larger NDS designs require faster server hardware, more server RAM, and more available bandwidth between servers.

Here are some guidelines for working with NDS replicas (depending on hardware):

- Have three replicas for any given partition of the tree.
- Allow no more than 15 to 35 child partitions per parent.
- Avoid lots of replication across a wide area network.
- Have a single server contain no more than 10 to 20 replicas.

Here are some guidelines for working with partitions:

- Create partitions based on geographic areas.
- Allow partitions to contain no more than 1000 to 3500 objects.
- Do not allow partitions to span your wide area network unless you have plenty of available bandwidth.

And finally, here are some guidelines for good NDS tree design:

- Build the top of the NDS tree based on your wide area network infrastructure.
- Design the lower parts of your NDS tree based on organizational or departmental needs.

The main limiting factors you face when designing a larger, complex NDS tree structure include the power of your server hardware (RAM and CPU speed), the number of replicas, the size of each replica, the number of objects in each replica, the speed of LAN and WAN links between servers that have replicas, and how often the NDS data changes.

NOTE For a complete discussion on preparing your NDS for ZENworks, see the "Designing NDS for ZENworks" white paper on Novell's ZENworks Web site at www.zenworks.com.

Installing the ZENworks Starter Pack

11.1 Install ZENworks

1. From the NetWare 5.1 Client CD-ROM, let AutoRun do its thing, or run the \WINSETUP program from the CD-ROM.
2. Click ZENworks, and then answer Yes to the license agreement.
3. Select the Typical Install type.
4. Select the Tree and NetWare servers on which to install ZENworks, and then click Next.
5. Click Next to confirm the installation settings.
6. Click Finish to complete the setup.

ZENworks is installed from a client and needs to be installed only once for each NDS directory tree. The NDS software is located on the NetWare 5.1 Client software CD-ROM. When you insert this CD-ROM, it should auto-play and display the ZENworks Starter Pack and Clients menu. That's where the screen in Figure 11.1 came from.

FIGURE 11.1

Menu, with a side of sales pitch

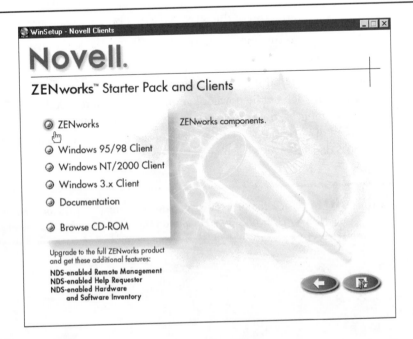

If the CD-ROM does not auto-play or if you are installing across the network, from the CD-ROM drive, run \WINSETUP from the root of the CD. Notice that the installation screen uses the Pointing Finger, just like a Web page. You can't see Novell's intelligent installation on this screen, unfortunately. The cursor changes only when run over ZENworks, Windows NT/2000 Client (this shot came from the GW2K-NT station), Documentation, or Browse CD-ROM. WINSETUP knows which system this runs on and won't let you install the wrong client.

I clicked ZENworks, which led me to a page of Starter Pack Components. Number one on the list was Install Starter Pack, which I clicked. After warning me to quit other Windows tasks, and asking me to confirm the license agreement, with an extra screen warning me that the Starter Pack contains only a subset of the full ZENworks package, the system finally offered the installation screen.

ZENworks offers three installation types: Typical, Compact, and Custom. Being the curious type, I always choose Custom.

The first screen you see after choosing Custom asks you to select the products you want to install, and I chose everything. There's more disk space on the Compaq ProLiant server than I can ever fill, so why not load them all, as in Figure 11.2?

PART

II

FIGURE 11.2

*Loading everything
for ZENworks*

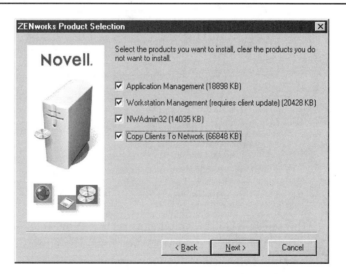

Managing the
Network

You can choose from the following:

- The Application Management (snAppShot) software
- The Workstation Management software

- The 32-bit NetWare Administrator program

- The NetWare 5.1 client software for future download

I recommend checking all these; I especially like to keep a copy of the client software on the server.

 TIP To use the Desktop Management software, the clients must have updated NetWare client software.

Select your components and click Next to display the Part Selection screen. Novell again asks you to select which parts you want to install, but in this case "everything" means some different things. In Figure 11.3, I said yes to everything.

FIGURE 11.3

Again, choosing everything

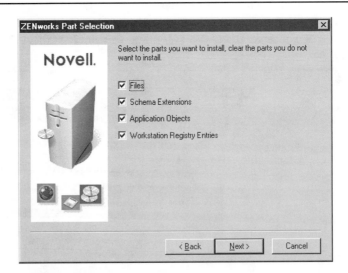

This screen includes components such as the general files, schema extensions, application objects, and the workstation Registry entries. I recommend leaving all these options checked. Do you know whether you need the workstation entries? I'll bet you do.

Now, click Next to display a list of NDS trees and NetWare server names on which to install the software. Choose from any or all servers to host the ZENworks software. For now, I just loaded ZENworks to the ProLiant server.

The next screen asks for the languages you want to install, then checks out the network, the space on the designated server, and the NDS schema. Once satisfied, ZENworks displays a summary of the software and objects that are about to be installed. Click Next again to begin the installation; files are copied, and the NDS schema is extended.

My copy procedure seemed fraught with delay after I told the warning dialog to copy over the read-only files it found. Then the process slowed to a crawl, with intermittent bursts of speed. Anyway, after the files are copied, you'll see a screen similar to the one in Figure 11.4.

FIGURE 11.4

Setting up rights for users to register workstations

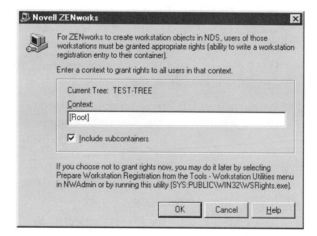

In order for workstations to be registered automatically, the user logging in at the workstation must be given the right to read and write workstation objects. This utility starts at [Root] (or whatever context you specify) and grants this permission. If you skip this step, you can always run this utility later.

TIP If you add new containers to NDS after installing ZENworks, run the WSRIGHTS.EXE utility again so that users are assigned the appropriate rights to the new containers.

If all goes well, a message appears telling you that all went well and that Workstation Auto-Registration rights were successfully set up. Finally, you are given the option of viewing the README.TXT file and the ZENworks setup log.

PART

II

Managing the
Network

Oops, not finally—there's one more step. A Congratulations dialog box appears to remind you to update the client software on all workstations.

New NDS Objects and Object Properties

Once ZENworks is installed, you will notice several new classes of objects that you can create using NetWare Administrator:

Application   Is used for setting up applications that will be used or installed through the NetWare Application Launcher.

Application Folder   Provides a way to organize applications that are presented to users through the NetWare Application Launcher.

Policy Package   Provides several types of policies, including Windows 3.1, Windows 95/98, and Windows NT user and workstation policies, and a Container Policy that controls the search policy for a particular container.

Workstation   Identifies workstations that have been registered and that the administrator has imported into NDS.

Workstation Group   Can be used to group together workstations for a common purpose such as to distribute applications or apply policies.

In addition to these new classes of objects, several existing objects have some new property pages associated with them. If you check the property page for the Organization or Organizational Unit objects, you will see six new property pages that are used by ZENworks, clipped out of their main window in Figure 11.5 for easier viewing:

Associated Policy Packages   Affect all users and workstations in this container.

Applications   Are programs that are set up for all users in this particular container.

Launcher Configuration   Lets the administrator customize the NetWare Application Launcher configuration for all users in this container.

Workstation Registration   Contains a list of all workstations that have been registered but have not yet been imported into NDS.

Workstation Tracking   Provides a property page for tracking moved or renamed workstations.

Workstation Filter   Allows the administrator to place restrictions on which workstations can be imported based on their IPX or IP addresses.

FIGURE 11.5

New pages for
containers in
NWAdmin32

The NDS Group object also has two new property pages associated with it. Figure 11.6 shows these two new page buttons, again separated from their encompassing window.

Associated Policy Packages   Allows the administrator to specify policy packages that affect members of this group.

Applications   Allows the administrator to assign applications only for members of this specific group.

FIGURE 11.6

New packages for
groups added by
ZENworks

Finally, the NDS User object has five new property pages associated with it. Aren't you glad all the page buttons in Figure 11.7 and the others are added to NDS automatically, rather than by hand?

Associated Policy Packages   Specifies which policy packages have been assigned to this particular user. A user can only have one Windows 3.x, Windows 95/98, and Windows NT package associated with it.

Effective Policies   This is my favorite property page. This page allows you to calculate this particular user's effective policies. For more information, see the "Viewing Effective Policies" section later in this chapter.

Applications   Allows you to assign applications to a specific user.

Launcher Configuration Allows you to customize the launcher configuration for a specific user.

Associated Workstations Allows you to associate user objects with a specific workstation.

FIGURE 11.7

Five new NDS user property pages, thanks to ZENworks

Creating Policy Packages

IN A HURRY

11.2 Create a New Policy Package

1. Using NetWare Administrator, highlight the container in which you want the policy to appear.
2. Press Insert, select policy package, and click OK.
3. Select the policy package type.
4. Enter the name for the policy package.
5. Check the type of policy to create.
6. Click the Details command button and set the policy details.
7. Click OK.

When you create a new policy package in NetWare Administrator, the Policy Package Wizard lets you select from seven types of policy packages (see Figure 11.8).

FIGURE 11.8

The available policy
packages

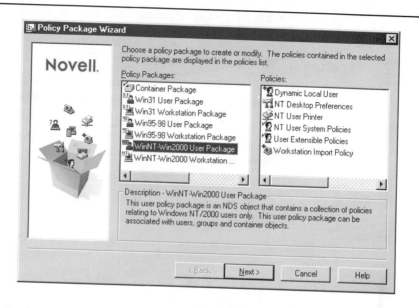

Each of these policy packages serves a specific purpose:

Container Package   Allows you to control the search order that sets the effective policies.

Win31 User Package   Sets policies for users working at Windows 3.1 workstations.

Win31 Workstation Package   Sets policies for Windows 3.1 workstations.

Win95-98 User Package   Sets policies for users working on Windows 95/98 workstations.

Win95-98 Workstation Package   Sets policies for Windows 95/98 workstations.

WinNT-Win2000 User Package   Sets policies for users working on Windows NT Workstation 4.

WinNT-Win2000 Workstation Package   Sets policies for Windows NT Workstation 4.

I could discuss the subtle nuances of each of these policy packages for dozens of pages, but that would probably not give you the specific information you need. So instead, I am going to walk you through creating a policy package for a Windows NT Workstation 4 user and a Windows NT Workstation. I hope this overview will give you enough information and an understanding of policy packages so that you can find the policy information you need.

Creating a Windows NT User Policy Package

First, let's create a simple Windows NT user policy that will be enforced when a user or users log in to a Windows NT Workstation. Follow these steps in the Policy Package Wizard:

1. Using NetWare Administrator, highlight the container in which you want the policy to be contained.

2. Press the Insert key or right-click the container and choose Create.

3. Choose Policy Package from the List object classes.

4. From the Policy Packages list, select WinNT-Win2000 User Package.

5. Enter a name for your policy package, such as **DESIGN Engineers WinNT Policy Package**.

6. Check one of the policies, then click the Details button.

7. Check Enable Dynamic Local User, then click Create.

Congratulations! You have just created your first policy package. It should appear similar to the one in Figure 11.9. All the policies in this package are disabled by default.

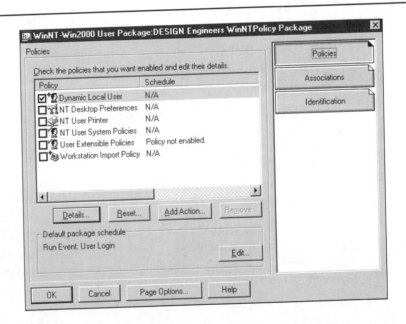

FIGURE 11.9

Windows NT user policies supported by the WinNT-Win2000 User Package

NetWare 5.0 with the earlier version of ZENworks showed the Policies screen separately from the Policy Packages screen. NetWare 5.1 and ZENworks 2.0 combine them in the cute screen shown back in Figure 11.8.

The screen in Figure 11.9 contains six policies. The penultimate policy, User Extensible Polices, which is not yet enabled, is the new one in ZENworks 2.0.

Creating a Local Windows NT Workstation User Account

IN A HURRY

11.3 Automatically Create a Local Windows NT Workstation User Account

1. Using NetWare Administrator, highlight the policy package that contains the NT User System Policy you want to modify.
2. Right-click the policy package, and then click the Details button.
3. Select the Dynamic Local User policy, and click the Details button.
4. Click the Enable Dynamic Local User checkbox.
5. Click OK.

To work with the Dynamic Local User policy, enable the policy by clicking its checkbox, and then click the Details button to open the Dynamic Local User dialog box, as shown in Figure 11.10.

The Dynamic Local User options allow a local user account to be created in the local Windows NT Workstation accounts database. If the Volatile User option is checked, the user account is removed when the user logs out. Many administrators like the idea of having local user accounts on the machines that they use most often. This allows them to log in locally if the network is not available.

On the bottom of the screen, you can specify the Windows NT Workstation local groups that the user will be made a member of when the account is created. Selecting the Custom button allows you to create specialized local groups on the Windows NT Workstation that have specific Windows NT user rights.

I like the idea of doing this even if it is just for the purpose of creating a local group that can do nothing but change the system time. By default, Windows NT Workstation users can't even change the time on their system. This is easily fixed using a Custom group configuration with the Windows NT User right called Change the System Time.

PART

II

Managing the Network

The Dynamic Local User options for the WinNT-Win2000 User Package

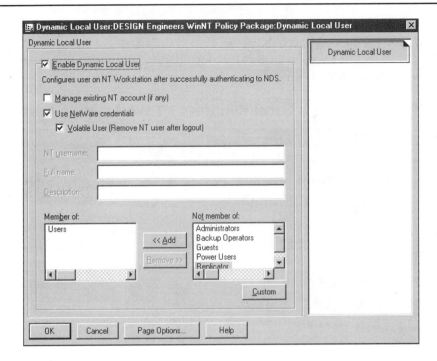

Using NT Desktop Preferences

IN A HURRY

11.4 Assign a Wallpaper through the NT Desktop Preferences Policy

1. Using NetWare Administrator, highlight the policy package that contains the NT User System Policy you want to modify.

2. Right-click the policy package, and then click the Details button.

3. Select the NT Desktop Preferences policy, and click the Details button.

4. Click the Display icon.

5. Click the Wallpaper checkbox.

6. Enter a path and filename for the .BMP file you want to use.

7. Click OK twice.

The NT Desktop Preferences policy allows you to set the preferences shown in Figure 11.11:

- Accessibility Options
- Console (Command Prompt)
- Display
- Keyboard
- Mouse
- Sounds

My favorite is Display. From within this choice, I can control the user's wallpaper, screen saver, and color scheme. Now I can play "network dictator." Do this if you're lonely and want some phone calls.

PART

II

Managing the
Network

FIGURE 11. 11

*NT Desktop
Preferences found in
the WinNT-Win2000
User Package*

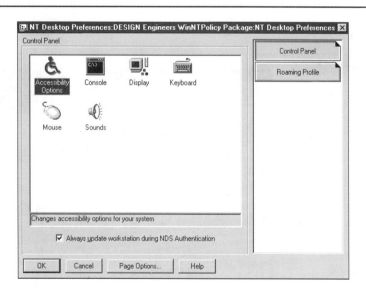

Assigning Roaming (Server-Based) Profiles

IN A HURRY

11.5 Assign Roaming Profiles to a User's Home Directory

1. Using NetWare Administrator, highlight the policy package that contains the NT User System Policy you want to modify.

2. Right-click the policy package, and then click the Details button.

Continued

IN A HURRY CONTINUED

3. Select the NT Desktop Preferences policy, and click the Details button.

4. Select the Roaming Profile property page.

5. Click the Roaming Profiles checkbox.

6. Click the Enable Storage of Roaming Profiles checkbox.

7. Click Store User Profile In User Home Directory.

8. Click OK twice.

The Roaming Profile property page (see Figure 11.12) of the NT Desktop Preferences policy allows you to specify a path for the Windows NT roaming (server-based) profile. You can specify whether the profile information is stored in the user's home directory or in some other directory located on a NetWare file server.

FIGURE 11.12

The Roaming Profile property page

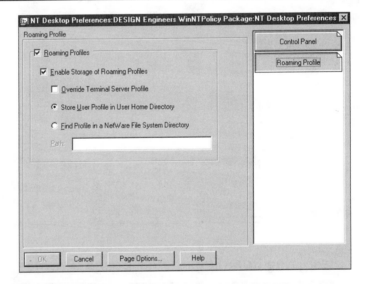

The advantage of roaming (server-based) profiles is that the user gets the same configuration, preferences, and settings regardless of the machine being used. The profile contains the user's desktop and application preferences.

 NOTE Windows NT Workstation roaming profiles and Windows 95/98 roaming profiles are not interchangeable. If you have users who work on both operating systems, they need separate roaming profiles.

Setting NT User Printer Policy

IN A HURRY

11.6 Assign a Printer to a User Policy

1. Using NetWare Administrator, highlight the policy package that contains the NT User System Policy you want to modify.
2. Right-click the policy package, and then click the Details button.
3. Select the NT User Printer policy, and click the Details button.
4. Click the Add button.
5. Browse the NDS directory for the printer you want to assign, select it, and click OK.
6. Click OK twice again.

Figure 11.13 shows the NT User Printer options. From here, you can assign the user-specific printers. Click the NetWare Settings button to specify NetWare printing options such as banner, form feed, hold, and so on.

FIGURE 11.13

NT User Printer policy information

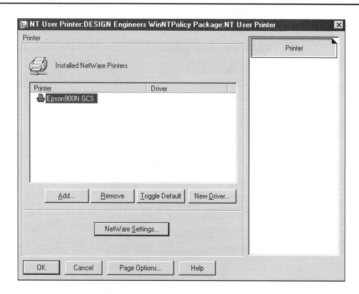

Setting NT User System Policies

IN A HURRY

11.7 Restrict the Run Command from the Start Menu on Windows NT Computers

1. Using NetWare Administrator, highlight the policy package that contains the NT User System policy you want to modify.

2. Right-click the policy package, and then click the Details button.

3. Select NT User System Policies, and choose Details.

4. Choose Shell ➤ Restrictions.

5. Check Remove Run Command From Start Menu.

6. Click the OK button twice.

One of the more powerful components is the NT User System Policies. If you have worked with the Windows NT System Policy Editor in the past, you will recognize these policies. Figure 11.14 shows two policies that were enabled for this policy package.

FIGURE 11.14

NT User System Policies

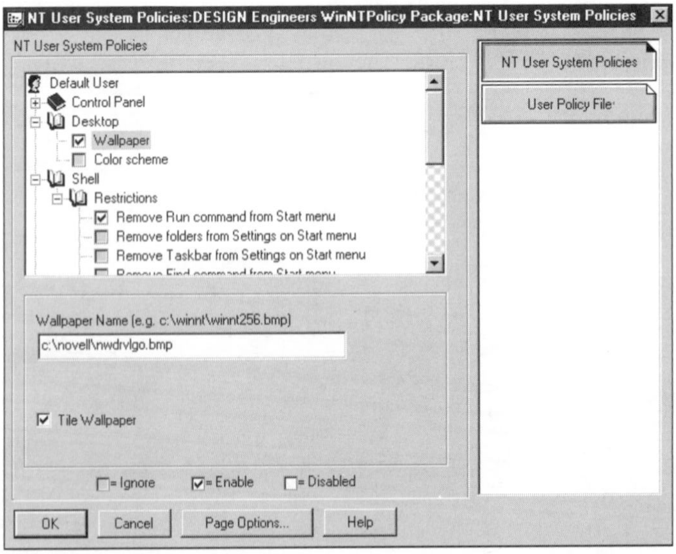

Checking the Wallpaper box assigns all users who are affected by this policy to use the wallpaper file `C:\NOVELL\NWDRVLGO.BMP`. (This file must be copied to that directory from the server, but it's cool to show, so it may be worth the trouble). Checking the Remove Run Command From Start Menu checkbox disables the Run command on the Start menu.

At the bottom of the screen are three checkboxes, showing the status of the selected policy:

- If the checkbox next to the policy is cleared, the policy is disabled.
- If the checkbox has a check in it, the policy is enabled.
- If the checkbox is grayed out, this policy is neither enabled nor cleared.

Table 11.1 lists some of the more useful NT User System Policies.

TABLE 11.1: COMMON AND USEFUL NT SYSTEM POLICIES

Location	Policy Name	Function
Control Panel ➤ Display	Restrict Display	Lets you choose which display property tabs are visible to the user, including Background, Screen Saver, Appearance, and Settings.
Desktop	Wallpaper	Sets the desktop wallpaper.
Desktop	Color Scheme	Sets the user's color scheme.
Shell ➤ Restrictions	Remove Run Command From Start Menu	Hides the Run command so that any user whom this policy affects won't be able to run programs.
Shell ➤ Restrictions	Remove Folders From Settings On Start Menu	Takes away the Control Panel and Printers folders from the Start menu.
Shell ➤ Restrictions	Remove Taskbar From Settings On Start Menu	Takes the Taskbar settings option out of the Settings folder on the Start menu.
Shell ➤ Restrictions	Remove Find Command From Start Menu	Removes the Find command from the Start menu.
Shell ➤ Restrictions	Hide Drives In My Computer	Removes drive letters from the My Computer folder.
Shell ➤ Restrictions	Hide Network Neighborhood	Removes the Network Neighborhood icon from the desktop.
Shell ➤ Restrictions	Hide All Items On Desktop	Removes all the items from the desktop, including My Computer.

PART

II

Managing the
Network

Continued ▶

TABLE 11.1 CONTINUED: COMMON AND USEFUL NT SYSTEM POLICIES

Location	Policy Name	Function
Shell ➢ Restrictions	Don't Save Settings At Exit	Prevents changes a user has made to the desktop from being saved.
System ➢ Restrictions	Disable Registry Editing Tools	Disables the use of REGEDIT.EXE and REGEDT32.EXE.
System ➢ Restrictions	Run Only Allowed Windows Applications	Lets you specify a list of authorized executable programs that this user can run.
Windows NT Shell ➢ Restrictions	Remove Common Program Groups From Start Menu	Removes the common program groups from the Start menu so that only the user's program groups appear.
Windows NT Shell ➢ Restrictions	Remove File Menu From Explorer	Removes the File menu choice from Explorer menus.
Windows NT Shell ➢ Restrictions	Remove The "Map Network Drive" And "Disconnect Network Drive" Options	Prohibits users from mapping and disconnecting mapped drives from Explorer.
Windows NT System	Disable Task Manager	Disables the ability to launch the Task Manager.
Windows NT System	Show Welcome Tips At Logon	Allows you to enable or disable the welcome tips.
ZAK Policies ➢ Windows NT ➢ Drives ➢ Restrictions	Show Only Selected Drives	Makes only the drive letters you have selected visible to the user.

 NOTE You'll find equivalent policies for Windows 95/98 users in the Win95-98 User Package.

Setting User Extensible Policies

New with ZENworks 2.0, the User Extensible Policies allow administrators to force policy actions at times other than login. The default remains User Login, but ZENworks engineers decided you needed more complexity.

11.8 Set User Extensible Policies

1. Using NetWare Administrator, highlight the policy package that contains the NT User System Policy you want to modify.
2. Right-click the policy package, then click the Details button.
3. Select User Extensible Policies, then click the Details button.
4. On the User Extensible Policies page, pull down the Schedule list to show the full range of options, then pick one.
5. If you chose Event, pull down the Event list and pick the event you wish from the list.
6. If you chose a calendar time, select the appropriate day and time for the policy to engage.
7. Click OK.

This action takes more time to explain than to demonstrate with a screen shot (check out Figure 11.15). The other options under Schedule are all date-dependent, such as day, week, month, year, or decade (just kidding). If you want to trigger a policy on an event, the second pick list box opens, as shown in Figure 11.15.

FIGURE 11.15

A wide choice of triggering events

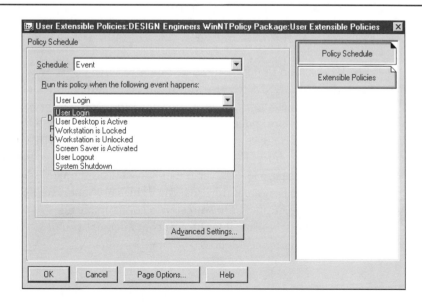

Managing the Network

PART

II

Why does ZENworks offer you a chance to pick an event, then pick User Login as the default event? So you can play with the Advanced Settings (see the big command button?). There are lots of controls here, allowing you to set the event to expire if it works, to handle things if it doesn't work, and to set time limits if things get slow. This is more complexity than I want right now, but some environments require serious control. This new version of ZENworks provides that level of serious control.

Setting the Workstation Import Policy

IN A HURRY

11.9 Specify a Selected Container for the Workstation Import Policy

1. Using NetWare Administrator, highlight the policy package that contains the NT User System Policy you want to modify.
2. Right-click the policy package, and then click the Details button.
3. Select Workstation Import Policy, and click the Details button.
4. On the Workstation Location property page, in the Create Workstations Objects In drop-down box, select Selected Container.
5. Browse the NDS tree and select the container in which you want the Workstation object to appear in the Path box.
6. Click OK.

The Workstation Import policy determines whether it is okay to import a workstation and where in the NDS tree the workstation is imported, and it also controls the auto-naming of workstations. Figure 11.16 shows the Workstation Naming page of the Workstation Import policy.

The default is the computer name concatenated with the IPX network address. You can use the IP address instead, as well as a variety of other types of names.

New on this page for this version of ZENworks is the Workstation Verification page button, on the bottom of the list at the right. This option verifies that the Workstation object was created in the directory a configurable number of minutes after the workstation first registered in the user container. Are you nervous that it won't happen? Set a timer to see if it does.

FIGURE 11.16

*The Workstation
Import policy
Workstation Naming
property page*

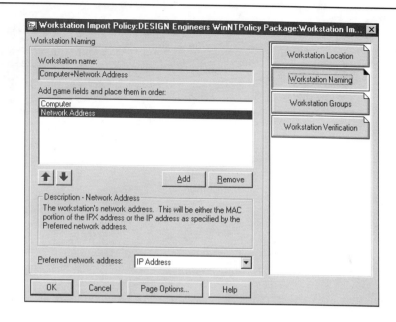

Assigning Policy Package Associations

IN A HURRY

11.10 Assign a Group of Users to a Policy Package

1. Using NetWare Administrator, highlight the policy package that contains the NT User System Policy you want to modify.

2. Right-click the policy package, and click the Details button.

3. Select the Associations property page.

4. Click the Add button.

5. Browse the NDS tree and find the group you want to assign to this policy package.

6. Click OK twice.

Don't forget to associate the policy package with users, groups, or containers. To do this, click the Associations property page button to display a list of the objects associated with this policy. In Figure 11.17, the group DESIGN Engineers.GCS has been associated with this policy.

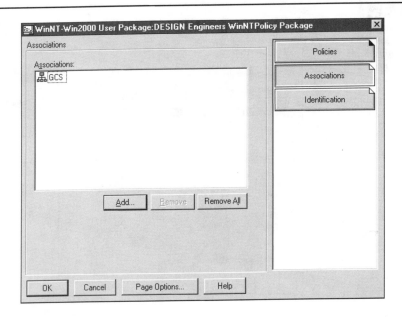

The Associations list could contain other users, groups, and NDS containers. If you forget to make associations, the policy will not be enforced. Only one policy package for each operating system (platform) can be enforced for a user, a group, or a container. For example, if you create a WinNT Workstation Package and associate it with a container, then only that WinNT Workstation Package can be associated with that container, although you could associate a Win95 and Win32 Workstation Package with the container as well.

Scheduling Events in the Policy Package

IN A HURRY

11.11 Create a Scheduled Action to Run CHKDSK Daily between Noon and 1:00 P.M.

1. Using NetWare Administrator, highlight the policy package that contains the NT User System Policy you want to modify.
2. Right-click the policy package, and click the Details button.
3. Click the Add Action button, enter the name of the action, and click Create.

Continued

IN A HURRY CONTINUED

4. Highlight the new Scheduled action in the Policy list, and then click the Details button.

5. Pull down the Schedule list box items.

6. Click the schedule you wish (User Logout Now).

7. Click the Actions page button on the right.

8. Enter the path and program name, the working directory, and any parameters. (For Windows NT, the path is `C:\WINNT\SYSTEM32\CHKDSK.EXE`.) Click OK.

9. Select the Policy Schedule page button. Make sure that Event is highlighted.

10. Click OK.

You may have noticed the Schedule section in Figure 11.9. You can create policy packages that run based on a schedule or some type of action. To create a Scheduled action, click Add Action on the Policies page to open the Create Scheduled Action dialog box. Enter a name for the Scheduled action, and click Create.

I am going to create a Scheduled action that runs the CHKDSK.EXE program every time the user logs out. After I create the name of the Scheduled action, it will appear in the list of policies. I can then select the policy name and click the Details button to open the Scheduled Action: Run CHKDSK Daily dialog box, as shown in Figure 11.18.

FIGURE 11.18

Setting item properties

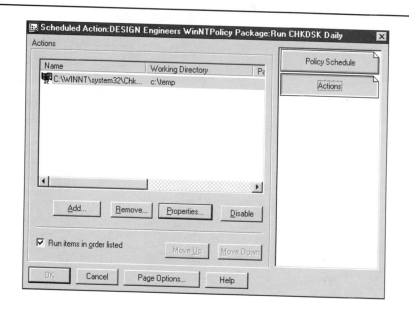

The Scheduled Action:Run CHKDSK Daily dialog box has two page buttons, Policy Schedule and Actions. You use the Policy Schedule property page to override the package default schedule and specify an alternative schedule that is defined for only this scheduled action. The Actions property page hides information about the program to be executed.

The Items Overview box in ZENworks 1.2 gave way to the Advanced Schedule consolidation—the Impersonation and Priority details now reside in this box. Advanced Schedule contains a list of the items that are scheduled to run. To view the properties of any of these items or to create a new item, click the Details button of the highlighted policy, set the triggering event, then click the Advanced Schedule button. You will see a page similar to the Advanced Schedule dialog box, shown in Figure 11.19.

FIGURE 11.19

*Advanced Schedule
properties*

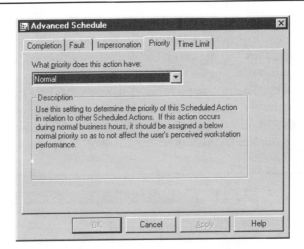

This dialog box displays the Scheduled action's priority level. Here, you can set the priority for the application when it is launched under Windows NT. You can choose from three priorities:

Normal   Covers most anything you want to run.

Above Normal   May interfere with applications running in the foreground by slowing them down.

Below Normal   Takes less CPU time, but may cause the action to complete more slowly.

The Impersonation tab in the Advanced Schedule window determines how the action will run on the workstation from the perspective of a security context. You have three choices:

Interactive User   Causes the action to run in the security context of the user who is currently logged in to that workstation.

System   Causes the action to run in the security context of the operating system (the Windows NT System Account). Depending on the type of program that is running, this account may not have permissions to complete the action.

Unsecure System   Is available only on Windows NT. You use this option if the action you are executing requires interaction with the currently logged-on user. Novell recommends not using this option unless you have no other alternative.

To add a new item to a list of actions, click the Add button in the Scheduled Action dialog box to open the Item Properties dialog box, shown in Figure 11.20.

FIGURE 11.20

Adding item
properties

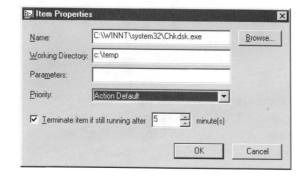

Enter the name of the program in the Name box, or click the Browse button to locate the program. The program can be on the NetWare server or on the machine's local hard disk. You can also specify a working directory, startup parameters, and this program's priority. If you leave the priority set at Action Default, the program will use the priority of the action. You can override the priority for this specific program.

The Terminate Item If Still Running checkbox allows you to set a time in minutes after which the action will be terminated if it has not yet completed. If it has not completed, it will be rescheduled to run at the next scheduled time.

 TIP   My advice to you is to make sure you leave enough time for the action to complete, or you'll waste your time setting up the action.

Figure 11.21 shows the Policy Schedule property page, which allows you to schedule how often or when the program runs.

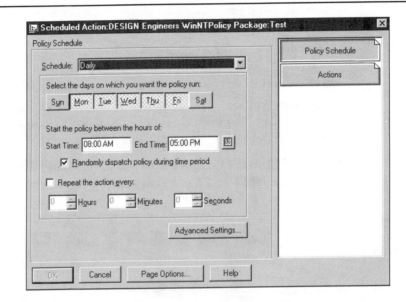

You can choose to run the action daily, weekly, monthly, or yearly. If a specific time interval is not an appropriate way to run this particular action, you can choose to run the action based on a specific event. Select Event in the Schedule field to open a drop-down list from which you can determine when the event occurs, as shown in Figure 11.22.

There are eight event choices for when the action will occur:

- Scheduler Service Startup
- User Login (the most common)
- User Desktop Is Active
- Workstation Is Locked
- Workstation Is Unlocked
- Screen Saver Is Activated
- User Logout
- System Shutdown

FIGURE 11.22

Other triggers for actions

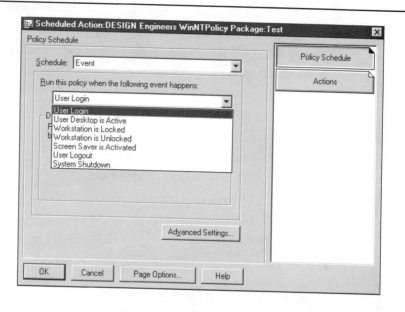

You use the Advanced Settings button of the Policy Schedule dialog box to control the finer details of scheduled events. If the action cannot be run for any reason, you can control what to do next. You have three choices:

- Disable The Action

- Retry Every Minute

- Ignore The Error And Reschedule Normally

In addition, you have the following options:

- Disable The Action After Completion

- Terminate If The Action Is Still Running After A Specified Number Of Minutes

- Randomly Dispatch Action During Scheduled Time Period

- Reboot After Completion

The WinNT-Win2000 Workstation Package

The WinNT-Win2000 Workstation Package allows you to configure settings that affect your Windows NT Workstations. There is a similar package for Windows 95/98 and for Windows 3.*x* clients. To create a policy package, follow these steps:

1. Using NetWare Administrator, highlight the container in which you want the policy to be contained.

2. Press the Insert key, or right-click the container and choose Create.

3. Choose Policy Package from the list of object classes.

4. From the Select Policy Package Type drop-down list box, select WinNT-Win2000 Workstation Package.

5. Click the type of policy to create from the list of policies.

6. Click the Next button.

7. Enter the name of the policy package, such as **DESIGN Dept NTW Policies**.

8. Choose the container in which to create the new policy, then click Next.

9. Click the policies to enable, then click Next.

10. Accept or change the associations for the new policy, then click Next.

11. Click the Create Another Policy Package button, or click Finish to create and/or modify the package.

ZENworks 2.0 expects administrators to make settings to a policy package during creation, rather than follow the path used in ZENworks 1.2, where there was a checkbox for Define Additional Properties. This saves time if you know what you're doing when you start (I hope you do by now). Figure 11.23 shows the summary screen of the Policy Package Wizard just before creating the policy.

FIGURE 11.23

The WinNT-Win2000 Workstation Package: DESIGN Dept NTW Policies summary box

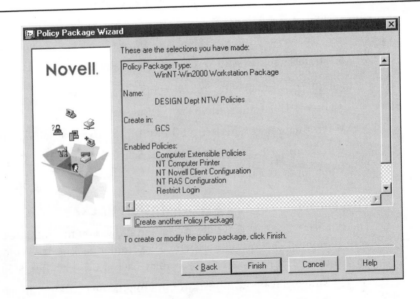

Just click Finish to create the policy and get ready to modify some of the parameters. Behold, Figure 11.24 shows the Policies page, exactly like the page in ZENworks 1.2, even though we reached this same place via a different route.

FIGURE 11.24

The WinNT-Win2000 Workstation Package dialog box

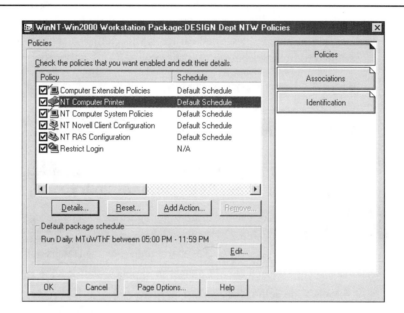

The Policies property page is where the real goodies are for this policy package, but I want to talk briefly about the other two property pages first. The Identification property page allows you to assign another name to this policy. You use the Associations property page to associate individual workstations, workstation groups, and container objects with this particular policy, just as we did earlier.

A workstation or a workstation group cannot be associated with more than one policy package for a particular platform. For example, the container DESIGN.SOMORITA cannot be associated with more than one WinNT-Win2000 Workstation policy, but it can be associated with one WinNT-Win2000 Workstation policy, with one Win95 Workstation policy, and with one Win31 Workstation policy.

The main WinNT-Win2000 Workstation Package screen shown in Figure 11.24 shows six policies:

- Computer Extensible Policies
- NT Computer Printer
- NT Computer System Policies

PART

II

Managing the
Network

- Novell Client Configuration
- NT RAS Configuration
- Restrict Login

You can edit policies, create additional actions, remove actions, and customize the schedule from this screen. The NT Computer Printer policies are similar to the NT User Printer policies described earlier in this chapter, except that the printers are assigned to the workstation that the policy affects rather than to a specific user.

Novell Client Configuration

IN A HURRY

11.12 Assign Workstations a Default Tree Name through the Novell Client Configuration Policy

1. Using NetWare Administrator, highlight the policy package that contains the NT User System Policy you want to modify.
2. Right-click the policy package, and then click the Details button.
3. Select the Novell Client Configuration policy, and click the Details button.
4. Select the Settings property page.
5. Click the Client item in the tree of configuration selections.
6. Click the Configuration button.
7. On the Client tab of the Novell Client Configuration dialog box, enter the tree you want to assign in the Preferred Tree field.
8. Click OK twice.

Let's take a look at the Novell Client Configuration policy. To display the details of this policy, highlight the policy in the policy window and click the Details button. Figure 11.25 shows the policy details on the left and the Novell Client Configuration dialog box on the right.

The Novell Client Configuration dialog box has two property pages (visible just over the top of the Novell Client Configuration active window):

- The Policy Schedule property page lets you set up a schedule that ignores the package policy defaults.
- The Settings property page lets you set policies relating to the client configuration.

FIGURE 11.25

The Novell Client
Configuration policy

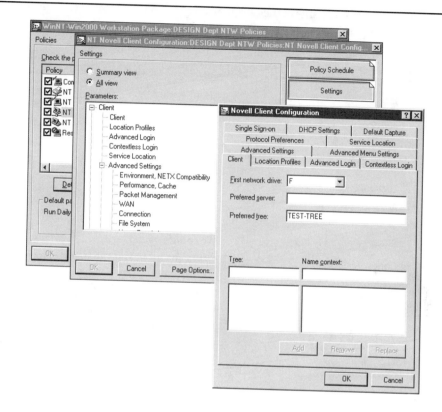

Remember all those settings you had to configure through the Control Panel (or, heaven forbid, the NET.CFG file)? As long as your clients are using the NetWare 5.1 client software, you can update those settings through the Novell Client Configuration policy. You can set policies for the following:

- NetWare 5.1 client configuration
- Workstation Manager
- NetWare/IP client software (included with the NetWare 5.1 client)
- Novell IP Gateway
- IPX Compatibility Adapter
- Storage Management System Target Service Agent (TSA)

To display the Novell Client Configuration dialog box, highlight the Client item in the Parameters tree and click the Configure button. The window on the right side in

Figure 11.25 shows the tabs that you can configure for the Novell client software. Table 11.2 lists these tabs and describes the parameters you can set with each one.

TABLE 11.2: NOVELL CLIENT CONFIGURATION PARAMETERS

Tab	Client Parameter
Client	First Network Drive
	Preferred Server
	Preferred Tree
Location Profiles	Location Profile Names
Advanced Login	Default Policy Support
	Tabs that appear in the NetWare Login dialog box
	Welcome screen bitmap and caption
Contextless Login	Tells NetWare to keep an index to login BILL by popping up a list of all BILLs and letting BILL choose
Single Sign-on	Enables NetWare's new Single Sign-on for easier access to network resources
DHCP Settings	Dynamic Host Configuration Profile settings for automatic IP address assignments
Default Capture	Print job settings such as Number Of Copies, Form Feed, Enable Tabs, Banner Settings, Hold, Keep, and Notify
Protocol Preferences	IP and IPX naming properties
Service Location	SLP (Service Location Protocol) Scope List
	Directory Agent List
Advanced Settings	Advanced client configuration settings
Advanced Menu Settings	Scores of control options over the user's view of the NetWare resources available

 TIP Did you know that you can customize your login screen? Using the Advanced Login property page, customize the Welcome screen bitmap and the caption for your network. This is one small way that you can help people feel more comfortable with the network.

The Advanced Settings tab of the Novell Client Configuration dialog box is shown in Figure 11.26. If you have worked with previous versions of NetWare, you will remember editing these settings in the NET.CFG file. I always forgot the correct syntax for many of these and had to look them up all the time. There are more settings here than any network will ever need. If something strange starts happening to a user, check here and see if you can control the problem. Otherwise, the default values almost always work.

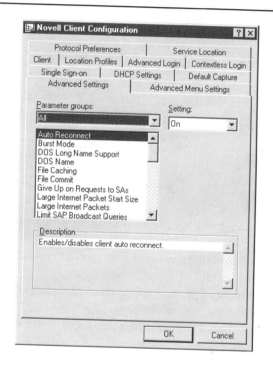

The Workstation Manager properties in the Novell Client Configuration parameters tree (see Figure 11.27) let you enable the Workstation Manager for a client, specify the tree name to be used and the NDS refresh rate, and determine whether volatile user caching is enabled.

The default for the NDS Refresh Rate is 540 minutes; the figure shows a more reasonable 30. There's barely a reason to use it if you're checking only every eight hours.

Volatile caching is used to store user credentials for a period of time. The next time the user logs in, the cached credentials can be used if the network is not available. The Workstation Manager parameters let you set the number of days that the volatile cache is maintained. The default number of days to cache volatile users was zero; I bumped it to 10.

PART

II

Managing the Network

*The Workstation
Manager configuration
properties*

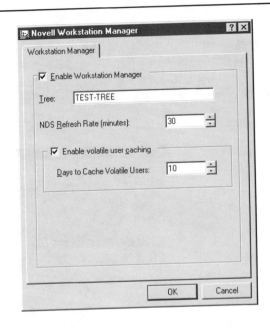

If you are using the Novell IP Gateway provided with IntranetWare 4.11 or if you are using BorderManager, the IP Gateway parameters will be of interest to you. In the Novell Client Configuration parameter tree, select Novell IP Gateway and click the Configure button.

Users of Novell's Storage Management Services (SMS) software can easily enable workstation Target Service Agents (TSAs). Select TSA Preferences from the Novell Client Configuration parameter tree and click the Configure button to open the TSA Preferences dialog box, shown in Figure 11.28.

In this dialog box you can configure the following TSA parameters on the workstation through this policy:

- Preferred server
- Protocol to be used
- Events to log
- Allow backup user
- Auto registration
- The drives that you want the backup server to back up across the network

PART

II

Managing the
Network

FIGURE 11.28

Target Service Agent
configuration

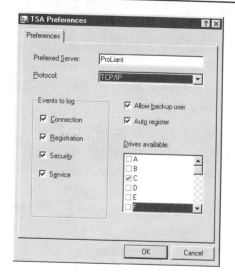

To display a summary of all the parameters that you set in the Novell Client Configuration policy (the ones that you changed from something other than a default parameter), click the Summary View radio button rather than the All View radio button on the Settings page. You will see a list of parameters that may or may not look like my parameters in Figure 11.29.

FIGURE 11.29

The Novell Client
Configuration parameters that you have
changed to something
other than the default

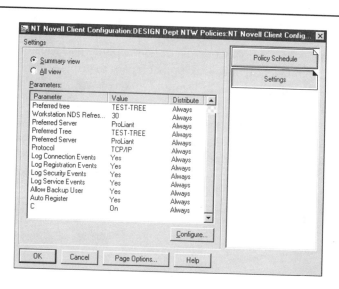

Establishing NT Computer System Policies

IN A HURRY

11.13 Set a Logon Banner Caption and Warning for Windows NT Workstations

1. Using NetWare Administrator, highlight the policy package that contains the NT User System Policy you want to modify.
2. Right-click the policy package, and then click the Details button.
3. Select NT Computer System Policies, and click the Details button.
4. Choose the NT Computer System Policies property page.
5. Choose Windows NT System ➢ Logon.
6. Click the Logon Banner policy.
7. In the Caption field, enter the Logon Banner dialog box caption.
8. In the Text field, enter the Logon Banner dialog box text.
9. Click OK.

The Windows NT Computer System Policies policy controls settings on the Windows NT Workstations that this policy affects. Highlight NT Computer System Policies and click the Details button to open the NT Computer System Policies dialog box, as shown in Figure 11.30.

You use the Policy Schedule property page to select a schedule for the NT Computer System policy that overrides the policy package's default schedule. Select the NT Computer System Policies property page to display the details we are looking for.

The policy shown in Figure 11.30 sets a Windows NT logon banner. This banner is a screen that pops up with the caption and text before displaying the login dialog box. Users must acknowledge this dialog box prior to proceeding. This allows you to display a warning message advising users that only authorized users can log in or some other such message. Many government systems require such a message. Figure 11.30 shows the default message from ZENworks. I suggest you put your own, friendlier, message in its place.

FIGURE 11.30

*The NT Computer
System Policies
dialog box*

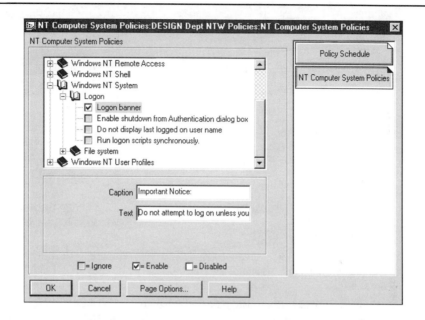

 NOTE   Do you welcome hackers to your system? A few years back, a hacker maliciously gained access to a company's computer system and got caught. The company attempted to prosecute the hacker but failed. The hacker's lawyer argued that the company's computer system had a logon message that said, "Welcome to the computer system!" and that the hacker should not be prosecuted. The judge agreed. Go figure!

Table 11.3 shows some other Windows NT Computer System policies that you can use to tighten security or custom configure the Windows NT Workstations on your network.

TABLE 11.3: SOME INTERESTING WINDOWS NT COMPUTER SYSTEM POLICIES

Location	Policy	Function
System ➤ SNMP	Communities	Sets the name(s) of the SNMP communities and the workstations this policy affects.
System ➤ SNMP	Permitted Managers	Sets the name or IP address of authorized SNMP management consoles.

Continued ▶

TABLE 11.3 CONTINUED: SOME INTERESTING WINDOWS NT COMPUTER SYSTEM POLICIES

Location	Policy	Function
System ➤ SNMP	Traps For Public Community	Sets the name or IP address of SNMP management consoles that will accept traps from the workstations that this policy affects.
System ➤ Run	Run	Specifies a program or programs that run when any user logs in.
Windows NT Network Sharing ➤ Sharing	Disable Peer To Peer Server	Disables the Windows NT Server and Browser services.
Windows NT Network Sharing ➤ Sharing	Create Hidden Drive Shares (Workstation)	Specifies whether hidden drive shares are created (C$, D$, ADMIN$, and so on) for Windows NT Workstations. The default is On.
Windows NT Network Sharing ➤ Sharing	Create Hidden Drive Shares (Server)	Specifies whether hidden drive shares are created (C$, D$, ADMIN$, etc.) for one Windows NT server. The default is On.
Windows NT Shell ➤ Custom Shared Folders	Custom Shared Program Folders	Specifies a location that contains shared program items. Everyone who uses workstations that this policy affects will see these program items.
Windows NT Shell ➤ Custom Shared Folders	Custom Shared Desktop Icons	Specifies a location that contains a shared desktop. Everyone who uses workstations that this policy affects will see these items on their desktops.
Windows NT Shell ➤ Custom Shared Folders	Custom Shared Start Menu	Specifies a location that contains shared Start menu items. Everyone who uses workstations that this policy affects will see these items on their Start menus.
Windows NT Shell ➤ Custom Shared Folders	Custom Shared Startup Folder	Specifies a location that contains shared startup program items. Everyone who uses the workstations that this policy affects will have these programs launched when they log in.
Windows NT System ➤ Logon	Logon Banner	Specifies a banner caption and text that the user must acknowledge before being presented with the login dialog box. You can use this to further secure a workstation.
Windows NT System ➤ Logon	Enable Shutdown From Authentication Dialog Box	Specifies whether a user can shut a system down without first logging in.

Continued ▶

	TABLE 11.3 CONTINUED: SOME INTERESTING WINDOWS NT COMPUTER SYSTEM POLICIES	
Location	**Policy**	**Function**
Windows NT System ➤ Logon	Do Not Display Last Logged On User Name	Specifies that the login name field should be cleared so that the next person who tries to log in at this workstation will not see who worked there earlier. You can use this to further secure a workstation.
Windows NT System ➤ File System	Do Not Create 8.3 File Name for Long File Name	Turns on or off the automatic creation of short filenames when a long filename is created.
Windows NT System ➤ File System	Allow Extended Characters In 8.3 Character File Names	Enables users to put extended characters in short filenames.
Windows NT System ➤ File System	Do Not Update Last Access Time	Specifies whether Windows NT will update a file's last access time when it is accessed.

 TIP You'll find similar policies for Windows 95/98 in the Win95-98 Workstation Package.

Configuring NT RAS   The NT RAS Configuration policy allows administrators to configure the Dial-Up Networking client for the workstations that this policy affects. Highlight NT RAS Configuration in the list of policies, and click the Details button to open the NT RAS Configuration dialog box, as shown in Figure 11.31.

FIGURE 11.31

RAS policy configuration

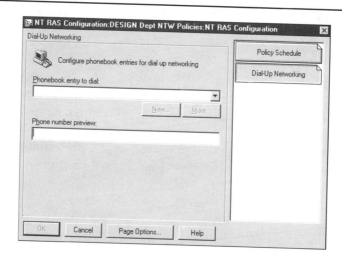

PART II

Managing the Network

This dialog box has two property pages:

- Use the Policy Schedule property page to set up a schedule for this policy.
- Use the Dial-Up Networking property page to create new Dial-Up Networking entries.

In order to configure the NT RAS, the Dial-Up Networking software must be installed on the system on which you are running NetWare Administrator. From the Dial-Up Networking property page, you can create new Dial-Up Networking entries. In order for these policies to be enforced on workstations that are covered by this policy package, the Dial-Up Networking software must also be installed on the Windows NT Workstations.

Personally, I much prefer other ways to connect from outside into the network. It's not that I don't trust NT security—it's, well, I guess it's that I don't trust NT security.

Restricting Login to a Workstation

IN A HURRY

11.14 Deny Access to a Group of Users through the Restrict Login Policy

1. Using NetWare Administrator, highlight the policy package that contains the NT User System Policy you want to modify.
2. Right-click the policy package, and then click the Details button.
3. Select the Restrict Login policy, and click the Details button.
4. In the Deny Login From column, click the Add button.
5. Browse the NDS tree and select the group that should not be allowed to log in at this workstation.
6. Click OK.

Using the Restrict Login policy, an administrator can specify which users, groups, or containers of users are allowed to log in at workstations covered by the policy package. Highlight the Restrict Login policy and click the Details button to open the Restrict Login dialog box, so you can see something similar to Figure 11.32. This dialog box has only one property page, Login Restrictions.

FIGURE 11.32

*Restricting logins
to policy-controlled
systems*

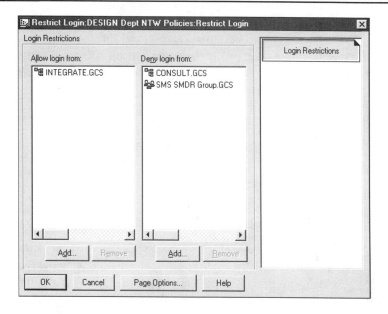

Effective Policies

IN A HURRY

11.15 View a User's Effective Policies

1. Using NetWare Administrator, browse the NDS tree and locate the user you are interested in.
2. Right-click the User object, and click Details.
3. Choose the Effective Policies property page.
4. In the Platform drop-down list box, select the operating system.
5. Click the Effective Policies button.
6. Highlight the policy you want, and click the Package Details button to browse through the effective policies.
7. Click Cancel twice to exit.

Effective policies are similar to effective rights in NDS. They are the sum of all enabled policies in all policy packages that affect a particular user. Policies are applied starting with the User object and then looking "up" the directory tree. A policy associated with a specific object takes precedence over policies associated with a group, and policies associated with a group take precedence over policies assigned to an Organization or an Organizational Unit object.

You can control the order in which policies are applied by creating a Container Package. To do so, follow these steps:

1. In NetWare Administrator, highlight the container in which you want this object to appear.

2. Press Insert, or right-click the container and choose Create.

3. From the list of object classes, choose Policy Package to open the Create Policy Package dialog box, just as you did in the earlier examples.

In the Create Policy Package dialog box, be sure that Container Package is selected in the Select Policy Package Type drop-down list box. In the Name field, enter a descriptive name for the policy package, check the Define Additional Properties checkbox, and click Create to open the Policy Search dialog box, as shown in Figure 11.33.

FIGURE 11.33

Checking the new container policy

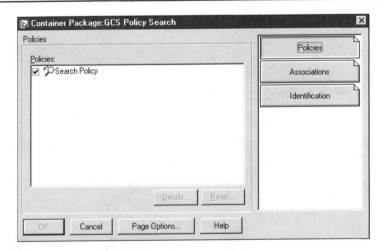

The only policy in the Policies list should be the Search Policy. To enable this policy, click the checkbox next to Search Policy. On the Associations property page, be sure to associate this policy with the appropriate container(s).

Select the Policies button to open the Policies property page, highlight Search Policy, and click the Details button to open the Search Policy dialog box. Here you can control the level to which the search policy applies, such as the Root, Organization, or Organizational Unit. To check or change the order in which policies are applied, as shown in Figure 11.34, click the Search Order button to open the Search Order property page.

FIGURE 11.34

Verifying search order

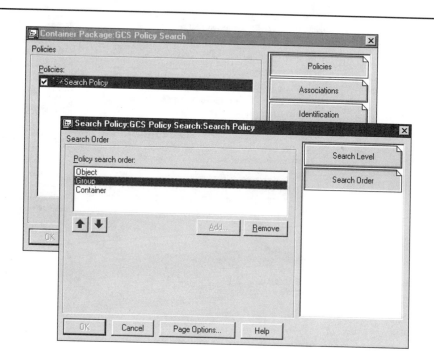

PART

II

Managing the Network

The default search order is Object, Group, and then Container. You can change the order or remove any of these from the order.

Viewing Effective Policies
To view a user's effective rights, follow these steps:

1. In NetWare Administrator, highlight the User object.
2. Display the details of that User object.
3. Open the Effective Policies property page.
4. In the Platform drop-down list box, select the operating system.
5. Click the Effective Policies button.

The effective policies for this user will be calculated and displayed in a list similar to the one you see in Figure 11.35. At this point, you can highlight any policy and view its details by clicking the Package Details button.

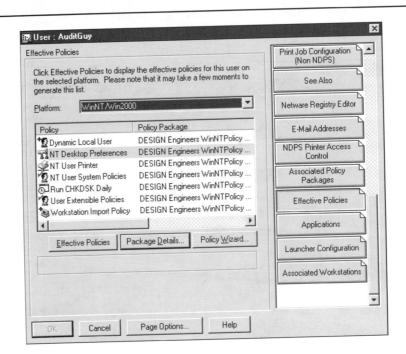

Deploying Software Remotely

ZENworks includes a tool called the Application Launcher that assists in software distribution. I will cover the Application Launcher shortly, but first let's take a look at software distribution. The real magic behind remote software distribution is an amazing tool called snAppShot, which creates a template of the application installation.

NOTE Those wanting to get an overview of how difficult this task can be should check out an article I did for *Network World* at http://www.nwfusion.com/reviews/ 0906rev.html. ZENworks was not included in the article because software distribution is not the program's focus, unlike the five products reviewed for *Network World*.

Software distribution programs like snAppShot track all activity on a workstation when an application is installed, including all new files and their locations, Registry settings, and modifications to Windows .INI, AUTOEXEC.BAT, and CONFIG.SYS files.

The administrator chooses a location for these files (usually on a server), and the snAppShot utility creates a configuration file called an Application Object Template (.AOT) file. It also tracks any files that were added to the workstation and copies them to this directory, giving each a number and an extension of .FIL (for example, 1.FIL, 2.FIL, 3.FIL, and so on).

The administrator then creates an NDS object that represents the new application and stores that template. This object is associated with groups of users so that those users can click on the application icon when it appears on their desktop and install it to their local workstations. The icon is deployed using the Application Launcher.

Creating a snAppShot

IN A HURRY

11.16 Create a snAppShot of an Application

1. Before installing the new application, run the SYS:PUBLIC\SNAPSHOT\SNAPSHOT .EXE program.
2. Select Standard.
3. Provide the NDS object name and an icon title for the application.
4. Provide a location for the snAppShot files to be created.
5. Confirm the name of the .AOT file that will be created.
6. Select the drives you want to scan for changes.
7. Click Next and wait for the scanning to complete.
8. Install the new application normally.
9. Continue with the snAppShot process.
10. Provide a path to the .AXT file.
11. Wait while the differences are scanned, the different file is created, and the application files are copied.

When ZENworks is installed on a server, it creates a new subdirectory, SYS:PUBLIC\SNAPSHOT, that contains the snAppShot software and supporting files. The SNAPSHOT.EXE program will auto-detect whether you are running 16-bit Windows or 32-bit Windows and launch the correct supporting software (SNAPPE16.EXE or SNAPPE32.EXE).

When you launch SYS:PUBLIC\SNAPSHOT\SNAPSHOT.EXE, you will see a screen similar to the one in Figure 11.36, which presents you with five options:

- Run a **Standard** discovery using the default settings.

- Run a **Custom** discovery that lets you specify which disk drives, files, folders, Registry hives, and shortcuts you want to include or exclude during the discovery process. This option is for advanced users.

- Run an **Express** discovery that uses a preferences file, which you created during a previous discovery session.

- Choose **Getting Started** for information about using snAppShot.

- **Exit** the snAppShot program.

FIGURE 11.36

The opening screen for the snAppShot application

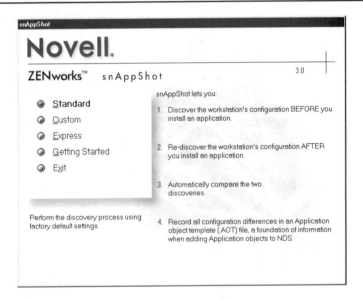

For most installations or for administrators who are new to snAppShot, the Express choice should work nicely. When you click Express, you are presented with a screen that asks for the NDS Application object name and the Application icon title, as shown in Figure 11.37.

FIGURE 11.37

The Novell Application Launcher snAppShot name screen

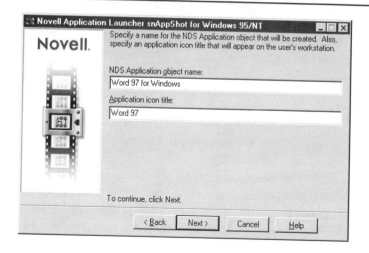

The NDS Application object name is the name that will appear in the NDS tree, and the Application icon title is the title of the icon that the user will see on his or her desktop or Start menu when used with the Application Launcher. In my example in Figure 11.37, I am creating an NDS Application object named Word 97 for Windows, and the application's icon title will be Word 97. If it matters, I'm avoiding Word 2000 because of the program bloat and various sticky problems users have with the program.

Click Next to open the dialog box shown in Figure 11.38; this dialog box asks you for the application's file locations.

FIGURE 11.38

Specifying the location on the server for the files that snAppShot is going to discover

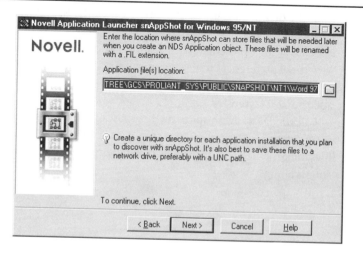

Novell moved the default file location from a local drive to a UNC (Universal Naming Convention) name on a unique location on the server. Not quite unique enough for me, however. The default location offered, the \SYS\PUBLIC\SNAPSHOT directory, provides no individual user information. Since Microsoft's convoluted Registry and system file guarantees that no two systems will ever look the same, I made a subdirectory for the user, NT1 (the first person using NT 4.0 Workstation software).

New for the UNC path is the inclusion of the tree, making the full file location \\TEST-TREE\GCS\PROLIANT_SYS\PUBLIC\SNAPSHOT\NT1\Word97. It looks worse than it is in practice. For those of you who are new to UNC names, this file is located in the TEST-TREE tree, GCS Organization container, PROLIANT_SYS: volume in a directory called \SNAPSHOT\NT1\WORD97. The files are hosted by the ProLiant server, although NDS allows volume names that may or may not have any reference to their host server. ZENworks uses the full NDS Application object name, Word 97 for Windows, as the default filename. Since I think that's too long, I must keep shortening the name to Word 97. See why you should read ahead, so you don't keep making the same mistakes I make?

Since NT1, the unique directory, did not exist, snAppShot gracefully asked if I wanted the directory created. If you made a typo, now's a good chance to fix your mistake before it gets cast in file system concrete.

When you again click Next, you are prompted for a name and location for the .AOT file. I see no reason to specify any location other than the location that contains the other files discovered by the snAppShot process for the NT1 machine, so I accept the defaults (after deleting the "for Windows" part) and click Next.

ZENworks then presents you with a list of drives that you want snAppShot to scan. To add drives to this list, click the Add button. To remove drives from this list, highlight the drive you want to remove and click the Remove button. When you've finished, click Next.

You are then presented with a summary of the options you have selected. You can save these preferences to use when generating other snAppShot packages later by clicking the Save Preferences button. I chose NT1 as the filename, letting snAppShot add the .INI extension.

Clicking Next again starts the first pass of the snAppShot process, which includes scanning the folders and files, Windows shortcuts, .INI files, system configuration files, and the Registry. Figure 11.39 catches the process as the entries-scanned number zooms along.

FIGURE 11.39

*Scanning the NT1
systems*

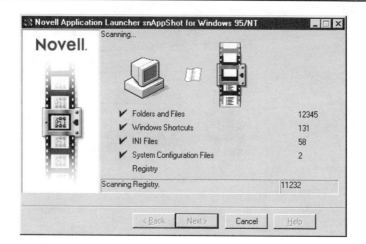

This scanning process could take a few minutes if the local hard disk contains a large number of files or a large amount of data or if the Registry already has a large number of entries. When the pass is finished, an instructional screen appears, along with a big command button named Run Application Install. A note reminds you to remember the file locations given earlier in the process, because you'll need them again. Click the Run Application Install button and away you go, or rather, here comes the application.

Now it is time to run the application installation. The next screen offers you the opportunity to run the installation program from this dialog box. When I click the Run Application Installation button, I am presented with a dialog box from which I can run the setup program for the application I am installing, in this case, Word 97.

Install the application just as you normally would. Take note of the directory in which the application is installed; you'll need this information later. Later, you can also enter user-specific information such as name, e-mail address, license number, and so on.

 TIP   If the application installation requires the computer to be rebooted, the snAppShot program will pick up where it left off when you reboot.

Once the application installation is complete, return to the snAppShot program and click Next. You will be prompted for the path to which you installed the new program, as shown in Figure 11.40.

FIGURE 11.40

Providing the path to the application I just installed

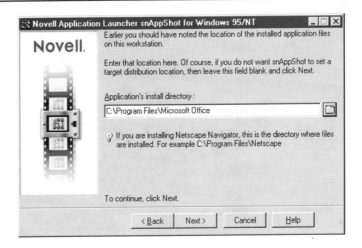

Click Next again to start another discovery pass (see Figure 11.41), this time generating a "picture" of the system after the new software installation. When the second "picture" is taken, snAppShot then compares the two pictures and creates what Novell engineers call a *delta* file (nothing to do with rivers—*delta* means change). This is an .AXT file that contains the differences between the before picture and the after picture. The .AXT file is placed in the directory on the server you specified during the first phase of the snAppShot installation.

The scanning screen looks just like Figure 11.39 except for one small difference: the word *Rescanning* appears in the upper-left corner of the screen, rather than *Scanning*.

After the delta file is created, you will see the screen shown in Figure 11.41, which contains a summary of the steps that were performed and a checklist of additional steps you need to take to distribute the application.

Notice the Print command button? It's not a bad idea to print this screen your first time or two through this process.

NOTE The process of creating the delta file can take a long time, depending on the number of changes, the size of the program that was installed, and the amount of data. When I installed Word 97, generating the data file took 45 minutes and placed 189 files taking up 45MB of disk space on the server in the PROLIANT\SYS:SNAPSHOT\NT1\WORD97 directory.

FIGURE 11.41

*The details of creating
an .AXT file*

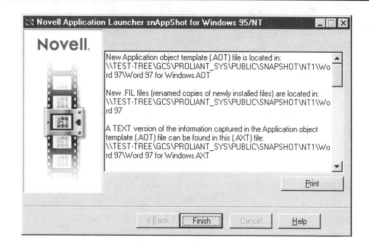

The .AXT file is a text file that contains all the changes that will be applied to configuration files and the Registry and that will be applied to any machine to which this application is distributed. This file uses a number of *macro object variables* (or sometimes just called *macros*) that are used when launching or installing this application. The Application Launcher can also use these object variables in Application Launcher Macros; Table 11.4 shows a list of some of the common object variables.

**TABLE 11.4: SOME OF THE OBJECT VARIABLES (MACROS) USED IN APPLICATION LAUNCHER
MACROS AND THE SNAPSHOT .*AOT* FILES**

Object Variable	Description
%SOURCE_PATH%	Location of source files, usually on the server
%TARGET_PATH%	Location where files will be installed
%*WinDir%	Location of Windows directory, such as C:\WINNT or C:\WINDOWS (Note: the asterisk [*] is required.)
%*WinSysDir%	Directory of the Windows system directory, such as C:\WINNT\ SYSTEM32 or C:\WINDOWS\SYSTEM
%*WinDisk%	Disk drive on which Windows NT or Windows is installed
%*TempDir%	Windows temporary directory, such as C:\TEMP
%*Desktop%	Directory that contains the user's desktop data
%*CommonDesktop%	Directory that contains the command desktop data
%*Personal%	Directory that contains the user's personal directory

Continued

TABLE 11.4 CONTINUED: SOME OF THE OBJECT VARIABLES (MACROS) USED IN APPLICATION LAUNCHER MACROS AND THE SNAPSHOT *.AOT* FILES

Object Variable	Description
%*Recent%	Directory that contains links to the user's most recently used documents
%*StartMenu%	Directory that contains the links and items on the Start menu
%*CommonStartMenu%	Directory that contains the links and items on all users' Start menus
%Favorites%	Directory that contains a user's favorite links and files
%NetHood%	Directory that contains items that are found in the user's Network Neighborhood folder
%Startup%	Directory that contains a user's links and programs that start when the user logs in
%CN%	NDS user Common Name attribute
%Given Name%	NDS user Given Name attribute
%Surname%	NDS user Surname (family name) attribute
%Home Directory%	NDS user Home Directory attribute

NOTE You can use many other variables, including many of those used in NetWare login scripts. See the ZENworks help files for more information.

Creating an Application Object for Application Launcher

The Application Launcher serves a couple of purposes:

- To deploy new applications to the user's desktop that were imaged using snAppShot.
- To place preexisting applications on the user's desktop or Start menu.

Now let's take a look at what it will take to deploy this new image of Word 97 to the users' desktops.

Creating an Application Object in NDS Using the Data That the snAppShot Tool Created

PART

II

Managing the Network

IN A HURRY

11.17 Create an Application Object Using the snAppShot Data

1. Using NetWare Administrator, browse the NDS directory and locate the container in which you want the Application object to appear.
2. Right-click the NDS container and choose Create.
3. Select Application.
4. Choose to create the application using an .AOT/.AXT file.
5. Provide the path to the data that the snAppShot utility created, preferably using UNC names.
6. Confirm the Application object name, source path, and target path. Click Next.
7. Click Finish.

First, we need to create an NDS Application object to represent Word 97. Follow these steps:

1. Using the NetWare Administrator program, highlight the container in which you want this object to appear.
2. Press Insert, or right-click the container and choose Create to open the New Object dialog box.
3. Choose the Application object and click OK. A screen remarkably similar to Figure 11.42 will appear.

The Create Application Object dialog box gives you three choices:

- Choose Create A Simple Application Object (No .AOT/.AXT File) to create an Application object that represents a pre-existing application either on the server or on local hard drives.
- Choose Create An Application Object With An .AOT/.AXT File to create an Application object from a previously created snAppShot image.
- Choose Duplicate An Existing Application Object to copy a previously created Application object.

FIGURE 11.42

Choices, always choices

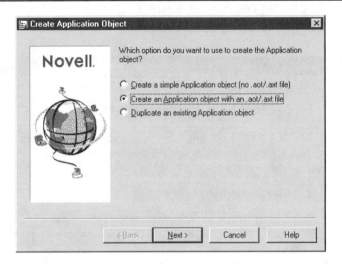

Since we are going to create an Application object for my previously created Word 97 snAppShot, I will select the second choice, Create An Application Object With An .AOT/.AXT File. When you click Next, you will be asked for the location of either the .AOT or the .AXT file. You can click the Browse button to locate the .AOT or .AXT object. Once you locate and select the file, click Next to display the screen shown in Figure 11.43.

FIGURE 11.43

Notice that the information has already been filled in for you.

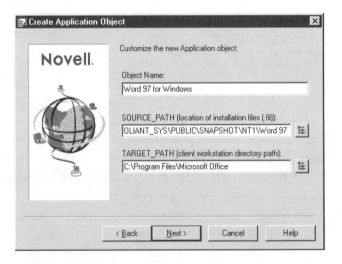

You will notice in Figure 11.43 that the Object Name, SOURCE_PATH, and TARGET_ PATH fields have already been filled in for you. The Create Application Object Wizard pulled this information from the .AXT file. Unless you need to make changes (unlikely and ill-advised) to this information, click Next.

The next screen summarizes the details of the object you are about to create and provides two checkboxes. You can either display details after creation or create another Application object after this one. These options are mutually exclusive. When you click Next again, the object is created.

This may take a few minutes if the snAppShot files (the .AOT and .AXT files) are very large because the information from these files is loaded in the NDS database. You will see a cute animated screen with a progress bar at the bottom and an application box becoming colorized as it flies through a screen.

The NDS Application Object

Once the Application object is created in the Novell Directory Services database, locate the object in your NDS tree and view its details. You will be impressed! Someone at Novell spent a lot of time planning and developing this feature. Take a look at Figure 11.44, which shows just the Identification property page for the Word 97 for Windows Application object.

PART

II

Managing the
Network

FIGURE 11.44

*The Application object
identification for the
Word 97 for Windows
application*

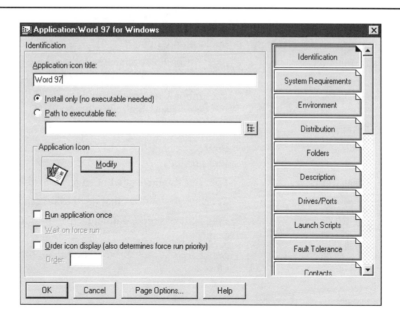

The Application object has 24 property pages! Table 11.5 lists each of these and describes their major functions.

TABLE 11.5: APPLICATION OBJECT PROPERTY PAGES AND THEIR MAJOR FUNCTIONS

Property Page	Property Page Contents
Identification	Specifies the Application icon title.
	Defines the path to the application.
	Sets the Application icon.
System Requirements	Defines which operating systems can use this application and which version of that operating system can use this application.
	Specifies the minimum amount of RAM and processor type that a machine must have to run this application.
	Specifies a minimum amount of disk space that the computer must have on its local drives.
Environment	Sets the application's command-line parameters.
	Sets the application's working directory.
	Sets to run normal, minimized, or maximized.
	Creates a log file for this application and specifies the log file location.
	Specifies that resources the application uses, such as drive mappings and server connections, should be cleaned up when the application terminates.
Distribution	Sets distribution options, including showing distribution progress and prompting the user before starting distribution.
	If a reboot is necessary after the application installs, either prompts the user or automatically reboots.
Folders	Allows you to create subfolders in the Application Launcher.
Description	Provides a place for a description of the services that this application provides.
Drives/Ports	Specifies the drives that need to be mapped for this application.
	Specifies the printers that need to be captured for this application.
Launch Scripts	Sets a list of script commands that are run when the application is launched.
	Sets a list of script commands that are run when the application is closed.

Continued ▶

TABLE 11.5 CONTINUED: APPLICATION OBJECT PROPERTY PAGES AND THEIR MAJOR FUNCTIONS

Property Page	Property Page Contents
Fault Tolerance	Sets fault-tolerant options so that if the primary path to an application is unavailable, the user will be redirected to another location.
	Sets load balancing so that a user uses the least busy copy of an application if more than one server in the local site has a copy of that application.
Contacts	Sets up a list of NDS users that a person can contact when encountering a problem with this application.
Associations	Grants multiple users, groups, or container objects the right to see and use this Application object.
Administrative Notes	Contains notes for the administrators. End users cannot see these notes.
Macros	Defines macros (variable names) that can be used by scripts or other Application object properties.
Environment Variables	Doesn't work with Windows 3.x systems, but allows you to set PATH statements and the like.
Registry Settings	Allows you to view and change the Registry settings for this application. These were imported from the .AXT file that was generated when the snAppShot application was run.
INI Settings	Lists .INI files and the changes that will be made to those .INI files when this application is installed or run on a computer.
Application Files	Views files and directories that will be installed when the application is set up.
	Adds, modifies, or deletes other applications that are required for a particular application.
Text Files	Adds, modifies, or deletes changes that need to be made to a workstation's text files such as the CONFIG.SYS and AUTOEXEC.BAT files.
Schedule	Sets up a schedule when the application is available and unavailable.
Icons/Shortcuts	Configures application shortcuts that will be placed on the Start menu, program folders, desktop, or elsewhere on the local drive.
File Rights	Grants rights to files and directories when this Application object is associated with a user or group. The rights are removed when the Application object is disassociated.
Termination	Specifies one of four methods by which an application is terminated when it is no longer available:
	Sends message to close application.

Continued ▶

PART

II

Managing the
Network

TABLE 11.5 CONTINUED: APPLICATION OBJECT PROPERTY PAGES AND THEIR MAJOR FUNCTIONS

Property Page	Property Page Contents
Termination	Sends message to close and then prompts to save data.
	Sends message to close, prompt to save data, and then forces close.
	Sends message to close and then forces close with explanation.
Application Site List	Lets administrators set up a site list so that users can execute the closest copy of an application. This is especially useful if you have users who work in offices separated by a wide area network.
Reporting	Specifies whether you wish to keep a log file of the application installation, including distribution success/failure and launch success/failure.

Though I won't go into detail about all of these objects, I will look at some of the more useful Application properties.

System Requirements

When you get ready to deploy an application remotely, you want to make sure that the workstations to which you are deploying can actually handle the application. That is the job of the System Requirements property page of the Application object, as shown in Figure 11.45.

FIGURE 11.45

System requirements for the Word 97 for Windows application

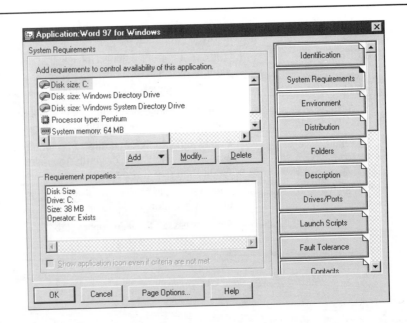

Novell changed this screen dramatically from ZENworks 1.2 to ZENworks 2.0 with NetWare 5.1. Earlier, more information about system details appeared on this screen. Now, more information hides under each of the items listed in the top window. I added the Processor Type and System Memory by clicking the Add button, choosing from the pop-up menu, and deciding the details myself. ZENworks figured out the disk space necessary of 38MB—but remember that amount is only for Microsoft Word, not the entire Office suite. Notice that I require 64MB of RAM and a minimum of a Pentium-class machine to run Word 97 for Windows. Such a machine is underpowered by today's standards, I know, but not everyone needs killer machines with 3D turbo graphics just to type company memos.

System Environment

Another useful property page is the Environment property page. It lets me specify details about the environment in which the application should run. Figure 11.46 shows the environment settings for my Word 97 for Windows application.

PART

II

Managing the Network

FIGURE 11.46

Word 97 for Windows environment settings

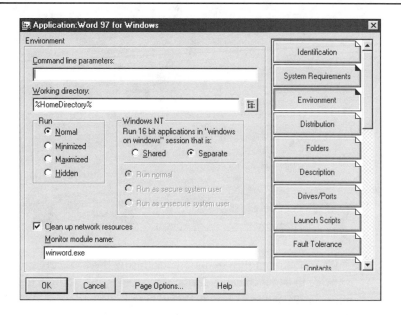

You can specify any command-line parameters, working directory, logging directory, and network cleanup. Notice that the working directory used to support a macro (variable), but it now demands an actual directory. I specified that resources should be cleaned up when the application terminates. I must provide a program name to monitor so that application termination can be determined, so I specified WINWORD.EXE.

Application Schedule

Do you have applications that you want users to run only during certain times of the day? Although Word 97 probably does not qualify as one of those, I have had a few programs that I would like to have been able to shut off after a certain time of the day. Click the Schedule button to open the Schedule property page, where you can specify when the application is available. Your choices are None, Range Of Days, or Specified Days. If you select None, the application is available all the time. In my example in Figure 11.47, I have specified Range Of Days.

FIGURE 11.47

The days and times that the Word 97 for Windows application will be available

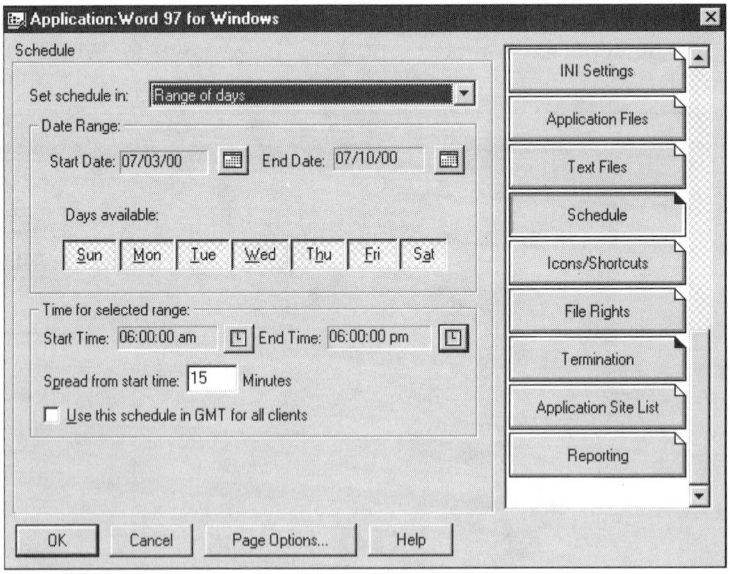

Planning for a full system upgrade during the company holiday, I scheduled the software to be unavailable during the week of July 3, 2000. If anyone comes to the office, or dials in from home, they will be unable to run Word 97 for Windows and possibly complicate a system upgrade.

If you try to access this application outside of its availability range, you will be unable to run it. If you are using the application when the time is up, you will be terminated based on the behavior set in the Termination page, with the following options:

None   No enforcement.

Send Message To Close Application   Trust the user to comply.

Send Message To Close Then Prompt To Save Data   A stronger message.

Send Message To Close Then Force Close With Explanation   Take that, users!

Application Icons and Shortcuts

Ever wonder who decides where to put icons and shortcuts for Windows applications? Is someone flipping a coin and saying, "Okay, heads, we put the icon on the desktop; tails, we bury it in several layers of menus"? Maybe it's just me.

The snAppShot utility figured out where the installation of Word 97 created every icon and shortcut and recorded that information. When the Application object is created, this information is moved into the NDS database and is visible in the Icons/Shortcuts property page of the Application object, as you can see in Figure 11.48.

FIGURE 11.48

Viewing shortcut properties

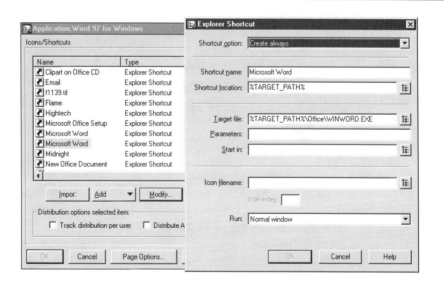

In Figure 11.48, you can see on the left side the Icons/Shortcuts page for my Word 97 for Windows Application object. I have highlighted one of the shortcuts and clicked the Modify button. You can see the Explorer Shortcut dialog box on the right side of Figure 11.48. Remember those macros I listed earlier (the ones I insist on calling variables)? Here is one place they come in to use.

The Shortcut Location is listed as %TARGET_PATH%, but the shortcut will appear on the Start menu in the Programs folder. The first time it appears at the bottom of the list, but after you reboot the system the list gets arranged alphabetically.

NOTE   One annoying thing that Word 97 does during installation is put a pesky shortcut on everyone's desktop that gives you the option of installing Internet Explorer. If you don't want this shortcut on all your users' desktops, simply delete it from the Icons/Shortcuts list!

Associating Applications

IN A HURRY

11.18 Associate a Group of Users with an Application Object

1. Using NetWare Administrator, highlight the Application object that you want to modify.
2. Right-click the Application object and choose the Details button.
3. Select the Associations property page.
4. Click the Add button.
5. Browse NDS and find the group you want to assign to this Application object.
6. Click OK twice.

I still don't think that Associations is the right name for this property page, but (sigh) no one asked me. I would have called it Authorized Users or Rights or Permissions or something. The Associations property page lets you assign permissions to use this Application object (see Figure 11.49).

You can assign User, Group, and Organizational Unit objects to this Application object. When assigning containers, you get to choose whether the association is to the workstations or the users in the container. The default, users, should be kept in most cases.

FIGURE 11.49

Who can use this Application object?

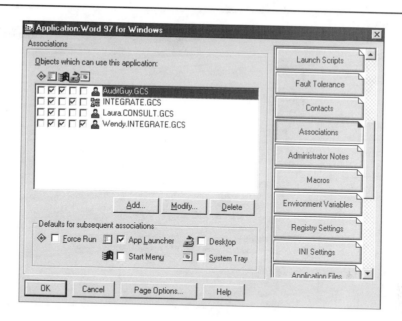

 TIP When you start creating applications and application folders, simply as an organizational technique, you might want to create an Organizational Unit under the container in which your User, Group, and other NDS objects are located. Call this Organizational Unit container something like Applications. This will keep your containers less cluttered. You will be glad you did.

The Two Flavors of Application Launcher

The programs that affect the end-user side of Application Launcher come in two separate colors:

- Application Launcher Window
- Application Launcher Explorer

The Application Launcher Window, shown in Figure 11.50, is an application that incorporates the applications you were assigned by the Application Launcher with applications that are already on the Start menu and the Programs menu. This program is launched by running the program SYS:PUBLIC\NAL.EXE.

The Application Launcher Window and applications that Novell provides

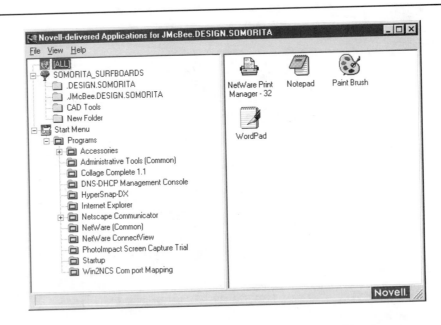

In Figure 11.50, I have highlighted the ALL object at the top of the applications directory tree in the left pane of the window. In the right pane, you can see the applications that were assigned by the Novell Application Launcher. In the left pane of the Application Launcher Window, I have opened the directory tree SOMORITA_SURFBOARDS and see groups as well as application folders. If my User object has been assigned any applications specifically, I will see those as well.

The Application Launcher Explorer incorporates Novell-delivered applications on the Start menu, the desktop, and the system tray. Figure 11.51 shows a Windows NT desktop after running the Application Launcher Explorer (SYS:PUBLIC\NALEXPLD.EXE).

The changes to the desktop may actually be subtle. In the system tray, you will notice a new icon representing the Notepad application. The Start menu will have the shortcuts, and the desktop will have new shortcuts for applications that were set up for the Application Launcher.

 TIP If you end up with duplicate icons in the system tray, on the desktop, and in menus, check to make sure that you are not launching multiple copies of the NALEXPLD.EXE program. This is the program that loads the Application Launcher Explorer (NALDESK.EXE).

PART

II

Managing the
Network

FIGURE 11.51

*The Windows NT
desktop after running
the Application
Launcher Explorer*

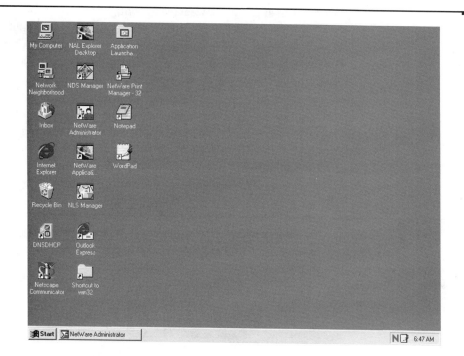

Assigning Applications to the Application Launcher

IN A HURRY

11.19 Assign a Previously Created Application to the Application Launcher

1. Using NetWare Administrator, highlight the Organization or Organizational Unit container for which you want to configure the Application Launcher.

2. Right-click the container object and choose Details.

3. Select the Launcher Configuration tab.

4. Click Add and browse the NDS directory for the applications you want to add.

5. Click the appropriate checkboxes for the places you want the object to appear: Application Launcher, Desktop, or System Tray.

6. Click OK.

Now that we have an application, we have to configure the Application Launcher to support those applications in the NDS directory. You configure the Application Launcher at the Country, Organization, or Organizational Unit container. You can also assign applications at the User and Group object levels. For simplicity's sake, I will look only at the Organizational Unit level. By default, this will provide applications through the Application Launcher for all users in that container.

Figure 11.52 shows the Applications property page of the Organizational Unit Apps (I told you to make a special container). From here, you can add and remove applications that you want available to everyone in this Organizational Unit. (Of course, the users must have been associated with the Application object when it was created. Otherwise, the users have no permissions to see or run the application.)

FIGURE 11.52

Applications that will be delivered to clients using the Application Launcher Window or Application Launcher Explorer

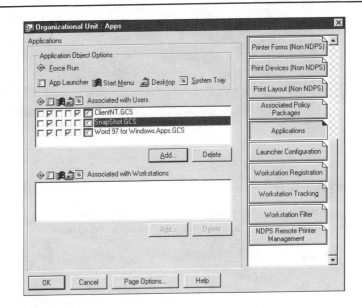

Notice in Figure 11.52 that there are five checkboxes for each application. The first checkbox column, Force Run, represents an application that will automatically run. The remaining columns of checkboxes represent the places where you want the object's shortcut to appear.

- The Force Run checkbox will start the application whether the user wants it or not.
- The App Launcher checkbox indicates that the application will appear in the Application Launcher Window. By default, all applications appear in the Application Launcher Window.

- The Start Menu checkbox indicates that the application will appear on the user's Start menu.

- The Desktop checkbox puts the application shortcut on the user's desktop.

- The System Tray icon, of course, indicates that the application will have a shortcut in the system tray.

 TIP Remember: Country, Organization, Organizational Unit, Group, and User NDS objects have an Applications page.

Customizing the Application Launcher Configuration

You can customize the Application Launcher configuration at the Country, Organization, Organizational Unit, and User NDS object levels, but not at the Group object level. To customize the Application Launcher configuration, view the details of the object you want to configure and open the Launcher Configuration property page. Figure 11.53 shows the Organizational Unit Apps container's Launcher Configuration property page, with the appropriate default values.

PART II

Managing the Network

FIGURE 11.53

The Launcher Configuration property page for the Apps container

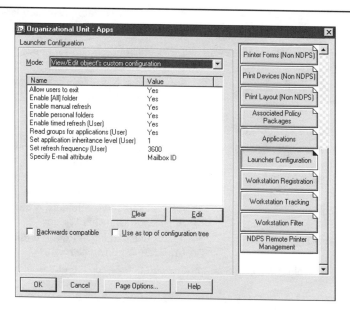

Notice the Mode drop-down list box near the top of the screen in Figure 11.53. You can view configurations in three modes:

- View Configuration Tree
- View Object's Effective Settings
- View/Edit Object's Custom Configuration

Figure 11.53 shows the View/Edit Object's Custom Configuration mode. From this mode on the property page, you can set the configuration mode for the object at this particular level. By default, the box is cleared, but if you click the Edit button, you will see the Launcher Configuration dialog box, where all these values listed in Figure 11.53 came from.

This dialog box has three property tabs—General, Window, and Explorer—that let you set properties for Application Launcher. The settings include Yes, No, **Unset**, and Custom. Table 11.6 describes the custom settings and their default values.

TABLE 11.6: APPLICATION LAUNCHER CUSTOM SETTINGS AND DEFAULTS

Setting	Explanation	Default Value
Allow Users To Exit	Allows users to exit the Application Launcher	Yes
Enable Manual Refresh	Allows users to manually refresh the icons	No
Enable Personal Folders	Allows users to create personal folders	No
Enable Timed Refresh	Enables use of the timed refresh setting	No
Read Groups For Applications	Looks at Group objects for applications assigned to them	Yes
Set Application Inheritance Level	Sets the number of levels up the tree that Application Launcher will "walk" looking for applications	1
Set Refresh Frequency	Sets the time between timed refreshes	3600 seconds
Specify E-mail Attribute	Sets which NDS User object property is used as an e-mail address	Mailbox ID
Display Start Menu	Includes the Start items and Programs menu folders in the Application Launcher Window	Yes
Enable Folder View	Allows users to view folders in the Application Launcher Window	Yes
Enable Log In	Allows users to log in from the Application Launcher Window File menu	Yes
Expand Folder View On Startup	If enabled, expands the entire folder subtree	No

Continued ▶

TABLE 11.6 CONTINUED: APPLICATION LAUNCHER CUSTOM SETTINGS AND DEFAULTS		
Setting	**Explanation**	**Default Value**
Save Window Size And Position	Saves the window settings and current position	Yes
Display Icon On Desktop	Places the Application Launcher Explorer icon on the desktop	Yes
Name Icon On Desktop	The name of the Application Launcher Explorer icon that Application Launcher puts on the Windows 95/98 or Windows NT desktop	Application Explorer

Effective Application Configuration Settings

IN A HURRY

11.20 View Effective Application Launcher Configuration

1. Using NetWare Administrator, highlight the object for which you want to view the effective Application Launcher configuration.
2. Right-click the object and choose Details.
3. Select the Launcher Configuration window.
4. In the Mode drop-down list box, select View Object's Effective Settings.
5. Click Cancel to exit.

If a value remains **Unset** up the tree through all the parent objects, the default values shown in Table 11.6 are set. Application Launcher will "walk" up the tree in search of configuration values of the next parent until it reaches the top of the tree or until it reaches a container that you have designated by checking the Use As Top Of Configuration Tree checkbox, shown near the bottom of the screen in Figure 11.53.

To determine the effective value, let's look at a quick example. Table 11.7 shows which values are overridden. Remember that the User object's Application Launcher configuration will override a configuration at a container level. This example comes from a working, rather than a lab, network.

TABLE 11.7: HOW EFFECTIVE SETTINGS ARE DETERMINED			
Object Name	**Allow Users to Exit**	**Enable Personal Folders**	**Set Refresh Frequency**
Somorita	No	Yes	*
.design.somorita	No	*	300
.jmcbee.design.somorita	Yes	No	3600
Effective Settings	Yes	No	3600

*Blank counts as unset.

You can also view the user's or container's effective configuration from the Launcher Configuration property page of that container. Figure 11.54 shows user JMcBee's effective configuration.

FIGURE 11.54

User JMcBee's effective Application Launcher configuration

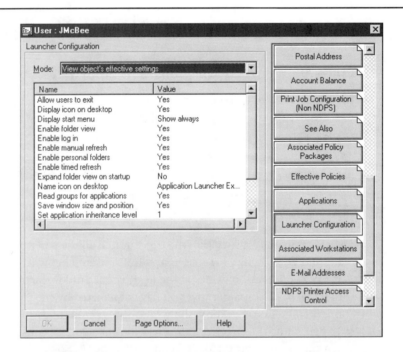

To view a user's or container's effective configuration, display the details of the object and select the Launcher Configuration property page. In the Mode drop-down list box, select View Object's Effective Settings.

If you want to view a summary of the settings at each level of the configuration tree, a handy feature is the Launcher Configuration property page's Mode: View Configuration Tree option, which displays the options at the current level up through the top of the tree. Figure 11.55 shows this configuration tree.

FIGURE 11.55

User JMcBee's configuration tree

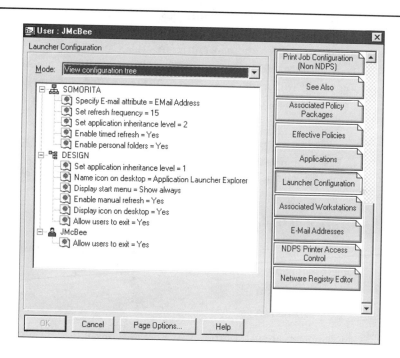

PART

II

Managing the Network

Launching the Application Launcher

Now that you have your applications configured through Application Launcher, the next dilemma you face is how all those workstations automatically load the NAL.EXE (Application Launcher) or NALEXPLD.EXE (Application Launcher Explorer).

The easiest way is to put the commands in the login script (just be careful not to launch them twice). Here is a sample command to put in the login script:

```
@\\RELL\SYS\PUBLIC\NAL.EXE
```

Remember that NAL will automatically launch the correct 16-bit or 32-bit program depending on the client's operating system platform. To launch the Application Launcher Explorer (which includes items on the Start menu, desktop, and system tray), put a command similar to this in the login script:

```
@\\RELL\SYS\PUBLIC\NALEXPLD.EXE
```

Other methods include adding a shortcut to a common Start menu using system policies that run the programs or setting up a scheduled event that launches when the user logs in.

Earlier Versions of Application Launcher

If you have been using an earlier version of NetWare Application Launcher, you need to know some things. Application Launcher 2.5 (included with NetWare 5.0) introduced new macros and new entries for .AOT files. Although NAL is backward compatible with older .AOT files, older versions of the NetWare Application Launcher are not compatible with applications and .AOT files created with the newest version of snApp-Shot. You should plan to upgrade your users so that they can all go to the new version at the same time.

 TIP   For more information about compatibility and upgrading older versions of NAL, see the ZENworks home page at www.novell.com/products/zenworks/.

Managing Workstations

Since installing ZENworks, you have probably noticed two new objects in the Create Object dialog box:

- Workstation
- Workstation Group

These objects are part of the Desktop Management (formerly known as Workstation Manager) features of ZENworks.

When you incorporate Desktop Management features with your other ZENworks features, you can assign policies to workstations and restrict users to specific workstations. With the full version of ZENworks (available through your Novell reseller), you can also handle workstation inventory and remote control.

Getting Workstations in the NDS Directory

IN A HURRY

11.21 Register a Workstation with the Directory

1. For Windows 3.1, run the program SYS:PUBLIC\WSREG16.EXE.
2. For Windows NT Workstation and Windows 95/98, run the program SYS:PUBLIC\WSREG32.EXE.

If you try to create a new Workstation object, you will receive a message telling you that the workstation should be registered and then imported. Workstations can be registered automatically or manually. Naturally, I prefer the automatic method whenever I can have my way, but first, let's take a quick look at the manual method.

Workstations need to have their preferred server or NDS tree configured when the client is installed and should be running the NetWare 5.1 client software. To register a workstation with the NDS directory, you can run two programs:

- WSREG32.EXE registers Windows NT and Windows 95/98 workstations.

- WSREG16.EXE registers Windows 3.1 workstations.

The user can launch these programs from a login script, or if you are using policy packages, you can create a scheduled action. The user who runs this program must have the Write right to the NDS container's WM: Registered Workstation attribute. You can either add this right manually or use the SYS:PUBLIC\WIN32\WSRIGHTS.EXE program.

If you are like me, you want as many things around you as possible to be automatic. You can add workstation registration to that list—provided that during the installation of your Windows 95/98 and Windows NT clients (sorry, no Windows 3.1 support), you left the Workstation Manager enabled. Figure 11.56 shows the Novell client installation options for the NetWare 5.1 client. You must select the Novell Workstation Manager option in order to get Workstation Manager support.

FIGURE 11.56

Novell client installation options

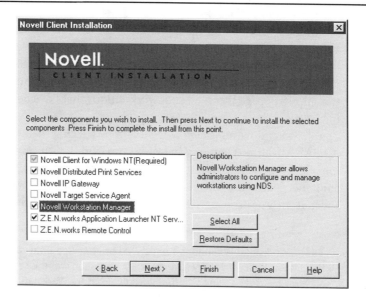

When a user logs in using the NetWare 5.1 client, the workstation is registered automatically. Before you register workstations, be sure that you have a Workstation Import policy set. The Workstation Import policy is part of the Windows 95 and Windows NT User System Policy Packages. It lets you define the container to which workstations will be imported and specify how the workstation name will be generated. See the section "Setting NT User System Policies," earlier in this chapter, for more information.

Importing Workstations

IN A HURRY

11.22 Import Workstations That Have Been Previously Registered

1. Run the program SYS:PUBLIC\WIN32\WSIMPORT.EXE.
2. Enter the name of the container from which you want to import previously registered workstations.
3. Click OK.
4. Click Close when the import process is complete.

Once the workstation is registered with NDS, it is the administrator's job to create the Workstation objects by running the Import utility. You can do this in a number of ways. To import all the workstations that have been registered in a specific container, use the SYS:PUBLIC\WIN32\WSIMPORT.EXE utility. You can launch this utility from NetWare Administrator by choosing Tools ➤ Import Workstations.

The other way to import workstations is from the Container object in which the workstation was registered. In Figure 11.57, the GCS container's Workstation Registration property page shows a list of workstations that have been registered but not yet imported.

You can remove a selected workstation by clicking the Remove button (or the Remove All button), or you can import the workstation by clicking the Import button. Clicking the Import button creates a new Workstation object in the directory container specified in the Workstation Import policy that was part of the policy package that the user who registered the workstation was assigned.

 TIP Workstations cannot be registered or imported until you have created a Workstation Import Policy. If you try to register a workstation without setting the policy, you will get an error message telling you that you must have a Workstation Import policy. For more information, see the "Setting the Workstation Import Policy" section earlier in this chapter.

FIGURE 11.57

*Workstations that are
ready to be imported*

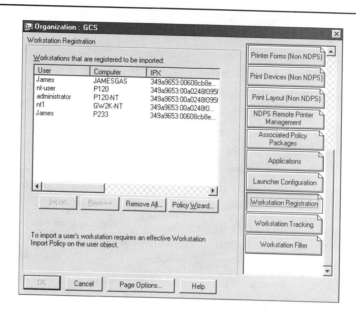

The Workstation object name is also determined by the Workstation Import policy. The workstation that I imported in Figure 11.57 will be created with a Workstation object name that consists of the workstation name and the network address. This is the default, but the naming rules can be modified in the Workstation Import policy. Figure 11.58 shows the Identification property page for the real-world workstation WS-NOVELL00104b740350 that I just imported.

FIGURE 11.58

*Details of a newly
imported Workstation
object and additional
details entered on
the Identification
property page*

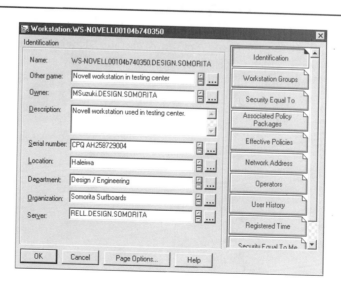

The Workstation object has 10 property pages:

Identification　Provides fields for additional information about the workstation, such as owner, description, serial number, location, department, organization, and server.

Workstation Groups　Allows the administrator to assign the workstation to one or more workstation groups.

Security Equal To　Assigns this workstation permissions equivalent to objects in this list.

Associated Policy Packages　Allows one Windows NT/2000, Windows 95/98, and Windows 3.1 policy package to be assigned to this workstation. Only one policy package for each platform can be assigned to a workstation.

Effective Policies　Allows the administrator to view the effective policies for this workstation from all sources, including the container and workstation groups.

Network Address　Lets you view the current network address or addresses.

Operators　Permits administrators to assign users to have operator permissions to this workstation.

User History　Lets you view a list of the most recent users of this workstation.

Registered Time　Lets you see what time this workstation is currently set to.

Security Equal To Me　Lets you assign other objects to have permissions equal to this object.

The Workstation Filter

Figure 11.59 shows the Workstation Filter property page for the DESIGN Organizational Unit. The purpose of the Workstation Filter is to specify, based on network address, which workstations can be imported. If you click the Add button, you can add additional filters to the list.

You can specify filters based on the IP or IPX address. If the list is left blank, by default any IP and IPX addresses can be imported.

FIGURE 11.59

*Viewing and adding
workstation filters*

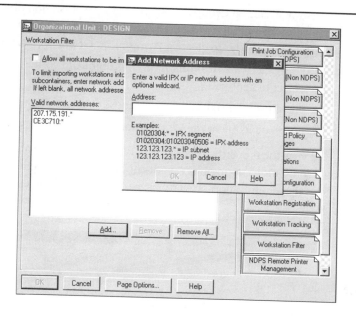

Creating Workstation Groups

IN A HURRY

11.23 Create a Workstation Group

1. Using NetWare Administrator, highlight the container in which you want the Workstation Group object to appear.

2. Right-click the container object and choose Create.

3. In the Create Object dialog box, choose Workstation Group and click OK.

4. Enter a name for the Workstation Group and check the Define Additional Properties checkbox.

5. Click the Create button.

6. Select the Members property page.

7. Click the Add button to add Workstation objects to this group.

8. Click the OK button when finished.

You use Workstation Groups to organize your Workstation objects in logical categories for purposes such as assigning a policy package to a whole group of workstations simultaneously. To create a Workstation Group object, follow these steps:

1. Using NetWare Administrator, highlight the container in which you want the object to appear.

2. Press Insert, or right-click and choose Create.

3. Enter the name of the Workstation Group and click OK.

To view the properties of a Workstation Group, use NetWare Administrator to locate the Workstation Group object, right-click the object, and choose Details. Figure 11.60 shows the Identification property page of the Workstation Group object.

FIGURE 11.60

The Workstation Group object's Identification property page

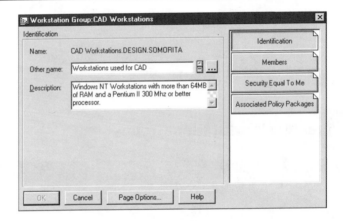

The Workstation Group object has four property pages:

Identification   Has fields for an additional name and a description of the group.

Members   Contains a list of currently imported workstations that are members of this Workstation Group.

Security Equal To Me   Contains a list of objects that have been assigned security equal to this object.

Associated Policy Packages   Contains a list of the policy packages assigned to this Workstation Group. A Workstation Group can have one Windows NT/2000, one Windows 95/98, and one Windows 3.1 Workstation policy package assigned to it. It cannot have two policy packages for the same platform (for example, two packages for Windows 95).

Trends in Software Metering and Licensing

Some of you will remember earlier versions of software such as Lotus 1-2-3 that required a "key" disk to activate the software. This disk ensured that you used only a single copy of the software. Many software packages that incorporated key disks were also network-hostile (not to mention user-hostile). Early makers of PC software wanted to ensure that you purchased every copy of software that you actually used. As the PC network grew in popularity, the concept of key disks became more and more impractical due to the complexity of implementing it on a variety of platforms.

Today, off-the-shelf software is more network-friendly; only in specialized software will you find keys, activation codes, or dongles required (a *dongle* is a hardware device that attaches to the PC's parallel port). Friends in the software business during the height of this madness tell me half or more of their support calls concerned problems with dongles or key disks. However, this made tracking software usage more difficult and opened a whole new cottage industry—software metering.

As early as NetWare 2.1, there were third-party tools to track concurrent usage of software. These tools ensured that your network software usage did not exceed the number of copies you actually purchased.

Early versions of these programs did have their flaws. Many early software-metering packages did not recognize when a workstation had locked up and had to be rebooted, thus keeping a software license active even when it was no longer being used. These early programs also had problems tracking applications that were installed on the local hard drive of networked workstations.

PART

II

Managing the
Network

Did You Purchase Every Piece of Software You Use?

Does your organization own every piece of software that it is using? Can you prove it? Do you have the license agreement and invoice records for the purchase of this software? Did you know that you could be fined up to $100,000 for *each* piece of software you do not have licensed legally? You can also be fined up to $250,000 and sentenced to five years in jail for copying software and giving it to a friend!

Software piracy is no joke! I know people who have experienced the penalties first hand, and I advise you to make sure your network is in compliance now. What can you do?

- Collect all your license agreement documents and keep them in a safe place.
- Keep copies of all invoices for software purchases.

Continued ▯▶

CONTINUED

- Periodically audit your software usage to make sure you are not exceeding your authorized usage levels or exceeding the number of licenses you can use.

- Read and understand the license agreement documents. I have had to read a few of these documents three times in order to make sense of them, but in the end, I am glad I did as I have a better understanding of what the license permits me to do.

- Questions? Contact the software vendor and enlist their help to ensure that you purchase the correct number of copies and that you use them correctly.

The best place of find out more about software piracy is the Software Publishers Association Web page at `www.spa.org`. Here you will find information about software piracy laws as well as other useful information such as forms and templates to help you set up your own software usage policy and Internet usage policy documents.

Those readers interested in the state of the art when I last reviewed these packages for *Network World* are welcome to check out `http://www.nwfusion.com/reviews/0809rev.html` for my thoughts in general and for particular packages. Again, ZENworks wasn't included because these applications did metering only; ZENworks pays the price again for crossing so many product boundaries.

Software-tracking programs have improved greatly over time, but still lack any sort of standardization. Now that is all changing.

Novell Licensing Services

Metering and licensing are two parts of the same coin. *Metering* tracks which software is being used and by whom. *Licensing* works with metering to set the usage levels of software products. Most metering software shows usage by concurrent users, which is what most software vendors track. Good metering software will also provide reports of application usage after the fact.

Novell, Gradient, IBM, and Microsoft have developed the LSAPI (Licensing Service Application Programming Interface). This specialized API (Application Programming Interface, a way software vendors write programs that other programs can access) provides a common interface for developers to manage execution of their products by electronic license certificates.

Novell has included with NetWare 5.1 the new Novell Licensing Services software. Novell Licensing Services (NLS) includes server-based software and components that integrate with NetWare Directory Services to help you license and meter software. Features include the ability to track applications launched from a network client's hard disk and to provide usage reports. As software vendors start using the LSAPI when developing applications, software packages will be able to communicate directly with the NLS service, but in the interim, NLS can also meter non-NLS applications.

These advances, and more to come, show improvement in the handling of network applications. It wasn't so long ago that companies had to keep closets full of single-user applications, such as Lotus 1-2-3, because the vendor didn't provide a network license. Now, a major application without network pricing and licensing is becoming, thank goodness, an anomaly. Except for Microsoft Office, of course. Microsoft pushes mightily to force every computer in every company to have an individual license for Office, just in case that user ever decides to use the program.

Novell Licensing Service Basics

When you start working with NLS, you need to be aware of some basics:

NLS Clients   Applications that can communicate directly with the NLS service. The application can be on a client workstation or at a NetWare server.

Non-NLS Clients   Applications that do not have the ability to communicate directly with NLS services. Most applications on the market today fall into this category.

License Service Providers   NetWare Loadable Modules (NLMs) that respond to requests from LSAPI-compliant applications for licenses or licensing information. This service is provided on the NetWare server by the NLSLSP.NLM. Although you only need one server running this NLM on your entire network, I recommend at least one server providing this support in each geographic location.

NLS Manager   A graphical utility that lets you browse the licenses that are currently installed and report on license usage.

License Certificates   NDS objects that are installed when an NLS-aware application is licensed. License Certificates are installed into NDS in License object containers. License Certificates can be installed through NetWare Administrator or the NLS Manager.

Metered Certificates   Allow you to track applications that are not LSAPI-compliant. Applications that are not LSAPI-compliant must be metered using the Application Launcher.

Envelopes   Bundles of licenses that allow you to install multiple licenses at one time, such as if you purchased a suite of applications or if you like your NetWare server and client licenses on one disk.

License Catalog   Uses the Catalog Service to provide frequently updated information about licensing.

Creating a License Certificate

11.24 Create a License Certificate

1. Using NetWare Administrator, choose Tools ➤ Novell Licensing Services ➤ Add Licenses.
2. Choose License File or License Metering.
3. Browse for the path and filename for the `.NLF` envelope file.
4. Select the NDS License Certificate and read the description.
5. Select the context (if necessary).
6. Click Add.

For LSAPI-aware applications, the software vendor will provide files that contain the activation key and software information. This information needs to be imported into the NDS directory. Novell uses the Licensing Services for their own protection, as well as for granting server and user licenses through the system.

The NLS Manager program disappeared with NetWare 5.0; all functions have been rolled into NetWare Administrator, as shown in Figure 11.61. This program can be used in Windows 95/98 or Windows NT.

FIGURE 11.61

Installing a License Certificate using Novell Licensing Services

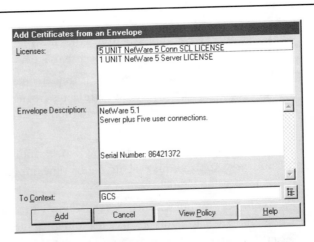

To create a new License Certificate using NLS, first choose Tools ➤ Novell Licensing Services ➤ Add Licenses. The screen that appears will look similar to the one in Figure 11.61.

Browse your disks to find and select the path to the .NLF file. The .NLF file acts as an envelope and contains the actual license files. It also contains a link to the activation password file. This activation password file contains the activation key (a string of numbers and letters) that enables the software to be used. Next, click Browse and select the NDS container in which you want the License object to appear, and then click OK.

Creating a Metered Certificate

IN A HURRY

11.25 Create a Metered Certificate

1. Using the Netware Administrator utility, choose Tools ➢ Novell Licensing Services ➢ Add Licenses.
2. Choose License Metering and click OK.
3. Enter the software publisher's name, product name, and version.
4. Select an NDS container for the Metered Certificate.
5. Enter the number of licenses you have purchased.
6. Enter the number of grace license units.
7. Select an update interval.
8. If multiple launches from a single workstation count as one license, check that checkbox.
9. Click OK.

PART

II

Managing the Network

You create Metered Certificates for applications whose usage you want to track but that are not LSAPI-compliant. However, you can also use Metered Certificates to track applications that are LSAPI-compliant. To create a Metered Certificate object in the NDS directory database, use NetWare Administrator. Choose Tools ➢ Novell Licensing Services ➢ Add Licenses ➢ License Metering. The Create A Metered Certificate dialog box, as shown in Figure 11.62, will appear.

The Create A Metered Certificate dialog box requires that you enter the name of the application publisher, the product name, and the software version. Although you enter these separately in the dialog box, they are combined to create a directory name. In the example in Figure 11.62, the directory name would be Microsoft+Word for Windows+97.

Enter an NDS directory context, the number of licenses purchased, grace license units, and update interval. If the application can be launched multiple times from the same workstation but count as only one used license, check the Multiple Launches At A Workstation Use Just 1 License checkbox.

FIGURE 11.62

Creating a Metered Certificate for an application that is not LSAPI-compliant

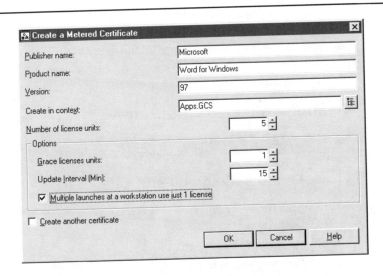

The Grace Licenses Units box allows you to specify the number of copies of software that can be running above and beyond the total number you have purchased. This gives you time to go out and purchase more. If you are unsure whether your software allows this, contact the vendor and leave the Grace Licenses Units field at zero until you are sure. This means that only the total number of licenses you have purchased will be allowed to use the software. Use Grace Licenses Units if rebooted clients hold licenses until they time out and declare themselves eligible once again.

Reporting on License Usage

IN A HURRY

11.26 Generate a License Listing and Usage Report

1. Using the Netware Administrator utility, choose Tools ➤ Novell Licensing Services ➤ Generate License Reports.

2. Click OK to use the default search of the current tree from the Organization level down.

3. Click the License Usage Report icon for more details.

One of the greatest features of Novell Licensing Services is the ability to view reports on license usage. This is important in determining future license purchases and making sure that you do not over-purchase licenses.

To view license usage information, use NetWare Administrator. Choose Tools ➤ Novell Licensing Services ➤ Generate License Reports. Not much to do here besides clicking OK to scan the tree from the Organization level down. If you created License Catalogs earlier, click that tab, but the easiest way to get the most information comes by accepting the defaults. Figure 11.63 shows some of the NetWare licenses in place on the lab network.

FIGURE 11.63

A screen listing the current NetWare licenses

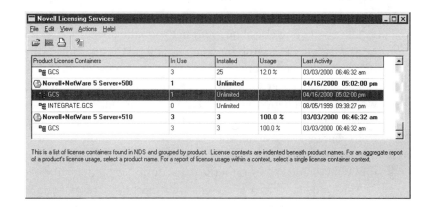

See the little chalkboard icon between the file open icon and the print icon at the top left of the report? That opens the License Usage Report.

The License Usage Report dialog box has two property pages or tabs: Graph and Summary. The Graph page, shown in Figure 11.64, is by far the easiest to understand. You can use this graph as proof to your boss that you are hitting your license ceiling (or that you purchased too many). The Summary page includes information such as current usage, peak usage, and the dates and times when your requirements exceeded your current allocation.

FIGURE 11.64

A graph of the license usage information for a NetWare license

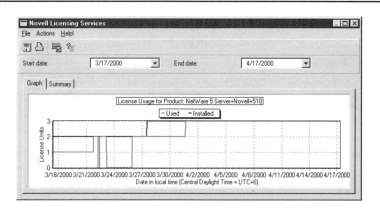

PART

II

Managing the Network

Server-Based Application Guidelines

Although I don't really like putting application software on workstation local hard drives, Microsoft Windows gives you little choice in the matter (most of the time). There are still occasions when it's possible to put users' applications on the server hard drives. Questions then arise about where to put programs, data, and system files. There are no hard-and-fast rules about where to put anything, so this is my general rule: protect your data.

Like everything else about your network, the directory structure for your applications is unique. The setup for your server-based applications will be based on your preferences, the preferences of your users, and, most of all, the dictates of your application. We'll go over some guidelines for your directory structure, but don't get upset when you must bend the rules to fit your situation.

The most important guideline is this: keep your application programs separate from your data. Many network administrators keep their applications on one volume and let users keep their data on another volume. For example, the database application is on volume APPS:, and the data controlled by that database is on DATA:.

This guideline makes good sense in almost every case. If you mingle the applications and the data, something will happen to one or the other. If users have Delete rights for a data directory in the same directory structure as the application programs, something will be erased. Guaranteed.

If your tape backup system is unable to capture everything in one tape, it may be able to back up the data in one tape if it is separate from the application programs. Separating the data and programs also means you need to back up only the data and/or application volumes when something changes.

Although it's possible to choose which directories are copied in a backup operation, it's easier to back up a volume. Your backup parameters take more time to set up and are more prone to errors if you must thread in and around your directories to cover everything.

Take a look at Figure 11.65 for a simple example of separating your data from your programs. This setup uses the RELL server, with one 2GB disk divided into three NetWare volumes.

The SYS: volume holds all the NetWare operating system files and utilities, the NetWare Java programs, and the working directories for printing. You can see the NetWare system directories on RELL_SYS. The APPS: volume in the example holds the Microsoft Office network installation and the GroupWise software. On the DATA: volume, under MSOFFICE, are the directories for the Office software, templates, clipart, and more.

FIGURE 11.65

*A simple but effective
method for separating
your application pro-
grams from your data*

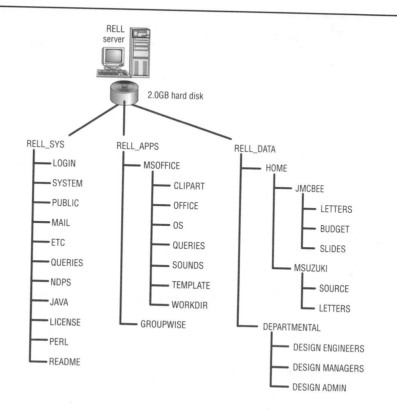

 TIP Unless your network karma is excellent, I am betting that you will wish you had allocated more disk space to one volume than to another. I have done this more times than I like to recall. I make the DATA: volume too large and the APPS: volume too small or vice-versa. This is one more argument for purchasing much more disk space than you think you will need. You will always need more.

I like the idea of putting all my applications on a separate volume. If you don't have lots of applications, you might be better off with all the applications on the SYS: volume. Calling a volume APPS:, for instance, makes several things easier. All drive mappings can point to the same volume, so it's easy to remember. It also adds one more level of separation for your tape backup process.

TIP If you put your application files on the SYS: volume, make sure that you still have plenty of disk space available. I like to have at least 250MB of disk space available on my SYS: volume, more if I am using that volume to spool print jobs. Low disk space can cause problems for your server, including server crashes.

In our example, the DATA: volume holds the HOME directories for users. This is where all the home directories are automatically placed when a new user is created. In Figure 11.65, you can see the directories for JMcBee and for MSuzuki (of course, your network will have more than two users—this is just to give you the idea).

Since these are home directories, users can organize them any way they wish. Your users' home directories will be around the jobs they must deal with in their workday. User JMcBee may have directories named LETTERS, BUDGET, and SLIDES (for presentations). MSuzuki may have SOURCE, for source code files, and LETTERS.

When the end of the day rolls around and it's time for backup, the most important volume is DATA:. The valuable data is there, where people are creating and using information. If space is tight on the tape for the backup, the APPS: and SYS: volumes could be skipped most of the time. Application files and the NetWare system files change rarely. It may seem like you need a software upgrade every day, but it's not really true.

It's not unusual to go a step farther down this road and keep the applications and data files on separate servers. Figure 11.66 shows this arrangement. RELL_APPS: is on the left, with the MSOffice and GroupWise subdirectories. You can see the program subdirectories within. The other server, GARCIA, has the HOME and Departmental data directories on GARCIA_DATA:.

FIGURE 11.66

Applications here, data there

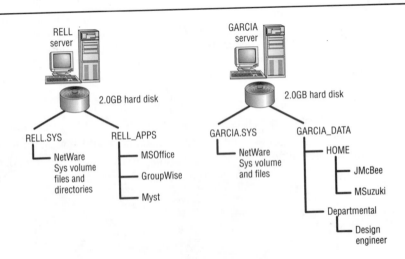

This arrangement also helps balance the load on servers a bit. If your server handles both the applications and the data files, there will be quite a bit of traffic. Multiply this scenario by the number of applications serving the users on your network, and you can imagine the traffic load. The ability of NetWare to support large numbers of concurrent users makes it tempting to load the server with all sorts of application and data directories.

Consolidating Application Licenses

If your workgroups have only a single server and are spread too far apart to use a central server, you have no option for tuning as we just discussed. Worse, you may need to buy many small licenses for network applications rather than one large license. It's more expensive to buy 10 packages, each supporting 10 users, than one package to support 100 users.

However, if your one-server workgroups are all on the same network, the advantages of NetWare may help you in a way you might not have considered. With earlier versions of NetWare, the one-server workgroup made sense because of the high management overhead of mapping each user to several different servers. It was done all the time, of course, but tracking user MSuzuki across six servers meant six times as much work as leaving the user on one server. With NetWare 5.1 and Novell Directory Services, however, you can track user MSuzuki across as many servers as you want, with a single login. Even more important for your social life, this can be done with a single administration step.

Let's go over an example considering three departments: Accounting, Graphics, and Legal. Each has 30 users. Each department has specific software licensed for those 30 users. But what about the general applications that these 90 users need? Why buy three network versions of Paradox, if all 90 users need access to Paradox? We know the Legal department needs access to the legal database, but doesn't everyone need a word processor? Why buy three separate licenses?

Figure 11.67 shows one way to share the load and save some money. The Accounting users must access the Solomon accounting package, but no one else cares about that. So they have a 30-user license for Solomon. The 30 users in the Graphics department need CorelDraw, and the 30 users in the Legal department need access to the Legal database. Nothing unusual here. Then there is the question of buying three licenses each for a word processor, database, and e-mail package (one each for every department).

FIGURE 11.67

Coordinating server application licenses

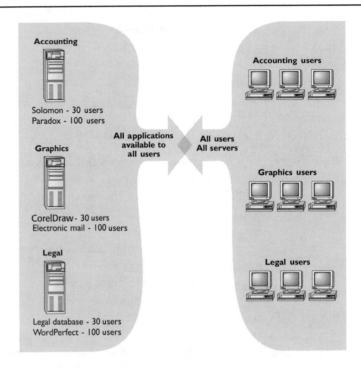

Accounting

Solomon - 30 users
Paradox - 100 users

Graphics

CorelDraw - 30 users
Electronic mail - 100 users

Legal

Legal database - 30 users
WordPerfect - 100 users

All applications available to all users

All users
All servers

Accounting users

Graphics users

Legal users

But the horizontal applications can be shared easily. Everyone needs word processing, so the Legal department server holds a 100-user license of WordPerfect. This lets all users in all three departments have access to one network copy of WordPerfect, rather than three separate ones. The same scenario is repeated on the Graphics department server, where the e-mail application is stored. Accounting also helps out by hosting the Paradox database, again with a 100-user license.

With NetWare 3.x, you needed to create and manage each user in each department on three different servers. With NetWare 4 and NetWare 5.1, users can connect to the Directory Services database and be granted access to their job-specific applications and the horizontal applications: one login, three servers, six applications.

As we've seen in earlier chapters, there's no reason each department can't be its own Organizational Unit. The three departments could also be one large Organizational Unit with three separate groups. Either option, or some other arrangement you may come up with, works for me as long as it works for you.

Access Rights for Application Directories

The default rights for all users to new directories are Read and File Scan (for servers in the same container as the user). These allow everyone to see the directories but not take any action in those directories. The primary action we want to avoid is a user accidentally deleting a file or two hundred. And, as you may have already discovered the hard way, the first step in virus control is keeping users (and hence viruses) from modifying executable files.

Managing Access Rights in Application and Data Directories

Keeping our application programs separate from the data generated by those programs forces us to manage the access rights separately. This time, multiple management steps are a good thing. We want all users to have enough rights to read and execute the application programs, but not to be able to make other file-system changes. Data directories require that appropriate users have full user rights, which I consider Read, Write, Create, Erase, and File Scan. These rights allow the users as much control over the directory on the server as they have on their own hard disks.

The model for these settings is the NetWare system itself. The PUBLIC directory contains all the utility files for users. Every user has access to PUBLIC and must have the ability to find and run each program there. However, since this is a system directory, you don't want anyone to change the files by deleting them or modifying the access rights. As PUBLIC provides Read and File Scan rights to everyone, so should you provide those rights to the application programs.

Applications differ, of course, and the final determination must be made by the application programs. If the installation routine demands more rights, such as the ability to create and delete temporary files in the application directories, you have no choice but to make those changes. But it will be worth a few minutes of testing to see if you can create and delete the temporary files elsewhere. Often, you can satisfy an application's need for a place to work with temporary files with this DOS setting:

```
SET TEMP=C:\TEMP
```

 TIP If you are using Windows NT Workstation and have formatted the local hard drives with the NTFS file system, you have the ability to prevent users from deleting files or even writing to directories on the local hard disk. Make sure that users have the correct Write permissions where they need them, though.

PART

II

Managing the Network

If you make use of the power users in a department as administrative helpers, check their rights to these application directories. They will often need full file access and control rights to administer the applications. This also means they should be made virus-aware, since they have both the ability (file rights) and attitude (let's load this new utility and see if it helps) to introduce a virus to the network.

Setting Rights to an Application Directory

IN A HURRY

11.27 Grant Rights to Application Directories

1. As the Admin user or equivalent, start NetWare Administrator.

2. Highlight the directory to set user or group rights.

3. Click the right mouse button to open the submenu and choose Details.

4. Click the Trustees Of This Directory button.

5. Click Add Trustees to open the Select Object dialog box.

6. Highlight the user, group, or container that needs rights to the application directory, and click OK.

7. Check the appropriate access rights (Read and File Scan are suggested).

8. Click OK to save and exit.

Applications do a good job of creating directories and distributing their files (sometimes all over the place), but they don't set rights for your users. You must do this, but because of rights inheritance, you need only adjust the top of the application's directory structure. You can also use the Application Launcher to set up application trustee rights.

The recipient of these rights may be an individual user, several users, a group, a container, several groups or containers, or the entire network. Since the Microsoft Office directory is our example, and it contains horizontal applications used by everyone, the example here is for the entire network to be granted access.

Figure 11.68 shows the MSOffice subdirectory chosen in the RELL_APPS: volume. The dialog box for the directory shows the [Public] object being granted trustee rights to Read and File Scan the MSOffice directory. As you can see in the display, the AAMSSTP, Bitmap, Cdonline, Clipart, and other Microsoft Office subdirectories are directly under the MSOffice directory. Everyone will also have the same Read and File Scan rights to these subdirectories.

FIGURE 11.68

Granting [Public] the
right to use Office

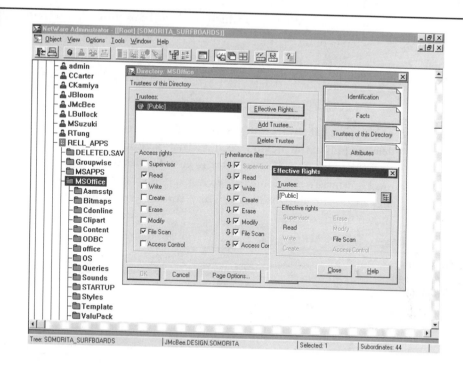

In the lower-right corner of Figure 11.68, you can see the Effective Rights dialog box, which I opened to illustrate the exact rights available. The Effective Rights dialog box isn't updated until you save the rights assignment settings and open the same view again.

More details for granting trustee rights to various network users and groups are discussed in Chapter 9.

Protecting Application Programs and Data Files

Your application programs must be protected from a variety of disasters. Some of these you have control over; some you don't. Those that you have control over include:

- Accidental deletion
- Intentional deletion
- Users allowed access to these files
- Concurrent program users as per the license agreement

Some of the disasters over which you have less control, or no control at all, include:

- Server or disk failure
- Catastrophe
- Application and data theft
- Software updates

We looked at a way to stop authorized users from accidentally (or intentionally) deleting files in the previous section. That method applies to users and their rights to access the files. There is also a way to give the files themselves some self-defense mechanisms. The attributes (often called *flags*) that can be given to directories and files are described in Chapter 9, which covers network security. The file attributes are shown in Figure 11.69.

FIGURE 11.69

*File attributes for
WINWORD.EXE*

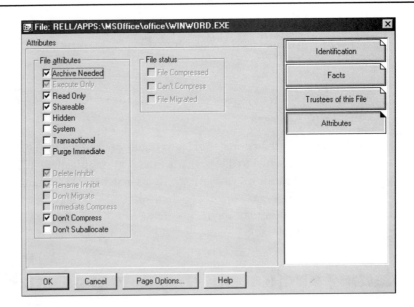

All these attributes (except Execute Only) can be changed by someone with the Modify right. That is why the manual strongly cautions you about granting the Modify right to anyone except administrative-level users.

Several of these attributes provide excellent self-defense for your files and directories. The most common flag used to protect files is Read Only. When a file is marked Read Only/Shareable, multiple concurrent users can read and execute the program, but none of them can delete, rename, or write to the file.

File Attributes As a Safety Device

IN A HURRY

11.28 Set File Attributes with NetWare Administrator

1. Log in as the Admin user or equivalent.
2. Using NetWare Administrator, browse to the directory where the file attributes need to be changed.
3. Right-click the file you want to change and click Details.
4. Select the Attributes property page.
5. Click the Read Only and Shareable attributes.

If you're familiar with the DOS ATTRIB command, just think of NetWare Administrator as the ATTRIB command with a few more options. DOS files have a Read Only switch as well. There is more reason to use this type of file protection in a shared environment.

See Figure 11.69, in the previous section, for a list of the file attributes provided by NetWare Administrator. Novell still provides a command-line utility, called FLAG, for changing NetWare file attributes. This utility can be useful in many circumstances. To read more about FLAG, check out Appendix E.

Changing Directory and File Ownership

IN A HURRY

11.29 Modify Directory and File Ownership

1. Log in as the Admin user or equivalent and start NetWare Administrator.
2. Highlight the directory or file to be modified in the browse window.
3. Click the right mouse button and choose Details.
4. Click the Facts button.
5. Click the Browse button at the right end of the Owner field.
6. Choose the owner from the Select Object dialog box and click OK.
7. Click OK to save and exit.

PART

II

Managing the
Network

The process for changing file and directory ownership is similar to that for changing file and directory rights. This time, let's use NetWare Administrator for the task.

Why would you want to change the owner of a file or a directory? Two reasons come to mind. One is to make tracking the evolution of the network clearer to whomever follows you in your present job. If the owner of a questionable file or directory is Bob, the future administrator has no idea if Bob was a user or an administrator. If the owner is Admin, there's no question.

The second reason to change file ownership applies to those companies that allocate disk space to users. When Bob creates a directory and copies files there, as in a typical software installation, all that file space counts against his budget. That's not fair to good old Bob, so you should change the file's owner value to Admin.

 TIP Another good reason to change ownership is that occasionally I stumble across an application that requires its program or data files to have an owner. The programs simply stop running if the owner of the file is deleted from NDS. It is a good idea for applications to be owned by the Admin user.

Figure 11.70 shows the screen in NetWare Administrator that you use to set the owner of the MSOffice directory from JMcBee to Admin. Although you can name the owner of files and directories, one does not influence the other. After changing the directory's owner, you must change the owner for all the files in the directory. You can't tag multiple files; each must be done individually.

You cannot type the name of the owner in the field. You must click the Browse button at the end of the field to get to the Select Object dialog box. This prevents any typos that could cause confusion and ensures that the entire owner's name, including context, is correct.

Changing Ownership with FLAG

Since you can't change the ownership of multiple files at once using NetWare Administrator, you can still use the FLAG command. Good old FLAG does the trick with a fistful of files (and even files in subdirectories) at once. For example, to change all the files in the current directory and subdirectories to have Admin as the owner, from the command line, type:

```
FLAG *.* /name=Admin /s /c
```

No muss, no fuss.

FIGURE 11.70

Transferring title to the directory

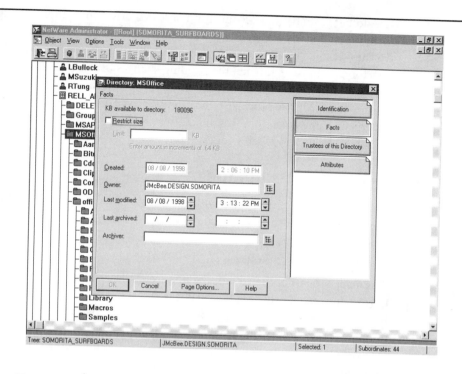

If you're curious as to who owns which files, just typing **FLAG** at the DOS prompt will list the filename, DOS and NetWare attributes, status, and owner. Subdirectories in the current directory will be listed with their owners as well. You can see why I think FLAG is a great utility.

Application Administration Tricks

Perhaps *trick* has the wrong connotation for this section. We aren't pulling rabbits out of hats, but we would like to make life as easy as possible for network clients. Don't think of tricks as in cheating, but tricks as in a clever way to circumvent small irritations.

One customer of mine has a subdirectory named COMMON, to which everyone on the network has full rights. This makes for a low-tech bulletin board, where anyone can put a file for one or more other employees to use. There is no guarantee that the file won't be out-of-date, so it's not the most reliable means of collaboration, but they make it work. Everyone understands the limitations of sharing in this manner, and the people work with one another.

Another customer has become fond of search drives for company budget and word-processing templates. The directories are set up like the PUBLIC directory, with the files set to RoSh (Read Only/Shareable). All files used must be saved in a different directory, of course. But when the wording changes in some contract paragraph, the network administrator places the changed file in the shared CONTRACTS directory in place of the superseded file. Now that all users have been trained to always pull their boilerplate paragraphs from this directory rather than an old contract, changes are available quickly and reliably for everyone.

Drive-Mapping Techniques

There are a couple of nice tricks with the MAP command that you might find useful. If your users have local hard disk directories to be searched before the network drives should be searched, use a command like:

```
MAP INS S16:=RELL_SYS:PUBLIC
```

This maps S16 rather than S1 for the first search drive, placing the MAP drives after all the existing search drives set by the PC's PATH statement. Using just MAP without the INS command puts this search-drive reference in the first position of the DOS environment space, overwriting what is there already. When you exit the network, the overwritten PATH commands will not be replaced. Using INSERT (INS) in the MAP command avoids this problem.

Some other interesting uses of the MAP command include providing you with the ability to replace an existing search map with a new one. To do this, use a command like:

```
MAP S1:=RELL_SYS:PUBLIC
```

You can also use the MAP command to insert a new search drive mapping at the beginning of the PATH by typing a command like:

```
MAP INS S1:=RELL_SYS:PUBLIC
```

If you have placed all the Windows 3.1x files on the PC, putting network search drives before the Windows directory will create extra, and unnecessary, network traffic. Worse, it will slow response for the user. The exception is the PUBLIC directory; you may want to use MAP INS S1 to place all the NetWare utilities at the forefront of the PATH statement.

If you have several drives to map, use the S16 drive setting for each. The first one will be drive Z:, then drive X:, and so on. The next lowest search number is assigned with each subsequent mapping.

Mapping drives to volumes in other contexts is easy, once you remember the Alias objects for the volumes from different contexts. I always forget to set up an Alias object the first time when mapping a volume from a server in another context. Of course, when I test the login script and see the error messages, I slap my forehead and say, "D'oh!" Then I explain to the customers looking over my shoulder how that was a lesson for them, so they would always remember to use the Alias object. (Most of them fall for it.)

The other option is to use Directory Map objects. These work like Alias objects, but they should be created only once and placed in a high container for everyone to reference easily. We'll get to that information in just a bit.

From the command line, erasing a drive mapping is simple. Type

```
MAP DEL H:
```

and you're finished.

If you prefer to make a new mapping for drive H: without deleting the previous mapping, you'll get a question prompt. When you map a local drive letter (A: through E: are normally set aside for DOS) to a network drive, you'll also get a question prompt. Just a quick check to remind you that if you redirect drive C: to the network, you won't be able to see your own hard disk until you delete the mapping.

Windows NT and Windows 95/98 clients have made mapping drives even easier using just the My Computer and Network Neighborhood icons. Simply right-click on either of these icons to display their context menu. Then choose the Novell Map Network Drive option. You will see the Map Drive dialog box shown in Figure 11.71.

FIGURE 11.71

Mapping drives using the Map Drive dialog box

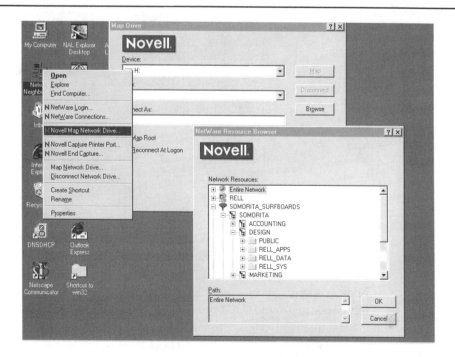

In the Map Drive dialog box are checkboxes that will specify that the drive you are mapping is reconnected at logon, a root drive, or a search drive. If you click the Browse button, you can browse the network, servers, or NDS tree looking for volumes and directory maps.

Mapping a Fake Root

The MAP ROOT command was developed as a response to problems with network-unaware applications in the early days. Many programs expected to be placed on the local hard disk, from the root of the hard disk. They refused to install to a subdirectory. A fake root drive was needed.

So Novell added the MAP ROOT option to help fool those applications. For example, to set drive H: to look like the root of my private home directory, I can type

```
MAP ROOT H:=RELL_DATA:HOME\Jgaskin
```

Instead of using the MAP utility, I can right-click the Network Neighborhood icon, select Novell Map Network Drive to open the Map Drive dialog box (see Figure 11.72), choose H: in the Device box, type **RELL/DATA:HOME/JGASKIN** in the Path box, click the Map Root checkbox, and click Map.

FIGURE 11.72

Mapping a fake root in the Map Drive dialog box

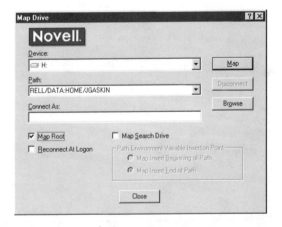

Any old-fashioned applications will happily install there, thinking they are in fact at the root of the hard disk. You can abbreviate the ROOT to just R in the command if you wish.

Another advantage, especially for home directories like this, is that the volume subdirectory designated as the ROOT becomes the highest directory that drive letter can see. In the example, the DOS CD .. command to move to the parent directory would not work to move to the USERS directory. Some companies use MAP ROOT for this feature alone, even if all their applications understand network directory installation.

Using Directory Maps

A Directory Map object is a leaf object that refers to a directory on a volume, somewhat like an Alias object. Any directory can be used as the object that is referenced by the Directory Map. These may be used in login scripts and from the command line.

A Directory Map is helpful when you have applications that you upgrade regularly or in situations where you want a single point of reference to a directory that changes. When change inevitably comes, you need only change the directory reference in the Directory Map object, not in every login script.

For example, one of my customers (like many other companies) uses the Microsoft Word word processor. When Word 97 came out, superseding Word 95, the administrator didn't want to automatically delete the 95 version at the site. So we installed the 97 version on a new volume. Was this a disaster, changing all the various references to reflect the new location of Word? Not at all. Changing the Directory Map object, referring to the new Word version in its new location, allowed us to reference Word as always, but have it point to the new location.

See Figure 11.73 for a reminder of creating a Directory Map object. The browse window on the left shows the location of MSOffice programs. The window on the right shows the NDS container location of the Directory Map to be created as the reference point.

PART

II

Managing the Network

FIGURE 11.73

Referencing Microsoft Office

Some Application Guidelines

Fortunately, the understanding of networks among software developers is growing and has been for several years. With more applications available than ever before, custom-fitting each to a network would be impossible. But several trends have pushed software into being more network-friendly.

First, Windows 3.1x provides a means for thousands of the products released over the last few years to work on the network by accepting the foundation provided by Microsoft. You might argue that there are better foundations for the software industry (like those used by our friends in the Unix community), but better a well-known foundation than nothing.

Second, Novell has been steadily providing software support for third-party vendors from the beginning. Over the years, application growth for NetWare networks has been tremendous.

The good part of all this is that applications will get more network-aware over the coming years. The bad part is that the new features of applications, including sound and video components, will require more robust networks and increased throughput. Looks like job security for NetWare administrators to me.

Microsoft Windows

Microsoft's Windows has become the standard for Intel-powered desktop computers, just as NetWare has become the standard network to connect those computers. Windows of various flavors and NetWare must work together smoothly.

Unfortunately, the burden of making Windows behave on the network falls to Novell, since Microsoft is busy trying to sell its own networking products. The good part of this has been that it forced Novell to develop client software for Windows that is far better than the software that Microsoft provides.

Windows 3.1x

I wondered about discussing Windows 3.1x in this book since so many people are moving to Windows 95/98 and Windows NT/2000. As I am continually reminded, however, many people (millions) are still using Windows 3.1, so I decided to discuss Windows 3.1x.

Discussions abound whether to place the Windows application components on the server or leave them on the local hard disk. The good points of putting them on the server are that it saves disk space on local drives, it makes Windows upgrades easier, it's more secure from user accidents, and it's easier to share groups of applications.

The negative points are that it increases network traffic, it causes some application installation hassles, and it forces you to delete Windows from newly purchased PCs.

Software cost doesn't enter into this argument. Microsoft provides no network license for Windows version 3.1. Every user must have a full copy of the program to be legal. Microsoft's Windows for Workgroups version 3.11 does have network licenses available, however.

The slim majority opinion favors running Windows 3.1*x* from the server. There is a caveat, however. The local configuration files are stored best on a local machine, and more important, the local hard disk is used for the swap file. Running the temporary memory workspace back to the server tremendously increases network traffic.

Just because the majority prefer to run Windows 3.1*x* from the server doesn't mean you should. It doesn't make sense to delete a working copy of Windows 3.1*x* from new computers. Laptop users can't argue this; they must run Windows locally. Personal applications can be configured for users of the network version, but it's always easier for the users to control their own desktop. It may not be easier for you as the administrator, but that's another story.

Use the SETUP /A option from the Windows 3.1*x* installation disks to load the program files to a shared directory on the server. You should label this shared directory something like WIN_NET, WINSHARE, WINPROG, or WINAPPS. If you use the SYS:\APPS structure, you would wind up with SYS:\APPS\WIN_NET for the program files. After copying the files, mark them all Read Only and Shareable using the FLAG command. This will keep the files from being deleted accidentally and will prevent anyone from putting a configuration file in this directory by mistake.

Each NetWare client that needs to receive a copy of Windows 3.1*x*, or that will upgrade its local copy, should run SETUP from that WIN_NET directory. If the workstation will run Windows 3.1*x* from the local hard disk, just the straight setup is used. If the workstation will run the bulk of the Windows programs from the server, the SETUP /N (for network) command should be given.

With SETUP /N, individual configuration files are copied to the local station. This makes it easy to set up the \TEMP directory and the local disk file used as part of the virtual memory feature. Each user running Windows 3.1*x* from the server must have a search drive pointing to the shared Windows files, such as:

```
MAP INS S16:=SYS:\WIN_NET
```

If you already had NetWare 4.1*x* client files installed on the PC before Windows 3.1*x* was installed, you will need to reinstall those NetWare client files. The NetWare Windows support files aren't copied to the local machine if Windows isn't already present. The client file installation program takes care to check with you before overwriting network configuration files.

You can have Windows 3.1*x* group files that can be shared by everyone on the network. After creating a group on your Windows workstation using Program Manager, copy the file with the .GRP extension to the shared Windows directory. This lets everyone see that .GRP file, but first you must edit the PROGMAN.INI file on each station. Under the [Groups] heading, add the name and network location of the .GRP file, as in:

```
[Groups]
Group11=\\RELL_SYS:\WINFILES\SCHEDULE.GRP
```

This brings up an interesting point with Windows 3.1*x* drive letters. Windows 3.1*x* warns you each time you set up a network application stored on the server. It's as if Windows 3.1*x* is trying to tell you that the network isn't reliable, so you should store everything locally. With many Windows 3.1*x* users sharing your network, the login scripts must be consistent so each program icon looking to drive N: will find the appropriate executable file. Windows 3.1*x* gets even weirder than usual when the drive mapping isn't consistent.

Another caution: your clients must log in to NetWare before starting Windows 3.1*x*. This is obviously the case for those using the shared network version, but it is also important for those running Windows 3.1*x* from a local hard disk. (But an exception is that you can use NWUSER to make your drive mappings and printer connections after Windows 3.1*x* is started.)

 TIP If you wondered about Novell's sense of humor, the old version of the NetWare Control Panel for Windows 3.1 allowed you to click the Novell logo in the upper-left corner. If you had a sound board, you would hear a Max Headroom voice stuttering, "N–N–NetWare."

Windows 95/98

All this goes out the window (literally) when we start discussing Windows 95 and Windows 98. Microsoft has made it nearly impossible to run Windows 95/98 from a server; many system files demand to be local. To compound the hassle, Windows 95/98 is impossible to install across the network by copying a set configuration to an empty disk. This was tricky but possible with Windows 3.1*x*.

You may hear of people devising complicated scripts to copy the Windows 95/98 files into the proper places in the proper ways without going through the official download and installation process. However, none I've heard about save enough time to make up for the retrofits necessary on the machines that don't accept the down-loaded files gracefully.

NOTE Why is downloading a Windows 95/98 installation impossible? We can't blame Microsoft entirely, because some of the problem comes from the Plug-and-Play technology users have been demanding. Your operating system must be tightly tied to your hardware if Plug and Play has a prayer, and Windows 95 took that to heart. Yes, there may be ways to support Plug and Play yet still support downloaded systems, but then we get to the problem of long filenames. How do you copy directory names like "Program Files" to a DOS-only hard disk? This can't easily be done. Give up trying to mass-install Windows 95/98, because life is too short to waste banging your head against the Microsoft wall. Even some of the utilities built just to mass-install Windows have problems with Microsoft's unique ID attached to every machine.

You can, however, use a NetWare CD-ROM drive as the source drive for a workstation Windows 95/98 installation or upgrade. Copying the files across the network will probably be faster than any but the speediest local CD-ROM drives. The only caution is to make sure that the CD-ROM drive is available for application upgrades and Windows modifications after the initial installation. Any time you add something to a Windows 95/98 system, you probably will need the CD-ROM drive once again.

TIP For more information on automating the installation of Windows 95/98, see the Windows 95 or Windows 98 Resource Kits or the Microsoft Web site at www .microsoft.com. Also check out the Windows 95 Batch Setup program.

Windows NT Workstation, Windows 2000 Professional

If Windows 95/98 was "almost" impossible to run from the network, Windows NT/2000 Workstation is beyond impossible. Windows NT cannot be run across the network; you must have a local hard disk. Windows NT Workstation is a different beast from Windows 95/98 and should be treated as such. I have grown to love Windows NT both at home and in the office. It is robust, scalable, stable (at least for Microsoft), and powerful.

Windows NT also cannot be installed by creating an image of Windows NT on the server and copying it down to individual machines. There are utilities on the market

PART

II

Managing the
Network

that will assist you with this and even some that Microsoft has come almost to the point of endorsing, but none that are officially supported by Microsoft.

 TIP For more information on automating the installation of Windows NT Workstation, see the Windows NT Workstation Resource Kit.

My experience with Microsoft is that if they don't officially support something, I am wary of it. What this means is that when you call Microsoft Technical Support, they are going to say, "Gee, we don't support that option/hardware/software/procedure. Why don't you call us back and let us know how you fixed the problem."

 NOTE There are huge books written on the subject of Windows NT. Sybex author Mark Minasi has a series of excellent books on Windows NT networking, including *Windows NT Complete, Mastering Windows NT Server*, and *Mastering TCP/IP for NT Server*. For more information on these titles, visit the Sybex Web site at www.sybex.com.

General Application Hints

There's no better advice than to read the manuals for multiuser applications that will be installed on your network. However, you must read the instructions with a level of skepticism and wariness. Many programs provide the bare rudiments of network installation details, and it's up to you to fill in the gaps of their network knowledge. Let's go over some quick rules and guidelines. Remember, it may be multiuser software, but it's your network. Don't let some manual rework your network plan without a fight.

Here are some general tips relating to applications on your network:

- Install all applications as the Admin user. This keeps the ownership straight, and there are some programs that look for the SUPERVISOR or Admin user, not an equivalent.

- Observe the license restrictions on all software. To do otherwise is stealing. If you fudge, bad karma will cause your server to crash the evening before your vacation.

- When possible, provide drive mappings for applications. Since most new applications run under Windows, organize your volumes so that each volume is referenced by its own drive letter. This makes the group setups within Windows much easier.

- Smart network programs allow the use of UNC (Universal Naming Convention) path names.

- Feel free to use the MAP ROOT command to fool stupid programs that demand a root directory.

- Directory Map objects can help ease installation problems or hard-to-find subdirectories.

- Flag application directories Read Only and Shareable (if appropriate).

- Make groups for each set of users who need an application. Feel free to have a WP group, a Presentations group, a Spreadsheets group, and all the rest.

- Assign Read and File Scan rights to these application groups for their respective applications.

- Be sensitive when things look unreasonable; dig deeper. WordPerfect won't let you set the initial font on a network printer, but it will let you set this on the same printer if you say it's a stand-alone printer. Does that make sense? Actually, yes. You don't want each user resetting the printers every which way. What looks stupid at first is really clever programming.

Application Aggravation

I am sensitive to the wails from software developers about how hard it is to keep track of all the different network types and write software to fit. I really am. But I also have some marketing advice for these developers: grow up, get clever, and grab market share.

NetWare customers want applications to run better with NetWare than they do on a stand-alone computer. Guess what? The good programs do. As a network administrator, you can tell the companies that do a good job with networked applications that you appreciate their hard work. You can also tell those companies that don't do a good job that you aren't interested in buying poorly written software.

How about this slogan: "If you don't network, I don't buy." Think that will get their attention?

CHAPTER **12**

Teaching Your Clients to Use the Network

F irst, a reminder: your clients don't like the network as much as you do. They don't like computers as much, either. Hardware and software either bore or terrify them. Don't take it personally.

You may teach, but you can't make them all learn. Some will learn and do well. Those are your future power users. Others will learn enough to do their job and will even figure out a few things on their own. This group will be the bulk of your user community. A few will regard computerization as a modern version of the biblical plague of locusts and will never learn enough to go beyond basic skills. If your company didn't require employees to use computers before you added the network, expect one or two people to quit their jobs rather than learn how to do something new. As grim as it may sound, this is normal.

To prepare for this situation, you and your management must plan how to handle the user community. Change is stressful, and changing to NetWare 5.1—even though this network runs better and is easier to use than what you had before—will stress some people.

Preparing the User Community

Your management has some questions to answer. First of all, what are the top three client issues? These issues will be a major part of the reason for the new network or the network upgrade. What of value to the users will this new system provide? See if you can rank the answers in order of importance. Let's start with the most important reason for the system.

Is providing the users an easy graphical interface the most important reason? How about increasing disk space? Maybe combining several departments onto one server?

The top user priority for the new system will guide you in presenting the network to your users. If a graphical interface is important, because all your workstations now support Windows 95/98, show them how easy it is to access resources anywhere with Network Neighborhood. If disk space is the hook, tell users about the home directories and room for more archived files and online information. If several departments are moving to the same server, or just the same container, show how much easier finding and using network resources are with NetWare 5.1.

The worst case is learning that your boss had no user benefit in mind when the new network was approved. Be prepared for the users to gripe and complain as you change their system for no tangible benefit. Better yet, quickly figure a benefit, and show the users how their situation has improved. This isn't cynical; it's making the best of a bad situation.

Now that your boss has weaseled out of the first question, here's another: What's the proposed ratio of user training compared with support staff responsibilities? The more training the users receive, the fewer support headaches for you and your compadres. Less user training, more headaches. No training, order aspirin by the pound.

Remind your boss that there are several kinds of training to be discussed. Network training is obvious, since you're installing a new system. How much network training? Here are some of your options:

- Send everyone on the new system out for training.
- Have a trainer come in and teach everyone.
- Send a few users out for training.
- Have a trainer come and teach a few users.
- Train one person from each department yourself.
- Throw everyone to the network wolves.

Unfortunately, the last choice is often the first choice. I wish I could tell you this has never happened, but users are thrown into new systems all the time. If this happens at your place, you have my condolences.

Remember, we haven't talked about application training yet. Nor have we mentioned desktop operating system training. The more computer training of any kind your network clients have, the better off they (and you) are.

Imagine a pie chart. The complete pie is your goal. The more training for the users, the less staff time filling the rest of the chart. More training, less support staff needed. More training, higher office productivity, and a bonus for your boss. Maybe you should explain things that way.

PART

II

Managing the Network

The Client's View of Your Network

There's a famous old map from the Middle Ages, charting what little knowledge people had of the world. The coastline of Europe was not too bad, but after about 100 miles of ocean, no one knew anything. With a dramatic flair, the mapmaker wrote this at the edge: "Beyond here, there be monsters."

Most of your users don't have a good idea what the network is, where it is, or how it works. That's why, when you point out the file server sitting under a table, they're disappointed. Something that causes as much trouble as a network should be big and complicated-looking. Perhaps downsizing companies should buy mainframe facades, with little motors keeping the big tape reels jerking along. That would impress people.

Continued

> **CONTINUED**
>
> Those users who do claim to know about networking probably mean the Internet. Don't be disappointed if they talk about "logging in" by starting AOL.
>
> Your network clients see only their computer and their printer when they look at the network. The rest of the network is something strange and, as far as some users are concerned, filled with monsters.

Clients and the NDS Tree

Object-oriented views of the world have been rare. NetWare 5.1 is probably one of a few object-oriented programs that will be widely distributed.

I know that network management stations have used objects for years, as have programmers. The trade magazines are full of object-oriented, client/server, user-friendly, fault-tolerant, Information Superhighway stories, but the typical NetWare user doesn't read those stories. The idea of inheritance never occurred to your users, unless a rich relative was ill.

This attitude will require you to present the new network landscape to your users in ways that directly help their daily activities. You should talk about the NDS tree and how it works, but the moment you see symptoms of the MEGO (My Eyes Glaze Over) disease, you should stop. Go straight to hands-on help with the tools they need to do their work. After a bit, you will see that the users are able to stand more explanation before their eyes roll up in their heads, and you will gradually teach them more than you ever thought possible. But don't rush it.

Go over the analogies and illustrations used earlier in this book for examples. Make up your own examples that apply to your business to supplement what's in this book and the manuals.

Use examples of physical items, like describing the NDS tree as a hallway, with Organizations as big rooms off the main hallway, and Organizational Units as smaller rooms off the larger rooms or smaller hallways. [Root] can be the building lobby, with all hallways running from there. Leaf objects such as users and printers and servers are things placed in various rooms. See Figure 12.1 for this example.

On the left, we have the NDS tree. The [Root] object is at the top of everything, with Organizations leading from it. There can be many Organizations, of course, but here we show two. The Organizational Units can be contained only within Organizations or other Organizational Units; they cannot be installed in the [Root] object.

FIGURE 12.1

Making the virtual tangible

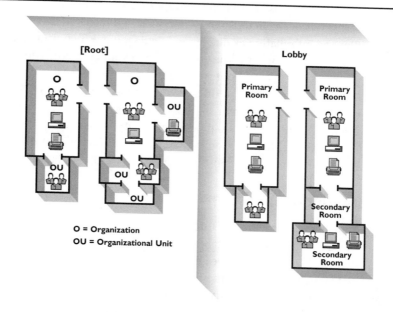

On the right, we have a lobby representing [Root], supporting the primary rooms. Only the primary rooms open from the lobby. Secondary rooms branch off the primary rooms, and often a secondary room supports attached secondary rooms of its own. As with Organizational Units, a secondary room may actually hold more than a primary room. Think of the anteroom leading to a ballroom as an example of this.

Icons for people, groups, computers, and printers are scattered around both drawings. It's easy to imagine real people and other objects in a real room. The same arrangements, with people and their supporting equipment, have the same look when placed in Organizations and Organizational Units. After all, Organizations and Organizational Units are just containers, as are rooms.

Finding Help

Help is always important in life. Sometimes you need help when you least expect it.

NetWare is complex and powerful. This means your users (and you) will need help on a regular basis. Does asking for help make you appear stupid? No, you appear stupid when you ignore help while struggling with a problem.

Novell's primary help resource is their Web site, www.novell.com. Here you'll find Lynx support for those Unix systems without a graphical interface and a ton of information on Novell, as well as bug fixes, updated software, and so on.

FTP (File Transfer Protocol) is supported from the same server as the Web server, with a mirror site in Germany. Try `ftp.novell.com` or `ftp.novell.de` for a list of files and information available for downloading. When using anonymous FTP, be sure you give anonymous as the user name and your entire Internet address (for example, `james@gaskin.com`) as your password.

`Comp.sys.novell` leads off a group of non-moderated, Novell-specific newsgroups on the Internet. The traffic is heavy (100+ messages a day) and comes from all over the world. Since there's no moderator or sub-newsgroups, everything is currently piled into one big heap. You may be assured, however, that the messages you see come from some of the most technically savvy folks in PC networking.

Using Electronic Manuals

Remember the problems I listed with paper as a technology exchange medium back in Chapter 8? Novell has taken these comments to heart (okay, they did this independently of me) and now releases all documentation electronically with NetWare 5.1.

Manuals are fine, but they are difficult to share. If a person borrows your manual, you can't use that same manual unless you're looking over that person's shoulder—not too practical. Ever take a manual home, then forget to bring it back? Ever lose a manual? Ever go through six manuals trying to find the notes you made on one page? These problems are eliminated with the new electronic manuals provided with your NetWare operating system. All the documentation is in HTML format, so you can view it with any Web browser. The search and printing features, however, work better (they claim) with Netscape Navigator. Not only do you need Navigator, you need version 4.5 or higher, which supports Java.

The documentation can be read from:

- A workstation CD-ROM drive
- A NetWare server CD-ROM drive set up as a NetWare volume

You can run both of these systems at one time if you have two CDs. Setting up the documentation on a stand-alone workstation is recommended if this is your first NetWare 5.1 installation. This gives you a chance to read the manuals before you start your installation. It also is useful if the server is down. I highly recommend that you keep a copy of the documentation on your own workstation, if you have the CDs available.

Installing and Using the Documentation

Now that you are sold on the value of online documentation, how do you install it? How is it used? Many people have difficulty with online documentation (from anybody, not just Novell), yet it is becoming more and more prevalent. Practice is the key to using it efficiently and quickly. Start now and it will soon become your friend. (A little too strong, right? OK, try to get used to it before things go down the toilet and you're desperate.)

Novell changed the rules with NetWare 5.1's documentation. You no longer have the option of running the documentation from a hard disk somewhere. At least I haven't figured out how to do it yet, and I tried using NCOPY (NetWare file attributes carry over and cause problems) and XCOPY (no attribute problems, but the main index.htm file forces most references to the CD). Novell forces you to mount the CD as a volume on a server, which isn't a bad idea, really, or connect to their Web site for documentation. Actually, the online option may be the best, because changes actually get put into the files on their Web site.

"Installing" may be a slight misnomer, but you will have to mount the documentation as a volume. We'll call that installation, OK?

Running the Documentation Viewer

Loading the Documentation CD into a Windows 95/98/NT/2000 workstation with AutoRun engaged will pull open a splash screen that replaces the old NetWare 5.0 screen, but with no choices. Load the CD, and it turns your workstation into a personal Web server just for viewing the documentation.

Seems odd to me, too, but I must admit this is easier to do, and more reliable, than the NetWare 5.0 documentation. None of the PCs I checked had trouble with this process, even the older 120MHz Pentium systems. Technically, Novell demands that you have a browser supporting Java and JavaScript and 24MB of RAM (64MB of RAM recommended).

Mount the Documentation CD on a NetWare 5.1 server. All you need to do is put the CD into the server's CD-ROM drive and type **CDROM** on the system console.

Map a drive to the CD volume, and change directory to the NOVDOCS directory. There await three directories and one file. Make sure to close your browser before starting to view the documentation. The documentation viewer will want to start the browser itself. Execute RUNME.EXE to start the viewing process.

Although the Web site documentation works with Internet Explorer (IE), the local documentation has a heavy preference for Netscape. Figure 12.2 shows the Windows NT system running Internet Explorer to load the documentation, but I had more trouble getting to the documents on this and another system with IE. May be my problem, but remember this warning. It worked, but it took more time and caused more frustration.

The opening screen after the RUNME.EXE program starts

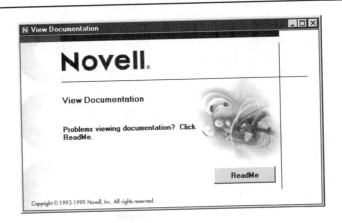

Nice splash screen, right? I'm sorry that the blues and greens in the water/universe being poked by a finger don't come through in print.

Notice the ReadMe button. Click it to see a small but somewhat useful readme.txt file from the CD. More up-to-date information awaits on the Novell Web site.

Moving along, the same splash screen stays up, but the text inside changes. The next message tells you that the Documentation Search Engine is now registering and to please wait (as if you have a choice). Luckily, this screen doesn't last long, but it does alert you to one of the nice features of the documentation. See all in Figure 12.3.

Status message during documentation load

Another new message follows, with yet another hint of powers to come. What does Figure 12.4 show? Your PC, while supposedly running a document viewer program, now becomes an HTTP Server. In essence, you're now sitting at a Web server, albeit one with a single mission: displaying documentation.

FIGURE 12.4

HTTP Server loading

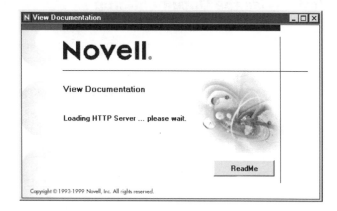

The next warning message tells you that the system is automatically loading an HTML browser. Your client's default browser will start. If you don't have a copy of Netscape, you can find one on the documentation CD. Since you are sitting at a Windows PC, you already have Internet Explorer, whether you want it or not.

Once the documentation display starts, the status message inside this dialog changes once again, as shown in Figure 12.5. In NetWare 5.0, the warning said, "Netscape browser is running." NetWare 5.1, however, says only that an HTML browser is running. Whether Novell dialog writers have given up on Netscape, or they expect you to be running a different browser entirely, remains to be seen. Anyone for opera? (www.opera.com).

FIGURE 12.5

Leave your CD in and your drive mapped to the server volume holding the CD.

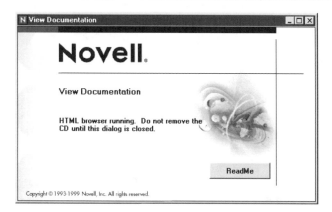

No need to display the last screen that appears when you close the documentation browser application. It just says, guess what, that the documentation is unloading.

How to Use the Documentation

Figure 12.6 shows the opening screen of the manuals in Internet Explorer 5 (I told you it was possible, just more trouble). You can work in several ways.

FIGURE 12.6

The opening screen of the manuals

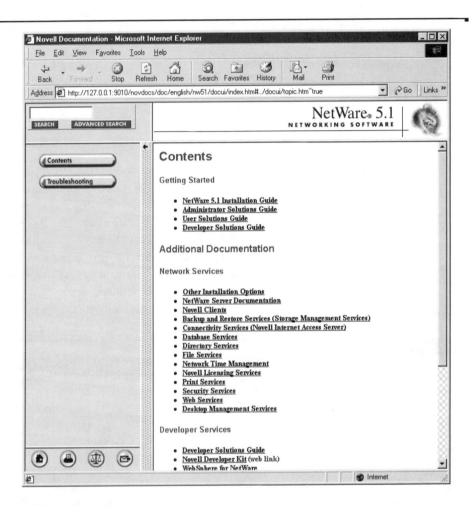

You'll notice the two buttons on the left side of the figure. Then you'll see that the top-left frame holds a text search window and the top-right frame shows the NetWare documentation banner. All the real goodies pop up in the bottom-right frame, which dominates the screen (as it should).

Notice the small arrow at the intersection of the four frame lines? Click there, and the largest frame will expand to fill the entire area. The thick separator bar will remain, with the black arrow reduced to a tab, which pops the left frame back open when clicked.

See the four small buttons on the bottom left of the screen? Down there in their own frame? They remain with all framed views, even when the left frame fills with the section's table contents. Here's what they mean:

House Really a home, because it's a Home key. Click that key anywhere, and you return to this screen.

Printer Opens a separate window to define which manual section you wish to print. See Figure 12.7 for details.

Scales Of justice, hiding the legal mumbo-jumbo gumbo.

Envelope Sends your comments to Novell.

Notice the URL in Figure 12.6, starting with `127.0.0.1`. That's the traditional "loopback" user in Unix, which means the local machine itself. Need any more proof that NetWare really does start a Web server on your local machine?

Click the Printer icon on the bottom left of the page, and a Java applet starts up to present the entire manual set, ready to print. All you need now is several reams of paper and a fast printer, right?

Printing a particular page or set of instructions doesn't insult your tech-hood, making a mockery of your life. It's smart, proactive planning, because you know at least three people will grab you for advice on your way to anywhere, so you'd better have the instructions written down.

PART

II

Managing the
Network

FIGURE 12.7

*Print window, slightly
exploded*

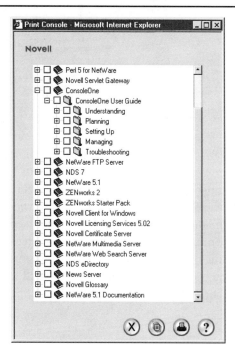

How to Search the Documentation

When time gets short and patience wears thin, the Search button awaits. I don't know if it will help, but it certainly can't hurt. Figure 12.8 shows the Search screen about to launch itself.

FIGURE 12.8

The Search screen

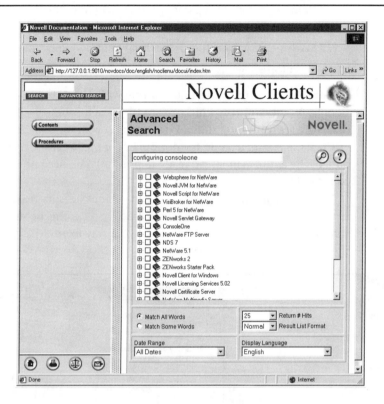

To find anything, simply type the word or phrase you are looking for in the text box and set your options. Typically, the defaults will serve you well, but you can modify them as needed and try interesting word combinations just for the fun of it.

Feel free to check the little boxes beside the book icons. When any of them are checked, the software searches only through the checked section or sections. If you feel confident that you know which book an item is in, you can cut down the time spent waiting by narrowing your search.

After you click Search, the main window will show your results. Note that the results are sorted by their relevance, as shown in the % column on the results page.

Do you need to see a list of topics with the start of paragraphs pulled from the documents, like in every other search engine? I didn't think so.

The main thing I want to say here is to play with it. Search for various words and phrases and get used to how the documentation works. The more time you spend getting comfortable with the system, the better off you will be in a pinch when the boss is staring over your shoulder.

Windows 95/98 Network User Support in NetWare 5.1

Windows 95/98 changed the rules for your NetWare connection in many ways. I've talked about a few of those ways already, and I'll talk about more of them later. This section will focus on the ways that the Windows 95/98 built-in client network utilities have eliminated the need for NetWare User Tools to be upgraded (at least in the minds of some Novell vice president).

TIP I can't begin to explain Windows 95/98 fully in this section, nor would I want to attempt such a feat. Instead, I'll refer you to *The Expert Guide to Windows 95* and *The Expert Guide to Windows 98*, both by Mark Minasi (published by Sybex). There is no shortage of Windows 95/98 books on the shelves, but I'm assuming you're past the initial learning curve and need some detailed, behind-the-scenes information. Minasi provides that in his books.

Do not make the mistake of enabling Windows 95/98's NetWare emulation software, File and Print Sharing for NetWare Networks. Microsoft, ever eager to bust Novell's chops, now emulates (but didn't license) the NCP codes necessary in an attempt to look like a NetWare 3.1*x* server. My objective opinion? It bites like hungry dogs in a butcher shop.

This section of the book is strictly about using Windows 95/98 workstations as network clients to NetWare servers. The next chapter will cover more Windows details, tackling NT and 2000. When I talked about printing, I mentioned sharing Windows 95/98-controlled printers as a replacement for NPRINTER, but that's as much Windows 95/98 networking as I like to use. With NDPS, even that may be going further than necessary. Any more will only cause problems; peer-to-peer networks require different management procedures and user training than do client/server networks such as NetWare.

The good news is that Windows 95/98 is a much better network client than Windows 3.1, and Windows 98 Special Edition does even better than the 95/98 first version. Features that many network managers have prayed for are included. You'll find concurrent multiple protocol support, graphical interfaces for the network protocol configuration screens, and enough multitasking support to make life almost bearable as a network client. Windows 95/98 isn't the ultimate desktop client by any means (reliability problems), but it's better than what we've had since NetWare started.

Before we look at all the NetWare client Windows 95/98 options, take a look at Figure 12.9, which shows the shortcut menu that appears when you right-click a tree. Compare that with Figure 12.10, which shows the same shortcut menu when a server is clicked instead, and with Figure 12.11, which shows the results of clicking a container object. First, let's talk about your choices, and then I'll sum them up in a table.

FIGURE 12.9

The shortcut menu for a tree

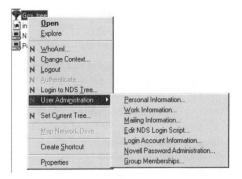

FIGURE 12.10

The shortcut menu for a server

FIGURE 12.11

*The shortcut menu for
a container*

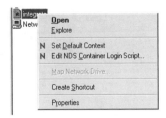

WhoAmI and NetWare Information

IN A HURRY

12.1 Use Network Neighborhood in Windows 95/98

1. Double-click the Network Neighborhood icon.

2. Right-click one of the servers or the NDS tree icon.

3. Click WhoAmI, Change Context, Logout, Authenticate, Login To Server (or NDS Tree, if you clicked the tree icon), or User Administration.

4. If you chose User Administration, click one of the seven submenu choices: Personal Information, Work Information, Mailing Information, Edit NDS Login Script, Login Account Information, Novell Password Administration, or Group Memberships. If you clicked a server, click Send Message; if you clicked a tree, click Set Current Tree.

5. If you right-click a container instead of a server or tree in step 2, you can then click Set Default Context or Edit NDS Container Login Script instead of the options in steps 3 and 4.

By combining the command-line program WhoAmI with the NetWare information feeds threaded into Windows 95/98, Client32 provides plenty of information. Look at the details given in Figure 12.12, pulled from the Compaq PROLIANT server connection.

FIGURE 12.12

*User Tools information
via Network
Neighborhood*

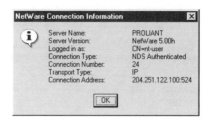

To reach this point, double-click the Network Neighborhood icon on the Desktop to open the Network Neighborhood application. Right-click a server or the NDS tree icon to display a drop-down menu that includes the following:

- WhoAmI

- Change Context

- Logout

- Authenticate

- Login to Server (or NDS Tree, if you clicked the tree icon)

- User Administration

If you chose User Administration, you can then select a submenu item:

- Personal Information

- Work Information

- Mailing Information

- Edit NDS Login Script

- Login Account Information

- Novell Password Administration

- Group Memberships

If you clicked a server, you can select Send Message; if you chose a tree, you can select Set Current Tree. Figure 12.12 is the result of clicking the WhoAmI menu option on a highlighted server.

While you receive the important information about your user name and primary server from Network Neighborhood, you also get some quick details that are sometimes useful. I learned that I was NDS-authenticated and connection number 24. The connection information doesn't do a user much good, but it is an easy way for you, the network administrator, to discover a user's connection number. This information is necessary if you must clear a hung connection (assuming that the Windows 95/98 workstation that you're currently using isn't the one causing the hung connection, of course). This is also a convenient way to find your IP address, since Windows 95/98 is not very forthcoming with that information except for reading the internal settings. This screen provides an IP address that's verified by a server, as this one is by the PROLIANT server.

Sending Messages within Network Neighborhood

Since Windows 95/98 offers rudimentary peer-to-peer network functions, you would expect users to be able to send messages to other workstations. Offered as a DOS command-line option since the beginning of NetWare, SEND is reincarnated once again under Client32.

Hiding within the same menu structure as WhoAmI is the Send Message option. Figure 12.13 shows this feature under Windows 95/98, with the new logo and all. One improvement over the Windows 3.*x* version of Send is the ability to select several users and send all the same message.

FIGURE 12.13

*Simple communica-
tions between users or
groups*

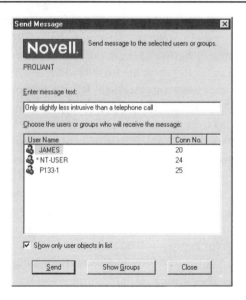

After sending this message to one of the available, logged-in network clients, a results screen appears on the sender's workstation. The screen, lacking in graphical interest, shows the target user's distinguished name, the connection number, and the status of the message. Status is a bit high-falutin' for a column heading, since the message is either "Sent" or "Not Sent," depending on whether the person has elected to block incoming messages. You do get informed, however, if the message made it to the user's screen.

Is this a valuable network feature? I suppose that if you were too lazy to pick up the phone and dial the interoffice number but energetic enough to open Network Neighborhood, type the message, find the person, and click the Send command button, this feature would be helpful. Of course, the phone gives you the option of leaving a voice-mail message. I'm afraid this type of instant messaging still reeks with the smell of AOL, chat rooms, and so much time wasted that many companies block instant messages.

Messages on the receiver screen must be manually cleared. If your message target is calculating some huge spreadsheet or reformatting a database when the message arrives, he or she will need to stop working and clear the message before continuing. You must then hope that your message carries more importance than the work it interrupted.

Logging In from Network Neighborhood

On the surface, the ability to log in from within Network Neighborhood makes no sense. If you don't activate all the network connections when you start Windows 95/98, how will Network Neighborhood know about your network?

Be that as it may, there are reasons to log in after Windows 95/98 is up and running. You may have a special login script set up on a particular server, such as for a "backup" user defined to operate the tape backup system for the network. You may have needed to close a DOS box because some program blew up, and now you want to reestablish your original network configuration. You may want to log in as a different person entirely to test some portion of the network configuration.

Regardless of the reason, it's possible to log in from within Windows 95/98. Figure 12.14 shows the regular Novell Login dialog box, the same one you see at the beginning of the Windows 95/98 boot process. The only difference between logging in then versus now is that now the server and tree names are grayed out, since you chose a server explicitly. The login process will proceed the same from here as it does during the initial Windows 95/98 boot sequence. Universal drive mappings will replace the existing mappings unless you specifically instruct the program otherwise.

FIGURE 12.14

*Log in here if
you want.*

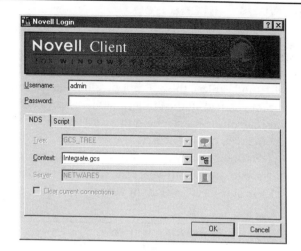

Logging Out

If you right-click a server or a tree, you can also choose to log out. If you want to log
out of a server but not the tree, you can do so. You will lose access to resources on that
server, but you will free a connection for someone else to use. If you try to log out of
the last server in a tree, however, the dialog box shown in Figure 12.15 will appear.

FIGURE 12.15

*Warning: you are
about to lose all con-
nection to the tree!*

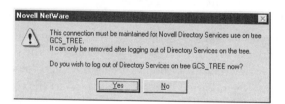

You will be warned that this is your connection to the tree and that if you continue, you will be logged out of the tree and lose access to resources on that server
and on the entire tree. If this is what you want, click Yes; otherwise, choose No.

Setting Your Current Tree

If you have multiple trees floating around (and remember from the discussion in Chapter 4 that neither Novell nor I recommend this practice), you may find from time to time that you need to access resources in another tree. In the old days (Net-Ware 4.10 and earlier), this was not possible, except through bindery connections. This meant you had all the Bindery Services issues to deal with and couldn't administer more than one tree at a time, and so on. Beginning with version 4.11, and improved in version 5, you can freely use resources in multiple trees. However, some applications haven't caught up with Novell yet and can be used by only one tree at a time. All you have to do, then, is select the tree that you want to make your current tree, right-click it, and select Set Current Tree. You'll see the dialog box shown in Figure 12.16.

FIGURE 12.16

Confirmation of current tree selection

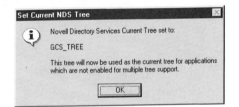

Setting Your Current Context

You may recall from earlier discussions that context is an object's position in the tree, and that is a permanent location, unless you move the object. Your *current* context, however, can vary at any time, much as you can change your current directory on a hard drive at any time. You may also recall that the way to do this at the command line is with CX. With Windows 95/98, however, you can do this graphically through Network Neighborhood. To do so, either select the container you would like to make your current context, right-click it, and select Set Default Context, or right-click the tree the context is in and choose Change Context. If you choose the container, you are finished, as that answers the question of which container you would like to be the current context. NetWare will simply provide a dialog box informing you that your change was successful. If, however, you select a tree and choose Change Context, you will be presented with the dialog box shown in Figure 12.17.

PART

II

Managing the
Network

FIGURE 12.17

*Enter your new
default context.*

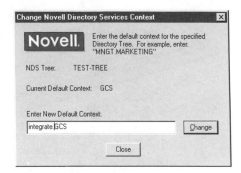

Notice the lack of any kind of Browse button in Figure 12.17. At least NetWare 5.1 added the small amount of help on the screen. Novell's presumption appears to be that if you want to browse for the context, you'll use Network Neighborhood. If you know where you want to go, however, and just don't want to go to a DOS prompt to use CX, simply select the tree and make the change.

User Administration

New in NetWare 5.0, with the new client, are the User Administration choices. In the past, simple user actions, such as editing their own user login script or changing a password that hadn't expired, required either your intervention or their getting into and using NWAdmin. Neither choice was good for most people. The new choices are wonderful for most people, although those who love to play, but have little knowledge of what they are doing, may get into more trouble now that they can right-click and edit their user login script. As I discussed in Chapter 10, however, there are ways to deal with this problem. Let's look at the seven actions that users can now take.

Personal Information

Users can now edit the information that describes them. With the dialog box shown in Figure 12.18, they can change their name or any portion thereof. Many users want to have correct information about them as part of their own object. They want their full name spelled correctly; they want their maiden name and so on to be available. Others don't want this information available at all. This information, by default, is in their hands, and they can maintain it. Now you don't have to update names when people get married, divorced, and so on. Let them do so.

FIGURE 12.18

The Personal Information dialog box

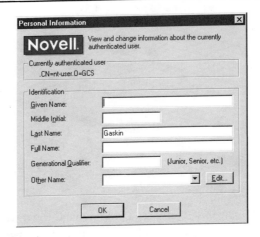

Work Information

In addition to updating their names, users can modify the things that define who they are at work. As Figure 12.19 shows, any user can change his or her title, job description, location, department, telephone number, or fax number. As I mentioned earlier, some users want this information up-to-date; others want greater privacy. Unless you need this information to be accurate and have the time to keep it up-to-date, let your users maintain this for you.

FIGURE 12.19

The Work Information dialog box

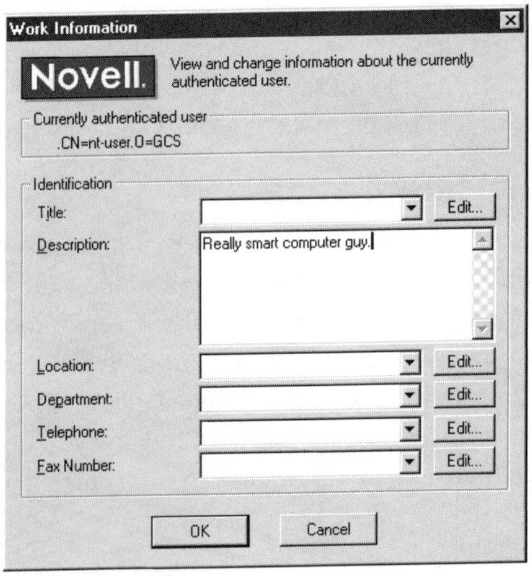

Mailing Information

NDS was designed so that most of the HR information for your company could be stored in NDS, with access available to everyone. This includes mailing addresses. In reality, few companies maintained and used the address information stored in NDS to mail things to their employees in the past. Today, however, more third-party products are taking advantage of these features within NDS. With the new Client32 software, any user can maintain this information, just as with the personal or work information. Figure 12.20 shows the dialog box associated with this choice.

The Mailing Information dialog box

Edit a Login Script

Users can now edit their own login scripts without going into NWAdmin. To do so, a user simply selects a server in the tree or selects the tree itself, right-clicks it, and chooses User Administration ➢ Edit NDS Login Script. Users with the Write right to a container's Login Script property can also edit the container's login script by simply right-clicking the container and choosing Edit NDS Container Login Script. In either case, the Edit Login Script dialog box shown in Figure 12.21 opens, and the user can write or modify a script. (Login scripts are covered in more detail in Chapter 7.) Changes to the script are verified through a dialog box asking whether to save the script: Yes, No, or Cancel.

PART

II

Managing the
Network

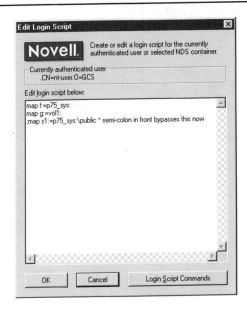

FIGURE 12.21

The Edit Login Script
dialog box

View Your Login Information, Including Account and Time Restrictions

Some of the things that users, particularly power users, may want to know are the restrictions placed on their accounts. The security conscious (some would say paranoid) may want to see when the account was last logged in. A user can get this information easily by selecting the server or tree, right-clicking it, and choosing User Administration ➤ Login Account Information. The biggest gotcha here is that you can only view, not change, any of this information, no matter how many rights you have. Figure 12.22 shows the User Login Administration dialog box, which appears when you make this choice.

As you can see from Figure 12.22, you can get such details as the following:

- Grace logins allowed and remaining
- Maximum simultaneous logins
- Account status

This summary screen shows users how their accounts are configured. Click the View Login Time Restrictions button to display login time restrictions. You'll find more information on these settings in Chapter 6.

FIGURE 12.22

Displaying login account information and restrictions

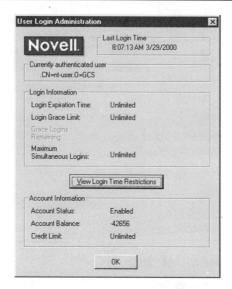

Dealing with Passwords and Password Issues

One of the biggest issues you will face is passwords. The User Password Administration dialog box in Figure 12.23, obtained by choosing the server or tree, right-clicking it, and choosing User Administration ➢ Novell Password Administration, is slightly more useful than the one that displays login account information. Not a lot more useful, since most of the data is still read-only, but a little. Users can still only view their password restrictions, such as if they are allowed to change their own password, if one is required, and if so, what the minimum length is, and so on. This information is not as useless as it seems. When users want to change their passwords or keep them in sync with other systems that have different restrictions, they can view what you have set up for them in NetWare as part of their planning. Or they can just use eDirectory and get a single sign-on to lots of systems.

The one thing that users can change here is their own password, by clicking the Change Password button. When they do so, a dialog box will prompt the user for his or her old password and new password, and a second line will confirm the new password to make sure the user typed it in correctly. This is a great new feature and ability, in my book.

Managing the Network

FIGURE 12.23

Viewing password-related settings and changing passwords

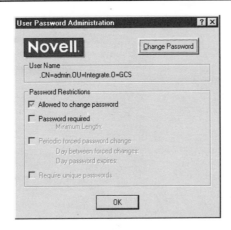

Group Membership

How many groups are you affiliated with? Could you name them all quickly? Net-Ware 5.1 gives the user easy access to that information. Simply select the server or tree, right-click it, choose User Administration ➤ Group Memberships to open the Group Membership dialog box, shown in Figure 12.24. This dialog box, like the last two in this category, is read-only. You can quickly locate all the groups to which you belong and see each group's distinguished name. You will not see, however, any Organizational Roles for which you are an occupant.

FIGURE 12.24

Group information

Summary of Shortcut Menu Features and Locations

Table 12.1 shows the various options in place, the purpose of each, and where each can be found.

TABLE 12.1: THE SHORTCUT MENUS

Menu Choice	Where Available	Purpose
WhoAmI	Tree, Server	Displays logged-in user's distinguished name, connection number, protocol, IP address, and so on
Change Context	Tree	Changes your current context
Logout	Tree, Server	Logs out of specified server or tree
Authenticate	Tree, Server	Authenticates to a tree
Login to NDS Tree or Server	Tree, Server	Logs in to a server or a tree
User Administration, Personal Information	Tree, Server	Allows changes to user names
User Administration, Work Information	Tree, Server	Allows changes to job title, location, phone number, and so on
User Administration, Mailing Information	Tree, Server	Allows changes to user's address information
User Administration, Edit NDS Login Script	Tree, Server	Allows user to create or edit his or her own login script
User Administration, Login Account Information	Tree, Server	Shows user account and time restrictions; read-only
User Administration, Novell Password Administration	Tree, Server	Displays password restrictions; read-only; and allows password changes
User Administration, Group Memberships	Tree, Server	Displays distinguished names of all groups to which the user belongs
Set Current Tree	Tree	Allows you to select your current tree, if multiple trees exist; for compatibility with some applications
Send Message	Server	Allows you to send a quick message to another user or group
Set Default Context	Container	Sets your current context to the selected container
Edit NDS Container Login Script	Container	Allows (with appropriate rights) the editing of the selected container's login script

PART

II

Managing the
Network

File System Operations in Windows 95/98

One of the major reasons for having a network is to access shared storage on servers. In the past, you had to do some file maintenance in DOS, some in Filer, and still some more in NWAdmin. This system required you to know not only what had to be done and how to do it, but where to go to find the tool to do the job. You can take care of most, if not all, file-management chores in Network Neighborhood, as shown in Figure 12.25.

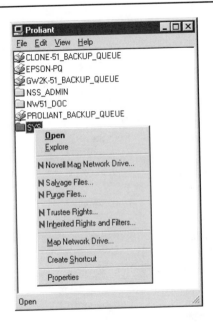

Now let's look at the four options that are Novell specific, beginning with a new capability in Network Neighborhood, NetWare Copy.

Copying Files the NetWare Way

NetWare Copy is a new feature that you can use to copy files, directories, or entire volumes from one place to another. You can copy only existing and/or newer files and keep or modify attributes when they are copied. NetWare Copy is essentially a graphical version of XCOPY. Microsoft has never come up with a graphical version of XCOPY, only COPY with a few extra capabilities (such as copying subfolders) from XCOPY's arsenal. I used to use the switches in XCOPY all the time to control what was going to be copied and how, and I missed a graphical way to do that, often reverting to a DOS prompt. Leave it to Novell to come up with what Microsoft should have had all along.

Right-click a volume or directory, and choose NetWare Copy to open the NetWare File Copy Utility dialog box, as shown in Figure 12.26.

FIGURE 12.26

The NetWare File Copy Utility dialog box

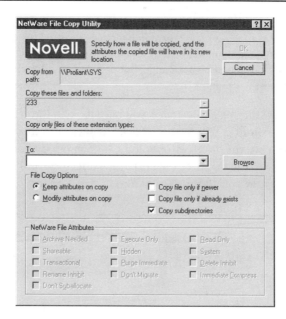

PART

II

Managing the Network

As you can see, you can do all those things I mentioned just a few paragraphs ago in an easy, graphical way. You can even copy entire volumes if you want to, and to keep the bandwidth requirements down, just copy existing or newer files. This is a great feature that Microsoft will probably be implementing soon. I highly recommend that you learn about it and use it; it will save you a lot of time and effort later.

Salvaging Deleted Files

Once you delete a file, what happens to it? Is it lost forever? No! NetWare keeps track of it and does not overwrite it with something else until it is out of free space. Even then, it starts overwriting files that have been deleted the longest (unless the files have been purged—more on that in a minute).

How do you get them back, then? In the old days you had to use a DOS command, Salvage, to get them back. This function was then integrated into Filer in DOS and added to NWAdmin. What does managing deleted files have to do with NDS? Not much. Nevertheless, that was where you had to go, unless you were a DOS person. Now, however, undeleting files is almost as easy as going to the Recycle Bin on the Desktop.

NOTE If you don't want deleted files to be salvaged, you can use a SET command to purge them immediately (Immediate Purge of Deleted Files). Not smart, unless you're close to the disk space edge, but possible. See Appendix C for a list of SET commands.

As Figure 12.27 illustrates, you need look no further than the Salvage utility included in the shortcut menus to get back any files from this directory. To access it, simply right-click the directory or volume (remember that deleted files *from deleted directories* will be in each volume's DELETED.SAV directory) and select Salvage Files. NetWare will then show you all the deleted files in that directory.

FIGURE 12.27

*Getting back a
deleted file*

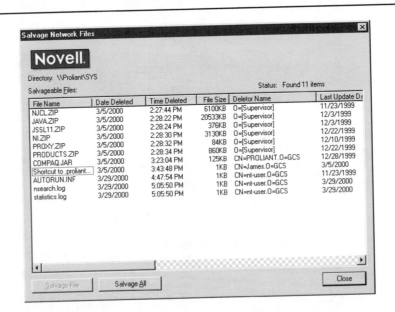

NetWare tracks a vast amount of information on the file. Figure 12.27 shows that for each file, the following information is maintained:

- File name
- Date and time deleted
- Size
- Deletor name (very useful when a user swears that he or she couldn't *possibly* have deleted that file—or to find out who actually did)

This is good information, but off the screen to the right is a wealth of additional information: Last Update Date and Time, Last Updater Name, Creation Date and Time, Owner, Last Archive Date and Time, Last Archiver, and Last Access Date.

To get a file back, simply select it and click Salvage File. To get all the files in this directory back, choose Salvage All. When you've finished, click Close.

Purging Files

If resurrecting files bothers you, you can slam that coffin door shut. Right-click a volume or a directory and choose Purge Files to open the Purge Network Files dialog box, shown in Figure 12.28. The difference between the Salvage dialog box and this one is the Salvage All or Purge All command button. Here you can flush all the deleted-but-not-forgotten files.

PART

II

Managing the
Network

FIGURE 12.28

Purging deleted files

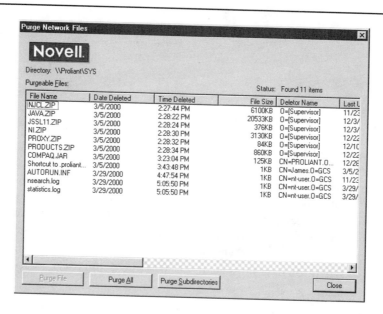

You have only a few choices here. To delete individual files, select them and choose Purge File. You can also purge all the files in this directory by choosing Purge All. To purge all the files in this directory, as well as *all files in all subdirectories* below this one, choose Purge Subdirectories. In either of the last two cases, a dialog box will appear confirming that this is what you want to do and reminding you that the action can't be undone. When you've finished, click Close. One last reminder: *purging files affects only already-deleted files*. It does not harm, in any way, any other file.

Mapping Drives from Windows 95/98

One of the things I have discussed extensively in other chapters is the need to map drives. In previous versions of the client, you essentially had the Windows 95/98 Map Network Drive command. This still exists, but now there are NetWare-specific ways to accomplish the same thing. Figure 12.29 shows what appears when you right-click a volume or directory and choose Novell Map Network Drive.

FIGURE 12.29

The Novell version of the Map Network Drive choice

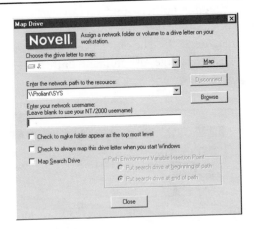

As you can see from Figure 12.29, from here you can choose what you want mapped (the default is what you right-clicked, but you can click Browse and choose any other path or type a different path in the Path text box). Once that selection is made, you can choose the drive letter that you want to use and specify whether to make the drive a search drive. You can also check the box to map the drive again when you start Windows, which serves the same function as the Reconnect At Login box you see when using the Windows Map Network Drive tool in Network Neighborhood. When you have finished in this dialog box, simply click Map.

Printing Is Here, Too

Not only can you map drives here, you can also take care of your printer captures. To do so, browse, if necessary, until you get to the printer or queue in question (for non-NDPS printers), right-click it, and select Novell Capture Printer Port to open the Capture Printer Port dialog box, shown in Figure 12.30.

FIGURE 12.30

Capturing a printer port

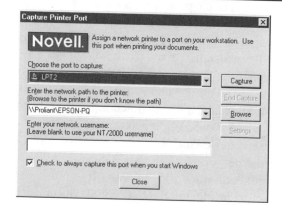

Notice that this dialog box looks a lot like the one in Figure 12.29. The process is similar: select the printer port (instead of the drive letter) and the path (if another one is desired, click Browse and go find it) and decide if you want to reconnect at login. If you do, check the box, just as you did when mapping a drive a minute ago or in NetWare User Tools when you clicked Permanent. When you have finished, click the Capture button. For information on the rest of the printing setup or how to use NDPS printing, see Chapter 8.

The last two screenshots are of an NT 4.0 client, so they have an extra text box labeled Enter Your Network Username and so on. These text boxes don't appear in the Window 95/98 versions of these utilities. At least, not yet.

NetWare User Tools: One-Touch Convenience for Windows 3.1*x*

Still stuck with Windows 3.1? I'm sorry. If you're not stuck with it, count your blessings and move on. If you are, accept my condolences and keep reading.

The best friend your Windows 3.1*x* users will have is the NetWare User Tools program, officially called `NWUSER.EXE`. The `NWUSER.EXE` program is loaded into the `\WINDOWS\SYSTEM` directory when NetWare client files are installed.

You will find the program in the Novell Client group after NetWare client installation. To run it, double-click the icon.

NetWare User Tools first appeared in Personal NetWare, the peer-to-peer networking product that replaced NetWare Lite. Since then, Novell has added a couple of polished edges, but the program has remained fundamentally the same. Since Windows 3.1 has long since faded away for most users, I'm surprised they actually included the program in NetWare 5.1. I guess Novell engineers were worried about those administrators like you, mired in old technology.

Personal NetWare was aimed at small workgroups without any network experience and without an on-site administrator. The simplicity of NetWare User Tools belies its sophistication and ability to function in all NetWare environments. With NetWare User Tools, you can see and make use of every level of NetWare resources, from Personal NetWare desktop peer servers, to NetWare 3.*x* servers, to NetWare 4.*x* and 5.*x* enterprise networks.

If you're still stuck using NetWare Tools, then you know about it. Novell doesn't even bother to add it to the NetWare 5.1 documentation CD, so I won't waste a lot of time or pages now.

Logging In from NetWare User Tools

You can log in to NetWare from the NetWare User Tools program. While in the program, selecting any resource from a server you are not already logged in to (but after all the NetWare client software has been run) opens the Login To NetWare dialog box. Figure 12.31 shows this dialog box for a NetWare 3.12 server.

Highlighting a server and clicking the Map command button or dragging the server from the Resources list into the Connections list also opens the Login To NetWare dialog box. This is a quick and straightforward login method.

You can connect as a guest or as a registered user. Since I am already logged in to several other servers, the system guesses that I want to log in to this server as user JAMES. If this is so, I need only provide a password and click OK or press Enter. The connection happens behind the scenes, and the server moves from the Resources list to the Connections list.

This is technically more of an attachment to a server than a login. You don't run a login script when you log in with NetWare User Tools. To make up for the lack of a login script, the program gives you the option to make permanent drive mappings and printer connections with NetWare User Tools. We'll look at those options in a bit.

FIGURE 12.31

Log in graphically.

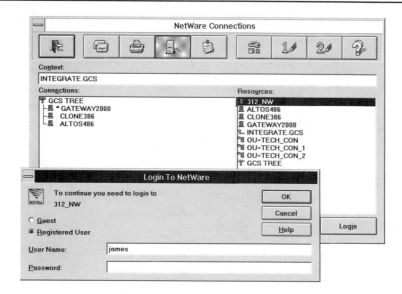

Mapping Drives

IN A HURRY

12.2 Map Drives with NetWare User Tools in NetWare

1. While in Windows 3.1*x*, start NetWare User Tools.

2. Click the command button in the top row next to the Exit button. The icon shows two external hard drives.

3. Drag a volume or a folder on a volume from the Resources list (on the right) and drop it on a drive letter, or highlight a drive letter and a volume and click Map.

4. If you are overwriting an existing mapping or mapping to a local drive, you will be asked to verify your intent.

5. Press Escape or click Exit.

PART

II

Managing the
Network

Forget the MAP command-line utility. Mapping drives with NetWare User Tools is quicker, graphical, and immune to typos. If you are running Windows 3.1*x*, this is the way to map drives. These drive mappings will be global, including DOS boxes under Windows 3.1*x*, if you have the Global Drives & Paths box checked in the NetWare Settings dialog box. This box is always checked if you have installed the Client32 files for DOS and Windows, but it is an option if you are still using the older DOS Requester (VLM) client. Figure 12.32 shows the NetWare Settings dialog box with the NetWare tab selected. The box you will need to check is in the 386 Enhanced DOS Sessions (VLM Client Only) section. The default is to have global settings.

FIGURE 12.32

The NetWare tab in the NetWare Settings dialog box

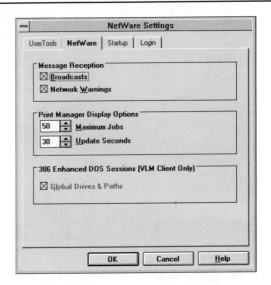

The first job is to locate the drive resource (meaning the volume or directory) that you want to map. The Resources list works like all the other browse windows in NetWare 5.1. If you are looking in one context, you see that context only. If you double-click a context, you change to that context. You can easily run up and down the NDS tree using NetWare User Tools.

The drag-and-drop method shows a little drive icon being pulled to the Drives list on the left side of the NetWare Drive Connections window. If you move the drive somewhere you can't legally drop it, the international circle-and-crossbar symbol covers the drive icon. See Figure 12.33 to witness the flying drive about to be dropped onto an empty drive letter.

Mapping a directory with NetWare User Tools

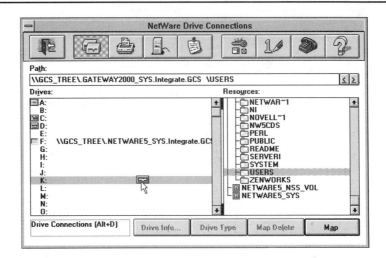

Once you see the volume you want to use, you may want to "map root" a drive to a particular directory. If so, double-click the volume name to open the directory listings. Double-click as many directory names as you need to drill down to the subdirectory for your mapping operation. When you find it, drag that particular directory to your desired drive letter.

Notice the directory path displayed in the Path text box. Here I'm mapping the K: drive to the Users directory so I can easily get to my home directories. The chosen directory will be set up as a regular drive mapping.

You can, however, adjust the map root directory if you desire. See the left and right arrows at the right end of the Path text box? Using these buttons, you can adjust the fake root setting for that drive letter. As you click the arrows, notice that a space appears between directories in the Path text box. This space indicates where the fake root is set. You must click the Map command button to force these new settings into effect.

As you change locations within directory structures, those changes are reflected in the NetWare User Tools display. After all, this is only a graphical front-end to the MAP command. All the MAP features you would expect are here, but they can be run with a mouse rather than a keyboard.

The Drive Info command button at the bottom of the NetWare Drive Connections window is a quick way to show your effective rights in a directory. When a mapped drive is highlighted, showing the path in the Path display, the Drive Info button becomes active. You can then either click the button or double-click the mapped drive. Either way, something along the lines of Figure 12.34 will appear.

PART

II

Managing the Network

FIGURE 12.34

*Checking your rights
the graphical way*

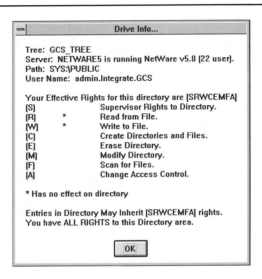

All rights are displayed here, but the appropriate ones for users with nonsupervisory rights will appear in a smaller window. The top of the Drive Info window provides the following information:

- Tree name
- Server name where the volume supporting the mapped drive resides
- NetWare version
- Number of licensed users
- The path of the directory of the rights being displayed
- The user's distinguished name

There are two other quick details to check in the NetWare Drive Connections window. First, notice the icon to the left of Drive Z:. See the little eyeglasses? Those indicate search drives. In Figure 12.33, Drive A:'s icon is supposed to resemble a floppy drive. Drive C: also has the eyeglasses, because it is another search drive (or in other words, there are directories on your hard drive that are part of the path).

Drive D: is my favorite. It looks like it's sticking out its tongue, doesn't it? That's really a CD-ROM drive, and the tongue is a CD-ROM disk. Who says pictures never distort reality?

Making Drives Permanent

IN A HURRY

12.3 Make a Drive Mapping Permanent with NetWare User Tools

1. While in Windows 3.1*x*, start NetWare User Tools.

2. Click the Drive Connections button in the top row next to the Exit button. The icon is two external hard drives.

3. Highlight the drive mapping to make it permanent, and click the Drive Type command button at the bottom of the dialog box.

4. Check the Permanent Drive box.

5. Choose OK. (Notice the change in the icon to the left of the drive letter.)

6. Press Escape or click Exit.

Mapping a drive permanently through NetWare User Tools works only after you have logged in and started Windows 3.1*x*. The permanent drive mapping is added to the `PROFILE.INI` file, which is stored in `C:\NOVELL\CLIENT32\PROFILE\LOC_x`, where *x* is the location number, usually 0 or 1. Locations allow you to log in easily from various locations, including on the LAN or across a dial-up link. The permanent drives are added to the [Permanent] section. The global drives setting makes sure this is carried through to the DOS boxes (for this location), however. All the `PROFILE.INI` manipulation is handled for you automatically.

 NOTE   I prefer to log in to the system and set the initial drives through the various login script options and use this feature only for changing and adding drive mappings. The reason for my preference is that any user can use NetWare User Tools and change drive mappings, including those that may already exist in various login scripts. This could potentially stop other programs from functioning correctly, meaning a trip to the user's desk. If you do your mappings in login scripts, however, if things get destroyed, all the user need do is log out and log in again and all is well.

Figure 12.35 shows the USERS subdirectory highlighted once again. Take a close look at the icon to the left of Drive K:. See the little dark line going through and dipping down for a bit (on the screen it would stand out better because that line is in

red)? That's supposed to represent a network cable connecting to this drive letter. A similar icon is used for network drive letters in File Manager.

FIGURE 12.35

Mapping a permanent USERS drive

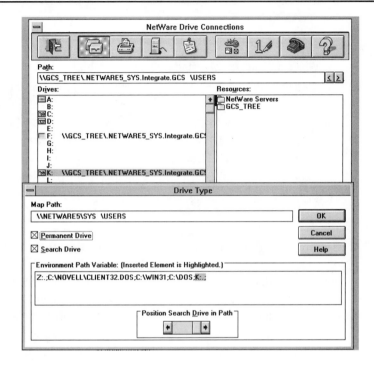

Permanent drive maps aren't permanent in any real way, since they're so easy to change. If you get tired of a permanent drive, just highlight the drive and click the Map Delete command button. This takes away the network drive icon and erases the setting from your PROFILE.INI file.

You may also have noticed the second checkbox in Figure 12.35, labeled Search Drive. As you can see from the screenshot, I have checked the box. When you check the box, it fills in the Environmental Path Variable: (Inserted Element Is Highlighted.) box with the DOS path, showing both local and network search drives. You can then choose the position of this drive in the path. To do so, simply click the left or right arrows in the Position Search Drive In Path area. This functionality cannot easily be duplicated with the MAP command. With MAP, you can choose the position in the path but not the drive letter, or you can choose the letter (as a regular mapping) and then change it to a search drive, but only as the last item on the path.

Controlling Printing

12.4 Set Up Network Printing with NetWare User Tools

1. While in Windows 3.1x, start NetWare User Tools.
2. Click the Printer command button (with the printer icon) in the top row.
3. Find the network printer you want to use in the Resources list. Move up and down the NDS tree if necessary.
4. Drag the printer or print queue to use over to the appropriate LPT port and drop it there, or highlight the desired printer or print queue and the LPT port and click the Capture command button.
5. Set any LPT settings necessary (in LPT Settings).
6. Press Escape or click Exit.

Just as the drive-mapping function in NetWare User Tools made me swear off the MAP command, so has the printing feature weaned me from CAPTURE, except in login scripts. You can use a number of command-line options when connecting to a new printer, and NetWare User Tools simplifies making these specifications.

The printer icon on the top line of command buttons is a lot more intuitive than the button for network drives (why is there an icon for a heartbeat monitor?). When you click the printer icon, the NetWare Printer Connections face of NetWare User Tools appears. Take a look at Figure 12.36 for the opening shot, as I capture LPT1 to Q1.

FIGURE 12.36

Dropping a printer

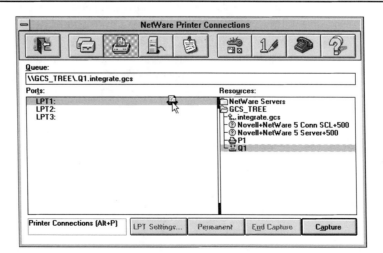

The process for setting up a printer connection is just like that for mapping drives. Everything in NetWare User Tools is fairly consistent (almost as if the programmers actually paid attention to the needs of the users—what a concept!).

You can drag-and-drop the printer or print queue onto the LPT port. Clicking the printer, the LPT port, and then the Capture button works just as well. Choosing either the printer or the print queue gives the same result.

To delete a print connection, use the same dragging-and-dropping or button-clicking procedures. You can just drag an existing printer connection and drop it back into the Resources list to disconnect (the CAPTURE/ENDCAP command). You can also highlight your printer connection and click the End Capture button.

Making Printer Connections Permanent

IN A HURRY

12.5 Make a Printer Connection Permanent with NetWare User Tools

1. While in Windows 3.1x, start NetWare User Tools.
2. Click the Printer command button in the top row.
3. Highlight the captured printer connection to make it permanent.
4. Click the Permanent command button at the bottom of the window. (Notice the new printer icon to the left of the printer port.)
5. Press Escape or click Exit.

Once again, a user has an easy way to make a permanent connection to a network resource without bothering the network administrator (whether it's the right resource, whether the correct printer is installed, and so on is another matter). Simply highlight the captured printer or print queue, and click the Permanent command button. The information is again written automatically to the PROFILE.INI file. It's available in DOS, but only after you start Windows 3.1x. Figure 12.37 shows a permanent printer connection.

Disconnecting a permanent printer is simple: highlight the printer and click End Capture. The PROFILE.INI file is modified, and the next time you start Windows, the printer you removed won't be configured.

FIGURE 12.37

A printer icon for a permanent printer connection

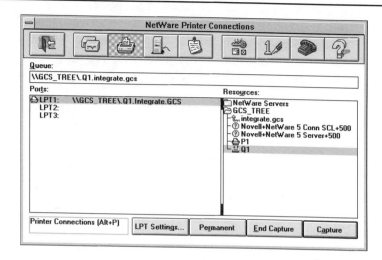

When you make a printer permanent, the LPT settings in place at the time you mark it permanent are kept. If you change the printer settings, use End Capture to disconnect the printer, and then recapture it to make the new settings permanent. (See the next section for information about adjusting the printer settings.)

NetWare Connections (Servers)

IN A HURRY

12.6 Make NetWare Server Connections with NetWare User Tools

1. While in Windows 3.1x, start NetWare User Tools.
2. Click the NetWare Connections button (the tall server case icon) in the top row.
3. Double-click the NetWare server or container object to use.
4. If necessary, log in to the server to make the resources available.
5. To check server information, click the NetWare Info command button.
6. To set or change your password to the highlighted server (or tree, if you are logged in to a tree), click the Set Pass(word) button.
7. To log out of the highlighted server, click the Logout button.
8. Press Escape or click Exit.

PART

II

Managing the Network

The NetWare Connections window of NetWare User Tools may be the first place you should go before doing anything new. If you aren't connected to the necessary servers or containers, you won't have access to the network resources you need. Use this screen to connect to NDS trees and servers.

If you try to use a network resource from a server that requires you to log in, the login screen will pop up automatically (as in Figure 12.31 earlier in this chapter), and your name will be listed as the user name. If you want to log in as a guest rather than as a registered user, you have that option. You can log in to the following objects:

- Tree
- NetWare NDS-Based Server
- NetWare Bindery-Based Server

Remember, this login is more like an attach; you don't run a login script. Most users log in before starting Windows 3.1*x* or use the new graphical login as they start Windows. The NET.CFG has a place under the NetWare DOS Requester section to set your starting context, preferred tree, and preferred server if you want. Although you don't log in only to a server in NetWare 5.1 as in NetWare 3, you can ask for a particular server to handle your login request, such as the server holding the master replica of the NDS database or one that is local to you.

Figure 12.38 shows the NetWare Connections window of NetWare User Tools, along with the results of pressing the NetWare Info command button. NETWARE5 is the head server in the network, at least at this time.

FIGURE 12.38

Checking NetWare Info for a server

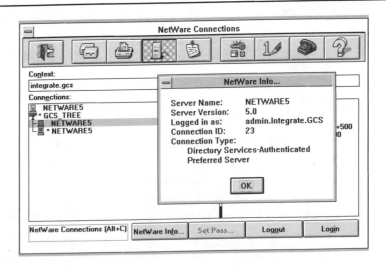

Your network resources are in the right-hand list, and your current connections are on the left. The command buttons across the bottom do the following:

NetWare Info   Shows server and network details for the object highlighted in the Connections list. The information will include:

- The NetWare version of the server
- Your login name
- Your connection number on that server
- Whether the connection is Directory Services, Personal NetWare, or Bindery
- If this is your preferred connection (from NET.CFG)
- If this is your current connection (denoted with an asterisk)

Set Pass(word)   Sets or changes your password for the highlighted tree or server. You will be asked to type the old password, type the new password, and retype the new password.

Logout   Logs out of the highlighted object in the Connections list.

Login   Logs in to the resource highlighted in the Resources list.

Notice the Login button at the bottom of the NetWare Connections window. In Figure 12.38, if you move the highlight bar up and down the Resources list, the Login button will become active for the server objects where you can log in. Otherwise, the button will be gray (inactive).

The asterisk by the NETWARE5 name (and its tree, GCS_TREE) indicates that this server (and since it is an NDS server, the tree it belongs to as well) is my current connection. Your view of network resources may change, depending on the information contained in your current server.

The information line just below the top icons now shows the context of your view of NDS. As you click the containers in the Resources list, the context text box reflects your changes. You may think you've lost some servers if you change your context and don't expand it to show all the resources.

The NetWare Set Password dialog box, shown in Figure 12.39, contains a wonderful new feature. If you look at the bottom of the dialog box, you will see a checkbox labeled Synchronize Password For All Connections. How many times have you logged in to a server that you don't use frequently only to forget what your password was six months ago? For servers you use every day, how much of a hassle is it for you to change the password on each every month? If you check this box, all other trees and bindery-based servers that you are currently connected to will change their password at the same time to whatever you put in this dialog box.

FIGURE 12.39

The NetWare Set
Password dialog box
with the Synchronize
Password For All
Connections box
checked

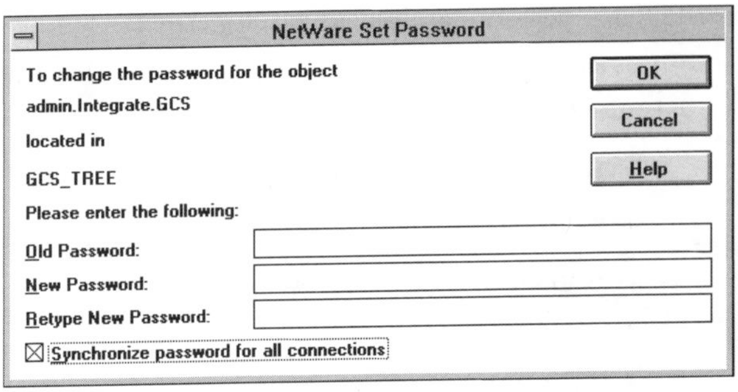

```
┌─────────────────────────────────────────────────────────┐
│ ─ │              NetWare Set Password                     │
├─────────────────────────────────────────────────────────┤
│  To change the password for the object      ┌─────────┐  │
│  admin.Integrate.GCS                         │   OK    │  │
│                                              └─────────┘  │
│  located in                                  ┌─────────┐  │
│                                              │ Cancel  │  │
│  GCS_TREE                                    └─────────┘  │
│                                              ┌─────────┐  │
│  Please enter the following:                 │  Help   │  │
│                                              └─────────┘  │
│  Old Password:      ┌──────────────────────────────────┐ │
│                     └──────────────────────────────────┘ │
│  New Password:      ┌──────────────────────────────────┐ │
│                     └──────────────────────────────────┘ │
│  Retype New Password:┌─────────────────────────────────┐ │
│                      └─────────────────────────────────┘ │
│  ☒ Synchronize password for all connections              │
└─────────────────────────────────────────────────────────┘
```

The Graphical Help Display

IN A HURRY

12.7 Using the NetWare User Tools Help System

1. While in Windows 3.1*x*, start NetWare User Tools.
2. Click the last icon in the toolbar, the large yellow question mark.
3. You will get help on whatever screen is active (drives, ports, and so on).
4. Close the Help screen when finished.

In developing an end-user tool for the smallest companies, NetWare User Tools designers obviously spent some time thinking about the Help system. These are not the usual tepid Windows 3.1*x* Help screens. The information is simple and straightforward, designed with the end user in mind. There are also many links to other places in the Help system for more information.

Teach Your Users Well

Each user has a job to do. Each job requires information and interaction. Your network is the conduit between the two. This situation does not gain the network, or even you, any respect when things work properly, just the chance to be blamed when things don't work to the user's advantage.

When users are unhappy, it's usually a management failure. Resources must be planned and deployed to support the users. If those resources, particularly your time and any necessary equipment, aren't available, the users become even more unhappy.

The animosity isn't personal, and it isn't deep. While it is aggravating, it's understandable. You get aggravated with your boss because tools you need aren't provided, don't you? When the network tool is not available, it's natural for the users to get mad at you, and it's safer for them than getting mad at their boss.

Track your user complaints. Half or more will be caused by something the users should know. The fact that they don't know usually has more to do with management priorities than user stupidity or apathy. Management's lack of priorities and support for you and your department will cause you more problems indirectly than any user will cause directly.

CHAPTER 13

Integrating NetWare 5.1 with Windows NT

Your network no doubt has at least one Windows NT system. If it doesn't today, it will tomorrow. You have no hope of converting those NT boxes to NetWare. In fact, you will have to fight to stop management from converting the NetWare boxes to NT. This chapter is for those of you who promised your bosses that you could manage both the NT and NetWare systems seamlessly without any complaints from the users (so maybe you stretched the truth a bit when you said "without any").

As you know, managing an environment with multiple NetWare and NT servers truly can be an administrative nightmare. How many of you have had to reset passwords on several different NT servers because a user forgot his or her password and there was no way to synchronize the change across multiple servers? Have you had to create several accounts on different systems for one user because he or she needed to use resources on each server? Do you listen to your users complain about needing to memorize multiple user names and passwords for all the different systems they use?

NetWare 4.*x* and NDS eliminated these problems by requiring a single login for all users connecting to an NDS tree. It also provided the NetWare Administrator utility to manage the trees and every server in the trees. Windows NT took a different approach. It established domains and domain controllers, each of which had to be managed individually to allow a user to access resources on a different NT Server. Microsoft claims that Active Directory, which is now available as part of Windows 2000, eliminates this problem. Active Directory does centralize network administration by storing resource information in a central database, but unfortunately its use is restricted to Windows clients. Its effectiveness is also limited by Microsoft's need to be backward compatible to prior versions of NT Server.

NetWare 5.0 made two products available to facilitate administration from the NetWare side: Novell Administrator for NT and NDS for NT. With the release of NetWare 5.1, Novell has eliminated the first product and upgraded NDS for NT into NDS Corporate Edition. The latest version of NDS, version 8, renamed NDS eDirectory, is an integral part of Netware 5.1. But the name change represents Novell's strategy to make NDS a standard directory service for networks other than NetWare, including improved support for LDAP. NDS eDirectory can be used with or without a Novell directory. NDS Corporate Edition, which is purchased separately from NetWare, integrates heterogeneous networks by making NDS schema available for Microsoft NT/2000 Server and UNIX servers running Sun Solaris or Linux.

 NOTE Active Directory is Microsoft's version of an active, distributed directory. This product was announced quite a while back but has just recently appeared as an integral part of Windows 2000. If Active Directory matches all the promise in the Microsoft announcement, it will be on par with NDS circa 1993—yes, six directory generations behind!

I am going to show you how you can manage your mixed NetWare and Windows NT environments without having to deal with anything except NDS. But first, for those of you who are new to NT management, I'll give you a crash course on Microsoft's entry in the network playing field.

Windows NT in a Nutshell

Before we get into the nuts and bolts of managing a mixed NT/NetWare environment, we need to go over some of the basics of a Windows NT Server and Windows NT Workstation environment. Of course, if you already know all this, you can jump right into the NDS Corporate Edition section. On the other hand, if you are new to the world of NT, read through this section, then get your hands on a book (or two or more) devoted to Windows NT Server—there is a whole lot more to it than I can cover in these few pages.

First, NT environments revolve around domains. A *domain* is a logical grouping of network servers and other computers. A Windows NT Server domain is illustrated in Figure 13.1.

PART

II

FIGURE 13.1

An NT domain

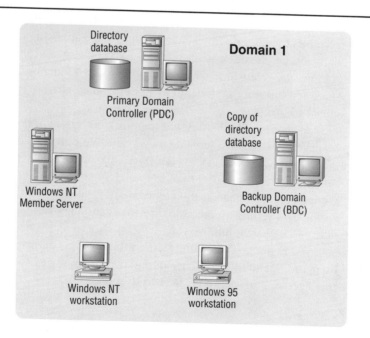

Managing the
Network

There are three roles a Windows NT server can have in a domain:

- A *primary domain controller* (PDC) contains the master database of user and resource accounts for NT Workstations in the domain. Each domain must have a PDC, and there can only be one PDC in a domain.

- A *backup domain controller* (BDC) stores copies of the directory database in case of failure at the PDC. If the PDC fails, a BDC can be promoted so that it is the new PDC for the domain. No changes are actually made to the BDC. All changes occur to the PDC. Login authentication can be handled by a BDC so users in a large domain benefit from multiple BDCs.

- A *member server* belongs to a domain but contains only resources for use by the domain. It does not hold any copies of the directory database. A complete reinstallation of NT Server is required if you want to change the status of a member server to a PDC or BDC.

The directory database I refer to above is the NT Security Accounts Manager, or *SAM*. The SAM is a domain-wide database, stored on the PDC and copied to the BDC, that holds information about users, groups, and computers in an NT domain. The maximum number of objects that should be defined in a single SAM is 40,000.

One of the key things to remember about the NT network environment is that there is no central point of administration. Both NT Workstation and NT Server require accounts to be set up for each user who will be accessing resources. For NT Server domains, you create domain and local users and local and global groups. For NT Workstation, you create local users, and local groups. Domains use trust relationships to share account information and to authorize the rights and permissions of users and global groups.

Management of NT users, groups, and domains requires several utilities: User Manager for Domains, Server Manager, and Windows Explorer. Each of these utilities is installed when you install NT Server and can be accessed by selecting Start ➢ Administrative Tools. User Manager for Domains allows you to manage users and groups, Server Manager is used for computer accounts, and Windows Explorer is your resource for setting up access to directories and files. NetWare does all that with one utility—NetWare Administrator.

If you're not familiar with NT, then the concepts of trust relationships, local and user groups, and file system rights and permissions need some explaining. Let's get that over with so we can get back to the good stuff.

Trust Relationships

A *trust relationship* is an administration and communication link between two domains. Trust relationships are necessary when you want to share resources among domains. Trusts must be created individually for each domain. Establishing trust relationships centralizes administration of your network. Users can log in from domains in which they do not have accounts, and users from one domain can use resources in another domain (such as printers) without an account in that domain.

There are two types of trusts:

- In a *one-way trust*, the *trusting* domain (the one that has the resources to be shared) lets users from other domains use its resources. The other domain is known as the *trusted* domain.

- In a *two-way trust*, both domains trust each other equally. As a result, users in each domain can access resources in both domains. A two-way trust is actually two one-way trusts because each trust must be configured independently. Two-way trusts allow a user to log in from either domain to the domain that actually contains that user's account. Each domain provides authentication services for users in the other domain.

I like to use a house-sitting analogy to explain the difference between the trusted and the trusting domains. If you are watching my house while I am on vacation and I give you my key, I am *trusting* you. Therefore, you are *trusted* by me not to abuse my faith in giving you access to my home (resources). In this example, you are the trusted domain and I am the trusting domain.

Trust relationships are not transitive. This means that if Domain A trusts Domain B and Domain B trusts Domain C, Domain A does *not* trust Domain C. A separate trust relationship needs to be created between Domain A and Domain C.

A domain can have up to 128 incoming trust relationships and an unlimited number of outgoing trust relationships. However, I wouldn't recommend that type of setup unless you enjoy pain. Just look at Figure 13.2 and tell me if you want to troubleshoot that!

When trust relationships exist between domains, you can place global groups from the trusted domain into local groups in a trusting domain. I'll clear up the global/local group distinction next.

FIGURE 13.2

*An NT domain
two-way trust*

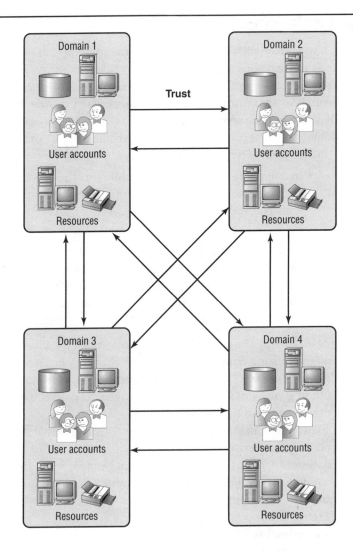

Global Groups and Local Groups

As I stated earlier, each NT computer—whether it is a PDC, BDC, member server, or NT Workstation computer—requires accounts. Each account must be given rights to use resources in the domain or at the NT Workstation computer. Rights can be assigned at either the user or group level. There are two types of groups:

- *Global groups* allow you, the administrator, to gather up all the user accounts that have common needs for resources in the domain. They are stored on domain controllers. A global group can contain only user accounts from its domain. It *cannot* contain local groups or other global groups. No rights can be assigned to global groups. They are strictly a way to organize your users.

- *Local groups* assign *permissions* (a fancy word for rights) to resources on local computers. They can contain user accounts and global groups from one or more domains that have trusts established with the local domain. All local groups are stored on the local computer's account database (don't forget to back up!).

 NOTE A Windows NT Server or NT Workstation can be used as a client PC at the same time as it is acting as a server. This is the reason that NT provides for local groups.

Let's look at an example. You are a member of Domain A. Your user account is User1. You need to have administrator rights to the domain. The NT network administrator would add your user account to the Domain Admin global group (a built-in group that comes with NT Server), which has already been added to the Administrators local group. After all that has been completed, you would be able to administer the domain.

Now that all the users, groups, and rights have been taken care of, the users will probably want to log in. To do this, each computer that will be authenticating to the domain to use its resources must have an account created. The quickest way to establish this account is through NT Server's Server Manager utility. From there, you tell the PDC the unique identifying name that has been assigned to the computer and is being broadcast by it. Then, each time a domain user logs in from that PC, that user can access domain resources.

NT File System and Permissions

Since I said this was "NT in a nutshell," I'm going to wrap this up with the NT file system as the final topic. Originally, the only file system that users in a Windows environment dealt with was the FAT (file allocation table). Permissions in FAT file systems can be assigned only at the directory that is the share point. No file-level security is available. This means that any user who walked up to a PC could do

PART

II

Managing the
Network

whatever he or she wanted to a file located on the local hard drive (unless it had a screen saver with a password enabled and active on it).

Since NT allows you to use the server PC as a client PC, additional security was needed at a file level. Thus was born *NTFS* (NT File System), which is the default file system for NT Server. It provides the only means for achieving file-level security on a local computer and really handles large disk drives well. It works best on hard drives over 400MB. Table 13.1 shows the individual NTFS permissions that are available.

TABLE 13.1: INDIVIDUAL NTFS PERMISSIONS FOR DIRECTORIES AND FILES

Individual NTFS Permissions	At a Directory You Can	At a File You Can
Read (R)	Display a directory name, attributes, owner, and permissions	Display file data, attributes, owner, and permissions
Write (W)	Add files and directories, change a directory's attributes, and display owner and permissions	Create or edit a file, display owner and permissions, change file attributes
Execute (X)	Make changes to a subdirectory, display attributes, and display the owner and permissions	Run a file if it is executable; display file attributes, owner, and permissions
Delete (D)	Delete a directory	Delete a file
Change Permission (P)	Change a directory's permissions	Change a file's permissions
Take Ownership	Take ownership of a directory	Take ownership of a file

 NOTE The person who creates a directory or file becomes the *owner* when you are using NTFS. The owner can *always* assign and change permissions on a directory or file.

Now, which of you wants to have to assign all those permissions every time someone needs to do something? I don't see any raised hands, so you'll be happy to know that NTFS comes with predefined standard or combination permissions to make your life a little easier.

Tables 13.2 and 13.3 indicate the standard permissions that most people use. These are combinations of the available individual NTFS permissions listed in Table 13.1. By default, the Everyone group has Full Control over shared directories.

TABLE 13.2: STANDARD DIRECTORY PERMISSIONS

Permission	On Directory	On File
No Access	None	None
List	Read (R), Execute (X)	Not specified
Read	Read (R), Execute (X)	Read (R), Execute (X)
Add	Write (W), Execute (X)	Not specified
Add & Read	Read (R), Write (W), Execute (X)	Read (R), Execute (X)
Change	Read (R), Write (W), Execute (X), Delete (D)	Read (R), Write (W), Execute (X), Delete (D)
Full Control	All	All

TABLE 13.3: STANDARD FILE PERMISSIONS

Permission	Individual Permission
No Access	None
Read	Read (R), Execute (X)
Change	Read (R), Write (W), Execute (X), Delete (D)
Full Control	All

 TIP Don't apply specific rights to an individual file in a directory unless you keep track of it somewhere. Try to place files that need more restrictive rights than have been applied to a directory in a directory with similar restrictions.

Now you're ready for the really cool stuff. Well, it's cool if you decided that managing all the NT details along with the NetWare accounts requires way too much work on your part on a daily basis.

PART

II

Managing the Network

Using NDS Corporate Edition

Using Novell's add-on product, NDS Corporate Edition, completely extends the schema of NDS to allow for a single, unified directory for administration. NDS Corporate Edition creates one object that contains all the NT and NDS information.

Once integrated, NDS can manage all NT domain requests made from NT Servers and Workstations. Each user will now have a single login and password that gains that user access to resources on both NetWare and NT servers. In fact, your users probably will not know (or care) where the resources are coming from—they will just click an application icon, and the program will start.

As an administrator, you can see how much easier this will make your life. Instead of managing two or more separate databases of users and resource information, you can now do it from one place—NDS. The NDS and NT domain databases are integrated into one NDS master database.

Have you ever been told that you need to remove all of a user's accounts from the network because that user no longer works for the company? How long did it take you? How many different NT Servers did you need to log in to? Were you sure you got them all? With NDS Corporate Edition, all you need to do is delete the NDS account for the user, and you have deleted all the accounts for that integrated user.

 NOTE Single login does not mean single point of failure. As long as you maintain your NDS replicas, the User object should always be available unless it has been deleted.

Another nice benefit is no more time spent configuring the typically complex domain trust relationships that are an integral part of NT networking. And you won't be asked to move a user from one domain to another because that person moved within the company and needs to be on a different NT server in another domain. If you've worked as an NT network administrator, you know moving a user from one domain to another means that you have to write down all the information, delete the account, and then re-create it in another domain.

That's the NT way. Now you are using NDS. NDS thinks of NT domains as groups to which NDS users can belong. It's a simple matter of changing someone's group access. A user can be a member of as many domains as his or her job requires.

In terms of security, this feature is the administrator's ultimate fantasy. In NT, administrative rights are granted on a per-domain, per-object basis. NDS grants administrative rights on a per-object basis only. If you want to grant someone administrative rights to a single printer, you can.

For those of you who need to convince your managers to allow you to purchase NDS Corporate Edition, you can sum this all up in their language. Just tell them that NDS Corporate Edition reduces the cost of ownership by reducing the amount of time spent administering the network by eliminating duplicate accounts.

NDS Corporate Edition Components

NDS Corporate Edition is made up of the following components:

- Novell NDS Corporate Edition Client
- Domain Object Wizard
- Novell SAMSRV.DLL
- NetWare Administrator
- Mailbox Manager for Exchange

Since each of these components plays an important role, let's take a closer look.

NDS Corporate Edition Client

The Novell Client is required for every NT Server machine that will be integrated into NDS. The client is automatically installed during the installation process for NDS Corporate Edition. Once installed, the client can access the NDS database from NT.

Domain Object Wizard

The Domain Object Wizard extends the schema of the NDS tree and migrates existing Domain objects from the NT SAM databases into NDS. You *do not* need to re-create the Domain objects again in NDS. It does it all for you!

The Domain Object Wizard is run only once. (Running it a second time allows you to uninstall NDS Corporate Edition, as you'll learn later in this chapter.) The Wizard will automatically start the first time your NT Server reboots after NDS Corporate Edition has been installed.

SAMSRV.DLL

Those of you who are not familiar with NT networking are probably wondering what SAMSRV.DLL is. In NT networking, an application that needs access to information from the NT domain makes a request to the file SAMLIB.DLL. Using remote procedure calls (RPCs), SAMLIB.DLL communicates with SAMSRV.DLL, which, in turn, accesses the

PART

II

Managing the
Network

NT SAM, where the domain database is stored. SAMSRV.DLL then performs the operation that has been requested.

NDS Corporate Edition renames the original SAMSRV.DLL file to MSSAMSRV.DLL and replaces it with a new one. The Novell SAMSRV.DLL redirects domain access calls to NDS, allowing NDS to complete requests from NT Servers, NT Workstations, and applications.

The Novell SAMSRV.DLL *must* be installed on every domain controller in the NT domain that you are integrating into NDS. It needs to be installed on a PDC and then on any BDCs in the domain(s).

NetWare Administrator and Mailbox Snap-ins

The last two components are NetWare Administrator and Mailbox Manager for Exchange. NDS Corporate Edition provides a snap-in to NetWare Administrator that allows you to administer Domain objects that have been migrated to the NDS tree. Another snap-in allows you to create, edit, and delete Exchange mailboxes from within NetWare Administrator. Any changes made in NetWare Administrator are automatically synchronized to the Exchange server.

NOTE The Mailbox Manager for Exchange does not automatically synchronize changes made in Microsoft's Exchange Manager to NDS. It does provide the ability to do manual synchronization. Look for future releases of NDS Corporate Edition to have automatic synchronization from Exchange. For more information about managing Exchange with NDS Corporate Edition, refer to the NDS Corporate Edition documentation from Novell.

Requirements for NDS Corporate Edition

For NetWare servers, you'll need the following to install NDS Corporate Edition:

- NDS Corporate Edition CD (available from your Novell reseller)
- NetWare 4.11 server(s) with NDS 5.99a or above with Support Pack 6 or above
- NetWare 4.2
- NetWare 5 with Support Pack 2
- Supervisor rights to the [Root] partition of each NDS tree you will be modifying
- 64MB or more of available RAM on each NetWare server containing a replica of the partition where you will be locating the NT domain

TIP If you are not sure how to calculate the required amounts of RAM for your environment, refer to Novell's Technical Information Document number 2932563 at support.novell.com.

Here are the requirements for your NT Server or NT Workstation machines:

- Windows NT Server(s) 4 with Service Pack 3.0 or higher, and an assigned IP address
- Administrator privileges to the domain
- Novell Client for Windows 95 3.0 or higher or Novell Client for Windows NT 4.5 or higher
- An NTFS volume in which to store NDS Corporate Edition

Installing NDS Corporate Edition

IN A HURRY

13.1 Install NDS for Windows NT

1. Log in to your Windows NT Server as Administrator.
2. Launch SETUP.EXE from the NT directory of the NDS Corporate Edition CD-ROM.
3. Select the Install Novell Directory Services option.
4. Read and accept the license agreement. The installation will copy all the required files.
5. Reboot your Windows NT Server when prompted to load the Novell NDS Corporate Edition Client, and launch the Domain Object Wizard.

First, you need to install NDS Corporate Edition on the NT domain's PDC. The PDC must be completed before any of the BDCs. Log in to your NT Server as Administrator.

 NOTE Remove any periods from domain names prior to installing NDS Corporate Edition. Any periods will be converted to underscores during the install.

Click the QuickStart button to display an installation manual in Adobe Acrobat format. When you are ready to install, launch SETUP.EXE from the NT directory on the NDS Corporate Edition CD-ROM and select the Install Novell Directory Services option. You'll see the opening screen shown in Figure 13.3.

FIGURE 13.3

*Beginning to install
NDS Corporate Edition
components*

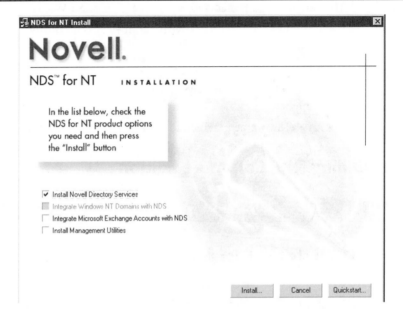

If you are not running the appropriate Novell client, the installation program will automatically update it from the CD and ask you to reboot the NT Server. Then the license agreement will appear, and you will be prompted for the license disk. Next, you will need to supply NDS information, including the name of your existing NDS tree and the context for this Server object. Finally, the installation process will copy files from the CD, and restart.

NOTE   If you are installing NDS Corporate Edition on a Citrix WinFrame product, refer to Novell Technical Information document number 2928433.

Running the Domain Object Wizard

IN A HURRY

13.2 Move NT Domains into NDS

1. After rebooting, log in to the NT Server as Administrator and to NDS as a user who has Supervisor rights to the [Root] of the tree.

2. Read the Domain Object Wizard's Welcome message and click Next.

3. Click Next to extend the schema.

4. Click the context Browse button to the right of the input field, select the context for your NT domain, and then click Next.

5. After the schema has been extended, click Next and then Search to begin the upload of NT objects.

6. In the Summary screen, review the Domain Object Wizard's findings and recommendations. Verify each user's status, change it if necessary, and then click Next.

7. At the Domain Object Wizard's final screen, optionally choose to view the log or documentation. Then click Finish.

8. Reboot when prompted.

9. Repeat this process for each BDC and PDC in your network that will be integrated. Remember that the PDC must be completed before the BDC.

Now that you have installed NDS Corporate Edition, you must integrate the NT Domain objects into NDS. To do this, you need the Domain Object Wizard. This will appear on your screen right after you reboot your NT Server and log in, as shown in Figure 13.4. If it does not launch automatically, select Start ➤ Programs ➤ Novell (Common) ➤ Domain Object Wizard.

To move existing NT domains into NDS, you need to know the name of the NDS tree and the context where the NDS is to be placed. You also need to have logged in to your NT Server as Administrator and logged in to NDS as a user with Admin rights to the tree into which you will be placing the NT Domain objects.

 WARNING Do not rename the domain or any computer acting as a PDC or BDC after you have installed NDS Corporate Edition.

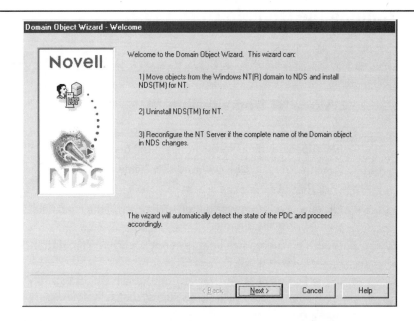

After you click Next in the Welcome screen, you're asked to select the NDS tree that you want to move the objects into. (If you have not logged in to NDS yet, you will be prompted to do so at this point.) In Figure 13.5, you can see that I've selected my SYBEX tree from the drop-down list.

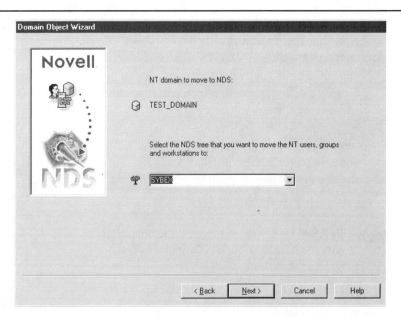

Next, the Domain Object Wizard will extend the NDS schema and create an NDS Domain object in the NDS tree you specified, as shown in Figure 13.6. The object will have the same name as your NT domain.

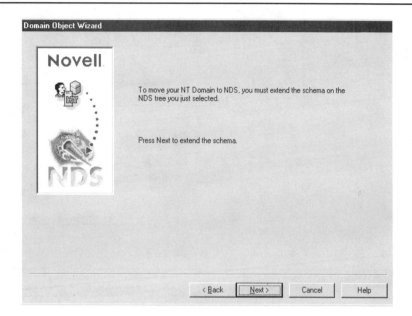

After the schema has been extended, the Wizard requires the NDS context for your NT domain and the default context for new NDS users, as shown in Figure 13.7. You can click the context Browse button located to the right of the input fields to find the context. If you already have a large NDS tree, I recommend creating a context specifically for use as a repository for NT objects. Then you will be able to see at a glance which objects are from NT. Often, the default context for new NDS users created in NT will be the same. Refer to your company's IS standards documents if you are not sure what to do. Notice that you can instruct the program to synchronize users who have been logging on to the NT domain to NDS.

Next, the Wizard will ask if you want to search NDS for any users who also exist in NT. Click Next, and then Search to begin the upload of NT objects. Once the search is complete, the Domain Object Wizard displays a summary of its findings and gives you a recommendation as to what to do with each user, as shown in Figure 13.8.

PART

II

Managing the
Network

FIGURE 13.7

Selecting your NDS context for your NT domain

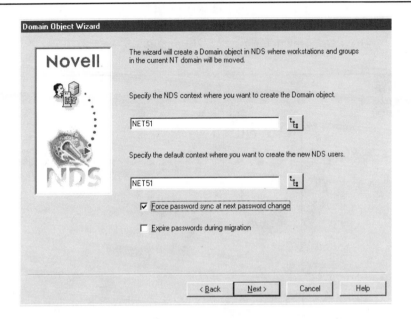

FIGURE 13.8

The Domain Object Wizard's summary and recommendations

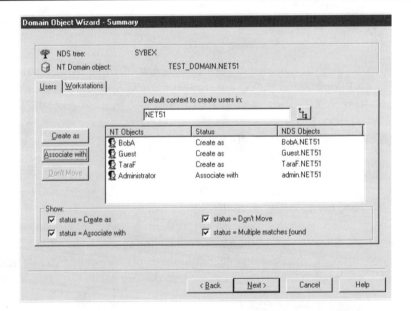

All NT user accounts will be created as NDS user accounts in the same context as your NT domain. The Domain Object Wizard will configure existing NDS user accounts so that they belong to the NT user groups to which the NT user belongs. This is known as being *associated*.

You can change any of the status assumptions made by the Wizard during discovery by selecting an NT user account and then changing the status with the buttons on the left side of the Summary window:

Create As   Use this button to reconfigure the creation of an NT user account in NDS after you've used the Don't Move button to prevent an NT user from being moved.

Associate With   This button allows you to manually specify which NDS user you want to associate your NT user to. This is very useful if you have different naming conventions on NDS and NT. Remember to tell the user which account name he or she will be using after migration.

 TIP   Associate the Administrator user with the NDS user Admin so that you need only log in as Admin to have administrative rights to NDS and the domain.

Don't Move   If you have an account that you do not want to migrate for any reason (for example, because that account is no longer in use), use this button to tell the Wizard not to migrate the NT user. Be aware that those user accounts will not be available to NDS after the migration is completed.

Resolve   If the Domain Object Wizard finds more than one NDS user account that matches an NT user account, this button will appear. Use this button to manually specify the NDS account with which you want to associate your NT user account.

At the bottom of the Summary window, the Show choices allow you to filter the summary list. If you have a number of accounts to be migrated, you might want to consider checking particular status boxes to show only those users to make the task of verifying more manageable. The default is to show all users.

Once you have verified all the users to be migrated and clicked Move, the Wizard completes the integration of the NT domain into NDS. You'll see an animated status screen that lets you know how the process is going, as shown in Figure 13.9.

PART

II

Managing the
Network

FIGURE 13.9

Watching NT objects move into NDS

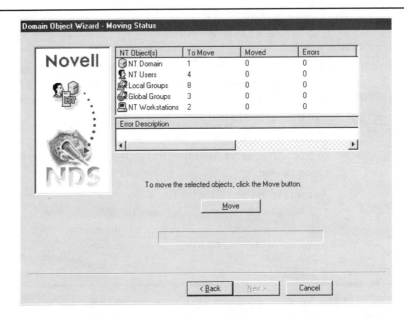

The Wizard will let you know when it's finished and will give you an opportunity to view the log file that was generated during the process and online documentation for NDS Corporate Edition, as shown in Figure 13.10. Figure 13.11 shows an example of a Domain Object Wizard log file (this file is stored as Move.log in the \WINNT\SYSTEM32 directory of your PDC).

FIGURE 13.10

Choices to view the log and documentation after the Domain Object Wizard finishes

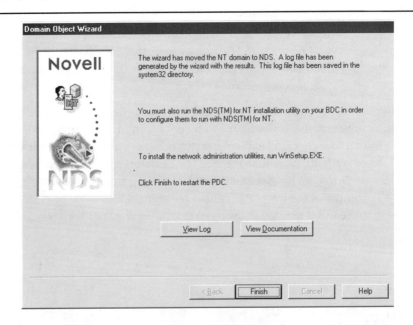

FIGURE 13.11

A sample Domain Object Wizard log file

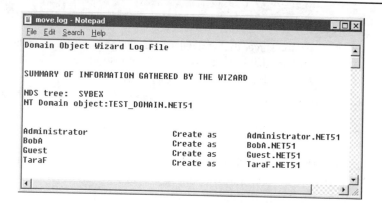

When you've finished viewing the log and/or documentation, click Finish. Then reboot when prompted.

 WARNING You must reboot the server when prompted. Otherwise, the new SAMSRV.DLL will not function correctly.

You should repeat this process for each BDC and PDC in your network that will be integrated. Remember that the PDC installation and integration process must be completed before you install NDS Corporate Edition on your BDCs.

Now you are ready to install the administration utilities provided on the NDS Corporate Edition CD.

Installing NDS Corporate Edition Management Utilities

IN A HURRY

13.3 Install NDS Corporate Edition Management Utilities

1. Log in to NDS as a user who has Supervisor object rights to the [Root] of the NDS tree.
2. Run WINSETUP.EXE from the NDS Corporate Edition CD-ROM.
3. Select Install NDS Corporate Edition Management Utilities.
4. Accept the license agreement.

Continued ▐▶

IN A HURRY CONTINUED

5. Verify the server that you will be installing to and the language you want to install. Make sure that both the NetWare Administrator and Domain Object Snap-in boxes are checked. Then click OK to begin the installation.

6. When the installation is completed, click Run NWAdmn32 to open NetWare Administrator.

The NDS schema has been extended to include an NT Domain object, and NT domain users have been migrated to become NDS users. In order to manage them with NetWare Administrator, you need to install the Domain Object Snap-in. Everything you just did would be useless without it, since the whole point was a single point of administration, wasn't it? If you don't install the Domain Object Snap-in, NT domains will appear as Unknown objects in NetWare Administrator.

 NOTE Windows NT will create a Registry entry for the user who installs the Domain Object Snap-in to NetWare Administrator. If anyone else logs in and tries to use NetWare Administrator, they will see Unknown objects where the domains were. If you are seeing Unknown objects, make sure you are logged in as the same user who installed the snap-in.

The NDS Corporate Edition installation program installs the NetWare Administrator and Domain Object Snap-in files in SYS:PUBLIC\WINNT. You can launch NetWare Administrator by running SYS:PUBLIC\WIN32\NWADMN32.EXE from Windows Explorer or from the Run dialog box (or you can create a shortcut to it on your desktop).

Yes, we need to go through that whole installation routine again, but it's fairly straightforward. Once again, log in to NDS as a user who has Administrator rights to the [Root] of the NDS tree. If you took my advice and associated the Administrator account with the Admin account, you will authenticate to NT and NDS using the same account. If you did not, then you will be authenticating as two different NDS users.

Load that NDS Corporate Edition CD into your CD disk drive (if it isn't still in there), and run SETUP.EXE from the NT directory. Select Install NDS Corporate Edition Management Utilities, and accept the license agreement. You can choose to install the utilities to the local drive of the NT Server or to a NetWare file server. When you make your selections, you'll be at the Setup Selections dialog box. Click OK to begin the installation. The current settings are summarized on the screen shown in Figure 13.12. Click Next to continue.

FIGURE 13.12

*Setting up NDS
Management Utilities*

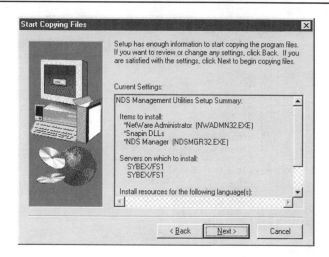

During the file-copy process, you may be informed that some of the files that are being copied are older than the files already on the server. I recommend *not* overwriting the newer files on the server, and so does Novell. So you should accept the default of No.

New programs will appear in your Novell menu. Click Start ➣ Programs ➣ Novell (Common) to access NetWare Administrator, ConsoleOne, and NDS Manager from your NT Server. Now you can see your NT Domain object in NetWare Administrator, as shown in Figure 13.13, and you're ready to leave NT's User Manager for Domains in the dust. Read on to discover the joys of NT user management through NDS.

NOTE   You may be prompted that you do not have the latest application launcher files. In this case, just highlight the displayed tree and click Modify to extend the schema for the application launcher files.

Configuring User Access

You can configure access to the NT domain in two ways: through the actual Domain object or through the User object. If you use the Domain object, you can only add members to the domain. If you use the User object, you can also configure group, application, and security options.

FIGURE 13.13

Ready to manage NT groups and users with NetWare Administrator

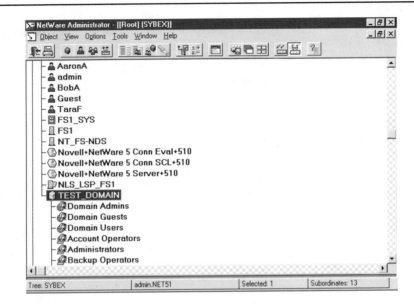

Let's see how NetWare Administrator handles NT domain users. In Figure 13.14, I have opened the User object BobA in NetWare Administrator. On the right side of the window, you can see that two options have been added: Domain Access and Domain User Settings (you'll need to scroll down the button bar to see these buttons). These are what you use to configure user domain access.

Selecting the Domain Access button shows all the domains and groups in the domains that a user has access to. From here, you can add a user to or delete a user from any domain that exists in the NDS tree. In Figure 13.15, you can see that BobA belongs to TEST_DOMAIN and is a member of Domain Users. To add the user to another domain, click Add and select the domain from the displayed list. To delete the user from a group, highlight the group and click Delete.

Clicking the Domain User Settings button brings up the window shown in Figure 13.16. You can specify a user profile or logon script, a home directory, and a specific workstation that the user may log on to. Settings configured here apply only to the NT platform. This window combines two windows from User Manager for Domains: User Environment Profile and Logon Windows NT Workstations. It completely eliminates the need to configure these NT-only properties from a separate utility.

FIGURE 13.14

*User properties with
Domain Access and
Domain User Settings
buttons*

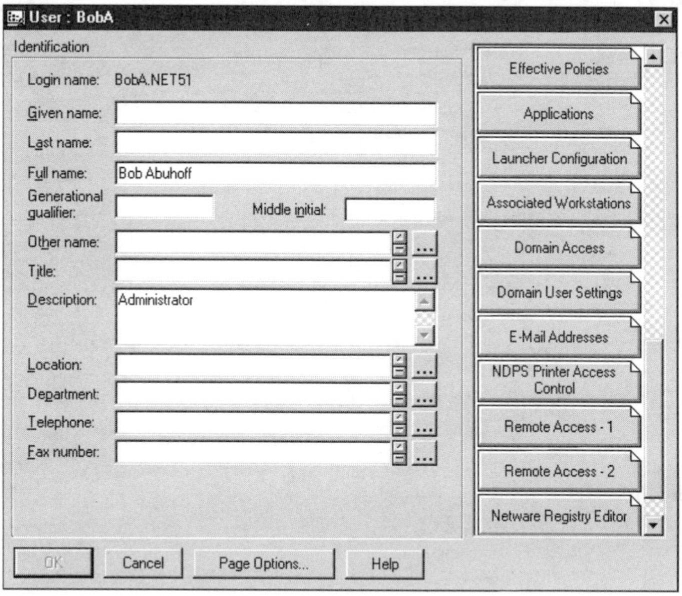

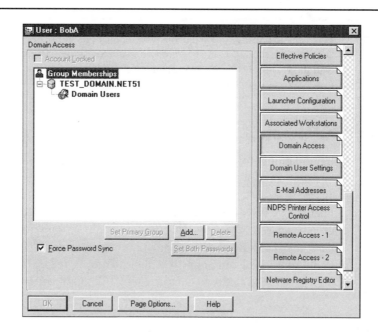

FIGURE 13.15

*Viewing a user's
domain access settings*

Viewing a user's NT settings

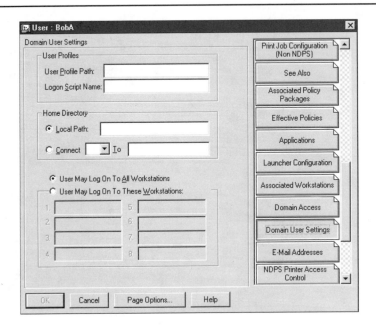

 NOTE To preserve password synchronization, users must change their password using the Domain Object Snap-in in NetWare Administrator or the password change utility provided with the Novell NT Client. Using anything else will cause the passwords to get out of sync.

So I've Migrated, Now What?

Congratulations! You have made your life easier. From now on, you will be using NetWare Administrator to manage user access to all network resources, including NT domains.

I bet you've been wondering if this means that you will never use NT utilities again. The answer is, sort of. The NT administration tools are still available for you to use, but they are now accessing domain information from NDS. Any domain requests made by an NT program or utility will be accomplished by NDS. NDS Corporate Edition gives NDS the ability to complete all NT domain requests without changing any existing NT applications or services that rely on the NT domain. This means that all NT utilities, tools, and trust relationships will work as they did before migration.

If you are addicted to User Manager for Domains and believe that your life will never be the same unless you get to use it every day, feel free to do so. All requests made by User Manager for Domains will be redirected to and filled by NDS. Keep in mind that although you can still use User Manager for Domains to configure NDS user access to NT domains, you *cannot* configure it to provide access to other NDS resources such as a printer or NetWare server. You'll have to launch NetWare Administrator for that. So why not just do it all from within NetWare Administrator?

 NOTE A user account cannot be managed in User Manager for Domains if it is longer than 20 characters or contains illegal characters. NetWare allows up to 64 characters for the login name, but you should limit the length if you think the user will become an NT user.

Configuring NT File and Print Access

The current version of NDS Corporate Edition does not provide for integration of NT File and Print Services. For now, the easiest way to grant NDS users access to NT File and Print Services is to make an NT group and then give access to that group using the NT utilities. After the group is created, any NDS user who needs access to those resources can be made a member of that group from NetWare Administrator.

For example, let's assume that we have an application on an NT Server that provides guidelines for writing screenplays, and we want to give user TaraF access to it. We would begin in NetWare Administrator by creating a new NT group called Writers, as follows:

- Right-click the Domain object and select Create.
- Click NDS Corporate Edition Local Group, then click OK.
- In the Local Group Name field, type **Writers**, then click Create.

Next, we launch Windows NT Explorer and create a directory called SCREENPLAYS. Then grant the Writers group the Read file permission to the SCREENPLAYS directory:

- Right-click the SCREENPLAYS folder and choose Properties.
- Click the tab marked Security, then click Permissions.
- Click Add, then click the Writers group.

- Confirm that the Type Of Access field says Read.
- Click Add, then click OK to add Writers to the list.
- Click OK again to add the Writers group to the Directory Permissions list.
- Click OK again, click Save, then click OK once more to close the dialog box.

Back in NetWare Administrator, give the NDS user TaraF access to the SCREENPLAYS directory on the NT Server by making her a member of the Writers group, as shown here:

- Double-click user TaraF to open her properties, then click the Domain Access page button.
- Click Add, then double-click the Domain object where you just created the directory.
- Double-click Writers in the Available Objects list, then click OK.

Now user TaraF is a member of the Writers group, as you can see in Figure 13.17. She has access to the screenplay program in the SCREENPLAYS directory on the NT Server (assuming that you installed the screenplay software, of course).

Wouldn't it be nice if Novell would add NT File and Print Services into the next release of NDS Corporate Edition? Then you could use NetWare Administrator to go through all the steps for you.

FIGURE 13.17

NDS Corporate Edition Local Group: Writers

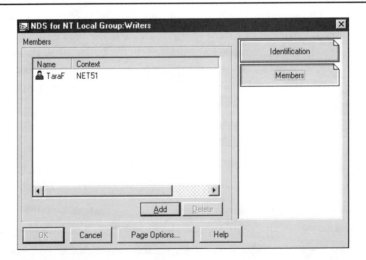

Uninstalling NDS Corporate Edition

IN A HURRY

13.4 Uninstall NDS Corporate Edition

1. Log in to your NT workstation as Administrator.
2. Select Start ➤ Programs ➤ Novell (Common) ➤ Domain Object Wizard.
3. Click Next at the Welcome screen.
4. Choose the uninstall option you want to use.
5. Click Finish to begin the uninstall process.
6. Reboot the server when prompted.

Why would you want to uninstall NDS Corporate Edition? Well, despite what a good product I think it is, it still may not work to your expectations. Another, perhaps more likely reason is that your managers change your company's policies and decide to go all NT, or if they're smart, all NetWare (and we all know that company policies change as often as help desk personnel).

I always recommend that installations or uninstallations of something that has network repercussions be done when no users are logged in and *after* you have confirmed a valid backup of the systems to be affected. Remember, Murphy's Law rules in the computer world, so protect yourself and the network.

 NOTE Any password information will be updated during the uninstall process.

There are two options for uninstalling NDS Corporate Edition:

Uninstall NDS Corporate Edition and revert to the original NT domain state. Everything will be put back the way it was before NDS Corporate Edition was installed. Any changes you have made will be lost. Any objects that were originally in the NT domain but *not* migrated to NDS when you installed NDS Corporate Edition will no longer be in the domain when you uninstall using this option.

Uninstall NDS Corporate Edition and include new NDS information in the NT domain. This option takes the current NT domain information from NDS and migrates it to the NT domain. If you have made changes to the domain since you installed NDS Corporate Edition, the new objects will be added to the NT domain.

PART

II

Managing the
Network

You must uninstall from any and all BDCs prior to uninstalling from the PDC.

To uninstall NDS Corporate Edition, you need to launch the Domain Object Wizard again. Log in to your NT Workstation as Administrator. (You do not need to log in to the network because the uninstall program will use the Domain object to log in to the network.) Then select Start ➤ Programs ➤ Novell (Common) ➤ Domain Object Wizard. Click Next from the Welcome screen. Since NDS Corporate Edition is already installed, the Wizard knows that you want to uninstall it and displays the screen shown in Figure 13.18. Choose the uninstall option you want to use, and then click Finish to begin the uninstall process. You will be prompted to restart the server for the changes to take place.

FIGURE 13.18

Uninstalling NDS Corporate Edition

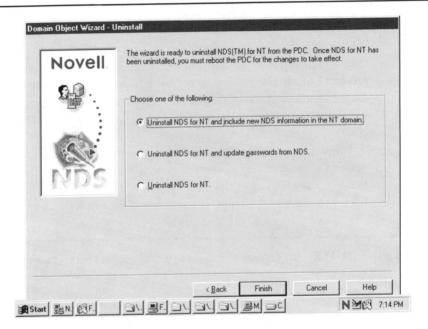

Once the uninstall process is complete, the NetWare console will display a message saying that the domain account has been deleted. The NT Server will also display a list of the changes that have been made during the removal process as it executes. The last message displayed will say that the domain has been restored to the Microsoft NT SAM.

If any errors occurred while uninstalling, you will be given an option to view the log file. You are then given the option to accept the uninstall process with the errors or to exit without finishing uninstalling. If you elect to exit, the uninstall routine will run the next time you reboot the NT Server.

The NDS Corporate Edition Client will not be uninstalled, but notice that you can no longer log in to any NetWare server. Use the Add/Remove Programs Control Panel to remove the client.

 NOTE If you made any permanent connections to the NetWare server or its resources, you may need to close them when NT attempts to connect to them on startup.

Remember to verify your domain database and the NDS database prior to allowing users to log back in to the network.

Better NT Management

You read all about the different solutions Novell offers for managing NT and now you are probably wondering what to do. I'll tell you. Convince your managers to go to a pure NetWare environment. (Don't we wish it were that easy!) If they laugh in your face, install NDS Corporate Edition and get your life back.

NDS Corporate Edition looks incredible. According to the Gartner Group, NDS Corporate Edition can lower the total cost of network ownership by 40 percent or more. Take that to management!

The biggest change to the NDS Corporate Edition product in the new version is the ability to place a replica of NDS on the NT server, thereby eliminating a failure point if access to the NetWare servers is unavailable. It will also provide management of NT file shares, increased scalability, enhanced password synchronization, and the ability to run Novell's ZENworks management solution on NT.

Basically, with the current version, Novell provides better management of Windows NT than Microsoft does. Future versions are expected to support NT Server 2000 and Active Directory Services. I don't know about you, but I'm looking forward to Novell making NT as easy to manage as NetWare is.

PART III

NetWare, TCP/IP, and the Internet

LEARN:

- *NetWare 5.1 TCP/IP support*

- *DHCP and DNS support*

- *NetWare 5.1 and remote access*

- *NetWare 5.1 enhancements and special features*

- *Troubleshoot your network*

CHAPTER 14

NetWare 5.1 TCP/IP Support

A lthough Novell has supported TCP/IP in some form or fashion since Net-Ware 3, TCP/IP has never figured prominently into NetWare until 5.0. NetWare always used Novell's proprietary network protocol, IPX/SPX, for most network communications. In NetWare 5.1, however, things have changed in a big way.

NetWare 5.0 was a significant milestone for Novell as it was the first release of Net-Ware that supported a pure IP environment. In NetWare 5.0, all NetWare Core Protocols (NCPs) used the TCP/IP transport protocol. NetWare 5.0 clients and servers did not encapsulate IPX information in TCP/IP packets.

NetWare 5.1 goes even further into the world of TCP/IP than 5.0. How? No traces of IPX/SPX are left on the network after you choose IP as the default protocol during installation. Want a detail? HTTP (Hypertext Transfer Protocol, the protocol powering the World Wide Web) now functions as a core protocol inside NetWare.

If you want to simplify your network and run a single protocol, you can run TCP/IP exclusively, never introducing IPX/SPX. This can lower wide area network bandwidth requirements, simplify supporting routers, and increase client and server interoperability with non-NetWare platforms.

Even if your only experience is with NetWare LANs, you're probably familiar with TCP/IP and have probably even had to work with it. If you have been working on a network that has more than just NetWare servers and clients or if you have had to connect your network to the Internet, you have worked with TCP/IP. No discussion of TCP/IP goes very far without including some discussion of the Internet because TCP/IP and the Internet have grown up together. The TCP/IP standards were developed in part because of the specific needs of the Internet and the Internet community.

If you already feel comfortable with terms such as *IP addressing, default gateways, subnet masks,* and *routing,* you can skip the first part of this chapter and head straight to the section called "NetWare 5.1 TCP/IP Components." However, if you feel you need a refresher course on TCP/IP terminology, read on and prepare for TCP/IP enlightenment!

But First, a Little Background

Way back when the world was young and dinosaurs (IBM mainframes) ruled the computer room, Novell Data Systems was working on the first microcomputer file servers. This was in the late 1970s and very early 1980s. Our friends at Novell had to choose a network protocol for client-to-server communication. They decided to develop their own protocol (based on Xerox XNS) and called it IPX/SPX (or Internetwork Packet eXchange/Sequenced Packet eXchange).

Soon NetWare (and IPX) was everywhere. NetWare was fast and fairly easy to deploy (those long hours—or days—of waiting for a disk to COMPSURF are now fading from my memory). Better yet, NetWare was a piece of cake from the network's perspective. Plug in the server and the clients and it worked!

NetWare originally flourished in the small departmental LANs, later spread through medium-sized businesses, and then eventually spanned the enterprise throughout large companies all over the world. But through it all, the IPX/SPX protocol remained king of LAN protocols (at least from the Novell administrator's perspective).

Some have often questioned Novell's wisdom of developing a proprietary protocol back in the early 1980s when TCP/IP already existed, but not me. TCP/IP was an also-ran to XNS at the time and was far from becoming mandatory in the world of Unix systems. I wince when thinking back to a few years ago when I first started working on TCP/IP networks and the difficulty I had in deploying my first IP networks. At that time, I certainly appreciated the ease with which an IPX network could be set up.

About early 1994, depending on who is doing the estimates, this thing called the World Wide Web started to take shape, at least from a mainstream perspective. The Internet had already existed in some form for almost 20 years but was mainly used by academics, the government, and research institutions.

The protocol used by the Internet then and now is TCP/IP. Internet law officially mandated Internet Flag Day, January 1, 1983, as the day when only TCP/IP-driven systems were allowed on the Internet. If you want to talk to other computers on the Internet and WWW, you must use TCP/IP.

It's no secret that the Internet has captured the imagination of the world. Your network users are bugging you about getting faster Internet access on one side, and sales and marketing are hollering for you to get them a faster Web server on the other. Luckily for you, NetWare 5.1 with TCP/IP makes all the Internet connections you need, both as a client of Internet resources and as a provider of those resources.

Today, TCP/IP supports small, medium, and large corporate networks as well as the Internet. Organizations that must support both TCP/IP and IPX/SPX invest a lot of time and effort to make sure their systems interoperate correctly.

As early as 1990, Novell was including basic TCP/IP support and later supported interoperability functions such as printing and file sharing with Unix and other TCP/IP hosts. In 1993, Novell released NetWare/IP, which allowed NetWare clients to use TCP/IP instead of IPX/SPX to connect to their NetWare servers; nevertheless, many components of IPX had to remain in place for years.

PART

III

Netware, TCP/IP, and the Internet

TCP/IP Overview

Early NetWare succeeded partly because IPX/SPX handled all network addressing details. Detailed knowledge of the transport protocol was unnecessary. Unlike with IPX/SPX, however, if you are going to build networks based on TCP/IP, you must have a good understanding of TCP/IP. Nestled in among all the buzzwords about IP addressing, subnet masking, routing, ports, sockets, and services is an incredibly powerful and versatile network protocol.

Let's first take a look at the history of TCP/IP and at some of the major standards bodies that control TCP/IP, and then let's hash out some of the buzzwords.

 NOTE On a TCP/IP network, all computers (routers, devices, and other gateways) are referred to as *hosts*.

Looking Back at TCP/IP

Would you believe that TCP/IP is a product of the cold war? It is—well, sort of. In 1969, DARPA (U.S. Department of Defense Advanced Research Projects Agency) funded a research and development project to design a packet-switched network that would allow the DOD's many dissimilar computer systems around the country to communicate reliably. The goal was to allow computer systems to be distributed throughout the country and thus make the DOD network less vulnerable to a nuclear attack. If a single site were destroyed, the remainder of the computers on this distributed network would continue to operate.

The result of this effort was the Network Control Program, also called NCP. This early predecessor to TCP/IP has been modified, upgraded, and improved continually over the years and gives us today's version of TCP/IP.

Significant Events in the TCP/IP and Internet Timeline

- 1969: The DOD funds research and development for TCP/IP.
- 1970: ARPANET starts using NCP.
- 1972: The first Telnet specification is introduced.
- 1973: File Transfer Protocol (FTP) is introduced.

Continued

CONTINUED

- 1974: TCP is introduced.
- 1975: IP addressing and routing standards are published.
- 1976: The DOD establishes TCP/IP as a standard.
- 1977: ARPANET switches from NCP to TCP/IP.
- 1983: TCP/IP is designated as the only protocol for the Internet, and Berkeley Unix implements TCP/IP.
- 1984: DNS (Domain Name System) is introduced.
- 1985: NSFNET is created, using a 56Kbps backbone.
- 1989: 100,000 hosts are connected to the Internet.
- 1991: The NSF allows commercial use of the Internet.
- 1993: The Mosaic Web browser is released.
- 1996: 12,800,000 hosts are connected to the Internet.

Why does my history of TCP/IP also include information about the Internet? Because they are so tightly interwoven and because the standards bodies that control TCP/IP standards are the same standards bodies that control the Internet standards.

Over the years, the Internet and networks connected to it have gone by many names, including:

- ARPANET—Advanced Research Projects Agency Network
- MILNET—Military Network
- NSFNET—National Science Foundation Network
- CSNET—Computer Science Network
- NIPRNET—Non-Classified IP Routed Network

 NOTE If you know TCP/IP, you understand how the Internet works. Quite simply, the Internet is just a large TCP/IP network.

Who Controls TCP/IP and Internet Standards?

If you have worked in the networking industry for long, you have already heard about many standards organizations, such as IEEE (Institute of Electrical and Electronics

PART

III

Netware, TCP/IP, and the Internet

Engineers), ISO (International Organization for Standardization), ANSI (American National Standards Institute), and CCITT (Consultative Committee International Telephone and Telegraph). Each of these organizations coordinates certain standards. I am sure the world would be a much simpler place if we had only one standards body, but we don't (sigh). Now I am about to add some other organizations to this list.

NOTE The CCITT (Consultative Committee International Telephone and Telegraph) is part of the ITU (International Telecommunications Union), which is a branch of the United Nations. The CCITT produces recommendations rather than compulsory standards. Some of these recommendations include ISDN (Integrated Services Digital Network), X.400 (messaging), and X.500 (directory services).

The TCP/IP suite of protocols is managed by a group of volunteers from all over the world called the Internet Society (ISOC). The Internet Society is a global organization that was created in 1992 to be responsible for internetworking technologies and applications on the Internet. Its principal purpose is to encourage the development and availability of the Internet.

Part of the Internet Society is the Internet Activities Board (IAB), a technical advisory group. The Internet Activities Board is responsible for setting Internet standards, publishing RFCs, and overseeing the Internet standards process. The IAB oversees three task forces:

- The Internet Engineering Task Force (IETF) is responsible for developing technical solutions to problems and new challenges as they arise on the Internet and developing Internet standards and protocols.

- The Internet Corporation for Assigned Names and Numbers (ICANN), at www.icann.org, oversees the assignment of unique protocol identities that are used on the Internet, such as TCP and UDP port numbers, which I will explain shortly. ICANN superseded the Internet Assigned Numbers Authority (IANA).

- The Internet Research Task Force (IRTF) is the research and development arm of the Internet Society and is responsible for TCP/IP-related research projects.

NOTE See RFC 1120 for more information about the IAB and its task forces.

> ⚠️ **TIP**   You'll find a complete listing of RFCs at www.isi.edu/rfc-editor/.

Standards, Meetings, RFCs, and More Meetings

TCP/IP and all Internet functions are standardized in a series of documents called *RFCs* (Request for Comments), but not all RFCs actually become standards. TCP/IP standards are not developed by committee, such as the IEEE or the ITU, but rather by consensus.

Throughout this book, you will see references to RFCs that contain more information about a specific feature or function. An RFC describes how a specific function is supposed to work on a TCP/IP network. Not all RFCs are entirely technical in nature, as you will see in Table 14.1.

TABLE 14.1: SOME COMMON REQUESTS FOR COMMENTS

RFC Number	What It Contains
768	UDP (User Datagram Protocol)
791	IP (Internet Protocol) and IP addressing
793	TCP (Transmission Control Protocol)
821	SMTP (Simple Mail Transport Protocol)
950	Subnetting
959	FTP (File Transfer Protocol)
1034 / 1035	DNS (Domain Name System)
1118	Hitchhikers Guide to the Internet
1157	SNMP (Simple Network Management Protocol)
1178	Choosing a name for your computer
1700	Assigned numbers (TCP and UDP port numbers)
1793	A primer on the Internet and TCP/IP tools
1883	IPv6 (also known as IPng–IP Next Generation)
1918	IP addresses allocated for private networks (networks that will never connect to the Internet)
1939	POP3 (Post Office Protocol v3)
2026	The Internet standards process
2324	HyperText Coffee Pot Control protocol (I'm not kidding.)

PART

III

Netware, TCP/IP, and the Internet

Anyone can write an RFC and submit it to the Internet community for consideration to become a standard. If you have an idea about something you would like to see TCP/IP do, write it up as an RFC and submit it to the Internet community. <grin> If you are interested in writing an RFC, you can find an RFC that explains the steps for writing an RFC (RFC 2223).</grin>

Documents are usually submitted by members of the Internet Society to the Internet Engineering Task Force but sometimes also directly to the RFC editor. The documents are reviewed by a technical expert, a task force, or the RFC editor and then assigned a classification, which can be one of the following:

Required All TCP/IP gateways, hosts, and devices must implement this RFC. (It is uncommon for newer RFCs to be classified as Required.)

Recommended All TCP/IP gateways and hosts are encouraged but not required to implement this RFC. Recommended RFCs are usually implemented.

Elective Implementation is optional. Application will probably not be widely used.

Limited Use Not intended for general use.

Not Recommended Not recommended.

Once the RFC is assigned a classification and a number, it goes through development, testing, and acceptance if it is being considered as a standard. During this process, technical experts review the RFC and provide feedback to its author. The Internet Standards Process refers to these stages as *maturity levels*:

Proposed Standard (maturity level 1) The RFC is considered stable and well understood. Enough people have technically reviewed it, and there is enough interest to warrant making it a standard.

Draft Standard (maturity level 2) The RFC has now been tested and reviewed. It is clear and concise, and implementation details are understood.

Internet Standard (maturity level 3) The RFC has been thoroughly reviewed by the Internet community. Its implementation is well understood, and it is generally believed that it will provide significant benefit to the Internet community.

Once an RFC is published, it is assigned a number. The number never changes. If updates or new technology need to be incorporated into a particular RFC, a new RFC number is created. The IAB Official Protocol Standard is a document that the IAB publishes quarterly; it indicates the most current RFC numbers for each protocol.

Common Protocols

TCP/IP is not a single protocol but a series of protocols that transport data and provide network services. Table 14.2 lists some of the common protocols and their functions.

TABLE 14.2: COMMON TCP/IP PROTOCOLS AND THEIR FUNCTIONS

Protocol	What It Does
IP (Internet Protocol)	Addresses and delivers packets. Similar to IPX.
TCP (Transmission Control Protocol)	Establishes a connection between two hosts and provides acknowledgments of packets being received. Used when reliable packet delivery is essential.
UDP (User Datagram Protocol)	Delivers packets to the host, but does not establish a connection first. Does not acknowledge packet receipt. Used in an environment where 100 percent reliable delivery is not necessary. The choice to use UDP or TCP is the application developer's, not the network administrator's.
ICMP (Internet Control Message Protocol)	Controls errors on IP networks. The PING command also uses ICMP.
ARP (Address Resolution Protocol)	Takes a known host's IP address and learns the host's hardware (MAC) address if the host is on the same network. If the host is remote (on the other side of a router), ARP learns the MAC address of the router instead.
FTP (File Transfer Protocol)	Transfers files between two hosts. To transfer a file, you also need FTP server and client software.
SMTP (Simple Mail Transport Protocol)	Transfers simple, 7-bit character messages between SMTP client software and SMTP server software.
HTTP (Hypertext Transfer Protocol)	Transfers Web pages between a Web server and a Web browser on a client.
DNS (Domain Name System)	Allows a client to look up the IP address of a host based on its name.
TELNET (Terminal Emulation Network)	Allows TELNET client software to connect to a host running TELNET server software, log in, and run programs on the machine running the TELNET server.

These are by no means the only protocols that TCP/IP supports. Many times, these protocols work together. For example, if you were to take a protocol analyzer such as

PART

III

Netware, TCP/IP, and the Internet

the Network Associates' Sniffer or Novell's LANalyzer and look at network traffic such as Web server traffic, you would see an IP datagram carrying a TCP segment that was carrying HTTP data. In the HTTP data portion of the frame would be the actual Web page information. Figure 14.1 shows how this works.

FIGURE 14.1

Protocols encapsu-lated inside other protocols

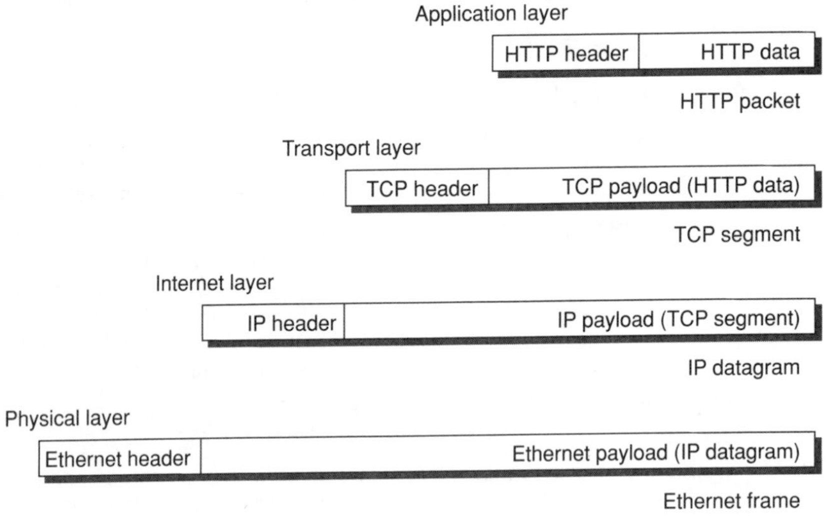

Application layer

HTTP header	HTTP data

HTTP packet

Transport layer

TCP header	TCP payload (HTTP data)

TCP segment

Internet layer

IP header	IP payload (TCP segment)

IP datagram

Physical layer

Ethernet header	Ethernet payload (IP datagram)

Ethernet frame

To understand this relationship a little better, it's helpful to look at the TCP/IP net-work model. You may be familiar with the International Organization for Standard-ization (ISO) seven-layer OSI (Open System Interconnection) model. The OSI model describes, in a perfect networking world, how two hosts communicate and how each layer is handled by a specific networking component. The TCP/IP—or DOD—model is an equivalent four-layer model that describes how two TCP/IP hosts communicate. Table 14.3 lists the four layers and some of the protocols that reside at each layer.

TABLE 14.3: TCP/IP LAYERS AND PROTOCOLS

Layer	Protocols That Work at This Layer
Application	HTTP, TELNET, FTP, DNS, STMP
Transport	TCP, UDP
Internet	IP, ICMP, IGMP, ARP
Network	Ethernet, Token Ring, ATM, Frame Relay, PPP, SLIP

At the Internet layer, IP is responsible for delivering packets. At the Transport layer, TCP can be used for connection-oriented, reliable delivery of data, or UDP can be used for quick, low-overhead delivery of data. The application developer chooses which protocol (UDP or TCP) to use.

How does TCP or UDP know what kind of data it is carrying from one host to another? The simple answer: a database lookup system in Cleveland. But here's a little more technical answer.

Each Application-layer protocol such as HTTP or TELNET is assigned a specific, unique number. In TCP/IP terms, this is called a *port* number. I like to think of a port as the address of a particular piece of software. When a client application connects to a server application, it needs to know the server's IP address, the transport protocol it uses (TCP or UDP), and the application's assigned port number.

Armed with all this information, the client application can create a socket, or endpoint of communication. The socket identifies a specific program running on a particular computer.

So now when one of your snobby TCP/IP friends says to you <superior attitude>, "I have just changed my Web server's default port to 8080" </superior attitude>, you can respond with <smirk>, "Then how do your Web browsers establish the correct socket?" </smirk>. Okay, I will stop trying to make TCP/IP humor.

Fortunately, we don't normally have to assign port numbers. The developer of your Web browser knew that the standard Web server operates on port 80. RFC 1945 describes how to build a Web server. The Internet Assigned Numbers Authority (IANA) assigned the port number for the Web server application before ICANN took over.

These assigned numbers are also referred to as Well Known Ports and are in the range 0 to 1023. Ports can actually range from 0 through 65,535, but only the lower 1024 ports are assigned by the IANA. Private or limited-use applications can use the upper port range. Table 14.4 shows some common TCP and UDP port numbers. For a complete listing of common ports, see RFC 1700.

TABLE 14.4: COMMON TCP AND UDP PORT NUMBERS AND THEIR USAGE

Port Number	Use
13	Daytime
17	Quote of the Day
21	FTP
23	TELNET
25	SMTP

Continued ▶

TABLE 14.4 (CONTINUED): COMMON TCP AND UDP PORT NUMBERS AND THEIR USAGE	
Port Number	**Use**
53	DNS
80	HTTP
110	POP3
119	NNTP (newsgroups)
135	RPC Endpoint Mapper
139	NetBIOS Session Service
389	LDAP (Lightweight Directory Access Protocol)
524	NetWare Control Protocol

Types of Frames on an IP Network

If you use a network analyzer on your network, you will see one of three types of frames:

- Directed
- Broadcast
- Multicast

A *directed frame* is the network manager's friend. It has the IP address of the host to which it is directed. No other host on the network has to open the frame and examine the contents to see if the frame is meant for it. In the IPX/SPX world, a frame is considered directed if it has the network address and the MAC address of the destination node.

Most network managers consider *broadcast* a four-letter word. This is because a broadcast frame must be opened by every client on the segment on which the frame originated. In an IPX/SPX world, routers usually forward broadcasts to other subnets. In a larger network, broadcasts can easily consume a large chunk of the network's available bandwidth.

Multicasting is becoming popular as more applications take advantage of it. *Multicast frames* are used with applications such as chat or video conferencing in which everyone sees everyone else's pictures or words. Without multicasting, the conference server would have to re-broadcast every frame it sends to every person in the conference. Using multicast, the software that the online participants are using registers itself as part of a specific group address, called a *multicast address* (this address is provided to the client by the server). When the server sends out frames, it sends them out to the multicast group. All routers between the client and the server must support multicasting. The addresses that multicasting uses are Class D addresses, by the way, which range from 224.*x.y.z* through 239.*x.y.z*.

IP Addressing

You might expect to see "TCP/IP Addressing" as the heading here, but "IP Addressing" is more correct. In most circles, TCP/IP addressing and IP addressing mean the same thing, but that's not technically correct. The Internet Protocol (IP) is responsible for addressing and routing frames.

As long as you remember a few basic rules about IP addressing, you will always come out okay. So take a deep breath, and let's dive in.

First, an IP address is a 32-bit binary number. Remember, that is the way your computer sees it. So that we can more easily read and work with this number, we break it into four 8-bit chunks, called *octets*:

```
11001100 10111011 00101110 00001100
```

This is a valid IP address as far as your computer is concerned. Kind of difficult to read, isn't it? But if we break the 32 bits in to four octets and then convert these octets to decimal, suddenly it is not so difficult to read, though still a little difficult to remember. In decimal, the address is:

```
204.187.46.12
```

This notation is also called *dotted-decimal*. IP addresses are broken into two parts:

- Network address
- Host address

You can tell which part of the address is the network address and which part of the address is the host address based on the class of the address (at least until we get into subnetting).

Characteristics of IP Address Classes

IP addresses are categorized in five classes. Each class's address has certain rules that govern its use and certain characteristics that make it recognizable as part of a specific class.

PART

III

Netware, TCP/IP, and the Internet

Class A Addresses

Class A networks are by far the largest of the network classes. With almost 17 million hosts per network, these networks can accommodate the largest organizations in the world, such as the U.S. government, Hewlett Packard, and IBM (and Novell). No more Class A networks are available.

- Begin with 1.0.0.0 and go through 127.0.0.0.
- 126 possible networks (127.0.0.0 is reserved).
- 16,777,216 hosts per network.
- Default subnet mask is 255.0.0.0.
- First octet is reserved for the network number.
- Second, third, and fourth octets indicate the host ID.

Class B Addresses

Class B networks are also quite large; with the capacity of more than 16,000 hosts per network. Class B networks are used by large organizations or divisions of giant corporations. All Class B addresses are assigned.

- Begin with 128.0.0.0 and go through 191.255.0.0.
- 16,384 possible networks.
- 65,534 hosts per network.
- Default subnet mask is 255.255.0.0.
- First and second octets represent the network number.
- Third and fourth octets indicate the host ID.

Class C Addresses

Class C addresses are the only addresses available today, and most companies can't even get their own Class C address anymore.

- Begin with 192.0.0.0 and go through 223.255.255.0.
- 2,097,152 possible networks.
- 254 hosts per network.
- Default subnet mask is 255.255.255.0.
- First, second, and third octet represent the network.
- Fourth octet indicates the host ID.

Class D Addresses

Class D addresses are not assigned to hosts, but rather are used in multicasting.

- Begin with 224.0.0.0 and go through 239.255.255.0.
- Not used for assigning addresses to hosts.
- Used for multicast applications.

Class E Addresses

Class E addresses are used neither for hosts nor for multicasting. They are reserved and considered experimental.

- They begin with 240.0.0.0.

Other Address Rules

Now that you know the rules for the address classes, you need to know a few other basic rules about valid and invalid addresses:

- No octet is ever above 255.
- Network address 0.*x.y.z* is invalid.
- Network addresses 224.*x.y.z* and above are invalid.
- The network address 127.*x.y.z* is reserved and is never used.
- A host address cannot end in zeros.
- A host address cannot end in 255.

Table 14.5 contains some examples of valid and invalid addresses. The octet that makes the address invalid is in boldface.

TABLE 14.5: EXAMPLES OF VALID AND INVALID IP HOST ADDRESSES	
Valid Addresses	**Invalid Addresses**
10.247.210.75	**0.**107.210.89
198.66.12.253	**225.**47.42.23
128.72.194.1	213.79.186.**0**
223.0.43.181	147.201.34.**255**
1.88.101.6	**127.**0.67.197

PART

III

Netware, TCP/IP, and the Internet

In addition, you need to remember the following:

- An address that ends in zero refers to the network itself.

- An address that ends in 255 refers to that network's broadcast address.

- The address 127.0.0.1 does not represent a specific host; network 127 is reserved for diagnostic functions and is sometimes called a *loopback address* (the address loops back to the same system).

- The address 0.0.0.0 is a special address and is referred to as the *default route*. You will see this address when working on a router or a routing table.

NOTE Sigh! In the good old days when we just used IPX/SPX on our networks, the only network addresses we had to worry about were the network addresses on the servers (and maybe third-party routers). IPX/SPX host addressing uses the media access control (MAC) address of the computer's network interface card.

Okay, so is this all there is to an IP address? Well, basically yes, but things do get a little stickier. Let's say that you have to convert your existing 300-node IPX/SPX network to be part of your corporate TCP/IP. What type of address will work? Can you use a Class C address? No, a Class C address can accommodate only 254 hosts.

Through an amazing stroke of luck, you work for an organization that has the Class B network address 191.180.0.0. Remember, the 0.0 in the host octets refer to "this network." This Class B address will give you a single network with 65,534 hosts. You have some room to grow, for sure.

But wait, you look at your network diagram and realize that you actually have two segments on your network, separated by a router. You really need two networks. What are the chances that you are going to be able to get a second Class B network? Since all Class B addresses are now allocated, none. What if you could break that single Class B network into two smaller networks? You can! The key is something called a *subnet mask*.

Subnet Masks

Up until now, IP addressing has not been too hard, right? Remember a few basic rules about which numbers you can use and which numbers you cannot, and you are ready to go. The subnet mask is always the tricky part. If you are going to manage a network of more than a single subnet, you are going to have to work with subnet masks.

Of all the problems in networking, TCP/IP subnet design and numbering are the worst. NetWare folks new to TCP/IP feel stupid when trying to understand subnets and subnet masks for the first time. Don't feel stupid; feel normal. Some of the brightest network gurus I know struggled with TCP/IP addressing and subnet masking.

Subnetting allows a complex local network to be seen as a single network from the outside. You might want to divide one network into two or more smaller networks for any of the following reasons:

- You have to connect multiple media, for example, Token Ring and Ethernet segments or remote networks.

- You want to reduce congestion. More nodes per network means more traffic. Segmenting the network keeps local traffic local and reduces overall congestion.

- You want to isolate networks for troubleshooting. Using several smaller networks greatly reduces the chance that a single failure somewhere can take down the entire network.

- You want to optimize your IP address space. Dividing a Class A or B address over smaller subnetworks makes efficient use of your available network addresses.

Each subnetwork behaves as if it were independent. An IP router is used to connect the two subnetworks. Routing between nodes on different subnetworks remains transparent to the users. Routing tables, maintained by each node or router, shield the users from the details.

The subnet mask allows hosts on an IP network to determine whether a destination host is on the local network segment or on a remote network. If the destination host is on a remote network, the source host sends the frame to a router to be forwarded. The subnet mask does this by identifying which part of the IP address represents the network and which part identifies the host. Let's look at the address we were assigned above and its default subnet mask:

```
Network Address: 191.180.0.0
Subnet Mask:     255.255.0.0
```

This is a standard Class B network address. The first two octets represent the network, and the second two octets represent the host. As I mentioned, a computer sees an IP address as a 32-bit binary number, not as the dotted decimal format we see above.

The computer also sees the subnet mask in binary. The subnet mask tells the computer that every "1" in the subnet mask is part of the network address. Here are our network address and subnet mask in binary:

```
Address: 10111111 10110100 00000000 00000000
Mask:    11111111 11111111 00000000 00000000
```

PART

III

Netware, TCP/IP, and the Internet

The default subnet mask indicates that all the bits in the last two octets can be used for hosts.

Now let's complicate matters just a little. You actually have two networks of 150 hosts each, rather than one large network of 300 hosts; so you can't use a single network number. You actually need two. Using a subnet mask, you can break your large network into smaller pieces.

Let's use a subnet mask of 255.255.255.0 for this Class B address and see what we come up with. First, here it is again in binary:

```
Address: 10111111 10110100 00000000 00000000
Mask:    11111111 11111111 11111111 00000000
```

This tells us that all bits in the third octet can be used for network numbers (or subnets). This gives us 254 possible combinations of subnet numbers with 254 hosts on each subnet.

So 191.180.1.0 is a subnet, 191.180.2.0 is another subnet, 191.180.3.0 is another subnet—all the way up to 191.180.254.0, which is the last subnet. Some hosts and routers will let you use 191.180.0.0 and 191.180.255.0 as valid subnets, but not all.

NOTE When we start working with subnets, we have to revise one of the IP host address rules that I gave you earlier. The rule said that an IP host address cannot be all zeros or all 255s. The real rule is that an IP host address cannot be all zeros or all ones. Remember to think about it in binary. That is the way that the computer sees it. Host addresses with all zeros refer to the network address, and host addresses with all ones refer to the network's broadcast address.

There, that wasn't too bad, was it? We broke your single large Class B network into 254 smaller networks. But, as with everything, there is always a more complicated side. In the above example, we used the entire third octet to represent the subnet ID. What if we required more than 254 hosts per subnet? Our example gave us a maximum of 254 hosts per network.

We can use a custom subnet mask to define how much of the IP address is for the network and how much is for the host address. Let's go back to our 191.180.0.0 example. Let's say we need four networks with 500 hosts on each network. We are going to have to select a subnet mask that produces this many networks and this many hosts per network.

Here is a shortcut that I use to calculate the required subnet mask. First, take the number of subnets you require, in our case, four. Convert this number to a binary number. Four would be 100 in binary. How many ones and zeros did that take to represent in binary? Three, correct? Write out three ones. That gives you 111. Fill this number out to eight places with zeros, and you get 11100000.

Convert this 1110000 number to decimal, which gives you 224. The subnet mask will be 255.255.224.0. All of the first two octets represent the network number, and the first three bits of the third octet represent the network. The next five bits of the third octet and all eight bits of the fourth octet represent host IDs.

How many possible networks does this give us? Well, if the first three bits of the third octet can form network numbers, it would give us two to the third power minus two, or six possible network numbers. Why subtract the two? Not all hosts and routers support subnet numbers using all zeros or all ones.

How many hosts per network does this give us? Five bits from the third and eight bits from the fourth can be combined to form host addresses. That is 13 bits total. Two to the power of 13 gives us 8192 less two, or 8190 possible hosts. We subtract the two because the host ID still can't be all zeros or all ones.

What complicates custom subnet masking is that because we humans read IP addresses in decimal, it is not easy to recognize which portion of the IP address is the host portion and which portion is the network portion. In our example, we got six networks. Table 14.6 shows the binary combinations for subnet numbers in the third octet and the resulting decimal subnet numbers.

TABLE 14.6: IP NETWORK NUMBERS USING AN IP NETWORK NUMBER OF 191.180.0.0 AND A SUBNET MASK OF 255.255.224.0

Third Octet in Binary	Resulting Network Number
000 00000	Possibly invalid (subnet is all zeros)
001 00000	191.180.32.0
010 00000	191.180.64.0
011 00000	191.180.92.0
100 00000	191.180.128.0
101 00000	191.180.160.0
110 00000	191.180.192.0
111 00000	Possibly invalid (subnet is all ones)

Now we have six subnets. If all the hosts and routers on our network support a subnet number with all zeros or all ones, we actually have eight subnets. Most newer

TCP/IP software for hosts and routers do support a subnet number with all zeros and all ones, but if you are not sure, consult your software or router vendor.

We now need to determine the valid host addresses for each subnet. Table 14.7 shows one of the subnets and its valid IP host addresses. The subnet is 191.180.32.0, and the subnet mask is 255.255.224.0. We will skip all combinations of the host addresses for the obvious reasons (there are 8190 of them).

TABLE 14.7: IP ADDRESSES WITH A CUSTOM SUBNET MASK

Address in Binary	Address in Decimal
10111111 10110100 00100000 00000000	191.180.32.0 (Network)
10111111 10110100 00100000 00000001	191.180.32.1
10111111 10110100 00100000 00000010	191.180.32.2
10111111 10110100 00100000 00000011	191.180.32.3
Continue incrementing addresses	
10111111 10110100 00100000 11111111	191.180.32.255
10111111 10110100 00100001 00000000	191.180.33.0
10111111 10110100 00100001 00000001	191.180.33.1
Continue incrementing addresses	
10111111 10110100 00111111 11111101	191.180.63.253
10111111 10110100 00111111 11111110	191.180.63.254
10111111 10110100 00111111 11111111	191.180.63.255 (Broadcast)

NOTE After years of trying to fake subnet addressing, I finally did the research and came up with exactly which subnet masks go with which network addresses. The reason these network numbers work is the subject of an entirely separate book. The best freely available information that I've seen on TCP/IP subnetting is on 3Com's Web site (www.3com.com). Look for the white paper "Understanding IP Addressing: Everything You Ever Wanted to Know." Be warned: it's involved and often complicated, but great.

TIP If you're after still more information, here are two books you might want to include in your personal library: *TCP/IP Illustrated, Volume I: The Protocols*, by W. Richard Stevens (Addison Wesley); and *TCP/IP Network Administration*, by Craig Hunt (O'Reilly & Associates).

IPv6 (a.k.a. IPng)

When IP addressing was developed in the 1970s, no one ever dreamed that we would come close to running out of IP addresses, nor did anyone estimate the massive growth of the Internet. The Internet has grown exponentially, and we are close to exhausting our supply of available IP addresses. For several years now, the IETF has been working on solutions to this problem.

The current IP addressing scheme is known as *IPv4*, or IP version 4. It uses 32-bit addresses and, if used perfectly, would provide about 3.6 billion hosts. But IP addresses are used nowhere near perfectly. In fact, a tremendous number of IP network addresses have been allocated and never used. Therefore, the IETF has implemented several measures to help prevent waste of IP addresses, including CIDR, which I'll discuss later in this chapter.

The IETF is also working on a long-term solution to the IP address shortage. Since the early 1990s, there have been a number of proposals and efforts for addressing limitations and expanding the IP version, including the following:

- TCP and UDP with Bigger Addresses (TUBA)
- Common Architecture for the Internet (CATNIP)
- Simple Internet Protocol Plus (SIPP)

IP Next Generation, or IP version 6, is actually a compilation of many proposals, specifications, and efforts to expand IPv4. IPv6, as it currently stands, provides several improvements:

- Expanded IP addressing and routing
- Better options support and simplified IP header
- Support for time-dependent traffic (such as video)
- Improved security and privacy features
- Support for IP mobility

An IPv6 address is 128 bits! This is 4 billion times 4 billion addresses or, if you just have to know, 340,282,366,920,938,463,463,374,607,431,768,211,456 possible host addresses. IPv6 addresses are broken into 16 octets and written in hexadecimal as eight octet pairs separated by colons (you don't want to see this in binary, trust me). Here's an example of a valid IPv6 address:

```
(4A3F:AE67:F240:56C4:3409:AE52:440F:1403)
```

Clearly, this is a big change for TCP/IP and Internet users, but the change will be gradual. It will first be implemented on the Internet backbone and then on the larger ISPs. It will be years before this change affects our own networks.

PART

III

Netware, TCP/IP, and the Internet

TIP   For more information on IPv6, see RFC 1883.

IP Routing

Here is another topic that you could dedicate your life to. Cisco Systems, the world's largest provider of routers, for example, offers weeks of training on internetworking and routing. Simply put, a *router* takes frames that are sent to it and makes a decision about where to forward the frame. Unlike a bridge or a switch, a router understands the protocols that it is routing. All versions of NetWare since version 3 are capable of acting as an IP router.

When an IP host gets ready to send a frame to another host, it examines the destination host's IP address and compares it with its own IP address and subnet mask. If the IP address is on a remote network, the frame is sent to the router, and the router decides how to route the frame.

Routing Protocols

A routing protocol's job is to allow a router to inform other routers about routes that it is aware of. It does this by either broadcasting or multicasting, depending on the routing protocol. An interior routing protocol is used within an autonomous system. Basically, an interior routing protocol allows routers within your private internetwork to share routing and network information. NetWare 5.1 supports two major *interior routing protocols*:

- RIP (Routing Information Protocol)
- OSPF (Open Shortest Path First)

RIP was originally developed at Xerox, as were many common technology gadgets, including Ethernet, the graphical user interface, and the mouse. And you thought all they made was photocopiers. But I digress.

The RIP implemented for TCP/IP networks is similar to the RIP used by IPX/SPX on NetWare servers since the beginning of time. RIP is easy to configure and works fine on smaller networks, but has problems on networks of more than 16 hops. The hop count is incremented by one each time an IP datagram crosses a router. RIP starts taking a long time to update routers within the internetwork because it works on the basis of broadcasts. If a new network is added or a route becomes unavailable on the network, the routers farther away may not learn about this change for several minutes; this problem is called *slow convergence*.

In addition, a router using RIP selects routes with the lowest hop count as the ideal route; this is because RIP is a *distance-vector* routing protocol. The number of hops does not always indicate the fastest route.

 TIP For more information about RIP, see RFC 1058.

For larger networks, you should consider using the OSPF (Open Shortest Path First) routing protocol, which is a *link-state* routing protocol. It favors faster routes, updates other routers about network topology changes quickly, and reduces the possibility of routing loops.

OSPF is very different from RIP. Routers running RIP broadcast information about the network to all their neighboring routers. An OSPF router shares information with other routers about its adjacent routers only, thereby allowing other routers to build routing tables based on information that is sent to them. You can configure OSPF routers for certain areas of the network or for the entire internetwork.

Naturally, since OSPF is so much faster, more versatile, and more powerful, it is more difficult to configure. My advice: seek professional help.

 TIP For more information about OSPF, see RFC 2178.

Classless Inter-Domain Routing (CIDR)

To help prevent the total depletion of available IP addresses, the Internet authorities had to come up with a way to allocate blocks of IP networks. Instead of giving out an entire Class B address to an organization that has only 1500 hosts, an Internet service provider (ISP) issues a block of addresses that could be used as Class C addresses, but that are actually part of Class B. Since all Class B addresses have been depleted, ISPs can give out a smaller chunk of the Class B that they have been allocated.

For example, instead of giving an organization the entire 186.45.0.0 Class B network, the ISP would give you 186.45.32.0, 186.45.33.0, 186.45.34.0, 186.45.35.0, 186.45.36.0, and 186.45.37.0 (where you would use a subnet mask of 255.255.255.0). These look like six Class C addresses that give you 254 hosts per network, don't they?

PART

III

Netware, TCP/IP,
and the Internet

Well, from your perspective, they are six Class C addresses. Internet service providers call this *supernetting.*

Here's the problem that then arises: the ISP that gave you those addresses must put four separate entries in its routing table on its routers in order to route network traffic to you. In a short time, these routing tables would become huge. The routers that service the Internet backbone would need hundreds of megabytes of RAM to accommodate all the Class C addresses on the Internet; remember, there are more than 2,000,000 of them! The amount of work required to maintain these addresses across hundreds of routers would be prohibitive.

To prevent overwhelming the Internet's routers, Classless Inter-Domain Routing (CIDR; pronounced "cider") was developed. Before CIDR, we relied exclusively on the IP address to tell us the class of the IP address. Now, we use the subnet mask for this purpose. Essentially, IP networks are no longer bound by the class definitions. The subnet mask can also have *fewer* bits in it than the default subnet mask.

This technique allows an ISP to collapse all entries for a network into one single router entry. The ISP can put a single entry in its routing tables that would look something like 186.45.32.0, with a subnet mask of 255.255.248.0. If you work in a Network Operations Center (NOC) supporting hundreds of subnets or if you work for an Internet service provider, you will probably see CIDR in use. Otherwise, people are just going to use the term in your presence and assume you know what they are talking about.

 TIP Classless Inter-Domain Routing is defined in RFCs 1518 and 1519. See RFC 1338 for more information on supernetting.

A New Convention and Another Example

When you get an IP network address from your provider, typically you also receive the subnet mask you are suppose to use, for example, 198.69.176.0/ 255.255.255.0. This has long been standard notation for IP network addresses and subnet masks.

Several years back, I supervised the connection of a small network to the Internet. The ISP wanted to know how many hosts required IP addresses and what growth I expected. I said that I needed 28 hosts on this network. They e-mailed me the IP network address that I was to use. I was expecting something like the example above. What I got was 202.18.193.64 / 27. Does this make sense to you? At the time, it surely did not make sense to me. I had a number of theories (all wrong) about what the 27 meant. I finally swallowed my pride and called to ask.

This is a newer convention for writing the IP network address and subnet mask. The 27 identifies how many "1" bits are in the subnet mask. A subnet mask with 27 bits looks like this (I have put spaces on each octet boundary):

11111111 11111111 11111111 11100000

The subnet mask in decimal is 255.255.255.224, which is what I was used to seeing. This mask tells me that only the last five bits of the IP address are available for hosts. This gives me two to the fifth possible IP host addresses, or 32 possible hosts, but I have to subtract two, since I cannot use the combination of all zeros and all ones. My first available host was 208.18.193.65, and my last host was 208.18.193.94.

Planning an IP Network

Planning a TCP/IP network is more complicated than planning an IPX/SPX network because you have to worry about not only unique network numbers but also unique host numbers. In addition, when planning each subnet, you have to make sure you have enough IP host addresses to go around. If you are lucky, someone may hand you a list of addresses to use; as long as you use these addresses, nothing goes wrong.

However, it is just as likely that planning your IP internetwork will be delegated to you, the new NetWare 5.1 internetworking and IP guru.

I like to divide this network-planning dilemma into two scenarios. First, someone is giving you your addresses; second, you have to select your own addresses. Regardless of the scenario, you need to know how many hosts you have on each network.

How Many IP Host Addresses Do You Need?

Think about your existing IPX/SPX network for just a minute. How many nodes does it have? Are you sure that is all? I have plugged some rather strange things into IP and IPX/SPX networks. On an IP network, they all require an IP host address in order to communicate with the rest of the network. Here are some examples:

- File and application servers (NetWare, Windows NT, Unix)
- Clients (DOS, Windows, Macintosh, OS/2, Unix)
- Print servers (including devices such as the HP JetDirect)
- Interfaces on your routers
- Hubs, bridges, switches, UPS, and other manageable devices

PART

III

Netware, TCP/IP, and the Internet

Caltech has a Coke machine on the Web (check it out at `rutabaga.caltech.edu`). I have also seen refrigerators, coffeepots, weather collection devices, and a hot tub plugged into a network.

Armed with this impressive list of devices, be sure you know about all the devices attached to your network. By the way, if your network has a hot tub attached to it, I want to come work with your company.

 NOTE Each host on your IP network must have a unique IP host address. If you accidentally assign a host a duplicate IP address, generally both hosts get an error message, and the second host that tries to use the address does not work. However, some older systems will actually crash or stop working if they detect a duplicate address. Plan carefully, and keep notes.

How Many Networks Do You Require?

In addition to discovering the maximum number of hosts per network, you need to ascertain how many IP networks you will need. How many IPX/SPX networks do you currently have? One of the most common mistakes people make when planning IP networks is to forget the "network" between two routers on the Internet. As you can see in Figure 14.2, three network numbers are required because of the "router" network and because each interface on the router must have an IP host address.

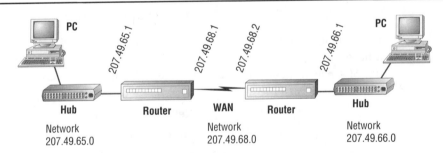

FIGURE 14.2

Three networks, two Ethernet and one "router"

Note that each router interface has an IP address.

Two routers that are separated by a dialup, an ISDN, or a leased-line circuit will require an IP network between them. This "router" network will require only two hosts, but it is still a separate network.

The "router" network rule is no longer hard and fast because many router vendors have proprietary software that eliminates the necessity for a router network. These are sometimes called *network-to-network* connections, but each router vendor has their own name for it.

Who Assigns Your IP Network Addresses?

Where do you go for an official IP network address? If your network is going to connect to the Internet, you must plan your address space carefully. IP network and host addresses that you use cannot be used anywhere else on the Internet. The organization that controls who gets which addresses (and also assigns domain names) is InterNIC (`rs.internic.net`).

In years past, if you wanted to put your network on the Internet, you had to contact InterNIC and get an allocation of IP addresses. Today, IP network addresses are allocated by Internet service providers. Your ISP has a block of addresses for customers. When you arrange with your ISP to connect to the Internet, have the following information at hand:

- The number of hosts that require an IP address
- The number of networks you have
- Your estimated growth potential

Don't expect your ISP to give you more IP addresses than you absolutely need. Remember, we are in the middle of an IP address shortage; they are rationing. If you cannot justify the number of addresses you are requesting, don't expect to get them.

If your network is part of a larger corporate, government, or academic network, your IP address will come from "upstream." Addresses will be assigned by the head of your network.

What if you never expect to connect your network to the Internet? See the "Private Networks" section, later in this chapter.

Networks Connected to a Larger Network (and the Internet)

If your IP network will connect to a larger network, you must coordinate with the "powers that be," usually the folks who are responsible for connecting your network to the other networks or providing backbone services.

They may give you a block of IP addresses and expect you to handle all network and host address assignments yourself. More than likely, though, you will have to coordinate with the upstream support organization. They will assign each network on

PART

III

Netware, TCP/IP,
and the Internet

your LAN a network address and may possibly require that you assign each specific host (client and server) a specific IP address.

This approach certainly limits your flexibility, but it also leaves no room for confusion regarding IP host addresses and subnet masks.

Private Networks

Some IP networks will never connect to the Internet. These networks are defined as private by RFC 1918. If your network is private, you can assign your networks and hosts anything you want, right? Well, you can. However, RFC 1918 specifies that certain IP network addresses never be assigned to any network on the Internet. These network addresses are set aside for private use. The Internet routers will not route data to these IP addresses. RFC 1918 sets aside a single Class A network, 16 Class B networks, and 255 Class C networks. Here are the addresses:

- 10.0.0.0
- 172.16.0.0 through 172.31.0.0
- 192.168.0.0 through 192.168.255.0

Why should you use one of these addresses? You don't have to, but if you plan to access the Internet in the future through software such as Novell's BorderManager, a proxy server, or a network address translator, you should use network addresses that do not appear anywhere on the Internet. Besides, 10.0.0.1 for your first network device sticks in your memory better than 192.168.212.1.

BorderManager, Proxy Servers, and Network Address Translators

Network managers who would never have dreamed of connecting to the Internet even as recently as two years ago now consider Internet connectivity essential. What is driving this trend? Companies want Internet mail and Web servers. In the future, more business will be conducted over the Internet, including the exchange of orders and inventory information as well as the buying and selling of goods and services. From the typical business perspective, the Internet is just entering the pre-adolescent stage of self-discovery and rebellion.

So what is so terrible about the Internet today? I am not opening the security can of worms here, but how about security? How about the occasional wholesale failure of a particular chunk of the Internet? Okay, okay, the Internet does not often fail completely, but my connection grinds to an intolerably slow pace at times. Let's not ignore the fact that you may not be able to get IP addresses for every host on your network.

Security procedures are getting better. The infrastructure of the Internet continues to be upgraded (both from the reliability perspective as well as speed). Tools to monitor and restrict access to the Internet are getting better and better. The IP address shortage will continue, but hope appears on the horizon. Most company Web sites have upgraded from brochure-ware to singing and dancing e-commerce money-grabbers.

In 1997 Novell released BorderManager, which has been widely received. This product combines several earlier products, including a DHCP server, a DNS server, and a product that had two names, the NIAS (NetWare Internet Access Server) or the IPX/IP Gateway.

You can use BorderManager, proxy servers, and network address translators to control what your users are accessing on the Internet and to protect your network from nefarious people on the Internet who might do your system harm.

BorderManager allows you to continue using IPX/SPX as your network protocol, and the BorderManager server connects to the Internet on behalf of your clients. You can restrict usage based on user, time, and the sites to which users can connect. BorderManager is tightly integrated with the NetWare Directory Service.

A *proxy server* acts in a similar fashion to BorderManager in that it is the only device on your network that actually has a connection to the Internet. Users from your private network connect to the Internet through the proxy server, and it connects to the Internet on their behalf.

A *network address translator* (NAT) is software (and a server) that converts internal (private) IP addresses to official IP addresses and forwards packets to the Internet. You assign a host a private IP address on the private IP network; when the host must communicate with the Internet, the NAT converts the private IP address to a public IP address as the IP datagram passes through the NAT.

Tunneling

Whether you realize it or not, tunneling happens all the time on today's networks. *Tunneling* is the process of encapsulating one protocol inside another and passing it over the network. For example, when you are communicating with a Web server, your computer is speaking IP, but the IP datagram is carrying a TCP segment (sometimes called its *payload*), and the TCP segment is carrying HTTP data.

I set up a wide area network several years ago in which the routers' software supported only TCP/IP. Even if the software had supported IPX/SPX, the routers connected two offices through the Internet. The primary purpose was to give employees access to the Internet. After the network was up and running, my client asked, "Oh,

PART

III

Netware, TCP/IP,
and the Internet

by the way" (I always hate that), "how can I map a drive to the server in the other office?"

The options were to convert everyone to the newly released NetWare/IP product or to implement IPX tunneling. The client did not want to move to NetWare/IP.

My client's NetWare servers did support TCP/IP, so I loaded the TCP/IP support and loaded the IPTUNNEL.NLM, which allowed me to specify a virtual IPX network over the Internet. Clients in both offices could now see and map drives to the servers in both offices. When a client mapped a drive, the client sent IPX data to the NetWare server running IPTUNNEL. The NetWare server encapsulated the IPX data in an IP datagram and forwarded it to the NetWare server in the other office running IPTUNNEL, where the IPX data was taken out of the IP datagram and placed back on the network as an IPX frame. This really nifty feature was completely transparent to the end users, and the client thought I was a genius (I kept my mouth shut and didn't ruin the impression).

Many routing vendors in addition to Novell support tunneling, and you may find it useful in your bag of network tricks.

NetWare 5.1 eliminates tunneling completely if you choose an all-IP network setup. Client-to-server and server-to-server communications all happen over IP, with no IPX involved.

NetWare 5.1 TCP/IP Components

At the core of the NetWare TCP/IP services on a NetWare 5.1 server is the TCPIP.NLM. This NLM is located in the SYS:SYSTEM directory. Other NetWare TCP/IP components include:

- Native IP support for NetWare (NWIP.NLM)
- Domain Name System (DNS) name server software (NAMED.NLM)
- Dynamic Host Configuration Protocol (DHCP) server software (DHCPSRVR.NLM)
- Simple Network Management Protocol NLM file (SNMP.NLM)
- SNMP Event Logger NLM file (SNMPLOG.NLM)
- TCP/IP Console NLM file (TCPCON.NLM)
- IP Static Route Configuration NLM file (IPCONFIG.NLM)
- ICMP Echo NLM files (PING.NLM and TPING.NLM) for diagnostics
- BootP Forwarder NLM file (BOOTPFWD.NLM)
- IP Filter Support (IPFLT.NLM)

Unix gurus will find familiar files such as HOSTS, NETWORKS, PROTOCOL, and SERVICES in the SYS:ETC directory. Sample IP data files are installed in the SYS:ETC\SAMPLES directory.

NetWare TCP/IP supports both Novell and third-party applications. Third-party products are supported through the TLI (Transport Layer Interface) used by the AT&T-developed STREAMS or the BSD 4.3 Sockets interface. Figure 14.3 shows how the software pieces plug together.

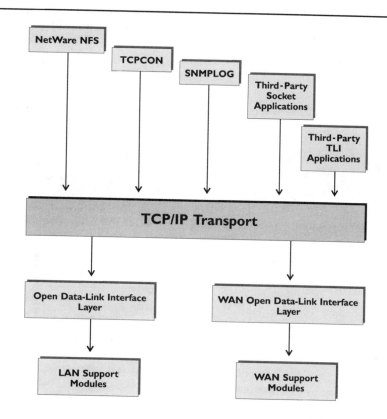

FIGURE 14.3

TCP/IP support in NetWare

Since the Unix and Internet folks in your organization will want to know the depth of NetWare's TCP/IP support, let's go down the list of services. Table 14.8 summarizes NetWare's TCP/IP support services.

PART

III

Netware, TCP/IP,
and the Internet

TABLE 14.8: NETWARE'S TCP/IP SUPPORT SERVICES

Service	Function
TCP/IP Application Support	Provides a transport interface for higher-level network services, such as NetWare NFS. Both TCP and UDP transport services are provided.
Native IP Client Support	NetWare clients can now communicate with NetWare 5.1 servers using the IP protocol exclusively.
Domain Name System	Provides a database of computer names and their IP addresses. Allows a client to look up the IP address of any system on the network.
Dynamic Host Configuration Protocol	Enables the NetWare server to assign IP addresses, subnet masks, and router addresses to clients automatically when the client boots.
Service Location Protocol	Provides clients the ability to locate services on an IP network. Similar to the Service Advertising Protocol (SAP).
File Transfer Protocol Server	Allows the NetWare server to interact with FTP clients for file transfer.
Trivial File Transfer Protocol	Allows TFTP clients to transfer files to and from the NetWare server.
Network Information Services	A distributed database of user and group information that is used specifically by NetWare NFS Services.
Network File System	Allows Unix clients to access NetWare volumes.
Unix to NetWare Printing	Provides bi-directional printing support for Unix and NetWare users.
Netscape Enterprise Web Server	Allows a NetWare server to support a full-featured Web server, with all the bells and whistles you need.
IP Routing	Forwards IP traffic from one network to another. Novell's TCP/IP software supports link-state, distance-vector, and static routing.
RIP (Routing Information Protocol)	Uses the distance-vector algorithm for routing operations and decisions. Most TCP/IP networks still use RIP.
OSPF (Open Shortest Path First)	Uses the link-state algorithm for routing operations and decisions.
Static Routing	Manually configures routes, dictating the routers used to reach remote destinations. Static routing may be used exclusively or in addition to dynamic routing protocols.

Continued ▶

TABLE 14.8 CONTINUED: NETWARE'S TCP/IP SUPPORT SERVICES

Service	Function
Router Discovery	Used by routers to advertise their presence on a network, similar to the way NetWare servers use SAP to announce themselves.
Variable Subnetwork Support	NetWare 4.1x and up allow different-sized subnetworks through support of variable-length subnet masks.
Directed Broadcast	A broadcast sent to all hosts on a particular IP network or subnetwork; often used to find or announce services.
BOOTP Forwarding	Used by some systems to discover their IP address and sometimes load other information, such as their operating system. This is similar to the Get Nearest Server packet sent by NetWare clients as they attempt to log in. The questioning host broadcasts a BOOTP request; routers may either block these requests or pass them to the appropriate network if the BOOTP server is on another network. Four BOOTP servers can be referenced.
TCP/IP Network Management with SNMP	Simple Network Management Protocol is the most popular TCP/IP management protocol. All the Unix-based management systems use SNMP as their primary protocol.
Internetworking Configuration Utility	INETCFG is the menu-driven utility we've seen when setting up AppleTalk. INETCFG replaces the LOAD and BIND commands in the AUTOEXEC.NCF file and provides interactive menus for configuration.
Permanent Connections	Links to other systems can be configured during initialization to stay up continually. If the line drops, the connection is automatically retried for reconnection.

In the old days (NetWare 3.x), you had to load many of the NLMs yourself. Don't let the list in Table 14.8 make you nervous. Most of your work will be done within INETCFG, and you won't need to worry about loading the right NLM at the right time. The TCP/IP system modules will take care of that themselves.

The services listed in Table 14.8 are not the only TCP/IP services, but they are a starting point for providing IP support for your clients.

PART

III

Netware, TCP/IP,
and the Internet

Native IP Support for NetWare Clients

The most significant new feature in NetWare 5.0 was the inclusion of "pure" IP support for NetWare clients. Pure in the sense that clients and servers no longer require an IPX encapsulation (or tunneling) to move IPX information to the server. The advantages of this for many NetWare users include:

- Consolidation to a single protocol rather than running two or more
- More efficient use of network bandwidth
- Lower support costs due to supporting only one protocol
- Allows connectivity for remote users over a wide range of systems
- Backward compatibility with IPX/SPX-specific applications

Novell accomplished this by modifying the NetWare Core Protocol (NCP) to be independent of a specific protocol. NCPs can now use IPX/SPX, TCP, and UDP for delivery. The NetWare 5.1 operating system was modified to remove any dependencies on IPX. Novell also modified the NDS structure to incorporate the Domain Name System (DNS) for naming of devices (and IP address resolution).

Service Location Protocol

The *Service Location Protocol* (SLP) provides service discovery, thereby replacing the service discovery function of the Service Advertising Protocol (SAP). This can eliminate large amounts of broadcast traffic found in larger NetWare networks. The SLP service provides backward compatibility for applications and services that rely on SAP discovery.

SLP registers information in a database that clients can query when looking for a specific service. Services register with SLP when they are brought up, but they do not continue to register themselves, as SAP does. With SAP, the service defaulted to re-registering itself every 60 seconds.

 TIP   For more information about the Service Location Protocol, see RFC 2165.

Compatibility with Existing IPX/SPX Networks

Novell used IPX from the early beginnings of NetWare. Though proprietary, it became a de facto standard for networking. Third-party developers have written thousands of applications to work with IPX/SPX networks. Will these applications continue to function if you move to the IP protocol exclusively?

Not to worry. Your existing IPX/SPX applications will continue to work as always. Clients that have been updated to use TCP/IP only can still communicate with services that speak only IPX/SPX.

Novell recognized that it would be impossible for many networks to simply switch from one protocol to another overnight, especially given the complexity of many modern networks. These migrations must occur over time.

IPX compatibility mode is a NetWare 5.1 feature that allows you to gradually migrate from an IPX or a NetWare/IP network to native IP. Most applications should work just fine over IP, but a small percentage of applications may not. In these cases, the developer of the application may have attempted to access IPX/SPX directly rather than following recommended programming conventions. For this reason, the compatibility mode detects that it is necessary to use IPX services, and it encapsulates IPX in an IP frame.

As time goes by, the need for compatibility mode will probably diminish because developers will clean up their applications and make them NetWare 5.1-friendly. IPX compatibility mode consists of three components:

- Compatibility mode drivers
- The Migration Agent
- The Bindery Agent

Compatibility Mode Drivers

Compatibility mode drivers (CMDs) consist of a client component and a server component. These drivers are loaded by default but are used only if required. On a NetWare 5.1 server, the CMD is viewed as a network adapter. You can bind both the IP and IPX protocols to the compatibility mode adapter, and it acts like a router when IPX packets need to be sent within the server. If it is not being used, the CMD is idle and uses no resources.

When the CMD is loaded on a NetWare server with the gateway option on, it is linking IP to the IPX world. These compatibility functions are all transparent to the end user.

The Migration Agent

The *Migration Agent* (or *Migration Gateway*) provides two translations. First, it translates IPX packets to IP (and vice versa), and second, it translates information between the two NetWare 5.1 naming and discovery services, SLP and SAP. The Migration Agent connects an IPX network and an IP network; however, it is needed only if there are both IPX and IP networks.

PART

III

Netware, TCP/IP,
and the Internet

The Migration Agent is necessary for communication between IP and IPX networks because NetWare 5.1 supports both natively. NetWare/IP worked differently; it encapsulated IPX frames in IP frames. All the server had to do was de-encapsulate the frame to get IPX information back. In the NetWare 5.1 world, the service information must be extracted from the IP frame and re-transmitted in an IPX frame in order for IP clients to communicate with IPX services. Figure 14.4 shows the Migration Agent sitting on the network between IPX and IP hosts.

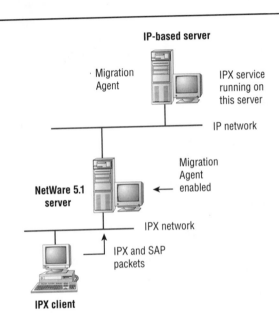

FIGURE 14.4

The Migration Agent handling conversion of data between IP and IPX clients

Only one Migration Agent is needed on small networks. Medium to larger networks may require servers running the Migration Agent. When planning a larger network, each LAN should have a server running the Migration Agent. For information on how to configure a server to run the Migration Agent, see the section "Setting Up IPX Compatibility Mode."

The Bindery Agent

The *Bindery Agent* allows for compatibility with NetWare 2.x and 3.x bindery-based clients. This service is necessary if you still have services running on NetWare 2.x or 3.x servers or if you have applications that require Bindery Services. The Bindery Agent creates static bindery objects in the NetWare Directory Service so that applications that require Bindery Services think there is a bindery.

Setting Up IPX Compatibility Mode

The good news is that compatibility mode drivers are loaded by default; there is nothing the administrator must do to enable CMD either on the client or the server. However, you need to take a few additional steps to enable the Migration Agent and the Bindery Agent.

To enable the Migration Agent, load the compatibility mode drivers module (SCMD .NLM) with the /G option. Your network requires only a single NetWare 5.1 server running the Migration Agent. In a multi-segment network, load the Migration Agent on any segment that has IPX clients, applications, or services.

To enable the Bindery Agent, create a new NDS Organizational Unit. For example, in the organization called SOMORITA, create a container called BINDERY. At a NetWare 5.1 server running the Migration Agent, set the bindery context. For the SOMORITA example, type **SET BINDERY CONTEXT=.BINDERY.SOMORITA**. Then load the BINDGATE.NLM. The server that runs the BINDGATE.NLM must also have a read/write replica of the partition where you created the bindery container.

To populate other NetWare 5.1 servers that don't have the Bindery Agent loaded, put a read/write replica of the partition that contains the bindery container on those servers, and set the bindery context as described above.

Installing TCP/IP on NetWare 5.1

When configuring TCP/IP on a NetWare server, you must use the INETCFG.NLM rather than doing it the old-fashioned way and putting all your LOAD statements directly in the AUTOEXEC.NCF. The INETCFG.NLM provides you with an easy interface for configuring TCP/IP protocol support and binding IP to the network interfaces.

Using INETCFG to Configure TCP/IP

Before you start, have the following information at hand:

- The server's IP address and subnet mask
- The IP address of the server's default gateway (router)
- The IP address of the nearest DNS name server (optional)

If you have used the INETCFG utility to configure IPX/SPX in the past, the utility has already loaded all your networking LOAD and BIND statements from the AUTOEXEC.NCF file and put them in its own database.

PART

III

Netware, TCP/IP,
and the Internet

If this is the first time you have run INETCFG, it will prompt you to transfer the LAN driver, protocol, and remote-access commands to the configuration files maintained by INTECFG. You must answer Yes to this question. All networking-related commands in the AUTOEXEC.NCF file will be transferred to INETCFG, and they will be commented out (with a # symbol) in your original AUTOEXEC.NCF.

Figure 14.5 shows the main menu of the INETCFG program, which includes the following options:

Boards   Configures new and existing network interfaces and WAN boards.

Network Interfaces   Configures individual interfaces for WAN boards only. LAN cards do not need to have this choice configured.

WAN Call Directory   Configures WAN connections. Not required for LAN boards.

Protocols   Configures protocols such as IPX/SPX, TCP/IP, and AppleTalk.

Bindings   Configures bindings to associate protocols with specific network interfaces.

Manage Configuration   Configures SNMP parameters and allows you to configure Remote Console access and TELNET access.

View Configuration   Displays the console commands that will be executed whenever the server boots or reinitializes.

Reinitialize System   Reloads the LAN and WAN configuration.

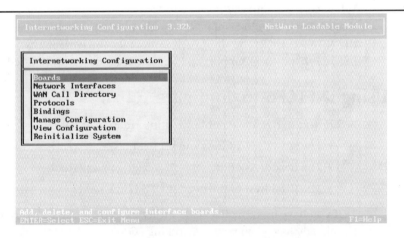

FIGURE 14.5

Internetworking Configuration (INETCFG) main menu

Configuring Protocols

14.1 Enabling TCP/IP Support on NetWare 5.1

1. At the server console, type **LOAD INETCFG**.

2. Choose Protocols ➤ TCP/IP.

3. Set the TCP/IP Status selection to Enabled.

4. Exit and save your changes.

For purposes of configuring TCP/IP support, we will be concerned primarily with two menu choices from the INETCFG main menu: Protocols and Bindings. Choose Protocols ➤ TCP/IP to open the TCP/IP Protocol Configuration screen, as shown in Figure 14.6.

FIGURE 14.6

The TCP/IP Protocol Configuration screen

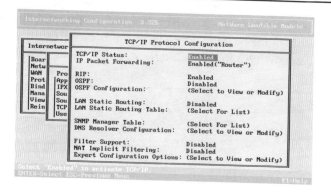

First, enable TCP/IP by changing the TCP/IP Status selection to Enabled. For a standard configuration, you need not change the remaining items. If you are using your NetWare server to route IP packets, see the "Using NetWare 5.1 for TCP/IP Routing" section, later in this chapter.

PART

III

Netware, TCP/IP, and the Internet

Binding TCP/IP to Network Interfaces

IN A HURRY

14.2 Bind TCP/IP to a Network Interface

1. From the INETCFG menu, choose Bindings.
2. Press Insert to create a new binding, and select TCP/IP.
3. In the Bind To box, select A Network Interface, and then select the Network interface to which you want to bind TCP/IP.
4. Enter the IP address and subnet mask.
5. Exit and save the configuration.
6. Reinitialize the system or reboot for this to take effect.

Your next task is to bind TCP/IP support to your network interfaces. Choosing Bindings displays the Protocol To Interface/Group Bindings list. If you are modifying an existing binding, highlight it and press Enter. Otherwise, press Insert to display a list of supported protocols; choose TCP/IP. In the Bind To box, select A Network Interface, highlight the board to which you want to bind TCP/IP, and press Enter to open the Binding TCP/IP To A LAN Interface dialog box, as shown in Figure 14.7.

FIGURE 14.7

Binding TCP/IP to a board

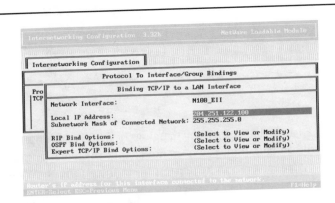

Enter the IP address and the subnet mask for this specific adapter. NetWare will automatically fill in the subnet mask value, but in hex, so it will show FF.FF.FF.0. This will freak out Unix people, so change it to 255.255.255.0 and make it match the rest of the world.

Unless you are using your NetWare servers as routers, you will not need to configure the RIP and OSPF Bind Options. The Expert TCP/IP Bind Options allow you to change your frame type, but unless your network is a really special case, you should leave it at Ethernet_II. Except in very special cases, none of the Expert options should be changed.

Configuring TCP/IP Manually

Okay, so we have just configured TCP/IP using INETCFG, and in my humble opinion, it us much easier to configure than to remember all the console commands that have to be entered in the AUTOEXEC.NCF file. However, for those of you who are console command people, here is a sample of what we just configured:

```
LOAD TCPIP
LOAD N100 NAME=N100_EII FRAME=ETHERNET_II SLOT=7
BIND IP TO N100_EII ARP=YES, MASK=255.255.255.0 ADDRESS=204.251.122.100
```

Using TCPCON to View TCP/IP Statistics

To monitor the TCP/IP protocols, Novell provides the TCPCON.NLM, which allows you to view information about protocols, routing, the routing table, and SNMP traps that have been logged. Figure 14.8 shows the TCPCON main menu.

FIGURE 14.8

*TCP/IP Console
(TCPCON)*

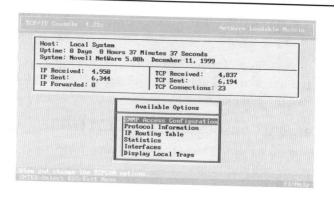

The information on the main screen lets you view how many IP datagrams and TCP segments have been received by this particular NetWare server. If the server is configured as an IP router, you can also view the IP datagrams that have been routed (IP Forwarded).

PART

III

Netware, TCP/IP,
and the Internet

Notice an anomaly about NetWare 5.1: the System text in the top box of the screen says this is NetWare 5.00h, dated December 11, 1999. That's really the date of Net-Ware 5.1's release, so this is the 5.1 version of TCPCON.

From the main menu, you have six choices:

SNMP Access Configuration   View and change the current SNMP Access configuration.

Protocol Information   View information about the EGP, ICMP, IP, OSPF, TCP, and UDP protocols, including current TCP and UDP connections.

IP Routing Table   View the current IP routing table.

Statistics   View protocol statistics for EGP, ICMP, IP, OSPF, TCP, and UDP protocols.

Interfaces   View statistics for the LAN, WAN, and logical network interfaces.

Display Local Traps   View the local SNMP log if the SNMPLOG.NLM is loaded.

Other TCP/IP Components

NetWare 5.1 ships with some additional components that provide interoperability with Unix and other TCP/IP network hosts:

- FTP Server for transferring files between the NetWare server and FTP clients (now administered through the NetWare Web Manager)

- XCONSOLE Server services for allowing NetWare administrators to gain access to the NetWare server console from X Window systems or through TELNET clients

If you were an IntranetWare 4.11 user, you will recall that DNS was also supported. It is still supported, but installed differently. For more information on DNS support in NetWare 5.1, see Chapter 15.

Remote Console Support via TELNET

The XCONSOLE.NLM allows an administrator to use the TELNET program to display a text screen. This utility was originally intended to allow administrators from X Window systems to access the NetWare server console, but it allows an administrator to TELNET from any platform.

To enable TELNET and XCONSOLE support, use the UNICON utility. From the UNICON utility, choose Start/Stop Services, press the Insert key, and choose XConsole Server.

 TIP   In order for the TELNETD (TELNET Daemon) to work properly, the REMOTE.NLM must also be loaded.

Using NetWare 5.1 for TCP/IP Routing

If your NetWare server has more than one network interface card, it is possible to enable IP Routing between the networks. In addition, you can choose from several routing protocols. The server should have two network interfaces configured, and both should have valid IP addresses and subnet masks configured.

To enable routing, use the INETCFG utility. Choose Protocols ➤ TCP/IP, and set IP Packet Forwarding to Enabled ("Router"). Figure 14.6, earlier in this chapter, shows this menu.

On each network segment, configure the client to use the IP address of the server as the default gateway.

Using NetWare 5.1 to Build an IP Tunnel

Earlier I mentioned that you can move IPX/SPX packets through an IP-only network by creating an IP tunnel. Figure 14.9 shows how this works. This is different from the old method of faking a TCP/IP packet, since NetWare now uses real TCP/IP packets and bundles IPX inside them when necessary.

FIGURE 14.9

IPX/SPX tunneled through an IP-only network

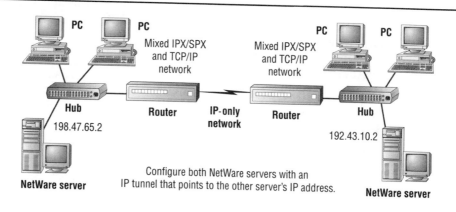

To do this, you must enable IPS tunneling on both NetWare servers. In INETCFG, choose Protocols ➤ IPX ➤ Tunnel IPX Through IP ➤ Enabled. Then provide the IP address of the server on the other side of the IP network.

Packets destined for the other IPX network will automatically be encapsulated in an IP packet and forwarded to the other server, where it is de-encapsulated. This is not designed for large throughput scenarios, as it places an additional load on the servers that are handling the tunneling operation.

TCP/IP Printing Support

NetWare 5.1 changed the rules on all the TCP/IP printing support, and those rules did not make the cut for the distribution CD. Unfortunately, that means those of you who are interested in printing back and forth between NetWare and Unix systems must download the upgrade from the Novell Web site when it becomes available.

Future truth: NetWare 5.1 includes bi-directional printing capabilities with Unix and TCP/IP printers. Users on Unix systems, or any system that supports the LPD (line printer daemon) protocol, can print to a NetWare print queue, and NetWare print queues can be redirected to Unix-based printers or IP network printer interfaces such as the HP JetDirect card.

Unix-to-NetWare Printing

The Unix-to-NetWare print service takes jobs that were sent to the NetWare server from Unix or other LPD protocol clients and places them in the appropriate NetWare print queue. A NetWare print server then takes over and forwards the job to the appropriate printing device.

Printers that are to be accessible for Unix users should be configured in the UNICON utility. The first step is to make the printer available to accept LPD print jobs. This process is called *exporting*. When you export a printer, you can make it available to all hosts or only a few.

NetWare-to-TCP/IP Printing

NetWare-to-TCP/IP printing takes a print job that has been sent to a NetWare print queue and directs it to a TCP/IP printer (essentially and interchangeably, a Unix printer).

Before configuring NetWare-to-Unix printing, be sure to complete the items on this checklist.

- Create at least one NetWare print server that will serve as the print server for jobs being sent to the Unix side.
- Create the NetWare printers that represent Unix printers.
- Create the NetWare print queues that you want redirected to the Unix system.
- If you are printing to a Unix host, have the Unix administrator create a user account with permissions to print to your desired printing devices. Create this account in the UNICON users list.
- In the SYS:ETC\HOSTS file, enter the IP address and host name of the Unix system to which you are planning to print.

Lightweight Directory Access Protocol

Lightweight Directory Access Protocol (LDAP) provides the rules and commands for accessing information such as user names, addresses, phone numbers, and e-mail addresses stored in an X.500-compatible directory service such as Novell Directory Services (NDS). X.500, by the way, is a series of *recommendations* from the International Telecommunications Union (ITU) on building a directory service.

Today, many larger organizations may have several directories. The NetWare Directory Service is one of these; others include the mainframe user accounts database, your e-mail system's directory, the Unix account database, your company phone directory (which is probably in hard copy), the human resources database, and other sources of information about people and users within your company. The vision of the future is to incorporate all these directories into a single database of information. Computer systems can use this directory when authenticating users, users can use it when looking up a phone number or mailing address, and people from outside your organization can use it to look up your e-mail address.

LDAP moves one step in that direction by providing a standard way to query and update directory databases. LDAP was originally developed as a front-end for accessing X.500 directory services. X.500 defines its own *Directory Access Protocol* (DAP) for clients to use when contacting directory servers. DAP is a heavyweight protocol that runs over a full OSI stack and requires a significant amount of computing resources. LDAP runs directly over TCP and provides most of the functionality of DAP at a much lower computing cost.

LDAP uses TCP port 389 for normal communications and TCP port 636 for secure communications using SSL (Secure Sockets Layer).

 NOTE To find out more information about the LDAP, check on the Web at `http://www.novell.com/nds/ldap.html`.

Configuring LDAP Support

During installation of NetWare 5.1, you are presented with a list of choices, including LDAP Services and NDS Catalog Services. By default, LDAP Services and NDS Catalog Services are installed.

LDAP is configured and ready to run with the default settings as soon as it is installed. No real customization is necessary; however, you may want to configure some custom options. When LDAP is installed, some additional objects appear in the

PART

III

Netware, TCP/IP, and the Internet

NDS directory (see Figure 14.10). These objects will be located in the same context as the server on which LDAP is installed.

LDAP Server object   This object stores configuration for a specific NDS server. This object's configuration includes searching limits, TCP port assignments, log file options, server console screen logging options, and LDAP catalog options.

LDAP Group object   This object stores configuration data that can be applied to a single server or to a group of servers. The object's configuration includes defining which portion of the NDS tree can be searched, defining a list of servers this configuration covers, specifying access control, and defining LDAP to NDS attribute and class maps.

LDAP Catalog object   This object defines the catalog database that is stored in the directory. The catalog is a flat-file database that contains a snapshot of the NDS database.

User Mailbox property   The User Mailbox property page does not appear as an object in the directory, but rather as a new tab for a User object. This tab allows you to enter e-mail addresses for a user. This address will be displayed when an LDAP client queries information about this user.

FIGURE 14.10

LDAP objects from the directory tree

These objects should appear in your NDS tree with the correct icons next to them. If they appear but do not have the correct icons or if you cannot display the properties of the object, you do not have the correct NetWare Administrator snap-in modules loaded.

Here's where Novell engineers have dropped the ball big time. Perhaps they're distracted trying to make ConsoleOne better than NetWare Administrator, but having to edit Registry keys and copy files from distribution CDs to make LDAP work ranks as inexcusable.

To cover Novell's lack of proper installation procedures, make sure that you have the correct snap-in modules loaded, and check the directory from which you are running the NetWare Administrator program. It should contain the files `DSCATMGR.DLL` and `LDAPSNAP.DLL`.

If these files are not in this directory, you need to copy them from your NetWare 5.1 server CD-ROM. For example, let's say you need these files in the `SYS:PUBLIC\WIN32` directory. You must copy the following files from the NetWare 5.1 server CD-ROM:

- Copy `\PRODUCTS\NLDAP\SYS\PUBLIC\WIN32\SNAPINS\LDAPSNAP.DLL` to `SYS:PUBLIC\WIN32`.

- Copy the `\PRODUCTS\NLDAP\SYS\PUBLIC\WIN32\SNAPINS\NLS\ENGLISH` directory to `SYS:PUBLIC\WIN32`.

- Copy `\PRODUCTS\CATALOG\SYS\PUBLIC\WIN32\DSC*.DLL` to `SYS:PUBLIC`.

- Copy `\PRODUCTS\CATALOG\SYS\PUBLIC\WIN32\SNAPINS\DSCATMGR.DLL` to `SYS:PUBLIC\WIN32`.

- Copy the `\PRODUCTS\CATALOG\SYS\PUBLIC\WIN32\NLS\ENTLISH` directory to `SYS:PUBLIC\WIN32\NLS\ENGLISH`.

You should also make sure that these snap-ins are properly registered in the Windows 95/98 or Windows NT Registry. If the `DSCATMGR.DLL` and `LDAPSNAP.DLL` entries do not exist, follow these steps to add them:

1. If you are using Windows NT, run `REGEDT32.EXE`; if you are using Windows 95/98, run `REGEDIT.EXE`.

2. Locate the Object DLLs WINNT key in `HKEY_CURRENT_USER\Software\NetWare\Parameters\NetWare Administrator\Snapin`.

3. Choose Edit ➢ Add Value.

4. In the Value Name box, enter **DSCATMGR.DLL**.

5. In the Data Type list box, make sure that REG_SZ is displayed, and then press Enter.

6. In the String field, enter **DSCATMGR.DLL**.

7. Repeat steps 4 through 6, substituting **LDAPSNAP.DLL** for **DSCATMGR.DLL**.

LDAP Security

By default, all users can connect anonymously and query the directory using the [Public] object. They can see any object to which the [Public] object has access. To tighten security, you may want to create an LDAP proxy user and assign only to that user the permissions to the objects, containers, and properties that you want people to view using LDAP.

To create an LDAP proxy user and assign the LDAP Group object using the Net-Ware Administrator utility, follow these steps:

1. In NDS, create a user called, for example, LDAP_Proxy_User.

2. Set this user so that it cannot change its own password and do not assign it a password.

3. Give the LDAP_Proxy_User the Browse object rights to the containers that you want anonymous users to be able to access. Also give this user Read and Compare rights to all properties (or only to the properties you want visible).

4. Select the LDAP Group object, and assign LDAP_Proxy_User to be the proxy user in the Proxy username field.

Querying the NDS Directory Using an LDAP Client

To query the NetWare 5.1 NDS database, you need an LDAP client. Both Netscape Communicator and Microsoft Internet Explorer provide an address book utility that allows you to query an LDAP directory service. Here is the procedure for configuring the Netscape Messenger's address book to query an LDAP directory.

1. Launch Netscape Messenger.

2. Choose Communicator ➢ Edit ➢ Preferences.

3. Under the Mail & Groups option, choose Directory ➢ New.

4. Enter a description for the NetWare server and the IP address or fully qualified domain name. If you want to narrow your search to specific organizational units, you can specify the container name in which to search. You should usually not have to change the LDAP port number.

To perform a directory query, from the Netscape Messenger's Communicator menu, choose Address Book. This displays the Search dialog box. Click the Directory button and choose the directory server you want to search in the Search For Items box, as shown in Figure 14.11. Enter the name you want to search for and click Search.

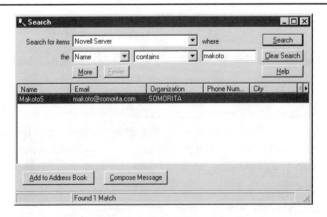

The NetWare Enterprise Web Server

Novonyx is a joint venture between Netscape and Novell whose primary goal is to rework Netscape servers to run on NetWare while leveraging NDS. The FastTrack Web Server for NetWare showed up first and shipped with NetWare 4.11/IntranetWare. The NetWare Enterprise Web Server is a full-featured Web server that runs as an NLM under NetWare. Some of its features include:

Simple Administration   Enterprise Web Server is administered via the Web. You can configure it from any place on the network that has a Web browser.

Open Standards   Enterprise Web Server supports standard HTML documents as well as standard application-development environments such as PERL, CGI scripting, JavaScript, and NetBasic Scripting.

Security   NetWare Enterprise Web Server supports Secure Sockets Layer (SSL) and allows administrators to restrict which pages users can access. Security is integrated with NDS.

This section is intended to give you only an overview of the NetWare Enterprise Web Server. The installation and quick setup may make you believe the NetWare Enterprise Web Server is a snap to deploy, but don't be fooled. Web server building information and hints fill many books, some as big as this. There's no room here for Web building; I'm just trying to cover the essentials and start you down the right road.

Installing Enterprise Web Server

The easiest way to install the Enterprise Web Server comes during NetWare installation. But if you skipped it, or forgot the settings of administration port numbers and can't get into your Web server now, re-installation won't hurt too much.

Adding the Enterprise Web Server is a definite upgrade for NetWare 5.1 over NetWare 5.0, which has the FastTrack Web Server. Think of the FastTrack Server as a departmental server, with the Enterprise Web Server able to handle, well, the Enterprise. Along with e-commerce, simple Web publishing from any user, and clustering software for the servers themselves, the Enterprise Web Server can become an unstoppable mega-server (see my adventures later with the Compaq Cluster Server).

Put the Operating System CD in the server's CD-ROM drive or otherwise make it available somewhere on the network. Switch to the X Server graphical console on the server and run the Install program. The Install program appears when you click the

PART

III

Netware, TCP/IP,
and the Internet

Novell button in about the same place that Microsoft puts the Start button on Windows 95/98/NT.

The Install program will assume that you want to access the A: floppy drive, as if anything today can be installed via a single floppy. Old habits die hard, I suppose. Click the Resource browse button and highlight NW51 in the left window, assuming you have the CD mounted in the server's CD-ROM drive. If you're accessing the CD across the network, you'll have to search and find it because I can't see it from here; you're on your own.

Once you highlight NW51 on the left side of the Install screen, PRODUCTS.NI will pop up on the right side. That's the file holding all the NetWare product details on the CD. Highlight that file, click OK, and wait for a bit (ConsoleOne is slow even on the killer Compaq dual and quad processor servers you'll see later). The Component screen appears to let you check the NetWare Enterprise Web Server box once more, and you're off.

You'll go right to the NDS Authentication Login screen. Security counts, as always, and you must prove that you're authorized to add software to the server. Provide an appropriate user name (Admin works best) and the password, and keep going.

You must configure the port settings for client browsers to connect to the Web server. The default port for normal use is 80, as in www.novell.com:80 (the 80 is assumed, since it's the Web default). The secure port connection offered is 443; change it if you know what you're doing and why you're changing it, or accept the default.

You may keep your current Web server settings or overwrite them. If you're reinstalling because you forgot something earlier, it's probably safest to overwrite everything and get a clean set of configuration files.

Get out your paper and pencil, because the Web Manager port number (2200 came up every time here) is the port number you must remember in order to configure the Web server later. Change this port if you wish, but write it down before you forget, or you'll have to reinstall all over again. The paranoid among us will change this port every month or so to keep security a bit higher and foil any hackers who guessed the access port number earlier.

Once again, you're offered a summary screen showing the Enterprise Web Server and Server Manager, which gets pulled in automatically. Accept the listing, and choose Customize if you wish some extra masochism and aggravation. Otherwise, click Finish and get some coffee while 115+MB of files slide from your CD to your server disk.

Here's what you need to know and/or remember for installation:

- The server's IP address and Web server name, such as www.gaskin.com.

- A TCP port number for the Web server. The default is port 80, which you should probably keep.
- A TCP port number for the administration server. This number is randomly assigned for you, but you can change it. You will use this port number to connect to the server for administration tasks by typing it at the end of the URL, such as www.gaskin.com:2200.

Once you confirm the settings, the software creates new directories under SYS:NOVONYX\SUITESPOT, which contain the Web server software, scripts, and default content directories.

Configuration

To configure and fine-tune your NetWare Enterprise Web Server, you must access it through a Web browser using the Admin port that you either chose or accepted as the default during installation. Figure 14.12 shows the main menu for NetWare Enterprise Web Server. From this menu, you can configure the server.

FIGURE 14.12

The General Administration screen for an Enterprise Web Server

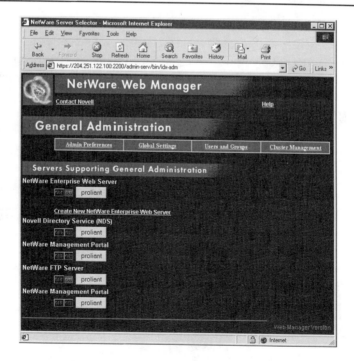

PART

III

Netware, TCP/IP, and the Internet

The General Administration section of the NetWare Web Manager page has four top-level command buttons. Table 14.9 lists these buttons and describes their functions.

TABLE 14.9: GENERAL ADMINISTRATION FUNCTIONS

Button	Functions
Admin Preferences	Shuts down the server.
	Changes the admin TCP port number.
	Restricts the superuser's access.
	Enables and sets security settings.
	Displays access and error logs.
Global Settings	Configures Directory Services to authenticate users through NDS or LDAP.
Users And Groups	Creates and manages Web server users and groups.
Cluster Management	Sets up and manages clustered Web servers.

Near the bottom of Figure 14.12 are five buttons showing the name of this particular server, in this case, PROLIANT. Clicking PROLIANT takes you to another page that has the options shown in Figure 14.13. Table 14.10 explains the server setting options for the choices across the top bar. Submenus run down the left side of the screenshot.

FIGURE 14.13

Server configuration option buttons

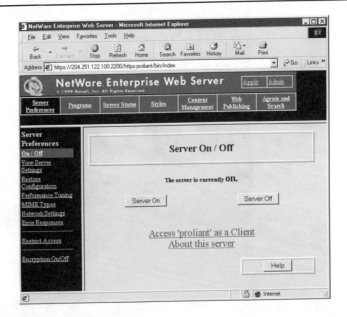

TABLE 14.10: SERVER CONFIGURATION BUTTONS

Button	Function
Server Preferences	Shuts down the server.
	Displays server settings.
	Tunes server performance.
	Changes the server name, IP address, and mail and news server names.
	Restricts access to the server for the superuser.
	Turns on encryption.
	Defines customized error messages.
Programs	Defines CGI directories and file types.
	Activates server-side JavaScript capabilities.
Server Status	Displays the access log.
	Displays the error log.
	Monitors current activity.
	Changes log preferences.
	Generates usage reports.
Styles	Creates, edits, and assigns styles.
Content Management	Defines the default document directory.
	Defines additional document directories.
	Sets up URL forwarding.
	Defines virtual hardware and software servers.
	Defines document footers.
	Defines proxy server cache values.
Web Publishing	Easy, collaborative access for NetWare users to place, access, edit, and manage files on remote Web servers.
	WebDAV (Web Distributed Authoring and Versioning) offers another method of file collaboration while retaining file protections.
Agents and Search	Special software applications that track document changes, directory changes, time-related events, and special search routines for indexing and information collection.

PART

III

Netware, TCP/IP,
and the Internet

Starting and Shutting Down the Web Server

The NetWare Enterprise Web Server should automatically load when the NetWare server it is running on is restarted. You should shut down the server from the administrative interface, but you can execute an .NCF file (NSWEBDN.NCF) from the server console prompt that will also shut down the server.

To restart a server that has been offline, use `NSWEB.NCF`.

Locating Web Documents

The default location for HTML and graphics files on my sample server, PROLIANT, is `SYS:NOVONYX/SUITESPOT/HTTPS-PROLIANT/DOCS`. This path will be different, of course, for each server name. You may want to put these files in another location, such as `SYS:WEBDOCS` or something else, depending on which users you want to give access to update the Web content.

To change the default document directory, use the administrative interface, select the server name, click the Content Management button, and then select Primary Document Directory.

Virtual Servers

The virtual server feature allows you to host multiple Web sites on a single server. You configure two options from within the Content Management option of the administrative interface:

- The Software Virtual Server
- The Hardware Virtual Server

The Software Virtual Server option allows you to specify URL names and a document directory associated with that URL. All URLs have the same IP address. The Web server scans the incoming URL request for defined domain names and returns the appropriate content for that Web site.

The Hardware Virtual Server option allows the administrator to assign different Web sites to different IP addresses. Each IP address is then assigned its own document directory. This option is more reliable than the software option, since the browser that is connecting must be able to forward the fully qualified domain name of the site it is requesting; some older browsers do not.

The NetWare FTP Server

NetWare 5.1 includes an FTP (File Transfer Protocol) Server from NetWare 4.11 and the (stupidly named) IntranetWare product release. Incredibly, the first NetWare FTP server could accept requests from any FTP client (such as Unix users), convert the request into IPX format, and fetch files from NetWare servers not even running TCP/IP, much less any FTP server software.

But since FTP doesn't come with a fancy graphical interface and support e-commerce by verifying credit cards online, few people care about it anymore. But the ones who do will be pleased to see how Novell has made their FTP life easier with NetWare 5.1.

FTP Server Now Tucked Cleanly into the Enterprise Web Server

Traditionally a command-line product with arcane server configuration details, Novell's new FTP Server now sits happily within the NetWare Enterprise Web Server management utilities. Look back at Figure 14.12, and you'll see something you may have missed before: the NetWare FTP Server command button, the fourth one down under Servers Supporting General Administration. The FTP Server is up and running in the earlier figure, even if you didn't notice it.

The first screen that appears after clicking the PROLIANT FTP Server command button is the On/Off screen. Pretty dull fare. However, the second screen, shown in Figure 14.14, has some decent information to peruse.

FIGURE 14.14

FTP Server General Settings

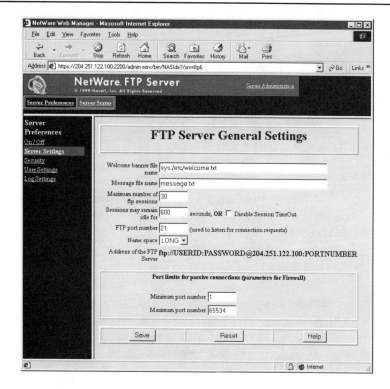

PART

III

Netware, TCP/IP, and the Internet

The Netscape engineers did a good job laying all this out for the Novell/Novonyx engineers to grab, didn't they? Clear and straightforward, just like FTP itself.

The Welcome Banner File Name portends a grandiose entrance, when all that really appears is a small text message like "Welcome to NetWare FTP Server PROLIANT" or something similar. FTP clients just need some indication that their requested connection has opened and awaits their next command.

The default maximum number of concurrent FTP sessions—30—appears more generous than necessary, unless FTP activity drives this server. The same goes for 600 seconds of idle time—way too much. The FTP port number of 21 shouldn't be changed unless every user comes from your own network, and changing the port number will heighten security. Long filenames, as opposed to brain-dead DOS short filenames, make Unix and Macintosh clients feel welcome.

FTP clients traditionally give their own name and use their e-mail address as their password. The NetWare FTP Server, however, takes advantage of NDS if necessary and builds NDS values of UserID and Password right into the default FTP Server address. Those values are configurable, as you will soon see.

The next screen for the FTP Server, Security, is pretty dull. How many times will you let a user or hacker give the wrong address before locking them out? Set the number, and the Security page is finished.

The User Settings screen offers more fun, however, as you can see in Figure 14.15. Setting the default home directory to SYS:\PUBLIC may not be smart (trust me), so change that value the first thing.

One critical decision concerns whether anonymous FTP clients are to be allowed into your server. The default is Yes, but you can change this easily. Of course, nothing in the FTP standard forces people to submit their real name and e-mail addresses to FTP servers. Check your FTP log files, and you'll find plenty of muscles@rophy.com and lost@sea.com to confuse the issue.

If you do allow anonymous access, please don't let them play around in your PUBLIC directory. Aside from any potential damage, how will you ever find uploaded files among the 200 files already churning inside PUBLIC? Make your own FTP directory, and keep things organized.

Did you notice the Server Status command button on the top of the page? This button just opens log files so you can read them without digging out a text editor and scrolling and scrolling and scrolling and scrolling.

Yes, the FTP Server software can help you do some things, especially when used with automatic file transfers between offices. Short script files can take a report's output, initiate an FTP session back to headquarters, and squirt the file over there without a single person touching the keyboard—or even being in the building for that matter.

Try some FTP. You might be amazed how nice a clean, unpretentious utility feels after years of browser bloat.

FIGURE 14.15

Controlling user access to the FTP Server

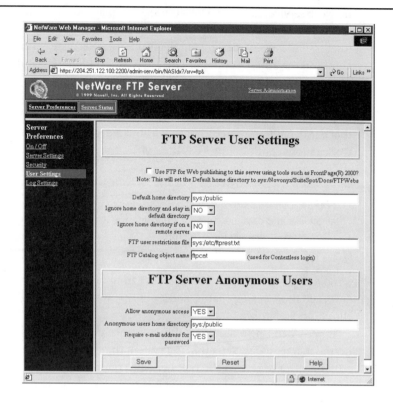

TCP/IP Networks, Firewalls, and Security

If you are going to access the Internet, security must become a larger concern. I rarely read about hacker attacks on NetWare servers. Without exception, these few attacks required access to the NetWare server's console or Admin-level access. In short, it was an inside job; or at the very least, someone got inside to do the hacking. Once you connect your NetWare servers to an IP network that is connected to the Internet, you will lose peace of mind. Don't get me wrong—NetWare is fairly secure. But no operating system that is connected to the outside world is 100 percent secure. And every system connected to the Internet has multiple server applications running that administrators may not even remember, such as TELNET or trivial FTP servers.

Even if a hacker cannot gain access to your data, your servers may be subject to *Denial of Service* (DoS) attacks. This type of attack crashes or otherwise renders a specific network service unusable. DoS attacks have plagued the Unix community for years and are becoming prevalent in the Windows NT world as well. No matter how much forethought Novell's design engineers put into NetWare 5.1, people are looking for chinks in the armor. Sooner or later, they will find one, or at least that's what you tell your boss in order to get the money you need for protection.

Furthermore, what is preventing your Windows 95/98/NT/2000 clients from installing their own TCP/IP services, such as Web and FTP servers? Microsoft makes that the default on some systems, without a decent security warning. When client workstations start offering TCP/IP services, they become vulnerable to attacks as well.

 NOTE I have read several security studies that state that between 50 and 80 percent of all attacks and data loss come from inside the network. Something to keep in mind when planning your security infrastructure.

So how do you protect your network from outside evil? Well, if your network has "official" IP addresses, that is, addresses that were assigned by an Internet authority, the choice is a firewall.

Exactly defining a firewall is difficult since many solutions from many vendors are on the market today. A *firewall* is a system (hardware and software) that allows the administrator to restrict the types of data coming into the network and the types of data going out. It serves as a filter of sorts.

Work with me here for a minute. Let's say a firewall acts like the U.S. Customs Service does at international airports; you are the IP datagram and the United States is the network. You are allowed to bring only certain things into the country, and you can take only certain things out of the country. When you pass through customs, an inspector checks to make sure that what you are carrying is not on the restricted list. There may even be restrictions on which countries you can arrive from. Try coming into the United States carrying Cuban cigars or coming into the United States from North Korea and see how much attention you generate.

A simple firewall does this job by examining three parts of the packet (IP datagram):

Source Address   Where did this packet come from? Is this source address permitted to talk to my network?

Destination Address   Where is the packet going? Is the computer for which this packet is destined allowed to receive data from outside? Is that computer allowed to receive this particular type of data?

Port Number   What application type generated this packet? Is this type of application permitted to come into or leave this network?

You might enable all network computers to use the World Wide Web but allow only specific computers to use FTP. Furthermore, you might restrict access to www.amazon-chicks.com or www.dudes-from-baywatch.com. The firewall enforces these restrictions for you.

Do You Need a Firewall?

If the answer to the following two questions is yes, you need a firewall:

- Is your network connected to the Internet and using official IP addresses?
- Is your organization the least bit concerned about the security and reliability of your network?

If the answer to the second question is no, you have nothing to worry about (except keeping your resume ready, because your management is obviously bonkers). If you answered yes (and I hope you did), it is time to start planning some type of firewall. One of the functions of Novell's BorderManager product is a firewall, by the way.

How Can You Protect Your Network?

Well, the list is long, but here is a start:

- For all operating systems you use, follow a security list or bug-fix list.
- Do not install unnecessary services on your servers. If a NetWare server handles only file and print services, do not install Web services or an FTP server on it.
- Restrict your users' computers so that users cannot install additional services on their desktops.
- Use strong passwords, consisting of upper- and lowercase letters, numbers, and special characters. Ensure that users do not put their passwords on a sticky note next to their monitor.
- Watch for Denial of Service attacks. These manifest themselves as computers mysteriously crashing or not letting people log in or attach.
- Beware of the PING of death (PING is discussed in more detail in the next section). A malevolent person can use PING functions to send a PING request that is larger than 65,536 bytes (the default size is 64 bytes). This can cause some systems to crash or hang.

TCP/IP Problems and Troubleshooting

On networks that are as complicated IP networks, you will occasionally have a problem that requires debugging. The TCP/IP suite includes some excellent tools for diagnosing problems.

What Is My IP Configuration?

First things first. Be sure that your IP host address, subnet mask, default gateway, and DNS addresses are exactly what they are supposed to be. Each platform has a utility that allows you to verify this:

- On NetWare servers, use the console CONFIG command.
- On Windows 95/98 computers, use the WINIPCFG graphical utility.
- On Windows NT Workstations, use the command-line utility IPCONFIG.

If these utilities do not report a correct IP address, fix this before you continue. Possible problems include incorrect addresses or the software not being installed.

Can I Communicate with Other IP Hosts?

The universal utility for testing whether you can communicate with other IP hosts is PING (Packet Internet Grouper). PING uses the ICMP protocol to send a diagnostics message (an echo) to another host. When the other host receives the echo message, it sends an echo reply to the sending host.

On Windows 95/98 and Windows NT Workstation hosts, PING is a command-line utility. At the console of the NetWare server, it is an NLM with a C-Worthy interface. To properly locate a communications problem, follow these steps:

1. Ping your internal software address (or loopback address). Type **PING 127.0.0.1.**
2. Ping your own IP address. Type **PING 198.67.201.157**.
3. Ping another host on your own network.
4. Ping your default gateway. Type **PING 198.67.201.1**.
5. Ping a host on another network. Type **PING 137.15.225.18**.

If you cannot ping your internal software address or your own IP address, your software is probably not installed correctly. If you cannot ping another host on your own network, check your IP address and subnet mask. If you cannot ping hosts on other networks, confirm that your default gateway is correct.

Checking Your Default Route

Your client computers have a routing table even if they have only a single network interface card. Windows 95/98 and Windows NT Workstation computers have a command utility called ROUTE.EXE that allows you to display and manipulate your computer's routing table. To display the routing table, type **ROUTE PRINT**. Here is sample output for a host whose IP address is 10.1.1.50:

Network Address	Netmask	Gateway Address	Interface	Metric
10.1.1.0	255.255.255.0	10.1.1.50	10.1.1.50	1
10.1.1.50	255.255.255.255	127.0.0.1	127.0.0.1	1
10.255.255.255	255.255.255.255	10.1.1.50	10.1.1.50	1
127.0.0.0	255.0.0.0	127.0.0.1	127.0.0.1	1
224.0.0.0	224.0.0.0	10.1.1.50	10.1.1.50	1
255.255.255.255	255.255.255.255	10.1.1.50	10.1.1.50	1
0.0.0.0	0.0.0.0	10.1.1.1	10.1.1.50	1

How do you read this stuff? Well, starting at the top is the network address 10.1.1.0. This indicates a route to get to this network through interface 10.1.1.50. The address 0.0.0.0 is the route for all addresses that do not have a route in the routing table; if there is no default route, send the packet to 10.1.1.1, which is the default gateway (or router).

Other TCP/IP Diagnostic Utilities

One of my personal favorites for diagnosing problems is the Trace Route utility, or TRACERT.EXE. Here is some sample output:

```
C:\>tracert www.novell.com
Tracing route to www.novell.com [137.65.2.11]
over a maximum of 30 hops:
  1   181 ms   180 ms   160 ms  hnl-nimitz1.inix.com [207.175.193.5]
  2   160 ms   180 ms   180 ms  medusa.inix.com [207.175.193.1]
  3   150 ms   160 ms   181 ms  GW1.HAW2.Alter.Net [137.39.3.138]
  4   200 ms   241 ms   230 ms  ATM2.SF01.Alter.Net [137.39.74.101]
  5   240 ms   230 ms   251 ms  ATM3.SC1.ALTER.NET [146.188.146.150]
  6   220 ms   241 ms   240 ms  ATM2.PA.ALTER.NET [146.188.146.121]
  7   220 ms   230 ms   221 ms  paix.bbnplanet.net [137.39.250.246]
  8   241 ms   220 ms   240 ms  su-bfr.bbnplanet.net [4.0.1.49]
  9   241 ms   230 ms   240 ms  paloalto.bbnplanet.net [4.0.2.214]
 10   330 ms   241 ms   250 ms  131.119.26.94
 11   260 ms   240 ms   241 ms  Cache.Provo.Novell.COM [137.65.2.11]
Trace complete.
```

Should You Move to TCP/IP As an Internal Network Protocol?

Should you consider moving to a single network protocol? Is Internet connectivity enough to move your network to TCP/IP? We know that TCP/IP becomes mandatory when discussing Internet and Web access. What about when moving your NetWare clients to NetWare servers? Let's consider once again the advantages and disadvantages of TCP/IP.

Advantages

- Support—more system support across more systems than any other protocol.
- Great WAN protocol—the de facto remote networking protocol suite. The only protocol suite allowed on the Internet.
- Size and speed—small and fast on PCs. Low-overhead Windows protocol stacks are getting faster than ever.

Disadvantages

- Installation is painful. Planning and addressing issues and the configuration necessary on every client make TCP/IP much more difficult to administer than IPX/SPX.
- Network routing is complicated. Configuration must be done carefully to avoid problems.

If your organization is already heavily invested in TCP/IP networking and you are tasked with making the clients communicate with TCP/IP hosts, you have a good argument for using TCP/IP for your servers as well. Reducing the complexity of your network overall is a noteworthy goal. Networks that support both IPX and TCP/IP are inherently more complex to support than a TCP/IP-only network.

If you are going to commit to using TCP/IP as a network protocol, you should commit to moving completely to TCP/IP and make it your goal to remove IPX clients and services from the network. New network-management products appear almost daily for TCP/IP, but almost never for IPX anymore.

Once IPX is eliminated from the network, you will have also eliminated broadcasts associated with RIP (Routing Information Protocol) and SAP (Service Advertising Protocol), which can only help your WAN performance.

And since many router vendors sell their routers and routing software based on the protocols supported, this can mean big savings for larger organizations that no longer have to purchase IPX/SPX support. One routing software vendor I am aware of charges approximately $500 more per router to include IPX/SPX routing support.

It all comes down to money and time, doesn't it? As good as IPX/SPX was and still is, the world has gone TCP/IP.

CHAPTER <u>15</u>

DHCP and DNS Support

T he administrator of a TCP/IP network faces two challenges:
- Assigning IP addresses
- Managing computer names

As you saw in Chapter 14, IP addressing is no trivial matter; it requires adequate planning, both before and after deploying an IP-based network. If an IP address, subnet mask, or default gateway address is entered incorrectly, the host computer does not communicate properly with the rest of the network. Without an accurate database of computer names and their associated IP addresses, network users cannot communicate with hosts throughout the network.

IP management tasks for a running network fall into two categories.

IP Address Distribution and Management   This involves assigning IP addresses and other IP host address parameters, such as the subnet mask, default gateway, and domain name server addresses. It also involves keeping track of which computer has which IP host addresses and making sure that you do not get duplicates.

Name Resolution   You must assign friendly names (sometimes called *host names* or *aliases*) to computers on your network so that their IP addresses can be easily found. Host name resolution is a critical part of a network's operation.

NetWare 5.1 includes two features that help network managers with IP addressing and name database issues:

- Domain Name System (DNS)
- Dynamic Host Configuration Protocol (DHCP)

What Are DNS and DHCP?

Domain Name System (DNS) and Dynamic Host Configuration Protocol (DHCP) are actually two completely separate technologies, but they complement each other.

An Overview of DNS

The *Domain Name System* (DNS) is a hierarchical name space very similar to the Novell Directory Services (NDS) database that allows a network administrator to register computer names. This name space is represented in one or more DNS servers that hold pieces of the name space database. In a large DNS system, the pieces of the name space can be spread (distributed) across many servers and thus decentralized. The pieces of this distributed database are similar to partitions of the NDS database, yet they are not as automated and controlled as NDS.

Once a host is registered with the DNS, other hosts can query the DNS, using the host's name, and the DNS will return the IP address of the host in question. If you have worked on a TCP/IP network or the Internet, you have used a DNS, and you may not even be aware of it. When you launch your Web browser and type www.novell.com in the address box, your client is using a DNS to look up the IP host address of Novell's Web server. Without DNS, you would have to remember the IP addresses of every IP-based computer you connect to.

NetWare 5.1 integrates the DNS name space data directly in with the NDS database. The administrator can configure a NetWare 5.1 server to be a DNS name server.

 NOTE I discuss DNS more thoroughly in the "Understanding the Domain Name System" section later in this chapter. If you would like more information about DNS, including the standards behind DNS, take a look at RFCs 1034 and 1045.

 NOTE Looking for an RFC? They are all full-text-indexed and searchable on the Web at www.isi.edu/rfc-editor.

Who Should Use DNS?

In a word, everyone. Connecting to other hosts by entering their IP address rather than a friendly name is just too difficult. Whether your network is a private network or you are connected to the Internet, using DNS is critical to providing an easy-to-use network.

An Overview of DHCP

The *Dynamic Host Configuration Protocol* (DHCP) is going to be your best friend if your job is managing a pool of IP addresses. As the name implies, it dynamically assigns IP addresses to hosts that need them. To use DHCP, you must have at least the same number of available IP addresses as you have hosts. When a host boots, it broadcasts a message to the local network segment, requesting an IP address. A DHCP server takes an IP address (and the applicable subnet mask) from a pool of available IP addresses and offers it to the client.

PART

III

Netware, TCP/IP, and the Internet

The administrator can configure the DHCP server to offer not only an IP address and a subnet mask, but also the default gateway address, the IP address of a DNS server, and other options that the client may require. Further, the administrator can specify that certain IP addresses be given only to certain clients and that other clients be denied IP addresses from the pool of available IP addresses.

The DHCP server stores a database of which computers have which IP addresses, thus making the administrator's job a little easier by relieving him or her of the task of tracking this information. Using DHCP greatly reduces the administrative overhead typically associated with managing IP networks. And since all the information is entered in the DHCP server ahead of time, common configuration errors, typographical errors, and duplicate IP addresses are eliminated.

Novell has integrated the management functions of DHCP into a Java-based, snap-in module for the NetWare 5.1 administrator utility called the DNS/DHCP Management Console. Further, the administrator can configure a NetWare 5.1 server to be a DHCP server.

 NOTE If you have worked on TCP/IP- and Unix-based networks, you'll be interested to know that DHCP is an extension of BOOTP (Bootstrap Protocol). I discuss DHCP in depth later in this chapter in the "Understanding Dynamic Host Configuration Protocol" section. BOOTP is defined in RFC 1532. DHCP was originally defined in RFCs 1533, 1534, 1541, and 1542. It has been updated in RFCs 2131 and 2132.

Who Should Use DHCP?

Since DHCP makes configuration much easier and less prone to mistakes, you should strongly consider using it to assign your IP addresses. Organizations that have managed IP addressing by hand for years may be reluctant to turn over their IP address allocation to an automated process. However, if you were part of this manual management process, you appreciate the difficulty involved in managing IP addresses by hand.

If your computers move from one subnet to another, you'll want to consider using DHCP. With the manual method, every time a computer is moved, it has to be reconfigured with a new IP address to reflect its new subnet. DHCP automates this process.

If you have problems keeping track of which hosts have which IP addresses or if you have duplicate IP addresses being assigned, you definitely need to consider using DHCP.

One possible security concern you may hear from the "by hand" folks is that anyone can plug a computer into any segment on your network and get a valid IP address. Do you not have security? How often does someone have the opportunity to get physical access to your network infrastructure so that they could request an IP address? If your answer suggests that this is truly a major security issue, you can configure DHCP to allocate IP addresses only to previously defined hosts, using a DHCP feature called *static allocation of addresses*. Then put locks on the doors and hire security guards.

Understanding the Domain Name System

IP addresses are not exactly easy to remember. Even in the early days of the Internet, some method had to be devised so that we mere mortals would not have to memorize the IP addresses of all the computers we used. It is much easier for us to remember names.

By 1984, the Internet (then it was still called the ARPAnet) had only about 1000 hosts. To make it easier for people to find a specific computer's IP host address, the Stanford Research Institute's Network Information Center (SRI-NIC) in Menlo Park, California, maintained a simple text file called the HOSTS.TXT file. Each line of the file had an IP host address and the host's friendly name, or alias. The file was updated with the newest computers that were connected to the Internet once or twice a week. Other sites on the ARPAnet periodically downloaded the latest version of this file. This was a simple solution to a simple problem.

However, it became apparent that the Internet was growing at a rate that would prohibit the use of the HOSTS.TXT file in the future:

- The file was getting large; the larger it got, the longer it took to search for a specific computer.

- As more and more hosts were added to the Internet, the file had to be updated several times daily.

- SRI-NIC was a single point of failure, since they maintained the only master copy of the file.

These and other problems led the governing body of the ARPAnet to come up with a better solution for providing host-name-to-IP-host-address resolution, or simply hostname resolution—a distributed, hierarchical name space. This name space would have a root and would branch to different parts of the name space in a way similar to NDS. Each branch of the DNS tree is similar to an NDS Organizational Unit (OU).

No single DNS name server would contain the entire database; rather, the database would be distributed to many name servers throughout the Internet to provide better performance as well as fault tolerance. This works in much the same way that replicas of an NDS partition work. Pieces of the NDS database can reside on many NetWare servers.

Components of the Domain Name System

The Domain Name System is broken into three distinct components:

- Resolvers
- Name servers
- Name space

Each component has its specific purpose. DNS is not only a service, but it is also an Application-layer protocol.

Resolvers and Name Servers

The first component of DNS is the *resolver*. Any host on an IP network that may need to look up a domain name is called a resolver. The resolver sends queries to the second component of DNS, the *name server*. The resolver first attempts to contact the name server using the User Datagram Protocol (UDP), but if the network does not reliably deliver the data using UDP, it can resort to using TCP for guaranteed delivery of the packets.

The resolver and the name server are analogous to Directory Assistance (411). The resolver sends a request to the name server to look up a phone number (IP address) based on a name. The name server has access to a database of every phone number in the world. The name server searches through these "phone books" and returns to the client the requested number. In the case of DNS, the phone book that the name server uses is the domain name space itself.

The Domain Name Space

The third component of the Domain Name System is the *domain name space*. This is the actual database of computer names and their IP addresses. To allow for this database to be broken up and placed in many locations, a hierarchical structure was created. At the top of this structure is the *root*. Off the root are *top-level domains*, which set up the initial distribution of this database. Some of the top-level domains are listed in Table 15.1. (There are scores of other top-level domains that I don't mention here.)

TABLE 15.1: SOME TOP-LEVEL DOMAIN NAMES	
Domain	**Domain Function**
.arpa	Special reverse lookup domain
.ca	Canada
.com	Commercial organizations
.edu	Educational organizations
.gb	Great Britain
.gov	U.S. government
.jp	Japan
.mil	U.S. military
.net	Internet service providers
.org	Nonprofit organizations
.us	United States

The responsibility for each of these top-level domains can be delegated to a separate entity, and, more important, the database can be distributed to many name servers. The database is distributed partly by servers called *root servers*. The InterNIC maintains 13 name servers, distributed around the world, that are the authorities for these top-level domains. Specifically, these root servers know how to contact the name servers for each of the top-level domains.

 NOTE   All name servers have a list of the root servers' names and IP addresses.

Each top-level domain has name servers that are the authority for the particular domain. These name servers are also distributed throughout the world and are typically operated by governments. The name servers for the .gov, .com, .edu, .net, .arpa, and .com top-level domains are operated by the InterNIC; the .mil domain is maintained by the U.S. military agency, DISA (Defense Information System Agency).

Registering Your Domain

To become part of the Internet domain name space, you must register your domain name with the authority that controls your particular top-level domain. Once this is done, you will be given a *second-level domain*, such as novell.com.

The agency or authority that is registering your domain name needs to know a few things. For example, when you register a commercial domain within the United States, you must provide the InterNIC with the following information:

- The domain name you are requesting
- Technical, administrative, and billing contact information
- The IP host address of at least two name servers that will be the authority for your domain name

The IP addresses of two name servers are important; one serves as a backup in case the other is unavailable. These name servers will contain your host information. For example, if you register somorita.com (a fictitious company) as a domain name, the .com name server only knows the IP address for a name server that will be the authority for your domain somorita.com. Your name server actually contains all the host data for your domain, such as www.somorita.com, ftp.somorita.com, mail.somorita.com, and so on.

If your organization is already registered as a second-level domain, but you want further divisions of your domain, you need to register with whomever maintains the name server for your organization. This person can create subdomains of your second-level domain, such as pipeline.somorita.com or sunset.somorita.com. The name server that is the authority for these subdomains does not have to be the same name server as for the second-level domain.

Domains versus Zones

A zone of authority is the portion of the domain name space for which a particular name server is responsible. Figure 15.1 illustrates a second-level domain (somorita.com) with a name server that is the authority for that particular zone. There are two additional subdomains, design.somorita.com and testing.somorita.com. Both use a different name server as their authority. Server DUKE's zone of authority is for the somorita.com zone; it also has name server records that point to the subdomains. Server RELL's zone of authority is the design.somorita.com zone.

Breaking your domain across multiple subdomains, name servers, and zones of authority can help improve performance, provide better fault tolerance, and distribute management functions. For example, in Figure 15.1, the person assigned to administer the hosts in the design.somorita.com domain may be different from the person who administers somorita.com. As with NDS, administrative tasks can be distributed across Organizational Units.

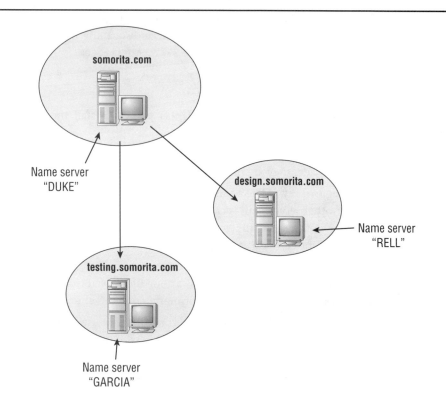

FIGURE 15.1

An example of a second-level domain with two subdomains and name servers in each

somorita.com

Name server "DUKE"

design.somorita.com

Name server "RELL"

testing.somorita.com

Name server "GARCIA"

In a traditional DNS world, the actual domain data, such as the host names and their associated IP addresses, are stored in a text file called a *zone file* or a *zone database file*.

NOTE The Domain Name System has a hierarchical structure just like the Novell Directory Services database. DNS zones and objects are represented in the NDS hierarchy as NDS objects, but their position in the NDS hierarchy has no relation to their true DNS hierarchy. You must use the DNS/DHCP Management Console to see the DNS hierarchy correctly.

Fully Qualified Domain Names

When using the Domain Name System, unfortunately, you cannot just use a name such as www or server1 because hundreds of thousands of people would want to use those names. Instead, each layer of the hierarchical name space has a name. To refer to a host, we call it www.somorita.com rather than just www. This is a *Fully Qualified Domain Name* (FQDN). Hundreds of thousands or millions of computers may be called www, but there will be only one www.somorita.com.

The Types of Name Servers

In a traditional DNS environment (Unix), you can install and configure five types of DNS servers:

Primary   Contains the master copy of a particular zone file. When changes are made, they are made to this server.

Secondary   The administrator can configure a server to copy a zone file from another server. This is called a *zone transfer*. The secondary name server keeps a copy of the zone file in case it is needed or for decentralization of the data. A machine can be a secondary name server for one zone file and a primary name server for another.

Master   Any server that has a zone file copied from it can be considered a master server. This can be a primary name server or a secondary name server.

Caching-Only   Contains no zone files, but users still query it for host names. When it learns a host name and address, it caches this information for a set amount of time.

Forwarder   When configuring a name server, you can define other servers as forwarder servers. When your name server cannot resolve a name, it checks with one of the forwarder servers rather than going through a standard name resolution and checking with the root servers.

Novell's DNS Innovations

Novell's NetWare 5.1 DNS name server can interoperate in a traditional DNS environment as a primary, a secondary, or a caching-only name server, but Novell has implemented an innovative approach to zone files and DNS data. The DNS data are stored in the NDS database and distributed to all servers that have a replica of the partition that contains the DNS data. Any NetWare server can be a DNS server. Since there is only one copy of the DNS zone information, there is no need to designate a primary or secondary name server. Nor does the DNS administrator need to worry about zone transfers, since NDS synchronization takes care of this automatically.

However, if your NetWare DNS system must be a secondary server or a primary server for another system's DNS, such as Unix, you can designate a server to operate in "compatibility" mode.

Understanding DNS/DHCP Services Licensing

NetWare License Service (NLS) manages the NetWare DNS/DHCP services licenses. You can install licenses through the server-based graphical user interface, the server console utility NWCONFIG, or the NetWare Administrator utility. The DNS/DHCP server software includes a server license certificate and an address license certificate for use with DHCP.

Each IP address that DHCP manages must have a license. You can determine the number of DHCP licenses you need by counting all the addresses that are managed by DHCP subnet address ranges and the statically configured IP addresses that the server assigns.

Name Server Queries

Earlier, I mentioned that no single name server in DNS contains a copy of the entire domain name space database. Two types of DNS name resolution make this possible:

Recursive   Resolvers (clients) do recursive queries. When doing a recursive query, the resolver says to the name server, "Give me the IP address of this host name. If you don't know the answer, go find out. Don't delegate the task to someone else."

Iterative   Name servers typically do iterative queries. As Figure 15.2 shows, if the name server cannot answer the query from its own zone databases or cache, it consults with a root server, which refers the query to a top-level server, which in turn refers it to a second-level domain server. Finally, the name server reaches an authority for the zone in question. That authoritative server returns the answer to the originating name server, and that server returns the answer to the resolver.

Essentially, all queries are done on the basis of referrals. When the client in Figure 15.2 queries the name server for www.somorita.com in step 1, the client's name server goes out to the root in step 2 and asks for a name server to handle queries about the .com domain. In step 3, the root name server responds with a referral to a .com domain name server, and the client's name server contacts that .com server in step 4, getting the response in step 5. In step 6, the client's name server contacts somorita.com's name server and asks for the IP address of www.somorita.com. The name server responds in step 7, and the client's name server responds to the client in step 8 with an IP address for the requested host.

PART

III

Netware, TCP/IP,
and the Internet

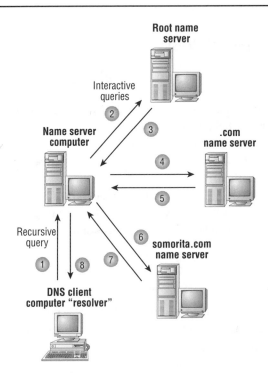

 NOTE Essentially, DNS operates on the basis of referrals. The client asks for a name to be resolved. If the client's name server does not know the answer, it checks with a series of other servers. The client thinks that its name server is a genius and knows everything, but in actuality, the client's name server just knows the right places to look.

When the client server gets an answer from the name server at Somorita, it puts that information in its own *cache*. The name server at Somorita determines how long that entry can remain in the cache. You don't want to keep entries in the cache too long because the IP address of the host in question could change. The administrator of the server controls how long you can keep an entry in the cache by setting a *time to live* (TTL) for entries on the Somorita name server. When an entry's TTL expires, a name server that holds that entry in the cache must discard it. If that particular entry is requested again, the name server must once again resolve the name.

Inverse Queries/Reverse Lookups

A special-purpose domain has been set aside in the DNS name space called the `in-addr`
`.arpa` zone. This zone is used for *inverse queries*, which allow a client to look up a
Fully Qualified Domain Name (FQDN) based on a known IP address. It is common
for mail servers to deny access to IP addresses that do not have a registered domain
name. Some application servers, such as FTP servers, will not allow a client to log in
unless it has a registered FQDN, and the application server can do an inverse query
using the client's IP address.

Though this looks like smoke and mirrors, it is really simple. The secret is that each
IP network address is registered with the InterNIC, as are domain names. Typically,
the ISP that supplies your IP addresses will either take care of this or will assist you in
creating the proper zones.

Remember, domain names get more specific when reading from right to left, and
IP addresses get more specific when reading from left to right. For this reason, the
domain names in a *reverse query file* are reversed. For example, if you have IP address
`207.188.53.0` for your network, your inverse query zone will be `53.188.207.in-`
`addr.arpa`. Notice that the IP address is reversed and that `in-addr.arpa` is added to
the right side of the address.

When you create zones in the NetWare 5.1 DNS/DHCP Management Console, you
must remember that you also have to create reverse lookup zones for any IP addresses
you are managing.

DNS Resource Records

A *resource record* (RR) is an entry in a zone file that identifies a certain attribute about
a host, a domain, or an IP address. There are many types of resource records, but I'll
limit the discussion here to the major types:

A   An address, which is also called a *host* record. This record identifies the IP
address for a specific host name.

CNAME   The canonical name, also known as an *alias*, allows you to associate
several names with a single host.

PTR   Used in reverse lookup files and servers as a *pointer* to the name of a host
based on its IP address. Its format is the IP host address in reverse, and it also
contains the host name associated with that IP address.

MX   The Mail Exchanger record lets mail servers know which servers in your
domain will accept or transfer mail. If you are going to exchange SMTP mail,
you must have an MX record.

SOA   The Start of Authority record is usually the first line (and usually spills over onto several lines) of a zone database file. It identifies the name server name and the name server contact and includes information about caching and zone transfers. This record is required.

NS   The name server record lists name servers that service this particular zone file. This list contains a list of all secondary servers that transfer a copy of this zone file.

The NetWare 5.1 DNS/DHCP Management Console creates the NS and SOA records for you automatically. You won't always have this luxury on other systems.

Traditional DNS Files

A traditional DNS runs on Unix systems. The zone data are placed in text files, and these files are usually located in the /ETC directory. You will find four types of files on a Unix system that is running a name server:

Zone database   Also called just *zone files*, these files contain the host information as well as other data, such as name servers and mail exchanges for a specific domain.

Reverse lookup   To handle inverse queries successfully, you will need a reverse lookup file for each IP network address whose hosts you manage. These files contain the PTR records that provide IP-address-to-host-name lookups.

Cache   Contains a listing of the names and the IP addresses of the root servers. This file is not normally updated often.

Boot   Found on BIND (Berkeley Internet Named Daemon) DNS servers, this file tells the name server software where to find zone database files, reverse lookup files, and the cache file.

This has been a quick tour through the Domain Name System, but it should get you started.

 NOTE   If your job responsibilities require that you manage a large DNS system or that you integrate with Unix systems, you'll need a more thorough understanding of DNS. A truly great DNS reference is *"DNS and BIND" Help for Unix System Administrators* by Paul Albitz and Cricket Liu, published by O'Reilly and Associates.

How Does DNS Differ from NIS?

DNS provides IP addresses for host names. *NIS* (Network Information Services) is another distributed database that provides common information for network use, such as user and group information. Originally developed by Sun, this service was first called "yellow pages," but it turns out that British Telecom owns the rights to that name. Some longtime NIS users still refer to it as "yp."

Similar to NDS, NIS uses the database of users and groups to validate access to network resources, especially Sun's NFS (Network File System). The tables of information are called *NIS maps*, which are controlled by the master NIS server.

The NIS domain is controlled by this NIS server. NIS domains consist of local network connections only and generally cover a single network. The domain names are flat, rather than hierarchical as in DNS, and the rules for these names are not as strict. Each domain must have a unique name. NIS and DNS domains may overlap, but it's not necessary.

In an NIS domain, there is only one master server. There are also *replica servers* (just as in NDS) for fault tolerance, but the databases are all read-only. Called *slaves* in NIS, these subordinate systems periodically query the master server for updates.

IntranetWare 4.11, NetWare 5.0, and NetWare 5.1 all support NIS so that NetWare can interoperate in an NFS environment. Novell has a product called NFS Server that is sold separately. To enable NIS support in NetWare 5.1, use the server console utility UNICON.NLM. For more information, see the Novell documentation.

Understanding the Dynamic Host Configuration Protocol

One of the major annoyances associated with an IP network is managing the IP host addresses for all the clients on the network. If client computers never moved from one subnet to another and hard drives were not replaced, managing IP addresses would be simpler. Managing client computers is further complicated because other IP parameters, such as the IP address of the default gateway and the domain name server, occasionally change.

In a traditional IP network, an administrator or a technician must visit each computer and manually make these changes. Once the changes are made, they must be tracked. You must have a way to track which computer has which IP address and where that computer is located. You must do this to ensure that you never allocate the same IP address twice and to ensure that you don't end up with IP addresses that never get used.

BOOTP (Bootstrap Protocol)

BOOTP (Bootstrap Protocol) was developed so that diskless workstations could start up and automatically get an IP address. Since these workstations are diskless, they also need an operating system when they start up. With BOOTP, a diskless workstation could read an image file of the appropriate operating system. The administrator assigned a specific IP address and a specific boot file to the client.

This is nothing new to Novell gurus who have worked with diskless workstations for years. BOOTP is merely the standard that the Unix community follows. BOOTP is defined in RFC 1532.

 NOTE Do you know why we "boot" a computer? Sometimes you may feel like kicking one, but that is not the reason. Old-timers called starting up a computer "bootstrapping" because of the complexity of starting some older minicomputers and mainframes. It was like pulling the computer up by its bootstraps. Over the years, it got shortened to just "booting."

DHCP Basics

Dynamic Host Configuration Protocol (DHCP) is an extension of BOOTP that was designed to allow centralization and management of a pool of available IP addresses. When a client requests an IP address, the DHCP server checks to see if an IP host address is available for that client. If so, the server sends the client an IP host address, a subnet mask, and possibly other information, such as the IP address of the client's router and domain name server. The server can be configured to give the IP address to the client indefinitely or for a specific period of time called the *lease period*.

The advantages of DHCP include the following:

- The management of available IP addresses is centralized.

- The DHCP server automatically tracks which clients have which IP addresses.

- Configuration errors are less likely.

- If a client moves to another subnet, it automatically gets an address on the new subnet.

- The likelihood of assigning duplicate IP addresses is eliminated.

DHCP works best in an environment in which you have at least as many available IP host addresses as you have clients that require IP addresses. To force DHCP to reuse IP addresses if they are not currently in use, you can configure incredibly short lease periods (20 minutes, for example). If a computer using an IP address is shut down, that IP address can be used by another client within 20 minutes.

Those suffering from a chronic shortage of IP addresses should check the possibility of using a private internal network-addressing scheme. Using 10.0.0.0, an address illegal on the Internet, internally gives you plenty of addresses (millions and millions, actually). Then use Network Address Translation (NAT) to convert the address of outgoing packets to your legal, but too small, network address.

 WARNING If TCP/IP is your only network protocol and a client cannot lease an IP address, it will *not* be able to communicate with the network. Not a good thing.

How DHCP Works

DHCP uses the *UDP* (User Datagram Protocol) as a network transport, and it uses UDP ports 67 and 68, which BOOTP also uses. To request an address for the first time, the client and the server send back and forth a series of four broadcasts:

DHCP Discover   The client broadcasts to the network an IP lease request.

DHCP Offer   All DHCP servers that saw the DHCP Discover broadcast extend an IP lease offer via another broadcast.

DHCP Request   The client accepts the first IP lease offer it receives and broadcasts back an IP lease selection. Feeling slightly rejected, the other DHCP servers that proposed an IP address withdraw their offer.

DHCP Ack   When the server whose offer was accepted receives the DHCP Request broadcast, it sends the client an IP lease acknowledgment that lets the client know it can have the IP address. The DHCP Ack packet may also contain options such as default gateway and name server addresses. The server records the IP address as being leased to that client.

If a DHCP server does not respond to the initial DHCP Discover broadcast frame, the client rebroadcasts the DHCP Discover three more times at approximately 9, 13, and 16 seconds. If no server responds after these four attempts, the client rebroadcasts DHCP Discover frames every five minutes.

Once a client has a lease for an IP address, it keeps that address until the end of the lease period. By default, at 50 percent of the way through the lease, the DHCP client contacts the DHCP server using a directed frame and asks to renew the lease. If the server does not respond, the client tries again at 87.5 percent of the way through the lease.

The release process takes two frames and consists of the following:

DHCP Request   In this particular DHCP frame, the client informs the server that it wants to renew its lease.

DHCP Ack   If the client is allowed to keep the lease, the server responds and allows the client to renew its lease. The lease period starts back over at the full lease length at this time. Any updated options, such as a new router or name server address, are also refreshed at this time.

If for some reason the server cannot renew the lease on the address because it is no longer valid, the DHCP server issues a DHCPNACK (negative acknowledgment) message. This causes the client to issue a DHCP Discover and to attempt to lease a new address.

DHCP clients keep their IP addresses even when they are shut down. However, when a DHCP client restarts, it does renew its lease during reboot. If the DHCP server is not available when the client reboots, it keeps its existing address as long as the lease still has time left on it.

DHCP supports three methods of allocating IP host addresses:

Dynamic DHCP   DHCP clients are assigned IP addresses from a pool, or subnet address range, of available addresses.

Dynamic BOOTP   BOOTP clients are assigned IP addresses from a pool of available addresses, and the DHCP server can provide a boot file with which the client can boot. This is in contrast to traditional BOOTP servers that assign IP addresses statically (each client is given a specific IP address).

Static allocation   DHCP or BOOTP clients are given a specific IP address based on their MAC address. This is sometimes called a reservation and should not be confused with manually configuring each client one machine at a time.

Planning a DHCP Installation

Before deploying DHCP, you need to gather some information about your network. Here is a sampling of questions that you need to answer:

• What are the IP network addresses for each subnet?

• How many hosts are on each subnet?

- Where are the NetWare 5.1 servers and what are their IP addresses?
- What are the IP addresses for routers and the DNS name servers?
- What are the IP addresses, MAC addresses, and names of any computers that must have the same IP host address all the time?
- Should any hosts be denied IP addresses?
- Do you have sufficient IP host addresses for all clients?
- Will each segment have its own DHCP server?

This information affects the scopes of addresses, the scope options, and the number of servers that you deploy. Additional considerations include whether DHCP servers exist on the opposite side of routers from the clients they serve and whether any redundancy is required.

DHCP Broadcasts and Routers

If you put your DHCP server on one segment and the clients that it serves on another segment, how do the DHCP client broadcasts reach the DHCP server? Since DHCP lease requests occur via broadcasts and routers do not forward broadcasts, network designers face a problem, which also existed for the designers of the original BOOTP protocol.

This problem is solved by using a special software program that you can find on most routers called a *BOOTP relay agent* (or sometimes called a *forwarder*). The BOOTP relay agent is configured with the IP address of nearby DHCP servers. It listens for DHCP broadcasts and forwards them to the DHCP on behalf of the client. From the perspective of the DHCP client, the relay agent looks like a DHCP server.

If you are using your NetWare server for IP routing, you may need to use BOOTP relay on your server. NetWare 5.1 supports DHCP relay as an NLM (NetWare Loadable Module). To enable BOOTP relay on your NetWare server, use the BOOTPFWD.NLM. It has three startup options:

SERVER= Specifies the IP address of the nearest DHCP server.

LOG= Specifies whether the BOOTPFWD.NLM creates a log to the console or a file.

FILE= Specifies a log file name.

Here is an example statement that loads BOOTP relay support on your NetWare 5.1 server:

```
LOAD BOOTPFWD SERVER=204.187.99.2 LOG=YES FILE=SYS:ETC\BOOTPFWD.LOG
```

If your NetWare 5.1 server is going to support BOOTP relay, this statement should be included in your server's AUTOEXEC.NCF file after the protocol BIND and LOAD statements.

WARNING Do not load `BOOTPFWD.NLM` and the DHCP server on the same NetWare server. Both applications require UDP port 67. Only one application at a time can occupy that port.

How Many DHCP Servers Are Required?

An easy question to ask, but not an easy one to answer. No hard and fast rule says that you must have a DHCP server for *x* number of clients. You should ensure that DHCP servers are near the client computers they serve. Since DHCP is administered centrally through the NDS database, administration is not a problem. Any NetWare 5.1 server can run the DHCP server NLM, but you must assign it a subnet address range; only one server can service a specific subnet address range.

Though you could configure a single DHCP server for thousands of users through-out your corporate intranet, this would probably generate a lot of unnecessary net-work traffic, and IP address distribution would have a single point of failure. On the other hand, you could configure a DHCP server for every little 10-node segment on your LAN. Though managing DHCP is easy, this is probably taking distribution of the DHCP servers to the other extreme.

An ideal distribution is a single DHCP server for each larger geographic area, such as a regional office. When I have more than about 300 users per office, I designate a second server in that office as a DHCP server to provide some backup and redundancy.

 TIP Each DHCP server will have to read and write from the NDS schema whenever addresses are leased or leases are renewed. To maximize performance, these servers should have a Read/Write replica of the partition of the NDS database on which the Sub-net Address Range object is created.

Plan for Some Redundancy

For fault-tolerance purposes, you may want to assign addresses for a specific subnet to two different servers. A good rule of thumb is to assign 75 percent of the available addresses to the closest DHCP server and to assign the remaining 25 percent to the second-closest server. The scopes should not overlap; if they do, you risk assigning duplicate IP addresses.

In Figure 15.3, we have two DHCP servers. SERVER1 is on subnet one, and SERVER2 is on subnet two. The IP network address for subnet one is 198.55.201.0, so we assign the DHCP server on subnet one the range of 198.55.201.10 through 198.55.201.193. We assign the subnet address range 198.55.201.194 through 198.55.201.254 to the DHCP server on subnet two. The DHCP server on subnet two can assign IP addresses for subnet one if the DHCP server on subnet one is not available. Notice that I started the first subnet address range with address .10, rather than address .1; this is so that I can manually assign IP host addresses for my router and servers.

FIGURE 15.3

Two segments with a router and two servers, using the 75/25 rule

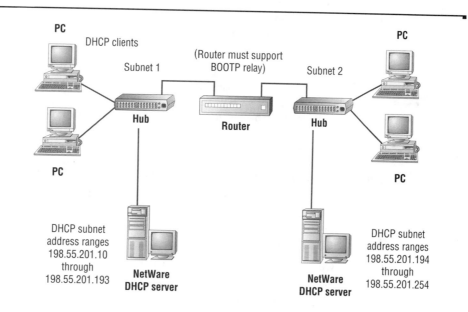

Lease Considerations

When planning scope options, one of your choices is the lease period. The lease period controls how long a client can keep a lease before it has to contact the server and extend the lease. The default lease period is three days. The client contacts the server halfway through the lease in order to renew the lease. If the DHCP server is not available at halfway through the lease, the client tries again at seven-eighths ($7/8$ or 87.5 percent) of the way through the lease.

You can use only the maximum number of available IP addresses. For example, if you have 254 available IP host addresses and 500 computers that require IP addresses, only 254 hosts can be using IP addresses at a single time. Make absolutely sure that you have enough IP addresses for all computers that will be simultaneously active on the network.

If your organization has a night shift and a day shift and each person has his or her own computer, you could find yourself with a shortage of IP addresses. In such a case, set short lease periods. Then, when a client is not active, the server makes its IP address available again at the end of the lease.

Novell recommends a lease period of 15 minutes in an environment that is extremely low on IP addresses. However, if the DHCP server is down for more than 15 minutes, clients will give up their IP addresses. In addition, 15-minute lease periods result in additional traffic since the client will be issuing a request to keep the address every seven and a half minutes (50 percent of the way through the lease).

 TIP Your life will be much simpler if you have enough IP addresses for every computer. Inevitably, if you do not have enough IP addresses for everyone, you are going to have computers that will not be able to connect to the network because they cannot lease an IP address.

If you have sufficient IP addresses, consider longer lease periods. A lease period of 10 days ensures that even if the DHCP server becomes unavailable for several days, clients will still have IP addresses.

DHCP Scope Options

When DHCP servers lease an IP address to a client, DHCP automatically provides a subnet mask. The administrator can also specify additional client options, providing the client supports them. Some of the more useful options include the following:

Number	Name	Description
3	Router	Sets the client's default gateway (router) IP address
6	Domain Name Server	Sets the IP address for the client's DNS name server
15	Domain Name	Sets the client's DNS domain name
44	NetBIOS over TCP/IP Name Server	Used typically in a Microsoft environment to look up NetBIOS computer names
46	NetBIOS over TCP/IP Node Type	Used typically in a Microsoft environment to set the order in which a client attempts to resolve a NetBIOS name

Number	Name	Description
62	NWIP Domain Name	Used only by NetWare/IP to set the NWIP domain name
63	NWIP Options	Used only by NetWare/IP to set options such as the NWIP primary DSS, preferred DSS, and nearest servers
85	NDS Server	Sets the default server IP address for the NetWare client
86	NDS Tree	Sets the default NDS tree name for the NetWare client
87	NDS Context	Sets the default NDS context for the NetWare client

 NOTE A complete list of all DHCP options is available in the NetWare 5.1 documentation. You can also view these with the DNS/DHCP Management Console by clicking the Global Preferences button.

There are dozens of other DHCP options, though most of them are not used by NetWare clients. For a complete list of DHCP options, see the NetWare 5.1 documentation or RFC 2132. Developers can add their own options, as Novell has done with options 62, 63, 85, 86, and 87. By taking advantage of these options, you can avoid additional visits to configure each client manually.

Installing DNS and DHCP Support

NetWare 5.1 takes a rather revolutionary step forward by incorporating DHCP and DNS database information in the NDS database. This information is managed by a Java-based utility that can run as a stand-alone or as a snap-in to the NetWare Administrator utility; this is the DNS/DHCP Management Console. Traditionally, DNS information is stored in text files (called *zone files*). Previous versions of NetWare DNS support used Btrieve database files, but NetWare 5.1 incorporates the zone information directly into the NDS database where it is distributed to all NetWare servers that contain a replica of an NDS partition. This is accomplished by extending the NDS schema. Even though the database is incorporated into the NDS, the NetWare 5.1

name server can maintain backward compatibility with other DNS systems, such as Unix DNS servers.

DHCP information is typically stored on a single DHCP server in a local database. NetWare 5.1 stores the DHCP data, such as available IP addresses and which computers have which IP addresses, in the NDS database. Like all other data in the NDS database, these data are distributed throughout servers that contain a replica of the NDS database.

Novell BorderManager includes DNS and DHCP servers; these products use a Btrieve database to store DNS and DHCP information rather than NDS. The NetWare 5.1 DNS and DHCP servers evolved from the BorderManager DNS and DHCP servers.

 NOTE DHCP and DNS are new technologies to many NetWare administrators. Before inflicting these technologies on users, create a lab and test for the results you expect.

Requirements

To install the DNS/DHCP software, the server should be configured (and tested) to use TCP/IP (see Chapter 14) and should have 128MB of RAM, though if you are planning to use the server-based graphical user interface, you should plan to have even more RAM. The person who installs the software should have Admin equivalence.

Understanding the NDS Extensions for DNS and DHCP

During installation, the NDS schema is modified to support DNS and DHCP object types. The installation process also adds three new NDS objects to the NDS database: the RootServerInfo Zone, Group, and Locator objects. You should place these objects in a container that is accessible from and replicated to all servers on the network that will use DNS and DHCP services. You can create these objects in either an Organization object or an Organizational Unit. Only one RootServerInfo Zone, Group, and Locator object will exist in an NDS tree.

The *RootServerInfo Zone* object contains the names and IP addresses of all the root servers on the Internet. Your DNS servers will refer to these name servers if they cannot answer a name query. You should never need to edit the root server information; the root server names and IP addresses do not change.

The *Group* object is a standard NDS group object. DNS and DHCP servers get their rights to other DNS/DHCP data within the tree through the group object. The *Locator* object is a custom object that contains the DNS and DHCP default options for all servers, DHCP and DNS server lists, zone names, and subnet information.

One approach is to create an Organizational Unit that will contain all DNS and DHCP objects, such as the Group and Locator objects, but also subnets, zones, and resource records.

Plan to locate your DNS and DHCP servers so that they adequately serve the user community they were designed to support. The DNS and DHCP servers should be geographically close to the clients and users they serve. Ensure that you have an NDS replication strategy in place so that the container that holds the DNS and DHCP objects is replicated to more than one server. This is especially important if you have a wide area network, since a WAN failure could isolate part of your network; replicating the DNS and DHCP information is important.

Place replicas of DNS and DHCP information so that the servers are adequately load balanced. As you can see in Figure 15.4, if you have NetWare 5.1 servers on a network segment, place DNS Name Services and DHCP Services close to the clients they serve. This can help reduce WAN traffic and improve response time to clients.

FIGURE 15.4

DNS and DHCP servers located throughout a WAN

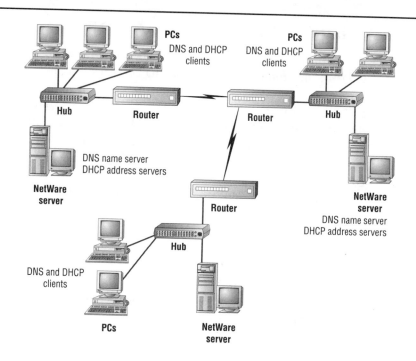

DNS and DHCP Use NDS to Store Objects

DNS and DHCP use the NetWare Directory Services database to store objects relating information such as:

- DNS server information
- DNS zones
- DNS resource records
- DCHP server information
- DHCP scopes and scope address records
- DHCP restrictions and other addressing information

 NOTE Even though the DNS and DHCP objects are stored and are visible in the NDS hierarchy, they can be modified only through the DNS/DHCP Management Console.

Installing DNS/DHCP Support

During the NetWare 5.1 server installation, one of the options that the graphical user interface will prompt you for is installing DNS/DHCP support. The files are installed automatically, even if you do not check this option. This option merely extends the NDS schema to support DNS and DHCP. You can skip installing DNS/DHCP support during the server installation and install it later using the DNIPINST server utility. If you choose to install DNS/DHCP support when the server is installed, you will be prompted for the Locator object, Group object, and RootServerInfo Zone object contexts.

The procedure to enable the NDS schema needs to be done only once per NetWare Directory Services tree. As mentioned earlier, before running the installation utility, you may want to create an Organizational Unit to hold all DNS/DHCP information. In my example, I create a container called OU=DNS-DHCP.O=SOMORITA.

If you did not choose to install DNS/DHCP support during the server installation, you can install DNS/DHCP support for the NDS schema by typing **LOAD DNIPINST** at the NetWare server console prompt. When asked to log in to NDS, provide an administrator-level user ID and password.

NOTE Be sure that the container you specify exists. If it does not exist, you will get an error, but the utility will think it has installed the Global and Locator objects. You can remove the schema extensions and start over, as I have had to do on a few occasions. At the server console prompt, type **LOAD DNIPINST –R** to remove the schema extensions.

The next screen you will see is the NDS Context Query Form, which prompts you to enter an NDS directory context in which to install the RootServerInfo Zone, Group, and Locator objects.

In our example, enter **OU=DNS-DHCP.O=SOMORITA** for the RootServerInfo Zone object, the Group object, and the Locator object and press Enter. You will receive a message stating that the NDS schema extensions have been added successfully.

 NOTE The Organizational Unit OU=DNS-DHCP must exist when you start this installation.

When completed, the NDS schema will have been extended to include these three new objects in the NDS Organizational Unit that you specified. In my example, these are in the OU=DNS-DHCP.O=SOMORITA container.

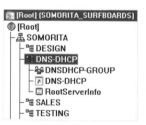

Once you have extended the NDS schema, use the NWADMIN utility to give users who need DNS/DHCP management privileges Read/Write rights to this object.

And, finally, ensure that the partition that holds the DNS/DHCP objects is replicated to all parts of the network that will use DNS and DHCP services.

PART

III

Netware, TCP/IP,
and the Internet

Installing and Using the DHCP and DNS Administrator

The new Java-based DNS/DHCP Management Console must be installed on any workstation that will perform DNS/DHCP administration. This utility runs under Windows 95/98/NT/2000. To install it, follow these steps:

1. From the `SYS:PUBLIC\DNSDHCP` installation subdirectory, run SETUP to copy the files to your local hard disk and place a shortcut on your desktop.

2. When asked if you want to install the snap-in for the NetWare Administrator, enter the location of your NWADMIN program.

3. When installation is complete, reboot the computer.

Using the DNS/DHCP Management Console

The DNS/DHCP Management Console has two functions:

- Managing DNS data
- Managing DHCP data

As you can see in Figure 15.5, this utility has two tabs, one for managing DNS data, or *DNS Service*, and one for managing DHCP data, or *DHCP Service*. Within each tab are three panes. The left pane is for managed objects, the right pane is for the properties of that object, and the bottom pane lists the DHCP or DNS servers that have been configured.

FIGURE 15.5

The DNS/DHCP Management Console

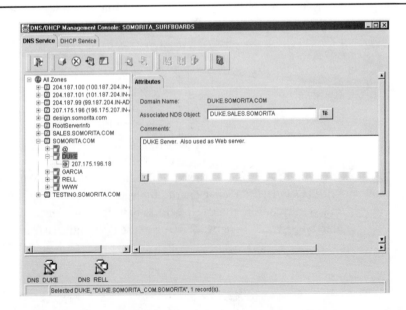

You can run the DNS/DHCP Management Console from within NetWare Administrator or as a stand-alone. To launch this program, from the NWADMIN utility, choose Tools ➤ DNS/DHCP Management Console, or run C:\PROGRAM FILES \NOVELL\DNSDHCP\ DNSDHCP.EXE. To run the program, you must be logged in to the NDS tree that you want to manage. This utility can manage only a single NDS tree at a time.

The DNS/DHCP Management Console Toolbar

This utility has no drop-down menus, only buttons on the toolbar found across the top of each tab. Each button has "fly-by help," or "rollover help." If you point the mouse at a button and hold for about a second, a small box displays text describing the button.

DNS Service

The buttons are slightly different for the DNS Service and DHCP Service tabs. Figure 15.6 shows the DNS Service toolbar, and Table 15.2 describes its functions. Not all functions on the toolbar are enabled at all times; when a button is grayed out, it is not available.

FIGURE 15.6

The DNS/DHCP Management Console DNS Service toolbar

TABLE 15.2: THE DNS SERVICE TOOLBAR BUTTONS AND THEIR FUNCTIONS

Button	Function
Exit	Exits the application
Create	Creates objects
Delete	Deletes objects
Save Data To NDS	Saves current changes
Tree Refresh	Refreshes current screen
Import DNS Database	Imports text-based zone files
Export DNS Database	Exports zone to a text file
View Events/Alerts	Displays name server alerts and events
View Audit Trail Log	Displays name server audit trail
Start/Stop Service	Stops or starts the highlighted DNS server
Help	Displays online help

PART

III

Netware, TCP/IP, and the Internet

The bottom pane of the DNS Service tab contains the DNS name servers. The servers listed identify NetWare 5.1 servers in your organization that will function as name servers. You can create the server object in any context. If there are already DNS zones created, you can specify which zones handled by this server will enter forwarding server lists.

In the left pane of the DNS Service tab, you will find the following object types:

Zone Identifies a specific domain, such as `somorita.com`. The zone contains resource records, such as host records and aliases. When you are creating a zone, don't forget that you create a reverse lookup zone (`in-addr.arpa` zone) to accompany any IP addresses you are managing. The Authoritative DNS Servers list contains the names of NetWare DNS servers that will resolve queries for this zone. The Dynamic DNS Server is the server that is used for backward compatibility with other DNS name servers and is used for tracking dynamically registered host names.

Resource Record Can be created within a Zone object. Each resource record contains a piece of information about something within a zone—host, mail server, or alias. For a complete list of supported zones, see the NetWare 5.1 documentation.

To create new DNS objects, click the Create button. What you can create depends on what is selected in the left pane:

- If you selected All Zones, you can create DNS servers and zones.
- If you selected Zone, you can create resource records or DNS servers.

DHCP Service

You use the DHCP Service tab to manage subnets and subnet address ranges. Figure 15.7 shows the DHCP Service toolbar, and Table 15.3 describes its functions.

The DNS/DHCP Management Console DHCP Service toolbar

TABLE 15.3: THE DHCP SERVICE TOOLBAR BUTTONS AND THEIR FUNCTIONS	
Button	**Function**
Exit	Exits the application
Create	Creates objects
Delete	Deletes objects
Save Data To NDS	Saves current changes
Tree Refresh	Refreshes the data on screen
Global Preferences	Sets DHCP global options
Import DHCP Database	Imports data from previous Novell DHCP data files
Export DHCP Database	Exports data to other Novell DHCP formats
View Events/Alerts	Displays DHCP alerts
View Audit Trail Log	Displays DHCP audit trail
Start/Stop Services	Stops or starts the highlighted DHCP server
Help	Displays online help

You'll find the following objects in the left pane of the DHCP Service tab:

Subnet   Identifies a range of available IP addresses. Each subnet must contain its own unique name.

Subnet Address Range   Found under Subnet Objects and identifies ranges of available IP addresses.

IP Address   Found only under the Subnet Object, this object identifies a specific IP host address that should be leased to a specific computer only (by its MAC address).

Subnet Pool   Optional, but can be used to logically group a number of subnets. Subnet pools are most commonly used when several subnet numbers are assigned to a single physical subnet, such as in an environment that is using a *virtual LAN* (VLAN).

At the bottom of the DHCP Service tab, you will find a list of DHCP servers. This list identifies NetWare 5.1 servers that can act as DHCP servers.

PART

III

Netware, TCP/IP,
and the Internet

To create new DHCP objects, click the Create button. What you can create depends on what you select in the left pane:

- If you select Our Network, you can create subnets, subnet pools, and DHCP servers.
- If you select Subnet, you can create subnet address ranges, IP addresses, and DHCP servers.
- If you select Subnet Address Range, you can create a DHCP server.
- If you select Free Addresses, you can create IP addresses and subnet address ranges.

Setting Up and Managing a NetWare 5.1 DNS

Novell's NetWare 5.1 DNS is a shift from a traditional Unix DNS. There is no longer the concept of a primary name server and secondary name servers. The DNS data (zone files) are now stored in the Novell Directory Services (NDS) database. This data is replicated to all servers that have a replica of the NDS partition that contains the DNS data. However, the NetWare DNS name server can interoperate with traditional name servers such as those running on Unix.

To best explain how to set up a DNS server, zones, and resource records, let's take our fictitious company and build it a Domain Name System based on NetWare 5.1.

Sample Company Requirements

Somorita Surfboards has moved to NetWare 5.1 and TCP/IP, and plans to connect its private network to the Internet. The private network consists of three subnets in two locations, Haleiwa and Pipeline. One requirement is a Web server for the entire company. In addition, each department should be able to build its own internal Web server, and anyone on the Internet should be able to connect to these servers.

The company has two locations and three NetWare 5.1 servers, one for each department—Sales, Testing, and Design. The company's ISP has provided Somorita with three full Class C network addresses and a small chunk of a Class C network address for the router network between the two locations.

Figure 15.8 illustrates the layout of Somorita's network, and Table 15.4 shows the network number assignments.

FIGURE 15.8

The Somorita
Surfboards network

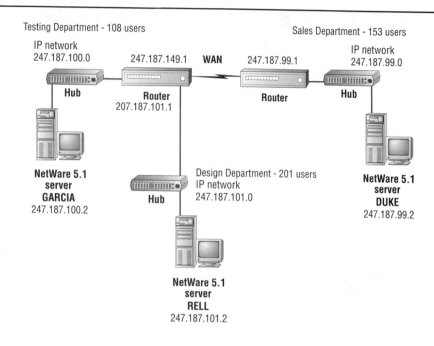

TABLE 15.4: NETWORK NUMBER ASSIGNMENTS FOR EACH DEPARTMENT			
Department/Subnet	**Location**	**Network Number**	**NetWare Server Name**
Sales	Haleiwa	204.187.99.0	DUKE
Testing	Pipeline	204.187.100.0	GARCIA
Design	Pipeline	204.187.101.0	RELL

The heads of departments and the president of the company have told you that they want to be able to access the Web servers for the company using the names in Table 15.5.

TABLE 15.5: FULLY QUALIFIED DOMAIN NAMES FOR WEB SERVERS

Department	Web Server URL
Company Wide	www.somorita.com
Sales	www.sales.somorita.com
Testing	www.testing.somorita.com
Design	www.design.somorita.com

The company is on a limited budget. You can't buy additional hardware, so the NetWare 5.1 servers that are functioning as file and print servers for each department are going to have to function also as Web servers.

Table 15.6 lists the IP host addresses for each of our NetWare 5.1 servers.

TABLE 15.6: NETWARE 5.1 SERVER IP ADDRESSES

Server Name	IP Address	Server Location
DUKE	207.187.99.2	Haleiwa
GARCIA	207.187.100.2	Pipeline
RELL	207.187.101.2	Pipeline

Now that we have our requirements, let's get busy setting up our servers.

Registering Your Domain

One of your first tasks is to contact one of the licensed registrar companies to register your domain name. For our fictitious company, we are going to request somorita.com. Here is the information we must have when we connect to the registration Web site (www.nsi.com or www.register.com, for example) to register our domain:

- Domain name requested
- E-mail address
- Organization name and mailing address
- Administrative, technical, and billing contact information
- Primary server host name (for example, duke.somorita.com)

- Primary server IP address (for example, 207.187.99.2)
- Secondary server host name (for example, rell.somorita.com)
- Secondary server IP address (for example, 207.187.101.2)

Notice that I assigned one of the Somorita servers to be the primary name server and one of them to be the secondary. It does not matter which I choose, since all three of my servers will be running naming services.

 TIP When designating primary and secondary servers, plan to locate secondary servers on a separate network from the primary server. In an environment that is connected to the Internet, I locate my primary server on my network. I ask my Internet service provider (ISP) to maintain a secondary server for me. Their name server will then do a zone transfer from my primary server periodically so that it has the latest information for my domain. This does not require additional hardware at the ISP's location; they can use one of their existing DNS servers to host a secondary zone for me. However, don't be surprised if they expect a small fee for their trouble.

Within a few days, your domain name will be functional, and you will receive a bill from the registrar for $70 (usually), which covers the first two years. Subsequent renewals are $35, and I recommend paying these bills on time; otherwise, your domain name might be turned off and be up for grabs before you find the buried invoice.

 NOTE In the past, the InterNIC charged $100 for name registrations and $50 for renewals, but this changed April 1, 1998. New registration companies, particularly those offering hosting services as well, often discount the name registration fee.

Creating a DNS Server

IN A HURRY

15.1 Create a DNS Name Server

1. Highlight the All Zones object in the left pane of the DNS/DHCP Management Console.
2. Click the Create button, choose DNS Server, and click OK.

Continued

3. Select the NetWare server that will host this name server from the NDS tree.

4. Enter this server's host name and a domain name.

5. Click the Create button.

Although you can create a DNS zone prior to creating a DNS server, I highly recommend creating the DNS Server object first. If you create the DNS Server object first, the zones will be easier to create because you will have to provide less information about each zone object.

You have decided to set up each server in your organization as a name server. To designate NetWare 5.1 servers as valid name servers, you use the DNS/DHCP Management Console. If your organization has more than one NDS tree, be sure that you are logged in to the correct tree.

 NOTE You need to run DNIPINST only once per NDS tree.

You must now decide where in the NDS tree you will create the DNS Server objects. For our example, we will put the DNS server objects in each department's Organizational Unit. Follow these steps:

1. In the DNS/DHCP Management Console, select the DNS Service tab.

2. In the left pane, select All Zones or an existing zone.

3. Click the Create button, choose DNS Server, and click OK to open the Create DNS Server dialog box:

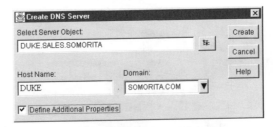

4. Select the NetWare Server object from the NDS tree.

5. Enter a unique host name in the Host Name field for this server. Since I am setting up server DUKE, I would enter DUKE in this field.

6. In the Domain field, enter a domain name or select a domain name from the drop-down menu. This should be the domain that this server will reside in, such as SOMORITA.COM.

7. Check the Define Additional Properties checkbox if necessary.

8. Click Create.

DNS Server Object Properties

A DNS Server object has four tabs:

Zones   Displays a list of zones that this server has been configured to resolve. Zones are assigned to a server through the Zone object. This tab also has a Comments field where you can enter a maximum of 256 characters of information about this server.

Forwarding List   Defines which DNS name server this server will forward name resolution requests to if this server does not have an answer. If you have nothing in these lists, the name server forwards queries to the root servers. To add entries to this list, click the Add button and enter the desired name server's IP address.

No-Forward List   Displays a list of domain names for which you do not want to send queries. To add entries to this list, click the Add button and enter the name of the domain for which you do not want to resolve names.

Options   Sets Event logging (None, Major, or All) and specifies whether to enable an audit trail log.

In the bottom pane, you will now see a Server object called DNS_DUKE. To add other NetWare 5.1 servers, simply repeat this process. To modify a server, highlight it in the bottom pane to display its properties in the right pane.

Creating a Zone

IN A HURRY

15.2 Create a DNS Zone

1. In the left pane of the DNS/DHCP Management Console, highlight the All Zones object.

2. Click the Create button, select Zone, and click OK.

3. Select the NDS context in which you want the Zone object to appear.

Continued

IN A HURRY CONTINUED

4. Enter the zone name in the Zone Domain Name field.

5. Assign this zone an Authoritative DNS Server in the Assign Authoritative DNS Server drop-down box.

6. Click the Create button.

Although you can create DNS zones without first creating a DNS server, I recommend that you create at least one DNS server in your NDS tree prior to creating the first DNS zone. Also, before creating DNS zones or servers, you must install the DNS/DHCP extensions described earlier in this chapter. You can install these during server installation or by running the DNIPINST.NLM program at the server console. For more information, see the section "Installing DNS and DHCP Support" earlier in this chapter.

First, we'll create our main domain name, somorita.com. In the left pane, highlight the All Zones object, click the Create button, and then choose Zone to open the Create Zone dialog box:

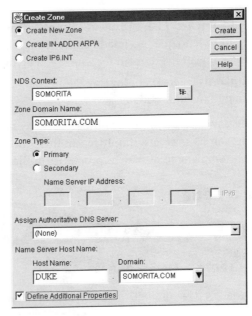

Now follow these steps:

1. Make sure that the Create New Zone radio button is selected.

2. Click the Browse button, and select the NDS context in which you want this object to appear.

3. In the Zone Domain Name box, type **somorita.com**.

4. Make sure that the Primary radio button is selected.

5. Assign the name server that will host this domain in the Assign Authoritative DNS Server field. If this is the first zone you have created and you have no DNS servers created yet, you can assign this later.

6. If you have not created your first DNS server, in the Domain field enter the domain name of the DNS server, such as **somorita.com**.

7. Click the Define Additional Properties checkbox, if necessary.

8. Click Create.

To configure other attributes about this zone, highlight the zone name (somorita .com) in the left pane. Figure 15.9 shows the Attributes tab for the somorita.com zone. Here you specify whether the zone is primary or secondary. Servers managed by NetWare NDS will always be primary, which is the default. From this tab, you can assign any of your DNS servers to answer queries for this zone in the Authoritative DNS Servers list. You can also assign a Dynamic DNS Server. This server is used to manage dynamic DNS data and is used if other non-NetWare 5.1 name servers will perform zone transfers from this server.

FIGURE 15.9

DNS Zone attributes

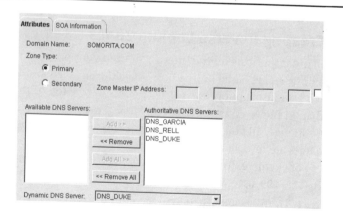

You use the SOA Information tab (or Start of Authority) to specify the current version of the zone information and the secondary server zone transfer information. You should not have to change any of the Serial Number information; the NetWare DNS handles that internally. In the E-mail Address box, enter the e-mail address of the administrator of this zone. The correct form uses periods, even though you are used to seeing an @ sign between the user name and the domain name.

 WARNING Do not change the SOA record's serial number manually if you are managing your DNS through NDS. NDS keeps this record up-to-date and correct. Changing it can cause non-NetWare DNS name servers to fail to perform zone transfers.

If you configured external name servers to transfer zone information from this zone, the Interval values may be important to you. These fields control communication between the secondary and the primary servers.

A value that will prove useful is the Minimal Caching field. It controls how long another name server keeps one of your resource records in its cache before it discards it and has to query your server again if it needs that information. The default is 24 hours.

 TIP Do not forget to create reverse lookup zones for each IP network that you are supporting. To create a reverse lookup zone, from the DNS/DHCP Management Console, choose Create ➢ Zone, click the Create IN-ADDR.ARPA radio button, and then enter the NDS Context and the IP network number and assign the Authoritative DNS server, if necessary.

Creating Reverse Lookup Zones

In order for hosts on the Internet or even your private intranet to be able to look up a host's name based on the host's IP address (called an Inverse Query), your name servers must support *reverse lookup zones*. I have found this to be much harder in Unix than in the NetWare DNS/DHCP Management Console. Though the name looks a little strange, all you are really doing is creating a zone in which the IP addresses and names are reversed.

For example, to create a reverse lookup zone for the hosts on the IP network 204.187.99.0, follow these steps:

1. In the DNS/DHCP Management Console, make sure you are viewing the DNS Service tab. Highlight the All Zones object in the left pane.

2. Click the Create button, choose Zone, and click OK.

3. Click the Create IN-ADDR.ARPA radio button.

4. Select the NDS container that will contain this zone object.

5. Enter the IP address in the IP Address box, such as 204.187.99.0.

6. Assign an Authoritative DNS Server to resolve queries for this zone.

7. If you have not created your first DNS server yet, enter the host name of the DNS server in the Name Server Host Name box, and enter the DNS server domain name in the Domain drop-down box.

8. Check Define Additional Properties if necessary.

9. Click Create.

Reverse Lookup Domain Names

Reverse lookup domain names vary, depending on the class of the IP address in use:

- The Class A network 12.0.0.0 will have a reverse lookup zone named 12.IN.ADDR.ARPA.
- The Class B network 178.79.0.0 will have a reverse lookup zone named 79.178.IN-ADDR.ARPA.
- The Class C network 204.178.99.0 will have a reverse lookup zone named 99.178.204.IN-ADDR.ARPA.

Creating Secondary Zones

Secondary zones are zones that are actually managed on another server. In the case of the NetWare DNS server, these zones are managed by a system external to NetWare, such as a Unix system. You create a secondary zone if you want your NetWare servers to maintain a copy of the zone and periodically update that copy using a *zone transfer*.

For example, I need to host a zone name for a domain called NORTHSHORE.COM on my server, but the primary server is on Unix at another site on the Internet. I create a secondary zone and provide the IP address of the server that has the primary zone. Here are the steps:

1. In the DNS/DHCP Management Console, make sure you are viewing the DNS Service tab. Highlight the All Zones object in the left pane.

2. Click the Create button, choose Zone, and click OK.

3. Make sure that the Create New Zone radio button is selected.

4. Select the NDS context in which this zone object will appear.

5. Enter the zone domain name, in this case, **NORTHSHORE.COM**.

6. Select the Secondary radio button.

PART

III

Netware, TCP/IP, and the Internet

7. Enter the IP address of the server that is the primary location of the zone information.

8. Select one of your DNS servers to resolve addresses for this zone in the Assign Authoritative DNS Server drop-down box.

9. Enter the Host Name and Domain Name.

10. Select Define Additional Properties if necessary.

11. Click Create.

Your server will transfer the zone from the primary server based on the Refresh interval defined in the zone information on the primary server. This Refresh interval is stored in the SOA record. The default for NetWare is 180 minutes, but this can vary greatly depending on the person who creates the primary zone.

Subdomains

Now we need to create *subdomains* (sometimes called *child domains* or *child zones*) under our somorita.com domain. Specifically, we need to create sales.somorita.com, testing.somorita.com, and design.somorita.com. To create a subdomain under a parent domain, in the left pane, highlight the zone for which you want to create a subdomain. Click the Create object, and then choose Zone to open the Create Zone dialog box. The procedures are the same as those for creating a zone.

Once the zone is created, the parent zone must contain *glue records* or *glue logic*. These are records that point to the name server that hosts the child zone. This means that there must be an NS (Name Server) record and an A (Address) record for the name servers that will resolve queries for the child zone. Without these records, the parent name server cannot refer queries to other name servers. For more information on creating NS and A records (resource records), see the following section in this chapter, called "Creating Resource Records."

Creating Resource Records

IN A HURRY

15.3 Create a Host (A) Resource Record

1. Highlight the zone name in which you want the record to appear in the left pane of the DNS/DHCP Management Console.

2. Click the Create button, choose Resource Record, and click OK.

3. Confirm that the A radio button is selected.

4. Enter the host's name and its IP address.

5. Click the Create button.

Now that we have created zones, we must add hosts to them. You will be working with three major types:

- Host records (A records)
- CNAME records (aliases)
- MX records (Mail Exchanger records)

Another type of record that you may have to create is the NS (Name Server) record, which is used to point to a name server for a specific domain. These are used when creating child zones (or subdomains).

For all hosts, you first create an A record. Follow these steps:

1. In the left pane, highlight the zone in which you want the record to appear.

2. Click the Create button, choose Resource Record, and click OK to open the Create Resource Record dialog box:

3. In the Domain box, enter the host name.

4. Click the radio button that corresponds to the type of record entry (A, CNAME, or Others). If you click Others, you can select from a list.

5. In the IP Address boxes, enter the IP address for the host.

6. Click the Create button.

Once the object is created, you can enter additional comments about the object by clicking Define Additional Properties, or if it corresponds to a particular NDS object, you can also associate this resource record with that NDS object.

 NOTE All NetWare servers should have an A record created for them, and this record should be associated with that server's NDS object.

IN A HURRY

15.4 Create Host Alias (CNAME) Records

1. Highlight the zone in which you want the alias to appear in the left pane of the DNS/DHCP Management Console.
2. Click the Create button, select Resource Record, and click OK.
3. Click the CNAME radio button.
4. Enter the alias for the host in the Host Name field.
5. In the Domain Name Of Aliased Host box, enter the Fully Qualified Domain Name of the host for which this CNAME is an alias.
6. Click the Create button.

Our final step is to create aliases for our servers so that we can use them as Web servers. For example, the DUKE server will host our www.somorita.com server. Since we already have an A record for it, we'll need to create an alias. Follow these steps:

1. Highlight the somorita.com zone in the left pane of the DNS/DHCP Management Console.

2. Click the Create button, choose Resource Record, and click OK to open the Create Resource Record dialog box:

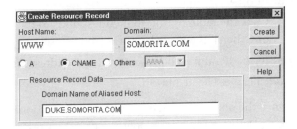

3. Select the CNAME radio button.

4. In the Host Name box, enter **WWW**.

5. In the Domain Name Of Aliased Host box, enter the Fully Qualified Domain Name for the actual host name, **duke.somorita.com**.

6. Click the Create button.

Once the Resource Record object is created, you can view the properties of this object by highlighting the Resource Record object in the left pane of the DNS/DHCP Management Console. The right pane will provide you with a text box to enter a comment and a box that will let you select an object from the NDS directory that this Resource Record represents.

Figure 15.10 shows the DNS/DHCP Management Console after creating DNS servers, DNS zones, and Resource Record objects. The DNS servers appear across the bottom pane of this window, the zones and resource records are on the left side of the window, and the attributes for the currently highlighted object are on the right side of the window.

FIGURE 15.10

The DNS/DHCP Management Console after configuring DNS servers, zones, and hosts

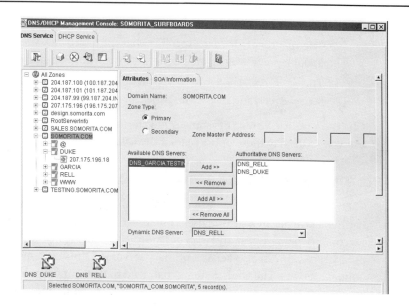

Enabling the NetWare 5.1 Server to Support Name Services

Once you define the servers in the DNS/DHCP Management Console and assign the zones, you can enable NetWare 5.1 to support Name Services. To do so, at the server type **LOAD NAMED.NLM** and press Enter.

You can use the following options with NAMED.NLM, which may prove useful for troubleshooting:

- The –h and –? options display help.
- The –v option allows the NLM to load in verbose mode and provides a troubleshooting screen. To load Name Services in verbose mode, type **LOAD NAMED.NLM –V** and press Enter.

PART

III

Netware, TCP/IP, and the Internet

- The −s option displays the current status of the NAMED.NLM program after it is loaded. The syntax is LOAD NAMED −S.

- The −i option reinitializes a currently running NAMED.NLM.

- The −l option allows the NAMED.NLM to bypass its own login and log in to NDS as an administrator. If you use this option, you provide a login name and password. Use this option only if the name server will not start any other way. Run DSREPAIR to repair the NDS Name Server object.

- The −m <zonefile.dat> specifies that NAMED.NLM should import the specified zone file and create a new zone.

- The −u <zonefile.dat> specifies that the NAMED.NLM should update information about a previously created zone with the information in <zonefile.dat>.

- The −r <zone.com> tells NAMED.NLM to remove all information in the database for zone.com and delete the zone.

The NAMED.NLM supports some other startup options for managing zones from the server. To display these options, load the NAMED.NLM with the -? or -h option.

Interoperability with Unix Name Servers

The NetWare 5.1 DNS Name Server NLM can interoperate with other name servers as either a primary or a secondary name server. NetWare 5.1 Name Services can act as a secondary name server and load data into NDS via a zone transfer with a Unix primary server. It can also act as a primary server for Unix systems that need to be secondary servers. The Unix systems that need to be secondary servers are configured to do a zone transfer with a NetWare 5.1 name server that you define as the *Dynamic DNS Server*. The Dynamic DNS Server is a server that the administrator has defined for a specific zone. It maintains the information needed if a zone transfer is requested.

If the Dynamic DNS Server is on a system that will act as a primary server for other name servers, its job is to make sure that the DNS data from the NDS database is available and up-to-date when a secondary server requests a zone transfer. If the Dynamic DNS Server is on a NetWare system that is acting as a secondary, it is responsible for connecting to a primary server and transferring data into NDS.

There can only be one NetWare server defined as a Dynamic DNS Server for each zone.

Configuring a Primary Server

To define a NetWare server as a primary server from which other systems can transfer zones, you must configure one zone at a time. Using the DNS/DHCP Management Console, in the left pane, highlight the zone that you want to transfer to a secondary server.

At the bottom of the window (see Figure 15.11), in the Dynamic DNS Server box, select the server to which secondary servers will connect to transfer zones.

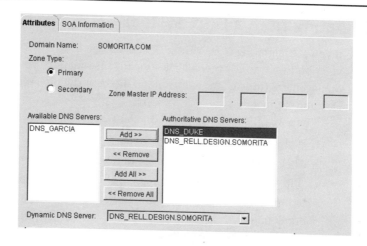

You do not need to do this for other NetWare 5.1 DNS servers to resolve queries for this zone. Instead, select the server name and add it to the Authoritative DNS Servers list so that other NetWare DNS servers can service queries for this zone.

Configuring a Secondary Server

A time may come when you merely want to transfer data from a Unix name server to your NDS.

If your DNS server is a secondary server, any zone data that NDS contains is read-only. If you want the ability to modify the data yourself, your NetWare server must be the primary server.

You use NetWare name servers as secondary servers if your DNS servers are already running under Unix and you don't want the hassle of moving them to NetWare 5.1 DNS (or you are not given that responsibility). For purposes of redundancy and better performance, you can transfer these zones to your NetWare 5.1 name servers. To change a primary server to a secondary server, follow these steps:

1. In the left pane, highlight the zone you want to transfer.

2. In the Zone Attributes property page, change the zone type from Primary to Secondary.

3. Enter the IP address for the server that has the original zone file (the Zone Master IP address).

The server you define as the Dynamic DNS Server will transfer data from the other server into NDS based on an interval that the other server administrator defined in the SOA record.

Migrating from a Unix System

If you are migrating from a Unix DNS name server to a NetWare 5.1 name server and you don't want to re-enter all the zone file information, you can use the DNS/DHCP Management Console to import files that are in the BIND (Berkeley Internet Named Daemon) format.

To import a file into your NetWare 5.1 DNS data, follow these steps:

1. Highlight the All Zones selection.

2. Click the Import DNS Database button.

3. When prompted, enter the filename, the NDS context in which the zone object will be created, and the name of the server that will service queries for this domain.

Configuring Clients to Use DNS

Once DNS services are configured and running, you will need to configure your client computers to use a DNS server. This is really quite simple in comparison to getting the DNS server up and running. You must enter the IP address (or addresses) of the DNS servers that you want the client to query. For Windows 95/98 clients, this is done from the DNS Configuration tab of the TCP/IP Properties dialog box:

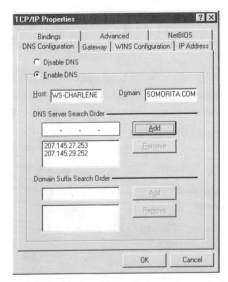

To view the TCP/IP Properties dialog box, choose Control Panel ➢ Network ➢ TCP/IP <for your network adapter> ➢ Properties ➢ DNS Configuration. Note that you can enter several IP addresses in the DNS Server Search Order field. The client will use only one of these, generally the first one in the list. It will resort to a second DNS server only if the first one is not available.

The host name is the computer name. Though it can be different, to keep things simple, I don't change the host name to be different from the computer's name. You should also enter a domain name in the Domain box.

The domain name is used in host name resolution if you attempt to contact a host without providing a fully qualified domain name. The TCP/IP software adds the domain name from the Domain box to the host name. For example, if I go to the command prompt and type **PING RELL**, but do not put a domain name after RELL, my TCP/IP software will contact my DNS and ask for the IP address of RELL.SOMORITA.COM. This is, of course, provided I have SOMORITA.COM entered in the Domain box.

 TIP You can automatically assign the Domain Name Server IP addresses and the domain name using the DHCP scope option. Keep reading for more information!

For Windows NT clients, assign the IP address of a DNS server by choosing Control Panel ➢ Network ➢ Protocols ➢ TCP/IP ➢ Properties and then selecting the DNS tab. For Unix systems, the information is generally entered in a file in the /etc directory called RESOLV.CONF or something similar.

Setting Up and Managing a NetWare 5.1 DHCP Server

The steps for setting up a DHCP server are similar to those for setting up a DNS server. Before setting up your first DHCP server, plan your IP address allocation carefully. To see how this works, let's take a look at our sample company and its requirements.

Sample Company Requirements

You are the network administrator for Somorita Surfboards; you have decided that DHCP will be the best way to allocate the IP addresses that your ISP has given you. You collect information about each subnet in your organization and the assigned IP address for that subnet and format this information in a table similar to Table 15.7.

PART

III

Netware, TCP/IP, and the Internet

For a detailed look at Somorita's intranet, refer to the network diagram in Figure 15.8, earlier in this chapter.

TABLE 15.7: SOMORITA SURFBOARD'S IP NETWORK INFORMATION					
Location	**Function**	**Number of Hosts**	**Network Address**	**Default Gateway**	**Nearest DNS**
Haleiwa	Sales	153	204.187.99.0	207.187.99.1	204.187.99.2
Pipeline	Testing	108	204.187.100.0	207.187.100.1	204.187.100.2
Pipeline	Design	201	204.187.101.0	207.187.101.1	204.187.101.1

The DHCP server automatically assigns the following IP options:

- IP address and subnet mask
- Default gateway address
- Nearest domain name server
- Default NDS tree name
- Default NDS tree context
- Nearest NetWare server's IP address

Since we have plenty of IP host addresses available for all hosts, we will use the default lease period for IP addresses, which is three days. If we had a shortage of IP host addresses, we would reduce the lease time to possibly even a few hours so that unused IP addresses would quickly return to the pool of available IP addresses.

Setting Global Preferences

Global preferences are settings that affect all DHCP servers throughout your NDS directory tree. To view your global preferences, follow these steps:

1. In the DNS/DHCP Management Console, select the DHCP Service tab.

2. Click the Global Preferences button.

You can use the Global DHCP Options tab to set DHCP options that will be sent to all clients that lease IP addresses from any DHCP server.

 NOTE DHCP options for a specific scope or IP address will override any global options you set up.

One of our requirements is that all clients that get an IP address from this DHCP server also be assigned the NDS Default Tree name. Since this will be universal for all clients, we will set this as a Global DHCP Option. Follow these steps:

1. Click the Modify button to open the Modify DHCP Options dialog box:

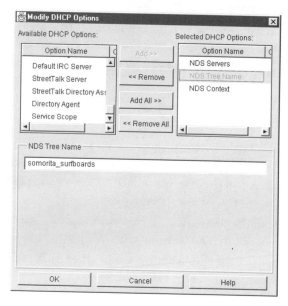

2. Scroll through the Option Name list, select NDS Tree Name, and click Add.

3. In the NDS Tree Name box, enter **SOMORITA_SURFBOARDS**.

The second page is the Global DHCP Defaults page. From this page, you can set up a list of computers, based on their MAC addresses, that should not be leased an IP address from any DHCP server.

 NOTE   When you add MAC addresses to this list, be sure you enter them in the following format (colons included): 00:60:97:23:D4:C6:28.

The final Global Preferences page is the DHCP Options Table, which lists the available DHCP options and lets you define your own DHCP options.

PART

III

Netware, TCP/IP, and the Internet

Creating DHCP Servers

15.5 Create a DHCP Server

1. In the DHCP Service tab of the DNS/DHCP Management Console, highlight the Our Network object, click the Create button, choose DHCP Server, and click OK.

2. Browse NDS, select the NetWare 5.1 server that will run DHCP server services, and then click OK.

3. Click Create.

The first task is to define which of our NetWare 5.1 servers will support DHCP servers. Since each department will use a subnet and have its own NetWare server, we will define each of those servers as a DHCP server and define a range of available addresses for that subnet. Follow these steps:

1. In the DNS/DHCP Management Console, select the Name Service tab, and then select the Our Network tab.

2. Click the Create button, choose the DHCP server, and click OK to open the Create DHCP Server dialog box:

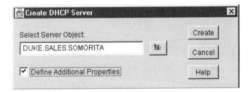

3. Browse NDS, select the server that will run DHCP server services, and click OK.

4. Select Define Additional Properties, if necessary, and click Create.

When you create the DHCP Server object, the DHCP Server properties box is displayed in the right pane. It has two property pages:

- The Server property page lists the subnets and subnet address ranges serviced by this particular server, and it has a comment field.

- The Options property page lets you set SNMP trap options, set audit trail options, and define IP allocation options for mobile users. In this case, *mobile users* are users who may move their computer from one subnet to another. The options are:

  - Disallow mobile address users

  - Allow mobile users but delete a previously assigned address

  - Allow mobile users, but do not delete a previously assigned address

At the bottom of the Options property page is a Ping Enabled checkbox. If this option is enabled, the DHCP server will ping an IP address before leasing it to ensure that the address is not in use.

Creating a Subnet

IN A HURRY

15.6 Create a Subnet

1. Using the DNS/DHCP Management Console, highlight the Our Network object, click the Create button, select Subnet, and click OK.
2. Enter a name for the Subnet object.
3. Select an NDS context in which the Subnet object will appear.
4. Enter the subnet's IP network address and subnet mask.
5. Select the NetWare 5.1 Server object from NDS that will be the default server for this subnet.
6. Click Create.

Subnets contain subnet address ranges and static IP addresses that have been reserved for specific hosts. Before creating static IP addresses or subnet address ranges, we need to create subnets. Follow these steps:

1. Highlight the Our Network object in the left pane, click the Create button, select Subnet, and click OK to open the Create Subnet dialog box.

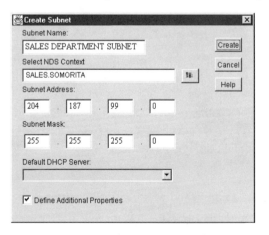

2. In the Subnet Name box, enter a name for the subnet.

PART

III

Netware, TCP/IP, and the Internet

3. In the Select NDS Context box, enter an NDS context for the Subnet object.

4. Enter the subnet address and subnet mask.

5. In the Default DHCP Server drop-down list, select the NetWare 5.1 server that will run this subnet.

6. Select Define Additional Properties if necessary.

7. Click Create.

Once you create the subnet, other properties are available for the Subnet object in the right pane. You can use the Addressing tab to assign a DNS zone name and domain name in which hosts will appear, using the NetWare 5.1 Dynamic DNS features. You should create these before using this feature. Also on this tab, you can assign a default DHCP server and make this subnet part of a subnet pool.

You use the Subnet Options tab to set the lease time and to set BOOTP parameters, such as server address, server name, and the boot file name that the BOOTP clients will use.

Use the Other DHCP Options tab to set DHCP options for all hosts on this subnet. These options will override the DHCP global options.

Creating Subnet Address Ranges

The *subnet address range* is the actual pool of addresses from which the DHCP server assigns an IP address. Because a subnet address range is contained under a subnet, you must first create the subnet.

IN A HURRY

15.7 Create a Subnet Address Range

1. Using the DNS/DHCP Management Console, highlight the subnet for which you want to create a subnet address range, click the Create button, choose Subnet Address Range, and click OK.

2. Enter a name for the subnet address range.

3. Enter the IP address range that you want this Subnet Address Range to support, and then click Create.

To create a subnet address range, follow these steps:

1. Using the DNS/DHCP Management Console, highlight the subnet that will contain the subnet address range.

2. Click the Create button, choose Subnet Address Range, and click OK to open the Create Subnet Address Range dialog box:

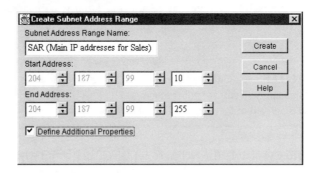

3. In the Subnet Address Range Name box, enter a name.

4. Choose the starting and ending IP addresses.

5. Select Define Additional Properties if necessary.

6. Click Create.

After you create the subnet address range, other options available in the right pane include the Range Type list box, which has several options:

Dynamic BOOTP   Indicates that IP addresses in this range are dynamically assigned to BOOTP clients.

Dynamic DHCP With Automatic Host Name Generation   Indicates that IP addresses in this subnet address range will be allocated to DHCP clients and that a name will be automatically generated for those clients in the DNS zone chosen for the subnet.

Dynamic DHCP   Indicates that IP addresses will be leased to DHCP clients.

Dynamic BOOTP and DHCP   Indicates that IP addresses will be leased dynamically to both BOOTP and DHCP clients.

Excluded   Indicates that all IP addresses in this range are not to be leased.

 NOTE Excluded subnet address ranges and IP addresses will not be leased to any computer. This is useful if you have manually configured a computer and its address exists right in the middle of a range of addresses that you want to use.

PART

III

Netware, TCP/IP,
and the Internet

Depending on the option, you can choose what the automatically generated host name starts with and whether to automatically register computer names with the DNS when the client gets an IP address. Finally, you can specify which DHCP server handles this particular scope. The default is the server that was chosen for the subnet.

 NOTE A subnet can contain multiple subnet address ranges. You might want to use this option if you are going to assign 75 percent of your addresses to one DHCP server and 25 percent of them to a second DHCP server.

How well does the NetWare 5.1 DHCP match up with other "official" DHCP servers running on Unix or Linux? Take a look at the graphic from a cool departmental Linux-based server from Rebel.com, the NetWinder OfficeServer.

Notice the similarities? DHCP servers must do the same things, whether on NetWare or Linux or Unix. Set the subnet address and subnet mask, set the IP address pool range, and set the lease time. This is another example of the value of standards: the same jobs on different server platforms work pretty much the same way.

Creating IP Address Records

IP address records are contained in either a subnet or a subnet address range. These record types allow you to assign the same IP address to a specific computer each time it leases an address. Novell refers to this as a *manual address assignment,* though some systems call this a *reservation.* You must know the client's MAC address in order to assign it a dedicated IP address. You can also use IP addresses to exclude individual IP addresses that should not be leased.

IN A HURRY

15.8 Create an IP Address Record

1. Using the DNS/DHCP Management Console, highlight the subnet or subnet address range in which you want to create the IP address, click the Create button, choose IP Address, and click OK.

2. Enter the IP address.

3. Using the Assignment Type drop-down box, specify whether the IP address is an exclusion or a manually configured address.

4. If it is a manual address, enter the MAC address for the client in the MAC Address field.

To create an IP Address object, follow these steps:

1. Using the DNS/DHCP Management Console, highlight the subnet or subnet address range in which you want to create the IP Address.

2. Click the Create button, choose IP Address, and click OK to open the Create IP Address dialog box:

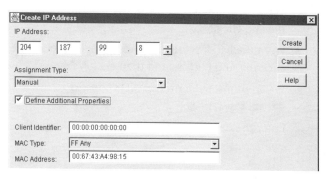

TIP If the IP Address option does not appear, you have not selected a Subnet object.

3. In the IP Address boxes, enter the IP address.

4. In the Assignment Type list box, specify whether the object is an exclusion or a manual address.

After you create the IP address, other options are available for the IP Address object on three tabs:

Addressing Use this tab to configure a client identifier, MAC address type, and MAC address. When entering the MAC address, be sure to enter it in the format 00:60:97:A4:71:C2. You can also use this tab to enter a host name for this computer, specify whether it participates in Dynamic DNS updates, and identify an NDS object with this object.

Usage Use this tab to specify IP address leasing options.

Other DHCP Options Use this tab to specify DHCP options that are set only for this client.

Importing DHCP Information from Previous Versions of Novell DHCP Server

You can use the DNS/DHCP Management Console to import information from Novell DHCP Server 2 or 3. To do so, follow these steps:

1. In the DNS/DHCP Management Console, select the DHCP Service tab.

2. In the left pane, highlight the Our Network object.

3. Click the Import DHCP Database toolbar button.

4. When you are prompted for the location of the DHCP database file, choose the file and click Next.

5. From the list of subnets found in the file, select the subnets you want to import, click the Add button, and then click Next.

6. When prompted, enter an NDS context to use for creating the subnet and subnet address ranges.

7. Enter the name of a NetWare 5.1 server that will service these subnets.

Dynamic DNS

Dynamic DNS is the result of integrating the DHCP server and the DNS data stored in the DNS database. In a traditional DNS environment, the DNS zone files had to be updated every time a client's IP address changed. If all clients are assigned static IP addresses, this is not a problem. However, if client IP addresses change often, such as when you are using DHCP, updating zone files manually is not an option.

You can configure NetWare 5.1 DHCP servers to automatically update the DNS data in NDS whenever a client is given an IP address. This includes creating a host (A) record and a reverse lookup (PTR) record. Both records are needed so that DNS clients can do nametoIPaddress resolution as well as IPaddresstoname resolution (reverse lookups).

To configure this support, you must enable it at the subnet address range level. Follow these steps:

1. In the DNS/DHCP Management Console, select the DHCP Service tab.

2. In the left pane, highlight the subnet address range.

3. In the right pane, select the Addressing tab, and then choose Always Update On for the DNS Update option. Also, specify an existing DNS zone that will include these names.

Let's say that you created a DHCP subnet address range and turned on Dynamic DNS for this zone. You assigned all leased IP addresses to the SOMORITA.COM zone. Since a name is assigned to computers running Windows 95/98 and Windows NT, a computer whose name is KAHUNA2 would automatically have a Fully Qualified Domain Name of KAHUNA2.SOMORITA.COM.

For clients that do not have assigned names, such as DOS clients, you can configure the DHCP server to automatically assign the client a name. This feature is also enabled at the subnet address range level.

When an IP address is assigned, the DHCP server updates the resource records for the appropriate zone. It also stores the lease time in the DNS information. If the IP address lease is not renewed or if the client releases its IP address, the DNS server automatically deletes the A and PTR records associated with that client from the DNS zone files at the end of the lease.

Enabling the DHCPSRVR.NLM

After you create your DHCP servers, subnets, and subnet address ranges, you need to load the DHCPSRVR.NLM. To do so, at the NetWare console, type **LOAD DHCPSRVR** and press Enter. Naturally, you will want to put this line in the AUTOEXEC.NCF file so that it loads each time the NetWare server starts.

PART

III

Netware, TCP/IP,
and the Internet

The DHCPSRVR.NLM has some load options that you can use for diagnostics and testing:

- The -d option turns on a console background screen of diagnostic information. It has three flags:

    -d1   Turns on a background screen to display DHCP activity.

    -d2   Turns on the background screen to display DHCP activity as well as debugging statements.

    -d3   Turns on the background screen, displays the debugging information, and writes a log of activity to the SYS:ETC\DHCPAGNT.LOG text file.

- The -p option sets the interval in minutes that the DHCPSRVR.NLM uses to poll NDS for changes.

- The -s option forces the server to read from and write to the master replica.

Here is a sample command that will load DHCPSRVR.NLM with a background activity screen and check for changes every five minutes:

```
LOAD DHCPSRVR -D2 -P5
```

Configuring Clients to Use DHCP

The final step in configuring a client to use the DHCP server to get IP addresses is to enable it in Control Panel on the same tab that you would have entered a TCP/IP address and subnet mask.

In Windows 95/98, choose Control Panel ➢ Network ➢ TCP/IP <for your network adapter> ➢ Properties to open the TCP/IP Properties dialog box, and select the IP Address tab:

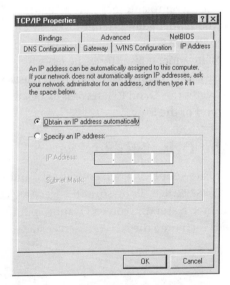

To use DHCP, click the Obtain An IP Address Automatically button.

For Windows NT clients, the procedure is similar. Choose Control Panel ➤ Network ➤ Protocols ➤ TCP/IP ➤ Properties. From this screen, click the Obtain An IP address From A DHCP Server button. Procedures vary for other clients that support DHCP.

Troubleshooting Common DNS and DHCP Problems

Although DNS and DHCP can help reduce your administrative load, there may be times when something just doesn't work right. You need to have a bag of troubleshooting tricks. Since DNS and DHCP are separate systems, there are separate troubleshooting tools for each.

Troubleshooting DNS Problems

DNS-related problems will manifest themselves quite clearly. Clients will not be able to resolve IP addresses from host names. This may include not only your internal clients, but also clients connecting from the Internet that may need to resolve your host names.

Let's look at a few possible problems and the steps you can take to resolve them:

A client cannot resolve host names.
- Verify connectivity to the network.
- Use the PING utility and ping another host's IP address.
- Check to see if the client can ping other host names.
- Verify that the client computer has the correct IP address of a valid name server.
- Confirm that the name server in question is indeed active.
- Ping the IP address of the name server.
- Try changing to a different name server's IP address.

Clients cannot access a specific host.
- Confirm that the host has been added as a host in your DNS tables.
- If you are using secondary name servers, verify that the secondary server has done a zone transfer from the primary (designated) server.

Clients or mail servers can't connect to certain hosts on the Internet.
- Check to make sure that they can access other hosts on the Internet.
- Verify that the client or mail server has a reverse query (PTR) record in the in-addr.arpa zone. Many FTP servers and mail servers will not allow clients to connect to them unless the host can do a reverse lookup of the client's IP address.

Client computers can do name resolution for hosts within your network, but not for hosts on the Internet.

- Verify that the name servers are communicating outside your own LAN.
- Ensure that your name servers are forwarding queries to one another only and not to the Internet root servers.
- Be sure that you have a list of the Internet root name servers in your NDS tree.

Client computers on the Internet cannot resolve your host names.
Verify with the InterNIC that they are pointing to the correct DNS server's IP addresses. You can verify your InterNIC registration information on the Web at rs.internic.net.

Client computers can resolve computer names in your main domain, but they cannot resolve computer names in the subdomains.
Be sure that the A and NS records at the parent domain match the A and NS records at the subdomains, and be sure that the IP addresses are correct for the name servers.

The name server program (NAMED.NLM) will not load.

- Ensure that TCP/IP is loaded and bound to an adapter. The NetWare Console command CONFIG can help you verify this.
- Be sure that you have sufficient memory on the server.
- Verify that the particular NetWare server has been configured as a name server in the DNS/DHCP Management Console.

Other Problems

Years ago, when you called Novell Technical Support with a problem, they invariably suggested one of three things:

- Upgrade
- Add RAM
- Add COMPSURF

A good rule of thumb for strange problems related to DNS is "reload and DSREPAIR." If you have problems relating to DNS, such as error messages that the name server generates to the console or messages indicating that it is not reading a particular zone object, try these two things:

- Unload and reload the NAMED.NLM.
- Run DSREPAIR.

In addition, turn on the console debug screen for the NAMED.NLM by loading it with the –v option (type **LOAD NAMED –V** and press Enter). This displays information such as DNS queries that the server is handling and automatic maintenance.

NSLOOKUP

Your number-one troubleshooting tool for DNS-related problems is NSLOOKUP, a utility that can perform a number of queries for you.

 NOTE Windows NT includes a command-line NSLOOKUP utility, but Windows 95/98 does not. You can find many other shareware utilities on the Internet.

Under Windows NT, NSLOOKUP has two modes of operation:

- Interactive, which allows you to type commands that NSLOOKUP interprets
- Batch, which you use from the command line

Both modes use the same command-line options.

Using NSLOOKUP, you can do the following types of searches:

- Host (A) records
- CNAMES (aliases)
- Mail Exchanger (MX) records
- Name server (NS records)

For example, to look up an address record for the host DUKE.SOMORITA.COM, use the following command:

```
NSLOOKUP -Q=A DUKE.SOMORITA.COM
Server:    rell.somorita.com
Address:   204.187.101.2
Name:      duke.somorita.com
Address:   204.187.99.2
```

Notice that the name server that resolved the request was RELL.SOMORITA.COM. Get to know the NSLOOKUP utility; it's a great time-saving tool when debugging DNS problems.

Troubleshooting DHCP Problems

When a client does not lease an IP address, this problem is also quickly and painfully obvious, especially if TCP/IP is the only network protocol. Without an IP address, the client cannot communicate with the IP network.

Windows 95/98 and Windows NT workstations are quite helpful when this problem occurs. The user receives a message indicating that a DHCP server could not be found and that an IP address could not be leased. Here are some sample problems and resolutions.

A client cannot lease an address.

- Verify physical connectivity to the LAN.
- Be sure that an IP address is available on the client's subnet.
- Confirm that there is not an exclusion for this particular client.

A client gets a duplicate IP address, indicating that another client has probably had that address manually configured.

Using the DNS/DHCP Management Console, select the DHCP server that has the particular scope from which the address came, and then select the Options property page. At the bottom of the right pane, select the Ping Enabled checkbox. This causes the DHCP server to check to see if the address is already being used before leasing it. This will increase the time it takes to lease an address by a few seconds.

Using IPCONFIG

Windows NT and Windows for Workgroups include a command-line utility called IPCONFIG that will prove especially useful when troubleshooting DHCP problems. Windows 95 and Windows 98 also provide the same utility in a graphical form called WINIPCFG. Using this utility, you can view your current IP configuration, release an IP address, or force your client to renew its lease on an IP address. IPCONFIG has four command-line options:

/ALL   Displays all the available IP configuration information.

/RENEW   Forces renewal of a DHCP lease.

/RELEASE   Forces the client to release an IP address that it had leased.

/HELP or **/?**   Displays online help in case you forget these options.

Figure 15.12 shows the WINIPCFG utility from Windows 98. You can renew or release IP addresses with this graphical utility.

Using Log Files

The DHCPSRVR.NLM creates a text log file, SYS:ETC\DHCPSRVR.LOG, if the −d3 option is used when the server NLM is loaded. You can use this log file to track possible problems. Console alerts are logged to the SYS:SYSTEM\SYS$LOG file.

FIGURE 15.12

The Windows 98
WINIPCFG IP utility for
reporting your TCP/IP
configuration

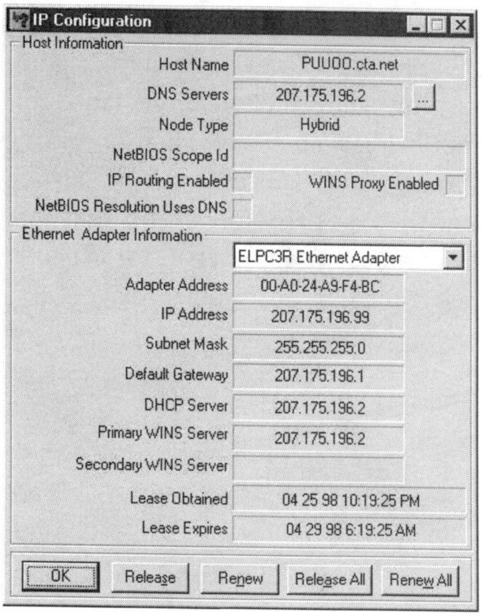

Console Messages

We all know that it is difficult to see every message that appears on the server console screen, especially if the messages are passing by quickly. You can use CONLOG.NLM to capture information and messages that appear on the NetWare server console. For an explanation of the CONLOG.NLM and how to use it, see Chapter 16.

Auditing

You can also use the DNS/DHCP Management Console to view events and details. To view events and alerts from a specific name server, highlight the DHCP server in the bottom pane of the DHCP Service tab of the DNS/DHCP Management Console. Then click the View Events/Alerts toolbar button.

Auditing uses CSAUDIT to track historical data and helps you diagnose problems. When auditing is enabled, all leased addresses, renewed leases, and rejected addresses are tracked in a Btrieve database.

SNMP Events

If you are using an SNMP management system, you can configure the DHCP server to generate SNMP traps. By default, the DHCP server generates traps for major events. A major event represents critical events that should not be ignored, such as server startup or shutdown errors.

The other options are No Traps and All Events. Choosing All Events generates traps for warnings and minor events and should not be turned on unless your server is experiencing problems and you need to diagnose them using the SNMP management system. Warning events include server faults that were recovered automatically and IP addresses not being available for clients. Minor events include something such as a client "declining" an IP address.

To change the types of SNMP events that are generated, in the DNS/DHCP Management Console, choose the server for which you want to change the event status, and then select the Options property page.

PART IV

Taking Advantage of Special Network Features

LEARN:

- NetWare 5.1 and remote access

- Using NetWare 5.1 enhancements and special features

- Troubleshooting your network

CHAPTER 16

NetWare 5.1 and Remote Access

Today, remote access is an important part of most networks. NetWare 5.1 includes support for remote users to dial in to the server, and it supports modem pooling, which allows users on the LAN to access shared modems. This support is made possible through three separate components, which run as additional services on a NetWare server:

Point-to-Point Protocol Remote Node Service (PPPRNS) Allows remote computers, such as Windows 95/98, Windows NT/2000, and Unix clients, to connect to the network through a modem, an ISDN line, or an X.25 network.

NetWare Asynchronous Services Interface Connection Service (NCS) Allows network workstations running Windows 3.x/95/98/NT/2000 to access shared modems by redirecting COM port data across the network to a modem that the client has acquired. When the client has finished using the modem, it is returned to the pool of available modems.

AppleTalk Remote Access Service (ARAS) Allows Macintosh clients using AppleTalk Remote Access client software to access the network and AppleShare services running on NetWare servers or other AppleTalk resources.

These features are part of the Novell Internet Access Server 4.1 (NIAS). If you have used NetWare Connect in the past, you are already familiar with this product; Novell has simply renamed it to Novell Internet Access Server. In this chapter, I will review how to configure a basic remote access server for dial-in access and for allowing users to dial out through the network.

An Overview of Remote Access

Since the early days of the mainframe, the ability to access a computer remotely has been important. Traditional remote access solutions for LANs have typically been *remote control* solutions. Software such as Carbon Copy or pcANYWHERE has allowed users to access a network by taking control of a host computer connected directly to the network. The applications execute at the host computer, and the host computer processes all data. The only data that actually come across the phone line are keystrokes and screen updates.

On the other side of the coin are *remote node* solutions. A remote node solution allows a remote PC to function as if it were directly attached to the LAN. File and application data are transferred over the remote node link to the remote PC just as if it were connected directly to the network. The applications execute at the remote computer, and the remote computer processes the data.

 WARNING An important consideration when implementing remote node solutions is that applications stored on a remote server must be downloaded across the remote node link. This can be excruciatingly slow, even on a 56Kbps modem. Remote node users should have the applications installed on their local hard drives for better performance.

Remote Access Connection Types

NetWare 5.1 remote access services allows for clients to connect to the server through a variety of connection types:

Public Switched Telephone Network (PSTN) A fancy name for your standard, analog telephone line. Telecommunications folks sometimes call this POTS (plain old telephone service). The maximum throughput that public telephone networks will support is 53Kbps due to FCC regulations.

Integrated Services Digital Network (ISDN) A special telephone line that supports digital connections. A Basic Rate Interface (BRI) ISDN line supports two 64Kbps data channels plus a single 16Kbps channel used for control and signal management. A Primary Rate Interface (PRI) supports 23 data circuits at 64Kbps each and a single 64Kbps channel for control and signal management. ISDN lines are more expensive than PSTN lines but provide faster and more reliable connections.

X.25 Packet-Switched Network A public, packet-switched network, requiring special hardware and leased lines for connection. Maximum speed on an X.25 network ranges from 64 to 128Kbps.

Remote Access Clients

Novell provides support for a diverse range of clients to dial in to a NetWare remote access server as well as support for clients to dial out to remote hosts and bulletin board systems through the remote access server's pool of available modems. The following dial-in clients are supported:

- Windows 95/98 Dial-Up Networking client
- Windows NT 4 Dial-Up Networking client

PART

IV

Special Network Features

- Windows NT 3.51 Remote Access Services client

- LAN Workplace 5 dialer

- Novell Mobile Services (for Windows 95 and Windows 3.*x*)

- Apple Remote Access client

Later in this chapter in the "Configuring Remote Access Clients" section, we'll look at how to set up a typical Windows 95/98 client to dial in to the NetWare remote access server.

NetWare 5.1 includes support for network clients to share the modems on the remote access server for dialing out to remote hosts, bulletin boards, and online services through NASI (NetWare Asynchronous Services Interface) Connection Service (NCS). We'll look at how to configure NCS in the "Setting Up Modem Pool Clients" section.

Novell Internet Access Server Components

The *Novell Internet Access Server 4.1* (NIAS) is actually a number of separate components, each providing specific remote access services:

Novell Internet Access Server Configuration (NIASCFG.NLM)   The Net-Ware server console utility that is used to install and configure remote access services, install and configure routing services, monitor remote access ports, and monitor communications protocols.

NetWare Connect Supervisor (NWCSU.NLM)   The NetWare server console utility configuration support as well as security, licensing, network management, auditing, logging, and port status functions.

NetWare Connect Service Selector (NWCSS.NLM)   Negotiates client requests with AIO (Asynchronous Input/Output) to assign ports and route incoming calls to appropriate services.

NetWare Connect Configuration (NWCCON.NLM)   Configures and manages remote access.

NetWare Administrator snap-in for remote access   Allows management of remote access information for servers and users.

Point-to-Point Protocol Remote Node Service (PPPRNS)   Provides the support required for PPP clients, such as Microsoft Dial-Up Networking clients, to connect to the server using the TCP/IP (Transmission Control Protocol/Internet Protocol) or IPX/SPX (Internetwork Packet Exchange/Sequenced Packet Exchange) protocols.

NASI Connection Service (NCS)   Provides the ability for a network workstation to have remote access to a port on the server, thus allowing modem pooling. The workstation can then dial out using third-party applications. NetWare 5.1 includes support for PC and Macintosh users to dial out through NCS client software.

AppleTalk Remote Access Service (ARAS)   Allows remote Macintosh clients using Apple's AppleTalk Remote Access software to dial in and become remote node clients.

ConnectView   Allows Novell Internet Access Servers and NetWare Connect 2.0 servers to be managed from a Windows network workstation.

Remote Access Management Agent (RAMA)   Allows the remote access server to be managed by any SNMP (Simple Network Management Protocol) management console and Novell's ConnectView software.

Asynchronous Input/Output (AIO)   Provides an interface among the communication ports, the remote access services, and the communication drivers. AIO is hardware independent but works in concert with software that is written for hardware such as AIOCOMX.NLM, which provides access to the server's built-in serial ports. Third-party vendors also provide drivers to access their multiport serial boards, ISDN adapters, and other hardware.

NetWare Remote Access Server Security

When you give a network access to the outside world, security is an important issue. You must take steps to prevent unauthorized access. As the administrator of your remote access system, you want to be able to control the following:

- Which users can dial in to the remote access server
- Which users can dial out using the modem pool
- Which times the remote access services are available
- Which resources users can access on the network

In addition, NetWare remote access services allow the use of a separate remote client password. This is an especially nice feature if you are concerned that a user's remote password may be compromised, but you do not want that compromised password to affect that user's LAN account. The remote client password is used for Password Authentication clients but not by NetWare Challenge Authentication Protocol (NWCAP) clients.

PART

IV

Special Network
Features

Configuring NetWare 5.1 Remote Access Services

Now that you are familiar with the components of NetWare 5.1 remote access services, let's look at how to install and configure the components to prepare a NetWare 5.1 server for remote dial-in and to allow users to share the modems on the server for dialing out.

Before installing the software, be sure that your modems are connected to the server. If you are using multiport serial boards or modem cards such as Digi International's Acceleport or Acceleport MODEM solutions, be sure that these hardware devices are installed correctly. Any external modems you plan to use should be connected to the serial ports or the multiport serial boards and powered on.

Are You Getting the Best Performance from Your Modem?

Most of today's personal computers include serial ports (or *com* ports). However, PCs that are more than three years old may have a UART (Universal Asynchronous Receiver/Transmitter). The UART is a microchip that controls communications between the computer and the computer's serial ports. An older UART may be able to operate the serial port only at speeds less than 19.2Kbps. External modems (even that snazzy new 56Kbps modem) will operate at 19.2Kbps or less!

To check the type of UART installed on your PC or server, boot the computer to a copy of MS-DOS, run the MSD program, and check the Com Ports option. The UART Chip Used line should contain 16550, which is a 16-bit chip. If the chip type contains 8250, it is an older, 8-bit chip, and you might want to consider installing a third-party serial port board. This is a good rule of thumb for both servers and PCs.

Installing Remote Access Services

Remote Access Services (RAS) must be installed during the initial installation of NetWare 5.1. The GUI setup prompts for options that include RAS.

If you skip the RAS setup during initial installation, you can add it later by inserting the NetWare 5.1 System CD and running NWCONFIG at the console. Pace the NetWare OS CD in the server and load CD-ROM support by typing **CDROM** at the console. The NLM will load if it has not already been running in memory. Then, enter the command **VOLUMES**, which will list the names of the volumes mounted on your server, including the CD-ROM, which you have activated. Choose Product Options ➢ Install A Product Not Listed from the subsequent page. The system will ask you to specify the path of the CD, which contains the files for remote access services. It defaults to the floppy disk drive, so press F3 to specify a different path, then type in the name of the CD-ROM volume to replace A:\ and press Enter (my CD-ROM volume was NW51). There will be a pause as your server reads the installation files into memory, and then it will display a Windows-type options box in the Graphical Console page. Select Novell Internet Access Server, and then click the Next button. Click the Finish button on the following screen to complete the installation. The next time you run NWCONFIG, the NIAS module will be listed as an installed product.

Configuring Remote Access Services

You configure and install remote access services through the server console utility NIASCFG.NLM. The first time you run NIASCFG.NLM, you will be informed that in order for NIAS to operate properly, all driver LOAD and BIND commands must be migrated from the AUTOEXEC.NCF file to the NETINFO.CFG file, which is managed by INETCFG. Press Enter to instruct the program to automate this process. Ignore any error messages reporting duplicate LOAD and BIND statements until the process has been completed. Reboot the server to activate the changes in NETINFO.CFG.

In addition to migrating your LOAD and BIND commands to the NETINFO.CFG file, the NetWare Directory Services (NDS) schema are extended to include remote access properties and the CONNECT object. To do this, from the NIASCFG main menu, choose Configure NIAS ➢ Remote Access. You must provide an administrative-level user name and password.

During the initial configuration, you will also be asked whether you have any synchronous adapters such as X.25 or ISDN adapters. This does not include ISDN terminal adapters, which you should install as modems. If you are using only asynchronous adapters (serial ports or multiport serial boards), answer No at this point.

 TIP NIASCFG will ask you to identify your serial adapter(s) in order to install the AIO drivers. A list will appear, which includes various Digiboards and other digital port devices. Choose whatever is appropriate, or, if you're using a standard serial port attached to your server's motherboard, select Serial Port (Comx). Then you will be asked to name the port and identify its I/O address, interrupt (IRQ), and speed. It's best to leave the speed at the default setting. This setting is influenced by the UART in your server. Next, NIASCFG will attempt to auto-detect any modems you have installed, but you can skip this stage if you want to do it later. If you can plan your remote access server so that you use identical modems on all ports, you will save yourself many hours of troubleshooting and reconfiguration.

Next, you'll be asked which services you want the remote access server to load automatically. These include:

ARAS   AppleTalk Remote Access Service

NCS   NASI (NetWare Asynchronous Services Interface) Connection Service

PPPRNS   Point-to-Point Protocol Remote Node Service

RAMA   Remote Access Management Agent

When selecting PPPRNS, you must select which protocols will be used with PPP, either IP or IPX:

- If you select IPX, enter the IPX network address of the PPPRNS service.
- If you select IP, enter the IP address and subnet mask of the PPP service.

You can also control whether to use header compression, and you can assign a range of IP addresses to the PPP clients. If IP packet forwarding has been disabled on this server, you will be prompted to run the INETCFG program and enable it. If you do not want to support remote IP or IPX clients, you can also delete these protocols from this menu.

 NOTE   To enable IP forwarding in INETCFG, from the main Internetworking Configuration menu, choose Protocols ➢ TCP/IP ➢ IP Packet Forwarding, and select Enabled ("Router").

To configure ARAS, AppleTalk must be installed on the remote access server.

Figure 16.1 shows the Remote Access Options menu of NIASCFG.NLM, which will be activated by the automated installation process. To get to this menu later, at the server console, type **LOAD NIASCFG**, and then choose Configure NIAS ➢ Remote Access.

FIGURE 16.1

The Remote Access Options menu from the NIASCFG.NLM program

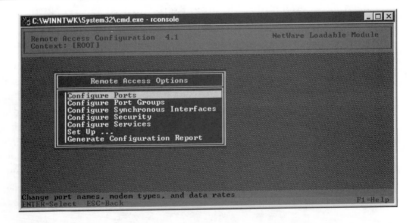

From the Remote Access Options menu, you have the following choices:

Configure Ports   Use to configure port names, modem types, port group membership, port link parameters such as speed and flow control, applications that are allowed to use this port, and application parameters.

Configure Port Groups   Use to create groups of ports and to assign specific ports to those groups. A modem or port can be a member of more than one group. You can assign specific services such as PPPRNS or NCS to a group of ports.

Configure Synchronous Interfaces   Use to configure synchronous interfaces such as X.25 or ISDN interfaces (except ISDN terminal adapters, which are treated like modems).

Configure Security   Use to configure which ports a user can access, which services (such as NCS or PPPRNS) a user can access, which ports a service can use, user specific parameters (which can also be modified through NetWare Administrator), user remote client passwords, and remote client password restrictions. By default, all users can use any service.

Configure Services   Use to configure NCS and PPRNS services, including service security parameters.

Set Up   Use to configure new serial ports and multifunction serial adapters. You can specify which ports are used for dial-in, which ports are used for dial-out, and which ports are used for both. In addition, you can set a directory context, set server information, and define audit trail parameters.

Generate Configuration Report   Use to configure a report about remote access services configuration, including which services are enabled, who can use those services, port definition information, port usage and group assignment, remote access password restrictions, system defaults, and detailed configuration information for each service that is enabled. After your remote access server is installed and configured properly, run this report and keep a copy for documentation purposes.

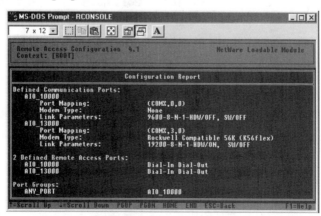

PART

IV

Special Network
Features

During the initial installation of remote access services using the NIASCFG.NLM program, you are prompted for the information necessary to get the remote access server up and running. If things change, such as modems, serial ports, or service configuration requirements, you can make modifications from the NIASCFG program in the System Setup Options menu, as shown in Figure 16.2. To get to this menu, from the NIASCFG main menu, choose Configure NIAS ➤ Remote Access ➤ Set Up.

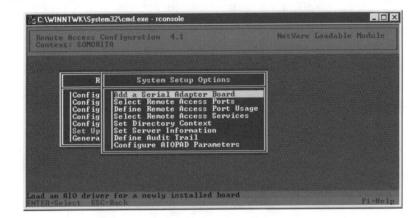

The administrator of the server can use the System Setup Options menu to fine-tune the remote access server parameters and configure security:

Add a Serial Adapter Board   Use to add multiport serial boards, modem cards, and, of course, drivers for a standard serial port (AIOCOMX). You can define settings manually or have NetWare automatically detect new hardware.

Select Remote Access Ports   Use to define which ports to use for NIAS if you do not want to use the total number of ports installed.

Define Remote Access Port Usage   Use to define a port for dial-in access only, dial-out access only, or both.

Select Remote Access Services   Specifies which remote access services are enabled: AppleTalk Remote Access Service (ARAS), NASI Connection Service (NCS), Point-to-Point Protocol Remote Node Service (PPPRNS), and Remote Access Management Agent (RAMA).

Set Directory Context   Specifies the current NetWare Directory Services (NDS) context.

Set Server Information   Specifies server location and description, which can be useful on configuration reports or from a remote SNMP management console.

Define Audit Trail   Use to enable or disable auditing and to specify what time audit logs are archived, how long archive logs are maintained, and how many days are stored in a specific audit log file.

Configure AIOPAD Parameters   Use to set X.25 packet assembler/disassembler parameters if X.25 support has been installed.

The most common tasks for a remote access server administrator include adding serial adapters from the Add a Serial Board Screen:

```
          What kind of serial adapter do you have installed?
 AIO driver for Microdyne's WNIM2000 and WNIM4400 4-port AIO adapters
 Comtrol(tm) RocketPort/RocketModem(tm)
 Digi Acceleport C1/C2 AIO Driver (Digi_C1C2)
 Digi International Acceleport Xr 920 Driver (ISA)
 Digi International Acceleport Xr 920 Driver (PCI)
 Digi International APR-4 Driver
 Digi International Avanstar Xp Driver (PCI)
 Digi International C/X and C/X [MC]
 Digi International EPC/X and EPC/X [MC]
▼Digi International Xe, Xi, Xe [MC], Xi [MC] Driver
```

From this screen, you can insert serial port drivers (Serial Port [COM*x*]) or multiport serial boards such as Digi International Acceleport boards.

Customizing Remote Access Services

If you skipped this step during the question-and-answer phase of the first-time installation, you will also need to enable the remote access services. To enable remote access services in NIASCFG, from the main menu, choose Configure NIAS ➤ Remote Access ➤ Set Up ➤ Select Remote Access Services to display a list of the remote access services and indications of whether they are enabled:

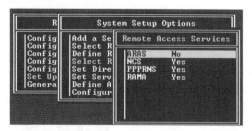

You can use this menu to enable or disable ARAS, NCS, PPPRNS, and RAMA; they are all disabled by default. To enable AppleTalk Remote Access Service (ARAS), the AppleTalk protocol must be installed on the remote access server. ARAS, NCS, and

RAMA are all enabled from this menu but have no other configuration options. The PPPRNS menu selection opens another menu from which you can configure the IP and the IPX protocols.

The IPX protocol requires only that an IPX network address be entered for the PPPRNS service. The IP selection requires a few additional parameters, as shown in Figure 16.3.

FIGURE 16.3

The PPPRNS parameters for IP

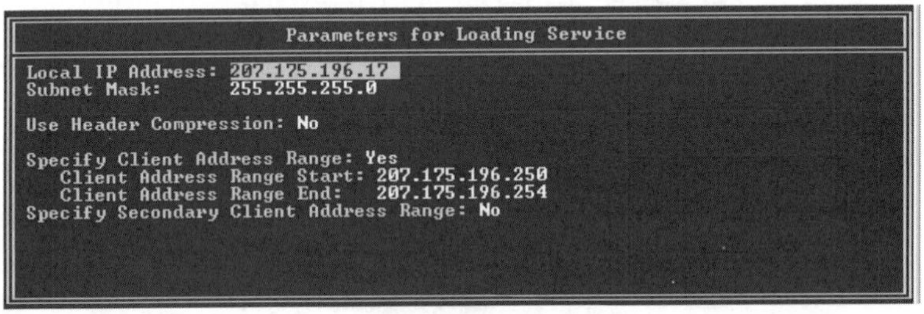

```
                         Parameters for Loading Service
 Local IP Address: 207.175.196.17
 Subnet Mask:      255.255.255.0

 Use Header Compression: No

 Specify Client Address Range: Yes
     Client Address Range Start: 207.175.196.250
     Client Address Range End:   207.175.196.254
 Specify Secondary Client Address Range: No
```

If you are planning to support IP over PPPRNS, on the form shown in Figure 16.3 you must provide the IP address and subnet mask for the PPP remote node service, specify whether to enable header compression, and supply the IP addresses that will be assigned to clients. The client IP addresses must be on the same subnet as the local IP address.

There are two separate places to enter IP addresses on this form. The Specify Client Address Range field assigns an address to each client when they connect automatically. The Specify Secondary Client Address Range field allows an administrator to assign IP addresses from this range to specific users.

Stub Subnetting

The IP address that you enter in the Local IP Address field is the IP address of the virtual PPPRNS interface. This IP address must be on a different IP network or subnet from the local area network interface. If you have only a single Class C network, for example, you can use variable subnetting to create a "stub" subnetwork.

For example, the LAN subnet is assigned the IP address 204.198.17.0 and a subnet mask of 255.255.255.0. The NetWare server that is supporting the remote access server is using IP address 204.198.17.2.

Continued

CONTINUED

Let's say you have four modems for which you need IP addresses plus the virtual IP network address. You need to take a small chunk of the Class C network and build a stub network.

You assign the local IP address as 204.198.17.33 and the subnet mask as 255.255.255.240. This assigns an IP address block of 14 available IP host addresses (204.198.17.33 through 204.198.17.46). Remember, you can't use the .32 address (address of the network), and you can't use the .47 address (the .32 subnet broadcast address).

Assign the client address range 204.198.17.34 through 204.198.17.37, and you will still have a few addresses left over for the secondary address range if you want to allow clients to request a specific IP address.

This method of stub-subnetting actually allocates a few more addresses than necessary, but that is just the way subnet addressing works. You must take care not to assign the addresses in the stub-subnetwork to hosts on the LAN. For more information on subnetting and IP addressing, see Chapter 14.

 TIP If the IP subnet address that you assign to your PPPRNS is on a different network or subnet from the LAN subnet, be sure that the routers in your intranetwork know the correct route to that subnet.

When all the changes are saved, restart the server so that all the services and protocols bind properly.

Configuring the NASI Connection Service

You may need to customize a few additional parameters for the NASI Connection Service (NCS). From the main NIASCFG utility menu, choose Configure NIAS ➤ Remote Access ➤ Configure Services, and then select NCS to display the NCS Configuration Options menu:

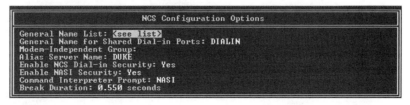

PART

IV

Special Network
Features

You use the NCS Configuration Options menu to set the following options for the NASI Connection Service:

General Name List Allows you to create lists of port groups. These names should not exceed eight characters.

General Name For Shared Dial-In Ports Allows you to select the general dial-in ports group.

Modem-Independent Group Allows you to configure groups of ports so that they are independent of a specific modem make or manufacturer. All modems in this group should support the same set of modem commands.

Alias Server Name Allows you to establish the name that this server will be known as to NCS users; it should be eight characters or fewer. The default is the first eight characters of the server name.

Enable NCS Dial-In Security If enabled (the default setting), users are required to provide their remote client password.

Enable NASI Security If enabled, users are required to enter their NetWare password.

Command Interpreter Prompt Allows you to set the NASI Command Interpreter prompt that is displayed when users start an application that supports NASI basic functions. The default is NASI.

Break Duration Allows you to set the time that NASI waits before sending a break signal to the remote host. Some minicomputers and mainframe hosts require that you send a break signal before starting to log in. The default is 0.550 seconds.

Configuring Point-to-Point Remote Node Service

You may need to customize some options for the Point-to-Point Remote Node Service (PPPRNS). From the NIASCFG main menu, choose Configure NIAS ➤ Remote Access ➤ Configure Services and then select PPPRNS to open the PPPRNS Configuration Options menu:

From the PPPRNS Configuration Options menu, you have the following options:

Configure Security   Allows the remote access server administrator to choose the types of authentication security that can be used. The choices include NetWare Connect Authentication Protocol (NWCAP), Password Authentication Protocol (PAP), and Challenge Handshake Authentication Protocol (CHAP). NWCAP is the default setting.

Configure ISDN Short Hold Parameters   Allows the administrator to set when an ISDN client will disconnect if it is inactive and to set the maximum call that the server will recognize that the client is in "short hold" mode before clearing the connection. This allows ISDN clients to disconnect while idle and to reestablish the connection when needed, thus saving ISDN per-minute charges, if they apply, and freeing ISDN lines for others to use.

Configure PPP Multilink   Allows users to connect from a single remote computer over multiple telephone lines, thus providing higher throughput. The ISDN folks call this *channel bonding*.

Set IPX Parameters   Allows specific users to be assigned IPX addresses and a home server. These parameters can also be assigned through the NetWare Administrator program. I will discuss this in the "Configuring Remote User Parameters" section, later in this chapter.

Set IP Parameters   Allows specific users to be assigned the IP address of a Domain Name Server and a domain name. BOOTP clients can be assigned the IP address of a TFTP (Trivial File Transfer Protocol) server from which they can download their boot file.

TIP   When configuring security for the PPPRNS service, enable the Challenge Handshake Authentication Protocol (CHAP) and Password Authentication Protocol (PAP) if you plan to support Windows 95/98, Windows NT/2000, or Unix clients.

Setting Up Security

Once you configure the ports and modems on the remote access server, security is your next concern. To secure the network from unauthorized access, you need to understand which users need access to which services. To configure security on the

PART

IV

Special Network
Features

remote access server, from the NIASCFG main menu, choose Configure NIAS ➤ Remote Access ➤ Configure Security to display the Configure Security menu.

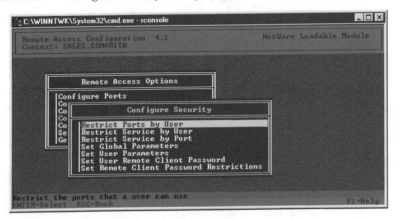

From the Configure Security menu, you have the following options:

Restrict Ports By User   Allows users to be authorized to use only specific ports. The default allows any user to use any port.

Restrict Service By User   Allows users to be restricted to specific services (ARAS, NCS, PPPRNS, and RAMA). The default allows any user to use any service.

Restrict Service By Port   Allows a service to use only specific ports.

Set Global Parameters   Allows you to set the global parameters shown in Figure 16.4 for the entire server. These parameters control how long a user can be connected, the idle timeout, and dial-back mode, and they restrict dial-out users (users of the NASI Connection Service [NCS]) to certain telephone numbers. These parameters can be overridden for an Organizational Unit or for a specific user.

Set User Parameters   Allows the administrator to set parameters for a specific user, including remote client restrictions, dial-back mode, and dial-out phone number restrictions. These parameters can also be set through the NetWare Administrator utility described in the "Configuring Remote User Parameters" section, later in this chapter.

Set User Remote Client Password   Allows the administrator to set a specified user's remote client password. The remote client password can also be set through the NetWare Administrator utility.

Set Remote Client Password Restrictions   Allows you to set restrictions for remote client passwords, such as invalid login attempts, minimum password length, and whether to require long passwords (more than eight bytes). Since this is a global setting, it will affect all remote passwords.

FIGURE 16.4

Remote access service Global Parameter options

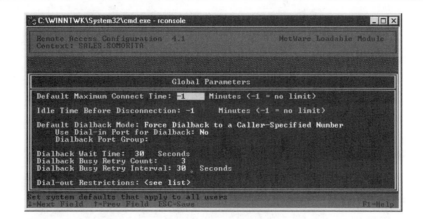

Configuring the NetWare Administrator Program

Novell includes a NetWare Administrator snap-in program that allows you to manage the remote user parameters more easily than you can using the NIASCFG program. After NIAS has been set up, you should be able to see the Remote Access property pages for the Country, Locality, Organization, and Organizational Unit.

Configuring Remote Access for NDS Containers

You can set remote access properties for all users in an NDS container, such as an Organizational Unit, by accessing the Remote Access property tab. This tab is shown in Figure 16.5 and is the same for the Organization, Locality, and Country containers.

PART

IV

Special Network Features

FIGURE 16.5

You can set remote access properties for each Organizational Unit.

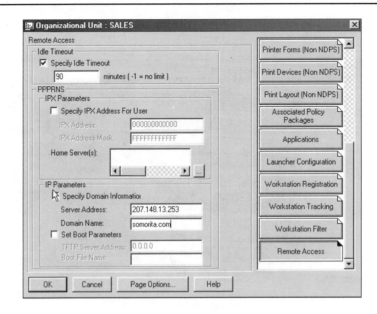

The remote access properties at the container level allow the following parameters to be set for all users in that container:

Specify Idle Timeout Specifies how long a user can remain connected but idle. If no activity is detected during the specified timeout period, the remote user is disconnected.

IPX Parameters Allows the administrator to specify a unique hexadecimal network address between one and eight characters that creates a virtual network of remote clients. The virtual network helps reduce the number of broadcasts that are sent to the remote clients. The administrator can also specify a home server for the users in this container.

IP Parameters Allows the administrator to specify the IP address of the domain name server, the domain name of the remote client, and the BOOTP (Bootstrap Protocol) parameters for a remote client. (BOOTP is not common, and you will probably not use it.)

Configuring Remote User Parameters

In addition to configuring all clients based on the container in which they are located, the administrator can also override that configuration on a per-user basis. The NWCADM32.DLL snap-in provides two remote access property tabs for the User object in NetWare Administrator:

- Remote Access–1
- Remote Access–2

The Remote Access–1 property page, shown in Figure 16.6, allows the administrator to control remote client password properties, maximum connect time, idle time-out, and dial-back parameters and includes a button that allows the administrator to change the user's remote client password.

PART

IV

Special Network Features

FIGURE 16.6

The Remote Access–1 property page for a NetWare user as seen in the NetWare Administrator program

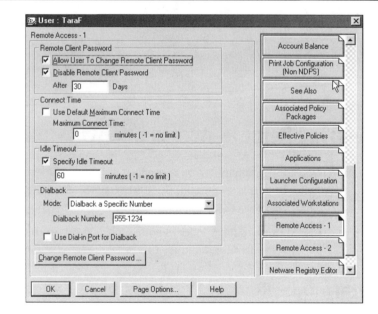

Figure 16.7 shows the Remote Access–2 property page, which allows the administrator to restrict the AppleTalk zones that an AppleTalk Remote Access Server user can access and to set IPX parameters, the IPX home server, and IP parameters.

FIGURE 16.7

The Remote Access–2 property page for a NetWare user as seen in the NetWare Administrator program

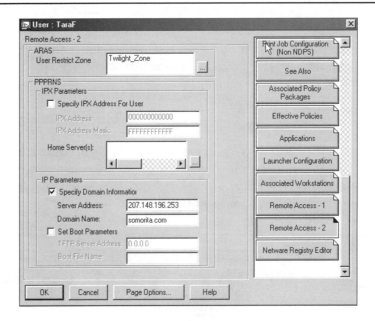

Configuring Remote Access Clients

After you configure remote access services and users, you need to configure the remote access clients. In this section, I'll discuss two types of remote access server clients:

- Point-to-Point Remote Node Service clients, such as Windows 95/98 clients
- NASI Connection Service clients, such as users on the LAN who need to access a shared modem for dial-out purposes

Setting Up a Remote Windows 95/98 Client

To configure a Windows 95 or Windows 98 client to dial in to a NetWare 5.1 remote access server, you use Microsoft Windows Dial-Up Networking (sometimes called DUN). The client is essentially the same under Windows 95 and Windows 98; it is also very similar under Windows NT/2000.

If the remote client needs to map drives to NetWare servers and use NetWare printers, you also need to install the Novell NetWare Client software or the Microsoft Client for NetWare Networks software. It is possible to configure remote clients just to use TCP/IP for access to your intranet servers, such as Web servers and FTP servers.

You'll find Dial-Up Networking in the My Computer folder on Windows 95/98/NT/2000. You can also open it in Windows 95 and Windows NT/2000 by choosing Start ➤ Programs ➤ Accessories ➤ Dial-Up Networking. You can open it in Windows 98 by choosing Start ➤ Programs ➤ Accessories ➤ Communications ➤ Dial-Up Networking.

If Dial-Up Networking is not installed, put your Windows 95/98 CD in the drive, and follow these steps to install it:

1. Choose Start ➤ Settings ➤ Control Panel ➤ Add/Remove Programs ➤ Windows Setup.

2. Select Communications.

3. Check Dial-Up Networking, and click OK.

To configure Windows 95/98 Dial-Up Networking, simply open the Dial-Up Networking folder and choose Make New Connection to start the Make New Connection Wizard. You will be asked for the name of the connection and for a device to be used with the connection, such as a modem or ISDN adapter. You will then be prompted for the country, area code, and phone number. This is all the information that you will be required to fill in for a new connection

To customize this connection, right-click on it in Dial-Up Networking and choose Properties. Your connection's properties will be displayed in four configuration tabs. Figure 16.8 shows the General tab for a dial-up connection called Somorita Surfboards RAS Server.

PART

IV

Special Network Features

FIGURE 16.8

The General tab for a Dial-Up Networking connection in Windows 98

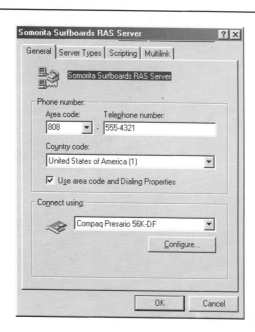

From this tab, you can configure the area code, country dialing code, and telephone number of the remote server you are calling. If you have configured Windows Telephony properties, you can use the Area Code and Dialing properties. In addition, you can select which modem or synchronous adapter you want to use for this connection.

Figure 16.9 shows the Server Types tab, which contains more advanced options. From this tab, you can specify the type of dial-up server. You have the following choices:

- NRN: NetWare Connect version 1 and 1.1
- PPP: Internet, Windows NT Server, Windows 98
- SLIP: Unix connection (to systems that don't support PPP)
- Windows for Workgroups and Windows NT 3.1

 TIP Leave the server type configured as a PPP: Internet, Windows NT/2000 Server, Windows 98 for almost all the connection types you are going to support, regardless of whether you are calling in to NetWare remote access services, Windows NT remote access services, or an Internet service provider.

FIGURE 16.9

The Server Types property tab for a Dial-Up Networking connection in Windows 98

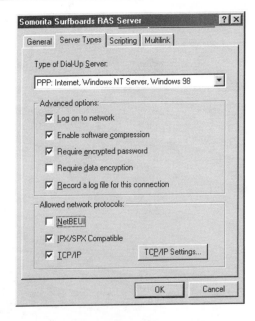

The Server Types property tab also allows some additional configuration and customization options:

Log On To Network   Dial-Up Networking will attempt to log on using the user name and password that you used when you logged in to Windows 98. If your dial-up server uses a different user name and password, you will need to provide them.

Enable Software Compression   Specifies whether to attempt to use software compression. This option will improve performance if both client and remote access server are using compatible compression techniques.

Require Encrypted Password   This option works only if the remote access server you are connecting to supports the same password-encryption mechanism that the client supports. If this option is checked, your client will accept or send only encrypted passwords. Windows 95/98, Windows NT/2000, and NetWare remote access services support a couple of common password-encryption methods: Challenge Handshake Authentication Protocol (CHAP) and Password Authentication Protocol (PAP).

Require Data Encryption   Specifies that the client will send only encrypted data. If the remote access server does not support the client's data-encryption method, the client will not be able to connect to the server. Currently, the Windows Dial-Up Networking client supports data encryption only when it is connecting to a Windows NT 3.5*x* or 4 remote access server.

Record a Log File for This Connection   Requires the client to create a Point-to-Point Protocol (PPP) log file for the connection. This log file is found in the \WINDOWS directory and is useful in troubleshooting authentication and connection issues.

Allowed Network Protocols   Specifies which protocols the client will attempt to use when connecting over the PPP link. The NetWare remote access server supports IPX/SPX and TCP/IP only, so you can disable NetBEUI. If you select TCP/IP, you can specify an IP address and domain name server IP addresses.

The Scripting tab allows you to set up a script to execute during login, and the Multilink tab allows you to specify additional modems and phone numbers to dial when connecting with this server. Multilink will improve your overall throughput but requires additional hardware.

PART

IV

Special Network
Features

WARNING When using remote access services, keep in mind that your network connection is going to be very slow. A 33.6Kbps or 56Kbps connection works well for copying smaller files and surfing the Web; however, retrieving large files and executing applications that are stored on the server you dialed in to are not recommended. Test each application that you want your users to run remotely before deploying it.

Setting Up Modem Pool Clients

The official name is, of course, NetWare Asynchronous Services Interface (NASI) Connection Service (or just NCS for short), but I have always called this *modem pooling*. Simply put, many network clients can share a group of modems located in the server. A client can "acquire" a modem when it needs one, and when the client is finished, the modem is once again available.

The Win2NCS (Windows to NASI Connection Service) software finds available modems, authenticates the user to the modem pool, and acquires a modem. It redirects data that would normally be sent to the COM port across the network to a modem controlled by the NASI Connection Service located on the remote access server (a.k.a. Novell Internet Access Server).

This software enhances security by allowing the administrator to limit who can do what, and also it helps reduce abuses from users who might install their own modems. One network that I worked on had no official dial-in or dial-out support, but the phone supervisor would connect individual phone lines for any user who asked for one. Within a year, we had a few dozen "rogue" modems connecting people to our network.

The NASI Connection Service supports the following clients:

- Windows 95/98 through Win2NCS
- Windows NT/2000 through Win2NCS
- Windows 3.x through Win2NCS
- Apple Macintosh through Mac2NCS

Remote Control

You may have noticed that I have made virtually no mention of NetWare 5.1 support of remote control. Remote control technology allows a remote client using software such as Symantec's pcANYWHERE to dial in to a computer running the pcANYWHERE software and "take over." Technically, Novell does not provide a remote control solution.

Continued

CONTINUED

However, if you need remote control-type solutions, you can still use the Novell Internet Access Server solution.

To do this, you use a combination of both the dial-in services and the dial-out services. In the simplest example, a PC on the LAN acquires a modem port and initializes the software to answer. A remote user then establishes a connection to that modem port with the client software. There are more complex solutions, of course, but this gives you a general idea of how it works.

Installing the Win2NCS Client Software

The Win2NCS software is located on the NetWare client CD-ROM, and the Macintosh Mac2NCS software is included with the Macintosh client software.

 TIP I recommend copying the Win2NCS software to a volume on a NetWare server so that any client PC can easily access it. My favorite location is SYS:PUBLIC\WIN2NCS. The software is on the NetWare client CD-ROM in the \PRODUCTS\WIN2NCS directory.

Ideally, you should install the Win2NCS software on a PC that is running the Novell NetWare Client software, but the Microsoft Client for NetWare Networks should work as well. If you have previously installed an older version of Win2NCS software, uninstall it before installing the new version.

To install the software, run the SETUP program, which is in the \WIN2NCS client software directory. The setup program is the same for Windows 3.*x*, Windows 95/98, and Windows NT/2000. During setup, you have two choices: Express or Custom. Express merely asks you to confirm the location of the software (C:\WIN2NCS by default). Custom also asks how the configuration files should be managed. Here are your options:

Configuration file is created in installed directory Option #0. Choose this option if Win2NCS software is installed locally and multiple users will not share the workstation. The default filename and location are C:\WIN2NCS\NCS.INI.

Configuration files are based on logged in name Option #1. Choose this option if the Win2NCS software is installed in a shared location. The files are named with the prefix USR and end with .INI (for example, USR2.INI).

Files are assigned to users according to either their NDS name or their bindery login name.

Configuration files are always on drive C   Option #2. Choose this option if the Windows software and the Win2NCS software are installed on the server and you want the user's configuration file to be stored locally. It will be stored in the root of the C: drive.

Configuration files are always in Windows directory   Option #3. Choose this option if each user has a private Windows directory and the Win2NCS software is installed in a shared location. The NCS.INI file is stored in the Windows directory or automatically created if one does not exist.

Configuration files are based on user name   Option #4. Choose this option if both the Windows software and the Win2NCS software are stored in a shared location. This choice is similar to *Configuration files are based on logged in name*, as each user has a unique configuration file created.

Automating the Win2NCS Software Installation

If you need to install the Win2NCS software on many workstations, you will not want to do so individually. You can easily automate the installation. If you have not already copied the \WIN2NCS software from the client CD-ROM, you should do so.

Create a text file called SETUP.INI, and put it in the SYS:PUBLIC\WIN2NCS subdirectory (my preferred location). The setup program looks for SETUP.INI and, when it finds it, takes the installation options found in this file.

The SETUP.INI file has three basic components:

Networked   Chooses the installation type, 0 through 4, described above.

InstallPath   Sets the drive and subdirectory in which to install the software.

COMx   Selects which ports are chosen or how ports are chosen and assigned to specific COM ports.

Here is a simple example of a SETUP.INI file that installs the software to C:\WIN2NCS, creates configuration files in the installed directory, and assigns COM3 dynamically and COM4 to any available port on server DUKE.

```
Networked = 0
InstallPath = C:\WIN2NCS
COM1 = UNMAPPED
COM2 = UNMAPPED
COM3 = DYNAMIC
COM4 = DUKE,ANY_PORT,?????????????
```

Using the WIN2NCS Software

Once Win2NCS is installed on a workstation, you can use it to assign modems to specific ports on your workstation. To configure the Win2NCS software, choose Start ➤ Programs ➤ Win2NCS Com Port Mapping ➤ Win2NCS. This launches the Win2NCS Mapping Utility, as shown in Figure 16.10.

FIGURE 16.10

The Win2NCS Mapping Utility

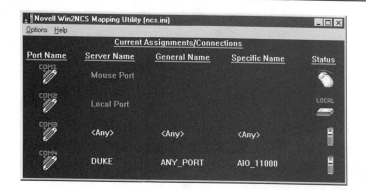

Figure 16.10 shows four ports mapped on this computer. The COM1 port is assigned to the mouse, and the COM2 port is assigned as a local port. Win2NCS will not use either of these COM ports. Port COM3 is assigned to <Any>, which means the first available modem is assigned when an application attempts to use that port. Port COM4 is assigned to a specific port on server DUKE.

You can configure and customize the Win2NCS software using the Options menu:

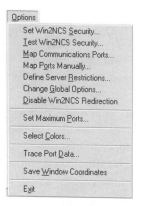

These options will be stored in your configuration file.

Once you set the options, you can define modems in Windows 95/98 or Windows NT/2000, even though they are located on the NetWare remote access server.

To install a new modem under Windows 95/98 or Windows NT/2000, choose Control Panel ➤ Modems ➤ Add to open the Install New Modem dialog box:

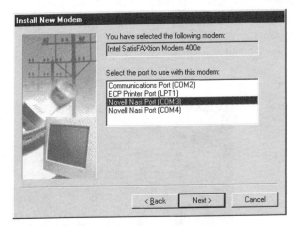

Application software that requires modem access will automatically acquire a modem when the software needs a modem and will release the modem when the software is through.

Monitoring Your Remote Access Server

Monitoring your remote access server is also important, whether you want to see the ports currently in use, to audit usage, or to bill for usage. A number of mechanisms are in place for auditing the usage of the Novell Internet Access Server (NIAS).

Monitoring and Managing Ports

Using the NIASCFG utility, you can view all port information and reset ports. From the NIASCFG main menu, choose View Status for NIAS ➤ Remote Access ➤ Display Port Status to display the port list. The list in Figure 16.11 shows all the active ports, their current status, which service is using that port, the user who is using the port, and how long that user has been connected.

From this screen, I can highlight a specific port and display the full NDS user name, port status, maximum connection limit, and modem type. The Status column will contain one of the following options.

Acquired   Acquired by remote access.

AcquiredOther   An application other than remote access acquired the port.

Answering   Answering an incoming call.

Broken   The modem port or the modem is not initialized.

Connected   Remote connection successfully established.

Connecting   Remote connection in progress.

Dialing   Remote access is dial-out.

Disconnected   The connection was terminated.

Idle   The port is available.

Initializing   The port is being reset.

Shutdown   Remote access server is shutting down.

Startup   Remote access server is still starting.

Unavailable   Configuration or modem problem. No modem attached.

Waiting   Ready for incoming calls.

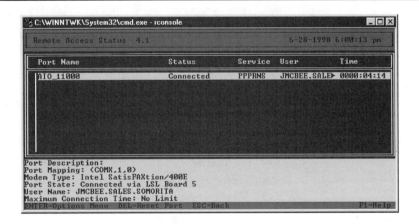

FIGURE 16.11

The NIAS Remote Access Status screen displaying active ports

Highlight a port and press Enter to display the Port Operations menu:

You can use this menu to display real-time port statistics on each port. Here are the options:

Display Port Statistics   Displays detailed information about port settings and port statistics.

Start Trace On Port   If a modem, port, or application is having problems, you can log all activity on this port and modem to a file.

Reset Port   If the port is not responding, if a user needs to be kicked off, or if the port just needs to be reinitialized, you can reset it. If it is currently in use and needs to be reset, you must choose Reset Port ➤ Unconditional Reset Of Port.

Identify Port   This is a useful feature if you have a large bank of modems and you want to identify a modem. This feature toggles the port's DTR signal, which causes the modem's TR or DTR light to blink. The port cannot be in use when this option is chosen.

Terminal Mode   Use this feature if you want to display a terminal window to send commands to the port and see the responses. The port cannot be in use when this option is chosen.

Configure Port   Displays the port configuration, including the modem type.

Other Options in NIASCFG

In addition to displaying the port status from within the NIASCFG utility, you have other options for managing the remote access server. Choose View Status For NIAS ➤ Remote Access to open the Status Options menu. You have the following options:

Display Service Status   Displays the status of the NASI Connection Service (NCS), Point-to-Point Protocol Remote Node Service (PPPRNS), AppleTalk Remote Access Service (ARAS), and Remote Access Management Agent.

Display Alerts   Displays a list of remote access alerts.

Display Audit Trail   Displays information about service startup and shutdown, user login, port name, ports used for dial-out, and telephone numbers used for dial-out.

Using ConnectView

NetWare 5.1 includes ConnectView, which allows you to perform a variety of monitoring, auditing, and accounting tasks. I could easily devote a couple of chapters to ConnectView, but since I don't have the space, I at least wanted to introduce you to the program.

ConnectView is a Windows application that allows you to manage multiple Novell Internet Access Server and NetWare Connect 2 remote access servers from a single seat. Figure 16.12 shows the main screen.

FIGURE 16.12

The main screen of the ConnectView program

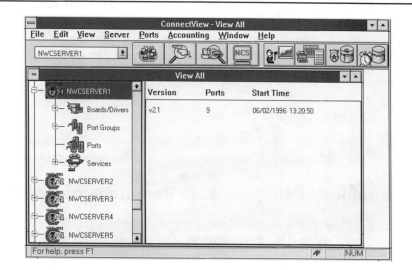

You can use ConnectView to do the following:

- Monitor all remote access servers centrally
- Graphically display remote access server port status
- Centrally start and stop remote access services
- Create usage reports and bill users for remote access service usage
- Generate alerts and audit trail reports
- Generate trend analysis reports of usage

ConnectView Requirements

To run ConnectView, you must be running Windows 3.*x*, Windows 95, or Windows 98. ConnectView will not run under Windows NT. The Setup program for ConnectView is on the remote access server's SYS: volume in SYS:PUBLIC\CVIEW\NLS\ENGLISH\DISK1.

During installation, it adds the BREQUEST.EXE file to either the Windows 3.*x* AUTOEXEC.BAT file or the Windows 95/98 WINSTART.BAT file.

The workstation should have a recent version of the NetWare client software on it and should have at least 6MB of free disk space. Any NIAS or Connect 2 server that is going to be managed by ConnectView should have the BSPXCOM.NLM and the NCMA.NLM loaded.

Troubleshooting Remote Access Services

Remote connectivity never causes problems. <Very big grin> However, it is still a good idea to have an arsenal of troubleshooting tools and techniques at your disposal. We can break these troubleshooting tools into two categories:

- Server based
- Client based

Both the server and the client have some helpful tools, procedures, and log file options to help you track down even the most annoying problems.

Troubleshooting NetWare Remote Access Servers

The process of troubleshooting the remote access services at the server level takes place either at the server console or from a workstation connected to the server that can examine the log files created by the server.

Here are some questions you should ask yourself when starting the remote access service troubleshooting process:

- Am I using server equipment and serial interface equipment that is certified by Novell labs? Choosing the right client and server modems can save you a lot of heartache.

- Do any of the IP or IPX addresses I am assigning to the PPPRNS conflict with an IP or IPX network address on the LAN?

- Are my serial adapters, ISDN boards, multiport serial adapters, or X.25 adapters configured properly and not interfering with other hardware devices?

- Have I tried to restart the server? (Restarting is one of my favorite troubleshooting suggestions! <grin>)

- Do I have the latest .LAN, .LDI, and NIAS (remote access service) patch files from Novell?

- Does the telephone line really work? (Invest $10 in a small phone you can use for testing.) Verify that the phone number for this phone line really rings this particular phone line. (Don't laugh. I see this happen a lot!)

TIP If you are receiving a specific error code and cannot track down what it means or why it is popping up, your first line of defense is the Novell Knowledgebase on the Web at support.novell.com. This extensive database of problems, solutions, and patches has saved me from hours of unnecessary troubleshooting more than a few times.

Verify That PPPRNS Services Are Loaded

Checking to make sure that the Point-to-Point Protocol Remote Node Services are loading is important. If these services are not loaded or being bound to a protocol, dial-in users will not be able to connect and communicate with the network. A quick way to check this is to use the NetWare server console command CONFIG.

You should see all the network interfaces you have loaded, including at least one instance of PPPRNS*xx*, loaded. For example, if you don't see PPPRNS01 loaded with either IPX or IP bound to it, check to make sure it is being loaded and that the protocols are being bound to it.

Use the CONLOG.NLM

You first need to make sure that all the NLMs are loading properly. You can do this by watching them all go racing by on the server's console screen during boot-up, or you can write a log of this activity to a text file. Since the information on the console screen usually loads faster than mere mortals can read, I recommend getting a log of console activity.

The CONLOG.NLM captures all messages generated to the server's console screen while CONLOG is loaded and puts them in a file (SYS:ETC\CONSOLE.LOG by default). The CONLOG.NLM has many startup options that you can use. I am going to give you an example of my personal favorite CONLOG options and leave it to you to refer to the utilities portion of the NetWare documentation to find others.

Place the following command in the AUTOEXEC.NCF file directly after the SERVER NAME command. You want it as close to the top of the AUTOEXEC.NCF as possible so that it can log as much activity as possible.

```
LOAD CONLOG SAVE=SYS:ETC\CONSOLE.BAK MAXIMUM=512 ENTIRE=YES
```

This command loads the CONLOG.NLM, creates a backup file of the previous SYS:ETC\CONSOLE.LOG called SYS:ETC\CONSOLE.BAK, sets the maximum file size for log files to 512KB, and captures the entire screen, including anything that was directly above the LOAD CONLOG command.

PART

IV

Special Network Features

You can also use the UNLOAD and LOAD CONLOG commands if you are getting ready to perform a specific task and want a smaller CONSOLE.LOG file that contains only the messages for that task.

You can scan this file with a text editor from a workstation, or you can use the EDIT.NLM and read the console log from the server.

You can also view the CONSOLE.LOG file from the NIASCFG utility. From the main NIASCFG menu, choose Configure NIAS ➤ Protocols and Routing ➤ View Configuration ➤ Console Messages.

Some specific areas to look for in this file, with regard to remote access, include when the NWCSS.NLM, PPPRNS.NLM, NCS.NLM, and AIO.NLM files are loading.

View a Configuration Report

Just so configuration problems don't sneak by you, run a configuration report from the NIASCFG main menu. Choose Configure NIAS ➤ Remote Access ➤ Generate Configuration Report. You can view this report on the screen or print it out from the text file that it creates on the SYS: volume in the NWCRPT.TXT file.

Verify that there are no error or warning messages in this file. Also make sure that all the services, modems, and ports are configured that you expect to be configured.

Client Authentication Problems

I could not decide if this section belonged with client issues or server issues, but since it has to be fixed on the server, I put it here. When a client connects to the NetWare remote access server, it has to authenticate.

Windows 95/98 and Windows NT clients require either the Password Authentication Protocol (PAP) or the Challenge Handshake Authentication Protocol (CHAP). These authentication protocols are turned off by default.

To enable them, from the NIASCFG main menu, choose Configure NIAS ➤ Remote Access ➤ Configure Services ➤ PPPRNS ➤ Configure Security to open the PPPRNS Configuration screen:

```
                          PPPRNS Configuration

Enable Security:  Enable
    NetWare Connect Authentication Protocol (NWCAP):  Yes
    Password Authentication Protocol (PAP):   Yes
    Challenge Handshake Authentication Protocol (CHAP):   Yes
```

Perform a Modem Port Trace

If you have a modem that is not initializing or applications that do not properly use a remote access server port, the NIASCFG utility allows you to capture all activity that occurs with that port, whether it was generated by the client, the modem, or the host.

To start a port trace, use the NIASCFG utility. From the NIAS main menu, choose View Status for NIAS ➤ Remote Access ➤ Display Port Status. Choose the port you want to trace, and then click Start Trace On Port. You will be prompted for the name of the trace file. If you do not provide a path, it will be saved in the root of the SYS: volume.

When you are finished with your trace, use the Stop Trace On Port option to stop tracing and save the file. When the file is saved, you can use the client utility, VIEWTRC.EXE, to convert the file to an ASCII text file for viewing.

Other Remote Access Server Diagnostic Utilities

There is a whole slew of other diagnostic utilities that get into a lot of detail. I will list these utilities here for you, but I recommend that you refer to the Novell documentation in the section "Novell Internet Access Server Management and Optimization" for additional information. These utilities are designed to capture data real-time to log files and allow you to analyze it later.

 WARNING These utilities capture very detailed information.

CAPITRCE.NLM Captures and displays communication that occurs between the CAPI (Communications Application Programming Interface) Manager and its upper and lower layers. Used when debugging ISDN problems.

DTRACE.NLM Captures and displays communications between an ISDN switch and the US Robotics ISDN Allegra adapters.

FRTRACE.NLM Captures and displays information about Frame Relay circuits and data that is crossing those circuits. This utility is used when the NetWare server is acting as a router to a Frame Relay network.

PPPTRACE.NLM Captures, decodes, and displays Point-to-Point Protocol information. This is useful when diagnosing authentication problems as well as protocol negotiation problems.

X25TRACE.NLM Captures and displays X.25 traffic for diagnosing problems such as X.25 hardware configuration and X.25 network traffic.

Troubleshooting Remote Client Problems

Troubleshooting client-related remote access problems is tough, especially considering how many times the remote access user is not in the same location that you are. I have a terrible time helping remote users solve problems because I am much better at solving problems if I am actually at the computer that is having them.

PART

IV

Special Network Features

The Best Offense Is a Good Defense

Everyone has heard that one before, right? What does it have to do with remote access? I realize that you may not have the luxury of doing these things, but if you can, you'll be immensely better off. Here are some defensive tactics:

- Standardize the modem types that are used on company-owned remote computers.
- If users buy their own modems, provide them with a list of supported modems (modems that you have tested yourself).
- Test the dial-out features of all official company PCs, such as laptops, that need remote access before they go out the door.
- When remote users have problems, ask them to bring their computer and modem into your office or helpdesk for testing and problem diagnostics. Some of you are already saying this is a bad idea, since it opens your helpdesk to becoming a tech support organization for your user's home computers. If you do this, be sure you lay down the rules to your users.

Your remote client problems generally fall into two categories:

- Configuration
- Authentication

Before starting off on your troubleshooting journey, ask yourself the following questions:

- Is the client using the correct logon name and password? Remember, Windows 95/98, Windows NT/2000, and Unix clients must use their remote client password, not their NetWare password, when connecting remotely.
- What type of modem is the client using? Is it installed correctly?
- Does the client have either the Novell NetWare Client software or the Microsoft Client for NetWare Networks installed? One of these is required if the client is going to connect to drives on the NetWare servers.
- Is the client configured with the correct telephone number?
- Have you tried using another modem?

Authentication Problems

In the Connect To dialog box, be sure that users enter their full NDS name in the User Name box, such as JMCBEE.SALES.SOMORITA. If their context is the same as the NDS context in which the remote access server is located, they can simply enter their logon name.

When using Windows 95/98 and Windows NT/2000 clients, users commonly make the mistake of using their NetWare password. When connecting with these clients, the remote client must use their remote client password. This password also expires without warning, so users should be educated about its use.

As I mentioned earlier, be sure that the server supports the correct authentication protocols. It should support Challenge Handshake Authentication Protocol (CHAP) and Password Authentication Protocol (PAP). You can check this on the server in the NIASCFG utility. From the main NIAS menu, choose Configure NIAS ➤ Remote Access ➤ Configure Services ➤ PPPRNS ➤ Configure Security.

Another option is to turn on logging for the client. This creates a file called C:\WINDOWS\PPPLOG.TXT. This can help you to verify that a client is connecting properly. To turn on logging, display the Dial-Up Networking folder, right-click the dialing entry you want to record a log file for, choose the Server Types tab, and check the Create Log File box.

PART

IV

Special Network
Features

CHAPTER 17

Using NetWare 5.1 Enhancements and Special Features

N etWare 4.*x* and 5.0 introduced many new features and benefits that changed the way people look at and use NetWare. With this newest version, Novell continues its tradition of improving server performance and reliability. Novell Directory Services has been fortified with new administrative features. Also significant is Novell's attempt to transform NetWare 5.1 into a major application platform. A number of new APIs have been made available to encourage alliances with hardware and software developers. This effort focuses on several areas, including Java, Internet applications, printing devices, storage, backup, and security.

This chapter highlights some previously existing NetWare features and introduces some NetWare 5.1 enhancements. Some of these are features, and some are benefits. These are my definitions: a *feature* is something the system does; a *benefit* is something positive you get from that feature.

I organized the topics in this chapter roughly in order of how valuable I feel these features are to the greatest number of users. However, each network is unique. What turns you on may leave the network manager in the next building cold. Hot features—the ones that provide real benefits—tend to change over time. What you care little about today may become very important when it solves a problem for you tomorrow.

NetWare 5.1 Enhancements

Before I start talking in depth about NetWare 5.1 enhancements, I want to take a moment and introduce you to some features that are covered elsewhere in this book. For many of you, these features won't provide any additional benefits, but I am betting that an equal number of you will be just as excited about these features as I am.

Native TCP/IP Support

Over the years, Novell has been increasing support for TCP/IP technologies. Starting with NetWare 3, basic TCP/IP routing support was included. Later, products such as LAN WorkPlace and LAN WorkGroup provided client connectivity to TCP/IP-based hosts. The NetWare/IP product then gave network administrators the ability to run TCP/IP-based clients, although IPX/SPX was still encapsulated in an IP datagram. NetWare 5.0 introduced native IP support, and NetWare 5.1 finishes that trip by making HTTP (HyperText Transfer Protocol, used for Web server-to-client communications) a core service. NetWare Core Protocol (NCP) data is transported natively via IP. This is a significant enhancement if you support both TCP/IP and IPX/SPX networks—and an even bigger deal if your company wants to be all TCP/IP. See Chapter 14 for more information.

Domain Name Service (DNS) and Dynamic Host Configuration Protocol (DHCP)

When managing a TCP/IP network, network administrators are faced with two significant challenges:

- Tracking IP addresses
- Resolving computer names to their current IP addresses

NetWare 5.1 now provides both a Dynamic Host Configuration Protocol (DHCP) server to automatically allocate IP host addresses to IP clients and a Domain Name Service (DNS) to manage the database of computer names and their IP host addresses. I discuss these in Chapter 15.

Netscape Enterprise Web Server for NetWare 5.1

NetWare 5.1 ships with the Netscape Enterprise Web server for creating, publishing, and serving Web documents. This full-featured Web server runs as a NetWare 5.1 NLM and provides Web publishing services, Web-based administration, and secure Web services. For more information on the Netscape Enterprise Web Server for NetWare 5.1, see Chapter 14.

ZENworks (Zero Effort Networks)

NetWare 5.1 includes the ZENworks Starter Kit, which is part of Novell's desktop management tool suite. This suite provides tools for distributing software, managing software, managing workstations, and administering workstations. These tools can reduce the amount of time that administrators spend managing their networks, installing software, and troubleshooting problems. Using ZENworks is covered in Chapter 11.

Oracle 8i for NetWare 5.1

You can easily find a bookcase full of books about Oracle, so anything I tell you in a book about NetWare will certainly be incomplete. However, I am mentioning it so that you realize it is part of the product and available to you. This product is tightly integrated with Novell Directory Services and takes advantage of NetWare's multitasking, multiprocessing, and I/O capabilities. This product is easy to install and comes with a preconfigured and pretuned database to help you quickly get up and running with this next-generation database server. A five-user license is included with NetWare 5.1.

NetWare Distributed Print Services (NDPS)

Years ago, one of the main reasons that small and medium-sized offices installed networks was to share printers. Network printing—print drivers, queues, printers, print servers, and the general hassle of troubleshooting network printers—has traditionally been a major pain in the neck for network administrators.

Novell, along with companies such as Xerox and Hewlett-Packard, has moved network printing forward once again with NetWare Distributed Print Services (NDPS). The goal of NDPS is to make network printers easier to install and manage while increasing their performance. I discuss NDPS in depth in Chapter 8.

NetWare Specialized Features

This section is my dumping spot for features that just did not quite fit anywhere else in the book. Those of you who have worked with NetWare 3.x or 4.x will recognize many of these features. NetWare 5.1 improves upon many of these as well. You will even see a few new features, such as virtual memory support.

File Name Space

By default, NetWare volumes support the DOS file-naming convention; however, NetWare has had the ability to support files from other operating systems for a long time. As far back as NetWare 2.15, NetWare supported Macintosh clients and files. This feature allows clients such as Macintosh computers to save files to a server volume; the files appear as native Macintosh files to the Macintosh user. PC users can also see the file, but they see it as if it were a DOS file. If both the PC user and the Macintosh user are using an application that creates a common data file format, they can share the file.

To support additional name spaces on a server volume, you must first load the appropriate supporting module (these files are NetWare Loadable Modules, but they end with .NAM instead of .NLM). Once the name space support module is loaded, you must configure each volume to support that name space.

NetWare 5.1 supports four name space modules:

DOS   The default name space on NetWare volumes. DOS is automatically supported.

LONG   Supports OS/2, Windows 95/98, and Windows NT/2000 clients, since these operating systems can store files with names longer than the traditional DOS eight-point-three (8.3) character filename limitation. NWCONFIG now automatically adds LONG name support to volumes it creates.

MAC   Used by Macintosh clients connecting to the NetWare server through services for Macintosh. This name space module file is MAC.NAM. For more information on NetWare/Macintosh connectivity, see Appendix E.

NFS   Used by Unix and other NFS clients through the NetWare NFS Server software. Although the name space module is included with NetWare 5.1, you must purchase the NetWare NFS Server software separately. The name space module file is called NFS.NAM.

Adding Name Space Support

You load the name space support modules from the STARTUP.NCF file using the LOAD command. To load the MAC name space, place the following command into the STARTUP.NCF file:

```
LOAD MAC
```

The first time the name space is loaded, you must add the name space support to any volume that is going to support those files. You need only do this once. For example, to enable the NetWare volume VOLUME1 to support the MAC name space, at the server console prompt, type:

```
ADD NAME SPACE MAC TO VOLUME1
```

To verify that the name space has been added to a NetWare volume, use the server console command VOLUMES to display a list of all mounted volumes and the name spaces they support.

 NOTE   To remove a previously installed name space without deleting the volume, use the server utility VREPAIR.NLM.

Repairing a Damaged Name Space

The VREPAIR.NLM utility automatically repairs NetWare volumes with the DOS name space, since this is the default name space. However, if a volume has other name spaces associated with it, the VREPAIR name space support modules must be available. There is a separate VREPAIR support module for each name space:

- V_LONG is used to repair volumes with long name spaces.
- V_MAC is used to repair volumes with Macintosh files.
- V_NFS is used to repair volumes with NFS files.

If required, these modules will be loaded automatically by the VREPAIR.NLM program. It is a good practice to make sure that these files are on the server's local hard disk (C:\NWSERVER by default) as well as in the SYS:SYSTEM directory. My rule of thumb is that they should be in the same location as VREPAIR.NLM.

Novell Storage Services and Name Spaces

I'll talk about Novell Storage Services later in this chapter in the section "Novell Storage Services (NSS)." NSS volumes automatically support all name spaces.

Server Memory Management

NetWare 5.1 requires that the file server have a minimum of 48MB of RAM. If you are planning to use the Java-based, graphical console, you should plan on at least 256MB of RAM (minimum 128MB). Other application services based on Java can up the RAM requirements even more.

The server works with its available resources to respond to clients' file and print requests, NLM applications, Java applications, and NetWare's own demands. Do not allow your server to become short on memory.

Novell developed a logical memory-addressing scheme that minimizes memory fragmentation during its daily routines. This memory-addressing scheme allows NetWare to allocate more memory than is physically present. This is called *virtual memory*, which I discuss later in this chapter in the section "Using Virtual Memory."

Low-memory conditions can abend the server or result in sluggish performance. The administrator can isolate problem applications with the MONITOR utility and optimize memory usage on the server with setting parameters and console commands.

Figure 17.1 shows a partial list of NLMs that are loaded on NetWare 5.1 server PRO-LIANT. To view memory usage on the file server, load the MONITOR.NLM utility, and choose Available Options ➤ Loaded Modules. Active NLMs will be listed at the bottom of the screen. As you scroll through them, pertinent information is displayed above. Press Enter for details about an individual module. To disable a module and free the memory it is using, press F4.

Memory Management Rules of Thumb

When dealing with NetWare servers, more RAM almost always equals better performance. This is especially true if the server acts as a file and print server. Here are a few rules of thumb that I follow with respect to server memory:

- Don't keep the Java-based, graphical user interface loaded on the server console if it is not in use.
- Don't load the Java components if they are not going to be used.

- Don't load unnecessary name space modules or add name space support to volumes that do not require that particular name space.

- Avoid loading unnecessary NLMs.

- If the server's Long Term Cache Hits value drops below 90 percent, add additional RAM. (You'll find more on this in the next section.)

FIGURE 17.1

The MONITOR.NLM *loaded modules list*

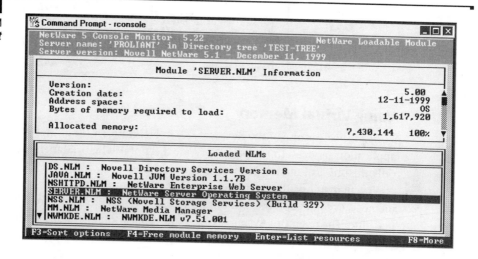

When people ask me how much RAM a server should have, I generally try to overestimate. The March 1997 edition of Novell's *AppNotes* has an excellent article, "Optimizing intraNetWare Server Memory," on estimating how much memory a server requires. Though the article was written for intraNetWare, many of the concepts and planning numbers are the same. You can find this article on the Novell developer Web site at developer.novell.com/research/appnotes.htm.

Does My Server Need More RAM?

When people ask me if a server needs more RAM, I tend to answer yes without even looking first. I am half joking, but I am a big fan of making sure servers have plenty of RAM. There is also a point of diminishing returns that occurs when your server has sufficient memory and just can't effectively use any more. Your boss is probably not going to share my enthusiasm for adding RAM indiscriminately and will ask you for hardcore numbers.

As I mentioned, a good guideline is the Long Term Cache Hits statistic. To display this value, use the MONITOR utility at the server. From the main MONITOR screen, press Tab to display the General Information statistics. If the Long Term Cache Hits value is below 90 percent, you should add additional RAM.

```
                        General Information
         Utilization:                          2%
         Server up time:                 1:20:35:23
         Online processors:                       1
         Original cache buffers:             15,822
         Total cache buffers:                 5,145
         Dirty cache buffers:                     0
         Long term cache hits:                  97%
         Current disk requests:                   1
         Packet receive buffers:                128
         Directory cache buffers:                31
         Maximum service processes:             570
         Current service processes:              19
         Current connections:                     5
         Open files:                            152
```

Using Virtual Memory

Virtual memory is one of the new features in NetWare 5.*x* that is designed to support application services. In the past, NetWare has not used virtual memory, but rather only the physical memory found in the machine.

Virtual memory allows applications and programmers to access very large blocks of memory, even beyond the amount of memory that is physically installed in the machine. The operating system assigns the application a range of virtual memory and maps the application's virtual memory addresses to blocks (or pages) of memory that are physically in RAM.

When the amount of physical memory that an application requires exceeds the amount of memory in the machine, the operating system creates temporary files that extend actual RAM in the server. When a user sends a request to the server to open a file or runs a query or a report on a database, data is placed in active RAM, using some of the available pool of resources on the system. The file server saves recent requests to RAM to speed response time.

To increase RAM efficiency, NetWare transfers data that is in low demand to temporary files, or swap files, which will be accessed when needed. NetWare maintains a translation table that tracks usage of RAM data, helping it to make decisions about swapping files to disk. The amount of swapping that NetWare does could possibly decrease the system's performance, since CPU and disk resources are required to manage the swapping operation, but it can also help overall system performance by making more memory available to applications that need it. If you ascertain that your server is swapping too often, it may be time to add additional memory to the server.

 NOTE The NetWare server operating system and the server's modules do not use virtual memory because they cannot be swapped out to disk.

Modules that are loaded into protected memory spaces and programs that run as part of the Java Virtual Machine use virtual memory. These programs and the data they access are subject to being swapped out to disk.

Tuning Virtual Memory

By default, NetWare creates a swap file in the SYS: volume. You can create one swap file on each volume. Type **HELP SWAP** at the server console to display the options for the SWAP command. Actually, it doesn't matter which volume you store swap files on, since any RAM data can be stored in any swap file found on any volume. Use the fastest and largest hard drives for your swap files for the best results. To add or delete a swap file on volume 1, type the following at the server console prompt:

```
SWAP ADD VOL1
SWAP DEL VOL1
```

To control the minimum and maximum sizes of a swap file, you use options with the SWAP command, as in the following example:

```
SWAP ADD VOL1 MIN=5 MAX=100 MIN FREE=100
```

The default minimum size (MIN) is 2MB, and the maximum (MAX) swap file can use all available disk space on the volume. The MIN FREE parameter specifies the amount of space to be left on the volume; if you don't specify, the default is 5MB. The MIN and MAX parameters are in megabytes (millions of bytes).

To modify an existing swap file, use the PARAMETER option:

```
SWAP PARAMETER SYS MIN=5 MAX=100 MIN FREE=100
```

When a volume is dismounted, the swap file is deleted. Add swap commands to your AUTOEXEC.NCF file if you want them to be available whenever the server is reset.

To display statistics about a server's virtual memory information, use the MONITOR utility. Choose MONITOR ➢ Virtual Memory, and then press the Tab key to display the full Virtual Memory Information statistics:

```
          Virtual Memory Information
  Page-in requests, total:          7,691
  Page-in requests per second:          0
  Page-out requests, total:        12,160
  Page-out requests per second:         0

  Swap pages, total:                7,680
  Swap pages, free:                    12
  Swap pages, reserved:             7,677

  Page faults, total:              34,322
  Page faults per second:               0
```

Server Self-Tuning for Better Performance (and How to Improve It)

NetWare's flat memory model allows processes that need more memory to be assigned more memory. This happens automatically, without any intervention on your part.

Each time the server is restarted, the settings that were adjusted during operation are set back to the defaults. You can change the defaults to more accurately reflect the performance profile of your server after it has had time to tune itself. The tuning happens fairly quickly, but not as quickly as it would have if the right values were in place when the server started. Many administrators don't need to adjust their systems. In certain situations, though, a certain amount of fine-tuning is helpful.

I'll describe some parameters for Directory Cache Buffers and File Caches that you might want to fine-tune. Caches work under the assumption that users make multiple requests of active files, for example, in saving and resaving a document or in searching for data in a database. So, a file server saves recent requests in RAM to speed response time.

NetWare allocates a minimum of 20 directory cache buffers of 4KB each, which saves the names of requested files in server memory. Each cache buffer contains 32 entries linked to 32 files. This is appropriate for small workgroups. The default maximum value for cache buffers is 500, or about 2MB. The maximum value is 200,000. To increase the level of directory cache buffers, type the following SET commands at the console prompt, and add them to STARTUP.NCF so that your system uses them every time the server boots:

SET MINIMUM DIRECTORY CACHE BUFFERS=2000

SET MAXIMUM DIRECTORY CACHE BUFFERS=4000

Optionally, you can use the MONITOR utility at the server console to set server parameters, but I prefer the new NetWare Management Portal, so I tend to use that. However, the MONITOR utility is probably where you are now, so try that. To set these parameters from the MONITOR utility, choose MONITOR ➢ Server Parameters ➢ Directory Caching, locate the parameter you want to set, and make the change.

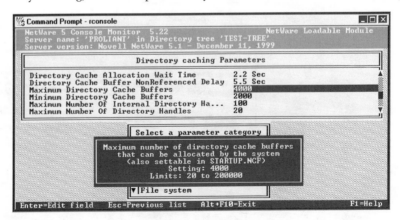

Each NetWare volume maintains a Directory Entry Table (DET) of files stored there. Each type of name space used on the system adds a directory entry for each file, so DOS, NFS, and LONG name spaces require three names for each file. Therefore, a directory cache buffer that contains 32 entries would account for only 10 files.

NetWare will try to accommodate multiple DET entries by self-adjusting the directory cache buffers. After a few weeks, look at Directory Cache Buffers on MONITOR's General Information screen to view the highest number of buffers allocated. Use that value to set the minimum, and add 100 for the maximum setting. If you need to add a name space type, use the formula below, and then use the SET commands I described earlier:

```
# of names space * high value in MONITOR = minimum cache buffers
minimum + 100 = maximum
```

Check the MONITOR screen regularly to get an idea of your performance profile during heavy network traffic sessions. Make a note of those settings. Then go back to Chapter 10 and check out how to use the SERVMAN or NetWare Management Portal utilities so that you can change as many SET parameters as necessary. You can use the MONITOR utility's Server Parameters function to adjust parameters easily. Chapter 11 has some suggestions for optimizing your server for certain operations.

 NOTE In earlier versions of NetWare, the server-based program SERVMAN allowed you to set parameters on the NetWare server. This functionality has been incorporated into the MONITOR utility and the NetWare Management Portal.

Old Network and Disk Adapters

Older ISA and microchannel network and disk adapters cannot access memory above 16MB. To make sure that these devices have enough memory below 16MB, allocate sufficient buffers below 16MB with a server command. Add the following line to your STARTUP.NCF file:

```
SET RESERVED BUFFERS BELOW 16 MEG = 200
```

 NOTE You must reboot before this option takes effect.

My personal feeling about older, slower adapters is that you should not be using them. Let's face it—servers that support the newer, faster PCI bus are inexpensive these days as are PCI network and disk adapters. Dump those old boards today.

Memory Protection

Starting in NetWare 4.1, it was possible to load certain NetWare server-based applications into a protected memory space, which was called a *domain*. The advantage of this is that applications running in protected memory space do not interfere with the server operating system. I cannot tell you how glad I was when this feature was announced. I have caused a server to abend more than a few times while running tape-backup software or database utilities at the server console.

The NetWare operating system, device drivers, and core services run in an address space that is sometimes called the *OS address space*, the *kernel address space*, or *Ring 0*.

In NetWare 5.1, the memory-protection feature is called a *protected address space*. Some operating systems call this memory space the *user address space* or *Ring 3*. Any application operating in a protected address space cannot interfere with applications running in other protected address spaces, nor can these protected applications interfere with the NetWare operating system. You can use this address space to load NLMs that are problematic or that have not been thoroughly tested.

Although most applications can run in a protected address space, some must run in the OS address space. These include:

- SERVER.EXE
- LAN and disk device drivers
- NSS file system
- MONITOR.NLM
- Applications or modules that were not designed to run in a protected address space

Loading Applications into Protected Memory

You create protected memory spaces at the server console, and you load modules into these spaces from either the server console prompt or through the AUTOEXEC.NCF. When you create a new address space, it is automatically assigned a name that starts with ADDRESS_SPACE and ends with a unique number. For example, the first address space created would be ADDRESS_SPACE1, the second address space would be ADDRESS_SPACE2, and so on.

Features of NetWare 5.1's protected address space include:

- Modules loaded into protected address spaces are part of the server's virtual memory system and are subject to being swapped out to disk if the code the module is using is not currently in use.

- If you use the RESTART option when creating protected address spaces, the system will automatically close up an address space, clean up the address space's resources, restart the address space, and reload the modules if the address space abends.

- If you load a module into a protected address space that requires other supporting modules, such as CLIB, those supporting modules are loaded into the same protected address space.

- NLMs can be loaded multiple times, even if they were designed to be loaded only once, as long as they are loaded into separate protected address spaces.

When you load modules into a protected address space, NetWare assigns whatever memory the module may require. As other modules are loaded into this space, it can grow as necessary. However, the maximum size of any NetWare 5.1 protected address space is 512MB.

There are a number of console commands for creating, manipulating, and unloading modules in protected address spaces; these are described in Table 17.1.

TABLE 17.1: PROTECTED ADDRESS SPACE COMMAND OPTIONS

Command	Description
LOAD PROTECTED *module_name*	Loads *module_name* into a new protected address space called ADDRESS_SPACEx.
LOAD RESTART *module_name*	Loads *module_name* into a new protected address space with restart functionality.
LOAD ADDRESS SPACE = *space_name module_name*	Loads *module_name* into an address space called *space_name*. You can use this command if you want to create your own address space names or if you want to load additional modules into the same address space.
PROTECT *filename.ncf*	Runs the *filename.ncf* file and loads all NLMs that are loaded in that .NCF file into a protected memory space called FILENAME.NCF.
PROTECTION RESTART *space_name*	Adds the restart functionality to the memory space called *space_name*.
PROTECTION NO RESTART *space_name*	Removes the restart functionality from the memory space called *space_name*.
UNLOAD ADDRESS SPACE = *space_name module_name*	Unloads the module *module_name* from the protected memory space *space_name*.
UNLOAD ADDRESS SPACE = *space_name*	Unloads all modules from the protected address space *space_name*.
UNLOAD KILL ADDRESS SPACE = *space_name*	Removes the address space without unloading the modules first. Use this only if you cannot unload the modules in the space first.

Here are some examples of using NetWare 5.1 protected memory space. To load the NetWare BTRIEVE.NLM into a protected memory space, type

```
LOAD ADDRESS SPACE=BTRIEVE BTRIEVE.NLM
```

Once this is loaded, to load the BSPXCOM.NLM file into the same address space, type

```
LOAD ADDRESS SPACE=BTRIEVE BSPXCOM.NLM
```

To enable the restart capability for the BTRIEVE address space, type

```
PROTECTION RESTART BTRIEVE
```

If you want to load both these modules into the BTRIEVE protected address space each time this NetWare server restarts and to enable the restart capability, enter the three previous commands into the server's AUTOEXEC.NCF file.

Viewing Address Space and Virtual Memory

To view information about which modules are loaded and which virtual memory spaces these modules are loaded into, use the server console command MODULES. This displays the module name, the version, the date, and the address space into which the module is loaded.

To display a list of all protected address spaces, at the server console prompt, use the PROTECTION command. This generates a list of all address spaces that have been created, along with the module names loaded into those address spaces.

Additional information about virtual memory is available through the server's MONITOR utility. To display virtual memory from the MONITOR utility, choose Monitor ➤ Virtual Memory ➤ Address Space. This displays a list of address spaces (see Figure 17.2) and information about them. Highlight any address space and press Enter to display a list of NLMs that are loaded into that particular address space.

FIGURE 17.2

*Address space infor-
mation shown by the
MONITOR utility*

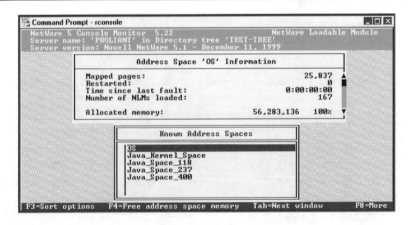

Symmetric Multi-Processing (SMP)

NetWare 5.1, like NetWare 4.x, supports *Symmetric Multi-Processing*, or *SMP*. This means that a computer with multiple processors will provide increased performance for servers that have a busy CPU. In years past, I have maintained that SMP capabilities were not terribly important in a NetWare environment. Even on servers with many hundreds of users, the server CPU was rarely the system bottleneck. Generally, the system bottleneck on a file and print server turns out to be memory, the network interface card, or the disk channel.

However, in today's NetWare network, the NetWare server is doing much more than acting as a simple file and print server. NetWare 5.1 servers now host application services such as Web servers and database servers as well as run Java applications. These services running on the NetWare server will contribute to the need for faster (or more) processors.

NetWare 5.1 automatically detects multiprocessor systems. Unlike NetWare 4.x, the new version of SMP now shares the same kernel for single and multiprocessor systems, and servers can employ as many as 32 processors, as compared with the previous four-CPU limit.

What's the Big Deal?

SMP allows the server to run multithreaded processes simultaneously on different processors. Since many of NetWare 5.1's core processes, such as RSA encryption, routing ODI (Open Data-Link Interface), and C-library (CLIB) functions, are multithreaded applications, the performance of multiprocessor servers will be enhanced. A NetWare server with multiple CPUs will have more capacity to handle single-threaded programs since processing power is shared in parallel.

Enabling SMP on Your Server

NetWare 5.1 will automatically load SMP when it recognizes that more than one CPU have been installed in a server. To inspect multiprocessor settings on your server, open the MONITOR utility at the server in question, and then choose Available Options ➤ Server Parameters ➤ Multiprocessor.

 NOTE The default value for the Auto Start Processors setting is On.

File Compression: Buy One Disk, Get Two Disks' Worth of Space

My friends at Novell report that *file compression* is the most exciting feature to small enterprises that have limited financial resources. Larger enterprises, with limited administrator resources, tend to be more excited about NDS. I guess that covers the spectrum; everyone has either too little money or too little time (or both).

File compression has these characteristics:

- Automatically enabled on all NetWare volumes
- Activated by volume, directory, or file
- Able to get better than 2:1 compression on some files
- Can be set to compress files after any amount of time you wish
- Can be archived (but the files must be restored to a volume that supports compression)

On volumes that have been upgraded from earlier NetWare versions, file compression is set to On by default. Earlier NetWare versions left compression Off, but now it's enabled unless you specify otherwise.

The File Compression Process

Files are compressed in the background, and an internal NetWare 5.1 operating system process handles the compression. The file compression process goes this way:

- The system verifies that compression is enabled on the volume.
- The system verifies that compression is enabled in the directory and for the file to be compressed.
- The file to be compressed is examined.
- If more than 2 percent of the disk space will be saved (the setting for the amount of disk space is configurable) by compressing the file, the compression process begins by creating a temporary file describing the original file.
- The compressed file is checked for errors.
- If the file verifies correctly, the original and compressed files are swapped (the original becomes the temporary file and is purged as needed for space).

If an error occurs or if there is a power failure, the file compression process is stopped, and the compressed file won't replace the original file. In other words, the original file is kept, and no compression is performed until the next pass.

You have these choices about how file compression is handled:

- Files can be decompressed the first time they are read.
- Files can be decompressed the second time they are read within a set time limit.
- Files can stay compressed.

The options allow you to keep active files from being compressed, eliminating the extra overhead to read a compressed file and maximizing throughput.

Compression is much more intensive than decompression, so schedule the compression at a time when there is no network activity, such as midnight. You can enable file compression on a volume any time. You can suspend (disable) compression with a SET command or by using the MONITOR utility's Server Parameters menu. Novell engineers recommend that you leave compression on at the volume level and then selectively turn off compression at the file or directory level using NetWare Administrator.

To compress a file immediately or to check on the status of a compressed file using the NetWare Administrator program, choose the file you want to compress by highlighting the volume in the NDS directory tree. Navigate down through the NetWare volume and subdirectories to find the file, right-click it, choose Details, and select the Attributes button:

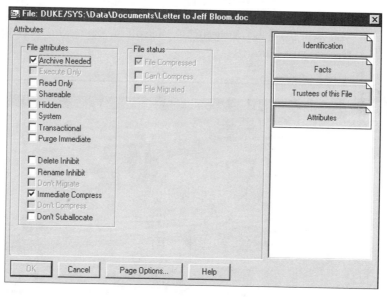

The File Attributes box lets you change all the file's attributes, including the compression attribute. The File Status box will also let you know if the file is currently compressed, is migrated, or can't be compressed.

WARNING If you do disable file compression, many files may need compressing all at once when you turn it back on. Schedule this procedure carefully to avoid affecting your server performance.

Checking File Compression Status

IN A HURRY

17.1 Check File Compression Statistics

1. Open NetWare Administrator and highlight the volume to check.
2. Right-click the volume and choose Details.
3. Click the Statistics command button on the right side of the dialog box.

NetWare Administrator provides an easy way to check the status of compressed files. You can see these charts from NetWare Administrator in the example in Figure 17.3. To view this information, use NetWare Administrator. Highlight the volume name you want to check on, right-click the volume name, choose Details, and then select the Statistics button.

FIGURE 17.3

Statistics for volume DUKE_SYS

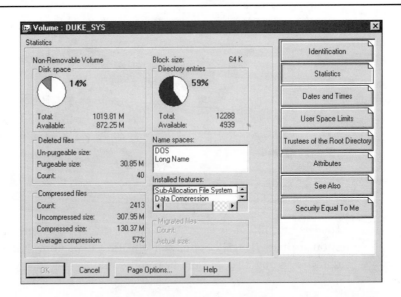

Is compression worthwhile? Take a look at the numbers on the screen in Figure 17.3. Notice that 872MB of disk space is available on the volume (shown as the total under the first circle graph to the left). Under the Compressed Files heading in the bottom-left corner, notice that the uncompressed size of the files on this volume is listed as 307MB, but when these 2413 files were compressed, they represented only 130MB of disk space. Do you count an extra 177MB of files on this volume that wouldn't be there without compression? So do I. Do you see why Novell says you can get as much as 60 percent extra disk space by using file compression? Your actual mileage may vary, depending on the types of data that are stored on the disk. Word-processing files and spreadsheets tend to compress really well, but files such as executables and some images do not compress as much.

File Compression Management

These are the only reasons to disable compression for a volume:

- There's too little memory in the server to support the compression overhead.
- All files are active data files, and production speeds demand the best possible performance.

If these reasons don't apply to your situation, you should use compression on each volume.

Compression management involves two steps:

1. Enable a volume to support compression. This is automatically set to On during the creation of the volume.

2. Activate compression per volume, directory, or file.

Generally, compression is enabled and activated per volume, but you can turn compression off without reworking your volume. When you do so, no more compression will take place on that volume until you turn compression back on.

The default setting is to compress a file after seven days of inactivity. If that doesn't work for you, adjust it to any interval you wish. Check Chapter 2 for the details on setting compression options during initial volume setup.

Improved Performance of Peripheral Devices

Ever alert for more TLAs (three-letter acronyms), in NetWare 4.11 Novell introduced *NPA (NetWare Peripheral Architecture)*. Although this is not a new feature, if you are moving to NetWare 5.1 from a version of NetWare prior to NetWare 4.11, you should be aware of NPA. NPA makes it easier for developers to add and support different storage devices and their associated controllers. There are two levels to NPA: one for the controller board in the system and the other for the device attached. The NPA.NLM file, which is loaded during the initial server boot sequence, handles all this.

The Media Manager is a database built into NetWare that tracks all peripheral storage devices and media attached to the server. In earlier NetWare versions, the single interface between the NetWare operating system and the hardware was a .DSK file (a device driver file with the .DSK extension). No matter how many devices were connected to one host adapter board in the server, only one .DSK file could be used to connect the systems.

As you might guess, today's modular world demands more layers in between the operating system and the hardware. More is better in this case because several layers make it easier to upgrade the driver for one storage device without messing up another storage device. The new layers are:

HAM (Host Adapter Module)   The driver controlling the host adapter hardware. Each HAM is adapter-specific and may be supplied by either Novell or the third-party manufacturer of the adapter. HAM drivers route requests across the bus to the specific adapter required.

HAI (Host Adapter Interface)   Programming hooks (APIs) within the NPA that provide a means of communication between the HAM and the Media Manager.

CDM (Custom Device Module)   The storage-device component software that handles details with the HAM. CDMs are normally supplied by the device manufacturer, although common ones are supported directly by NetWare. One CDM must be loaded for each physical device; for example, you'll need four CDMs for four devices attached to one HAM. To set this up during installation, you will need to use the Custom Installation routine.

CDI (Custom Device Interface)   APIs within the NPA that provide a means of communication between the CDMs and the Media Manager.

Are these new modules worthwhile? Yes, especially as more vendors get with the NetWare 5.1 development program. If everyone making storage devices follows the rules laid out in the NetWare development guidelines, storage devices of all kinds will be less trouble to install and they will provide higher performance. Even if the third-party vendors don't do their part, this modular technique allows Novell engineers to make improvements more easily than ever before.

Block Suballocation Saves Even More Space

A *block* is the smallest amount of disk space that can be allocated on a NetWare volume. The installation program assigns a block size for each volume, but you can change the default. The smaller the block size, the more memory required of the operating system. For that reason, some network managers override the installation suggestions and use the maximum block size, 64KB, for servers with limited RAM.

Block suballocation combines overflow file fragments from several files in a single disk block. If a 65KB file is copied to a volume with 64KB blocks, two blocks are required. That one file takes away almost twice the disk space necessary. If this happened with NetWare versions prior to NetWare 4, you were just out of luck—and out of disk space sooner than you should be.

Starting with NetWare 4, however, block suballocation places 512-byte pieces of files in a block with other overflow file pieces. Our 65KB file suddenly takes only 65KB of disk space—64KB for one block, and two 512-byte pieces in another block with other overflow files. This is just another way to stretch your disk drive dollar, courtesy of Novell.

You configure suballocation at the volume level when creating the volume, but you can override the configuration at the file attribute level by enabling the Don't Suballocate file property.

SMS: Storage Management Services and SBACKUP

In NetWare 4, Novell introduced new storage management capabilities called *SMS* (*Storage Management Services*). The SMS system is independent of the backup-and-restore hardware and the file systems (DOS, OS/2, Macintosh, Windows, or Unix) being backed up. SMS describes the architecture provided by NetWare to support reliable cross-platform backup-and-restore procedures. It's up to the product manufacturers to implement SMS (and many of them do).

SIDF (System Independent Data Format) describes a common way for data to be read and written from media. Normally, a backup tape made with Seagate software is worthless when loaded into a server running Cheyenne backup software, for example. However, companies that follow the SIDF guidelines can read and write any other SIDF-compliant tape or optical disk.

The SIDF Association is working with other standards organizations, such as ANSI (American National Standards Institute), ECMA (European Computer Manufacturers Association), and ISO (International Organization for Standardization), to ratify SIDF as a true industry standard. Although SIDF began as part of Novell's SMS strategy, the idea of cross-platform backup media is too valuable for one company alone, and Novell has turned over SIDF to the SIDF Association.

In NetWare 5.1, Novell improves on SMS by enhancing the backup server abilities. Some new features with NetWare 5.1's SMS include:

- Protocol independence; you can use either TCP/IP or IPX/SPX to back up remote servers.

- NDS for name resolution rather than the Service Advertising Protocol (SAP).

- Support for backing up files larger than 4GB.
- Ability to back up a server's local DOS partition.
- Support for backing up remote Windows 95/98/NT/2000 workstations.
- Windows 95/98/NT/2000 graphical user interface for managing backups.
- NetWare server console backup utility for managing backups from the server console.
- Concurrent job support if you have multiple backup devices.

Backup Solutions

If you have a new network, your dealer should have provided a backup solution for your servers when the system was installed. Not having a reliable file backup system is beyond imprudent; it is sheer folly. If you are setting up your system yourself without the help of a dealer or consultant, go *directly* (do not pass GO, do not collect $200) to a reseller or dealer and buy a tape backup system before another sunset.

One of my favorite third-party backup-and-restore systems is Legato Networker (from Legato Systems in Palo Alto, California), primarily because it uses SMS, backs up multiple systems at one time, and supports both NetWare and Unix systems during the same tape backup. Other companies are providing many of these same features. One of the highest backup rates belongs to the Micron NetFRAME DataJET: 100MB a minute, or 12GB per hour, under the right conditions.

Look around for a tape backup system, both hardware and software, that protects your network data well enough to make you comfortable.

Components of the NetWare 5.1 SMS

NetWare 5.1 Storage Management Services is not a single program, but a collection of NLMs that provide various services. SMS is a modular architecture that allows vendors to incorporate their own components. Figure 17.4 shows some of the components that are part of a NetWare 5.1 SMS system. Some of these are located on the server that is actually running the Storage Management Engine (this is where the backup media are located), and other components are located on other machines on the network.

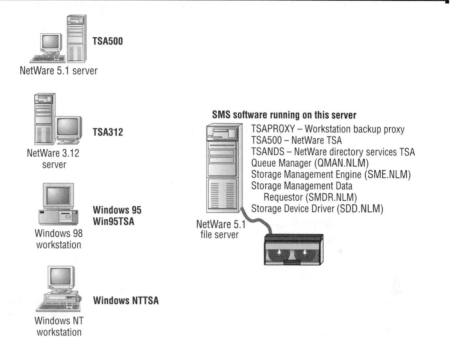

FIGURE 17.4

The components of NetWare 5.1 Storage Management Services

This collection of components and software includes:

- SME.NLM (Storage Management Engine), which includes the enhanced SBACKUP software utility that provides backup and restore functions.

- SMDR.NLM (Storage Management Data Requester), which manages communications between SME and TSAs (Target Service Agents).

- SMSDI (SMS Storage Device Interface), which manages communications between SBACKUP and storage devices and media.

- Device drivers (IDE.DSK, TAPEDAI.DSK, AHA2940.DSK), which handle the physical and mechanical operations of storage devices. They act on commands passed through SMSDI from SBACKUP.

- NetWare server TSAs (such as TSA500.NLM, TSA410.NLM, and TSA312.NLM), which manage communications asking for data from SME to the NetWare server holding the data. They then return the data through SMDR to SME, which passes it to the physical device.

- NetWare server DOS partition TSADOSP.NLM, which allows the backup software to back up the local server's DOS partition.

- Database TSAs (such as TSANDS), which manage communications between the server hosting SBACKUP and the database on the server hosting the data, then back through the SMDR to SBACKUP.

- Workstation TSAPROXYs (such as TSADOS, Win95 TSA, and Windows NT TSA), which manage communications between the SME host server and the workstation holding the data to be backed up. You can install the Windows 95/98 and Windows NT TSAs when you install the client software. The TSAPROXY manages a list of workstations available to be backed up. The workstations regularly send "I'm alive" packets. You must load the TSAPROXY.NLM in order to support remote workstations.

- Windows 95/98 and Windows NT Novell Storage Management Service program (SYS:PUBLIC\NWBACK32.EXE).

- NetWare server utility SBCON.NLM, which allows you to manage and schedule jobs from the NetWare server console.

 NOTE In earlier versions of NetWare, the SMS backup engine was contained in the SBACKUP.NLM program. NetWare 5.1 does not have an SBACKUP.NLM. Novell often refers to the enhanced SBACKUP capabilities, but these features are actually in the SME.NLM, SMDR.NLM, and SMSDI.NLM programs.

Understanding the Role of the TSA

The Target Service Agent, or TSA, is a software program that runs on any computer on the network, acting as an agent that communicates with SME on the host server. TSAs are loaded on the host server, target servers, and clients. The TSA advertises the presence of a target to the server so it can be backed up. TSAs are designed specifically for the server and client operating systems:

- TSA500—NetWare 5.1 host server
- TSA410—NetWare 4.11 and 4.10 target server
- TSA312—NetWare 3.12 target server
- TSANDS—NDS database
- W95TSA—Windows 95/98 client
- NTTSA—Windows NT workstation
- MACTSA—Macintosh client
- GWTSA—GroupWise data

Using Storage Management Services

SMS now offers scheduling capabilities, workstation backup, and customization options. Enhanced SBACKUP copies data files to tape and generates log and error files that are saved to a specified directory on the host server.

The Novell documentation lists vendors of SME-compliant hardware; check with your NetWare resellers for their recommendations. You should always use certified backup hardware.

SMS standards are almost a requirement now for backup product vendors. They must meet these standards in order to properly back up and restore NetWare 5.1 information. However, there is a difference between backing up NetWare 5.1 data and backing up NDS.

The additions in NetWare 5.1 that affect backup systems include extra attributes and flags on the files. The backup system must understand and handle compressed and non-compressed files without a hiccup.

NDS is a different story altogether (at least it is when speaking of multiple servers on a network). There are no database files with special attributes to back up. The NDS database is replicated across multiple network servers. If there is a problem with NDS on a server, the last thing you should do is restore some NDS files from a backup tape.

The active replicas on other servers in your network will copy their NDS information to your problem server over time. Several management tools available in NetWare Administrator allow you to move or copy replica information. From the server console, DSREPAIR offers several ways to rebuild or copy a damaged NDS database on one server. When a server suffers a catastrophic failure, rebuild NDS through these methods if at all possible.

 NOTE If you want confirmation that you're not as prone to stupidity as I am under stress, look back in Chapter 10 and read about when I deleted the SYS: volume holding the master replica of [Root] for my network. Believe it or not, I recovered the network without restoring a tape backup of NDS. If I can resurrect NDS after deleting the main replica, you can resurrect NDS as well.

If none of the above methods works, reinstall NDS; then go back through the previous suggestions to force other servers to update your problem server with the latest NDS changes. DSREPAIR is probably the best place to start re-synchronizing the NDS database information. Although it may not be your first choice, it is important to have NDS on tape as an additional safety net for your network.

Installing Storage Management Services on the Backup Server   During installation of the NetWare server, you should choose to install Storage Management Services as one of the optional components for which you are prompted. All this does, though, is copy files from the NetWare 5.1 CD-ROM to the NetWare server's SYS: volume. The files on the CD-ROM are in the \PRODUCTS\SMS directory.

 NOTE   The NetWare server that is going to host the backup device or devices should have at least an extra 4MB of RAM available.

When you load the SMDR.NLM the first time, you will be asked for two pieces of information:

- The SMDR context, which is the NDS context where the SMDR object will be created.
- The SMDR group context, which holds the SMDR Group object that is used when searching for multiple SMDR servers.

You will then be asked to provide an Admin-level user ID and password. The default for both of these is the container in which the NetWare Server object resides.

This procedure will create a configuration file called SYS:ETC\SMS\SMDR.CFG. This file has the two pieces of data you provided above. If you need to change the SMDR object or SMDR Group object context, I recommend deleting the file. You can also recreate the SMDR.CFG file by typing **LOAD SMDR NEW** at the server console prompt. When the SMDR.NLM is reloaded, you will be asked to re-create it.

Next you have to configure the queue manager module, QMAN.NLM. When you configure QMAN for the first time, you will be asked some QMAN configuration questions. The first question you must answer is the SMS job queue context. This is the NDS context in which the queue object will be created. The default is the NDS context in which the NetWare server object resides.

The second request is for the name of the backup queue. For example, if the backup server's name is DUKE and the backup server's context is OU=SALES.O=SOMORITA, the default backup queue name would be CN=DUKE Backup Job Queue.OU=SALES. O=SOMORITA. You will also be prompted to enter an Admin-level user and password.

This process creates a file called SYS:ETC\SMS\SBACKUP.CFG that the QMAN.NLM program uses. If you need to re-create the backup queue or change the parameters, you can delete this file and reload QMAN.NLM; you will be prompted for the information again. You can also type **LOAD QMAN NEW** at the server console to re-create the file.

The final step is to add all the correct statements to your STARTUP.NCF file and AUTOEXEC.NCF file. Table 17.2 shows sample lines from the files for a NetWare 5.1 server that has the tape drive on an Adaptec 2940 SCSI host adapter and whose administrator wants to back up the NDS database, the NetWare 5.1 file system, remote workstations, and the local DOS partition.

TABLE 17.2: ADDITIONS TO THE STARTUP.NCF AND AUTOEXEC.NCF FILES TO SUPPORT STORAGE MANAGEMENT SERVICES	
Filename	**Load Statements***
STARTUP.NCF	LOAD AHA2940.HAM SLOT=4
	LOAD SCSIHD.CDM
AUTOEXEC.NCF	LOAD TSANDS
	LOAD TSA500
	LOAD TSAPROXY
	LOAD TSADOSP
	LOAD QMAN

*These statements should be included in existing files.

The queue manager (QMAN) NLM manages the job scheduling; it will automatically load the SMDR.NLM and supporting NLM files.

Configuring Windows 95/98/NT/2000 Workstations   Don't forget to load any required TSAs on workstations or other NetWare servers. The Windows 95/98/NT/2000 workstation clients give you the option of installing the SMS software. You can do this during the NetWare client installation by checking the Novell Target Service Agent choice during a custom installation.

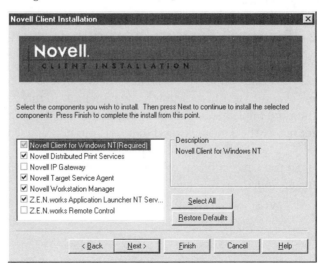

After you install the SMS software, you can configure and customize properties. For example, to configure the Windows NT TSA software, choose Control Panel ➤ Network ➤ Services, highlight Novell Target Service Agent, and click the Properties button to open the TSA Preferences dialog box:

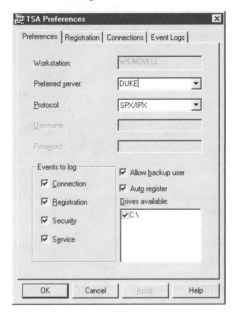

Here you can configure the preferred server, the default protocol, and event logging, specify which drives are available to be backed up, and more. The Windows 95/98 Target Service Agent is similar.

Tape "Restore" System Procedures

Years ago, I had a boss who used to say, "Customers don't buy tape backup systems; they buy tape restore systems. They just don't realize it." This quote has stuck with me over the years because it is really profound. To this day, this quote affects my planning and implementation of any backup system. The bottom line is that you have to make sure the data you expect to be on your backup media is really there and that you can get it off. I could fill a chapter with tape backup horror stories.

So you have your tape drive installed and tested. Now you are ready to start backing up your data. You now face these questions:

- What should I back up each day?
- How many tapes should I use?

- Is just doing backups enough?
- Am I ready to face my boss if I need to restore important data but am unable to?

These are all important questions—especially the last one. It is time to start planning your "restore." Even if you never end up restoring a single byte of data thanks to duplexed disks or RAID 5 drive arrays, you need to be prepared.

Here are some tape "restore" system hints:

- When installing a new tape system, test all options. Run large backups and restores.
- Rotate your backup media. Don't use the same tape night after night.
- Retire tapes when they reach a certain age. I don't trust 4mm or 8mm tapes for very long. I retire 8mm tapes after 25–40 uses and 4mm tapes after 50–75 uses. DLT and other $1/4$-inch technologies can typically be used longer. If you are not sure, check with the manufacturer of your tape drive.
- Purchase data grade tapes.
- Check your backup logs daily.
- Do a bimonthly test restore.
- Always do a verification pass when data is backed up.
- If you can, do a full backup of your servers every night. I recognize that this is not possible on many systems, but it is usually my goal when setting up a system.

A Sample Tape Rotation

I could spend the next 20 or 30 pages discussing possible tape rotation strategies. It is also quite possible that you already have an adequate tape rotation strategy. This rotation strategy will not work for all systems, but I have found it to be sufficient for most systems. Table 17.3 shows the tapes that I use.

TABLE 17.3: TAPES REQUIRED FOR THE SAMPLE ROTATION		
Daily Tapes	**Weekly Tapes**	**Monthly Tapes**
Monday–Even	Friday–First	January
Monday–Odd	Friday–Second	February
Tuesday–Even	Friday–Third	March
Tuesday–Odd	Friday–Fourth	April
Wednesday–Even	Friday–Fifth	May

Continued ▶

TABLE 17.3 (CONTINUED) : TAPES REQUIRED FOR THE SAMPLE ROTATION		
Daily Tapes	**Weekly Tapes**	**Monthly Tapes**
Wednesday–Odd		June
Thursday–Even		July
Thursday–Odd		August
		September
		October
		November
		December

The daily tapes are used over a two-week period. On Monday the 7th, I use the Monday–Odd tape, but on Monday the 14th, I use the Monday–Even tape. On the first Friday of the month, I use the Friday–First tape, on the second Friday of the month, I use the Friday–Second tape, and so on.

I select a day during the month that I do the monthly backup—usually the first day of the month. However, if you support a system that has an accounting, order-entry, or some other type of system that does a month-end close, you might want to select either the day before or the day after that close occurs. I also allocate a few backup tapes in my library just for "special" occasions, such as accounting systems and database repair.

 TIP The whole reason we back this data up is in the event of a disaster. The disaster may be a failed hard disk, or it could be something as dramatic as a flood or a computer room fire. It is a good idea to store at least some backup tapes in another location. I try to keep my Friday tapes stored in an alternate location, whether this is a special off-site storage company or just my briefcase.

Scheduling Backups

To schedule backups, you need to have read and file-scan privileges for those files and directories you want to back up. There are three backup methods:

Full   Copies all files in selected volumes and directories, clearing the archive bit for each file.

Differential   Copies all files changed since the last backup and does not clear the archive bits.

Incremental   Copies all files changed or added since the last full or incremental backup, clearing the archive bit for each.

You can create and save data sets that list specific directories and/or files to be backed up. Use the Exclude option to choose most of the files or NDS tree and omit a small portion. Use the Include option to add particular files and directories. You can actually combine the two options to create your data set. Name the set to save and reuse it.

You can mix and match backup methods on successive days. Differential and incremental sessions have the advantage of speed, since they do not work on all files and may be suitable on a daily basis. But the most complete method is, of course, a full backup. Since enhanced SBACKUP will not copy active files, it's best to schedule backup sessions at times of no or low activity. Remember that your backup will help you to restore your system to its prior state when you make major changes, as well as restore your users' data and applications.

Optimizing SBACKUP

The SBCON.NLM program allows you to manage backup operations from the console of the NetWare server. After activating SBACKUP, you can use the options on the SBCON main menu (see Figure 17.5).

FIGURE 17.5

The SBCON main menu

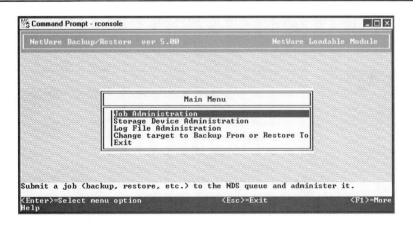

Job Administration   Displays a submenu that allows you to do backups, restores, and verification passes.

Storage Device Administration   Configures tape drive properties.

Log File Administration   Allows you to view session activity and errors from the log files and to configure the default location for the log files.

Change Target To Backup From Or Restore To   Specifies the target drive for backup-and-restore sessions.

Choosing Job Administration displays the Select Job menu:

From here, you have the following options:

Backup   Selects files and directories to be copied from a hard disk drive to tape.

Restore   Selects files that had been backed up to tape to restore to a hard drive, if files have been damaged or lost.

Verify   Checks backed-up files on tape with originals on a hard disk to make sure they were backed up correctly.

Create Session Files   Creates session files from data on a selected device.

Current Job List   Ddisplays a list of all pending and active jobs in the backup queue.

You can also activate SBACKUP at a Windows 95/98 or Windows NT/2000 workstation with a graphical user interface (shown in Figure 17.6). Locate and run NWBACK32.EXE in the Public directory on the SYS: volume.

The Novell Storage Management Service (NWBACK32.EXE) graphical user interface

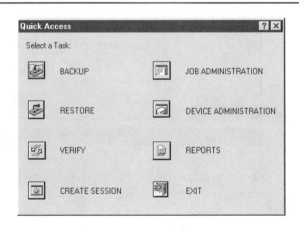

The Quick Access screen gives you the following options:

Backup   Selects files and directories to be copied from a hard disk drive to tape.

Restore   Selects files that had been backed up to tape to restore to a hard drive, if files have been damaged or lost.

Verify   Checks backed-up file sizes on tape with originals on a hard disk.

Create Session   Records session activity and errors in a log file for later reference by the backup operator.

Job Administration   Lists scheduled jobs, which can be viewed or modified.

Device Administration   Configures tape drive properties.

Reports   Prints sessions and log files.

Storage Management Services Log Files

SMS creates two types of files:

- Log
- Error

By default, these files are in the SYS:SYSTEM\TSA\LOG directory, although you can change this in the SBCON.NLM utility. To do so, from the SBCON main menu, choose Log File Administration to open the Error/Log File Administration menu:

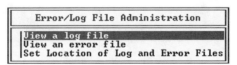

Select Set Location Of Log And Error Files, and enter a valid path for the log files. You can also view these log files from the same menu that allows you to change their default location.

Novell Storage Services (NSS)

Novell Storage Services (NSS) was a new feature of NetWare 5.0. During the NSS beta testing period, when I first started reading about NSS and tinkering with it, I experienced two distinctly separate emotions: excitement and dread. I was excited about this great new feature, and I dreaded figuring out a way to explain it to others. Although this is a rather simplistic way to look at it, Novell Storage Services allows an administrator to combine areas of free space from empty partitions, NetWare volumes, and even CD-ROMs together into one large, logical volume.

When designing NSS, Novell had specific goals in mind:

- To create volumes that could hold millions of files
- To eliminate the current file and volume size restrictions
- To ensure that servers running NSS would be backward-compatible with the NetWare file system (NWFS)
- To ensure that even large volumes could be quickly repaired and mounted
- To optimize the use of server memory
- To be modular and versatile and to support new generations of storage

I don't think that saying NSS is a revolutionary step forward in storage systems is an exaggeration. NSS employs logical rather than physical partitions to better manage storage by pooling free space on all storage devices. It handles large volumes with files up to 8 terabytes and large numbers of files, much more than traditional NetWare volumes. It takes less time to mount and rebuild NSS volumes—less than a minute in most cases. Multiple name spaces share the same storage space under NSS.

The first volume on the server, SYS:, must be a traditional NetWare file system (NWFS) volume, but any others can be NSS volumes. Table 17.4 compares traditional NetWare file system volumes with NSS volumes.

TABLE 17.4: COMPARISON OF NETWARE FILE SYSTEM VOLUMES AND NOVELL STORAGE SERVICES VOLUMES

Topic	NetWare File System (NWFS)	Novell Storage Services (NSS)
Volumes	64 mounted volumes	253 mounted volumes
	8 segments per volume	No maximum segments
		1 terabyte volume size
		8 terabyte volumes (32-bit system)
		8 exabyte volumes (64-bit system)
File size	32-bit file system that limits files to 4GB	64-bit file system that allows files up to 8 terabytes
Number of files	Up to 16 millions files, though only 2 million with all name spaces loaded	Up to 1 trillion files
Maximum open files	100,000 per server	1,000,000 per server
Characters used	ASCII double-byte	UNICODE (provides better internationalization support)
Volume mount or repair time	Large NWFS volumes can take a long time to mount and hours to repair.	NSS volumes can be mounted and repaired quickly.

Continued ▶

Topic	NetWare File System (NWFS)	Novell Storage Services (NSS)
TABLE 17.4 (CONTINUED): COMPARISON OF NETWARE FILE SYSTEM VOLUMES AND NOVELL STORAGE SERVICES VOLUMES		
Memory usage	NWFS volumes with many files can consume a large amount of server RAM.	NSS volumes offer improved memory usage.
Maximum subdirectory depth	100 directory levels	Limited only by the client operating system

Novell Storage Services Architecture

In order that you can better understand Novell Storage Services, I need to introduce you to some terms related to NSS and the modular NSS architecture. This may also give you a better idea of what is in store for NSS in the future. Figure 17.7 illustrates the NSS modular architecture and shows where some of these components fit.

FIGURE 17.7

Novell Storage Services components

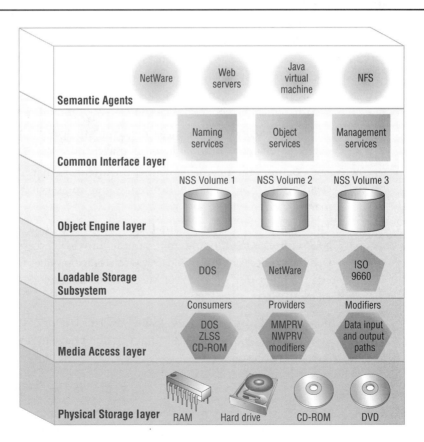

Here's what the various layers, interfaces, and modules do:

- The Physical Storage layer provides the only physical part of this chain. Until something new comes around (optical storage cubes sound pretty cool), NetWare supports RAM, magnetic drives or silicon-based drives that mimic hard drives, CD-ROMs, and DVDs. As new storage media appear, NSS will handle them.

- The Media Access layer (MAL) provides access to the actual storage media. It manages an *object bank*, which is responsible for the storage manager and storage object registration. The storage managers access the actual media. There are three types of storage managers: consumers, providers, and modifiers.

  - The Consumer Storage Manager takes ownership of storage space types such as free space, DOS partitions, and CD-ROM space.

  - The Provider Storage Manager manages storage objects such as the NetWare file system (NWFS) and DOS partitions. NSS has two types of providers: NWPRV for NetWare volumes and files and MMPRV for IBM partitions and files.

  - The Modifier Storage Manager manages the storage information by changing the input and output data paths.

- The Loadable Storage Subsystem layer provides the files that define the various file systems that NSS uses, such as DOS, NetWare, and ISO 9660 (CD-ROMs). Future LSS modules could include the Windows NT file system, Macintosh file system, optical jukeboxes, DVD, NFS Gateway, and other file systems.

- The Object Engine layer manages the actual storage resources. It provides a high degree of reliability, optimal memory usage, and performance.

- The Common Interface layer defines the interfaces that the semantic agents use to access the object engine. It provides naming services, object services, and management services.

- The Semantic Agents layer contains the loadable modules that provide access to NSS services. One module, for example, provides access for NetWare clients. Other modules might provide access to storage services for clients such as Web clients, Microsoft SMB (Server Message Block) network clients, NFS (Network File System), or others.

Confused? Don't worry if you are; I sure was. This is a lot of layers, modules, and interfaces to absorb. The bright side is that you don't have to understand the architecture to create an NSS volume.

Managing Novell Storage Services

Novell Storage Services are automatically installed when you install NetWare 5.1. To load NSS, at the server console type **LOAD NSS** (or just **NSS**). This starts the necessary NetWare Loadable Modules (NLMs).

 TIP You will find that Novell has eliminated the need to type LOAD for many operations that used to require it. Now, if you just type the name of the NLM you want to load, NetWare 5.1 will automatically load it. It is hard to teach an old dog new tricks, so you will catch me using the LOAD command quite often. Also, this way I don't get spoiled when I have to work on earlier versions of NetWare.

The NSS module has a number of command-line options; many of these are shown in Table 17.5. Some of these require the slash key; others do not. You can use the slash key for all commands, though, so this is what I tend to do. This way, I am always consistent and don't have to think about which options require the backslash and which ones do not.

TABLE 17.5: SOME NSS COMMAND-LINE OPTIONS

Option	Description
\Help	Displays a list of options
\Exit	Dismounts all NSS volumes and unloads NSS and all NSS supporting modules
\Version	Displays the current version of NSS
\Modules	Displays all NSS support modules loaded and their current version
\Menu	Enters the NSS configuration menu
\Status	Displays all NSS configuration information
\Volumes	Displays a list of all currently available NSS volumes
\Activate=*NSS_volume_name*	Switches *NSS_volume_name* to the active state
\Deactivate=*NSS_volume_name*	Switches *NSS_volume_name* to the inactive state
\Maintenance=*NSS_volume_name*	Switches *NSS_volume_name* to the maintenance state
\VerifyVolume=*NSS_volume_name*	Checks *NSS_volume_name* physical integrity
\RebuildVolume=*NSS_volume_name*	Repairs *NSS_volume_name*

Continued ▶

TABLE 17.5 (CONTINUED): SOME NSS COMMAND-LINE OPTIONS

Option	Description
\AutoVerifyVolume=*NSS_volume_name*	Sets *NSS_volume_name* to be automatically verified during each startup
\StorageAlarmThreshold=	Sets the value in megabytes that will trigger a storage warning if the disk space drops below that value
\StorageAlarmReset=	Sets the value in megabytes that will reset a low storage warning
\(No)StorageAlertMessages	Turns on or off storage alert warnings to all users
\(No)CacheBalance	Turns on or off the cache balancing
\CacheBalance	Set the percentage of free memory that is used for the NSS buffer cache
\Salvage=*NSS_volume_name*	Enables salvage of deleted files for *NSS_volume_name*
\NoSalvage=*NSS_volume_name*	Disables salvage of deleted files for *NSS_volume_name*

You can also use the NetWare console command VOLUMES to display information about currently mounted NSS volumes. Here is a sample of what the VOLUMES command will display on a NetWare 5.1 server with NSS and CD-ROM support loaded:

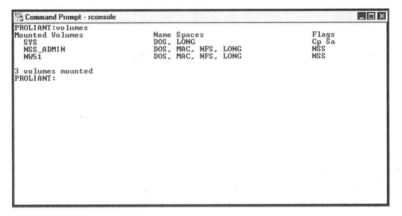

The NW51 volume is actually a CD-ROM. If you load NetWare CD-ROM support, it is now provided through HSS.

NOTE All the NSS-supported volumes include all name space modules; the NetWare file system volume includes only DOS and LONG name spaces.

Creating an NSS Volume   To create an NSS volume, you can use either the NWCONFIG program or the NSS menu. I prefer the NSS menu simply because it does not prompt me for an NDS login and password every time I want to create a volume or do any sort of volume maintenance. To get to the NSS Administration menu from the console prompt, type **NSS /MENU.**

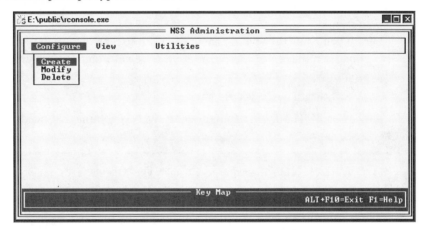

You have three choices: Configure, View, and Utilities. To create a volume, choose Configure ➤ Create ➤ One Step Configuration, and enter a name for this new NSS volume. This creates a new NSS volume and assigns all areas of free space to it.

If you want to incorporate space from an existing NetWare volume, you must choose the Advanced Configuration option rather than the One Step Configuration option. From the Advanced Configuration menu, you can update provider information, assign ownership of free space to a consumer, create a new storage group, and create a new NSS volume.

TIP Although it is possible to do so, Novell recommends against using free space from your NetWare SYS: volume as part of an NSS volume.

If you choose the Advanced Configuration option, you must take the following steps in the correct order. If you do not, the NSS volume will not be created.

1. Assign ownership of any free space you want to use.

2. Create a new storage group from the free space you assigned.

3. Create a new NSS volume from the new storage group you created.

Repairing an NSS Volume   Novell Storage Services includes a Rebuild command-line option specifically for repairing corrupt or damaged NSS volumes. You can access this option through the NSS menu. At the server console prompt, type **NSS /MENU**. Choose Utilities ➤ Rebuild NSS Volume, and then choose the NSS volume you want to rebuild.

If you know the volume name you want to repair, you can perform the entire operation from the server console prompt. To repair a damaged volume, from the console prompt type

```
NSS /REBUILD=NSS_VOLUME_NAME
```

The *NSS_VOLUME_NAME* argument is the NSS volume that needs to be repaired.

 WARNING   The NetWare 5.1 utility `VREPAIR.NLM` does not work with NSS volumes.

Backing Up an NSS Volume   Although any type of tape backup system can back up the NSS volume, Novell highly recommends you use a backup that is compatible with the NetWare Target Service Agent (TSA500). Backups using older versions of the TSA are not efficient when backing up large files.

NetWare 5.1 ships with an enhanced SBACKUP utility that works well with NSS.

A Few Words about NSS and Fault Tolerance   If you create large NSS volumes and store critical information on them, you should make sure you have two things on your side:

• Reliable, consistent tape backups

• Disk fault tolerance

RAID 5 arrays as well as duplexed or mirrored partitions can be incorporated into an NSS volume. Either make sure you have a consistent way to restore your data or include disk fault tolerance in your server designs. Remember that an NSS volume may reside across many disks. If any one of these disks fails, you risk losing all your data.

NLSP: Improved Routing for Your WAN

IPX/SPX is the Rodney Dangerfield of network protocols—it don't get no respect. This is especially true if you have a TCP/IP person as part of your management team. As you saw in the chapters concerning protocols (Chapters 1 and 14), Novell's IPX/SPX takes a lot of abuse, especially from TCP/IP people. People who don't understand why the protocol generates so much traffic over low-bandwidth WAN links complain about IPX/SPX. But rather than blame IPX/SPX, you must really blame RIP (Routing Information Protocol), SAP (Service Advertising Protocol), and NCP (NetWare Core Protocol) for the overhead traffic.

Why Use NLSP?

Novell developed *NLSP* (*NetWare Link Services Protocol*) to replace RIP and SAP. Loaded as an NLM program on NetWare 3.11 and later, NLSP provides the following advantages over RIP and SAP:

Improved routing   RIP-based routers know about only the next router, not the network. NLSP knows the layout of the entire network and lets routers make more intelligent choices when routing traffic.

Reduced network overhead   Routers using RIP periodically broadcast their entire routing table to keep other RIP devices up-to-date. Although these broadcasts keep all routers in sync, they are broadcast regardless of whether the network changes. NLSP systems send broadcasts only when the network changes (the link state changes). Rather than using general broadcast packets, NLSP uses multicast packet addresses, meaning that only routers need to pay attention to these broadcasts. All other network devices can safely ignore the multicast NLSP packets.

Low WAN overhead   NetWare servers send an SAP broadcast every 60 seconds, containing their entire service database. NLSP eliminates SAP packets by sending broadcasts only when a service changes. Unlike SAP, NLSP uses a reliable packet that contains both IPX network and services information.

Faster data transfer   NSLP uses IPX header compression to reduce packet sizes across WAN links. NLSP also supports load balancing between parallel paths. If more equal-cost paths exist between network nodes, NLSP can support as many parallel paths as you allow, or you can disable load splitting.

Parallel paths   NLSP supports two or more paths between two network nodes. This is impossible under the spanning-tree routing used in traditional Ethernet networks, as an example. Using multiple paths between NLSP nodes (often called *load splitting*) provides fault-tolerance and higher performance.

Increased reliability   NLSP regularly checks all links for the data integrity of the link. When a link fails, NLSP quickly switches to an alternate link. It then updates the network routing diagrams stored in each node, informing all devices of the change in connection status.

Lower CPU usage   RIP and SAP sending and receiving require a fair amount of routing overhead in the host computer. NLSP cuts down this overhead because of the reduced need for broadcasts. Link-state protocols such as NLSP do take more time than RIP to figure the best packet routes, but this overhead is small compared with the RIP broadcast overhead.

Better support for larger NetWare networks   Packets using RIP may go through only 15 hops between their source and destination addresses; NSLP supports a maximum of 127 hops. This allows bigger networks automatically, even before you add the growth of network nodes possible through NLSP's hierarchical addressing. NLSP can easily support thousands and thousands of networks and servers.

Superior manageability   NLSP uses a standardized management interface based on SNMP (Simple Network Management Protocol). A single NLSP router can provide the network manager with a complete network topology map.

Backward-compatible   NLSP and RIP-based routers can easily exist on the same network. Your RIP-to-NLSP conversion can proceed in phases, and you don't even need to reboot NetWare servers and routers after enabling NLSP.

Support for multiple networking media   NLSP provides end-to-end data delivery over Ethernet, Token Ring, and point-to-point links. Any media supported by a NetWare server will support NLSP, including the drivers for the NetWare server.

Optional link-cost assignment   You can manually assign a cost to each NLSP link and allow NLSP to choose the most efficient path for each packet. A NetWare server/router may be designated as more expensive than a dedicated router. When available, NLSP will route packets across the dedicated router, using the NetWare server/router only as a backup. For WAN links, a T1 line would be designated as less expensive than a 56K connection, making NLSP automatically route packets across the high-speed link if possible.

In a smaller, purely local network, the RIP and SAP overhead is not a concern. In a mixed LAN/WAN environment, you have an incentive to activate NLSP, especially if your WAN links are not high-speed. If you have a large, local network with multiple routers, you may gain an advantage by adding NLSP to support more than 15 hops between source and destination addresses. Very large local networks (with more than

400 network numbers) must be segmented into NLSP routing domains in a hierarchical design.

Before converting your network to NLSP, check out the *NetWare Link Services Protocol In-Depth* booklet from Novell. Your dealer can order one. NLSP information is provided in the "IPX Upgrade" part of the NetWare Online Documentation. This section also covers adding the IPX upgrade, including NLSP, to a pre-NetWare 5.1 server.

You can also find more information in a Novell AppNote called "NetWare Link Services Protocol: An Advanced Theory of Operations" in the November 1995 issue of *AppNotes*. Go to the Web at developer.novell.com/research.

Planning Your Move to NLSP

Novell offers several products to migrate an internetwork to NLSP. Choose your solution according to your organization's network topology—number of segments, number of servers, WAN links, third-party routers, and so on.

- Novell Internet Access Server 4 is a combination of NetWare Multiprotocol Router 3.1 and NetWare 4.11. This product is included with NetWare 5.1.

- NetWare Multiprotocol Router3.1 adds routing for IPX, TCP/IP, and AppleTalk on NetWare 3.12 and 4.*x* servers.

- NetWare 4.1 or 4.11 IPX Upgrade for NetWare Servers upgrades the IPX stack for NetWare 3.12 servers to provide NSLP routing.

Server-Based Java Support

NetWare 5.1 continues Novell's commitment to making NetWare a Java development platform and to Java-based administration. You'll notice this the first time you install NetWare 5.1, since the server installation tool is a Java GUI (this trend started with NetWare 5.0). The NetWare installation experience has been transformed to a wizard-driven procedure that collects information about protocols, configurations, and NDS and generates a customized network environment.

ConsoleOne is a Java application that loads at the server or at Windows workstations. With its mouse-enabled, Windows-style graphical look, ConsoleOne makes much of NWAdmin's functionality available at the server. Novell plans to offer snap-in modules to incorporate all its management tools into ConsoleOne's unified interface, including NWAdmin, ManageWise, ZENworks, GroupWise, BorderManager, and NDS for NT.

The Novell Upgrade Wizard is another example of the Java influence in NetWare 5.1. This utility upgrades the NetWare 3 bindery, printers, and data to NetWare 5.1. It also verifies system options and identifies potential problems for the upgrade process.

JavaBeans for Novell Services

With NetWare 5.1, Java developers, Webmasters, and script programmers can take advantage of NetWare services using JavaBeans as the server programming interface. They can use Java to build server console applications, server-side Java applications called *servlets,* and CGI programs. Novell provides two JavaBean objects that abstract NetWare services and data sources:

- The NWDirectory Bean allows programmers to access the Novell Directory Services database.
- The NWSession Bean allows programmers to access features relating to network sessions, such as login features and file services.

Additional support related to Java and server application development includes Java database connectivity (JDBC) and the Novell Trader, an object broker architecture based on CORBA. Platforms such as CORBA allow the development of cross-platform, distributed computing applications.

Additional Security-Related Features

NetWare 5.1 provides security APIs and services that allow developers to use cryptographic services and authentication systems rather than providing their own cryptographic services.

Cryptographic Services

The *Novell International Cryptographic Infrastructure* (*NICI*) is a modular framework that can use various cryptography mechanisms. The *Controlled Cryptography Service* (*CCS*) API is an important aspect of NICI, providing developers with the capability to integrate cryptographic algorithms with their applications. The United States currently limits the length of cryptographic keys to 40 bits, although European countries allow 128-bit keys. NICI can recognize both 128- and 40-bit cryptographic keys within an application, so that applications can be used anywhere in the world, regardless of local ordinances.

Secure Authentication Services (SAS)

NetWare 5.1 extends version 4.11's C2-certified capabilities with *Secure Authentication Services*, or *SAS*. The SAS API will support new authentication techniques as they are developed. NetWare's SAS supports the Internet standard, Secure Socket Layer (SSL) version 3.

Public Key Infrastructure Services (PKIS)

NetWare 5.1's *Public Key Infrastructure Services* (*PKIS*) supports public key cryptography and digital certificates, which can be stored and managed by new objects in the NDS tree.

The *Certificate Authority Object* (*CAO*) contains the public key, private key, certificate, and other information. The *Key Material Object* (*KMO*) represents a private key in encrypted form. The Security Container is created when SAS is installed. It holds security-related objects.

 NOTE For more information about NetWare cryptographic and security services, check out Novell's developer Web site at developer.novell.com.

SNMP: A Management Solution

SNMP (Simple Network Management Protocol) is widely used for TCP/IP networks and Unix hosts. Because of this, many people mistakenly believe SNMP is a TCP/IP-only management solution. This is not true.

The developers made sure that SNMP was transport-protocol neutral. As management becomes more critical to PC networks, SNMP systems will become available for IPX-only networks. The only restriction today is marketing, not technology.

A Bit of SNMP History

SNMP was developed by four gentlemen over dinner in Monterey, California, in March 1987. Two of the gentlemen were working in universities, and the other two worked for a leading Internet service provider. Being engineers, the group developed the SGMP (Simple Gateway Monitoring Protocol) in two months.

By August 1988, SNMP (the spiffed-up subsequent protocol that improved upon SGMP) was a reality. The protocol details were officially declared an Internet draft standard, meaning they were completed, implemented, and under production at several companies.

In April 1989, SNMP became recommended, making it the de facto operational standard for managing TCP/IP networks and internetworks. More than 30 vendors displayed products at the InterOp trade show in San Jose, California, in October 1989. SNMP had officially become "The Protocol" when speaking of network management.

Continued

CONTINUED

In enterprise networks, SNMP is still The Protocol and shows no signs of slowing down. Although SNMP was developed to be small enough to run in an IBM XT (at least, the Agent part), it isn't used on many PC-only networks. This probably won't change any time soon. Most of the serious management consoles for SNMP are Unix systems, and they are designed and priced for large networks, not for small and medium LANs.

Now waiting in the wings is SNMP version 2, adding some capabilities and security to SNMP. Unfortunately, the two SNMP camps are fighting about security details, so the IETF has yet to release an official SNMP version 2. NetWare server and client software will be compatible with any updated SNMP management consoles that support SNMP version 2; management is too important for companies to drop the ball at the start of a new version.

SNMP for the NetWare 5.1 Server

Network and object details for SNMP are kept in a .MIB (Management Information Base) file. Since NetWare 5.1 is object-oriented, the idea of SNMP managing objects rather than computers and printers should not cause you any mental strain.

Each device to be managed runs a small bit of software called the SNMP Agent. The agents monitor certain functions depending on the device hosting them. When some event happens, the agent sends a message to a predetermined address. The SNMP management console software collects these traps and uses them to monitor the health of the network.

The NetWare server can easily run the SNMP Agent software, and that capability is included in the TCP/IP software. You can add TCP/IP support without SNMP, but if you're in an enterprise network with SNMP management consoles, your servers deserve to be monitored.

Management consoles are most often Unix workstations with special software. The most popular management software is by Sun and HP. These systems may cost close to $100,000 when fully configured—overkill for a NetWare-only network. However, if you have a graphical management package for your wiring concentrators, you have a subset of an SNMP management console.

SNMP.NLM handles the agent chores for SNMP management consoles and also helps control the TCP/IP module for the TCPCON.NLM utility. The community name used during SNMP message authentication must be provided before SNMP starts. The default community name is *public*, used for read-only SNMP activities. Therefore, no SNMP management console can change any parameter on the NetWare server.

The `INETCFG.NLM` allows you to configure the SNMP parameters from the SNMP Parameters menu, which is shown in Figure 17.8. To change these parameters, from the main INETCFG menu, choose Manage Configuration ➤ Configure SNMP Parameters.

PART

IV

Special Network Features

FIGURE 17.8

The SNMP Parameters menu

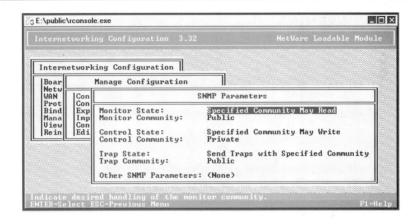

You can configure three community name options from the SNMP parameters screen:

Monitor Community   Determines which SNMP management consoles can read this information.

Control Community   Determines which SNMP management consoles can write (change) this information.

Trap Community   Designates where traps will be sent (management consoles to inform of changes).

Each option in INETCFG has three choices:

- Any community can access the server (read or write).
- No community can access the server.
- Only specified communities can have access.

The default option leaves read authority for the public community.

Also from the INETCFG Manage Configuration menu, you can choose Configure SNMP Information to open the General SNMP Information For This Node menu:

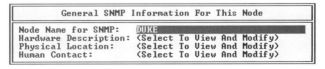

Here, you can enter information that an SNMP management console would see when it queries this particular agent. This includes the server's name, contact information, location, and a description of the system hardware.

 WARNING If you are going to activate SNMP, you should go directly to your Unix system administrator and work out the details. There are no NetWare-only SNMP packages, so this isn't something you get into just as a lark. If you start SNMP, you must have a large network with active network management.

Although NetWare Management Systems (NMS) can use SNMP clients, check the installation of NMS before you add SNMP to the server. With a NetWare-only network, there is no need for the SNMP overhead.

Hot Plug PCI and Configuration Manager

The first time that I saw Hot Plug PCI, I said to myself, "This will make life easier!" And it does! Hot Plug PCI gives you the ability to replace or upgrade PCI cards such as network boards while the server is running. You can start yanking PCI cards out of your server while it is online.

The hardware must support Hot Plug PCI, and you must make sure that three things properly support it:

- The operating system
- The device drivers
- The server hardware

NetWare 5.1 does support Hot Plug PCI, but you must have the supporting software from your server vendor. You'll find a lot of good information about Hot Plug PCI on Compaq's Web site at www.compaq.com, or contact your server vendor. For an example of Compaq's Hot Plug PCI support in action, check out Figure 17.9.

One new feature of NetWare 5.1 helps track the current server configuration. The Configuration Manager detects the hardware configuration of devices that support auto-detection on the following hardware buses: PCI, EISA, MCA, and PnP ISA. If a hardware change is detected, NetWare automatically loads the appropriate configuration NLM.

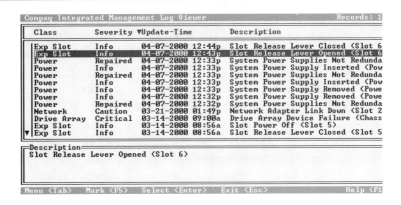

FIGURE 17.9

*Hot Plug details on
the first and last two
entries in the log file*

NetWare 5.1 Web Enhancements

Some have called NetWare 5.1 the version when Novell finally filled in all the gaps
and added a premier Web server to go along with their award-winning file and print
services. Microsoft's Windows NT with Internet Information Server has claimed, with
at least a little bit of justification, the file/print/Web server triple crown. The days of
Microsoft NT/2000 being a better Web server platform than NetWare are now, officially (I just said so), over.

Several upgraded Web server applications are included with NetWare 5.1, along
with a few applications that are brand new. Let's take a look at them, and see where
they will help your company the most.

NetWare FTP Server

Enough detail about the NetWare FTP Server appeared in Chapter 14 for you to get
the idea so that you could set up the server if you're familiar with FTP. If you're not
familiar with FTP and skipped the information in Chapter 14 because you don't see
why you'd want an FTP Server running on your NetWare server, keep reading and I'll
try to show you why.

First of all, as mentioned in Chapter 14, if one NetWare server has an FTP Server
running, you can "reach through" that server and get files from any other NetWare
server on your network. This unusual feature comes courtesy of Novell's server-to-
server communications capabilities and the use of NDS for authentication.

Have you ever been at home and desperately needed a file from work? This trick offers savvy network administrators a way to retrieve a file (I wouldn't trust too many users to handle the details). If you want to fetch a file from an office server that's not on the Internet and runs only IPX, and your only connection is through the Internet, let me show you how to do it.

You can navigate to a remote server, or fetch or put a file directly on the remote server. Let's navigate to one and show a directory.

Connect to your FTP Server via the command line with the FTP client program included with Windows 95/98/NT/2000 (limited though it is), and authenticate to NDS by giving a NetWare user name and password.

Then, use the CD (Change Directory) command to connect to the remote, non-FTP server through NDS. Why does CD work? In the Unix and NFS world, remote file systems are treated like local file systems. This is very handy; it's too bad that Microsoft's view of the world is so limited that they didn't know how to "emulate" that technology.

Look at Figure 17.10 for an example session reaching through an FTP Server to another NetWare server.

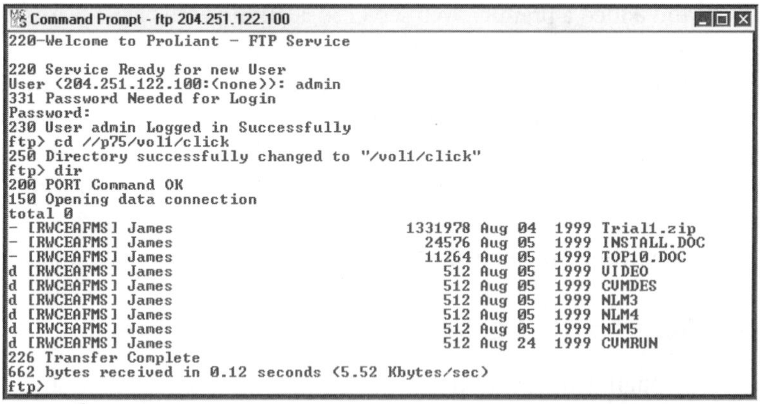

FIGURE 17.10

Connect to PROLIANT, reach through to P75

```
Command Prompt - ftp 204.251.122.100                        _ □ ×
220-Welcome to ProLiant - FTP Service

220 Service Ready for new User
User (204.251.122.100:(none)): admin
331 Password Needed for Login
Password:
230 User admin Logged in Successfully
ftp> cd //p75/vol1/click
250 Directory successfully changed to "/vol1/click"
ftp> dir
200 PORT Command OK
150 Opening data connection
total 0
- [RWCEAFMS] James                   1331978 Aug 04  1999 Trial1.zip
- [RWCEAFMS] James                     24576 Aug 05  1999 INSTALL.DOC
- [RWCEAFMS] James                     11264 Aug 05  1999 TOP10.DOC
d [RWCEAFMS] James                       512 Aug 05  1999 VIDEO
d [RWCEAFMS] James                       512 Aug 05  1999 CUMDES
d [RWCEAFMS] James                       512 Aug 05  1999 NLM3
d [RWCEAFMS] James                       512 Aug 05  1999 NLM4
d [RWCEAFMS] James                       512 Aug 05  1999 NLM5
d [RWCEAFMS] James                       512 Aug 24  1999 CUMRUN
226 Transfer Complete
662 bytes received in 0.12 seconds (5.52 Kbytes/sec)
ftp>
```

See the list of commands and responses? You can't see the command opening the connection within the screen, but Windows NT shows the command in the top status line of Figure 17.10. I put the Welcome message in the system by creating a WELCOME.TXT file in the SYS:\ETC directory.

Notice one other interesting thing about this FTP server pass-through: P75 is a Net-Ware 5.0 server, not a 5.1 server. It's not connected to the Internet. It does happen to use TCP/IP to communicate, but FTP pass-through works over IPX (I know because I've done it before).

Of course, command-line applications like FTP are passe, and no user will ever willingly use one. Luckily, a variety of graphical FTP clients are available.

Let's look at one of the best FTP client programs, WS_FTP Pro from Ipswitch, Inc. (http://www.ipswitch.com). Figure 17.11 shows the opening screen of a client FTP connection to the FTP Server on the Compaq ProLiant here in the lab.

FIGURE 17.11

One of several viewing options for WS_FTP Pro

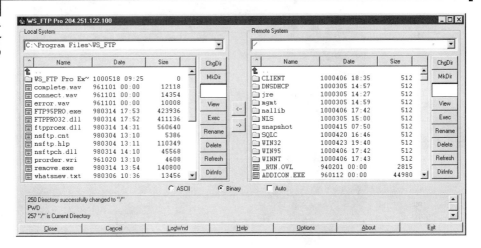

Is PUBLIC a dumb location for a default directory for FTP service? You bet. Change that location immediately, if you really plan to use FTP, to something where critical client and system files aren't hanging out for all to see. The easiest way to change this setting is to use the Netscape-derived NetWare Server Administration utility. Let's change the directory setting, as shown in Figure 17.12.

Once the Server Administration screen is up on your browser, click the NetWare FTP Server command button. The settings in Figure 17.12 are on the User Settings page, so click that link on the left side of the first FTP Server screen.

Can you think of any directories that would be better for anonymous FTP clients than PUBLIC? I sure can. Create a SYS:\FTP directory for users and you won't be wondering what happened to some of your PUBLIC files.

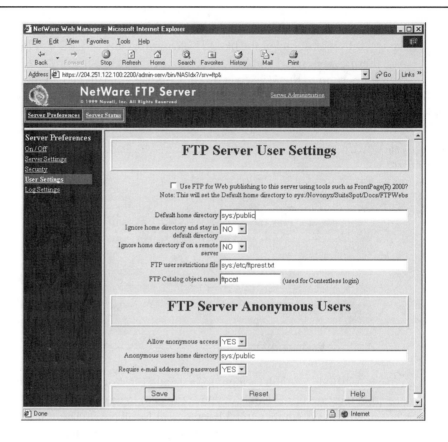

NetWare MultiMedia Server

I'll bet you didn't know that you needed a multimedia server, did you? The file and print server has taken on some new responsibilities.

Using *RTSP* (*Real Time Streaming Protocol*), the NetWare MultiMedia Server provides efficient delivery of streamed multimedia over IP networks. Do you think it works over IPX? Maybe so, if you used an IPX/IP gateway product, but the RealPlayer application expects to ride upon IP, so don't make your life complicated. Either use IP or don't try the MultiMedia Server.

File formats supported (today) include .WAV (digital audio), .MP3 (more digital audio, causing all sorts of copyright problems on the Internet), and .RM (RealVideo). There still isn't enough support for some popular protocols, but this is okay for a start.

The documentation says to install the NetWare MultiMedia Server during the main installation or use NWCONFIG to install it later. When I tried NWCONFIG, it kicked into the ConsoleOne install utility in the graphical server screen. So you may as well save yourself the trouble and start your installation process there.

There's nothing to installation: simply check the box, say Yes a few times, and agree to let the installation program copy the NetWare Web Manager utility again, so as to include the multimedia pieces. The process is rather dull, actually.

After the files are copied, you must return to the colon prompt for the System Console and type **media** to load the NLM. You may, if you're feeling paranoid, type **protect media** to load it into protected memory.

The documentation also tells you to edit the SYS:\ETC\MEDIA.CFG file to provide the location of the media files. You can do that if you want, but the default location of SYS:\PUBLIC\MEDIACONTENT gets written into the configuration file during installation, so you needn't bother.

Unload (umedia) and reload (media) the NetWare MultiMedia Server to make sure that the file locations are read by the server application. Then start your RealPlayer G2 program, run the welcome program ERIC.RM, which was loaded to your server automatically, and get the popcorn ready. See Figure 17.13 for a preview.

FIGURE 17.13

Eric says hello, streaming across your network.

It's good of Dr. Eric Schmidt, Chairman and CEO of Novell, to say hello. I've had the pleasure of meeting him, and he seems like a nice guy. Even though I conned him into writing a cover blurb for my *BorderManager* book published by Sybex, when he may have believed it was being printed by Novell Press, he was still polite.

What's the upside of the NetWare MultiMedia Server? When one of your users gets a copy of a certain video with an angry cubicle dweller taking out his frustrations on his monitor, maybe he'll use the MultiMedia Server to show it to everyone. It will run faster and won't clog your e-mail server or line out to the Internet.

You can configure all this for .MP3 audio files as well, but I'm not going to help you. Your office is noisy enough without sounds of stolen songs screeching through cheap PC add-on speakers.

Want another nice trick? You can control the NetWare MultiMedia Server through the Server Administration Web interface.

NetWare News Server

A news server comes courtesy of the Netscape/Novonyx Enterprise Web Server software. Netscape has a decent news server, and you get it free.

Of course, killjoys may point out that you can get free news servers for Linux systems as well and skip the cost of a NetWare operating license. But what fun would that be?

News servers add a tremendous value to a company when used properly. Not by downloading newsgroups like alt.fetish.dirtyfeet.yucky, but by creating internal discussion groups to share corporate knowledge. Let's go to the sidebar to see how.

Free Groupware with NetWare 5.1

Did you know NetWare 5.1 includes free groupware with every license? Nope, not GroupWise, but something easier, less complex to configure, and already familiar to most users.

The term *collaborative computing* now claims official buzzword status, especially when tied with the recent buzzwords *Web-enabled* or *thin-client*. It all boils down to sharing information within a closed group, capturing the give-and-take common with e-mail exchanges while structuring and archiving the information into a useful package.

Enough teasing: NetWare 5.1 includes an NNTP server software module. *Network News Transfer Protocol* (*NNTP*) sounds complex, but it powers the lowest common denominator of Internet interaction: news groups. Some 50,000 news groups (or more, and growing every day) are available through your Internet Service Provider, ranging from discussions in high-level organic chemistry to ways to kill Barney, the purple TV dinosaur for children.

Continued

> **CONTINUED**
>
> NNTP servers start easily and run with little administrative overhead. If you can handle NetWare, you can handle a news server in your sleep. However, a small investment of your time in news server setup can pay big dividends for your company.
>
> Jon Udell was editor of *Byte Magazine* and authored *Practical Internet Groupware* for O'Reilly & Associates publishing. I spoke with him recently while doing research for an article about groupware. Here's what he had to say:
>
> "The information that's the lifeblood of a company is not in a data warehouse, but in all the message traffic between people. People live in e-mail. Documents have value, not just because of the information inside, but because of the context wrapped around the documents and contained information."
>
> Yes, e-mail lists and CC: lists can help, but the information scatters to hard disks here and yon. News servers collect and retain all the messages in a central site. Any index server offers a quick way to archive the material into a useful storehouse of corporate information.
>
> Company discussion lists open the doors for everyone to participate and share their knowledge with the group. If your company is like most, real knowledge is hard to find and should be preserved whenever possible. Your NetWare 5.1 NNTP server will help, and it's free.

This sidebar came from a column I did for ITworld's weekly newsletter (`http://www.itworld.com`). They say that the copyright belongs to them, but since I didn't sign their overly restrictive contract at this writing, the information is still mine to use as I wish. So I wish to put it here.

Installation and Configuration

Once again, go to the ConsoleOne GUI installation routine, and check the box to install the NetWare News Server. Of course, if you installed it during the primary server installation, you're ahead of me.

You'll get a couple of unusual questions at the start of installation, which will reaffirm that you're doing an Internet product installation. You must provide your SMTP host name (for outgoing mail from news clients) and an e-mail address for an administrator (for daily reports).

There are no NWCONFIG or other C-Worthy utilities to use with the NetWare News Server, since it's an imported product. Go straight to the Netscape, excuse me, NetWare Web Manager General Administration screen (`http://www.servername.com:2200`), and click the NetWare News Server 3.52 command button.

The first screen offers a chance to start and stop the server. You must start the server the first time because the installation routine doesn't start it. You'll have to make some other configuration changes before starting.

Be careful when you start this NetWare News Server because the first full newsgroup download will choke your Internet connection, downloading thousands of messages from 20,000 newsgroups. Novell recommends 1GB of RAM and a 20GB hard disk allocation to support a full newsgroup presentation to your clients.

My advice? Leave the full newsgroups to your ISP, and don't encourage users to waste valuable work time reading hobby newsgroups. Set up one or two simple newsgroups for internal use only, and enjoy the benefits of shared knowledge properly archived for future reference.

Those of you interested in running a full newsgroup feed through NetWare can be my guest, but I can't help you with all the details.

NetWare 5.1 Developer Services

You can't push NetWare 5.1 as a full Web server solution unless developer support applications are included. Inside the NetWare box, you'll find three CDs: Oracle 8i for NetWare (server), Oracle 8i for NetWare (clients), and IBM's WebSphere. On the WebSphere disk is WebSphere Studio, the design application for WebSphere.

These are big deals for NetWare sites planning to run their commercial Web sites on a server platform that doesn't crash with each slam of the computer room door. They are also major programming tools, which have spawned several hundred pounds of technical books describing how to program Web sites in ways far beyond my abilities as a networking, but not programming, expert.

IBM WebSphere

Check out `developer.novell.com/websphere/` for the latest product details and updates of WebSphere. Novell didn't buy WebSphere from IBM; they just helped IBM port WebSphere to the NetWare server platform. Adding NetWare to their supported server list just about filled every checkbox for WebSphere platforms; most Internet-type servers already had WebSphere support.

Once again, the GUI Installation routine starts the process. You'll find plenty of files to copy, because this is a serious application.

How serious? The documentation says, "IBM WebSphere for NetWare combines a portable, Java-based Web application server with the industry's strongest network platform. The Novell implementation of WebSphere supports the development and deployment of open, distributed, enterprise-level Internet applications that provide a high level of scalability, reliability, performance, security, and manageability."

Yeah, that quote is a little heavy on the marketing speak, but WebSphere offers considerable power to back up Web applications and has been integrated into NDS.

While not exactly a bait-and-switch sales pitch, there is a stronger version of WebSphere available if the Version 3.0 Standard version of WebSphere included with NetWare isn't enough. WebSphere Version 3.0 Advanced supports Enterprise JavaBeans for stronger CORBA implementations to use to map to portable Java technologies.

If you are scratching your head, you aren't a programmer and won't have a clue what do to with all this stuff. Call over your programmers and show the WebSphere CD to them, and see if they get excited. If they do, install WebSphere and let them get to work on it.

IBM WebSphere Studio

An application server like WebSphere does little good if you can't build or customize applications for it. Enter WebSphere Studio.

A team-oriented product, WebSphere Studio allows your entire Web team to build powerful Web sites leveraging the WebSphere Application Server. The propaganda, excuse me, valuable marketing literature, says Studio combines easy-to-use wizards with graphical Java development tools. That doesn't mean I can program with it, because I can't.

If you can program, you'll love WebSphere and WebSphere Studio. If you can't program, call your programmers over and show them the Studio along with WebSphere. They will get excited and run gleefully off to build something that you will then have to install and support. Good luck.

Oracle8i

Novell included Oracle 8 in NetWare 5.0, and now they upped the version to Oracle 8i (little i for Internet, of course). Again, this is a powerful developer tool, able to build databases that support entire large companies, and it's packed into the red NetWare box. And I can't use this one, either.

There may not be a bigger, more powerful, or more accepted enterprise database than Oracle. There may not be one more complex, either, but that's a different story. Again, Novell packs a best-of-breed application into the red box.

The Novell documentation sends you straight to the Oracle Web site for details about Oracle on NetWare, so I'll do the same. Again, gather your programmers, and if they react with horror, hide the Oracle CDs. If they jump up and down with joy, beef up your server. Oracle runs big databases, and your current server is not, I promise, strong enough for a serious Oracle application on top of everything you're already running.

Adventures in Cluster Land

NetWare Cluster Services costs extra ($4,995 per server), which makes it the only real optional product I'll describe in much detail. I don't normally spend much time on optional products, because there's so much to cover with normal NetWare features. But I had the chance to play with a mega-server from Compaq and write an article for *Network World* comparing building your own cluster of servers against buying a pre-configured cluster.

Am I being pushy putting this story in here? Maybe, but I think you can learn some interesting things from the article. Besides, it was too much fun to see it run once and disappear into landfills. At least this way, people will have to throw two things into landfills to get rid of this article.

The following is more than just the article; it includes some extra information, extra comments, and no editing by *Network World*. Therefore, I claim this as my copyright (no one else seems to be rushing to claim it), and I can run it here if I want. So there!

Two Options for NetWare Cluster Services

"Mission-critical" today means Web server uptime at many companies, especially since Web site outages now make national news headlines. But even if your company doesn't make headlines during every Web site hiccup, you still lose revenue and customer goodwill during every minute of downtime.

Once management agrees to spend the time and money necessary to increase server uptime, the modern network manager faces multiple options. Put all your eggs in one basket with a new mega-server? Distribute applications across multiple servers, each with standby capability? Set up server clusters? If clustering appeals, do you use your existing servers, buy new servers and cluster them together yourself, or buy pre-configured clusters?

Then come the software choices. Should you stick with something you know? Follow the hot fad and hope it works for you? Bet your company's Web site on newly released server software? (Any ideas which products I'm referring to with the last two sentences? Linux and Windows 2000 would be good guesses.)

For this test, we narrowed down the questions by using NetWare 5.1 as the server operating system, supporting the included Netscape Enterprise Web Server. NetWare servers have a strong track record of reliability earned by measuring uptime in years, not days. The Netscape Enterprise Web Server shipping with NetWare 5.1 is the third generation of NetWare/Netscape server application, and it has been tweaked to use NDS (Novell Directory Service) for easier management and security.

NetWare 5.1 SMP (Symmetrical Multi-Processor) support now handles up to 32 processors under the basic NetWare license. Novell just upgraded their NetWare Cluster Services software to version 1.01 to support NetWare 5.1. This new combination caps nearly a decade of fail-proofing started by Novell with their SFT (System Fault Tolerant) software in NetWare 3.

The remaining questions are simple. First, how hard is NetWare Cluster Services to install and use? We tested by installing the software on existing lab servers. Second, should you roll your own cluster or buy a preconfigured system, such as the one provided for us by Compaq?

Installation and Configuration

NetWare generally installs easily, albeit more slowly recently with Novell's new insistence on the new Java-based graphical user interface. However, mashing four existing NetWare 5.1 servers into a cluster required more work than anticipated. Note that clustering demands that TCP/IP be installed on each NetWare server to handle IP addressing used for fail-over support, but that isn't a problem since TCP/IP has become the default protocol choice. Installing new management utilities and extra configurations, along with assigning the new clustering licenses, took more time than expected.

Novell now includes a Certificate Authority with Secure Authentication Services, primarily for Enterprise Web Server users. Yet a known error with older SAS files and the Enterprise Web Server required several Web Server deletions and re-installations. Perhaps it's my fault, but user licensing errors come and go on a seemingly random basis. (Could it be all the strange stuff I do to these servers during testing? Probably so.)

These errors helped me reach the conclusion that combining existing servers takes more time and is more trouble than starting from scratch. Adding a Storage Area Network to an existing network involves plenty of other technical considerations and requires software modifications and new hardware for all cluster servers.

Actually installing the NetWare Cluster Service software went fairly easily, until the Web Server/SAS problem. A Windows 95/98/NT/2000 client handles the installation honors, after the Novell-recommended upgrade of the network client software and adding a new version of ConsoleOne, the Java-based management utility. After rebooting the servers (a rare occurrence for NetWare server installations), each server searched for, and found, the others ready to cluster. From CD insertion to clustering took about an hour.

The ProLiant Cluster for NetWare 5 from Compaq avoided all those problems. Although lab policy blocks vendor technician involvement unless the tech does every installation for every customer, Compaq does send a tech out to set up each ProLiant Cluster of this size.

Nothing is left out of the Compaq system when delivered. NetWare is installed (Compaq has long been tightly connected to Novell), the Storage Area Network runs as various NetWare volumes, and extra Compaq utilities add to the ease of management. The stand-alone ProLiant 3000 server was easier to install than a regular NetWare server because the Compaq SmartStart utility handles many hardware details during installation.

Once the existing servers reboot and start up as cluster-enabled, the Novell CMON (Cluster MONitor) screen appears, showing each server in the cluster and a few other details. Check out Figure 17.14 for an update.

FIGURE 17.14

Quick display of clustered servers

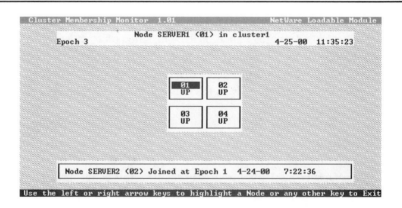

This screen loads automatically on clustered servers. The updated ConsoleOne utility includes a Cluster object (added automatically) and a new screen showing cluster-specific information. Figure 17.15 shows the new cluster logo made from the balls laid off from the old Novell N logo.

FIGURE 17.15

*ConsoleOne shows
the Compaq cluster.*

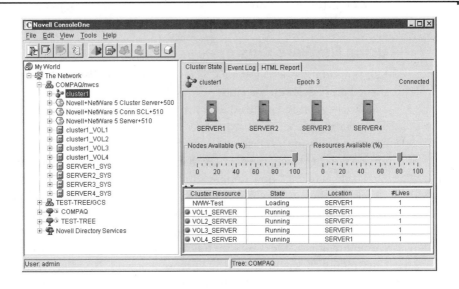

ConsoleOne's Cluster Policies page is plain but important. Start Mode (the default is Automatic) groups the cluster resources (applications) from each server into the assigned cluster upon booting. Failover Mode (the default is Automatic) tells the resource to automatically move to the next assigned server in case of failure. Fallback Mode (again, Automatic is the default) tells the resource whether to migrate back to the original server when it reappears or just stay put.

You can set a Quorum number so cluster resources don't start loading until just some or all (your choice) of the cluster servers are online. A checkbox on the Cluster Policies page allows you to bypass the Quorum rule and load the resources on the first server available. This option makes sense when a stout server with plenty of horse-power handles the majority of the load and spreads critical applications to other, smaller servers in case of a failure.

Shared volumes must be up and running—and accessible to each NetWare server—before starting the cluster installation. Novell has strict rules about placing cluster information on certain disks, but the installation notes cover the needed details well.

Novell includes templates for cluster resources such as Enterprise Web Server, GroupWise, Oracle 8i, and Novell Distributed Print Services. The templates are a good start, but installation still requires you to edit several text files, including load and unload scripts for resource startup and shutdown. Cluster-enabled applications must utilize the shared volume to allow other servers to pick up in case of fail-over or migration. The exceptions are certain applications like GroupWise, which can't use shared volumes. Again, read the installation notes carefully.

Using NetWare Clusters

Most important, does NetWare Cluster Services work? Yes, and quite well; once configured properly, both the lab servers and the Compaq cluster servers send keep-alive and watchdog packets across the network to verify that all servers and cluster resources are operating properly. If hardware or cluster-enabled software goes down, the next assigned server in the cluster takes over the stranded applications within a few seconds. Web clients will never know that the delay isn't a typical Internet traffic jam.

"Load balancing" now implies automatic sharing of the application load, and Novell misuses the term slightly. Rather than true load balancing, NetWare Cluster Services makes it easier than ever before to migrate applications from one server to another without client interruption. Do you want to add a new server to the cluster with more horsepower? You can migrate cluster applications to the new server with three mouse clicks rather than an afternoon of work. The Cluster Resource Manager dialog box shifts applications between servers in much less than a minute. Do you need hardware maintenance? You can migrate the applications, do the maintenance, then migrate the applications back to their original server. This results in less hassle for you and zero downtime for your clients.

Internal NetWare clients using file and print services do require some client software adjustment, mainly to support swapping from one server to another in case of failure or migration. Nothing serious, but you should record these configuration file changes as another reason to get an automatic software rollout utility.

It's hard to tell where the NetWare services stop and the Compaq value-added services start on the ProLiant Cluster. Each rack-mounted server pulls out on rails to provide access to the PCI connectors. Novell supports hot-plugged PCI slots, and so does the Compaq hardware, so who gets credit for the easy replacement of a network interface card while the server is running?

Compaq gets the credit for quickly restructuring data when we pulled a 9.1GB drive from the SAN (Storage Area Network) during operation. Early RAID systems taxed the server tremendously when rebuilding data from a failed drive, but the ProLiant Cluster barely bumped up the NetWare utilization level.

Web-based Compaq Management Agents cover every server hardware detail from any client with a browser and a password. On the server console, added utilities include the Compaq Integration Maintenance Utility, Compaq Software Support Utility, Compaq Online Configuration for the Fibre Array, and the Compaq Power Subsystem Utility, all indistinguishable from the NetWare utilities. Figure 17.16 shows just one of the many online screens available from Compaq.

FIGURE 17.16

*Software version
information with great
detail*

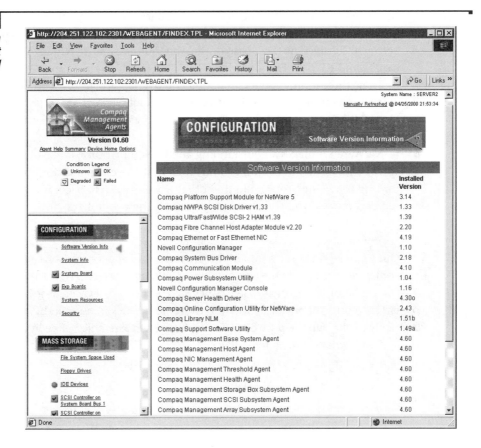

NetWare Cluster Services offers a variety of options to parcel out the applications during a failure. Applications on one server can all go to a second server or be spread to multiple servers. The same holds true for control over shared NetWare volumes. Each cluster resource can be configured differently from any other resource, if you want to take the time and effort. One server can fail over to one server, one can fail to many, many can fail to one, or many can fail to many. This flexibility comes from NetWare, not the hardware. However, the faster you can resolve hardware problems, the better. By comparison, your car's spare tire works fine, but you want to use it as little as possible.

Cluster Quibbles

Perhaps it's just early in the NetWare Cluster Services product cycle, but the lack of utility support and lack of templates for non-Novell applications are troublesome.

NetWare installation and management, even for a relatively small addition like the 1MB of Cluster Services files on the various NetWare servers, still bounced around between ConsoleOne (Java-based), NetWare Administrator (Windows 95/98/NT/2000-based), and NWCONFIG (DOS-based).

These three utilities offer competing and overlapping features on one hand, with painful restrictions on the other. ConsoleOne looks great, but the Java utility crawls around like Windows NT on a 486, even running on a quad-processor Pentium III at 550 MHz with a gigabyte of RAM and no other load.

NetWare 5.1 makes an outstanding application platform, and Novell wisely tries to spread that word. But couldn't some other, non-Novell applications have templates for load balancing? You would think that Novell's push to become a Web applications server company would push development for these templates.

Pricing

Our Compaq support team frankly worried about price comparisons between their pre-configured cluster and the cost of adding NetWare Cluster Services to existing servers. "Our solution is not inexpensive," they said honestly. They were worried that the apparent high price for one ticket for everything would stick in our minds, rather than accurately totaling up the price of a comparable system assembled piece by piece.

Here's what Compaq included:

- four PL6400R/550MHz-w/4 2MB processors each
- one RA41000 Storage Enclosure
- twenty 9.1GB Ultra2 drives (two drives per server and one populated array)
- four 64-bit/66MHz StorageWorks fibre channel Host Bus Adapter Kits (Persian)
- one 7-port FC hub
- one 7-port FC hub mounting kit
- one 22U rack (9122)
- one 6-port KMM Switch box
- six KMM cables (2M)

The exact price: $167,110. Yes, that seems like a lot, but we must avoid comparing apples to oranges.

Apples to apples, matching the Compaq 6400R cluster we tested requires four servers capable of supporting four Intel Pentium III XEON processors and up to 4GB of RAM. Each tested 6400R server has dual power supplies; pull one out and the server never blinks. Hot Plug PCI support allows you to add or remove network cards without taking the server down. Hot-swappable redundant hard disks allow you to add or remove storage any time. You can't find these systems at Joe's Computer Shack.

NetWare's reliability lulls some people into believing that any clone desktop PC can become a server. Yet the first step up either the horsepower or reliability scale illustrates the limits of cheap PC servers. Dual- or quad-processor-capable systems are not found on the bargain table, and high-quality storage costs more than the use-three-years-and-replace IDE drives in many new computers today.

Speaking of storage, the Compaq 4100 Storage Area Network pushes hot-swappable storage capacity into the terabyte range. Fiber Channel SANs with high-throughput Ultra/Fast/Wide SCSI-2 drives and controllers stand at the top end of performance, reliability, and price charts from every manufacturer.

Roll Your Own or Buy A Cluster?

The Intel-based, multi-processor server market gets more crowded each day. Compaq made some of the earliest heavy-duty NetWare servers, but history counts for little in today's market. Every one of Compaq's major competitors have similar hardware products in their catalog, all claiming to be "the best."

While every hardware vendor claims high availability on their marketing brochures, detailed examination of the technical specifications can show a different story. The Compaq ProLiant 3000 performs quite well in the stand-alone tower case, although the size and shape are more those of a small metal hope chest than a tower. The Compaq ProLiant Cluster for NetWare performs even better in the heavy rack enclosure that tucks four powerful servers, a Storage Area Network, and the attendant controllers and cables for all of the above in a sturdy package two feet wide, three feet deep, and almost four feet tall (and very, very, heavy). Every support module comes in pairs, pulls out while the system stays running, slides smoothly back into place, and locks down into a single block of solid server.

Another apparent pricing disadvantage for clusters concerns the bundled-in software expense. Hardware catalogs highlight software prices, but the software needed to power any cluster for NetWare adds up quickly. A basic NetWare 5.1 license is $1,345, and 100 more users cost an additional $10,745. NetWare Cluster Services software runs $4,995 per cluster node (the tested Compaq cluster came with $19,980 of cluster software alone). You must purchase software for your own cluster, and you must include that software total in your comparison figures to be fair to the preconfigured cluster.

Companies realizing the value of a never-fail server system should also recognize the value of setting up new servers from scratch rather than mashing together existing servers as we did. Clean server installations are less trouble, and new servers more often match the horsepower needs at hand rather than taking the servers that are available.

Adding up the convenience of a complete, ready-to-go cluster with highly available hardware in a single convenient package pushes our vote toward the ProLiant Cluster for NetWare. Adding in the Compaq utilities such as SmartStart and Compaq Management Agents makes the vote even more strongly in favor of a ProLiant Cluster.

How I Did It

Compaq provided us a complete ProLiant Cluster for NetWare, including all hardware and software. We took four existing servers (Compaq ProLiant 3000, Pentium 120 clone of undetermined origin, and two Gateway2000 Pentium 120 systems, all with 128MB of RAM) running NetWare 5.1 and added the NetWare Cluster Services software. Performance wasn't the issue; we tested installation, configuration, and management. Novell provided all network software. Infrastructure components came from 3Com (EtherLink III network adapters) running through a LinkSys 24 port SNMP-managed hub.

Using the Enhancements

Some of the enhancements I discussed in this chapter are part of the core NetWare 5.1 product, and some are highly specialized and of interest to only a few customers. File compression is the most popular of all enhancements, since you get something (more space for files) for almost nothing (some server RAM).

If you don't use any of the extra enhancements, such as HSM or SNMP, don't feel bad. Most NetWare users don't take advantage of all these technologies.

But don't you feel smart using an operating system with more horsepower than you'll ever need? Too many NetWare competitors offer the opposite; horsepower is promised, but the release date of these features keeps fading into the distant mists of the future.

It's a common statement that most users leave 80 percent of their application programs unexplored. In other words, users are happy using only 20 percent of the product's power. NetWare doesn't use that ratio; more like 70 percent of the power is used by everyone, with 30 percent reserved for those with special needs. Few, if any, customers ever need more PC LAN features and horsepower than NetWare delivers.

The third-party additions, particularly from Netscape/Novonyx, make a huge difference in the functionality of your NetWare server. Critics who rated Windows NT higher than NetWare because of Internet applications must rethink their position. Of course, if they had an open mind, they wouldn't be so thrilled with Microsoft to start with, but that's another personal diatribe we don't have time for right now.

If you see features here that you like and think you want to incorporate into your own network, experiment with them on a pilot system first before putting them to work on your production network, as you would with anything new.

CHAPTER 18

Troubleshooting Your Network

No matter how carefully you plan, how carefully you build your network, and how carefully you train your users, things will go wrong. In fact, things going wrong is a normal part of your network operations. When things don't go wrong, you should worry.

When something on the network is not working properly, you must change hats from strategic thinker to ambulance driver. Even if the problem is not much of a problem to the network as a whole, the affected user needs to be reassured. Psychology is important. When users have a problem, they don't want to hear that it isn't a big problem, because it is big to them. They want to hear that you understand their problem and are working to fix that problem. They will be reasonable (probably) if you acknowledge their distress ("I feel your pain") and inform them of your actions to resolve the problem.

A Troubleshooting Scene

Let's look at a troubleshooting situation as a scene from a movie, or, more appropriately, a sitcom.

(SCENE: Irate user who can't boot his computer to the network.)

YOU: "What's the problem?"

USER: "Your stupid network is broken." (User registers disgust and waves an arm toward the defunct computer.)

YOU (sitting at the computer): "Your hard disk seems to be dead."

This is the time many network managers try to defend their network, pointing out that the user's problem is caused by and limited to the user. Your "stupid" network had nothing to do with this problem. However, resist this urge. The user is angry, and he will now be embarrassed. Anything you say in defense of the network will be seen by the user as "rubbing my nose in it."

YOU: "Let me configure a boot floppy, so you can get logged in to the network. We'll order a new hard disk for you, and I'll let you know when it arrives so we can install it at your convenience."

USER: "Thanks for your prompt attention to this matter. I apologize for disparaging the network, but I was upset by this disk failure. Please forgive me. Allow me to buy you lunch today in apology."

Continued ▶

CONTINUED

(ACTION: Glowing sunshine warmly colors the scene. Birds sing. Flowers bloom. Theme music swells.)

Perhaps this scenario is a bit far out, even for Hollywood. But the idea of not defending your network against an angry user is a good one. Angry people often need to blow off steam, and you're a good target. You aren't the boss, so you can't fire them. You aren't an immediate coworker, so the user won't be embarrassed every morning afterward. You are a fairly safe target for the user's anger. Anything you say in defense of your network, or that insinuates that the problem is self-caused, will only make the user angrier. This is a "no-win" situation for you, at least in the short term.

Letting the user win doesn't make you a doormat. The network administrator's favorite fable is "The User Who Cried Wolf" for good reason. You will soon learn which users howl the loudest with the smallest problems. When several problems arrive at once, as they often do, you may safely put these users at the bottom of the help list. After all, you have already documented your multiple quick responses, right? How can they complain if they were served quickly many times and only served slowly when a larger network crisis appeared? Well, they will complain, but no one will listen to them, because you have documentation. That's the beauty of CYAWP (Cover Your A** With Paper).

General Troubleshooting Tips

What changed? This is my first question when a problem appears. Something almost always changes. Computer hardware has gotten so reliable that it's rare to find outright physical failures. Disk drives still wear out and power supplies still die, but hardware failure will not be a problem at the top of your list of aggravations.

I contend that you don't manage a network; you manage network changes. If nothing is changing, there's no troubleshooting to do. When nothing changes, you can focus on the future and try to keep up with your computer trade magazines. When you're adding users, software, and hardware, there will always be something to fix.

There are, however, occasions when a hardware component does cause your problem, even if it isn't a component failure. How about someone moving a wiring concentrator plug from a UPS to a wall plug? When the power blips and takes your concentrator offline, is that a component failure? Yes, and no. Something changed, and you can't blame that on component failure.

Many network managers have developed a "Top Ten" list of troubleshooting or prevention tips. Rather than stopping at ten, here's everything I could find, think of, or steal. Let's start with preventive measures.

Prevention Tips

The following are some prevention strategies you can try.

Ask your management to decide on a downtime "comfort level."
The faster you want to resurrect the network, the more money you must spend in preparation. A maximum of a few minutes of downtime can be guaranteed by using NetWare SFT III (System Fault Tolerance, level III) and by having backup hardware for every system wiring component. Downtime will stretch to several hours if you have some, but not all, of your replacement equipment available. Downtime will stretch to a day or more if you rely completely on outside resources.

Have your management decide which users must get back to work first.
In case of a serious network problem, you may be able to support only a few users. Which users will those be?

Know what you have.
Inventory all your network hardware and software. How else will you buy spare parts and get updated replacement drivers?

Expect everything and everyone to let you down.
If you expect the worst, you're prepared for anything. You're also pleasantly surprised almost all the time, since the worst rarely happens.

Anything that can fail *will* fail.
Be prepared for any LAN component to fail, be stolen, or be tampered with.

Know your component failure profiles.
On a server, failures are likely to be (in order): disks, RAM, the power supply, or network adapters. The same applies to a workstation, but only one user is inconvenienced.

Balance your network to eliminate as many single points of failure as possible.
Many network administrators spread every workgroup across two wiring concentrators, so one failure won't disable an entire department. You can also spread a group's applications across multiple servers, which is easy to do with NetWare 5.1.

Spend the money necessary to back up your system every night.
The quickest way to recover from corrupt or lost data files is by using a complete backup made the night before. Most restores will be user files deleted by accident. The previous night's tape will solve that problem.

Test your backup and restore software and hardware.
How long does it take to completely restore a volume with your backup hardware and software? You can't bring a replacement hard disk online until the restored files are in place.

Duplicate system knowledge among the administrative staff.

If a person, even you, is the single point of failure, take precautions. I know you feel you're always there, but do you want to come back from your honeymoon to replace a disk drive? Start some cross-training.

Your suppliers will let you down sometime, somehow.

Support organizations have problems, too. Don't bet the ranch on your dealer stocking a replacement drive that they "always" have. If you must have one without fail, have it on your shelf.

Find sources of information before you need them.

Check out Novell's Web site, and participate in NetWare-oriented bulletin board services and Internet newsgroups. The more you know, and the more places you can go for quick information, the better off you are.

Document everything far more than you think necessary.

Write down everything about your network, then fill in the blanks. Assume that your manager must recover the network while you're on your honeymoon. Will your documentation provide the manager with enough information? If some or all of your documentation is stored electronically, reprint the information after every substantial change and store the paper in a safe location.

Keep valuable network information in a safe.

Your password, some backup tapes, boot disks, software licenses, proof of purchase forms, and a copy of your network documentation should be in a safe—literally. Only network administrators and your manager should have access to this safe.

Make your network as standardized as possible.

Hardware and software consistency is not the hobgoblin of small minds; it's the savior of the harried administrator. Standardized CONFIG.SYS, AUTOEXEC.BAT, and NET.CFG files make life easier. It may be impossible to keep them consistent, but try. Find a good network adapter card and stick with it. Make as few different Windows Desktop arrangements as you can.

Make a detailed recovery plan in case of a partial or complete network disaster and test your recovery plan.

Companies with workable recovery plans stay in business after a disaster. Those with no recovery plans are rarely in business two years after the disaster. But you'll never be sure that the plan works until the plan is tried. Do you want to try the plan after office hours in a test or while the CEO is looking over your shoulder? Test the plan as well as the people involved.

Put step-by-step instructions on the wall above every piece of configurable equipment.

Every server, gateway, or communications box should have a complete operational outline on the wall above the equipment. It should cover all steps necessary for a computer novice to take the system down and/or bring the system back up. Large companies with a night support staff will find this particularly useful.

Tips for Solving Problems

Network problems can be both physical (cable) and virtual (protocols). This makes troubleshooting more fun than normal.

No matter how prepared you are, something will go wrong. It's nothing personal—it's just life. When faced with a problem, the following hints may be of some help.

What changed?

I said this at the beginning, but it's worth repeating. When there's a problem, 99 percent of the time, somebody changed something somewhere. Scientists have disproved the idea of "bit rot," where software that did work goes sour and mutates into software that doesn't. However, it's common for workstation software to be pushed beyond its capabilities or to be modified by new applications. But that is a change, isn't it?

When you hear hoofbeats, look for horses before you look for zebras.

Check the simple things first; hoofbeats are more likely to come from horses than from zebras (at least in Texas, where I'm writing this). Is the plug in the wall? Is the power on? Is the monitor brightness turned up (I once drove across town in a snowstorm to turn up the brightness on a Unix system monitor)? Is this the right cable? Is the cable plugged in on both ends? Is a connection loose? You get the idea—nothing is too simple to verify before going on to the next step.

Isolate the problem.

Does this problem happen with other machines? Does it happen with this same user name? Will this system work on another network segment? Will the server talk to another workstation?

Don't change something that works.

If you change a configuration parameter and that doesn't fix the problem, change the parameter back to what it was. The same goes for hardware. No use introducing new variables from new hardware or software while you're still trying to find the problem.

Let me say this again: if you change something and it doesn't fix your original problem, change it back. It may look okay now, but you will more often than not mess up more than you fix if you change things all over the place.

Check your typing.

Typos in the configuration files will cause as much of a problem as the wrong command. Your software won't work well if your path includes \WINCOWS rather than \WINDOWS.

Read the documentation.

Equipment documentation may not be good enough, but it's better than nothing. Print out the readme files from the installation disks and keep the printout with the manuals. It's much easier for manufacturers to put crucial manual modifications in the readme file than in the manual.

Look for patches.

Check Novell's Web site for files to update your troublesome hardware. Call the vendor of third-party products for new drivers for network adapters and drive controllers.

Refer to previous trouble logs.

Keep a log of problems and solutions for your network. Even a new problem may be related to an old problem you've solved before.

Trust, but verify, everything a user tells you.

People interpret the same events different ways. What is unnoticed by a user may be a crucial bit of information for you. If a user tells you a screen looks a certain way, take a look for yourself.

Call your NetWare dealer early in the process.

Buying your NetWare hardware and software from a local dealer gives you the right to call and ask for help. This is especially true during and just after installation. If you have a good relationship with your dealer, the support people should answer specific questions (such as, "Does this network adapter have a different driver when used in the server?") without charge. Be prepared to pay for support if your questions are open-ended ("Why doesn't this server talk to the workstation?") or you request a technician to come and look at your system.

Check out a Novell Support Connection CD-ROM.

Tons of information are on every disk. Patches, white papers, compatibility reports, and tips of all kinds are there if you look.

Call Novell technical support.

It's better to spend the money on 1-800-858-4000 than to leave your network down for a second day. But don't call until you've gone through the documentation, the Novell Web site, and all local support resources. It's embarrassing to find out during a paid support call that the solution is in the manual.

Do things methodically, one by one.

Don't make a "brilliant" leap of deductive reasoning; that's a high-risk/high-reward procedure. Las Vegas casinos are rich because suckers play long odds. Keep following the plan, and don't try to be a hero.

Learning Your Network's Normal Operation

Do you know what your car sounds like when it's working properly? Do you know the beeps and buzzes your computer makes as it boots? Do you know how your body feels as you struggle out of bed?

Of course you do. You know these things from regular repetition. More important, you know that when one of those sounds or feelings is not right, something needs to be checked out.

Your network is the same way. You must learn how it is when it's normal so you can quickly tell when it isn't normal.

Several obvious things help you track the details of your network's normal operation.

Paper, in this case network documentation, is more necessary than you may imagine. You have about 2000 items to remember for every user. If you have lots of users, learn to write down everything, or every day will be a rough day.

An activity log is vital to managing large networks. This log doesn't need to be fancy, just consistent. If you keep the log on paper, you should regularly put it in a database to organize and comment on the results of each action. Having it available on the system makes it easier for other administrators to share.

Help desk software is becoming inexpensive enough for small- and medium-sized companies. By tracking every support call from users, you maintain a single database with all trouble calls listed, cataloged, and indexed. Most important, this type of software tracks and shares the little, but aggravating, configuration details for many software packages that cause your network problems. If you have more than two network managers, you can benefit from help desk software.

Networks are often judged harshly by old mainframers, since one or more stations or printers may be unavailable at any one time. To some, especially those who wish to cast aspersions on your network, this will count as downtime and be held against you. Don't let them define downtime to fit their terms. In fact, let's define downtime and another type of network time:

> **Downtime**   Time when a network service or resource is unavailable to any user.

> **Crosstime**   Time when a service object, such as a printer, is down, but the user has easy options to use comparable services.

If a server is down, but all users can log in through NDS, they are not down. The few users who need access to volumes on the down server do suffer downtime; everyone else suffers crosstime. Routing to another printer in place of your normal printer is not downtime; it's crosstime.

You should track the times that resources are down, but you must put this information into context. If you have 10 servers, and one server is down for one day, your servers are 90 percent available that day. If that is the only down day in a 30-day month, the monthly total for server availability is 99.67 percent available (299 available server days divided by 300 possible server days). This is very acceptable, even to mainframe bigots.

PART
IV

Special Network
Features

 TIP If the mainframe people give you too much trouble, ask for their remote-access uptime. It's usually lousy. They'll blame it on the phone lines. Just laugh and walk away.

Of the 2000 details you must track for users, about 1950 of them are tied to their workstations, especially if they run a Windows operating system. Don't feel bad if you never feel in control of Windows workstations on your network. With the added complexity that comes with the Registry, it is often difficult to get a handle on exactly what is happening on a particular computer. Thank you, Microsoft, for foisting on us a system where every new application overwrites critical system files for other applications.

Regardless of the hassle factor, you must make some baseline of your workstations, servers, and network in general. You might want to check some of the third-party server management software available, but you can also monitor your network fairly well with the tools NetWare provides.

Tracking Normal Server Performance

It's easy to ignore the server when it's running as it should. You have so many other little problems, such as printers that act strangely and users who behave even more strangely, that you leave the server alone.

Although it's easy not to pay attention to the server, it isn't advisable. You must spend a few minutes now and then checking on the server when it's running well so you'll have some idea what it should look like under normal circumstances. Believe me, when it's down and you can't figure out why, you'll wish you had a few screenshots and configuration files saved in a notebook on your desk (hint, hint).

The MONITOR Program

MONITOR is your best bet for tracking server performance during the day. Many network managers leave this screen on all the time. Even the snake-like screen saver (SCRSAVER.NLM) indicates server activity. The longer and faster the snake gets, the more server activity going on.

When the MONITOR program is running, four important performance indicators are evident from the General Information screen:

Utilization Shows how much CPU time is being spent servicing the network. This is half of the network load, with disk activity being the other half. If this number regularly stays over 50 percent for more than a minute or two at a time, you need more horsepower. It's possible for this number to run over 100 percent, so don't overreact if you see 103 percent utilization sometime.

Total Cache Buffers   The lower this number, the slower file performance will be. If less than half of your cache buffers are in the Total category, you need to get more RAM.

Current Service Processes   This number indicates outstanding read requests. When a read request comes in but there is no way to handle it immediately, a service process is created to perform the read as quickly as possible. Having too few cache buffers will run up this number. If you have plenty of RAM but increasing service processes, you need disk channel help. Upgrade the controller or disk, or move high-load applications to another server.

Packet Receive Buffers   These buffers hold packets from workstations until they can be handled by the server. They will be allocated as needed, but a gradually increasing number indicates that the server isn't keeping up with the load. Two thousand buffers are allocated automatically to support the Enterprise Web Server.

Figure 18.1 shows the MONITOR main screen, with the General Information window open to show all statistics. You can press Tab to shrink or expand this window. Shrink it to use the Available Options menu.

FIGURE 18.1

The standard server performance check

NOTE   There is an interesting note about the screen shown in Figure 18.1. Do you see the Directory Cache Buffers entry, showing 170? This number started at 23, then after about one minute of uptime, it increased to 50, then kept going. Just a bit of server self-tuning information. You can set this parameter; the details are back in Chapter 10.

The other screen you may leave open in MONITOR is the Disk Cache Utilization Statistics view. You can see the Disk Cache Utilization menu choice at the bottom of

Figure 18.1. If the Long Term Cache Hits figure stays above 90 percent, you have a server that's well configured for file service.

You should take a few screenshots of your server's MONITOR screen now and then. Using RCONSOLE makes this easy (old-timers used to scratch the numbers in stone tablets, since there was no way to capture a server console screen to a printer before RCONSOLE). Make a few of these screenshots for each server now and then, with a notation of the date and time. (See Chapter 10 for information about using RCONSOLE.) Connections and open files are shown at the bottom of the window. Both of these are good load indicators for referencing the server activity.

Server Log Files

NetWare automatically creates three server log files, and one more is optional:

SYS$LOG.ERR   Contains file server errors and general status information. This log file is stored in the \SYSTEM directory and can be viewed with NetWare Administrator or any file viewer.

VOL$LOG.ERR   Shows volume errors and status information. This file is stored in the root of each volume and can be viewed with a file viewer.

TTS$LOG.ERR   Has information about TTS (Transaction Tracking System). This file is stored in the root of each volume with TTS active and can be viewed with a file viewer.

CONSOLE.LOG   Keeps a copy of all console screen messages. It is started by this line in the AUTOEXEC.NCF file: LOAD CONLOG. This log file is stored in the \SYS:ETC directory and can be viewed using INETCFG or with a file viewer.

The SYS$LOG.ERR file is normally checked using the NetWare Administrator program, but this viewer can't show a long log file. The beginning of the log file will not be shown, on the assumption that you are more interested in immediate history. If you wish to see the entire log file, you must use a text viewer.

Figure 18.2 shows the error log file for TEST_SERVER displayed in NetWare Administrator. The bottom button on the right of the dialog box opens this view. Horizontal and vertical scroll bars are available to allow you to see more of the file.

Notice that items that are not normally considered errors are tracked in this file. The first two messages complain that the NetWare Cluster Services licenses have expired. The last two entries indicate that an RCONSOLE connection was granted and cleared for the workstation at the particular network address.

The volume log, VOL$LOG.ERR, is created automatically and stored in the root of each volume. There are no special viewers or ways to reach this log except to read it with a text tile, but you won't need to read it often. Figure 18.3 shows an example volume log in the life of a lab server. It's up, it's down, it's up, it's down, it's up. Mostly up.

FIGURE 18.2

Errors and server information

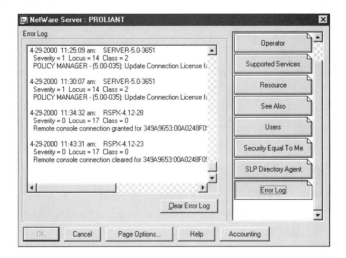

FIGURE 18.3

Volume log

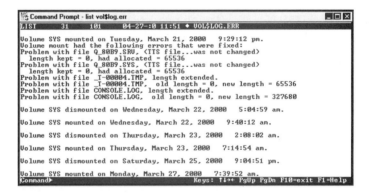

Most of your volume log will look like this yo-yo. It may stretch over several years, since many volumes stay mounted for months at a time.

Notice the errors listed in the volume log at the top of the screen. There were no real problems, but files were enlarged to hold more information. The term "errors" may be a bit harsh, but you can see that everything got cleaned up and all is well.

The last automatic log file, TTS$LOG.ERR, is activated only on those servers where TTS is enabled. If TTS is started, the log is started. Those servers without TTS enabled will not have the log file.

TTS guarantees that transactions are completely finished or completely undone back to the pre-transaction state. The log file lists times and data file names rolled back because of an incomplete transaction. This file won't have much inside it, except a time and date stamp of when TTS was started or shut down. These times will match those in the volume log.

CONSOLE.LOG is a bit different. It keeps a copy of all console messages that normally scroll by quickly as the server boots. Figure 18.4 shows a part of the CONSOLE.LOG file.

FIGURE 18.4

Console comments in a file

This viewer is in the INETCFG utility, loaded at the server console. To see the file, type **LOAD INETCFG** at the console or go through RCONSOLE, choose View Configuration, and then choose Console Messages. All the messages sent to the console are tracked here.

As the screen in Figure 18.4 says, the log is shown Read-Only. You can open the log in the \SYS:ETC directory with a file viewer if you wish. You can also use a text editor to make notes about the log process before you print the log for safekeeping.

Server Configuration File Copies

Printing logs for safekeeping is a good idea. Having a clean server boot record may come in handy someday when you're trying to re-create a load sequence for a long list of NLMs.

The log files just mentioned are easy to find and print. There are a couple of other quick options, as well. Figure 18.5 shows the option to copy all SET parameters to a file.

The MONITOR utility offers a chance to copy all parameters to a file every time you leave the Select A Parameter Category menu of the Server Parameters option. When you choose to copy all parameters to a file, the SETCMDS.CP file is copied to the SYS:\SYSTEM directory. That location is the default, but you can change that path. Once the file location is chosen, every SET command is listed with the current setting.

FIGURE 18.5

Take advantage of this option.

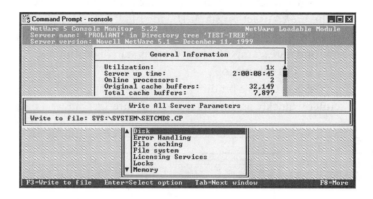

There isn't any help information in this file, and the file is more than 5KB of ASCII text, but it's good to have. Some of the SET parameters can be a real problem if they are incorrect. Having a clean copy of the parameters for each of your servers is handy if a problem should arise.

The AUTOEXEC.NCF file is kept in the \SYS:SYSTEM directory. It's easy to find, so you have no excuse not to make a quick printout of it every time it changes. Put it in the server notebook. Keep the old ones, so you can return to a former configuration if necessary.

The easiest way to get a copy of STARTUP.NCF is while the server is down. This file is kept in the \NWSERVER directory of the DOS partition by default. You may have placed it in a different directory during installation, but I asked you not to at the time. So look in \NWSERVER first. If it is there, copy it to floppy disk and print it later. Your alternative is to look at it in the INSTALL program (choose NCF File Options, then Edit STARTUP.NCF File). From there, you can print the screen.

If you have used the INETCFG utility to manage your protocols, the AUTOEXEC.NCF file will have all the protocol statements commented out with the number sign (#). There is a message telling you to check the INITSYS.NCF and NETINFO.CFG files in the \SYS:ETC directory. There is also a warning in the message not to edit those files directly, but to use the INETCFG utility. However, you can certainly print these files and put the printouts in your server notebook.

Tracking Normal Workstation Details

An easy place to check the performance of a workstation is through the MONITOR screen on a server. When you choose Connection Information and press Enter on the user connection name, a screen similar to the one shown in Figure 18.6 will appear.

FIGURE 18.6

*A healthy, active
workstation connection*

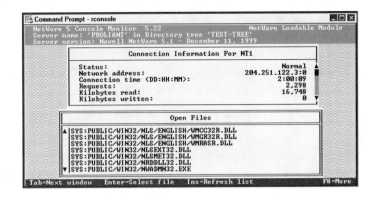

What does this tell us? Well, first, if you see the user's name on the connection list, the network connection must be in fairly good shape. The connection time is listed, as is the number of requests made from the workstation to the server. The resulting kilobytes read and written are shown, and these three numbers are updated in real time.

The second window shows open files, and again, this number is updated in real time. If you press Enter on a filename, the Record Lock Information window will pop up. If the user stops an application or otherwise closes files, those changes will appear immediately in the window.

NOTE Notice the identifying address for the workstation: 204.251.122.3. It's odd for an old NetWare dog like me to see an IP address there, but I can still learn a new trick now and then.

Go back to Chapter 5 for details about workstation installation and setup. For this section, we're assuming the workstation did work at one time and has now developed a problem.

Workstation Configuration File Copies

During installation of each workstation or shortly thereafter, it's a good idea to make a backup copy of the important configuration files. For Windows 95 computers, this means creating an Emergency Boot Disk either during the installation of the operating system or through the Add/Remove Programs applet in the Control Panel. This principle is continued for Windows NT Workstation computers, except that the disk is called the Emergency Repair Disk (ERD). In Windows 98, the disk is called the Emergency System

Disk, but it performs the same function. Each of these creates a disk that contains the configuration information for the computer and can be used during the repair processes in the event that you experience the dreaded catastrophic failure.

Yes, these workstation disks are just one more thing to keep track of, but they will come in handy. As these disks start piling up, your urge to develop and enforce a standard workstation configuration will grow.

The NET.CFG File (DOS and Early Windows Clients)

The NET.CFG file (installed in the \NWCLIENT directory by default) controls the interaction between the network hardware and software and your DOS, Windows, or OS/2 workstation. Installation details should have been taken care of already, but sometimes new network servers or new software packages cause problems.

If you have the same adapter in each workstation, the NET.CFG file may be mass-produced and copied to each station during installation. Remember to check the PRE-FERRED TREE settings if you have more than one tree. The name context must be tracked as well as any other modifications you use in your network configuration.

Client32 software running under Windows 95/98/NT doesn't require a NET.CFG file. Client32 software running on a DOS or Windows 3.1x system will still have this file, however.

NT Workstation Utilities

If you have NT Workstations in your network, you have some extra tools for determining how those workstations are operating: Performance Monitor and Windows NT Diagnostics.

 NOTE Since this is a book about NetWare, not NT, this is not the place to find full coverage of the Performance Monitor and Windows NT Diagnostics utilities. For details, refer to the NT online documentation or one of the many books devoted to NT.

Performance Monitor is used to track NT counters that monitor all aspects of the computer, from the percentage of CPU time being used by applications to the number of packets being sent through a network interface. It displays the information retrieved from these counters in a real-time chart, as shown in Figure 18.7.

To start Performance Monitor, select Start ➤ Programs ➤ Administrative Tools (Common) ➤ Performance Monitor. You can add counters to the chart by clicking the plus sign on the menu bar and selecting the appropriate object and counter. An *object* is a system component, such as the network interface or processor. A *counter* is a particular function of that object that is tracked, such as the number of bytes transmitted per second.

FIGURE 18.7

*The Windows NT
Performance Monitor*

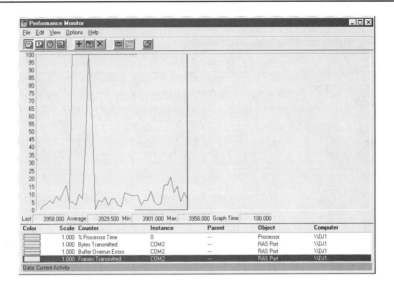

 NOTE   Some objects in Performance Monitor allow you to track more than one instance of the object. These occur when there is more than one of a particular object installed in a system, such as multiple hard disks, network interfaces, or processors.

Here are some of the more useful counter and object pairs to track with Performance Monitor:

Memory–Page Faults/sec   The average number of page faults per second for the current processor instance. If this number is more than double what you see during normal operation, it's time to put more RAM in your computer.

Network–Bytes Total/sec   The total amount of traffic through the computer's network adapter, both inbound and outbound. When this counter begins to approach the theoretical maximum for your network medium, it's time to consider increasing the speed of your network or dividing it into separate segments.

Network–Output Queue Length   The number of packets awaiting transmission across the network. If there are more than two packets queued at any particular time, network delays are likely and a network bottleneck should be investigated.

Processor–%Processor Time   The percentage of time since Performance Monitor started that the CPU has been busy handling non-idle threads. If this counter is continuously greater than 80 percent, the machine is heavily taxed and steps should be taken to alleviate the load.

As you can imagine, there are many, many more counters than the ones listed here. The best way to make the most of Performance Monitor is to take the time to familiarize yourself with all the available objects and counters.

 TIP There are two objects that relate to the operation of the hard disks in your system: Physical Disk and Logical Disk. Because of their tax on system performance, these counters must be enabled manually and should be disabled immediately after the measurements are taken. To enable the disk counters, run DISKPERF –Y from a command prompt and reboot the computer. To disable the counters, run DISKPERF –N.

Windows NT Diagnostics is a utility that provides information about the configuration of devices in the computer as well as information about the driver and the operating environment for the computer. This is read-only information. The executable for Windows NT Diagnostics is WINMSD. (For those of you who have worked with the MSD program for DOS-based computers, WINMSD will look familiar.)

To run WINMSD, select Start ➢ Programs ➢ Administrative Tools (Common) ➢ Windows NT Diagnostics. You'll see the Version tab, as shown in Figure 18.8.

FIGURE 18.8

The Version tab of Windows NT Diagnostics

This Gateway2000 P120 with 128MB of RAM functions as both NT 4.0 Server and Workstation. Each of the nine tabs displays various information about the computer:

Version   Shows information about the version of NT installed and its registration.

System   Displays more detailed information about the system, such as the BIOS revision and the type of processor(s) installed.

Display   Displays information about the video adapter and driver.

Drives   Displays information about all drives connected to the computer. Click the Properties button to see the properties for each drive.

Memory   Displays information about the physical memory in the system and its virtual memory.

Services   Displays information about the status of all services and devices.

Environment   Displays the environment settings for the local user and the entire system.

Network   Displays network configuration information and statistics.

Resources   Displays information about all IRQs, I/O ports, DMS channels, and memory addresses used in the system. This might be the most useful of the NT Diagnostics tabs, particularly when you are installing new hardware. Check this tab first to determine which resources are available.

Windows Program Problems

Windows of any flavor is a royal pain to manage. Configuration files are scattered through at least two (and sometimes more) directories. Mysterious .DLL (Dynamic Link Library) files, program code pieces that are used by every Windows application, are scattered everywhere as well. When you think everything is working fine, something blows up.

Moving to Windows 95 didn't help as much as I had hoped. The best we can get is rebooting every two days rather than twice a day as with Windows 3.1x. Windows 98 crashes slightly less than Windows 95, but it still leaks memory like an old farm shed leaks rainwater. Windows NT is not based on DOS, but there is still a lot of work to be done in stabilizing the operating system.

If you still have Windows 3.1x workstations on your network, one handy tip is to keep all the .INI, .GRP, and .DAT files on every Windows 3.1x system backed up to a separate directory. On my system, I have a SAVE.BAT file in the \WINDOWS directory. The file contents are as follows:

```
copy c:\windows\*.ini c:\windows\save
copy c:\windows\*.grp c:\windows\save
copy c:\windows\*.dat c:\windows\save
```

Running this file before each software installation gives me a fighting chance against some of the poor installation procedures I've seen. The .DAT files, especially REG.DAT, help Windows keep track of programs that are registered with the Windows system. If the REG.DAT file is damaged, you'll have problems. You should have a backup copy.

Running most of the Windows 3.1 program files from the server helps control some of the random catastrophes, but not all of them. Each user will add some little Windows program, and you won't know about it until it destroys something and prevents that user from connecting to the network. Then you'll get that plaintive call, along with the vow that he or she hasn't added anything to the system (and you'll also believe that the cow jumped over the moon).

There's little we can do to stop Windows from being changed constantly. All we can do is try to make it easy to recover from whatever weird program clobbered the system this time. Some self-defense tactics include the following:

- Keep the Windows applications on the server.

- Keep the Windows 3.*x* .INI and .GRP files on the server whenever possible.

- Keep the Windows 95/98/NT Profiles on the server whenever possible.

- Remind the users that Windows needs to be rebooted now and then.

- Provide as complete a set of productivity tools as possible. Having e-mail, group scheduling, word processing, fax software, database, PIM (Personal Information Manager), spreadsheet, and modem utilities available as shared server resources eliminates 90 percent of the ill-behaved applications that users want to add themselves.

- Make sure the swap file is installed on each local hard disk, not across the network.

 NOTE   A *swap file* is a technique used by the Windows virtual memory system to increase program workspace by considering part of the hard disk to be just like RAM. The performance is much slower, of course, but at least the programs don't crash for lack of workspace.

- Set FILES=30, BUFFERS=30, and FILE HANDLES=80 as a minimum in an Windows workstation's CONFIG.SYS file.

Tracking Normal Network Performance

When Network General released their Sniffer products in the late 1980s, I worked for a company that sold them. Every customer I visited had the same question: "How busy is my network?" At the time (1988), Sniffers cost between $15,000 and $32,000 and came in a Compaq 286 luggable that weighed more than 20 pounds (and did a major number on your shins if you didn't carry it carefully).

People still want to know how busy their network is, but they don't need to spend thousands of dollars unless they want special protocol decoders and intelligent network analyses. If you just want to see how many packets are whizzing through your network and which stations are generating those packets, software-only traffic monitors are readily available.

Novell makes LANalyzer, a Windows-based system that has a long history. The product has a wonderful gas gauge display that shows activity in easily understood formats. It's well worth checking out.

Other companies make competitive software-only analyzers. Some other products I'm familiar with are Intel's LANDesk, Triticom's LANdecoder32, and even Microsoft's Network Monitor, which is included with Windows NT. EtherPeek, TokenPeek, and LocalPeek from the AG Group do the same job from both Macintosh and Windows platforms. The Sniffer, now part of Network Associates, still carries the high-end lead banner (a personal feeling, not based on exhaustive testing), but there is plenty of competition in all price ranges.

Component Failure Profiles

That's an ugly phrase, "component failure," but it does happen. Your job as network administrator includes figuring out what will fail when and how to fix it quickly.

Guide to Managing PC Networks by Steve Steinke, with Marianne Goldsmith, Michael Hurwicz, and Charles Koontz (published by Prentice-Hall PTR), is a book about managing PC networks of all kinds. This book includes one section that has details of expected faults in a mythical network. The graphs don't list exact percentages, but I can guess fairly well. What are the causes of network downtime? In order, these are the reasons for downtime and the percentage each item is responsible for:

47 percent	Cabling or physical infrastructure
20 percent	Servers
13 percent	Drivers, network operating system
13 percent	Improper configuration
3 percent	Routers
2 percent	Hubs
2 percent	Wide area links

Do you believe these numbers? I would like to see the data behind these statistics because I would bet that cable problems cause more than half of the network downtime. Some studies rate cabling as the cause of 90 percent of network downtime, but those studies are paid for by people who are selling either high-grade cable or physical plant management products. See the section about cabling problems later in this chapter for some tips.

One area this list doesn't address is users, since they aren't a component that will fail. However, they will cause plenty of downtime, one way or the other.

Part of the relatively low failure rate for cabling may be explained by another chart in the book, named "Causes of Cabling Fault Events on a Mythical Network." Once again, here are my estimates of the percentages:

88 percent	Coax Ethernet
8 percent	Token Ring
4 percent	10BaseT Ethernet

These numbers I do believe without question. Anyone who has ever crawled under desk after desk looking for the loose BNC thin Ethernet connector that is causing the network problems is a strong advocate for 10BaseT Ethernet. Fortunately, none of the popular cabling schemes being promoted today are a shared-bus system like coax Ethernet.

On the server itself, the breakdown of breakdowns goes this way:

69 percent	Disk drives
18 percent	RAM
11 percent	Network interface boards
2 percent	Power supply

This list makes sense. The two highest failure rates belong to the only moving part (disk drive) and the part most sensitive to overheating (RAM). However, it isn't only heat that will cause RAM to stop a server. The cause can be voltage fluctuations, components running beyond their specifications, or just plain component failure.

Common Workstation Problems and Solutions

You will have more problems from users running Windows than from DOS, Macintosh, Unix, or OS/2 users. But you knew that already, didn't you? Primarily, Windows presents the most problems because it's the most popular platform and because it must track the most variable hardware and software resources.

NOTE Novell support actually had a disproportionate amount of tech support people dedicated to OS/2 during the rollout of NetWare 4.10. But IBM's fading desktop fortunes have changed that statistic for NetWare 5.1.

Some problems and solutions are common to all PC workstations. Again, we're assuming a workstation was working, then developed a problem. Questions about installation are covered in the appropriate chapters about that workstation type.

The following sections cover the most common workstation problems and provide some suggestions for solving them.

Workstation Can't Connect to the Server

The following are typical workstation connection problems and some solutions to try.

Check the workstation cable to the wall.

Many patch cables that run between the workstation and the wall plug have been kicked out of their sockets. Others have been rolled over by a desk chair one too many times.

Check that the plug for the patch cable is plugged into the wall. My friend Greg Hubbard says all 10BaseT Ethernet cards should have a speaker. That way, when you plug the Ethernet card into a phone plug, you'll hear the dial tone and realize your mistake. (Of course, if your phone still uses RJ-11 jacks, the ones that are smaller than 10BaseT RJ-45 connectors, this won't be a problem.)

Check the link between the wall plug and the wiring closet. Has anyone added cabling anywhere in that part of the building? It's common for new cabling installation to bump and loosen old cabling.

Is the port on your wiring concentrator working? Switch the problem connection with a known good connection into a known good port.

Check the frame type.

Has the NET.CFG file on a Windows 3.1 workstation been amended? How about protocol details under the Networking program in later versions of Windows? Is this workstation now trying to reach a new server? The default frame type for Personal NetWare and some early versions of NetWare 4 was not Ethernet 802.3. Since NetWare has used that frame type since the beginning of time, many managers forget to check frame types. The same may be happening with the move to TCP/IP in many companies.

Verify the login name and password.

Wrong login names or passwords will obviously prevent a user from connecting to the server. If the user can't remember his or her password, change it immediately.

Check for a locked account.

With intruder detection, stations may be locked out of the network after a configurable number of unsuccessful login attempts. When a user comes to you with a password problem, check to see if the account is locked.

Verify that all the workstation files were loaded properly.

Error messages go by fast, and sometimes they are missed by users. Changes in the workstation may use some network memory.

Make sure the network adapter is seated properly.

Adding a card to one slot often loosens cards in other slots. Remember that a card can look well seated from outside the case but actually be disconnected. Patch cables, when tugged on, can loosen network adapters.

Check any routers, bridges, and hubs.

WAN links are much less reliable than LAN links. If you're trying to reach a remote network service, always assume the WAN link is at fault before changing anything at the workstation.

WAN links take longer, and some workstations may time out before reaching the remote server and getting authenticated properly. Increase the SPX timeout value.

Routers, both local and remote versions, sometimes get flaky on one port or another. Test other connections running through the same router in the same manner. You may need to check the router and reset a port.

Wiring hubs rarely fail, but they sometimes become unplugged. Check to see if other computers connected to the same hub are able to communicate. Hubs are also liable to run out of space, and the wiring plan gets reworked on the fly to add another station or two. When this happens, your station may be left out of a concentrator altogether.

Verify that the server sees the workstation's request.

Use the TRACK ON command on the server to monitor requests from clients. If you know the client's MAC address, you can watch the server monitor to ensure that connection requests are received and the server responds.

Reboot the workstation.

This can't hurt, and you'll be amazed at what a reboot can fix.

Workstation Can't Use an Application

The following are workstation application problems and some solutions to try.

Find out what changed at the workstation.

Some new utility may have changed the AUTOEXEC.BAT or CONFIG.SYS file. A new Windows application may have modified the Registry. All applications have potential for disaster.

Check the user's rights.

Does the user have the trustee rights to run the application? If you assign trustee rights to the directory and not the file, this shouldn't be much of a problem. This problem usually occurs with new applications, because few applications properly handle setting the rights for the users. Make sure to check all the application directories created by the installation. It is becoming common to place some directories for the same application on the same level of the directory tree, rather than placing all the directories under one main directory. You may need to grant rights to another directory or two so that the user has rights to use some of the application files in the oddly placed directory.

Be careful after upgrading an application. The rights will probably be the same in the existing directories, but a new directory or two is often added during an upgrade. You'll need to grant trustee rights to those directories as well.

Check the flags.

Most applications should have flags set to Read-Only and Shareable. Data files will be marked Shareable and Write, but the application must support multiple-user file access.

Upgraded applications will need to be checked, since new files in the new version will probably not have the proper flags set. Verify your tape-restore procedure, since some vendors don't copy the extended file attributes NetWare uses to set the flags. An application that was Read-Only when backed up may become Normal (Read, Write, Erase, and so on) after being restored by tape. If someone then accidentally erases some files, the application won't work.

Check the user's current directory.

Many users never understand the drive redirection used by NetWare. When you ask where a problem is for them, they'll say, "drive K:." Make sure drive K: still points to the same subdirectory. New users are especially vulnerable to changing directories within a drive mapping without realizing what they've done.

Check the application's need for installing at the volume root.

Some applications demand to be placed in the root directory. Others don't but have a limit of how deep they can be installed in a directory structure. Some say they can be installed anywhere, but references to other directories are based on indexing from the root of the directory. You will need to use fake root mapping if any of these problems occur.

Does the application need NetBIOS?

Some applications, even on NetWare, still require NetBIOS. Check that out, and load NetBIOS on a test workstation. If NetBIOS is used and has worked before, verify that the workstation is loading NetBIOS properly. Workstation changes may have ruined some necessary client files.

If NetBIOS is needed, set up batch files so NetBIOS can be loaded and then unloaded after the application is exited. No use wasting more RAM than you need to for NetBIOS.

Verify that the application files are not mangled and that the application isn't missing some files.

If an application is corrupted, you must reinstall it. In a Windows application, the .DLL files may be missing or some users may be picking up old versions of them through poor search mapping.

Check for file handles and SPX connections.

Database programs in particular often eat lots of file handles. Check the application's documentation in the off chance that the writers have done their job and listed this information. Verify that the number of file handles in NET.CFG matches the number in CONFIG.SYS.

See if the application directory looks empty.

This means that the user doesn't have rights to the directory. Check the rights of the container or group for the user before making a change for one user alone.

Workstation Shows "Not Enough Memory" Errors

The following are typical memory problems and some solutions to try.

Check to see what has changed.

If a working network client suddenly has too little memory, something has changed. Check drivers and other TSR (terminate-and-stay-resident) programs in the workstation.

Move all network drivers and other TSRs to high memory if possible. With MS DOS, run the MEMMAKER program after all network client files are loaded. Rerun MEMMAKER after every change to the workstation client files.

Unload sneaky resident programs.

Some applications, such as fax and e-mail programs, sometimes leave little notification programs or utilities to fax from within your application on workstations. These can take up memory without explaining their presence to the user.

Modify the VLM load files.

If this workstation doesn't need BIND support, don't load that VLM. You may also go through and select to load just the VLM components needed for your network.

Beware of the network client software upgrade.

New driver and client files often require more room than the previous versions. You may wish to postpone an upgrade for some workstations that are critically short of memory. Make a note of those workstations in your network logs.

Beware of new video boards.

Video boards and network interface cards often fight over particular memory location in PCs.

Beware of new monitors.

High-resolution monitors can force a video board to a higher resolution requiring more memory. Then the upper memory for a network driver won't be available, forcing the driver to load low. The result is "RAM Cram." Run MEMMAKER after any new hardware or software is added to a workstation.

Windows Doesn't Work Right

The following are typical Windows problems and some solutions to try.

Find out what has changed.

Everything in Windows affects everything else. Users are constantly adding utilities, screen savers, and wallpaper, all of which can mess up something else.

Sometimes, the user is not at fault. Demo software under Windows now often adds .DLL files, modifies the Registry, and loads more fonts into the local Windows system. Did anyone ask for this? No. Do you need to fix it? Yes.

Believe me, something is always changing in Windows. As much as you're tempted, you can't always blame Microsoft for this. Every application vendor has its problems, and some problems aggravate Windows more than others.

Get a good uninstall program for Windows. Many applications, even when they uninstall themselves, don't clean up behind themselves very well.

Windows 95/98 is better, as the application guidelines now require an uninstall program. Programmers don't always follow that advice, of course, being programmers. However, what Microsoft giveth, Microsoft taketh away. Windows 95 hides what's going on "under the covers" more than Windows 3.1x did. Check out *Expert Guide to Windows 98* by Mark Minasi, Eric Christiansen, and Kristina Shapar (Sybex, 1998) for more detailed help than you'll find in the manuals.

Restart Windows daily.

Microsoft has not yet stopped the memory leaks within Windows. Applications regularly leave fewer resources available after they unload. Windows doesn't need to leak, but careless programming is everywhere.

Check System Resources before and after loading an application for an idea of the application's resource needs. Then check again after the application is unloaded. It's likely that you'll have fewer resources than when you started.

Check to see if the user has logged in from the wrong workstation.

Shared Windows files on the server make great sense and save time for administration, but they are dependent on the right workstation configuration. If a user logs in from a different workstation, details such as the permanent swap file will be different on the different machine.

Check for new fonts.

Many applications add special fonts to Windows. Each font loaded takes memory and slows performance. If your workstations have little RAM, pare down the fonts. One font family can take enough resources away for an application to have trouble where it didn't have trouble before.

Don't use wallpaper if memory is critical.

Wallpaper may take just enough memory to cause trouble in RAM-deficient systems. Until you can add more memory or upgrade the workstation, strip out all nonfunctional pieces of MS Windows.

Printing Problems

The following are typical printing problems and some solutions to try.

Verify that the proper printer or print queue is captured properly.

With Windows 95/98/NT printing choices, it's easy for users to pick the wrong printer by accident. Verify that the chosen printer is the correct printer. It's best to use a login script to assign the default printers for your network and discourage too much printer experimentation among users.

Verify that the job is in the print queue and that a print server is connected.

Use NWADMIN to check the status of the print queue. See if the job has actually arrived and whether the correct print server is attached to the queue. In most cases, the job will arrive in the queue, but the print server is not processing the job.

Check the print job configuration.

If you have multiple print job configurations, verify that the proper one is still used by the user. This is something else that is easy to change by accident with NetWare User Tools. Under Windows 95/98, verify these settings through the Printers Control Panel (Properties).

Check the printer hardware.

Is the printer plugged into the print server? Can other users print to this printer? Are the proper paper and font cartridge (if used) in place?

Check which page description language was used in the print job.

Sending PostScript output to a non-PostScript printer guarantees problems and the need to reset the printer. Do the users understand the different types of printers they have available and how to send print jobs to those printers?

Stop the 20-second print screen hangup.

When the Shift–Print Screen key combination is pressed on a network workstation without a local printer, about 20 seconds goes by until DOS gives up on the local printer. Until then, the station appears to be dead. If this is a problem for some users, add this line to the NET.CFG file:

```
LOCAL PRINTERS=0
```

 NOTE There seems to be a problem with the Notification setting for printers under NetWare Administrator. Several times, I have been unable to stop notifications from printers by using the tools in NetWare Administrator. However, PCONSOLE always stops the incessant notifications about a turned-off printer.

Common Server Problems and Solutions

Let me summarize the NetWare manuals' advice on server problems: add more RAM. The manuals provide quite a bit more help than that, of course, but more RAM is a constant mantra for NetWare servers. I have regularly suggested that you add RAM whenever possible, so take this as another polite request. Save yourself the headache—*get more RAM*.

As servers support more users, more RAM is necessary. As more NLMs are loaded, more RAM is necessary. More disk space means more RAM.

Some applications, such as the NetWare NFS Services, demand a ton of RAM on their own (20 to 24MB of RAM just for NFS Services). Want to tune your Netscape Enterprise Web Server? RAM demands jump from 128MB to 256MB. More insidious is the RAM-creep of little programs and utilities that gradually eat your available cache buffers until you reach rock bottom.

Your servers are the core of the network. Server hardware is not a place to save a few pennies. When your boss complains about the cost of quality components in the server, amortize the cost across all potential server users. The more users you expect to support, the less investment per user a quality server will require. And this isn't just sales talk. Your server is an investment in the knowledge-sharing infrastructure necessary to propel your company into the future.

NetWare is a resilient operating system, and server hardware is more reliable today than ever before. Even before you start considering mirrored or duplexed disk drives or a clustered system, off-the-shelf computer components work faster and longer today than ever before. However, this is of little comfort as you stand before a dead server, with the howling mob at your back. Problems do happen. You must learn to manage these problems before and after they occur.

Server Availability: A Management Decision

Your management decides how available your servers will be. Your job is to maintain service to the agreed-upon level. How available is that?

The quick answer is 24-7, meaning every hour of the day, seven days a week. Do you need this? Think about the answer. When will you do maintenance? Must you keep the system available during tape backup? How will you add a new disk drive to a server?

Guarantee that your network will be available during normal business hours. If you have no one in the office at 3:00 A.M., why does the network need to be available? Would it be reasonable for your network to be generally available, but with no guarantees, after 7:00 P.M. and before 7:00 A.M.?

Every system needs maintenance. If your network must be up overnight, pick one window of time on the weekends or during an evening for maintenance. Network management demands accessibility to the servers, including taking them down now and then.

WARNING If you work in a large company, network-hostile mainframe bigots will track every minute a server is down. They will point to the fact that your network is unavailable more than the mainframe. Remember, mainframes don't need to shut down to add new disks. I hope your situation isn't this bad, but such hostility happens in some companies. Mainframers are feeling a bit unloved lately (with good reason, perhaps) and will spend a lot of energy to discredit the networks that are replacing mainframes. Be prepared.

The Hardware Scale and the Costs

Even if your network consists of one server and 15 users, management personnel must decide how much availability they are willing to pay for. Nothing is certain with computers, but more guaranteed uptime translates into more cost.

Any chart showing dollars in the computer business is suspect, since prices generally fall. Those prices that don't fall reliably, such as the cost of memory chips, tend to gradually fall with occasional spikes to weaken the hearts of purchasing managers everywhere. Hard drives today are amazingly inexpensive, and the prices continue to drop. Today, you are able to get large (6 or 8GB) IDE drives for about the same price as a 500MB drive only a few years ago.

The ascending hardware listing is explained this way:

Peer-to-peer networks   Low cost, low numbers of users supported comfortably. This is the wrong book for you if you want information about peer-to-peer networks, but they are inexpensive.

Desktop PCs as dedicated servers   Common choice for low-end servers. Desktop PCs don't have as much space for hard disks or RAM. Power supplies are sometimes inadequate for multiple disk drives.

Mirrored or duplexed drives   Disk mirroring (two drives, one controller) and disk duplexing (two drives, two controllers) improve performance and provide protection against a single disk failure stopping your server. With the dropping cost of hard drives, it's hard to justify trusting your network to a disk drive as a single point of failure.

PC server models   Extra space for drives, more RAM, and beefier power supplies help these systems look and act more like servers. Always in a tower case, these systems look more expensive and rugged, making management happier with the investment.

RAID storage systems   RAID (redundant array of inexpensive disks) systems go further to eliminate the disk as a point of failure and add performance. These systems are often able to swap hard drives while the server is running, eliminating downtime due to a bad disk.

Servers on steroids   Companies such as Compaq, HP, Acer, Dell, and AST (among others) are placing their servers at the top of the food chain. Diagnostic software and hardware offer a level of control and management unattainable with regular PC servers. Many of these systems now offer multiple processors, boosting horsepower even higher if your software is able to use the extra CPUs.

Clustered servers   The new replacement for SFT III, clusters primarily aim at keeping critical applications, such as Web servers, available. I've had the fun of playing with a killer Compaq ProLiant cluster, and I must say proper use of such equipment will eliminate downtime completely. But Novell, with NetWare Cluster Services 1.01, charges $5,000 per clustered-server license, so only the critical apps will pass budget muster.

The further up the scale you go, the more money you must invest in your network. This extra investment buys peace of mind and better performance. Management must make the decision on the proper amount of investment for your network. See if you can find a subtle way to remind the people making the decisions that you can't get a Rolls Royce for a go-cart price.

Operating System and RAM Problems

The following are typical operating system and RAM problems and some solutions to try.

Abend messages occur.

An abend (abnormal end) is a system shutdown due to an internal error of some sort. The best course of action after an abend is to write down the abend error message number and look it up in the System Messages section of the online documentation. Reboot the server, then check for sufficient RAM. Verify current versions of NLMs and drivers. If new hardware or software has been added, restart the server without the new component as a test. If all else fails, you may need to reload the operating system, but that doesn't happen often.

Users can't see server.

Check the frame type in use. Multiple frame types are easily supported, but both clients and servers must use a common frame type in order to communicate.

Check the LOAD and BIND statements to make sure nothing has changed. Some third-party utilities may un-BIND or un-LOAD drivers during installation or by accident. Driver errors may also cause a network interface card to disconnect.

Server can't see users or other servers.

Again, check the frame type in use. Also check the LOAD and BIND statements. Check that SAP (Service Advertising Protocol) is active and not disabled.

Verify network numbering of internal and external network numbers for the server. Driver errors may also cause a network interface card to disconnect.

Server goes up and down for no reason.

Check the power supply. This fails more often in a server than you might think. If your server UPS isn't doing the job, low voltage may cause the power supply to reset the computer motherboard. You should have a dedicated circuit for all your server equipment. Also, keep the cleaning crew from using AC plugs in the server area. I once saw a cleaning crew unplug servers to power their vacuum cleaners.

Server Memory

As I've said many times before, the main thing to do when you're low on RAM is to buy more RAM quickly. Here are some suggestions for freeing some server memory temporarily (until you can add more memory to the server):

- Type **REMOVE DOS** or **SECURE CONSOLE** to release the DOS memory in the server for the file cache.

- Forcibly purge files with FILER or NetWare Administrator to free the directory entry table space.

- Unload NLM programs that are not needed, such as MONITOR (often left up). The X Server Graphical Console eats a ton of memory and may be the only reason you need the Java Virtual Machine loaded, which requires another ton of memory.

- Dismount volumes that are not being used (this suggestion is straight from the manual, as if you have extra disks hanging off your server that no one needs).

- Turn off block suballocation and specify a 64KB block size on volumes. This requires the volume to be reinitialized, meaning all data on the volume must be backed up and restored. This measure saves RAM but is a lot of trouble, takes the server offline for quite a while, and runs a slight risk of losing data. However, you might try it if you need to add a new volume with the smallest RAM impact possible. This method does use quite a bit more disk space, especially if you turn off file compression to save that RAM as well.

- Move volumes from this server to a different server with more RAM.

Disk Errors

For volume dismounts and other disk problems, try the following:

- If you have an external disk subsystem, verify that the power is on and the cables are still connected.

- Check for error messages on the console. Ordinary disk errors will force a volume to dismount.

- Verify settings for the controller and driver combination.

- Check for increased numbers of Hot Fix redirection areas used. Increasing Hot Fix numbers generally indicate your disk is dying and should be replaced. The manual offers instructions on increasing the Hot Fix redirection area; I say dump the drive or at least reformat it and start all over.

- Run VREPAIR on the volume. This loads from the console, and if your SYS: volume is having a problem, you will need to reference the file on the DOS partition or the floppy. Run VREPAIR at least twice each time you use it.

- Load INSTALL and choose Disk Options, then Perform Surface Test, then the drive to check. You should try to run the nondestructive test first, but be aware that this takes hours and your server will be unavailable this entire time. If a bad block is found, the disk test will shut down. Your last option before throwing the disk away is to reformat the disk and restore the software. You do have a current backup, right?

Running out of disk space is a problem you don't want to have. Don't let this sneak up on you. If it happens to your SYS: volume, the server usually shuts down. Even if it isn't your SYS: volume, it still causes extra work and other hassles.

Check your volume space regularly. To produce a quick report on your current volume, use this command:

```
NDIR /VOL
```

This replaces the VOLINFO command from NetWare 3.*x*. Figure 18.9 shows the command and result for the ALTOS486 SYS: volume.

FIGURE 18.9

Good space left, good compression

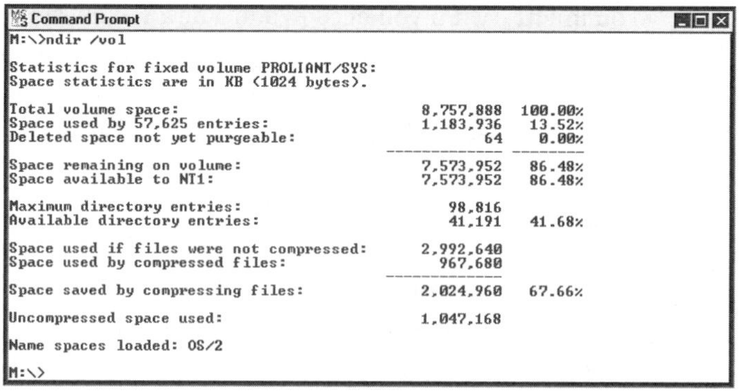

```
Command Prompt                                                    _ □ ×
M:\>ndir /vol

Statistics for fixed volume PROLIANT/SYS:
Space statistics are in KB (1024 bytes).

Total volume space:                        8,757,888    100.00%
Space used by 57,625 entries:              1,183,936     13.52%
Deleted space not yet purgeable:                   64      0.00%
                                          ----------
Space remaining on volume:                 7,573,952     86.48%
Space available to NT1:                    7,573,952     86.48%

Maximum directory entries:                    98,816
Available directory entries:                  41,191     41.68%

Space used if files were not compressed:   2,992,640
Space used by compressed files:              967,680
                                          ----------
Space saved by compressing files:          2,024,960     67.66%

Uncompressed space used:                   1,047,168

Name spaces loaded: OS/2

M:\>
```

When space becomes a serious concern, type **PURGE /ALL** for each volume. If the command-line PURGE doesn't clear enough space, use FILER or NetWare Administrator to delete unnecessary files still taking up directory entry table space. Change the Minimum File Delete Wait Time SET parameter to 0 so that files can be purged immediately. This stops them from being kept whole and salvageable on the volume.

For Coax Ethernet or ARCnet Users

If you have coax Ethernet, or worse, ARCnet, you no doubt turned to this troubleshooting chapter quickly. Let me tell you what you may or may not want to hear: *upgrade.*

You have been told this several times before. You know this is necessary every time you crawl under a desk to check a BNC connector. You know coax ages, gets brittle, and breaks time after time. You just need to convince your management.

Continued

CONTINUED

Put the boss's secretary on the worst coax leg of your network. This isn't dishonest, but it is in your self-interest. Every time you go up to the executive area to fix the network (again and again), be sure you know how much it will cost to replace the coax Ethernet with 10BaseT Ethernet. Basically pennies, nowadays.

The per-port cost of 10BaseT concentrators is ridiculously low for plain-vanilla products. Today, you can purchase a "network in a box," which includes a small Ethernet hub (five ports) and two NICs, for around $100. Micro transceivers that will convert the AUI (Attachment Unit Interface) 15-pin plug to 10BaseT wiring cost $30 or less each as well. If you have any volume to speak of, you should be able to convert each coax user for about $50. Remember that number when you're crawling under the secretary's desk, and repeat it to the boss when you emerge.

Cabling Problems

As mentioned in this chapter, cabling causes lots of network problems. Vendors of new cable will tell real horror stories of old cable and the problems it caused. Introduce those vendors to your boss.

As was also mentioned earlier in this chapter, coax Ethernet causes more than 20 times the number of network outages than are caused by 10BaseT Ethernet. Log your time spent chasing cable problems for two weeks, and then figure out the cost of those problems in your time alone. This is especially effective if your company is faced with a need to hire more network technicians. Replacing the cable will probably keep down your head count.

The first step when your network is having problems is to check all cables to make sure that they are plugged in. Don't laugh. Cables that aren't plugged in never work. Here are some other suggestions for avoiding cable problems:

- Find a cable contractor you like and stick with that contractor. Cabling consistency counts for a lot. If you find a cabling contractor who does good work, tests the cables with digital equipment, and offers a good warranty, you're lucky. Don't switch contractors for a few cents per foot.

- Buy quality cable. Cheap cable is good for telephones but not for data networks. High-speed systems in development now will push quality cable and will quickly overload cable not up to par. Buy the best cable (Level 5 and above) now, and you're covered for the foreseeable future.

- Declare a truce with any hostile telecom folks in your company. Some companies have telecom and datacom departments that are openly hostile. If your company is that way, I'm sorry. Go to management and request a meeting with all parties involved. If you can get over your differences, you will find that the telecom folks can be a great help.

- Verify cable distances, especially on new runs. All UTP (unshielded-twisted pair) cable networks have a length limit, usually 100 meters (300 feet plus a little). Going slightly beyond that limit will cause random problems. Going far beyond that limit will stop the connection entirely. There are third-party products that extend the cabling distance over UTP. Buy one of those, or just add a powered wiring concentrator to help cover the extra distance.

- Take care to avoid interference for your cable runs. Strong interference will blitz your cable and disrupt your network. Did you ever hear stories about networks that always went down at dusk? The cable was routed by a light switch. When that light was turned on, the cable interference overloaded the network and blocked all the packets.

- Provide UPS systems for all powered wiring components. In a blackout, your server and your desktop machine will likely continue on battery power. But if the wiring concentrator is powerless, how will you connect to the server from your workstation?

Monitoring Network Cable Performance

The best way to stop network downtime remains preparation, and knowing what your network does regularly may be the most critical part of your preparation. Let's look at another method of cable-related preparation you may not have considered.

Wiring hubs have gotten far smarter while getting far cheaper. One of the hubs used in my lab is from LinkSys (www.linksys.com), and they included an SNMP module to manage the 24-port hub. Check out the details in Figure 18.10, and we'll discuss some of them.

The top frame of the browser reflects the front of the hub. Yes, the active lights on the left and the colored port plugs on the right mean something and change in real time. Plugs with 10BaseT connections are green, the 100BaseT links are blue.

Most of the informative details opened by the menu choices in the left frame are text oriented, with tables of packet details and the like. These are interesting on a micro level but are not too graphically pleasing.

FIGURE 18.10

*Physical network
details unfolding every
five seconds*

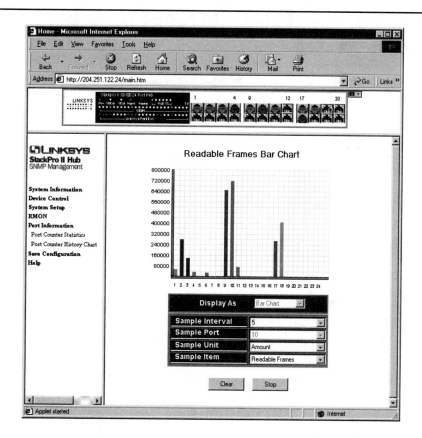

The screenshot in Figure 18.10, however, colors port summary information with five-second updates (configurable). The tallest (those with the most packets) ports are the servers in this picture, and they should be in your network as well. If one of those server bar lines drops down to nothing, your phone will magically start ringing. It happens every time.

SNMP modules add a couple hundred dollars to the cost of the 24-port hub but are worth it for at least your servers. LinkSys engineers allow you to control up to six 24-port hubs with one SNMP module, spreading the couple hundred dollars across 144 connections. That's getting too cheap to pass up. Show this page to your tightwad boss, and see if that helps loosen the budget strings at least a little.

Tell Your Boss: Prior Planning Prevents Poor Performance

Every decision made during the design and implementation of your network impacts the performance and reliability of that network. Some of these choices are easy to evaluate: a fast Pentium-based server will perform better than a low-end 486 system. Other design choice ramifications don't appear until something has blown up, taking your network and peace of mind with it.

Keep in mind crosstime (as opposed to downtime) and explain the idea to your management. The option to support network clients through alternative servers and other resources is a sign of network flexibility, not fallibility.

Building fault-tolerance for your network means more work and more money. It's also the only way to guard against downtime. Mirrored or duplexed disk drives are a quick, easy example. If one drive dies, the other one keeps going without missing a beat. Try that in a server with a single disk.

What can your boss do to help the troubleshooting process? Provide money for training (you and your users). Provide network analysis and management tools. Provide spare parts.

The best your boss can provide is a reasonable atmosphere. High expectations are met with high resources. Low resources lead to low results. Your management must make the decision on how important the network is and then provide resources accordingly.

In a typical company, management will try to force high expectations from low resources. That's possible for a time, especially if you're smart and work hard. However, one day the lack of spare parts and support tools will catch up to you. Your network will be down for at least one day. Your boss will try to blame you. Don't let that happen; point to the empty shelf labeled spare parts. Keeping a copy of your rejected proposals for network upgrades won't hurt, either.

PART V

Appendices

APPENDIX <u>A</u>

Upgrades, Migration, and Windows 95/98 Client and Server Installation Support

M any buyers of NetWare 5.1 will be current NetWare customers. That has been the case with previous NetWare upgrades, and it will be the case in the future. Once you're a NetWare customer, you tend to remain a NetWare customer (much to Microsoft's chagrin).

Being a NetWare customer doesn't mean that you automatically upgrade with every NetWare release. This causes Novell engineers some problems because they must support users back on NetWare 3, as well as those running NetWare 5.1. This wide range of supported NetWare versions has created several upgrade options, which are the subject of the second half of this appendix.

First, however, I want to discuss Client32 for Windows 95/98. I'll describe how to install it and how to configure the client once it is installed.

Upgrading Windows 95/98 Clients to NetWare's Client32, Version 3.00

Novell's Client32 family of products, available for DOS and Windows 3.1*x*, 95, 98, and NT/2000, are the clients of choice for connection to NetWare networks. They offer many more features and capabilities than Microsoft's clients. You may ask, "Why bother installing Novell's client when Microsoft's client is on the operating system CD for 95, 98, NT, and 2000?" The answer is simple: Microsoft has nothing to gain by giving you a powerful, full-featured client. Microsoft needs to provide connectivity with Novell servers for marketing reasons, but it would much rather you use NT/2000 Server instead of NetWare. Novell, on the other hand, has a vested interest in providing you the best possible client to keep you as a customer.

In this section, I'll discuss installing and configuring Client32, and I'll discuss the Windows 95/98 version of the client. Other installations are similar. For complete information and for other versions of the client or other operating systems, see the online documentation.

Installing Client32

Installation is about as simple as it can get. You have several options, all discussed in the online documentation, to automate rolling out the client to many users. They include the Automatic Client Upgrade (ACU) and several options for installing Client32 while Windows 95/98 is being installed. I will focus on running the setup program and understanding how it works.

Inserting the NetWare Client CD into a CD-ROM drive in a Windows 95/98/NT/2000 system with AutoRun enabled pops open a new Novell client splash screen, as shown in Figure A.1. Only the options that can be installed on the target computer will be highlighted when running the cursor over the text, as the Windows 95/98 Client popup text shows in the figure.

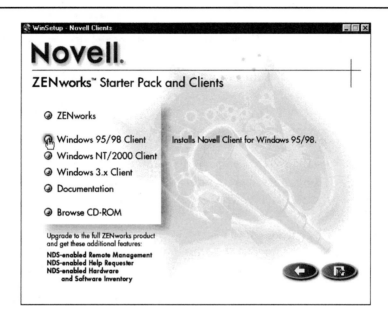

Another option, if you don't have the AutoRun toggle set to start each new CD automatically, is to run `WINSETUP.EXE` on the Client CD. You'll see a fairly typical license agreement (does anyone read those things?). Click Next to display the Welcome screen, shown in Figure A.2.

As you can see, you have two choices here:

- Typical
- Custom

When you select Typical, the default button in the bottom of the screen is Install. If you are installing the client for the first time, you can choose the directory in which to install (take the default). If you are upgrading, the client is installed in the directory where it was installed previously (which should be the default).

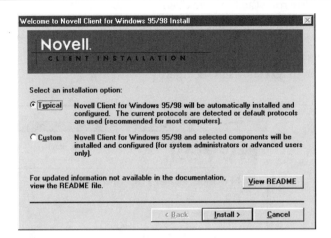

Check out the View README command button at least once. Here you'll learn interesting stuff, such as the fact that the installation won't work on the original Windows 95 release. If you've been putting off that workstation upgrade, your delay time has run out.

There are no more choices for you when you choose Typical: the installation takes off, using IPX and IP for the protocols, and using all the IP configuration information within Windows. Your next move is to reboot to activate the new client.

I suggest you try the Custom option, at least until you feel comfortable with the client choices NetWare provides. For one thing, I feel helpless when the dialog box pops up saying "removing existing client software" and I can't stop the process, when I haven't even been told exactly what the process includes. I don't want you to feel helpless, so learn what's happening, then choose Typical if it works for your network.

Protocol choices come in the next screen after choosing the Custom installation. As you can see, you can choose to communicate with NetWare servers over the following:

- IP Only (and optionally remove IPX if it is installed)
- IP With IPX Compatibility
- IP And IPX
- IPX

Unless you are sure that you have a pure IP or IPX environment and it's certain to stay that way, I would choose IP And IPX (the default) to ensure access to all servers. The memory used by adding IPX to your client mix won't ruin anything and may eliminate a problem or two with some legacy software. Figure A.3 shows all, with the IP Only box checked to better show the Remove IPX If Present option.

FIGURE A.3

Protocol choices aren't forever, but are most conveniently made here.

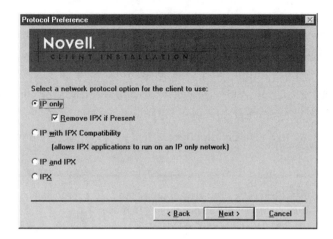

Click Next, and you are asked if you want to default to an NDS or a bindery connection when logging in (NDS is the default). Unless you have only NetWare 3 servers (in which case you probably aren't reading this book), leave the default NDS selected and click Next to display the Optional Components screen, shown in Figure A.4.

FIGURE A.4

Custom choices for clients

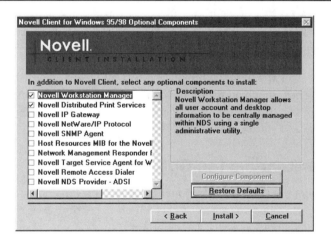

Selecting Custom in the Welcome screen installs the core client and the following options:

- Novell Workstation Manager
- Novell Distributed Print Services (NDPS) client

The documentation describes these options in detail, so I will give you only a brief overview. Before I do that, though, I want to point out that you can modify these settings later. Here are the steps:

1. In Control Panel, choose Network.

2. Choose Add ➤ Service ➤ Novell, and select the component you want to modify.

3. To add a component, enter its location.

4. To delete a component, select it and choose Remove.

 WARNING You are not prompted before removing anything, so be sure to select the correct component before clicking Remove.

You can add or remove all components, except for the Novell NDS provider, ADSI, in this manner. You can install the ADSI provider only during setup. To configure an optional component (if possible; some are not), simply select it, click Properties, and modify the settings in the dialog box.

 NOTE I won't discuss the configuration options here, but you'll find some of them in the body of this book, and you'll find all of them in the online documentation.

Click the Install command button, and watch files load and semi-informative dialog boxes tell you what's happening. Then cross your fingers and reboot. Well, that's not fair. Installation improvements by Novell almost always guarantee success. (Almost always.)

Understanding the Options

From the Optional Components screen, you can choose from among several components. When you select one, you'll see a description of it in a box on the right. Let's briefly look at each of these options.

Novell Workstation Manager

This component allows user and desktop settings to be centrally stored and managed. Users can access their personal settings anywhere on the network, but at the cost of downloading (possibly across WAN links) profile information. This is a great option for central control and, therefore, is selected by default. It is similar to NT Workstation Manager described in Chapter 13.

Novell Distributed Print Services (NDPS)

This component is the client portion of the NDPS system that allows you to browse for printing resources and automatically download and install drivers for printers as they are used. Unless you are not installing NDPS and have no plans to do so, select this option. For more information, see Chapter 8.

Novell IP Gateway

This was a big deal before Microsoft loaded TCP/IP onto every client (without proper security settings or help information, may I kvetch), and Novell and other vendors made special gateway servers that translated IPX packets into TCP/IP for Internet connections. This component is rarely used now, even though using IPX internally with an IP gateway provides the highest internal security possible.

Novell NetWare/IP Protocol

This component is for compatibility with the old NetWare/IP options and servers. If you have IP only on your NetWare 5.1 servers, you don't need this component.

Novell SNMP Agent

As you may recall from earlier discussions, the Simple Network Management Protocol (SNMP) allows you to request information from a workstation from a central network monitoring station (called a *management console*). In addition, it allows a workstation to notify a management console about an unusual event. If you have SNMP and a management console (such as ManageWise) installed, select this option. See Chapter 17 for more information.

Host Resources MIB for the Novell Client

This component allows the management console to request inventory information (such as CPU, amount of RAM, and so on) and have the client reply. If you have SNMP and a management console (such as ManageWise) installed, select this option. See Chapter 17 for more information.

Network Management Responder for the Novell Client

With this component, you can extend the information that the SNMP agent with the Host Resources MIB returns.

PART

V

Appendices

Network Target Service Agent for Windows 95/98

This component allows you to back up a workstation's hard drive during the normal backup process for your servers. You will not normally advertise this fact to your clients, as one of the benefits of using a network is central storage and backup. If your clients know they can store anything on their local drives and still have them backed up, they will, and then they will bother you whenever something gets deleted, damaged, and so on. With rare exceptions, I would not make this capability known, nor would I want to do it if possible.

Novell Remote Access Dialer

NetWare provides several ways to dial into or across the Internet, and this checkbox enables those options. However, VPNs (Virtual Private Networks) may be a better option than each client fending for itself across the Internet.

Novell NDS Provider—ADSI

Microsoft has come up with a new method of doing what NDS has done for years and is calling it *ADSI* (Active Directory Services Interface). It appears in Windows 2000, but since Microsoft hasn't released version 1.1 as of this writing, the marketing hype has remained unfulfilled. Oh yeah, there are lots of security problems, too. This client allows ADSI client applications to access data stored in NDS, such that the client application doesn't have to be aware of whether the server being accessed is based on ADSI or NDS. I would install this choice for compatibility with future ADSI-aware applications. Remember, this is the only option that you cannot add or remove after setup.

Novell used to include Remote Control agents in this screen with NetWare 5.0. That feature now comes as part of ZENworks, and therefore it no longer gets installed with the standard NetWare client.

Once you make all your selections, click Install to install them. When you have finished, click Reboot to restart your computer so that all the changes can take effect. You don't have to cross your fingers anymore, since this process works almost all the time, but you may bite your lip with apprehension if you wish.

Configuring the Client

Once the client is installed and operating, you may want to modify some of the options you installed or change some of the parameters for an installed option. To do so, follow these steps:

1. Choose Control Panel ➢ Network.

2. Select the component you want to modify.

3. Choose Properties.

NOTE Help is available by clicking the ? in the upper-right corner of the dialog box or by clicking the Help button. It is also available, in great detail, in the online documentation.

The component that you will be modifying most often is the core component of the client. You do so by choosing Novell NetWare Client ➤ Properties to open the Novell Client Configuration dialog box, which you can see in Figure A.5. You can also find this same dialog box by right-clicking the big red N on the taskbar and choosing Novell Client Properties.

FIGURE A.5

More client properties than a landlord

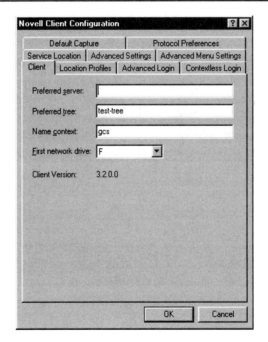

As you can see, this dialog box has nine tabs:

Client This tab is the most used. Here you can specify the preferred server and/or tree, the default name context, and the first network drive.

Location Profiles Here you can specify locations that are useful if a user travels or if multiple users share a computer. Each profile tracks items such as user name and context to make it easier for users to log in.

Advanced Login   If you want to give users more control over the login process, this is the place to do so. The four checkboxes here give the user some additional options:

- Show Location List On Login
- Show Advanced Button On Login
- Show Variables Button On Login
- Show Clear Connections On Login

Contextless Login   Here you can enable contextless login and specify which catalogs will be used to enable this feature. By default, all available catalogs are used. For more information on catalogs, see Chapter 5.

Service Location   This tab allows you to configure how the client will get information from the Service Location Protocol (if you are using TCP/IP). You can find more information on this in Chapter 14.

Advanced Settings   The only one of these 11 settings that you may need to modify is to change the File Cache Level from 3 (lots of cache) to 1 (not so much cache) for RAM-limited stations.

Advanced Menu Settings   This is the place where all the old NET.CFG options are set, as well as many new ones. You'll rarely need this tab, but it is very handy when you are directed to change a parameter to fix some problem. There are 61 parameters here.

Default Capture   Here you can specify the default capture settings, such as banners, form feeds, and so on, so that when a login script simply has Capture P=Printer, your preferred settings are used. I like to set defaults here as well as in every login script, explicitly specifying any options that I want (even those that I set as defaults). You'll find more information on printing in Chapter 8; login scripts are covered in Chapter 7.

Protocol Preferences   Here you can specify your primary (or first choice) protocol as IP or IPX. To resolve server names to IP or IPX addresses, you can specify which methods should be used and in what order.

As I mentioned, this is only a brief overview of what is available. Many of the options in this section and the previous one are discussed elsewhere in the book, and references have been made to them. The Novell Web site online documentation is the source of the latest, as well as the most detailed, information.

Options for Upgrading Your Server

Depending on your current system, you can use one of the following methods to upgrade to NetWare 5.1:

The NetWare 5.1 Installation Program   The INSTALL.BAT program offers an easy way to upgrade your NetWare 3.1*x* or NetWare 4.1*x* server to NetWare 5.1. With this option, there is little difference between upgrading and installing a new server.

Novell Upgrade Wizard   The Novell Upgrade Wizard, running on a Windows 95/98/ NT/2000 client workstation, copies bindery information and server data between a NetWare 2, 3, or 4 server to the new NetWare 5.1 server. The data on the older NetWare server is only copied, not changed. Bindery entries are migrated to NDS objects. This option used to be called an Across-the-Wire Migration.

Let me say this for the first of many times: no matter how you upgrade your server, make at least two (2) copies of all data that will be migrated. Any information of value on the earlier version of NetWare that you want to use under NetWare 5.1 should be backed up to tape or rewritable optical disks. Doing both would be an excellent safety measure.

Am I paranoid? Yes, always, especially about server disk operations. Make a backup before doing any operation that affects a server disk. Converting to a new version of NetWare is no different: back up or be sorry. That's such a good line, let's say it again: back up or be sorry.

Okay, back to your options for upgrading. Which of these routes makes the most sense for your situation? Here's a matrix that should give you some guidance.

From NetWare Version	Hardware (same or different)	Recommendation
NetWare 2.*x*	Different	Novell Upgrade Wizard
NetWare 3.*x*	Same (are you sure?)*	INSTALL.BAT
	Different	Novell Upgrade Wizard
NetWare 4	Same	INSTALL.BAT
	Different	Novell Upgrade Wizard

*Are you sure that you want to use the same hardware? See the next section, "Before You Upgrade Your Server, Think Again," for cautions.

PART

V

Appendices

Remember, there are two pieces to your upgrade: the bindery information (in the case of NetWare 2 and NetWare 3) and NDS information (in the case of NetWare 4), and the data on the server.

Before You Upgrade Your Server, Think Again

I want to distinguish between upgrading your network operating system to NetWare 5.1 and upgrading your existing physical server to NetWare 5.1. The first is usually a good idea; the second is often not.

When you bought your old server, say the server now running NetWare 3.12, you bought the best hardware you could afford. If you're lucky, and price wasn't an option, you got a serious server with lots of RAM, a big hard disk, and as fast a processor as possible (486/50 was a popular model at the time). The serious server likely had an EISA (Extended Industry Standard Adapter) bus, or perhaps it was an IBM model using a MicroChannel bus. Today, unfortunately, this setup doesn't even make a good workstation.

Look what has happened to each of your server's features:

RAM   16MB used to be plenty for a server; now that amount is barely adequate for a workstation running anything more powerful than Windows 3.1x. Retail PCs often come with 32MB or more of RAM; your server should start at 128MB and increase RAM quickly.

Hard disk   1GB was a big disk for early NetWare 3.x. Today, PCs bought at office supply stores and WalMart have 6GB (and larger) hard disks.

Hard disk controller   SCSI (Small Computer Systems Interface) controllers were the rage as NetWare 3.x became popular. Today, SCSI-2 and Fast and Wide SCSI multiply the throughput of your SCSI adapter. EIDE (Enhanced IDE) drives and controllers have broken the 512MB disk-size barrier and offer great speed and throughput, although SCSI is still preferable.

486 processor   NetWare 3.x ran well on a 486, even on a processor slower than 50MHz. However, the number of NLMs has grown, and the addition of Java and a GUI at the server places more pressure on the server processor than ever before. Your average users would be insulted to get a PC with "only" a Pentium II processor. A fast Pentium II (or Pentium III) processor is necessary for any server supporting more than a workgroup.

EISA or MicroChannel bus   MicroChannel has been officially stopped by IBM; no other vendors seriously supported it. EISA unofficially died. PCI (Peripheral Component Interconnect) bus slots and corresponding adapters are winners in the server bus race. PCI slots provide the throughput necessary for the 100Mb Ethernet adapters becoming more popular, and they support the Gigabit Ethernet cards arriving today.

CD-ROM drive   Does your old server have a bootable CD-ROM drive? Bet it doesn't.

What does all this mean? Your old server is way underpowered today. Upgrading the server would probably take too much money, especially if your motherboard doesn't support high-capacity RAM modules. Your old disk controller is outdated, so just getting a bigger disk won't help enough. Besides, new servers are becoming more affordable as disk prices plummet and the cost of Pentium processors is forced lower by their new processor competitors.

Face it, your old server needs to be retired.

Of course, you must read this with your particular situation in mind. If you have a P/60 with 64MB RAM, 2GB hard disk, and an ISA network adapter supporting 20 non-power users, your server has some life left—as an underpowered e-mail client. That configuration is not even adequate for a workgroup server today.

What can you do with it? If your server is the same configuration (or close) as the example, it will work as a low-end workstation or spare computer.

How Data Migrates

The first thing to do before migrating your data from an old server to a nice, new NetWare 5.1 server is to back up your data. Then back up that same data again, preferably with a different type of device so any errors in your hardware or software won't mess up two backups. If you do two backups with the same hardware and software, you might reproduce in the second backup any error made during the first backup.

Of course, if you are migrating to new server hardware, you'll have less fear and paranoia about your backup. If both the old and the new replacement server are up and running, any migration glitch is merely inconvenient rather than catastrophic. But even in the two-server scenario, you aren't absolved from the need to back up the original server. (Remember, back up or be sorry.)

Before any data-file migration, there are some things you must do in preparation for the big move:

- Delete unneeded files. No sense in taking old, worthless files to your nice, new server. If you want to consolidate some directories, the time to do so is before the migration.

- If you are upgrading from NetWare 2 or 3, run BINDFIX before migrating. BINDFIX will clean up the trustee rights and mail subdirectories of deleted users.

The Novell Upgrade Wizard utility allows you to choose which volumes to migrate. You can migrate all volumes or different volumes to different NetWare 5.1 servers. You might want to move files on one NetWare 2.x or 3.x server to several NetWare 5.1 servers. Any upgrade or other change is a good time to reorganize your network. Use the Novell Upgrade Wizard or INSTALL.BAT to move from NetWare 2, 3, or 4 servers.

The Novell Upgrade Wizard is a new utility that helps organize NetWare 2 and 3 bindery information into NDS format before migration. A Windows 95/98/NT/2000 management station is required when using the Novell Upgrade Wizard. The same tool facilitates file migration.

How File Attributes Migrate

The advantage of using the Novell Upgrade Wizard is the retention of all NetWare file attributes. If a file on a NetWare 3.x server is marked as Read Only and Shareable, it will transfer to the new system as Read Only and Shareable.

There are some new file attributes to consider: migration attributes and compression. The migration attributes do not concern the migration from one NetWare version to another, but the migration from the server hard disk to a near-line data storage facility.

After you run the Novell Upgrade Wizard, you must manually go through the files and directories on the NetWare 5.1 system and set any compression attributes. Don't trust the migration utility to read your mind when setting the compression attributes on the new files. Manually check each volume and directory after migration to ensure that attributes are set the way you want them. If you want the defaults, the migration utility is fine, but if you want to force immediate compression or to never allow a file to be compressed, you will need to set the attributes manually.

Upgrading Bindery Information

Since NetWare 3.x servers became the workhorses for most corporate networks, migrating the bindery information is critical. It's one thing to re-create the security profile for a dozen users after a migration, but quite another to re-create thousands of security profiles.

The largest area of concern is trustee rights. The Novell Upgrade Wizard will do much of the work for you, but you will (again) be forced to verify that the rights have been transferred properly.

System login scripts are not migrated. These have been replaced in NetWare 5.1 by Container login scripts. Since there may be several Container login scripts on every

NetWare 5.1 server, the earlier System login script has no direct correlation in NetWare 5.1.

User login scripts are transferred, but no corrections are made. The new names of servers and the changed directory structure will not be reflected in the transferred login scripts. You must manually make these changes in all login scripts.

Take special care with the directory paths in the new system. The volume names are probably the same in the NetWare 5.1 server as the older NetWare server in a one-to-one server upgrade. However, many companies use the upgrade as a chance to combine several older servers onto one new server or change the location of files and directories to reflect their new network design. In these cases, volumes will have new names and/or servers. These changes must be made in the login scripts.

With NetWare 3.*x*, multiple servers were available through the ATTACH command. NetWare 5.1 doesn't use the ATTACH command (although you may still use it in login scripts); NDS makes it easy to connect one user to many NetWare servers. All NetWare 3.*x*-specific login commands must be updated. Refer to the online documentation for details and issues when upgrading.

Where to Go from Here

The first place you should go from here is to telephone your NetWare reseller and buy a new server rather than upgrade your old server. The only possible exceptions are when upgrading from an earlier version of NetWare 4 to NetWare 5.1 or when you are placing the upgraded server into a light-duty situation. If you're coming from NetWare 3.*x*, your server is almost certainly too old and slow and limited in memory and hard drive space to make a satisfactory medium- or high-duty NetWare 5.1 server.

But since your budget or your boss (or both) may restrict your ability to buy the hardware you know you need, we must push onward. Right or wrong, you've got to get a system up and running.

Be sure to read the online documentation for the hardware requirements for a good NetWare 5.1 server. All the detailed information on installation and upgrading existing NetWare servers is in there. After you read Chapters 2 through 4 of this book, review the instructions there before beginning.

Upgrades Always Have a Hangup

There are lots of problems the manuals don't warn you about, of course. Whatever you think is adequate for your data backup procedures is probably not adequate. Go back and add one more backup or file copy of critical files.

Whatever time you have budgeted for the upgrade and changeover, increase the time. Double it if possible; more time will be needed than you imagine.

It isn't your fault (or mine) if it takes you longer to upgrade your existing system than you thought it would. You upgraders may have some information to "unlearn." Administrators new to NetWare 5.1 start without the baggage of remembering how things used to be and getting confused when NetWare 5.1 is different from the NetWare version they are using now.

Life is tough enough; don't make it harder by rushing into NetWare 5.1 before you check out the terrain. Every hour spent planning your upgrade or new installation will repay you tenfold in making your network a positive experience for your users.

APPENDIX **B**

How NetWare 5.1 Differs from Earlier Versions

Novell's NetWare has been the leader in local area networking for more than a decade. But this is the computer business, where the leader yesterday can be a follower tomorrow. Can we still say NetWare is the leading network operating system, even with all the competitors busily working to catch up and pass NetWare?

Yes, we can say NetWare is still the leader, in both installed server market share and product features. Novell engineers always aim to make networking easier for people trying to get their work done.

Would it surprise you if I said there were as many NetWare dealers as 7-Eleven stores? Well, there *are* twice as many NetWare dealers as 7-Eleven stores. You should not have any trouble finding a place to buy NetWare.

Of course, you may still be having trouble convincing your (shortsighted) boss to finally approve the purchase of NetWare 5.1. If so, read on.

Advantages of NetWare over Other Network Operating Systems

Novell engineered NetWare first and foremost to provide users access to files. Early on, the shared hard disk concept was forced by the high cost of mass storage. Later, as hard disk storage prices dropped, file sharing became important as a way to share information.

With more than a decade of improvements, NetWare provides file access faster, but with more control than any other network operating system. The file-caching scheme developed in the early days has consistently given better performance than mere hard drive improvements.

The use of cache buffers keeps important server resources in RAM. When one user reads a file, the file stays in server memory. If that same user, or another user, needs a piece of that file again, he or she gets immediate access. Server RAM is much faster than the fastest hard disk.

Another cache improvement pioneered by Novell was the "hashing" of directory information. Novell uses some of the cache memory in the server for a partial list of each file on the hard disk and the physical location of all files (via the FAT). Note that this occurs only for the traditional file format volumes, not for the newer NSS (Novell Storage Services) volumes. This cache eliminates the time spent in reading the directory off the hard disk. When a file is requested, the first physical movements of the hard disk drive-heads are to the file, not to the directory to ask directions for the file location. The new NSS format offers even better performance with even larger volumes.

These are examples of NetWare's advanced control of server memory. All the caching in the world runs out sooner or later, of course, and the hard disk must be used. Once again, NetWare engineers have been thinking of improvements for more than a decade.

Early hard disks were large, slow, and expensive. The IBM XT originally shipped with a 10MB hard disk, and people wondered if they would ever fill it.

One way Novell turbo-charged hard disk access was through "elevator seeking." Elevators go all the way up and then all the way down. This reaches all the waiting riders in the most efficient manner.

Hard disks, in most operating systems, however, service file requests in the order they are received. When taken to extreme, this leads to *thrashing*, where the heads whip back and forth. Back when I started, the disks were so big and heavy the server would rock back and forth unless it was on a solid table.

By queuing up the hard disk requests (possible because of the directory hashing), NetWare engineers implemented elevator seeking for the file server hard disk. Rather than service requests in the order received, NetWare accesses files in the direction the disk heads are already moving. Figure B.1 illustrates how elevator seeking works.

PART

V

Appendices

FIGURE B.1

Elevator seeking services files in order of location.

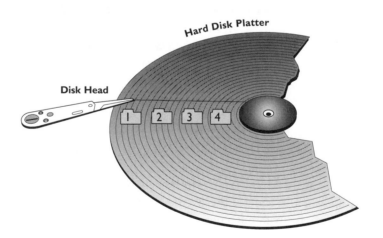

Hard Disk Platter

Disk Head

Order of File Request: 4213
Order of File Service: 1234

These technical advantages give NetWare a performance advantage over competing networks. One other important success factor for Novell has been the developers' philosophical approach to the networking business.

Ray Noorda, president of Novell from 1983 to 1994, rescued Novell Data Systems from bankruptcy in the early 1980s and turned it into Novell, Inc. An important goal for Mr. Noorda was to grow the networking business, not just Novell. Following the old adage that "a rising tide lifts all boats," Noorda pushed Novell to support every interface card and computer on the market. Alliances were made with and technical information was shared between other companies that were, to all appearances, rivals of Novell. An example is Novell's strong support of 3Com's outstanding Ethernet cards, even while 3Com was selling a competing network operating system.

The term Noorda used was *co-opetition*, a combination of cooperation and competition. For the world of PCs and PC networking, this was amazing. Don't expect your Unix friends to be impressed, however. The Internet was grown and developed in exactly the same way, except the entire Unix and WAN industries share information—not a bad model.

Advantages of NetWare 5.1 over NetWare 3

NetWare 3.*x* is the world's leading network operating system. Whether you count total server licenses, clients supported, third-party support, or dollars invested by clients, NetWare 3.*x* tops every measurement. Millions of users every workday rely on one or more NetWare 3.*x* servers.

Designed to be the best departmental network operating system, NetWare 3.*x* has succeeded. But between the time NetWare 3 premiered in 1989 and today, the world of networking has grown tremendously. While this is a book on NetWare 5.1, and obviously this version of the product has many, many advantages that are discussed both in this appendix and in the rest of the book, Novell still sells and supports NetWare 3. In fact, early in 1998, just a few months before NetWare 5.0 was due to ship, Novell released version 3.2. This is one of the great strengths of Novell: the company supports and enhances its older products as well as the latest and greatest version. Your investment is secure with Novell. Compare this with other companies and their approach. When was the last time you saw an improvement for Windows 3.*x*? Can you even buy through normal distribution channels any version of Microsoft Office 4? You can still get NetWare 3.2.

Whereas NetWare 3.*x* was built for the department, the world now demands an enterprise-wide network solution. Companies that used to depend on the mainframe to offer information to geographically dispersed locations now demand that capability from their network operating systems.

Customers demand more from their servers today. Some of today's requirements were impossible for even the largest mainframe 20 years ago. Requirements today include the following:

- Servers that support a thousand concurrent users
- Servers that support many thousands of potential users
- Support for DOS, Windows, OS/2, Macintosh, and Unix clients
- Internet connections and access control
- Applying Internet-based technologies to internal networks
- Improved WAN performance
- Multiple-language support on one server
- Automatic hard disk compression
- Ability to communicate with mainframe and Unix systems

Some of the features needed by large corporations are supported by NetWare 3.*x*. But consider this analogy: although a DC-10 can carry groups of people through the air, the Concorde designers applied new thinking to the requirements and revolutionized jet travel with more speed and style. NetWare 5.1 also improved upon NetWare 3.*x* by adding both new technology and new ways of helping users reach their networking goals. Here is a summary of some of the features NetWare 5.1 offers to improve your network and their advantages for your users (more are discussed under the improvements from version 4 to version 5):

- File compression and block suballocation stretch your disk drive investment.
- NLMs (NetWare Loadable Modules) in protected mode reduce server downtime and provide multiple-language support.
- With NDS (Novell Directory Services), users have a global view of the network rather than a server-centric view.
- New and enhanced server and workstation utilities are provided for both DOS and Windows users, including new 32-bit utilities for Windows 95, 98, NT, and 2000.
- The NetWare client software includes workstation support for DOS and Windows clients. Single network login allows users access to an enterprise network after authentication.
- The Netscape Enterprise Web server provides an easy way to create an intranet and to provide information on the Internet.
- IBM's WebSphere Application Server software supports the Enterprise Web Server and includes the WebSphere Design Studio software.

PART

V

Appendices

- The server installation procedure includes a step-by-step installation Wizard to help with the installation, and the Novell Upgrade Wizard offers an easy-to-use, GUI interface to smooth the migration to NetWare 5.1.

- New features and enhancements to NetWare print services allow more flexible printing, especially with NDPS (Novell Distributed Print Services).

- SMS (Storage Management Services) and TSAs (Target Service Agents) add sophisticated control of backups, both of clients and servers. Also new is a Windows 95/98 GUI for setting up the backups.

- SNMP (Simple Network Management Protocol) support allows for standards-based network management from many vendors.

- HCSS (High-Capacity Storage System) adds an optical disk library, called a juke-box, to the NetWare server.

- Packet Burst Protocol and Large Internet Packets speed WAN connections. Multiple protocols are supported in the client and server. NLSP (NetWare Link Support Protocol) provides better routing support, and the MPR (Multi-Protocol Router) adds full WAN control to your NetWare server.

- The new online documentation, viewable with any Web browser, includes functions for complex searches (with the Netscape browser) as well as browsing for information.

- TCP/IP support is now part of NetWare natively; IPX is no longer encapsulated (or tunneled) in IP packets, for better performance.

- HTTP (Hypertext Transfer Protocol), the protocol for Web server communications, is a kernel-level service in NetWare 5.1.

- DNS (Domain Name Service), DDNS (Dynamic DNS), and DHCP (Dynamic Host Configuration Protocol) support is tied to NDS. DDNS support allows clients to get IP addresses from a DHCP server and then automatically update the information in DNS with the current IP address.

- A GUI (graphical user interface) is now available at the server. You can now do much of your administration from the server itself, without having to go anywhere else. Many have wanted this for years, although I must admit I prefer to administer from my office rather than from a dark server closet.

- A five-user version of Oracle 8i (a SQL database) is included with NetWare 5.1. You have a powerful server-based database program included; if you like it and want to use it, you can purchase additional licenses. It also uses NDS for administration and single login to both NetWare and Oracle.

Your Choice: DOS or Windows Management Utilities

When Novell started, networking management of competitors' products meant command-line utilities and cryptic text files. Novell provided a clean and fairly straightforward utility interface. It was DOS, of course, since this happened in the early 1980s. Some DOS utilities still exist, but their numbers are dwindling with each NetWare version.

That interface has served Novell well over the years. It's a model for many third-party vendors who make their screens look as much like NetWare as possible. The DOS interface (called the "C-Worthy" interface, named after the compiler used) is now even cleaner and more informative than before.

If you prefer DOS, you will be greeted by the familiar C-Worthy interface with some upgrading. See Figure B.2 for a look at the new Volume Statistics screen now inside the FILER administration utility. The DOS commands are covered in Appendix E.

PART

V

Appendices

FIGURE B.2

The DOS look and feel of NetWare administration

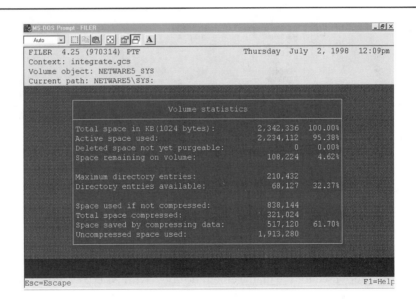

But it's still DOS, and some people don't like that as much as Windows. That alone is a good reason to move to Windows, but even more important is that the handling of objects works better with a GUI. Since NetWare 5.1 is now object-oriented and flexible, the drag-and-drop capabilities provided by Windows ease management tasks more than ever. And the Client32 platform running on Windows 95, 98, NT, and

2000 makes 32-bit utilities a reality. More horsepower on the management workstation means better performance.

With full graphics at every step, the NetWare Administrator program under Windows shows more information more quickly than is possible with the DOS utilities. Notice in Figure B.3 how the information concerning the NETWARE5_SYS volume is clearer than that shown in Figure B.2.

FIGURE B.3

*The new look
of NetWare
administration*

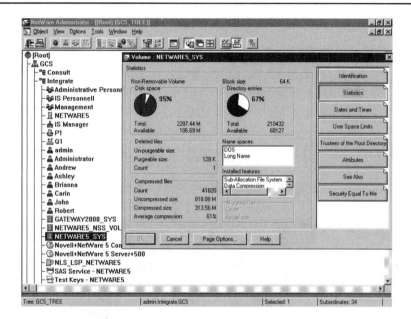

Similar options exist for the users, but an extra twist has been thrown in. Whereas the users had only a DOS interface in NetWare 3 (except for 3.20, to which a Windows interface was added for many functions), they have both starting in NetWare 4, and this continues in version 5. NETUSER is an extension of the DOS C-Worthy interface used for the management utilities. With NETUSER, even the newest user can easily attach to network printers, send messages, and change drive mappings. The corresponding Windows 3.1*x* program is NetWare User Tools. This is even easier for users to navigate. Once you enable its hot key, you can call the NetWare User Tools program from anywhere within Windows 3.1*x* with the touch of the F6 key (or another key you assign). Users can "mouse about," dragging and dropping for printer control, sending and receiving messages, and mapping drives. Only the Windows 3.1*x*

users still have NetWare User Tools, since Windows 95, 98, and NT 4 all come with Network Neighborhood.

Windows 95/98/NT/2000 clients perform the same functions within Network Neighborhood or Windows Explorer. The Client32 additions to Windows 95, 98, NT, and 2000 even allow users to map drives and configure printers, all from their Windows Desktops.

File Compression and Other File System Enhancements

No matter how much disk space you have, you will run out one day. That's a guarantee in the computer business. Now that "feature-bloat" and "code creep" have pushed standard word processors to require more than 250MB of space, that day will come sooner than you imagine. Your budget may not be ready.

Applying the techniques learned in providing file compression in Novell DOS 7 and packing installation programs onto fewer disks, NetWare 4 premiered the first file-server background compression. Unlike the compression program you may have on your own computer disk, this system is optimized for the file server. For your desktop system, the scales are balanced for good on-the-fly compression and decompression.

Software developers have choices to make during product development. There's no free lunch in software development; the code that crunches the files down the smallest takes longer to decompress the files. Conversely, the code that expands files the fastest doesn't get the best compression ratio.

Your desktop system uses software written to crunch the file as well as it can in the time allotted. But it can't crunch too much, because then the file retrieval would be slower when you need it later. So you get a compromise.

On the NetWare server, other options are available. There's no need to worry about crunching the file in real time, for several reasons. Since the server has enough disk space to support many people, the file compression is not mandatory the instant you save the file. Because the system is shared, you may be saving a file at your desk that the person in the next cubicle is busy opening. There is no sense in wasting server CPU cycles crunching and expanding the same file at the same time, is there?

NetWare engineers developed software that focuses on reducing file-opening time. When people want a file, they want it now. Besides, NetWare has a reputation to protect when it comes to file service, and quick response to file requests is an important part of that reputation.

File compression is done by another set of software, separate from the file-expansion software. Two important details optimize performance. First, you can set the delay (in days) for a file to be untouched before being compressed from 0 days (at the next

PART

V

Appendices

compression cycle, which you can configure) and 100,000 days (obviously a joke unless you plan on checking back in 273 years). The default is 14 days before compression.

After choosing your compression delay, you can choose how you will deal with compressed files that are read by a user or by an application. You can always leave them in compressed mode, you can always leave them in uncompressed mode, or you can cheat. The third option is to leave the file compressed if it's only read one time in the 14 days, but leave it uncompressed if it's read twice in that time period. Figure B.4 shows the duality of file compression.

FIGURE B.4

File compression: read in haste, compress at leisure.

Compression

Dedicate plenty of **CPU** horsepower.
Run compression at midnight when the server is not busy.

Decompression

Use as little **CPU** horsepower as possible,
since files will be read during the workday.

One quick note about another space-saving feature: suballocation of disk blocks. *Suballocation* (which is not undersea ship deployment for the Navy) allows NetWare to have large blocks of data (as much as 64KB in one block), which speeds file retrieval. But if you save a 64.5KB file, another entire 64KB block is needed, of which 63.5KB are wasted. NetWare 5.1 (on traditional-style volumes) allows suballocation of the disk block size, down to 512 bytes (0.5KB) and groups these leftover file pieces in one large block. Suballocation allows our 64.5KB file to take one 64KB disk block and one 512-byte section of a second block. This approach is much more efficient.

The biggest new feature relating to the file system is NSS, Novell Storage Services. It uses much, much less memory when a volume is mounted, allows for billions of files and directories, and allows for file sizes up to 8TB (that's about 8000GB!). Volumes now mount in seconds, not minutes, and are also repaired in seconds, not minutes to hours for large volumes. You are also allowed many more volumes with NSS. You may also choose to mount the server's DOS partition(s) for updates, upgrades, troubleshooting, and so on.

Server Performance

File servers are getting bigger and faster, almost as fast as our demands on them are growing. Four recent PC innovations are supported by NetWare 5.1 to increase the workload your server can handle.

- NetWare 5.1 supports the PCI (Peripheral Component Interconnect) bus developed by Intel. PCI cards communicate directly with the CPU in either 32 or 64 bits at a time. Bus-mastering PCI cards can perform some tasks concurrently with the CPU for even greater timesaving. NetWare supports 66MHz, 100MHz, and faster PCI busses.

- Hot Plug PCI is an extension to the PCI standard. This technology allows you to add and remove PCI cards while the server is running. Currently, you must take the server down, often at an inconvenient time (for you—like 2 A.M. on Saturday), replace the troubled component, and then test the repaired or upgraded component to make sure it still works. Let's say, for example, that one of your three NICs has gone bad. With Hot Plug PCI, you simply open the case, pull the card, replace it with a spare, and move on—all the while the two remaining NICs are servicing the needs of the clients. This works great in a system like our Compaq loaners, built for hot-swapping card ease.

- NetWare 5.1 now supports I2O (Intelligent Input/Output), an industry-wide standard to move I/O processing off the CPU and onto dedicated processors. This allows the CPU to do other tasks, such as service client requests for information or manage printing. NetWare is one of the first operating systems to support this new standard.

- NetWare 5.1 supports multiple CPUs right out of the box (as many as 32 of them). In the past, a separate kernel (the core operating system files) was needed to support this feature; now it is integrated into one kernel. If your server is running slowly, adding another CPU may be just the ticket to speed up performance without buying another computer.

Memory Management

In NetWare 3, memory was segmented into five "pools." After studying the NLMs on the market, however, Novell engineers learned that a single, flat memory space provides both better performance and easier memory allocation routines (imagine that!). "Garbage collection" routines, which are programs that find released but unused bits of memory and gradually work them back into the system, work better in this memory model as well.

Another memory improvement is segmented memory areas to store unknown or suspect NLM applications. Memory in Intel-based computers (since the 386) is divided into four rings, from 0 (the closest to the CPU and most powerful ring) to 3 (the least powerful ring). Ring 3 memory leaves gaps between applications and protects the Ring 0 application memory space from interruption.

With new or suspect NLMs in Ring 0, your server can be slowed or even stopped by an NLM not behaving properly. Placing these NLMs elsewhere greatly reduces the chance of the rogue NLM affecting the rest of the server.

There is a significant performance penalty for Ring 3 operations. Some network administrators place all new NLM applications (that support being loaded into Ring 3— some don't) in Ring 3 for a few weeks. If there are no problems, they can move them into the trusted memory area with all the other well-behaved NLMs. This offers a way to protect your server and still provide the best possible performance.

The biggest new feature in this area is the support for virtual memory. Virtual memory means using some space on the hard drive as if it were physical memory. With Novell's new focus on making NetWare 5.1 not only a fast file and print server, but an application server as well, a mechanism was needed to support the applications (such as a Web server or a database server) and their memory needs in a potentially memory-short situation. Virtual memory has been used for years in Unix and now has made it to NetWare as well.

Server Self-Tuning

While running, the server software constantly adjusts the memory available, directing extra memory where it will do the most good. This shows in all the variable settings in the MONITOR.NLM program, which runs on the server console.

The good news is that the system tunes itself; the bad news is that it will not remember those settings the next time you reboot the server. The settings will gradually move back to the most efficient levels, but you can help them along.

Check the MONITOR screen, and make a note of items that affect performance, such as the number of directory cache buffers. The range is 20 to 200,000, with a default of 500. If your server shows a number far from the default, especially toward the low end or approaching the high end, use SET command parameters (see Appendix C) in your AUTOEXEC.NCF file or MONITOR (see Chapter 10) to place the buffers at this value (plus a little extra for "wiggle" room) on server startup. This puts your server into a more efficient mode immediately.

Advantages of NetWare 5.1 over NetWare 4

There are many improvements in NetWare 5.1 over NetWare 4, but many people focus on the ones concerned with NDS. In NetWare 5.1, NDS is more flexible, easier to install, and easier to reconfigure.

Confused? Need help? The new Web-based electronic documentation has the answers.

Directory Service Improvements

No matter how well you plan, your company structure changes. With the new tools for NDS, it won't be difficult to change your network to match.

NDS Manager provides a graphical environment for many normal NDS chores. Common tasks such as partitioning the NDS tree, finding and fixing errors that crop into the NDS database, and removing servers from the tree can all be done from here, in a graphical manner. I discussed NDS Manager in Chapter 10.

ZENworks (Zero Effort Networks) allows you to control software distribution (replacing NAL, the NetWare Application Launcher) and do some workstation management. NetWare 5.1 ships with the ZENworks Starter Pack; to get additional functionality, you need to purchase the full version.

New Installation Options

If your network is small, some of the power of NDS is no advantage to you. If you won't get all the power, why should you go through the configuration?

With NetWare 5.1, an Installation Wizard steps you through the entire process, with defaults along the way to make selecting options even easier. About halfway through, the process goes graphical for the first time ever in NetWare. See Chapter 3 for more information.

The physical act of installation is also now easier. You can install from a CD-ROM attached to the server, from a CD-ROM anywhere on the network, or from another file server (if it has a copy of much of the CD-ROM). You can also boot from the installation CD-ROM, speeding the installation process even more.

New NDS Configuration Options

The NWADMN32 (or more officially, NetWare Administrator for Windows) program has new features. You may, starting with NetWare 5.0, see and administer multiple trees.

NDS Manager allows you to move a container, change and manage partitions and replicas, and perform many of the DSREPAIR functions. You will be surprised at how much you can manage without ever leaving your Windows 95, 98, NT, or 2000 workstation.

Printing Enhancements

Counting on the ability of smarter printers, Novell has unveiled Novell Distributed Print Services (NDPS). Using the network for two-way communications between printers and servers makes printing decisions easier for users.

Printer Agents combine the functions of print queue, print server, and spooler into one technology. NDPS helps prepare networks for the day when printers anywhere on the Internet can be addressed as NetWare system printers.

One of the best features of NDPS is that it will automatically download the correct printer driver for a printer based on the user's operating system. NDPS ships with support for Windows 3.1x, 95, 98, and NT printer drivers. The user browses for a printer, selects it, and the driver is installed and configured to use that printer. NDPS even allows the user to search the tree for printers with specific capabilities and print to any printer in the tree (assuming that he or she has sufficient rights to use the printer).

A great feature for the non-NDPS-based printing system is the Print Layout Page option in the print server information. With one click, you can display a graphic diagram of that server's print queues, printers, and print jobs in the queue. Red exclamation points (!) highlight any problems with any of the components. You can use this feature to see whether the print server is loaded, whether a printer is not functioning, and so on.

New Storage and Backup Options

No one has enough storage, whether we're talking closets or network disk space. *HCSS* (High-Capacity Storage System), while included in NetWare 4.1x, is still a great feature that needs to be discussed here and may be new depending on your previous operating system. HCSS helps add storage space by adding jukebox systems of optical media into the NetWare file system of the server. Users treat the optical media the same way they do any other server volume, using the same software and commands.

In NetWare 5.1, multiple drives are supported in a jukebox. Improvements mean more efficient jukebox information retrieval and less time spent importing the information into the NetWare file system. Customization is now possible, with the new parameters you can set for HCSS.

As I mentioned in the section on new features from NetWare 3, the new front end for backup is a Windows 95/98/NT/2000 program that allows you to schedule backups. You can centrally schedule all backups, as well as manage centrally, because the information is stored in NDS. It is also protocol independent, allowing you to back up IP or IPX servers and workstations. The new version of SMS supports NSS as well, of course.

NetWare Peripheral Architecture

Novell has always supported more server hardware than any other network vendor. Keeping that lead is the purpose behind NPA (NetWare Peripheral Architecture, sometimes also referred to as NWPA).

NetWare disk drivers are now separated into two parts:

- HAM (Host Adapter Module)
- CDM (Custom Device Module)

The HAM is the interface to the host adapter hardware (the card in the server). The CDM drives any hardware devices attached to that adapter.

This was done in the past with a single .DSK file. The advantage of NPA is scalability. Before, any hardware change required a new driver file, which could present problems with other installed devices. With NPA, all you need for new hardware is the CDM for that particular piece of equipment. While technically not new in NetWare 5.1, it is, however, the only supported disk driver type. The .DSK drivers are no longer supported.

PART

V

Appendices

Web (HTML) Documentation

ElectroText and DynaText are now gone. In their place is HTML (Hypertext Markup Language) documentation, designed to be read from any Web browser. Although Netscape Navigator 4.*x* is preferred and gives you additional capabilities, any Web browser will do. You have heard that before about "new, improved" software, but it's true this time.

ElectroText was limited to Windows readers; DynaText was limited to Windows and Macintosh users. Any client for which a browser is available can now view the Web documentation. The look and feel, as well as the graphics, translate into the same picture on all platforms.

Netscape Enterprise Web Server

Bundled with NetWare 5.1 is Netscape Enterprise Web Server. If you're not involved with the Internet, you may wonder what all the fuss is about. Let me tell you.

Web servers, and the Netscape Web Server in particular, rely on a standardized client and server communications protocol called HTTP (HyperText Transfer Protocol). Web servers provide information in small pieces that the client, no matter what operating system, formats and presents based on the browser software running on the client.

Most of the information provided by Web servers is documents. Well, what's the best network operating system in the world for providing files to intelligent clients quickly and reliably? That's right, NetWare.

Enterprise Web Server includes the ability to connect to remote hosts, remote NetWare servers, local NetWare servers, and most databases running on TCP/IP hosts. Easy script language samples provided by Novell make your Web experience simple and straightforward, even if you're new to the Web world.

Even more exciting, the Web Server can rely on NDS for security. Authorized clients can browse NDS through their Web clients, viewing your entire network directory structure in HTML look and feel. This is accomplished with LDAP (Lightweight Directory Access Protocol), which is a stripped-down (lightweight, get it?) version of DAP (Directory Access Protocol), which is x.500 (the protocol on which NDS is based). LDAP version 3.0 support is included and enhanced in NetWare 5.1 as well.

Netscape Client Software

NetWare 5.1 includes a fully licensed version of Netscape Communicator 4.7. This is shipped to allow you to view the online documentation, as well as for Web browsing in general.

MPR (Multi-Protocol Router)

Another included feature is the MPR. Also a separate product not long ago, MPR now works with your server for connection to your Internet service provider or in a traditional way for telecommunication connections. You can list multiple call locations, allowing back-up connections to your remote offices. This powerful feature is included with the basic package.

How the Global Directory Helps Users

You, my reader friend, are an unusual person. You not only understand computers, you like them. You like working with them and playing with them. Unfortunately, some people believe computers are just tools to use as a means of producing other work. I know that seems strange, but it's true.

One consequence of this attitude is a low tolerance for computer interaction. These people refuse to learn how a computer system works. They have this idea that the computer should support them, not the other way around.

This type of user is the biggest beneficiary of NDS. Users no longer need to remember server names, volume names, print queue and print server names, or anything else of a technical nature. With the new client software for both DOS and Windows, users can see and connect to resources without having a clue where these things are physically located.

Many administrators copied login scripts and user names between NetWare 3.x servers so that the users could automatically attach to multiple servers. This is no longer necessary. Although this looks like a much better benefit for you than the users, it does help them.

When resources are added (a new color laser printer, for example), users can use them immediately, without waiting for you to configure a dozen different server user lists. Advertise the new Printer object, and all users can see and use it at their whim. With NDPS, even the drivers are automatically installed.

The client programs included with NetWare 5.1 help computer-phobic users. A single network view is available through both DOS and Windows, where all the network resources appear. Even the most cantankerous users will be forced to admit that everything they need is within easy reach.

PART

V

Appendices

APPENDIX <u>C</u>

NetWare 5.1 SET Commands

This appendix describes a few of the SET commands and parameters, which are grouped in 16 categories:

- Communications
- Directory caching
- Directory Services
- Disk
- Error handling
- File caching
- File system
- Licensing Services
- Locks
- Memory
- Miscellaneous
- Multiprocessor
- NCP (NetWare Core Protocol)
- Service Location Protocol (SLP)
- Time
- Transaction tracking

The parameters not described here are those that are infrequently used or otherwise not generally modified. See the online documentation for more information about these parameters. The values shown are defaults.

You will rarely need to change any of these SET parameters during normal use. NetWare has come a long way, and many of these settings are dynamic in NetWare 5.1. Change a setting only in response to a specific problem or when directed by support personnel.

Take a look at Figure C.1, showing the new way to view and change SET commands.

The URL in the picture is slightly misleading. Connect to your server using the IP address followed by a colon and 8008. After logging in to the NetWare Management Portal, some of the links change their port number. You don't have to worry about it.

Contrast the new with the old, shown in Figure C.2. The old C-Worthy interface still lives, and probably will for quite some time.

FIGURE C.1

Web browsers are now the SET command portal.

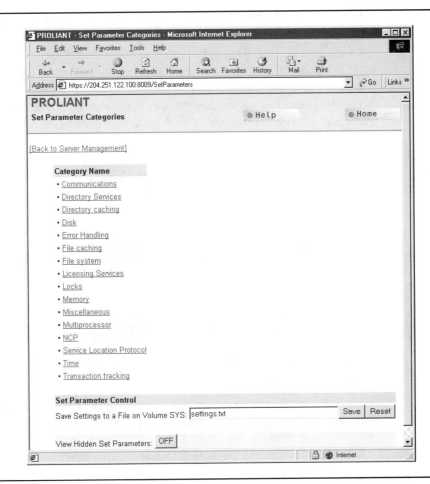

FIGURE C.2

The old SET command interface

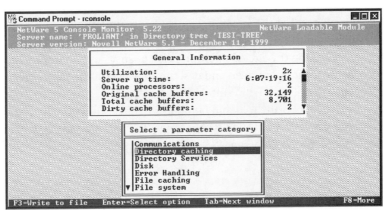

You should recognize this interface as the MONITOR program. This screen hides beneath the Server Parameters menu item on the front screen of MONITOR.

Unfortunately, Novell has yet to incorporate all the goodies of Server Parameters into the Management Portal. While the browser interface gives two bits of helpful information not found in MONITOR (the owner NLM of the setting, and when items can be changed and whether they will stay at the new setting or not), the help screens aren't as good. The help screens in MONITOR–Server Parameters tend to give a bit more information.

Communications SET Commands

```
Load Balance Local LAN = Off
```

This parameter enables or disables load balancing of requests. Load balancing is spreading the load (for client requests, login authentication, and so on) across all the servers in the LAN.

Directory Caching SET Commands

```
Dirty Directory Cache Delay Time = 0.5 Sec
```

This parameter sets the minimum time before a dirty (changed) directory cache buffer is written to the disk. Longer delay times give slightly better performance but increase the chances of corrupted directory entry tables. The range for this setting is 0 to 10 seconds. A setting of 0 is not advised, since it slows performance.

Let's use this setting to show the differences in the new (Web interface) versus the old (Server Parameters) SET commands access method. Figure C.3 shows the Web method.

Notice that the values in Figure C.3 are underlined, indicating a hyperlink. Clicking a value opens the Change Value dialog box.

Clicking the circled question mark opens the Help information. It would make sense if the help screen and description were on the same screen as the settings, but they're not, at least in this version.

The C-Worthy (old and familiar) interface shows the help and/or description on the same screen as the list of settings. To change a setting, you must, of course, select it and hit the Enter key.

FIGURE C.3

Click a question mark to see more details or click a value to open the Change Value screen.

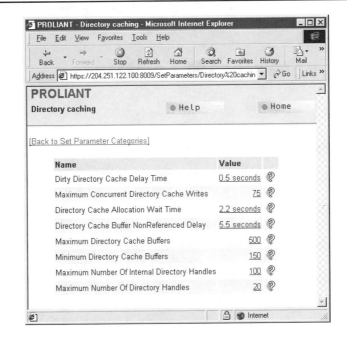

FIGURE C.4

Changing SET parameters the old fashioned way

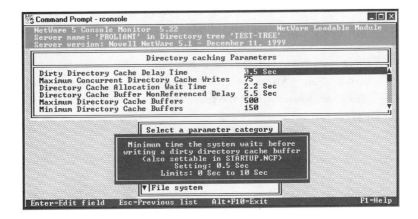

```
Maximum Concurrent Directory Cache Writes = 10
```

Concurrent writes aren't actually concurrent, unless you have multiple drives. The idea is to group write requests for each sweep of the disk head across the disk platters.

The range for this setting is 5 to 500. Higher numbers make for more efficient writes but less efficient reads, and vice versa.

Directory Services SET Commands

```
NDS Trace to Screen = Off
```

When set to On, this parameter displays NDS events on the server console screen.

```
NDS Trace to File = Off
```

When set to On, this parameter sends NDS events to a trace file. The default file is SYSTEM\DSTRACE.DBG, but that can be changed when starting the NDS log file (see NDS Trace Filename). The maximum size of the trace file is about 500KB, after which new information overwrites the oldest.

```
NDS Trace Filename = SYSTEM\DSTRACE.DBG
```

This parameter is the default value for the NDS trace file mentioned previously. The maximum path length for the complete filename, including the path, is 254 characters. It is always stored on the SYS: volume.

Disk SET Commands

```
Enable Disk Read After Write Verify = Off
```

Enable this portion of Hot Fix if you have a single disk or multiple disks that are not mirrored. If your disks are mirrored and reliable, you can gain extra speed by setting this parameter to Off. Disable this parameter for disks and drivers that perform their own read-after-write verification to avoid doing this verification twice. This setting affects disks loaded after the parameter is changed; put it in your STARTUP.NCF file for regular use.

```
Ignore Disk Geometry = Off
```

This setting allows creation or modification of nonstandard and otherwise unsupported partitions. The default is Off.

 WARNING Setting Ignore Disk Geometry to On may have drastic, negative consequences for any other file system (such as FAT or NTFS).

Error Handling SET Commands

```
Server Log File Overflow Size = 4194304
```

This parameter sets the maximum file size for the SYS$LOG.ERR file. The range for this setting is 65,536 to 4,294,967,295 bytes. When this value is reached, the action specified in Server Log File State occurs.

```
Server Log File State = 1
```

This parameter specifies what happens when the SYS$LOG.ERR file grows larger than the set limit. The settings are 0 = do nothing, 1 = delete the log file, and 2 = rename the log file.

File Caching SET Commands

```
Read Ahead Enabled = On
```

During sequential file access, such as reading block number one of a large file, NetWare assumes that you are going to read blocks two, three, four, and so on. When this parameter is set to On, the system reads these blocks ahead of the actual read request from the application. This setting can greatly improve access time, because when the actual read request does come in, the next disk block is already in RAM, waiting.

```
Read Ahead LRU Sitting Time Threshold = 10 Sec
```

This setting tells NetWare that if the cache LRU (Least Recently Used) time is below the set time, not to perform the read-ahead block feature. The range for this setting is 0 seconds to 1 hour.

File System SET Commands

```
Minimum File Delete Wait Time = 1 Min 5.9 Sec
```

Files deleted are not gone until purged. This is a wonderful feature, especially when you immediately realize that you have deleted drive F: when you meant drive A:. This parameter says that a file must be salvageable at least this long, even when the volume is full and users have no new space. If there is plenty of room on the volume, a file may be salvageable for weeks. The range for this setting is 0 seconds to 7 days.

```
File Delete Wait Time = 5 Min 29.6 Sec
```

The `Minimum File Delete Wait Time` setting defines the minimum wait time; this setting is for the normal wait time, and the same situation applies. If the file is deleted but there is plenty of room on the volume, it will not be purged for quite a while. When the volume finally fills with regular and purgeable files, the oldest purgeable files are erased first. The range for this setting is 0 seconds to 7 days.

Licensing Services SET Commands

```
Dirty Certificate Cache Delay Time = 1 minute
```

This parameter sets the minimum time that the Licensing Services will wait before writing a dirty (changed) certificate to the NDS database. The range for this setting is 1 minute to 1 hour.

```
NLS Search Type = 0
```

This parameter specifies how far up the tree Licensing Services will search for a license certificate. The settings are 0 = all the way to the [Root] and 1 = to the top of the partition (the partition root) only.

Locks SET Commands

```
Maximum Record Locks per Connection = 500
```

This parameter sets how many record locks one workstation can use at a time. Check this value in the MONITOR screens. The range for this setting is 10 to 100,000.

Memory SET Commands

```
Average Page In Alert Threshold = 2000
```

A page in occurs when the virtual memory (VM) system needs data returned to memory that has been paged out to disk. An alert will be issued at the console when the average over the last five seconds exceeds this value. If this is a frequent problem, it means either that your server needs to offload a process that is consuming RAM or that more RAM is needed. The range is 1 (which is far too low—you will get a lot of alerts) to 4,294,967,295.

```
Memory Protection No Restart Interval = 1
```

When an address space crashes (or faults), NetWare may automatically try to reclaim its resources and restart the server software if `Memory Protection Fault Cleanup` is set to On. If this process occurs more than once in the specified number of minutes, you should stop this process because server resources and time are being wasted. Setting this value disables this feature, potentially wasting valuable time.

Miscellaneous SET Commands

```
Sound Bell for Alerts = On
```

This parameter sets the console to beep or not when an alert appears. My first change on every new server is to set this parameter to Off.

```
Replace Console Prompt with Server Name = On
```

This parameter places the server name to the left of the console prompt (a colon :).

Multiprocessor SET Commands

```
Auto Start Processors = On
```

If this parameter is set to On, all secondary CPUs will be started (and therefore used) when the PSM (Platform Support Module) is loaded. If it is set to Off, you must enter the command START PROCESSORS to activate them. Unless you suspect a problem with a CPU, leave it On.

NCP SET Commands

```
NCP File Commit = On
```

Some NetWare-aware programs prefer to force files to write to disk before receiving confirmation of the success of the write. Normal files are placed in the cache, and the cache responds to the application with verification, even though the file hasn't actually been placed on the disk. The default setting of On allows this forced writing.

```
Display NCP Bad Component Warnings = Off
```

Poorly written programs may not handle NetWare system calls properly. This setting allows (On) or prevents (Off) alert messages from going to the console.

```
NCP Packet Signature Option = 1
```

NCP packet signatures are a security feature that uses embedded identification in the packets to guarantee identity. The values and their definitions for the server are 0 = no packet signatures ever, 1 = packet signatures at the request of the client, 2 = packet signatures if the client can and wants to (but don't force them), or 3 = force packet signatures. If either the client or the server is set to 3 and the other is set to 0 (or is unable to do packet signatures), a connection between them will not be possible. Packet signatures use CPU resources and slow performance on both ends of the network transactions. Few situations require this level of security.

Service Location Protocol SET Commands

```
SLP SA Default Lifetime = 3600
```

This parameter controls how long a service will remain registered (without an update) with the SLP. In an unstable environment, you should reduce the number; in a highly stable one, you could increase it. The range is 0 to 65,535 seconds.

Time SET Commands

```
TIMESYNC Configuration File = SYS:SYSTEM\TIMESYNC.CFG
```

This parameter sets the location of the TIMESYNC.CFG file. You can have a maximum of 255 characters in the full path name.

```
TIMESYNC Configured Sources = Off
```

This parameter specifies the time sources for this server to listen to. When this is set to On, the server ignores SAP time sources and listens only to those sources listed in the TIMESYNC.CFG file.

Transaction Tracking SET Commands

```
Auto TTS Backout Flag = On
```

When this parameter is set to On, it automatically answers all prompts and performs any necessary TTS backout procedures upon booting the server. This parameter must be set in STARTUP.NCF if used.

SET Little

A repeat of the earlier warning: you won't need to mess with these SET parameters very often. Earlier NetWare versions required more fiddling with these settings, but NetWare has matured, and developers are better at following NetWare application guidelines.

You'll rarely need these parameters, but check them all out at least once. You never know what the future will hold, and you may have to SET yourself a parameter one day.

PART

V

Appendices

APPENDIX **D**

DOS-Based NetWare Clients and Utilities

like to think that the average network today consists of Windows 95/98/NT and a few Windows 2000 computers. As I am reminded often enough, though, many networks have not upgraded from Windows 3.1 or even DOS. And there is nothing wrong with this. As long as the computer performs its job adequately and effectively, it does not have to be a Pentium III 1000MHz system with 512MB of RAM running Windows 2000.

The current clients for Windows 95/98/NT/2000 are discussed in Chapter 5. These are the 32-bit network clients that you should be using in newer installations of NetWare.

However, I think it is important to discuss the non-Client32 DOS and Windows 3.x client, which I call the VLM client. Anyone who is deploying new workstations should be aware of the DOS portion of this client software. The older client software is important from three perspectives:

- When installing workstations, connecting to the network for the first time is simpler when using the older client software. Often, the software you need to connect to the server will fit on a single floppy.

- Older software may make non-standard network function calls and may not be compatible with the newer Novell NetWare Client32 software.

- Some older network interface cards and network interface card drivers may not work with the newer Novell NetWare Client 32 software.

Although it shipped with NetWare 4, the simpler VLM client is no longer shipping with NetWare 5.*x*. However, you can download this client from the Novell Web site at support.novell.com. Download the Client 2.71 package, just under 9MB, and pay attention to the notice that this is the last DOS/Windows 3.1 client to be produced. This is the client software discussed in this appendix.

Let's set the record straight right now: it's nearly impossible to create a single boot disk to connect a DOS machine to a NetWare server. It's possible, but only barely, with much more work than it's worth.

If you have DOS and/or Windows 3.1 clients, use their existing NetWare client to connect to a server and install the new software from the server. Since most of the older PCs running DOS and Windows 3.1 don't have CD-ROM drives, connecting using the old NetWare client and upgrading is just about your only option.

Using the new NetWare client software for Windows 95/98 and Windows NT changes the rules quite a bit. Chapter 5 covers installing and using the new NetWare client software.

NOTE The DOS and Windows 3.*x* VLM client software does not support connecting to a NetWare server through TCP/IP. Your server should support IPX/SPX for these clients. It is possible to connect to a NetWare server running TCP/IP with these clients, but you must be using client software provided with NetWare/IP. You will find TCP/IP parameters for the NET.CFG file that are used with the TCP/IP driver from Novell LAN Workplace and LAN Workgroup.

Client Files Required for Client32 Clients

Here are the contents of the STARTNET.BAT file created by the DOS installation routine of NetWare 5.1:

```
@ECHO OFF
C:
SET NWLANGUAGE=ENGLISH
C:\NOVELL\CLIENT32\NIOS.EXE
LOAD C:\NOVELL\CLIENT32\NBIC32.NLM
LOAD C:\NOVELL\CLIENT32\LSLC32.NLM
LOAD C:\NOVELL\CLIENT32\CMSM.NLM
LOAD C:\NOVELL\CLIENT32\ETHERTSM.NLM
LOAD C:\NOVELL\CLIENT32\3C5X9.LAN FRAME=ETHERNET_802.2 PORT=300 ISA
    RXEARLY=NO
LOAD C:\NOVELL\CLIENT32\TRANNTA.NLM
LOAD C:\NOVELL\CLIENT32\IPX.NLM
LOAD C:\NOVELL\CLIENT32\SPX_SKTS.NLM
LOAD C:\NOVELL\CLIENT32\CLIENT32.NLM
```

The total disk space of these required files comes to over 1.1MB, meaning nearly a full disk. Add the requirements for the files referenced in the CONFIG.SYS and AUTOEXEC .BAT files, such as memory managers, SMARTDRV for drive caching, and SHARE, and you can see there may not be enough room no matter how much you curse as the COPY program beeps with an error message.

Each program is a TSR (terminate-and-stay-resident) program, meaning it must be loaded from DOS before starting any GUI applications. The files can load in upper memory (just like every other TSR fighting for space up there).

PART

V

Appendices

NET.CFG Means Client Network Configuration for DOS and Windows 3.*x* Clients

The NET.CFG file is a small ASCII file, normally stored in the \NOVELL\CLIENT32 directory, in which you specify custom settings for the NetWare client software on that particular workstation. NET.CFG is workstation-centric; each PC workstation will have its own NET.CFG file, not a shared version somewhere on the network. This is somewhat similar to the AUTOEXEC.BAT file that configures each PC upon startup. NET.CFG configures the workstation-to-network interface.

No, NetWare doesn't do the "right thing" and expect that an older system running DOS or Windows 3.1 has only ISA cards installed. The default is NOT ISA—so go carefully and adjust the network interface card parameters during installation, or be frustrated.

Standard NET.CFG Options for Typical Clients

During DOS and Windows 3.*x* client software installation, the installation program creates a default NET.CFG file and places it in either \NOVELL\CLIENT32 or the directory you specified to hold all client programs. The file's important lines look similar to these:

```
Link Driver 3C5X9
    FRAME Ethernet_802.2
    PORT 300
    INT 3
```

And:

```
; This is the driver default
;
    FRAME ETHERNET_802.2
    PROTOCOL IPX E0 ETHERNET_802.2
```

 WARNING Each line in the NET.CFG file, including the last, must have a hard return at the end. If you leave off the hard return on the last line, that setting or instruction will be ignored. I promise you will pull your hair trying to figure out what is wrong; I did.

There are many parameters with multiple settings inside NET.CFG, but most are not necessary under normal circumstances. Most parameters concern network interface card settings and NetWare DOS Requester options.

Rules for modifying NET.CFG are much like those for editing AUTOEXEC.BAT. You can add comments, beginning with a semicolon flush on the left margin. Imagine the NET.CFG file listed previously after the switch from Ethernet 802.3 to Ethernet 802.2. It might look like this:

```
Link Driver 3C5X9
 INT 10
 PORT 300
;  FRAME Ethernet_802.3
  Frame Ethernet_802.2
NetWare DOS Requester
FIRST NETWORK DRIVE = F
; New frame type installed 10/16/99
; Kim W
```

This example shows a good form in client management: it leaves a record of what was changed, when it was changed, and who changed it. Obviously not a real-world example.

Of the long list of NET.CFG parameters and settings, six are the most popular:

- EXCLUDE VLM=*path_vlm/vlm_name.VLM* specifies a .VLM file that VLM.EXE should not load. This parameter causes any .VLM file listed in the VLM.EXE program default load table or in the VLM=*vlm_path/vlm_name.VLM* parameter to not load when the VLM.EXE program runs. You must specify the complete filename, including the .VLM extension. You must list this parameter after the NetWare Protocol section. For example, the following lines exclude printing support, security, and management diagnostics:

```
EXCLUDE VLM=C:\NWCLIENT\PRINT.VLM
EXCLUDE VLM=C:\NWCLIENT\SECURITY.VLM
EXCLUDE VLM=C:\NWCLIENT\NMR.VLM
```

- FIRST NETWORK DRIVE=*A–Z* sets the first network drive to the letter of choice when the NetWare DOS Requester makes a connection to the NetWare server. This parameter accepts only the drive letter and not the colon. The default setting is the first available drive letter.

- NAME CONTEXT=*"name_context"* allows you to set your current position in the NDS tree structure. This parameter applies only to workstations connecting to a NetWare 4 network. The default is the root, which may cause confusion if duplicate user names exist. The quotation marks are required in this parameter setting. An example is

```
NAME CONTEXT="OU=INTEGRATE.O=GCS"
PREFERRED SERVER=312_NW
```

- PREFERRED TREE=*any_tree_name* sets the tree you want to connect to first in a NetWare 4 network if you have multiple trees. If the tree specified has a server with a free connection, the NetWare DOS Requester attaches to that tree (obviously, this option is not necessary in a single-tree network). An example is

  ```
  PREFERRED TREE=MARKETING
  ```

- SHOW DOTS=[ON/OFF] sets whether the . and .. entries appear in directory listings. The NetWare server doesn't have directory entries for . and .. as DOS does. To see . and .. in directory listings, use SHOW DOTS=ON. File Manager utilities will be hindered if you can't move to a parent directory or subdirectory. The default setting is OFF. Setting SHOW DOTS=ON makes NetWare behave more like pure DOS for utilities and applications.

The most popular options vary per network, of course. If none of these look applicable, don't feel bad. If these don't cover your special circumstances, read the help screens (and your old NetWare manuals) to see many more options for the NET.CFG file.

Link Support Options

The Link Support section of the NET.CFG file can be used to configure the number and size of the receive buffers, the size of the memory pool buffers, and the number of boards and stacks used by the Link Support Layer (LSL). You can also use this option to configure the LSL environment for managing Named Pipes and NetBIOS sessions.

The parameter

```
BUFFERS number_of_buffers[buffer_size]
```

configures the number and size of receive buffers that the LSL will maintain. For example

```
LINK SUPPORT
 BUFFERS=15 2800
```

sets fifteen, 2800-byte buffers.

The number of communication buffers must be large enough to hold all media headers and the maximum data size. If you make many connections, you should increase the number of buffers to improve performance. See the manufacturer's specifications for the settings available for third-party protocol stacks.

Buffer size is optional. The minimum size for IPX is 618 bytes. The buffer number multiplied by the buffer size (plus the header information) cannot be greater than 65,536 bytes. For example, 20 buffers multiplied by 1514 bytes equals 30,280 bytes.

The other Link Support option parameter is

```
MEMPOOL number
```

Some protocols use this option to configure the size of the memory pool buffers that the LSL program will maintain. For example

```
LINK SUPPORT
MEMPOOL=1024
```

sets memory pool buffers at 1024 bytes.

Protocol IPX Options

Use the Protocol IPX options of the NET.CFG file to change the default value of the parameter settings for the IPX protocol. For example, a protocol usually binds to the first network board it finds. The BIND parameter forces the protocol to bind to the boards you specify. The parameter

```
PROTOCOL IPX
 BIND=NE2000
```

binds to one NE2000 board.

The parameter

```
PROTOCOL IPX
 BIND=NE2000 #2, #3
```

binds to boards 2 and 3. Board numbers are displayed when you load the network board drivers. Note that the equal sign is optional; you could enter the command as just

```
BIND NE2000
```

PART

V

Appendices

Remaining DOS Utilities

Not quite all the NetWare DOS utilities are gone, but most are. There are nine utilities useful to an administrator like you, but only a couple useful to a user.

CAPTURE

Back when networking was new and DOS remained clueless about how to deal with printers not tied directly to the PC, CAPTURE saved the day for NetWare clients. CAPTURE fooled DOS into thinking a printer was waiting at LPT1:, but really it was the NetWare client software redirecting the print output to the NetWare print server.

Still visible in the Red N taskbar menu, CAPTURE provides easy ways to set the printer and multiple printout details via a command line. Novell may not dare show you the command line from the taskbar N, but it's still there.

All the options available through the taskbar Settings command button are available through the command line. A couple of examples:

CAPTURE /?	Help screens
CAPTURE P=P1	Capture to network printer 1
CAPTURE Q=Q1	Capture to print queue Q1
CAPTURE EC or CAPTURE ENDCAP	Stop capture
CAPTURE /SH	Show captured printer settings

You may no longer use the command ENDCAP to stop the capture. Rely on one of the two options listed above. Users will rarely have need of this utility.

NPRINT

Used to print existing files directly to a network printer, NPRINT offers the networked version of the DOS PRINT command (remember that?). You can list several files on one command line as long as the filenames are separated by commas. All the CAPTURE settings concerning the number of copies and the like are supported by NPRINT:

NPRINT /? Help screens

Users will almost never use NPRINT, and they didn't use it all that much back in the old days, either.

CX

Context hit the NetWare world like a water balloon, making a big mess everywhere as people grappled with the idea of object-oriented networking. Clever login scripts, the NetWare Application Launcher, and the Universal Naming Convention support (such as \\PROLIANT\PROLIAN_SYS) have just about eliminated the need for CX for administrators and made the utility completely obsolete for users:

CX /? Help files

The one value of CX to modern administrators comes when quickly obtaining a list of certain objects within a context helps a troubleshooting situation. CX /T will print out a list of major objects in the container, and other options will give more depth.

FLAG

Early on, setting file attributes for certain files for ill-designed networking applications appeared to be black magic. Files had to be a wild mixture of shareable and non-shareable to guarantee file integrity.

Such problems are behind us, but FLAG remains. When do I use FLAG? When I want to delete an entire directory structure and some read-only files somewhere screw up the deletion process.

Try using FLAG *.* N to set all the files to Normal, which for NetWare is Read and Write, including delete and modify rights. If a file inside the directory structure tree has the Read Only attribute set, FLAG will cure it. This is true on NetWare hard drives, of course, not personal computers.

LOGIN and LOGOUT

Yes, the command line allows a user to log in or log out, believe it or not. Users won't believe that either of these actions are possible unless they click a command button, but they are possible.

LOGIN by itself will prompt for a user name. LOGIN and the user name (LOGIN james) will bypass the question.

LOGOUT clears the network decks. If you wish to log out only from a particular server for some reason, you can do so by specifying the same (LOGOUT proliant).

MAP

MAP is another command-line utility users won't believe. (You mean I have to type the name of the server? Yuck!) Yes, users are spoiled, and that's good. If this networking stuff were as easy as the marketing blurbs promise, you and I both would be looking for work.

MAP F:=PROLIANT_SYS: is the command to link Drive F: to the root of SYS: on PROLIANT. Type **MAP** from any command line to see the existing mapped drives, and copy those examples. Users won't do this, particularly since they can achieve the same result with graphical utilities such as the N on the taskbar or Network Neighborhood.

PURGE

PURGE is not an eating disorder, but a way to clear files that have been deleted but are still hanging around on the disk in case you want to SALVAGE them. (Oops, SALVAGE is no longer. Use FILER or NWADMN32 to reclaim deleted files.)

RIGHTS

Here's the utility to check or modify trustee assignments or inherited rights filters for volumes, directories, and files. Typing RIGHTS on a command line by itself will tell you the rights you have, which will be all of them for Admin users or equivalent.

PART

V

Appendices

File rights used to be a big problem, because installation routines weren't smart enough to handle the RIGHTS command. New applications wouldn't respond properly, or they would tell users that a file wasn't there, because they had no rights to that file or directory. Today, however, this utility is another one hanging around after its time is over.

As with the DOS ATTRIB utility, you add rights with a + (plus) and delete them with a – (minus).

SETPASS

Quickly, go to your NetWare servers and delete SETPASS from the SYS:\PUBLIC directory on each and every server. Security controls are bad enough without users changing passwords to all sorts of things, leaving no trail and no chance for help desk people to figure out what the heck they did.

Are your users always smart enough to set their own password? Do you let them change the password all the time? How will you help them when they call and complain that they can't remember their password?

Nobody likes passwords (even administrators, although we realize that users have no business changing their password to something we can't control). If a user (it will happen) resets their password and forgets it, they can't change it back.

Do yourself a favor, and your users too, for once, and declare that SETPASS doesn't exist. If a user says they read about it, blame Novell and their policy of doing away with DOS utilities.

Don't let your users play with SETPASS. If you do let them, don't come crying to me.

A Word of Advice for Managers Dealing with DOS and Windows 3.1 Clients

Don't change anything on these clients. These people either don't like to change or they refuse to change. Otherwise, they would have changed already.

If you can't leave the old NetWare server supporting the (no doubt) custom applications running on these old workstations, copy the files over carefully to the new NetWare servers. Take care that all drive mappings and the rest match exactly what these users had before the upgrade.

Repeat: don't change anything on these old clients. The grief and frustration will overwhelm any supposed productivity gains. Trust me, you don't want to upgrade DOS and Windows 3.1 clients if you can possibly avoid it.

APPENDIX E

Using Macintoshes with NetWare 5.1

Novell was the first desktop LAN company to support Apple's Macintosh computer. First released in December 1988, NetWare's support for Apple networking became the preferred high-performance server operating system for Macintosh networks.

In NetWare 4.1, the Macintosh became a full citizen in a NetWare network. Starting with NetWare 4.1, Novell included the MacNDS client software, which uses the IPX protocol to connect Macintosh clients directly to native NetWare 4 servers. The native Macintosh interface could now take advantage of all NetWare server NDS functions and use the IPX network rather than AppleTalk.

NetWare 5.1 is a milestone release for Novell in many respects, with its native TCP/IP support, a new management interface, and more. Another thing that makes this release noteworthy is that Novell continues to unbundle the Macintosh file and print services; this first happened with NetWare 5.0. In order to provide a more Macintosh-savvy product, Novell has licensed Prosoft Engineering, Inc., a long-time Macintosh developer, to develop, distribute, and support NetWare for Macintosh file server services and NetWare for Macintosh client software.

This new product will provide new features for the Macintosh client and will be optimized for Apple's latest operating system, Mac OS 9, and the newest G4 computers. The enhanced client will also include support for TCP/IP networking, enhanced security services, and Novell Storage Services (NSS).

NOTE For more information on the Prosoft Macintosh support product for NetWare 5.1, visit the Prosoft Engineering Web site at www.prosofteng.com. You can also visit the companion pages to *Mastering NetWare 5.1* on the Sybex Web site for updated information on the Prosoft Engineering product when it is released. Point your browser to www.sybex.com and click Catalog to search for this book's components.

Before we get to the Prosoft specifics, I thought I would give you a brief introduction to some Macintosh concepts and networking terms.

Network Services for the Macintosh

NetWare for Macintosh software (a group of NLM programs) provides these capabilities:

- Macintosh users can share files with non-Macintosh users.
- Macintosh users can send print jobs to NetWare queues.
- Non-Macintosh users can send print jobs to AppleTalk printers on AppleTalk networks.

Don't get too excited by that first point; the Macintosh is still a completely different computer from the PC. You can share files between Macintosh systems and non-Macintosh systems, but this only helps when the applications on each client can read and understand the file's structure. There is no magic translator built into NetWare that enables a Macintosh to run PC software or vice versa. However, many application programs are realizing the value of a common file format, regardless of the client operating system.

The Coming of the Common File Format

WordPerfect was the first major software vendor to guarantee that an application file from one client could be used by any other WordPerfect client on any other platform.

The state of desktop computing interoperability when WordPerfect made this cross-platform file sharing a reality was dismal. Clients supported by WordPerfect included the TI PC, the Victor 9000, the DEC Rainbow, and the AT&T 6300, each with its own unique version of DOS. The idea of connecting WordPerfect's first platform, Data General, or any Unix systems in a meaningful way was essentially impossible.

Today, the world is a much more integrated place. Many of the major software applications have a common file format, or they can read and write other file formats without needing a separate conversion step. So the easy connection of Macintosh, OS/2, Unix, and PC clients to a NetWare 5.1 network makes even more sense today than in the mid-1980s.

PART

V

Appendices

Macintosh Networking Crash Course

If you are a PC person faced with Macintosh networking decisions, you need a bit of background. A grip on your patience won't hurt, either. Macintosh systems take a different approach to networking, but all the systems will work together.

The Macintosh was truly network-ready from the beginning. It included a built-in LocalTalk network port that you could use to communicate with Macintosh file servers (called AppleShare servers) and any printer on the LocalTalk network. In 1985, when most PC users were not even dreaming of connectivity, the Macintosh was already network-aware.

Let's get a few basic terms under control. Everyone likes it better when outsiders learn the lingo, and Macintosh networking lingo is different from NetWare terminology.

AppleTalk   The proprietary protocol suite from Apple Computer that provides a peer-to-peer network architecture. Ease of installation is a moot point; AppleTalk is standard on every Macintosh. Each device on the network must have a unique address within the range set for the network.

AppleTalk node   An addressable device on a network, such as a computer, printer, or server.

AppleTalk stack   The suite of AppleTalk protocols that supports functions, such as file and print services.

AppleTalk internetwork   Two or more AppleTalk networks connected by AppleTalk router(s). The routers and supporting protocols are necessary to find machines on the other sides of routers.

AppleTalk zone   A logical grouping of nodes. Any grouping is allowed, much like an Organizational Unit in NetWare. The zones often are grouped as Organizational Units, collecting nodes and network resources by geographical area, departmental use, or function.

AppleTalk router   Hardware and/or software that connects AppleTalk networks so that all nodes in each network can find and use resources from the other network.

AppleTalk Phase 2   Released in 1989. Some new services were added, and some old services were extended. Some of the advantages include support for more than 254 nodes per network and for up to eight AppleTalk networks connected by the AppleTalk Internet router.

Extended AppleTalk network   An AppleTalk network that supports Phase 2 extensions, such as zone lists and network ranges. Novell documentation often refers to this as an *extended network*.

Non-extended AppleTalk network   An AppleTalk network that does not support Phase 2 extensions.

Configuring Networking on the Macintosh

If you are a PC person, you need to be familiar with a few Macintosh features in order to set up the Macintosh to use the network properly. The first is the Apple menu. This is the colorful Apple logo in the upper-left corner of the screen. The Windows 95/98 Start button is similar to the Apple menu, but the Apple menu had a 10-year head start.

The next feature is the AppleTalk Control Panel. To get to the AppleTalk Control Panel, choose the Apple menu ➤ Control Panel ➤ AppleTalk. From this screen, you can configure the interface that the Macintosh will use to communicate with the network. On a typical Macintosh, the choices may include the following:

- LocalTalk port
- EtherTalk (Ethernet) port
- TokenTalk (Token Ring) port
- Modem port (if a modem is installed)
- Infrared port (for Apple PowerBooks)

AppleTalk can only be configured to use one interface at a time.

The final item is the Chooser, which is the equivalent of the Windows 95/98 Network Neighborhood. From the Chooser, you can select which server volumes you have on your Macintosh desktop and which network printer you are using.

AppleTalk, EtherTalk, TokenTalk, and the Seven Layers of OSI

A nicely layered protocol, AppleTalk fits well into the OSI (Open Systems Interconnection) network model. Let's take a look at this from the bottom up and remember the discussions in the first chapter about IPX and TCP/IP as we go through these layers.

At the Physical and Data Link layers (1 and 2):

- Ethernet—ELAP (EtherTalk Link Access Protocol), which is Apple's version of 10Mbps Ethernet. Phase 1 is modeled on Ethernet 2.0 (different from Ethernet 802.3). Phase 2 is modeled after Ethernet 802.3. This is now the default network connection for Macintosh computers made after 1989.

- FDDI—FLAP (FDDITalk Link Access Protocol), which is Apple's implementation of the 100Mbps FDDI (Fiber Distributed Data Interface) networking standard.

- TokenTalk—TLAP (TokenTalk Link Access Protocol), which is Apple's support for both the 4Mbps and 16Mbps Token Ring from IEEE 802.5 and IBM, respectively. Only Phase 2 supports TokenTalk.

- LocalTalk—LLAP (LocalTalk Link Access Protocol), which is Apple's 230Kbps network for AppleTalk, shipped with every Macintosh since the original unit. The cable is UTP, with RS-422 connectors or small DIN connectors.

- Serial (RS-422)—ARAP (AppleTalk Remote Access Protocol), which is for remote connections over a serial line, such as over a modem.

PART

V

Appendices

At the Network layer (3):

- AARP (AppleTalk Address Resolution Protocol), which maps network addresses to physical addresses.
- DDP (Datagram Delivery Protocol), which prepares packets for the network.

At the Transport layer (4):

- RTMP (Routing Table Maintenance Protocol), which is a mechanism for routers to exchange information concerning routes and building each router's connection table. Internetworks use RTMP constantly.
- AURP (AppleTalk Update Routing Protocol), which is similar to RTMP, but sends updates only after a network change.
- AEP (AppleTalk Echo Protocol), which is similar to TCP/IP PING. It bounces packets off another node to ensure that data can be transmitted.
- ATP (AppleTalk Transaction Protocol), which provides reliable request and response for transaction reliability.
- NBP (Name Binding Protocol), which connects device names with network addresses. It is transparent to the user and to the Macintosh Chooser application.

At the Session layer (5):

- ADSP (AppleTalk Data Stream Protocol), which sets a full-duplex data connection between two nodes for reliable delivery.
- ASDSP (AppleTalk Secure Data Stream Protocol), which provides extra security for ADSP.
- ZIP (Zone Information Protocol), which associates zone names with network addresses and uses queries to maintain the network information when new zones are added. ZIP provides a means of finding a particular node in a large internet.
- ASP (AppleTalk Session Protocol), which adds reliability to ATP.
- PAP (Printer Access Protocol), which allows Macintosh clients to connect to print services on the network.

At the Presentation and Application layers (6 and 7):

- AFP (AppleTalk Filing Protocol), which is an Application-level protocol to allow file and printer sharing.
- PostScript, which displays and prints output language.

You should be able to see many similarities between TCP/IP, IPX/SPX, and AppleTalk. The original LocalTalk network for Macintosh systems had too little horse-power to be much more than a printer-sharing network, but EtherTalk and TokenTalk have made the Macintosh a contender in the corporate market.

Macintosh Network Addresses and Zones

Somewhat similar to IP addressing, each AppleTalk network is assigned a unique num-ber, and each node in that network refers to that number. Packets addressed to a node must provide both the network and node addresses in the following format:

```
network#.node#
```

The network number is two bytes; the node number is only one.

When a node connects to an AppleTalk network, a number is assigned for the node number. The station remembers that number and tries to use it again the next time the station connects to the network. If the station can't use the same number, it will look for the next available number to use.

The network numbers are a little more involved. The advance in Phase 2 allows each network multiple network numbers for a single network. Each network number can support a maximum of 253 network nodes.

The network range for extended networks is expressed as two numbers, such as 1000 to 1010. These numbers in the range must be unique. Another network cannot use the same range or overlap any of the first network's address. You multiply the number of addresses in the range, in this case 10, by the 253 allowable addresses for nodes, for a possibility of 2530 individual nodes. There is no limit to network range, but you should keep the size down to maintain performance.

AppleTalk routers must always connect networks with different numbers. There-fore, a network can't come back around and route to itself by accident or connect to networks with conflicting network numbers. AppleTalk bridges must connect network segments with the same number range.

A zone is more a group than a physical limitation. Although the name *zone* implies a geographical area, any node may belong to many zones or not belong to any zone. The zones may cross network boundaries and contain nodes from many networks. The name usually indicates the zone's function, such as ACCOUNTING, SALES, or GRAPHICS. Quite often, the Chooser and other applications use zones to organize devices into groups for easy reference. Zones also tend to have a server as part of the zone. The zone acts as a top-level organizer in the Chooser.

A zone list may contain as many as 255 zone names. One zone is configured as the default zone. New workstations connecting to the network send an NBP broadcast request. A router will continue broadcasting the packets and even forward them to another zone name if necessary.

Here is a sampling of what happens when your Macintosh comes on the network:

- Your Macintosh sends out NBP request packets (similar to a NetWare client sending "get nearest server" packets when starting).

- Routers send the NBP requests to networks associated with the selected zone name. These requests will be sent to other networks as necessary.

- Routers directly connected to a network associated with the selected zone broadcast the NBP request to every node in the zone.

- Services in the selected zone send NBP reply packets to the original Macintosh. The service names of available resources are displayed in the Chooser.

The network range for AppleTalk Phase 1 is a single number (for example, 12-12). NetWare for Macintosh supports AppleTalk Phase 1. But if your systems were bought within the last few years, AppleTalk Phase 2 is probably all you need to worry about.

Preparing to Install Macintosh Services

Above and beyond the amount of server resources necessary to support your disk space and concurrent users, another ration of RAM is needed for the Macintosh NLMs. Here's the official version of required memory resources for the NetWare 4 product:

- 1MB for NLMs, but subtract 500KB if BTRIEVE is already loaded on your server. I would bump this up by a couple of extra MB just to be on the safe side.

- 12KB per active AFP session.

- 10KB per Macintosh connection.

- 20KB per ATPS (AppleTalk Print Services) print server.

- 20KB per ATPS spooler.

- 10KB per concurrent ATPS spooler user.

- 20KB per ATXRP (AppleTalk eXtender Remote Printer) printer.

The important numbers are the 1MB for the NLMs and the 10KB for each Macintosh on the network. Throw in a handful of RAM for each printer and print user, and you need at least 2MB no matter how few Macintosh clients you have. I always try to estimate on the cautious side when planning memory requirements, so I think I would start with about 5MB of additional RAM, even for a minimal number of clients. Remember, RAM makes the world go 'round—or at least makes your network go 'round faster. If you need to support Macintosh clients, make the department with the Macintoshes throw some server memory into the deal.

Let's get some of the official business out of the way. The NLMs are loaded (and function) by server, not by network. The support for Macintosh filenames is done by volume, not by server.

Be aware that Macintosh systems almost always use the frame type ETHERNET_ SNAP (Sub-Network Access Protocol, a variant of an 802.2 packet). This frame type is not normally used with PCs and Unix systems, so it may not be configured on any of your server network interface boards. The documentation is not always clear about this, and it is a tidbit of information you may not even know about if you have never worked with a Macintosh network.

If you assume that the frame type will be added automatically, as I did, or that the Macintosh will see the 802.3 or 802.2 frame types, you will waste a day trying to figure out why the Chooser in the Macintosh client doesn't see any zones or your Net-Ware server. This warning comes from personal experience. You may configure MacIPX a different way, but it's difficult to get your first Macintosh connected to gain access to the Macintosh client files until you get your frame type under control.

Configuring the AppleTalk Stack

Before installing Macintosh services, you should configure the AppleTalk protocol. You can configure the NetWare 5.1 server to support AppleTalk even without the Prosoft services for Macintosh. This is done through the INETCFG (Internetworking Configuration) program. You can reach this screen by typing **LOAD INETCFG** at the server console prompt.

The seven Internetworking Configuration menu items are as follows:

Boards   Add, delete, and configure interface boards. For each board in the server, configure the board name, interrupt, I/O base address, node address (to override the setting on the interface board), number of retries to redo a failed transmission, memory base address if used by the board, and a space for a comment.

Network Interfaces   Configure the network interfaces on configured boards. If there is more than one board, this screen allows you to choose the board on which to make future modifications.

WAN Call Directory Add, delete, and modify WAN call destinations. This item is used only if a WAN driver is installed in the server.

Protocols Configure the Network-layer protocols, such as IPX, TCP/IP, and AppleTalk. Allows you to view the enabled or unconfigured protocols on the server. For AppleTalk, choose to configure AppleTalk and set the details in the AppleTalk Configuration screen.

Bindings Connect a particular protocol to a particular network interface. Opens the Configured Protocol To Network Interface Binding screen, allowing you to connect a protocol to an interface.

Manage Configuration Configure other server information not included above. Set SNMP (Simple Network Management Protocol) details, export or import the configuration to a disk, configure the remote access profile for this server, and edit the AUTOEXEC.NCF file.

View Configuration View in Read-Only mode the various configuration commands used in the AUTOEXEC.NCF and INETCFG.NCF files. You can also view the console log.

Several of these options are of no use in setting up AppleTalk. Let's go through the ones that we need now.

The Boards and Network Interfaces Options

If you have more than one network adapter in the server, you must choose which one to use. That happens in the Network Interfaces menu item. If that's your situation, choose the board that will connect to the network with the Macintosh computers.

The Protocols Option

Figure E.1 shows the submenu that appears when you choose Internetworking Configuration ➤ Protocols.

Along with AppleTalk and IPX, the other choices on the Protocol Configuration menu are:

Source Route End Station Enables the Source Routing Router (ROUTE.NLM) program for Token Ring and/or FDDI network adapters.

TCP/IP Sets the details for TCP/IP protocol support on this server. (See Chapter 14 for details.)

User-Specified Protocol Load List A place to load miscellaneous NLM files to perform other functions not covered with the previous choices.

FIGURE E.1

*Preparing to configure
the AppleTalk protocol*

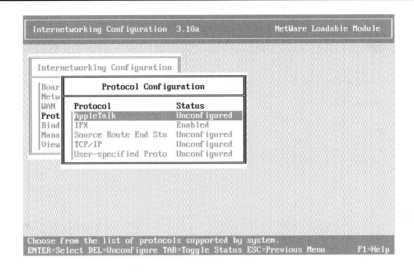

Now you need all the AppleTalk zone and network number information you gathered before starting. Three tables present the descriptions and options for three different network setups. Figure E.2 shows the middle configuration described by the NetWare electronic documentation.

FIGURE E.2

*The middle-road
AppleTalk
configuration*

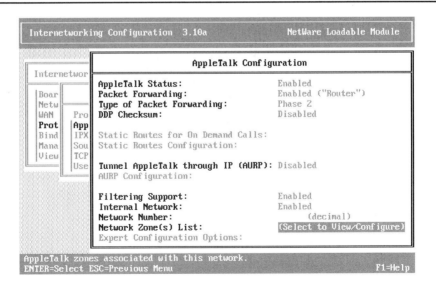

Table E.1 shows the default settings and options for these fields.

TABLE E.1: APPLETALK CONFIGURATION FIELDS

Field	Description
AppleTalk Status	Starting state. If this setting is Enabled, AppleTalk will activate during system startup. Disabled leaves the configuration intact but not active. The default is Enabled once you open this screen.
Packet Forwarding	Decides whether the server acts like a Macintosh workstation (end node) or a router. If it acts like a router, nodes can access services on other networks. The default is Disabled (end node).
Type Of Packet Forwarding	NetWare for Macintosh is a Phase 2 router but will work with a Phase 1 router if your network dictates. Transition forced Phase 2 restrictions to comply with Phase 1 routers, particularly limiting the network range to one (4–4, not 4–6) and a single zone name. This appears only if Packet Forwarding is Enabled. The default is Phase 2.
DDP Checksum	DDP (Datagram Delivery Protocol) is used to deliver packets between nodes on different subnetworks. This setting depends on your settings for existing nodes and routers. The default is Disabled.
Static Routes For On-Demand Calls	Listing of particular addresses to contact when demanded.
Static Routes Configuration	Route addressing and location details.
Tunnel AppleTalk Through IP (AURP)	AURP (AppleTalk Update Routing Protocol) uses a link-state algorithm to determine routes through an internetwork. AURP allows you to connect separate AppleTalk networks through a TCP/IP tunnel, similar to IP Tunnel for NetWare. TCP/IP must be fully configured before AURP can be activated and configured. The default is Disabled.
Filtering Support	Allows you to filter AppleTalk using the FILTERCFG program. The default is Disabled.
Internal Network	Allows the server to support AppleTalk applications. When this is enabled, applications can choose between having the application get an address on the internal network or one of the bound LAN interfaces. The default is Disabled.
Network Number	Sets the internal network number to a unique number for your AppleTalk network. The range is one to 65,279.

Continued ▶

	TABLE E.1 (CONTINUED): APPLETALK CONFIGURATION FIELDS	
Field	**Description**
Network Zone(s) List	Zone name(s) with one to 32 characters, including any printable characters and embedded spaces. Type the zone name(s) as used in your network. The case you use in typing the name is the case that will be displayed on the Macintosh nodes later. You will need to set one of the zones as the default zone.
Expert Configuration Options	Name of the vendor providing AppleTalk over X.25 on the other peer. The options are Novell, Cisco, and Other.

When you make your choices and press the Escape key, you will have a chance to write all the changes made in this screen into a configuration file. But the protocol won't do you any good until it's bound to a network interface card. That's what the Bindings option lets you do.

The Bindings Option

Figure E.3 shows where the AppleTalk protocol is bound to a network interface. In our example, it's bound to an Ethernet card that uses the NE2000 driver supplied by Novell.

PART

V

Appendices

FIGURE E.3

Adding AppleTalk to the protocol mix

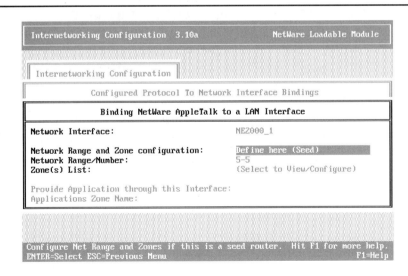

```
Internetworking Configuration  3.10a          NetWare Loadable Module


   ┌ Internetworking Configuration ┐
   ├────────────────────────────────────────────────────────────┤
   │     Configured Protocol To Network Interface Bindings        │
   ├────────────────────────────────────────────────────────────┤
   │      Binding NetWare AppleTalk to a LAN Interface            │
   │                                                              │
   │ Network Interface:                    NE2000_1               │
   │                                                              │
   │ Network Range and Zone configuration: Define here (Seed)     │
   │ Network Range/Number:                 5-5                     │
   │ Zone(s) List:                         (Select to View/Configure)│
   │                                                              │
   │ Provide Application through this Interface:                  │
   │ Applications Zone Name:                                      │
   └────────────────────────────────────────────────────────────┘


 Configure Net Range and Zones if this is a seed router.  Hit F1 for more help.
 ENTER=Select ESC=Previous Menu                                    F1=Help
```

We reached this point by choosing the Bindings option back on the Internetworking Configuration menu. This is where you return after saving the earlier AppleTalk configuration information.

If one of the previously configured IPX protocol frame types does not include ETHERNET_SNAP, configure that before starting the AppleTalk protocol configuration. Press the Insert key at the Configured Protocol To Network Interface Bindings screen, seen in the background in Figure E.3. The menu doesn't say whether you have ETHERNET_SNAP configured, so you must check each IPX protocol interface already defined for this frame type.

Once the ETHERNET_SNAP detail is taken care of, press Insert again to add the AppleTalk protocol bindings. The Network Range And Zone Configuration field needs the same information provided in the last section—in our case, a seed router, because this is the first AppleTalk router on our network. The Network Range/Number field needs a different number from the 10 we used previously. The 10 was used as an internal network number; this is for external use. The Zone(s) List field works the same way: enter the zone name you provided earlier. Then press the Escape key twice to return to the Internetworking Configuration menu once again.

The Manage Configuration and View Configuration Options

The penultimate choice on the Internetworking Configuration menu offers a way to manage the configurations. Currently, we don't need to edit the AUTOEXEC.NCF, because the INETCFG program moves the protocol and bindings part of the AUTOEXEC.NCF to another file (NETINFO.CFG in SYS:ETC), which is reached only by the INETCFG program.

The last choice, View Configuration, offers a chance to see all your newly configured INETCFG commands. You may peruse them in a group or separated into LAN, WAN, Protocol, and Protocol Bind Commands submenus. When you've finished perusing, press Escape.

You will be warned that changes made in the INETCFG program are not active until the system is rebooted. This makes sense, because all the changes happen in the AUTOEXEC.NCF file and other startup files such as INETCFG.NCF. Select Yes to Exit Configuration. And remember—you must reboot for anything new to happen.

Adding the Macintosh Name Space

Though you may have chosen which NetWare volumes will support Macintosh files during installation, you may later need to add additional volumes. By default, NetWare volumes do not support Macintosh files. Macintosh file support is handled by the MAC.NAM program, which should be loaded in the STARTUP.NCF file.

You should make sure that the SYS:SYSTEM directory has a copy of this file in it. If other volumes have the name space configured, the startup programs may not be able to find the MAC.NAM program. By default, the installation program puts this file in the C:\NWSERVER directory in the DOS partition. Once the SYS: volume becomes active, the server startup directory may no longer be seen; the DOS partition of the server is not available to the NetWare server software. Make life simple by copying the MAC.NAM program to the SYS:SYSTEM directory if the installation program has not already placed it there. Once there, it will always be found whenever you try to start the Macintosh name space on any volume for that server.

Support Pack 2 for NetWare 5.0 added a file called V_MAC.NLM. This program is used by VREPAIR (Volume Repair) to fix Macintosh volume-related problems. There used to be a copy of this file in the SYS:SYSTEM directory and a copy in the C:\NWSERVER directory, but now there's only one in C:\NWSERVER.

The quickest way to add Macintosh name space support to a volume is to use the server console prompt. You need to do this only once per volume. For example, say you want to add Macintosh name space support to a volume called USER1. First, make sure that the MAC.NAM program is loaded, and then at the server console prompt, type

```
ADD NAME SPACE MAC TO USER1
```

The disk will crunch and churn for a couple of minutes, and then it will return you to the colon prompt.

 WARNING Do not add Macintosh support to a volume that is nearly full, because there won't be room to add the extra overhead for the filename translation. Also, do not add Macintosh support to a volume supporting only one or two Macintosh clients if you can avoid it. The performance impact will be higher than if you moved a few extra directories to a volume that already supports the Macintosh.

NetWare 5.1 for AppleShare from Prosoft Engineering

I have to admit, I'm surprised that Novell dumped their Macintosh support with the release of NetWare 5.0, since that came close to the release of the iMac and a resurgence of Macintosh fortunes in the workplace. Yes, I know that all the Web additions to NetWare 5.1 support all clients, including Macs. But I must tell you: it grates painfully to run my wife's Macintosh through a Windows NT 4.0 server because it converts PostScript output for HP LaserJet printers. I'm writing a NetWare book and listening to my wife connect through NT? That's not right. Novell; you blew it.

Be that as it may, the Prosoft people seem well equipped to mash NetWare into a fine AppleTalk server and to provide excellent NetWare client software for Macintosh systems. I just believe that Novell's distance from Macintosh today reeks of a strategic error and a surrender to Windows NT, which I hate to see on any basis. But enough kvetching for now. Let's see some software.

Making NetWare 5.1 Service Macintosh Clients

After reading most of this heavy book, you should realize that I prefer to make changes as seldom as possible. Prosoft Engineering products offer the choice of making a NetWare server an AppleTalk server without changing any clients whatsoever. I prefer this method to using their NetWare client for Macintosh, even though I have only a single Macintosh to integrate. But my wife gets really aggravated when I mess with her computer, so I'll add AppleTalk support to the PROLIANT server and not have to touch her computer at all. That's definitely the safest option.

Before you start with the Prosoft installation, verify that all the NetWare AppleTalk functions are configured following the examples earlier in this appendix. We'll use the NetWare control programs for management in just a bit.

If you haven't used any Macintosh support previously, feel free to overwrite any printer definitions and the like. You won't have any configurations to save, and the Prosoft drivers are better than what ships with NetWare 5.1.

You may install this product from the CD-ROM by loading the CD into the server drive, or take the easy way out (my favorite) and copy the files to the NetWare server in question. There are only 18MB of files on the CD, so you should have room.

From NWCONFIG, choose Install Products Not Listed under the Products menu heading. Follow the Prosoft directions and point NWCONFIG to the (in my case) SYS:\PROSOFT\PRODUCTS\NWMAC directory. Files will zoom by (not many, though), and you'll have to make some choices. They're easy choices, as illustrated in Figure E.4.

The Macintosh name space will be added to your volume, files will churn even more than before, and you'll come to the AppleShare Configuration screen. Take a look at Figure E.5 for those details.

FIGURE E.4

Easy installation questions

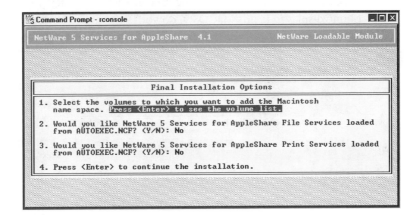

FIGURE E.5

Your window into MacLand

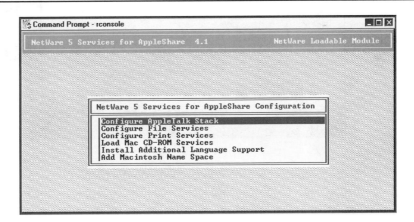

The first choice, Configure AppleTalk Stack, pops you back into INETCFG to verify all the things we did earlier. Remember my earlier note about configuring ETHERNET_ SNAP? If you don't do it, you will pull hair by the double handfuls, so check that con- figuration carefully. Your Macs won't see your servers if you don't have the right pro- tocol for them.

There are three small files to put on your Mac clients, but they don't change the Mac nearly as much as the full Prosoft NetWare Clients for Macintosh change things. Use the CD, and you'll quickly get the files copied and your Macintosh ready to go.

And go it does. Take a look at Figure E.6. You don't often see a full NetWare server volume displayed inside Mac OS 9, do you?

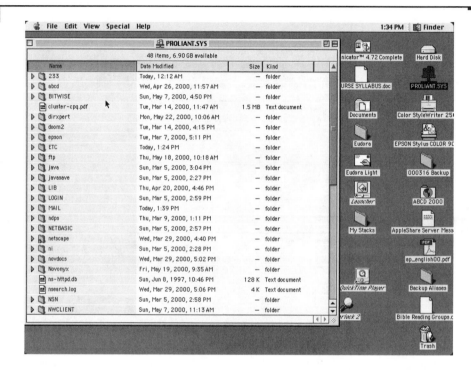

Sorry you can't see the ProLiant icon on the right of the screen, toward the top. It's the PROLIANT.SYS icon, and it shows a little red apple on the folder. I suppose it's red for NetWare. The same icon is on the header for the primary window, but it's pretty small there. And you can't tell what color the network line is in this screen shot (red).

Helping Macintosh and PC Users Work Together

Many PC people like to harangue Apple people for their arrogance. Do they suppose no one in the PC side of computing has an ego? I can point them to, oh, at least three or four PC company executives and/or owners with egos the size of small cities. At least a couple of these people have egos the size of large countries.

Besides, if your ideas really are better than everyone else's, are you being arrogant or just truthful? The first Macintosh came loaded with friendliness before user interface meant anything to anyone. The existing systems at that time had no user interface; there was an empty screen daring you to guess what to do. Whether the Apple design crew developed the interface themselves or borrowed the ideas from our friends at Xerox PARC is not part of this discussion. That's a whole other book.

The problem, of course, comes when either someone else trumps your idea or when you have a new idea that's not better, just different. Can you objectively look at your idea and the competing ideas and honestly judge between them? Sadly, history answers no to that question. Worse, some people start to reject ideas simply because their company didn't develop them, refusing to take advantage of advancing technology.

So it happened with Apple. The science of human/computer interfacing has caught up to them. The price/performance computing curve passed them long ago, although the iMac product line puts the prices of equivalent PC and Macintosh systems closer than ever before.

A lot has changed with Apple over the past several years, but they still produce interesting and unusual products and facilitate interesting results by Macintosh users. Adding them to your NetWare client mix will only help.

PART

V

Appendices

APPENDIX **F**

Recommended Reading

T he books listed here are those that I used as references while writing this book. I've included a few brief descriptions, so you can get an idea of whether you will benefit from reading these books (in addition to the one you're holding in your hands now, of course).

General Reading

Mastering Local Area Networks, Christa Anderson and Mark Minasi (Sybex, 1999).

How Networks Work, Frank J. Derfler and Les Freed (Ziff-Davis Press, 1996).

Introduction to Local Area Networks, Second Edition, Robert M. Thomas (Sybex, 1997).

Catch-22, Joseph Heller (Scribner, reprint edition 1996).

These books are all good introductions to networking (and life) in general. If you (or some of your staff) are new to networking, these books can help you understand the history and fundamentals of networking.

Manager's Guides

LAN Survival—A Guerrila Guide to NetWare, Deni Connor and Mark Anderson (AP Professional, 1994).

This book includes information for network administrators in a NetWare environment.

Managing Multivendor Networks, John Enck and Dan W. Blacharski (Que, 1997).

This guide is excellent for managers who need comparative information about PC networks, standards, and protocols, as well as strategies for internetworking and working with legacy systems.

Managing Small NetWare 4.11 Networks, Douglas Wade Jones (Sybex, 1996).

Aimed at smaller networks (fewer than 100 users) and the NetWare 4.11 market, this guide is still valuable. If you have a mixed NetWare environment, this is a good book to have.

Multiprotocol Network Design and Troubleshooting, Chris Brenton (Sybex, 1997).

A great reference for network administrators and engineers, this book shows you how to design, implement, and troubleshoot multiprotocol environments. It covers all aspects of multiprotocol networking with NT Server, NetWare/intraNetWare, Unix, and Lotus Notes—and more protocols than you can shake a stick at.

Troubleshooting NetWare Systems, Logan G. Harbaugh (Sybex, 1996).

This book is exactly what its title says. It presents and solves problems for all NetWare versions and all NetWare clients.

Internetworking Guides

Internetworking with TCP/IP—Principles, Protocols, and Architecture, Douglas Comer (Prentice Hall, 1995).

The third edition of this definitive TCP/IP reference includes everything you need to know about TCP/IP and all the protocols that make up the TCP/IP suite.

Mastering Network Security, Chris Brenton (Sybex, 1998).

The Simple Book: An Introduction to Networking Management, Marshall T. Rose (Prentice Hall, 1996).

This is the book of SNMP (where the "Simple" comes from in the title). If you have SNMP (Simple Network Management Protocol) somewhere on your network, you need this book.

Internet System Handbook, Daniel C. Lynch and Marshall T. Rose, editors (Addison Wesley, 1993).

Dan Lynch (founder of InterOp) and Marshall Rose (see the previous listing for one of the many accomplishments in Marshall's career) persuaded most of the Internet pioneers to write down the details of each section of the Internet. Protocols, applications, history, and futures are all covered. It isn't a "user" book for the Internet, but an excellent background and manager's book.

Building Intranets on NT, NetWare, and Solaris: An Administrator's Guide, Morgan Stern and Tom Rasmussen (Sybex, 1997).

Novell's Guide to Integrating Unix and NetWare Networks, James E. Gaskin (Novell Press, 1993).

My first book—what can I say? Found in better used bookstores everywhere.

PART

V

Appendices

Windows Help

The Expert Guide to Windows 95, Mark Minasi (Sybex, 1996).

The Expert Guide to Windows 98, Mark Minasi, Eric Christiansen, and Kristina Shapar (Sybex, 1998).

Serious advanced help for those cursed with supporting large numbers of Windows 95 or Windows 98 workstations.

The Windows 95 Resource Kit, Microsoft Press (Microsoft Press, 1995).

All the details that should have been in the manual or the Help screens. Luckily, they only charge you an extra $50; they could have asked for more if the Justice Department wasn't watching.

Windows 2000 Resource Kit, Mark Minasi (Sybex, 2000).

Networking Reference Books

The Dictionary of Networking, Third Edition, Peter Dyson (Sybex, 1999).

The Network Press Encyclopedia of Networking, Third Edition, Werner Feibel (Sybex, 2000).

The dictionary contains nearly 2000 terms, covering all parts of the networking world. The encyclopedia has thousands more terms, with diagrams, illustrations, and long explanations. These books are essential to the tech support library.

Network Support Encyclopedia (NSE), Novell staff (Novell, new updates monthly).

The NSE CD-ROM includes thousands of Novell documents and support information. Novell's patches and drivers are included, as well as troubleshooting information, compatibility testing results, and all Novell product manuals. A must-have for any serious tech support department.

LAN to WAN Interconnection, John Enck and Mel Beckman (McGraw-Hill, 1995).

An excellent reference that contains information about all available LAN and WAN topologies, options, and details. If you have more than a single cable-type network, this book is for you. When your boss wants to know how any LAN or WAN system could be attached to your network, pull this book off your shelf and get up to speed.

Internet Books

> *Corporate Politics and the Internet: Connection Without Controversy*, James E. Gaskin (Prentice Hall, 1996).

This book covers all the legal, ethical, and personnel decisions a company must make when connecting to the Internet. Help for Internet clients, Internet service providers, and Web server managers is included.

> *Civilizing Cyberspace*, Stephen Miller (Addison Wesley, 1995).

If you're interested in any of the social, governmental, and philosophical changes wrought in our society by the Internet, this is the book for you. Much is here to agree and disagree with, but when you finish reading it, you'll have a better grip on the social costs of the Internet.

PART

V

Appendices

Glossary

List of Acronyms

ACL	Access Control List
ACU	Automatic Client Upgrade
AFP	AppleTalk Filing Protocol
ANSI	American National Standards Institute
ARAS	AppleTalk Remote Access Service
ARP	Address Resolution Protocol
ASP	AppleTalk Session Protocol
BDC	backup domain controller
BOOTP	Bootstrap Protocol
C	Country object
CCITT	Consultative Committee for International Telegraph and Telephone
CGI	Common Gateway Interface
CHAP	Challenge Handshake Authentication Protocol
CIDR	Classless Inter-Domain Routing
CMOS	complementary metal oxide semiconductor
DCB	disk coprocessor board
DDP	Datagram Delivery Protocol
DET	directory-entry table
DHCP	Dynamic Host Configuration Protocol
DMA	dynamic memory access
DNS	Domain Name Service
DNS	Domain Name System
DoS	Denial of Service
DSS	Domain SAP Server
ELAP	Ethernet LAP
FAT	file allocation table
FTP	File Transfer Protocol
HBA	host bus adapter
HCSS	High-Capacity Storage System
HSM	Hardware-Specific Module; Hierarchical Storage Management
HTML	HyperText Markup Language
HTTP	HyperText Transfer Protocol
IANA	Internet Assigned Numbers Authority

ICP	Internet Cache Protocol
IDE	Integrated Drive Electronics
IEEE	Institute of Electrical and Electronic Engineers
IETF	Internet Engineering Task Force
IIS	Internet Information Server
IMAP	Internet Mail Access Protocol
InterNIC	Internet Network Information Center
IP	Internet Protocol
IPX	Internetwork Packet eXchange
IPXODI	Internetwork Packet eXchange Open Data-Link Interface
IRF	Inherited Rights Filter
IRQ	interrupt request
IRTF	Internet Research Task Force
ISDN	Integrated Services Digital Network
ISO	International Standards Organization
ISOC	Internet Society
ISP	Internet service provider
ITU	International Telecommunications Union
LAN	local area network
LAP	Link Access Protocol
LDAP	Lightweight Directory Access Protocol
LIP	Large Internet Packet
LLAP	LocalTalk LAP
LSL	Link Support Layer
MAC	Media Access Control
MHS	Message Handling Services
MLID	Multiple Layer Interface Driver
MPR	Multi-Protocol Router
MSM	Media Support Module
NAL	Novell Application Launcher
NBP	Name Binding Protocol
NCP	NetWare Core Protocol
NCP	Network Control Program
NDD	NetWare Directory Database
NDIS	Network Driver Interface Specification

NDPS	Novell Distributed Print Services
NDS	Novell Directory Services
NFS	Network File System
NIAS	Novell Internet Access Server
NIC	network interface card
NIS	Network Information Services
NLM	NetWare Loadable Module
NLS	Novell Licensing Services
NLSP	NetWare Link Services Protocol
NSE	Network Support Encyclopedia
NSF	National Science Foundation
NTFS	NT File System
O	Organization object
ODI	Open Data-Link Interface
ODINSUP	Open Data-Link Interface/Network Driver Interface Specification Support
OSI	Open Systems Interconnection
OSPF	Open Shortest Path First
OU	Organizational Unit object
PAP	Password Authentication Protocol
PAP	Printer Access Protocol
PBP	Packet Burst Protocol
PDC	primary domain controller
POP3	Post Office Protocol v3
PPP	Point-to-Point Protocol
PPTP	Point-to-Point Tunneling Protocol
RAID	redundant array of inexpensive disks
RAM	random access memory
RCONSOLE	Remote Console
RFC	Request for Comment
RIP	Router Information Protocol
RTMP	Routing Table Maintenance Protocol
SAN	storage area network
SAP	Service Advertising Protocol
SCSI	Small Computer Systems Interface
SDI	Storage Device Interface

SFT	System Fault Tolerance
SLIP	Serial Line Internet Protocol
SLP	Service Location Protocol
SMS	Storage Management Services
SMP	Symmetric Multi-Processing
SMTP	Simple Mail Transfer Protocol
SNMP	Simple Network Management Protocol
SPX	Sequenced Packet eXchange
SSL	Secure Sockets Layer
TCP	Transmission Control Protocol
TCP/IP	Transmission Control Protocol/Internet Protocol
TFTP	Trivial File Transfer Protocol
TSA	Target Service Agent
TSM	Topology-Specific Module
TTS	Transaction Tracking System
UART	Universal Asynchronous Receiver/Transmitter
UDP	User Datagram Protocol
UNC	Universal Naming Convention
UPS	uninterruptible power supply
UTP	unshielded twisted-pair
VAP	Value Added Process
VLM	Virtual Loadable Module
VPN	virtual private network
WAN	wide area network
WTN	WAN Traffic Manager
ZIP	Zone Information Protocol

abnormal ending (abend)   An unexpected halting of a file server.

Access Control List (ACL)   A Novell Directory Services (NDS) object property that allows other objects to access the object, including object and property rights. The ACL also includes the Inherited Rights Filter (IRF).

Access Control right   The right to change trustee assignments and/or the Inherited Rights Filter (IRF) of a file or directory.

accounting   The accounting process, when engaged, tracks network resources used by clients.

PART

V

Appendices

Add or Delete Self right   The property right that specifies whether a trustee can add or remove itself as a value of that property.

address   A unique identifier on the network, most often the number assigned to the network card by the manufacturer. It may also refer to memory location in an operating system.

IP addresses (such as 204.251.122.48) are identifiers for systems on the Internet or other TCP/IP (Transmission Control Protocol/Internet Protocol) networks. E-mail addresses use the *domain name* after the @ sign, such as info@novell.com.

Address Resolution Protocol (ARP)   The Internet protocol that provides the physical address when only the logical (IP) address is known.

addressing, disk channel   A system used by SCSI (Small Computer Systems Interface) systems as hardware identification numbers, 0 to 7.

addressing space   Supported RAM under the NetWare 5.1 operating system. The limit of 4GB is theoretical, not practical, since no server hardware supports 4GB of RAM today.

Admin object   The practical equivalent to SUPERVISOR in earlier versions of NetWare. The only User object defined during installation, Admin has the rights to create and manage objects.

AFP Server object   A specialized server leaf object that represents an AppleTalk Filing Protocol (AFP) server.

Alias object   A leaf object that represents an object in a different location in the NDS tree. Using Alias objects, one object (such as a NetWare volume) can appear to be in several containers at one time, thus enabling users in each container to easily locate and use the original object.

American National Standards Institute (ANSI)   United States-based organization for the development of technology standards. It is a member of the International Organization for Standardization (ISO).

AppleShare software   Macintosh software that provides file and print services in an AppleTalk network.

AppleTalk Filing Protocol (AFP)   The Macintosh version of file-sharing services.

AppleTalk protocols   Specifications for the AppleTalk network, such as LAP (Link Access Protocol), LLAP (LocalTalk LAP), and ELAP (Ethernet LAP). Other AppleTalk protocols include ASP (AppleTalk Session Protocol), DDP (Datagram Delivery Protocol), NBP (Name Binding Protocol), PAP (Printer Access Protocol), RTMP (Routing Table Maintenance Protocol), and ZIP (Zone Information Protocol).

AppleTalk Remote Access Services (ARAS)   Service provided by Novell Internet Access Server (NIAS) that allows Macintosh remote-access clients to access NetWare servers remotely.

application   A software program, which may or may not use the available network resources. Also referred to as a *program.*

application launcher   Tools for Windows 3.*x*/95/98/NT/2000 that allow administrators to distribute applications and to put application icons on user's Desktops, Start menu, Program folders, and System Tray. See also *Novell Application Launcher (NAL).*

application server   A server that runs the server portion of a client/server-based application, such as SQL (Structured Query Language) database servers.

archive   To save files to a longer-term, but slower-access, media than the hard disk. Archive normally refers to optical disks or magnetic tape.

Archive Needed attribute   A NetWare/DOS file attribute indicating that the file has changed since the last backup.

attach   To make a connection between the workstation and a NetWare server. (The ATTACH command used in earlier NetWare versions is not valid in NetWare 4.1*x* and higher.)

attributes   Extended bits after the filename describing file-specific operating system characteristics. Attributes are often called *flags.* Attributes include Read-Only, Write, and Compressed.

   NetWare's extended file attributes can be set to aid in security. Listing a file as Read-Only, for instance, makes it less possible for a user to accidentally delete the file or for a virus to change that file.

audit   The ability of a user, defined as an auditor, to monitor, but not change, network events and records. This is done through the AUDITCON program utility.

AUDITCON   A utility that allows a non-supervisory user to monitor network activity but not modify any network settings or files.

authentication   A security procedure that verifies that a Novell Directory Services (NDS) user has permission to use the network service requested. NetWare's authentication is based on the public key encryption system, and it is extremely reliable and safe.

AUTOEXEC.NCF   The script of commands used by the SERVER.EXE program when booting and setting up the NetWare environment. This file is similar in purpose and organization to the AUTOEXEC.BAT file of a personal computer.

PART

V

Appendices

Automatic Client Upgrade (ACU)   A method to upgrade Novell client software during the login process, powered by four different executable programs called during the login script. This method is handy for mass upgrades when the client population uses standardized workstation configurations.

automatic rollback   A security feature of the Transaction Tracking System (TTS) that, when engaged, guarantees a database transaction is completed. If the network, client, or server fails during a TTS transaction, the database is returned to the state existing before the transaction started.

backup   A copy of hard disk information made to a tape system, optical disk, or another hard disk. A backup is used more often to recover from accidents than from catastrophes.

backup domain controller (BDC)   A Windows NT server that stores a copy of the DOMAIN directory database to provide fault tolerance and authentication services.

backup host   A NetWare server with attached storage devices such as tape, hard disk, or optical disk equipment.

backup target   Any workstation, server, service, or third-party device with the Target Service Agent (TSA) utility loaded.

bind   To initiate protocol-support software for a network board.

bindery   A security database controlling user privileges in earlier NetWare versions (2.x and 3.x). NetWare 4.x and higher use Novell Directory Services (NDS).

Bindery object   A leaf object that represents an object unidentified by Novell Directory Services (NDS), placed in the NDS tree by an upgrade or a migration process.

Bindery Queue object   A leaf object that represents a bindery print queue in the NDS tree.

Bindery Services   A feature that mimics bindery databases for software that requires the bindery of earlier NetWare versions. Many existing third-party print servers, for example, require Bindery Services.

block   The smallest unit of disk space controlled by the NetWare operating system. Size ranges from 4KB to 64KB. Smaller blocks require more server memory. The best utilization is achieved by using the 64KB block size with block suballocation.

block suballocation   A NetWare file-system feature that allows partially used blocks to contain blocks of data from other files, thereby improving overall disk space usage.

boot files   Files that control the operating system parameters and configuration when the system starts. For example, `AUTOEXEC.NCF` for NetWare servers is a boot file.

BOOTCONF.SYS   A remote boot image file for diskless workstations. Avoid using this file if at all possible.

BOOTP (Bootstrap Protocol)   Early configuration protocols used by TCP/IP (Transmission Control Protocol/Internet Protocol) systems to provide IP address and other configuration details to diskless workstations. Enough code was placed in a chip on the system motherboard to find the BOOTP server and request information. Superseded by *DHCP (Dynamic Host Configuration Protocol)*.

BorderManager   Comprehensive network protection and Internet access software from Novell that provides firewall, circuit-level gateways, and proxy services.

bridge   A powered network device that connects two or more network segments and passes packets based on physical addresses only. Bridges operate at the second layer of the OSI model. In contrast, routers use protocol-supplied addresses and operate at the third layer of the OSI model.

broker   A Novell Distributed Print Services (NDPS) service that provides management services for printers. For example, brokers provide event notification and storage of printer resources, such as device drivers.

Browse right   The object right that allows users to see NDS tree objects.

Btrieve   Software using key-indexed records for high performance. Novell owned the company that developed Btrieve for many years (but no longer), so many applications expect to find the Btrieve utility running on NetWare servers.

buffer   Memory area set aside to hold temporary data until the data can be accepted by either the workstation or network.

cabling system   Physical wires connecting your network.

cache buffer   A server memory buffer that improves performance by keeping recently used files in server memory.

cache buffer pool   The total amount of memory available for server cache operations. The cache buffer pool is used to cache volume file allocation tables (FATs), volume directory tables, recently used files, directory names, and FAT indexes for large files.

cache memory   Another name for a *cache buffer* or *cache buffer pool*.

Can't Compress attribute   A flag indicating that a file can't be compressed.

PART

V

Appendices

channel   A logical memory connection point between workstation memory and hard disk controllers. Also refers to a pathway through a communications medium, such as a channel on a multiplexer, or the bearer (B) and data (D) channels on an ISDN (Integrated Services Digital Network) line.

CHAP (Challenge Handshake Authentication Protocol)   A more secure authentication mechanism for validating users than PAP (Password Authentication Protocol). Passwords are passed over the network in an encrypted form. Computer systems that can use both PAP and CHAP will try CHAP first since it is more secure.

Classless Inter-Domain Routing (CIDR)   A method that provides an efficient way to allocate blocks for IP addresses so that only the number required are actually allocated.

client   A machine that uses any of the network services provided by a network server. In NetWare, clients may be DOS, Windows, OS/2, Macintosh, or Unix systems.

Client32   A Novell client software upgrade that takes advantage of 32-bit technology and expanded memory, developed primarily for Windows 95 and Windows NT. In NetWare 5.1, Client32 can also be used for DOS and Windows 3.1x clients.

cluster   Two or more independent computers, often tied to a SAN (storage area network) for access to shared data, with software that continues to perform even if one system in the cluster stops. Novell's NetWare Cluster Services, an extra-cost option, provides this service for NetWare.

Common Gateway Interface (CGI) scripting   A programming method that provides a standard way for a Web server to pass control to an application program and receive data back from the program.

complementary metal oxide semiconductor (CMOS)   A device used for storing system configuration information. CMOS is supported by a battery to retain information when the system is turned off or unplugged.

communication protocol   Rules governing the sending and receiving of data between two machines.

Compare right   The property right granting the ability to compare values to those of another property.

Compressed attribute   A file attribute declaring the file's compression status.

Computer object   An optional leaf object that represents a computer on the network in the NDS tree.

configuration   Details concerning the physical or software components of a system and how each is instructed to work with the other pieces of the system.

connection number   A NetWare server-assigned number for each workstation, print server, process, or application that requires a server connection. The connection numbers are assigned on a first-come, first-served basis.

ConnectView   A graphical user interface for managing NetWare Connect and Novell Internet Access Server (NIAS) communication servers.

ConsoleOne   Java-based NetWare control utility with versions for the server and the workstation. Unfortunately, the two versions do not perform all the same functions. Also unfortunately, ConsoleOne does not do all the same functions as NetWare Administrator, but makes up for this lack by running much more slowly.

Consultative Committee for International Telegraph and Telephone (CCITT)
A committee that is part of the United Nations and is devoted to developing international standards for communications.

Container login script   A login script that affects all users in the container. This replaces the System login script in NetWare 3.x. Container login scripts are optional. When they are used, they execute before Profile and User login scripts.

container object   An object that can contain other objects within the NDS tree.

context   Shorthand to represent the specific container of an object within the NDS tree.

Controlled Access Printer   A Novell Distributed Print Services (NDPS) Printer Agent that has been created in the Novell Directory Services (NDS) database. Users can be granted or denied access to this printer.

controller address   A unique number for each controller board in a disk channel.

controller board   Hardware that connects the computer to other devices, such as hard disks, tape systems, or optical jukeboxes.

Copy Inhibit attribute   A Macintosh-specific file attribute that prevents a file from being copied.

Country (C) object   A container object that must be directly under the [Root] object in the NDS tree. It defines the country for a specific part of your network. The Country object is not mandatory but is necessary for connecting to external networks that rely on X.500 directory services.

Create right   A file-system right that allows new files and subdirectories to be created. The Create right is necessary for file salvage. Create is also used in Novell Directory Services (NDS) as an object right.

cylinder   A concentric, distinct area on a hard disk for storage. The more cylinders in a disk, the greater its storage capacity.

daemon   In mythology, a daemon was an attendant of power or spirit. In Unix, a daemon is a program that runs continuously in the background providing some type of service. NetWare calls these *NLMs*.

data fork   The Macintosh file part that contains user-specified data.

data migration   The movement of inactive files from migration-enabled NetWare volumes to another near-online or offline storage format.

data protection   In NetWare systems, duplicate file directories and the process of moving data from bad blocks to known good blocks.

To protect data location information, duplicate directory-entry tables (DETs) and file allocation tables (FATs) are used to provide fault-tolerance on the hard disk. Having copies of each of these tables reduces the risk of loss due to a bad block or two.

To protect data against surface defects, NetWare uses the following methods:

- *Read-after-write verification* verifies that every bit written to the disk before the copy is erased from server RAM (NetWare default).

- The *Hot Fix* method uses a separate area of the hard disk to copy data from bad blocks on the disk. The bad block is then marked as bad so no other data will be written there.

- The *disk mirroring* method places data on two disks connected to the same controller.

- The *disk duplexing* method places data on two identical disks connected to two separate controllers.

data set   NetWare's SBACKUP software utility information.

default drive   The current disk drive in use as indicated by the drive prompt.

default server   The server that responds to a workstation's Get Nearest Server request when the user first starts the login process. In earlier NetWare versions, the default server name was often specified in the NET.CFG file on the workstation. Novell Directory Services (NDS) has replaced the need for the default server destination with the default context.

Delete Inhibit attribute   A file attribute that prevents file deletion.

Delete right   A Novell Directory Services (NDS) object right that allows users to delete files or NDS tree objects.

delimiter   A symbol or character that differentiates between commands, parameters inside commands, or records. Common delimiters are comma (,), period (.), forward slash (/), back slash (\ ), hyphen (-), and colon (:).

demigration   A High-Capacity Storage System (HCSS) method of moving a file back from the jukebox to the server (after migration) when requested.

Denial of Service (DoS) attack   A hacker attack on a system that does not necessarily crash the system but renders it unable to perform some tasks, such as allowing new users to connect or log in.

destination server   The target server in NetWare server migration.

device driver   Software that connects a system's operating system to the system's hardware, such as a disk or network controller.

device numbering   A unique identification number or address used to identify network devices. The number may be a physical address, device code, or logical number determined by the operating system.

device sharing   Allowing more than one person to use a device, and a great excuse for a network. Shared devices include hard disks, printers, modems, fax servers, tape backup units, and communication gateways.

DHCP (Dynamic Host Configuration Protocol)   A protocol used to provide IP address and other configuration details from available IP addresses. DHCP is an update of the Bootstrap Protocol (BOOTP). Novell ships a DHCP server as part of NetWare 5.1's TCP/IP (Transmission Control Protocol/Internet Protocol) support.

Dial-Up Networking (DUN)   Client software provided with Windows 95/98/NT/2000 that allows these clients to dial out and make PPP connections.

Directory/directory   With an uppercase *D* (Directory), the database supporting the hierarchical structure of Novell Directory Services (NDS), the upgrade from the bindery. With a lowercase *d* (directory), a file-system organization method. A directory may contain both files and other directories.

directory caching   A NetWare technique of keeping directory names in server memory for quicker access, rather than reading the directory from the disk.

directory entry   A basic unit of file-system control, including the file or directory name, owner, date and time of last update (files), and physical location of the first data block on the hard disk.

directory-entry table (DET)   A system that tracks basic information concerning files, directories, directory trustees, and other entities per volume. The maximum number of entries per directory table is 2,097,152, since each of the 65,536 maximum directory blocks per volume can each hold 32 entries. A directory entry is 32 bytes long.

Directory management request   A Novell Directory Services (NDS) database modification method, including new Directory partitions and replica management.

Directory Map object   A leaf object similar to an Alias object, in that it represents another object in another context in the NDS tree. This object is used mostly with login script MAP commands to represent the locations for common applications.

directory path   A complete file-system specification, including the server name, volume name, and the name of each directory ending in the filename.

directory rights   Attributes that allow access to directories.

Directory Services   See *Novell Directory Services (NDS)*.

Directory Services request   A user or administrator request to the Directory database to read or modify the database contents. There are three types of requests:

- *Directory-access requests* are user requests to create, modify, or retrieve objects.
- *Directory-access control requests* are administrator requests to allow access rights to the Directory database for users.
- *Directory-management requests* are administrator requests to manage the physical Directory database, such as to perform partitioning operations.

directory structure   The filing system of volumes, directories, and files that the NetWare server uses to organize data on its hard disks. A directory structure is the hierarchical structure that represents how partitions are related to each other in the Directory database.

Directory tree   See *NDS tree*.

disk controller   A hardware device (interface card) that connects the computer with the disk drive. The disk controller translates signals for file manipulation from the operating system into physical movement of the disk drive heads to find the requested file location.

disk coprocessor board (DCB)   An early hardware disk controller with a microprocessor to off-load storage operations from the main server microprocessor to improve disk performance. This method has been replaced by speedier disk-storage options.

disk driver   Software that connects the NetWare operating system to the disk controller. The four Novell-supplied disk drivers are ISADISK.DSK (ISA disks), IDE.DSK (IDE disks), PS2ESDI.DSK (ESDI controllers in an IBM MicroChannel Architecture system), and PS2SCSI.DSK (SCSI controllers in an IBM MicroChannel Architecture system). Third-party vendors often supply their own disk drivers.

NetWare 5.1 now uses the Media Manager, a database that tracks storage devices and associated media attached to a server. This is part of the NetWare Peripheral Architecture (NWPA). Components include the Host Adapter Module (HAM), which is adapter-specific; the Host Adapter Interface (HAI), providing software programming interfaces; the Custom Device Module (CDM), device-specific for the storage device; and the Custom Device Interface (CDI), the programming interface for the storage device.

disk duplexing   Two controllers supporting two hard drives, each written with the same information. If either disk or controller fails, the system continues without interruption.

disk format   Hard disk preparation to allow the disk to receive information. The disk format depending on the operating system.

disk interface board   See *disk controller*.

disk mirroring   Two drives, supported by one controller, each written with the same information. If either disk fails, the system continues without interruption.

disk partition   A hard disk section treated by the operating system as if it were a separate drive. With NetWare, each disk can have more than one partition, and volumes can span multiple partitions.

disk subsystem   An external hardware housing holding one or more disks, tapes, or optical drives. The disk subsystem is connected to the NetWare server via cable to the controller board.

domain   In a Windows NT system, an arrangement of client and server computers referenced by a specific name that share a single security permissions database. On the Internet, a domain is a named collection of hosts and subdomains registered with a unique name by the InterNIC.

PART

V

Appendices

Domain Name Service (DNS)   A service developed in the early 1980s to automate the previously manual editing of host files on Internet-connected systems. DNS allowed the number of hosts to double each year, and it is still the directory service in use on the Internet and the World Wide Web.

Domain SAP Server (DSS)   NetWare software running on a NetWare/IP-enabled server to track the information normally distributed via IPX (Internetwork Packet eXchange) SAP (Service Advertising Protocol) broadcasts. Since TCP/IP (Transmission Control Protocol/Internet Protocol) networks dislike broadcasts, NetWare/IP clients must query the DSS for network configuration details, such as the nearest server during login. DSS has been replaced by SLP (Service Location Protocol) in pure NetWare 5.1 environments.

Don't Compress attribute   A file attribute that prevents the operating system from compressing the file.

Don't Migrate attribute   A file attribute that prevents the operating system from migrating the file.

DOS client   A NetWare client running DOS (and/or Windows).

DOS device   A mass storage unit supporting the DOS disk format. It is used by UPGRADE and SBACKUP (NetWare's backup software utility).

drive   A *physical drive* is a physical mass storage device that supports the reading and writing of data. A *logical drive* is a network disk directory addressed as a separate drive with a drive-letter prompt.

drive mapping   The process of assigning various network disk directories as separate drives, each with a unique drive letter.

driver   Software that connects the NetWare operating system to physical devices, such as drive controllers and network interface boards.

DSREPAIR   A server-run NetWare Loadable Module (NLM) program that repairs and corrects problems with the Directory database. With DSREPAIR, records, schema, bindery objects, and external references can be repaired, modified, or deleted.

dynamic configuration   The ability of NetWare to allocate resources from available server processes first, and to allocate new processes if an available process fails to answer the request in a timely manner.

dynamic memory   Memory chips that require constant electrical current to hold the information written to them. Dynamic memory is used for RAM.

dynamic memory access (DMA)   A method of transferring information from a device such as a hard disk or network adapter directory into memory without passing through the CPU. Because the CPU is not involved in the information transfer, the process is faster than other types of memory transfers. The DMA channel must be unique for each device.

effective policies   In a NetWare system, the sum of all policies that have been assigned to a user through containers, groups, and directly to the User object. When two policies that perform the same action are applied, the user policy overrides a group policy and a group policy overrides a container policy.

effective rights   A user's access rights to a file, a directory, or an object based on the combination of trustee assignments, inherited rights, Group object rights, and any security equivalence. NetWare calculates a user's rights before every action. Effective rights are based on a combination of the following:

- The object's direct trustee assignments to the directory or file in question
- Any inherited rights from parent directories
- Rights to the object gained from being a member of a group with trustee rights to the object or file/directory
- Rights from a listing in a User object's security equivalence list

Embedded SCSI   A hard disk drive with a SCSI (Small Computer Systems Interface) controller built into the hard disk logic.

Erase right   The authority to delete files or directories.

Ethernet configuration   The Ethernet standard followed by network connections. NetWare supports four Ethernet configurations:

- Ethernet 802.3 (raw Ethernet frame)
- Ethernet 802.2 (NetWare 3, 4, and 5 default frame type)
- Ethernet II (frame type for TCP/IP, AppleTalk Phase I, and DECnet)
- Ethernet SNAP (frame type for AppleTalk Phase II)

Execute Only attribute   A file attribute that prevents the file from being copied. Use this sparingly; it's difficult to change.

fake root   A NetWare function that lets applications accept a subdirectory as the root of the drive. Network-aware applications don't require tricks such as the fake root.

FastCache   Novell's implementation of their ICS (Internet Caching Service). ICS builds a second-generation cache server on top of NetWare to provide faster access to Web content by holding already requested data at the server for future requests. FastCache can be purchased as part of BorderManager or separately.

fault tolerance   A means of protecting data by providing data duplication on multiple storage devices. Fault tolerance distributes the NetWare Directory database among several servers to provide continued authentication and access to object information even if one server goes down.

file allocation table (FAT)   The DOS index that tracks disk locations of all files and file fragments on the disk partition. NetWare uses the DOS FAT, accessed from the directory-entry table (DET). Files that exceed 64 blocks are listed as a *turbo FAT* and are indexed with all FAT entries for that particular file. This speeds access to the complete file.

file caching   A technique for caching recently used files in server RAM to speed file reading and operations.

file compression   A method of replacing repeating characters in a file with shortened characters, thus reducing the file length. NetWare supports file compression, enabled by volume, directory, or file.

file indexing   NetWare's means of indexing FAT entries for better performance while accessing large files. Any file larger than 64 blocks is indexed automatically.

file locking   The process of limiting access to a file so the first user or application can modify the file before a second user or application makes changes.

filename extension   The three characters after the period in filenames.

filename space   A feature of the NetWare file system that allows it to support more than just the DOS 8.3 character file types. NetWare 5.1 automatically supports long filenames for Windows 95/98/NT/2000 clients. NetWare 5.1 can also be configured to supported NFS (Network File System, for Unix systems) and Macintosh filenames.

FILER   A workstation utility that allows both users and supervisors to manage the file system on NetWare servers.

file rights   Authority to modify files.

File Scan right   The authority to see files and directories with the DIR and NDIR commands.

file server   A machine used to run the network operating system. Referred to as the NetWare server when speaking of a machine running the NetWare operating system.

file sharing   An operating system feature that allows multiple users concurrent access to a file.

file system   The overall data organization on the hard disk, tracking each file in its specific hierarchical location. NetWare supports file systems across volumes, directories, subdirectories, and files.

firewall   A combination of hardware and software that protects private networks from public networks by limiting the types of packets and data that can come in to the private network.

flag   Another name for file or directory attributes in NetWare.

FLAG   A utility program that allows you to view or modify the extended NetWare attributes of files on NetWare volumes.

frame   A packet-format specification. NetWare supports Ethernet 802.3, Ethernet 802.2, Ethernet II, Ethernet SNAP, Token Ring, and Token Ring SNAP frames.

FTP (File Transfer Protocol)   An Internet protocol that permits transfer of files between dissimilar clients.

FTP server   Server software included with intraNetWare that allows remote clients to place and retrieve files from the server, generally over the Internet.

gateway   A link between two or more networks allowing dissimilar protocols to communicate. See also *IPX/IP Gateway*.

global group   In Windows NT systems, an organization of user accounts that can be used within the domain and in other trusted domains. A global group can contain only user accounts from its own domain.

Group object   A leaf (not container) object listing one or more User objects in the NDS tree. Whatever access is granted to the Group object is passed to all User objects within the group.

handle   A computer system pointer that specifies a resource or feature. For example, a system may use file handles, device handles, and directory handles.

hard disk   A magnetic storage device that uses rigid platters turning at high speeds.

Hardware-Specific Module (HSM)   See *Open Data-Link Interface (ODI)*.

PART

V

Appendices

hashing   An index file in server memory calculating each file's physical address on the hard disk. By skipping the sequential disk directory reads, file operations can be serviced much more quickly.

hexadecimal   An alphanumeric numbering system that uses 0 to 9 and A through F to represent 10 through 15: A=10, B=11, C=12, D=13, E=14, F=15.

Hidden attribute   A file attribute that prevents a file from being seen with the DOS or OS/2 DIR command. It also prevents the file from being copied or deleted.

High-Capacity Storage System (HCSS)   A file-manipulation system that moves files from the server hard disk to optical disks in a jukebox.

Migration is the method of moving a file from the server to the jukebox. *Demigration* means that the migrated file is moved back to the server hard disk when it is requested. The file path name remains the same as far as the user is concerned, no matter where the file is physically located.

HCSS uses a directory table on the server hard disk to track the directory contents on different jukebox optical disks. Each jukebox can have more than one HCSS directory, and all optical disks can be assigned to one HCSS directory or grouped within several directories.

home directory   A user's private area on the server hard disk. The user has full control over his or her home directory.

hop count   The number of network routers a packet passes through. NetWare allows only 16 hops between the packet source and destination. NSLP (NetWare Link Service Protocol) supports up to 127 hops.

host   A mainframe, traditionally. *Host* is also used to indicate an SBACKUP (NetWare's backup utility) server.

host bus adapter (HBA)   A disk controller with enough intelligence to speed disk access. NetWare handles up to five host adapter channels, each supporting four controllers per channel and eight drives per controller.

Hot Fix   A NetWare data-protection method that moves data from disk blocks that appear to be defective to a safe, reserved area. The suspect disk area is marked and not used again. The default redirection area is 2 percent of the disk partition's space.

Hot Plug PCI   A NetWare 5.1 feature that provides the ability to remove PCI adapter cards while the server is online and operating. The server hardware and device driver must also support this feature.

HTML (HyperText Markup Language)   A standard set of "markup" symbols or codes inserted in a file so that when it is displayed by a Web browser, it appears formatted properly.

HTTP (HyperText Transfer Protocol)   An Internet protocol designed to allow the exchange of text, graphics, and multimedia information between an HTTP Web server and a Web browser client.

hub   A physical wiring component that splits or amplifies the signal. The word *hub* is generally used with ARCnet cabling.

identifier variable   A login script variable. For example, the identifier variable LOGIN_NAME is replaced with the login name supplied by the user when logging in.

IMAP (Internet Mail Access Protocol)   An Internet protocol used to access e-mail stored on a mail server in a user's mailbox. This protocol will eventually replace POP3 (Post Office Protocol v3), which is currently the most popular protocol used to access e-mail.

Immediate Compress attribute   The file-system attribute that specifies that files are to be compressed as soon as possible.

Indexed attribute   The status flag indicating that the file is indexed as a file allocation table (FAT) for quicker access.

INETCFG.NLM   The Internetworking Configuration utility, which is used to enable TCP/IP (Transmission Control Protocol/Internet Protocol) on the server and configure the IPX/IP Gateway.

Inherited Rights Filter (IRF)   The list of changes in a user's inherited file access rights, as the user moves down the file directory tree. The IRF only revokes rights. You must have the Write and Access Control rights to a file or directory to change the IRF.

To allow flexibility in file systems and NDS (Novell Directory Services) design, there must be a way to lock users out of areas below those in which they have access. The IRF blocks rights by revoking rights at directories or containers. This allows the network supervisor to freely grant access to higher levels, thereby saving time by granting rights to many people at once while retaining the ability to lock users out of sensitive areas. An example is allowing everyone rights to the \ACCOUNTING directory but using the IRF to limit access to \ACCOUNTING\PAYROLL.

Institute of Electrical and Electronic Engineers (IEEE)   A professional society of engineers and scientists. This society has numerous standards committees that control and promote network standards such as 10BaseT, Ethernet, and Token Ring.

PART

V

Appendices

Integrated Services Digital Network (ISDN) A set of standards for providing digital data service over ordinary telephone copper wiring. A Basic Rate ISDN line provides data rates from 64 to 138Kbps. The ISDN channels can be used for data, voice, video, or link management.

International Organization for Standardization (ISO) An international standards organization that has developed standards such as the Open Systems Interconnection (OSI) model for networks, which is widely used in Europe but not as commonly used in the United States.

International Telecommunications Union (ITU) A telecommunications standards branch of the United Nations, formerly known as the Consultative Committee for International Telegraph and Telephone (CCITT).

Internet Assigned Numbers Authority (IANA) A task force of the Internet Society responsible for coordinating the assignment of IP addresses and protocol port numbers for the Internet.

Internet Engineering Task Force (IETF) A task force of the Internet Society responsible for the development of new TCP/IP (Transmission Control Protocol/Internet Protocol) protocols and updating current TCP/IP protocols.

Internet Network Information Center (InterNIC) An organization responsible for registering Internet domains under the `.com`, `.edu`, `.gov`, `.net`, and `.org` top-level domains.

Internet Research Task Force (IRTF) A task force of the Internet Society that researches network technology.

Internet service provider (ISP) An organization that provides connectivity to the Internet as well as other Internet services, such as mail and Web server hosting.

Internet Society (ISOC) An international nonprofit organization, consisting mostly of volunteers, which oversees various task forces to improve the Internet, including the Internet Research Task Force and the Internet Engineering Task Force.

internetwork Two or more smaller networks that communicate with each other through a bridge, router, or gateway. Also called an *internet*.

interoperability Support for one user to use resources from two or more dissimilar networks. Advances such as ODI (Open Data-Link Interface) and TCP/IP (Transmission Control Protocol/Internet Protocol) support in the server make interoperability easier, but interoperability is not automatic.

intranet A local network infused with Internet technology. For most companies, this means Web servers and clients used for connections within the company network, rather than outside to the Internet. NetWare supports this function well.

IntranetWare - intraNetWare Novell's name-mistake bundle that included the operating system, the Web Server, NetWare/IP, the Multi-Protocol Router (MPR), and the IPX/IP Gateway (Novell Internet Access Server) with NetWare 4.11. The name emphasizes the value of an existing NetWare network, now infused with Web and Internet technologies. Thankfully, the intraNetWare name was dumped after a single release, and every box of NetWare now includes Internet technology.

IP (Internet Protocol) Part of the TCP/IP (Transmission Control Protocol/Internet Protocol) protocol suite. IP is similar to IPX (Internetwork Packet eXchange) in that it makes a best-effort attempt to deliver packets but does not guarantee delivery. TCP is required for that step, as SPX (Sequenced Packet eXchange) is required in NetWare.

IP address The four-byte address, which must be unique in the entire Internet if connected, that identifies host network connections. Normally seen in the dotted-decimal format, such as 204.251.122.12. Internet committees oversee IP address coordination and distribution.

IPX (Internetwork Packet eXchange) The Novell-developed and Xerox Network Services (XNS)-derived protocol used by NetWare. Addressing and routing for IPX is handled by NetWare, unlike the corresponding functions in TCP/IP (Transmission Control Protocol/Internet Protocol).

IPX external network number The unique network number that identifies a single network cable segment. The IPX (Internetwork Packet eXchange) network is defined by a hexadecimal number of from one to eight digits (1 to FFFFFFFE). A random number is assigned during installation, or the installer can specify the external network number.

IPX internal network number The unique network number that identifies a NetWare server. Each server on a network must have a unique IPX (Internetwork Packet eXchange) internal network number. A random number is assigned during installation, or the installer can specify the internal network number for each server.

IPX internetwork address A 12-byte number (24 hexadecimal characters) made up of three parts: a four-byte IPX (Internetwork Packet eXchange) external network number, a six-byte node number (derived from the interface card's unique address), and a two-byte socket number.

PART

V

Appendices

IPX/IP Gateway   Generically, any software that converts datagrams from IPX (Internetwork Packet eXchange) to IP (Internet Protocol). There are at least a dozen vendors that sell IP translation gateways, most of which are focused on the NetWare market.

Specifically, IPX/IP Gateway is the name of Novell's IP translation software running under NetWare 4.*x* and higher versions and included as part of intraNetWare.

IPXODI (Internetwork Packet eXchange Open Data-Link Interface)   The client software module that accepts data from the DOS requester, attaches a header to each data packet, and transmits the data packet as a datagram.

JavaBeans   An object-oriented programming interface from Sun Microsystems that lets programmers develop reusable applications or program building blocks, called *components*.

JavaScript   An interpreted programming or scripting language from Netscape now used by many Web sites to add functionality to Web browser clients.

jukebox   A clever updated meaning for the old musical device, a jukebox for NetWare is a device holding multiple optical disks, which plays one or more at a time as requested by the operating system. Capacity for jukeboxes ranges from two disks and one reader to hundreds of disks and a dozen readers.

LAN driver   Software in the server and workstation that interfaces the physical network board to the machine's operating system.

Large Internet Packet (LIP)   A feature that allows packets going through routers to have more than 576 bytes. The small packet size was a limitation of ARCnet packets, and NetWare defaulted to the small size in case ARCnet was on the other side of the router. Because the use of ARCnet is dwindling, this restriction has been lifted.

LDAP (Lightweight Directory Access Protocol)   An emerging Internet protocol that allows client software to query a directory database in a standard fashion, regardless of the type of directory database or the platform it is stored on.

leaf object   A Novell Directory Services (NDS) object that can't contain other objects. Examples are users, volumes, printers, and servers.

license certificate   A piece of paper entitling you to use software you have purchased (or obtained legally) under the conditions outlined. Novell Licensing Services (NLS) also creates License Certificate objects in the Novell Directory Services (NDS) directory to represent NLS-enabled applications.

License Services Application Programming Interface   An application programming interface (API) that allows application developers to use Novell's Licensing Services (NLS) to control usage and metering of applications that are used on the network or on workstations where the application is installed locally but the workstation is connected to the network.

Link Support Layer (LSL)   The client and server software between the LAN drivers and the communications protocols. The LSL allows more than one protocol to share a network board.

loadable module   An executable file with the extension .NLM (for NetWare Loadable Module) that runs on the server. NLMs can be loaded and unloaded without taking the server down.

local area network (LAN)   A network connected by physical cables, such as within a floor or building.

local groups   In a Windows NT system, an organization of user accounts and/or global groups used to assign permissions to resources on local computers. They can contain user accounts and global groups from one or more domains that have trust relationships established with the domain.

log in   The process by which a user requests and receives authentication from the operating system and then is able to use network resources. Login scripts configure details such as printer setup and drive assignments.

LOGIN directory   SYS:LOGIN, a default NetWare directory, created during installation. The directory contains LOGIN and NLIST utilities to support users who are not yet authenticated.

login restrictions   User restrictions that control certain network security parameters. Login restrictions include the workstation a user is allowed to log in from, the time of day, and whether the user is allowed to have more than one active connection to the network.

login script   An ASCII text file that performs designated commands to configure a user's workstation environment. The login scripts are activated when the user executes the LOGIN command.

   Container login scripts set general parameters for all users in a container and execute first. *Profile login scripts* also set parameters for multiple users, but only for those users who specify the Profile script. This script executes after the Container script. *User login scripts* set parameters for individual users and are the least efficient for administrators to use.

PART

V

Appendices

login security   An aspect of NetWare security. The NetWare supervisor establishes login security by using the LOGIN command to control who can access the network. Users must be authenticated by Novell Directory Services (NDS) by use of the login name and the correct password (although they are optional, passwords are strongly recommended). Passwords travel between the client and server in an encrypted mode, so network protocol analyzers cannot capture any passwords.

log out   To disconnect from the network. The LOGOUT command does not remove the Novell client software from workstation memory.

Macintosh client   A NetWare desktop client using a Macintosh computer.

MAIL directory   SYS:MAIL, a default NetWare directory created by the system during installation. Earlier NetWare versions stored each user's login script in his or her personal mail directory; now login scripts are a property of the User object.

MAP   A command-line utility that checks drive assignments and allows users to modify those assignments. If MAP commands are placed in a login script, they can assign drive letters to directory paths during the login process.

Media Access Control (MAC) address   A unique address assigned to the network adapter hardware.

Media Manager   NetWare functions that abstract backup storage device control, allowing applications to address different storage devices without using device-specific drivers.

Media Support Module (MSM)   See *Open Data-Link Interface (ODI)*.

member server   A Windows NT server that is part of a domain but does not contain the directory database for the domain. It provides resources for use by the domain.

memory   A computer's internal storage under control of the operating system, generally called random access memory (RAM) in desktop computers. The storage and retrieval speed of RAM is more closely matched to that of the CPU than any other system storage.

memory allocation   Segmenting random access memory (RAM) for specific purposes such as disk caches, extended memory, and application execution space. NetWare has replaced the five memory allocation pools with a single, more efficient memory pool.

Message Handling Services (MHS)   Early (NetWare 2.*x* through 4.10) e-mail integration and coordination software. MHS provided a standard means of connecting disparate e-mail systems. The focus on Internet technologies, including the intraNetWare product, has moved the LAN e-mail world to Internet standards, leaving MHS behind.

message packet   A basic unit of transmitted network information.

message system   The set of Application Program Interfaces (APIs) running on top of IPX (Internetwork Packet eXchange), which facilitate messages between nodes on the network.

Metered Certificate   A Novell Licensing Services (NLS) directory object that helps track usage and provide metering for applications.

Migrated attribute   A NetWare file indicator showing whether a file has migrated through Hierarchical Storage Management (HSM) off the server hard disk.

migration   The process of moving bindery and other data from earlier NetWare servers or a different network operating system to NetWare 5.1. Part of a High-Capacity Storage System (HCSS) method of moving a file from the server to the jukebox (*migration*) and, when requested, back to the server hard disk (*demigration*).

Migration Agent   NetWare 5.1 software that converts packets from IPX (Internetwork Packet eXchange) clients into IP (Internet Protocol) packets that are destined for IP servers.

Modify bit   A status file attribute that indicates whether the file has been changed since the last backup. This bit is used by backup systems such as SBACKUP to know which files to protect when a partial backup is used. Commonly known as the *Archive bit*.

Modify right   Authority to change file or directory names or attributes.

MONITOR   The utility that displays the primary NetWare server information screen. MONITOR tracks the state of the server and, to a lesser extent, the state of the network. As a NetWare Loadable Module (NLM), it executes only at the server.

multilink   Provides the ability for Dial-Up Networking clients the ability to use more than one modem or Integrated Services Digital Network (ISDN) channel when connecting to a Novell Internet Access Server (NIAS). Also called *channel bonding*.

Multiple Layer Interface Driver (MLID)   See *Open Data-Link Interface (ODI)*.

PART

V

Appendices

multiport serial adapter A serial adapter port that provides one, two, four, eight, or more high-speed asynchronous ports. Some of these adapters include built-in modems.

Multi-Protocol Router (MPR) An expansion of Novell's long-time ability to route multiple protocols through the NetWare server operating system. Sold separately for awhile, MPR is included with NetWare starting with the intraNetWare/4.11 product. Any currently available WAN connection, up through T1 lines, may be controlled by WAN boards in a NetWare server running the MPR software.

multiserver network A physical network with more than one server. Internet-works have more than one network connected by a router or gateway.

name context The location of an object in the Novell Directory Services (NDS) tree.

name space The ability of a NetWare volume to support files from non-DOS clients, including Macintosh, OS/2, FTAM (Open Systems Interconnect), and Unix (Network File System, or NFS) systems. Each client sees files on the file server in its own file format. A Macintosh client will see a file as a Macintosh file, while an OS/2 user will see that same file as an OS/2 file.

Name space support is enabled per volume. NLMs with an extension of .NAM are loaded to provide the filename translations. The ADD NAME SPACE command is nec-essary for each volume, after the appropriate name space NLM is loaded (for example, LOAD NFS, then ADD NAME SPACE). This process creates multiple entries for each file in the name space of the volume's file system.

Name spaces cannot be removed without using the VREPAIR utility or by deleting the volume and creating a replacement volume without the name space.

National Science Foundation (NSF) A United States government agency that has funded the development of a cross-country backbone network as well as regional net-works designed to connect scientists to the Internet. It operates the National Science Foundation Network (NSFNET).

NCP (NetWare Core Protocol) The NetWare Presentation-layer protocol and pro-cedures used by a server to fulfill workstation requests. NCP actions include manipu-lating files and directories, changing the Directory, printing, and opening programming connections (*semaphores*) between client and server processes. The process of starting and stopping a connection between the workstation and server is indelicately called creating and destroying a service connection.

NCP Packet Signature The NetWare security feature that allows each workstation to add a special "signature" to each packet going to the server. This signature changes with every packet, and this process makes it nearly impossible for another station to pretend to be a station with more security privileges.

NetWare Cluster Services   Optional product that links up to 32 NetWare servers into a cluster for hardware and software fault tolerance. Cluster resources, such as Web servers and databases, will automatically transfer from a stopped NetWare server to an assigned operational server.

NDS for NT   An add-on product from Novell that allows the integration and management of Windows NT domains from within NetWare Administrator.

NDS Manager   A graphical utility included with NetWare and intraNetWare that includes parts of the older Partition Manager client application and the DSREPAIR console NLM (NetWare Loadable Module) application. All partition and replica operations, except major repairs, are supported by NDS Manager.

NDS tree   Container objects and all the leaf objects that make up the hierarchical structure of the Novell Directory Services (NDS) database. Also known as a *Directory tree*.

NetBIOS   A peer-to-peer networking application interface used by IBM and Microsoft. Also a naming standard for computer names on Microsoft networks.

NETBIOS.EXE   The client networking file that emulates NetBIOS, the peer-to-peer network application interface used in IBM or IBM-inspired networks. The INT2F.COM file is necessary when the NETBIOS.EXE file is used.

NET.CFG   The client workstation boot file that contains configuration and setup parameters for the client's connection to the network. This file functions like the DOS CONFIG.SYS file and is read by the machine only during the startup of the network files.

NETSYNCx   Two utility programs for NetWare 3 and NetWare 4 servers (NETSYNC3 and NETSYNC4, respectively) that allow NetWare 3 servers to be managed by Novell Directory Services (NDS).

NetWare Administrator   The primary program for performing NetWare 4.1x and higher supervisory tasks. This application is fully graphical and runs within Windows supporting a 32-bit NetWare client.

NetWare DOS Requester   Client software for DOS and Windows computers. The DOS Requester replaces the earlier NetWare shell software. Modules of the DOS Requester provide shell compatibility for applications. See also *Virtual Loadable Module (VLM)*.

PART

V

Appendices

NetWare/IP Server modules and client software that replace IPX (Internetwork Packet eXchange) as the transport protocol between NetWare clients and NetWare servers by encapsulating the IPX information inside an IP (Internet Protocol) datagram. NetWare 5.1 supports NCP (NetWare Core Protocol) natively over IP, so this functionality is no longer necessary in a pure NetWare 5.1 network.

NetWare Loadable Module (NLM) A program that executes at the NetWare server. NLM programs are loaded at the command line, by one of the configuration programs, such as AUTOEXEC.NCF, or by another NLM. Types of NLMs include disk drivers (.DSK extension), LAN drivers (.LAN extension), name space (.NAM extension), and utilities/applications (.NLM extension).

NetWare Management Portal New, browser-based management utility included with NetWare 5.1 that focuses primarily on server-centric control. Handy and much faster than ConsoleOne, it allows remote management through the Internet.

NetWare NFS Services A collection of NetWare Loadable Modules (NLMs) that allows a NetWare server to participate in Unix networks as both a Network File System (NFS) client and server.

NetWare operating system The operating system developed by Novell in the early 1980s to share centralized server resources with multiple clients. The seven important features of the NetWare operating system are directory, file, print, security, messaging, management, and routing services.

NetWare partition A disk partition on a server hard disk under control of NetWare.

NetWare Requester for OS/2 NetWare Requester software for OS/2 clients provides the same NetWare client functions as those provided by the NetWare DOS Requester.

NetWare Runtime A specialized version of the NetWare operating system that allows only a single concurrent client. This is used most often as a platform for communication or application servers that provide their own user authentication. NetWare Runtime servers support all NetWare Loadable Modules (NLMs), both from Novell and third-party vendors.

NetWare server An Intel (or equivalent processor) based PC running the NetWare operating system.

NetWare server console operator A user authorized by the Admin or equivalent supervisory personnel to run server and print server software. Standard management tasks, such as print server loading and unloading or checking a file server using MONITOR, can be done by console operators.

NetWare Server object   A leaf object representing a NetWare server in the NDS tree.

NetWare Tools/NetWare User Tools   The Windows 3.1x-based graphical user utility provided with NetWare. NetWare User Tools (NWUSER) allows any user to see available network resources, map drives, add or change printing assignments, and send messages.

NetWire   The online information service accessed through CompuServe. Marketing and product information is available, as are patches, fixes, and helpful technical support files. All the information in NetWire on CompuServe is also included in Novell's Internet offerings: `ftp.novell.com` or `www.novell.com`. NetWire's days are numbered (if it's not gone by the time you read this), so make it a habit to use the Web site.

network backbone   A special network generally connecting only specialized devices such as servers, routers, and gateways. The backbone is a separate cabling system between these devices, isolating the backbone from regular client/server traffic.

network board   See *network interface card.*

network communication   Data exchanged in packet format over a defined network.

Network Driver Interface Specification (NDIS)   A process similar to Open Data-Link Interface (ODI) that allows a workstation to support multiple protocols over one network interface card. This was developed by 3Com, Microsoft, and Hewlett-Packard and released before Novell released the ODI drivers. ODINSUP (ODI NDIS Supplement) supports NDIS drivers under ODI when necessary.

Network File System (NFS)   File-sharing software developed by Sun Microsystems and considered to be the standard file-sharing protocol for Unix networks.

Network Information Services (NIS)   A naming and administration system developed by Sun Microsystems that is similar to the Domain Name Service (DNS). NIS is most commonly used in the Unix community.

network interface card (NIC)   A network board, card, or adapter (choose your term) that connects a device with the network cabling system. More recent Novell documentation favors network board rather than NIC or adapter; other companies and references are less restrictive.

network node   An intelligent device attached to the network. Traditionally, nodes are servers, workstations, printers, routers, gateways, or communication servers. However, other devices such as fax machines, copiers, security systems, and telephone equipment may be considered network nodes.

PART

V

Appendices

network numbering   A unique numbering scheme to identify network nodes and separate network cable systems. IPX (Internetwork Packet eXchange) automatically adds the node number for the client, while the server installation process sets the network cable segment number (IPX external network number) and the address of the server (IPX internal network number). TCP/IP (Transmission Control Protocol/Internet Protocol) networks require the installer to set and maintain all network addresses.

network printer   A printer that is attached to either the network cabling, file server, or workstation and is available for use by any network client.

network supervisor   A traditional term for the person responsible for the network, or a portion thereof (subadministrator). Also called the network administrator. Truly, a hero for the modern age.

Network Support Encyclopedia (NSE)   The CD-ROM–based information resource including Novell patches, fixes, drivers, bulletins, manuals, technical bulletins, compatibility testing results, press releases, and product information.

NETX   The Virtual Loadable Module (VLM) under the client DOS Requester that provides backward-compatibility with the older versions of the NetWare shell.

NLSP (NetWare Link Services Protocol)   A routing protocol designed by Novell that exchanges information about the status of the links between routers to build a map of the internetwork. Once the network map is built, information is transferred between routers only when the network changes. *Router Information Protocol* (RIP), the previous method for routers to exchange information, requires regular broadcasts that add network traffic. Using NLSP reduces routing traffic across WAN links. NLSP uses RIP to communicate with NetWare clients.

node number   Similar to a network number, a node number generally refers to a client machine only. Under NetWare, node numbers are based on the unique, factory-assigned address (Ethernet and Token Ring) or the card's configurable address (ARCnet and Token Ring cards supporting Locally Administered Addresses, or LAA).

Normal attribute   The default setting for NetWare files, indicated by a specific file-system attribute.

Novell Administrator for Windows NT   Software that allows the synchronization of Windows NT and NetWare accounts.

Novell Application Launcher (NAL)   A utility for managing applications presented to NetWare clients. The NetWare administrator defines which applications are available for the users and provides an icon group for the users. Different startup and shutdown scripts may be used for extra application control. NAL uses the Universal Naming Convention (UNC), reducing the need for more drive letters and their attendant management.

Novell Asynchronous Services Interface Communications Services (NCS)   A service of the Novell Internet Access Server (NIAS) (and formerly NetWare Connect) that provides network modem sharing.

Novell Client32   See *Client32*.

Novell Directory Database (NDD)   The database that stores and organizes all objects in the NDS tree. The objects are stored in a hierarchical structure, mimicking the hierarchical arrangement of NDS (Novell Directory Services) itself.

Novell Directory Services (NDS)   The distributed security and network resource-locating database released with NetWare 4.*x* and higher versions to replace and upgrade the bindery. The database in NDS is distributed and replicated among multiple servers for fault tolerance and high performance. Network resources controlled by NDS include users, groups, printers, volumes, and servers.

This database works on the network level, not per server. NDS allows access to network resources independent of the server holding those resources. With the bindery, each user was required to know the server responsible for each network service. NDS allows users to access resources without knowing the server responsible for those resources.

Users no longer establish a link to a single server in order to log in. Users are authenticated (logged in and verified) by the network itself through NDS. The authentication process provides the means for the client to communicate with NDS, as well as to check the security profile of each user.

Novell Distributed Print Services (NDPS)   Novell's next-generation printing architecture that centralizes and standardizes usage, service, and management of the printer. The NDPS architecture consists of Printer Agents, Brokers, NDPS Managers, and Gateways.

Novell Internet Access Server (NIAS)   The server software module that translates data requests from a client running on IPX (Internetwork Packet eXchange) to TCP/IP (Transmission Control Protocol/Internet Protocol) for connection to the Internet or TCP/IP host.

There are two pieces to this technology, one at the client and one at the server. The client software includes a special version of Winsock that "spoofs" the TCP/IP client software, such as Netscape, into believing the client is running the TCP/IP protocol stack. In reality, only IPX is running at the client.

The server portion of the Winsock software converts the data transport protocol from IPX to IP for connection to the TCP/IP systems. Outgoing packets are assigned port numbers in addition to the IP address of the NIAS, which is shared by all systems. Incoming packets, identified by their port numbers, are routed back across IPX to their original stations.

Novell Licensing Services (NLS)
A Novell Directory Services (NDS) management feature that tracks application use to ensure that you have enough valid licenses for the number of concurrent users for each application.

Novell Storage Management Services (SMS)
Services provided by Novell for backing up and restoring local data as well as data on remote servers. See also *Storage Management Services*.

Novell Storage Services (NSS)
Services provided by Novell to create large areas of storage that can reside on many different types of storage media.

NT File System (NTFS)
The native file system for Windows NT, which provides the ability to place file-level security on a Windows NT Server or NT Workstation machine.

object
In NetWare 5.1, a Novell Directory Services (NDS) database entry that holds information about a network client or another resource. The categories of information are called *properties*. For example, a User object's mandatory properties are login name and last name. The data in each property is called its *value*.

NetWare objects include users, printers, servers, volumes, and print queues. Some of these are physical; some are virtual, like the print queue and groups of users. Container objects help manage other objects. Leaf objects, such as users, printers, volumes, and servers, are the end nodes of the NDS tree.

Containers (called *branches* in some other systems) are Country (C), Organization (O), and Organizational Unit (OU) objects. A container object can be empty. Leaf objects can't contain any other objects.

Object names consist of the path from the root of the NDS tree down to the name of the object. The syntax is *object.container.container.root*. There may be one or more containers in the middle section. Typeless names list just the names (LPRATT.CONSULT.MLD). Typeful names list the designators (CN=LPRATT.OU=CONSULT.O=MLD). An advantage of NetWare 5.1 over earlier versions of NetWare is that it allows the constant use of typeless names.

object rights   Rights granted to a trustee over an object. An example is the Create object right for a container object, which allows the trustee to create new objects in that container.

Open Data-Link Interface (ODI)   Novell's specification, released in 1989, that details how multiple protocols and device drivers can coexist on a single network interface card without conflict. The ODI specification separates device drivers from protocol stacks. The biggest advantages of ODI over the Network Driver Interface Specification (NDIS) are speed and size. ODI routes packets only to the appropriate frame type, rather than to all frame types as in NDIS. The major components of the ODI architecture are as follows:

- Multiple Layer Interface Driver (MLID) is a device driver that manages the sending and receiving of packets to and from a physical (or logical) network. Each MLID is matched to the hardware or media and is therefore unique.

- Link Support Layer (LSL) is the interface layer between the protocol stacks and the device driver. Any driver may communicate with any ODI-compliant protocol stack through the LSL.

- Media Support Module (MSM) is the interface of the MLIDs to the LSL and the operating system. This module handles initialization and runtime issues for all drivers.

- Topology-Specific Module (TSM) is the software layer that handles a specific media type, such as Ethernet or Token Ring. All frame types are supported in the TSM for any media type supported.

- Hardware-Specific Module (HSM) is the software layer that handles adapter startup, reset, shutdown, packet reception, timeouts, and multi-cast addressing for a particular interface card.

Open Data-Link Interface/Network Driver Interface Specification Support (ODINSUP)   Refers to the interface that allows both ODI and NDIS protocol stacks to exist on a single network interface card.

Open Shortest Path First (OSPF)   A routing protocol developed for large, complex TCP/IP (Transmission Control Protocol/Internet Protocol) networks.

open systems   Technically, a goal of guaranteed interoperability between disparate operating systems. Marketing has recast this term to mean any system that can be coerced to communicate with TCP/IP (Transmission Control Protocol/Internet Protocol). Realistically, open systems utilize Internet and Web technologies to support any client connecting to any server.

PART

V

Appendices

Open Systems Interconnection (OSI) model   A reference model for the layering of common functions in a telecommunications system. This model consists of seven layers that define how an ideal network operates. These layers include Application, Presentation, Session, Transport, Network, Data Link, and Physical.

optical disk   A high-capacity disk storage device that writes or reads information based on reflecting laser light for bits, rather than reading magnetic fluctuations as on a standard hard or floppy disk. Disks may be read-only (a CD-ROM), read-once (a WORM, for Write Once Read Many), or fully rewritable.

optical disk library   A jukebox, which is an optical disk reader with an auto-changer that mounts and dismounts optical disks as requested.

Organization (O) object   The container object below the Country (C) object and above the Organizational Unit (OU) object in an NDS (Novell Directory Services) tree. Organization objects can contain Organizational Unit objects and leaf objects.

Organizational Role object   In an NDS tree, a leaf object that specifies a role within an organization, such as Purchasing Manager or Workgroup Leader. The Organizational Role object usually has special rights, and these rights tend to rotate among different users as job responsibilities change.

Organizational Unit (OU) object   The container object below the Organization object in an NDS tree. The Organizational Unit object can contain other Organizational Unit objects or leaf objects.

OS/2 client   A computer running NetWare client software for the OS/2 operating system (remember that?). OS/2 clients can perform almost all the same user and administrative operations that DOS or Windows workstations can perform.

packet   A block of data sent across the network; the basic unit of information used in network communications. Service requests, service responses, and data are all formed into packets by the network interface card driver software before the information is transmitted. Packets may be fixed or variable length. Large blocks of information will automatically be broken into appropriate packets for the network and reassembled by the receiving system.

Packet Burst Protocol (PBP)   The NetWare version of the TCP/IP (Transmission Control Protocol/Internet Protocol) *sliding windows* feature. Rather than send one packet to acknowledge the receipt of one packet, PBP acknowledges multiple packets at one time. This improves the performance of NCP (NetWare Core Protocol) file read and writes, especially across WAN connections.

NetWare 3.1 requires additional NetWare Loadable Modules (NLMs) loaded at the server and some configuration at the client. NetWare 5.1 has PBP built into both the server and client software automatically.

packet receive buffer   The memory area in the NetWare server that temporarily holds arriving data packets. These packets are held until the server can process the packets and send them to their proper destination. The packet receive buffer ensures that the server does not drop arriving packets, even when the server is heavily loaded with other operations.

paging   A NetWare performance feature that takes advantage of the Intel 80386 and above architecture to group memory into 4KB blocks of RAM. The NetWare operating system assigns memory locations in available 4KB pages, then uses a table to allow the noncontiguous pages to appear as a logical contiguous address space.

PAP (Password Authentication Protocol)   Used by PPP (Point-to-Point Protocol) dial-in systems to authenticate users. The user ID and password are sent over the telephone line in unencrypted format.

parent directory   In a file system, the directory immediately above any subdirectory.

parent object   An object that holds other objects. In Novell Directory Services (NDS), an Organization is a parent object for all included Organizational Unit and leaf objects.

parity   A simple form of error checking in communications.

partition   In a hard disk, a section treated by the operating system as an independent drive. For example, there are DOS and NetWare partitions on a server hard disk.

In Novell Directory Services (NDS), a partition is a division of the NDS database. A partition consists of at least one container object, all the objects therein, and all the data about those objects. A partition is contained in a replica. Partitions contain only NDS information; no file-system information is kept in a partition.

Partitions are useful for separating the Directory to support parts of the network on different sides of a WAN link. Multiple partitions are also advised when the network grows to include many servers and thousands of NDS objects. More partitions keep the NDS database closer to the users and speed up lookups and authentication.

The [Root] object at the top of the NDS tree is the first partition created during installation. New partitions are created with the NDS Manager (NetWare 4.11 and above), NetWare Administrator (NetWare 4.10), or PARTMGR utility. Each partition must contain contiguous containers. The partition immediately toward the [Root] of another is called that partition's *parent*. The included partition is referred to as the *child partition*.

password   The most common security measure used in networks to identify a specific, authorized user of the system. Each user should have a unique password. NetWare encrypts the login passwords at the workstation and transmits them in a format only the NetWare server can decode.

path   The location of a file or directory. An *absolute* path is the complete location of a file or directory, listed from the root of the drive through each directory and subdirectory and ending with the filenames. A *relative* path is from the current location.

PCONSOLE   The DOS utility that allows supervisors to control the NetWare printing system. With PCONSOLE, printers, print queues, and print servers can be created, modified, assigned, and deleted.

Perl   A scripting language similar to C, but with many Unix functions such as sed and awk.

permissions   Used for access control in Windows NT systems, similar to file-system rights in NetWare.

physical memory   The random access memory (RAM) in a computer or server.

Point-to-Point Protocol Remote Node Service (PPPRNS)   A service of the Novell Internet Access Server (NIAS) (and formerly NetWare Connect) that allows remote PPP (Point-to-Point Protocol) clients to dial in to NetWare servers. It also allows connectivity to other services on the network on which the NIAS server resides.

POP3 (Post Office Protocol v3)   An Internet protocol for retrieving e-mail from a mailbox located on a server.

port   A *hardware port* is the termination point of a communication circuit, as in parallel port. A *software port* is the memory address that specifies the transfer point between the microprocessor and a peripheral device.

power conditioning   The method used to protect electronic equipment from power fluctuations. Power conditioning can work by suppressing, isolating, or regulating the electric current provided to that equipment.

PPP (Point-to-Point Protocol)   A protocol for communication between two computers using a serial interface, typically a personal computer connected by telephone line to a server. PPP is commonly used to connect to the Internet via modem.

PPTP (Point-to-Point Tunneling Protocol)   A protocol that allows corporations to extend their own corporate network through private "tunnels" over the public Internet. Effectively, a corporation uses a wide area network as a single large local area network. A company no longer needs to lease its own lines for wide area communication but can securely use the public networks.

primary domain controller (PDC)   A Windows NT Server that contains the master directory database. The PDC serves as the administration point for the domain. There is only one PDC for each domain.

Primary time server   The NetWare server that provides time information to Secondary time servers and workstations. Primary time servers must synchronize time with at least one other Primary or Reference time server.

print device   Any device that puts marks on paper or plastic, such as a laser, dot-matrix, or inkjet printer or a plotter. NetWare's defined print device files have a .PDF extension and can be configured by using the NetWare Administrator or PRINTDEF utility.

print device mode   The sequence of printer commands (or print functions, control sequences, or escape sequences) that control the appearance of the printed file. Print device modes can define the style, size, boldness, and orientation of the typeface. Modes are set by using the NetWare Administrator or PRINTDEF utility.

print job   Any file in a print queue waiting to be printed. Once the print server forwards the print job to the printer, the print job is deleted from the queue.

print job configuration   Characteristics that define how a job is physically printed, rather than how the printed output looks on the page. For example, a print job configuration may specify the printer the job will print on, the print queue the job is sent through, the number of copies to print, or the use of a banner page.

print queue   The directory on a volume that stores print jobs waiting for printer assignment. In NetWare 5.1, the print queue directory may be stored on any volume. Earlier NetWare versions (including NetWare 4 servers in bindery mode) limit the print queue to the SYS: volume. Print queue capacity is limited only by disk space. Print queues can be created by using either the NetWare Administrator or PCONSOLE utility.

print queue operator   A user with additional authority to manage the print queue. Print queue operators can edit the status of print jobs, delete print jobs, change the service mode, or modify the print queue operational status. This is an excellent job for subadministrators.

print queue polling time   The interval between print server status checks of the print queue for jobs. Users can modify the time period.

PART

V

Appendices

print server   In a NetWare server, the PSERVER.NLM software moves print jobs from the print queue to the appropriate network printer. NetWare print servers can service up to 256 printers and associated print queues.

Third-party print servers are small hardware devices that connect directly to the network cabling and support one or more printers remotely from the file server. Printing performance is increased by using remote print servers rather than printers attached to the file server itself.

Print Server object   The leaf object that represents a network print server in the NDS tree.

print server operator   A user granted extra authority to manage a print server. Rights include the ability to control notification lists, supported printers, and queue assignments.

printer   Any device that puts marks on paper or plastic, such as a laser, dot-matrix, or inkjet printer or a plotter. A network printer can be attached to the file server or an external print server. In Novell Directory Services (NDS), Printer objects are independent of the Print Queue and Print Server objects.

Printer Agent   Represents a Novell Distributed Print Services (NDPS) Printer object. It replaces the Print Queue, Printer, and Print Server objects found in traditional NetWare printing models.

printer definition   The control characters, specific to the printer model, that interpret the commands to modify printed text.

printer form   A print system option that allows users to specify which type of paper (letter, legal, memo, and so on) to use for any print job. Each defined printer form is given a unique name and number between 0 and 255. Printer forms may be specified in the print job configuration or with the command-line printer utilities NPRINT and CAPTURE. The mounted form must match the requested form or the print job won't print.

Printer object   The leaf object representing a physical printer on the network in the NDS tree.

private key security   See *public key/private key security*.

privilege level   The rights granted to users or groups by the NetWare Administrator program. These rights set the level of network access for that user or group.

Privilege level also refers to the microprocessor access level determined by the Intel architecture for 80386 and higher microprocessors. Four levels are defined: 0 through 3. NetWare uses the 0 and 3 levels. These levels, also known as *protection rings*, are controlled by the NetWare memory domains.

Profile login script A special type of login script that can be applied to several users with identical login script needs. Profile login scripts are not mandatory. They execute after the Container login script but before the User login script.

Profile object The special leaf object that represents the Profile login script in the NDS tree.

program A software program, which may or may not use the available network resources. Also referred to as an *application*.

prompt An on-screen character(s) that awaits your input. Examples are the DOS prompt, the OS/2 prompt, and the colon prompt of the NetWare server console.

property A piece of information, or characteristic, of any Novell Directory Services (NDS) object. For example, User object properties include login name, last name, password restrictions, and similar information.

property rights Rights to read, create, modify, or delete properties of a Novell Directory Services (NDS) object.

protected memory address space An area of memory that is protected from programs that are not part of that memory space. Programs in a specific memory space cannot interfere with programs in other memory spaces. This prevents one NLM from crashing another (or the entire operating system).

protected mode The mode in 80286 and higher Intel processors that support multitasking and virtual memory management. This mode is the default used by processors. They switch to real mode only when forced to emulate the earlier 8086 processor functions. In protected mode, 80286 processors can address up to 16MB of memory. 80386 and higher processors can address up to 4GB of memory.

protection ring See *privilege level*.

proxy server A server that acts as an intermediary between a workstation user and the Internet so that the enterprise can ensure security, administrative control, and caching service. A proxy server is associated with or part of a gateway server that separates the enterprise network from the outside network and a firewall server that protects the enterprise network from outside intrusion.

Public Access Printer A Novell Distributed Print Services (NDPS)-compatible printer that has been installed on the network but not yet created as an object in Novell Directory Services (NDS) and is therefore available to everyone on the network.

PART

V

Appendices

PUBLIC directory   One of the NetWare system directories created during installation. PUBLIC stores NetWare utilities and files for use by all clients. The default login script for DOS users maps a search drive to SYS:PUBLIC, with Read and File Scan rights granted automatically.

public files   Files kept in the SYS:PUBLIC directory, placed there during NetWare installation. These include all command-line utilities, Help files, and printer definition files.

Public Key Infrastructure Services (PKIS)   A service supported by Novell that allows developers to take advantage of a public/private key infrastructure rather than writing their own public/private key systems.

public key/private key security   An encryption mechanism that employs two unique keys for encrypting data. The publicly available key is used to encrypt the data, and the private key is used to decrypt the data. The public key cannot be used to decrypt data that it has previously encrypted.

Public Switched Telephone Network (PSTN)   The public telephone network, sometimes called POTS (for Plain Old Telephone Service). The telephone network in the United States is limited to a maximum transmission speed of 53Kbps by the FCC.

Public trustee   A special NetWare trustee, used only for trustee assignments. It allows objects in Novell Directory Services (NDS) that do not have any other rights to have the effective rights granted to the [Public] trustee. This works similarly to the user GUEST or group EVERYONE in earlier NetWare versions. [Public] can be created and deleted, just like any other trustee. The Inherited Rights Filter (IRF) will block inherited rights for the [Public] trustee.

Rather than use the [Public] trustee to grant rights to large groups of objects, it's more secure to grant those rights only to a container object. The difference between the two options is that rights granted to a container object are only passed to those objects in the container, while [Public] rights go to all objects.

Purge attribute   The file-system attribute that allows the NetWare operating system to completely erase a directory or file that has been deleted.

random access memory (RAM)   The main system memory in a computer addressed by the operating system. RAM is used for the operating system, applications, and data. The memory is dynamic, and the information contained in RAM is cleared when power is discontinued.

RCONSOLE   The NetWare utility (Remote Console) that echoes the server console to a DOS workstation. This ability is also included in the NetWare Administrator program under the Tools drop-down menu.

Any function that can be done at the server console can be done via RCONSOLE. Before running RCONSOLE, however, the server must have the following commands in the `AUTOEXEC.NCF` file, or they must be entered at the colon prompt:

```
LOAD REMOTE password
LOAD RSPX
```

read-after-write verification   The method used by NetWare to guarantee the integrity of data written to the hard disk. After data is written to the disk, it is compared to the data still held in memory. If it matches, the memory is cleared. If the data does not match, the hard disk block is marked as "bad" and the Hot Fix feature redirects the data to a known good block in the Hot Fix Redirection area.

Read-Only attribute   The file-system attribute indicating that the file can be read, but not modified, written to, or deleted.

Read right   The file-system right that allows a user to open and read files.

real mode   The 8086 emulation mode in 80286, 80386, and 80486 Intel processors. Real mode is limited to 1MB of RAM address, as the 8086 itself is limited, and no multitasking is possible.

record locking   The operating system feature that prevents more than one user from modifying a record or file at the same time.

recursive copying   Copying the complete contents of a directory or directory structure, using the recursion property that enables a subroutine to call itself. For example, XCOPY and NCOPY use recursive copying to copy all files in a directory structure.

Reference time server   A NetWare server that provides the network time to Primary and Secondary time servers and workstations.

Remote Access Management Agent (RAMA)   A service of the Novell Internet Access Server (NIAS) that allows NIAS servers to be managed by management consoles such as Novell's ManageWise.

remote boot   The process of booting a workstation from the files on a NetWare server rather than from a local drive.

remote workstation   A personal computer linked to the LAN by a router or through a remote asynchronous connection. Remote workstations can be either stand-alone or part of another network.

Rename Inhibit attribute   The file-system attribute that prevents a file or directory from being renamed.

Rename right   The authority for an object to change the name of an object. This technically changes the Name property.

replica   A copy of a Novell Directory Services (NDS) partition, used to eliminate a single point of failure, as well as to place the NDS database closer to users in more distant parts of the network. There are three types of replicas that can be managed:

- The Master replica is the primary replica, created during installation. A Master replica of the [Root] partition is stored in a hidden directory on the SYS: volume of the first file server installed.

- The Read/Write replica is used to read or update the database. Actions such as adding or deleting objects or authenticating users are handled by the Read/Write replicas. There should be at least two Read/Write replicas for each partition, to ensure that the Directory will function if one or two of the servers that hold replicas are unavailable.

- The Read-Only replica is the least powerful replica, used to access or display NDS database information, but unable to support changes. (Read-Only replicas are generally not very useful.)

Subordinate Reference replicas are maintained by the system. They cannot be modified by a user (even the supervisor).

Replica synchronization is the process of a partition's replicas exchanging information to stay up-to-date. When a change is made to one replica, the synchronization process guarantees that all other replicas obtain the same information as soon as it is practical.

Request for Comment (RFC)   An Internet or other technical standard or formal document that is the result of committee drafting and subsequent review by interested parties. As an Internet standard, the final version of an RFC becomes an established document that cannot be changed. (However, subsequent RFCs may supersede or elaborate on all or parts of previous RFCs.)

resolver   Name given to a Domain Name Service (DNS) name server client.

resource fork   A Macintosh-specific file portion that contains Macintosh-specific windows and icons, as well as the file resources.

resource tag   An operating system function call that tracks NetWare server resources. Screens and memory allocated for various tasks, as well as the memory resources used by NetWare Loadable Modules (NLMs), must be tracked so that the resources can be made available to the operating system once the NLMs are stopped or no longer require the resource.

resources   Technically, any part of the network, including cabling, concentrators, servers, gateways, and the like. Practically, resources are the components on a network that are desired by the network clients. Under this definition, resources tend to be server volumes, gateways, printers, print queues, users, processes, and the security options of a network.

restore   To replace a file or files from the backup media onto the server hard disk. This is done when the file or files on the server hard disk have been erased or corrupted by accident (most commonly) or when an entire disk's worth of files needs to be replaced after a disk failure.

ribbon cable   Flat cable with each conductor glued to the side of the other conductors rather than twisted around each other. This type of cable is used most often for internal disk and tape drive connections.

rights   Privileges granted to NetWare users or groups of users by the Admin user (or equivalent). These rights determine all functions the user can perform on the system, including reading, writing, creating, deleting, and modifying files and directories.

Trustee assignments grant rights to specific directories, files, or objects. An object with a trustee assignment to a directory, file, or another object is called a *trustee* of that directory, file, or object.

Each object maintains a list of which other objects have rights to the object in the Access Control List (ACL).

Directory rights apply to the directory in the NetWare file system in which they were assigned, as well as to all files and subdirectories in that directory. Rights flow downhill. By granting trustee rights to the top level of a directory, the trustee has the same rights to all files and subdirectories.

Rights can be reassigned or modified by the Inherited Rights Filter (IRF) in lower levels of the directory tree. These rights are part of the file system only and have no relevance to Novell Directory Services (NDS) objects.

The following types of rights apply to a NetWare network:

- File rights apply to only the file to which they are assigned. Trustees may inherit file rights from the directory containing the file.

- Object rights apply to only NDS objects. These rights do not affect the properties of the object, just the object itself.

- Property rights apply to only the properties of NDS objects. These rights may be assigned to each property, or a default set of rights may be assigned to all properties.

A trustee must have the Access Control right to a directory or file before granting directory or file rights to other objects. A trustee must have the Write, Add or Delete Self, or Supervisor right to the ACL property of the object before granting other objects property or object rights to the object.

RIP (Routing Information Protocol)   A widely used protocol that allows routers to communicate with one another to share routing information. RIP is most effective for smaller, private networks.

root container   The highest container in an NDS tree partition. The partition and replicas are named after the applicable root container.

root directory   The highest directory level in a directory structure. The root directory is the volume in NetWare, and all directories are subdirectories of their volume.

[Root] object   The highest object in an NDS tree. The purpose of the [Root] object is to provide an access point to different Country and Organization objects. Rights granted to the [Root] object are granted to the entire NDS tree. The [Root] object holds no information; it merely acts as a reference point.

router   A combination of hardware and software that examines the internet or network layer of a datagram in order to make a decision about the best route that datagram should take to get to its destination. The router maintains tables of available routes and forwards the datagram on based on the optimal route. Routers function at the third layer of the OSI model.

salvageable files   Files that have been deleted by a user or application but are still tracked by NetWare. The FILER utility shows the list of salvageable files and can recover files if they have not been overwritten on the server disk.

If the directory that contained a deleted file was also deleted, the file is saved in a system directory labeled DELETED.SAV in the volume's root directory.

Deleted files can be purged, eliminating any chance of salvage. If the NetWare server runs out of available allocation blocks on the volume, it will start purging files to make room for new files. The files are deleted on a first-deleted, first-purged basis.

SAP (Service Advertising Protocol)   The NetWare protocol that allows servers of all types to broadcast their available services across the network. Routers and other NetWare servers receive and track these broadcasts to keep their router information tables up-to-date.

NetWare clients begin each login process by broadcasting a Get Nearest Server SAP packet. The first server that responds will become the server the workstation attaches to before continuing the login process.

Because of the traffic generated by SAP, most WAN routers now offer the capability of filtering SAP broadcasts. SAP filtering can also be activated on the NetWare server.

SBACKUP   A software utility that provides the means for NetWare backup and restore operations.

scheduled action   An event that is scheduled to run using ZENworks policies and Workstation Manager tools. The action can be any program, such as a SCANDISK, virus scan, or application installation.

schema   Novell Directory Services (NDS) database design components, hidden from direct manipulation. Applications that use NDS may modify and expand the schema; for example, the schema is extended when the IPX/IP Gateway adds new objects to the NDS database.

SCSI (Small Computer Systems Interface)   The industry standard that sets guidelines for connecting peripheral storage devices and controllers to a microprocessor. SCSI (pronounced "scuzzy") defines both the hardware and software requirements for the connections. The wide acceptance of the SCSI standard makes it easy to connect any disk or tape drive to any computer.

SCSI bus   Another name for the SCSI (Small Computer Systems Interface) interface and communications protocol.

SCSI disconnect   A feature in NetWare that allows communications with SCSI (Small Computer Systems Interface) disks to be more efficient by informing the disk of upcoming input/output (I/O) requests.

search drive   A designated drive used by the operating system to look for a requested file that is not found in the current directory. Search drives allow users working in one directory to access application and data files in other directories. NetWare allows up to 16 search drives per user.

search mode   A specification that tells programs how to use search drives when looking for a data file. When an .EXE or .COM file requires support files, the file-open request is made through the operating system. This request may or may not specify a path to the support files. When a path is specified, that path is searched. If no path is specified, the default directory is searched first. If the files are not found, the Novell client software uses the search mode of the executable file to determine whether or not to continue looking in the search drives.

Secondary time server   A NetWare server that requests and receives time information from another server, then provides that time information to requesting workstations.

secret key encryption   An encryption mechanism that employs a single key (or password) to encrypt data. The same key is used to decrypt the encrypted information.

Secure Sockets Layer (SSL)   Program extensions created by Netscape that manage the security of data crossing a network by encrypting the data. SSL can be implemented between many different types of clients and servers, including Web browser and mail clients.

security   The operating system controls used by the network administrator to limit user access to network resources. The six categories of NetWare security are login security, trustees, rights, inheritance, attributes, and effective rights.

security equivalence   The assignment of one set of rights to an object that has the same needs as another object. Security equivalence is a quick way to give the same access privileges to two or more objects, but it should be used with extreme caution.

Being a member of a group list gives a user the same trustee rights as those granted to the Group object. The same security equivalence is granted to all users listed in the occupant list of an Organizational Role object.

Each object also receives an "implied" security equivalence to its own container. If the container is granted the Supervisor right to a volume, all users in that container will also have the Supervisor right to that volume.

semaphore   A file-locking and control mechanism to facilitate control over the sharing of files. Semaphores with byte value 0 allow file sharing; byte value 1 locks the file while in use. Semaphores are also used to limit the concurrent number of users for applications. When the user count is reached, the semaphore blocks any more users from gaining access until a current user closes the file.

serial port   A hardware port. IBM PCs and compatible computers generally come with COM1 and COM2, which transmit data one bit at a time. Serial ports are primarily used for a modem or a mouse on the workstation. In the past, these ports were used on file servers for serial printers. Today, most printers are parallel printers, so it is rare to see a serial printer attached to a file server.

serialization   The process of branding each NetWare operating system with a unique serial number to prevent software piracy. If two NetWare servers discover (through non-filterable broadcasts) that both are using software with the same serial number, copyright violation warnings are shown at the server console and at each connected workstation.

server   A *NetWare server* is a PC providing network resources through the use of the NetWare operating system.

A *print server* is a device that routes print jobs from a print queue and sends them to a printer. The print server may be software in a file server or workstation, or a stand-alone unit attached to the network cabling. The Novell Directory Services (NDS) object that represents this device is referred to as a Print Server object.

A *time server* is a NetWare server that provides time to network clients and is capable of providing time for other servers. All NetWare servers are time servers of some type (Primary, Secondary, Single Reference, or Reference).

A *Web server* is a software system based on HTTP communications to send HTML-enabled documents to Web client systems. Novell's Web Server is included with intraNetWare.

server console   The information screen for the NetWare server operating system. Monitoring traffic levels, setting configuration parameters, loading additional software NetWare Loadable Modules (NLMs), and shutting down the server must be done at the server console.

The physical keyboard and monitor on the file server are the primary server console. The RCONSOLE utility allows a DOS session on a network client to echo the server screen and redirect keyboard input across the network.

server protocol   An inaccurate shorthand method of referring to NCP (NetWare Core Protocol). NCP is used on more devices than just the server.

SERVMAN   The server-based utility that provides an interactive front end to NetWare's SET commands. SERVMAN configures the AUTOEXEC.NCF, CONFIG.SYS, and TIMESYNC.CFG files through the traditional NetWare menu interface. Starting with NetWare 5.0, SERVMAN folded into MONITOR under the Server Parameters setting. All the SERVMAN functions can be done just as well, starting with NetWare 5.1, through the NetWare Management Portal browser interface.

Shareable attribute   The file-system extended attribute for NetWare that allows more than one user to access a file concurrently.

short machine type   A short (four letters or fewer) identifier specified in the NET.CFG file. The default is IBM. The short machine type is used specifically with overlay files, such as IBM$RUN.OVL for the DOS windowing utilities.

Single Reference time server   A NetWare server that provides time to workstations and Secondary time servers. The Single Reference name comes from the fact that a server so designated is the single source of time for the network. This is the default for the first server in an NDS tree.

SLIP (Serial Line Internet Protocol)
An Internet protocol used for dial-up connections. It is used to transfer IP (Internet Protocol) datagrams across a dial-up link.

PART

V

Appendices

SLP (Service Location Protocol)   An Internet protocol used for automatic discovery of resources on IP (Internet Protocol) networks. The equivalent of this protocol on IPX/SPX (Internetwork Packet eXchange/Sequenced Packet Exchange) networks is the SAP (Service Advertising Protocol). NetWare 5.1 implements SLP when using TCP/IP (Transmission Control Protocol/Internet Protocol).

SMTP (Simple Mail Transfer Protocol)   An Internet protocol standard used for transporting e-mail messages across the Internet from SMTP clients to SMTP servers.

snAppShot   A program used to take a "picture" of a workstation both before an application is installed and afterwards. Once the before and after pictures are taken, a differences file is created and stored (usually on the server). The Novell Application Launcher (NAL) can then install that application to other workstations automatically or repair missing files on a workstation that already has the application installed.

SNMP (Simple Network Management Protocol)   An Internet protocol that defines functions for monitoring and managing devices on an IP (Internet Protocol) network.

socket   The destination point within an IPX (Internetwork Packet eXchange) packet on a network node. The socket number is part of an IPX internetwork address. Many sockets, such as those used by NCP (NetWare Core Protocol), are reserved by Novell. Third-party developers may also reserve socket numbers by registering their intentions with Novell.

source routing   The IBM method of routing data across multiple networks by specifying the route in each frame. The end stations determine the route through a discovery process supported by source-routing bridges or routers.

There are two types of source routing:

- In *single-route broadcasting*, designated bridges pass the packet between source and destination, meaning only one copy of each packet arrives in the remote network.

- In *all-routes broadcasting*, the packet is sent through all bridges or routers on the network. This results in many copies of the same frame arriving at the remote network—as many frames as there are bridges or routers.

sparse file   A file with at least one empty block, often created by databases. Some operating systems will write any file to disk in its entirety, even if only 12 bytes were written. NetWare copies only the last block to disk, tracking the application's request and saving time and disk space. The NCOPY utility will not copy sparse files unless forced to with the /f option.

SPX (Sequenced Packet eXchange)   The part of NetWare's transport protocol suite that guarantees packet delivery at the protocol level. If an SPX packet is not acknowledged within a specific amount of time, SPX retransmits the packet. In applications that use only IPX (Internetwork Packet eXchange), the application program is responsible for ensuring that packets are received intact. Because of the guaranteed nature of SPX, this protocol is often used for backup systems based in workstations.

STARTUP.NCF   The first of two boot configuration files on a NetWare server. The STARTUP.NCF file primarily loads and configures the disk driver and name space support. Some SET parameters may also be set through this file. It is located on the DOS partition and in the directory where SERVER is executed.

station   Usually, station is short for *workstation*, but it can refer to any intelligent node connected to the network.

Storage Device Interface (SDI)   SBACKUP (NetWare's backup software utility) routines that are used to access various storage devices. If more than one storage device is attached to the host server, SDI supplies a list of all devices.

Storage Management Services (SMS)   NetWare services that support the storage and retrieval of data. SMS is independent of file systems (such as DOS, OS/2, Unix, or Macintosh) and the backup and restore hardware.

SMS NLMs and other software modules that run on NetWare servers include the following:

- *SBACKUP* provides backup and restore capabilities.
- *Storage Management Data Requester* (SMDR) sends commands and information between SBACKUP and Target Service Agents (TSAs).
- *Storage Device Interface* sends commands and information between SBACKUP and the storage devices.
- *Device drivers* control the mechanical operation of storage devices and media under orders of SBACKUP.
- *NetWare server TSAs* send requests for SBACKUP-generated data to the NetWare server where the data resides, then return requested data through the SMDR to SBACKUP.
- *Database TSAs* send commands and data between the SBACKUP host server and the database where the data to be backed up resides, then return the requested data through the SMDR to SBACKUP.

PART

V

Appendices

- *Workstation TSAs* send commands and data between the SBACKUP host server and the station where the data to be backed up resides, then return the requested data through the SMDR to SBACKUP.

- Workstation Manager accepts "I am here" messages from stations available for backup. It keeps the names of these stations in an internal list.

STREAMS The common interface between NetWare and transport protocols that need to deliver data and requests for services to NetWare. STREAMS makes protocols, such as IPX/SPX (Internetwork Packet eXchange/Sequenced Packet eXchange), TCP/IP (Transmission Control Protocol/Internet Protocol), SNA (Systems Network Architecture), and OSI (Open Systems Interconnection) transport protocols, transparent, allowing services to be provided across internetworks.

NetWare can install the protocols of your choice (if your applications support these protocols), and the service to the user will be unchanged.

The following are NetWare STREAMS and related NLMs:

- STREAMS.NLM contains the STREAMS application interface routines, the utility routines for STREAMS modules, the log device, and a driver for Open Data-Link Interface (ODI).

- SPXS.NLM provides access to the SPX (Sequenced Packet eXchange) protocol from STREAMS.

- IPXS.NLM provides access to the IPX Internetwork Packet eXchange) protocol from STREAMS.

- TCPIP.NLM provides access to the TCP (Transmission Control Protocol) and UDP (User Datagram Protocol) protocols from STREAMS.

- CLIB.NLM contains the function library required by some NetWare Loadable Modules (NLMs).

- TLI.NLM provides the Application Program Interface (API) that sits between STREAMS and applications.

strong password A password that has a combination of letters, numbers, and special characters. Strong passwords are more difficult to guess and are less susceptible to "dictionary" type password-guessing programs.

subdirectory A directory contained within another directory in a file system.

subnet mask An IP address technique used to differentiate between different TCP/IP (Transmission Control Protocol/Internet Protocol) networks. Each client must have a subnet mask, so it will know the exact network address range. The format is in dotted decimal. The most common subnet mask is 255.255.255.0 (often shown by NetWare in hex as ff.ff.ff.00).

subnetwork   A network that is part of a larger network and connected by a router. From the outside, the subnetwork's identity is hidden, and only the main network is visible, making addressing simpler.

Supervisor right   The file-system trustee right that conveys all rights to directories and files. The Supervisor object right grants all access privileges to all objects and all rights to the property when speaking of property rights.

   Misuse of the Supervisor right may be the single largest security hole in many networks. Grant Supervisor privileges with extreme caution.

surface test   A hard disk test that scans for bad blocks. The NetWare INSTALL program offers two surface tests: destructive and nondestructive. These may be run in the background on a dismounted hard disk so you can keep the server up, but the server performance will be impacted. Although the nondestructive test works the vast majority of the time, it is best to never perform hard disk operations until the disk has two fresh backups.

Symmetric Multi-Processing (SMP)   A computer system (and the operating system) that can take advantage of more than one CPU. It is "symmetric" because the work is automatically divided evenly among all the CPUs rather than certain types of work being assigned to individual CPUs.

synchronization   *Replica synchronization* is the process of ensuring that Directory partition replicas contain the same information as that of the other replicas in the partition.

   Time synchronization is the process of ensuring that all servers in an NDS tree agree on the time.

System attribute   The file-system attribute that specifies that files or directories are only to be used by the operating system.

SYSTEM directory   The directory created during installation on each server that contains the NetWare operating system files. Also included are NetWare Loadable Modules (NLMs), the AUTOEXEC.NCF file, and many of the NetWare utilities used by the Admin user to manage the network. The name of this directory is SYS:SYSTEM and should not be changed.

System Fault Tolerance (SFT)   A process of protecting information on the server by providing multiple storage devices. If one storage mechanism fails, the data will be

PART

V

Appendices

safe on the alternate storage device. This may range from duplicated file allocation table (FAT) entries all the way to completely redundant server hardware.

System Independent Data Format (SIDF)   A tape format designed to allow interoperability among different vendors' tape backup products.

System login script   In NetWare 3, the login script that affected all users on the server. In NetWare 4.*x* and higher, the System login script has been replaced by the Container login script.

System Policies   A feature of ZENworks that allows parameters that affect a user's settings, preferences, and restrictions or a workstation's configuration to be stored centrally. These policies are then enforced centrally by a combination of the Novell client Workstation Manager software and Novell Directory Services (NDS).

tape backup unit   A tape drive that copies information from hard disks to tape.

target   Any local storage device on the network that should be backed up and is running the Target Service Agent (TSA) software. The target may be the same server that holds the backup system, another server, or a workstation.

During the merger of two NDS trees, the tree that retains its tree name and [Root] partition is called the *target tree*.

Target Service Agent (TSA)   Software running on a workstation or server that allows Novell Storage Management Services (SMS) compatible tape backup software to see and back up these workstations, servers, and databases. TSA resources are categories of data created by each TSA. These may be major resources or minor resources, depending on the TSA.

TCP (Transmission Control Protocol)   The Internet protocol that provides reliable, connection-oriented delivery of data between a client and a server. TCP requires that a connection be negotiated with the client and the server first; then it requires acknowledgments of data transmitted.

TCP/IP (Transmission Control Protocol/Internet Protocol)   The primary, industry-standard suite of networking protocols, and the only protocol allowed on the Internet since 1983.

TCP/IP is built upon four layers that roughly correspond to the seven-layer OSI model. The TCP/IP layers are process/application, host-to-host, internet, and network access.

NetWare TCP/IP refers to the collection of NetWare Loadable Modules (NLMs) that add support for TCP/IP onto the NetWare server. Routing can be enabled, as can RIP (Router Information Protocol) to support that routing. One advantage of TCP/IP support in the NetWare server is the ability for IPX Internetwork Packet eXchange) packets to travel across a TCP/IP-only network by using IP (Internet Protocol) tunneling.

The NetWare TCP/IP suite of protocols is a necessary foundation for all Network File System (NFS) products from Novell. The NetWare TCP/IP suite provides both the 4.3 BDS Unix socket interface and the AT&T Streams Transport Layer Interface (TLI).

TCP/IP support at the NetWare server is particularly important for the new Internet-enabled NetWare. The Web server relies on TCP/IP to communicate with the Internet and intranet clients. Older NetWare IPX clients can use the IPX/IP Gateway providing TCP/IP at the gateway server to provide the TCP/IP protocol stack necessary for connection to TCP/IP hosts, either locally or on the Internet. More recent Windows and NetWare clients include TCP/IP support automatically.

Telnet An Internet protocol providing terminal emulation to remote systems using TCP/IP (Transmission Control Protocol/Internet Protocol). All TCP/IP applications today use fancier emulation, but basic Telnet functionality provides the foundation for them all.

termination The process of placing a specific resistor at the end of a bus, line, chain, or cable to prevent signals from being reflected or echoed, causing transmission problems. Typical devices that need terminating resistors include hard disk drives and SCSI (Small Computer Systems Interface) devices.

TFTP (Trivial File Transfer Protocol) A subset of the FTP (File Transfer Protocol) suite, used without any security measures such as passwords. TFTP is rarely used today, but it was a mainstay of automated file-transfer functions, such as e-mail transfer.

time synchronization The method of guaranteeing that all servers in an NDS tree report the same time. Any Novell Directory Services (NDS) function, such as a password change or renaming of an object, requires an NDS time stamp.

The *time stamp* is the unique code that includes the time and specifies an event. The NDS event is assigned a time stamp so the order of events may be recounted.

NDS uses time stamps to do the following:

- Establish the order of events (such as object creation and partition replication)
- Record "real-world" time values
- Set expiration dates on accounts, passwords, and other items

The time server software specifies each NetWare server as either a Single Reference, Primary, Reference, or Secondary time server.

Time source servers must find each other. The two ways to do so are SAP (Service Advertising Protocol) and custom configuration. Primary, Reference, and Single Reference servers use SAP to announce their presence on the network by default. Primary and Reference time servers also use SAP packets to determine which other servers to poll in order to determine the network time. Secondary time servers use SAP information to pick a time server to reference. SAP is easy to install and works without regard to the network layout. It does create a small amount of network traffic.

Alternatively, you can set up a custom configuration. Specific time servers that a particular server should contact may be listed. You can also specify that a server should ignore SAP information from other time sources and that it shouldn't advertise its presence using SAP.

The network supervisor retains complete control of the network time environment using this method. However, the custom configuration method does require extra planning and installation time.

topology   The physical layout design of network components, such as cables, workstations, servers, and concentrators. There are three design options when planning your network topology:

- *Star networks* have end nodes that are connected directly to a central concentrator but not to each other (used for ARCnet and 10BaseT Ethernet).

- *Ring networks* have all nodes cabled in a ring; a workstation's messages may need to pass through several other workstations before reaching the target station or server (used by IBM's Token Ring network and followers).

- *Bus networks* have all nodes connected to a central cable (called a *trunk* or *bus*). The electrical path of a 10BaseT Ethernet network is really a bus.

Topology-Specific Module (TSM)   See *Open Data-Link Interface (ODI)*.

Transaction Tracking System (TTS)   A standard, configurable feature on NetWare servers that protects database applications. By "backing out" of any incomplete transactions resulting from a network failure, the system guarantees to return the database to the state it was in before the interrupted transaction.

Transactional attribute   The file-system attribute that indicates Transaction Tracking System (TTS) is protecting this file.

trustee   A User or Group object that has been granted access to an object, a file, or directory. A *trustee assignment* determines how a user can access an object, directory, or file.

A *trustee list* is kept by each directory, file, and object. This list includes those objects that can access the object, file, or directory. The trustee list is kept in the object's ACL property.

Rather than granting trustee rights to multiple objects one at a time, you can grant them to a group of users. Trustee assignments granting access for the group enable each individual user to have the same trustee rights as the group.

A *[Public] trustee* is a special case that grants the trustee rights of [Public] to all users. Users who try to access an object, directory, or file without explicit rights still have the rights granted to the [Public] trustee.

Rights are the access levels assigned to an object to a directory, file, or object. Trustee assignments grant to an object the rights to other objects. Assign the right to the trusted object, not the trustee. For example, to grant LYNNE the right to delete a Print Queue object, make LYNNE a trustee of the Print Queue object, not the Print Queue object a trustee of LYNNE.

trusted domain   In a Windows NT system, the domain that has permissions to use resources in another domain.

trusting domain   In a Windows NT system, a domain that lets remote users and global groups in the trusted domain use its resources.

turbo FAT index table   The special file allocation table (FAT) index created when a file exceeds 64 blocks and the corresponding number of FAT entries. NetWare creates the turbo FAT index to group all FAT entries for the file in question. This turbo FAT index allows a large file to be accessed quickly.

typeful name   The complete Novell Directory Services (NDS) path name for an object, including the container specifiers. An example is CN=Terry.OU=Consult.O=Pratt. This was the default in earlier versions of NetWare 4.

typeless name   The complete Novell Directory Services (NDS) path name for an object, excluding the container specifiers. An example is Terry.Consult.Pratt.

UDP (User Datagram Protocol)   The Internet protocol that provides best-effort delivery of data on an IP (Internet Protocol) network. Unlike TCP (Transmission Control Protocol), UDP does not require acknowledgments or an initial connection prior to transmitting data.

UIMPORT   A DOS utility (User Import) for adding user names and details into Novell Directory Services (NDS) from an external database. The information must be placed in ASCII format.

unbind   To remove protocol-support software from a network board.

Unicode   A 16-bit character code, defined by the Unicode Consortium, that supports and displays up to 65,536 different unique characters. With Unicode, multiple language characters can be displayed with a single code. Different Unicode translation tables are needed when you change code pages.

All objects and their attributes in the Novell Directory Services (NDS) database are stored as Unicode representations. Clients use only a 256-character code page comprised of eight-bit characters. The Unicode pages and translations are one of the reasons you must define a country code for different locales. These Unicode files are necessary for each language and translation table:

- `437_UNI.033` translates the specific code page to Unicode.
- `UNI_850.033` translates Unicode to the specific code page (page 437, supporting English, French, and German, among others).
- `UNI_MON.033` handles the proper display of upper and lowercase letters.

UNICON   The server utility (Unix Console) used to configure and manage NetWare/IP.

uninterruptible power supply (UPS)   A power backup system that every server should have. The UPS maintains power to an attached device when source AC power is disrupted. There are two types of UPS:

- An online UPS monitors the power going through the unit. The power goes through the internal battery that feeds power to the protected device. These systems are more expensive but do an excellent job of smoothing out rough power before providing power to the end device.
- An offline UPS monitors the power line and becomes activated when the power drops. There is a tiny lag before the UPS can kick in completely.

NetWare includes UPS serial port support, which allows you to connect your UPS directly into the server's serial port.

Universal Asynchronous Receiver/Transmitter (UART)   Serial port controller chips that control the flow of data between the CPU and the serial port. Older PC UARTs could not transfer data to the serial ports of a PC any faster than 9600 baud. Newer PCs should have at least a 16,550 UART chip.

Unix client   A NetWare client running the Unix operating system.

Unknown object   The leaf object that represents an object that Novell Directory Services (NDS) cannot identify. This object is either corrupted or is an object that has become unstable after a partitioning operation. If this is the case, the Unknown object will become known as the partitioning settles down. If the Unknown object remains, delete it.

unloading   To stop NetWare Loadable Modules (NLMs) and remove them from Net-Ware's operating system memory. This is done with the UNLOAD command.

unshielded twisted-pair (UTP)   Cable with two or more pair of wires twisted together and wrapped with a plastic sheath. Each individual wire is twisted around its mate; the more twists, the less interference. Originally used for telephone wiring, UTP is now the LAN wire of choice. Various grades of cable run from the low end (level 3 is telephone wire) to the high end (level 5), supporting high-speed data transmissions.

upgrade   The process of converting your network operating system from an earlier version of the operating system to a more current version. Many customers will upgrade from NetWare 3.*x* to NetWare 4.*x*, or NetWare 4.*x* to 5.

Migration refers to the process of upgrading to NetWare 5.1 using one of the following methods:

- The Across-the-Wire upgrade transfers the network information from an existing server to an existing NetWare 5.1 server on the same network.
- The Same-Server method upgrades the network information on the same server hardware.

UPS monitoring   The connection between a NetWare server and an attached uninterruptible power supply (UPS) that allows the NetWare server to know when the UPS becomes active after power has been lost. When the UPS becomes active, the system sends a signal to the NetWare server, and the server notifies users of the backup power situation. A timeout may be specified, giving the users time to close their files and log out. When the time expires (and the power has not returned), the NetWare server closes all open files and shuts itself down properly.

User login script   The login script specific to the user and the environment set up for that user. A User login script might include specific drive mappings or an extra printer connection for a special job. User login scripts execute after the Container and Profile login scripts. Adding the NO DEFAULT option in a Container script bypasses the User login scripts.

User object   The leaf object in Novell Directory Services (NDS) that signifies a person on the network. The following facts are important when dealing with User objects:

- The login name is the name the user logs in with, and it is mandatory.
- You may assign a user to Group objects, which means that the user inherits the rights assigned to that group.

PART

V

Appendices

- Home directories are the user's personal space on the server hard drive. It is easiest to group all the home directories into one directory or one volume, if there are many to support.

- Trustee rights are the user's rights to access specific directories and files (other than those assigned by the system).

- Security equivalence is a quick way to give one user the same rights as another user.

- User login scripts are the configurable script for individuals. Login scripts for individual users will take a great deal of your management time; avoid them if possible.

- Account management options are available for workgroup administrators to perform some network supervisory jobs without being granted full Supervisor status. You may grant the Supervisor object right to one user to manage other User objects and fulfill specific functions, such as checking and updating user addresses and telephone numbers.

- User account restrictions are the quickest security control for all users. Restrictions can be placed on everything from the time of day users have access to the system to the number of bytes they may use on the server hard disk.

user template   A feature that allows a new User object to inherit default property values based on predefined information. This speeds the creation of many users at one time, especially if these users share details such as account restrictions, locations, fax numbers, and so on.

utilities   Programs that have a specific purpose and add specific functionality to an operating system. NetWare utilities are included for DOS, Windows, and OS/2 clients. Utilities that execute on the server and are listed as NetWare Loadable Modules (NLMs) are run from the console colon prompt. Examples of NLMs are MONITOR, INETCFG, and NWCONFIG. The server NLMs add LAN drivers, disk drivers, name space support, and other low-level network utilities to the NetWare operating system. Workstation utilities execute on a client workstation and are .COM or .EXE files.

Value Added Process (VAP)   First-generation NetWare Loadable Modules (NLMs) that ran on NetWare 2.x.

Virtual Loadable Module (VLM)   The modular, executable client program that connects each DOS workstation with the NetWare server. There are many VLMs called by the VLM.EXE program; some add new NetWare client features and others ensure backward-compatibility.

There are two types of VLMs: *child VLMs* and *multiplexor VLMs*. Child VLMs support particular implementations of a logical grouping. For instance, there is a child VLM for each NetWare server type:

- NDS.VLM is for Novell Directory Services (NetWare 4.x and higher) servers
- BIND.VLM is for bindery-based servers (prior to NetWare 4.x)
- PNW.VLM is for NetWare desktop-based servers (Personal NetWare)

Multiplexor VLMs are the multiplexing modules that route network calls to the proper child VLM.

virtual memory   Temporary storage on the local hard disk. Operating systems that support virtual memory can swap data out of real memory (RAM) to the local hard disk. This allows these operating systems to appear to have more RAM available than just the physical RAM installed. Virtual memory is important for application servers, but using the virtual memory too much can affect performance.

virtual private network (VPN)   A data network that makes use of public data networks such as the Internet. Virtual private network software typically encrypts data while it is crossing public networks.

volume   A logical grouping of physical hard disk storage space. A NetWare volume is fixed in size and is the highest level in the NetWare directory structure, similar to the DOS root directory. Each volume is represented by a Volume object in the Directory.

A NetWare server can support as many as 64 volumes. These volumes may be divided logically on a single hard disk, as a single volume per hard disk or as a single volume spanning multiple hard disks. The first and only mandatory volume is labeled SYS: and includes the NetWare system and client support files. Other volumes can have names between two and 15 characters in length.

A volume must be "mounted" by NetWare in the following sequence:

- The volume becomes visible to the operating system.
- The volume's file allocation table (FAT) is loaded into memory. Each file block of data takes up one entry in the FAT. Because of this, volumes with a smaller block size require more server memory to mount and manage.
- The volume's directory-entry table (DET) is loaded into memory.

volume definition table   The table that tracks volume-segment information, including volume name, volume size, and volume segments on various server hard disks. The volume definition table is required for each NetWare volume and is created by the system during volume initialization.

PART

V

Appendices

Volume object   The leaf object that represents a volume on the network in the NDS tree. The Volume object's properties store information concerning the NetWare server holding the physical volume and the volume name.

volume segments   The physical division of a volume. A volume may be composed of up to 32 volume segments; the maximum number of segments on a single NetWare disk partition is eight.

Volumes can have multiple physical segments spanning multiple hard disks. This allows you to create larger volumes, with NetWare maintaining the volume definition table to track all the segments. Be aware that if one drive of a volume fails, the entire volume must be re-created. For this reason, some networks prefer to stick with a one-disk, one-volume philosophy.

wait state   The period of time a microprocessor does nothing but wait for other processes. For instance, slow memory forces many wait states on a fast CPU.

wait time   The number of seconds the uninterruptible power supply (UPS) will wait before signaling to the attached NetWare server that normal power is lost. The Net-Ware server then sends a message to all workstations warning their users to log out.

watchdog   Packets sent from the server to make sure a workstation is still con-nected. Watchdog packets are sent until the workstation responds or the server clears that connection.

Web server   A software system based on HTTP (HyperText Transfer Protocol) com-munications to send HTML (HyperText Markup Language)-enabled documents to Web client systems. Novell and Netscape ported the Netscape Enterprise Web Server to NetWare via their joint venture, Novonyx.

wide area network (WAN)   A network that communicates long distance across non-physical media, such as public or private telephone lines, satellites, or microwaves. Traditionally, a WAN includes modems connecting different LANs (local area networks) across leased telephone lines.

Winsock   Software that resulted from a vendor group meeting in 1991 to provide a single, standard application platform separate from the underlying network transport protocol. The top part of the Winsock software residing on a client machine interfaces with a TCP/IP (Transmission Control Protocol/Internet Protocol) application, such as Netscape. The bottom part of Winsock interfaces with the TCP/IP protocol stack on the machine, regardless of the TCP/IP developer.

workstation   A personal computer connected to a NetWare network. The term *workstation* may also refer to a Unix or OS/2 machine. Synonyms are client, station, user, or end node.

workstation import   The step that an administrator goes through to take workstations that have been registered with a Novell Directory Services (NDS) container and import them into NDS as Workstation objects.

workstation registration   An automatic process when a user logs in from a network workstation. The workstation is automatically registered with the container object in which the user that logged in exists. The workstation remains in a list of registered workstations until the administrator imports them into Novell Directory Services (NDS).

Write right   The file-system right that allows a user to open and write to files. Also, the property right that allows a user to add, change, or remove any values of the property.

XCONSOLE   A utility included with server TCP/IP (Transmission Control Protocol/Internet Protocol) support that allows a remote VT100 (or equivalent) terminal or terminal emulation program to run RCONSOLE.

XON/XOFF   The handshaking protocol that negotiates the sending and receiving speeds of transmitted data to ensure that no data is lost.

X/Open   A group formed by competing and cooperating vendors in 1984 to ensure that standards were fair to all companies, not dictated by market share. As Unix has waned in public consciousness, so has X/Open. Novell granted the UnixWare name and reference code technology to X/Open in 1994 for continued sharing of Unix standards.

ZENworks   A collection of tools and Novell Directory Services (NDS) objects that allow administrators to manage workstations, distribute software, control network workstation configurations, and enforce restrictions on users. Novell provides the ZENworks Starter Kit with NetWare 5.1.

zones   An arbitrary group of nodes on an AppleTalk internetwork. Zones divide large internetworks into manageable groups. Clients can belong to only one zone at a time, and that zone is determined automatically when that node connects to the network.

Zone names may be up to 32 characters in length. In a network without routers, the zone is invisible to all clients. In a network with routers, the zone names are converted to addresses by NBP (Name Binding Protocol) and ZIP (Zone Information Protocol). A Zone Information Table is maintained by each router. A NetWare server can act as a router for AppleTalk.

PART

V

Appendices

INDEX

Note to the Reader: Page numbers in **bold** indicate the principal discussion of a topic or the definition of a term. Page numbers in *italic* indicate illustrations.

G

M

N

Q

R

U

X

Z